GEORGE THOMAS KURIAN

is an editor, publisher, lexicographer, and historian. He holds an M.A. in history and archaeology. He served as editor-in-chief of Indian Universities Press before emigrating to the United States in 1968. Until 1976 he was associate editor of the World Book Encyclopedia Dictionary. His publications include *Dictionary of Indian English* (I.U.P., 1966), *Dictionary of American Book Publishing* (Simon & Schuster, 1975), *Children's Literary Almanac* (G.K. Reference Books, 1973), and *Historical and Cultural Dictionary of India* (Scarecrow, 1976), *Worldwide Markets for English-language Books* (Knowledge Industry Publications, 1977), *Encyclopedia of The Third World* (2 vols., Facts On File, 1978), and *The Book of World Rankings* (Facts On File, 1979).

OTHER LAUREL BOOKS OF INTEREST

DICTIONARY OF ART
Eleanor S. Greenhill

DICTIONARY OF MUSIC
Theodore Karp

DICTIONARY OF FOREIGN TERMS
Mario Pei and Salvatore Ramondino

DICTIONARY OF THE OCCULT AND PARANORMAL
J. P. Chaplin

DICTIONARY OF PSYCHOLOGY
J. P. Chaplin

DICTIONARY OF SCIENCE
Siegfried Mandel

Dictionary of Biography

George Thomas Kurian

A LAUREL ORIGINAL

To
my father,
Thomas K. George,
this book is
admiringly and respectfully
dedicated.

A Laurel Edition
Published by
Dell Publishing Co., Inc.
1 Dag Hammarskjold Plaza
New York, New York 10017

ISBN: 0-440-31889-0

Printed in the United States of America

First printing—September 1980
DESIGN: RFS Graphic Design, Inc.

Introduction

The Laurel Dictionary of Biography is designed as a desk reference book of biographical information. It includes over 3000 biographical entries drawn from all ages and countries and is specially geared to the needs of students who require encapsulated information in an easily consultable form.

Names are as important as words in the modern world and a knowledge of the achievements of men and women whose lives are significant in the history of the world, particularly the Western world, is as essential to a literate person as a good vocabulary.

The first question in any biographical dictionary is also the most obvious: Why are certain persons included while others are not? Selection of 3000 from among the 1,500,000 people of whom some form of biographical information is known to exist in the printed form in the English language was the most onerous part of the compilation. Given the stark limitations of space in a concise dictionary, the process of selection became a rigorous discipline consisting of both the formulation of criteria and their application to each entry. There is, of course, an uncontroversial nucleus of biographees who form the hard core of entries in a biographical dictionary. But there is a vast array of secondary names, and they present a problem for which there is no entirely satisfactory solution. There are limitations inherent in any type of selection process and no selection can be entirely flawless or nonsubjective. The editor craves the indulgence of those readers who may find that one or another of their favorite personalities have not been included.

The basic selection was made from a master checklist compiled from the indexes of major encyclopedias and dictionaries, including a few general dictionaries of biography. The effort was directed toward establishing not only those names that have universal significance but also those that possessed special significance in certain areas of human endeavor. The entries in this dictionary are restricted to persons who find a place in all or most of the consulted encyclopedias and dictionaries.

Since fame is always subject to the vagaries of public opinion, some of the names included may sound unfamiliar to modern readers. They were selected on the basis of the esteem in which they were once held rather than current critical estimate of their achievements. Another general rule was to restrict to the minimum representation of names from the fields of arts and sports—often lumped together under the rubric of celebrities—whose reputations are, more often than not, ephemeral and rarely outlast their lifetimes.

The second question concerns the structure, size, and type of the entries. In view of the special nature of biographical material, some uniformity in arrangement and typographical consistency were seen as necessary. The actual structure of each entry is explained in the Guide to the Use of the Dictionary. Basically, the structure conforms to the pattern of a dictionary rather than that of an encyclopedia, and the effort has been to provide factual data rather than evaluative data. Eight elements common to all entries are, in order: name (with variants, title, pseudonyms); pronunciation; birth date (and death date); birth place; nationality; profession; career and principal achievements; principal publications or creative works. This order has been modified where modification was necessary for purpose of clarity of presentation. The length of each entry is determined by the nature of each biographee's life or the nature of material available and is in no way an index of his or her importance.

Abbreviations have been reduced to the minimum. All years are A.D. unless indicated as B.C.

Tuckahoe, New York
October 3, 1979

GEORGE THOMAS KURIAN

Guide to the Use of the Dictionary

The mechanical details of each entry are, for all practical purposes, self-explanatory. Yet, an understanding of the organization and special features is necessary for making effective use of the Dictionary.

Names Full information is supplied about the names of persons. The names themselves appear in bold face and are followed by (where applicable) prenames, surnames, maiden surnames, alternative names or variants, pseudonyms, titles or honorifics, all in italic. Where a nickname or pseudonym is used as the entry heading, the real name is given in italic.

Dates Birth and death dates are printed in full; other dates are usually abbreviated. Dates of both birth and death are given wherever available. Where one date is not available the other is prefixed with a *b*. (for born) or *d*. (for died). A question mark accompanies uncertain dates. Where only the general period of a person's existence is known it is indicated by *fl*. (flourished in) followed by the century.

Titles Titles of books and periodicals are shown in italic.

Abbreviations *b*. born (in). *c*. circa. *d*. died (in). *fl*. flourished in.

Composite Entries and Hidden Entries Members of a single family or members of a dynasty bearing the same name are treated in composite entries, where the subjects are usually, but not necessarily, described in chronological order. All entries following the leading entry are known as hidden entries.

Cross References Variants, alternative names, nicknames, and titular names are cross-referenced.

Order of Entry Names are entered by alphabetical order in directory style, with the surname followed by a comma and the prename. Names beginning *Mc* are alphabetized as if spelled *Mac*. Names containing the abbreviation *St.* are alphabetized as if *Saint* were spelled in full. Common usage has been the guide in determining whether or not connective elements such as *de, van,* and *von* are treated as part of the surname; in most cases they are disregarded for the purpose of alphabetization.

Pronunciation Scheme The symbols used in pronunciation are as follows:

ā *as in* age
ă *as in* add
â *as in* care.
ä *as in* father
ȧ *as in* ask
ch *as in* chair
ē *as in* eat
ĕ *as in* end
g *as in* get
ī *as in* ice
ĭ *as in* ill
j *as in* jet
K *as in German* ich, ach
L *as in Spanish* olla *and Italian* figlio
N *as in French* bon
ō *as in* open
ŏ *as in* odd
ô *as in* order

oi *as in* oil
o͞o *as in* food
o͝o *as in* foot
ou *as in* out
sh *as in* she
th *as in* thin
t͟h *as in* then
ū *as in* cube
ŭ *as in* up
û *as in* furl
ü *as in French* tu
y *as in* yet
z *as in* zebra
zh *as the* z *in* azure
ə *indeterminate vowel as in the unstressed syllables of* *a*bout, tak*e*n, penc*i*l, lem*o*n, circ*u*s

A

Aakjaer *(ôk yər),* **Jeppe** 1866–1930. Danish lyric poet and novelist. *b.* Jutland. Author of *Bondens Søn* (1899), *Vredens Børn; et Tyendes Saga* (1904), and *Rugens Sange* (1906).

Aalto *(äl tō),* **Hugh Alvar Henrik** 1898–1976. Finnish architect and furniture designer. *b.* Kuortane, near Helsinki. Taught in U.S. (1940–46); returned to Finland after World War II; designed sanatorium at Viipuri, Baker House at M.I.T., the Sunila Pulp Mill at Kotka, and other buildings.

Aaron *(âr ən)* (Old Testament) First high priest of the Hebrews. Eldest son of Amram and Jochebed of the tribe of Levi, and brother of Moses; with Moses, led the Israelites out of Egypt and was consecrated high priest on Mount Sinai; believed to have died at age 123 at Mount Hor.

Aasen *(ô sən),* **Ivar Andreas** 1813–96. Norwegian philologist and lexicographer. *b.* Orsta. Devised national language known as Landsmaal by standardizing various dialects; popularized the language through his own works, particularly *Grammar of the Norwegian Dialects* (1848) and *Dictionary of the Norwegian Dialects* (1850).

Abba Arika *(ȧb ä ȧ rè kä)* also called Rab. c175–247. Jewish haggadist and one of the principal authors of the Babylonian Talmud; founder of the Academy at Sura on the Euphrates, which flourished for nearly eight centuries as one of the greatest intellectual centers of Israel.

Abbad I *(äb bäd)* full name: Abbad ibn-Muhammad abu-'Amr. *d.* 1042. Cadi and founder of Abbadide dynasty of Seville; ruler of Seville (1023–42).

Abbas *(ăb bäs)* full name: al-Abbas ibn-Abd-al-Muttalib. c566–652. Arab merchant and paternal uncle of Muhammad. One of the principal promoters of Islam and progenitor of the Abbassid dynasty.

Abbas I the Great 1557–1628. Shah of Persia (1586–1628). Defeated the Uzbeks near Herat (1597) and the Turks at Basra (1605) and Sultanieh (1618); expanded Persian Empire by capturing Kandahar (1625), Hormuz (1622), and Baghdad (1623); introduced many internal reforms.

Abbe *(ăb ē),* **Cleveland** 1838–1916. American meteorologist. *b.* New York, N.Y. Director of Cincinnati Observatory (1868–73) and meteorologist of U.S. Weather Bureau; pioneered weather forecasting and the use of standard time throughout U.S.; called the Father of the Weather Bureau. Author of *Report on Standard Time* (1879), *Merchanics of the Earth's Atmosphere* (1910), *Relation Between Climate and Crops* (1901), and *Basis of*

Long-Range Forecasting (1902).

Abbe *(äb ĕ),* **Ernst** 1840–1905. German physicist and industrialist. *b.* Eisenach. Director of optical research with Carl Zeiss (1866); partner (1875); head of the firm (1888); invented the Jena glass and the Abbe refractometer.

Abbey *(ăb ĭ),* **Edwin Austin** 1852–1911. American painter and illustrator. *b.* Philadelphia, Pa. Began career on staff of *Harper's Weekly;* illustrated editions of Shakespeare and Goldsmith; executed mural *Quest of the Holy Grail* for the Boston Public Library and murals for British Houses of Parliament and state capitol at Harrisburg, Pa.; official painter at coronation of Edward VII (1902).

Abbot *(ăb ət),* **George** 1562–1633. English prelate. *b.* Guildford, Surrey. Archbishop of Canterbury (1611–33); one of the translators of the New Testament in the Authorized Version of the Bible; vice-chancellor of Oxford University (1600–1605).

Abbott *(ăb ət),* **Jacob** 1803–79. American Congregational clergyman and author of children's books. *b.* Hallowell, Me. Founder and first principal of Mount Vernon School in Boston, one of the first women's academies in U.S.; after the phenomenal success of *The Young Christian,* retired to devote himself to writing. Author of over 180 books, including the 28-volume Rollo Series; father of Benjamin, Austin, and Lyman Abbott.

Abdallah ibn-Yasin *(ȧb dool lä ĭb'n yä sēn) d.* c1058. Founder and spiritual leader of the Almoravides, a Berber people of North Africa whom he converted to Islam. His successors conquered much of the territory between the Sahara and ancient Gaetulia with Marrakesh as capital.

Abd-al-Malik *(ȧb do͝ol mȧ lĭk)* c646–705. Fifth Ommiad caliph of Baghdad (685–705). United Islam and engaged in a protracted war against Byzantine emperors; established Arabic as official language and coined the first purely Arabic currency.

Abd-al-Mumin *(ȧb do͝ol mo͞o mĭn)* also ABDUL MUMIN. c 1101–63. Arab chieftain and founder of the Almohade dynasty. Assumed title Caliph and extended his rule over Morocco, Córdoba, Almeria, Granada, Tunis, and Tripoli.

Abderhalden *(äp dėr häl dĕn),* **Emil** 1877–1950. Swiss chemist and physiologist. Director of the Halle Physiological Institute (1911); discoverer of norleucine and proteinases; editor of *Handbuch der Biologischen Arbeitsmethoden* (9 vols.).

Abd-er-Rahman III *(ȧd do͝or rä män)* full name: ABD-ER-RAHMAN AL-NASIR. 891–961. Ommiad emir of the Western Emirate of Córdoba. Assumed title Caliph (929); united Muslim Spain under a strong central government; extended its boundaries through successful campaigns against Fatimids and kings of León and Navarre; patronized arts and sciences and made Córdoba a great center of learning.

Abdul Baha *(ȧb do͝ol bă hä)* real name: ABBAS EFFENDI. 1844–1921. Bahai leader. Son of Baha Ullah, founder of Bahai sect; exiled and imprisoned by Turks at Acre (1868–1908); released by Young Turks and assumed leadership of

Bahai movement; knighted by the British (1920) as Sir Abdul Baha Bahai.

Abdullah ibn-Hussein *(äb do͞ol lä ĭb n hoo sĭn)* 1882–1951. King of Jordan (1946–51). *b.* Mecca. Son of Hussein, a Hashemite leader who was crowned king of Hejaz; one of the Arab leaders in revolt against Turkey; amir of Trans-Jordan (1921); king (1946); ally of Great Britain and organizer of the Arab Legion; assassinated (1951).

Abdul-Wahhab *(äb do͞ol wä häb)* 1691–1787. Muslim reformer and founder of Wahabi sect. Launched his puritanical movement in Nejd to restore the traditions of primitive Islam.

Abe *(ä bĕ),* **Nobuyuki** 1875–1953. Japanese general. *b.* Ishikawa prefecture. Twice prime minister of Japan (Aug.–Sept. 1939; Sept. 1939–Jan. 1940); governor general of Korea (1944–45).

Abel *(ā bəl),* **Sir Frederick Augustus** 1827–1902. English chemist. *b.* Woolwich. Professor of chemistry at Royal Military Academy (1851–55); war department chemist (1854–88); inventor of cordite (with James Dewar) and Abel tester for determining flash point of petroleum. Author of *Gun-cotton* (1866) and *Electricity Applied to Explosive Purposes* (1884).

Abel, John Jacob 1857–1938. American endocrinologist and physiological chemist. *b.* Cleveland, Ohio. Professor of pharmacology at Johns Hopkins (1893–1932); isolated epinephrine and pituitary hormone and first produced insulin in its crystalline form.

Abelard *(ăb ə lärd),* **Peter** 1079–1142. French theologian and logician. *b.* near Nantes. Student of William of Champeaux and Roscellin of Compiègne; founded own school at Melun (1101); teacher of philosophy in Paris (1117–21); cited before Synod of Soissons on charge of heresy (1121) and compelled to burn his *Introductio ad Theologiam;* retired to Nogent-sur-Seine and continued teaching in a hermitage known as Oratory of the Paraclete; became Abbot of St. Gildas-de-Rhuys in Brittany (1124–35); withdrew to Cluny as an ascetic; accused of heresy at the Council of Sens by Bernard of Clairvaux and condemned by the Council (1141) and by the pope (1142). Abelard's famous love affair with his pupil Héloïse, niece of Fulbert, the canon of Notre Dame, led to his castration at the hands of Fulbert's hirelings. A rationalist and dialectician, Abelard espoused a modified form of nominalism known as conceptualism, which held that universals exist only as concepts in the mind of man or God. His principal works include *Nosce Teipsum, Sic et Non, Historia Calamitatum Mearum,* and *Glossulae super Porphyrium.*

Abercrombie *(ăb ər krŏm bĭ),* **Lascelles** 1881–1938. British poet, playwright, critic, and scholar. *b.* Ashton-on-Mersey, Cheshire. Professor of English literature at universities of Leeds (1922–29) and London (1929–35). Author of *Interludes and Poems* (1908), *Emblems of Love* (1912), *Twelve Idylls* (1928), *Deborah* (1913), *An Essay Towards a Theory of Art* (1922), *Principles of Literary Criticism* (1932), and *Principles of English Prosody* (1923).

Abercromby *(ăb ər krŏm bĭ),* **Sir**

Ralph 1734–1801. British general. *b.* Menstry, Scotland. Commander-in-chief of expeditionary force that conquered St. Lucia and Trinidad (1795–96); defeated French at Alexandria (1801) but was fatally wounded.

Abernathy *(ăb ər năth ĭ),* **Ralph David** 1926–. Black American leader and clergyman. Early leader for desegregation of the South; close associate of Martin Luther King, Jr.; one of organizers of The Southern Christian Leadership Conference (1957); house and church bombed (1957); vice-president of SCLC (1965); succeeded King as president of SCLC (1968) after King was assassinated.

About *(ȧ bo͞o),* **Edmond François Valentin** 1828–85. French novelist and dramatist. *b.* Dieuze. Author of *Le Roi des Montagnes* (1856), *Madelon* (1863), *L'Homme a l'Oreille Cassée* (1861), *Le Nez d'un Notaire* (1862), and *Alsace* (1872).

Abraham *(ā brə hăm)* (Old Testament) First patriarch of the Jews and, through his son Ishmael, progenitor of the Arabs. Believed to have lived in the 15th or 16th century B.C.; according to tradition, buried in cave of Machpelah at Hebron.

Abraham ibn Daud *(ā brə hăm ĭb n dä wo͝od)* 1110–80. Jewish philosopher and historian. *b.* Toledo, Spain. Author of *Sepher Haqabala (Book of Tradition)* and *'Emunah Ramah (Sublime Faith).*

Absalom *(ăb sə lŏm)* (Old Testament) Third son of David. Murdered his brother Ammon, rebelled against his father, and was defeated and slain by Joab.

Absalon *(äp sä lôn)* also AXEL. 1128–1201. Danish prelate and statesman. Archbishop of Lund (1178–1201); counselor to Waldemar I and Canute VI; commander of expeditions which defeated Wendish pirates (1168) and Pomeranian fleet (1184), and conquered Estonia.

Abu-al-Atahiyah *(ä bo͞ol ä tä hĭ yä)* 748–828. Arab poet. *b.* Anbar in Mesopotamia. Courtier of caliphs al-Mamun and Harun al-Rashid; developed a simple verse form to replace the archaic qasida or elegy; known as the father of Arab sacred poetry.

Abu-al-Faraj Al-Isfahani *(ä bo͞ol fä räj äl ĭs fä hä nĕ)* 897–967. Arab historian and anthologist. *b.* Isfahan, Persia. Author of *Kitab al-Aghani (Book of Songs),* a treasury of Arab poetry and history, valuable as a sourcebook of Arab antiquities.

Abu-Bakr *(ä bo͞o bäk ər)* also ABU BEKR; original name: ABD-AL-KAABA; called AL-SIDDIK (the Faithful). 573–634. First caliph of Islam (632–34). *b.* Mecca, Arabia. Father of Ayesha, Muhammad's wife; accompanied Muhammad on the Hegira; completed first written record of the sayings of the Prophet, which formed the basis of the Koran; succeeded Muhammad as leader of Islam (632); fought successfully against Persia and Byzantium.

Abu-Hanifah *(ä bo͞o hä nē fä)* real name: AL-NUMAN IBN-THABIT. 699–768. Muslim jurist. *b.* Kufa, Mesopotamia. Founder of the Hanafite school of Muslim law.

Abulfeda *(ä bo͞ol fĭ dä),* **Ismail ibn Ali** 1273–1331. Arab prince and historian. *b.* Damascus, Syria. Fought against Crusaders (1285–

98); served Mamaluke sultan al-Nasir (1298); governor of Hama, Syria (1310–31); given title Sultan (1320). Author of *An Abridgment of the History of the Human Race,* a valuable sourcebook on Saracenic history up to 1200.

Abul Kasim *(ä bo͞ol kä sĭm)* Arabic name: ABU-AL-QASIM KHALAF IBN-'ABBAS AL-ZAHRAWI; Latin name: ALBUCASIS. *d.* 1013. Arab surgeon. *b.* Córdoba, Spain, Author of *al-Tasrif,* a medical encyclopedia in 30 sections.

Abul Kasim Mansur. *See* **Firdausi**

Abu-Tammam *(ä bo͞o tăm mäm)* full name: ABU TAMMAM HABIB IBN-AWS. 807–45. Arab Christian poet. *b.* near Lake Tiberias, Syria. Author of *Diwan,* a collection of his poetry, and *Hamasa,* a collection of early Arab poetry.

Achenwall *(ä Kĕn väl),* **Gottfried** 1719–72. German scholar. *b.* Elbing, Prussia. Professor of philosophy and law at University of Gottingen; founder of the science of statistics.

Acheson *(ăch ə sən),* **Dean Gooderham** 1893–1971. American lawyer and statesman. *b.* Middletown, Conn. U.S. Secretary of State under Harry S. Truman (1949–53); took a leading part in discussions which led to the signing of the Atlantic Pact. Author of *Present at the Creation* (1969), *A Citizen Looks at Congress* (1957), and *An American Vista* (1956).

Achillini *(ä kēl lē nē),* **Alessandro** 1463–1512. Italian anatomist and philosopher. Professor of both philosophy and medicine at Universities of Bologna and Padua; one of the first to dissect cadavers; called the second Aristotle.

Acton *(ăk tən),* **Lord** full name: JOHN EMERICH EDWARD DALBERG-ACTON; FIRST BARON ACTON OF ALDENHAM. 1834–1902. English historian. *b.* Naples, Italy. Regius Professor of Modern History at Cambridge (1895–1902); editor of *Cambridge Modern History;* author of *Lecture on the Study of History* (1895) and *Lectures on the French Revolution* (1910); leader of the liberal Roman Catholics who opposed papal infallibility.

Adalbert *(äd äl bĕrt),* **Saint** 955–97. Bohemian prelate and nobleman. Bishop of Prague; preached gospel among Hungarians, Poles, and Prussians; murdered in Pomerania by a heathen priest; also known as Apostle of the Prussians.

Adam *(ăd əm),* **Robert** 1728–92. Scottish architect and furniture designer. *b.* Kirkcaldy. Architect to King George III (1762–68); with his brothers James and William built the Adelphi, off the Strand in London. The Adam style of furniture design is noted for its delicate and classic motifs such as wreaths, paterae, honeysuckle, and fan ornaments.

Adam de la Halle *(ä däɴ dē lä äl)* also ADAM LE BOSSU. c1235–85. French dramatist and narrative poet. *b.* Arras. Composer of lyrics, motets, rondeaus, and operas. Author of *Le Jeu de la Feuillée,* the earliest French comedy, and *Le Jeu de Robin et Marion,* the earliest French comic opera.

Adams *(ăd əmz),* **Henry Brooks** 1838–1918. American historian. *b.* Boston, Mass. Grandson of John Quincy Adams. Assistant professor of history at Harvard and editor of *North American Review.* Author of *History of the United States* (9 vols.,

1889–91), *Mont-Saint-Michel and Chartres* (1904), *The Education of Henry Adams* (1906), *A Letter to American Teachers of History* (1910), and *The Life of Albert Gallatin* (1879).

Adams, James Truslow 1878–1949. American historian. *b.* Brooklyn, N.Y. Author of the Pulitzer-Prize-winning *Founding of New England* (1921), *The Epic of America* (1931), *The March of Democracy* (2 vols., 1932–33), and *The Living Jefferson* (1936); editor-in-chief of *The Dictionary of American History* (1940).

Adams, John 1735–1826. Second president of the U.S. *b.* Braintree, Mass. Delegate from Mass. to First and Second Continental Congresses (1774–78); proposed election of Washington as commander-in-chief; served on committee that drafted Declaration of Independence; commissioner to France and minister to United Provinces (1778–85); envoy to Great Britain (1785–88); negotiated treaty of peace with Great Britain (1782); vice-president of U.S. (1789 and 1792); president of U.S. (1796); on seeking reelection, defeated by Jefferson (1800). Author of *Defence of the Constitutions of the United States Against the Attacks of Mr. Turgot* (3 vols., 1787–88). His son, John Quincy Adams, was sixth president of the U.S. *The Life and Works of John Adams* (10 vols., 1850–56) was edited by his grandson, Charles Francis Adams.

Adams, John Couch 1819–92. English astronomer. *b.* Lidcot, Cornwall. Discoverer, along with Leverrier, of the planet Neptune (1845–46); professor of astronomy at Cambridge (1858); published tabulation of moon's parallax and paper on secular acceleration of moon's mean motion.

Adams, John Quincy 1767–1848. Sixth president of U.S. *b.* Braintree, Mass. Son of John Adams, second president of U.S. Minister to the Netherlands (1794–97) and to Prussia (1797–1801); senator from Mass. (1803–1808); minister to Russia (1809–14); member of the commission which negotiated Treaty of Ghent (1814); minister to court of St. James (1815–17); secretary of state (1817–25); elected president of U.S. by House of Representatives (1825); defeated by Andrew Jackson for second term (1828); representative in Congress (1830–48); author of *Memoirs,* edited by Charles Francis Adams (12 vols., 1874–77).

Adams, Samuel 1722–1803. American revolutionary. *b.* Boston, Mass. Leader of the radical party in the Mass. legislature (1765–74); organized Committee of Correspondence (1772); led agitation culminating in Boston Tea Party; delegate to first and second Continental Congresses (1774–78); signer of Declaration of Independence; member of Congress (to 1781); governor of Mass. (1794–97).

Adams, William Japanese name: Anjin Sama (the Pilot). 1575–1620. English navigator. *b.* Gillingham, near Chatham. First Englishman to reach Japan when his ship, the *Charity,* arrived at Kyushu (1600); rose in favor at Japanese court and became advisor to the shogun (1600–1620); married a Japanese woman and received an estate near Yokosuka and the rank of samurai; obtained trading station for the

English at Hirado (1613); commanded voyages to Cochin China (1617–18) and Siam (1616).

Addams *(ăd əmz),* **Jane** 1860–1935. American social worker and pacifist. *b.* Cedarville, Ill. Founded Hull House, a social settlement at Chicago (1889) and served as its head until 1935; president of International Congress of Women (1919); worked to secure social justice for minorities, immigrants, women, and children; shared Nobel Peace Prize with Nicholas Murray Butler (1931); author of *Democracy and Social Ethics* (1902), *Newer Ideals of Peace* (1907), *Twenty Years at Hull House* (1910), *A New Conscience and an Ancient Evil* (1911), *The Second Twenty Years at Hull House* (1930), and *The Excellent Becomes the Permanent* (1932).

Addington *(ăd ĭng tən),* **Henry** title: First Viscount Sidmouth. 1757–1844. British statesman. *b.* Reading. Entered Parliament (1783); Speaker (1789–1801); prime minister (1801–1804); concluded Treaty of Amiens (1802); home secretary (1812–21); unpopular for his repressive measures.

Addison *(ăd ĭ sən),* **Joseph** 1672–1719. English essayist and statesman. *b.* Milston, Wiltshire. Served in various posts under Whig ministries; secretary for Ireland (1715); lord commissioner of trade (1716); secretary of state (1717–18). His essays in *The Spectator* and *The Tatler* are regarded as models of English prose style, distinguished by grace and subtlety of humor; his drama in blank verse, *Cato,* achieved great popularity for its defense of Whig principles.

Ade *(ād),* **George** 1866–1944. American humorist and playwright. *b.* Kentland, Ind. Author of *Fables in Slang* (1900), *In Babel* (1903), *Single Blessedness* (1922), and plays *The Sultan of Sulu* (1902), *The County Chairman* (1903), and *Father and the Boys* (1907).

Adelard *(ăd ə lärd)* also Æthelhard. c1116–c1142. English mathematician and scientist. *b.* Bath. Translated Arabic treatises on trigonometry and algebra into English; author of *De Eodem et Diverso* and *Questiones Naturales.*

Adenauer *(ä dən ou ər),* **Konrad** 1876–1967. German statesman. *b.* Cologne, West Germany. Lord mayor of Cologne (1917–33); dismissed from all offices by Nazis (1933) and twice arrested (1934; 1944); reinstated as lord mayor (1945); founded Christian Democratic Union (1945); chancellor of West Germany (1949–63); took a leading part in rebuilding West Germany after World War II.

Adler *(äd lər),* **Alfred** 1870–1937. Austrian psychologist and psychiatrist. *b.* Penzing-Vienna. At first, a prominent member of the Freudian group; from 1911, developed his own theory of individual psychology based on the inferiority complex; established School of Individual Psychology at Vienna and founded the *Journal of Individual Psychology* (1914); became visiting professor of medical psychology at Long Island College of Medicine in N.Y. (1932); author of *Practice and Theory of Individual Psychology* (1918), *Study of Organ Inferiority and Its Psychical Compensation* (1917), *The Science of Living* (1929), *Education of Chil-*

dren (1930), and *The Pattern of Life* (1930).

Adler, Felix 1851–1933. American reformer and educator. *b.* Alzey, Germany. Immigrated to U.S. (1857); professor of political and social ethics at Columbia from 1902; founder of N.Y. Society for Ethical Culture (1876) and New York City's first free kindergarten (1878); author of *Creed and Deed* (1877), *Life and Destiny* (1903), *Religion of Duty* (1905), and *An Ethical Philosophy of Life* (1918).

Adrian *(ā drĭ ən)* also Hadrian. Name of six popes:

Adrian I *d.* 795. Pope (772–95). Presided over Second Nicene Council which upheld veneration of images (787); allied with Charlemagne to drive back the Lombards.

Adrian II Pope (867–72). Passed sentence of deposition on Photius, patriarch of Constantinople.

Adrian III, Saint Pope (884–85).

Adrian IV 1100–1159. Pope (1154–59). *b.* Langley, Hertfordshire, England. Abbot of monastery of St. Rufus near Avignon (1137); succeeded Pope Eugenius III; first and only Englishman to sit on the throne of St. Peter; gave Ireland to Henry II of England; began long conflict between the papacy and the Hohenstaufens by insisting upon papal supremacy against Frederick Barbarossa.

Adrian V Pope (1276).

Adrian VI 1459–1523. Pope (1522–23). Bishop of Tortosa and grand inquisitor of Aragon (1516); created cardinal by Leo X (1517); as pope, failed to check the Reformation and the rise of Turkish power.

Adrian, Edgar Douglas 1889–. English physiologist. *b.* London. Co-winner of Nobel Prize for medicine (1932) for discoveries relating to the function of neurons. Author of *The Basis of Sensation* (1928).

Ady *(ŏ dĭ),* **Endre** 1877–1919. Hungarian lyric poet. *b.* Erdmindszent. Leader of modernist symbolist movement; began career with the publication of *Uj versek (New Poems)* (1906).

AE. *See* **Russell, George William**

Aegidius of Assisi *(ə jĭd ĭ əs əv äs sē zē)* also Blessed Giles. *d.* 1262. Friar and companion of St. Francis of Assisi by whom he was called "The Knight of Our Round Table." His sayings were collected and published as *Dicta (The Golden Words of Blessed Brother Giles).*

Aeschines *(ĕs kə nēz)* 389–314 b.c. Athenian orator. Opponent of Demosthenes; advocated appeasement of Philip of Macedon; compelled to flee Athens; established school of eloquence in Rhodes; died at Samos.

Aeschylus *(ĕs kə ləs)* 525–456 b.c. Greek tragic dramatist. *b.* Eleusis. Fought in Persian Wars and wounded at Marathon; won 13 first prizes in the annual competitions at Athens (484–468); finally defeated by Sophocles; left Athens for Sicily, where he died; of approximately 90 plays only seven survive: *The Suppliants, The Persians, Seven Against Thebes, Prometheus Bound,* and the Orestean trilogy, *Agamemnon, Choephoroi,* and *Eumenides.*

Aesop *(ē səp)* c620–c560 b.c. Legendary Greek fabulist and reputed author of *Aesop's Fables.* According to tradition he was a native of Phrygia and a born slave who lived in Lydia at the court of King Croesus.

Æthelhard. *See* **Adelard**

Affonso o Grande. *See* **Abuquerque, Affonso de**

Aga Khan I *(ä gə kän)* real name: Hasan Ali Shah. 1800–1881. Head of Ismaili Muslim community; descendant of Muhammad; fled Persia after quarrel with the Shah and settled in India; granted the title of Highness.

Agassiz *(əg á sē),* **Alexander** 1835–1910. American zoologist. *b.* Neuchatel, Switzerland. Son of Louis Agassiz. Conducted many zoological and oceanographic expeditions; director of Museum of Comparative Zoology at Harvard (1860–98); author of *Revision of the Echini* (1873), *Embryology of the Starfish* (1864), *A Catalogue of North American Acalephae* (1865), and *North American Starfishes* (1877).

Agassiz, Jean Louis Rodolphe 1807–73. American naturalist, biologist, geologist, paleontologist, and ichthyologist. *b.* Môtier-en-Vully, Switzerland. Professor of natural history at Neuchâtel (1832–45); arrived in U.S. (1846); professor of zoology and geology at Harvard (1848–73); established Museum of Comparative Zoology at Harvard (1859); with his wife, Elizabeth Cary Cabot, established Agassiz School for Girls, predecessor of Radcliffe College (1855); founded Anderson School of Natural History on Penikese Island, Buzzards Bay, Mass., one of the earliest marine biological stations (1873). Author of *The Fishes of Brazil* (1829), *Recherches sur les Poissons Fossiles* (5 vols., 1833–34), *History of the Fresh Water Fishes of Central Europe* (1839–42), *Critiques sur les Mollusques Fossiles* (1840–45), *Nomenclator Zoologicus* (1842–46), *Geological Sketches* (1853–54; 1864–65), and *Contributions to the Natural History of the United States* including *Essay on Classification* (4 vols., 1857–62).

Agatha *(ăg ə thȧ),* **Saint** d. 251. Sicilian Christian martyr. *b.* Catania or Palermo. Virgin tortured and killed by the Prefect Quintilianus, whose advances she had spurned; patron saint of Malta. Feast day: Feb. 5.

Agathocles *(ə găth ō klēz)* 361–289 B.C. Sicilian tyrant. *b.* Thermae. Seized power (316); crossed Mediterranean to attack Carthage (310); invaded Italy and Corcyra (300–295).

Agee *(ā jē),* **James** 1909–55. American playwright and critic. *b.* Knoxville, Tenn. Author of *Let Us Now Praise Famous Men* and *A Death in the Family.*

Agesander *(ăj ə săn dər)* also Agesandros. *fl.* 1st century B.C. Greek sculptor. Native of Rhodes; with Athenodorus and Polydorus carved the Laocoön, now in the Vatican.

Agnes *(ăg nĕs),* **Saint** *d.* 304. Roman Catholic virgin martyr. Patron saint of maidens. Feast day: Jan. 20.

Agnew *(ăg nū),* **Spiro Theodore** 1918–. American politician. *b.* Baltimore, Md. Governor of Md. (1967); vice-president of U.S. (1969–73); resigned in disgrace on bribery charges.

Agnon *(äg nŏn),* **Shmuel Yosef** 1888–1970. Israeli writer. *b.* Buczacz, Poland. Noted for his trilogy on European Jewry *Bridal*

Canopy (1931), *A Guest for the Night* (1939), and *Days Gone By* (1945), as well as novellas, including *In the Heart of the Seas* (1933); awarded Nobel Prize for literature with Nelly Sachs (1966).

Agramonte *(ä grä môn tā),* **Aristides** 1869–1931. Cuban bacteriologist and pathologist. *b.* Puerto Principe (now Camagüey). Member of U.S army board that discovered the transmission of yellow fever by the mosquito *Aëdes calopus.*

Agricola *(à grĭk ō là),* **Gnaeus Julius** 37–93. Roman general and statesman. *b.* Forum Julii (now Frejus), France. Quaestor in Asia (63); governor of Aquitania (74–78); consul (78); as governor of Britain extended Roman dominion in seven campaigns to the north of Forth; circumnavigated Britain for the first time, discovering it to be an island.

Agricola, Johannes real name: JOHANNES SNEIDER, later SCHNITTER; also called MAGISTER ISLEBIUS. 1492–1566. German Protestant theologian. *b.* Eisleben, Saxony. One of the founders of the Reformation; disciple of Luther; broke from him in 1536 on the issue of Antinomianism, which he supported; author of collection of German proverbs (1528–48).

Agrippa *(à grĭp à),* **Marcus Vipsanius** 63–12 B.C. Roman general and statesman. *b.* Rome. Son-in-law of Emperor Augustus; suppressed revolt in Aquitania (38); consul (37); defeated Sextus Pompeius Magnus at Mylae and Naulochus (36); defeated Antony's fleet at Actium (31); governor of Syria (23); shared the tribuneship with Augustus (from 18).

Aguinaldo *(ä gē näl dō),* **Emilio** 1869–1964. Filipino revolutionary. *b.* near Cavite, Luzon. Led insurrections against Spain (1896–98) and U.S. (1899–1901); captured by General Frederick Funston (1901); joined Japanese puppet government during World War II.

Ahab *(ā hăb)* *d.* c853 B.C. Seventh king of Israel (c875–853 B.C.). Son of King Omri; through diplomacy and alliances brought peace to the kingdom; repulsed Shalmaneser at Karkar (854); killed in battle against Benhadad of Damascus; introduced Phoenician forms of worship into Hebrew religion through the influence of his wife Jezebel.

Ahmad Shah Durrani *(ä măd shä do͞or rä nē)* 1724–73. Amir of Afghanistan (1747–73). Chief of the Abdali Afghan tribe; commander of the bodyguard of Nadir Shah, after whose assassination he retired to Afghanistan, where he founded the kingdom of Kandahar; invaded India six times (1748–52); defeated the Mughal emperor (1756); destroyed the Maratha power at the Battle of Panipet (1761); acquired great wealth through plunder.

Aidan *(ā dən),* **Saint** *d.* 651. Irish monk of Iona or Hii and first bishop of Lindisfarne. With the help of King Oswald, founded the Northumbrian Church.

Aiken *(ā kən),* **Conrad Potter** 1889–1973. American poet and critic. *b.* Savannah, Ga. Author of books of poetry *Earth Triumphant* (1914), *Priapus and the Pool* (1922), *Time in the Rock* (1936); novels *Blue Voyage* (1927), *King Coffin* (1935), *The Conver-*

sation (1940); awarded Pulitzer Prize (1929) for *Selected Poems* and National Book Award (1953) for *Collected Poems;* published autobiographical *Ushant* (1952).

Ainsworth *(ānz wûrth),* **William Harrison** 1805–82. English novelist and publisher. *b.* Manchester. Editor of *Bentley's Miscellany, Ainsworth's Magazine,* and *New Monthly.* Author of 39 novels, including *Rookwood* (1834), *Jack Sheppard* (1939), *Tower of London* (1840), *Guy Fawkes* (1841), *Windsor Castle* (1843), *The Flitch of Bacon* (1854), and *Boscobel* (1872).

Airy *(âr ĭ),* **George Biddell** 1801–92. English astronomer royal (1835–81). *b.* Alnwick. Appointed professor of astronomy at Cambridge (1828) and director of Greenwich Observatory (1835); determined the mean density of the earth; discovered an inequality in the motions of Earth and Venus. Author of *Autobiography* (1896).

Aitken *(āt kən),* **Robert Grant** 1864–1951. American astronomer. *b.* Jackson, Calif. Director of Lick Observatory (1930–35); awarded gold medal of the Royal Astronomical Society (1932) for his discovery of over 3000 double stars.

Aitken, Robert Ingersoll 1878–1949. American sculptor. *b.* San Francisco, Calif. Works include McKinley Monument in Golden Gate Park, San Francisco; George Rogers Clark Monument at the University of Virginia; and busts of Thomas Jefferson, Daniel Webster, Benjamin Franklin, and Henry Clay in the Hall of Fame.

Aitken, William Maxwell. *See* **Beaverbrook, Baron**

Akahito *(ä kä hē tō),* **Yamabe No** *fl.* 8th century. Japanese poet. Exponent of the *uta;* regarded as one of the twin stars of the golden age of Japanese poetry.

Akbar *(ăk bər)* also called AKBAR THE GREAT; real name: JALAL-UD-DIN MUHAMMAD. 1542–1605. Third Mughal emperor of India (1556–1605). *b.* Umarkot, Sind. Consolidated Mughal power by annexing Rajput kingdoms, Gujarat, Bengal, Kashmir, Sind, and Berar; established a sound administrative system; built Fatehpur Sikri as capital (1570–85); promulgated new syncretic religion known as Din Ilahi; achievements recorded in *Akbar-namah* by Abu-l-Fazl.

Akhenaten. *See* **Ikhnaton**

Akibaben, Joseph *(ȧ kĭ vä bĕn jōzəf)* c50–132. Jewish rabbi and martyr. As teacher of the rabbinical school at Jaffa, laid the foundations of the Mishnah; supported Bar Cocheba's revolt against the Romans (132); captured and flayed alive.

Alain de Lille *(ȧ lăN də lēl)* 1128–1202. French monk and theologian. Author of the satirical poem *De Planctu Naturae* and the encyclopedic poem *Anticlaudianus.* Known also by the title Doctor Universalis.

Alamgir. *See* **Aurangzeb**

Alaminos *(ä lä mē nōs),* **Antonio** also ANTON. 1499–1520. Spanish navigator. Accompanied Columbus as pilot on two of his voyages (1499 and 1502); discovered the Bahama Channel (1520).

Alarcón *(ä lär kôn),* **Hernando de** *b.* c1500. Spanish explorer. *b.* Trujillo. Sailed up the Gulf of California (1540) to assist Coronado's expedition to southwestern

U.S.; first West European to explore the Colorado River.

Alarcón, Pedro Antonio de 1833–1931. Spanish writer and diplomat. *b.* Guadix, Granada. Member of the Cortes and the Royal Spanish Academy; founded radical journal *La Redención;* published *El Eco de Occidente* and edited *El Látigo;* best known for his novels *El Nino de la Bola* (1880) and *El Sombrero de Tres Picos.*

Alarcón y Mendoza, Juan Ruiz de c1580–1639. Spanish dramatic poet. *b.* Taxco, Mexico. Emigrated to Spain (1600); member of the Council of the Indies from 1626. Author of *La Verdad Sospechosa* (adapted by Corneille as *Le Menteur*), *El Semijante de sí Mismo, Las Paredes Oyen, El Examen de Maridos,* and *Ganar Amigos.*

Alaric I *(ăl ə rĭk)* c370–410. King of the Visigoths. *b.* Peuce, an island in the Danube. Commander of Gothic auxiliaries under Emperor Theodosius; left Roman service; king of the West Goths (395); invaded Greece (395–96); appointed governor of Illyria by Emperor Arcadius; invaded upper Italy but defeated by Stilicho at Pollentia (402); invaded Italy (408) a second time and successfully captured and sacked Rome (410).

Alba. *See* **Alva**

Alban *(êl bən),* **Saint** *d.* 304. First British martyr. Stoned to death near St. Albans for sheltering a Christian priest. Feast day: June 22 (Catholic); June 17 (Anglican).

Albategnius; Albatenius. *See* **Battani, al-**

Albéniz *(äl bā nēth),* **Isaac** 1860–1909. Spanish composer and pianist. *b.* Comprodón. Student of Franz Liszt; official pianist to the queen of Spain; composer of operas, zarzuelas, and piano pieces based on folk melodies, of which the best known are *Iberia* and *Catalonia.*

Alberoni *(äl bā rō nē),* **Giulio** 1664–1752. Cardinal and prime minister of Spain (1715–19). *b.* Parma, Italy. Invaded Sardinia, leading to the Quadruple Alliance (1719) of England, France, Austria, and Holland; exiled from Spain following disastrous war; died in Rome.

Albert *(ăl bərt)* German name: ALBRECHT; also known as the PIOUS. 1559–1621. Cardinal and archduke of Austria. Third son of Emperor Maximilian II; brought up at the Spanish court and trained for the Church; made cardinal (1577) and archbishop of Toledo (1584); viceroy of Portugal (1594–96); stadtholder of the Netherlands (1596); relinquished holy orders and married the infanta Isabella (1599); defeated by Maurice of Nassau at Nieuport, Flanders (1600); concluded 12-year truce with Netherlands.

Albert, Prince full name: ALBERT FRANCIS CHARLES AUGUSTUS EMMANUEL OF SAXE-COBURG-GOTHA. 1819–61. Prince consort of England. *b.* Schloss Rosenau, near Coburg, Germany. Married Queen Victoria (1840); took active role in promotion of arts and sciences; regarded as prime mover of Great Exhibition of 1851.

Albert I full name: ALBERT LEOPOLD CLEMENT MARIE MEINRAD. 1875–1934. King of Belgium (1909–34). *b.* Brussels. Led Belgian forces in World War I and later directed Belgium's postwar reconstruction and currency stabilization.

Albertus Magnus *(ăl bûr təs măg nəs)*, **Saint** also called ALBERT THE GREAT and DOCTOR UNIVERSALIS; real name: ALBERT, Count VON BOLLSTADT. c1200–1280. German scholastic philosopher. *b.* Lauingen, Swabia. Taught in various schools in Paris and Cologne, where Thomas Aquinas was his pupil; appointed provincial of the Dominicans in Germany (1254); bishop of Ratisbon (1260); retired to his convent at Cologne (1262) to devote himself to philosophic studies; noted as an interpreter of Aristotle and for his extensive knowledge of physical sciences. Author of *Summa Theologiae* and *Summa de Creaturis;* canonized and named Doctor of the Church (1932).

Albinus. *See* **Alcuin**

Albrecht. *See* **Albert**

Albuquerque *(ăl bə kûr kē)*, **Affonso de** also known as AFFONSO O GRANDE (Affonso the Great). 1453–1515. Founder of the Portuguese Empire in the East. *b.* Alhadra, Spain. Appointed viceroy of Portuguese Indies (1506); captured Goa (1510); established Portuguese suzerainty in Ceylon, Ormuz, and Malacca; recalled by King Emanuel (1515). Author of *Commentaries.*

Alcaeus *(ăl sē əs)* c611–580 B.C. Greek poet of Mytilene. Invented Alcaic meter. His lyrics in the Aeolic dialect dealt with politics and love; only fragments of the 10 books of odes ascribed to him survive.

Alcibiades *(ăl sĭ bī ə dēz)* c450–404 B.C. Athenian statesman and general. *b.* Athens. Nephew of Pericles and disciple of Socrates; leader of the radical party against Nicias (421); commander of Athenian League against Sparta in Peloponnesian War (420–418); commander of expedition against Sicily (415); accused of profanation, escaped to Sparta, where he induced Ionians to revolt against Athens; exiled from Sparta to the court of the Persian satrap Tissaphernes (412); recalled by Athenian army at Samos, which he led to victory over the Spartans at Cynossema, Abydos, and Cyzicus, thus restoring Chalcedon, Byzantium, and the dominion of the sea to Athens; returned home in triumph (407); again forced into exile following defeat at Notium (406); assassinated on the orders of Lysander of Sparta (404).

Alcmaeon *(ălk mē ŏn) fl.* 6th century B.C. Greek physician and philosopher. *b.* Crotona, Italy. Regarded as the father of Greek medicine; contemporary and disciple of Pythagoras; discovered the Eustachian tubes and the optic nerve; first to make anatomical dissections; recognized the brain as the central organ and explained sleep and sense impressions.

Alcott *(ôl kət)*, **Amos Bronson** 1799–1888. American transcendentalist philosopher and teacher. *b.* Wolcott, Conn. Father of Louisa May Alcott. Established cooperative community at Fruitlands, Mass. (1844), later abandoned; appointed superintendent of schools, Concord, Mass. (1859); founded Concord Summer School of Philosophy and Literature (1879). Author of *Observations on the Principles and Methods of Infant Instruction* (1830), *The Doctrine and Discipline of Human*

Culture (1836), *Concord Days* (1872), *Ralph Waldo Emerson* (1865), and *Record of a School* (1835).

Alcott, Louisa May 1832–88. American author. *b.* Germantown, Pa. Daughter of Amos Bronson Alcott. Raised in Boston, Mass., mostly educated by father; supported family through journalism; achieved fame as author of *Little Women* (1868), which attained long-lasting popularity. Other works include *Hospital Sketches* (1863), *An Old Fashioned Girl* (1870), *Little Men* (1871), *Jo's Boys* (1886).

Alcuin *(ăl kwĭn)* also ALBINUS; Anglo-Saxon name: EALHWINE; surname: FLACCUS. 735–804. English prelate and leader of the revival of European learning. *b.* York. Settled at Aachen (Aix-la-Chapelle) at the invitation of Charlemagne; served as abbot of Ferrières and Troyes and head of the palace school; led opposition to the adoptionist heresy at the Council of Frankfort; as abbot of Tours (796–804) presided over the foremost Carolingian school; author of numerous works on language, rhetoric, theology, and hagiology.

Aldenham, First Baron of. *See* **Acton, Lord**

Aldrich *(ôl drĭch),* **Nelson Wilmarth** 1841–1915. American financier and statesman. *b.* Foster, R.I. Member of House of Representatives (1878–81) and Senate (1881–1911); sponsored or influenced passage of McKinley Tariff Act (1890), Silver Purchase Act (1890), Anti-Trust Act (1890), Gold Standard Act (1900), Payne-Aldrich Tariff Act (1909), and Aldrich-Vreeland Currency Act (1908).

Aldrich, Thomas Bailey 1836–1907. American editor and writer. *b.* Portsmouth, N. H. Editor of *Every Saturday* (1865–74) and *Atlantic Monthly* (1881–90). Author of *The Story of a Bad Boy* (1870), *Prudence Palfrey* (1874), *The Queen of Sheba* (1877), and *Stillwater Tragedy* (1880).

Aldus Manutius *(ôl dŭs mȧ nū shĭ ŭs)* Latin name: TEOBALDO MANNUCCI or MANUZIO. 1450–1515. Italian printer and scholar. *b.* Bassiano. Founded Aldine press (1490) in Venice to bring out fine editions of Greek and Latin classics; invented italic type face (1501); founded New Academy of Hellenic Scholars (1500). The Aldine firm lasted through three generations.

Alekhine *(ŭ lyā kyĭn),* **Alexander** Russian name: ALEKSANDR ALEKSANDROVICH ALEKHIN. 1892–1946. Russian chess master. *b.* Moscow. Twice world chess champion (1927–35; 1937–46). Author of *My Best Games of Chess: 1923–1937.*

Alemán *(ä lā män),* **Miguel** full name: MIGUEL ALEMÁN VALDÉS. 1902–. Mexican statesman. *b.* Sayula. Began career as labor attorney; governor of Veracruz (1936–40); president of Mexico (1946–52).

Alembert *(ȧ län bâr),* **Jean Le Rond d'** 1717–83. French philosopher and mathematician. *b.* Paris. Secretary of French Academy (1772–83) and co-founder and editor of Diderot's *Encyclopédie.* Author of *Traité de Dynamique* (1743), *La Précession des Équinoxes* (1749), *Différents Points Importants du*

Système du Monde (1754), *Opuscules Mathématiques* (8 vols., 1761–80), and *Oeuvres Littéraires* (5 vols., 1821).

Alessandri Palma *(ä lā sän drē päl mä)*, **Arturo** 1868–1959. Chilean statesman. *b.* near Linares. As president of Chile (1920–25), attempted many reforms but was deposed by an army revolt; later reelected president (1930–38).

Alexander I *(ăl ĕg zăn der)* Russian name: ALEKSANDR PAVLOVICH. 1777–1825. Emperor of Russia (1801–25). *b.* St. Petersburg. Introduced sweeping reforms and encouraged education and science; joined coalition against Napoleon (1805); present at Battle of Austerlitz and joined Prussia against Napoleon (1806); forced to sign Treaty of Tilsit following defeats at Eylau and Friedland (1807); led coalition against France following Napoleon's invasion of Russia and subsequent retreat; active in battles of Dresden and Leipzig (1813); entered Paris with allies (1814); present at Congress of Vienna (1815) and others that followed; formed Holy Alliance (1815); became increasingly reactionary and unpopular.

Alexander II Russian name: ALEKSANDR NIKOLAEVICH. 1818–81. Emperor of Russia (1855–81). Concluded Treaty of Paris (1856) which ended Crimean War; emancipated serfs (1861); reorganized judicial, military, and civil administrations; extended boundaries of Caucasus and Central Asia (1868–81); suppressed Polish insurrection (1863–64); assassinated by nihilists (1881).

Alexander II real name: ANSELMO BAGGIO. *d.* 1073. Pope (1061–73). Founder of Patarine party, which favored celibacy of the clergy.

Alexander III real name: ORLANDO BANDINELLI. *d.* 1181. Pope (1159–81). *b.* Siena, Italy. Engaged in long struggle with Emperor Frederick Barbarossa which ended with the emperor's defeat at Legnano (1176) and reconciliation at Venice (1177); contest with Henry II of England, murderer of Thomas à Becket, ended in king's acknowledgment of papal supremacy and the canonization of Becket.

Alexander VI real name: RODRIGO LENZUOLI BORGIA. c1431–1503. Pope (1492–1503). *b.* Xativa, near Valencia, Spain. Nephew of Pope Calixtus III, by whom made cardinal (1476); elected pope through bribery; issued bill dividing New World between Spain and Portugal (1493); joined Holy League with Emperor Maximilian I, aligning Milan, Venice, and Spain against Charles VIII of France (1495); ordered execution of Savonarola (1498); instituted censorship of books (1501); noted as the patron of Michelangelo, Raphael, and Bramante, he was given to intrigues and luxury and had many mistresses and natural children.

Alexander VII real name: FABIO CHIGI. 1599–1667. Pope (1655–67). *b.* Siena, Italy. Promulgated bill against Jansenists (1665); lost Avignon in conflict with Louis XIV (1662); enlarged Sapienza and Vatican libraries and built St. Peter's Colonnade, designed by Bernini.

Alexander Nevski *(nĕv skĭ)* c1220–63. Russian hero and patron saint of St. Petersburg. Prince of Novgorod (1238); defeated Swedes (1240) on the Neva and Teutonic Knights on Lake Peipus (1242); became grand duke of Kiev and Novgorod (1246) and of Vladimir (1252). Though a vassal of the Tartars, he fostered their friendship and secured a reduction in the tribute paid to them.

Alexander of Tunis, Earl full name: HAROLD RUPERT LEOFRIC GEORGE ALEXANDER. 1891–1969. British soldier. *b.* Tyrone, Ireland. General Officer Commanding, Burma (1942); commander in chief of the Middle East (1943); field marshal and supreme allied commander, Mediterranean theater (1943–45); captured Rome (1944); governor general of Canada (1946–52); minister of defense (1952–54). Author of *Memoirs* (1962).

Alexander the Great 356–323 B.C. Macedonian ruler and conqueror of the world. *b.* Pella, Macedonia. Trained by Aristotle; succeeded to throne of Macedon at age 20 on the assassination of his father, Philip; conquered Thrace and Illyria and destroyed Thebes (335); crossed the Hellespont (334); defeated the Persians at Granicus and Issus; occupied Damascus and destroyed Tyre (332); overran Palestine and Egypt; built Alexandria (332); the first of over 70 communities founded by him; won another decisive victory over the Persians at Arbela (Gaugamela) (331); gained control of Babylon, Susa, and Persepolis; overthrew the Scythians on the banks of Jaxartes (329); subdued Sogdiana (328); proceeded to India, crossing the Indus near modern Attock; overthrew Porus, the king of Hydaspes (326); returned through Indus Valley and Baluchistan to Babylon when his men refused to follow him further; died of fever and fatigue at Babylon at age 33; called the greatest general in history by Napoleon.

Alexanderson *(ăl ĕg zăn dər sən),* **Ernst Frederik Werner** 1878–1975. American engineer and inventor. *b.* Uppsala, Sweden. Emigrated to U.S. (1901); joined General Electric Company (1902); holder of over 200 patents in radio and television; inventions include high-frequency alternator, multiple-tuned antenna, vacuum-tube telephone transmitter, and tuned radio-frequency receiver.

Alexis I *(ä lĕk sĭs)* Russian name: ALEKSEI MIKHAILOVICH. 1629–76. Czar of Russia (1645–76). Waged war with Poland and acquired possession of Smolensk and eastern Ukraine; suppressed peasant revolt led by Stenka Razin (1669–71); extended frontiers eastward in Central Asia; codified laws of various provinces and thus prepared the way for the Europeanization of Russia under his son, Peter the Great.

Alexius *(ȧ lĕk sĭ ŭs)* also called GRAND COMNENUS. c1180–1222. Emperor of Trebizond (1204–22). Grandson of Byzantine emperor Andronicus I; gained control of Trebizond (later established as an independent empire) when Constantinople was captured by Crusaders (1204); founded dynasty that lasted more than 250 years (1204–1461).

Alfaro *(äl fä rō),* **Eloy** 1864–1912. Ecuadorian statesman. *b.* Monte Cristi. Led insurrection against President Luis Cordero and declared himself dictator (1895) and president (1897–1901); led second uprising (1906) against President Lisardo García and became president under a new constitution (1907–11); administration marked by separation of church and state and construction of the Quito-Guayaquil railway.

Alfieri *(äl fyâ rē),* **Vittorio** 1749–1803. Italian tragic dramatist and satirist. *b.* Asti. Wrote the tragedy *Cleopatra,* produced in 1775; moved to Florence (1776) to study Tuscan dialect; published 21 tragedies, six comedies, and the tragelomedia *Abele,* a mixture of tragedy and opera. His *Opere* (22 vols.) includes an epic in four cantos, an autobiography, poetry, and satires.

Alfonso *(ăl fŏn sō)* **I** Portuguese name: AFFONSO HENRIQUES. c1110–85. First king of Portugal (1139–85). Son of Henry of Burgundy, Count of Portugal; wrested the throne from his mother and became sole ruler (1128); freed Portugal from León and was crowned first king; captured Lisbon (1147); defeated the Moors at Ourique (1139) and Santarem (1146).

Alfonso III also called ALFONSO THE GREAT. 848–912. King of Asturias and León (866–910). Fought over 30 campaigns and gained numerous victories over the Moors; occupied Coimbra and extended territories from the Duero River to the Guadiana River; forced to abdicate in favor of his son Garcia.

Alfonso X also called ALFONSO THE WISE and ALFONSO THE ASTRONOMER. 1221–84. King of León and Castile (1252–82). *b.* Burgos, Spain. Twice candidate for the office of Holy Roman Emperor; waged wars with Moors (1261–66); united Murcia with Castile; forced to abdicate in favor of his son Sancho (1282); promulgated the code *Las Siete Partidas,* the basis of Spanish jurisprudence; author of the Alphonsine tables of planetary observations; regarded as the founder of Castilian national literature.

Alfred *(ăl frĕd)* also called ALFRED THE GREAT. 849–99. King of England (871–99). *b.* Wantage, Berkshire. Youngest son of Ethelwulf, king of the West Saxons. After several campaigns, inflicted decisive defeat on the Danes at Ethandun in Wiltshire (878); by the Treaty of Wedmore, compelled the Dane leader Guthrum to receive baptism and to acknowledge the supremacy of Alfred; took and fortified London (886); received the submission of the East Anglians and Northumbrians and thus became overlord of all England; waged defensive war with the Danes under Hasting (892–96) effecting their withdrawal; by improving navy, gained an advantage over the Vikings; reformed the fyrd, or national militia, so that half the shire force was always ready for military service; compiled code of laws by collecting the best enactments of earlier kings; brought famous scholars to court and encouraged learning; translated from Latin the *Epitome of Universal History* by Paulus Orosius, the *Consolations of Philosophy* by Boethius, and the *Pastoral Rule* of Gregory the Great.

Alfvén *(äl vān),* **Hannes** 1908–. Swedish physicist. Co-winner (with Louis Néel) of Nobel Prize in physics (1970) for work in plasma physics.

Alger *(ăl jər),* **Horatio** 1832–99. American clergyman and writer. *b.* Revere, Mass. Author of 119 popular books for boys, including *Ragged Dick* (1867), *Luck and Pluck* (1869), *From Canal Boy to President* (1881), most of them dealing with rags-to-riches themes.

Ali *(ä lē)* Arabic name: ALI IBN-ABI-TALIB; called by Shiites SHER-I-KHUDA (the Lion of God). c600–661. Fourth caliph of Islam (656–61). *b.* Mecca, Arabia. Cousin and son-in-law of Muhammad and one of his first converts; opposed by Abu-Bakr (Muhammad's immediate successor), Ayesha (Muhammad's wife), and Muawiyah (founder of the Ommiads); succeeded Othman as caliph (656); defeated armies of Ayesha (656) and Muawiyah (657); assassinated by Kharijites (661); venerated as a martyr by his followers who comprise the Shiite sect.

Ali Mohammed of Shiraz. *See* **Bab**

Al-Khowarizmi *(äl Kōō wä rēz mē),* **Mohammed ibn-Musa** c780-c845. Arab mathematician. *b.* Khwarizm (now Khiva), U.S.S.R. Author of *Al-Jabr wa'l Muqabalah,* from which the word *algebra* is derived. The word *algorithm* is a corruption of his name. Known as the FATHER OF ALGEBRA.

Allamand *(à là mäN),* **Jean Nicholas Sebastien** 1713–87. Swiss physicist. *b.* Lausanne. Professor of philosophy at University of Leiden; first to explain phenomenon of Leyden jar.

Allen *(ăl ən),* **Ethan** 1738–89. American Revolutionary soldier. *b.* Litchfield, Conn. Served in French and Indian Wars; settled in Vermont (c1769); organized militia known as the Green Mountain Boys; with Benedict Arnold, captured Fort Ticonderoga (1775); taken prisoner by British after unsuccessful attempt to take Montreal (1775–78); exchanged, and on return made a major general on Vermont militia; pressed Vermont's claims for statehood at Second Continental Congress (1778). Author of *A Narrative of Col. Ethan Allen's Captivity* (1779) and *Reason the Only Oracle of Man* (1784).

Allen, William 1532–94. English cardinal. *b.* Rossall, Lancashire. Opposed accession of Queen Elizabeth; forced to flee to Louvain (1561); founded English Catholic seminary at Douai (1568); moved to Reims (1578), where he began work on the Douay version of the Bible; founded seminaries at Rome (1575–78) and Valladolid (1589); created cardinal (1587) by Pope Sixtus V; appointed Vatican librarian by Pope Gregory XIV. Author of *Letters* (1582).

Allen, William Hervey 1889–1949. American writer. *b.* Pittsburgh, Pa. Author of *Anthony Adverse* (1933), *Towards the Flame* (1926), *Action at Aquila* (1938), *The Forest and the Fort* (1943), *Bedford Village* (1945), and *Israfel* (1926).

Allenby *(ăl ən bĭ),* **Edmund Henry Hynman** Title: VISCOUNT ALLENBY OF MEGIDDO AND FELIXSTOWE. 1861–1936. British soldier. *b.* Suffolk. Served in Boer War (1899–1902); commanded Egyptian Expeditionary Force which took Jerusalem (1917); won a great victory at Megiddo (1918) which led to the fall of Damascus and Aleppo and the Turkish capitulation; high commissioner for Egypt (1919–25).

Allison *(ăl ĭs n),* **Fred** 1882–. American physicist. *b.* Glade Spring, Va. Professor of physics at Alabama Polytechnic Institute; devised the magneto-optic analytical method which led to the discovery of element 87 (francium) and element 85 (astatine).

Allouez *(à lwā),* **Claude Jean** 1622–89. Jesuit missionary and explorer. *b.* St. Didier, France. Came to Canada (1658); explored the country around Lake Superior (1665-75) and established missions there.

Almagro *(äl mä grō),* **Diego de** c1475–1538. Spanish soldier and conquistador. *b.* Aldea del Rey. Joined Francisco Pizarro's expedition to Peru, meeting him at Cajamarca (1533); quarreled with Pizarro, but later reconciled; sent to conquer Chile and was made governor (1535); returned and captured Cuzco by surprise (1537); finally defeated by Hernando Pizarro at Las Salinas, taken prisoner, and strangled (1538).

Almeida-Garrett *(äl mā ē thà gär rĕt),* **Visconde de** title of João Baptista da Silva Leitão. 1799-1854. Portuguese poet and dramatist. *b.* Oporto. Participated in revolt of 1820; exiled but permitted to return (1826); minister of interior under Dom Pedro; pioneered romantic movement in Portuguese literature. Author of the epic *Camões,* the poem *Dona Branca* (1826), historical prose dramas, such as *Auto de Gil Vicente* (1838) and *Frei Luiz de Sousa* (1844); worked to found the national theater.

Aloysius *(ăl ō ĭsh əs),* **Saint** real name: Luigi Gonzaga. 1568–91. Italian Jesuit and nobleman. *b.* Castiglione, near Mantua. Renounced marquisate and entered Society of Jesus (1585); during plague at Rome, devoted himself to the care of the sick, becoming infected and dying at age 23; canonized (1726); declared patron of youth by Pope Benedict XIII (1729).

Alp Arslan *(älp ärs län)* original name: Mohammed. 1029–72. Seljuk sultan (1063–72). Succeeded his father, Daud, as ruler of Khurasan (1059) and his uncle, Toghrul Beg, as ruler of Persia; subdued Georgia and Armenia (1064); conquered Aleppo; defeated and took Byzantine emperor Romanes Diogenes prisoner at Manzikert (1071); established Seljuk empire of Rum.

Alva *(äl vä),* **Duke of** also Alba; real name: Fernando Alvarez de Toledo. 1508–82. Spanish governor of the Netherlands (1567–73). *b.* Piedratita. Became general at age 26 and commander in chief at 30; led forces of Charles V to victory over the Elector of Saxony at Mühlberg (1547); commanded imperial forces in Italy against the pope and the king of France (1553–59); sent to the Netherlands by Philip II to suppress revolt; set up the Council of Troubles, which executed over 18,000 persons; defeated William of Orange and Prince Louis and entered Brussels in triumph (1568); returned to Portugal (1573); led expedition to Portugal which defeated Dom Antônio and occupied Lisbon (1580).

Alvear *(äl vā är),* **Carlos María de** 1789–1853. Argentine leader in war for independence. *b.* Misiones territory, Uruguay. Present at surrender of Montevideo (1814);

succeeded Gervasio Antonio Posadas as dictator (1815); deposed by army (1820); commanded Argentine forces against Brazilians in Uruguay (1826) and won at Ituzaingó (1827); banished from Argentina by dictator Juan Manuel de Rosas.

Alvarado *(äl vä rä thō)*, **Pedro de** Indian name: TONATIUH (the Sun). 1485–1541. Spanish general. *b.* Badajoz. Accompanied Hernando Cortes in the conquest of Mexico; present at the seizure of Montezuma; escaped Indian insurgents in Mexico City by leaping across a great gap in a causeway (known as Alvarado's leap); led expedition against Utitlán and burned the city (1524); founded Guatemala (1524); appointed governor of Guatemala (1530); headed another expedition (1534) against Quito; conquered Honduras; went to Mexico (1540) to subdue a revolt in Jalisco.

Alzon *(äl zôn)*, **Emmanuel Marie Joseph Maurice Daudé d'** 1810–80. French religious. Founder at Nîmes of the religious order known as Augustinians of the Assumption (1844).

Amadeo *(ä mä dâ ō)*, **Giovanni Antonio** also OMODEO. c1447–1522. Lombard sculptor. *b.* Pavia, Italy. Principal works include facade of the Cerosa at Pavia, tomb of San Lanfranco at Pavia, chapel and tomb of Bartolommeo Colleoni at Bergamo, cupola of the cathedral at Milan, and monument to Medea Colleoni at Basella near Bergamo.

Amati *(ä mä tē)* Family of Italian violinmakers of Cremona in the 16th and 17th centuries, of whom the most important were ANDREA AMATI (1520–1611), his brother NICOLO AMATI (1568–86), Andrea's sons ANTONIO (1550–1638) and GERONIMO (1551–1630), Geronimo's son NICOLÒ (1596–1684) and grandson GERONIMO (1649–1740).

Ambrose *(ăm brōz)*, **Saint** Latin name: AMBROSIUS. 340–97. Bishop of Milan and one of the fathers of the Catholic Church. *b.* Trier, Germany. Elected bishop of Milan (374); opposed Arianism; presided over Synod of Aquileia (381), which deposed Arian prelates Palladius and Secundianus; during the Gallic occupation of Milan, melted down church vessels to help the poor; won universal respect for having turned Emperor Theodosius away from his church door for his massacre in Thessalonica and having restored him only after severe penance; introduced the Ambrosian chant and Ambrosian ritual. Author of treatises *De Spiritu Sanctu, De Mysteriis, De Officiis Ministrorum* and hymns, such as *Veni Redemptor Gentium* and *Deus Creator Omnium.*

Amenemhet *(ä mĕn ĕm hĕt)* also AMENEMHAT, AMMENEMES. Name of four kings of the XII Dynasty (Theban) of ancient Egypt:

AMENEMHET I. Founder of the dynasty (2000–1970 B.C.); built temple of Amon in Thebes and pyramid at El Lisht.

AMENEMHET II. Third king of the dynasty (1938–1903 B.C.); son of Sesostris I; led expeditions to Sinai and Nubia.

AMENEMHET III. Sixth king of the dynasty (1849–1801 B.C.); son of Sesostris III; constructed Lake Moeris and the Labyrinth.

AMENEMHET IV. Seventh king of the dynasty (1801–1792 B.C.)

Amenhotep *(ä měn hō tĕp)* also AMENOPHIS. Name of four kings of the XVIII Dynasty (Diospolite) of ancient Egypt:

AMENHOTEP I. Second king of the dynasty (c1557–1540 B.C.); son of Ahmose I. Waged successful campaigns in Ethiopia, Nubia, Libya, and Syria.

AMENHOTEP II. Seventh king of the dynasty (1448–1420 B.C.); son of Thutmose III; victorious in Palestine and Euphrates region; commemorated in inscription at Amadah in Nubia.

AMENHOTEP III. Ninth king of the dynasty (1411–1375 B.C.); son of Thutmose IV; greatest ruler of the middle kingdom, whose empire extended from Mesopotamia to Ethiopia; developed Thebes as imperial capital; built many monuments and edifices, including temples at Gebel Barkal, Luxor, and Soleb, the Colossi at Memnon, and the hypostyle hall at Karnak.

AMENHOTEP IV. *See* **Ikhnaton**

Ames *(āmz),* **Fisher** 1758–1808. American statesman. *b.* Dedham, Mass. House of Representatives (1789–97); supported Hamilton's Federalist policies; opposed Madison's proposal of commercial war with Britain. Author of *The Dangers of American Liberty* (1805).

Amherst *(ăm ərst),* **Jeffrey** title: BARON AMHERST. 1717–97. British soldier. *b.* Sevenoaks, Kent. Sent by William Pitt to North America (1758); led British forces that took Louisburg from the French; commander in chief of North America; captured Ticonderoga and Crown Point (1759) and Montreal (1760); governor general of British North America (1760–63): baron (1787); field marshal (1796).

Amherst, William Pitt title: EARL AMHERST OF ARAKAN. 1773–1857. British colonial administrator. Governor general of India (1823); waged successful campaign against Burma (1824–26).

Amici *(ä mē chē),* **Giovanni Battista** c1786–c1863. Italian optician and astronomer. *b.* Modena. Invented dioptric achromatic microscope that bears his name (1827); developed reflecting telescope and polarization apparatus; director of Florence Observatory (from 1835).

Amiel *(ȧ myĕl),* **Henri Frédéric** 1821–81. Swiss philosopher. *b.* Geneva. Professor of aesthetics and moral philosophy at Academy in Geneva (from 1849). Author of *Fragments d'un Journal Intime* published after his death and regarded as a model of introspective writing.

Amman *(äm än) or A men (ä mən),* **Jacob** Swiss Mennonite bishop. Founded sect known as Amish or Amish Mennonites; seceded from Mennonite Church in Switzerland and Alsace (1693–97).

Ammonius *(ă mō nĭ ŭs)* surname: SACCAS. c175–242. Egyptian philosopher of Alexandria. Founder of Neoplatonism; taught Plotinus, Longinus, and Origen.

Amos *(ā mŏs)* (Old Testament) Minor Hebrew prophet of the 8th century B.C.; native of Tekoa, near Bethlehem, and contemporary of Isaiah and Hosea.

Ampère *(äN pâr),* **André Marie** 1775–1836. French scientist. *b.* Polémieux, near Lyons. Professor of mathematics at École Polytechnique (1809) and Collège de France (1824); discovered relationship between magnetism and electricity (Ampère's law), the basis of the science of electrodynamics; invented astatic needle; the ampere, or unit of electrical current, is named after him. Author of *Observations Électrodynamiques* (1822) and *Théorie des Phénomènes électrodynamiques* (1830).

Amr ibn-al-As *(äm ro͞ob nĭl äs)* also Amru. c594–664. Arab general. Koreish tribesman converted to Islam (629); served as general entrusted with the conquest of Syria (633) during caliphate of Abu-Bakr; sent by Caliph Omar I to subjugate Egypt (639); defeated Egyptians at Heliopolis (640); governor of Egypt (642–44); put down revolt in Alexandria (646) and extended Muslim influence into Tripoli; sided with Muawiyah against Ali after the death of Caliph Othman; appointed vice-regent of Egypt (658–64).

Amundsen *(ä mo͞on sĕn),* **Roald** 1872–1928. Norwegian explorer. *b.* Borge. Navigated Northwest Passage on the *Gjöa* and determined the exact location of magnetic north pole (1903–1906); sailed to Antarctic in the *Fram* and discovered South Pole (1911); successfully crossed the Northeast Passage in the *Maud* (1918–20); lost at sea (1928) on flight to rescue Umberto Nobile, whose *Italia* had crashed in the Arctic. Author of *My Life as an Explorer* (1927), *South Pole* (1912), and *Northwest Passage* (1908).

Anacreon *(ȧ năk rē ŏn)* c563–c478 B.C. Greek lyric poet. *b.* Teos, Asia Minor. Composed flowery and graceful poems in praise of the muses, wine, and love at courts of Polycrates of Samos and Hipparchus of Athens. His verse form was later widely imitated and called Anacreontic.

Anaxagoras *(ăn ăk săg ō răs)* c500–428 B.C. Greek philosopher. *b.* Clazomenae, Ionia. Taught in Athens (c462-432) until charged with impiety and exiled; teacher of Pericles, Thucydides, and Euripides; introduced the atomic theory which held that all matter existed in the form of atoms or seeds and that order was produced out of chaos by intelligence or nous; also taught that men and animals were born of moist clay and that heavenly bodies were pieces of the earth which broke away.

Anaximander *(ă năk sĭ măn dėr)* 611–547 B.C. Greek philosopher and mathematician. *b.* Miletus. Pupil of Thales; taught that the primary principle is an eternal and indeterminate substance from which all things arise and to which all things return, that perpetual motion creates opposites and reconciles them in a continuing cycle; also said to have discovered the obliquity of the ecliptic, the sundial, and the gnomon, and to have invented cartography.

Anaximenes *(ăn ăk sĭm ē nēz) fl.* 6th century B.C. Greek philosopher. *b.* Miletus. Disciple of Anaximander; held that the first principle is air, and all things are derived from its expansion and contraction.

Anchieta *(ăN shē â tə),* **José de** 1533–97. Portuguese Jesuit missionary. *b.* Canary Islands. Sent to Brazil (1553), where he founded a school for the conversion of Indians. Author of the first grammar of a native language (1595) and the earliest poems and plays in Brazilian literature; called Apostle of Brazil.

Andersen *(ăn dər sən),* **Hans Christian** 1805–75. Danish writer. *b.* Odense. Early poverty redeemed by talent for writing, which brought him to the notice of rich patrons, such as King Frederick VI; published his earliest volume of verse in 1830, followed by *Travelling Sketches* (1833), *The Improvisatore* (1835), *O.T.* (1836), and *Only a Fiddler* (1837); his fame rests on his many series of fairy tales, of which the first volume was published (1872) as *Eventyr.*

Anderson *(ăn dər sən),* **Carl David** 1905–. American physicist. *b.* New York, N.Y. Co-winner of the Nobel Prize for physics (with Victor Franz Hess) for discovery of positron (1936).

Anderson, Marian 1902–. American concert contralto. *b.* Philadelphia, Pa. Began career as a singer (1925); notable in operatic arias and Negro spirituals; awarded the Spingarn medal (1935).

Anderson, Maxwell 1888–1959. American playwright. *b.* Atlantic, Pa. Wrote historical and tragic dramas, some of which are in free-form blank verse; works include *What Price Glory* (1924), *Elizabeth the Queen* (1930), *Mary of Scotland* (1933), *Valley Forge* (1934), *High Tor* (1936), *Key Largo* (1939), *Anne of the Thousand Days* (1948), and *The Bad Seed* (1955); awarded Pulitzer Prize for *Both Your Houses* (1933).

Anderson, Sherwood 1876–1941. American poet and writer. *b.* Camden, Ohio. Began as a paint factory manager in Elyria, Ohio, later an advertising copywriter in Chicago; published first novel, *Windy McPherson's Son* (1916); and received national recognition with *Winesburg, Ohio* (1919); other works include *Mid-American Chants* (1918), *Many Marriages* (1922), *Dark Laughter* (1925), *Beyond Desire* (1933), *Home Town* (1940), and *Sherwood Anderson's Memoirs* (1942).

Andreev *(ŭn dryā yĕf),* **Leonid Nicolaevich** also ANDREYEV. 1871–1919. Russian novelist and playwright. *b.* Orel. Published first short story *They Lived* (1899); won friendship of Maxim Gorki; opposed Bolshevik government and forced to flee to Finland; died in poverty. Works include *The Red Laugh* (1904), *The Seven Who Were Hanged* (1909), *Anathema* (1909), *Silence and Other Stories* (1910), *He Who Gets Slapped* (1916) and *S.O.S.* (1919).

Andrew *(ăn drōō),* **Saint** (New Testament) One of the twelve apostles of Jesus and brother of Simon Peter; suffered martyrdom by crucifixion on an X-shaped cross which is named after him; patron saint of Scotland and Russia. Feast day: Nov. 30.

Andrewes *(ăn drōōz),* **Lancelot** 1555–1626. English scholar and prelate. *b.* Barking. Dean of Westminster (1601); bishop of Chichester (1605); bishop of Ely (1609); bishop of Winchester (1618); chaplain to Elizabeth I, James I, and Charles I; one of the translators of the Authorized Version of the Bible. Author of *Tortura Torti* (1609) and *Manual of Private Devotions.*

Andrews *(ăn drōōz),* **Roy Chapman** 1884–1960. American naturalist and writer. *b.* Beloit, Wis. Took part in or headed expeditions to Alaska (1908), Borneo (1909),

Korea (1911), and Central Asia (1914–30); discovered remains of *Baluchitherium*, the largest land mammal known to have existed; director of American Museum of Natural History (1935–41). Author of *Across Mongolian Plains* (1921), *On the Trail of Ancient Man* (1926), *The New Conquest of Central Asia* (1932), *Ends of Earth* (1929), *Meet Your Ancestors* (1945), and *Heart of Asia* (1951).

Andros *(ăn drəs),* **Sir Edmund** 1637–1714. British colonial governor in America. *b.* Guernsey Island. Governor of New York (1674), Dominion of New England (1686–89), and Virginia (1692–97); antagonized the colonists, who revolted and imprisoned him (1689), but later acquitted of all charges.

Anfinsen *(ăn fĭn sən),* **Christian Boehmer** 1916–. American biochemist. *b.* Monessen, Pa. Co-winner of the Nobel Prize for chemistry (1972) with Stanford Moore and William Stein.

Angela Merici *(än jā lä mā rē chē),* **Saint** 1474–1540. Italian religious. *b.* Desenzano del Garda. Founded Ursuline order of Roman Catholic nuns (1535); canonized (1807).

Angell *(ān jəl),* **Sir Norman** original name: RALPH NORMAN ANGELL LANE. 1872–1967. English pacifist and writer. *b.* Holbeach. Rancher, prospector, and journalist in U.S. until 1898; Labor member of Parliament (1929–31); awarded Nobel Peace Prize (1933). Author of *The Great Illusion* (1910), *America's Dilemma* (1940), and *After All* (1952).

Ångström *(ông strəm),* **Anders Jonas** 1814–74. Swedish physicist and pioneer spectroscopist. *b.* Lödgö. Professor of physics at University of Uppsala from 1858; keeper of Uppsala Observatory, and secretary to Royal Society (from 1867); demonstrated the presence of hydrogen in sun's atmosphere (1862); mapped the solar spectrum (1869); discovered the Ångstrom line in the spectrum of aurora borealis (1867); published *Optiska Undersökningar,* which laid the foundations of spectroscopy; the Ångstrom unit, used in the measurement of light wavelength, is named after him.

Animuccia *(ä nē mo͞ot chä),* **Giovanni** also called FATHER OF THE ORATORIO. 1500–1571. Italian composer of sacred music. *b.* Florence. Maestro di cappella (choirmaster) at the Vatican from 1555; composed *Laudi Spirituali.*

Anna Ivanovna *(ȧn nŭ ĭ vȧ nộv nŭ)* 1693–1740. Empress of Russia (1730–40). Daughter of Ivan V; married (1710) Frederick William, the Duke of Courland; elected to the throne by Supreme Council (1730), but decimated the Council and declared herself autocrat; surrounded herself with German favorites of whom her paramour Biron was the leader; conducted campaign against Turks, gaining Azov by the Treaty of Belgrade (1739); gained ascendancy over Poland through intervention in the War of Polish Succession (1733–35).

Anne *(ăn)* 1665–1714. Queen of Great Britain and Ireland (1702–14). *b.* London. Daughter of James II; married (1683) George, Prince of Denmark; dominated by the Duke and Duchess of Marlborough and later Abigail Masham; principal events of reign were union of England and Scotland and War of the Spanish Succession; name associated with a graceful style of furniture and the neoclassic Augustan Age of English literature.

Anouilh *(ȧ noo ē)*, **Jean** 1910–. French dramatist. *b.* Bordeaux. Author of *Le Voyageur Sans Bagage* (1938), *Le Bal des Valeurs* (1938), *La Sauvage* (1938), *Eurydice* (1942), *Antigone* (1946), *Médée* (1946), *L'Invitation au Château* (1948), *Becket* (1961), and *Poor Bitos* (1963).

Anquetil-Duperron *(äNk tēl dü pĕ rôN)*, **Abraham Hyacinthe** 1731–1805. French orientalist. *b.* Paris. Translator of the *Zend-Avesta* (1771) and the *Upanishads* (1778).

Anschar *(ăns kär)*, **Saint** also ANSCHARIUS, ANSGAR, ANSGARIUS, ANSKAR; called APOSTLE OF THE NORTH. 801–65. Frankish Benedictine missionary to Denmark, Sweden, and Germany. *b.* near Amiens, France. First bishop of Hamburg-Bremen (857).

Anselm *(ăn sĕlm)*, **Saint** 1033–1109. Archbishop of Canterbury and scholastic philosopher. *b.* Aosta, Italy. Became abbot of Bec in Normandy (1078); appointed archbishop of Canterbury (1093); a long struggle with William Rufus and Henry I over right of investiture led to two periods of exile, but compromise was reached (1107). Author of *Monologion, Proslogion, Cur Deus Homo, Meditations,* and *Letters;* canonized (1494). Feast day: Apr. 21.

Anson *(ăn sən)*, **George** 1697–1762. English admiral. *b.* Shugborough Park. Commander of a squadron of six ships sent to attack Spanish territories on the Pacific coast of South America (1740); fleet reduced by storms to one ship, but captured Spanish treasure ship *Nuestra Señora de Covadonga* with booty of £500,000 (1743); circumnavigated the world (1740–44); defeated French fleet off Cape Finisterre; as first lord of the admiralty (1751–56, 1757–1762) reorganized the navy; created admiral of the fleet (1761).

Antalcidas *(ăn tăl sĭ dăs)* *fl.* 4th century B.C. Spartan commander. Defeated Athenian fleet near the Hellespont with Persian king Artaxerxes II; imposed the Peace of Antalcidas (386), causing all of Asia Minor including Cyprus and Clazomenae to become Persian territories, while all but three Greek city-states became independent.

Antheil *(ăn tīl)*, **George** 1900–1959. American composer and pianist. *b.* Trenton, N.J. Pupil of Ernest Bloch and Constantin von Sternberg; gained attention in the musical world with his *Ballet Mécanique* which used mechanical pianos and eccentric percussion instruments; other compositions include *Zingareska* (1922), *American Symphony* (1937), *Symphony No. 4* (1943), *Symphony No. 5* (1945), the operas *Transatlantic* (1929) and *Helen Retires* (1932), the ballet *Dreams* (1935), and musical scores for films *Once in a Blue Moon* and *The Scoundrel.* Author of *Bad Boy of Music* (1945).

Anthemius *(ăn thē mĭ ŭs)* **of Tralles** *(trăl ēz)* *fl.* 6th century. Greek architect. *b.* Tralles, Lydia. Architect of Church of Saint Sophia in Constantinople (532–37).

Anthony *(ăn thō nĭ),* **Saint** also ANTONY, ANTHONY THE GREAT, ANTHONY OF THEBES. c251–c350. Egyptian hermit and founder of Christian monasticism. *b.* Coma. Withdrew into desert and spent 20 years in ascetic exercises; gathered disciples and established first monastery in Christian history at Fayum (c305); emerged from seclusion only twice, to encourage martyrs (311) and to attack the Arians; life and holy deeds recorded by Saint Athanasius. Feast day: Jan. 17.

Anthony, Susan Brownell 1820–1926. American women's suffrage leader. *b.* Adams, Mass. Organizer and president, National (later American) Woman Suffrage Association (1892–1900); organized the International Council of Women (1888) and the International Woman Suffrage Alliance (1904); active in movements for temperance, abolition of slavery, and coeducation; elected to American Hall of Fame (1950); coauthor of *History of Woman Suffrage* (6 vols., 1881–1900).

Anthony of Padua *(păd ū ȧ),* **Saint** 1195–1231. Franciscan friar and theologian. *b.* Lisbon, Portugal. Taught at Montpellier, Toulouse, and Padua; according to legend, preached to a school of fish when men refused to hear him; claimed a vision in which he embraced the infant Christ; canonized by Pope Gregory IX (1232). Feast day: June 13.

Antigonus I *(ăn tĭg ō nŭs)* also called ANTIGONUS CYCLOPS or MONOPHTHALMOS. c382–301 B.C. King of Macedonia (306–301) B.C. General under Alexander the Great; received provinces of Phrygia Major, Lycia, and Pamphylia; attempted to become master of Asia Minor and Syria through incessant wars; assumed title King (306); defeated and slain at Ipsus (301) by a coalition including Seleucus and Lysimachus.

Antiochus I *(ăn tī ō kŭs)* also called ANTIOCHUS SOTER (the Savior). 324–261 B.C. Seleucid king of Syria (280–261 B.C.). Son of Seleucus I Nicator; victorious over Gauls in Asia Minor (275) and gained his surname; waged wars with Ptolemy II of Egypt and Eumenes I of Pergamum; killed in battle.

Antiochus II also called ANTIOCHUS THEOS (the Divine). 286–247 B.C.). Seleucid King of Syria (261–247 B.C.). Son of Antiochus I; gained his surname by expelling the tyrant Timarchus from Miletus; waged ruinous war with Ptolemy II of Egypt; lost Bactria to Diodotus and Parthia to Arsacids.

Antiochus III also called ANTIOCHUS THE GREAT. 241–187 B.C. Seleucid king of Syria (223–187 B.C.). Son of Seleucus II; subdued rebellious governors of Medea (220), Persia (220), and Asia Minor (215–213); recovered Armenia (212); made peace with Ptolemy Epiphanes, to whom he betrothed his daughter Cleopatra, giving as dowry the provinces of Coele-Syria and Palestine won at Battle of Paneas (198); conquered Thracian Chersonese from Macedonia (196); gave asylum to Hannibal (195); warred with Romans (192–189); defeated successively at Thermopylae (191), Magnesia (190), Chios (191), and Myonnesus (190); purchased peace by giving up Asia Minor and paying tribute.

Antiochus IV also called ANTIOCHUS EPIPHANUS (the Illustrious). *d.*

163 B.C. Seleucid king of Syria (175–163 B.C.). Son of Antiochus III. Waged successful war with Egypt and defeated Ptolemy VI and VII (171–168); reconquered Armenia; declared Judaism illegal (168); took Jerusalem by storm and desecrated the Temple (170); provoked Jewish revolt under Mattathias, father of the Maccabees (167).

Antipater *(ăn tĭp ə tər)* 398–319 B.C. Macedonian ruler. Appointed regent of Macedonia during Alexander the Great's expedition to the east (334); suppressed revolt in Sparta under Agis III by victory at Megalopolis (331); became joint ruler of Macedonia with Craterus on the death of Alexander.

Antipater also called ANTIPATER THE IDUMAEAN. *d.* 43 B.C. Procurator of Judea (47–43 B.C.). Father of Herod the Great; ally of Pompey and Caesar.

Antiphanes *(ăn tĭf ə nēz)* c408–c334 B.C. Greek comic poet and playwright. Settled in Athens (387); author of over 200 plays.

Antisthenes *(ăn tĭs thə nēz)* c444–371 B.C. Athenian philosopher. Founder of Cynic school; disciple of Gorgias and Socrates.

Antoninus *(ăn tō nī nŭs)*, **Saint** real name: ANTONIO PIEROZZI; also ANTONIO DE' FORCIGLIONI. 1389–1459. Italian Dominican friar. *b.* Florence. Participated in Council of Florence (1439); archbishop of Florence (1446); canonized by Pope Adrian VI (1523). Author of *Summa Theologica* (1477), *Summa Confessionalis*, and *Summa Historialis*.

Antoninus Pius *(pī ŭs)* full name: TITUS AURELIUS FULVUS BOIONIUS ARRIUS. 86–161. Emperor of Rome (138–61). *b.* Lanuvium, Italy. Consul (120); adopted by Hadrian as heir and successor (138); reign remarkable for internal peace and prosperity and encouragement of art and learning.

Antony *(ăn tō nĭ)*, **Mark** Latin name: MARCUS ANTONIUS. c83–30 B.C. Roman triumvir. Member of an old patrician family; protégé of Julius Caesar; became successively quaestor, augur, and tribune of the plebs (50); expelled (47) from the curia and fled to Caesar in Gaul, who made this a pretext for civil war; commanded Caesar's army at Pharsalus (48); after Caesar's death (44), roused the populace against his assassins; formed second triumvirate with Lepidus and Octavian (43); with Octavian, defeated Republican army at Philippi (42); in division of Roman world, took the East (40–36); from 40 B.C., lived chiefly at Alexandria with Cleopatra; defeated by the Parthians (36); deprived of power by the Roman Senate (32); defeated by Octavian at Actium (31); fled to Egypt and committed suicide (30).

Anwari *(ăn vă rē)* full name: AUAD-UD-DIN ALI ANWARI. *fl.* 12th century. Persian poet. *b.* Khurasan. Author of *Divan*.

Anza *(ăn sä)*, **Juan Bautista de** 1735–88. Spanish explorer. *b.* Fronteras, Mexico. Led expedition to Alta California (1775–76); founded San Francisco; governor of New Mexico (1777); colonies founded by him on the Colorado River wiped out by Yuma Indians (1781).

Apelles *(ȧ pĕl ēz)* *fl.* 4th century B.C. Greek painter. *b.* Ionia. Considered greatest painter of the ancient world; celebrated for portraits of Alexander, Archelaus, Clitus, and Antigonus; painted Aphrodite rising from the sea for the temple of Aesculapius at Cos; none of the paintings are extant.

Apion *(ā pĭ ŏn)* *fl.* 1st century. Greek grammarian. *b.* Libya. Headed deputation sent by citizens of Alexandria to complain against the Jews to Emperor Caligula; wrote diatribes against Jews refuted by Josephus in *Contra Apioneum;* wrote tale of Androcles and the lion and commentary on Homer.

Apollinaire *(à pô lē nâr),* **Guillaume** full name: GUILLAUME APOLLINAIRE DE KOSTROWITSKY. 1880–1918. French surrealist poet. *b.* Rome, Italy. Settled in Paris; wrote avant-garde poems, novels, and plays, such as *Le Poète Assassiné* (1916), *La Femme Assise* (1920), *Les Mamelles de Tirésias* (1917), *Couleur du Temps* (1920), *Alcools* (1913), and *Calligrammes* (1918); writings characterized by bizarre fantasies.

Apollinaris *(à pŏl ĭ nâr ĭs)* **of Laodicea** *(lā ŏd ĭ sē à)* *d.* 390. Bishop of Laodicea. With his father, rewrote parts of the Bible in the form of Greek classics to circumvent Emperor Julian's prohibition on teaching Greek literature; opposed Arianism; founder of Apollinarianism, a doctrine denying the human nature of Christ; condemned as a heresiarch by Council of Constantinople (381).

Apollonius *(ăp ŏ lō nĭ ŭs)* **of Tyana** *(tī à nà)* *fl.* 1st century. Greek neo-Pythagorean philosopher. *b.* Tyana, Asia Minor. Traveled in Babylon, Persia, and India; gained knowledge of magic and the occult; set up school at Ephesus; gained fame as a miracle-worker and was patronized by Emperor Vespasian.

Appert *(à pâr),* **François** 1750–1841. French chef. Devised process for preserving food by heating and hermetically sealing in cans. Author of *Art of Preserving Animal and Vegetable Substances* (1811).

Appleseed, Johnny. *See* **Chapman, John**

Appleton *(ăp əl tən),* **Sir Edward Victor** 1892–1965. English physicist. *b.* Bradford. Awarded Nobel Prize in physics (1947) for the discovery of a layer of electrically charged particles in the upper atmosphere (Appleton layer); professor of natural philosophy at Cambridge (1936–39); secretary of Department of Scientific and Industrial Research (1939–49); president of British Association (1953).

Apraksin *(ŭ prà ksĭn),* **Count Feodor Matveyevich** 1671–1728. Founder of Russian navy. Entered service of Czar Fyodor III; favorite of Peter the Great; governor of Archangel (1692); chief of the admiralty (1700–1706); defeated Swedish forces at Poltava (1709); captured Viborg (1710), Helsingfors, and Borgo (1713); secured Baltic Provinces and Russia by the Treaty of Nystad (1721).

Apuleius *(ăp ū lē yŭs),* **Lucius** *fl.* 2nd century. Roman satirist. *b.* Madaura, Nubia. Best known for the satirical work *The Golden Ass* or *Metamorphoses;* also wrote *De Magia,* or *Apologia,* on magic and alchemy.

Aquinas *(à kwī năs),* **Saint Thomas** also called ANGELIC DOCTOR, FATHER OF MORAL PHILOSOPHY, PRINCE OF SCHOLASTICS. 1225–74. Italian theologian. *b.* Rocca Secca.

Entered Dominican order (1243); pupil of Albertus Magnus at Paris (1245–48) and Cologne (1248); taught successively at Cologne (to 1252), Paris (1252–56, 1268–72), and Rome (1259–68); systematized the theology accepted as official by the Catholic Church (1879); founded philosophical system known as Thomism; canonized by Pope John XXII (1323); proclaimed doctor of the church (1567) and patron of Catholic schools (1880). Author of *Summa Theologica,* considered one of the most brilliant philosophical works of all time, and *Mass for Corpus Christi,* containing some of the finest Christian hymns; other works include *Summa de Veritate Catholicae Fidei Contra Gentiles, Questiones Disputatae, Quodlibeta, Catena Aurea,* and *Opuscula Theologica.*

Arago *(ȧ ră gō),* **François** full name: Dominique François Jean Arago. 1786–1853. French scientist. *b.* Estagel. Appointed director of Paris Observatory (1830); made important contributions to electromagnetism and optics; formulated law of polarization; discovered magnetic property of rotation; investigated and supported Jean Fresnel's undulatory theory of light; had prominent role in July Revolution of 1830; minister of war and marine in the provisional government (1848); abolished slavery in French colonies; opposed Louis Napoleon and refused to take oath of allegiance to him (1851).

Arany *(ô rən y),* **János** 1817–82. Hungarian poet. *b.* Nagyszalonta. Secretary of Hungarian Academy (1865–79); regarded as one of the greatest Hungarian poets. Author of the epic *Toldi* trilogy, *King Buda's Death, The Siege of Murány,* and translations of Aristophanes and Shakespeare.

Aratus *(ȧ rā tŭs)* **of Soli** *(sō lī)* c315–c245 B.C. Greek poet. *b.* Soli, Cilicia, Asia Minor. Court poet of Antigonus II of Macedonia and Antiochus I of Syria; *Phenomena,* a didactic poem on astronomy and weather signs in 1154 verses, proved immensely popular with the Romans; his invocation to Zeus was quoted by St. Paul in his speech on Mars' Hill at Athens.

Arbuthnot *(är bŭth nŏt),* **John** 1667–1735. Scottish wit. *b.* Arbuthnot. Physician to Queen Anne; joined Jonathan Swift, Alexander Pope, John Gay, and Thomas Parnell to form the Scriblerus Club (1713). Author of *The History of John Bull* (1712) and *The Memoirs of Martinus Scriblerus,* published in Pope's *Works* (1741), both satires of contemporary pedantry and politics.

Arcadius *(ä kā dĭ ŭs)* c377–408. First emperor of the Eastern Roman Empire of Byzantium. *b.* Spain. Son of Emperor Theodosius; received eastern half of the empire as his share, while the western half fell to his brother Honorius; left the actual governing to Queen Eudoxia, prefects Rufinus and Anthemius, and the eunuch Eutropius.

Archilochus *(ăr kĭl ŏ kŭs)* c714–c676 B.C. Greek lyric poet. *b.* Paros, Cyclades. Regarded as inventor of iambic and trochaic meters and the poetic form called epode; author of hymns, elegies, and lampoons.

Archimedes *(ăr kĭ mē dēz)* c287–

212 B.C. Greek mathematician and engineer. *b.* Syracuse, Sicily. Important contributions to mechanics and hydrostatics; discovered equal relationship of the weight of a body immersed in fluid and the weight of fluid displaced (the Archimedean principle); invented the endless screw and the Archimedes screw; devised the lever and various engines of war, used against the Romans during the siege of Syracuse (214–212 B.C.).

Archipenko *(ŭr kyĭ pyān kô),* **Aleksandr Porfirievich** 1887–1964. American sculptor. *b.* Kiev, Russia. Emigrated to U.S. (1924); leader of modern abstract sculpture; noted for use of unusual materials.

Archytas *(är kī tăs) fl.* 400–350 B.C. Greek general, mathematician and Pythagorean philosopher. *b.* Tarentum, Italy. Contributed to study of acoustics and theory of proportion; doubled the cube; invented the pulley; first to distinguish harmonic progression.

Ardashir I *(är dȧ shĭr)* Old Persian form: ARTAXERXES. Sassanid king of Persia (c226–241). Conquered Kerman and Susiana; defeated and killed Ardavan, the last Parthian emperor (226); founded Sassanian Empire with the title King of Kings; established capital at Ctesiphon; proclaimed Zoroastrianism as the official religion.

Arenski *(ŭ ryān skû ĭ),* **Anton Stepanovich** 1861–1906. Russian composer. *b.* Novgorod. Student of Rimsky-Korsakov; composer of church music, two symphonies, and three operas: *A Dream on the Volga* (1892), *Raphael* (1894), and *Nal and Damayanti* (1899).

Aretino *(ä rā tē nō),* **Pietro** 1492–1556. Italian satirist. *b.* Arezzo. Served as hired wit at court of Leo X, Clement VII, Giovanni de'Medici, Francis I, and Charles V, gained nickname Scourge of Princes from his attacks on the rich and powerful; finally settled in Venice, where his friends included Titian. Works included *Ragionamenti* (1532–34), *La Cortegiana* (1534), *Orazia* (1546), and *La Talenta* (1550).

Argand *(är gȧN),* **Aimé** 1755–1803. Swiss inventor. *b.* Geneva. Invented the Argand lamp with a circular wick that admits a current of air in the center.

Ariosto *(ä rē ôs tō),* **Ludovico** also LODOVICO. 1474–1533. Italian poet. *b.* Reggio. Entered service of Cardinal Ippolito d'Este (1503); began work on *Orlando Furioso,* a Roland epic considered one of the masterpieces of Renaissance literature and forming a continuation of Boiardo's *Orlando Innamorato;* left the cardinal for service to his brother Alfonse d'Este, Duke of Ferrara (1517); as governor of Garfagnana (1522) suppressed an insurrection of outlaws; retired to Ferrara (1525), where he composed his comedies and revised *Orlando.* Works include *La Cassaria* (1508), *Gli Suppositi* (1509), *Il Negromante* (1520), and *La Lena* (1529).

Aristarchus *(ăr ĭs tär kŭs)* **of Samos** *(sā mŏs)* c280–264 B.C. Greek astronomer. Member of the Alexandrian school; regarded as first to maintain that earth revolves around the sun and on its own axis; wrote a treatise on the sizes and distances from earth of the sun and moon.

Aristarchus of Samothrace *(săm ō*

thrās) also called CORYPHAEUS OF GRAMMARIANS. c217–c145 B.C. Greek grammarian and scholar. *b.* Samothrace. Successor to Aristophanes of Byzantium as librarian of the Alexandrian library; founder of school of philology known as Aristarcheans; editor of Homer, Hesiod, Pindar, Aeschylus, and Sophocles; chiefly known for arranging the Iliad and Odyssey in 24 books.

Aristides *(ăr ĭs tī dēz)* also ARISTEIDES, ARISTIDES THE JUST. c530–c468 B.C. Athenian statesman. *b.* Athens. One of 10 Greek generals at Marathon (490); elected chief archon of Athens (489–488); opposed naval policy of Themistocles and advocated reliance on the army; ostracized (c483); returned and took part in the Battle of Salamis (480-79); shared victory at Plataea with Pausanius (479); commanded Athenian squadron off Byzantium (c478); took active role in Delian Confederacy by assessing contributions of members; died in poverty.

Aristipus *(ăr ĭs tĭp ŭs)* c435–c386 B.C. Greek philosopher. *b.* Cyrene, Africa. Pupil of Socrates; taught philosophy at Athens and Aegina; founded Cyrenaic or Hedonistic school of philosophy, which held that pleasure is the only end of life.

Aristophanes *(ăr ĭs tŏf ȧ nēz)* c448–c380 B.C. Athenian dramatist. Regarded as the greatest Attic comic genius; said to have written 54 plays, of which 11 survive: *The Acharnians* (425), *The Knights* (424), *The Clouds* (423), *The Wasps* (422), *The Peace* (421), *The Birds* (414), *Lysistrata* (411), *The Thesmophoriazusae* (411), *The Frogs* (405), *The Ecclesiazusae* (393), and *Plutus* (388). Works characterized by imagination, wit, and satire; as a political and social critic, attacked intellectual decadence, political corruption, and newfangled ideas.

Aristophanes of Byzantium *(bĭ zăn shĭ ŭm)* c257–c180 B.C. Greek philologist and critic. *b.* Byzantium. Pupil of Zenodotus and Callimachus; librarian of the Alexandria Museum; editor of Homer, Hesiod, Alcaeus, Anacreon, Pindar, Plato, and other Greeks; as a lexicographer, compiled word lists, introduced diacritical marks, systematized accentuation, and punctuation of Greek; regarded as the greatest philologist of antiquity.

Aristotle *(ăr ĭs tŏtl)* also called THE STAGIRITE. 384-322 B.C. Greek philosopher. *b.* Stagira. Studied under Plato at Academy at Athens (367–347); carried on zoological studies at Mytilene (345–343); tutor of Alexander the Great (345-335); returned to Athens and opened Lyceum or Peripatetic School (335–322); forced to leave Athens by Anti-Macedonians; died in Chalcis (322). Made contributions to every department of knowledge; regarded as the founder of logic and comparative anatomy; undertook first systematic study of meteorology, chemistry, evolution, psychology, geometry, and constitutional law; outlined scientific classification of knowledge; works divided into six classes: (1) on logic, including the two books of *Organon;* (2) on natural science, including *Physics, On the Heavens, On Beginning and Perishing, Parts of Animals, Generation, On the Soul,* and *On Plants*; (3) on philosophy, including *Metaphysics*; (4)

on ethics, including Nicomachean Ethics and *Politics*; (5) on aesthetics, including *Rhetoric* and *Poetics*; and (6) miscellaneous writings, including *Problems* and *Constitution of Athens;* books transmitted to Europe in Arabic translations dominated Western thought and science until the 18th century.

Arius *(ȧ rī ŭs)* c256–336. Greek heresiarch. *b.* Alexandria, Egypt. Founder of Arianism, which maintained that Christ was only a created and finite being, a combination of divine Logos and human body subordinate to God; excommunicated and deposed by the Synod of Alexandria (321); reinstated and absolved at Council of Bithynia (323); condemned and anathematized at Council of Nicaea (325); banished to Illyria; recalled (336), but died before being readmitted to the sacraments.

Arkwright *(ärk rīt),* **Sir Richard** 1732–92. English inventor and pioneer of the Industrial Revolution. *b.* Preston. Invented the cotton-spinning frame (1769); set up first mill driven by horses (1768); with Jedidiah Strutt established stocking factory at Cromford using water power (1771); used steam engine at Nottingham (1790); granted numerous patents for improvements in machinery (1775).

Arlen *(är lĕn),* **Michael** original name: DIKRAN KOUYOUMDJIAN. 1895–1956. British-Armenian novelist. *b.* Roustchouk, Bulgaria. Author of *The Green Hat* (1924), *Man's Mortality* (1933), *The Crooked Coronet* (1937), and *The Flying Dutchman* (1939).

Arminius *(är mĭn ĭ ŭs)* also ARMIN, HERMANN. 17 B.C.–A.D. 21. German chieftain and hero. Chief of Cherusci tribe; served in Roman legions (1-6); returned home and led a Cherusci revolt against Varus; in a three-day battle in Teutoburg Forest, annihilated the entire Roman army; pushed back Roman frontier from the Elbe to the Rhine; defeated by Germanicus Caesar in two campaigns (15–16) but managed to maintain independence; overthrew Marbo, head of the Marcomanni.

Arminius, Jacobus real name: JACOB HARMENSEN or HERMANSZ. 1560–1609. Dutch theologian. *b.* Oudewater. Ordained (1588); professor of theology at Leiden (1603); founder of branch of Protestant theology known as Arminianism, the basis of Remonstrant and Laudian sects and Wesleyan, Baptist, Methodist, and Congregationalist churches; opposed Calvinist doctrine of predestination and taught that God bestows universal redemption on all who repent of their sins and believe in Jesus Christ.

Armour *(är mər),* **Philip Danforth** 1832–1901. American industrialist. *b.* Stockbridge, N.Y. With brother Herman Ossian, organized Armour & Company, meatpackers (1870); as its president, introduced refrigeration, methods of waste-recycling, and canned meats; founded Armour Institute of Technology (1893).

Armstrong *(ärm strông),* **Daniel Louis** known as LOUIS ARMSTRONG; called SATCHMO. 1900–1971. American jazz musician. *b.* New Orleans, La. Exponent of Dixieland style of jazz; composed and sang jazz versions of popular songs. Author of *My Life in New Orleans.*

Armstrong, Neil Alden 1930–. American astronaut. *b.* Wapakoneta, Ohio. Chosen as an astronaut (1962); commanded Gemini VIII (1966); with Edwin Aldrin and Michael Collins, commanded successful moon-landing expedition of Apollo XI; first man to set foot on an extraterrestrial body (1969).

Armstrong, William George title: BARON ARMSTRONG OF CRAGSIDE. 1810–1900. English inventor. *b.* Newcastle. Inventor of improved hydraulic engine (1840); an apparatus for producing electricity from steam (1842); hydraulic crane (1845); the Armstrong gun with a barrel built of successive wrought-iron coils and a new design for breech-loading and rifling (1855); a 6-inch breech-loading gun with a cylinder wound with high tension wire; founded Elswick Engineering Works (1847), which later merged with Vickers' Sons and Company to form Vickers Armstrongs, Ltd. (1927).

Arnold *(är nəld),* **Benedict** 1741–1801. American Revolutionary War army officer and turncoat. *b.* Norwich, Conn. Aided in capture of Fort Ticonderoga (1775); made brigadier general (1775) for gallantry at the siege of Quebec; fought with distinction at Battles of Ridgefield and Saratoga; promoted to major general (1777); placed in command of Philadelphia (1778); court-martialed and reprimanded for private use of militia (1779); began treasonable negotiations with Sir Henry Clinton, British commander in chief in North America; obtained command of West Point (1880); arranged to betray West Point to the British; fled to British lines when plot was discovered; given command in the Royal Army and led raids on Virginia (1780) and Connecticut (1781); settled in England after the war and spent last years in obscurity and poverty.

Arnold, Sir Edwin 1832–1904. English poet. *b.* Gravesend. Principal of Deccan College, Poona, India (1856–61); chief editor of *Daily Telegraph* (1873–1904). Best known as author of *Light of Asia,* an epic poem on the life of Buddha (1853); other works include *Poems Narrative and Lyrical* (1853), *The Light of the World* (1891), and *East and West* (1896).

Arnold, Matthew 1822–88. English poet and critic. *b.* Laleham. Son of Thomas Arnold; lay inspector of schools (1851–83) and professor of poetry at Oxford (1857–67). Fame as a critic rests on *On Translating Homer* (1861), *On the Study of Celtic Literature* (1867), *Essays in Criticism* (1865, 1888), *Culture and Anarchy* (1869), and *Literature and Dogma* (1873); poetical works include *Empedocles on Etna and Other Poems* (1853), and *New Poems* (1867); theological studies include *St. Paul and Protestantism* (1870) and *Last Essays on Church and Religion* (1877).

Arnold, Thomas 1795–1842. English scholar and educator. *b.* East Cowes, Isle of Wight. Took holy orders (1818); as headmaster of Rugby school (1828–42) provided strong impetus to development of modern public school system; appointed Regius Professor of History at Oxford (1841). Author of six volumes of sermons, *History of Rome* (3 vols., 1838–43), and *Lectures on Modern History* (1842).

Arnold of Brescia *(brā shä)* 1100–1155. Italian religious reformer. *b.* Brescia. Student of Abelard in Paris; denounced corruption of clergy and aroused the people of Brescia against their bishop; banished from Italy by Innocent II (1139); condemned and reprimanded by Council of Sens (1140); took refuge in Zurich (1140–43); assumed leadership of republican faction in Rome and drove Pope Eugene into exile; struggled for ten years for government reform on the model of the ancient republic; power broken by Pope Adrian IV who, with the support of Frederick I Barbarossa, laid an interdict on Rome and drove out the republicans; arrested and hanged (1155).

Arnoldson *(ȧr nəld sôn),* **Klas Pontus** 1844–1916. Swedish pacifist. *b.* Gotebörg. Member of Riksdag (1882–87); advocate of permanent neutrality; shared Nobel Peace Prize (1908) with Fredrik Bajer. Author of *Hope of the Centuries, a Book on World Peace* (1900).

Arp *(ärp),* **Jean** also HANS. 1887–1966. French artist. *b.* Strasbourg. One of the founders of the Dada movement in Zurich (1916); best known for organic abstract sculptures based on natural forms in wood, metal, and stone.

Árpád *(är päd)* *d.* 907. National hero of Hungary. Magyar chief and founder of Árpád dynasty; led Magyars into Hungary (c884).

Arrhenius *(ȧr rā nĭ əs),* **Svante August** 1859–1927. Swedish scientist. *b.* Wijk. Professor of physics at University of Stockholm (1895); director of the Nobel Institute for Physical Chemistry (from 1905); awarded Nobel Prize in chemistry for theory of electrolytic dissociation in conductivity of solutions (1903). Author of *Immunochemistry* (1907), *Worlds in the Making* (1908), *Quantitative Laws in Biological Chemistry* (1915), and *Destinies of Stars* (1918).

Arriaga *(ȧr ryȧ gȧ),* **Manuel José de** 1842–1917. Portuguese statesman. *b.* Horta, Azores. Rector of University of Coimbra; leader in revolution of 1910; elected first constitutional president of Portugal (1911–15); resigned presidency following coup d'état (1915).

Arrian *(ăr ĭ ăn),* **Flavius** also ARRIANUS. *fl.* 2nd century. Greek historian. *b.* Nicomedia, Asia Minor. Appointed prefect of Cappadocia (131–37); archon of Athens (147–48). Author of *Anabasis of Alexander, Indica, Periplus of the Euxine,* and editor of the *Encheiridion* and *Diatribai* of Epictetus.

Arrom, Cecilia Francisca Josefa de. *See* **Caballero, Fernán**

Arrow *(ăr ō),* **Kenneth Joseph** 1921–. American economist. *b.* New York, N.Y. Co-winner of Nobel Prize in economics with John Richard Hicks for theory of general economic equilibrium (1972).

Arsonval *(ȧr sôɴ vȧl),* **Jacques Arsène d'** 1851–1950. French physicist. *b.* Borie. Pioneer in electrotherapy; invented reflecting galvanometer (d'Arsonval galvanometer); investigated high-frequency oscillating current (d'Arsonval current); devised the d'Arsonval instrument for measuring direct current of electricity.

Arthur *(är thər)* *fl.* 6th century. Legendary British king. Central hero of the Arthurian cycle of romance; believed to have led the Christian Cymri against the pagan Saxons and won a great victory at the Mount of Badon (516); probably died at the Battle of Camlan (537).

Arthur, Chester Alan 1830–86. 21st president of the U.S. *b.* Fairfield, Vt. Republican vice-president (1880) and became president on Garfield's death; administration (1881–85) marked by modernization of navy and passage of Pendleton Civil Service Reform Bill (1883).

Asbury *(ăz bĕr ĭ)*, **Francis** 1745–1816. American Methodist Episcopal bishop. *b.* Handsworth, England. Appointed John Wesley's superintendent in America (1772); recalled to England by Wesley (1775) but disobeyed order; took active role in formation of American Methodist Episcopal Church (1779–84); consecrated superintendent (1784); assumed title Bishop (1785); held office until death (1816).

Asch *(äsh)*, **Sholem** also SHALOM or SHOLOM. 1880–1957. Yiddish writer. *b.* Kutno, Poland. Settled in U.S. (1914). Author of *The Mother* (1930), *The Three Cities* (1933), *The War Goes On* (1936), *Song of the Valley* (1939), *The Nazarene* (1939), *Children of Abraham* (1942), *The Apostle* (1943), *East River* (1946), *Mary* (1949), and *Moses* (1951).

Asclepiades *(ăs klē pī ă dēz)* **of Bithynia** *(bĭ thĭn ĭ ă)* *fl.* 1st century B.C. Greek physician. *b.* Prusa, Asia Minor. Settled in Rome; maintained that disease is caused by disorder of the corpuscles and recommended a system of therapy consisting of diet, exercise, bathing, and wine.

Ashurbanipal *(ä sho͞or bä nē päl)* also ASSURBANIPAL; Greek form: SARDANAPALUS; in Old Testament: ASENAPPAR. Sargonide king of Assyria (668–c626 B.C.). Son of Esarhaddon and grandson of Sennacherib, quelled revolt of brother Shamash-shum-ukin, viceroy of Babylonia; captured and destroyed Susa (646–640); defeated Cimmerians and Elamites; reign marked by prosperity and splendor, flourishing art and literature, and the collection of great cuneiform library at Ninevah.

Ashurnasirpal II *(ä sho͞or nä zĭr päl)* also ASSURNASIRPAL. King of Assyria (c884–c859 B.C.). Greatest of Assyrian conquerors whose victorious and bloody expeditions extended imperial dominions westward; rebuilt Calah as royal capital.

Asoka *(ȧ sō kȧ)* full name: ASOKAVARDHANA; also DEVANAMPIYA and PIYADARSHIN. *d.* 232 B.C. Indian ruler. Third emperor of the Maurya dynasty of Magadha (273–232); waged a bloody war with Kalinga (261) but was sickened by the violence; embraced Buddhism; devoted next 31 years to the propagation of Buddhism; sent Buddhist missionaries to all kingdoms of Asia; convoked Buddhist Council of Pataliputra; caused edicts to be inscribed on rocks and pillars throughout India.

Asquith *(ăs kwĭth)*, **Herbert Henry** title: EARL OF OXFORD AND ASQUITH. 1852–1928. British statesman. *b.* Morley. Entered Parliament (1886); home secretary (1892–95); chancellor of the exchequer (1905–1908); prime minister (1908–16); term marked by restriction of veto power of House of Lords, passage of Welsh Disestablishment Act, and declaration of war against Germany (1914); created earl (1925); resigned leadership of Liberal Party (1926). Author of *Memories and Reflections* (1928).

Assemani *(äs sā mä nē),* **Giuseppe Simoni** 1687–1768. Syrian Orientalist. *b.* Tripoli, Syria. Keeper of Vatican library; obtained several hundred valuable manuscripts on two journeys to Middle East. Author of *Bibliotheca Orientalis Clementino-Vaticana* (1719–28).

Asser *(äs ər),* **Tobias Michael Carel** 1838–1913. Dutch jurist. *b.* Amsterdam. Professor of law (from 1876) at University of Amsterdam; co-winner (1911) of Nobel Peace Prize (with A.H. Fried). Author of *La Codification du Droit International Privé* (1901) and *Arbitrage International Entre les États-Unis d'Amérique et la Russie* (1902).

Astaire *(ȧ stâr),* **Fred** original name: FRED AUSTERLITZ. 1899–. American dancer and actor. *b.* Omaha, Neb. Made debut (1916) with sister Adele, his partner until 1932; starred in musical comedies with original tap-dance routines, such as *Gay Divorcee, Roberta, Top Hat,* and *Carefree.*

Aston *(ăs tən),* **Francis William** 1877–1945. English scientist. *b.* Birmingham. Known for work on isotopes and investigation of isotopic structure of elements; invented mass spectrograph; awarded the Nobel Prize in chemistry (1922); the Aston dark space in electronic discharges is named after him. Author of *Isotopes* (1922) and *Mass Spectra and Isotopes* (1933).

Astor *(ăs tər),* **John Jacob** 1763–1848. American magnate. *b.* Waldorf, Germany. Immigrated to U.S. (1784); entered fur trade (1787); incorporated American Fur Company (1808) and Pacific Fur Company (1810); monopolized fur trade in Great Lakes and Mississippi region with the South West Fur Company (1811); invested in Manhattan real estate; entered China trade (1815); withdrew from business (1834); left a fortune estimated at $20 million, of which half a million was a bequest to the Astor Library (now New York Public Library).

Asturias *(äs to͞o ryäs),* **Miguel Angel** 1899–1974. Guatemalan writer. Awarded Nobel Prize in literature (1967).

Atahualpa *(ăt ȧ wäl pä)* also ATABALIPA. 1502–33. Last Inca ruler of Peru. Seized kingdom on death of his father Huayna Capac (1525); captured by Spaniards under Pizarro (1532), to whom he offered a room full of gold in exchange for freedom; condemned to death and killed by strangulation (1533).

Athanasius *(ăth ȧ nā shĭ ŭs),* **Saint** also ATHANASIUS THE GREAT, FATHER OF ORTHODOXY, ATHANASIUS CONTRA MUNDUM. c296–373. Greek patriarch. *b.* Alexandria, Egypt. Took part in Council of Nicaea (325); chosen patriarch of Alexandria (326); became most notable defender of orthodoxy against Arianism; exiled five times (335, 340, 356, 362, 365). Author of *Defense Against the Arians, Discourses Against the Arians, History of the Arians,* and On *the Decrees of the Nicene Synod.*

Athelstan *(ăth əl stăn)* 889–940. King of West Saxons and Mercians (924–40). Grandson of Alfred; crowned (924); conquered Cornwall, Wales, and Northumbria and invaded Scotland (933 or 934); defeated combined army of Welsh, Scots, and Danes at Brunanburh (937).

Atherton *(ăth ər tən),* **Gertrude Franklin** *née* HORN. 1857–1948. American writer. *b.* San Francisco, Calif. Author of *The Californians* (1898), *The Conqueror* (1902), *Tower of Ivory* (1910), *Black Oxen* (1923), *The Sophisticates* (1931), *Golden Peacock* (1936), *The House of Lee* (1940), and *The Horn of Life* (1942); president of the American National Academy of Literature (1934).

Atkinson *(ăt kĭn sən),* **Sir Harry Albert** 1831–92. New Zealand statesman. *b.* Broxton, England. Immigrated to New Zealand (1853); served in wars against Maori tribesmen; entered New Zealand Parliament (1861); prime minister (1876–77, 1883–84, 1887–91); responsible for the abolition of provincial governments.

Attar *(ăt ər),* **Farid ud-din** also ATHAR; real name: MOHAMMED IBN-IBRAHIM. 1119–c1209. Persian poet and mystic. *b.* Nishapur, Iran. Author of over 40 poetical works dealing with Sufi philosophy, of which the most important are *Mantiq ut-Tair (The Language of Birds), Pandnamah (Book of Counsel),* and *Bulbul Namah (Book of the Nightingale).*

Atticus *(ăt ĭ kŭs),* **Titus Pomponius** 109–32 B.C. Roman Epicurean philosopher and bibliophile. *b.* Rome. Withdrew to Athens (85); returned to Rome (65) on invitation of Sulla; intimate friend of Cicero, Pompey, and Caesar; best known for editing and publishing collection of 396 epistles addressed to him by Cicero.

Attila *(ăt ĭ lȧ)* called THE SCOURGE OF GOD. C406–53. King of the Huns (433-53). Began career of conquest (445); extended sway over Germans and Slavs; overran and devastated all countries between Black Sea and the Mediterranean (447); defeated Emperor Theodosius II in three engagements and exacted tribute of 6,000 pounds of gold; invaded Gaul (451), but suffered defeat at Châlons-sur-Marne by combined armies of the Roman general Aëtius and the Visigoths Theodoric and Thorismond (451); invaded northern Italy, but retired without sacking Rome on plea of Pope Leo I (452); died on return to Pannonia (453).

Attlee *(ăt lē),* **Clement Richard** title: VISCOUNT PRESTWOOD. 1883–1967. British statesman. *b.* Putney. Entered parliament (1922); succeeded George Lansbury as leader of Labor party (1935); joined War Cabinet as lord privy seal (1940–42) and deputy prime minister (1942–45); prime minister (1945–51); took part in Potsdam Conference (1945); administration marked by nationalization of coal industry, civil aviation, cable and wireless services, railways, road transport, and steel; the introduction of national health service; and the granting of independence to India (1947) and Burma (1948); in foreign policy supported NATO and Western Alliance.

Auber *(ōbâr),* **Daniel François**

Esprit 1782–1871. French composer. *b.* Caen. Regarded as the founder of French grand opera. Works include *La Muette de Portici* (which signaled the Brussels uprising of 1830), *Fra Diavolo, Le Philtre, Le Dieu et la Bayadère, Les Diaments de la Couronne, La Bergère Châtelaine,* and *Le Domino Noir.*

Auchinleck *(ôkĭn lĕk),* **Sir Claude John Eyre** 1884–. British general. *b.* Aldershot. Began career in Egypt and Mesopotamia (1914–19); commanded Peshawar Brigade in North West Frontier Province, India (1933–36); commander in chief in India (1940–41; 1943); commander in chief in Middle East (1942); created field marshal (1946).

Auden *(ô dən),* **Wystan Hugh** known as W. H. AUDEN. 1907–73. Anglo-American poet. *b.* York, England. Member of group of radical poets which included Stephen Spender, C. Day Lewis, Christopher Isherwood, and Rex Warner; early works such as *Poems* (1930), *Spain* (1937), and *Journey to a War* (1939) reflect socialist sympathies; immigrated to U.S. (1939); converted from liberal-humanism to Anglican faith; appointed to chair of poetry at Oxford (1956). Other works include *The Orators* (1932), *The Dance of Death* (1933), *Look Stranger* (1936), *Another Time* (1940), *The Double Man* (1941), *For the Time Being* (1944), *Collected Poems* (1945), *The Age of Anxiety* (1947), *Nones* (1951), and *The Shield of Achilles* (1955); also collaborated with Christopher Isherwood on three plays and wrote libretto to *The Rake's Progress* (1951); works characterized by verbal dexterity and moral passion.

Audubon *(ô do͞o bŏn),* **John James** 1785–1851. American ornithologist. *b.* Cayes, Santo Domingo. Natural son of Jean Audubon and a Creole woman; sent to America (1804) to manage father's estate near Philadelphia; migrated westward to Louisville, Cincinnati, and elsewhere; began painting birds from life; sent to jail for debt and declared bankrupt (1819); voyaged down the Ohio and Mississippi (1820) adding to collection of bird illustrations; sailed to England (1826) and held successful exhibitions at Liverpool and Edinburgh. Published *Birds of America* (1827–39) in elephant folio consisting of 435 hand-colored copperplate engravings and *Ornithological Biography* (5 vols., 1831–39).

Augereau *(ōzh rō),* **Pierre François Charles** title: DUC DE CASTIGLIONE. 1757–1816. French general. *b.* Paris. Served with distinction in Italian campaign; took part as leader in coup d'état of 18 Fructidor; fought at Lodi, Jena, Eylau, and Leipzig; created marshal of the empire (1804) and duke (1808); survived fall of Napoleon and served Louis XVIII.

Augier *(ō zhyā),* **Guillaume Victor Émile** 1820–89. French dramatist. *b.* Valence. His *Théâtre Complet* (7 vols., 1890) includes *Gabrielle* (1849), *Mariage d'Olympe* (1855), *Les Effrontés* (1861), *Maître Guérin* (1864), *Lions et Renards* (1869), *Madame Caverlet* (1876), *Les Fourchambault* (1878); elected member of French Academy (1857).

Augustine *(ô gŭs tēn)*, **Saint** Latin name; AURELIUS AUGUSTINUS. 354–430. Church father. *b.* Tagaste, Numidia. Son of Saint Monica; became a professed Manichaean in youth; went to Milan as teacher of rhetoric and came under the influence of Saint Ambrose (383); became a Christian through a mystic experience and received baptism at the hands of Ambrose (387); returned to Tagaste and was ordained (391); consecrated bishop of Hippo (395); championed orthodoxy against Pelagians, Donatists, and Manichaeans; expounded ideas that shaped the spirit of the Christian Church for centuries. Author of *Confessions* (397) and *The City of God* (413–26); died during siege of Hippo under the Vandals (430). Feast day: Aug. 28.

Augustine, Saint also AUSTIN, APOSTLE OF THE ENGLISH. *d.* 604. First archbishop of Canterbury. Prior of Benedictine monastery of St. Andrew at Rome; chosen by Pope Gregory I (596) to lead 40 missionaries to England; received by Ethelbert, king of Kent, and his Christian queen Bertha and installed at Canterbury (597); converted Ethelbert and thousands of his subjects; consecrated bishop of the English at Arles (597) and archbishop (601); set up the dioceses of London, Rochester, and York.

Augustus *(ô gŭs tŭs)* full name; GAIUS JULIUS CAESAR OCTAVIANUS. 63 B.C.–A.D. 14. First emperor of Rome. *b.* Velitrae, Italy. Son of Gaius Octavius and Atia and adopted son and heir of Julius Caesar; after death of Caesar, gained control of Rome through the influence of Cicero (44); formed second triumvirate with Antony and Lepidus (43); with Antony defeated Brutus and Cassius at Philippi (42); defeated Sextus Pompey in Sicilian War (38–36); defeated Antony and Cleopatra at Battle of Actium (31) and became sole ruler of the Roman dominions; made princeps senatus (28); closed temple of Janus and proclaimed universal peace (27); received title of Augustus (exalted) and became de facto emperor; enlarged empire through victories in Spain, Pannonia, Dalmatia, Gaul, and Asia, but suffered a crushing reverse when Roman legions under Varus were annihilated by the Germans under Arminius; presided over the Golden Age of Latin literature known as the Augustan Age; beautified Rome with marble edifices; the eighth month of the year (Sextilis) was renamed August in his honor; toward end of reign beset by domestic sorrow and failing health; appointed Tiberius as heir and successor; died in Nola, Campania (14).

Aurangzeb *(ô rŭng zĕb)* also ALAMGIR (Conqueror of the World). 1618–1707. Sixth Mughal emperor of India (1659–1707). Seized throne after imprisoning his father, Shah Jehan, and killing his three brothers; enlarged Mughal empire to its furthest boundaries in west, east, and south; sapped the empire's strength through ruinous wars and alienated non-Muslim communities through intolerance.

Aurelian *(ô rē lĭ ăn)*, **Lucius Domitius** also AURELIANUS; called RESTITUTOR OOBIS. c212–75. Roman emperor (270–75). *b.* Sirmium, Pannonia. Of obscure birth; rose from the ranks to high military office; elected emperor by the army on the death of Claudius; repulsed the Alemanni and Marcomanni (271); defeated Zenobia, queen of Palmyra, and razed her capital (271–73); quelled rebellion in Egypt (273); reconquered Gaul and Britain from Tetricus (274); erected walls and fortifications around Rome.

Auriol *(ô ryôl),* **Vincent** 1884–1966. French statesman. *b.* Revel. Entered Chamber of Deputies as a socialist (1914); member of first and second Léon Blum cabinets; active in the Resistance (1942–43); following liberation, elected president of the two constituent assemblies and the National Assembly; one of the principal framers of the Constitution of the Fourth Republic; first president of the Fourth Republic (1947–54).

Austen *(ôs tən),* **Jane** 1775–1817. English novelist. *b.* Steventon. Spent first 25 years at the parsonage of Steventon, where her father was rector; later lived at Bath, Southampton, Chawton, and Winchester. Wrote six great novels: *Sense and Sensibility* (1811), *Pride and Prejudice* (1813), *Mansfield Park* (1814), *Emma* (1816), *Persuasion*, and *Northanger Abbey* (1818); works characterized by irony, sensitivity, humor, and richness of detail.

Austin, Saint. *See* **Augustine, Saint**

Austin *(ôs tĭn),* **Alfred** 1835–1913. English poet laureate (1896–1913). *b.* Leeds. Editor of *National Review* (1883–95); poet laureate (1896). Author of 20 vols. of verse including *The Season; A Satire* (1861), *The Human Tragedy* (1862), *The Conversion of Winckelmann* (1897), and *Autobiography* (1911).

Austin, Stephen Fuller 1793–1836. Founder of Texas. *b.* Wythe County, Va. Successfully negotiated colonization of Texas with Mexican government (1821); directed its governing until 1827; undertook mission to Mexico City to demand statehood (1833); detained and imprisoned (1834–35); commissioner to U.S. from provisional government of Texas (1835–36); secretary of state of Republic of Texas (1836).

Avenol *(äv nôl),* **Joseph Louis Anne** 1879–1952. French statesman. Official in French finance ministry (1905–19); appointed deputy secretary-general and secretary-general (1932–40) of the League of Nations.

Averroës *(ȧ vĕr ō ēz)* also AVERRHOËS; full Arabic name: ABU-AL-WALID MUHAMMAD IBN-AHMAD IBN-RUSHD. 1126–98. Spanish-Arabian philosopher. *b.* Córdoba, Spain. Cadi of Seville, Córdoba, and Morocco; stripped of all honors and banished as a heretic under al-Mansur (1195); made important contributions to jurisprudence, astronomy, grammar, and medicine, but best known for commentaries on Aristotle's writings; tried to develop an Islamic philosophy of religion by interpreting Koran in the light of Aristotle; upheld doctrine of Universal Reason and denied immortality of the individual; his ideas, known as Averroism, profoundly influenced Christian scholasticism.

Avicenna *(ăv ĭ sĕn ȧ)* full Arab name; ABU-ALI AS-HUSAYN IBN-SINA. 980–1037. Arab physician and writ er. *b.* near Bukhara, Central Asia.

Court physician to several sultans at Khiva and Isphahan; vizier at Buyid court at Hamadan; wrote over 100 works on medicine, theology, philosophy, logic, and mathematics, of which *The Canon of Medicine* is the most important; as a philosopher, espoused Aristotelian and Neoplatonic ideas.

Ávila *(ä vē lä),* **Juan de** c1500–69. Spanish preacher. *b.* Almódovar del Campo. Gained a vast following during a 40-year mission in Andalusia. Author of *Epistolario Espiritual* (1578). Also known as Apostle of Andalusia.

Avogadro *(ä vō gä drō),* **Count Amedeo** 1776–1856. Italian scientist. *b.* Turin. Professor of physics at University of Turin (1834–50); originator of Avogadro's Law, which states that equal volumes of gas at equal temperatures contain equal numbers of molecules.

Avon, Earl of. *See* **Eden, Sir Robert Anthony**

Axelrod *(ăk səl rŏd),* **Julius** 1912–. American biochemist. *b.* New York, N.Y. Co-winner of Nobel Prize in physiology and medicine with Bernard Katz and Ulf von Euler (1970).

Ayala y Herrera *(ä yä lä ē ĕr rĕ rä),* **Adelardo Lopez de** 1828–79. Spanish politician and playwright. *b.* Guadalcanal, Spain. Elected to the Cortes (1857); rose to become minister of colonies (1875), and president of chamber of deputies (1878). Works include *Un Hombre de Estado* (1851), *Castigo y Perdón* (1851), *Los Dos Guzmanes* (1851), *Rioja* (1854), *El Tanto por Ciento* (1861), *El Nuevo Don Juan* (1863), and *Consuelo* (1878).

Ayolas *(ä yō läs),* **Juan de** *d.* 1537. Spanish explorer. Lieutenant of Pedro de Mendoza on expedition to Argentina (1535); assumed command when Mendoza returned to Spain; sailed up Río de la Plata and Paraguay river; built fort at the site of Asunción; ambushed by natives while returning home.

Azaña *(ä thä nyä),* **Manuel** full name: MANUEL AZAÑA Y DIEZ. 1880–1940. Spanish statesman. *b.* Alcalá de Henares. Founder of liberal political group Acción Republicana (1930); participated in overthrowing the monarchy (1931); prime minister (1931–33); attempted reforms that incensed army and clergy; imprisoned during Catalonian revolt (1934); elected president (1936); driven into exile by civil war (1939).

Azeglio *(ä dzâ lyō),* **Marchese Massimo Taparelli d'** 1798–1866. Italian statesman. *b.* Turin. Son-in-law of Alessandro Manzoni; leader in Risorgimento and Revolution of 1848; premier of Sardinia (1849–52). Author of historical novels *Ettore Fieramosca* (1833) and *Nicolò de' Lapi* (1841), autobiography, *I Miei Ricordi* (1873), and polemic writings.

B

Baal Shem-Tov *(bȧ ȧl shām tōv)* real name: ISRAEL BEN ELIEZER; also (from his initials) BESHT. c1700–1760. Jewish teacher. *b.* in Ukraine. Founder of Hasidism; by profession a shohet (slaughterer of kosher meat), teacher, and tavern keeper; performed acts of healing with herbal remedies; taught communion with God through ecstatic worship; proclaimed religion as a form of joy; his oral sayings and parables constitute the basis of Hasidism.

Bab *(băb)* full name: MIRZA (or SAYID) ALI MOHAMMED OF SHIRAZ; called BAB ED-DIN (the Gate of Faith). 1819–50. Founder of Babism (1844). *b.* Shiraz, Iran. Proclaimed himself a prophet equal to Muhammad and announced imminent arrival of a messiah; quickly gained a large following, imprisoned and condemned to death as a heretic, executed in public square of Tabriz (1850); mission continued by Bahaullah, who was accepted by the surviving Babists as the prophesied manifestation (1863).

Babbage *(băb ĭj),* **Charles** 1792–1871. English mathematician. *b.* Totnes. Lucasian Professor of Mathematics at Cambridge (1829–39); helped found the Statistical and Astronomical societies; devised a calculating machine and an ophthalmoscope and worked on a table of logarithms. Author of *On the Economy of Machinery and Manufactures* (1832).

Babbitt *(băb ĭt),* **Irving** 1865–1933. American teacher and scholar. *b.* Dayton, Ohio. Professor of French literature at Harvard (from 1912); founder (with Paul Elmer More) of movement known as New Humanism. Works include *Literature and the American College* (1908), *The New Laokoön* (1910), *Rousseau and Romanticism* (1919), and *Democracy and Leadership* (1924).

Babbitt, Isaac 1799–1862. American inventor. *b.* Taunton, Mass. Discoverer of the antifriction-bearing metal (an alloy of tin, copper, lead, and antimony) known as Babbitt metal, used in high-speed machinery.

Baber *(bä bər)* also BABUR, BABAR; real name: ZAHIR-UD-DIN MOHAMMED. 1483–1530. Mughal emperor of India (1526–30) and founder of Mughal dynasty. Grandson of Timur; at age 12, succeeded his father as king of Fergana (1495); conquered Samarkand (1497) and Kabul (1504); led army into India and defeated Ibrahim Lodi, Afghan sultan of Delhi, at Battle of Panipat (1526); occupied Delhi and Agra; defeated Rajput leader Rana Sangram Singh of Mewar (1527); destroyed Afghan power in Bihar and Bengal at Battle of Gogra (1529); wrote *Memoirs*.

Babes *(bä bĕsh),* **Victor** 1854–1926. Romanian bacteriologist. *b.*

Vienna, Austria. Worked at Pasteur Institute at Paris on protective properties of serum from an immunized animal; described granular bodies known as Babes-Ernst bodies found in the protoplasm of bacteria; discovered genus of protozoan parasites called *Babesia;* demonstrated ability of bacteria to penetrate skin and mucosa.

Babeuf *(bă bûf),* **François Nöel** also BABOEUF; pseudonym: GRACCHUS BABEUF. 1760–97. French communist and revolutionary. *b.* St. Quentin. Founded journal *Tribune du Peuple* during French Revolution, advocating theories of absolute equality and community of property known as Babouvism; organized conspiracy against the Directory; betrayed and sentenced to the guillotine (1797). Author of *Cadastre Perpétuel* (1789) and *Du Système de Population* (1794).

Baccio della Porta. *See* **Bartolomeo, Fra**

Bach *(bäĸ),* **Johann Sebastian** 1685–1750. German composer and organist. *b.* Eisenach. Son of Johann Ambrosius Bach; began career as violinist in chamber orchestra of Prince Johann Ernst at Weimar (1703); organist at Arnstadt (1703); organist at Mühlhausen (1707); court organist and violinist at Weimar (1708); Kapellmeister to Prince Leopold of Anhalt-Köthen (1717); cantor, Thomasschule, and director of university music at Leipzig (1723); honorary Kapellmeister to the Duke of Weisenfels (1729); honorary court composer to the elector of Saxony (1736); became totally blind in 1749. Composed both secular and religious music for solo performance and for vocal and instrumental combinations, including about 300 church cantatas (of which 200 survive) a mass in B minor, oratorios, the St. Matthew Passion and the St. John Passion, six Brandenburg concertos, 48 preludes and fugues, *The Well-Tempered Clavier,* sonatas, fantasias, toccatas, suites, partitas, the Goldberg Variations, *The Musical Offering* (on a subject given by Frederick the Great); concertos, capriccios, and *Art of Fugue.* He sired twenty children, of whom ten died in infancy; four sons became eminent musicians: WILHELM FRIEDEMANN (1710–84), composer and organist at Dresden and Halle; KARL PHILIPP EMANUEL (1714–88), composer and director of church music, Hamburg; also chamber musician to Frederick the Great; JOHANN CHRISTOPH FRIEDRICH (1732–95), composer and Kapellmeister at Bückeburg; and JOHANN CHRISTIAN (1735–82), composer and cathedral organist, Milan, and music master to Queen Charlotte Sophia of London.

Back *(băk),* **Sir George** 1796–1878. English explorer. *b.* Stockport. Accompanied Sir John Franklin on three expeditions: to the Spitzbergen region (1818), the Coppermine River and the Arctic coast of America (1819–22), and the Mackenzie River (1825–27); conducted two more Arctic expeditions; on the first (1833–35) discovered Artillery Lake and the Great Fish (or Back) River; made admiral (1857). Wrote *Narrative of the Arctic Land Expedition to the Mouth of the Great Fish River* (1836) and *Narrative of an Expedition in H.M.S. Terror* (1838).

Bacon *(bā kən),* **Francis** title:

BARON VERULAM OF VERULAM, VISCOUNT ST. ALBANS. 1561–1626. English philosopher and statesman. *b.* London. Called to the bar (1582); entered Parliament (1584); commissioned to prosecute erstwhile benefactor Earl of Essex (1601); gained favor of James I; knighted (1603); appointed commissioner for the union of England and Scotland (1604); solicitor general (1607); attorney general (1613); privy councillor (1616); lord keeper (1617); lord chancellor (1618); raised to peerage (1618); found guilty of bribery and corruption and banished from Parliament and court (1621); as a philosopher, was instrumental in founding a new system of investigation and a philosophical tradition based on inductive reasoning and observation; held that truth is not derived from authority and that knowledge is the fruit of experience; advocated a reform of learning called the Great Instauration. Works include *Essays* (1597), *Advancement of Learning* (1605), *De Sapientia Veterum* (1609), *Novum Organum* (1620), *History of Henry VII* (1622), *Apophthegms New and Old* (1624), *Phenomena Universi* (1622), *De Dignitate et Augmentis Scientiarum* (1623), *Maxims of the Law* (1630), and *Reading on the Statute of Uses* (1642).

Bacon, Nathaniel 1647–76. American revolutionary. *b.* Friston Hall, England. Immigrated to Virginia (1673); dissatisfaction with Governor John Berkeley's Indian policy caused Bacon to lead an expedition against Pamunkey Indians; arrested on return to Jamestown for unauthorized raids into Indian territory; pardoned, but declared an outlaw on organizing another expedition; in an incident known as Bacon's Rebellion (1676), seized and burned Jamestown in retaliation.

Bacon, Roger also DOCTOR MIRABILIS OR THE ADMIRABLE DOCTOR. c1214–c1294. English friar and philosopher. *b.* Ilchester. Educated at Oxford and Paris; joined Franciscan order (1250); confined in Paris for ten years either because of infirmity or as punishment for heresy (1257); wrote *Opus Majus,* a general treatise on the sciences, at the request of Pope Clement IV (1266); condemned as heretical (1277) by Franciscan Council and again confined (until 1292); appreciated as an encyclopedist who stressed unity of knowledge, utility of learning, and experimental investigation; made few actual inventions but foresaw such developments as circumnavigation of the world, flight, motor boats, gunpowder, and magnifying glass; suggested a revised calendar; later gained reputation as a wonder worker and magician. Author also of *Opus Minus, Opus Tertium,* and *Compendium Philosophiae.*

Baden-Powell *(bā dən pō ĕl)* **of Gilwell** *(gĭl wĕl),* **Baron** real name: ROBERT STEPHENSON SMYTH. 1857–1941. British founder of Boy Scout movement. *b.* London. Joined the army; served in India, Afghanistan, Ashanti, and Matabeleland; won fame as defender of Mafeking against Boers (1903); general of South African constabulary (1900–1903); inspector general of cavalry (1903–1907); founder of Boy Scouts (1910) and (with sister Agnes) of Girl Guides (1910). Author of *Cavalry Instruction*

(1895), *The Matabele Campaign* (1896), *Sketches in Mafeking and East Africa* (1907), *Scouting for Boys* (1908), and *Lessons of a Lifetime* (1933).

Baedeker *(bā dĭ kər),* **Karl** 1801–59. German publisher. *b.* Essen. Founded imprint (1827) at Coblenz; issued first travel guidebook (1829); moved to Leipzig (1872); name associated with series of travel handbooks covering most countries.

Baekeland *(bāk lənd),* **Leo Hendrik** 1863–1944. American chemist. *b.* Ghent, Belgium. Emigrated to U.S. (1889); invented a synthetic resin called Bakelite and Velox photographic paper usable with artificial light; president of the Bakelite Corporation (1910–39); considered one of the founders of U.S. plastics industry.

Baer *(bâr),* **Karl Ernst von** 1792–1876. Estonian biologist. *b.* Piep. Professor of zoology at Königsburg (1819) and director of Anatomical Institute; librarian of Academy of Sciences of St. Petersburg (1834); noted for researches in embryology; discovered human ovum and the notochord; formulated biogenetic laws governing embryonic development. Chief works are *Über Entwicklungsgeschichte der Thiere* (2 vols., 1828–37) and *Untersuchungen Über die Entwicklung Fische* (1835).

Baeyer *(bâ yər),* **Johann Friedrich Wilhelm Adolf von** 1835–1917. German chemist. *b.* Berlin. Professor of chemistry at Strasbourg (1872) and Munich (1875–1915). Conducted fundamental experiments in organic chemistry; synthesized dye indigo and nitrosophenol; discovered phthaleins, formulated strain theory, which explains the stability of organic rings; demonstrated the mechanism of photosynthesis and condensation of phenols and aldehydes. Author of *Memoirs;* won Nobel Prize in chemistry (1905).

Baffin *(băf ĭn),* **William** 1584–1622. English navigator. *b.* London. Pilot of the *Discovery,* dispatched by Muscovy Company of London to North America in search of Northwest Passage (1615); discovered Baffin Bay and Lancaster, Jones, and Smith sounds (1616); led voyages to the East (1616–21); killed at the siege of Ormuz (1622).

Bagehot *(băj ŭt),* **Walter** 1826–77). English economist and political scientist. *b.* Langport. Entered banking (1852); succeeded father-in-law, James Wilson, as editor of *Economist* (1860). Author of *The English Constitution* (1867), *Lombard Street* (1873), *Physics and Politics* (1869), *Literary Studies* (1879), and *Economic Studies* (1880).

Bahaullah *(bă hă o͞o lă)* real name: MIRZA HUSAYN ALI. 1817–92. Persian religious leader. *b.* Tehran, Iran. Became disciple of the Bab (1850); persecuted and exiled; founded Bahai sect at Acre, Palestine (1863); claimed to be the divine manifestation promised by Bab and assumed title Bahaullah (Splendor of God).

Bailey *(bā lē),* **Liberty Hyde** 1858–1954. American horticulturist. *b.* South Haven, Mich. Professor of horticulture at Cornell and director of Cornell College of Agriculture (1888–1913); donated the Liberty Hyde Bailey Hortorium to Cornell (1935). Author of *Principles of Fruit Growing* (1897), *Evolution of Our Native Fruits* (1898), *Outlook to Nature* (1905), and *Nature-Study Idea* (1903); editor of *Cyclopedia of American Horticulture* (1900–1902) and *Cyclopedia of American Agriculture* (1907–1909).

Bailey *(bā lĭ),* **Francis** 1774–1844. English astronomer. *b.* Newbury. Made fortune as a broker and retired from business to study astronomy; helped found Royal Astronomical Society (1820); revised star catalogues; described phenomenon known as Baily's beads, which are bright spots on moon's disk during total eclipse of the sun (1836); calculated mean density of the earth.

Bain *(bān),* **Alexander** 1818–1903. Scottish psychologist. *b.* Aberdeen. Professor of logic and English literature at Aberdeen University (1860–80); lord rector (1880–87); developed empirical school of psychology based on physiology. Chief works include *The Senses and the Intellect* (1855), *The Emotions and the Will* (1859), *Mental and Moral Science* (1868), *Logic* (1870), *Mind and Body* (1872), *Education as a Science* (1879), and *Autobiography* (1904); founded the periodical *Mind* (1876).

Baird *(bârd),* **John Logie** 1888–1946. British inventor. *b.* Helensburgh, Scotland. Inventor of the first television mechanism, called Televisor, and an apparatus for seeing in the dark by means of invisible rays, called Noctovisor; demonstrated first true television image with a 240-line mechanically scanned system (1926).

Bajer *(bī ər),* **Fredrik** 1837–1922. Danish statesman. *b.* Vester Egede. Founded Danish Peace Union (1882) and International Peace Bureau in Bern, Switzerland (1891); shared Nobel Peace Prize (1908) with Klas Arnoldson.

Baker *(bā kər),* **George Pierce** 1866–1935. American teacher. *b.* Providence, R.I. Professor of English at Harvard (1905–24); gained reputation as the head of the 47 Workshop, a course in playwriting; professor of the history and technique of drama and director of the University Theater at Yale (1925–33); taught Philip Barry, Eugene O'Neill, Sidney Howard, and Thomas Wolfe. Author of *The Development of Shakespeare as a Dramatist* (1907), *Technique of Drama* (1915), and *Dramatic Technique* (1919); edited series of plays and Elizabethan texts.

Baker, Sir Herbert 1862–1946. English architect. *b.* Kent. Designed Groote Schuur near Cape Town; Union House, government buildings, and cathedral in Pretoria; Secretariat and Parliament House in New Delhi, Rhodes House at Oxford, and Bank of England and South Africa House in London. Author of *Architecture and Personalities* (1944).

Baker, Sir Samuel White 1821–93. English explorer. *b.* London. Founded agricultural colony at Nuwara Eliya, Ceylon (1848); explored Blue Nile region (1861); discovered Lake Albert Nyanza (1864); commanded expedition (1869–73) organized by the pasha of Egypt for suppression of slave trade and annexation of equatorial regions. Author of *Eight Years' Wanderings in Ceylon* (1855), *The*

Albert Nyanza (1866), *The Nile Tributaries of Abyssinia* (1867), and *Ismailia* (1874).

Bakst *(băkst),* **Léon Nicolaevich** original name: ROSENBERG. c1867–1924. Russian painter and designer. *b.* St. Petersburg. Settled in Paris (1906); became scenic artist and costume designer for Diaghilev's Ballet Russe (1909); won international recognition with his rich and exuberant stage settings for *Cleopatra, Scheherazade, Salome, Daphnis and Chloe, Boris Godunov,* and *Istar.*

Bakunin *(bŭ kōō nyĭn),* **Mikhail Aleksandrovich** 1814–76. Russian anarchist. *b.* Torzhok. Left Russia (1840); forcibly repatriated for role in the Dresden insurrection of 1849; exiled to Siberia (1855); escaped and returned to Europe via Japan and U.S. (1861); devoted later years to incessant revolutionary activity; attempted abortive uprising at Lyons (1870); as leader of anarchists, opposed Karl Marx at Hague Congress of the First Communist International (1872), but was outvoted and expelled; developed atheism and collectivism as the principal tenets of Bakuninism in *God and State* and other writings.

Balaguer y Cirera *(bä lä gĕr ē thē rā rä),* **Victor** 1824–1901. Spanish poet, historian, and statesman. *b.* Barcelona. Keeper of archives of Barcelona (1854) and professor of history at University of Barcelona; minister and senator (from 1872); became leading figure in Catalan renaissance. Published historical studies *Historia de Cataluña y de la Corona de Aragón* (1860–63) and *Historia Política y Literaria de los Trovadores* (6 vols., 1877–80), *Don Juan de Serravalle* (1875), and poetry, *El Trovador de Montserrat* (1850), *Poesías Completas* (1884), and the epic trilogy *Los Pirineos* (1892).

Balakirev *(bŭ lȧ kyĭ ryĕf),* **Mili Alekseevich** 1837–1910. Russian composer. *b.* Nizhni Novgorod (now Gorki). Founded (with Modest Moussorgsky, Nicolai Rimsky-Korsakov, and Aleksandr Borodin) the Free School of Music (1861); conductor (1867–70) of the Royal Russian Musical Society and director (1883–94) of the Imperial Capella Society. Principal compositions include *Tamara* and *Russia* (symphonic poems) and *Islamey* (piano piece).

Balanchine *(băl ən chĭn),* **George** original name: GEORGI BALANCHIVADZE. 1904– . American choreographer. *b.* St. Petersburg, Russia. Ballet master with the Ballet Russe of Sergei Diaghilev (1924–29); immigrated to New York (1933); helped organize the Ballet Theater (1946), known from 1948 as the New York City Ballet; created a neoclassical style of ballet typified in *Concerto Barocco, Ballet Imperial, Four Temperaments,* and *Orpheus.*

Balbo *(bäl bō),* **Count Cesare** 1789–1853. Italian statesman and historian. *b.* Turin. Associate of Camillo Cavour and one of the founders of Risorgimento; first premier of Piedmont (1848). Italian studies include *Storia d'Italia sotto ai Barbari* (1830), *Vita di Dante* (1839), and *Delle Speranze d'Italia* (1843).

Balboa *(băl bō ȧ),* **Vasco Nuñez de** 1475–1519. Spanish explorer. *b.* Jerez de los Caballeros. Sailed to America (1500) with expedition of

Rodrigo de Bastidas; settled as a planter in Hispaniola; founded town of Darien, the first Spanish settlement in continental America, and became provisional governor (1511); discovered Pacific Ocean (1513) and took possession of it in the name of King Ferdinand of Spain; quarreled with Pedrarias Dávila, the new governor of Panama; accused of sedition, condemned, and executed (1519).

Balbuena *(bäl bwā nä),* **Bernardo de** 1568–1627. Spanish poet. *b.* Valdenpeñas. First bishop of Puerto Rico; claimed by Mexico as one of her greatest poets because of the epic *La Grandeza Mejicana* (1609). Also wrote *El Bernardo o La Victoria de Roncesvalles* on the life of Bernardo del Carpio (1624) and a pastoral classic, *Siglo de Oro en las Selvas de Erífile* (1608).

Balch *(bôlch),* **Emily Greene** 1867–1961. American social scientist. *b.* Jamaica Plain, Mass. President of Women's International League for Peace and Freedom (from 1936); co-winner of Nobel Peace Prize (1946) with John R. Mott. Author of *Our Slavic Fellow Citizens* (1910), *Approaches to the Great Settlement* (1918), and *Refugees as Assets* (1939).

Baldovinetti *(bäl dō vē nät tē),* **Alessio** also Balduinetti. 1427–99. Italian painter. *b.* Florence. Leading artist of early Florentine Renaissance; executed series of frescoes for Church of Santa Trinità at Florence; noted also for beautiful mosaics.

Baldwin I *(bôld wĭn)* 1058–1118. King of Jerusalem (1100–1118). Brother of Godfrey of Bouillon, whom he accompanied on the First Crusade; enlarged the Latin kingdom by conquering Acre (1104), Beirut (1109), and Sidon (1110).

Baldwin, Stanley title: Earl Baldwin of Bewdley. 1867–1947. English statesman. *b.* Bewdley. Entered Parliament (1908); succeeded Bonar Law as prime minister (1923); held office for three terms (1923–24, 1924–29, 1935–37); administration marked by settlement of General Strike of 1926, abdication of King Edward VIII (1936), and India Act of 1935; also remembered for settlement of war debts with U.S. after World War I. Author of *Classics and the Plain Man* (1926), *On England and Other Essays* (1926), and *An Interpreter of England* (1939).

Balfe *(bălf),* **Michael William** 1808–70. Irish composer. *b.* Dublin. Best known for opera *The Bohemian Girl* (1843); other works include *Siege of Rochelle* (1835), *The Maid of Artois* (1836), *Joan of Arc* (1837), *Falstaff* (1838), *Maid of Honor* (1847), *Sicilian Bride* (1852), *Rose of Castile* (1857), and *Satanella* (1858).

Balfour *(băl fo͝or),* **Arthur James** title: Earl of Balfour. 1848–1930. English statesman. Entered Parliament (1874); became first lord of the treasury and leader in the Commons (1891–92, 1895–1900); prime minister (1902–1905); premiership witnessed the end of South African War and passage of Education Act; served under Lloyd George as foreign secretary (1916–19); issued Balfour Declaration that the British government favored the establishment in Palestine of a national home for Jewish people without prejudice to the civil and religious rights of other communities; attended Paris Peace Conference and Washington Disarmament Conference (1922). Author of *Defense of Philosophic Doubt* (1879), *The Foundations of Belief* (1895), *Theism and Humanism* (1915), and *Theism and Thought* (1923).

Ball *(bôl),* **Frances** also MOTHER FRANCES MARY THERESA. 1794–1861. English religious. Founder (1822) of order of Loretto Nuns, first in Dublin, later in all English-speaking countries.

Ball, Hugo 1886–1927. German religious writer. *b.* Pirmasens. One of the founders of Dadaism in Zurich. Author of *Zur Kritik der Deutschen Intelligenz* (1919), *Das Byzantinische Christentum* (1923), and *Folgen der Reformation* (1924).

Ballance *(băl əns),* **John** 1839–93. New Zealand statesman. *b.* Glenavy, Ireland. Moved to New Zealand (1865); served in Maori Wars; entered Parliament (1875); became leader of the Liberal Party (1889) and premier (1891–93); initiated such social reforms as progressive income and land taxes.

Ballou *(băl lo͞o),* **Hosea** 1771–1852. American clergyman. *b.* Richmond, N.H. Joined Universalists (1791) and became circuit preacher; through untiring efforts made Universalism a major religious force in New England. Edited *Universalist Magazine* (1819–28) and *Universalist Expositor* (from 1830); wrote the influential *Notes on the Parables* (1804) and *Treatise on the Atonement* (1805).

Balmer *(bäl mər),* **Johann Jakob** 1825–98. Swiss physicist. *b.* Lausanne. Discovered the Balmer formula concerning the frequencies of radiation in the hydrogen spectrum and the Balmer series, a series of radiations emitted by electrons, appearing in spectra of white stars as bright lines spaced at regularly decreasing intervals from red to violet.

Balmont *(bȧʟ mənt),* **Konstantin Dmitrievich** 1867–1943. Russian poet. *b.* Gumnishchi. Settled in Paris (1918); produced many tuneful and light lyrics on symbolist themes; translated Shelley and Whitman into Russian. Works include *Under the Northern Sky* (1894), *Silence* (1898), *In Boundless Space* (1895), *The Liturgy of Beauty* (1905), and *The Bird of Flame* (1907).

Balzac *(bȧl zȧk),* **Honoré de** 1799–1850. French novelist. *b.* Tours. Achieved success with *Le Dernier Chouan* (1829), the first of over 350 works to bear his name; nearly 100 novels form part of a grand cycle called *La Comédie Humaine* (1842) including masterpieces such as *Père Goriot, Les Illusions Perdues, Les Paysans, Les Marana, La Femme de Trente Ans, La Cousine Bette, Eugénie Grandet,* and *Une Ténébreuse Affaire;* also wrote series of Rabelaisian stories entitled *Contes Drolatiques;* considered a founder of the realist school and one of the world's greatest novelists.

Balzac, Seigneur **Jean Louis Guez de** c1597–1654. French writer. *b.* Balzac. Protégé of Louis, Cardinal de la Valette and Cardinal Richelieu; gained reputation as master of rhythmic and balanced prose style exemplified in *Lettres* (1624), *Le Prince* (1631), *Discours* (1644), *La Barbon* (1648), *Socrate Chrétien* (1652), and *L'Aristippe ou de la*

Cour (1658); elected to French Academy (1634).

Bancroft *(băn krôft),* **George** 1800–1891. American historian. *b.* Worcester, Mass. Studied for the ministry at Harvard and history at Göttingen; established Round Hill School for Boys at Northampton, Mass., on Pestalozzian principles (1823); active in Democratic politics; secretary of navy (1845–46) under Polk and founder of U.S. Naval Academy at Annapolis; minister to Great Britain (1846–49); minister to Germany (1867–74); fame rests on monumental *History of the United States* (10 vols.) completed in 1874. Other works incude *Literary and Historical Miscellanies* (1855) and *History of the Formation of the Constitution of the United States* (2 vols., 1882).

Bancroft, Hubert Howe 1832–1918. American publisher and historian. *b.* Granville, Ohio. Founded publishing house H.H. Bancroft and Company in San Francisco (1858); undertook encyclopedic project entitled *West American Historical Series* (39 vols., 1875–90); donated library of over 60,000 rare volumes to University of California. Other works include *Resources of Mexico* (1893), *The New Pacific* (1900), and *Retrospection, Political and Personal* (1910).

Bancroft, Richard 1544–1610. English prelate. *b.* Farnworth. Bishop of London (1597); succeeded John Whitgift as archbishop of Canterbury (1604); active at the Hampton Court conference; combated spread of Puritanism; supervised translations of the Bible for the Authorized Version.

Bandinelli *(băn dĭ nĕl lĭ),* **Bartolommeo or Baccio** 1493–1560. Italian painter and sculptor. *b.* Florence. Works include the statues *Hercules and Cacus* outside the Palazzo Vecchio, *Adam and Eve* at the National Museum in Florence, and bas-reliefs in choir of Florence cathedral.

Banér *(bȧ nār),* **Johan** also BANIER, BANNER. 1596–1641. Swedish general. *b.* Djursholm. In Thirty Years' War, took part in campaigns against Russia and Poland under Gustavus Adolphus; commanded Swedish forces in Germany (1632); made field marshal after death of Gustavus Adolphus (1634); victories at Wittstock (1636) and Chemnitz (1639).

Banks *(băngks),* **Sir Joseph** 1743–1820. English botanist. *b.* London. Accompanied Captain James Cook's first expedition in the *Endeavour* (1768–71); elected president of Royal Society (1778–1820) and French Institute (1802); helped found colony of New South Wales; donated library and herbarium to British Museum.

Banting *(băn tĭng),* **Sir Frederick Grant** 1891–1941. Canadian research physician. *b.* Alliston. Conducted research on the pancreas at University of Toronto (1921); with Charles H. Best, discovered insulin, a hormone now used as specific remedy for diabetes (1922); shared Nobel Prize in physiology and medicine (1923) with J. J. R. Macleod; professor of medical research at University of Toronto (1923–41).

Banting, William 1797–1878. English undertaker. Author of diet system known as Bantingism; in pamphlet entitled *A Letter on Corpulence* (1863), recommended a diet for weight reduction consisting of lean meats and abstinence from fats, starch, and sugar.

Bantock *(băn tək),* **Sir Granville** 1868–1946. English composer. *b.* London. Principal of School of Music at Birmingham; professor of music at University of Birmingham (1908–34). Composed operas, symphonic poems, suites, and vocal and chamber music, including *Omar Khayyam, Atlanta in Calydon,* and *Hebridean Symphony.*

Banville *(bäɴ vēl),* **Théodore Faullain de** 1823–91. French poet and dramatist. *b.* Moulins. Gained reputation as musical lyricist and witty parodist with *Les Cariatides* (1841), *Le Cousin du Roi* (1857), *Diane au Bois* (1864), *Gringoire* (1866), *Odes Funambulesques* (1857), *Contes Bourgeois* (1885), *Mes Souvenirs* (1882), and *Dans la Fournaise* (1892); for mastery of ballades and rondels known as roi des rimes.

Baradai *(băr ȧ dī),* **Jacob** *d.* 578. Syrian religious leader. *b.* Edessa. Consecrated bishop of Edessa (c543); founded Monophysite Jacobite Church and through tireless efforts transformed it into a major Eastern church with a patriarchate at Antioch.

Baranov *(bŭ rȧ nôf),* **Aleksandr Andreevich** 1746–1819. Russian–Alaskan fur trader. Founded trading colony on Bering Strait (1796); built fortress on Baranov Island; first governor of Russian America (until 1818).

Bárány *(bä räɴ'),* **Robert** 1876–1936. Austrian pathologist. *b.* Vienna. Worked at University of Uppsala on the vestibular apparatus; name associated with the caloric differential test for the function of the labyrinth and with the pointing test for circumscribed lesions of the cerebellum; received Nobel Prize in medicine (1914).

Barat *(bȧ rȧ),* **Saint Madeleine Sophie** 1779–1865. French religious. *b.* Joigny. Founder of Society of the Sacred Heart of Jesus (1800).

Barbara *(bär bȧ rȧ),* **Saint** *fl.* 3rd or 4th century. Christian martyr. According to *Martyrologium Romanum Parvum,* daughter of Dioscorus, a heathen nobleman of Nicomedia in Bithynia, who betrayed and beheaded her for her conversion to Christianity; patroness of artillerymen. Feast day: Dec. 4.

Barbarossa. *See* **Frederick I**

Barber *(bär bər),* **Samuel** 1910–. American composer. *b.* West Chester, Pa. Early compositions essentially traditional and neoromantic, such as *Dover Beach* (1931), *Overture to School for Scandal* (1932), and *Adagio for Strings* (1936); later music characterized by dissonance and achromaticism, such as *Capricorn Concerto* (1944), the ballet *Medea* (1946), *Piano Sonata* (1948), and *Hermit Songs* (1952); wrote the opera *Vanessa,* performed at Salzburg Festival (1958); winner of Prix de Rome (1935), Pulitzer Prize for music (1958, 1963) and New York Music Critics' Award (1946).

Barbirolli *(bär bĭ rōl ĭ),* **Sir John** 1899–1970. British conductor. *b.* London. Violoncellist and soloist with International String Quartet (1920–24), conductor of New York Philharmonic Orchestra (1936–38); conductor of Halle Orchestra (1938–58).

Barbusse *(bär büs),* **Henri** 1873–1935. French writer. *b.* Asnières. Achieved recognition with *Le Feu* (1916), an antiwar novel that won the Prix Goncourt. Other works include *Pleureuses* (1895), *Les Suppliants* (1903), *L'Enfer* (1908), and *Le Judas de Jésus* (1927).

Bar Cocheba *(bär kōk vä),* **Simon** also BAR KOKHBA, BAR COZIBA. *d.* 135. Jewish revolutionary. Led insurrection against Emperor Hadrian (132–135) and was proclaimed king; defeated and slain in a holocaust in which half a million Jews were slaughtered and Jerusalem was razed.

Bardeen *(bär dēn),* **John** 1908–. American physicist. *b.* Madison, Wis. Awarded Nobel Prize in physics (1956) with William Shockley and Walter Brattain for discovery of the transistor; won second Nobel Prize in physics (1972) with Leon N. Cooper and John R. Schrieffer.

Bardesanes *(bär dĭ sā nēz)* also BARDAISAN. 154–223. Syrian Church leader and hymnologist. *b.* Edessa. Founder of Gnostic sect named Bardesanists; regarded as the earliest Syriac writer and founder of Syriac poetry.

Barents *(bä rĕnts),* **William** *d.* 1597. Dutch navigator and explorer. Commander of several Dutch expeditions to Novaya Zemlya and Spitzbergen in search of Northeast Passage to China; discoverer of Spitzbergen (1596); Barents Sea and Barents Island named after him.

Bar-Hebraeus *(bär hē brē ŭs),* **Gregorius** Arabic name: ABU-AL-FARAJ IBN-AL-IBRI; also ABULFARAJ; Latin form: ABULFARAGIUS, 1226–86. Syrian prelate and scholar. *b.* Malatya, Armenia. Son of a Jewish-Christian physician; became monk at Antioch (c1243); bishop of Aleppo (1252); archbishop of Eastern Jacobites (1264); regarded as greatest writer in Syriac literature. Works include *Chronicle,* a history of the world; *Ausar Raze,* a scriptural commentary; commentaries on Aristotle; and an autobiography.

Baring *(bâr ĭng),* **Evelyn** title: EARL OF CROMER. 1841–1917. Comptroller general of France and England in Egypt (1879); British agent and consul-general in Egypt (1883–1907); aided in modernization of Egypt by promoting land, educational, legal, and railway reforms. Author of *Modern Egypt* (1908), *Ancient and Modern Imperalism* (1910), and *Abbas II* (1915).

Baring-Gould *(bâr ĭng gōōld),* **Sabine** 1834–1924. English clergyman and author. *b.* Exeter. Author of *Lives of the Saints* (15 vols., 1872–77), *Curious Myths of the Middle Ages* (1866–68), *The Book of Werewolves* (1865) and the famous hymn "Onward Christian Soldiers."

Barkla *(bärk lä),* **Charles Glover** 1877–1944. English physicist. *b.* Widnes. Wheatstone Professor of Physics, University of London (1909–13); professor of natural philosophy, Edinburgh University (1913–44); won Nobel Prize in physics (1917).

Barkley *(bär klĭ),* **Alben William** 1877–1956. American statesman. *b.* in Graves County, Ky. Senator from Kentucky (1926–49); Senate majority leader (1937–46); vice-president of U.S. (1949–53) under Harry S Truman.

Barlach *(bär läk),* **Ernst** 1870–1938. German artist. *b.* Wedel. leading exponent of German expressionism in drama and art; best known as sculptor in wood, bronze, and stone. Principal works include *Ehrenmal* (1927) in the cathedral at Güstrow and war monuments at Magdeburg (1929) and Hamburg (1930); works condemned by Nazis as subversive; soon after age 40, began writing plays, of which the most famous are *Der Tote Tag* (1912), *Der Arme Vetter* (1918), *Die Echten Sedemunds* (1920), and *Der Findling* (1922).

Barnabas *(bär nȧ bəs),* **Saint** surname of JOSES or JOSEPH. *d.* 61. Apostle of Christian Church. Taught with Paul at Antioch and accompanied him on first missionary journey to Cyprus and Asia Minor; after disagreement with Paul, went to Cyprus and was martyred there. Feast day: June 11.

Barnard *(bär nərd),* **Christiaan Neethling** 1922–. South African surgeon. Performed first successful human heart transplant (1967).

Barnard, Edward Emerson 1857–1923. American astronomer. *b.* Nashville, Tenn. Astronomer at Yerkes Observatory (1895–1923); discovered fifth satellite of Jupiter and 16 comets.

Barnard, Frederick Augustus Porter 1809–89. American educator. *b.* Sheffield, Mass. President of University of Mississippi (1856–61); president of Columbia College (1864–89); Barnard College is named after him.

Barnard, Henry 1811–1900. American educator. *b.* Hartford, Conn. Directed reorganization of public school systems of Conn. (1839) and R.I. (1843); first U.S. commissioner of education (1867–70); editor of *American Journal of Education* (1855–82) and *Library of Education* (52 vols.).

Barnardo *(bär när dō),* **Thomas John** 1845–1905. British physician and social worker. *b.* Ireland. Noted for work in rescuing and training destitute children; from 1867 established several homes for destitute children (now known as Dr. Barnardo's Homes); institutions incorporated (1899) as the National Institution for the Reclamation of Destitute Waif Children.

Barnes *(bärnz),* **Albert Coombs** 1873–1951. American art collector and discoverer of argyrol. *b.* Philadelphia, Pa. Founded (1902) A.C. Barnes Company, which manufactured argyrol; assembled one of the most notable collections of modern French art; established Barnes Foundation at Merion, Pa., with an endowment of $10 million, to afford free schooling in art to deserving students.

Barnum *(bär nəm),* **Phineas Taylor** 1810–91. American showman. *b.* Bethel, Conn. Opened American Museum of Curios in N.Y. (1842), introducing the famous dwarf General Tom Thumb (Charles S. Stratton); sponsored Jenny Lind's concert tour of U.S. (1850); established circus (1871) ballyhooed as "The Greatest Show on Earth"; joined with rival James Anthony Bailey to form (1881) Barnum and Bailey Circus, whose principal attraction was an elephant named Jumbo; mayor of Bridgeport (1875). Author of *Struggles and Triumphs, or Forty*

Years' Recollections (1869).

Baroja y Nessi *(bä rô hä ē nĕ sē),* **Pío** 1872–1956. Spanish writer. *b.* San Sebastian. Author of over 70 volumes of novels and essays on Basque life, the best known of which are *La Casa de Aizgorri, El Mayorazgo de Labraz, Zalacaín el Adventurero, La Dama Errante, La Ciudad de la Niebal, El Árbol de la Ciencia,* and *Memorias de un Hombre de Acción.*

Barrie *(băr ĭ),* **Sir James Matthew** 1860–1937. Scottish novelist and playwright. *b.* Kirriemuir. Began career with a series of autobiographical novels including *The Little Minister* (1891), *Margaret Ogilvy* (1894), and *A Widow in Thrums* (1889); turned to writing plays (from 1890) characterized by whimsy and fantasy. Principal works include *Peter Pan* (1904), *Walker, London* (1893), *Quality Street* (1902), *The Admirable Crichton* (1904), *Little Mary* (1904), *What Every Woman Knows* (1908), *Der Tag* (1914), *Dear Brutus* (1917), and *Shall We Join the Ladies?* (1922).

Barrow *(băr ō),* **Henry** *d.* 1593. English religious reformer. One of the founders of Congregationalism; follower of Robert Browne; imprisoned for rejecting ecclesiastical and legal authorities; hanged at Tyburn as a recusant.

Barrow, Isaac 1630–77. English scholar and mathematician. *b.* London. Appointed first Lucasian Professor of mathematics at Cambridge (1663–69); taught Isaac Newton and was later succeeded by him; served as chaplain to Charles II and master of Trinity College. Author of *Lectiones Opticae et Geometricae* (1669) and several theological works, including treatise on *Pope's Supremacy* (1680).

Barrow, Sir John 1764–1848. English geographer and explorer. *b.* Dragley Beck. Explored parts of China and Africa (1792–1803) as secretary to Lord Macartney, the British ambassador to China and, later, governor of the Cape of Good Hope; on return to England, founded Royal Geographical Society (1830) and promoted Arctic explorations; Barrow Straits, Point Barrow, and Cape Barrows are named after him. Author of *Travels in China* (1804), *Travels in South Africa* (1804), *History of Arctic Voyages* (1818), and *Autobiography* (1847).

Barry *(băr ĭ),* **Sir Charles** 1795–1860. English architect. *b.* London. Noted as designer of the Houses of Parliament, the Reform Club, and the Travellers' Club.

Barry, John 1745–1803. American naval commander. *b.* Tacumshane, Ireland. In Revolutionary War, as commander of *Lexington* and *Alliance,* captured the British ships *Edward* (1776) and *Atalanta* and *Trepassy* (1781).

Barrymore *(băr ĭ mōr),* **Maurice** real name: HERBERT BLYTHE. 1847–1905. English actor. *b.* Agra, India. Won acclaim as the leading man opposite Madame Modjeska, Lily Langtry, Olga Nethersole, and Minnie Maddern Fiske; husband of actress GEORGINA EMMA DREW and father of three great actors: LIONEL, ETHEL, and JOHN.

Barth *(bärt),* **Heinrich** 1821–65. German traveler. *b.* Hamburg. Traveled through North Africa, Palestine, Syria, Asia Minor, and Greece (1845–55); discovered

Binue River (1851); crossed Great Desert and continued explorations in Central Africa. Described journeys in *Journeys Through the Border Lands of the Mediterranean* (1849) and *Journeys and Discoveries in Northern and Central Africa* (1855–58).

Barth, Karl 1886–1968. Swiss theologian. *b.* Basel. Established theological reputation with commentary on St. Paul's Epistle to the Romans (1919); professor of theology at Göttingen, Münster, and Bonn (1921–35); dismissed on refusal to take unconditional oath to Hitler; professor of theology at Basel (1935–62); developed the crisis and dialectical schools of theology on the basis of man's finiteness and God's infinite grace. Author of *Knowledge of God and the Service of God* (1938), *Church Dogmatics* (1958), and *Credo* (1935).

Bartholdi *(bär tôl dē),* **Frédéric Auguste** 1834–1904. French sculptor. *b.* Colmar. Noted for such monumental figures as *Liberty Enlightening the World* (The Statue of Liberty) on Bedloe's Island in New York Harbor (1885) and the *Lion of Belfort* (1870–71).

Bartholomew *(bär thŏl ō mū),* **Saint** One of the 12 apostles of Jesus Christ, believed to be identical with Nathanael; said to have preached the Gospel in Mesopotamia, Persia, Egypt, Armenia, and Phrygia and suffered martyrdom by being flayed alive. Feast day: Aug. 24.

Bartlett *(bärt lĕt),* **Robert Abram** 1875–1946. Arctic explorer. *b.* Brigus, Newfoundland. Master of Robert Peary's ship *Roosevelt* on expeditions of 1905–1906 and 1908–1909; commander of the *Karluk* under Vilhjalmur Stefansson in the Canadian government expedition (1913–14); led expeditions to Greenland (1917), Baffin Island (1927), and Labrador (1929). Author of *Last Voyage of the Karluk* (1916) and *The Log of Bob Bartlett* (1928).

Bartók *(bŏr tōk),* **Béla** 1881–1945. Hungarian composer. *b.* Nagyszentmiklós. Professor of piano (1907–12) at Royal Hungarian Musical Academy in Budapest; received recognition as composer with the ballet *The Wooden Prince,* the opera *Duke Bluebeard's Castle,* and the *Second String Quartet* (1918); collected over 6,000 Slavic folk tunes, published them in *Hungarian Folk Music,* and incorporated their vigorous rhythms and melodies in his own work; driven into exile by Nazi occupation of Hungary and settled in U.S. (1940). Other works include *The Miraculous Mandarin, Concerto for Orchestra,* concertos for piano and violin, *Mikrocosmos* (1935), and vocal works.

Bartolommeo *(bär tō lōm mâ ō),* **Fra** original name: BARTOLOMMEO DI PAGOLO DEL FATTORINO; properly: BACCIO DELLA PORTA; also called IL FRATE. 1475–1517. Italian religious painter of the Florentine school. *b.* Savignano. Student of Piero di Cosimo; became Dominican monk and gave up painting on the death of Savonarola, whose cause he had espoused; resumed art (1504) through the influence of Raphael, a lifelong friend and associate. Principal works include *The Last Judgment of St. Mark, Marriage of St. Catherine, St. Sebastian, Christ at Emmaus, Assumption,* and *Madonna and the Saints.*

Bartolus *(bär tō ləs)* Italian name: Bartolo da Sassoferrato. 1314–57. Italian jurist. *b.* Sassoferrato. Regarded as one of the greatest legal minds of the Middle Ages; professor of law at Perugia (from 1343). Works include *On Procedure, On Evidence,* and *Commentary on the Code of Justinian.*

Barton *(bär tən),* **Clara** full name: Clarissa Harlowe Barton. 1821–1912. Founder and first president of American Red Cross. *b.* Oxford, Mass. Organized relief work for the wounded in the Civil War; set up military hospitals during Franco-Prussian War (1870–71); superintended relief work at Strasbourg (1871), Paris (1872), Constantinople (1896), and during Spanish-American War (1898) and Boer War (1899–1902); campaigned for U.S. participation in the International Red Cross; first president of American National Red Cross Society (1882–1904). Author of *History of the Red Cross* (1882) and *Story of My Childhood* (1907).

Barton, Sir Edmund 1849–1920. Australian statesman. *b.* Sydney. Campaigned (from 1890) for a federated Australia and was a member of constitutional conventions (1891, 1897–98); formed first federal ministry (1900); first prime minister of Australian Commonwealth (1901–1903); on resignation, appointed judge of the high court (1903-20).

Bartram *(bär trəm),* **John** 1699–1777. American botanist. *b.* Chester County, Pa. Founded (1728) first botanical garden in America at Kingsessing, near Philadelphia; described by Linnaeus as the greatest contemporary natural botanist; appointed honorary botanist to King George II of England.

Baruch *(bä ro͞ok),* **Bernard Mannes** 1870–1965. American businessman. *b.* Camden, S.C. Made a fortune in the stock market; devoted later life to public service as advisor to presidents; served on many national commissions such as National Defense Council (1916), War Industries Board (1918–19), Supreme Economic Council (1919), American Peace Commission (1919), special commission on rubber (1942), and U.N. Atomic Energy Commission (1946–47); formulated Baruch Plan for the control of atomic weapons. Author of *My Own Story* (1958) and *The Public Years* (1961).

Basil *(băz əl),* **Saint** also Basilius, Basil the Great. 329–79. Greek Church father. *b.* Caesarea, Asia Minor. Entered monastic life (361); ordained presbyter (364); bishop of Caesarea and metropolitan of Cappadocia (370–79); emerged as vigorous supporter of orthodoxy against the Arians; reorganized monasticism by emphasizing work, charity, and communality rather than asceticism. Wrote many liturgies, homilies, commentaries on the scriptures, and polemical works, including *De Spiritu Sanctu, Moralia,* and *Regulae.*

Basil I also Basil the Macedonian. c813–86. Byzantine emperor (867–86) and founder of Macedonian dynasty. Raised by Emperor Michael III to rank of co-emperor (866); sole ruler (867) after causing Michael's death; reign marked by improvement of financial administration, expulsion of Saracens from Italy, and codification of laws called *Constitutiones Basilicae* or *Basilica;* regarded as one of the strongest and greatest Byzantine rulers.

Basilides *(băs ĭ lī dēz)* *d.* c140. Syrian Gnostic. *b.* Syria. Founder of the Basilidian Christian sect; claimed possession of secret traditions of the Apostle Peter which he elaborated into a system of philosophy and cosmogony; wrote commentaries on the Gospels in 24 books, of which extracts are extant.

Baskerville *(băs kər vĭl),* **John** 1706–75. English typographer. *b.* Sion Hill. Began experiments in typography (about 1750); served as printer to Cambridge University (1758–68); introduced modern typefaces with long and level serifs and contrasting upstrokes and downstrokes; pioneered innovations in paper and ink; issued over 55 books including editions of Vergil, Milton, the Bible, and Latin authors.

Basov *(bä sôf),* **Nikolai Gennadievich** 1922–. Russian physicist. Professor at Lebedev Physics Institute in Moscow; co-winner of Nobel Prize in physics (1964) with C. Townes and A. Prochorov for work on laser beams.

Bates *(bāts),* **Henry Walter** 1825–92. English naturalist. *b.* Leicester. Accompanied A.R. Wallace to the Amazon (1848) and spent 11 years collecting 8000 new species of plants and insects that were transported to England in 1859; published (1861) a theory of natural selection explaining a phenomenon now called Batesian mimicry. Author of *The Naturalist on the River Amazon* (1863).

Bates, Herbert Ernest 1905–1974. English writer. *b.* Rushden. Highly regarded novelist and short-story writer. Principal works include *Fair Stood the Wind for France* (1944), *The Jacaranda Tree* (1949), *The Scarlet Sword* (1951), and *The Darling Buds of May* (1958).

Batista y Zaldívar *(bä tēs tä ē säl dē vär),* **Fulgencio** 1901–73. Cuban statesman. *b.* Banes. Took part in revolution (1933) against President Gerardo Machado; led coup against Carlos Céspedes; appointed chief of staff of army by the Government of Five, which made him a virtual dictator; served as president (1940–44, 1952–59); deposed by Fidel Castro and sent into exile (1959).

Battani, al- *(ăl băt tä nē)* Arabic name: ABU-ABDULLAH MUHAMMAD IBN-JABIR AL-BATTANI; Latin name: ALBATEGNIUS or ALBATENIUS. c850–929. Arab astronomer. *b.* Haran, Turkey. Regarded as one of the greatest astronomers in Islamic history; wrote treatise based on 40 years of research (877–918), later translated into Latin and Spanish.

Baudelaire *(bō dlâr),* **Charles Pierre** 1821–67. French poet. *b.* Paris. Gained fame with a volume of verse, *Les Fleurs du Mal* (1857), a seminal work of symbolist and modern poetry; established himself as a leader of the Decadents, a group concerned with aestheticism and the macabre in human emotions; translated the writings of Poe and De Quincey; took to drink and drugs and spent last days stricken with paralysis and poverty. Other works include *Petits Poèmes en Prose* (1869), *Art Romantique,* and *Curiosités Esthétiques* (1868–69).

Baum *(bäm),* **Lyman Frank** 1856–1919. American playwright and writer. *b.* Chittenango, N.Y. Author of *The Wonderful Wizard of Oz* (1900) and 13 other *Oz* stories that have acquired a permanent place in children's literature.

Baum *(boum),* **Vicki** 1888–1960. American novelist. *b.* Vienna, Austria. Emigrated to U.S. (1931). Author of *Grand Hotel* (1931), *And Life Goes On* (1932), *Men Never Know* (1935), *A Tale from Bali* (1937), *Shanghai* (1939), *Grand Opera* and *Helene* (1942), *Mortgage on Life* (1946), and *Danger from Deer* (1951).

Baumé *(bō mā),* **Antoine** 1728–1804. French chemist. *b.* Senlis. Inventor of the Baumé hydrometer, two scales used in measuring liquids (the Baumé scales), and new processes for dyeing, refining saltpeter, and making sal ammoniac. Author of *Éléments de Pharmacie* (1792) and *Chimie Expérimentale et Raisonnée* (1773).

Baumgarten *(boum gär tən),* **Alexander Gottlieb** 1714–62. German philosopher. *b.* Berlin. Founder of the science of aesthetics; professor of philosophy at Frankfurt an der Oder (from 1740). Author of *Metaphysica* (1739) and *Aesthetica Acromatica* (1750–58).

Baur *(bour),* **Ferdinand Christian** 1792–1860. German theologian. *b.* Schmiden. Founder of Tübingen school of theology; professor of theology at Tübingen (from 1826); first to apply methods of historical research to the study of apostolic Christianity. Author of *Das Manichäische Religionssystem* (1831), *Die Christliche Lehre von der Dreieinigkeit* (1841–43), *Paulus* (1845), *Kritische Untersuchungen über die Kanonischen Evangelien* (1847), *Das Markus-Evangelium* (1851) and other works.

Baxter *(băks tər),* **Richard** 1615–91. English nonconformist clergyman. *b.* Rowton. Ordained (1638); served as chaplain in Cromwell's army (1645); appointed royal chaplain at Restoration (1660) but forced to leave English Church on the passage of Act of Uniformity (1662); permitted to return to preaching by Act of Indulgence (1672); accused of libeling the Church in *Paraphrase of the New Testament* (1685) and imprisoned for 18 months. Other works include *Saints' Everlasting Rest* (1650), *Called to the Unconverted* (1657), and *Reliquiae Baxterianae* (1696).

Bayard *(bȧ yär; bā ərd),* **Chevalier de** original name: PIERRE TERRAIL. c1473–1524. French national hero. *b.* Grenoble. Fought in the Italian campaigns of Charles VIII, Louis XII, and Francis I; displayed extraordinary valor at battles of Guingate (1513), Marignano (1515), and in the defense of Mezières (1521); known as *Chevalier sans peur et sans reproche.*

Bayle *(bâl),* **Pierre** 1647–1706. French philosopher. *b.* Carlat. Regarded as the founder of rationalism; elected to the chair of philosophy at the Protestant Academy in Sedan (1675) and in Rotterdam (1681); launched the journal *Nouvelles de la Republique des Lettres* (1684); emerged as a champion of religious toleration and freedom of thought; dismissed for his beliefs (1693); devoted himself to compilation of *Dictionnaire Historique et Critique* (1696).

Bayliss *(bā lĭs),* **Sir William Maddock** 1860–1924. English physiologist. *b.* Wolverhampton. Professor of physiology at University College, London (from 1912); made important discoveries regarding nervous mechanisms, innervation of the intestine, and venous and capillary pressures; devised saline injection treatment for surgical shock; discovered (with Ernest Henry Starling) the hormone secretin, which governs functioning of the pancreas. Author of *The Nature of Enzyme Action* (1908), *Principles of General Physiology* (1914), *The Vasomotor System* (1923), and other books.

Beadle *(bē dəl),* **George Wells** 1903–. American biologist. *b.* Wahoo, Neb. Cowinner of Nobel Prize in physiology and medicine (1958) with Edward L. Tatum and Joshua Lederberg.

Beard (bērd), **Charles Austin** 1874–1948. American historian. *b.* Knightstown, Ind. Professor of politics at Columbia (1907–17); director of Training School for Public Service (1917–22); a founder of the New School for Social Research. Author of (with James Harvey Robinson) *The Development of Modern Europe* (1907), *American Government and Politics* (1910), *American City Government* (1912), *Economic Interpretation of the Constitution* (1913), (with W.C. Bagley) *History of the American People* (1918), and *Economic Basis of Politics* (1922); (with wife, MARY RITTER) *History of the United States* (1921), *The Rise of American Civilization* (1927), and *America in Midpassage* (1939).

Beard, Daniel Carter 1850–1941. American illustrator, writer, and founder of the Boy Scout movement in U.S. *b.* Cincinnati, Ohio. Teacher of drawing at Woman's School of Applied Design (1893–1900); head of the department of woodcraft at Culver Military Academy. Author of *American Boys' Handy Book* (1882), *American Boys' Book of Camplore and Woodcraft* (1920), and *Wisdom of the Woods* (1927).

Beardsley *(bērdz lĭ),* **Aubrey Vincent** 1872–98. English illustrator. *b.* Brighton. In book illustration, gained recognition with fantastic drawings and posters for *Yellow Book* magazine and a series of books, including *Morte d'Arthur,* Oscar Wilde's *Salome, Rape of the Lock, Mlle de Maupin,* and *Volpone*; published *Book of Fifty Drawings* in black and white, a work remarkable for its capricious and asymmetric style.

Beaufort *(bō fərt),* **Sir Francis** 1774–1857. English sailor. *b.* Navan, Ireland. Entered Royal Navy (1787); surveyed coast of Asia Minor, described in *Karamania, or a Brief Description of the South Coast of Asia Minor* (1817); appointed hydrographer to the navy (1829–55); devised the Beaufort scale for measuring wind velocity.

Beaumarchais *(bōmär shā),* **Pierre Augustin Caron de** 1732–99. French playwright. *b.* Paris. Followed his father's profession as a clockmaker; devised a new escapement, which brought him to the notice of court of Louis XV;

enlarged fortune by two marriages to rich widows and the partnership of a rich banker; published bitter satire on the judicial system, *Mémoires du Sieur Beaumarchais par Lui-même* (1774–78), inspired by his litigation with the heirs of his partner; gained fame as a dramatist with comedies *Le Barbier de Séville* (1775) and *Le Mariage de Figaro* (1784); financed supplies for American colonists during War of Independence; died in relative poverty.

Beaumont *(bō mŏnt),* **Francis** 1584–1616. English dramatist. *b.* Grace-Dieu. Intimate friend of Ben Jonson and John Fletcher; began (1606) a productive collaboration with Fletcher in creating 52 dramatic works, including *The Knight of the Burning Pestle* (1613), *The Scornful Lady* (1616), *The Maid's Tragedy* (1619), *Philaster* (1620), and *The Coxcomb* (1647); regarded as the sole author of *The Woman Hater* (1607).

Beaumont, William 1785–1853. American surgeon. *b.* Conn. Investigated the digestive process through observing the exposed stomach of a Canadian patient with an unhealed gunshot wound; after 235 experiments, demonstrated the function of gastric juices; published results in *Experiments and Observations on the Gastric Juice and the Physiology of Digestion* (1833).

Beauregard *(bō rə gärd),* **Pierre Gustave Toutant** 1818–93. American Confederate general. *b.* near New Orleans, La. Served with distinction in Mexican War; appointed superintendent of West Point (1860); resigned on the secession of Louisiana to enter Confederate Army as brigadier general (1861); bombarded and captured Fort Sumter (1861); raised to rank of general after Battle of Bull Run; commanded army at Shiloh, Charleston, and Drury's Bluff (1864); surrendered with Joseph Johnston (1865).

Beauvoir *(bō vwär),* **Simone de** full name: SIMONE LUCIE ERNESTINE MARIE BERTRAND DE BEAUVOIR. 1908–. French novelist, feminist, and existentialist. Close associate of Jean-Paul Sartre. Her book *The Second Sex* (1953) is a ringing denunciation of women's place in society and established her as a leading feminist; her principal works include *The Mandarins* (1943), *All Men Are Mortal* (1954), *The Blood of Others* (1948), *Memoirs of a Dutiful Daughter* (1958), *Prime of Life* (1962), *Force of Circumstance* (1963), and *the Coming of Age* (1972).

Beaverbrook *(bē vər brŏŏk),* **Baron** original name: WILLIAM MAXWELL AITKEN. 1879–1964. British publisher. *b.* Maple, Canada. Amassed fortune in Canada by consolidation of cement mills; went to Britain and entered parliament; minister of information under Lloyd George (1918); entered publishing by taking over *Daily Express* (1919), *Evening Standard* (1929) and by founding *Sunday Express* (1921); member of Churchill's war cabinet (1940–42); lord privy seal (1943–45). Author of *Canada in Flanders* (1916), *Success* (1921), *Politicians and the Press* (1925), *Politicians and the War* (1928, 1932), and *The Decline and Fall of Lloyd George* (1963).

Beccaria *(bāk kä rē ä),* **Cesare Bonesana, Marchese di** 1738–94.

Italian economist and jurist. *b.* Milan. Anonymously published the influential *Tratto dei Delitti e delle Pene* (1764), denouncing capital punishment and advocating educational methods for prevention of crime; held chair of political philosophy at Milan (from 1768); published lectures anticipating social theories of Malthus and economic theories of Adam Smith.

Becket *(bĕk ĕt),* **Thomas à** 1118–70. English ecclesiastic and archbishop of Canterbury. *b.* London. Appointed chancellor on accession of Henry II (1115); proved himself a brilliant minister, skilled diplomat, and courageous knight; raised to see of Canterbury (1162); gave up courtly ways and became ascetic and zealous defender of the Church; defied the sovereign by refusing to accept Constitutions of Clarendon drawn up by Henry to codify allegiance of church to the state (1164); induced by Pope Alexander III to submit; forced to leave the country by king's continued antagonism (1164); returned to England (1170) amid rejoicings of the people following reconciliation; provoked the king by excommunicating the bishops who had crowned Prince Henry without sanction of the primate; murdered by four knights who wished to rid the king of "this turbulent priest" (1170); canonized (1172); under public pressure, Henry did penance at his tomb (1174), which was later destroyed under Henry VIII (1538). Feast day: Dec. 29.

Beckett *(bĕk ĕt),* **Samuel** 1906–. Irish writer. *b.* Dublin. Resident in Paris (from 1932), writing principal works in French; through novels and plays, developed theme of existential despair caused by pointlessness of human strivings and hopes; awarded Nobel Prize in literature (1969). Works include *Waiting for Godot* (1956), *Endgame* (1957), *Molloy* and *Malone Dies* (1958).

Becquer *(bĕ kər),* **Gustavo Adolfo Dominguez** 1836–70. Spanish poet. *b.* Seville. Author of *Leyendas Españolas,* a collection of prose tales written in macabre style, comparable to Poe and Hoffman, and many volumes of lyrical love verses including *Volverán las Oscuras Golondrinas, Olas Gigantes que Os Rompéis Bramando,* and *Cuando Me Lo Contaron Sentí el Frío.*

Becquerel *(bĕ krəl),* **Antoine César** 1788–1878. French physicist. *b.* Châtillon-sur-Loing. One of the founders of science of electrochemistry and first to use electrolysis for isolating metals from their ores; invented thermoelectric needle for measuring internal body temperatures. Author of *Traité d'Électro-chimie* (1843) and *Traité de Physique.* His son ALEXANDRE EDMOND (1820–91), noted for research in the fields of optics, diamagnetism, and solar radiation, also devised a phosphoroscope; grandson ANTOINE HENRY (1852–1908), with Pierre and Marie Curie, received Nobel Prize in physics (1903) for discovery of Becquerel rays, which made possible the isolation of radium and marked the birth of nuclear physics.

Beddoes *(bĕd ōz),* **Thomas Lovell** 1803–49. English poet. *b.* Clifton. Dispirited by the failure of his early work *The Bride's Tragedy* (1822), began a strange wandering life on the Continent; engaged (from 1825) in the writing of *Death's Jest-Book or The Fool's Tragedy,* a macabre drama characterized by spectral imagery but redeemed by scattered passages of haunting beauty; selections from writings published posthumously as *Poems* by Thomas Kelsall.

Bede *(bēd),* **Saint** also BAEDA or BEDA. 673–735. English historian and theologian. *b.* near Monkwearmouth. Regarded as greatest scholar of his time and as the father of English history; spent entire life at Benedictine monastery at Jarrow teaching and writing; made Doctor of the Church by Pope Leo XIII. Principal works include *Historia Ecclesiastica Gentis Anglorum, De Sex Aetatibus Mundi, Historia Abbatum, De Natura Rerum,* and *De Temporum Ratione;* known as The Venerable Bede.

Bedier *(bā dyā),* **Charles Marie Joseph** 1864–1938. French scholar in medieval studies. *b.* Paris. Established reputation with prose rendering of *Roman de Tristan et Yseult;* developed theory in *La Formation des Légendes Épiques* (4 vols., 1908–13) that French epic songs were composed in monasteries along Crusaders' routes and sung for the benefit of pilgrims.

Beebe *(bē bē),* **Charles William** 1877–1962. American naturalist. *b.* Brooklyn, N.Y. Curator of ornithology (from 1899) at N.Y. Zoological Society; led scientific expeditions to Nova Scotia, Central America, South America, the Himalayas, and Borneo; conducted oceanographic surveys in Bermuda waters with a specially designed bathysphere. Author of *Galapagos* (1923), *Jungle Days* (1925), *Beneath Tropic Seas* (1928), *Half Mile Down* (1934), *Book of Bays* (1942), and *High Jungle* (1949).

Beecham *(bē chəm),* **Sir Thomas** 1879–1961. English conductor. *b.* St. Helens. Established and conducted New Symphony Orchestra (1906–1908) and Beecham Symphony Orchestra (1908–10), giving first performance of concert works by Delius; as impresario, produced 120 works and introduced Diaghilev's Russian ballet to British audiences; conductor and director of Covent Garden (from 1932); conductor of Metropolitan Opera in New York City (1943); founded Royal Philharmonic Orchestra (1947) and conducted at Glyndebourne (1948–49); instrumental in popularizing the works of Sibelius, Strauss, and Stravinsky.

Beecher *(bē chər),* **Henry Ward** 1813–87. American Congregational preacher and reformer. *b.* Litchfield, Conn. As pastor of Presbyterian Church in Indianapolis (1839–47) and Plymouth Congregational Church in Brooklyn (1847—87), became a powerful and influential spokesman for abolitionism and women's suffrage; raised and equipped volunteer regiment at outbreak of Civil War; founded and edited the *Independent* and the *Christian Union.* Author of *Lectures to Young Men* (1844), *Summer in the Soul* (1858), *Freedom and War* (1863), *Aids to Prayer* (1864), *Yale Lectures on Preaching* (1874), and *Evolution and Religion* (1885).

Beerbohm *(bēr bōm),* **Max** full name; SIR HENRY MAXIMILIAN BEER-

BOHM. 1872–1956. English critic and caricaturist. *b.* London. Succeeded Shaw as drama critic of *Saturday Review* (until 1910); retired to Rapallo, Italy. Author of contemporary caricatures, novels, parodies, and essays, including *Twenty-five Gentlemen* (1896), *The Poet's Corner* (1904), *Observations* (1925), *Zuleika Dobson* (1911), *Christmas Garland* (1912), *The Happy Hypocrite* (1897), *More* (1899), *And Even Now* (1920), *Variety of Things* (1928), and *Mainly on the Air* (1947).

Beernaert *(bār nàrt),* **Auguste Marie François** 1829–1912. Belgian statesman. *b.* Ostend. Shared Nobel Peace Prize (1909) with Baron d'Estournelles de Constant for role in Hague International Peace Conferences of 1899 and 1907.

Beers *(bērz),* **Clifford Whittingham** 1876–1943. American founder of mental hygiene movement. *b.* New Haven, Conn. Published *A Mind That Found Itself* (1908), a record of his mental breakdown and subsequent recovery; devoted himself to the promotion of mental hygiene science; founded Conn. Society for Mental Hygiene (1908), National Committee for Mental Hygiene (1909), American Foundation for Mental Hygiene (1928), International Commission for Mental Hygiene (1930), and International Foundation for Mental Hygiene (1931).

Beethoven *(bā tō vən),* **Ludwig van** 1770–1827. German composer. *b.* Bonn. Joined orchestra of elector of Cologne (1783); sent to Vienna to study under Haydn, Albrechtsberger, and Salieri (1792); spent remaining life in Vienna except for brief excursions; troubled by increasing deafness (from 1798) and became totally deaf by 1819; career divided into three periods: the first period (1792–1802) included the three trios dedicated to Haydn, the first two symphonies, the Sonate Pathétique, the Pastoral Sonata, the Violin Sonata in C Minor, and the six String Quartets; the second period (1802–12) included the Third *(Eroica),* Fourth, Fifth, Sixth *(Pastoral),* Seventh, and Eighth Symphonies, the Violin Concerto in D, the Leonore overture, and the music to *Egmont;* the third period (1813–27) included the orchestral fantasia *The Battle of Vittoria (The Battle Sympthony),* the Ninth or Choral Symphony, the Missa Solemnis, three piano sonatas, and the last four quartets; music characterized by many innovations, including the chorus in the finale of a symphony, changing the minuet into the scherzo, and multiplication of key relationships of the movements; regarded as greatest composer in history of music.

Behan *(bē ən),* **Brendan Francis** 1923–64. Irish writer. *b.* Dublin. Won recognition with *The Quare Fellow* (1956) based on his prison experiences as a member of I.R.A.; developed talent for caricature and bawdry in *The Hostage* (1959), the autobiographical *Borstal Boy* (1958), and *Brendan Behan's Island* (1963).

Behrens *(bā rəns),* **Peter** 1868–1940. German architect. *b.* Hamburg. Regarded as one of the pioneers of modern architecture; designed A. E. G. turbine factory in Berlin, other industrial buildings, and the abbey of St. Peter at

Salzburg; as a teacher of architecture and applied arts at Düsseldorf, Vienna, and Berlin, taught Walter Gropius and Le Corbusier.

Behring *(bā rĭng),* **Emil von** 1854–1917. German bacteriologist. *b.* Hansdorf, Prussia. As professor of hygiene at Marburg, conducted important researches in immunization; awarded Nobel Prize in medicine (1901) for discovery of bovovaccine and antitoxins for diphtheria and tetanus.

Bekesy *(bā kā shĭ),* **Georg von** 1899–1972. Hungarian-American physiologist. *b.* Budapest, Hungary. Regarded as an authority on aural physiology; immigrated to U.S. (1949); awarded Nobel Prize in medicine (1961).

Bekhterev *(byāк tyĭ ryəf),* **Vladimir Mikhailovich** 1857–1927. Russian neuropathologist. *b.* Ssarali. Founded psychoneurological institute at St. Petersburg (1907); made important contributions to the study of experimental psychology and the classification of insanity; Bekhterev's fibers in the cerebral cortex, Bekhterev's disease (Ankylosing spondylitis), Bekhterev's nucleus of the vestibular nerve, and Bekhterev's reflexes are named after him. Author of *Psyche und Leben* (1908), *Das Verbrechertum im Lichte der Objectiven Psychologie* (1914), *General Principles of Human Reflexology* (1932), and other books.

Belalcázar *(bā läl kä thär),* **Sebastián de** also BENALCAZAR; real name SEBASTIÁN MOYANO. c1499–1550. Spanish conquistador. *b.* Benalcaz. Joined expedition of Pedro Arias de Avila to Nicaragua; took part in Pizarro's conquest of Peru (1532); defeated Inca general Rumi-ñaui at Riobamba and captured Quito (1533); invaded Popayán in Colombia and carried Spanish arms to the north (1533); founded city of Guayaquil; appointed governor of Popayán (1538).

Belinski *(byĭ lyēn skĭ),* **Vissarion Grigorievich** 1811–48. Russian critic. *b.* Fribourg, Switzerland. Editor of *Moscow Observer* (1838–39) and contributor to *Annals of the Fatherland* and *Sovremennik* of St. Petersburg; abandoned early romanticism for didacticism and realism; laid foundation of Russian literary criticism with *Survey of Russian Literature Since the 18th Century* (1834); liberal political and social ideas influential on later writers.

Belisarius *(bĕl ĭ sâr ĭ ŭs)* c505–65. Byzantine general. *b.* Germania, Illyria. Regarded as greatest general in Eastern Roman Empire. Commander of eastern army under Justinian I; defeated Persians (530); suppressed revolt of the Green Faction in Constantinople (532); defeated Vandals in Africa (533–34) and Ostrogoths in Italy (535); conquered Sicily and Southern Italy (535–37); occupied Rome (536) and Ravenna (540); repelled Persian army of Chosroes (541–42); command against Goths in Italy (544) but replaced by Narses (548); emerged from retirement to save Constantinople from the Huns (559); spent last years in disfavor.

Bell *(bĕl),* **Alexander Graham** 1847–1922. American inventor. *b.* Edinburgh, Scotland. Immigrated to U.S. (1871) as a teacher of speech to deaf-mutes using his father ALEXANDER MELVILLE BELL'S system of visible speech; invented the telephone (1876), the photophone (1880), and a recorder for Edison's phonograph (1887); made important contributions to early science of aviation; established (1890) American Association to Promote the Teaching of Speech to the Deaf.

Bell, Sir Charles 1774–1842. Scottish anatomist and surgeon. *b.* Edinburgh. Discovered functions of sensory and motor nerves in the brain (1807); conducted studies of gunshot wounds; held chair of surgery at Edinburgh (from 1836); Bell's palsy, a form of facial paralysis, is named after him. Author of *Anatomy of the Brain* (1811), *System of Comparative Surgery* (1807), *Nervous System of the Human Body* (1830), and other books.

Bellamy *(bĕl à mĭ)*, **Edward** 1850–98. American writer. *b.* Chicopee Falls, Mass. Best remembered as author of *Looking Backward* (1888), a Utopian and socialist novel describing the world as it might be in the year 2000.

Bellarmine *(bĕl är mĭn; -mēn)*, **Robert** Italian name: ROBERTO FRANCESCO ROMOLO BALLARMINO. 1542–1621. Italian cardinal and theologian. *b.* Montepulciano. Noted as chief defender of Catholic Church in 16th century; elected to chair of theology at Louvain (1570); appointed rector of Roman College (1592), cardinal (1599); archbishop of Capua (1602); took part in revision of the Vulgate (1591); proclaimed Doctor of the Church and canonized (1931). Author of famous defense of papal power *Tractatus de Potestate Summi Pontificis in Rebus Temporalibus* (1603).

Bellay *(bĕ lā)*, **Joachim du** 1522–60. French poet. *b.* Liré. Joined group of poets known as the Pléiade; published *Défense et Illustration de la Langue Française* as the manifesto of the group (1549) advocating classical models of composition. Wrote *L'Olive* (sonnets to his mistress) and the sonnet collections *Les Antiquités de Rome* and *Les Regrets.*

Bellingshausen *(bĕl ĭngs hou zən)*, **Fabian Gottlieb von** Russian name: FADDEI FADDEEVICH BELLINGSGAUSEN. 1778–1852. Russian explorer. *b.* Oesel Island. Commander of Russian expedition to Antarctica (1819-21) that discovered and named Peter I Island and Alexander I Island; Mount Bellingshausen and Bellingshausen Sea are named after him.

Bellini *(bāl lē nē)* Family of Venetian painters: IACOPO OR JACOPO. c1400–c1470. Painted a wide range of subjects; works include *The Crucified One, Annunciation,* and *Adoration of the Kings.*

GENTILE. c1427–1507. Son of Iacopo. Official painter to the Venetian state and sultan of Constantinople. Works include *Preaching of St. Mark.*

GIOVANNI. c1430–1516. Son of Iacopo. Known principally for altarpieces and madonnas whose sensuous light and color became the hallmark of the Venetian school. Works include *Self-Portrait, The Feast of the Gods,* and the *Pietà* at Rimini; taught Titian, Giorgione, and Palma Vecchio.

Bellini, Vincenzo 1801–35. Italian operatic composer. *b.* Catania, Sicily. Won recognition with *Adel-*

son e Salvina (1824) and *Bianca e Fernando* (1826); settled in Paris (1833); composed a number of operas, including *La Sonnambula* (1831), *Norma* (1832), and *I Puritani* (1834).

Belloc *(bĕl ŏk),* **Hilaire or Hilary** full name: JOSEPH HILARY PIERRE BELLOC. 1870–1953. English writer. *b.* Paris, France. Became naturalized British subject (1902) and member of Parliament (1906–10); established reputation as a master of English prose with a Roman Catholic viewpoint. Works include *Bad Child's Book of Beasts* (1896), *The Modern Traveller* (1898), *Danton* (1899), *Robespierre* (1901), *The Path to Rome* (1902), *The Servile State* (1912), *Europe and the Faith* (1920), *The Jews* (1922), *History of England* (1925–31), *Richelieu* (1929), *Wolsey* (1930), *Cromwell* (1934), *Napoleon* (1932), *Characters of the Reformation* (1936), *The Great Heresies* (1938), and *The Last Rally* (1940).

Bellow *(bĕl ō),* **Saul** 1915–. American writer. *b.* Lachine, Canada. Moved to U.S. (1924); published first novel *The Dangling Man* (1944); won National Book Award (1955) for *The Adventures of Augie March* (1953), *Herzog* (1964), and *Mr. Sammler's Planet* (1970), and Pulitzer Prize (1976) for *Humboldt's Gift.* Other works include *The Victim* (1947) and *Henderson the Rain King* (1959).

Bellows *(bĕl ōz),* **George Wesley** 1882–1925. American artist. *b.* Columbus, Ohio. Noted for such realist paintings of the American scene as *Stag at Sharkey's, Emma and her Children, Portrait of My Mother, Polo Game at Lakewood, Up the Hudson, North River,* and *Gramercy Park;* influential as a teacher at the Art Students League in New York City and Chicago Art Institute; also did book illustrations and lithographs.

Belmonte *(bĕl môn tā),* **Juan** 1892–. Spanish bullfighter. *b.* Seville. Entered the ring at Madrid (1913); through legendary skill and courage, established reputation as greatest contemporary bullfighter.

Belzoni *(bāl tsō nē),* **Giovanni Battista** 1778–1823. Italian archaeologist. *b.* Padua. Explored Egyptian antiquities (1815–19) and discovered tomb of Seti I at Thebes, cleared temple of Abu Simbel, found the ruins of Berenice on the Red Sea, opened second pyramid at Giza, excavated temple at Idfu, and transported the colossal bust of Rameses to the British Museum. Published *A Narrative of the Operations and Recent Discoveries Within the Pyramids. . . .* (1820).

Bemelmans *(bē məl mənz),* **Ludwig** 1898–1962. American artist and writer. *b.* Meran, Austria. Immigrated to U.S. (1914). Works include *Hansi* (1934), *My War with the U.S.* (1937), *Life Class* (1938), *Madeline* (1939), *Small Beer* (1939), and *I Love You, I Love You, I Love You* (1942), illustrations and articles to *The New Yorker* and other magazines.

Benavente y Martínez *(bā nä vān tā ē mär tē nāth),* **Jacinto** 1866–1954. Spanish dramatist. *b.* Madrid. Beginning with *El Nido Ajeno* (1893), developed new genre of Spanish drama whose main elements are satire, characterization, and dialogue; awarded

Nobel prize in literature (1922). Major plays include *La Malquerida* and *Los Intereses Creados.*

Benchley *(bĕnch lĭ),* **Robert Charles** 1889–1945. American humorist. *b.* Worcester, Mass. On staff of New York *Tribune, Vanity Fair, New York World, Life,* and *New Yorker.* Published collections of humorous essays in *Of All Things* (1921), *Love Conquers All* (1922), *Pluck and Luck* (1925), *The Early Worm* (1927), *The Treasurer's Report* (1930), *From Bed to Worse* (1934), *My Ten Years in a Quandary* (1936), *Inside Benchley* (1942), *Chips Off the Old Benchley* (1949).

Bendl *(bĕn dəl),* **Karel** 1838–97. Czech composer. *b.* Prague. Composed cantatas, choral compositions, chamber music, and masses, but principally operas, including *Lejla, Břetislav and Jitka, Stary Zenich, Indicka Princezna,* and *Cĕrnahorci.*

Benedict of Nursia *(bĕn ə dĭkt əv nûr shĭ ȧ),* **Saint** c480–c543. Italian monk. *b.* Nursia. Founder of the Benedictine order and Western monasticism; withdrew at age 14 to a grotto near Subiaco to practice asceticism; gathered community of monks and established monastery at Monte Cassino (529). Wrote the *Regula Monachorum* (515), the manual of monasticism in the Western church. Feast day: Mar. 21.

Benes *(bĕ nĕsh),* **Eduard** 1884–1948. Czech statesman. *b.* Kožlany. Collaborator with Thomas Masaryk in Czech nationalist movement; headed Czech delegation to Peace Conference (1919–20); foreign minister (1918–35); prime minister (1921–22); member of Council of League of Nations (1923–27); architect of Little Entente and coauthor of Geneva Protocol (1924); president of the republic (1935–38; 1945–48), president of Czech government-in-exile in London (1940-45).

Benét *(bĕ nā),* **Stephen Vincent** 1898–1943. American poet. *b.* Bethlehem, Pa. Brother of William Rose Benét. Author of Pulitzer-Prize-winning *John Brown's Body* (1928), *Ballads and Poems* (1931), *The Devil and Daniel Webster* (1937), *Thirteen O'Clock* (1937), *Tales Before Midnight* (1939), *Western Star* (1943), and other books.

Benét, William Rose 1886–1950. American editor and poet. *b.* Fort Hamilton, N.Y. Brother of Stephen Vincent Benét; on editorial staff of *Century Magazine* (1911–18), New York *Evening Post Literary Review* (1920–24), and *Saturday Review,* which he helped found (1924). Published poetry and novels including *The Falconer of God* (1914), *The Great White Wall* (1916), *Man Possessed* (1927), *Starry Harness* (1933), *Golden Fleece* (1935), *The Dust Which Is God* (1941; won Pulitzer Prize in 1942), *The Stairwary of Surprise* (1947), *The First Person Singular* (1922), and *The Flying King of Kurio* (1926); edited *Reader's Encyclopedia* (1948).

Ben-Gurion *(bĕn go͞or yôn),* **David** real name: DAVID GREEN. 1886–1973. Israeli statesman. *b.* Plonsk, Poland. Emigrated to Palestine (1906); helped organize Jewish Legion against the Turks; general secretary of General Federation of Jewish Labor, the Histadrut (1921–33); leader of Mapai

Party (from 1930); proclaimed independence of Israel (1948); prime minister (1949–53; 1955–63).

Benjamin of Tudela *(bĕn jȧ mĭn əv to͞o thā lä)* *d.* 1173. Jewish traveler. *b.* Navarre, Spain. Author of *Massa'ot,* an account of his travels in France, Italy, Greece, Palestine, Persia, China, Egypt, and Sicily (1159–73); generally regarded as first western traveler to reach China.

Benn *(bĕn),* **Gottfried** 1886–1956. German poet. *b.* Mansfeld. Began writing as an expressionist and nihilist, but later became a Nazi and, after 1945, a pessimist, thus matching the moods of 20th-century Germany. Author of *Morgue* (1912), *Fleisch* (1916), *Schutt* (1924), *Gehirne* (1917), *Vermessungsdirigent* (1919), *Nach dem Nihilismus* (1932), *Kunst und Macht* (1934), and *Statische Gedichte* (1948).

Bennett *(bĕn ĕt),* **Arnold** full name: ENOCH ARNOLD BENNETT. 1867–1931. English novelist. *b.* near Hanley. Began career as a journalist; from 1900 devoted himself exclusively to writing; fame rests on *The Old Wives' Tale* (1908), the *Clayhanger* trilogy (1910–16), *Riceyman Steps* (1923), *Buried Alive* (1908), dramatized as *The Great Adventure* (1913), and *Imperial Palace* (1930).

Bennett, James Gordon 1795–1872. American publisher. *b.* Keith, Scotland. Founded New York *Herald* (1835); remained its editor until retirement (1867). Control passed to his son JAMES GORDON BENNETT (1841–1918), whose most spectacular exploit was sending Henry M. Stanley to find David Livingstone, reported missing in Africa; also promoted yachting, automobile and airplane racing, and the polar expedition of George W. DeLong (1879–81).

Bennett, Viscount Richard Bedford 1870–1947. Canadian statesman. *b.* Hopewell. Entered Canadian Parliament (1911); head of Conservative Party; prime minister (1930–35); convened Ottawa Imperial Conference (1932), which adopted a system of empire trade preference known as the Ottawa Agreement.

Bennett, Sir William Sterndale 1816–75. English composer. *b.* Sheffield. Teacher at Royal Academy of Music (1839) and its principal (from 1868); founded Bach Society (1849); conducted London Philharmonic Orchestra (1856–66). Compositions include *Naiads* (1837), *The May Queen* (1858), *Paradise and the Peri* (1862), and *Woman of Samaria* (1867).

Benoît de Sainte-Maure or Sainte-More *(bə nwȧ də sănt môr)* *fl.* mid-12th century. French trouvère. *b.* Sainte-Maure. Author of *La Chronique des Ducs du Normandie* (c1180), a poem of 45,000 lines dedicated to his patron, Henry II of England, and *Roman de Troie,* a poem of 30,000 lines based on works of Dares Phrygius and Dictys Cretensis, which was a sourcebook on the Troilus and Cressida legend used by Boccaccio, Chaucer, and Shakespeare.

Bentham *(bĕn thəm),* **Jeremy** 1748–1832. English philosopher. *b.* London. Called to the bar (1772); laid foundation of utilitarianism with publication of *Introduction to the Principles of Morals and Legislation* (1789); held that morality is determined by utility, that laws should be socially useful, and that the goal of government is to promote "the greatest happiness of the greatest number"; exerted great influence on legal reform through his writings, especially *Fragment on Government* (1776), *Rationale of Punishment and Rewards* (1825), *Rationale of Judicial Evidence* (1825), and *Constitutional Code* (1827); helped found *Westminster Review* (1823).

Bentinck *(bĕn tĭngk),* **Lord William Cavendish** 1774–1839. British colonial administrator. Governor general of Bengal (1828–33); governor general of India (1833–35); administration marked by introduction of English language as medium of instruction in Indian schools and colleges, the abolition of *sati*, and the suppression of thugs.

Bentinck, William Henry Cavendish title: THIRD DUKE OF PORTLAND. 1738–1809. English statesman. *b.* Bulstrode. Entered Lord Rockingham's cabinet (1765); lord lieutenant of Ireland (1782); leader of Whig Party; prime minister (1783; 1807–1809); home secretary under William Pitt (1794–1801); lord president of the council (1801–1805).

Benton *(bĕn tən),* **Thomas Hart** 1889–1975. American painter. *b.* Neosho, Mo. Specialized as an American scene painter; dramatized midwestern America in vigorous murals and portraits. Among best-known works are *Contemporary America, The Arts of Life in America, History of Indiana, History of Missouri, Louisiana Rice Field, Susanna and the Elders, Threshing Wheat, Cotton Pickers, Lonesome Road, Homestead,* and *The Music Lesson.* Author of *The Artist in America,* a record of a ten-year trip through the South and West (1937); nephew of THOMAS HART BENTON (1782–1858), U.S. Senator (1821–51).

Ben-Yahuda *(bĕn yə hōō dȧ),* **Elieser** 1858–1922. Jewish scholar. *b.* in Lithuania. Immigrated to Palestine (1881); helped popularize Hebrew as national language of the Jews by modernizing its vocabulary; compiled *The Dictionary of Ancient and Modern Hebrew* (16 vols., unfinished at death).

Benz *(bĕnts),* **Karl Friedrich** 1844–1929. German automotive engineer. *b.* Karlsruhe. Constructed two-stroke model engine and founded Benz & Company in Mannheim for its manufacture; devised triple-axle steering gear and invented the differential and battery ignition with spark induction; built first car (1885); merged with Daimler's firm to form Mercedes-Benz (1926).

Béranger *(bā räɴ zhā),* **Pierre Jean de** 1780–1857. French lyricist. *b.* Paris. Composer of such popular patriotic songs as *Le Roi d'Yvetot* and *Le Vieux Drapeau,* extolling Republicanism and Bonapartism. Author of *Ma Biographie* (1858).

Berdyaev *(byər dyȧ yəf),* **Nikolai Aleksandrovich** 1874–1948. Russian philosopher. *b.* Kiev. Exiled as an anti-Communist (1922); founded Academy of the Philosophy of Religion in Berlin (1922) later transferred to Paris; expounded a Christian-apocalyptic philosophy in *Dostoievsky* (1934), *Freedom and the Spirit* (1935), *The Destiny of Man* (1937), *The Meaning of History*

(1936), *Solitude and Society* (1938), *Spirit and Reality* (1939), and *Dream and Reality* (1951).

Berenson *(bĕr ən sən),* **Bernhard** also BERNARD. 1865–1959. American art critic. *b.* Vilna, Lithuania. Reputation as leading authority on Italian Renaissance art; works in this field include *Venetian Painters of the Renaissance* (1894), *Florentine Painters of the Renaissance* (1896), *Central Italian Painters of the Renaissance* (1897), *The Study and Criticism of Italian Art* (1901), *Essays in Mediaeval Art* (1930), and *Aesthetics and History in the Visual Arts* (1949); also published *Sketch for a Self Portrait* (1949).

Bergh *(bûrg),* **Henry** 1811–88. American philanthropist. *b.* New York, N.Y. Founder of American Society for the Prevention of Cruelty to Animals (1866); major force in founding Society for the Prevention of Cruelty to Children (1875); son of CHRISTIAN BERGH (1763–1843), shipbuilder.

Bergius *(bĕr gē oos),* **Friedrich** 1884–1949. German industrial chemist. *b.* Goldschmieden. Developed the Bergius Process for the conversion of coal to oil by hydrogenation and the conversion of wood to sugar by hydrolysis; shared (with Karl Bosch) Nobel Prize in chemistry (1931).

Bergman *(bėrg mȧn),* **Ingmar** 1918–. Swedish film director. *b.* Uppsala. Manager of Sweden's Royal Dramatic Theater; won acclaim with impressionistic films rich in metaphor and subtle photographic nuances. Works include *Summer with Monika* (1953), *The Seventh Seal* (1956), *Wild Strawberries* (1957), *Persona* (1965), *Cries and Whispers* (1972), and *Scenes from a Marriage* (1974).

Bergson *(berg'sôN; -sən),* **Henri** 1859–1941. French philosopher. *b.* Paris. In *Creative Evolution* (1907), *Essai sur les Données Immédiates de la Conscience* (1889), *Matière et Mémoire* (1897), *L'Énergie Spirituelle* (1920), *Durée et Simultanéité* (1922), and other works, attacked mechanistic materialism by postulating the principle of *élan vital* as the creative force underlying change and evolution; held that *élan vital* can be apprehended only through intuition of the phenomenon of duration or experienced time; awarded Nobel Prize for literature (1927).

Bering *(bā rĭng),* **Vitus Jonassen** also BEHRING. 1680–1741. Danish navigator. *b.* Horsens. Entered the service of Peter the Great; appointed to lead expedition to North Pacific; sailed from Kamchatka (1728), following the coast to the northeast point of Asia; traversed Bering Strait and proved that Asia and America are separate land masses; explored west coast of America (1741) but forced to return by sickness and storms; died on the island of Avatcha; Bering Island, Bering Strait, and Bering Sea are named after him.

Berkeley *(bûrk lĭ),* **George** 1685–1753. Irish bishop and philosopher. *b.* Kilkenny. Bishop of Cloyne (1734); founder of the philosophic system known as Berkeleianism, based on subjective idealism and phenomenalism; held that matter exists only through perception and that divine mind and perception makes possible the continued existence of material objects. Principal works include *Three Dialogues*

Between Hylas and Philonous (1713) *A Treatise Concerning the Principles of Human Knowledge (1710), Essay Towards a New Theory of Vision* (1709), and *Alciphron, or The Minute Philosopher* (1732).

Berlin *(bûr lĭn),* **Irving** real name: ISRAEL BALINE. 1888–. American composer. *b.* Russia. Beginning with *Alexander's Ragtime Band* (1911), composed lyrics and music for over 1000 songs, including *"God Bless America," "White Christmas," "Easter Parade," "Blue Skies," "Oh, How I Hate to Get Up in the Morning," "Russian Lullaby,"* and *"Because I Love You";* furnished scores for such musicals as *Ziegfeld Follies, As Thousands Cheer, Annie Get your Gun,* and *Call Me Madame.*

Berlioz *(bĕr lyôz),* **Louis Hector** 1803–69. French composer. *b.* La Côte-Saint-André. One of the founders of program music and the musical genre dramatic symphony; compositions innovative in structure, melody, rhythm, and instrumentation. Chief works are *Symphonie Fantastique* (1830), *Harold in Italy* (1834), *Romeo and Juliet* (1839), *The Infancy of Christ* (1854), *Damnation of Faust* (1846), *Beatrice and Benedict* (1862), *Les Troyens* (1858), *Roman Carnival.* Author of *Evenings with the Orchestra* (1852), *Memoirs* (2 vols., 1870), and *Treatise on Orchestration* (1844).

Bernadette of Lourdes *(bĕr nȧ dĕt əv loord),* **Saint** real name: BERNADETTE SOUBIROUS. 1844–79. French visionary. *b.* Lourdes. Claimed to have received 18 apparitions of the Blessed Virgin Mary at the Massabielle Rock from February 11 to July 16, 1858; instructed by the Virgin to make known the miraculous healing power of the waters of a fountain in the grotto; became a novice of the Sisters of Charity at Nevers (1866); beatified (1925); canonized (1933). Feast day: Feb. 11.

Bernadotte, Jean Baptiste Jules. *See* **Charles XIV (Sweden)**

Bernanos *(bĕr nȧ nôs),* **Georges** 1888–1948. French Catholic writer. *b.* Paris. Author of religious works concerned with sin and salvation, such as *The Star of Satan* (1940) and *Diary of a Country Priest* (1937).

Bernard *(bĕr nȧr),* **Claude** 1813–78. French physiologist. *b.* St.-Julien. Held chair of general physiology at College de France (1854) and chair of experimental physiology (from 1855); conducted important research in functions of the liver and pancreas, the working of the sympathetic nervous system, alimentary canal secretions, changes of blood temperature, and oxygen in arterial and venous blood. Published *Leçons de Physiologie Expérimentale* (1865) and other works.

Bernard of Clairvaux *(bĕr närd əv klĕr vō),* **Saint** 1090–1153. French ecclesiastic. *b.* Fontaines. Founder (1115) and first abbot of Cistercian monastery of Clairvaux in Champagne; instrumental in election of Pope Innocent II; principal advisor to Pope Eugene III; led successful opposition to the rationalistic heresies of Peter Abelard and Arnold of Brescia; called for a second crusade at the Council of Vézelay (1146). Writings consist of over 400 epistles, 340 sermons, and 12 treatises, including *On the Steps of Humility and Pride, On the Love of God, On Grace and Free*

Will, and *On Conversion;* canonized (1173); named Doctor of the Church by Pope Pius VIII. Feast day: Aug. 20.

Bernard of Menthon *(mäɴ tôɴ),* **Saint** 923–1008. Swiss churchman. *b.* Savoy. Founded hospices of the Little and Great St. Bernard passes and a community of Hospitallers to give aid to travelers in the Alps; patron saint of mountaineers. Feast day: May 28.

Bernhardt *(bûrn härt),* **Sarah** original name: Henriette Rosine Bernard. 1844–1923. French actress. *b.* Paris. Made debut at Comédie Français (1862); superb performances in *Le Passant, Ruy Blas, Hernani,* and *Phèdre* earned her the title "divine Sarah"; found greatest roles in *La Tosca, Froufrou,* and *La Dame aux Camélias;* also appeared in *Gismonda, La Princesse Lointaine, L'Aiglon, Fédora, Théodora,* and *Adrienne Lecouvreur;* made several American and Continental tours (after 1880); purchased Théâtre de la Renaissance (1893) and founded the Théâtre Sarah-Bernhardt (1899); starred in two silent films (1912). Published *Autobiography* (1912).

Bernini *(bĕr nē nē),* **Giovanni Lorenzo** 1598–1680. Italian sculptor. *b.* Naples. Succeeded Carlo Maderna as papal architect. Designed fountains of Piazza Navona, Trevia, and Berberini, the grand staircase of the Vatican, bronze baldacchino, the tombs of Urban VIII and Alexander VII, colonnades in the apse and piazza of St. Peter's, and Jesuit church of S. Andrea al Quirinale; three best-known sculptures are *David, Apollo and Daphne,* and *Rape of Proserpine.*

Bernoulli *(bĕr no͞ol ē; bĕr no͞o yē)* Family of Swiss mathematicians:

Jacques or Jakob (1654–1705). Professor of mathematics at University of Basel (from 1687); discovered properties of logarithmic spiral, improved differential calculus, established principles of calculus of probability, described Bernoulli's numbers, first used the term *integral,* and solved the isoperimetrical problem.

Jean or Johann (1667–1748). Professor of mathematics at University of Basel (from 1705); worked on exponential calculus.

Daniel (1700–1782). Professor of mathematics at St. Petersburg (1723); returned to Basel to become professor of, successively, anatomy, botany, and physics (1733); solved an equation proposed by Riceti known as Bernoulli's equation; chief work was *Hydrodynamica* (1738).

Berthelot *(bĕr tē lō),* **Pierre Eugène Marcelin** 1827–1907. French scientist and statesman. *b.* Paris. Founder of thermochemistry and organic chemistry; first to synthesize methane, acetylene, formic acid, ethanol, and benzene; pioneered in explosives; held chair of organic chemistry at Collège de France (1861–1907); served as life senator (1881), minister of public instruction (1886–87), and minister of foreign affairs (1895–96).

Berthollet *(bĕr tô lĕ),* **Comte Claude Louis** 1748–1822. French chemist. *b.* Talloires. One of the professors and founders of l'École Polytechnique; with Antoine Lavoisier, conducted researches on gunpowder and devised system of chemical nomenclature; discovered the important properties of chlorine, carbon, and potassium chlorate. Works include *Essai de Statique Chimique, Éléments de l'Art de la Teinture,* and (with Lavoisier) *Méthode de Nomenclature Chimique.*

Bertillon *(ber tē yôɴ; bû tĭ lŏn),* **Alphonse** 1853–1914. French anthropologist. *b.* Paris. Chief of department of identification of Paris police; devised Bertillon system (1880) for identifying criminals by means of anthropometric measurements; investigated handwriting analysis.

Berzelius *(bər zē lĭ əs),* **Baron Jöns Jakob** 1779–1848. Swedish chemist. *b.* Westerlösa. Developed modern system of chemical symbols; discovered thorium, selenium, and cerium; prepared table of atomic weights; isolated calcium, barium, strontium, columbium, silicium, and zirconium; advanced atomic theory by determination of atomic and molecular weights; originated electrochemical theory. Author of *Lärebok i Kemien* and other books.

Besant *(bĕz nt),* **Annie** *née* Wood. 1847–1933. British theosophist. *b.* London. Associated with Charles Bradlaugh in the free thought and population control movement; joined Theosophical Society as pupil of Madame Blavatsky (1889); became president and high priestess (1907–33); instrumental in establishing Central Hindu University at Benares (1898); president of Indian National Congress (1917); organized India Home Rule League. Wrote extensively on theosophy and India.

Besht. *See* **Baal Shem-Tov**

Bessel *(bĕs əl),* **Friedrich Wilhelm** 1784–1846. German mathematician and astronomer. *b.* Minden. Director of observatory at Königsburg (from 1813); made first authenticated measurement of a star's distance by determining the parallax of 61 Cygni; calculated orbit of Halley's comet (1804); predicted the existence of dark stars and a planet beyond Uranus; systematized Bessel functions, used in astronomy and mathematical physics.

Bessemer *(bĕs ə mər),* **Sir Henry** 1813–98. English engineer. *b.* Charlton. Invented the Bessemer process (1856–58) for making steel from pig iron by using blast air to oxidize impurities in molten iron.

Bethe *(bā tĕ),* **Hans Albrecht** 1906–. American physicist. *b.* in Germany. Immigrated to U.S. (1935); awarded Nobel Prize in physics (1967) for researches in astrophysics and nuclear physics.

Betjeman *(bĕch ə măn),* **John** 1906–. English poet. *b.* London. Poet laureate of England (1972). Author of *Mount Zion* (1933), *New Bats in Old Belfries* (1940), *Collected Poems* (1958), *Summoned by Bells* (1960), and *High Low* (1966).

Beveridge *(bĕv ər ĭj),* **William Henry** title: Baron Beveridge of Tuggal. 1879–1963. English economist. *b.* Rangpur, India. Director of London School of Economics (1919–37); master of University College at Oxford (1937–45); president of Royal Statistical Society (1941–43); principally associated with the Beveridge Report (1942) which recommended a comprehensive scheme of social security for all British citizens without income limit. Author of *Insurance* *for All* (1924), *Full Employment in a Free Society* (1944), and *India Called Them* (1947).

Bevin *(bĕv ĭn),* **Ernest** 1881–1951. British labor leader and statesman. *b.* Winsford. Pioneer of modern trade unionism; consolidated 45 unions into the Transport and General Workers' Union and became its general secretary (1921–40); chairman of Trades Union Congress (1936–37); member of Churchill's war cabinet as minister of labor and national service (1940–45); secretary of state for foreign affairs in Attlee's cabinet (1945–51). Author of *The Job to be Done* (1942).

Bewick *(bū ĭk),* **Thomas** 1753–1828. English wood engraver. *b.* Cherryburn. Among his finest works are illustrations for Gay's *Fables,* (1779), *Select Fables* (1784), *General History of Quadrupeds* (1790), *History of British Birds* (2 vols., 1797–1804), and *Aesop's Fables* (1818).

Beyle, Marie Henri. *See* **Stendhal**

Bèze *(bâz),* **Théodore de** 1519–1605. French Protestant theologian. *b.* Vézelay. Professor of theology and rector of Academy at Geneva (1559); with Calvin, leader of Reformation in France; succeeded him as leader of church of Geneva; presided at synods of French Protestants at La Rochelle (1571) and Nîmes (1572). Best known legacy is the Latin New Testament.

Biddle *(bĭd əl),* **John** 1615–62. Founder of English Unitarianism. *b.* Wotton-under-Edge. Imprisoned (1645–52, 1662) for publicly rejecting the deity of the Holy Ghost; banished to Scilly Islands (1655–58) for publishing the heretical *Twofold Catechism* (1654); died in prison.

Bienville *(byăN vēl),* **Jean Baptiste Le Moyné Sieur de,** 1680–1768. French colonizer. *b.* Longueuil. Governor of Louisiana (1701–1713, 1718–26, 1733–43); founder of Fort Louis (1702), Mobile, Ala., (1710), and New Orleans, La. (1718).

Bierce *(bērs),* **Ambrose Gwinnett** 1824–c1914. American writer. *b.* Meigs County, Ohio. Journalist in San Francisco (1868–72, 1876–99), England (1872–76), and Washington, D.C. (from 1899); acquired reputation as a caustic and satirical writer. Wrote *The Fiend's Delight* (1872), *Cobwebs from an Empty Skull* (1874), *Tales of Soldiers and Civilians* (1891), *Fantastic Fables* (1899), and The Devil's Dictionary (1906); disappeared in Mexico (1913).

Billroth *(bĭl rōt),* **Albert Christian Theodor** 1829–94. Austrian surgeon. *b.* Bergen, Germany. Professor of surgery at Zurich (1860–67) and Vienna (1867–94); pioneer in military surgery; performed first excision of the larynx (1874) and first intestinal resection (1881).

Binet *(bēn nĕ),* **Alfred** 1857–1911. French psychologist. *b.* Nice. Founder and director of laboratory of physiological psychology at Sorbonne (1889); devised (with Theodore Simon) tests for measuring intelligence, known as Binet-Simon tests (1905). Author of *La Psychologie du Raisonnement* (1886), *L'Étude Experimentale de l'Intelligence* (1903), and *Introduction à la Psychologie Expérimentale* (1894).

Binyon *(bĭn yən),* **Laurence** 1869–1943. English poet and critic. *b.* Lancaster. Chief of Oriental prints and paintings at British Museum (1913–33); contributions to art criticism include *Painting in the Far East* (1908), *Japanese Art* (1909), and *Drawings and Engravings of William Blake* (1922); established reputation as poet with *Lyric Poems* (1894), *Collected Poems* (1931), *Odes* (1901), *The Praise of Life* (1896), *Porphyrion and Other Poems* (1898), and *The Death of Adam* (1903).

Birdseye *(bûrdz ī),* **Clarence** 1886–1956. American food technologist. *b.* Brooklyn, N.Y. Developed method for quick-freezing food (1923); held over 250 patents related to dehydration of food and incandescent reflector lamps.

Bismarck *(bĭz märk),* **Prince Otto Eduard Leopold von** also BISMARCK-SCHÖNHAUSEN; called THE IRON CHANCELLOR. 1815–98. German statesman. *b.* Schönhausen. Entered Prussian United Diet (1847); became outspoken royalist and opponent of liberalism; Prussian ambassador to German Diet at Frankfurt (1849), where he called for consolidation of German peoples under Prussia; ambassador to Russia (1859) and France (1862); president of Council of Ministers, and foreign minister (1862); defeated Denmark in Schleswig-Holstein War (1864), Austria in Seven Weeks' War (1866), and France in Franco-Prussian War (1870–71); organized North German confederation under Prussian leadership (1866); created German Empire (1871) and annexed Alsace-Lorraine; internally, initiated economic and social reforms, protective tariffs, and public ownership of industries; engaged in protracted struggle with Catholic Church known as *Kulturkampf;* presided over Congress of Berlin (1878) and formed Triple Alliance (1882); resigned over disagreement with Wilhelm II (1890). Author of *Reflections and Reminiscences* (1898).

Bivar, Rodrigo Díaz de. *See* **Cid, the**

Bizet *(bē zĕ),* **Alexandre César Léopold** also GEORGES BIZET. 1838–75. French composer. *b.* Paris. Best known for the opera *Carmen* (1875). Other works include *Les Pêcheurs de Perles* (1863), *La Jolie Fille de Perth* (1867), and *L'Arlésienne* (1872).

Björnson *(byûrn sən),* **Björnstjerne** 1832–1910. Norwegian writer. *b.* Kvikne. Director of the theater at Bergen (1857–59) and Christiania theater (1865–67); editor of *Aftenbladet* (1859) and *Norsk Folkeblad* (1866); active in politics as a liberal Republican; early works dealt with Norwegian peasant life, but later wrote plays on social themes. First novel was *Synnöve Solbakken* (1857), followed by *Arne* (1858), *A Happy Boy* (1860), *The Fisher Maiden* (1868), *Magnhild* (1877), *Flags are Flying in Town and Port* (1884), and *In God's Way* (1889); major dramas were *Between the Battles* (1857), *Lame Hulda* (1858), *King Sverre* (1861), *Sigurd the Bastard* (1862), *Mary Stuart in Scotland* (1864), *The Newly Married* (1865), *A Bankruptcy* (1875), *The Editor* (1875), *The King* (1877), *The New System* (1879), *Beyond Human Power* (1883), and *Paul Lange and Tora Parsberg* (1898); Norwegian national anthem is taken from his

Poems and Songs (1870); awarded Nobel Prize in literature (1903).

Black *(blăk),* **Joseph** 1728–99. Scottish chemist. *b.* Bordeaux, France. Professor of anatomy and chemistry at Glasgow (1756) and of medicine and chemistry at Edinburgh (1766); developed theory of latent heat and laid foundation on the subject of specific heats (1760); conducted research on causticity of lime and alkalies.

Blackett *(blăk ət),* **Patrick Maynard Stuart** 1897–1974. British physicist. *b.* London. Professor at Birkbeck College, London (1933–37), Manchester University (1937–53), and Imperial College of Science (1953–65); first to photograph (1925) nuclear collisions using an improved Wilson cloud chamber; discovered the positron (1932); investigated cosmic rays and mesons; awarded Nobel Prize in physics (1948). Author of *The Methodology of Operation Research* (1943) and *The Military and Political Consequences of Atomic Energy* (1948).

Blackmore *(blăk mōr),* **Richard Doddridge** 1825–1900. English novelist. *b.* Longworth. Began writing novels with *Clara Vaughan* (1864) followed by 15 other works, of which the best known is *Lorna Doone* (1869).

Black Prince, the. *See* **Edward of Woodstock**

Blackstone *(blăk stōn),* **Sir William** 1723–80. English jurist. *b.* London. Held first Vinerian chair of English law at Oxford (1758); returned to successful law practice; member of Parliament (1761); king's counsel (1761); solicitor-general to the queen (1763). Published *Commentaries on the Laws of England* (4 vols., 1765–69), one of the most celebrated expositions of English law.

Blackwell *(blăk wĕl),* **Elizabeth** 1821–1910. American physician. *b.* Bristol, England. First woman doctor of medicine in U.S.; immigrated to U.S. (1832); graduated from the Medical School in Geneva, N.Y. (1849); opened private dispensary in N.Y. (1850) which later became the New York Infirmary and College for Women; returned to England (1869) where she helped found the London School of Medicine for Women, serving as its professor of gynecology until 1907.

Blackwood *(blăk wo͝od),* **Frederick Temple Hamilton-Temple** titles: MARQUIS OF DUFFERIN AND AVA, BARON CLANDEBOYE. 1826–1902. English statesman. *b.* Florence, Italy. Governor general of Canada (1872–78); ambassador at St. Petersburg (1879–81) and Constantinople (1881–82); commissioner in Egypt (1882–83); governor general of India (1884–88); annexed Upper Burma to British Indian Empire (1885); ambassador to Rome (1889–1891) and Paris (1891–96).

Blaeu *(blou),* **Willem Janszoon** also BLAEUW or BLAUW. 1571–1638. Dutch mapmaker and astronomer. *b.* Alkmaar. Founded publishing firm noted for its maps, atlases, and globes. Author of *Novus Atlas* (1634–62); business continued by sons JAN and CORNELIUS and by Jan's son, WILLEM.

Blake *(blāk),* **Robert** 1599–1657. English admiral. *b.* Bridgewater. Joined Parliamentarians (1640); defended Bristol, Lyme, and Taunton against Royalists (1643–

45); appointed to command of the fleet (1649); pursued and destroyed Prince Rupert's squadron; crippled Dutch fleet and shattered naval supremacy of Holland (1652–53); sailed into Mediterranean (1654–55) and made British presence felt at Cadiz, Leghorn, Naples, and Tunis; burned the Spanish West Indian fleet at Santa Cruz (1657); regarded as one of the greatest English admirals.

Blake, William 1757–1827. English poet, painter, and mystic. *b.* London. Wrote some of the finest lyrics in the English language in *Songs of Innocence* (1783) and *Songs of Experience* (1794); developed system of visionary mythology in the Prophetic Books which included *Book of Thel* (1789), *The Marriage of Heaven and Hell* (1791), *The Gates of Paradise* (1793), *The Vision of the Daughters of Albion* (1793), and *The Song of Los* (1795); produced a series of engravings and etchings to illustrate Edward Young's *Night Thoughts* (1797), Robert Blair's *The Grave* (1808), *The Book of Job* (1820–26), and works by Mary Wollstonecraft (1791), as well as his own writing.

Blanc *(blän),* **Jean Joseph Charles Louis** 1811–82. French socialist. *b.* Madrid, Spain. Began career as a journalist; founded *Revue du Progrès* (1839); established reputation as socialist theoretician with *Organisation du Travail* (1840), advocating state socialism and cooperative workshops; published *Histoire de Dix Ans 1830–40* (1841) attacking Orleanists; member of provisional government of 1848; accused of fomenting disturbances and forced to seek refuge in England (1848); completed *Histoire de la Révolution Française* (12 vols., 1847–62) and several polemical works; returned to France (1871) and was elected deputy to the National Assembly.

Blasco-Ibáñez *(bläs kō ē bä nyāth; -nyās),* **Vicente** 1867–1928. Spanish writer. *b.* Valencia. Imprisoned and exiled for republican sympathies. Prolific output includes *La Barraca* (1898), *Cañas y Barro* (1902), *The Shadow of the Cathedral* (1903), *Blood and Sand* (1908), *The Four Horsemen of the Apocalypse* (1918), and *El Papa del Mar* (1926).

Blavatsky *(blȧ văt skĭ),* **Helena Petrovna** *née* HELENA HAHN. 1831–91. Russian occultist and theosophist. *b.* Ekaterinoslav. Acquired interest in occult through travels in Tibet and India; with Henry Steel Olcott, founded Theosophical Society in N.Y. (1875) with a branch at Bombay (1879); claimed supernatural powers; deemed fraudulent by Society for Psychical Research. Author of *Isis Unveiled* (1876), *The Secret Doctrine* (2 vols., 1888), *The Key to Theosophy* (1889), and *The Voice of Silence* (1889).

Blériot *(blā ryō),* **Louis** 1872–1936. French aviator. *b.* Cambrai. First to cross the English Channel in a heavier-than-air machine (1909).

Bleuler *(bloi lər),* **Eugen** 1857–1939. Swiss psychiatrist. *b.* Zollikon. Professor at University of Zurich (1898–1927); carried out important research on dementia praecox; introduced the term *schizophrenia* (1913). Author of *Dementia Praecox or Group of the Schizophrenias* (1911), *The Theory* *of Schizophrenic Negativism* (1912), and *The Textbook of Psychiatry* (1924).

Blicher *(blē kər),* **Steen Steenson** 1782–1848. Danish lyric poet and novelist. *b.* Vium, Denmark. Collected poems and stories, including *The Migratory Birds* and *Twelve Stories,* regarded as among the gems of Danish literature; translated Ossian into Danish (1807–1809).

Bligh *(blī),* **William** 1754–1817. English admiral. *b.* Plymouth. Sailed with Captain Cook on second voyage (1772–74); appointed commander of the *Bounty* (1787) on voyage to Tahiti to collect breadfruit trees; antagonized the crew by harsh, tyrannical conduct and provoked mutiny; in one of the most famous incidents in naval history, was set adrift in an open 23-foot boat with 18 men, few provisions, and no chart, yet managed to reach Timor, 3618 miles away; appointed governor of New South Wales (1805–1808), but was arrested and imprisoned by his own soldiers; vice-admiral (1814).

Bloch *(blôk),* **Ernest** 1880–1959. American composer. *b.* Geneva, Switzerland. Immigrated to U.S. (1916); directed Cleveland Institute of Music (1920–25) and San Francisco Conservatory of Music (1925–30); composed chiefly on Jewish themes. Works include *Schelomo* (1916), *Macbeth* (1903), *Jezebel* (1918), symphonic poems, sonatas, and *Sacred Service.*

Bloch, Felix 1905–. American physicist. *b.* Zurich, Switzerland. Immigrated to U.S. (1934); professor of theoretical physics at Stanford (from 1934); shared Nobel Prize in physics (1952) with E.M. Purcell for work in measurement of magnetic fields in atomic nuclei.

Bloch, Konrad Emil 1912–. American biochemist. *b.* in Germany. Immigrated to U.S. (1936); professor of biochemistry at Harvard (from 1954); shared (with Feodor Lynen) Nobel Prize in physiology and medicine (1964) for work on cholesterol and fatty acid metabolism.

Blok *(blôk),* **Aleksandr Aleksandrovich** 1880–1921. Russian poet. *b.* St. Petersburg. Influenced in early life by mysticism of Vladimir Soloviev, which inspired his first book of poems, *Verses About the Lady Beautiful* (1904); moved to realism in *Nocturnal Hours* (1911); idealized October Revolution in *The Twelve* and *The Scythians* (1920); later disillusioned with Communism.

Blondel *(blôɴ dĕl),* **François** title: SIEUR DES CROISETTES. 1617–86. French architect. Director of French Academy of Architecture; principal work was the triumphal arch at Porte St.-Denis. Work continued by nephew JACQUES FRANÇOIS BLONDEL (1705–74), who designed city reconstruction in Metz and Strasbourg and who authored *L'Architecture Française* (1752–56) and *Cours d'Architecture Civile* (1771–77).

Bloomfield *(bloo͞m fēld),* **Leonard** 1887–1949. American philologist. *b.* Chicago, Ill. Professor of German and linguistics, Ohio State University (1921–27); professor of Germanic philology, University of Chicago (1927–40); revolutionized linguistics with *An Introduction to the Study of Language* (1914) and *Language* (1933); held that language study must be centered in forms and sounds of spoken language; stressed practical applications in *Outline Guide for the Practical Study of Foreign Languages* (1942); helped found Linguistic Society of America; also published *Menomini Texts* and *Plains Cree Texts.*

Blücher *(blü kər),* **Gebhard Leberecht von** title: PRINCE OF WAHLSTATT; nickname: MARSHAL VORWÄRTS (Marshal Forward). 1742–1819. Prussian field marshal. *b.* Rostock. Entered cavalry as lieutenant after two years in Swedish service (1758); retired to farming (1770); rejoined army as major (1787) and took part in Dutch and French campaigns; distinguished himself at Auerstädt (1806); defeated by French at Lübeck; on outbreak of War of Liberation, placed in command of Prussian army (1813), and fought in battles of Lützen, Bautzen, and Haynau; cleared Silesia through victories at Katzback and Möckern; defeated Napoleon at Laon and entered Paris (1814); given command of Prussian army on Napoleon's return from Elba (1815); severely defeated by French at Ligny, but helped win battle at Waterloo (1815); occupied Paris.

Blum *(bloom),* **Léon** 1872–1950. French statesman. *b.* Paris. Joined French Socialist party under guidance of Jean Jaurès (1902); elected to Chamber of Deputies (1919) and leadership of Socialist party; helped form Popular Front (1934); as premier (1936–37, 1938) carried through social reforms and monetary devaluation; interned by Germans during World War II; headed interim government (1946–47). Author of *Les Nouvelles Conversations de Goethe Avec Eckermann* (1901) and *Stendhal et le Beylisme* (1914).

Blumenbach *(bloo mən bäk),* **Johann Friedrich** 1752–1840. German naturalist. *b.* Gotha. Founder of science of physical anthropology; professor of medicine and anatomy at University of Göttingen (1776–1835); through pioneering studies in craniology, introduced five racial classifications of humans: Caucasian, Mongolian, Ethiopian, American, and Malayan. Author of *Handbuch der Vergleichenden Anatomie und Physiologie* (1804).

Boas *(bō ăs),* **Franz** 1858–1942. American anthropologist. *b.* Minden, Germany. Began ethnological research on Indians of North America (1886); professor of anthropology at Columbia (1899–1937); curator of anthropology at Museum of Natural History in N.Y. (1901–1905); pioneered mass-scale analysis of anthropometric data. Author of *The Growth of Children* (1896), *Changes in Form of Body of Descendants of Immigrants* (1911); *The Mind of Primitive Man* (1911), *Primitive Art* (1927), *Anthropology and Modern Life* (1928), *Race, Language and Culture* (1940); editor of *Handbook of American Indian Languages* (2 vols., 1911–22).

Boccaccio *(bōk kät chō),* **Giovanni** 1313–75. Italian writer. *b.* Paris, France. Began writing in verse and prose at Naples, where he fell in love with Maria d'Aquino ("Fiammetta"), daughter of Robert d'Anjou, king of Naples; lived subsequently in Florence (1340), Ravenna (1346), and Forlì (1348);

formed lasting friendship with Petrarch (1350); as Florentine ambassador, visited Rome, Avignon, and Brandenburg; lecturer on Dante at Florence (1373). Author of the *Decameron* (1353), a classic of Italian prose, and other works, including *Il Filocopo* (1331–38), *Il Filostrato* (1338), *La Teseide* (1341), and *Il Corbaccio* (1354).

Böcklin *(bûk lēn),* **Arnold** 1827–1901. Swiss painter. *b.* Basel. Known for allegorical and romantic landscapes embodying mythological figures of nymphs and satyrs. Noted works include *The Island of the Dead, The Sacred Grove,* and *The Elysian Fields.*

Bode *(bō də),* **Johann Elert** 1747–1826. German astronomer. *b.* Hamburg. Director of Berlin Observatory (1786–1825); catalogued 17,240 stars and nebulae in *Uranographia* (1801); codified Bode's law, a formula expressing relative distances of planets from the sun.

Bodin *(bô dăɴ),* **Jean** 1530–96. French political philosopher. *b.* Angers. Supported absolute monarchy in *Les Six Livres de la République* (1576) and religious liberty in *Colloquium Heptaplomeres* (1857); also published a philosophy of history, *Methodus ad Facilem Historiarum Cognitionem* (1566).

Bodmer *(bōd mər),* **Johann Jakob** 1698–1783. Swiss critic. *b.* Greifensee. With Jakob Breitinger, founded and edited influential journal *Die Discourse der Mahlern* (1721–23); helped spread interest in English literature through translation of *Paradise Lost* into German; discovered and edited Middle High German classics, including *Nibelungenlied* (1757) and *Minnesänger* (1748).

Bodoni *(bə dō nē),* **Giambattista** 1740–1813. Italian type-designer and printer. *b.* Saluzzo. Designed modern typeface known as Bodoni, characterized by contrasting dark and light lines and level serifs; published editions of classics, widely admired for their elegance though not for their accuracy. Author of *Manuale Tipografico* (1818).

Boethius *(bō ē thĭ əs),* **Anicius Manlius Severinus** c480–c524. Roman philosopher. Magister officiorum and consul under Theodoric the Goth (510); accused of treason, stripped of office, imprisoned, and executed (524). Wrote *The Consolation of Philosophy* while facing death in prison at Pavia; regarded as the first of the scholastics and as commentator on Aristotelian philosophy.

Bohl von Faber, Cecilia. *See* **Caballero, Fernán**

Böhm-Bawerk *(bûm bä vĕrk),* **Eugen** also Böhm von Bawerk. 1851–1914. Austrian economist. *b.* Brünn. Minister of finance (1895, 1897–98, 1900–1904); co-founder and leading exponent of the Austrian school, an economic theory based on concept of final utility. Author of *Kapital und Kapitalzins* (1884–89) and *Einige Strittige Fragen der Kapitalstheorie* (1900).

Böhme *(bû mĕ),* **Jakob** also Böhm, Boehme, Boehm, Behmen. 1575–1624. German mystic. *b.* Altseidenberg. Principal works include *Aurora, oder die Morgenröte in Aufgang* (1612), *Von den Drei Prinzipien des Göttlichen Wesens* (1619), *Mysterium Magnum* (1623), and *Der Weg zu Christo*

(1624); writings condemned as heretical because they explained existence of evil by postulating divine dualism.

Bohr *(bōr),* **Niels Henrik David** 1885–1962. Danish physicist. *b.* Copenhagen. Held chair of theoretical physics at University of Copenhagen (1916); director of Copenhagen Institute for Theoretical Physics (1920); advisor to Manhattan Project at Los Alamos (1944–45); formulated Bohr theory of atomic structure and Bohr theory of nuclear fission, laying groundwork for modern nuclear science; awarded Nobel Prize in physics (1922). Author of *On the Application of the Quantum Theory to Atomic Structures.*

Boiardo *(bō yär dō),* **Matteo Maria** title: CONTE DI SCANDIANO. 1434–94. Italian poet. *b.* Scandiano. Fame rests on incomplete chivalric romance *Orlando Innamorato* (1486), a narrative poem of 69 cantos, in which the legend of Roland is recast in ottava rima; the theme was developed and completed by Ariosto in *Orlando Furioso.*

Boileau-Despréaux *(bwä lō dā prā ō),* **Nicolas** 1636–1711. French critic. *b.* Paris. Began as satirist with *Satires* (1660–66); established reputation as critic with *L'Art Poétique* (1674); published nine epistles on Horatian model (1669–77); royal historiographer with Racine (1677). Other works include *Lutrin* (1674) and *Réflexions Critiques sur Longin* (1693); introduced standards of literary criticism and composition; gained the title "lawgiver of Parnassus."

Boleyn *(bo͞ol ĭn),* **Anne 1507–36.** Second queen consort of Henry VIII. Daughter of Sir Thomas Boleyn, Earl of Wiltshire; mistress of Henry VIII (1527); secretly married him (1533); declared legal queen (May 1533) on Cranmer's annulment of Henry's marriage to Catherine of Aragon; gave birth to the future Queen Elizabeth (1533); arrested, charged with adultery and incest, and beheaded (1536).

Bolingbroke *(bŏl ĭng bro͝ok),* **Henry St. John, Viscount** 1678–1751. English statesman. *b.* Battersea. Entered Parliament (1701); secretary for war (1704–1708); foreign secretary (1710); negotiated Treaty of Utrecht (1713); fled to Continent on accession of George I (1714); attainted (1715); pardoned and allowed to return (1723); associated with Pope, Swift, and other men of letters; intrigued unsuccessfully against Robert Walpole; returned to France (1735). Author of *Reflections on Exile, Letters on the Study of History* (1752), and *Idea of a Patriot King* (1749).

Bolívar *(bō lē vär),* **Simón** known as EL LIBERTADOR. 1783–1830. South American revolutionary and statesman. *b.* Caracas, Venezuela. Revolutionary against Spain under Francisco de Miranda; captured Caracas (1812–13) and Bogotá (1814), but defeated and forced to take refuge in Jamaica; made repeated forays on Venezuela (1816–17) and captured Angostura (1817); defeated Spanish forces at Boyacá and liberated New Granada (1819); elected president of Greater Colombia, comprising Colombia, Venezuela, and New Granada (1819); defeated Spaniards at Carabobo (1821); marched to Quito and added Ecuador to the

Republic (1822); drove Spaniards from Peru after victories at Junín and Ayacucho (1824); dictator of Peru (1824–27) and perpetual protector of Bolivia, a separate republic established in upper Peru in his honor; returned to Bogotá when Peru and Bolivia declared against him; resigned presidency of Colombia when Venezuela and Ecuador seceded (1830).

Böll *(bûl),* **Heinrich** 1917–. German writer. *b.* Cologne. Author of *The Train was on Time* (1949), *The Clown* (1963), and *Group Portrait with Lady* (1971); awarded Nobel Prize in literature (1972).

Bolland *(bô län),* **Jean de** 1596–1665. Belgian Jesuit hagiologist. *b.* Julemont. Editor (from 1643) of the great *Acta Sanctorum (Lives of the Saints),* a work continued after his death by his successors, known as Bollandists.

Boltzmann *(bōlts män),* **Ludwig** 1844–1906. Austrian physicist. *b.* Vienna. Professor of mathematics and physics at Gratz (1869, 1876), Vienna (1873, 1895), Munich (1890), and Leipzig (1900); contributed to kinetic theory of gases and statistical mechanics; established Stefan-Boltzmann law of radiation of a black body.

Bonaparte. *See* **Napoleon I**

Bonaventura *(bŏn à vĕn tū rà),* **Saint** also BONAVENTURE; real name: GIOVANNI DI FIDENZA. 1221–74. Italian scholastic philosopher. *b.* Orvieto. Professor of theology at Paris (1253), general of Franciscans (1256), bishop of Albano (1273); cardinal (1274); canonized (1482). Author of *Breviloquium, Centiloquium, Itinerarium Mentis ad Deum, Biblia Pauperum, Speculum Mariae Virginis,* and *Reductio Artium in Theologiam;* given the title Doctor Seraphicus; ranked sixth of great Doctors of the Church.

Bonheur *(bô nûr),* **Rosa** full name: MARIE ROSALIE BONHEUR 1822–99. French painter. *b.* Bordeaux. Noted for paintings of animals, of which the best known are *Tillage in Nivernais, Studies of Animals, Horse Fair,* and *Ploughing with Oxen.*

Boniface *(bŏn ĭ fās),* **Saint** original name: WINFRID OR WYNFRITH. c680–755. English missionary. *b.* Crediton. Abbot of Benedictine monastery at Nursling (717); commissioned by Pope Gregory II to preach to German tribes (718); established churches in Bavaria, Thuringia, Friesland, Hesse, and Saxony and baptized many; bishop (723), archbishop, and primate of Germany (732); occupied see of Mainz (746-754); resigned to resume missionary work in Friesland, where he was killed (755); known as Apostle of Germany. Feast day: June 5.

Bonnard *(bô nàr),* **Pierre** 1867–1947. French painter. *b.* Fontenay-aux-Roses. Joined group called Les Nabis, which included Jean Vuillard and Maurice Denis; style influenced by Japanese prints, Paul Gauguin, and Toulouse-Lautrec; founder of Intimiste school of painting. Painted interiors, landscapes, and nudes, characterized by subtle rendering of soft, warm colors. Prolific output included *Dancers* (1922), *Fishing Boats* (1929), *Open Window on the Sea* (1933), *Boulevard des Batignolles* (1939), and *Vase of Flowers* (1943).

Boole *(bōōl),* **George** 1815–64. English logician and mathematician. *b.* Lincoln. Pioneer of modern symbolic logic through use of mathematical symbolism to express logical processes; advanced his theories in *Mathematical Analysis of Logic* (1847) and *Laws of Thought* (1854); made contributions to mathematics in *Treatise on Differential Equations* (1859) and *Treatise on the Calculus of Finite Difference* (1860).

Boone *(bōōn),* **Daniel** 1734–1820. American pioneer and frontiersman. *b.* Berks County, Pa. Made early trips to Ky. (1767, 1769–71), later guiding settlers there (1775); blazed the Wilderness Road and built a fort at present-day Boonesboro (1775); moved to western Va. (1788–98); immigrated to Missouri, then a Spanish possession (1799).

Booth *(bōōth),* **William** known as GENERAL BOOTH. 1829–1912. English preacher. *b.* Nottingham. Minister of Methodist New Connexion (1852–61); became an independent revivalist; founded Christian Revival Association, a mission in London's East End (1865), developed it on military lines, and renamed it Salvation Army (1878); established branches worldwide. Author of *In Darkest England* (1890). Work carried on by sons WILLIAM BRAMWELL (1856–1929) and BALLINGTON (1859–1940), and daughters EMMA MOSS BOOTH-TUCKER (1860–1903) and EVANGELINE CORY (1865–1950).

Bopp *(bōp),* **Franz** 1791–1867. German linguist. *b.* Mainz. Founder of comparative philology; professor at Berlin University (1821–64); published pioneering work *The Conjugation of the Sanskrit Verb* (1816), showing the common origin of Indo-European languages; numerous studies of languages culminated in *Comparative Grammar of Sanskrit, Zend, Greek, Latin, Lithuanian, Old Slavonic, Gothic, and German* (6 vols., 1833–52).

Borchgrevink *(bôrk grā vĕngk),* **Carsten Egeberg** 1864–1934. Norwegian explorer. *b.* Oslo. Immigrated to Australia (1888); member of first party to land on Antarctic continent (1894); commanded *Southern Cross* on first expedition to winter in Antarctica (1898–99); determined approximate position of south magnetic pole. Author of *First on the Antarctic Continent* (1901).

Borden *(bôr dən),* **Gail** 1801–74. American food processor and inventor. *b.* Norwich, N.Y. Developed process for condensing milk (1853); opened first American plant for producing condensed milk at Wassaic, N.Y. (1861); held patents for condensing cider, juices, and fruits.

Borden, Sir Robert Laird 1854–1937. Canadian statesman. *b.* Grand Pré, Nova Scotia. Leader of Conservative party in Canadian House of Commons (1901); prime minister (1911–20); represented Canada at Paris Peace Conference (1919) and on the Council of the League of Nations.

Bordet *(bôr dĕ),* **Jules** 1870–1961. Belgian bacteriologist. *b.* Soignies, France. Founder and director of Institut Pasteur in Brussels (1907); pioneer in serology and immunology; discovered bacterial hemolysis (1898) and the microbe of whooping cough (1906); described phagocytosis (1895), anaphylaxis (1913), and complement fixation (1900);

awarded Nobel Prize in medicine (1919). Author of *Studies in Immunity* (1909) and *The Theories of Blood Coagulation* (1921).

Borgia *(bôr jä),* **Cesare** 1476–1507. Italian nobleman. At age 17, created cardinal (1493) by his father, Pope Alexander VI; relinquished cardinalate (1498); granted duchy of Valentinois (1498) by Louis XII; married (1499) Charlotte d'Albret, sister of the king of Navarre; in two campaigns, made himself master of Romagna, Perugia, Siena, Piombino, and Urbino; created duke of Romagna; forced to surrender possessions to Pope Julius II (1503); arrested in Naples and sent to Spain as a prisoner (1504); escaped to Navarre; killed in siege of castle at Viana (1507).

Borgia, Lucrezia 1480–1519. Italian noblewoman. *b.* Rome. Daughter of Rodrigo Lenzuoli Borgia (Pope Alexander VI), who made three political marriages for her: to Giovanni Sforza, lord of Pesaro (1493), to Alfonso of Aragon, natural son of Alfonso II of Naples (1498), and to Alfonso of Este (1501), who became Duke of Ferrara (1505); known as a patroness of learning and art, her brilliant court including Ariosto, Titian, and Aldus Manutius.

Borgia, Rodrigo Lenzuoli. *See* **Alexander VI**

Borglum *(bôr gləm),* **Gutzon** full name: JOHN GUTZON DE LA MOTHE BORGLUM 1867–1941. American sculptor. *b.* Idaho. Designed and carved Mount Rushmore National Memorial portraying George Washington, Abraham Lincoln, Thomas Jefferson, and Theodore Roosevelt; other works include equestrian statue of General Sheridan in Washington, D.C., the *Mares of Diomedes* in the Metropolitan Museum of Art, and figures of the Apostles for Cathedral of St. John the Divine in N.Y.

Borlaug *(bôr lôg),* **Norman Ernest** 1914–. American agronomist. *b.* Cresco, Iowa. Launched "green revolution" by developing new crop strains of rice and wheat; awarded Nobel Peace Prize (1970).

Born *(bôrn),* **Max** 1882–1970. German physicist. *b.* Breslau. Professor of theoretical physics at Göttingen (1921–33); dismissed by Nazis and became British subject (1933); Stokes Lecturer in Mathematics at Cambridge (1933–36); Tait Professor of Natural Philosophy at University of Edinburgh (1936–53); important contributions to quantum physics; awarded Nobel Prize in physics (1954) with Walther Bothe. Author of *Die Relativitätstheorie Einsteins und Ihre Physische Grundlagen* (1922), *Atom Physics* (1935), and *Experiment and Theory in Physics* (1944).

Borodin *(bŭ rŭ dyēn),* **Aleksandr Porfirevich** 1834–87. Russian composer and chemist. *b.* St. Petersburg. Trained as a chemist, but devoted leisure time to musical composition. Works include the unfinished opera *Prince Igor,* three symphonies, and the symphonic poem *In the Steppes of Central Asia* (1880).

Borrow *(bŏr ō),* **George** 1803–81. English author and philologist. *b.* East Dereham. Noted for works on Romany language and gypsies, of which he considered himself an adopted member. Chief books include *The Zincali, or Gypsies of Spain* (1840), *The Bible in Spain* (1843), *Lavengro* (1851),

The Romany Rye (1857), *Wild Wales* (1862), and *Romano Lavo-Lil, or Word-Book of the English-Gypsy Language* (1874).

Bosanquet *(bō zən kĕt),* **Bernard** 1848–1923. English philosopher. *b.* Rock Hall. Professor of moral philosophy at St. Andrews (1903–1908); developed philosophical doctrines of Hegel and T.H. Green in *Logic, or Morphology of Knowledge* (1888), *A History of Aesthetics* (1892), *Philosophical Theory of the State* (1899), *Three Lectures on Aesthetics* (1915), and *Implication and Linear Inference* (1920).

Boscawen *(bŏs kō ən),* **Edward** 1711–61. English admiral. *b.* in Cornwall. Took part in naval actions off Porto Bello (1739), Cartagena (1741) and Cape Finisterre (1747); intercepted French fleet off Newfoundland, capturing two ships (1755); admiral (1758); led successful expedition against Cape Breton (1758); defeated French fleet in Lagos Bay (1759); known as OLD DREADNOUGHT.

Bosch *(bōsh),* **Carl** 1874–1940. German chemist. *b.* Cologne. Shared Nobel Prize in chemistry (1931) with Friedrich Bergius; developed Bosch process by which hydrogen is obtained from water, gas, and steam; adapted Haber process for the manufacture of fertilizers and explosives from atmospheric nitrogen.

Bosch *(bŏsh),* **Hieronymous** real name: HIERONYMOUS VAN AKEN or AEKEN; also JEROME BOS. c1450–1516. Dutch painter. *b.* Hertogenbosch. Excelled in surrealistic folk and allegorical religious canvases filled with fantastic and monstrous creatures. Best-known works include *The Temptation of St. Anthony* and *The Last Judgment.*

Bosco *(bôs kō),* **Don Giovanni** 1815–88. Italian ecclesiastic. *b.* in Piedmont. Founded oratory at Turin for the care and education of young men (1842), out of which the Salesian Order developed; canonized (1929).

Bossuet *(bô sü ĕ),* **Jacques Bénigne** 1627–1704. French ecclesiastic. *b.* Dijon. Renowned pulpit orator; tutor to the dauphin (1670–81), for whom he wrote *Discours sur l'Histoire Universelle* (1679); bishop of Meaux (1681). Wrote *Doctrine de l'Église Catholique* in defense of the Catholic Church, and *Politique Tirée de l'Écriture Sainte* in support of Divine Right of kings; other works include *Histoire Universelle* and *Oraisons Funèbres.*

Boswell *(bôz wĕl),* **James** 1740–95. Scottish biographer. *b.* Edinburgh. Cultivated the friendship of great men and kept private journal of his transactions; first met Samuel Johnson at a London bookshop (1763); toured Continent, introducing himself to Voltaire, Rousseau, and General Pascal Paolo, whom he later wrote about (1768); returned to London (1766) and was elected to Johnson's Club (1773); accompanied Johnson to the Hebrides, an account of which appeared as *The Journal of a Tour of the Hebrides* (1785); completed his acknowledged masterpiece, *The Life of Samuel Johnson* (1891), a biography without peer in the English language.

Botha *(bō tȧ),* **Louis** 1862–1919. South African statesman. *b.* Greytown. Member of Transvaal Volksraad; commanded Boer forces (1899) at Ladysmith, Colenso, and Spion Cop; succeeded

Joubert as commander in chief of Boer army (1900); later advocated cooperation with Britain; first prime minister of crown colony of Transvaal (1907); led Transvaal delegation to union convention; first premier of Union of South Africa (1910); put down De Wet's Rebellion (1914); conquered German South West Africa (1914–15).

Bothe *(bō tĕ),* **Walther** 1891–1957. German physicist. *b.* Oranienburg. Head of Max Planck Institute for Medical Research at Heidelberg (from 1934); shared Nobel Prize in physics with Max Born (1954) for work on the coincidence technique in counting processes.

Böttger *(bût gər),* **Johann Friedrich** also BÖTTCHER or BÖTTIGER. 1682–1719. German porcelain-maker. *b.* Schleiz. Discovered the chemical process by which Dresden china is made; established factory at Dresden, later moved to Meissen (1710); developed a reddish-brown stoneware (called Böttgerware) and perfected various glazes.

Botticelli *(bōt tə chĕl lĭ),* **Sandro** original name: ALESSANDRO DI MARIANO DEI FILIPEPI. c1444–1510. Italian painter. *b.* Florence. Pupil of Fra Filippo Lippi. Among best-known paintings are *Spring, Birth of Venus, Coronation of the Virgin, Madonna and the Child, The Life of Moses, The Temptation of Christ, Punishment of Korah, Dathan, and Abiram, Mars and Venus, Nativity, Annunciation, Calumny, The Adoration of the Magi,* and *Fortitude;* made a series of illustrations for the *Divine Comedy* for Pier Francesco de Medici; assisted in the decoration of Sistine Chapel on the invitation of Pope Sixtus IV; later became a follower of Savonarola.

Bougainville *(bōō gaɴ vēl),* **Louis Antoine de** 1729–1811. French navigator. *b.* Paris. Commander of first French expedition to circumnavigate the world (1766–69); visited Pacific Islands, including Bougainville; wrote *Voyage Autour du Monde* (1771); commanded several ships in American War of Independence; field marshal (1780); made senator, count, and member of Legion of Honor by Napoleon I: the flowering vine *Bougainvillaea* is named after him.

Boulanger *(bōō läɴ zhā),* **Georges Ernest Jean Marie** 1837–91. French general. *b.* Rennes. Aided in defense of Paris during Franco-Prussian War (1870–71); commanded French army of occupation in Tunis (1884); minister of war (1886–87); gained great popularity through military reforms and became identified with anti-German revanchists; known as the Man on Horseback from his mounted public appearances; led Boulangist movement uniting all opponents of Third Republic, including extremists; to forestall coup d'état; deprived of command by war minister (1888); deputy (1888); accused of conspiracy by cabinet of Tirard (1889); fled to Brussels; convicted of treason in absentia; committed suicide.

Boule; Boulle. *See* **Buhl**

Bourgeois *(bōōr zhwȧ),* **Léon Victor Auguste** 1851–1925. French statesman. *b.* Paris. President of Chamber of Deputies (1902–1904); president of Senate (1920–23); premier (1895–96); head of the French delegation to Hague Peace Conferences (1899, 1907), where he supported formation of a world court; one of the drafters of covenant of League of Nations (1919) and chairman of its first meeting; awarded Nobel Peace Prize (1920).

Bourget *(bōōr zhĕ),* **Paul** 1852–1935. French novelist. *b.* Amiens. Began as a poet with *La Vie Inquiète* (1875), *Edel* (1878), and *Les Aveux* (1881); in *Essais de Psychologie Contemporaine* (1883) and *Nouveaux Essais de Psychologie* (1886), explored the roots of French pessimism; wrote first novel *L'Irréparable* (1884), followed by *Cosmopolis* (1893), *Un Saint* (1894), *L'Étape* (1902), *Le Sens de la Mort* (1915), *Le Danseur Mondain* (1925), and *Nos Actes Nous Suivent* (1927); converted to Catholicism in 1880s and later works show mystical themes.

Bovet *(bô vĕ),* **Daniele** 1907–. Italian pharmacologist. *b.* in Switzerland. Awarded Nobel Prize in physiology and medicine for work on sulfa drugs, antihistamines, and muscle relaxants (1957).

Bowdler *(boud lər),* **Thomas** 1754–1825. English editor. *b.* Ashley. Published *Family Shakespeare* (10 vols., 1818) in an expurgated edition omitting those words and expressions "which cannot with propriety be read aloud in a family"; similarly edited the Old Testament and Gibbon's *Decline and Fall of the Roman Empire* (1826); the term "bowdlerize" now describes this process.

Boyd Orr *(boid ôr),* **Lord John** 1880–1971. British nutritionist. *b.* Kilmaurs. Director of animal nutrition research, University of Aberdeen (1914); director of Rowett Institute (1919); founder of Imperial Bureau of Animal Nutrition (1929); director-general of FAO (1945–48); awarded Nobel Peace Prize (1949). Author of *Food and the People* (1944), *The White Man's Dilemma* (1952), and *As I Recall* (1966).

Boyle *(boil),* **Robert** 1627–91. British physicist and chemist. *b.* Lismore Castle, Munster, Ireland. One of the first members of Invisible College, an association of Oxford intellectuals that became the Royal Society in 1645; studied pneumatics, specific gravity, metal calcination, crystallography, refraction, and sound; prepared phosphorus; invented a compressed-air pump; defined chemical element and chemical reactions, and distinguished between elements and compounds; advanced concept of atomism; isolated methyl alcohol; established the effect of atmospheric pressure on boiling point of water; formulated Boyle's law (1662), which states that a gas's pressure and volume are inversely proportional; worked to promote Christianity and founded the Boyle Lectures to that end. Author of *The Sceptical Chemist* (1661), *New Experiments Physico-Mechanical Touching the Spring of the Air and Its Effects* (1660), *Origin of Forms and Qualities According to the Corpuscular Philosophy* (1666), and *Memoirs for the Natural History of the Human Blood* (1684).

Bracton *(brak tən),* **Henry de** also, Bratton or Bretton. *d.* 1268. English cleric and judge. Author of *De Legibus et Consuetudinibus Angliae,* the earliest attempt at a systematization of English law.

Bradford *(brăd fərd),* **William** 1590–1657. Colonial governor. *b.*

Austerfield, England. Joined the nonconformist Brownists and moved to Amsterdam and Leiden in search of freedom of worship; sailed with Pilgrims on the *Mayflower* to New World and signed Mayflower Compact (1620); elected governor of Plymouth Colony (1621–32, 1635, 1637, 1639–43, 1645–56). Author of *History of Plimoth Plantation* (1856), a valuable sourcebook.

Bradford, William 1663–1752. American printer. *b.* Barnwell, England. Sailed with William Penn for New World (1682); settled in Philadelphia and set up the first press, issuing *America's Messenger* (1685); helped found first colonial paper mill (1690); moved to N.Y. (1693); appointed crown printer (1693–1742); official printer to N.J., Pa., N.Y., R.I, and Md.; founder of *New York Gazette* (1725), the first newspaper in N.Y.; son ANDREW (1686–1742) founded *American Weekly Mercury,* the first newspaper in Philadelphia; grandson WILLIAM (1722–91), known as "Patriot Printer of 1776," was founder of *Weekly Advertiser,* or *Pennsylvania Journal* (1742).

Bradley *(brăd lĭ),* **Francis Herbert** 1846–1924. English philosopher. *b.* Glasbury. Rejected scientific reductionism and utilitarianism and expounded a philosophy of absolute idealism in *Ethical Studies* (1876), *The Principles of Logic* (1883), *Essays on Truth and Reality* (1914), and his greatest work, *Appearance and Reality* (1893).

Bradstreet *(brăd strēt),* **Anne** *née* DUDLEY. 1612–72. American poet. *b.* Northampton, England. Came to Mass. with Puritans (1630); daughter of Thomas Dudley and wife of Simon Bradstreet, both later governors of Mass. (1679-86, 1689–92); published *The Tenth Muse Lately Sprung Up in America* (1650), the first poetic work by an American writer, and *Several Poems* (1678).

Brady *(brā dĭ),* **Mathew B.** c1823–96. American photographer. *b.* Townsend, N.Y. Known for photographs of Abraham Lincoln and for the photographic record of the Civil War known as *Brady's National Photographic Collection of War Views and Portraits of Representative Men* (1870).

Bragg *(brăg),* **Sir William Henry** 1862–1942. English physicist. *b.* Wigton. Professor of mathematics and physics, Adelaide University (1886–1908); Cavendish Professor, Leeds University (1909–15); professor of physics, University of London (1915–23); director of Royal Institution (from 1923); investigated crystal structure and X-ray spectra using X-ray spectrometer. Author of *Studies in Radioactivity* (1912), *X-rays and Crystal Structure* (1915), *The World of Sound* (1920), *Concerning the Nature of Things* (1925), and *The Universe of Light* (1933); awarded Nobel Prize in physics (1915) with son WILLIAM LAWRENCE (1890–1971), Cavendish Professor of Experimental Physics at Cambridge (from 1938) and author of *Crystalline State* (1934) and *The Atomic Structure of Minerals* (1937).

Brahe *(brä ə),* **Tycho** 1546–1601. Danish astronomer. *b.* Knudstrup, Sweden. Under patronage of Frederick II of Denmark built observatory Uranienborg on island of Hven (1580); entered service of

Emperor Rudolph II and settled in Prague (1599); discovered Tycho's Star in Cassiopeia (1572); by making exact observations with improved instruments, provided basis for laws of planetary motions discovered by his assistant Johannes Kepler; rejected Copernican system in favor of modified Ptolemaic system. Author of *Astronomiae Instauratae Mechanica* (1598).

Brahms *(brämz),* **Johannes** 1833–97. German composer. *b.* Hamburg. Moved to Vienna (from 1862); deeply influenced by Robert Schumann, who was instrumental in establishing his reputation; principal works include two serenades (1860), four symphonies (1876–86), the *Academic Festival* and *Tragic* overtures (1881), *Variations on a Theme of Haydn* (1873), a violin concerto (1879), choral works *German Requiem* (1868), *Rinaldo* (1869), *Rhapsody* (1870), *Schicksalslied* (1871), *Triumphlied* (1871), *Nänie* (1881), and *Gesang der Parzen* (1883); works characterized by classical musical forms and expressive melodies.

Braille *(brāl),* **Louis** 1809–52. French musician and teacher of the blind. *b.* Coupvray. Blinded at age three; as professor at Institution Nationale des Jeunes Aveugles, developed and improved Charles Barbier's method of writing and reading based on combinations of raised points, now known as Braille.

Bramante *(brä män tā)* real name: DONATO D'AGNOLO. 1444–1514. Italian architect. *b.* Monti Asdrualdo. Worked in Milan (1472–99); went to Rome serving Popes Alexander VI and Julius II; designed plan for rebuilding St. Peter's; introduced Renaissance style of architecture known as Bramantesque, examples of which are the circular Tempietto in the courtyard of San Pietro in Montorio, the long gallery connecting the old palace with the Belvedere at the Vatican, and the fort at Civita Vecchia.

Brancuşi *(brän ko͞osē),* **Constantin** 1876–1957. Romanian sculptor. *b.* Pestisani. Moved to Paris (1904); developed abstract and symbolist style using simple curved shapes. Best known works are *The Kiss, New-Born, Leda, Sleeping Muse, Prodigal Son, Mademoiselle Pogany, Bird in Space, The Miracle,* and *The Sea-Lions.*

Brandeis *(brăn dīs),* **Louis Dembitz** 1856–1941. American jurist. *b.* Louisville, Ky. Established early reputation as "people's counsel" for consistent defense of public interest against monopolies and large institutions; advocated liberal social legislation, especially minimum wage laws and freedom of expression; associate justice of Supreme Court (1916–39), appointed by President Wilson. Author of *Other People's Money* (1914), *Business, A Profession* (1914), and *The Curse of Bigness* (1934).

Brandes *(brän dəs),* **Georg Morris** original surname: COHEN. 1842–1927. Danish critic. *b.* Copenhagen. Taught at University of Copenhagen (1872–77, 1882–1902) and at Berlin (1877–82); as a disciple of Renan, Comte, Taine, Mill, and Spencer, introduced rationalism and radicalism into Danish literary criticism. Author of *Aesthetic Studies* (1868), *Main*

Currents in Nineteenth-Century Literature (6 vols., 1872–90), *Sören Kierkegaard* (1877), *Danish Poets* (1884), and *Recollections* (1906).

Brandt *(bränt)*, **Willy** real name: HERBERT FRAHM. 1913–. West German statesman. *b.* Lübeck. Joined Social Democratic party at age 17; fled (1933) and took Norwegian citizenship; returned to Germany (1945) and regained citizenship (1948); elected to *Bundestag* (1949); president of *Bundesrat* (1955–57); mayor of West Berlin (1957–66); leader of Social Democrats (1966); chancellor in a coalition government with Free Democrats (1969); initiated policy of *Ostpolitik* leading to rapprochement with Eastern bloc; awarded Nobel Peace Prize (1971); resigned over a spy scandal (1974).

Branting *(brän tĭng)*, **Karl Hjalmar** 1860–1925. Swedish statesman. *b.* Stockholm. Founder of Swedish Socialist party; premier (1920, 1921–23, 1924–25); Swedish representative on League of Nations Council (from 1922); cowinner of Nobel Peace prize (1921) with Christian Lange.

Braque *(bräk)*, **Georges** 1882–1963. French painter. *b.* Argenteuil. Cofounder with Picasso of classical cubism; produced sculptures, collages, and engravings, but principally known as painter of still lifes, nudes, and landscapes; developed highly original nongeometric abstract style, characterized by startling perspective and sharply defined shadows. Works include *Violin and Jug, Musicienne, Beach at Dieppe, Still Life with Playing Cards, Plums and Lemons,* and *Ateliers.*

Bratianu *(brä tĭ ä nōō)* Family of Romanian statesmen including: IOAN or ION 1821–91. *b.* Pitesci, Walachia. Principal founder of an independent Romania through the union of Walachia and Moldavia; leader of Liberal party; prime minister (1867–68, 1876–88); succeeded in office by brother DIMITRIE, 1818–92. ION, 1864–1927, Ion's son, prime minister for 12 years during the period 1909–27; premier and virtual dictator (from 1922); yielded office to his brother VINTILA, 1867–1930, prime minister (1927–28). CONSTANTIN 1889–c1950, led National Liberal party (from 1934); opposed both Antonescu and Communists.

Brattain *(brăt n)*, **Walter Houser** 1902–. American physicist. *b.* Amoy, China. Researcher at Bell Telephone Laboratories; shared Nobel Prize in physics (1956) with J. Bardeen and W. Shockley for work on semiconductors.

Braun *(broun)*, **Karl Ferdinand** 1850–1918. German physicist. *b.* Fulda. Professor of physics and director of Physical Institute in Strasbourg (from 1895); invented Braun cathode-ray tube; shared Nobel Prize in physics with Guglielmo Marconi (1909) for work on wireless telegraphy. Published *Wireless Telegraphy Through Water and Air* (1901).

Braun, Wernher von 1912–77. American space scientist. *b.* Wirsitz, Germany. Director of German rocket research station at Peenemünde, which launched V-2 rockets against Britain (1944); after World War II, surrendered to U.S. forces; became naturalized American and director of U.S. Army's ballistic missile agency at

Huntsville, Ala.; instrumental in launching first American satellite, the *Explorer*, at Cape Canaveral (1958).

Bray *(brā),* **Thomas** 1656–1730. English clergyman. *b.* Marton. Established parochial libraries in England and America, from which emerged the Society for the Promotion of Christian Knowledge (1699); founded Society for the Propagation of the Gospel in Foreign Parts (1701).

Brazza *(brȧ zȧ),* **Pierre Paul François Camille Savorgnan de** real name: BRAZZA SAVORGNANI. 1852–1905. French explorer. *b.* Rio de Janeiro, Brazil. Went to Africa (1875); explored Ogowe basin; discovered Alima and Likuala Rivers; sent by French government to Equatoria (1879); founded Franceville and Brazzaville; placed Makoko kingdom under French protection; explored Lalli and Niadi Rivers; commissioner of French Congo (1886–98); explored the Nkoni and Sanga Rivers.

Breal *(brā ȧl),* **Michel Jules Alfred** 1832–1915. French philologist. *b.* Landau, Rhenish Bavaria. Settled in Paris (1859); professor of comparative grammar at Collège de France (1866). Author of *Essai de Sémantique* (1897), a seminal work which helped found science of semantics.

Breasted *(brĕs təd),* **James Henry** 1865–1935. American Orientalist. *b.* Rockford, Ill. Professor of Egyptology and Oriental History at University of Chicago (1905–33); led archaeological expeditions to Egypt and Mesopotamia (from 1919), published *A History of Egypt* (1905), *Monuments of Sudanese Nubia* (1908), *Development of Religion and Thought in Ancient Egypt* (1912), *Conquest of Civilization* (1926), and *The Dawn of Conscience* (1933).

Brecht *(brĕкt),* **Bertolt Eugen Friedrich** 1898–1956. German playwright. *b.* Augsburg. Won Kleist Drama Prize (1922) for *Trommeln in der Nacht* and *Baal*; established reputation as major dramatist with *The Threepenny Opera* (1928); developed epic theater based on Marxist and antimilitaristic themes; fled Hitler's Germany (1933) and settled in U.S. (1941); published *Furcht und Elend des Dritten Reiches* (1945); left U.S. to become theater director in East Berlin (1948). Best-known plays include *Mother Courage and Her Children* (1941), *The Caucasian Chalk Circle* (1933), and *Puntilla* (1940).

Breckinridge *(brĕk ĭn rĭj),* **John Cabell** 1821–75. American statesman. *b.* Lexington, Ky. House of Representatives (1851-55); vice-president of U.S. (1857–61); presidential candidate of Southern Democrats (1860); Senator from Kentucky (1861); joined Confederate army (1861); major-general (1862); led Southern forces at Shiloh, Baton Rouge, Newmarket, East Tennessee, and Nashville; Confederate secretary of war (1865); escaped to Europe at end of Civil War, but returned (1868).

Breton *(brə tôN),* **André** 1896–1966. French man of letters. *b.* Tinchebray. Joined Dadaists (1919) and collaborated with Philippe Soupalt to write *Les Champs Magnétiques* (1921); helped found

Surrealist movement and wrote its manifesto; edited *La Révolution Surréaliste* (1924); joined Communist party (1930). Works include *The Soluble Fish* (1924) and *What is Surrealism?* (1934).

Breuer *(broi ər),* **Josef** 1842–1925. Austrian physician. *b.* Vienna. Made important contributions to neurology and psychoanalysis; developed the technique of questioning hysteric patients under hypnosis; coauthored with Sigmund Freud *Studien uber Hysterie* (1895).

Breuer, Marcel Lajos 1902–. Hungarian-American architect. *b.* Pécs, Hungary. Director, Bauhaus in Dessau (1925–28); practiced architecture in Berlin (1928–31) and London (1935–37); partner of Walter Gropius in Cambridge, Mass. (1937–42); associate professor Harvard (1937–46); pioneered functional furniture design in steel, aluminum, and plywood; designed Whitney Museum of American Art in New York City. Author of *Art in Our Time* (1939), *The Modern House* (1940), and *Design of Modern Interiors* (1942).

Breugel; Breughel. *See* **Brueghel**.

Brewster *(broo̅ stər),* **William** 1567–1644. American colonist. *b.* Scrooby, England. Leader of nonconformist sect known as Pilgrims that separated from Church of England (1606) and immigrated to the Netherlands (1608); printed religious tracts for dissenters (1609–19); obtained colonization grant for Pilgrims in New World; sailed to America on the *Mayflower* (1620); as chief religious leader of Plymouth Colony, guided them for many years.

Brezhnev *(brĕzh nyĕf),* **Leonid Ilyich** 1906–. Soviet statesman. *b.* Ukraine. Communist party chief in Ukraine, Moldavia, and Kazakhstan; elected to Central Committee (1952); president of Presidium and chief of state (1960); named first secretary of Communist party (1963); one of principal architects of *Westpolitik* or opening to the West, which led to U.S.-Soviet détente.

Briand *(brē äɴ),* **Aristide** 1862–1932. French statesman. *b.* Nantes. As a radical socialist, founded *L'Humanité* with Jean Jaurès (1904); sponsored the draft separating church and state (1905–06); served eleven terms as prime minister and sixteen as foreign minister between 1909 and 1929; advocated rapprochement with Germany; negotiated Locarno Accord (1925) and Briand-Kellogg Pact (1928); supported League of Nations and plans for European unity; awarded (with Gustav Stresemann) Nobel Peace Prize (1926).

Bridges *(brĭj əz),* **Robert Seymour** 1844–1930. English poet laureate. *b.* Walmer. Practiced medicine (1875–82) but abandoned it for poetry; wrote lyrics marked by metrical innovations; published such plays as *Nero* (1885), *Achilles in Scyros* (1890), and *The Feast of Bacchus* (1889), and the narrative poem *Eros and Psyche* (1885); edited *Yattendon Hymnal* (1895–99); critical works include essays on Keats and Milton; introduced Gerard Manley Hopkins to English public; founded Society for Pure English (1913), advocating spelling reform; poet laureate (1913); completed magnum opus, *The Testament of Beauty* (1929).

Bridget *(brĭj ət),* **Saint** also BRIGIT, BIRGITTA, BRIGITTA. c1302–73. Swedish nun. *b.* Finstad. Born into noble family; married Ulf Gudmarsson, a judge, and had eight children, one of whom was Saint Catherine; on death of husband (1344) founded monastery of Vadstena, where Brigittine Order was established (1370); made pilgrimage to Palestine (1373); canonized (1391); patroness of Sweden. Author of *Revelationes Stae Brigittae.* Feast day: Oct. 8.

Bridgman *(brĭj mən),* **Percy Williams** 1882–1961. American physicist. *b.* Cambridge, Mass. Professor at Harvard (from 1926); awarded Nobel Prize in physics (1946) for work on high pressure physics and thermodynamics. Author of *The Physics of High Pressure* (1931), *The Nature of Physical Theory* (1936), and *The Nature of Thermodynamics* (1941).

Bright *(brīt),* **John** 1811–89. English statesman. *b.* Rochdale. Entered Parliament (1843); with Richard Cobden, formed Anti-Corn Law League, which led to repeal of the corn laws; spokesman for free trade, religious freedom, electoral and financial reform; opposed Crimean War and Gladstone's Irish Home Rule policy; supported the North in American Civil War; president of Board of Trade (1868–70); chancellor of Duchy of Lancaster (1873–74, 1880–82). Author of *Speeches* (1867, 1869), *Letters* (1885), and *Diaries* (1930).

Bright, Timothy c1551–1615. English inventor of modern shorthand. *b.* near Sheffield. Practiced as physician (1586–90), but left to take holy orders. Author of *Characterie* (1588), on the art of shorthand, and *Treatise of Melancholie* (1586).

Brissot *(brē sō),* **Jacques Pierre** surname: DE WARVILLE. 1754–93. French Revolutionary leader. *b.* Quarville. Gained reputation as a jurist with *Theorie des Lois Criminelles* (1780) and *Bibliothèque des Lois Criminelles* (1782–86); elected to National Assembly (1789); founded *La Patriote Français*, organ of Republicans; emerged as leader of moderate Girondists, also called Brissotins, in the Convention; supported abolition of monarchy; guillotined (1793).

Britten *(brĭt n),* **Edward Benjamin** 1913–76. English composer. *b.* Lowestoft. During 1930s, collaborated with W.H. Auden on *Our Hunting Fathers, On This Island, Paul Bunyan*, and other works; first opera, *Peter Grimes* (1945), followed by *Billy Budd, Gloriana*, and *Turn of the Screw*. Works cover a broad range of vocal and instrumental compositions and include symphonies *Sinfonia da Requiem* and *Spring Symphony*, the song cycle *Seven Sonnets of Michelangelo*, the suite *A Young Person's Guide to the Orchestra*, and the chorales *A Ceremony of Carols, The War Requiem,* and *Cantata Misericordium.*

Broca *(brô cà),* **Paul** 1824–80. French anthropologist and neurosurgeon. *b.* Ste.-Foy-la-Grande. Discovered seat of articulate speech in brain's frontal lobe; devised methods of classifying hair and skin color and establishing ratio of brain to skull; founded Anthropological Society of Paris

(1859), School of Anthropology (1876), and French Association for the Advancement of Sciences (1872). Author of *Mémoires sur le Caractères Physiques de l'Homme Préhistorique* (1869) and *Instructions Craniologiques et Craniométriques* (1875).

Broglie *(brô glē)* French noble family, including:

VICTOR MAURICE 1647–1727. Marshal of France under Louis XIV.

FRANCOIS MARIE 1671–1745. Son of Victor Maurice, marshal of France under Louis XIV; led campaigns in Germany and Italy.

VICTOR FRANÇOIS 1718–1804. Son of François Marie, marshal of France; fought in Seven Years' War; minister of war under Louis XVI; on outbreak of French Revolution, emigrated from France and served under the English and Russians.

VICTOR CLAUDE 1757–94. Son of Victor Francois; president of Constituent Assembly (1791); adjutant general of army of the Rhine; defied National Convention and guillotined.

ACHILLE CHARLES LÉONCE VICTOR 1785–1870. Son of Victor Claude; peer of France; minister of the interior and of public instruction and worship (1830); minister of foreign affairs (1832–34, 34–36); author of *Souvenirs*.

JACQUES VICTOR ALBERT 1821–1901. Son of Achille, premier and minister for foreign affairs (1873–74); president of the council and minister of justice (1877); author of many historical works including *L'Église et l'Empire Romain au IVe Siècle* (1856–66).

MAURICE 1875–1960. Grandson of Jacques; physicist, noted for studies on X-rays, nuclear physics, and radioactive substances.

LOUIS VICTOR 1892–. Grandson of Jacques; nuclear physicist, awarded Nobel Prize for physics (1929) for research on quantum theory and discovery of the wave character of electrons.

Bromfield *(brŏm fēld),* **Louis** 1896–1956. American novelist. *b.* Mansfield, Ohio. Author of *The Green Bay Tree* (1924), *Early Autumn* (Pulitzer Prize, 1926), *The Strange Case of Miss Annie Spragge* (1928), *The Rains Came* (1937), *Night in Bombay* (1939), *Wild is the River* (1941), *Mrs. Parkington* (1943), *Colorado* (1947), *Mr. Smith* (1951), *Awake and Rehearse*, and *The House of Women*.

Brontë *(brŏn tē),* Name of three sisters who were important novelists of the 19th century; the passion and intensity of their stories added new vitality to the Victorian novel; known as much for dark penury of their lives as for their works; daughters of Patrick Brontë, curate of Haworth:

CHARLOTTE 1816–55. Pseudonym: CURRER BELL. Author of *The Professor* (1857), *Jane Eyre* (1847), *Shirley* (1849), and *Villette* (1853).

EMILY JANE 1818-48. Pseudonym: ELLIS BELL. Author of *Wuthering Heights* (1848).

ANNE 1820-49. Pseudonym: ACTION BELL. Author of *Agnes Grey* (1848) and *The Tenant of Wildfell Hall* (1848).

Brooke *(brook),* **Sir Alan Francis** title: VISCOUNT ALANBROOKE. 1883–1963. British general. *b.* Bagneres-de-Bigorre, France. Entered British army in Royal Field Artillery (1902); officer in Indian army in World War I; commander of antiaircraft forces (1938–39); commander of Second Corps, British Expeditionary Forces (1940); commander in chief of home forces (1940–41); chief of Imperial General Staff (1941); field marshal (1944); elevated to peerage (1945) and created viscount (1946). Churchill's principal military advisor; diaries formed the basis of Arthur Bryant's *Turn of the Tide* and *Triumph in the West*.

Brooke, Sir James 1803–68. First British raja of Sarawak. *b.* Varanasi, India. Entered service of East India Company (1825); created raja of Sarawak in return for aid to Raja Muda Hassim, uncle of sultan of Sarawak, in expedition against Dyak tribe (1841); suppressed piracy; governor of British-held Labuan Island, off Borneo (1847–51); retired and left Sarawak (1863); rajaship also held by nephew Sir Charles Anthony Johnson Brooke (1829–1917) and grandnephew Sir Charles Vyner (1874–1963).

Brooke, Rupert Chawner 1887–1915. English poet. *b.* Rugby. Traveled in Germany, Italy, America, Canada, and South Seas; saw service in Belgium (1914). Wrote *The Bastille* (1905), *Poems* (1911), *1914 and Other Poems* (1915), *Lithuania* (1915), *Letter from America* (1916); best remembered for his sonnet "The Soldier."

Brookings *(brŏŏk ĭngz),* **Robert Somers** 1850–1932. American philanthropist. *b.* Cecil County, Md. Founder of Institute for Government Research (1918), Institute of Economics (1922), and Robert Brookings Graduate School of Economics and Government (1924); all three were merged (1927) into the Brookings Institution, Washington, D.C.; president of governing body of Washington University (1897–1928). Author of *Industrial Ownership* (1925) and *Economic Democracy* (1929).

Brooks *(brŏŏks),* **Phillips** 1835–93. American Episcopal bishop. *b.* Boston, Mass. Curé in Philadelphia and Boston; bishop of Episcopal diocese of Mass. (1891); famous as pulpit orator and as author of "O Little Town of Bethlehem"; delivered the Yale Lectures on Preaching (1877).

Brooks, Van Wyck 1886–1963. American essayist. *b.* Plainfield, N.J. Editor of *The Freeman* (1920–24) and *American Caravan* (from 1927). Major works include *The Wine of the Puritans* (1909), *The Malady of the Ideal* (1913), *America's Coming of Age* (1915), *The Ordeal of Mark Twain* (1920), *The Pilgrimage of Henry James* (1925), and the five-volume *Makers and Finders* of which the first volume, *The Flowering of New England, 1815–1865*, won Pulitzer Prize for history (1937).

Brown *(broun),* **Charles Brockden** 1771–1810. American novelist. b. Philadelphia, Pa. Wrote seven Gothic novels, including *Wieland* (1798), *Ormond* (1799), *Arthur Mervyn* (1799–1800), and *Edgar Huntly* (1800); edited three magazines, wrote political pamphlets, and compiled a semiannual historical register; called father of the American novel.

Brown, John 1800–1859. American abolitionist. *b.* Torrington, Conn. A tanner by profession and father of 20 children in two marriages; conceived the idea of forcibly ending slavery (1839); moved to Kansas (1855) and became leader in antislavery struggle; executed five antiabolitionists at Pottawatomie; suffered loss of home and one son in reprisal; planned to establish stronghold in Va. for runaway slaves; with followers, went to Va. and captured U.S. arsenal at Harpers Ferry, later recaptured by Robert E. Lee; captured and executed; regarded as a martyr in the North and immortalized in the song "John Brown's Body."

Brown, Martha 1838–1916. American temperance movement leader. *b.* Baltimore, Md. Organized Prohibition party (1869); led National Conference and Prohibition and Woman Suffrage workers; founded National Woman's Christian Temperance Union (1874); also known as first woman editor of a secular magazine, *The Alliance.*

Brown, Robert 1773–1858. Scottish botanist. *b.* Montrose. Naturalist on Matthew Flinders's Australian expedition (1801–1805); curator of British Museum (from 1827); as librarian to Linnaean Society, promoted adoption of Jussieu's system of classification, and discovered *gymnospermae*; described phenomenon known as Brownian movement, the rapid movement of particulate matter suspended in a liquid; pioneer in fossil and pollination microscopy; called *Facile Princeps Botanicorum* by Alexander von Humboldt.

Browne *(broun),* **Sir Thomas** 1605–82. English physician and author. *b.* London. Established a fine stylist and natural philosopher with *Religio Medici*, *Pseudodoxia Epidemica, Hydriotaphia, or Urn Burial, The Garden of Cyrus, Miscellany Tracts, Letter to a Friend,* and *Christian Morals.* Writings dwelt on the mystery of death and out-of-the-way learning couched in baroque and elaborately periodic prose.

Browning *(broun ĭng),* **Elizabeth Barrett** maiden name: ELIZABETH MOULTON, later BARRETT. 1806–61. English poet, *b.* Coxhoe Hall, Durham. Invalided for many years due to a riding accident at age 15 and the trauma of watching her brother drown; married poet Robert Browning (1846) and resided in Florence, Italy, for remainder of life. During her lifetime her poems enjoyed critical praise and popularity. Principal works include *Prometheus Bound* (1833), *Seraphim, and Other Poems* (1838), *Poems* (1844), *Sonnets from the Portuguese* (1850), *Casa Guidi Windows* (1851), *Aurora Leigh* (1857), *Poems Before Congress* (1860), and *Last Poems* (1862).

Browning, John Moses 1855-1926. American firearms designer. *b.* Ogden, Utah. First patent on an improved rifle (1879); devised repeating rifle (1884), and later a magazine rifle, an automatic rifle, an automatic pistol, and a machine gun, all of which were widely used in World Wars I and II; assisted by brother JONATHAN EDMUND (1859–1939), who patented an improved model of the automatic rifle (1940).

Browning, Robert 1812–89. English poet. *b.* Camberwell. Married Elizabeth Barrett (1846); resided in Florence until her death (1861) and thereafter in London. Secured recognition as a great poet with

The Ring and the Book (1868–69), a story of a Roman murder case in blank verse; other principal works include *Pippa Passes* (1841), *Men and Women* (1855), *Dramatis Personae* (1864), *Fifine at the Fair* (1872), *The Inn Album* (1875), *Pacchiarotto* (1876), and *Dramatic Idylls* (1879); among his most famous poems are "Saul," "My Last Duchess," "The Bishop Orders His Tomb," "The Pied Piper of Hamelin," "The Guardian Angel," "Prospice," "Rabbi Ben Ezra," "De Gustibus," "A Death in the Desert," and "Andrea del Sarto."

Broz, Josip. *See* **Tito, Marshal**

Bruce *(bro͞os)* English earls of Elgin, including:

THOMAS 1766–1841. 7th EARL OF ELGIN AND 11th EARL OF KINCARDINE; British envoy to the Porte in Constantinople; arranged to convey the "Elgin marbles" from the Acropolis at Athens to British Museum.

JAMES 1811–63. 8th EARL OF ELGIN AND 12th EARL OF KINCARDINE; governor of Jamaica (1842); governor general of Canada (1847–54); viceroy of India (1862).

VICTOR ALEXANDER 1849–1917. 9th EARL OF ELGIN AND 13th EARL OF KINCARDINE; viceroy of India (1894–99); colonial secretary (1905–1908).

Bruce, Robert. *See* **Robert VIII.**

Bruce, Viscount Stanley Melbourne 1883–1967. Australian statesman. *b.* Melbourne. Member of House of Representatives (1918–29, 1931–33); prime minister (1923–29); Australian high commissioner in London (1933–45); representative on council at League of Nations (1933–35), president of council (1935).

Bruckner *(bro͝ok nər),* **Anton** 1824–96. Austrian composer. *b.* Ansfelden. Composer of nine symphonies (the last unfinished) and a large number of sacred and choral works, including a Te Deum; professor at Vienna Conservatory (1867–91); also an accomplished organist.

Brueghel *(brû gĕl)* also BRUEGEL, BREUGEL, or BREUGHEL. Family of Flemish painters including:

PIETER also called THE ELDER, THE DROLL, PEASANT BRUEGHEL. c1525–69. Received into Antwerp Guild of Master Painters (1551); toured France and Italy (1551–53); settled in Antwerp (1553–1563); moved to Brussels (1563) where he spent the remainder of life; portrayed Flemish peasants in vibrant colors.

PIETER also called THE YOUNGER, HELL BRUEGHEL. 1564–1638. Son of Pieter the Elder; portrayed infernal regions and its grim inhabitants.

JAN also called THE ELDER, VELVET BRUEGHEL, FLOWER BRUEGHEL. 1568–1625. Son of Pieter the Elder, painter of landscapes with mythological and Biblical figures.

JAN also called THE YOUNGER. 1601–78. Son of Jan the Elder; painter of landscapes.

Brummell *(brŭm əl),* **George Bryan** called BEAU BRUMMEL. 1778–1840. English gentleman. *b.* London. Gained a reputation in 19th-century fashionable society as an arbiter of taste and for exquisiteness of dress and manners; intimate companion of Prince of Wales, the future George IV, to 1813; retired to Calais to escape heavy gambling losses (1816); imprisoned for debt

(1835); died in an insane asylum.

Brunelleschi *(brōō nāl lās kē),* **Filippo** also BRUNELLESCO. c1377–1446. Italian architect. *b.* Florence. First great architect of the Renaissance; best known for design and construction of dome of Santa Maria del Fiore Cathedral in Florence (1420–61), largest dome in the world, measured diametrically. Other works include church of San Lorenzo in Florence, the Badia in Fiesole, the cloister in Santa Croce, the Pazzi chapel, Ospedale degl'Innocenti, and the Pitti Palace.

Bruno *(brōō nō),* **Giordano** 1548–1600. Italian philosopher. *b.* Nola. Entered Dominican Order (1563) but left (1576) because of disbelief in Catholic doctrines and repudiation of dogmatic authority; traveled widely on the Continent, lecturing and writing (1577–92); arrested in Venice (1592) by order of the Inquisition; burned as a heretic in Rome (1600). Writings expounded anti-Aristotelian and pantheistic philosophy; held that absolute truth is unattainable and that human knowledge is relative; championed Copernican heliocentric theory; influenced Leibnitz, Spinoza, Schelling, and Hegel; principal works include *Spaccio della Bestia Trionfante* (1584), *Della Causa, Principio et Uno* (1584), *Dell' Infinito Universo Emondi* (1584), and *De Monadi Numero et Figura* (1591).

Bruno of Cologne, Saint c1030–1101. German monk. *b.* Cologne. Priest (1055); head of episcopal school at Reims (1064–84); retired to the mountain wilderness of Chartreuse with six friends to found order of the Carthusians (1084); advised Pope Urban II in Rome (1090); established a monastery at Della Torre in Calabria (1091), where he died.

Brutus *(brōō tŭs),* **Marcus Junius** c85–42 B.C. Roman politician. A partisan of Pompey during the Civil War, but submitted to Julius Caesar after Pompey's defeat at Pharsala (48); pardoned and appointed governor of Cisalpine Gaul (46); praetor urbanus (44); joined Cassius and took part in assassination of Caesar (44); defeated by Octavian and Antony at Philippi (42); committed suicide.

Bryan *(brī ən),* **William Jennings** 1860–1925. American statesman, also known as The Commoner. *b.* Salem, Ill. Member, House of Representatives (1890–95); won Democratic party's presidential nomination (1896) with celebrated cross-of-gold speech; defeated by McKinley; champion of free silver and agrarian interests against Eastern establishment; renominated (1900) on antiimperialist platform; defeated by McKinley again; nominated again (1908), but defeated by Taft; secretary of state under Wilson (1913) but resigned (1915) as protest against American involvement in World War I; a compelling orator and writer, he was a popular lecturer on the Chautauqua circuit; editor in chief of *Omaha World-Herald* (from 1894) and editor of *Commoner* (1901–13); led prosecution in the Scopes trial (1925).

Bryant *(brī ənt),* **William Cullen** 1794–1878. American journalist and poet. *b.* Cummington,

Mass. As editor and co-owner of *New York Evening Post*, became influential, championing free soil, free speech, free trade, and abolition of slavery; as a poet, recognized through works, including *Thanatopsis* (1817), *To A Waterfowl* (1818), *The Fountain and Other Poems* (1842), *The White-Footed Doe and Other Poems* (1844), and *The Flood of Years* (1876).

Bryce *(brīs),* **Viscount James** 1838–1922. British historian and diplomat. *b.* Belfast, Northern Ireland. Regius Professor of Civil Law at Oxford (1870–93); Liberal Member of Parliament (1880–1907); undersecretary of foreign affairs (1886); president of board of trade (1894); chief secretary for Ireland (1905–06); British ambassador to U.S. (1907–13); one of the founders of League of Nations; member of Hague Tribunal (1913); president of British Academy (1907). Author of *The Holy Roman Empire* (1864), *The American Commonwealth* (1888), *Studies in History and Jurisprudence* (1901), and *Modern Democracies* (1921).

Buber *(bo͞o bər),* **Martin** 1878–1965. Jewish religious philosopher. *b.* Vienna, Austria. Editor of *Welt* (1901) and *Der Jude* (1916–24); professor of religion and ethics at University of Frankfurt (1924–33); director of Central Office for Jewish Adult Education (until 1938); escaped Nazis to become professor of social philosophy in Jerusalem (1938); his system of religious philosophy, based on I-Thou concept, defines relationships between man and God and man and man; pioneered in revival of Hasidic mysticism. Works include *Die Legende des Baalschem* (1907), *Ekstatische Konfessionen* (1908), *Völker, Staaten und Zion* (1916), *Mein Weg zum Chassidismus* (1918), *I and Thou* (1923), *Die Stunde und die Erkenntnis* (1936), *Between Man and Man* (1947), *Eclipse of God* (1952), and *Good and Evil* (1953).

Buchan *(bŭk ən),* **Sir John** title: Baron Tweedsmuir. 1875–1940. Scottish writer and statesman. *b.* Perth. Director of information (1917–18). Member of Parliament (1927–35); governor general of Canada (1935–40). Author of novels, biographies, and histories including *The 39 Steps* (1915), *Greenmantle* (1916), *The Three Hostages* (1924), *John McNab* (1925), *The Gap in the Curtain* (1932), *Sir Walter Raleigh* (1911), *Julius Caesar* (1932), *Sir Walter Scott* (1932), *Oliver Cromwell* (1934), and *Pilgrim's Way* (1940).

Buchanan *(bū kăn ən),* **James** 1791–1868. 15th president of U.S. *b.* Stony Batter, Pa. House of Representatives (1821–31); minister to Russia (1832–34); senator (1833–45); secretary of state (1845–49); minister to Great Britain (1853–56); president of U.S. (1857–61); failed to resolve conflict between North and South over slavery; favored maintenance of slavery and supported attempt to establish a slave state in Kansas; toward end of administration, S.C. seceded from the Union and the Civil War had virtually begun; collected papers, edited by J.B. Moore (12 vols., 1908-11).

Buchman *(bo͝ok mən),* **Frank Nathan Daniel** 1878–1961. American evangelist. *b.* Pennsburg, Pa. Founded the Oxford Group at Oxford (1921) to bring together young men dedicated to sustaining religious values in a world shattered by war; based on "world-changing through life-changing," it stressed improvement of character and emphasized principles of honesty, purity, unselfishness, and love; also known as Buchmanism, it spread to over 60 countries; began (1939) campaign for Moral Re-Armament (MRA), which attracted considerable membership after World War II.

Buchner *(bo͞ok nər),* **Eduard** 1860–1917. German chemist. *b.* Munich. Awarded Nobel Prize for chemistry (1907) for discovery that alcoholic fermentation is caused by zymase, an enzyme in yeast cells. Author of *Zymase Fermentation* (1903) and *Relations of Chemistry to Agriculture* (1904).

Buchner, Georg 1813–37. German poet. *b.* Goddelau. As student of medicine, became involved in revolutionary politics and published radical pamphlet, *Der Hessische Landbote;* forced to flee to Zurich. Wrote *Dantons Tod* (1835), *Leonce und Lena* (in manuscript), and *Wozzeck* (1837), which inspired an opera by Alban Berg.

Buck *(bŭk),* **Pearl** *née* SYDENSTRICKER. 1892–1973. American novelist. *b.* Hillsboro, W. Va. Daughter of Christian missionaries in China; spent early life as teacher in Nanking (1921–31). Best known for novels about China; author of *The Good Earth* (Pulitzer Prize, 1932), *Sons* (1932), *A House Divided* (1935), *The Mother* (1934), *The Exile* (1936), *Fighting Angel* (1936), *The Patriot* (1939), *Other Gods* (1940), *Dragon Seed* (1942), *The Dragon Fish* (1944), *Pavilion of Women* (1946), *God's Men* (1951), *The Hidden Flower* (1952), and *My Several Worlds* (1954); awarded Nobel Prize for literature (1938).

Buckingham *(bŭk ĭng əm)* English family of courtiers including GEORGE VILLIERS 1592-1628. 1st DUKE OF BUCKINGHAM. Gained notice of James I and rose in favor; knighted, raised to peerage as Viscount Villiers (1616), created Earl of Buckingham (1617), Marquis (1618), and Duke (1623); appointed lord high admiral and lord warden of Cinque Ports (1617); negotiated marriage of Charles I with Henrietta Maria of France but maintained ascendancy at court after Charles's accession (1625); urged James and Charles to wage disastrous wars with France and Spain; unpopular in Parliament after abortive expeditions against Cadiz, Rochelle, and Palatinate; charged by Parliament in a remonstrance, saved from impeachment by dissolution of Parliament; assassinated (1628).

GEORGE VILLIERS 1627–88. 2nd DUKE OF BUCKINGHAM. Son of First Duke; lost estates on outbreak of Civil War and fled into exile with Charles II; returned on Restoration; member of infamous Cabal; instrumental in fall of Clarendon; noted for wit, debauchery, and reckless temper; dismissed from court (1674), but restored to favor (1684); wrote many comedies, of which the wittiest is *The Rehearsal* (1671).

Buddha *(bo͝od dȧ),* **Gautama** real

name: SIDDHARTHA; also called SAKYAMUNI (Sage of the Sakya tribe) or SAKYASINHA (Lion of the Sakya tribe). c563–483 B.C. Indian philosopher and founder of Buddhism. *b.* Kapilavastu. Born to royal family of Sakya tribe; married at age 16; renounced luxury and became wandering monk to find an escape from the sufferings of old age, disease, and death (c534); spent six years practicing austerity and studying philosophy; achieved enlightenment under a bo tree near Bodh-Gaya; hence, the name Buddha, or Enlightened One; delivered first sermon at Deer Park in Sarnath; spent remainder of life preaching and converting thousands and organizing the Sangha or Buddhist Order; died at Kusinagara at 80. The highest goal of Buddhism is Nirvana; it affirms the Hindu concepts of karma and rebirth. Its Four Noble Truths are: There is suffering in life; this suffering has a cause; suffering must be caused to cease; and suffering can cease if one knows the right way. The Noble Eightfold Path consists of right beliefs, right aims, right speech, right conduct, right means of livelihood, right endeavor, right mindfulness, and right meditation.

Budé *(bü dā),* **Guillaume** Latin form: BUDAEUS. 1468–1540. French scholar. *b.* Paris. Appointed royal librarian by Francis I; built up library of Fontainebleau, which later became Bibliothèque National; instrumental in founding Collège de France (1530); fostered study of Greek classics, used textural criticism to study Roman law, and laid foundations of scientific philology. Author of *De Asse et Partibus Eius* (1514) and *De Transitu Hellenismi ad Christianum* (1534–35).

Budge *(bŭj),* **Sir Ernest Alfred Wallis** 1857–1934. English archaeologist. *b.* in Cornwall. Keeper of Egyptian and Assyrian antiquities in British Museum (1893–1924); conducted excavations in Nubia, Mesopotamia, and Egypt; translated and edited Egyptian and Assyrian texts, such as *Book of Paradise* and *Book of the Dead.*

Buffalo Bill. *See* **Cody, William Frederick.**

Buffon *(bü fôN),* **Comte Georges Louis Leclerc de** 1707–88. French naturalist. *b.* Montbard. Member of Academy of Sciences in Paris (1739); director (1739) of Jardin du Roi (now Jardin des Plantes); undertook monumental *Histoire Naturelle*, (44 vols., 1749–1804; completed by B.G.E. de Lacepède), a compendium of scientific knowledge; admitted to French Academy (1753) and delivered the famous *Discours sur le Style* as his inaugural address.

Bugenhagen *(bo͞o gən hä gən),* **Johann** also called POMERANUS or DR. POMMER. 1485–1558. German Lutheran leader. *b.* Wolin. Follower of Martin Luther (1520); professor of biblical exegesis at Wittenberg (1525); organized Protestant churches in Brunswick, Hamburg, Lübeck, Pomerania, Denmark, and Schleswig-Holstein (1528–42); translated Bible into Low German (1533).

Buhl *(bo͞ol),* **André Charles** also BOULLE or BOULE. 1642–1732. French cabinetmaker. *b.* Paris. Entered service of Louis XIV as royal furniture maker in Louvre Palace (from 1672); introduced buhlwork, a style of decorating furniture by inlaying metals, tortoiseshell, and mother-of-pearl on ebony or ebonized wood.

Buisson *(bü ē sôɴ),* **Ferdinand Édouard** 1841–1932. French educator. *b.* Paris. Professor of pedagogy at Sorbonne (from 1886); member of Chamber of Deputies (1902–14, 1919–24); president of the League of Human Rights and ardent supporter of League of Nations; awarded (with Ludwig Quidde) Nobel Peace Prize (1927).

Bukhari, al- *(ăl bo͞o ᴋä rē)* full name: Abu Abdallah Mohammed ibn-Ismail al Bukhari al-Jufi. 810-70. Iranian religious scholar. *b.* Bokhara, Uzbek Republic. Compiler of *Al-Sahih* (*The Genuine*), a collection of 7275 hadiths (traditions) that is the basis of Muslim law and second only to the Koran in holiness.

Bukharin *(bo͞o ᴋȧ ryēn),* **Nikolai Ivanovich** 1888–1938. Soviet politician. *b.* Moscow. Joined Bolshevik faction of Social Democratic party (1906) and became co-editor (with Lenin) of *Pravda;* after October Revolution, member of Central Committee of Communist party and Politburo; head of Third International (1926–29); expelled from Communist party (1929); readmitted and appointed editor of *Izvestia* (1934); purged and executed in treason trials (1938).

Bulfinch *(bo͝ol fĭnch),* **Charles** 1763–1844. American architect. *b.* Boston, Mass. Designed Mass. and Conn. state houses, Maine state capitol and other elegant buildings; appointed architect of Capitol (1817) in Washington, D.C., where he completed the western front. Father of Thomas Bulfinch (1796–1867), author of *The Age of Fable, Age of Chivalry, Legend of Charlemagne*, and other books.

Bulganin *(bo͝ol gȧ nyĭn),* **Nikolai Aleksandrovich** 1895–1975. Russian statesman. *b.* Gorki. Joined Communist party (1917); served in secret police (Cheka); chairman of Moscow Soviet (1933–37) and member of Military Council; created marshal for role in defense of Moscow; helped establish Communist regime in Poland; member of Politburo (1946); succeeded Stalin as minister of armed forces (1947); deputy premier (1949–53); minister of war under Malenkov (1953–55); premier (1955–58); ousted by Khrushchev; retired from public life.

Bülow *(bü lō),* **Prince Bernard von** 1849–1929. German statesman. *b.* Flottbeck. Son of a Prussian secretary of state for foreign affairs, Bernhard Ernst von Bülow (1815–79). Entered diplomatic service (1873); secretary of state for foreign affairs (1897–1900); imperial chancellor and president of council of ministers (1900–1909); prince (1905); took a leading part in Algeciras Conference (1906) following Moroccan crisis, caused fall of French foreign minister, Théophile Declassé; failed to establish friendly relations with England; resigned (1909). Author of *Imperial Germany* (1916), *Memoirs* (1931–32), and *Deutsche Politik* (1916).

Bultmann *(bo͝olt män),* **Rudolf** 1884–. German theologian. *b.* Wiefelstede. Professor of New Testament theology at University of Marburg (from 1921); through fundamental revisions of biblical criticism, demythologized New Testament. Author of *Der Stil der Paulinischen Predigt und die Kynisch-stoische Diatribe* (1910), *Die Geschichte der Synoptischen Tradition* (1921), *Jesus* (1926), and *Offenbarung und Heilgeschehen* (1941).

Bunau-Varilla *(bü nō vȧ rē yȧ),* **Philippe Jean** 1860–1940. French engineer. *b.* Paris. Chief engineer of Panama Canal under de Lesseps (1884); on de Lesseps project's failure, organized new company (1894), later sold to U.S.; won Theodore Roosevelt's support; engineered the revolution of 1903 in Panama; appointed minister from new republic of Panama to U.S.; negotiated Hay-Bunau-Varilla Treaty (1903) giving U.S. control of the Canal Zone. Author of *From Panama to Verdun* (1940).

Bunche *(bŭnch),* **Ralph Johnson** 1904–71. American diplomat. *b.* Detroit, Mich. Grandson of a slave; head of political science department at Howard University (from 1929); served with Office of Strategic Services (1941–44); State Department advisor on African and colonial matters (1944–45); head of trusteeship section of U.N. Secretariat (1946); successfully mediated U.N. truce in Palestine (1948) following assassination of Count Folke Bernadotte; awarded Nobel Peace Prize (1950).

Bunin *(bo͞o nyĭn),* **Ivan Alekseevich** 1870–1953. Russian poet and novelist. *b.* Voronezh. Settled in Paris after October Revolution, and works reflect old rather than new Russia. Best-known works are *The Village* (1923), *The Gentleman from San Francisco* (1922), and the autobiographical *The Well of Days* (1933); awarded Nobel Prize for literature (1933), the first Russian to be so honored.

Bunsen *(bo͝on zən),* **Robert Wilhelm** 1811–99. German chemist. *b.* Göttingen. Professor of chemistry at Kassel, Marburg, Breslau, and Heidelberg (1852-89); invented Bunsen burner, grease-spot photometer, carbon-zinc electric cell, ice calorimeter, and (with Roscoe) the actinometer. With G.R. Kirchhoff, discovered (1860) elements rubidium and cesium, devised a spectrometer for spectrum analysis, and pioneered in gas analysis and measurement with *Gasometrische Methoden.*

Bunyan *(bŭn yən),* **John** 1628–88. English religious writer and preacher. *b.* Elstow. Joined nonconformist Christian fellowship at Bedford (1653); began preaching (1655) in midland counties; led resistance of dissenters against established church; imprisoned (1660–72) for preaching without license; released under Declaration of Indulgence, but imprisoned (1673) as dissenter. In jail, wrote *Pilgrim's Progress*, the work which made him famous; also published 40 other books, including *Grace Abounding to the Chief of Sinners* (1666), *The Holy City, or The New Jerusalem* (1666), *The Life and Death of Mr. Badman* (1680) and *The Holy War* (1682).

Burbank *(bûr băngk),* **Luther** 1849–1926. American horticulturist. *b.* Lancaster, Pa. Through successful experiments in cross-fertilization, bred 618 new fruits, flowers, and vegetables at farm in Santa Rosa, Calif.; among varieties that he developed were Burbank potato, Shasta and Alaska daisies, blue Shirley poppy; Burbank, Calif., is named after him.

Burckhardt *(bo͞ork härt),* **Jakob** 1818–97. Swiss historian. *b.* Basel. Studied history of art at Berlin and Bonn; editor of *Basler Zeitung* (1844–45); professor at Zurich (1855–58) and Basel (1858–93); founded study of cultural history with *The Civilization of the Renaissance in Italy* (1860), followed by *Geschichte der Renaissance in Italien* (2 vols. 1867–78), *Griechische Kulturgeschichte* (4 vols., 1898–1902), and *Force and Freedom: Reflections on History* (trans. 1943); Nietzsche and Spengler are counted among his disciples.

Burghley, Baron. *See* **Cecil, William.**

Burke *(bûrk),* **Edmund** 1729–97. British statesman and political philosopher. *b.* Dublin, Ireland. Entered Parliament as member for Wendover (1765); spokesman of Whig party, his eloquent orations considered among the greatest in any language or in any Parliament; M.P. for Bristol (1774) and Malton (1781); advocated liberal treatment of American colonies in speeches "American Taxation" (1774) and "Conciliation with America" (1775); supported free trade with Ireland, Catholic emancipation, and Wilberforce's efforts to abolish slave trade; led prosecution in impeachment of Warren Hastings, governor general of India, with one of the most forceful orations of career (1786); opposed anarchy of French Revolution with *Reflections on the French Revolution* (1790) and *Letters on a Regicide Peace* (1795–97), which lost him Whig support and led to break with Charles James Fox; retired from Parliament (1794) and from public life (1795); ranks with Disraeli as founder of liberal conservatism and champion of constitutional government.

Burleigh, Baron. *See* **Cecil, William**

Burne-Jones *(bûrn jōnz),* **Sir Edward Coley** 1833–98. English artist. *b.* Birmingham. Began painting under influence of William Morris and D.G. Rossetti; became a principal exponent of Italianate Pre-Raphaelitism; paintings based on Arthurian romances and Greek myths. Best-known works include *The Days of Creation, The Beguiling of Merlin, The Mirror of Venus, Pan and Psyche, The Golden Stairs, The Depths of the Sea, Love and the Pilgrim, The Merciful Knight,* and *The Wine of Circe;* created woodcuts for Morris Kelmscott's *Chaucer*.

Burnet *(bûr nĕt),* **Sir Frank Macfarlane** 1899–. Australian physician. *b.* Traralgon. Director of Institute for Medical Research, Melbourne; contributed to development of immunity against viruses; shared Nobel Prize for physiology and medicine (1960) with Peter Medawar for research in the immunology of skin and organ grafts.

Burnett *(bûr nĕt),* **Frances Eliza** *née* HODGSON. 1849–1924. American novelist. *b.* Manchester, England. Immigrated to U.S. (1865) and settled in Tenn. Author of several plays and novels, but famous as a writer of children's books, including *Sara Crewe* (1888), *Little Lord Fauntleroy* (1886), *Little Saint Elizabeth* (1890), and *The Secret Garden* (1911).

Burns *(bûrnz),* **Robert** 1759–96. Scottish poet. *b.* Alloway. Began as farmer; beset by poor health, poverty, dissoluteness, and drink; planned to immigrate to Jamaica; to raise money for voyage, published *Poems, Chiefly in the Scottish Dialect* (1786); success induced him to stay in Scotland; lionized by Edinburgh society; bought farm at Ellisland and married Jean Armour, one of his many mistresses (1788); gave up farming again and became exciseman at Dumfries; flirted with radical ideas of French Revolution; wrote or adapted hundreds of songs for James Johnson's Scots Musical Museum and for George Thomson's *Scottish Airs with Poetry*; acknowledged after death as national poet of Scotland. Best-remembered lyrics are *Auld Lang Syne, Comin' thro the Rye, The Jolly Beggars, Tam o' Shanter, The Cotter's Saturday Night, Halloween, Holy Willie's Prayer, The Holy Fair, A Man's a Man for A' That, To a Mouse, The Twa Dogs, Mary Morison, Duncan Gray, Highland Mary, Ae Fond Kiss, Scots Wha Hae wi' Wallace Bled, Auld Rob Morris,* and *Tam Glen.*

Burr *(bûr),* **Aaron** 1756–1836. American statesman. *b.* Newark, N.J. Son of AARON BURR (1716–57), president of College of New Jersey, now Princeton University. Joined Revolutionary army and became a lieutenant colonel; resigned and entered law practice in N.Y. (1782); N.Y. attorney general (1789–91); Senator (1791–97); tied with Jefferson in electoral college for presidency (1800); lost on 36th ballot, but elected vice-president (1801–1805); killed Alexander Hamilton in duel at Weehauken, N.J. (1804); conspired with Gen. James Wilkinson to seize Spanish region in the Southwest to create new republic; betrayed by Wilkinson; accused by Jefferson of trying to dismember the Union; tried for treason (1807); acquitted; retired from politics and went (1808–12) to Europe; returned and resumed law practice; *Memoirs* were edited by Matthew L. Davis (2 vols., 1836–37).

Burroughs *(bûr ōz),* **Edgar Rice** 1875–1950. American author. *b.* Chicago, Ill. Best known as creator of Tarzan, the hero of an adventure series beginning with *Tarzan of the Apes* (1914), eventually extending to 23 volumes; wrote 36 other novels including *Princess of Mars* (1920) and *At the Earth's Core* (1922).

Burton *(bûr tən),* **Sir Richard Francis** 1821–90. British explorer and Orientalist. *b.* Torquay. Served in Indian army under Napier (1842); made pilgrimage to Mecca disguised as a pathan (1853); with John Speke, explored East Africa and Ethiopia (1853); discovered Lake Tanganyika; consul in Fernando Pó, Santos, Damascus, and Trieste (1861–72); visited Midian (1876–78) and (with Captain Cameroon) Gold Coast (1882); published over 30 volumes of travel narratives and translations, including *Scinde, or the Unhappy Valley* (1851), *Personal Narrative of a Pilgrimage to El Medinah and Meccah* (1855), *First Footsteps in East Africa* (1856), *Lake Regions of Central Africa* (1860), *A Mission to the King of Dahomey* (1864), *Explorations of the Highlands of Brazil* (1868), and a monumental annotated edition of the *Arabian Nights* (16 vols. 1885–88).

Burton, Robert Pseudonym; DEMOCRITUS JUNIOR. 1577–1640. English writer. *b.* Lindley. Vicar of St. Thomas at Oxford (from 1616) and of Segrave in Leicestershire (from 1630). Known principally as the author of *Anatomy of Melancholy*, a learned treatise on the causes, symptoms, and cure of melancholy, with quotations from classical writers (1621).

Bustamente *(bōōs tä mán tā),* **Anastasio** 1780–1853. Mexican general and statesman. *b.* Jiquilpán. Joined Spanish army against revolutionaries (1808); participated in Iturbide's march on Mexico City; member of provisional junta (1821); vice-president under Guerrero; overthrew Guerrero and became acting president (1829–32); deposed by Santa Anna (1832), but recalled, after his fall, for second term as president (1837–39).

Butenandt *(bōō tə nänt),* **Adolph** 1903–. German chemist. *b.* Wesermünde. Known for work on steroid sex hormones, leading to isolation of androsterone and oestrone and syntheses of testosterone and progesterone; awarded (with Leopold Ruzicka) Nobel Prize for chemistry (1939), but declined in accordance with Nazi directive.

Butler *(bŭt lər),* **Nicholas Murray** 1862–1947. American educator. *b.* Elizabeth, N.J. Professor of philosophy and education at Columbia (1890–1902); founder and first president of Teachers College (1886–91); founder of *Educational Review* (1891); president, of Columbia (1902–45), Barnard (1904–45), Bard (1928–45); chairman, Lake Mohonk Conference on International Arbitration (1907, 1909–12); president, Carnegie Endowment for International Peace (1925–45); shared Nobel Peace Prize (1931) with Jane Addams. Author of *The Meaning of Education* (1898), *The International Mind* (1912), *Scholarship and Service* (1921), *The Faith of a Liberal* (1924), *The Path to Peace* (1930), *Between Two Worlds* (1934), and *Across the Busy Years* (2 vols., 1939–40).

Butler, Samuel 1612–80. English satirist. *b.* Strensham. Best known as author of *Hudibras*, published in three parts (1663–78); a broad satire on Puritanism, it found immediate popularity and its octosyllabic couplets came to be known as hudibrastics; other writings published posthumously, including *Genuine Remains in Verse and Prose* (1759).

Butler, Samuel 1835–1902. English writer. *b.* Langar. Began as sheep farmer in New Zealand; described experiences in *A First Year in Canterbury Settlement* (1863); first important work was *Erewhon* (1872), a utopian novel, and its sequel, *Erewhon Revisited* (1902); sparred with Darwin in *Evolution: Old and New* (1879), *Unconscious Memory* (1880), and *Luck or Cunning* (1886), opposing theory of natural selection while accepting evolution; turned to literary criticism, publishing *The Humor of Homer* (1892), *The Authoress of the Odyssey* (1897), and *Shakespeare's Sonnets Reconsidered* (1899); as a musician, composed oratorios, gavottes, minuets, fugues, and a cantata; studied painting, and exhibited in British Museum, Royal Academy, and Tate Gallery; in his greatest novel, the autobiographical *The Way of All Flesh* (1903), raised iconoclasm to an art.

Byng *(bĭng),* **Julian Hedworth George, Viscount** 1862–1935. British general. Served in Boer War; commanded 9th Army Corps at Gallipoli and gained notice by skillful retreat from Dardanelles (1916); commanded Canadian Army Corps (1916–17) and Third Army (1917–18), capturing Vimy Ridge and breaking Hindenburg Line; governor general of Canada (1921–26); viscount (1926); field marshal (1932).

Byrd *(bûrd),* **Richard Evelyn** 1888–1957. American explorer. *b.* Winchester, Va. Commander (1925) of aviation unit in Navy-MacMillan Polar Expedition; flew with Floyd Bennett over North Pole (1926); flew over South Pole (1929); led expeditions to Antarctica (1928–30, 1933–35), discovering Edsel Ford Mountains and Mary Byrd Land; rear admiral (1930); led three U.S. government-sponsored expeditions to Antarctica (1939–40, 1946–47, 1955–56). Recorded missions in *Skyward* (1928), *Little America* (1930), *Discovery* (1935), and *Alone* (1938).

Byrnes *(bûrnz),* **James Francis** 1879–1972. American statesman. *b.* Charleston, S.C. House of Representatives (1911–25); Senator (1931–41); associate justice, Supreme Court (1941–42); director of economic stabilization (1942–43) and of war mobilization (1943–45); secretary of state (1945–47); governor of S.C. (1951–55). Author of *Speaking Frankly* (1947).

Byron *(bī rən),* **George Gordon Noel** title: 6th Baron Byron. 1788–1824. English poet. *b.* London. Raised by widowed mother (from 1791); educated at Harrow and Trinity College, Cambridge, where he published first volume of poems, *Hours of Idleness* (1807); came into great-uncle's title and estates (1798); married Anne Isabella Milbanke (1815), but separated within a year and after birth of daughter (1816); left England to travel on the Continent, espousing various causes; formed liaisons with several women, notably Jane Clairmont and Teresa, Countess Guiccioli; accepted invitation to join Greek insurgents in struggle for independence; set sail for Greece (1823) but stricken and killed by fever at Missolonghi (1824). Principal romances and verse-stories include *Childe Harold's Pilgrimage* (1812-17), *Lara* (1813–14), *The Prisoner of Chillon* (1816), *Don Juan* (1818), *Beppo* (1818), *The Lament of Tasso* (1817), *The Prophecy of Dante* (1821), *The Island* (1823), *Manfred* (1817), and *Mazeppa* (1819); also wrote such plays as *Cain, Marino Faliero, Sardanaplus, The Two Fascari* (all 1821), *Werner* (1823),

The Deformed Transformed (1824); and satires, such as *Vision of Judgment* (1822) and *English Bards and Scotch Reviewers* (1809); ranked, with Shelley and Keats, as a great Romantic poet.

C

Caballero *(kä bä lyā rō),* **Fernán** Pseudonym: CECILIA FRANCISCA JOSEFA DE ARROM, *née* BOHL VON FABER. 1797–1877. Spanish writer. *b.* Morges, Switzerland. Educated in Germany and returned to Spain (1813); thrice widowed; considered first modern novelist in Spain. Beginning with *La Gaviota* (1849), wrote 50 romances, including *La Familia de Alvareda* (1880) and *Clemencia* (1887).

Cabell *(kăb ĕl),* **James Branch** 1879–1958. American novelist. *b.* Richmond, Va. Served on various newspapers, including *New York Herald* (1899–1901) and *Richmond News* (1901); editor of *The American Spectator* (1932–35); author of *Jurgen* (1919), *Figures of Earth* (1921), *The High Place* (1923), *These Restless Heads* (1932), *Domnei* (1920), *The First Gentleman of America* (1942), *The Devil's Own Dear Son* (1949), and *Ladies and Gentlemen* (1934). Also wrote "Biography of Manuel" series.

Cabot *(kăb ət),* **John** 1450–98. Italian navigator. *b.* Genoa. Naturalized citizen of Venice (1476); settled in Bristol, England (1490); sailed (1497) in the ship *Mathew*, under letters-patent from Henry VII, in search of route to Asia; after 52 days, landed on Cape Breton Island; in second voyage (1498) reached Greenland and Baffin Island. Travels continued by son SEBASTIAN (1476–1557), who entered service of Ferdinand V of Spain as cartographer (1512–16); appointed by Charles V of Spain to command expedition to Moluccas by Strait of Magellan (1526); reached Brazil, sailed south, discovered Uruguay and Paraña Rivers, and explored La Plata (to 1530); in service of Spain (until 1547); published engraved map of the world (1544); returned to England (1547); founder and life governor of Merchant Adventurers of London (1551), which sent the two expeditions (1553, 1555–56) that opened northeast trade routes to Russia; inspector of the navy under Edward VI.

Cabral *(kȧ bräl),* **Pedro Alvares** 1460–1526. Portuguese navigator. In command of 13 vessels sent to East Indies by King Emanuel I of Portugal (1500–1501); went westward and discovered Brazil, taking possession of it for Portugal (although Vicente Yañez Pinzón had landed in northeast Brazil two months earlier); resumed voyage and reached Calicut on India's west coast (1500); erected a fort and established first commercial treaty between Portugal and India; returned to Lisbon (1501).

Cabrini *(kȧ brē nē)*, **Saint Frances Xavier** known as MOTHER CABRINI. 1850–1917. Roman Catholic religious. *b.* Sant' Angelo, Italy. Founded (c1874) Missionary Sisters of the Sacred Heart in Codogno; came to U.S. (1889) and established hospitals, orphanages, and schools; beatified (1938); canonized (1946) as first American saint; named (1950) patron saint of emigrants. Feast day: Dec. 22.

Cade *(kād)*, **John (Jack)** *d.* 1450. English rebel leader. Led Cade's Rebellion, a Kentish uprising during the reign of Henry VI; assuming the name of Mortimer and the title of Captain of Kent, led 40,000 followers in a march on London; defeated royal forces at Sevenoaks; entered London and held the city for two days; executed Saye-and-Sele and Crowmer, king's favorites; the uprising spent itself within a few days, and Cade was hunted down and killed at Heathfield.

Cadillac *(kăd əl ăk)*, **Sieur Antoine de la Mothe** 1658–1730. French explorer and official. *b.* Gascony. Went to America with French army (1683); led colonists in founding a settlement on Detroit River that became Detroit; antagonized Jesuits; arrested (1704); acquitted, but recalled from Detroit and appointed governor of Louisiana (1711); recalled to France (1716), spending last years in disappointment and disgrace.

Caedmon *(kăd mən)* *fl.* 7th century. First English Christian poet. Although illiterate, according to Bede, was divinely inspired to compose metrical paraphrases of the Bible; a nine-line hymn believed to be only extant fragment; later became inmate of abbey at Whitby.

Caesar *(sē zər)*, **Gaius Julius** c100–44 B.C. Roman statesman. Joined party of Lucius Cinna, opposed to Sulla (83); proscribed, remaining in Asia until Sulla's death (78); elected pontifex (74), quaestor (68), curule aedile (65), pontifex maximus (63), praetor in Spain (61), and propraetor (61); formed first triumvirate with Pompey and Crassus (60); elected consul (59), and proconsul in Gaul and Illyricum (58); conducted victorious campaigns (58–49) in the Gallic Wars, vanquishing the Helvetii and Ariovistus, the Belgic Confederacy, the Nervii, and the Veneti; invaded Britain, crossed Rhine, and defeated Vercingetorix; ordered by Pompey and Senate to disband and return to Rome, crossed river Rubicon and led army in civil war against Pompey, who was eventually defeated at Pharsalia (48); as an ally of Cleopatra, concluded Alexandrine War (49); defeated Pharnaces II at Zela (47); routed Pompeian generals, Scipio and Cato, at Thapsus (46), and defeated them at Munda (44); celebrated victories with four great triumphs in Rome; dictator (49–45); elected dictator for life (45); given titles "Father of the Country" and "Imperator;" declared divine and statue placed in temples; offered crown (44), but refused it; murdered by 60 disaffected patricians, including Brutus and Cassius, on the Ides of March (44); regarded as one of greatest Roman generals, and, next to

Cicero, one of finest Roman orators; established reputation as a historian with *Commentaries*, introduced Julian calendar, made important contributions to Roman law, architecture, and philology.

Cage *(kāj),* **John Milton, Jr.** 1912–. American composer. *b.* Los Angeles, Calif. Pioneered in avant-garde compositions based on electronic sounds and aleatoric music; composed *Imaginary Landscape No 4* (1951), *Water Music* (1952), and *Music for Amplified Toy Music* (1960).

Caine *(kān),* **Sir Thomas Henry Hall** 1853–1931. British novelist. *b.* Runcorn. Author of numerous novels dealing with Manx life, such as *The Deemster* (1887), *The Manxman* (1894), *The Christian* (1897), *The Woman Thou Gavest Me* (1913), and *Master of Man* (1921).

Calder *(kôl dər),* **Alexander Stirling** 1870–1945. American sculptor. *b.* Philadelphia, Pa. Son of ALEXANDER MILNE CALDER (1846–1923), Scottish-born sculptor who executed statues of Penn and Meade in Philadelphia. Principal A.S. Calder statues include Witherspoon, Whitman, Davies, Penn, Audubon, the Ericsson Memorial, and groups on the Washington Arch in N.Y.; father of ALEXANDER CALDER (1898–1976), American sculptor, best known for abstract sculptures (mobiles and stabiles) consisting of suspended constructions of wire and metal.

Calderón de la Barca *(käl də rôn də lä bär kä),* **Pedro** 1600–1681. Spanish playwright and poet. *b.* Madrid. In Spanish army (to 1630); summoned by Philip IV to court (1635); fought against Catalan rebels (1640); entered Order of St. Francis (1650); priest (1651); chaplain to Philip; regarded as Spanish dramatist and last of the Golden Age; author of 118 dramas, 72 *autos sacramentales* (religious plays) for Corpus Christi festival, and comedies, including *The Fair Lady, The Mock Astrologer, The Wonder-Working Magician, Life is a Dream, The Constant Prince, No Magic like Love,* and *The Weapons of Beauty.*

Caldwell *(kôld wĕl),* **Erskine Preston** 1903–. American writer. *b.* White Oak, Ga. Best known for novels and stories portraying poor whites in the South, as in *God's Little Acre* and *Tobacco Road*; correspondent in Moscow for *Life, PM,* and CBS; collaborated with wife MARGARET BOURKE-WHITE (1906–71) on documentary books on Russia and World War II.

Calhoun *(kăl ho͞on),* **John Caldwell** 1782–1850. American statesman. *b.* Abbeville, S.C. House of Representatives (1811–17); secretary of war (1817–25); vice-president of U.S. (1825–32) under John Q. Adams and Jackson; champion of states' rights during Nullification Controversy; set forth theory of states' rights in *Address to the People of South Carolina* (1831); Senator (1832–43, 1845–50); secretary of state (1844–45); asserted right of states to set aside unconstitutional federal laws and to secede if necessary; defended slavery and advocated dual presidency to safeguard interests of slave-holding states; organized Nashville Convention of 1850; regarded, with Henry Clay and Daniel Webster, as great American orator;

complete works published (6 vols., 1851–55).

Caligula *(kə lĭg ū lə)* real name: Gaius Caesar. 12-41. Roman emperor (37-41). *b.* Antium. Son of Germanicus and Agrippina, succeeded Tiberius as emperor and ruled with moderation for a year; suffered derangement through illness (38); thereafter, began orgy of senseless cruelty and tyranny; in fit of insanity, made his horse a consul and declared himself a god; assassinated by Praetorian guard, led by Cassius Chaerea.

Callimachus *(kă lĭm ə kŭs)* *fl.* 3rd century B.C. Greek scholar. *b.* Cyrene, Libya. Famous as chief librarian of Alexandrian Library; reputed to have written some 800 works, of which *Pinakes*, an annotated catalog of books, and *Aetia*, a collection of legends, are among extant fragments.

Calmette *(kăl mĕt),* **Albert Léon Charles** 1863–1933. French bacteriologist. *b.* Nice. Founder and director of Pasteur Institutes at Saigon (1891–93) and at Lille (1896–1919); developed an antisnakebite serum and a vaccine (with Guerin) against tuberculosis, called BCG (Bacillus Calmette-Guerin).

Calvin *(kăl vĭn),* **John** 1509–64. French Protestant theologian and reformer. *b.* Noyon. Embraced Reformation (c1528); banished from Paris (1533); went to Basel and published *Institutes of the Christian Religion* (1536); aided Guillaume Farel in setting up theocratic government at Geneva (1536); banished from city by Libertines (1538); recalled to Geneva (1541) to direct establishment of an absolute theocratic state; founded Academy at Geneva (1556); struggled to suppress heretics, one of whom, Servetus, was burned at the stake (1553); systematized Protestant doctrines known as Calvinism, which held that redemption is the free gift of God for the elect alone.

Calvin, Melvin 1911–. American chemist. *b.* St. Paul, Minn. Director of the bioorganic division of Lawrence Radiation Laboratory at University of California; awarded Nobel Prize in chemistry (1961) for work on photosynthesis.

Camões *(kə mōənsh),* **Luiz Vaz de** Anglicized form: Camoëns. 1524–80. Portuguese poet. *b.* Lisbon. Educated for the church at Coimbra, but did not enter holy orders; left Lisbon and served in army at Ceuta, Africa, losing an eye in battle; returned (c1550), but imprisoned (1552) for wounding a minor courtier; released on agreeing to leave for India; exiled in Goa and Macao (1553–69); returned to Lisbon (1570); published (1572) *Os Lusiades (The Lusiads)*, written in 1556; it was acclaimed as national epic of Portugal; also wrote sonnets, lyrics, and comedies.

Campanella *(käm pä nĕl lä)* **Tommaso** original name: Giovanni Domenico Campanella. 1568–1639. Italian philosopher. *b.* Stilo. Entered Dominican order at age 15; gained fame as a preacher; charged before Inquisition with heresy and conspiracy; imprisoned in a Neapolitan dungeon (1599–1626) and tortured; fled to France (1634) and gained patronage of Louis XIII and Richelieu. Wrote magnum opus, *Citta Del Sole*, in prison, describing a

Catholic utopia; other works include *Philosophia Sensibus Demonstrata*, (1591), *De Sensu Rerum at Magia* (1620), and *Universalis Philosophia* (1638); opposed Aristotelianism and tried to reconcile scholastic theology and scientific approach.

Campbell *(kăm bĕl),* **Alexander** 1788–1866. American clergyman. *b.* near Ballymena, Ireland. Immigrated to U.S. (1809); nondenominational preacher (1813–27); founded magazine *Christian Baptist* (1823), later *Millennial Harbinger* (1830); with followers, broke from Baptist Church and formed new denomination called Disciples of Christ, or Campbellites (about 1827); founded Bethany College at Bethany, W.V. (1840); published translation of Bible (1826), a hymnal (1828), and *The Christian System* (1839); doctrines advocated a simple form of Christianity, including adult baptism.

Campbell, Sir Colin title: BARON CLYDE; original surname: MACLIVER. 1792–1863. British general. *b.* Glasgow, Scotland. Served with distinction in Peninsular War (1810–13), in Chinese campaign (1842), Second Sikh War (1848–49), and battles of Alma River and Balaklava in Crimean War (1854–55); on outbreak of Indian Mutiny (1857), appointed commander in chief of India; suppressed mutiny (1858); elevated to peerage (1858); field marshal (1862).

Campbell-Bannerman *(kăm bĕl băn ər mən),* **Sir Henry** 1836–1908. British statesman. *b.* Glasgow, Scotland. Entered Parliament as Liberal (1868); financial secretary to war office (1871–74, 1880–82); secretary to admiralty (1882–84); chief secretary for Ireland (1884–85); secretary of state for war (1886, 1892–95); leader of Liberal party in House of Commons (from 1899); prime minister (1905–08); advocated reconciliation with Boer republics of South Africa and home rule for Ireland; led campaign against House of Lords.

Campi *(käm pə)* Italian family of artists in 16th-century Cremona, including:

GALEAZZO 1477–1536. Religious painter in the style of Boccaccino and Perugino.

ANTONIO c1530–91. Son of Galeazzo. Architect and painter; known for imitations of Correggio, such as *Birth of Christ* in Milan's Church of San Paolo; commissioned by Philip II to decorate the Escorial.

GIULIO 1502–72. Son of Galeazzo. Painter noted for frescoes in Santa Margherita and *Virgin and Child with Saints Celsus and Nazarus* for the Church of Sant'Abbondio, both in Cremona.

VINCENZO 1536–91. Son of Galeazzo. Painter noted for portraits and genre scenes.

BERNARDINO 1522–c1590. Possibly related to sons of Galeazzo. Painter who imitated Titian so well that it is difficult to distinguish authorship; painted frescoes in the cupola of the Church of San Sigismondo at Cremona, regarded as masterpiece; also painted *Descent from the Cross* and *Mater Dolorosa*; wrote *Parere Sopra la Pittura* (1584).

Campion *(kăm pĭ ŭn),* **Edmund** 1540–81. English Jesuit martyr. *b.* London. Ordained Anglican deacon (1569); espoused Catholic doctrines and fled to Douai; joined Society of Jesus in

Bohemia (1573); professor of rhetoric in Prague; returned to England (1580) as Catholic missionary; outlined opposition to Anglican faith in *Decem Rationes*; preached against the established church and gained many converts; arrested, found guilty of conspiracy and sedition, tortured and executed (1581); beatified (1886).

Camus *(kȧ mü)*, **Albert** 1913–60. French writer. *b.* Mondovi, Algeria. Active in French Resistance during World War II; edited left-wing paper *Combat* (1945–48). Works deal with meaninglessness and absurdity of existence and man's isolation in a world without values; awarded Nobel Prize in literature (1957); writings include *The Myth of Sisyphus* (1942), *L'Homme Révolté, The Stranger* (1942), *The Plague* (1947), *The Fall, Caligula* (1945), and *The Misunderstanding* (1945).

Canby *(kăn bĭ)*, **Henry Seidel** 1878–1961. American critic. *b.* Wilmington, Del. Influenced American letters as editor of *Saturday Review of Literature* (1924–36) and as chairman of board of judges of the Book-of-the-Month Club. Author of *Education by Violence* (1919), *Definitions* (1922, 1924), *Classic Americans* (1931), *The Age of Confidence* (1934), *Thoreau* (1939), and *American Memoir* (1947).

Candolle *(käN dôl)*, **Augustin Pyrame de** 1778–1841. Swiss botanist. *b.* Geneva. Founded natural system of botany with *Historia Plantarum Succulentarum* (4 vols., 1799–1803) and *Astragalogia* (1802); undertook botanical survey of France (1806–12); appointed to chair of botany at Montpellier (1810); professor of natural science at University of Geneva; directorship of Geneva Botanical Gardens (1816–34); completed *Regni Vegetabilis Systema Naturale* (2 vols., 1818–21); continued in *Prodromus Systematis Regni Vegetabilis* (17 vols.), the last ten volumes of which were written by his son ALPHONSE LOUIS PIERRE PYRAME DE CONDOLLE (1806–1893) and grandson ANNE CASIMIR PYRAME DE CONDOLLE (1836–1925).

Canning *(kăn ĭng)*, **George** 1770–1827. British statesman. *b.* London. Entered Parliament (1794); noted as brilliant orator; held government posts under aegis of his friend William Pitt the Younger (1796–99, 1804–1806); as minister for foreign affairs in Portland ministry (1807–10), planned seizure of Danish fleet at Copenhagen and advocated aggressive military stance against Napoleon; reappointed foreign ministry (1822); prime minister (1827); promoted British non-intervention in nationalistic movements in Europe and South America, which had enormous significance on the course of history; asserted British independence of Holy Alliance; first to recognize free states of Spanish America; supported Greece against the Turks; advocated greater religious and political freedom for Catholics and laid ground work for repealing the corn laws. His son, CHARLES JOHN, EARL CANNING (1812–62), succeeded Lord Dalhousie as governor general of India (1856–62); steered administration through Indian Mutiny (1857) and restored peace; appointed viceroy (1858); nicknamed "Clemency Canning."

Cannizzaro *(kän nəd dzä rō),* **Stanislao** 1826–1910. Italian chemist. *b.* Palermo, Sicily. Active in Sicilian Revolution; fled to France (1849); professor of chemistry at Alexandria (1851), Geneva (1855), Palermo (1861), and Rome (1871); discovered Cannizzaro reaction (1881) for obtaining alcohols from aldehydes; discovered cyanamide; established distinction between atomic and molecular weights using Avogadro's hypothesis.

Cannon *(kăn ən),* **Joseph Gurney** 1836–1926. American legislator. *b.* New Garden, N.C. Member of House of Representatives for 46 years (1873–91, 1893–1913, 1915–23); elected Speaker (1903); exercised dictatorial control over House procedures until displaced (1911); his high-handedness led to a successful bipartisan move to curtail Speaker's powers by enlarging Rules Committee membership (1910).

Canova *(kä nô vä),* **Antonio** 1757–1822. Italian sculptor. *b.* Possagno. Went to Rome (1779), where he spent remainder of life; curator of Vatican art under Pius VII (1802); to Paris to execute commissions for Napoleon (1802, 1805, 1810) and to recover art treasures taken from Rome (1815); created marquis of Ischia. Among principal works are *Venus and Adonis, Orpheus, Eurydice, Perseus with the Head of Medusa, Psyche Holding a Butterfly, Winged Cupid, Theseus Vanquishing the Minotaur, Cupid and Psyche, Hebe Pouring Nectar, Napoleon, Penitent Magdalen, Perseus, Venus, Three Graces, Paris, Daedalus and Icarus,* and *Hercules and Lichas.*

Canute II *(kȧ nūt),* also called CANUTE THE GREAT. 994–1035. King of England (1016–35), Denmark (1018–35), and Norway (1028–35). Succeeded father, Sweyn, as King of England (1014); claim opposed by Ethelred and son Edmund Ironside; undisputed ruler of England after death of Edmund (1016); divided kingdom into the earldoms of Mercia, Northumberland, Wessex, and East Anglia; developed into a pious, wise, just, and popular ruler; married (1017) Emma, widow of Ethelred; pilgrimage to Rome (1026–27); conquered Norway (1030) after death of Olaf; assumed crown of Denmark after death of Harold (1018).

Čapek *(chȧ pĕk),* **Karel** 1890–1938. Czech writer. *b.* Schwadonitz. Author of *R.U.R. (Rossum's Universal Robots;* 1920), in which the term "robot" first appeared. Other works include *The Makropoulos Secret* (1922), *The Power and the Glory* (1936), and (with brother, Josef) *The Life of the Insects* (1921) and *Adam the Creator* (1927).

Caracalla *(kăr ə kăl ə)* real name: MARCUS AURELIUS ANTONINUS; original name: BASSIANUS. 188–217. Roman emperor (211–17). *b.* Lyons, France. Ascended throne on death of father Septimius Severus as joint emperor with brother, Geta; caused assassination of Geta (212); proclaimed sole ruler by Senate; killed over 20,000 of Geta's followers, including the jurist Papinianus; extended full citizenship to free inhabitants of the empire; victorious against the

Alemanni; assumed the surname Alemannicus (213–14); built many public structures, including the Baths of Caracalla at Rome; reign marked by extortions and excesses; assassinated on an expedition against Parthians.

Caravaggio *(kä rä väd jō),* **Michelangelo Amerighi da** real name: MICHAELANGELO MERISI. 1565–1609. Italian painter. *b.* Caravaggio. Protégé of Cardinal de Monte in Rome; killed a friend in a gambling fracas and fled to Naples, and later to Malta and Sicily; considered founder and finest exponent of naturalism; used chiaroscuro to great effect. Principal works include *The Entombment of Christ, Card Players, Gipsy Fortune Teller, Christ and the Disciples at Emmaus, Death of the Virgin Mary, St. Matthew Writing the Gospel, Martyrdom of St. Sebastian,* and *Grand Master of the Knights of Malta.*

Cárdenas *(kär thə näs),* **Lázaro** 1895–1970. Mexican statesman. *b.* Michoacán. Joined revolutionary forces (1913) under Calles and Obregon; general (1924); governor of Michoacán (1928–32); president of Partido Revolucionario Nacional (from 1930); minister of interior (1931); minister of war and navy (1933); president (1934–40); administration marked by struggle with Catholic Church, inauguration of the Six-Year Plan, nationalization of foreign-owned oil companies, and secularization of education; minister of defense (1943–45).

Carducci *(kär do͞ot chē),* **Giosuè** 1835–1907. Italian writer. *b.* Valdicastello. Professor of Italian literature at Bologna (1861–1904); awarded Nobel Prize in literature (1906); regarded as national poet of modern Italy; complete editions of poetry issued in 20 vols., including *Odi Barbare, Rime a Ritme,* and *Satana e Polemiche Sataniche*; also published such critical studies as *Storia del Giorno de Parini* (1829) and *La Poesia Barbara nei Secoli XV e XVI* (1881).

Carey *(kâr ĭ),* **Mathew** 1760–1839. American publisher. *b.* Dublin, Ireland. Editor, *Freeman's Journal* and *Volunteer's Journal* (1780–84); immigrated to U.S. (1784); founded *Pennsylvania Herald* (1785), *Columbian Magazine* (1786), and *American Museum* (1787); entered book publishing (1785), first book publisher and bookseller in U.S.; author of *Autobiography* (1829); business handed down to son HENRY CHARLES CAREY (1793–1879), political economist and author of *Principles of Political Economy* (3 vols., 1837–40).

Carlyle *(kär līl),* **Thomas** 1795–1881. Scottish writer. *b.* Ecclefechan. Schoolmaster at Annan and Kircaldy (1814–18); married Jane Baillie Welsh and moved to Edinburgh (1826), to Craigenputtock (1828), and to London (1834), where he was known as "the Sage of Chelsea." Principal writings include *Sartor Resartus* (1833–34), *French Revolution* (1837), *Heroes and Hero Worship* (1840), *Chartism* (1839), *Past and Present* (1843), *Latter Day Pamphlets* (1850), *Oliver Cromwell* (1845), *History of Frederick the Great* (6 vols., 1858–65), and *Reminiscences* (2 vols., 1881); exerted profound influence on contemporary literature through powerful style and ethical and political ideals.

Carnegie *(kär nā gĭ),* **Andrew** 1835–1919. American industrialist and philanthropist. *b.* Dunfermline, Scotland. Immigrated to U.S. (1848); entered steel business (1865); principal owner of Homestead Steel works and other plants, consolidated into Carnegie Steel Company (1889); introduced Bessemer process to American steel production; merged with J.P. Morgan's U.S. Steel Corp. and retired (1901); devoted remainder of life to philanthropy; donated over $350 million to many organizations in Britain and U.S., including Carnegie Corporation of N.Y., Carnegie Foundation for the Advancement of Teaching, Carnegie Endowment for International Peace, Carnegie Institute of Pittsburgh, and Carnegie Institution of Washington, D.C.; also helped build many public library buildings and the Peace Palace at the Hague; wrote *Autobiography* (1920), *Triumphant Democracy* (1886), and *The Gospel of Wealth and Other Timely Essays* (1900).

Carnot *(kär nō)* Name of French family, including: LAZARE NICOLAS MARGEURITE 1753–1823. Statesman and general. *b.* Nolay. Member of Legislative Assembly (1791) and National Convention (1792); member of Committee of Public Safety (1793); organized Revolutionary Army and gained title of "Organizer of Victory" by repelling reactionary forces from the frontier; member of the Directory (1795–97) and twice its president; fled to Germany to escape coup of Fructidor (1797), but returned after 18th Brumaire; minister of war (1800–01); member of Tribunate (1802–07); heroically defended Antwerp (1814); minister of interior during Hundred Days (1815); exiled by Louis XVIII and lived remainder of life in Warsaw and Magdeburg.

NICOLAS LÉONARD SADI 1796–1832. Physicist. *b.* Paris. Developed Carnot cycle of engine thermal efficiency and the Carnot principle, an early version of the second law of thermodynamics; published *Réflexions sur la Puissance Motrice du Feu,* a pioneer work on heat (1824).

MARIE FRANÇOIS SADI 1837–94. Statesman. *b.* Limoges. Elected to National Assembly (1871); finance minister (1880–81, 1885–86); fourth president of French Republic (1887–94).

Caro *(kärō),* **Joseph ben Ephraim** also KARO. 1488–1575. Jewish Talmudic scholar. *b.* Toledo, Spain. Settled in Palestine after being expelled from Spain (c1535). Author of *Beth Joseph (The House of Joseph)* and *Shulcan Aruch (Arranged Tables),* authoritative works on Jewish civil and religious law.

Carpenter *(kär pĕn tẽr),* **John Alden** 1876–1951. American composer. *b.* Park Ridge, Ill. Best known compositions include the three ballets *Birthday of the Infanta* (1919), *Krazy-Kat* (1922), and *Skyscrapers* (1926), the suite *Adventures in a Perambulator* (1915), *Concertino* (1917), the tone poem *The Sea Drift* (1933), and *The Anxious Bugler* (1943).

Carpini *(kär pē nē),* **Giovanni de Piano** c1182–1252, Italian monk and traveler. *b.* near Perugia. Companion and disciple of Saint Francis of Assisi; leader of mission to khan of Tartary bearing a message from Pope Innocent IV seeking friendship; though the mission was not successful, the narrative of the journey, called *Liber Tartarorum*, is one of the most important accounts of Central Asia and the Mongols in the Middle Ages.

Carr *(kär),* **Sir Robert** *d.* 1667. English colonial governor. *b.* Northumberland. Appointed one of three commissioners to New England (1664); captured New Amsterdam from the Dutch and renamed it New York (1664); governor of Maine (1666–67).

Carrel *(kăr ĕl),* **Alexis** 1873–1944. French biologist. *b.* Sainte-Foy-lès-Lyon. Immigrated to U.S. (1905); worked at Rockefeller Institute for Medical Research (1906–39); awarded Nobel Prize in physiology and medicine (1912) for work on transplantation of organs; discovered method for suturing blood vessels and the Carrel-Dakin system of treating wounds. Author of *Man, the Unknown* (1935).

Carroll *(kăr ŭl),* **John** 1735–1815. American Catholic prelate. *b.* Upper Marlboro, Md. Educated in France; ordained as Jesuit priest (1769); returned to Md. after suppression of Jesuits in France (1774); bishop of Baltimore, the first American Catholic bishop (1790); archbishop of Baltimore (1808); founded Georgetown College (1791). Author of first Catholic book published in U.S., *Address to the Roman Catholics of the United States* (1784).

Carroll, Lewis pseudonym of Charles Lutwidge Dodgson. 1832–98. British writer. *b.* Daresbury. Took holy orders (1861), lecturer in mathematics at Oxford (1855–81); best known for *Alice's Adventures in Wonderland* (1865) and *Through the Looking Glass and What Alice Found There* (1872), both illustrated by John Tenniel; wrote three more books for children: *The Hunting of the Snark* (1876), *A Tangled Tale* (1885), and *Sylvie and Bruno* (1889); also published books on mathematics and a journal of a visit to Russia.

Carson *(Kär sən),* **Christopher** known as Kit. 1809–68. American trapper, guide, and Indian agent. *b.* in Madison County, Ky. Ran away from home (1826); frontiersman and hunter; John C. Frémont's guide on three expeditions (1842–45); credited with heroic exploits during Mexican War (1846); appointed Indian agent (1853); active in numerous campaigns against Indians during Civil War; given command of Fort Garland, Colo. (1866); resigned because of poor health (1867); published a highly romanticized autobiography (1858), *The Life and Adventures of Kit Carson, the Nestor of the Rocky Mountains.*

Carson, Rachel Louise 1907–64. American scientist and author. *b.* Springdale, Pa. Educated at Pennsylvania College for Women and Johns Hopkins University; studied the sea at Woods Hole; known for her books about the sea and nature; warned of dangers of misuse of chemicals such as DDT; sensitive style of writing and her thorough knowledge gained her a popular audience. Author of *Under the Sea Wind* (1941), *The Sea Around Us* (1951), and *Silent Spring* (1966).

Carter *(kär tər),* **Howard** 1873–1939. English archaeologist. *b.* Swaffham, Norfolk. Joined Egyptian archaeological survey (1890); assisted Flinders Petrie at Tell el-Amarna (1892); inspector-general of antiquities department of Egypt; collaborated with G.E. Herbert from 1907 in excavations in Valley of the Kings, leading to the discovery of the tombs of Hatshepsut, Amenhotep I, and Tutankhamen.

Carter, James Earl, Jr. 1924–. Thirty-ninth president of the United States. *b.* Plains, Ga. Graduated from the U.S. Naval Academy at Annapolis in 1942; entered the nuclear submarine program as an aide to Adm. Hyman Rickover; married Rosalynn Smith in 1946; on his father's death in 1953 resigned from the Navy and took over the family peanut farming and warehousing business; began political career with election to the Georgia senate in 1962; elected governor in 1970; as chairman of the Democratic Campaign Committee began building up grassroots support by tirelessly crisscrossing the country and entering all the presidential primaries; won 19 out of 31 primaries in a hard-fought campaign with a broad appeal to both blacks and whites, conservatives and liberals; gained Democratic presidential nomination on the first roll-call vote; in the 1976 presidential race defeated President Gerald R. Ford to become the first president from the Deep South since the Civil War; set the tone of his presidency by abjuring the pomp and circumstance of the imperial presidency and adopting a more homely style; as a born-again Christian and devout Baptist stressed moral imperatives, especially in the field of foreign affairs by linking U.S. aid to observance of human rights; suffered severe erosion in popularity as a result of inept handling of Congress and inability to curb inflation; achieved greatest triumphs in the signing of the Israeli-Egyptian peace treaty and the SALT II agreements, both in 1979.

Cartier *(kär tyā),* **Jacques** 1491–1557. French explorer. *b.* St. Malo. Made three historic voyages to Canada: explored the Gulf of St. Lawrence (1534); sailed up to Montreal (1535); and made an unsuccessful attempt to colonize Canada (1541–42).

Cartwright *(kärt rīt),* **Edmund** 1743–1823. English inventor. *b.* Marnham. Country parson (1779); after a visit to Arkwright's cotton mills at Cromford, devised and patented a power loom (1785); built a weaving mill (1787); patented a wool-carding machine (1789) and a steam engine using alcohol (1797); granted £10,000 by Parliament (1809).

Caruso *(kä ro͞o zō),* **Enrico** 1874–1921. Italian operatic tenor. *b.* Naples. First appeared on the Italian stage (1895) in *Faust*; later appeared in St. Petersburg, Buenos Aires, London, Milan, and New York; principal tenor of the Metropolitan Opera House until his death; repertoire included *Pagliacci, Rigoletto*, *La Bohème*, and 40 other operas; noted for the extraordinary power of his voice.

Carver *(kär vər),* **George Washington** 1864–1943. American scientist. *b.* near Carthage, Mo. Born of slave parents; received M.S. in agriculture at Iowa State College (1896); joined Tuskegee Institute as director of agricultural research (1896); developed hundreds of new products from peanuts, sweet potatoes, soybeans, and cotton wastes, which revolutionized the Southern economy.

Carver, John c1576–1621. English colonist. *b.* Nottinghamshire or Derbyshire. Led by nonconformist beliefs to emigrate from London to the Netherlands (1609); joined Pilgrims in Leiden as chief financial backer (1610); hired and outfitted the *Mayflower*; elected first governor of Plymouth colony (1620) negotiated treaty between English and Indian chief Massasoit (1621).

Casals *(kä säls),* **Pablo** 1876–1973. Spanish cellist, conductor, and composer. *b.* Vendrell. Professor at Barcelona Conservatory (1897); founded the Pau Casals Orchestra at Barcelona (1920); left Spain at outbreak of Civil War, never to return; founded annual festival of classical chamber music at Prades, France. Compositions include works for orchestra, piano, violin, cello, and organ, and the Christmas oratorio, *El Pesebre* (1960); established Casals Festivals in Puerto Rico (from 1957).

Casanova de Seingalt *(kä sä nô vä dā säN gäl),* **Giovanni Jacopo** 1725–98. Italian adventurer. *b.* Venice. Expelled from seminary (1741); after serving as secretary to Cardinal Acquaviva and as soldier in Venetian army, began roving as a preacher, gambler, alchemist, cabalist, musician, and glib sensualist; imprisoned as a spy in Venice, but managed a daring escape (1756); traveled through Europe, mingling with the rich and the powerful, including Marie Antoinette, Empress Catherine, Voltaire, von Haller, Frederick II, Mme. de Pompadour, Cagliostro, and the Pope; gained reputation as a charlatan and libertine; accepted post of librarian at Count Waldenstein's castle of Dux in Bohemia (1785), where he remained until his death. Author of *Memoires* (12 vols., 1826–38), which gained a certain notoriety.

Casement *(kās mĕnt),* **Sir Roger David** 1864–1916. Irish nationalist. *b.* Kingstown. British consular official in Africa and South America (1900–1913); denounced the atrocities against natives in Congo and Brazil; knighted (1912); returned to Ireland and worked for Irish independence (1913); on outbreak of World War I, went to Germany in an effort to raise an Irish liberation army among Irish prisoners of war; returned to Ireland in a German submarine and was arrested and hanged (1916) as a traitor.

Casimir *(kăz ĭ mĭr)* Polish royal family including:

CASIMIR I also called THE PEACEFUL and THE RESTORER. 1015–58. King of Poland (1034–58); driven out of kingdom by nobles and fled to Hungary; recovered crown with aid of Holy Roman Emperor Henry III; established Christianity as national faith of Poland.

CASIMIR II also called THE JUST. 1138–94. King of Poland (1177–94).

CASIMIR III also called THE GREAT

and THE PEASANTS' KING. 1309–70. King of Poland (1333–70); made peace with Teutonic Knights; defeated Lithuanians; protected peasants and Jews; codified laws of Great and Little Poland; established University of Cracow (1364).

CASIMIR IV 1427–92. King of Poland (1447–92); Carried on 13-year war (1454–66) with Teutonic Knights, ended it with the Peace of Thorn, giving Pomerania, West Prussia, and other territories to Poland; founded the Polish Parliament or Sejm (1467); long reign considered cultural golden age of Poland.

Caslon *(kăs lŏn),* **William** 1692–1766. English type designer. *b.* Cradley. Gun engraver and toolsmith by profession; designed old-style type faces noted for legibility and grace; caslon types very popular with printers until the end of 18th century; revived about 1850 by Chiswick Press, they are still used extensively.

Cassin *(kăs ĭn),* **René** 1887–1976. French statesman. *b.* Bayonne. Permanent head of Conseil d'État, the highest administrative tribunal in France (from 1944); awarded Nobel Peace Prize (1968) for work as president of U.N. Human Rights Commission (1946–68).

Cassirer *(kä sē rər),* **Ernst** 1874–1945. German philosopher. *b.* Breslau. Taught at universities of Berlin, Hamburg, Oxford, Goteburg, Yale, and Columbia (1905–45); one of the leaders of Marburg school of neo-Kantianism; explored relations between knowledge and perception and between language and symbols in *Substanzbegriff und Funktionbegriff* (1910), *Freiheit und Form* (1916), *Das Erkenntnisproblem in der Philosophie und Wissenschaft der Neueren Zeit* (3 vols., 1906–19), *Sprache und Mythos* (1925), *Descartes* (1939), *An Essay on Man* (1944), and *The Myth of the State* (1946).

Castiglione, Duc de. *See* **Augereau, Pierre François Charles**

Castlereagh *(käs l rā),* **Viscount** real name: ROBERT STEWART. 1769–1822. British statesman. *b.* Dublin, Ireland. Elected to Irish Parliament (1790); chief secretary for Ireland (1799–1801); resigned with William Pitt on George III's refusal to allow introduction of Catholic Emancipation bill; president of East India Board of Control (1802); war minister (1805–1806, 1807–1809); directed extension of war to Iberian Peninsula under Wellesley and the successful Elbe expedition; wounded in duel with Canning (1809); as foreign secretary and leader of House of Commons, led coalition against Napoleon (1812–22); represented Britain at Congress of Vienna (1814), at the Treaty of Paris (1815), and at Congress of Aix-la-Chapelle (1818); restrained a policy of retaliation against France by the Grand Coalition; arranged confinement of Napoleon at St. Helena; took own life on eve of Conference at Verona (1822).

Castriota, George. *See* **Scanderbeg.**

Castro *(käs trō),* **Fidel** 1927–. Cuban statesman. *b.* Mayari, Cuba. Led two unsuccessful risings against Fulgencio Batista (1953, 1956) before finally toppling him (1958); appointed premier (from 1959); with brother Raul, proclaimed a Marxist-Leninist state in

Cuba and expropriated all foreign-owned properties; survived the emigré invasion at the Bay of Pigs (1961) and the missile crisis (1962).

Cather *(kă thər),* **Willa Sibert** 1876–1947. American writer. *b.* Winchester, Va. One of most brilliant writers about the immigrant experience in the Midwest and prairie frontier. Managing editor of *McClure's Magazine* (1906–1912). Works include *O Pioneers* (1913), *My Ántonia* (1918), *One of Ours* (Pulitzer Prize, 1922), *A Lost Lady* (1923), *Death Comes for the Archbishop* (1927), *Shadows on the Rock* (1931), *Lucy Gayheart* (1935), and *Sapphira and the Slave Girl* (1940).

Catherine *(kăth ər ĭn)* Name of two Russian empresses:

CATHERINE I Russian name: EKATERINA ALEKSEEVNA; original name: MARFA SKAVRONSKAYA. 1684–1727. Empress of Russia (1725–27). *b.* Jakobstadt, Latvia. Of peasant origin; married a Swedish dragoon; captured by Russian soldiers at the fall of Marienburg (1702); became serf of Prince Menshikov; attracted notice of Peter the Great, becoming his mistress (1703); married Peter (1712); created empress (1724); succeeded Peter, as Catherine I (1725); established supreme privy council and Russian Academy of Sciences; sponsored naval expedition of Vitus Bering.

CATHERINE II Russian name: EKATERINA ALEKSEEVNA; real name: SOPHIA AUGUSTA FREDERICA OF ANHALT-ZERBST; also called CATHERINE THE GREAT. 1729–96. Russian empress (1762–96). *b.* Stettin, Prussia. Married Peter, later Peter III (1745); estranged from husband; deposed Peter, usurped the throne, and had dethroned emperor murdered (1762); continued the expansionist policies of Peter the Great; extended Russian frontiers by the Treaty of Kuchuk Kainarja (1774), the Treaty of Jassy (1792) with the Turks, the annexation of Crimea (1783), the partitions of Poland (1772, 1793, 1795); corresponded with Voltaire and the Encyclopedists, whose ideas she shared.

Catherine de Médicis *(kä trēn də mā dē sēs)* 1519–89. Queen of France. *b.* Florence, Italy. Queen of Henry II of France; mother of three French kings (Francis II, Charles IX, and Henry III). Daughter of Lorenzo de' Medici, Duke of Urbino; became the virtual ruler of the realm during reign of Charles IX (1560–74); attempted to hold balance of power between the Protestant Huguenots and the Catholic Guises; precipitated Wars of the Huguenots (1562) and ordered massacre of St. Bartholomew's Day (1572); unpopular through her intrigues and machinations.

Catherine of Aragon *(ăr ȧ gŏn)* 1485–1536. First queen of Henry VIII. *b.* Alcalá de Henares, Spain. Daughter of Ferdinand and Isabella of Spain; married Arthur, Prince of Wales (1501); on death of Arthur (1502) and before consummation of marriage, betrothed to Henry; married Henry (1509); gave birth to Mary (1516); regent during Henry's invasion of France (1513); separated (1526) while Henry sought to revoke the validity of marriage; marriage formally declared null by Archbishop Cranmer (1533); refused to yield title of queen and, a prisoner, spent remainder of life in austere devotions.

Catherine of Siena *(syâ nä),* **Saint** 1347–80. Italian religious. *b.* Siena. Dominican nun (1365); recorded visions and revelations in *Dialogue* and *A Treatise of Divine Providence;* believed to have borne Christ's stigmata on her body; prevailed upon Pope Gregory XI to end Babylonian Captivity at Avignon and return to Rome (1377); canonized (1461). Feast day: Apr. 30.

Catlin *(kăt lĭn),* **George** 1796–1872. American artist and author. Wilkes-Barre, Pa. Studied Indians of the West; painted series of portraits illustrative of Indian life and manners, now in the National Museum and in the American Museum of Natural History. Works include *Manners, Customs, and Condition of the North American Indians* (2 vols., 1841), *North American Portfolio* (1844), and *Life Among the Indians* (1867).

Cato *(kā tō),* **Marcus Portius** also CATO THE CENSOR, CATO THE ELDER. 239–149 B.C. Roman statesman. *b.* Tusculum, Italy. Served in Second Punic War and in capture of Tarentum (209), in Spain (194), and against Antiochus (191); elected quaestor (204), aedile (199), praetor (198), consul (195), censor (184), and ambassador to Carthage (150); led anti-Carthaginian party in Senate, concluding every speech with "*Ceterum censeo Carthaginem esse delendam*" ("For the rest, I am of the opinion that Carthage should be destroyed"); championed the virtues and high morals of the early republic, and tried to stem the tide of alien luxury and fashions; author of *De Agricultura, or De Re Rustica.*

MARCUS PORCIUS CATO surname: UTICENSIS; also CATO THE YOUNGER. 95–46 B.C. Roman philosopher and official. *b.* Rome. Great-grandson of Cato the Elder. Served under Gellius Publicola against Spartacus (72); military tribune in Macedonia (67); quaestor (65); tribune (62); praetor (54); sided with Cicero against Catiline and with Pompey against Caesar; took own life at Utica on learning of Caesar's victory at Thapsus.

Catt *(kăt),* **Carrie Chapman** *née* LANE. 1859–1947. American feminist leader. *b.* Ripon, Wis. Succeeded Susan B. Anthony as president of National American Woman Suffrage Association (1900–04, 1915–47); led successful campaign for the 19th Amendment to the Constitution; organized League of Women Voters; president of International Woman Suffrage Alliance (1904–23).

Catullus *(kȧ tŭl ŭs),* **Gaius Valerius** c84–54 B.C. Roman poet. *b.* Verona, Italy. Settled in Rome (c62) and became an intimate of Cicero, Caesar, Lucretius, the Metelli, Asinius Pollio, Cornelius Nepos, Calvus, and Hortensius; addressed love songs to Lesbia, identified with Clodia, wife of Quintus Metellus Celer; assailed opponents, including Caesar, with scurrilous wit; 113 extant poems include the "Attis," composed in galliambics, short lyrics, four longer poems, and a group of epigrams and elegies; considered greatest lyric poet of ancient Rome.

Cavell *(kăv əl),* **Edith Louisa** 1865–1915. English nurse. *b.* Norfolk. Served as first matron of

Berkendael Medical Institute in Brussels, a Red Cross Hospital during World War I; assisted over 100 Allied soldiers to escape during German occupation; arrested by Germans; confessed; condemned to death and shot by a firing squad (1915).

Cavendish *(kăv ən dĭsh),* **Henry** 1731–1810. English scientist. *b.* Nice, France. Devoted life to scientific investigation; regarded as founder of pneumatic chemistry; discovered nitric acid; first to combine oxygen and hydrogen to form water; determined specific gravity of hydrogen; devised experiment for measuring density of earth; anticipated later discoveries of Faraday and Coulomb on electricity; the famous Cavendish Laboratory at Cambridge is named after him.

Cavendish, Thomas c1555–92. English navigator. *b.* Trimlay St. Martin. Sailed from Plymouth on third circumnavigation of the world (1586) with three vessels, *Desire, Content,* and *Hugh Gallant*; ravaged Spanish towns and shipping on coasts of Mexico and South America; passed Strait of Magellan (1587), crossed Pacific and returned home with only one ship, the *Desire*, by way of Cape of Good Hope (1588); died at sea during a second voyage (1591) around the globe.

Cavour *(kä vo͞or),* **Conte Camillo Benso di** 1810–61. Italian nationalist and statesman. *b.* Turin. Established, with Count Cesare Balbo, the newspaper *Il Risorgimento* (1847); entered Sardinian parliament (1848); member of Azeglio's cabinet (1850–52); premier (1852); joined France, England, and Turkey against Russia (1854), and sent a contingent of Sardinian troops to Crimea (1855); represented Sardinia at Congress of Paris (1856); formed alliance with Napoleon III against Austria at Plombières (1858); successful war against Austria; resigned (1859) following the Peace of Villafranca between Napoleon and Austria, which left Venetia in Austrian hands; premier (1860–61); ceded Nice and Savoy to France in return for the acquiescence of France in unification of Northern Italy; aided Garibaldi in expedition against Sicily; achieved unification of all Italy excepting Rome and Venetia under Victor Emmanuel II (1861); set seal on career by summoning an Italian parliament.

Caxton *(kăks tən),* **William** c1422–91. English printer. *b.* Kent. Went to Bruges (1446), established as a mercer; governor of English Association of Merchant Adventurers in Bruges (1465–69); learned art of printing at Cologne (1471–72); in partnership with Colard Mansion, set up printing press in Bruges and printed (1474–75) first book in English, *Recuyell of the Historyes of Troye; The Game and Playe of Chesse* printed (1475); set up press in Westminster (1476) and issued *Dictes or Sayengis of the Philosophres* (1477), first book printed in England; printed over 100 books, of which over a third survive.

Cecil *(sĕs l; sĭs l),* **Edgar Algernon Robert** 1864–1958. English statesman. *b.* London. Entered Parliament (1906); undersecretary for foreign affairs (1915); minister of blockade (1916); assistant secretary of state for foreign affairs (1918); helped draft covenant of the League of Nations; member of Baldwin's cabinets as lord privy seal (1923–24) and chancellor (1924–27); president of the League of Nations Union; awarded Nobel Peace Prize (1937).

Cecil, Robert Arthur Talbot Gascoyne title: MARQUIS OF SALISBURY. 1830–1903. British statesman. *b.* Hatfield House. Entered Parliament (1854); secretary of state for India in Derby ministry (1866–67) and Disraeli ministry (1874–78); as foreign secretary (1878) accompanied Disraeli to Berlin Congress; leader of Conservative party on death of Disraeli (1881); prime minister and foreign minister (1885–86, 1886–92, 1895–1902); adopted imperialist policy abroad and anti-reform policy at home; annexed Burma, reconquered the Sudan, conducted Boer War (1899–1902); adopted conciliatory policy toward Turkey and secured treaty privileges in China.

Cecil, William BARON BURGHLEY; also BURLEIGH. 1520–98. British statesman. *b.* Bourn. Secretary to Somerset, lord protector (1548); secretary of state (1550); conformed to Catholicism under Queen Mary; chief secretary of state under Elizabeth (1558–72); lord high treasurer (1572–98); principal architect of the Elizabethan age; organized network of spies to suppress dissidents; created Baron Burghley (1571); succeeded by his son ROBERT CECIL, VISCOUNT CRANBORNE AND EARL OF SALISBURY (1563–1612) as secretary of state (1596–1608). Secured orderly succession of James I on Elizabeth's death; virtually controlled government until his death.

Cellini *(chĕ lē nē),* **Benvenuto** 1500–1571. Italian goldsmith and sculptor. *b.* Florence. Worked at Pisa (1516–17), Florence (1517–23), and Rome (1523–40) as metalwork artist for Pope Clement VII; assisted in defense of Rome against Constable de Bourbon (1527); imprisoned for murder of rival goldsmith; pardoned and set free by Pope Paul III; imprisoned (1538), escaped, recaptured, and pardoned; at court of Francis I (1540–44) and of Cosimo de' Medici (1545–71). Best-known works include *Perseus with the Head of Medusa, Nymph of Fontainebleu, Crucifixion*, and busts of Cosmo and Bindo Aldoviti. Author of *Autobiography* (1558), regarded as a classic.

Celsius *(sĕl sĭ əs),* **Anders** 1701–44. Swedish astronomer. *b.* Uppsala. Professor of astronomy at Uppsala (1730) and appointed director of the observatory (1740); devised centigrade thermometer, called Celsius thermometer (1742); published recorded observations on aurora borealis (1733); went to polar regions to measure the degree of meridian (1736).

Cervantes Saavedra *(sər vän tēz sä ä vā thrä),* **Miguel de** 1547–1616. Spanish writer. *b.* Alcalá de Henares. Went to Rome (1569) in service of Cardinal Giulio Acquaviva; (c1570–74); maimed in Battle of Lepanto (1571); in engagements at Navarino, Corfu, and Tunis; captured by Algerian corsairs while returning to Spain and imprisoned at Algiers (1575–80) until ransomed; went to Madrid and published first work, *Galatea*, a pastoral romance (1585); wrote 20 or 30 plays, of which only *La Numancia* and *Los Tratos de Argel* have survived; commissary to fleet at Seville; tax collector at Granada (1588–97); imprisoned for irregularities in bookkeeping (1597); wrote first part of *Don Quixote* in prison; published (1605, 1615); the book became phenomenally popular; at Valladolid (1604–1605); spent the remainder of life at Madrid. Minor works include *Viage del Parnaso* (1614), *Novelas Ejemplares* (1613), and *Persiles y Sigismunda* (1616).

Cézanne *(sā zàn),* **Paul** 1839–1906. French impressionist painter. *b.* Aix-en-Provence. Went to Paris (1861) on advice of Zola; sketched at Atelier Suisse; met impressionist painters; worked mainly at Aix and l'Estaque; exhibited at first and third impressionist exhibitions (1874; 1877); under influence of Pissarro, abandoned early somber and heavy technique; began foreshadowing cubism (1886) by painting from a rhythmic series of colored planes suggesting volume and depth through shading and modulation. Some works: *The Card Players, The Bathers, The House of the Hanged Man,* and *Bouquet of Flowers.*

Chadwick *(chăd wĭk),* **Sir James** 1891–1973. English physicist. *b.* Manchester. Assistant director of radioactive research at Cavendish Laboratory (1932–35); professor of physics at University of Liverpool (from 1935); chief British advisor to Manhattan Project (1943–45); scientific advisor to U.N. Commission on Atomic Energy (1946); awarded Nobel Prize in physics (1935) for discovery of neutrons (1932).

Chagall *(shə gàl),* **Marc** 1887–. Russian painter. *b.* Vitebsk. Studied under Bakst; went to Paris (1910) and formed Cubist group; held one-man show in Berlin (1914); left Russia permanently and settled in Paris (1922); lived in U.S. (1941–47). Works characterized by opulent colors and fantasies drawn from Jewish folklore; also known for theater panels, stained-glass windows, book illustrations, and lithographs; considered forerunner of surrealism; best-known works include *Adam and Eve, Banquet of Flying Colors, I and My Village, Village on Fire, Between Darkness and Light, Paris Through the Window, The Wedding,* and *The Graveyard.* Author of an autobiography, *Ma Vio* (1931).

Chain *(chān),* **Ernst Boris** 1906–. English biochemist. *b.* Berlin, Germany. Shared Nobel Prize in physiology and medicine with Alexander Fleming and H. Florey for work on penicillin (1945).

Chaitanya *(chī tŭn yà)* 1485–1527. Indian mystic. *b.* Nadia, Bengal. Renounced the world at age 24; adopted life of sannyasin, preaching the gospel of bhakti. Regarded as one of the founders of Vaishnava sect of Hinduism; believed by his followers (Caitanyas) to be an incarnation of Krishna; opposed caste distinctions and priestly rituals and taught the importance of devotion toward the deity.

Chaliapin *(shŭ lyà pyĭn),* **Feodor Ivanovitch** 1873–1938. Russian operatic basso. *b.* Kazan. First appeared (1893) as Mephistopheles in Gounod's *Faust* at Tiflis; thereafter sang in all major opera houses in Europe and America; left Russia (1927) and settled in Paris; appeared regularly at Metropolitan Opera House (1921–29); particularly distinguished as Boris Godunov and Don Quixote.

Chalmers *(chä mərz),* **Thomas** 1780–1847. Scottish divine. *b.* Anstruther. Professor of moral philosophy at St. Andrews (1823–28) and of theology at Edinburgh (1828–43); leader of an evangelical group of the Church of Scotland; led 470 ministers in founding the Free Church of Scotland (1843); principal of Free Church College of Edinburgh (1843–47). Author of *Natural Theology* (1823), *Institutes of Theology* (1847–49), and other works.

Chamberlain *(chām bər lĭn),* **Joseph** 1836–1914. British statesman. *b.* London. Retired from business to enter politics as a radical (1874); mayor of Birmingham (1873–76); Member of Parliament (1876); president of board of trade (1880–85); responsible for passage of Bankruptcy Bill (1883) and Patent Act (1883); president of local government board in third Gladstone cabinet (1886), but resigned in opposition to Home Rule Bill; leader (from 1891) of Liberal Unionists; colonial secretary in third Salisbury cabinet (1895–1903); steered Britain through Boer War and led postwar reconciliation; resigned in protest over the failure of government to grant tariff preferences to colonies; advocated imperial fiscal union and closer relations with the dominions; responsible for defeat of Unionist party under Balfour (1906); retired from public life (1906).

Chamberlain, Sir Joseph Austen called AUSTEN. 1863–1937. British statesman. *b.* Birmingham. Eldest son of Joseph and half brother of Neville; entered Parliament as Liberal-Unionist (1892); civil lord of admiralty (1895–1900); financial secretary to the treasury (1900–1902); postmaster general (1902–1903); chancellor of exchequer (1903–1906); secretary of state for India (1915–17); member of war cabinet (1918); chancellor of exchequer (1919–21); Conservative leader of House of Commons and lord privy seal (1921–23); helped negotiate Irish Free State treaty; foreign secretary (1924–29); received Nobel Peace Prize (with Charles G. Dawes) (1925) for role in bringing about the Locarno Pact; first lord of admiralty (1931). Author of *Peace in Our Time* (1928).

Chamberlain, Neville full name: ARTHUR NEVILLE CHAMBERLAIN. 1869–1940. British statesman. *b.* Edgbaston. Son of Joseph and half brother of Sir Austen; lord mayor of Birmingham (1915–16); entered Parliament (1918); chancellor of exchequer (1923–24); minister of health (1924–29); chancellor of exchequer (1931–37); chairman of Unionist party (1930–31); prime minister (1937-40); worked to avert world war by policy of appeasement, culiminating in Munich Pact (1938); declared war after German invasion of Poland; criticized for initial military reverses; yielded office to Churchill (1940).

Chamberlain, Owen 1920–. American physicist. *b.* San Francisco, Calif. Professor at University of California at Berkeley (from

1948); with Emilio Segré, awarded Nobel Prize in physics (1959) for discovery of antiprotons.

Chamisso *(shä mĭs ō),* **Adelbert von** original name: Louis Charles Adélaïde de Chamisso. 1781–1838. German naturalist and writer. *b.* in Champagne, France. Forced to flee to Prussia on outbreak of French Revolution (1790); returned to France (1806); joined the circle of Madame de Staël at Coppet, Switzerland; took up study of botany; botanist on *Ruik*, Otto von Kotzebue's scientific voyage around the globe (1815–18); keeper of Botanical gardens of Berlin; wrote *Peter Schlemihls* (1813); also wrote lyrics, collected and published as *Frauenliebe und Leben,* and later set to music by Robert Schumann.

Champlain *(shăm plān),* **Samuel de** c1567–1635. French explorer. *b.* Brouage. First visited New World as member of Spanish fleet (1599–1601); persuaded Henry IV of France to sponsor expedition; sailed to Gulf of St. Lawrence (1603); founded colony at mouth of St. Croix River in New Brunswick (1605) and another at Quebec (1608); discovered Lake Champlain (1609); sailed up Ottawa River, surveyed Lake Huron (1615), and reached the source of St. Lawrence; lieutenant of Canada 1612); captured by English fleet and imprisoned (1629–32); governor of New France (1633–35). Wrote about his travels.

Champollion *(shän pô lyon),* **Jean François** also called Champollion le Jeune. 1790–1832. French Egyptologist. *b.* Figeac. Devoted to study of Oriental languages; professor of history at Grenoble (1809–16); using the Rosetta Stone, deciphered Egyptian hieroglyphics according to a system he published in *Précis du Système Hiéroglyphique des Anciens Égyptiens* (1824); conservator of Egyptian collections (1826); accompanied scientific expedition to Egypt (1828–29); chair of Egyptology established for him at Collège de France (1831). Also published *Grammaire Égyptienne* (1836–41) and *Dictionnaire Égyptien* (1841–43).

Chancellor *(chăn sə lər),* **Richard** *d.* 1556. English sailor. Captain of *Edward Bonaventure*, and pilot of Willoughby's expedition (1553) in search of Northwest Passage through White Sea; separated from other ships and sailed into Archangel; traveled overland to Moscow; obtained valuable trade concessions at Russian court; established Muscovy Company on return to England (1554). Published account of experiences in Russia in Hakluyt's *Navigations*.

Channing *(chăn ĭng),* **William Ellery** 1780–1842. American clergyman. *b.* Newport, R.I. Minister of Federal Street Church in Boston (1803–42); famous for fervor and solemnity of sermons; leader of Unitarian group among New England Congregationalists, defended liberal humanitarianism against orthodoxy; organized Berry Street Conference of Ministers (1820), from which developed American Unitarian Association. Wrote a number of tracts on slavery including *Slavery* (1835), *The Abolitionist* (1836), and *Duty of the Free States* (1842).

Chaplin *(chăp lĭn),* **Charles Spencer** known as Charlie Chap-

LIN. 1889–1977. English film actor. *b.* London. A stage performer from childhood; went to Hollywood (1914) with Fred Karno's vaudeville act; made screen debut (1914) with Keystone Film Company; built studios (1918) and later became a founder of United Artists; in early comedies, adopted tilted derby hat, small mustache, baggy trousers, large shoes, and bamboo cane as hallmarks of supreme buffoonery; because of political differences, left U.S. (1952) and settled in Switzerland. Greatest films include *Easy Street, Shoulder Arms, The Kid, The Champion, The Gold Rush, The Circus, City Lights, Modern Times,* and *The Great Dictator*; knighted (1975).

Chapman *(chăp mən),* **George** c1559–1634. English playwright. *b.* near Hitchin. Dramatic works include *All Fools* (1598), *The Gentleman Usher* (1606), *Bussy d'Ambois* (1607), *May Day* (1611), *The Widow's Tears* (1612), *Caesar and Pompey* (1631), and *The Tragedie of Chabot, Admiral of France* (1639); completed Marlowe's fragment of *Hero and Leander* (1598); wrote poems such as *The Shadow of Night* (1594) and *Enthymiae Raptus* (1609); greatest achievement was translation of Homer (1616) as well as Petrarch, Hesiod, Juvenal, and Musaeus.

Chapman, John nickname: JOHNNY APPLESEED. 1774–1845. American pioneer. *b.* Leominster, Mass. Owned a large nursery in Pa.; wandered through Ohio, Indiana, and Illinois from 1800 to 1845 as missionary of Swedenborgian Church planting apple trees and tending orchards, dressed—according to legends—only in burlap bags with holes cut for head, arms, and legs; also scattered seeds of rattlesnake weed, catnip, hoarhound, and pennyroyal; subject of many folk tales and Vachel Lindsay's poem, *In Praise of Johnny Appleseed.*

Charcot *(shär kō),* **Jean Martin** 1825–93. French neurologist. *b.* Paris. Established neurological clinic at Saltpêtrière, Paris (1880); taught Sigmund Freud and Alfred Binet; experimented in treating mental diseases and hysteria with hypnotism; studied senile diseases, locomotor ataxia, and sclerosis (called Charcot's disease). Published collected works (9 vols., 1886–90), including *Leçons sur les Maladies du Système Nerveux.*

Chardin *(shär dăɴ),* **Jean Baptiste Siméon** 1699–1779. French painter. *b.* Paris. Elected to the Academy (1728); genre painter of peasant life and domestic scenes; often compared with Flemish and Dutch masters for his fine colors and sensitive treatment. Principal works include *Le Buffet, Les Tours de Carte, Le Jeune Violiniste*, and *L'Enfant au Toton.*

Charlemagne *(shär lə măn)* 742–814. King of the Franks (768–814) and emperor of the West (800–814). *b.* Aachen, Germany. Son of Pepin the Short, whom he succeeded as King of Neustria; became king of all Franks on death of his brother Carloman (771); began war against Saxons, culminating in defeat of Wittekind (785) and total subjugation and Christianization of Saxons (by 804); crossed Alps (773) and overthrew Lombard kingdom; crowned himself king of Lombards (774); led expedition against Arabs in Spain (778); defeated Avars and Wends (791–796); annexed Bavaria (778); pushed Danes back behind Eider River (808–10); crowned Carolus Augustus, Emperor of the Romans, by Pope Leo III (800); zealously promoted the Christian faith, education, agriculture, arts, and industries; patronized palace school at Aachen, founded by Alcuin, which became the cradle of the Carolingian Renaissance; established effective administrative and legal system; issued Capitularies, or collections of laws; exploits gave rise to cycle of medieval romances called *Chansons de Geste*.

Charles I *(Chärlz)* 1600–1649. King of England (1625–49). *b.* Dunfermline, Scotland. Second son of James IV of Scotland; heir to throne on death of Prince Henry (1612); married Henrietta Maria, Princess of France, who was permitted to be Catholic; succeeded to throne (1625); influenced by unpopular Duke of Buckingham, who was assassinated (1628); appointed William Laud and Thomas Wentworth (later earl of Strafford) as advisors; granted Petition of Right (1628); dissolved three Parliaments (1625–29); ruled without Parliament (1629–40), raising money through forced loans, poundage, tonnage, ship money and other illegal means of revenue; aroused John Hampden's passive resistance (1637); suffered reverses in French wars (1627); attempt to impose Anglican episcopacy on Church of Scotland led to invasion of Scotland and Treaty of Berwick (1639); summoned Short Parliament (1640) to obtain money for new invasion of Scotland, but was met with demand for redress of grievances; dissolved it only to summon Long Parliament (1640), yielding to demand it would be dissolved only by its own vote; Parliament impeached Strafford and Laud and abolished Star Chamber; precipitated Civil War by attempting to arrest five members who had sponsored the Grand Remonstrance (1642); left London and raised royal standard at Nottingham; defeated decisively by Parliamentary forces under Fairfax at Naseby (1645); surrendered to Scots at Newark and handed over by them to Parliament (1647); tried at Westminster (1648); condemned to death as tyrant and enemy of the nation; beheaded at Whitehall (1649).

Charles II 1630–85. King of England (1660–85). *b.* London. Assumed title of king on execution of father Charles I (1649); came to terms with Covenanters of Scotland and proclaimed king of Scotland (1651); defeated by Cromwell at Worcester (1651); fled to Continent; after fall of Protectorate, recalled to London and proclaimed king (1660); by Declaration of Breda, promised amnesty, liberty of conscience, and restoration of parliamentary rights; married Catherine of Braganza (1662); ruled for seven years with help of Earl of Clarendon, thereafter with the cabal consisting of Clifford, Arlington, Buckingham, Ashley, and Lauderdale; conducted Dutch Wars (1664–67, 1672–74); peace with Holland cemented by marriage of niece Mary to William, Prince of Orange; accepted subsidy from Louis XIV and concluded secret treaty with France (1670); sold Dunkirk to French (1662); forced to approve repressive measures against nonconformists such as Act of Uniformity (1662), Conventicle Act (1664), Five-Mile Act (1665), and Test Act (1673); reign witnessed Great Fire of London (1666) and Great Plague of London (1665); dissolved Parliament that enacted Habeas Corpus Act (1679), tried to exclude brother James, Duke of York, from succession; thereafter ruled absolutely; died without legitimate issue although fathered many children through his mistresses; set tone of the pleasure-loving Restoration period; patronized science, arts, and theater.

Charles Name of several kings of France including: CHARLES III called CHARLES THE SIMPLE. 879–929. Son of Louis II; king of France with Eudes (893–98); sole king (898–923); ceded Normandy to Rollo (911); became lord of Normandy; lost crown to Robert at Battle of Soissons (923).

CHARLES IV called CHARLES THE FAIR. 1294–1328. Son of Philip IV; king of France (1322–28).

CHARLES V called CHARLES THE WISE. 1337–80. Son of John II; king of France (1364–80); with Bertrand du Guesclin, suppressed free companies and recovered most territory lost to Edward III of England; founded Royal Library of Paris.

CHARLES VI called CHARLES THE WELL-BELOVED. 1368–1422. Son of Charles V; king of France (1380–1422); defeated Flemings at Rosebecque (1382); subject to fits of insanity and retired from active government (1392); struggle between regents led to war of Burgundians and Armagnacs; French defeated by Henry V at Agincourt (1415) and humiliated by Treaty of Troyes (1420).

CHARLES VII called CHARLES THE VICTORIOUS. 1403–61. Son of Charles VI; king of France (1422–61). Won back most of France from English, with the aid of Joan of Arc; crowned at Reims (1429); made peace with Philip of Burgundy (1435); entered Paris (1437); truce with England (1444–49); by Pragmatic Sanction (1438), recognized rights of Gallican Church and limited papal authority.

CHARLES VIII 1470–98. Son of Louis XI; king of France (1483–98); invaded Italy (1494); entered Naples in triumph (1495); driven out by Holy League of Ferdinand of Aragon, Maximilian I, and Italian forces.

CHARLES X 1757–1836. Brother of Louis XVI and Louis XVIII; king of France (1824–30); attempted to restore ancient régime with policy of extreme reaction; dissolved Chamber of Deputies and tried to govern by ordinances; overthrown by revolution (1830).

Charles Name of several Holy Roman Emperors including:

CHARLES II called CHARLES THE BALD. 823–77. Son of Louis I; king of France as Charles I (840–77) and Holy Roman Emperor (875–77). Received the crown of France on death of father; defeated brother Lothair at Fontenay (841); defeated brother Louis in Italy and thus became undisputed ruler of Holy Roman Empire; crowned emperor (875).

CHARLES III called CHARLES THE FAT. 839–88. Son of Louis the German; king of Germany (876–

87); king of France (884–87); Holy Roman Emperor (881–87); made humiliating treaty with Northmen; deposed by Arnulf (887).

Charles V 1500–1558. Son of Philip I of Spain; Holy Roman Emperor (1519–56); king of Spain (1516–56); ruler of Netherlands and Burgundy, Aragon, Navarre, Granada, Spanish dominions in America, Naples, Sardinia, and Sicily; defeated and captured Francis I of France at Pavia, forcing him to relinquish all claims (1525–26); hostilities ended with Treaty of Cambrai; renewed; concluded favorably to emperor (1529); a truce concluded with France and pope (1538) broken by invasion of France and imposition of unfavorable Peace of Crespy on Francis (1544); occupied Rome and made pope prisoner (1527); as undisputed master of Italy, crowned by pope at Bologna (1530); took field against the Turks; crushed corsair Barbarossa and captured Tunis (1535); at Diet of Augsburg (1530), confirmed Edict of Worms, leading Protestant princes to form Schmalkaldic League (1531); at Battle of Mühlberg (1547), defeated John Frederick I, elector of Saxony and one of the leaders of the League; by Treaty of Passau (1552) and Peace of Augsburg (1555), recognized freedom of reformed religion; resigned kingship of Netherlands and crown of Spain to son Philip II (1555–56) and Imperial crown to brother Ferdinand (1556); retired to a monastery at Yuste, Spain.

Charles VI 1685–1740. Son of Leopold I; Holy Roman Emperor (1711–40) and, as Charles III, king of Hungary (1712–40); as pretender to throne of Spain, precipitated War of Spanish Succession (1701–14); gave up claims to Spain and Spanish Netherlands by Peace of Rastatt (1714); conducted two campaigns against Turks, first concluded by Treaty of Passarowitz (1718), and second by Treaty of Belgrade (1739); issued Pragmatic Sanction (1713) to secure throne for his daughter Maria Theresa.

Charles Name of several kings of Sweden including:

Charles VIII called Karl Knutson. c1408–70. King of Sweden (1448–57, 1464–65, 1467–70) and of Norway (1449–50); engaged in continuous warfare with Danes.

Charles IX 1550–1611. King of Sweden (1604–11); ousted Sigismund of Poland and seized throne (1604); restored Protestantism as the state religion; began war with Poland (1600) and with Denmark (1611).

Charles X also Charles Gustavus. 1622–60. Son of John Casimir; King of Sweden (1654–60); won great victory over Poles at Warsaw (1656); invaded Denmark (1658); by Treaty of Roskilde (1658), won back extensive territories in Norway and South Sweden.

Charles XI 1655–97. Son of Charles X; king of Sweden (1660–97); after early reverses in war against Denmark, Netherlands, and Holy Roman Empire, gained favorable terms at Peace of Nijmegen (1678–79); acquired Pomerania by Treaty of Saint-Germain (1679); granted absolute power by Riksdag; undertook economic and administrative reorganization of Sweden.

Charles XII 1682–1718. Son of Charles XI; king of Sweden (1697–

1718); faced by hostile alliance of Denmark, Poland, and Russia, invaded Denmark and compelled Danes to accept Peace of Travendal (1700); routed Russians at Narva (1700); overran Poland, after defeating the Saxons and Poles of Klissow (1702); by Treaty of Altranstädt (1706) forced Augustus of Poland to sue for peace; installed (1704) Stanislas Laszczynski as king of Poland; invaded Russia and defeated Peter the Great at Smolensk (1707); after a severe winter, laid siege to Poltava with a depleted army and was defeated (1709); fled to Turkey to induce Porte to declare war on Russia, but was imprisoned until 1714; back to Sweden; purchased peace with Russia by surrendering Baltic provinces; invaded Norway (1716); killed by musket shot on battlefield.

CHARLES XIII 1748–1818. Son of Adolphus Frederick; king of Sweden (1809–18) and Norway (1814–18); accepted role as limited monarch under new constitution; made peace with Russia (1809) by giving up Finland; with Denmark (1809), and France (1810).

CHARLES XIV original name: JEAN BAPTISTE JULES BERNADOTTE. c1763–1844. King of Norway and Sweden (1818–44); entered French army (1780) as common soldier; became marshal of France under Napoleon (1804); named prince of Pontecarvo (1805) for heroic conduct at Austerlitz; elected crown prince of Sweden (1810); commanded army of the North against Napoleon at Leipzig (1813).

Charles Martel *(mär těl)* c689–741. Frankish ruler. Son of Pepin of Herstal and **grandfather** of Charlemagne; chosen duke by Austrasian Franks (714); became ruler of all Franks (720); in historic battle at Tours, crushed Muslim armies of Abd-er-Rahman and saved empire from Islam; established Frankish kingdom and Carolingian dynasty; on death (741), divided kingdom between his two sons, Carloman and Pepin the Short.

Chase *(chās),* **Salmon Portland** 1808–73. American jurist. *b.* Cornish, N.H. Began as abolitionist; in Senate as a Free-Soiler from Ohio (1849); Republican governor of Ohio (1855); secretary of the treasury (1861–64); devised national banking system (1863); chief justice of the United States (1864–73); presided over trials of President Andrew Johnson and Jefferson Davis.

Chateaubriand *(shȧ tō brē äN),* **Vicomte François René de** 1768–1848. French writer and statesman. *b.* Saint-Malo. Born of noble family; traveled in U.S. (1791–92) and wrote *Voyage en Amérique;* fought with emigrés on return to France; withdrew in exile to England (1793–1800); published *Essai sur les Révolutions* (1797); returned to France (1800); converted to Roman Catholicism (1802), wrote classic defense of the faith in *Le Génie du Christianisme* (1802); served in consular posts in Rome and Valais (1803–04); supported Bourbon's Restoration in a pamphlet *De Buonaparte et des Bourbons* (1814); created peer (1815); ambassador to Great Britain (1822); minister of foreign affairs (1823–24); wrote monumental autobiography *Mémoires d'Outre-Tombe* (6 vols., 1849–50); considered founder of romanticism; *Atala* and *René* are noted for rich, romantic style; other works include *Les Martyrs* (1809), *Les Adventures du Dernier des Abencérages* (1826), and *Les Natchez* (1826).

Chatterton *(chăt ər tən),* **Thomas** 1752–70. English poet. *b.* Bristol. Chiefly known for literary hoaxes written in a pseudo-medieval style, especially works purported to be by a 15th-century monk called Thomas Rowley (1765–69); contributed numerous satires, essays, stories, and epistles in the style of Junius to London periodicals; destitute and discouraged by rejections, committed suicide at age 18; acknowledged posthumously as a poet of considerable imagination and lyric power.

Chaucer *(chô sər),* **Geoffrey** c1340–1400. English poet. *b.* London. Began as a courtier; served in French campaigns (1359); undertook diplomatic missions to the Continent, meeting Boccaccio and perhaps Petrarch (1370–78); held petty offices under the crown; received pensions from Edward III, John of Gaunt, Richard II, and Henry IV. Principal works include *Book of the Duchess* (1369), *The House of Fame*, *The Parliament of Fowls*, *Troilus and Cressida*, *The Legend of Good Women* (1372–86), and *The Canterbury Tales* (c1387–1400); considered the first great poet in English; helped to establish English language as a literary vehicle; introduced iambic pentameter into English verse.

Chautemps *(shō täN),* **Camille** 1885–1963. French statesman. *b.* Paris. Leader of Radical-Socialist party; minister of interior (1924, 1932–33); minister of justice (1925–26); premier (1930, 1933–34, 1937–38); minister of public instruction (1931); minister of public works (1936); minister of state (1936); vice-premier (1938–40); member of first Pétain cabinet (1940–41); after liberation of France, convicted in absentia and deprived of citizenship.

Chekhov *(chā Kôf),* **Anton Pavlovich** 1860–1904. Russian writer. *b.* Taganrog. Studied medicine and qualified as a physician (1884); abandoned medicine for literature; published first stories (1886); cultivated friendship of Tolstoy and Gorki; early plays unsuccessful, but after the successful revival of *The Sea Gull* (1898) at the Stanislavsky Moscow Art Theater, wrote seriously for the theater, producing *Uncle Vanya* (1900), *The Three Sisters* (1901), and *The Cherry Orchard* (1904); stories portray sensitive and melancholy people struggling with life's frustrations and the erosion of the spirit as a result of this struggle.

Chénier *(shā nyā),* **André Marie de** 1762–94. French poet. *b.* Constantinople, Turkey. Only two poetical works published during his lifetime: *Le Jeu de Paume à David Peintre* and *Hymne aux Soldats de Châteauvieux*; enemy of the Jacobins because of his pamphlet against excesses of the Reign of Terror, *Avis au Peuple Français sur ses Véritables Ennemis;* guillotined (1794); considered the greatest writer of French classic verse since Racine and Boileau on basis of poems published after his death, including *La Jeune Captive* (1795), *La Jeune Tarentine* (1801), *Élégies*, and *Bucoliques*.

Chennault *(shĕ nôlt),* **Claire Lee** 1890–1958. American air force commander. *b.* Commerce, Ga. Joined U.S. Army Air Corps (1917); pioneered in use of parachute troops; resigned from U.S. Army to become air advisor to Chiang Kai-shek (1937); organized Flying Tigers to aid China and protect Burma Road (1941); headed U.S. air task force in China (1942–45); major general (1943); resigned (1945). Author of *Way of a Fighter* (1949).

Cherenkov *(chĕ rĕng kôf),* **Pavel Alekseevich** 1904–. Soviet physicist. Shared Nobel Prize in physics with I.M. Frank and I.Y. Tamm (1958) for work leading to discovery of the Cherenkov effect (the emission of blue light from water and other media when atomic particles pass through it faster than the speed of light).

Chesterfield *(chĕs tər fēld),* **Earl of** real name: PHILIP DORMER STANHOPE. 1694–1773. English statesman and man of letters. *b.* London. Entered Parliament (1716); succeeded father as Earl of Chesterfield (1726); ambassador to the Hague (1728–32, 1744); lord high steward (1730); lord lieutenant of Ireland (1745–46); secretary of state (1746–48); opposed policies of George II and Walpole; intimate of Voltaire, Pope, Swift, and Bolingbroke; earned Samuel Johnson's rebuke for ignoring prospectus of the *Dictionary*; in *Letters to His Son* (1774), tried to convey elegance, wit, and cynicism of his times in epigrammatical style.

Chesterton *(chĕs tər tən),* **Gilbert Keith** 1874–1936. English writer. *b.* Kensington. Began writing articles and reviews for periodicals; became Roman Catholic (1922) and a brilliant apologist for the faith; achieved popularity with fictional Father Brown, an amiable priest-detective; writings characterized by paradox, humor, and stylistic ebullience. Works include *Robert Browning* (1903), *The Man Who Was Thursday* (1908), *Orthodoxy* (1909), *Heretics* (1905), *The Innocence of Father Brown* (1911), *The Uses of Diversity* (1921), *Chaucer* (1932), *The Scandal of Father Brown* (1935), and *Autobiography* (1936).

Chiang Kai-Shek *(jē äng kī shĕk)* real name: CHIANG CHUNG-CHENG. 1887-1975. Chinese statesman. *b.* Fenghwa. Joined Revolutionary party of Sun Yat-sen while studying at Tokyo Military Staff College (1907–11); visited U.S.S.R. (1923); principal of Whampoa Military Academy (1924); on Sun's death, elected generalissimo of Southern Army (1925); established Kuomintang National government at Wuchang (1926), at Nanking (1927), and eventually at Peking (1928); president (1928–31); commander in chief (1932); chairman, Executive Yuan (1935–38, 1939–45); from 1927, sought to suppress Chinese Communist party; kidnapped by Chang Hsueh-liang at Sian (1936) and held prisoner for two weeks; on release, decided to unite with Communists against Japanese; as supreme commander of allied air and land forces, conducted war against Japan (1937–45); set up National government at Chungking; succeeded Lin Sen as Nationalist president (1943–49); on collapse of Kuomintang on the mainland, withdrew to Taiwan, where he set up a government aided by U.S. (1950). Author of *Summing Up at Seventy* (1957).

Chikamatsu Monzaemon *(chē kä mā tso͞o mōn zä ə mōn)* 1653–c1724. Japanese dramatist. Wrote over 100 five-act plays, most of them romances for the puppet stage; called the Shakespeare of Japan.

Chippendale *(chĭp ən dāl),* **Thomas** c1718–79. English furniture-maker. *b.* Otley. Set up carpentry shop (1753); designed neoclassical chairs, tables, desks, bookcases, cabinets, and settees in the graceful style that bears his name; worked most effectively in dark mahogany; published *Gentleman and Cabinet-Maker's Director* (1754), the first trade catalog of superior furniture, which exerted considerable influence on furniture-makers in England and U.S.

Chirico *(kē rə kō),* **Giorgio de** 1888–. Italian artist. *b.* Volos, Greece. First exhibited in Paris Salon d'Automne (1911); emerged as pioneer of surrealist movement and leader of Pittura Metafisica movement; helped found *Valori Plastici* (1918); from 1910, painted eerie dreamlike vistas of empty spaces and buildings, and, from 1915, semi-abstract geometric figures; designed settings for plays and ballets; abandoned surrealism (about 1950) and reverted to realism. Wrote *Hebdomeros* (1929) and *Memorie della Mia Vita* (1945); best-known works include *Nostalgia of the Infinite, The Enigma of the Oracle, Dream Flowers,* and *Metaphysical Interior.*

Chopin *(shô păɴ),* **Frédéric François** 1810–49. Polish composer. *b.* Zelazowa Wola. Published first work, a Rondo in C Minor, at age 15; gave concerts in Vienna, Munich, and Paris (1829); settled in Paris; began liaison with George Sand (1836) and lived with her (until 1847); died in Paris, wasted by consumption (1849). Compositions include mazurkas, polonaises, études, préludes, nocturnes, waltzes, sonatas, rondos, and a funeral march.

Chou En-lai *(jō ĕn lī)* 1898–1976. Chinese statesman. *b.* Huaian. Studied in Tientsin (1919); went to France (1920–22) and Germany (1923); on staff of Whampoa Military Academy at Canton (1924); a founder of Chinese Communist party; joined Sun Yat-sen (1924); took part in Shanghai and Nanchang uprisings (1927); expelled from Kuomintang and joined Kiangsi Soviet (1931); liaison between Chiang Kai-shek and Communist party during the War (1937); prime minister and foreign minister of People's Republic of China (1949–76).

Chrétien de Troyes *(krā tyăN də trwä)* c1150–c1190. French medieval writer. *b.* Troyes. First great writer of Arthurian romances weaving together Christian, Celtic, and Byzantine legends and myths. Extant works include: *Erec et Enide, Cligés, Lancelot, ou le Chevalier de la Charrette, Yvain, ou le Chevalier au Lion*, and *Perceval* (unfinished and continued by other poets).

Christie *(krĭs tē),* **Agatha Mary Clarissa** pseudonym: MARY WESTMACOTT. 1891–1976. English writer. *b.* Torquay. Creator of fictional detectives Hercule Poirot and Miss Marple; published nearly 100 detective novels, beginning with *The Mysterious Affair at Styles* (1920); successful as a playwright with many theater and film productions, including *The Spider's Web, Witness for the Prosecution*, and *The Mousetrap*.

Christina *(krēs tē nȧ)* 1626–89. Queen of Sweden (1632–54). *b.* Stockholm. Daughter of Gustavus II Adolphus; succeeded father under regency of five crown officials, primarily Axel Oxenstierna; came of age and crowned (1644); made peace with Germany and Denmark; patronized and brought to court artists and thinkers, including Caludius Salmasius, Hugo Grotius, and Descartes; antagonized nobility by eccentricities and refusal to marry; abdicated in favor of cousin, Charles Gustavus (1654); left Sweden and converted to Catholicism; tried unsuccessfully (1660, 1667) to regain throne.

Christophe *(krēs tôf)*, **Henri** 1767–1820. King of Haiti (1811–20). *b.* Grenada. A freed slave; aided Toussaint L'Ouverture in Revolution of 1791–93, which liberated Haiti; brigadier general; defended Cape Haiti against French (1802); commander under Dessalines (from 1803); joined Pétion in overthrowing Dessalines (1806); president (1807); proclaimed king of Haiti as Henri I (1811); engaged in civil war with Pétion, ruler of South Haiti; provoked uprising by tyranny and avarice; killed himself with a silver bullet (1820).

Chrysostom *(kris əs təm)*, **Saint John** c345–407. Greek Father of the Church. *b.* Antioch, Syria. Baptized and ordained as a reader (c370); monk in Syrian desert (374–80); deacon (381); priest (386); reputation as a great orator, named Chrysostomos ("golden-mouthed") for eloquence; archbishop of Constantinople (398–404); popular with people from bestowing church revenues on charity; undertook reform of clergy; antagonized Empress Eudoxia through denunciations of her vices; deposed and banished by Eudoxia to Nicaea, to Taurus mountains, and eventually (404) to Pityus. Complete works published in 13 vols. Feast day: Jan. 27.

Chuang-Tzu *(jōō äng dzŭ)* *fl.* 4th century B.C. Chinese Taoist philosopher. Considered to be most important exponent of the teachings of Lao-tzu; works translated into English by Herbert A. Giles (1926).

Churchill *(chûrch il)*, **Lord Randolph Henry Spencer** 1849-95. British statesman. *b.* Blenheim Palace. Son of 7th Duke of Marlborough and father of Sir Winston Churchill; married Jennie Jerome of N.Y. (1874); entered Parliament (1874); leader of dissident conservatives, known as the Fourth Party; as a founder of Primrose League, tried to promote progressive Toryism, called Tory democracy; secretary of state for India (1885–86); chancellor of the exchequer and leader of House of Commons in Salisbury's second ministry (1886); resigned.

Churchill, Winston 1871–1947. American novelist. *b.* St. Louis, Mo. Settled in New Hampshire. Author of historical novels *Richard Carvel* (1899), *Mr. Crewe's Career* (1908), *A Far Country* (1915), and *The Dwelling Place of Light* (1917); also wrote plays, religious works and travelogues.

Churchill, Sir Winston Leonard Spencer 1874–1965. British statesman. *b.* Woodstock. Eldest son of Sir Randolph Churchill; educated at Harrow and Sandhurst; entered army (1895); served in Cuba (1895), the North West Frontier Province in India (1897), Sudan (1898), and South Africa during Boer War (1899); entered Parliament as a Conservative (1901) but transferred allegiance to Liberal party (1906); undersecretary for the colonies (1905–1908); president of board of trade (1908–10); home secretary (1910–11); first lord of the admiralty (1910–15); organized Royal Navy for war, accelerating ship-building and establishing a naval war staff; directed creation of Royal Flying Corps, later, the Royal Air Force; accepted responsibility for Dardanelles disaster and resigned (1915); minister of munitions (1917); secretary for war and air (1919–21); secretary for colonies (1921–22); chancellor of the exchequer (1924–29); politically inactive (1929–39); appointed first lord of admiralty two days after declaration of war (1939); prime minister of coalition government (1940); with Franklin D. Roosevelt, drew up Atlantic Charter (1941); with Stalin and Roosevelt at Tehran (1943) and Yalta (1945), and with Truman and Stalin at Potsdam (1945), shaped map of postwar world; resigned as prime minister after Labor victory (1945); denounced Russian expansionism and coined the term *Iron Curtain*; promoted Atlantic unity and sponsored NATO and other free-world organizations; prime minister (1951–55); declined peerage, but accepted many other honors, including Nobel Prize for literature (1953); generally acknowledged as an important Englishman, whose profound sense of history, classic oratory, imagination, and patriotism shaped the course of 20th-century history. Author of *World Crisis* (4 vols., 1923–29), *Marlborough, His Life and Times* (4 vols., 1933–38), *My Early Life* (1930), *The Second World War* (6 vols., 1948–53), and *History of the English-Speaking Peoples* (4 vols., 1956–58).

Churriguera *(chōōr rē gā rä)*, **José** 1650–1723. Spanish architect. *b.* Salamanca. Royal architect to Charles II; created the baroque style known as Churrigueresque, the best example of which is the cathedral at Murcia, Spain.

Cicero *(sĭs ər ō)*, **Marcus Tullius** 106–43 B.C. Roman statesman. *b.* Arpinum, Italy. Learned rhetoric and law at Rome; toured Greece and Asia Minor (79–77); quaestor in Sicily (75); conducted impeachment of Verres, the corrupt propraetor of Sicily (70); aedile (69), praetor (66) and consul (from 63); *Orations Against Cataline*, foiled conspiracy of Lucius Catiline and the Catilinarians against the Republic; exiled by Publius Clodius (58) for killing some members of Cataline's group; recalled by Pompey (57); proconsul of Cilicia (51–50); joined Pompey against Caesar (49); pardoned by Caesar after Battle of Pharsalus (48); after assassination of Caesar, delivered the Philippics against Mark Antony (44–43); proscribed by Second Triumvirate and slain (43); extant works include orations, letters, books, and essays on rhetoric and philosophy including *Rhetorica, De Oratore, De Republica, De Legibus, Tusculanae Disputationes, De Officiis,* and *De Amicitia*; regarded as one of the greatest Latin stylists.

Cid, the *(thə sĭd)* Spanish form: EL CID CAMPEADOR (the Lord Champion); real name: RODRIGO DÍAZ DE BIVAR. c1040–99. Spanish hero. *b.* Burgos. Valorous warrior in service of Castilian kings Sancho II and Alfonso VI, until exiled by latter (1081); soldier of fortune under Spanish and Moorish flags; captured Valencia (1094), and thereafter ruled Valencia and Murcia (1094–99) until overthrown by the Almoravides; married Ximena, daughter of count of Oviedo; life and exploits became the subjects of ballads and epic poems such as *Song of the Cid, Rhymed Chronicle of the Cid*; and of later works like Castro y Bellvís' *La Mocedades del Cid* (1612), Corneille's *Le Cid* (1636), and Massenet's opera.

Cincinnatus *(sĭn sĭ nā təs),* **Lucius Quinctius** c519–438 B.C. Semi-legendary Roman statesman. Consul (c460); named dictator by the Senate (458) to rescue Rome from Aequians; victorious, but resigned and returned to his farm all within 16 days; idealized in Roman history as the model of Republican virtues.

Clarendon *(klăr ən dən),* **Earl of** real name: EDWARD HYDE. 1609–74. English statesman. *b.* Dinton. Member of Short and Long Parliament (1640); supported Popular party (until 1641), but opposed Grand Remonstrance and drafted king's reply and other royal manifestoes; headed royalist opposition as a member of Charles I's inner council until expelled by Parliament (1642); knighted and made chancellor of the exchequer (1643); in Prince Charles' retinue in Scilly and Jersey (1646–48); appointed lord chancellor by Charles in exile (1658) and confirmed in that post on Restoration (1660); virtual head of government (from 1660); enforced repressive Act of Uniformity; conducted disastrous foreign policy that led to war with Dutch and subservience to France; antagonized Parliament and fell victim to the Cabal; dismissed (1667); impeached for high treason; lived in exile until death in Rouen. Author of *History of the Rebellion in England* (3 vols., 1704–1707), *History of the Civil War in Ireland* (1721), and *Life of Edward, Earl of Clarendon* (3 vols., 1759).

Clarendon, Earl of real name: GEORGE WILLIAM FREDERICK VILLIERS. 1800–1870. English statesman. *b.* London. Appointed ambassador to Madrid (1833–39); lord privy seal under Melbourne (1839–41); president of board of trade (1846); viceroy of Ireland (1847–52); foreign secretary (1853–58, 1865–66, 1868–70); guided England through Crimean War and helped draft Declaration of Paris (1856).

Clark *(klärk),* **Champ** full name: JAMES BEAUCHAMP. 1850–1921. American legislator. *b.* Lawrenceburg, Ky. Member of House of Representatives from Mo. (1893–95, 1897–1921); Democratic minority leader (1907); led the House revolt against "Uncle Joe" Cannon and replaced him as Speaker (1911–19); leading contender for Democratic presidential nomination (1912).

Clark, George Rogers 1752–1818. American frontiersman. *b.* near Charlottesville, Va. Brother of William Clark; settled in Kentucky as surveyor; led expedition in Northwest country (Ill.); took Kaskaskia, Cahokia, and Vincennes; subsequently defended this region against Indians and British; during Revolutionary War eliminated British power in regions west of the Alleghenies. Wrote *Memoir* (1791), a sourcebook on the Northwest.

Clark, William 1770–1838. American explorer. *b.* in Caroline County, Va. Brother of George Rogers Clark; settled in Louisville, Ky.; in army expeditions against Indians (1791–96); present at Battle of Fallen Timbers (1794); resigned and retired to family estate (1796); joined Meriwether Lewis in his cross-continental expedition (1804–1806); resigned again from army (1807); superintendent of Indian affairs (1807); governor of Missouri territory (1813–21); coauthor of *History of the Expedition under the Command of Captains Lewis and Clark* (4 vols., 1893).

Claudel *(klō dĕl),* **Paul Louis Charles** 1868–1955. French poet. *b.* Villeneuve-sur-Fère. In French diplomatic service (from 1898); converted to Catholicism (1886); emerged as major Catholic symbolist poet; works include *Cinq Grandes Odes* (1910), *Le Messe là-bas* (1919), *Poèms de Guerre* (1915), *Tête d'or* (1889), *L'Otage* (1911), *Le Pain Dur* (1918), and *Le Père Humilié* (1920); elected to French Academy (1946).

Claudius *(klô dĭ əs)* Name of two Roman emperors: CLAUDIUS I full name: TIBERIUS CLAUDIUS DRUSUS NERO GERMANICUS. 10 B.C.–A.D. 54. Roman emperor (41–54). *b.* Lyons, France. Proclaimed emperor on assassination of nephew Caligula; reign marred by cruel excesses of wives (Messalina and Agrippina, whose son Nero was adopted as heir and successor); wrote several works in Greek and Latin now lost; built Claudian aqueduct; warred with Britain, Germany, and Syria and made Mauritania a province (42); believed to have been poisoned by Agrippina.

CLAUDIUS II full name: MARCUS AURELIUS CLAUDIUS; surnamed GOTHICUS. 214–70. Roman emperor (268–70). *b.* in Dardania or Illyria. Succeeded Gallienus as emperor (268); won two great battles, one over Alemanni in northern Italy (268) and the other over the Goths near Nis in Moesia (269).

Clausewitz *(klou zə vĭts),* **Karl von** 1780–1831. Prussian general. *b.* Burg. Entered Prussian army (1792); as chief of staff to General Thielmann (1814–18), took part in Battle of Waterloo; named to head German War School (1818); revolutionized the science of war and military tactics with *On War* (3 vols., 1833).

Clausius *(klou zē oos),* **Rudolf Julius Emanuel** 1822–88. German scientist. *b.* Köslin. Professor of physics at University of Bonn (from 1869); formulated second law of thermodynamics (1850); made important contributions to theories of gases and electrolysis; developed the concept of entropy.

Clay *(klā),* **Henry** 1777–1852. American statesman. *b.* in Hanover County, Va. Senator (1806–07, 1810–11, 1831–42, 1849–52);

Member, House of Representatives (1811–14, 1815–21, 1823–25); Speaker (1811–14, 1815–20, 1823–25); secretary of state (1825–29); war hawk of War of 1812; nicknamed Great Pacificator from defense of Missouri Compromise; National Republican party candidate (1832), and Whig Party candidate (1844) for president; supported John Quincy Adams in election of 1824; clashed with Andrew Jackson over chartering second Bank of the U.S.; resolved Nullification Controversy by submitting compromise bill (1833); secured passage of Compromise of 1850, which sought to prevent Civil War; called the Great Compromiser; regarded, with Daniel Webster and John C. Calhoun, as one of the triumvirate of American parliamentary orators; works published (7 vols. 1896).

Clemenceau *(klā mäN sō),* **Georges** 1841–1929. French statesman. *b.* Mouilleron-en-Pareds. Studied medicine (1862); traveled in U.S. as a French teacher (1866–69) and as correspondent; elected to National Assembly (1871); headed extreme left-wing Republicans and was nicknamed the Tiger for his savage polemics; helped found many journals, such as *La Justice* (1880), *L'Aurore* (1897), *Le Bloc* (1900), and *L'Homme Libre* (1913); defended Dreyfus and helped win him a new trial and exoneration; Senator (1902–20); minister of the interior (1906); premier (1906–1909); advanced separation of church and state; used troops to suppress miner's strike (1906); recalled to form coalition war cabinet (1917); led France to victory; as head of French delegation to Peace Conference at Paris (1919), adopted intransigent attitude toward Germany; elected to French Academy (1918); failed in presidential election (1920) against Paul Deschanel and retired to writing and lecturing; wrote *Grandeurs et Misères d'une Victoire* (1930) and *Au Soir de la Pensée* (2 vols., 1928).

Clemens, Samuel Langhorne. *See* **Twain, Mark**

Clement I *(klĕm ənt),* **Saint** also Clemens Romanus. c30–c97. Pope (88–97). First and one of the greatest apostolic fathers; believed by some to be the Clement mentioned by Paul in Philippians and numbered among the martyrs; author of numerous writings, now classed as pseudepigrapha, including *Epistles to the Corinthians* (95 or 96), which was part of the New Testament until the 5th century.

Clement of Alexandria full name: Titus Flavius Clemens. c150–c215. Greek Father of the Church. *b.* Athens. Came to Alexandria as a Christian convert; entered presbytery; head of Catechetical School (190); in writings, attempted to reconcile Platonism and Greek pagan philosophies with Christian theology; defended orthodoxy against Gnosticism although acknowledged some Gnostic ideas; left Alexandria during the persecution under Severus (203); extant writings include *Who is the Rich Man that is Saved?, The Tutor, Exhortation to the Greeks, The Missionary*, and *Miscellanies.*

Cleopatra *(klē ō pā trȧ)* **VI or VII** 69–30 B.C. Queen of Egypt (51–49, 48–30 B.C.). *b.* Alexandria. Daughter of Ptolemy **XI (Ptolemy**

Auletes); succeeded him as coruler of Egypt with her husband/brother Ptolemy XII (or XIV) (51–49); dispossessed, but regained throne with help of Julius Caesar; relinquished reins of government to younger brother Ptolemy XIII (or XV); became Caesar's mistress, living with him in Rome (46–44); after his assassination, returned to Egypt, murdered Ptolemy, and set up her son Cesarion as coruler; after battle of Philippi, met Antony in Cilicia (41) and won his love; Antony divorced Octavia (32) and incurred the hostility of Rome; defeated with Antony in naval battle at Actium (31); committed suicide; bore Antony three children, including ALEXANDER HELIOS and CLEOPATRA SELENE.

Cleveland *(klēv lənd),* **Stephen Grover** known as GROVER CLEVELAND. 1837–1908. 22nd and 24th president of U.S. (1885–89, 1893–97). *b.* Caldwell, N.J. Mayor of Buffalo (1881–82); governor of N.Y. (1883–85); first Democrat in 28 years to win presidency (1884); administration marked by moderate reforms; in 1888, secured popular majority but lost to Harrison in Electoral College; regained presidency (1892); secured repeal of Sherman Silver Law; used federal troops to put down Pullman strike (1894); invoked Monroe Doctrine in dispute between Great Britain and Venezuela over British Guiana. Published *Presidential Problems* (1904).

Clinton *(klĭn tən),* **Dewitt** 1769–1828. American statesman. *b.* Little Britain, N.Y. Son of JAMES CLINTON (1738–1812), general in the Revolutionary army. Member of N.Y. Assembly (1798); Member of N.Y. Senate (1798–1802, 1806–11), U.S. Senator (1802–1803); Mayor of New York City (1803–1807), 1810–11, 1813–15); governor of N.Y. (1817–21, 1825–28); sponsored construction of Erie Canal; as Peace party candidate, lost presidential election to Madison (1812).

Clinton, George 1739–1812. American statesman. *b.* Little Britain, N.Y. Delegate to Second Continental Congress (1775); brigadier general in Continental army (1777); governor (for 7 terms) of N.Y. (1777–95, 1801–1804); vice-president (for two terms) of U.S. (1805–12); uncle of DeWitt Clinton.

Clive *(klīv),* **Robert** title: BARON CLIVE OF PLASSEY. 1725–74. British general and founder of British Empire in India. *b.* Styche. Went to Madras, India, as minor employee of East India Company (1743); captured Arcot, capital of the Carnatic, holding it successfully for 11 weeks against superior native and French forces (1751), thereby establishing British predominance in southeast India; lieutenant governor of Fort St. David (1755); sent to Bengal to avenge Black Hole and to reestablish British supremacy (1756); recovered Calcutta and captured French settlement at Chandernagore; victorious over Suraj-ud-daulah, Nawab of Bengal, at Plassey (1757); established East India Company's protégé, Mir Jafar, as Nawab, receiving a gift from him of nearly £250,000; governor of Bengal (1758); at Battle of Biderra eliminated Dutch in Bengal and wrested Northern Circars from French; returned to England, hailed as "a heaven-born general," and created baron; returned to India (1765) after Battle of Buxar and obtained Dewani (grant) of provinces of Bengal, Bihar, and Orissa from Mughal emperor Shah Alam II; instituted many reforms in territorial administration; returned to England (1767); faced with Parliamentary inquiry; acquitted (1773); committed suicide.

Clovis I *(klō vĭs)* c466–511. Frankish king and founder of Merovingian dynasty. Succeeded father Childeric as king of Salian Franks; converted to Christianity by Queen Clotilda, a Christian princess of Burgundy (496); victory over Alamanni at Tolbiacum; took possession of country between Somme and Loire by overthrowing (486) Syagrius, the Gallo-Roman ruler, at Soissons; moved capital from Tournai to Soissons; defeated Burgundians (500) and Visigoths under Alaric II at Vouillé (507); ruled country extending to Bordeaux and Toulouse; moved court to Paris (507); on death, divided kingdom among four sons.

Cobbett *(kŏb ĕt),* **William** pen name: PETER PORCUPINE. 1763–1835. British political journalist. *b.* Farnham. Self-taught writer; enlisted in army and served in New Brunswick (1783–91); by exposing venality of three of his officers, obtained their court martial; in America (1792–1800); wrote pamphlets against Tom Paine and other radicals; twice prosecuted for libel; returned to England and started *Weekly Political Register* (1802); shifted from Toryism to radicalism; campaigned for reform; imprisoned (1810–12) for denouncing flogging in the army; as a farmer (1817–19), developed new techniques; Member of Parliament (1832); later became a radical socialist. Author of over 50 works including *Grammar of the English Language* (1818), *Rural Rides* (1830), *Porcupine's Works* (12 vols., 1801), *History of the Reformation* (1824–27), and *Advice to Young Men* (1830).

Cobden *(kŏb dən),* **Richard** 1804–65. English statesman and economist. *b.* Heyshott. Began as calico merchant; Member Parliament (from 1841); active in Anti-Corn Law League, repealing Corn Laws (1846); adherent of Manchester School, believing in minimum government at home and nonintervention in affairs of other nations; opposed Crimean War, Palmerston's China policy, and intervention in Denmark; organized international congresses to advocate settlement of issues by arbitration and gradual disarmament; as a step toward free trade and tariff reduction, negotiated commercial treaty with France (1859–60).

Cockcroft *(kŏk rôft),* **Sir John Douglas** 1897–1967. British nuclear physicist. *b.* Todmorden. Professor of natural philosophy at Cambridge (1939–46); chief superintendent of air defense research (1941–44); director of Atomic Energy Division of Canadian National Research Council (1944–46); director of Atomic Research Establishment at Harwell (1946); master of Churchill College at Cambridge (1956); shared Nobel Prize in physics with E.T.S. Walton for work on splitting atoms with protons.

Cocteau *(kôktō),* **Jean** 1889–

1963. French artist and writer. *b.* Maisons-Lafitte. Work touched many areas: as a novelist, wrote *Le Grand Écart* (1923), *Thomas l'Imposteur* (1923), *Les Enfants Terribles* (1923); as a playwright, wrote *The Infernal Machine* (1936), *Orphée* (1927), *Antigone* (1922), *La Belle et la Bête* (1945), *L'Aigle à deux Têtes* (1946); as a poet wrote *Poésie* (1916–23), *Allégories* (1941); as a ballet scenarist, wrote *Le Boeuf sur le Toit* (1920) and others for Diaghilev; as a filmmaker, produced *La Sang d'un Poète Orphée* (1949); *La Belle et la Bête* (1945); elected to French Academy (1955); wrote *Maalesh* (1950) and *Journals* (1957). Work characterized by surrealistic fantasy.

Coddington *(kŏd ĭng tən),* **William** 1601–78. English colonial governor. *b.* in Lincolnshire. Came to Mass. (c1630); supported Anne Hutchinson (1637); founder of Newport, R.I. (1639); governor of Providence Plantations and Rhode Island (1674, 1675, 1678).

Cody *(kō dĭ),* **William Frederick** known as BUFFALO BILL. 1846–1917. American plainsman and showman. *b.* Scott County, Iowa. Rider for Pony Express (1860); scout with 9th Kansas Calvary during Indian Wars, with Union Army during Civil War, and with 5th Cavalry during Sioux War; given nickname after killing nearly 5000 buffalo in 18 months to supply meat to workers on Kansas Pacific Railway; appeared as a rifleman on stage in Edward Z.C. Judson's Scouts of the Plains (1872); organized Buffalo Bill's Wild West Show (from 1883) and toured U.S. and Europe.

Coen *(ko͞on),* **Jan Pieterszoon** 1587–1629. Dutch colonial governor. *b.* Hoorn. Governor general of Dutch East Indies (1618–23, 1627–29); founder of Batavia (1619); considered founder of Dutch colonial empire in East Indies.

Cohen *(kō ən),* **Hermann** 1842–1918. German philosopher. *b.* Coswig. Founder of Marburg school of Neo-Kantianism. Author of *System der Philosophie* (1902), *Der Begriff der Religion im System der Philosophie* (1915), and other books.

Cohn *(kōn),* **Ferdinand Julius** 1828–98. German botanist. *b.* Breslau. Considered founder of bacteriology; first to demonstrate that bacteria are plants; professor at Breslau (from 1859) and founder (1866) of Institute of Plant Physiology; director (from 1872).

Coke *(ko͞ok),* **Sir Edward** 1552–1634. English jurist. *b.* Mileham. Called to bar (1578); solicitor general (1592); Speaker of House of Commons (1593); attorney general (1594); chief justice of Common Pleas (1606); chief justice of King's Bench and first lord chief justice of England (1613); prosecutor at trials of Essex, Southampton, Raleigh, and Gunpowder Plot conspirators; emerged (from 1606), as foe of royal prerogative and champion of national liberties, opposing encroachments by church and crown; dismissed from the bench; entered Parliament (1620); as leader of popular party, attacked monopolies and royal interference with parliamentary rights; imprisoned in the tower for nine months; continued opposition into reign of Charles I; inspired and drafted the Petition of Right and denounced Duke of Buckingham; legal fame rests upon the 13 parts of *Law Reports* (1600–1615) and the four *Institutes* (1628–44).

Colbert *(kôl bâr),* **Jean-Baptiste** 1619–83. French statesman. *b.* Reims. Began in service of Mazarin (1651); controller general of finance (1665); minister of marine and interior (1669); modernized France, purged dishonest administrators; rationalized and trebled tax collection; reorganized colonies in Canada, Martinique, and St. Domingo and founded new ones at Cayenne and Madagascar; created strong navy; streamlined civil code and introduced marine code; founded Academies of Inscriptions, Science, and Architecture; imposed protective tariffs and encouraged commerce and industry; *Lettres, Instructions et Mémoires* published (8 vols., 1862–82).

Cole *(kōl),* **George Douglas Howard** 1889–1959. English socialist. b. London. Professor of social and political theory at Oxford (from 1944); chairman (1939–46, 1948–50) and president (from 1952) of Fabian Society. Works on socialism include *The World of Labour* (1913), *Social Theory* (1920), *Organized Labour* (1924), *Socialism in Evolution* (1938), and *Fabian Socialism* (1943); coauthored (with wife Margaret) detective stories.

Coleridge *(kōl rĭj),* **Samuel Taylor** 1772–1834. English poet and critic. *b.* Ottery St. Mary. Planned, with Robert Southey, utopian community of pantisocracy in Susquehanna, Pa.; published first volume of poetry (1796); engaged in lecturing, journalism, and preaching in Unitarian chapels in Bristol; published liberal weekly *The Watchman*; began association with William and Dorothy Wordsworth, from which emerged *Lyrical Ballads* (1798), his contributions being *"Ancient Mariner"* and *"The Nightingale"*; visited Germany with the Wordsworths (1798–99); translated Schiller's *Wallenstein* (1800); settled in Lake District, but growing addiction to opium brought him near collapse; lectured on Shakespeare and literature (1808–19); published the periodical *The Friend* (1809–10); lived as a guest of James Gillman (from 1816), a physician who cured him of opium addiction. Published works included *Biographia Literaria* (1817), *Sibylline Leaves* (1817), *Aids to Reflection* (1825), *Table Talk* and *Confessions of an Inquiring Spirit*; best-known works include "Kubla Khan" (1816), "Christabel" (1816) and "Dejection: An Ode" (1802); returned to Orthodoxy and defended Christian doctrines; noted as exponent of German idealistic metaphysics and as a seminal Romantic poet.

Colet *(kŏl ət),* **John** c1467–1519. English Renaissance theologian. *b.* London. Studied in Paris and Italy; influenced by Savonarola (1493–96); ordained priest on return to England; lectured at Oxford (1496–1504); Dean of St. Paul's (1504–19); associated with humanists Guillaume Budé, Thomas More, Erasmus, William Grocyn, and Thomas Linacre; urged church reforms; accused of heresy, but protected by Archbishop William Warham; founded St. Paul's School (1509–12).

Colette *(kô lĕt)* Pen name of SIDONIE GABRIELLE CLAUDINE COLETTE. 1873–1954. French writer. *b.* Saint-Sauveur-en-Puisaye. Works characterized by sensitive and subtle portrayals of characters—often semiautobiographical—in critical developmental stages. Author of *Chéri* (1920), *La Fin de Chéri* (1926), *La Chatte* (1933), *La Retraite Sentimentale* (1907), *La Vagabonde* (1910), *Gigi* (1945), *L'Envers du Music-Hall* (1913), and the Claudine novels *Claudine â l'École* (1900), *Claudine à Paris* (1901), and *Claudine en Ménage* (1902). First woman president of Goncourt Academy; second to be grand officer in French Legion of Honor.

Colfax *(kōl făks),* **Schuyler** 1823–85. American politician. *b.* New York City, N.Y. Member, House of Representatives (1855–69); Speaker (1863–69); vice-president of U.S. (1869–73); retired following Credit Mobilier scandal (1873).

Coligny *(kô lē nyē),* **Gaspard de** 1519–72. French Huguenot leader. *b.* Châtillon-sur-Loing. Distinguished in Italian campaign under Duc d'Enghien (1544); admiral of France (1552); taken prisoner by Spaniards at St.-Quentin (1557–59); converted to Protestantism in prison; commanded Huguenot army on death of Louis I, Prince of Condé, at Battle of Jarnac (1569); victorious over Catholics at Arnay-le-Duc (1570), leading to peace of St.-Germain; supported Huguenot immigration to New World; aroused enmity of the Guise faction and Catherine de Medici because of growing influence over Charles IX; murdered in St. Bartholomew's Day massacre (1572).

Collins *(kŏl ĭnz),* **Michael** 1890–1922. Irish revolutionary leader. *b.* near Clonakilty. Took part in Easter Rebellion (1916); rose to high position in Sinn Fein; Member of Parliament (1918); helped adoption of declaration of independence and provisional constitution of 1919; minister of finance in Sinn Fein ministry (1919–22); aided De Valera in escaping from Lincoln jail; signed treaty in London setting up Irish Free State (1921); on the outbreak of civil war, led Irish Free State for ten days until mortally wounded in an ambush (1922).

Collins, William Wilkie 1824–89. English novelist. *b.* London. Known as father of the English detective novel. Wrote *The Woman in White* (1860), *The Moonstone* (1868), *The New Magdalen* (1873), *No Name* (1862), *The Dead Secret* (1857), and *The Guilty River* (1886); collaborated with Charles Dickens on *No Thoroughfare* (1867).

Colt *(kōlt),* **Samuel** 1814–62. American inventor. *b.* Hartford, Conn. Took out first patent for a revolver (1835); gained fame when revolver was adopted for U.S. army after Mexican War.

Colum *(kŏl əm),* **Padraic** 1881–1972. Irish poet and playwright. *b.* Longford. One of the founders of *Irish Review* and (with W.B. Yeats and Lady Gregory) of Irish National Theater (later Abbey Theater); immigrated to U.S. (1914); dramatic works include *The Land* (1905), *The Fiddler's House* (1907), *Thomas Muskerry* (1910), *Mogu the Wanderer* (1917), *The Miracle* *of the Corn* (1917), and *The Betrayal* (1920); poetic works include *Wild Earth* (1907), *Dramatic Legends* (1922), *Creatures* (1927), *Poems* (1932), and *The Story of Lowry Maen* (1937).

Columba *(kō lŭm bȧ),* **Saint** 521–97. Irish missionary. *b.* Donegal. Founded monastery schools at Derry (545), Durrow (553), and Kells (554), and monastery on Island of Iona (563); converted northern Picts, hence known as Apostle of Caledonia; wrote three hymns; one of three patron saints of Irish; said to have written over 300 books. Feast day: June 9.

Columbus *(kō lŭm bəs),* **Christopher** 1451–1506. Italian navigator; discoverer of New World. *b.* Genoa. Took to the sea at age 14; voyaged to Sierra Leone, Cape Verde Islands, Ireland, and Iceland; as early as 1474, conceived the idea of reaching India by sailing west; found Ferdinand and Isabella of Spain as patrons for the project; set sail from Palos, in command of three vessels, the *Santa Maria*, *Pinta*, and *Niña,* with a crew of 90 to 120 men (August 3, 1492); sighted land (called Guanahani by the natives and renamed San Salvador by Columbus; (thought to be Watling Island in the Bahamas) on October 12, 1492; planted a fortress colony at La Navidad; received home with great honor (1493); on second (1493) voyage, with 17 ships and 1500 men, discovered Dominica, founded Isabela, Haiti, the first European town in New World, and discovered Jamaica; on third voyage (1498) discovered Trinidad and the mainland of South America at the mouth of the Orinoco; arrested by Francisco de Bobadilla, the royal commissioner, and sent to Spain in chains but released on arrival in Spain; on fourth voyage (1502) sailed along Gulf of Mexico; discovered Honduras, but failed to find westward passage across Isthmus of Panama; returned to Spain (1504) and spent last days in poverty and neglect; literary works include *Letters* and *Journal*.

Comenius *(kō mē nĭ ŭs),* **John Amos** original name: Jon Amos Komensky. 1592–1670. Czech educational innovator. Member of Moravian Brethren; rector of Moravian school at Prerau (1614–16) and later taught at Fulnek (1618); driven by Spanish persecution into Leszno in Poland (1628); rector of a gymnasium (1636); bishop of Moravians (1632); visited England and Sweden to reform educational system (1641–42); bishop of Unity of Brethren (1648); taught at Sáros-Patak in Hungary (1650–55); returned to Leszno (1655), but when it was destroyed (1656) in Swedish-Polish War, moved to Amsterdam. Author of over 90 works in educational theory and practice including *Labryinth of the World, A Patterne of Universall Knowledge, Via Lucis, Pansrophiae Prodromus*, and *Orbis Sensualium Pictus*, the first picture book for children.

Commager *(kŏm ə jər),* **Henry Steele** 1902–. American historian. *b.* Pittsburgh, Pa. Professor of American history at Columbia (from 1939). Author of *The American Mind* (1950) and *The Era of Reform* (1960), editor of *Documents of American History* (2 vols., 1969), and co-author (with Samuel Eliot Morison) of *The*

Growth of the American Republic (3rd ed., 1942), among other works.

Commodus *(kŏm ō dəs),* **Lucius Aelius Aurelius** 161–192. Roman emperor (180–92). *b.* Lanuvium, Italy. Son and successor of Marcus Aurelius Antoninus; abandoned himself to a career of cruelty and dissipation after the murder of his father's advisors; vain about his physical prowess, often appeared in the amphitheater as a gladiator and in the guise of Hercules; strangled to death by the athlete Narcissus.

Compton *(kŏmp tən),* **Arthur Holly** 1892–1962. American physicist. *b.* Wooster, Ohio. Professor of physics at Washington University (1920–23); professor of physics at University of Chicago (1923–45); chancellor of Washington University (from 1945); shared Nobel Prize in physics with C.T.R. Wilson (1927) for discovery of Compton effect (increase in wave length of X-rays on collision with electrons) studied cosmic rays, properties of X-rays, and atomic chain reactions. Author of *X-Rays and Electrons* (1926), *The Freedom of Man* (1935), and *Human Meaning of Science* (1940).

Compton, Karl Taylor 1887–1954. American physicist. *b.* Wooster, Ohio. President of M.I.T. (1930–48); conducted important research in photoelectricity, ionization, radar, ultraviolet spectroscopy, the structure of crystals, and thermionic emission; brother of Arthur Holly Compton.

Comstock *(kŭm stŏk),* **Anthony** 1844–1915. American moral crusader. *b.* New Canaan, Conn. Secretary of Society for the Suppression of Vice; instrumental in securing state and Federal legislation prohibiting the use of the mails for sending obscene matter (1873); tracked down and helped convict a number of publishers of pornographic material. Author of *Frauds Exposed* (1880) and *Traps for the Young* (1883).

Comte *(kôNt),* **Auguste** full name: ISIDORE AUGUSTE MARIE FRANÇOIS XAVIER COMTE 1798–1857. French philosopher and founder of positivism. *b.* Montpellier. Systematized the radical ideas of his mentor, Saint-Simon, into a philosophy of positivism; after breaking with Saint-Simon (1824), continued to expound seminal theories of Positivist sociology in *Cours de Philosophie Positive* (6 vols., 1830–42), *Système de Politique Positive* (4 vols., 1851–54), *Discours sur l'Ensemble du Positivisme* (1848), *Catechisme Positiviste* (1852); *Testament* and *Lettres* were published posthumously.

Condé *(kôN dā)* French noble family whose members included:

LOUIS I 1530–69. Son of Charles de Bourbon, Duc de Vendôme, and younger brother of Antony of Bourbon, King of Navarre. Joined Huguenots and became their leader; in first civil war with the Guises, defeated and taken prisoner at Dreux (1562); in second civil war, slain at Battle of Jarnac (1569).

LOUIS II, DUC D'ENGHIEN; also called the GREAT CONDÉ. 1621–86. As commander of French forces in Thirty Years' War, won victories over Spanish at Rocroi (1643) and Lens (1648) and over the army of Holy Roman Empire at Nördlingen (1645); captured Dunkirk (1646); in War of the Fronde, defeated royal troops at Bleneau (1652) but was subsequently defeated at Paris and forced to conclude peace; defected to Spanish army and served against France for six years; pardoned and restored to former dignity by Treaty of Pyrenees (1659); conquered Franche-Comté (1668); fought last battle (1674) at Seneffe against William of Orange; succeeded Henry Turenne as commander of the army of the Rhine (1675) but soon retired.

Condillac *(kōN dē yak),* **Étienne Bonnot de** 1715–80. French philosopher. *b.* Grenoble. Expounded theory of sensationalism in *Essai sur l'Origine des Connaissances Humaines* (1746), *Traité des Systèmes* (1749), *Traité des Sensations* (1754), and other works; elected to French Academy (1768).

Condorcet *(kôN dôr sĕ),* **Marquis de** real name: MARIE JEAN ANTOINE NICOLAS CARITAT. 1743–94. French philosopher. *b.* Ribemont. Espoused radical ideas of Voltaire, Turgot, and Rousseau; supported the popular side during French Revolution; elected to Legislative Assembly (1791) and National Convention (1792); proscribed as a Girondist during Reign of Terror and died mysteriously in prison; set forth anticlerical and liberal democratic philosophy in principal work *Esquisse d'un Tableau Historique des Progrès de l'Esprit Humain* (1794).

Confucius *(kən fū shŭs)* Chinese form: K'UNG FU-TZU (Philosopher Kung); also K'UNG CH'IU. c 551–478 B.C. Chinese philosopher and religious teacher. *b.* Lu. Began career as teacher (531); chief magistrate of Chung-tu (501); elevated by Duke of Lu to minister of works, minister of crime, and prime minister (500–497); retired following a breach with the duke; spent 13 years traveling with a group of disciples; returned to Lu (484) and spent the rest of his life in literary undertakings; maxims recorded by disciples in *Analects*. Author of *Ch'un-chiu* and *Four Books;* teachings emphasize *jen* (sympathy) and the Golden Rule.

Congreve *(kŏn grēv),* **William** 1670–1729. English dramatist. *b.* Bardsey. Achieved success with a series of comedies noted for vigorous dialogue and brilliant wit, including *The Old Bachelor* (1693), *Double Dealer* (1693), *Love for Love* (1695), and *The Way of the World* (1700); also wrote the tragedy *The Mourning Bride* (1697).

Conrad *(kŏn răd),* **Joseph** original name: TEODOR JOSEF KONRAD NAECZ KORZENIOWSKI. 1857–1924. British novelist. *b.* Berdichev, Poland. Left Poland (1862); joined British merchant service (1878); became naturalized British subject (1886); retired from the sea to devote himself to writing (1894). Principal works include *Almayer's Folly* (1895), *The Nigger of the 'Narcissus'* (1897), *Lord Jim* (1900), *Typhoon* (1902), *Nostromo* (1904), *The Secret Agent* (1907), *Under Western Eyes* (1911), *Chance* (1914), *Victory* (1915), and *The Shadow-Line* (1917).

Constable *(kŭn stə bəl),* **John** 1776–1837. English painter. *b.* East Bergholt. Noted as painter of landscapes and rustic scenes; exerted considerable influence on Delacroix and other French artists, but obtained little recognition at home. Finest works include *Valley*

Farm, Cornfield, Hay Wain, The White Horse, Salisbury Cathedral, and *Arundel Mill and Castle.*

Constantine I *(kŏn stăn tīn)* full name: Flavius Valerius Aurelius Constantinus; called the Great. c274–337. Roman emperor (306–37). *b.* Naissus in Moesia (Yugoslavia). Son and successor of Constantius Chorus, emperor of the West; proclaimed emperor at York (306); defeated rival Maxentius in three battles; the last, at Milvian Bridge, (312) was notable for the legendary appearance of a flaming cross inscribed with the words *in hoc signo vinces* (in this sign, conquer); adopted the labarum as his standard; issued Edict of Milan (313) giving civil rights to Christians throughout the empire; as sole emperor of the West (until 323), consolidated the empire and strengthened the administration; defeated and killed Licinus, emperor of the East (324), and became sole emperor of the Roman world; established Byzantium as imperial capital and renamed it Constantinople (330), dedicating it to the Virgin Mary; promulgated Christianity as state religion (324); convened Council at Nicaea (325); accepted baptism shortly before death; regarded as a brilliant Roman administrator and military leader.

Cook *(kŏŏk),* **James** known as Captain Cook. 1728–79. English explorer and navigator. *b.* Marton. Entered the navy (1755); commanded the *Endeavour* on expedition to South Pacific; charted coasts of Australia, New Zealand, and New Guinea; completed circumnavigation of the globe by way of Cape of Good Hope (1768–71); on second voyage, the *Resolution* and *Adventure* sailed close to Antartic ice fields, visited Tahiti and New Hebrides, and discovered New Caledonia (1772–75); on third voyage (1776-79) in *Resolution* and *Discovery,* surveyed Pacific coast of North America as far as Bering Strait; turned back and returned to Sandwich Islands (Hawaii), where he was killed.

Coolidge *(kōō lĭj),* **John Calvin** 1872–1933. 30th president of U.S. (1923–29). *b.* Plymouth, Vt. Entered politics as Republican councilman in Northampton, Mass. (1899); governor of Mass. (1919–20); achieved national prominence by firm stand during Boston Police Strike (1919); won vice-presidency on the Republican ticket with Warren G. Harding; succeeded to presidency on death of Harding (1923); nominated and elected president (1924); at the end of term, retired and devoted his time to writing *Autobiography.*

Cooper *(kōō pər),* **James Fenimore** 1789–1851. American novelist. *b.* Burlington, N.J. Son of William Cooper, founder of Cooperstown, N. Y. Joined the navy as midshipman (1806) after expulsion from Yale for prankishness; retired (1811) to devote full time to writing; achieved fame with second novel *The Spy* (1821), followed by a series of adventure stories called the Leatherstocking tales, including *The Deerslayer* (1841), *The Last of the Mohicans* (1826), *The Pathfinder* (1840), *The Pioneers* (1823), and *The Prairie* (1827); lived in Europe (1826–33); on return wrote books critical of America, involving him in several libel suits.

Cooper, Leon N. 1930–. American physicist. *b.* New York, N.Y. Awarded Nobel Prize in physics with John Bardeen and John R. Schrieffer (1972) for research on superconductivity.

Cooper, Peter 1791–1883. American philanthropist. *b.* New York, N.Y. Built first American steam locomotive, the *Teakettle* or *Tom Thumb,* at Canton Iron Work, Baltimore, Md.; as president of New York, New Foundland, and London Telegraph Company and North American Telegraph Company, promoted the laying of the Atlantic cable; founded (1857–59) Cooper Union in New York City, offering free courses in science and art to the working classes.

Copernicus *(kō pûr nĭ kŭs),* **Nicolaus** Polish form: Mikolaj Kopernik. 1473–1543. Polish astronomer. Considered founder of modern astronomy. *b.* Toruń. Canon of cathedral of Frauenburg (1497); lectured on astronomy at Rome (1500); studied medicine at Padua (1501); received doctorate in canon law at Ferrara (1503); served patron/uncle Lucas Watzelrode, Bishop of Ermeland, as physican (1507–12); at Frauenburg, performed minor offices as vicar general, bailiff, tax collector, and judge; published epoch-making heliocentric theory of astronomy *On the Revolutions of the Heavenly Bodies* just before his death (1543).

Copland *(kōp lənd),* **Aaron** 1900–. American composer. *b.* Brooklyn, N.Y. Major compositions based on American folk themes and idioms as in the ballets *Billy the Kid* (1938), *Appalachian Spring* (1944), and *A Lincoln Portrait* (1942); works also include the play-opera *The Second Hurricane* (1937), symphonies, operas, piano pieces, and chamber music. Published *Composer from Brooklyn* (1953), an autobiography.

Copley *(kŏp lĭ),* **John Singleton** 1738–1815. American portraitist. *b.* Boston, Mass. Won election to Society of Artists of Great Britain with exhibition of *The Boy with the Squirrel* in London; up to 1774, painted New England portraits such as *John Hancock, Samuel Adams, Mrs. Thomas Boylston, Lady Wentworth,* and *Mrs. Robert Harper;* a Loyalist, left for England (1774) and settled in London; his British period consists of historical and Biblical pieces, including *The Death of Lord Chatham, The Siege of Gibralter, The Resurrection, Death of Major Peirson, Lord Cornwallis, The Red Cross Knight,* and *Earl of Mansfield.*

Cori *(kō rĭ),* **Carl Ferdinand** 1896–. American biochemist. *b.* Prague, Czechoslovakia. Immigrated to U. S. (1922); professor of biochemistry at Washington University of St. Louis (from 1931); awarded Nobel Prize in physiology and medicine (1947) with wife Gerty Theresa Cori and Bernardo Alberto Houssay for research on metabolism and enzymes of animal tissues.

Corneille *(kŏr nâ y),* **Pierre** 1606–84. French playwright. *b.* Rouen. Began career with comedy *Mélite* in Paris (1630); followed success with other comedies *Clitandre* (1631), *La Galerie du Palais* (1633), *La Place Royale* (1634), *L'Illusion Comique* (1636), and *La Menteur* (1643); turned to tragedies and achieved greater triumphs with *Médée* (1635), *Le Cid* (1636), *Horace* (1640), *La Mort du Pompée* (1643), *Héraclius* (1647), *Andromède* (1650), *Oedipe* (1659), and *Othon* (1664).

Cornell *(kôr nĕl),* **Ezra** 1807–74. American philanthropist. *b.* Westchester Landing, N.Y. Associated with Samuel Morse in developing magnetic telegraph; helped found telegraph companies and systems, eventually consolidated into the Western Union Telegraph Company (1856); with Andrew White, founded Cornell University, (1868); son ALONZO B. CORNELL (1832–1904) was governor of N.Y. (1879–83).

Cornwallis *(kôrn wŏl ĭs),* **Charles** title: FIRST MARQUIS CORNWALLIS. 1738–1805. English statesman and general. *b.* London. Entered army (1756) and served in Germany in Seven Years' War (1758–62); Member of Parliament (1760–63); major general and sent to American colonies with seven regiments (1776); helped defeat John Sullivan at Battle of Brandywine (1777); appointed second in command to Sir Henry Clinton (1788); defeated General Gates at Camden (1780) and General Greene at Battle of Guilford Court House (1781); forced to surrender to George Washington at Yorktown (1781); appointed governor general of India (1786); waged successful campaign against Tipu Sultan of Mysore and undertook civil and military reforms; retired (1793) and made marquis; viceroy of Ireland (1798–1801); crushed rebellion of 1798; supported Act of Union (1800) which joined Ireland and England; as ambassador to France, negotiated peace of Amiens (1802); governor general of India (1804); died at Ghazipur (1805).

Corot *(kô rō),* **Jean Baptiste Camille** 1796–1875. French painter. *b.* Paris. Paintings of landscapes and architectural subjects, done mainly at Barbizon in Forest of Fontainebleau and in Italy, and figures and portraits. Among his masterpieces are *Danse des Nymphes, Homère et les Bergers, Orphée, Joueur de Flûte, Matin Soirée, Paysage, Pastorale, Soleil Couchant dans le Tyrol, Le Repos, La Solitude, Biblis, Plaisirs du Soir,* and *Vue d'Italie.*

Correggio *(kō räd jō),* **Antonio Allegri da** 1494–1534. Italian painter. *b.* Correggio. Founded school of painting at Parma. Principal works include *Virgin Enthroned, The Ascension, Holy Family, Madonna, Zingarella, Marriage of St. Catherine, Holy Night, Ecce Homo, Il Giorno, Jupiter and Antiope, Education of Cupid, Reading Magdalene, Danae, Leda,* and frescoes in the convent of San Paolo at Padua; considered one of the greatest Italian painters of the Lombard school.

Cortes *(kôr tĕz),* **Hernando** 1485–1547. Spanish conquistador. *b.* Medellín. Sailed to New World (1504); commanded expedition against Mexico (1518); fought first battle at Tabasco and founded Veracruz; burnt his ships, began march on Tenochtitlán (Mexico City); subdued and gained alliance of independent Tlascalans; entered the city (1519) and was received with great honor by Montezuma who soon was a hostage;

left 150 men there under Pedro de Alvarado while he captured Panfilo de Narvaez at Cempoala; found Aztec nation in arms against Spaniards under Montezuma's brother Guatemotzin; tried to leave secretly (June 30, 1520), but was pursued and lost half his force and most of his treasure in a bloody battle; victorious over pursuers at Otumba; with Tlascalans, rallied forces and laid siege to Mexico City, which fell and was leveled (1521); governor and captain general of New Spain (1522); succeeded by Ponce de León (1526); returned to Spain (1528); received with high honor by Charles V; created Marquis of the Valley of Oaxaca; returned to New Spain as military captain general but not civil governor (1530); explored west coast, discovering lower California (1536); went back to Spain to seek support against rivals (1540); expedition against Algiers (1541); died in comparative obscurity in Seville; his body was conveyed to Mexico City (1629).

Cotton *(kŏt ən),* **John** 1584–1652. American Puritan divine. *b.* Derby, England. Pastor at Boston, England (1612–33); cited by William Laud for nonconformity and immigrated to Boston, Mass. (1633); head of Congregationalism in America; clashed with Anne Hutchinson and Roger Williams over primacy of religion, but upheld rights of civil magistrates over religious affairs. Wrote popular children's primer *Spiritual Milk for Boston Babes* (1646), *The Keyes of the Kingdom of Heaven* (1644), and *The Way of the Churches of Christ in New England* (1645).

Coubertin *(ko͞o bĕr tăN),* **Pierre** 1862–1937. French sportsman and educator. *b.* Paris. Revived Olympic Games in Greece (1894); founded International Olympic Committee (1894) and headed it (until 1925).

Coué *(kwā),* **Émile** 1857–1926. French psychotheraptist. *b.* Nancy. Pharmacist at Troyes; began study of hypnotism and autosuggestion (from 1901); developed psychotherapeutic system called Couéism and set up a clinic at Nancy (1910); introduced the formula "Day by day, in every way, I am getting better and better". Author of *Self-Mastery Through Conscious Autosuggestion.*

Coulomb *(ko͞o lôN),* **Charles Augustin de** 1736–1806. French physicist. *b.* Angoulême. Invented the torsion balance for measuring force of electrical attraction; established Coulomb's Law, which governs the forces existing between charged bodies; the coulomb, an electrical unit, named for him.

Courbet *(ko͞or bĕ),* **Gustave** 1819–77. French painter. *b.* Ornans. Founder of Realism, whose best works consisted of landscapes, seascapes, and everyday scenes; influenced by Flemish and Venetian masters; member of Commune of Paris (1871); directed destruction of the column in Place Vendôme; on fall of the Commune, escaped to Switzerland; most famous works include *Peasants of Flazey, Funeral at Ornans, Studio of the Painter, After-Dinner at Ornans,* and *The Stonebreakers.*

Cournand *(koor nänd),* **André Frédéric** 1895–. American physiologist. *b.* Paris. Immigrated to

U.S. (1930); taught at Columbia (from 1935); awarded Nobel Prize in physiology and medicine (1956) with W. Forssmann and D. W. Richards, Jr., for developing a technique for inserting catheter tube into the heart.

Cousin *(ko͞o zăN),* **Victor** 1792–1867. French philosopher. *b.* Paris. Taught at the Sorbonne (1815–17, from 1828); exponent of Scottish metaphysicians; after Revolution of 1830, active as member of Council of Public Instruction (1830), peer of France and director of École Normale (1832); minister of public instruction (1840); retired (1849). Principal works are *Fragments Philosophiques* (1826), *Du Vrai, Du Bien et Du Beau* (1858), and *Histoire Générale de la Philosophie* (1863); considered leader of Eclectic school of philosophy.

Coverdale *(kŭv ər dāl),* **Miles** 1488–1568. English biblical scholar. *b.* North Riding, Yorkshire. Joined Austin friars at Cambridge (1514–26); converted to Lutheranism through influence of Robert Barnes, who was later burned for heresy; left convent (1526) to devote himself to preaching; lived on the Continent (1531–35); published (1535) first English translation of the whole Bible with Apocrypha; sent to Paris by Thomas Cromwell to superintend printing of the Great Bible (1539); edited second Great Bible, or Cranmer's Bible of 1540; on Cromwell's fall, left England (1540); lived in Germany (1540–48); returned (1548) as chaplain to King Edward VI; Bishop of Exeter (1551); in exile (1553–59); resigned rectorate of St. Magnus (1566) objecting to enforced strict observance of the liturgy. *Letters* and other works edited by George Pearson (2 vols., 1844–46).

Coward *(kou ərd),* **Noel** 1899–1973. English playwright and composer. *b.* Teddington. Wrote a number of plays distinguished by witty dialog and satire: *The Vortex* (1923), *Fallen Angels* (1925), *Private Lives* (1930), *Blithe Spirit* (1941), *Peace in Our Time* (1947), and *Nude with Violin* (1956); produced a series of revues, and operettas *Bitter Sweet* (1929) and *Pacific 1860* (1946); films include *Brief Encounter* (1946) and *In Which We Serve* (1942). Author of the autobiographical *Present Indicative* (1937) and *Future Indefinite* (1954).

Cowper *(ko͞o pər),* **William** 1731–1800. English poet. *b.* Great Bekhamstead Rectory. Called to the bar (1754); suffered mental breakdown (1763); recovered and experienced religious conversion; moved to Olney, collaborating with curate John Newton in producing *Olney Hymns* (1779); under guidance of Lady Austen, wrote *The Task* (1785), acclaimed for its joy in nature, social concern, and patriotism; after 1786, translated Homer, Milton's Latin poems, and Italian and French poems; published last poem *The Castaway* (1798); also much admired for his *Letters.*

Cozzens *(kŭz ənz),* **James Gould** 1903–1978. American writer. *b.* Chicago, Ill. Published first novel, *Confusion* (1922); followed with *S. S. San Pedro* (1931), *Ask Me Tomorrow* (1940), *The Just and the Unjust* (1942), *By Love Possessed* (1958), and *Children and Others* (1965), among others.

Craigie *(krā gī),* **Sir William Alexander** 1867–1957. English lexicographer. *b.* Dundee, Scotland. Professor of Anglo-Saxon at Oxford (1916–25) and of English at Chicago (1925–35); joint editor (from 1901) of *Oxford English Dictionary;* editor of *A Historical Dictionary of American English* (1936) and *A Dictionary of the Older Scottish Tongue* (1931).

Cranach *(krä näK),* **Lucas** also KRANACH or KRONACH. 1472–1553. German painter. *b.* Kronach. Court painter to Elector Frederick the Wise of Saxony. Works include altarpieces, wood engravings, and portraits, associated with leaders of the Reformation, many of whom he painted; father of LUCAS THE YOUNGER (1515–86), painter.

Crane *(krān),* **Hart** full name: HAROLD HART CRANE. 1899–1932. American poet. *b.* Garrettsville, Ohio. Poetry marked by two images, the sea and the city; much of his work marked by brillance, most notably *The Bridge* (1930), which depicts the past, present, and future of America; victim of alcoholism, committed suicide. Works include *White Buildings* (1930), *The Bridge* (1930), and *Collected Poems* (1933).

Crane, Stephen 1871–1900. American writer. *b.* Newark, N.J. War correspondent for *New York Journal* and *New York World* during Greco-Turkish and Spanish-American wars; wrote poems, short stories, and novels, the best known of which is *The Red Badge of Courage* (1895).

Cranmer *(krăn mər),* **Thomas** 1489–1556. English ecclesiastic. *b.* Aslacton. Served on diplomatic missions to Rome and Spain on behalf of Henry VIII (1530–32); Archbishop of Canterbury (1533); instrumental in annulment of Henry's marriage to Catherine of Aragon (1533), Anne Boleyn (1536), and Anne of Cleves (1540); championed royal supremacy over Church of England; acquiesced in promulgation of Six Articles (1539) and in the persecution of Frith, Lambert, Friar Forest and others; during reign of Edward VI, supported reform of Church doctrines; promoted translation of the Bible into English; compiled the first *Prayer Book* (1549) and the Thirty-nine Articles (1552); on accession of Queen Mary (1555) arraigned for treason, convicted, excommunicated, degraded, and burned at the stake.

Crassus *(krăs əs),* **Marcus Licinius** surname: DIVES (the Rich). c115–53 B.C. Roman statesman. Served under Sulla in civil war against Marius; amassed fortune estimated at over 8000 talents (about $5 million) by speculating in properties confiscated by Sulla; as praetor, crushed the slaves' insurrection under Spartacus (71); elected consul with Pompey (70); censor (65); joined Caesar and Pompey to form first triumvirate (60); consul (55); governor of Syria (54); defeated and slain treacherously by Parthian general Surenas.

Cremer *(krē mər),* **Sir William Randal** 1838–1908. English pacifist. *b.* Fareham. Trade unionist and organizer of Carpenters' and Joiners' Union; as secretary (1871–1908) of Workingmen's Peace Association, helped develop International Arbitration League; Member of Parliament (1885–95,

1900–1908); editor of the journal *Arbitrator* (from 1889); awarded Nobel Peace Prize (1903).

Crick *(krĭk),* **Francis Harry Compton** 1916–. British biologist. With James Watson, constructed molecular model of the genetic material known as DNA (1953); with Watson and M. Wilkins, awarded Nobel Prize in physiology and medicine (1962).

Croce *(krō chā),* **Benedetto** 1866–1952. Italian philosopher. *b.* Pescasseroli. Founded bimonthly review *La Critica* (1902); developed anti-Hegelian phenomenology of the mind, postulating four complementary aspects of spirit: aesthetic, logical, economic, and ethical; identified history with philosophy and liberty; Senator (from 1910); minister of public instruction (1920–21); opposed Mussolini and promoted liberalism in postwar Italy. Principal works include *Historical Materialism and the Economics of Marx* (1914), *Philosophy of the Practical Economics and Ethics* (1913), *What is Living and What is Dead in the Philosophy of Hegel* (1915), *Philosophy of the Spirit* (1902–17), *La Letteratura della Nuova Italia* (6 vols., 1914–40), *History of Europe in the Nineteenth Century* (1933), and *History as the Story of Liberty* (1941).

Crockett *(krŏk ət),* **Davy** 1786–1836. American backwoodsman. *b.* Limestone, Tenn. Won spurs in Creek War under Andrew Jackson (1813–14); elected to Tennessee legislature (1821); U. S. House of Representatives (1827–31, 1833–35); took part in Texan War of Independence; died at Battle of the Alamo.

Croesus *(krē səs)* *fl.* 6 century B.C. King of Lydia (560–46). Ruled Greek principalities of Asia Minor; at height of power, thought to be one of the wealthiest men of the ancient world; defeated and imprisoned by Cyrus the Great (546).

Cromer, Earl of. *See* **Baring, Evelyn**

Crompton *(krŭmp tən),* **Samuel** 1753–1827. English inventor. *b.* Firwood. Invented the spinning mule (1779), revolutionizing the textile industry, though earning only £67 for him; granted £5000 by Parliament (1812) as a reward.

Cromwell *(krŏm wĕl),* **Oliver** 1599–1658. English statesman; lord protector of England (1653–58). *b.* Huntingdon. Member of Parliament (1628) active in Puritan cause; sat in Short and Long Parliaments (1640); on outbreak of Civil War, organized Ironsides and distinguished himself at Edge Hill (1642) and Marston Moor (1644); emerged as leader of extreme Independents against Presbyterian moderates; reorganized New Model Army and passed the Self-Denying Ordinance (1645); under Sir Thomas Fairfax, won victory over Royalists (1645); believed to have ordered seizure of Charles at Holmby (1647); routed Scottish troops under Hamilton at Preston (1648); brought Charles to trial and signed his death warrant (1649); established the Commonwealth; led punitive expedition against Ireland, extensively expropriating lands after ruthlessly suppressing resistance (1649); in final battles at Dunbar and Worcester (1650–51), defeated Royalist Scots under Charles II; dissolved Rump Parliament (1653) and its successor, **Little Parliament**; declared lord protector under an Instrument of Government that also established a Council of State; ruled by ordinances; offered crown by second Parliament (1656), but declined; reorganized Church of England and gave Scotland and Ireland representation in Parliament; triumphs in foreign policy; ended Dutch claims to naval supremacy in First Dutch War (1652–54); through Blake's naval victories, humbled Spain and Barbary pirates; acquired Jamaica and Dunkirk; concluded treaties with Portugal (1653), France (1655, 1657), Sweden, and Denmark; buried at Westminster Abbey with royal pomp; after Restoration, disinterred and hung at Tyburn, where he was buried.

Cromwell, Thomas title: EARL OF ESSEX. c1485–1540. *b.* Putney. Employed by Cardinal Wolsey as legal advisor, collector of revenues, secretary, and factotum (from 1514); Member of Parliament (1523); gained favor of Henry VIII and became privy councillor (1531), chancellor of the exchequer (1533), secretary of state (1534), vicar general (1535), lord privy seal (1536), knight of the garter (1537), lord great chamberlain (1539), and earl of Essex (1540); effected Act of Supremacy (1534) and dissolution of the monasteries (1536–39); though Catholic, engineered Protestantization of English Church and the Terror, in which More and other Catholics perished; incurred Henry's displeasure by promoting marriage with Anne of Cleves; accused of treason, attainted, and beheaded.

Crookes *(kro͞oks),* **Sir William** 1832–1919. English chemist and physicist. *b.* London. Conducted research on sanitation, radium, rare earths, diamonds, beetroot sugar, wheat, dyeing, calico printing, and psychical research; discovered thallium (1861); invented the radiometer, Crooke's tube, the spinthariscope, and protective goggles; founded *Chemical News* (1859) and edited *Quarterly Journal of Science* (1864). Author of *Select Methods of Chemical Analysis* (1871).

Cruikshank *(kro͞ok shăngk),* **George** 1792–1878. English caricaturist and illustrator. *b.* London. Developed unique and brilliant style of etching; the best examples of which appeared in *Peter Schlemihl* (1823), *Grimm's German Popular Stories* (1824–26), *Bentley's Miscellany* (14 vols., 1837–43), Dickens's *Sketches by Boz* (1836), *Ainsworth's Magazine* (1836–44), *The Scourge* (1811–16), *The Humorist* (1819–21), *Points of Honor* (1823–24), and *Italian Tales* (1824); later began a powerful series against alcoholism with *The Bottle* (1847), *The Drunkard's Children* (1848), and *Worship of Bacchus* (1862).

Cumberland *(kŭm bər lənd),* **Richard** 1631–1718. English philosopher. *b.* London. Bishop of Peterborough (from 1691); *De Legibus Naturae* (1672), written in refutation of theories of Thomas Hobbes, is considered the foundation of English Utilitarianism.

Cummings *(kŭm ĭngz),* **Edward Estlin** known as E E CUMMINGS. 1894–1962. American poet. *b.* Cambridge, Mass. Wrote poetry characterized by unconventional typography, rhythm, and grammar and the frequent omission of capital letters. Volumes include *Tulips and Chimneys* (1923), *XLI Poems* (1925), *&* (1925), *Is 5* (1926), *1×1* (1944), *Santa Claus* (1946), and *Collected Poems, 1923–1954* (1954); also wrote *Six Non-Lectures* (1953), *The Enormous Room* (1922), and *Him* (1927); noted as a painter.

Curie *(kü rē),* **Pierre** 1859–1906. French physicist. *b.* Paris. Professor at School of Physics and Chemistry at Paris (1895); professor at the Sorbonne (from 1900); established Curie's Law (1895), which governs the relationship between magnetism and absolute temperature; married (1895) MARIE CURIE maiden name: MARJA SKLODOWSKA. 1867–1934. Physical chemist. *b.* Warsaw, Poland. With Pierre, discovered radium and polonium, the radioactivity of thorium, and induced radioactivity in other substances; shared Nobel Prize in physics (1903) with husband and Becquerel; succeeded husband as professor at the Sorbonne (1906); received Nobel Prize in chemistry (1911) for isolation of metallic radium; mother of IRÈNE CURIE 1897–1956. French physicist. *b.* Paris. Married Frédéric Joliot–Curie (1926); professor at University of Paris (from 1937); director of Institut du Radium (from 1946); shared Nobel Prize in chemistry (1935) with husband Frédéric Joliot–Curie for research on induced reactivity. Author of *L'Existence du Neutron* (1932) and *La Chimie des Radioélements Naturels* (1946).

Currier *(kûr ĭ ər),* **Nathaniel** 1813–88. American lithographer. *b.* Roxbury, Mass. Set up business in N.Y. (1835); joined by J. Merritt Ives (1857) to form Currier & Ives; after death of the partners, firm was dissolved (1907); published prints portraying scenes and persons of 19th-century America.

Curtin *(kûr tĭn),* **John** 1885–1945. Australian statesman. *b.* Creswick. Labor Member of Parliament (1928–31, 1934–45); leader of the opposition (1935–41); prime minister (1941–45); led Australia through World War II.

Curtis *(kûr tĭs),* **Charles** 1860–1936. American statesman. *b.* North Topeka, Kan. Republican member of House of Representatives (1893–1909); senator (1907–13, 1915–29); vice-president of U.S. under Hoover (1929–33).

Curtiss *(kûr tĭs),* **Glenn Hammond** 1878–1930. American aviator. *b.* Hammondsport, N.Y. Won *Scientific American* prize (1908) for first flight of 1 km., the International Aviation Cup at Reims, France (1909) for flying 20 km., and grand prize at Brescia, Italy (1909) for flying 31.05 miles, all in record time; opened first flying school in U.S. (1909); demonstrated first seaplane (1912) and first heavier-than-air craft for translantic flight (1914); produced Jennies, Wasps, and NC4 seaplanes during World War I.

Curzon *(kûr zən),* **George Nathaniel** title: BARON CURZON OF KEDLESTON. 1859–1925. English statesman. *b.* Kedleston. Entered Parliament (1886); undersecretary of state for India (1891–92) and for foreign affairs (1895–98); viceroy of India (1898); introduced many reforms, some controversial, such as the partition of Bengal; resigned (1905) over difference of opinion with Lord Kitchener; joined Lloyd George's cabinet (1916); secretary of state for foreign affairs (1919–24); played a key role at Lausanne Conference (1922–23); wrote on international relations and university reform.

Cushing *(ko͞osh ĭng),* **Harvey Williams** 1869–1939. American surgeon. *b.* Cleveland, Ohio. Professor of surgery at Harvard (from 1911); developed new and important techniques in brain surgery. Author of *The Pituitary Body and Its Disorders* (1912), *The Life of Sir William Osler* (Pulitzer Prize, 1925), *From a Surgeon's Journal (1915–18)* (1936), and other books.

Custer *(kŭs tər),* **George Armstrong** 1839–76. American soldier. *b.* New Rumley, Ohio. After distinguished service in Union Army during Civil War, commanded 7th Cavalry (1876); killed with all members of his party during an expedition to pacify the Sioux and Cheyennes at Little Bighorn, in an action now known as Custer's Last Stand (1876). Author of *Wild Life on the Plains* (1874).

Cuvier *(kü vyā),* **Baron Georges Léopold Chrétien Frédéric Dagobert** 1769–1832. French naturalist. *b.* Monbéliard. Professor of natural history at Collège de France (1799); titular professor at Jardin des Plantes (1802); permanent secretary of Academy of Sciences (from 1803); councilor of state (1814); chancellor of University of Paris after Restoration; admitted to French Academy (1818); president of committee of the interior (1819–32); peer of France (1831); regarded as founder of comparative anatomy and paleontology; devised natural system of animal classification under four distinct phyla; opposed theory of evolution in favor of catastrophism; Principal works include *Leçons d'Anatomie Comparée* (5 vols., 1800–1805), *Tableau Élémentaire de l'Histoire Naturelle des Animaux* (1798), *Recherches sur les Ossements Fossiles* (1812), *Le Règne Animal Distribué d'Aprés son Organisation* (1817), *Les Ossements Fossiles des Quadrupèdes* (1812), and *Histoire Naturelle des Poissons* (1828–49).

Cyrano de Bergerac *(sē rä nō də bĕr zhə räk),* **Savinien de** 1619–55. French writer and duelist. *b.* Pērigord. Retired after brief service in army (1637–40) to devote himself to study ; fought over a thousand duels, perhaps on account of a monstrously large nose. Author of *Agrippine* (1653), *Le Pédant Joué* (1654), and two utopian satires: *Histoire Comique des États et Empires de la Lune* (1656) and *Histoire Comique des États et Empires de Soleil* (1662).

Cyril *(sĭr ĭl)* **of Alexandria, Saint** 376–444. Egyptian Father of the Church. *b.* Alexandria. Patriarch of Alexandria (412); as champion of Orthodoxy, led struggle against pagans and heretics, especially Novatians and Nestorians, triumphantly concluding at Council of Ephesus (431), which condemned Nestorius as a heretic; extant works (7 vols., 1638) include homilies and treatises on the Trinity and the Incarnation. Feast day: Jan. 28.

Cyril, Saint original name: CONSTANTINE; also called APOSTLE OF THE SLAVS. 827–69. Greek missionary. *b.* Thessalonica. With brother

Saint Methodius (826–85), evangelized Tartar Khazars, Bulgarians, Moravians, and other Slavs; translated gospels and liturgical works into Slavonic; devised Cyrillic alphabet. Feast day: July 7.

Cyrus *(sī rŭs)* **The Great** *d.* 529 B.C. Achaemenid king of Persia (550–529). Son of Cambyses; ascended throne of Anshan (558); dethroned Astyages, king of the Medes, and united Media and Persia (549); carried arms to Lydia, vanquished Croesus, and took Sardis, the Lydian capital (547–46); marched into Babylonia (538), which fell without struggle; treated Babylon and its king Nabonidus with magnanimity; permitted Jews in exile in Babylon to return to Jerusalem, helped to rebuild their temple, and returned to them sacred vessels that had been seized by Nebuchadnezzar; died in battle against the Messagetes near Caspian.

D

Daguerre *(dȧ gâr),* **Louis Jacques Mandé** 1787–1851. French painter and inventor of daguerreotype. *b.* Cormeilles. Scene painter in Paris; with Charles Bouton, opened Diorama in Paris (1822); devoted himself to perfecting a process for obtaining permanent pictures on copper plates coated with light-sensitive silver iodide and bromide; worked with Nicéphore Niepce (1829–33) and alone (until 1839); the discovery, known as daguerreotype, was ceded to the Academy of Sciences (1839).

Daimler *(dīm lər),* **Gottlieb** 1834–1900. German engineer and automobile manufacturer. *b.* Schorndorf. Invented an internal-combustion engine (1885); founded Daimler Automobile Company in Cannstatt (1890), which later merged with Benz & Company to form Daimler-Benz and Company, producers of Mercedes and other automobiles.

Dakin *(dā kĭn),* **Henry Drysdale** 1880–1952. English biochemist. *b.* London. Carried out important research at Herter Laboratory in New York City on the action of enzymes within the body; developed Dakin's Solution (0.5% solution of sodium hypochlorite) for treatment of wounds. Author of *Handbook of Chemical Antiseptics* (1917).

Daladier *(dȧ lȧ dyā),* **Édouard** 1884–1970. French statesman. *b.* Carpentras. Radical Socialist deputy (1919–40); succeeded Édouard Herriot as president of Radical Socialist party (1934); premier (1933, 1934, 1938–40); minister of foreign affairs (1934, 1940); minister of national defense (1936–40); one of the signatories of Munich Pact (1938); signed declaration of war against Germany, but resigned on eve of invasion of France (1940); imprisoned by Germans during World War II; returned to National Assembly (1946).

Dalberg-Acton, John Emerich Edward. *See* **Acton, Lord**

Dale *(dāl),* **Sir Henry Hallett** 1875–1968. British scientist. *b.* London. Director, Wellcome Physiological Research Laboratories (1904–14), National Institute for Medical Research (1928–42), Royal Institution of Great Britain (1942–46); secretary of the Royal Society (1925–35) and president (1940–45); with Otto Loewi, shared Nobel Prize in physiology and medicine (1936) for investigation of the action of acetylcholine in the transmission of nerve impulses.

Dalén *(dȧ lān),* **Nils Gustaf** 1869–1937. Swedish scientist and inventor. *b.* Stenstorp. Principal inventions include an automatic regulator for acetylene-gas lights, a hot-air turbine, compressors, air pumps, a pasteurizer and milking machine, and a method for dissolving acetylene in acetone; awarded Nobel Prize in physics (1912); blinded in an explosion (1913) but continued to experiment until his death.

Dalhousie *(dăl hōō zĭ),* **10th Earl and 1st Marquis of** full name: JAMES ANDREW BROUN RAMSAY. 1812–60. British statesman. *b.* Dalhousie Castle, Midlothian. President of board of trade (1845–47); governor general of India (1847); expanded Indian Empire, acquiring Punjab, Pegu, lower Burma, Satara, Jaipur, Sambalpur, Jhansi, Nagpur, and Oudh; suppressed various native customs; modernized civil service and opened it to British subjects of all races; established network of canals, roads, bridges, railways, and post and telegraph offices; considered greatest of the Indian proconsuls; retired (1856).

Dali *(dä lē),* **Salvador** 1904–. Spanish painter. *b.* Figueras. Experimented with avant garde styles of painting; became a principal exponent of surrealism (from 1928); paintings characterized by irrational imagery, meticulous detail, and dream symbolism; settled in U.S. (from 1940) and became a Catholic; collaborated with Luis Buñuel in producing such surrealist films as *le Chien Andalou* (1928) and *L'Age d'Or* (1930); best-known works include *The Persistence of Memory* (1931), *Nostalgic Echo* (1935), *Soft Self-Portrait with Grilled Bacon* (1941), *Portrait of Gala (1935), and Christ of St. John of the Cross* (1951).

Dallas *(dăl əs),* **George Mifflin** 1792–1864. American statesman. *b.* Philadelphia, Pa. Senator (1831–33); minister to Russia (1837–39); vice-president of U.S. (1845–49); minister to Great Britain (1856–61); negotiated Dallas-Clarendon Convention of 1856, settling U.S.-British differences in Central America. Author of *Letters of London* and a biography of his father, ALEXANDER JAMES DALLAS (1759–1817), secretary of the treasury (1814–16).

Dalton *(dêl tən),* **John** 1766–1844. English scientist. *b.* Eaglesfield. Conducted important investigations into gases and vapors; formulated Dalton's Law in *Absorption of Gas by Water and Other Liquids* (1805); first described color blindness or Daltonism (1794); established atomic theory on a firm basis (1803); arranged table of atomic weights (1803). **Published** ***Meteorological Obser-***

vations and Essays (1793) and *A New System of Chemical Philosophy* (1808–10, 1827).

Dam *(dàm),* **Carl Peter Henrik** 1895–1976. Danish biochemist. *b.* Copenhagen. Taught at University of Copenhagen (until 1941); immigrated to U. S. (1940) and became associate member of Rockefeller Institute of Medical Research (1945); awarded Nobel Prize in medicine with E. A. Doisy (1943) for discovery of vitamin K (1934).

Damien *(dà myăN),* **Father** original name: JOSEPH DE VEUSTER. 1840–89. Belgian Catholic missionary. *b.* Tremeloo. Missionary in Hawaii; voluntarily sought transfer to leper colony at Molokai, where he spent the remainder of his life caring for the lepers; contracted leprosy (1885) and died (1889).

Dampier *(dăm pĭ ər),* **William** 1652–1715. English navigator. *b.* East Coker. Went to sea (1668); joined plundering expeditions (1679, 1683) on coasts of Peru, Chile, and Mexico; sailed across the Pacific with Captain Swan, touching China, Philippines, Australia, and Nicobar Islands; returned to England (1691); described experiences in *New Voyage Round the World* (1697); circumnavigated the world (1699, 1707, 1711); explored coasts of Australia and New Guinea, discovering Dampier Strait and Dampier Archipelago; wrote an authoritative hydrographic treatise; during last voyage, rescued Alexander Selkirk, the original Robinson Crusoe.

Dana *(dā nà),* **Charles Anderson** 1819–97. American journalist. *b.* Hinsdale, N.H. Member of Brook Farm Colony (1841–46); editor of *New York Tribune* (1848–62); acquired *New York Sun* (1867) and developed it into one of the country's liveliest newspapers; with George Ripley, a Brook Farm associate, edited *The New American Cyclopedia* (16 vols., 1857–63) and *American Cyclopedia* (16 vols., 1873–76).

Dana, Richard Henry 1815–82. American writer. *b.* Cambridge, Mass. Went to sea (1834–36) and from New York to California around Cape Horn; the record of this voyage, *Two Years Before the Mast,* became a classic in American literature; distinguished as a maritime lawyer; wrote the standard admiralty manual *The Seaman's Friend* (1841); one of the founders of the Free-Soil party.

Daniel *(dăn yĕl)* (O.T.) One of the prophets; as a youth, carried off to Babylon as captive (605 B.C.); gifted with the power of interpreting dreams; read handwriting on the wall for Belshazzar; one of the three "presidents" of the empire under Darius; mysteriously delivered from the lion's den; influential under Cyrus; regarded as an embodiment of righteousness and wisdom.

Daniel, Arnaud also ARNAUT or ARNAULT. *fl.* 12th century. Provençal poet. *b.* Périgord, France. Member of court of Richard Coeur-de-Lion; gained fame as great master of love songs; introduced the sestina verse form later adopted by Dante and Petrarch.

D'Annunzio *(dän no͞on tsyō),* **Gabriele** 1863–1938. Italian author and nationalist. *b.* Francavilla al Mare. Hero of post-World War I

Italy because of his daring exploits, including the occupation of Fiume (1919); granted title of Prince of Monte Nevoso by Fascists (1924). Works characterized by decadence, affectation, and sensuous imagery; wrote poetry: *Primo Vere* (1879), *Canto Novo* (1881), and *Laus Mortis* (1927); short stories: *Le Novelle della Pescara* (1882–86); dramas: *La Giaconda* (1898), *Francesca da Rimini* (1902), and *La Nave (1908);* and novels: *Il Piacere* (1889), *Il Fuoco* (1900), and *La Leda Senza Cigno* (1916).

Dante *(dăn tĭ)* full name: DANTE (DURANTE) ALIGHIERI. 1265–1321. Italian poet. *b.* Florence. Active in politics of Florence; as a result of his allegiance to White Guelphs, banished from the city for life (1302); wandered on the Continent (1303–21) and died at Ravenna; around 1307, began writing *Divine Comedy,* regarded as one of the greatest of all poetic works; it recounts Dante's imaginary journey through Hell, Purgatory, and Paradise, presenting a synthesis of philosophy, theology, history, science, and art couched in exquisite and melodious language; other works include *Vita Nuova, Il Convivio,* and *De Vulgari Eloquentia.*

Danton *(däN tôN),* **Georges Jacques** 1759–94. French revolutionary. *b.* Arcis-sur-Aube. On outbreak of French Revolution, founded the Cordeliers, a radical political club; minister of justice in republican government; voted for death of the king (1793); president of Jacobin Club (1793); set up Revolutionary Tribunal and dominated nine-member Committee of Public Safety (1793); approved the purge of moderate Girondists; lost influence to the extremist Robespierre; arrested with Camille Desmoulins and, after a mock trial, executed (1794).

Darby *(där bĭ),* **John Nelson** 1800–1882. English ecclesiastic. *b.* London. Chief founder of the Plymouth Brethren, especially a sect known as Darbyites. Author of *Personal Recollections* (1831) and 30 other works.

Darius I *(dȧ rī us)* surname: HYSTASPIS, also called DARIUS THE GREAT. c550–486 B.C. Achaemenid king of Persia (521–486 B.C.). Ascended the throne after defeating the usurper Magian Gomates (Smerdis); suppressed two revolts in Babylonia and tore down its walls; waged a long campaign against the Scythians; extended borders to the Indus in the east and to Egypt in the south; sent two unsuccessful expeditions to punish Greece for the revolt of the Ionian cities; built Persepolis in Persia; established Zoroastrianism as state religion; reorganized the empire and divided it into 20 satrapies; introduced regular taxation, a postal system, uniform coinage, and new roads; left many inscriptions as records of reign.

Darrow *(dăr ō),* **Clarence Seward** 1857–1938. American lawyer. *b.* Kinsman, Ohio. Defense counsel in many prominent trials: for Eugene Debs in the Railroad Union case (1894); Nathan Leopold and Richard Loeb in their trial for murder of Bobbie Franks (1924); John Thomas Scopes, charged with teaching evolution in a Tennessee school (1925); and for the Negro defendants in the Scottsboro trial (1932).

Darwin *(där wĭn),* **Charles Rob-**

ert 1809–82. English naturalist. *b.* Shrewsbury. Grandson of ERASMUS DARWIN (1731–1802), English naturalist. Naturalist on *H. M. S. Beagle* on an around-the-world expedition (1831–36); based on knowledge of fauna, flora, and geology worldwide, began to formulate a theory of evolution by natural selection; secretary of Geological Society (1838–41); wrote preliminary paper (1844), but waited until 1857 to write to Asa Gray, American botanist, outlining his theories; received from Alfred Russell Wallace, English naturalist in the Moluccas, a memoir proposing a theory of natural selection identical with his own (1858); encouraged by Charles Lyell to present both his and Wallace's essays to the Linnaean Society (1858); published *The Origin of Species on the Basis of Natural Selection* (1859), marking a turning point in the history of science; developed the theory further in *Descent of Man* (1871), which introduced the concept of sexual selection and argued that the human race was descended from an animal of the anthropoid group. Other works include *The Expression of the Emotions in Man and Animals* (1873), *Insectivorus Plants* (1875), and *Climbing Plants* (1875).

Daudet *(dō dĕ),* **Alphonse** 1840–97. French novelist. *b.* Nîmes. Principal works include *Les Amoureuses* (1858), *Lettres de Mon Moulin* (1866), *Tartarin de Tarascon* (1872), *Let Petit Chose* (1868), *Jack* (1876), *L'Évangéliste* (1883), *L'Immortel* (1888), *Sapho* (1884), and *Le Soutien de Famille* (1898); published the autobiographical *Trente Ans de Paris* (1887) and *Souvenirs d'un Homme de Lettres* (1888); husband of JULIE ALLARD (1847–1940), poet; brother of ERNEST LOUIS MARIE DAUDET (1837–1921), historian and novelist; father of LEON DAUDET, (1867–1942), journalist.

Daumier *(dō myā),* **Honoré** 1808–79. French caricaturist. *b.* Marseilles. Artist on the staff of *La Caricature* and later *Charivari;* also produced nearly 4000 lithographs and 200 canvases, among them *Don Quixote* and *The Third Class Carriage.*

Davenant *(dăv ə nənt),* **Sir William** 1606–68. English poet and dramatist. *b.* Oxford. Began writing for the stage (1628); produced many plays, including the comedy *The Wits* (1633); poet laureate, succeeding Ben Jonson (1638); as a Royalist, imprisoned in the Tower during the Civil War, when he wrote the epic *Gondibert* (1650–52); released through Milton's intercession and in turn saved Milton's life after Restoration; created first opera in England, the *Siege of Rhodes* (1656), in which Mrs. Coleman was the first English actress; founded the Duke of York's Players.

David *(dā vĭd)* *d.* c960 B.C. Second king of Israel (c1000–960 B.C.). *b.* Bethlehem. Son of Jesse of tribe of Judah; at age 18, anointed king of Israel by the prophet Samuel; intimate with King Saul and his son Jonathan; slew the Philistine giant Goliath; outlawed by Saul; lived in cave of Adullam, near Gath; on death of Saul and Jonathan, gathered Judah to his scepter and ruled for seven years; on death of Saul's son, Ishbosheth, became king of all

Israel for 33 years; moved capital to Jerusalem, which he had taken from the Jebusites, and built his palace on its highest hill, Zion; subdued the Philistines, Moabites, Ammonites, Edomites, Amalekites, and the Aramaeans; last years clouded by the rebellion of Absalom and Adonijah; regarded as the sweet singer of Israel and the author of Psalms.

David, Jacques Louis 1748–1825. French painter. *b.* Paris. Founder of French classical school of painting; sympathized with the Revolution and was elected to National Convention (1792); voted for death of Louis XVI; member of the Committee of Public Safety and its artistic director; appointed court painter by Napoleon (1804); exiled to Brussels at the Restoration (1816). Principal works include *The Grief of Andromache, Rape of the Sabines, Coronation of Napoleon I, Leonidas at Thermopylae, The Assassination of Marat, Death of Socrates,* and *Brutus Condemning His Son.*

Davidson *(dā vĭd sən),* **John** 1857–1909. Scottish poet. *b.* Barrhead. Noted as an unconventional poet and playwright. Works include poetry, plays, and novels such as *Fleet Street Eclogues* (1893), *Ballads and Songs* (1894), *Bruce* (1886), *Scaramouch in Naxos* (1890), *Knight of the Maypole* (1903), *Perfervid* (1890), *Mammon and His Message* (1909), and *The Testament of John Davidson* (1908).

Davis *(dā vĭs),* **Jefferson** 1808–89. American statesman; president of the Confederate States of America. *b.* Christian (now Todd) County, Ky. Served in U.S. army (1828–35); member, House of Representatives (1845–46); Senator (1847–51, 1857–61); secretary of war (1853–57); leader of Southern States' Rights Party; asserted that Congress had no right to abolish slavery; resigned from Senate on secession of Miss. (1861); chosen president of Confederate States and inaugurated in Richmond, Va. (1862); faced increasing opposition from extreme States' Righters within the South; on the fall of the Confederacy, fled from Richmond, but was captured at Irwinville, Ga. (1865); imprisoned (until 1867); indicted for treason, but released without trial and granted amnesty (1868). Published *The Rise and Fall of the Confederate Government* (1881).

Davis, John also DAVYS. c1550–1605. English navigator. *b.* Sandridge. Undertook three Arctic voyages (1585–87) in search of Northwest Passage; discovered the Davis Strait; discovered Falkland Islands (1592); killed by pirates near Singapore (1604). Author of *World's Hydrographical Description* (1595) and *The Seaman's Secrets* (1594).

Davisson *(dā vĭ sən),* **Clinton Joseph** 1881–1958. American scientist. *b.* Bloomington, Ill. Engaged in research on electricity, magnetism, and radiant energy at Bell Telephone Laboratories (1917–46); with L. H. Germer, discovered diffraction of electrons by crystals (1927); awarded Nobel Prize in physics with George Paget Thomson (1937).

Davy *(dā vĭ),* **Sir Humphrey** 1778–1829. English chemist. *b.* Penzance. Assistant in Thomas Beddoes's Pneumatic Institute in

Clifton (1798); discovered effects of nitrous oxide (laughing gas); lecturer at Royal Institution, where his eloquence and personality attracted wide attention (1801); published *Elements of Agricultural Chemistry* (1813) and *On Some Chemical Agencies of Electricity* (1806); studied diamonds as carbons, alkalis and rare earths as compound substances, and hydrogen in acids; discovered potassium, sodium, barium, strontium, calcium, chlorine, and magnesium; invented the miner's safety lamp (1815); president of Royal Society (1820). Author of *Elements of Chemical Philosophy* (1812), *On the Safety-Lamp* (1818), and *Salmonia, or Days of Fly-fishing* (1828); collected works (9 vols., 1839–40).

Dawes *(dôz),* **Charles Gates** 1865–1951. American statesman and financier. *b.* Marietta, Ohio. Organized and was president (1902–21) and chairman (1921–25) of Central Trust Company of Chicago; first director of U.S. Bureau of the Budget (1920–21); president of international commission on German reparations which drew up the Dawes Plan (1924); vice president of U.S. (1925–29); U.S. ambassador to Great Britain (1929–32); head of Reconstruction Finance Corporation (1932); awarded the Nobel Peace Prize with Sir Austen Chamberlain (1925). Author of *Notes as Vice-President* (1935).

Daye *(dā),* **Stephen** c1594–1668. American printer. *b.* London. Immigrated to the Colonies (1638); set up printing establishment in Cambridge, Mass., on behalf of the widow of Jesse Glover, a dissenting clergyman; issued a broadside, *Oath of a Freeman (1639), the first piece of printed matter in English North America; published the Bay Psalm Book (1640), regarded as the first English book printed in the New World; business carried on by his son Matthew (1620–49).*

Deakin *(dē kĭn),* **Alfred** 1856–1919. Australian statesman. *b.* Melbourne. Entered Lower House at Victoria (1880); promoted movement toward an Australian federation; member of Federal House of Representatives (1901–1913); prime minister (1903–1904, 1905–1908, 1909–10).

Debussy *(dĕ bü sē),* **Claude Achille** 1862–1918. French composer. *b.* St. Germain-en-Laye. Leader of French musical impressionism; experimented with new harmonic combinations and techniques; compositions include *Pelléas et Mélisande* (1902), *Printemps* (1882), *L'Enfant Prodigue* (1884), *La Demoiselle Élue* (1888), *L'Après-midi d'un Faune* (1894), *Nocturnes* (1893–99), *La Mer* (1903–1905), *Rapsodie* (1905), *Images* (1906–12), piano pieces, preludes, etudes, and the songs *"Clair de Lune"* (1884) and *"Pierrot"* (1884).

Debye *(də bī),* **Peter Joseph Wilhelm** 1884–1966. American physicist. *b.* Maastricht, Netherlands. Director of Kaiser Wilhelm Institute for Physics in Berlin (1935); immigrated to U.S. (1940); head of department of physics at Cornell (1940–66); awarded Nobel Prize in physics (1936) for study of molecular structure; formulated the Debye equation, which relates dielectric constant, dipole moment, and temperature for gases.

Author of *Polar Molecules* (1928) and *Molekulstruktur* (1931).

Decatur *(də kā tər),* **Stephen** 1779–1820. American naval commander. *b.* Sinepuxent, Md. Joined navy as midshipman (1798); gained fame during Tripolitan War (1801–1805) by burning the frigate *Philadelphia,* which had been captured by the enemy; commodore (1810); commanded southeast naval forces in War of 1812; captured British *Macedonian* (1812) but was forced to surrender (1815); taken prisoner but released a month later; in the Algerian War of 1815, forced the dey of Algiers to cease tribute demands; killed in a duel (1820).

Decker, Thomas. *See* **Dekker, Thomas**

Defoe *(də fō),* **Daniel** 1660–1731. English writer. *b.* London. As political pamphleteer, served under four sovereigns (1688–1732); gained favor with William III with *True-Born Englishman* (1701); suffered imprisonment and pillory under Queen Anne for *Shortest Way with Dissenters* (1702); on release from prison, started *The Review,* published thrice weekly (until 1713); undertook secret spy missions promoting union with Scotland (1706–1707); supported Whigs (1708–10), but on Harley's return to power (1710) was back in Tory camp; *Appeal to Honor and Justice* (1715), after Harley's fall, was an apologia for his political ambivalence; began writing fiction (c1719); best-known work was *Robinson Crusoe* (1719), followed by *The Memoirs of a Cavalier* (1720), *Moll Flanders* (1722), *A Journal of the Plague Year* (1722), and *Roxana* (1724); published over 400 books and tracts altogether, written in remarkably simple and direct prose.

Deforest *(də fŏr əst),* **Lee** 1873–1961. American inventor. *b.* Council Bluffs, Iowa. Known as the father of radio for his invention of triple-electrode vacuum tube, the audion, and other fundamental devices; held over 300 patents in the fields of television, sound movies, radiotherapy, and facsimile transmission.

Degas *(dē gä),* **Hilaire Germain Edgar** 1834–1917. French painter. *b.* Paris. One of the leaders of the impressionists; works influenced by Japanese woodcuts and techqniues of photography; early period consists of oils, but later turned to pastels; favorite subjects included ballet dancers, racing scenes, and theater. Best-known paintings are *Miss Lola at the Cirque Fernando, Rehearsal of the Ballet, Dancer Lacing Her Shoe, Dancer at the Bar,* and *Cotton-Broker's Office.*

de Gaulle *(də gōl),* **Charles André Joseph Marie** 1890–1970. French statesman. *b.* Lille. Fought in World War I and took part in defense of Verdun (1916); wrote *Army of the Future* (1940), advocating reorganization of French army with greater emphasis on tanks and air support; brigadier general and undersecretary of state for national defense (1940); on fall of France, became head of Free French National Committee in England (1941); after Allied liberation of Paris, entered the city in triumph (1944); named head of provisional government by Constituent Assembly (1945–46); resigned; organized Rassemblement du Peuple Français (1947) to rally French people to his cause; premier (1958) during Algerian crisis; engineered establishment of Fifth Republic; president (1958) with extraordinary powers; granted independence to all French African colonies, including Algeria; developed an independent French nuclear deterrent; withdrew France from NATO; blocked Britain's entry into Common Market; re-elected president (1965); resigned (1967) when proposed administrative reforms were defeated in a referendum. Wrote *War Memoirs* (3 vols., 1954–59).

Dekker *(děk ər),* **Thomas** also DECKER. c1570–c1632. English dramatist. *b.* London. Prolific Elizabethan playwright, often in collaboration; wrote plays depicting lives of common people. Principal works include *The Shoemaker's Holiday* (1600), *Old Fortunatus* (1600), *Patient Grissel* (1603, with Chettle and Haughton), *The Spanish Moor's Tragedy* (1600, with Day and Haughton), *The Famous History of Sir Thomas Wyat* (1607, with Webster), *The Honest Whore* (1604, with Middleton), *Match Me In London* (1631), *The Witch of Edmonton* (1621, with Ford and Rowley); also published pamphlets.

Delacroix *(də lə krwä),* **Ferdinand Victor Eugène** 1798–1863. French painter. *b.* Charenton. Belonged to Romantic school of painting; rebelled against the academicism of the day, favoring loose drawings and bright, brilliant colors; specialized in historical and dramatic scenes and literary themes from Shakespeare and Tasso. Major works include *Dante and Vergil in Hell, The Massacre at Chios, The Execution of Faliero, Liberty Guiding the People, The Abduction of Rebecca, Algerian Women,* and *The Prisoner of Chillon;* also painted murals in the library of the Chamber of Deputies, in the Louvre, and in the library of the Luxembourg.

de la Mare *(də lə mâr),* **Walter John** 1873–1956. English poet and novelist. *b.* Charlton. Works include *Songs of Childhood* (1902), *The Return* (1910), *Peacock Pie* (1913), *Stuff and Nonsense* (1927), *The Fleeting* (1933), *Early One Morning* (1935), *Memory, and Other Poems* (1938), *Henry Brocken* (1904), *Memoirs of a Midget* (1921), *The Connoisseur* (1926), *On the Edge* (1930), and *The Lord Fish* (1933); also wrote books for children.

Delaroche *(də lȧ rôsh),* **Hippolyte Paul** 1797–1856. French painter. *b.* Paris. Belonged to eclectic school of painting; turned from landscapes to history and portraits; his best-known examples are *Death of Queen Elizabeth* (1827), *Joash Saved From Death by Jehoshabeth* (1822), and *Execution of Lady Jane Grey* (1834); also painted murals in the École des Beaux-Arts (1841).

Delbrück *(děl brük),* **Max** 1906–. American biologist. *b.* in Germany. Immigrated to U.S. (1937); taught at California Institute of Technology (from 1947); awarded Nobel Prize in physiology and medicine (1969) with A. Hershey and S. Luria.

Deledda *(də lěd dä),* **Grazia** 1875–1936. Italian author. *b.* Nuoro, Sardinia. Awarded Nobel Prize in literature (1926); wrote novels dealing with Sardinian life, including *Elias Portoliu* (1903), *L'Edera* (1904), *La Madre* (1920), *La Fuga in Egitto* (1926), and *Annalena Bilsini* (1928).

Delibes *(də lēb),* **Léo** 1836–91. French composer. *b.* St. Germain-du-Val. Composed the operas *Le Roi l'a Dit* (1873), *Jean de Nivelle* (1880), and *Lakmé* (1883), and the ballets *Coppélia* (1870), and *Sylvia ou la Nymphe de Diane* (1876).

Delisle *(də lēl),* **Guillaume** 1675–1726. French geographer. *b.* Paris. As royal geographer he published the first highly accurate world map (1700); considered the founder of modern geography and cartography; brother of JOSEPH NICOLAS DELISLE (1688–1768), founder of the school of astronomy in St. Petersburg and a pioneer in the study of solar coronas.

Delius *(dē lĭ ŭs),* **Frederick** 1862–1934. English composer. *b.* Bradford. Abandoned commercial career as an orange planter in Florida to study music in Leipzig (1886); lived in France (after 1890) and composed *Koanga* (1895–97), *A Village Romeo and Juliet* (1900–1901), *Florida* (1887), *Brigg Fair* (1907), *On Hearing the First Cuckoo in Spring* (1912), *Sea Drift* (1903), *A Mass of Life* (1904–1905), and *Songs of Farewell* (1930), as well as songs, concertos, and chamber music, some composed after he became blind and paralyzed.

De Long *(də lông),* **George Washington** 1844–81. American explorer. *b.* New York, N.Y. Commander of the *Jeannette* on an expedition to reach the North Pole through the Bering Strait (1879); ship trapped and crushed by pack ice (1881); the crew set out in three groups toward Siberia; De Long perished with all members of his group near the mouth of the Lena River.

Democritus *(də mŏk rĭ təs)* known as THE ABDERITE and THE LAUGHING PHILOSOPHER. *fl.* 5th century B.C. Greek philosopher. *b.* Abdera. Visited many countries in Asia and Africa in pursuit of knowledge; gained reputation as one of the most learned men of his day; expounded the mechanistic theory that the universe was composed of indivisible, indestructible, and invisible atoms which combined to form things without design; held that the soul died with the body and that pleasure was the sole end of ethics; only a few fragments of his work survive.

Democritus Junior. *See* **Burton, Robert**

De Morgan *(də môr gən),* **Augustus** 1806–71. English mathematician and logician. *b.* Madura, India. Professor of mathematics at University College, London (1828–31, 1836–66); developed formal or Aristotelian logic; discovered De Morgan's theorem; wrote extensively on mathematics and logic, including *Essay on Probabilities* (1838), *Formal Logic* (1847), *Trigonometry and Double Algebra* (1849), and *Budget of Paradoxes* (1872).

Demosthenes *(də mŏs thə nēz)* c383–322 B.C. Greek orator and statesman. *b.* Paeania. Entered public life as constitutional lawyer; member of popular assembly (355); as leader of the anti-Macedonian party, delivered a series of orations (the *Olynthiacs* and the *Philippics)* against the expansionist policies of Philip; member of the embassy which negotiated peace of Philocratus with Philip; when war broke out (340), sent Athenian fleet to the relief of Byzantium; during Amphictyonic War, persuaded Athenians to form alliance with Thebes, but allies were overwhelmed at Battle of Chaeronea (338); led unsuccessful rising on death of Philip (336); accused of embezzling money belonging to Alexander of Macedon in the Athenian state treasury; condemned (324) and forced into exile; recalled on death of Alexander (323) to lead another rising against Macedonians; fled into second exile when Antipater and Craterus captured Athens after Battle of Crannon (322); at Caluria took poison to avoid capture. Other major orations include *On the Peace, On the Embassy, On the Affairs of the Chersonese,* and *On the Crown.*

Denis *(də nē),* **Maurice** 1870–1943. French artist. *b.* Granville. Belonged to symbolist school of painting known as Nabis; inspired by religious painting of the Renaissance, founded the Studios of Sacred Art (1919). Author of *Théories* (1913), *Nouvelles Théories* (1921), and *Histoire de l'Art Religieux* (1939). Best-known paintings include *Descent from the Cross, Homage to Cézanne, Virgin and Child, Promenade,* and *Head of a Woman.*

De Quincey *(də kwĭn sĭ),* **Thomas** 1785–1859. English writer. *b.* Manchester. Contributed nearly 200 articles on many subjects to contemporary literary periodicals, such as *Blackwood's Magazine, Tait's Magazine,* and *London Magazine;* published only two books; addicted to opium at an early age and recorded his experiences in *Confessions of an English Opium Eater* (1821); other pieces of merit are *On Murder Considered as One of the Fine Arts, The English Mail Coach, The Spanish Military Nun, Suspiria De Profundis, Vision of Sudden Death,* and *Collected Writings* (14 vols., 1889–90).

Derby, Earl of. *See* **Stanley, Edward George Geoffrey Smith**

Derzhavin *(dyər zhä vyĭn),* **Gavriil Romanovich** 1743–1816. Russian poet. *b.* Kazan. Poet laureate at court of Catherine II; secretary of state (1791); imperial treasurer (1800); minister of justice (1802). Best-known poems include *Ode to God, Monody on Prince Mestcherski,* and *The Taking of Warsaw.*

Descartes *(dā kärt),* **René** 1596–1650. French philosopher. *b.* La Haye. After several years of military service and travel, settled in Holland, pursuing studies in philosophy and mathematics; established modern rationalist philosophy by extending a mathematical approach to metaphysical investigations; rejected scholasticism and based speculation on reason and the certitude of the mind as demonstrated in the dictum *Cogito, ergo sum* (I think, therefore I am); postulated mind/body dualism mediated by God; expounded system in *Discours de la Méthode* (1637), *Meditationes de Prima Philosophia* (1641), *Principia Philosophiae* (1644), *Traité des Passions de l'Âme* (1649), and *De l'Homme* (1664); made important contributions to mathematics; originated Cartesian coordinates and Cartesian curves, and founded analytical geometry; went to Sweden on invitation of Queen Christina and died of pneumonia five months later (1650).

Desmoulins *(dā mōō lăN),* **Camille** full name: LUCIE SIMPLICE CAMILLE BENOIT DESMOULINS; called PROCUREUR DE LA LANTERNE. 1760–94. French revolutionary leader. *b.* Guise. Incited crowds to storm the Bastille (1789), beginning the Revolution; wrote *Discours de la Lanterne aux Parisiens, La Philosophie au Peuple Français* (1788), and *La France Libre* as the spokesman of extreme republicanism; founding member of Cordeliers Club and published the revolutionary organs *Tribune des Patriotes* and *Révolutions de France et de Brabant* (1789–91); allied himself with Mirabeau and Danton; as member of National Convention led attack on Girondists with *Histoire des Brissotins;* joined Danton in urging moderation (1793); published *Vieux Cordelier* against Jacobins; arrested with Danton, and after a mock trial, was guillotined.

de Soto *(də sō tō),* **Hernando** also FERNANDO. c1496–1542. Spanish explorer. *b.* Jerez de los Caballeros. Accompanied Dávila to Darien and Pizarro to Peru; commissioned by Charles V to conquer Florida; governor of Cuba (1537); landed near Charlotte Bay on Florida coast with 1000 men (1539); lured by reports of gold, marched through southeast America fighting with Indians; discovered Mississippi River (1541); turned back after reaching Oklahoma; died on west bank of the Mississippi.

Dessalines *(dā să lēn),* **Jean Jacques** 1758–1806. Emperor of Haiti (1804–1806). *b.* Grande Rivière. Slave of a French planter whose name he assumed; joined insurrection of 1791; second in command to Toussaint L'Ouverture; subdued by Charles Leclerc (1802); headed another revolt with British aid (1803) and established a republic; governor general for life; emperor with title Jean Jacques I (1804); alienated followers by acts of savage cruelty; assassinated by Henri Christophe, who succeeded him.

de Valera *(dĕv ə lâr ə),* **Eamon** 1882–1975. Irish statesman. *b.* New York, N. Y. Commandant in Easter Uprising (1916); arrested and condemned to life imprisonment; released but arrested again (1918); escaped from prison and fled to U.S.; president of Sinn Fein (1917–26); president of Irish Volunteers (1917–21); president of Dáil Éireann (1919–20); resigned the latter and led opposition to Anglo-Irish Treaty (1921); formed (1924) Fianna Fáil, a party of militant Republicans; brought his party into Free State parliament (1927); won election (1932); president of executive council and minister of external affairs (1932–37); prime minister (1937–48); kept Ireland neutral during World War II; defeated (1948); prime minister (1951–54, 1957–59); resigned to accept presidency (1959); re-elected (1966); retired (1973).

de Vere *(də vēr),* **Aubrey Thomas** 1814–1902. Irish poet. *b.* Curragh Chase. Joined Catholic Church (1851); intimate with Browning and Tennyson; wrote numerous works on medieval lore and Irish history. Author of *Waldenses* (1842), *Poems: Sacred and Miscellaneous* (1854), *Legends of St.*

Patrick (1872), *St. Thomas of Canterbury* (1876), *Legends and Records of the Church and Empire* (1877), *Critical Essays* (3 vols. 1887–89), and *Recollections* (1897).

Devereux *(dĕv ə ro͞o),* **Robert** title: EARL OF ESSEX. 1566–1601. English statesman. *b.* Netherwood. As general of the horse, won spurs at Zutphen (1586); principal courtier of Queen Elizabeth (from 1588); commander of English forces sent to aid Henry of Navarre against the League (1591–92); captured Cadiz (1596) but unsuccessful against the Azores (1597–98); created earl marshal (1598); appointed lord lieutenant and governor general of Ireland (1599); aroused queen's ire by making truce with Hugh O'Neill, Earl of Tyrone, following defeat at Arklow; without authorization, returned to England to defend actions; stripped of offices; conspired with Charles Blount, Baron Mountjoy, and Henry Wriothesley against the queen; captured, tried for treason, and executed (1601); distinguished as a patron of letters and as a sonneteer.

De Vries *(də vrēs),* **David Pietersen** c1592–c1655. Dutch colonizer in America. *b.* La Rochelle, France. Partner in Dutch West India Company, which established a colony in Delaware; made several voyages to New World (1631, 1632–33, 1634–36, 1638–44); wrote an account of his travels in *Korte Historiael . . .* (1655); founded a Dutch colony on Staten Island and another near Tappan.

De Vries, Hugo 1848–1935. Dutch botanist. *b.* Haarlem. As professor at Amsterdam (1878–1918), continued Mendel's work on mutation in plants. Author of *Die Mutationstheorie* (1900–1903), *Plant Breeding* (1907), and other books.

Dewar *(dū ər),* **Sir James** 1842–1923. Scottish chemist. *b.* Kincardine-on-Forth. Professor of experimental philosophy at Cambridge (1875–1923) and of chemistry at Royal Institution (1877–1923); best known for inventing the Dewar flask, a container designed to keep liquid hot or cold; with Frederick Abel, discovered cordite; conducted important research into properties of matter at low temperatures; produced liquid and solid hydrogen and devised techniques for liquefying gases.

Dewey *(dū ĭ),* **John** 1859–1952. American educational philosopher. *b.* Burlington, Vt. Professor, University of Michigan (1884–88, 1889–94), Minnesota (1888–89), Chicago (1894–1904), and Columbia (1904–30); advocated progressive education based on students' needs and motivations, which led to entire system of education; in philosophy reformulated pragmatism in his theory of instrumentalism. Principal works include *Psychology* (1886), *School and Society* (1899), *Studies in Logical Theory* (1903) *How We Think* (1909), *Democracy and Education* (1916), *Reconstruction in Philosophy* (1920), *The Quest for Certainty* (1929), *Art as Experience* (1934), *Logic* (1938), and *Problems of Man* (1946).

Dewey, Melvil 1851–1931. American librarian. *b.* Adams Center, N.Y. Chief librarian at Columbia (1883–88), director of New York

State Library (1889–1906) and Library School in Albany (1887–1906); founded and edited *Library Journal* (1876–81) and *Library Notes* (1886–98); secretary of Spelling Reform Associaton (from 1876); promoted simplified spelling, using it in his works; helped found American Library Association (1876); developed Dewey Decimal System of book classification in *A Classification and Subject Index for Cataloguing and Arranging the Books and Pamphlets of a Library* (1876) and was instrumental in its adoption by American libraries.

De Witt *(də vĭt),* **Jan** 1625–72. Dutch statesman. *b.* Dordrecht, Leader of republican (oligarchic) party; strove to abolish office of the stadholder and adopted a policy of opposition to House of Orange; elected Grand Pensionary of Holland (1653); negotiated treaty with Cromwell that ended Anglo-Dutch War (1652–54); led Netherlands to victory in second Anglo-Dutch War (1665–67), concluded by peace of Breda; strengthened national finances and established Dutch commercial and maritime supremacy; procured passage of the Perpetual Edict depriving House of Orange of all offices (1667); negotiated Triple Alliance with England and Sweden against Louis XIV (1668); on invasion of United Provinces by France, forced to resign office; lynched with brother Cornelius (1623–72) by a mob at The Hague.

Diaghilev *(dyä gyĭ lyĕf),* **Sergei Pavlovich** 1872–1929. Russian ballet impresario. *b.* Perm. Editor of *Mir Iskousstva,* an art journal; joined Imperial Russian Theater, and, with Fokine and Bakst, produced ballets and operas distinguished by innovations in music, scenery, and costumes; founded the *Ballet Russe* company (1909), which triumphantly toured cities in Europe and America; associated with such great artists as Nijinsky, Stravinsky, Pavlova, Massine, Karsavina, Lifar, and Tchelichev.

Dias *(dē äsh),* **Bartholomeu** also Diaz. c1450–1500. Portuguese navigator. Placed in command of two vessels by King John II of Portugal (1486); sailed around southern Africa, following the coast to Algoa Bay; forced to turn back by disaffected sailors; discovered Table Mountain and the Cape of Good Hope, named by King John; accompanied da Gama's expedition (1497) to Cape Verde Islands; commander under Pedro Cabral, the discoverer of Brazil, but perished in a storm (1500).

Díaz *(dē äs),* **José de la Cruz Porfirio** 1830–1915. Mexican statesman. *b.* Oaxaca. Fought in Mexican War (1846–48), War of the Reform (1858–60) under Benito Juárez, and in successful struggle against Emperor Maximilian (1863–67); opposed President Juárez and his successor Sebastián Lerdo de Tejada; ousted the latter (1876) and installed himself as provisional president (1876–77); elected president (1877); reelected seven times (1884–1911); administration marked by economic prosperity and peace but lack of social progress; resigned office under pressure from Francisco Madero, Emiliano Zapata, and Pancho Villa; died in exile in Paris.

Dibelius *(də bā lĭ o͞os),* **Martin** 1883–1947. German theologian. *b.* Dresden. Professor of New Testament theology at University of Heidelberg (from 1915); one of the leaders of Formgeschichte school of theology. Author of *Die Geisterwelt im Glauben des Paulus* (1909), *Die Formgeschichte des Evangeliums* (1919), *Jesus* (1939), and *The Sermon on the Mount* (1940).

Dickens *(dĭk ĕnz),* **Charles John Huffam** 1812–70. English writer. *b.* Portsmouth. Spent childhood in poverty; after some schooling, served as an attorney's clerk, a reporter in House of Commons, and reporter for the *Morning Chronicle* (1835); published first book, *Sketches by Boz* (1836); followed with *Pickwick Papers* (1836); after establishing literary reputation, toured America (1842, 1867–68), Italy (1844–45), and Switzerland (1846); edited *Bentley's Miscellany* and published *Household Words* (1850) and *All the Year Round* (1859). Principal works include *Oliver Twist* (1837–39), *Nicholas Nickleby* (1836–39), *American Notes* (1842), *A Christmas Carol* (1843), *Martin Chuzzlewit* (1843–44), *Dombey and Son* (1846–48), *David Copperfield* (1849–50), *Bleak House* (1852–53), *A Tale of Two Cities* (1859), *Great Expectations* (1860–61), *Our Mutual Friend* (1864–65), and *Mystery of Edwin Drood* (unfinished, 1870); works characterized by humor, idealism, directness, and a deep sympathy for the downtrodden.

Dickinson *(dĭk ĭn sən),* **Emily Elizabeth** 1830–86. American poet. *b.* Amherst, Mass. Spent life in seclusion at Amherst; wrote over 1500 short and intensely personal poems, only seven of which were published during her lifetime; recognized as a fine original poet with the posthumous publication of *Poems* (1890, 1891, 1896), *Further Poems* (1929), *Unpublished Poems* (1936), *Poems: Centenary Edition* (1930), *The Single Hound* (1914), and *Bolts of Melody* (1945); work characterized by spiritual melancholy, extensive use of paradox, and metrical innovation.

Diderot *(dē drō),* **Denis** 1713–84. French encyclopedist. *b.* Langres. Began as a tutor and hack writer (1734–44) while studying science, language, and art; translated Robert James's *Dictionnaire Universel de Médicine, de Chimie, de Botanique* (6 vols., 1746–48); entrusted by Le Breton with the task of editing (with d'Alembert) an enlarged version of Chambers's *Cyclopaedia* (1751); headed project successfully (1751–72) and completed it in 35 volumes entitled *Encyclopédie, ou Dictionnaire Raisonné des Sciences, des Arts, et des Métiers;* work infused with spirit of the Enlightenment and the rationalism and skepticism of the philosophes; pioneered in art criticism in *Salons;* received financial support from Catherine II of Russia and visited Russia (1773–74) at her invitation; other works include plays, philosophical tracts, and letters.

Diefenbaker *(dē fən bā kər),* **John George** 1895–. Canadian statesman. *b.* Normanby. Entered Federal House of Commons (1940); leader of Progressive Conservative party (1956); prime minister (1957–63).

Diels *(dēls),* **Otto Paul Hermann** 1876–1954. German chemist. *b.* Hamburg. Professor of chemistry at University of Berlin (1904–16) and University of Kiel (1916–48); developed (1928), with Kurt Alder, a method of synthesizing benzene ring hydrocarbons, known as diene synthesis or Diels-Alder reaction; shared Nobel Prize in chemistry (1950) with Alder.

Diesel *(dē zəl),* **Rudolf** 1858–1913. German automobile engineer. *b.* Paris, France. Patented (1893) an internal combustion engine, known as Diesel engine, that could run on cheap crude oil; developed the engine in association with Friedrich Krupp and exhibited it in Munich (1898); established factory in Augsburg for producing Diesel engines (1899). Author of *The Theory and Construction of a Rational Heat Motor* (1893).

Diocletian *(dī ō klē shən)* full name: Gaius Aurelius Valerius Diocletianus; surname: jovius. 245–313. Emperor of Rome (284–305). *b.* Dioclea, Dalmatia. Proclaimed emperor by army at Chalcedon on death of Numerianus (284); adopted Maximian as co-emperor and later Galerius and Constantius Chlorus as subordinate associates called "Caesars"; divided empire into four regions, retaining Thrace, Egypt, Syria, and Asia as his provinces, with Nicomedia as capital; persecuted Christians throughout empire (303–13); restored tranquillity throughout his dominions; abdicated with Maximian and retired to Salona in Dalmatia.

Diogenes *(dī ŏj ə nēz)* c412–323 B.C. Greek Cynic philosopher. *b.* Sinope, Asia Minor. Went to Athens as a youth; studied under Antisthenes; practiced extreme asceticism; attracted considerable attention by his eccentricities, including living in a tub and once going out in broad daylight with a lighted lamp, looking for an honest man.

Dirac *(dĭ răc),* **Paul Adrien Maurice** 1902–. English physicist. *b* Bristol. Professor of mathematics at Cambridge (from 1932); shared, with Erwin Schrodinger, Nobel Prize in physics (1933) for work on quantum mechanics. Author of *Principles of Quantum Mechanics* (1930).

Disney *(dĭz nē),* **Walt** 1901–66. American animated-film producer. *b.* Chicago, Ill. Began as commercial artist; went to Hollywood and produced animated motion-picture cartoons including *Snow White and the Seven Dwarfs* (1937), *Pinocchio* (1940), *Fantasia* (1940), *Dumbo* (1941), *Bambi* (1942), *Lady and the Tramp* (1955), and *Sleeping Beauty* (1959); created cartoon characters that are part of American culture, such as Mickey Mouse and Donald Duck; later produced animal and nature films; created Disneyland, a fantastic amusement park, in Calif. (1955), and Disney World in Fla. (1971).

Disraeli *(dĭz rā lĭ),* **Benjamin** title: Earl of Beaconsfield; nickname: Dizzy. 1804–81. British statesman and author. *b.* London. Son of Isaac D'Israeli (1766–1848), a Jewish man of letters who baptized his four sons into the Anglican Church. After four unsuccessful elections, entered Parliament (1837) on Conservative ticket; leader of Young England Tories; supported Corn Laws and brought down Peel ministry for repealing them (1846); chancellor of exchequer (1852, 1858–59, 1866–68); carried Reform Bill of 1867, enfranchising all ratepayers; succeeded Derby as premier (1868); resigned after general election (1868); prime minister (1874–80); pursued aggressive foreign policy; annexed Fiji and the Transvaal (1874, 1877); warred against the Afghans and Zulus (1878–79); purchased controlling share of Suez Canal stock (1875); had Queen Victoria named Empress of India; elevated to peerage as Earl of Beaconsfield (1876); at Congress of Berlin (1878), obtained Cyprus and reduced Russian ambitions and Turkish territories; gained literary reputation with *Vivian Grey* (1826), *Coningsby* (1844), *Sybil* (1846), *Henrietta Temple* (1837), *Venetia* (1837), *Tancred* (1847), and other books and novels.

Dodgson, Charles Lutwidge. *See* **Carroll, Lewis**

Doisy *(doi zĭ),* **Edward Albert** 1893–. American biochemist. *b.* Hume, Ill. Head of department of biochemistry at St. Mary's Hospital, St. Louis (from 1924); conducted research on blood buffers; isolated vitamin K and the sex hormones theelol, theelin, and dihydrotheelin; synthesized vitamin K_1; awarded Nobel Prize in medicine with Henrik Dam (1943).

Dolci *(dōl chē),* **Danilo** 1925–. Italian social leader. *b.* Trieste. Devoted life to helping Sicilian poor by adopting Gandhian techniques of nonviolence and self-help; opposed by the government and the Mafia in his efforts to gain justice and better living standards for landless peasants. Author of *To Feed the Hungry* (1959); known as the Sicilian Gandhi.

Dole *(dōl),* **Sanford Ballard** 1844–1926. American statesman. *b.* Honolulu. Son of a missionary; elected to Hawaiian legislature (1884, 1886); led Bayonet Revolution (1887) which helped establish constitutional monarchy; associate justice of supreme court (until 1893); on the overthrow of Queen Liliuokalani (1893), chosen head of revolutionary provisional government; president, Republic of Hawaii (1894–98); on U.S. annexation of Hawaii first governor of Territory of Hawaii (1900–1903); judge of U.S. district court for Hawaii (1904–15).

Döllinger *(dûl ĭng ər),* **Johann Joseph Ignaz von** 1799–1890. German theologian and leader of Old Catholic movement. *b.* Bamberg. Professor of ecclesiastical history and canon law at University of Munich (1826–71); ordained Catholic priest (1822); staunch defender of papal supremacy (until 1857); excommunicated (1871) for opposition to decree of papal infallibility; summoned Congress of Munich, where Old Catholic Church was created. Author of *Kirche und Kirchen* (1861), *Papsttum und Kirchenstaat* (1861), *Papstfabeln des Mittelalters* (1863), *Die Reformation* (1846–48), *Akademische Vorträge* (1888–91), and other books.

Dolomieu *(dô lô myû),* **Déodat Guy Silvain Tancrède Gratet de** 1750–1801. French geologist and mineralogist. *b.* Dolomieu. First described the mineral dolomite, named after him (1791); accompanied Bonaparte on expedition to

Egypt (1798); conducted research on volcanic rocks. Author of *Philosophie Minéralogique* (1802) and other books.

Domagk *(dō mäk),* **Gerhard** 1895–1964. German chemist. *b.* Brandenburg. Director of I. G. Farben's research institute in Elberfeld (from 1927); demonstrated antibacterial properties of prontosil, forerunner of sulfa drugs; awarded Nobel Prize in medicine and physiology (1939), but declined the honor on Nazi directive.

Domenichino, Il *(ēl dō mā nē kē nō)* original name: DOMENICO ZAMPIERI. 1581–1641. Italian painter. *b.* Bologna, Italy. Belonged to the baroque classicist school of Lodovico Carracci; worked at Bologna, Rome, and Naples. Principal works include *Communion of St. Jerome, Diana and Her Nymphs, Adam and Eve, Saint Cecilia, Martyrdom of Saint Agnes,* and *Madonna of the Rosary.*

Dominic *(dŏm ĭ nĭk),* **Saint** original name: DOMINGO DE GUZMÁN. 1170–1221. Spanish friar. *b.* Calaruega. Canon of cathedral of Osma (1194); preached in Languedoc against the Albigenses (from 1204); founded Dominican order in Toulouse (1215); at the fourth Lateran Council (1216) received authorization for the order from Pope Honorius III; appointed *Magister Sacri Palatii* (Master of the Sacred Palace); canonized (1234). Feast day: Aug. 4.

Domitian *(dō mĭsh ən)* full name: TITUS FLAVIUS DOMITIANUS AUGUSTUS. 51–96. Third Flavian emperor of Rome (81–96). *b.* Rome. Succeeded brother Titus (81); built boundary wall between the Danube and the Rhine following successful war against the Chatti (83); suffered setbacks against the Dacians and Marcomanni (86–90); became despotic and cruel; assassinated by Stephanus in conspiracy with the empress Domitia.

Donatello *(dŏn ā tĕl ō)* real name: DONATO DI NICCOLÒ DI BETTO BARDI. c1386–1466. Italian sculptor. *b.* Florence. Worked at Rome, Padua, and Florence; considered one of the greatest artists of Renaissance and the founder of modern sculpture; invented the technique of shallow relief known as schiacciato. Principal works in Florence include *Zuccone, St. Peter, St. Mark, St. George and the Dragon, St. John the Evangelist, Magdalen,* and *Angel with Tambourine.*

Donatus *(dō nā tŭs)* known as THE GREAT. *fl.* 4th century. Bishop of Carthage (from 315). Elected by Christian Donatists in opposition to the Traditores (who escaped the Diocletian persecution by handing sacred books over to Roman persecutors); the Donatists, a schismatic group, held that the validity of the sacraments depended on the worthiness of the minister.

Donizetti *(dŏn ĭ zĕt ĭ),* **Gaetano** 1797–1848. Italian composer. *b.* Bergamo. Composed over 65 operas, including *Anna Bolena* (1830), *L'Elisir d'Amore* (1832), *Lucia di Lammermoor* (1835), *Lucrezia Borgia* (1834), *la Favorita* (1840), *La Fille du Régiment* (1840), and *Don Pasquale* (1843); works characterized by a wealth of melody.

Donne *(dŭn),* **John** 1573–1631. English poet. *b.* London. Abandoned Roman Catholicism and embraced Anglican Church; went on expeditions under Earl of Essex (1596, 1597) to Cadiz and Azores; court career as secretary to Thomas Egerton, lord keeper of privy seal, ended (1601) because of his clandestine marriage to Egerton's niece; gained favor of James I with *Pseudo-Martyr* (1610); received holy orders (1614); successively, royal chaplain, reader at Lincoln's Inn, and dean of St. Paul's (1621); gained fame as a preacher. Works include *Songs and Sonnets, Satires, Elegies, An Anatomy of the World* (1611); *Of the Progress of the Soul,* (1612), *Biothanatos* (1644), *Divine Poems* (1607), *Epithalamium* (1613), *Cycle of Holy Sonnets* (1618), and *Devotions* (1623); considered the greatest metaphysical poet; poetry characterized by wit, emotion, paradox, and imagery.

Doppler *(dōp lər),* **Christian Johann** 1803–53. Austrian scientist. *b.* Salzburg, Germany. Discovered principle known as the Doppler effect, which explains shifts in frequency when a source of sound or light vibration is approaching or receding from the observer (1842); Fizeau developed the Doppler Shift (1848) from this principle to explain the motions of stars and nebulae in an expanding universe.

Doré *(dô rā),* **Paul Gustave** 1833–83. French artist. *b.* Strasbourg. Illustrated books by Rabelais and others, including *The Wandering Jew* and *Contes Drolatiques de Balzac (1856), Don Quixote* (1863), the *Bible* (1865–66), *Paradise Lost* (1866), Tennyson's *Idylls of the King* (1867–68), La Fontaine's *Fables* (1867), and Dante's *Divine Comedy* (1861, 1868).

Doria *(dô ryä),* **Andrea** 1468–1560. Genoese admiral and statesman. *b.* Oneglia, Italy. As captain general of the galleys (from 1513), commanded Genoese fleet that defeated Turkish corsairs off Pianosa (1519); sided with Francis V (1524–28); transferred allegiance to Charles V (1528); liberated Genoa from the French, and set up independent republic under an aristocratic government; active in imperial campaigns against Turks; victorious at Patras (1532) and Tunis (1535); defeated by Turks at Algiers (1541) and Jerba (1560); forced to flee Genoa by Fieschi conspiracy (1547), but returned to regain power.

Dorr *(dôr),* **Thomas Wilson** 1805–54. American reformer. *b.* Providence, R. I. Entered R. I. Assembly (1834); leader of People's party, a reform movement for extending the franchise; drafted liberal constitution approved by a majority of state voters (1840); established parallel government claiming popular mandate; when followers were imprisoned by legal government, led 234 men ("Dorr's Rebellion") in an unsuccessful attack on Providence arsenal (1842); arrested, tried for treason, convicted, sentenced to hard labor for life, but released (1845) under general amnesty.

Dos Passos *(dŭs păs ŭs),* **John Roderigo** 1896–1970. American writer. *b.* Chicago, Ill. Works include *One Man's Initiation* (1919), *Three Soldiers* (1921), *Manhattan Transfer* (1925), *The 42nd Parallel* (1930), *1919* (1932), *The Big Money* (1936), *Adventures of a Young Man* (1939), *Number One* (1943), and *Chosen Country* (1951)

Dostoevski *(dŭ stŭ yăf skĭ),* **Fyodor Mikhailovich** 1821–81. Russian writer. *b.* Moscow. Left army career for literature (1844); published *Poor Folk* (1846); joined Petrashevski revolutionary group; arrested (1849), sentenced to death, and reprieved at the last moment; exiled to Siberia; pardoned (1859) and permitted to return to St. Petersburg; founded reviews *The Times* and *Epoch* which both failed; beset by epilepsy, financial worries, and gambling, but wrote some of the world's greatest literature, including *The Double* (1846), *Netochka Nezvanova* (1849), *Friend of the Family* (1859), *The House of the Dead* (1861), *The Insulted and the Injured* (1872), *Notes from the Underground* (1864), *Crime and Punishment* (1866), *The Gambler* (1866), *The Idiot* (1868–69), *The Eternal Husband* (1871), *The Possessed* (1871), *A Raw Youth* (1875), and *The Brothers Karamazov* (1880). Works characterized by Slavophilism, compassion, faith in Russian Orthodoxy, and psychological insights into abnormal human behavior; *Letters and Reminiscences* (translated 1923); achieved journalistic success with *Diary of a Writer* (founded 1876).

Doughty *(dou tĭ),* **Charles Montague** 1843–1926. English writer and traveler. *b.* Theberton Hall. Known principally for *Travels in Arabia Deserta* (1888); other minor works include *The Dawn in Britain* (1906), *Adam Cast Forth* (1908), *The Cliffs* (1909), *The Clouds* (1912), *The Titans* (1916), and *Mansoul* (1920).

Douglas *(dŭg ləs),* **Stephen Arnold** 1813–61. American statesman. *b.* Brandon, Vt. House of Representatives (1843–47); Senator (1847–61); supported principle of each state's deciding the question of slavery (known as popular or squatter sovereignty) in Kansas-Nebraska Bill (1854); broke away from pro-slavery wing of Democratic party; debated with Lincoln (1858); presidential candidate of northern Democrats (1860), but lost to Lincoln; supported Lincoln during Civil War.

Doumergue *(dōō mĕrg),* **Gaston** 1863–1937. French statesman. *b.* Aigues-Vives. Deputy (1893–1910); senator (1910–24, from 1931); premier (1913–14); president of Senate (1920–24); president of French Republic (1924–31); premier during Stavisky scandal (1934).

Doyle *(doil),* **Sir Arthur Conan** 1859–1930. British writer. *b.* Edinburgh, Scotland. Creator of fictional detective Sherlock Holmes, introduced in *A Study in Scarlet* (1887), and later appearing in *The Sign of the Four* (1889), *Adventures of Sherlock Holmes* (1891), *The Memoirs of Sherlock Holmes* (1893), *The Hound of the Baskervilles* (1902), *Return of Sherlock Holmes* (1904), *The Last Bow* (1917), and *The Casebook of Sherlock Holmes* (1917); other books included *Micah Clarke* (1888), *The White Company* (1890), and *A History of Spiritualism* (2 vols., 1929).

Drake *(drāk),* **Sir Francis** c1540–96. English navigator. *b.* Crowndale. Related to Sir John Hawkins, under whom he commanded the *Judith* (1567–68) on ill-fated expedition to Mexico; as commissioned privateer, led marauding expeditions against Spanish (1570–72); seized Nombre de Dios on Isthmus of Panama, burned Porto Bello, and crossed isthmus to reach Pacific shore (1572); started out to explore strait of Magellan (1577) with five vessels and 166 men; flagship *Golden Hind* separated from others by storm during passage through the Strait; plundered Spanish treasure ships and settlements on Pacific coast of South America; touched California coast, which he named New Albion and claimed for Queen Elizabeth; sailed across the Pacific and Indian Oceans, arrived in Plymouth (1580), completing first English circumnavigation of the world; knighted; on outbreak of war with Spain, commanded 25 ships (1585); took Santiago in Cape Verde Islands, Santo Domingo, Cartagena, and St. Augustine; burned 33 Spanish ships at Cadiz (1587); seized a rich Portuguese ship off the Azores; as vice-admiral under Lord Charles Howard, helped destroy Spanish Armada (1588); died on voyage from Plymouth to West Indies (1595).

Drayton *(drā tən),* **Michael** 1563–1631. English poet. *b.* Hartshill. Works include *Idea; The Shepherd's Garland* (1593), *Idea's Mirror* (1594), *The Baron's Wars* (1603), *England's Heroical Epistles* (1597), *Poems Lyric and Pastoral* (1606), *Polyolbion* (1622), *Nymphidia,* (1627), and *The Muses' Elysium* (1630).

Dreyfus *(drā fŭs),* **Alfred** 1859–1935. French soldier. *b.* Mülhausen. Artillery captain in French army; charged (1893–94) with treason in the *cause célèbre* known as the Dreyfus Affair; court-martialed, convicted, and imprisoned; conviction condemned as act of anti-Semitism by Zola in *J'Accuse* (1898); re-tried at Rennes (1899), condemned to ten years' imprisonment, but pardoned; completely exonerated by court of appeals (1906); restored to military rank and decorated with Legion of Honor; later fought in World War I, becoming brigadier general.

Drummond *(drŭm ənd),* **Sir Eric Henry** title: Earl of Perth, Viscount Strathallan. 1876–1951. British diplomat. *b.* Fulford. Entered foreign office (1900); secretary to various ministers (1908–19); first secretary general of League of Nations (1919–33); ambassador to Italy (1933–39).

Dryden *(drī dən),* **John** 1631–1700. English poet and dramatist. *b.* Northamptonshire. Panegyrized Cromwell in *Heroic Stanzas on the Death of Oliver Cromwell* (1659); joined Royalists after Restoration; celebrated accession of Charles II with *Astrea Redux* (1660) and *Panegyric on the Coronation* (1661); for next 20 years wrote heroic verse plays: *The Rival Ladies* (1663), *The Indian Queen* (1664), *The Indian Emperor* (1665), *Tyrannic Love* (1669), *Marriage à la Mode* (1673), *Amboyna* (1673), *All for Love* (1678), and *The Spanish Fryar* (1681): poet laureate and historiographer royal (1670); turned to satire against Whigs with *Absalom and Achitophel* (1681), *The Medal* (1682), and *MacFlecknoe* (1684); supported Anglicanism in *Religio Laici* (1682); converted to Roman Catholicism (1685) and published *The Hind and the Panther,* an apologia of the Catholic faith; other works include *Annus Mirabilis* (1667), *Essay of Dramatic Poesy* (1668), adaptations of Shakespeare, Milton, Chaucer, and Boccaccio, translations of Vergil, Juvenal, and Perseus, and *Fables, Ancient and Modern* (1699).

Du Barry *(dü bär ē),* **Comtesse** original name: MARIE JEANNE BÉCU. 1746–93. French adventuress. *b.* Vaucoleurs. Illegitimate daughter of a seamstress; went to Paris (1762); mistress of Jean, Comte du Barry (1764–68); mistress of Louis XV (1768–74); gained title through marriage to Guillaume, brother of Jean; influential at court, aided by duc d'Aiguillon; retired from court on death of Louis (1774); arrested by Jacobins (1793); condemned and guillotined by Revolutionary Tribunal.

Du Bois *(dōō bois),* **William Edward Burghardt** 1868–1963. American civil rights leader and author. *b.* Great Barrington, Mass. Professor of economics and history at Atlanta University (1896–1910); editor of *Crisis,* organ of NAACP (1910–32); professor of sociology at Atlanta (1932–44); editor of *Phylon Quarterly Review* (1940–44), *Studies of the Negro Problem* (1897–1911), and *Encyclopedia of the Negro* (1933–45). Author of *The Suppression of the Slave Trade* (1896), *John Brown* (1909), *The Negro* (1915), *Black Reconstruction* (1935), *Color and Democracy* (1945), *The World and Africa* (1947), and other books; advocated civil, political, and economic equality for blacks; active in Pan African Congresses; joined Communist party (1961).

Duccio di Buoninsegna *(dōōt chō dē bwô nēn sā nyä)* **c1260–c1320.** Italian painter. Founded Sienese school of painting; best known for altarpiece in cathedral of Siena; other works include *Annunciation, Christ Healing the Blind Man,* and *The Transfiguration.*

Duchamp *(dü shäN),* **Marcel** 1887–1968. French painter. *b.* Blainville. Brother of JACQUES VILLON (pseudonym of GASTON DUCHAMP), 1875–1963, French artist and engraver, and RAYMOND DUCHAMP-VILLON, 1876–1918, French cubist painter. A pioneer of dadaism; later associated with cubism, futurism, and surrealism; settled in U.S. (1924); editor of American art magazine *VVV* (1942–44). Principal works include *Coffee-Mill* (1911), *Nude Descending a Staircase* (1912), and *The Bride Stripped Bare by Her Bachelors, Even* (1915–23). Author of *Green Box* (1933).

Duchenne *(dü shĕn),* **Guillaume Benjamin Amand** 1806–1875. French physician. *b.* Boulogne. Pioneer in electrophysiology; founder of electrotherapeutics and neuropathology; first to describe locomotor ataxia and other muscular and nervous disorders. Author of *L'Electrisation Localisée* (1855) and *Physiologie des Mouvements* (1867).

Duchesne, Père. *See* **Hébert, Jacques René**

Ducommun *(dü kô mûN),* **Élie** 1833–1906. Swiss journalist and pacifist. Worked to promote pacifism as editor of *Revue de Genève* (1855) and as founder of International Bureau of Peace (1891); awarded, with Charles Gobat, Nobel Peace Prize (1902).

Dudevant, Baronne. *See* **Sand, George**

Dudley, *(dŭd lĭ),* **Robert** title: EARL OF LEICESTER. 1532–88. English courtier. Son of JOHN DUDLEY, DUKE OF NORTHUMBERLAND AND EARL OF WARWICK (c1502–53), joint regent and high chamberlain under Edward VI. Sentenced to death with father for plotting to place Lady Jane Grey on throne to succeed Edward VI; pardoned; gained affections of Elizabeth I, becoming chief courtier and privy councillor (1558); commanded English forces sent to aid States-General against Spaniards (1585); recalled (1587) and appointed captain general of the army to resist Spanish Armada (1588); as patron of arts and drama, founded company of players that later included Shakespeare.

Dufferin, Marquis of. *See* **Blackwood, Frederick Hamilton-Temple-**

DuGard, Roger Martin. *See* **Martin DuGard, Roger**

Du Guesclin *(dü gĕ klăN),* **Bertrand** called THE EAGLE OF BRITTANY. c1320–80. French soldier. *b.* near Rennes. Served under Charles of Blois in campaigns against the English and Pedro el Cruel; took part in defense of Rennes (1356–57), and in campaigns at Melun (1359), Cocherel (1364), Auray (1364), and Montiel (1369); Constable of France (1370); under Charles V, led campaigns that recaptured southern and western France from the English (1370–79).

Duhamel *(dü ȧ mĕl),* **Georges** pseudonym: DENIS THÉVENIN. 1884–1966. French writer. *b.* Paris. Author of more than 50 novels and plays including *Des Légendes, des Batailles* (1907), *L'Homme en Tête* (1909), *La Vie des Martyrs* (1917), *Civilisation* (1918, Prix Goncourt), *Les Hommes Abandonnés* (1923), *Le Cycle de Salavin* (4 vols., 1920–32), *The Pasquier Chronicles* (10 vols., 1937–41), *Light on My Days* (1948), *La Lumière* (1911), and *Combat* (1913).

Duke *(dūk),* **Benjamin Newton** 1855–1929. American industrialist. *b.* near Durham, N.C. With brother JAMES BUCHANAN DUKE (1856–1925), founded American Tobacco Company (1890) and British-American Tobacco Company, two of the largest tobacco concerns in the world; endowed Trinity College in Durham, which later became Duke University.

Dulles *(dŭl ĕs),* **John Foster** 1888–1959. American statesman. *b.* Washington, D.C. Grandson of JOHN WATSON FOSTER (1836–1917), secretary of state (1892–93). Attended Hague Conference (1907); advisor to President Wilson; principal U.S. spokesman on Reparations Commission (1918–19); U.S. representative at Berlin Debt Conferences (1933); advisor to Senator Vandenburg at U.N. charter conference in San Francisco (1947); secretary of state under Eisenhower (1952–59); developed concepts of massive retaliation and regional alliances of free nations against Communist aggression; sought to contain Soviet expansionism by policy of brinkmanship.

Duluth *(dŭ lo͞oth),* **Daniel Greysolon, Sieur** also DULHUT. 1636–1710. French explorer. Came to Canada (c1675); explored Lake Superior region and reached head of Lake Superior (1678–79); established the sites of Detroit and Fort William; took part in wars against

Senecas (1687) and Iroquois (1689); commanded Fort Frontenac (1695).

Dumas *(dü mà),* **Alexandre** also known as DUMÁS PÈRE. 1802–70. French writer. *b.* Villers-Cotterets. Wrote 277 novels and plays; believed to have been assisted by collaborators and researchers. Principal works include *Le Chevalier d'Harmental* (1843), *The Count of Monte Cristo* (1844–45), *The Three Musketeers* (1844), *Twenty Years After* (1845), *The Vicomte de Bragelonne* (26 vols., 1848–50), *Memoirs of a Physician* (1846–48), *The Countess of Charny* (19 vols., 1853–55), *The Forty-five* (1848), *The Black Tulip* (1850), *The She-Wolves of Machecoul* (1859), *The Two Dianas* (1846–47), *Henry III and His Court* (1829), *Antony* (1831), and *Napoleon Bonaparte* (1831). Published a daily newspaper devoted to literature, *Le Mousquetaire* (1853–57), converted into the weekly *Monte Cristo* (1857–60); published *Memoirs* (20 vol., 1852–54); father of: ALEXANDRE DUMAS, also known as DUMAS FILS. 1824–95. French writer. *b.* Paris. Achieved success as a novelist and dramatist with works such as *La Dame aux Camélias* (1848), *Diane de Lys* (1851), *Tristan le Roux* (1849), *La Dame aux Perles* (1854), *Le Demi-Monde* (1855), *La Question D'Argent* (1857), *Le Fils Naturel* (1858), *Un Pere Prodigue* (1859), *Les Idées de Mme Aubray* (1867), *Monsieur Alphonse* (1873), *Denise* (1885), and *Francillon* (1887).

Du Maurier *(dū mô rĭ ā),* **George Louis Palmella Busson** 1834–96. British illustrator and writer. *b.* Paris. Illustrator on the staff of *Once A Week, Cornhill Magazine,* and *Punch.* Author of *Peter Ibbetson* (1891), *Trilby* (1894), and *The Martian* (1896); creator of the character Svengali, a hypnotist.

Dunant *(dü näN),* **Jean Henri** 1828–1910. Swiss humanitarian. *b.* Geneva. After observing the wounded on the battlefield at Solferino, Italy (1859), inspired to write *A Souvenir of Solferino,* calling for an international code for wartime treatment of the sick, the wounded, and prisoners of war; effected conference at Geneva that adopted Geneva Convention (1864) and established International Red Cross; awarded Nobel Peace Prize with Frédéric Passy (1901). Author of *Fraternité et Charité Internationale en Temps de Guerre* (1864).

Dunsany *(dŭn sā nĭ),* **Baron** real name: EDWARD JOHN MORETON DRAX PLUNKETT. 1878–1957. Irish writer. Wrote tales, poems, and plays often dealing with fantasy and supernatural creatures, including *The Gods of Pegana* (1905), *The Evil Kettle* (1926) *Fifty Poems* (1929), *Patches of Sunlight* (1938), *The Gods of the Mountain* (1911), *A Night at an Inn* (1916), *If* (1921), *The Laughter of the Gods* and *Lord Adrian* (1933).

Duns Scotus *(dŭnz skō tŭs),* **John** also known as DOCTOR SUBTILIS. c1265–1308. Scottish scholastic theologian. *b.* Maxton. Joined Franciscan order; lectured at Oxford; known as founder of Scotism, an anti-Thomist scholastic system that sought to base Christian theology on faith and will rather than on speculation and reason; defended doctrine of Immaculate Conception; held that state obtains its sanction from consent of the people and that private property is contrary to natural law; complete works published by Luke Wadding at Lyons (12 vols., 1639).

Dunstan *(dŭn stən),* **Saint** c909–88. English ecclesiastic. *b.* near Glastonbury. Banished from court of Athelstan for practicing black arts; took monastic vows; recalled to court on accession of Edmund; abbot of Glastonbury (945); transformed abbey into great Christian center; chief advisor to Eldred (946–55); in exile in Flanders during reign of Edwy (955–59); recalled by Edgar; archbishop of Canterbury (961) and restored to power as chief royal advisor; introduced strict Benedictine rule; sought to integrate Danes and English into one nation, foster rule of law, abolish simony, and enforce payment of tithes; retired after Edward's murder and the accession of Ethelred II (978).

Dupin, Amandine Aurore Lueie. *See* **Sand, George**

Dupleix *(dü plĕks),* **Marquis Joseph François** 1697–1763. French colonial administrator. *b.* Landrecies. As governor general in India (1742–54) attempted to expand French empire; clashed with Robert Clive and English East India Company; made treaties with Nawab of Carnatic and Nizam of Hyderabad and organized native troops in European style; successfully withstood Admiral Boscawen's siege of his capital, Pondichéry; recalled (1754) to Paris on failure of policy; died in relative poverty.

Du Pont de Nemours *(dü pôn də nə moor),* **Pierre Samuel** 1739–1817. French economist. *b.* Paris. Gained reputation as economist of Physiocrat school; immigrated to U.S. (1799); returned to France (1802) but immigrated again to U.S. (1815); father of ÉLEUTHÈRE IRÉNÉE DU PONT (1771–1834), American industrialist and founder of E. I. Du Pont de Nemours & Company. Immigrated with father to U.S. (1799); established gunpowder works near Wilmington, Del. (1802–1804); succeeded as president of company by sons ALFRED VICTOR (1798–1856) and HENRY (1812–89) and great-grandsons THOMAS COLEMAN (1863–1930), PIERRE SAMUEL (1870–1954), IRÉNÉE (1876–1963), and LAMMOT (1880–1952). Other members of the family include VICTOR MARIE (1767–1827), brother of Éleuthère. Settled in U.S. after service in French legation in Washington (1787–96); on failure of his enterprises, joined the company. HENRY ALGERNON (1889–1906), U. S. Senator (1906–17).

Durant *(də rănt),* **William Crapo** 1861–1947. American industrialist. *b.* Boston, Mass. Founded Durant-Dort Carriage Company (1886), Buick Motor Car Company (1905), General Motors Company (1908), and Chevrolet Motor Company (1915); held controlling interest in General Motors (1915–20); after losing control of General Motors, founded Durant Motors (1921) and Industrial Rayon Corporation.

Dürer *(dü rər),* **Albrecht** 1471–1528. German painter. *b.* Nuremberg. Had studio (1497) after apprenticeship under Michael Wohlgemut; visited Venice (1505–1507) and Netherlands (1521); court painter to Emperor Maximilian I and Charles V of Spain; regarded as greatest engraver and woodcut artist and inventor of etching; as a friend of Luther and Melanchthon, sympathized with Reformation; copper plates include *Little Passion, The Knight, Death and the Devil, St. Jerome in His Study, Melancholia, The Prodigal Son,* and *Adam and Eve;* woodcuts include *Greater Passion, The Little Passion, Apocalypse,* and *Triumphal Arch;* paintings include *Adoration of the Trinity, Adam and Eve, Four Apostles, Feast of the Rosaries, Assumption of the Virgin, Adoration of the Magi, Crucifixion, Martyrdom of the Ten Thousand, Virgin Crowned by Two Angels,* three self-portraits, and *A Young Man;* writings included treatises on human proportion, fortifications, and measurement.

Durkheim *(dür kĕm),* **Émile** 1858–1917. French sociologist. Professor at Bordeaux and at the Sorbonne; believed that scientific methodology can be used in study of society; influenced by positivist philosophy of Comte; regarded as a chief founder of modern sociology; introduced statistics as a tool of sociological study. Works include *The Division of Labor in Society* (1893), *The Rules of Sociological Method* (1894), *Suicide* (1897), and *Elementary Forms of Religious Life* (1912).

Duryea *(do͞or yā),* **Charles Edgar** 1861–1938. American automobile manufacturer. *b.* near Canton, Ill. Built first automobile to use gasoline (1892); organized Duryea Motor Wagon Company in Springfield, Mass., which sold the first car in U.S. (1896); introduced pneumatic tires and invented a spray carburetor (1892); established Duryea Power Company in Reading, Pa. Considered as "father of the automobile."

Dutt *(dôt),* **Michael Madhu Sudhan** 1824–73. Indian poet. *b.* Sagandari, Bengal. Converted to Christianity; wrote poetry and plays in Bengali and English. Works include *Sarmishtha* (1858), *Krishna Kumari* (1858), *Padmavati* (1859), *Tillotama* (1860), and *Meghanad-Badha* (1861).

Du Vigneaud *(dū vēn yō),* **Vincent** 1901–1978. American biochemist. *b.* Chicago, Ill. Professor, George Washington University (1932–38) and Cornell (from 1938); conducted research on insulin, amino acids, hormones, and proteins; synthesized penicillin and oxytocin; described the structure of biotin; awarded Nobel Prize in chemistry (1955) for synthesizing two hormones of the pituitary gland.

Dvořák *(dvôr zhäk),* **Anton** 1841–1904. Czech composer. *b.* Nelahozeves, Bohemia. Gained recognition with cantata *Hymnus* (1873); influenced by Brahms, whose friendship provided stimulus and recognition; acclaimed for *Stabat Mater,* performed in London (1883); director of National Conservatory of Music, (1892–95); director of Conservatorium in Prague (1901–1904); introduced Slavonic folk elements and Bohemian forms into his music. Among his works are *The Pigheaded Peasants* (1874), *Vanda* (1876), *Dimitri* (1882), *Jacobin* (1889), *The Devil and Kate* (1888), *Slavonic Dances* (1878), *The Spectre's Bride* (1885), *St. Ludmila* (1886), and *From the New World* (1893).

Dwight *(dwīt),* **Timothy** 1752–1817. American clergyman. *b.* Northampton, Mass. Chaplain of Revolutionary army (1777–79); president of Yale College (1795–1817). Author of *Theology, Explained and Defended* (5 vols., 1818–19), *Travels in New England and New York* (4 vols., 1821–22), *The Conquest of Canaan* (1785), and *A Dissertation on the History, Eloquence, and Poetry of the Bible* (1772), regarded as literary model for the Hartford Wits; father of TIMOTHY DWIGHT (1828–1916), American clergyman and educator, president of Yale (1886–98).

E

Eadward. *See* **Edward the Confessor**

Eakins *(ā kĭnz),* **Thomas** 1844–1916. American painter. *b.* Philadelphia, Pa. Studied art in Paris (1866–70); taught at Pennsylvania Academy of Fine Arts (1873). Principal paintings include *Clinic of Dr. Agnew, Clinic of Dr. Gross, The Chess Players, The Writing Master, Between Rounds, Biglen Brothers Turning the Stakeboat, and Pair-Oared Shell;* sculptures appear on battle monuments in Brooklyn, N.Y., and Trenton, N.J.

Ealwhine. *See* **Alcuin**

Earhart *(âr härt),* **Amelia** 1898–1937. American aviator. *b.* Atchison, Kans. First woman pilot to fly across the Atlantic (with Wilmer Stutz and Louis Gordon) (1928); repeated feat solo (1932); flew from Honolulu to California (1935); believed lost in Pacific on a round-the-world flight attempt (1937). Author of *20 Hrs. 40 Mins.* (1928) and *Last Flight* (edited by husband G. P. Putnam, 1938).

Eastman *(ēst mən),* **George** 1854–1932. American inventor and pioneer in photography. *b.* Waterville, N.Y. Obtained patents for photographic coating process of dry plates (1879), flexible film with paper backing (1884), Kodak cameras (1888), color film, and film for motion pictures; founded Eastman Dry Plate and Film Company (1884), donated millions of dollars to University of Rochester, Rochester School of Music, and other institutions.

Ebert *(ā bərt),* **Friedrich** 1871–1925. German statesman. *b.* Heidelberg. Entered politics as trade union leader and Social Democratic journalist; elected to Reichstag (1912); leader of Social Democrats (1913); chancellor (1918); Reichspresident (1919); suppressed rightist putschs of Kapp and Hitler, and leftist revolt of the Spartacists.

Eccles *(ĕk ləz),* **Sir John Carew** 1903–. Australian physiologist. Awarded Nobel Prize in physiology and medicine (1963) with A. Hodgkin and A. Huxley for determining how impulses travel through the body's nervous system.

Echegaray y Eizaguirre *(ā chə gə rä ə ē ē ə thä gēr rā),* **Jose** 1832–1916.

Spanish playwright. *b.* Madrid. Professor of physics and mathematics at University of Madrid (1854–68, from 1905); member of the Cortes (1868); minister (1868–74, 1905); won fame as a dramatist, particularly for his play *El Gran Galeoto* (1881); awarded Nobel Prize in literature with Frédéric Mistral (1904). Other works include *La Esposa del Vengador* (1874), *Madman or Saint* (1876), *El Hijo de Don Juan* (1892), *La Duda (1898), El Loco Diós* (1900) *La Desequilibrada* (1903), and *A Fuerza de Arrastrarse* (1905).

Eckhart *(ĕk härt),* **Johannes** called MEISTER ECKHART. c1260–c1328. German mystic. *b.* Hocheim. Entered Dominican order; taught theology in Paris; provincial in Saxony (1303–11); vicar-general of Bohemia (1307); preached a form of pantheistic mysticism resembling the Neoplatonism of Plotinus, Vedanta, and Jewish and Islamic doctrines; arraigned for heresy (1325); defended orthodoxy before Pope John XXII; teachings condemned as heretical after his death (1329).

Eddington *(ĕd ĭng tən),* **Sir Arthur Stanley** 1882–1944. British astronomer. *b.* Kendal. Professor of astronomy at Cambridge (from 1913); director of Cambridge Observatory (from 1914); president of Royal Astronomical Society (1921–23); president of International Astronomical Union (from 1938); determined the Eddington number, or the total number of particles in the universe. Author of *Stellar Movements and the Structure of the Universe* (1914), *The Mathematical Theory of Relativity* (1923), *Stars and Atoms* (1927), *New Pathways in Science* (1935), *Relativity Theory of Protons and Electrons* (1936), and *The Philosophy of Physical Science* (1939).

Eddy *(ĕd ĭ),* **Mary Baker** maiden name: MARY MORSE BAKER. 1821–1910. American founder of Christian Science. *b.* Bow, N.H. Experienced spiritual healing of a severe injury sustained in a fall (1866); transformed this experience into the science of mental healing based on the Bible; expounded doctrine in *Science and Health* (1875), *Messages to the Mother Church* (1900–1902), *Christian Healing* (1886), and *Church Manual* (1895); chartered Church of Christ, Scientist (1879); founded The Christian Science Publishing Society (1898), publishers of *The Christian Science Monitor* and other journals.

Edelman *(ĕd əl mən),* **Gerald Maurice** 1929–. American biochemist. *b.* New York, N.Y. Awarded, with R. R. Porter, the Nobel Prize in physiology and medicine for work on immunology (1972).

Eden *(ē dən),* **Sir Robert Anthony** title: EARL OF AVON. 1897–1977. British statesman. *b.* Ferry Hill. Entered Parliament (1923); undersecretary in the foreign office, (1931–33); lord privy seal and privy councilor (1934–35); minister without portfolio for League of Nations affairs (1935); secretary of state for foreign affairs (1935–38, 1940–45, 1951–55); secretary of state for dominions (1939–40); secretary of state for war (1940); prime minister (1955–57); resigned over Chamberlain's policy of appeasement of Hitler and Mussolini (1939); led British delegation to San Francisco Conference (1945);

as prime minister, ordered disastrous Anglo-French invasion of Suez. Author of *Foreign Affairs* (1939), *Days for Decision* (1949), and *Memoirs* (3 vols., 1960–65).

Edgeworth *(ĕj wûrth),* **Maria** 1767–1849. Irish novelist. *b.* Blackbourton. Daughter of RICHARD LOVELL EDGEWORTH (1744–1817), English inventor and educator. Collaborated with father on *Practical Education* (1798) and *Essay on Irish Bulls* (1802). Author of over 20 volumes, including *Castle Rackrent* (1800), *Belinda* (1801), *Moral Tales for Young People* (1801), *Tales of Fashionable Life* (1809–12), *Leonora* (1806), *The Absentee* (1812), *Ormond* (1817), and *Helen* (1834).

Edinburgh *(ĕd ĭn bŭr ō),* **Duke of** title: PRINCE PHILIP MOUNBATTEN. 1921–. Consort of Queen Elizabeth II of England. *b.* Corfu, Greece. Son of Prince Andrew of Greece and Princess Alice and grandson of Prince Louis of Battenberg; joined Royal Navy (1939) and saw naval action during World War II; married Princess Elizabeth, heiress presumptive (1947); made member of the Order of the Garter and given the title of His Royal Highness; noted as sportsman and yachtsman.

Edison *(ĕd ĭ sən),* **Thomas Alva** 1847–1931. American inventor. *b.* Milan, Ohio. Received limited schooling and began as newspaper boy; learned telegraphy and worked as a telegraph operator in various cities; invented an electrical vote-recording machine (1868); established factory at Newark, N. J. (1876), later moving to Menlo Park, N.J. and Orange, N.J. (1887); patented over 1200 inventions, among them the automatic telegraph repeater, quadruplex telegraph, printing telegraph, electric pen, the mimeograph, the microphone, the phonograph, the Ediphone, the incandescent electric lamp, the electric valve, the kinetoscope, the alkaline storage battery, the motion picture camera, and the sextuplex telegraph.

Edward *(ĕd wərd)* Name of eight British kings:

EDWARD I 1239–1307. King of England (1272–1307). Active in struggle between his father (Henry III) and the barons; defeated and killed Simon Montfort, leader of the barons, at Evesham (1265); joined in Seventh Crusade (1270–72); succeeded to throne (1274); defeated Prince Llewelyn and annexed Wales (1276–84); subdued Scotland with victories over John de Baliol (1296) and William Wallace (1298); expelled Jews from England (1290); concluded Peace of Amiens with France (1303); convened Model Parliament (1295) representing the three estates; limited political power of barons by Statutes of Westminster (1275, 1285, 1290); established Royal Council (later the Star Chamber) and the three tribunals: the court of exchequer, the court of king's bench, and the court of common pleas; refused tribute to Rome and ended papal overlordship of England; established principle against arbitrary taxation without Parliamentary assent.

EDWARD II 1284–1327. King of England (1307–27). Fourth son of Edward I and first prince of Wales (1301–1307); provoked conflict with barons by falling under ascendancy of Piers de Gaveston;

compelled to accept government of the realm by baronial committee of 21 lords ordainers (1311) who kidnapped and executed Gaveston (1312); yielded actual power to Thomas, Earl of Lancaster (until 1322); with aid of new favorites Hugh le Despenser and his son, Edward, defeated the barons and killed Lancaster at the Battle of Boroughbridge (1322); led invasion of Scotland (1314), which ended in disastrous defeat at Bannockburn and the loss of Berwick (1318); concluded truce with Robert Bruce for 13 years (1323); dispossessed of crown by an army led by Queen Isabella, her lover Roger de Mortimer, and other disaffected nobles; imprisoned and murdered (1327).

EDWARD III 1312–77. King of England (1327–77). Son of Edward II; took reins of government after banishing his mother Isabella and executing Roger de Mortimer; invaded Scotland, defeating the Scots at Halidon Hill (1333); failed to place Edward de Baliol on Scottish throne; claimed crown of France through his mother Isabella (sister of Charles) and, in alliance with Flemings, Emperor Louis IV, and other German princes, began Hundred Years' War; brilliant victory at Sluys (1340) over French navy; with his son Edward the Black Prince, defeated French at Crécy and Poitiers (1346, 1356); took King John of France prisoner at Poitiers; conquered Calais and most of Normandy; renounced claim to French throne in exchange for Aquitaine (1360); on renewal of hostilities with Charles V, lost all possessions in France except Bordeaux, Calais, and Bayonne; defeated the Scots near Neville's Cross (1346) and took David II prisoner; later released David after a secret agreement in which he agreed to union of England and Scotland if he died without a male issue; reign marked by ravages of the Black Death (1348–49, 1361, 1369), consequent breakdown of feudalism, rise and progress of Lollardy, repudiation of papal authority, and cessation of payment of Peter's pence (1366), establishment of English as Parliament's official language, and growth of parliamentary power over the purse; toward end of reign turned over actual power to his mistress Alice Perrers and their son John of Gaunt.

EDWARD IV 1442–83. King of England (1461–70, 1471–83). Son of Richard Plantagenet, Duke of York; banished from England by Lancastrian King Henry IV; with his uncle Earl of Salisbury and cousin Earl of Warwick, invaded England and gained the crown, defeating Lancastrians at Mortimer's Cross (1461), Towton (1461), Hedgeley Moor and Hexham (1464); through marriage to Elizabeth Grey, gave offense to Warwick, who joined forces with Lancastrians to install Henry VI as king; fled to Flanders (1470) but returned next year to defeat Warwick and Queen Margaret at Barnet (1471) and Tewkesbury; with deaths of Warwick, Henry VI, Prince Edward (son of Queen Margaret), and George (Duke of Clarence), enjoyed undisputed power; secured freedom from parliamentary grants by annual subsidy from Louis XI; ruled thereafter as absolute monarch.

EDWARD V 1470–83. King of England (Apr.–June 1483). Son of Edward IV; murdered with his brother, the Duke of York, by order of the Protector Richard, Duke of Gloucester, later Richard III.

EDWARD VI 1537–53. King of England (1547–53). Son of King Henry VIII; succeeded to throne under regency of uncle Edward Seymour, Duke of Somerset, who invaded Scotland and defeated the Scots at Pinkie (1549); on execution of Somerset on charges of overambition (1552), fell under tutelage of John Dudley, Duke of Northumberland; reign witnessed publication of 42 articles of religion (1553) and introduction of the Book of Common Prayer (1549).

EDWARD VII 1841–1910. King of Great Britain and Ireland (1901–10). Son of Queen Victoria; called "the Peacemaker" for role in promoting international friendship.

EDWARD VIII 1894–1972. King of Great Britain and Ireland Jan. 20–Dec. 11, 1936). Son of George V; abdicated throne (1937) in order to marry Mrs. Wallis Simpson; thereafter known as Duke of Windsor; governor of the Bahamas (1940–45). Author of *A King's Story* (1951).

Edward of Woodstock known as the BLACK PRINCE; titles: FIRST DUKE OF CORNWALL, PRINCE OF WALES, PRINCE OF AQUITAINE AND GASCONY. 1330–76. *b.* Woodstock. Eldest son of Edward III; created duke of Cornwall (1337), the first duke in English history; fought in battle of Crécy (1346) and siege of Calais (1347); won victory at Poitiers (1356) and took John II of France prisoner; made prince of Aquitaine and granted all British possessions in southern France; with victory over Bertrand du Guesclin at Nájera, restored Pedro el Cruel to throne of Castle and León (1367); faced with revolt of French barons and renewal of hostilities with Charles V, took Limoges (1639) and massacred its inhabitants; struck with mortal illness; resigned possessions in France and returned to England; opposed Lancastrian Party at court.

Edward the Confessor also EADWARD. c1002–66. Last Anglo-Saxon king of England (1042–66). *b.* Islip. Son of Ethelred; succeeded Hardicanute as king (1042); reign marked by confict between national party, led by father-in-law Earl Godwin of Wessex, and the Norman party; broke with Godwin over election of Robert de Jumièges as archbishop of Canterbury, having set aside election of Aelfric, Godwin's relation; caused Godwin to flee England for refusing to punish the town of Dover; restored Godwin to power (1052) after invasion led by Godwin and son Harold; forced to yield to removal of his favorite, Tostig, Earl of Northumbria, when faced with revolt by Danes; celebrated for monkish piety; canonized (1161).

Edwards *(ĕd wərdz),* **Jonathan** 1703–58. American clergyman. *b.* East Windsor, Conn. Ordained (1727); succeeded grandfather Solomon Stoddard as minister in Northampton, Mass. (1728); resigned ministry (1750) over dispute concerning barring persons from communion who had not been properly converted; missionary to Indians in Stockbridge, Mass. (until 1758); president of College of New Jersey (now Princeton), but died within three months; considered one of the greatest intellects of New England Puritanism; upheld Calvinist doctrines of absolute divine sovereignty tempered only by grace; opposed Arminian doctrine of free will; led spiritual revival (1734–35) known as "the Great Awakening". Principal works include *Freedom of the Will* (1754), *A Narrative of Surprising Conversions* (1735), *A Treatise Concerning the Religious Affections* (1742–46), *The Great Christian Doctrine of Original Sin Defended* (1758), *Sinners in the Hands of an Angry God* (1741), *Charity and Its Fruits* (1751), and *The End for Which God Created the World* (1789).

Ehrlich *(ār lĭK)*, **Paul** 1854–1915. German bacteriologist. *b.* Strehlen. Head of Koch Institute for Infectious Diseases (1890); director of Institute for Serum Research in Dahlem (1896) and Institute for Experimental Therapy at Frankfurt-am-Main (from 1899); conducted research in hematology and immunity; developed methods for staining microscopic specimens; propounded lateral chain theory of immunology (1897), for which he was awarded (with E. Metchnikoff) the Nobel Prize in physiology and medicine (1980); discovered Salvarsan arsenicals (1910), long used in treating syphilis.

Eiffel *(ī fəl)*, **Alexandre Gustave** 1832–1923. French engineer. *b.* Dijon. One of the pioneers of aerodynamics; built Aerodynamics Laboratory at Auteuil (1912); best-known engineering works include the iron bridge over the Garonne River; the railroad bridge over the Douro in Oporto, Portugal; locks for French Panama Canal Company; the iron framework for Bartholdi's Statute of Liberty; the iron bridge over the Tardes; and the Eiffel Tower, 985 feet high, on the Champ-de-Mars in Paris (1887–89).

Eigen *(ī gĕn)*, **Manfred** 1927. German chemist. Shared Nobel Prize in chemistry with R. Norrish and G. Porter (1967).

Eijkman *(īk män)*, **Christiaan** 1858–1930. Dutch hygienist. *b.* Nijkerk. Director (1888–96) of Pathological Institute at Weltevreden, Dutch East Indies; professor of hygiene (1898–1928) at University of Utrecht; produced nutritional deficiency in fowl by feeding them polished rice exclusively; established essential role of vitamins in health; shared Nobel Prize in physiology and medicine with Sir F. G. Hopkins (1929) for discovery of vitamin B_1 (thiamine).

Einstein *(īn shtīn)*, **Albert** 1879–1955. German-American physicist. *b.* Ulm, Germany. Took Swiss nationality (1894); examiner at Swiss Patent Office (1902–1905); professor of theoretical physics at Zurich (1909–11, 1912–14), and Prague (1911–12); resumed German citizenship (1914); professor of physics at Berlin and director of Kaiser Wilhelm Physical Institute (1914–33); on Hitler's rise to power, was deprived of citizenship and left Germany; taught at Princeton (from 1934); became naturalized American citizen (1940). At age 26 (1905), published three papers that revolutionized physics: an explanation of the photoelectric effect on the basis of light quanta (photons), a theory of Brownian movement, and the special theory of relativity, demonstrating equivalence of mass and energy; awarded Nobel Prize in physics (1921) for theory of photoelectric effect; presented general theory of relativity (1913–16), which held that the curvature of space-time continuum was determined by gravitation defined as a field rather than a force; developed quantum theory of specific heat (1907), the Bose-Einstein statistics (1924–25), and studied emission and absorption of radiation (1917); completed work on unified field theory attempting to explain gravitation, electromagnetism, and subatomic phenomena in one set of laws; inspired creation of atomic bomb, but, after bombing of Hiroshima, became an advocate of pacifism and world government. Author of *The Meaning of Relativity* (1921), *Sidelights on Relativity* (1922), *Investigations on the Theory of the Brownian Movement* (1926), *Builders of the Universe* (1932), *On the Method of Theoretical Physics* (1933), *Why War?* (with Freud, 1933), and *The World As I See It* (1934).

Einthoven *(īnt hō vən),* **Willem** 1860–1927. Dutch physiologist. *b.* Samarang, Java. Professor of physiology at University of Leiden (1886–1927); made electrocardiography possible by perfecting the string galvanometer; awarded Nobel Prize in physiology and medicine (1924).

Eisenhower *(ī zən hou ər),* **Dwight David** 1890–1969. 34th president of U.S. *b.* Denison, Tex. Served in tank corps under Patton in World War I; member of U.S. Military Mission to the Philippines under MacArthur (1935–39); lieutenant general of U.S. forces in Europe (1942); commander of Allied forces in northwest Africa (1942); directed invasion of Sicily and Italy (1943); commander in chief of Allied forces in western Europe (1943); directed Normandy invasion and conquest of Germany (1945); general of the army (1944; permanently, 1946); U.S. army chief of staff (1945–48); president of Columbia University (1948–53); supreme Allied commander in Europe, NATO forces (1951–52); Republican president of U.S. (1953–61); helped arrange truce in Korea (1953); formulated Eisenhower Doctrine to aid Middle Eastern nations against Communism; took part in Geneva Summit Conference (1955); pursued moderate domestic policies at home, but sent Federal troops to Little Rock, Ark. (1957) to enforce school desegregation; restored to rank as five-star general (1961).

Eisenstein *(ī zĕn shtīn),* **Sergei Mikhailovich** 1898–1948. Russian film director. *b.* Riga, Latvia. Noted for contributions to the development of film techniques, especially montage, documentary realism, and impressionistic effects achieved through cutting and recutting. Major films include *Potemkin* (1926), *Ten Days That Shook the World* (1928), *Alexander Nevsky* (1938), and *Ivan the Terrible* (Part I, 1941); author of *Film Sense* (1943) and *Film Form* (1951).

Elgar *(ĕl gər),* **Sir Edward** 1857–1934. English composer. *b.* Broadheath. A master of musical technique, stands as as one of the most significant composers of late 19th and early 20th century music. Compositions include *The Dream of Gerontius* (1900), *The Apostles* (1903), *The Kingdom* (1906), *Pomp and Circumstance* (1902), *Enigma Variations* (1899), *In the South* (1904), *Light and Life, King Olaf, Caractatus,* and *Introduction and Allegro.*

Elias. *See* **Elijah**

Elijah *(ē lī jȧ)* also ELIAS. *fl.* 9th century B.C. Hebrew prophet, considered one of the greatest in the Old Testament; opposed Phoenician idolatry of King Ahab and Queen Jezebel; demonstrated miraculous powers by raising from the dead the son of the widow of Zarephath, calling down fire from heaven to consume a sacrifice to Jehovah, receiving sustenance from ravens, and by departing from earthly life by being carried to heaven in a chariot of fire.

Eliot *(ĕl ĭ ət),* **Charles William** 1834–1926. American educator. *b.* Boston, Mass. President of Harvard (1869–1909); introduced far-reaching changes in administration and curricula; added new graduate school of arts and sciences. Editor of the *Harvard Classics.*

Eliot, George pseudonym of MARY ANN or MARIAN EVANS. 1819–80. English novelist. *b.* Arbury Farm. Contributed to *Westminster Review,* later becoming its assistant editor (1851); met and formed lifelong intimate relationship with G. H. Lewes; achieved critical success with first story, *The Sad Fortunes of the Rev. Amos Barton,* the first of *Scenes from Clerical Life* (2 vols., 1858); followed with *Adam Bede* (1859), *The Mill on the Floss* (1860), *Silas Marner* (1861), *Romola* (1863), *Felix Holt the Radical* (1866), *Middlemarch* (1872), and *Daniel Deronda* (1876); also wrote poetry (1868–71); *Letters* were edited by G. S. Haight (7 vols., 1954–56).

Eliot, Thomas Stearns usually T.S. ELIOT. 1888–1965. British poet and critic. *b.* St. Louis, Mo. Settled in England (from 1914) and naturalized (1927); encouraged and influenced by Ezra Pound to publish first volume of verse, *Prufrock and Other Observations* (1917); edited *The Criterion,* an influential literary journal (until 1939); baptized and confirmed into Church of England (1927). Principal poetic works include *Poems* (1919), *The Waste Land* (1922), *The Hollow Men* (1925), *Journey of the Magi* (1927), *A Song for Simeon* (1928), *Ash Wednesday* (1930), *The Rock* (1934), and *Four Quartets* (1944), and are characterized by esoteric styles, obscure allusions, disassociations, and complex imagery. Plays include *Murder in the Cathedral* (1935), *The Cocktail Party* (1950), *The Family Reunion* (1939), *The Confidential Clerk* (1954), and *The Elder Statesman* (1958). Critical works include *The Sacred Wood* (1920), *An Essay of Poetic Drama* (1928), *Selected Essays* (1932), *The Use of Poetry and the Use of Criticism* (1933), *After Strange Gods* (1934), *Elizabethan Essays* (1934), *Essays Ancient and Modern* (1936), *What is a Classic?* (1945), and *Notes Toward the Definition of Culture* (1949); awarded Nobel Prize for literature (1948).

Elizabeth *(ə lĭz ə bĕth),* **Saint** 1207–31. German queen. *b.* Pressburg, Czechoslovakia. Daughter of Andrew II, king of Hungary; married Louis IV, Landgrave of Thuringia; gained reputation for charity and sanctity; on the death of Louis (1227), dispossessed by brother-in-law, retiring to monastery at Kitzingen with three children; though restored to her rights by followers of Louis, renounced royal life to spend her days in penance and service to the poor and sick; credited with many miracles; canonized (1235). Feast day: Nov. 19.

Elizabeth I 1533–1603. Queen of England and Ireland (1558–1603). *b.* London. Only daughter of Henry VIII and Anne Boleyn; educated by humanist teachers and adherents of the New Learning; brought up as a Protestant but remained indifferent to religion throughout her life; sided with sister Mary against Lady Jane Grey (1553); ascended throne on Mary's death (1558); established the Anglican Church in its present form with the Act of Uniformity (1559), making the Catholic Mass the Anglican Communion, and with the Act of Supremacy, making Elizabeth the Supreme Governor of the realm in spiritual matters (1559); appointed Matthew Parker archbishop of Canterbury (1559); made English the language of the church service; pursued policy of religious toleration; supported Protestant factions in France, Scotland, and Low Countries, but remained at peace with neighbors for 30 years; imprisoned Mary, Queen of Scots, (1568–87), and, faced with plots to enthrone her, signed warrant for her execution (1587); with help of the great English seamen Howard, Drake, Hawkins, and Frobisher, and a providential storm, defeated Spanish Armada (1588); failed to quell revolt in Ireland; passed Poor Laws (1597, 1601); maintained policy of moderate taxation and financial soundness; aided by such great counselors as William Cecil, Nicholas Bacon, and Francis Walsingham; remained unmarried, but had many favorites, most importantly Robert Dudley, Earl of Leicester, and Robert Devereux, Earl of Essex; presided over a brilliant and prosperous age in English history, noted for its literature, commercial expansion, colonization, and naval supremacy.

Elizabeth II full name: ELIZABETH ALEXANDRA MARY. 1926–. Queen of Great Britain and Northern Ireland (1952–). *b.* London. Daughter of King George VI; married Prince Philip, Duke of Edinburgh (1947); crowned (1953).

Ellsworth *(ĕlz wûrth),* **Oliver** 1745–1807. American jurist. *b.* Windsor, Conn. Delegate to Second Continental Congress (1777–84) and Constitutional Convention (1787); put forward Connecticut Compromise, providing for equality of state representation in the Senate; believed to have originated the phrase "United States"; chairman of committee that drew up bill setting up federal judiciary; Senator from Conn. (1789–96); chief justice of U.S. (1796–99); commissioner to France (1799–1800).

Emerson *(ĕm ər sən),* **Ralph Waldo** 1803–82. American philosopher. *b.* Boston, Mass. Pastor of

Second Unitarian Church in Boston (1829–32); resigned pulpit over heterodox views; went to Europe, meeting Wordsworth, Coleridge, and Carlyle; on return, settled in Concord, Mass.; gathered a circle of associates including Bronson Alcott, Jones Very, Henry David Thoreau, and Margaret Fuller; launched literary and philosophical movement known as Transcendentalism; outlined principal ideas in *Nature* (1836), *"The American Scholar"* (1837), and *The Address Before the Divinity Class of Cambridge* (1838); edited *The Dial* (1842–44); advocated supremacy of individual consciousness over formal religion; expounded mystical unity of nature; held that individualism and intuition are the best guides to morality; published *Essays* (1841–44). Other works include *Poems* (1847), *Representative Men* (1850), *English Traits* (1856), *The Conduct of Life* (1860), *Letters and Social Aims* (1876), *Natural History of Intellect* (1893); his *Journals* were edited by son Edward Waldo Emerson (10 vols., 1910–14).

Emin Pasha *(ĕ mēn pä shä)*, **Mehmed** real name: EDUARD SCHNITZER. 1840–92. German explorer and adventurer. *b.* Neisse. Born Jewish, converted to Protestantism (1846), and to Islam (1865); medical officer in Khartoum under General Charles Gordon (1876–78); governor of Equatorial Province with rank of bey (1878); isolated by Mahdi revolt (1888); rescued by H. M. Stanley (1889); entered (1890) service of German East Africa Company; with Stuhlmann and Langheld, explored central Africa; established the station of Bukoba in Tanganyika; murdered by Arabs near Nyangwe in Belgian Congo (1892); contributed to knowledge of African languages, anthropology, zoology, and botany.

Empedocles *(ĕm pĕd ō klēz)* c490–c430 B.C. Greek philosopher. *b.* Agrigentum, Sicily. Disciple of Pythagoras and Parmenides; held that the universe was made up of particles of earth, air, fire, and water; credited with miraculous powers and the ability to prophesy; ended life by throwing himself into the crater of Mount Etna to establish his divinity.

Endecott *(ĕn dĭ kət)*, **John** also ENDICOTT. c1589–1665. Colonial governor of Massachusetts. *b.* Chagford, England. One of six incorporators who, by royal charter, obtained the territory patent for Massachusetts Bay from Plymouth Council; sailed to America on the *Abigail* (1628); landed at Salem; acted as governor until arrival of John Winthrop (1630); governor (1644, 1649, 1651–53, 1655–64).

Enders *(ĕn dərz)*, **John Franklin** 1896–. American bacteriologist. *b.* West Hartford, Conn. Awarded, with T. H. Weller and F. C. Robbins, Nobel Prize in physiology and medicine (1954) for successfully growing poliomyelitis virus in tissue culture.

Engels *(ĕng əls)*, **Friedrich** 1820–95. German socialist. *b.* Barmen. Became interested in radical Owenite and Chartist movements on visit to Manchester (1842); met Karl Marx in Brussels (1844); active in Revolution of 1848 and fled to England on its failure; managed father's factory in Manchester (1850–69), residing in London (1870–95); collaborated with Marx on *The Communist Manifesto* (1848); active in First International (1864) and Second (1889). Other works include *The Condition of the Working Classes in England in 1844* (1845), *Landmarks of Scientific Socialism* (1878), *The Origin of the Family, Private Property, and the State* (1884), and *The Peasant War in Germany* (1926).

Ephraem *(ē frā ĭm),* **Saint** also EPHRAIM, EPHREM, EPHRAEM SYRUS. c306–c378. Syrian theologian. *b.* Nisibis, Mesopotamia. Lived in Edessa (from 363); gained great reputation for his orthodoxy, asceticism, and learning; wrote treatises, homilies, hymns, and commentaries on the Bible; given title of Doctor of the Church (1920).

Epictetus *(ĕp ĭk tē tŭs) fl.* 1st century. Stoic philosopher. *b.* Hierapolis, Phrygia. A freed slave in Rome; studied under Musonius Rufus and taught philosophy until banished by Domitian with other philosophers; settled in Nikopolis in Epirus; taught that the will is superior to the gods, and that wisdom consisted of patience, contentment, freedom, and self-renunciation; maxims preserved in eight books of commentaries and the *Enchiridion* of pupil Flavius Arrian.

Epicurus *(ĕp ĭ kū rəs)* c341–270 B.C. Greek philosopher. *b.* Samos. Established a school in Athens (306) and devoted himself to teaching; believed to have written over 300 works, of which only a few epistles and fragments, entitled *Principal Doctrines,* still exist; developed hedonistic and materialistic system of ethics called Epicureanism; held that philosophy's purpose was to rid men of fear of gods and death, that pleasure was the chief end of life, and that the gods are indifferent to human life; defined pleasure as the freedom of the body from pain and the soul from anxiety; developed atomistic theory of Democritus as basis of ethics.

Epstein *(ĕp stīn),* **Sir Jacob** 1880–1959. British sculptor. *b.* New York, N.Y. Settled in England (1905) and became a British subject. Works include 18 figures for British Medical Council Building (1907–1908), *Night and Day* (1929), the tomb of Oscar Wilde (1909), *Venus* (1917), *Christ* (1920), *Visitation* (1926), *Genesis* (1930), *Ecce Homo* (1934), *Adam* (1939), *Madonna and Child* (1950), and portraits in bronze of Churchill, Einstein, Eliot, Shaw, Conrad, and others. Author of *Let There Be Sculpture* (1940) and *The Sculptor Speaks* (1931); knighted (1954).

Erasmus *(ē răz məs),* **Desiderius** original name: GERHARD GERHARDS, GEERT GEERTS. c1465–1536. Dutch humanist. *b.* Rotterdam. Ordained priest (1492); studied in Paris (to 1498); lived in England (1498–99, 1505–1506, 1510–14), Paris (1500–1506), Louvain (1517–21), Basel (1521–29), and Freiburg im Breisgau (from 1529); met most of great scholars of the day; sought to rescue theology from scholastic pedantries, to reform church from within, and to promote revival of learning; first supported, but later opposed, Reformation. Works include *Adagia* (1515), *Enchiridion Militis Chris-*

tiani, Encomium Moriae (1509), *Colloquia* (1519), *De Libero Arbitro* (1523), and *Ciceronianus;* published annotated New Testament in Greek with Latin translation (1516) and the writings of St. Jerome (9 vols., 1519).

Eratosthenes *(ĕr ə tŏs thē nēz)* c276–c196 B.C. Greek scholar. *b.* Cyrene, Africa. Head of Alexandrian Library; considered as founder of scientific chronology and astronomical geography; measured the obliquity of the ecliptic and the magnitude of the earth; made catalog of 675 fixed stars; contributed to grammar, philosophy, history, and geometry; extant fragments of his works published (1822).

Ericson *(ĕr ĭk sən),* **Leif** also ERICSSON, ERIKSEN. *fl.* c1000. Norse mariner. Son of ERIC THE RED (*fl.* 10th century), founder of first Norse settlement in Greenland. Sailed from Greenland with 35 companions; discovered a land that he called Vinland, the modern identity of which has never been definitely determined.

Ericsson, John 1803–89. American engineer. *b.* Långbanshyttan, Sweden. After service in Swedish army, went to England (1826); patented first successful screw propeller (1836); immigrated to U.S. (1839); designed warship *Princeton* with engines and boilers located entirely below water line; during Civil War built the iron-clad warship *Monitor* for the Union navy; with its revolving gun-turret, it easily defeated the Confederate *Merrimac* (1862); other inventions include a caloric engine, a solar engine, and a torpedo boat.

Erigena *(ĕ rĭj ə nä),* **Johannes Scotus** original name: JOHANNES SCOTUS; pseudonym: JOHANNES ERIUGENA. c815–c891. Irish philosopher. Director of palace school at court of Charles the Bald (c847); introduced Neoplatonism into Europe with his translation of Dionysius the Aeropagite (c858); in the predestination controversy, defended the heterodox principle of free will; identified theology and philosophy and God and nature; held that nature was the ultimate unity manifesting itself in rational processes; condemned by Councils of Valence (855), Langres (859), Vercellis (1050), and Sens (1225); writings placed on the Index. Works include *De Divinis Praedestinatione* (c851) and *De Divisione Naturae (865–70).*

Erlanger *(ûr lăng ər),* **Joseph** 1874–1965. American physiologist. *b.* San Francisco, Calif. Professor of physiology at Washington University (1910–46); cowinner, with H. S. Gasser, of Nobel Prize in physiology and medicine (1944) for work on nervous fibers. Author (with Gasser) of *Signs of Nervous Activity* (1946).

Esarhaddon *(ē sär hăd ən)* *fl.* 7th century B.C. King of Assyria of Sargonid dynasty (681–669 B.C.). Son of Sennacherib; rebuilt Babylon and great palace at Ninevah; defeated Chaldaeans, Medes, Scythians, and Jewish rulers of Palestine; destroyed Sidon (676); conquered Egypt after defeating Tirhakah, third ruler of the Ethiopian dynasty, in Battle of Memphis (671); the inscription of 673 enumerates 22 kings as subject to his scepter.

Essex, Earl of. *See* **Cromwell, Thomas; Devereux, Robert**

Estournelles de Constant *(ĕs tōōr nĕl də kôNs täN),* **Paul Henry Benjamin Balluat, Baron d'** 1852–1924. French statesman. *b.* La Flèche. French delegate to The Hague Peace Conference (1907); cowinner with Auguste Beernaert of Nobel Peace Prize (1909).

Eucken *(oi kĕn),* **Rudolf Christoph** 1846–1926. German philosopher. *b.* Aurich. Professor of philosophy at Jena (from 1874); expounded an idealistic philosophy of ethical activism; awarded Nobel Prize in literature (1908). Works include *Geschichte und Kritik der Grundbegriffe der Gegenwart* (1878) and *Gesammelte Aufsätze zur Philosophie und Lebensanschauung* (1903).

Euclid *(ū klĭd)* *fl.* c300 B.C. Greek mathematician. Founded a school at Alexandria and taught there; laid groundwork of Euclidean geometry with 13 books of the *Elements,* a collection of postulates, theorems, rules, and problems; made contributions to theory of numbers and geometrical optics. Among other works are *Data, Phaenomena, Section of the Scale, Optics, Divisions of Superficies,* and the lost *Pseudaria, Conics, Surface-Loci,* and *Porisms.*

Eugene *(û zhân)* title: PRINCE OF SAVOY; full name: FRANÇOIS EUGÈNE DE SAVOIE-CARIGNAN. 1663–1736. Austrian general. *b.* Paris, France. On banishment of mother, Olympia Mancini, from France, entered service of Austrian Emperor Leopold I; commander in chief of imperial army against Turks (1696); defeated Turks at Senta (1697); on outbreak of War of Spanish Succession (1701–14), invaded Italy and won battles at Carpi and Chiari (1701) over the French; with Marlborough, shared victories at Blenheim (1704) and Oudenarde (1708); expelled French from Italy by victory at Turin (1706); triumphed at Malplaquet (1709), but then fortunes were reversed until Peace of Rastadt (1714) ended the war; in new war with Turks, defeated them at Peterwardein (1716) and Belgrade (1717); imposed Treaty of Passarowitz, which effectively put an end to Turkish power in east Europe.

Euler *(oi lər),* **Leonhard** 1707–83. Swiss mathematician. *b.* Basel. Invited to St. Petersburg by Catherine I and became professor of physics (1730) and mathematics (1733); director of mathematics at Academy of Sciences in Berlin (1741–66); returned to St. Petersburg (1766); made important contributions to algebra, trigonometry, analytic geometry, calculus, mechanics, astronomy, hydrodynamics, and optics; founder of higher mathematics and the calculus of variation; Eulerian equation and Euler's formula named after him.

Euler *(ĕ oo lər),* **Ulf Svante von** 1905–. Swedish physiologist. Cowinner of Nobel Prize in physiology and medicine with B. Katz and J. Axelrod (1970) for research on nerve and muscle functions.

Euler-Chelpin *(oi lər kĕl pĭn),* **Hans August Simon von** 1873–1964. Swedish chemist. *b.* Augsburg, Germany. Went to Sweden and accepted chair of physical chemistry at Stockholm (1898); did research on enzymes and chemistry of fermentation; isolated coenzyme I; with Arthur Harden, awarded Nobel Prize in chemistry (1929).

Euripides *(ū rĭp ĭ dēz)* *fl.* 5th century B.C. Greek playwright. *b.* Salamis. Produced first play, *Peliades,* at age 25; wrote 91 plays, of which 18 are extant; won first prize in five dramatic contests; lived in Athens (to 408) when he left for court of Archelaus, king of Macedonia, where he died (406). The 18 extant plays are *Alcestis, Medea, Hippolytus, Hecuba, Andromache, Ion, The Suppliants, Heracleidae, Mad Heracles, Iphigenia in Aulis, Iphigenia Among the Tauri, The Trojan Women, Helen, The Phoenician Women, Electra, Orestes, Bacchae,* and *Cyclops;* plays characterized by realism, religious skepticism, and extensive use of prologues and epilogues.

Eusebius *(ū sē bĭ əs)* **of Caesarea** surname: PAMPHILI. c264–c340. Palestinian ecclesiastical historian. *b.* Caesarea, Palestine. Bishop of Caesarea (from c314); attended Council of Nicaea and delivered panegyric oration welcoming Emperor Constantine; though a moderate Origenist, voted with Athanasians condemning the Arrians; later attended Synods of Antioch (330) and Tyre (335). Best known as author of *Ecclesiastical History* (10 books, 324) and *Chronicon,* a history of the world to 325; other works include *Preparatio Evangelica, Demonstratio Evangelica, Theophania,* and a life of Constantine; called "Father of church history."

Eustachio *(ā o͞o stä kyō),* **Bartolommeo** Latin name: EUSTACHIUS. c1520–74. Italian anatomist. *b.* San Severino. Professor of anatomy at Rome and physician to the pope; first to describe many internal organs such as the Eustachian tube and the Eustachian valve, the thoracic duct, the uterus, and the kidney. Published *Opuscula Anatomica* (1564) and *Tabulae Anatomicae* (1714); considered a founder of modern anatomy.

Eutyches *(ū tĭ kēz)* c384–c456. Greek heresiarch. Archimandrite in Constantinople; founded Monophysite sect whose chief doctrine was that Christ's humanity was absorbed by His divine nature; teachings condemned by Synod of Constantinople (448); deposed for heresy; reinstated by so-called "Robber Synod," the Council of Ephesus (449); condemned by Council of Chalcedon (451) and finally excommunicated and banished.

Evans *(ĕv ənz),* **Sir Arthur John** 1851–1941. English archaeologist. *b.* Nash Mills. Conducted (from 1898) excavations in Crete that led to the discovery of a pre-Phoenician script and the remains of the Minoan civilization, including the palace of Minos. Author of *Cretan Pictographs* (1896), *Further Discoveries of Cretan and Aegena Script* (1898), *The Mycenaean Tree* (1901), and books on Celtic Art and numismatics.

Evans, Herbert McLean 1882–1971. American anatomist and embryologist. Professor of anatomy (from 1915) and biology (from 1930) at University of California; director of Institute for Experimental Biology (from 1930); discovered vitamin E (1922) and 48 chromosomes in man (1918); isolated four hormones of the pituitary gland and produced endocrine disorders experimentally (1922); demonstrated that vascular trunks originated from capillaries (1909); determined action of vital dyes of the benzidine series; conducted research on physiology of reproduction and the relation between fertility and nutrition.

Evelyn *(ēv lĭn),* **John** 1620–1706. English diarist. *b.* Wotten. Best known for his *Diary,* covering the years from 1640 to 1706, an important sourcebook in British history; wrote over 30 other books on numismatics, architecture, politics, gardening, and other subjects.

Everest *(ĕv ər ĕst),* **Sir George** 1790–1866. British engineer. *b.* Gwernvale. Superintendent of Trigonometrical Survey of India (1823) and surveyor general of India (1830–43); Mount Everest is named in his honor.

Everett *(ĕv ər ĕt),* **Edward** 1794–1865. American statesman and orator. *b.* Dorchester, Mass. Professor of Greek at Harvard (1815); House of Representatives (1825–35); editor of *North American Review* (1820); governor of Mass. (1836–40); minister to court of St. James (1841–45); president of Harvard (1846–49); succeeded Daniel Webster as secretary of state (1852–53); Senator (1853–54); celebrated as an orator; delivered principal speech at dedication of national cemetery at Gettysburg (1863) preceding Lincoln's famous address; published *Orations and Speeches on Various Occasions* (4 vols., 1853–68).

Ewald *(ĭ väl),* **Johannes** also EVALD. 1743–81. Danish poet. *b.* Copenhagen. Established reputation as lyric poet with a poem on the death of King Frederick V (1766). Other works include the Biblical drama *Adam and Eve* (1769), the first Danish tragedy, *Rolf Krage* (1770), a heroic drama, *Balder's Death* (1773), and the festival drama *The Fishermen* (1779) containing the Danish national anthem, *"King Christian Stood by the Lofty Mast."*

Eyck *(īk),* **Jan van** c1389–c1441. Flemish painter. *b.* Maaseyck, Flanders. Brother of HUBERT (c1370–1426), painter. Court painter in service of John of Bavaria and Philip the Good; worked at Bruges and Ghent; best-known work is the altarpiece in the cathedral at Ghent (1432) with 24 panels, whose central motif is the *Adoration of the Lamb;* other works include *Giovanni Arnolfini and His Bride* and *Saint Francis Receiving the Stigmata.*

F

Fabius *(fā bĭ əs)* **Maximus Verrucosus, Quintus** surname: CUNCTATOR (the Delayer). *d.* 203 B.C. Roman general. Scion of one of the oldest Roman patrician families and grandson of QUINTUS FABIUS MAXIMUS RULLIANUS (*d.* c290 B.C.), dictator and victor of Third Samnite War. Consul (233, 228, 215, 214, 209); censor (230); head of Roman mission sent to demand reparations from Carthage (218); dictator and commander of Roman forces in Second Punic War (217); devised strategy of avoiding pitched battles in favor of harassing the enemy by constant skirmishes; recaptured Tarentum from Hannibal during final consulship.

Fabre *(fä br),* **Jean Henry** 1823–1915. French entomologist. *b.* St. Léon. Devoted life to the study of insects; known as the Insects' Homer for poetic style of writing; crowning work was *Souvenirs Entomologiques* (10 vols., 1925), parts of which have been translated into English as *The Life and Love of the Insect* (1911), *Social Life in the Insect World* (1912), *The Life of the Fly* (1913), and *Bumble Bees* (1915).

Fabricius Ab Aquapendente *(fə brĭsh ĭ əs ăb ăk wə pĕn dĕn tē),* **Hieronymous** Italian name: GIROLAMO FABRIZIO. 1537–1619. Italian surgeon and anatomist. *b.* Aquapendente, Italy. Succeeded Gabriel Fallopius as professor of anatomy at Padua (1562); teacher of William Harvey; described the valves of the veins. Author of *Opera Chirurgica* (1617).

Fahrenheit *(fä rĕn hīt),* **Gabriel Daniel** 1686–1736. German physicist. *b.* Danzig, Poland. Perfected the thermometer by using quicksilver instead of spirits; (1714); devised Fahrenheit temperature scale.

Fairbanks *(fâr băngks),* **Charles Warren** 1852-1918. American statesman. *b.* near Unionville Center, Ohio. Senator from Indiana (1897–1905); vice-president of U.S. (1905–1909).

Fairbanks *(fâr băngks),* **Douglas** original name: DOUGLAS ULLMAN. 1883–1939. American film actor. *b.* Denver, Colo. First appeared on stage in 1901; entered films (1915); best remembered for roles in *The Three Musketeers, Robin Hood, The Thief of Baghdad,* and *The Iron Mask;* headed own motion picture company (from 1916); married actress Mary Pickford; son DOUGLAS ELTON FAIRBANKS, JR., 1909–. American actor. *b.* New York. Appeared in numerous films, including *Catherine the Great, The Prisoner of Zenda, Little Caesar,* and *Gunga Din;* later became a diplomat in South America.

Falkner. *See* **Faulkner**

Falla *(fä lyä),* **Manuel de** 1876–1946. Spanish composer. *b.* Cadiz. Lived in Paris (1907–14) and, after Spanish Civil War, in Argentina. Principal compositions include *La Vida Breve* (1905), *Love the Magician* (1915), *The Three-Cornered Hat* (1919), *Nights in the Gardens of Spain* and *Master Peter's Puppet Show* (1923).

Fallopius *(fă lō pĭ əs),* **Gabriel** 1523–62. Italian anatomist. *b.* Modena. Professor of anatomy at Ferrara, Pisa, and Padua; first to describe the structure and function of the Fallopian tubes and other organs of the body; works published (3 vols., 1584).

Faraday *(făr ə dā),* **Michael** 1791–1867. English scientist. *b.* Newington Butts. Assistant to Sir Humphrey Davy (1813); succeeded Davy as professor of chemistry in Royal Institution (1827); discoveries include electromagnetic induction, electrostatic induction (1838), magnetization of light

(1845), diamagnetism (1846), identity of electricity from different sources (1833), relation of electricity and magnetic forces (1838), hydroelectricity (1843), magnetic rotary polarization (1846), relation of gravity to electricity (1851), and atmospheric magnetism (1851); also contributed to study of electrolysis, liquefaction of gases, catalysis, and the vacuum tube. Author of *Chemical Manipulation* (1827), *Experimental Researches in Electricity* (1844–55), and *Experimental Researches in Chemistry and Physics* (1859).

Farragut *(făr ə gŭt),* **David Glasgow** 1801–70. American naval commander. *b.* Campbell's Station, Tenn. Went to sea at age 10; first command aboard the *Ferret* (1821); captain (1855); appointed to command of West Gulf Blockading Squadron (1862); sailed up the Mississippi, past Forts St. Philip and Jackson, to defeat the Confederate flotilla and enable the capture of New Orleans; ran blockade of mines in Mobile Bay, defeated Confederate fleet under Franklin Buchanan, and took Forts Gaines and Morgan (1864); admiral (1866), a post created for him by a grateful Congress.

Faulkner *(fôk nər),* **William Harrison** original name: FALKNER. 1897–1962. American writer. *b.* New Albany, Miss. One of greatest American writers; known for original but complicated prose style. In series of novels located in the mythical town of Jefferson in Yoknapatawpha County, explored breakdown of social fabric of the Deep South; awarded Nobel Prize for literature (1949). Works include *Soldier's Pay* (1926), *Mosquitoes* (1927), *Sartoris* (1929), *The Sound and the Fury* (1929), *As I Lay Dying* (1930), *Sanctuary* (1931), *Idyll in the Desert* (1931), *Light in August* (1932), *Pylon* (1935), *Absalom, Absalom!* (1936), *The Unvanquished* (1938), *The Wild Palms* (1939), *The Hamlet* (1940), *Go Down, Moses and Other Stories* (1942), *Intruder in the Dust* (1948), and *Requiem for a Nun* (1951); won Pulitzer Prize for *A Fable* (1955) and *The Reivers* (1963).

Fawkes *(fôks),* **Guy** 1570–1606. English conspirator. *b.* York. Converted to Roman Catholicism; served in Spanish army in Flanders (1593); returned to England on accession of James I; conspired with Robert Catesby, Thomas Percy, Thomas Winter, John Wright, and other Catholics to blow up the House of Commons (1604); plot, known as the Gunpowder Plot, was discovered and he was caught in the gunpowder-filled cellar under Parliament (1605); arrested and tortured, tried, convicted, and executed with accomplices (1606). Nov. 5 is celebrated as Guy Fawkes Day.

Fénelon *(fān lôN),* **François de Salignac de la Mothe-** 1651–1715. French writer. *b.* Périgord. Ordained (1675); appointed by Louis XIV as tutor to grandson, the duc de Bourgogne (1689); for the edification of his charge, wrote *Fables, Dialogues des Morts,* and *History of the Ancient Philosophers;* archbishop of Cambria (1695); defended Madame Guyon, the quietist mystic, in *Maximes des Saints sur la Vie Intérieure,* but acquiesced when work was condemned by pope; most famous work, *Telemaque* (1699), offended the king, who thought it a satire on his court; lived in seclusion in diocese.

Ferdinand V of Castile *(fûr· dĭ nănd)* or FERDINAND II OF ARAGON; also called FERDINAND THE CATHOLIC. 1452–1516. *b.* Sos, Aragon. Son of John II of Navarre and Aragon; married Isabella, sister of Henry IV of Castile (1469); joint sovereign of Castile with Isabella (1474–1504); king of Sicily (1468–1516); king of Aragon as Ferdinand II (1479–1516); resumed wars against Moors and conquered Granada (1492); expelled Jews from Spain (1492); broke power of feudal lords and banditti by organizing Santa Hermandad (holy brotherhood); established Inquisition (1478–80); sponsored historic voyage of Columbus to New World (1492); formed Holy League, an alliance with the Pope, the Emperor, Milan, Venice, and England against Charles VIII of France; expelled French from Naples and crowned himself Ferdinand III of Naples (1504); on the death of Isabella (1504), proclaimed himself regent of Castile for daughter Juana, who was insane; married Germaine de Foix (1505); invaded and conquered Navarre and incorporated it with Castile (1515); divided the world with Portugal by Treaty of Tordesillas (1494); reign considered to mark the beginning of Spain's imperial power.

Fermi *(fār mē)*, **Enrico** 1901–54. Italian physicist. *b.* Rome. Professor of theoretical physics in Rome (1926–38), at Columbia (1939–45), and at Institute of Nuclear Studies in Chicago (from 1945); leading scientist in Manhattan Project; constructed first American nuclear reactor (1942); first to split the atom by bombarding it with neutrons; discovered element 93 (neptunium); investigated structure and behavior of atomic nuclei; awarded Nobel Prize in physics (1938).

Feuchtwanger *(foiKt väng ər)*, **Lion** 1884–1958. German writer. *b.* Munich. Fled (1933) Hitler's Germany; interned in France (1940); settled in U.S. (1940). Author of *The Ugly Duchess* (1923), *Success* (1930), *Josephus* (1932), *The Jew of Rome* (1935), *Paris Gazette* (1939), *Proud Destiny* (1945), *This is the Hour* (1951), and other books.

Feuerbach *(foi ər bäK)*, **Ludwig Andreas** 1804–72. German philosopher. *b.* Landshut. Son of PAUL JOHANN ANSELM VON FEUERBACH (1775–1833), celebrated German jurist. Abandoned Hegelianism for naturalistic materialism; held that God is only a self-projection of man; denied immortality, moral obligations, and all forms of external authority. Author of *Das Wesen des Christentums* (1840), *Das Wesen der Religion* (1845), and others (10 vols., 1846–66).

Feynman *(fīn mən)*, **Richard Phillips** 1918–. American physicist. *b.* New York, N.Y. Professor at California Institute of Technology; co-winner of Nobel Prize (1965) in physics (with J. Schwinger and S. Tomonaga) for work on quantum electrodynamics.

Fibiger *(fē bə gēr)*, **Johannes** 1867–1928. Danish pathologist. *b.* Silkeborg. Professor of pathology at Copenhagen (from 1900); first to experimentally produce cancer in rats; awarded Nobel Prize in physiology and medicine (1927).

Fichte *(fĭK tē),* **Johann Gottlieb** 1762–1814. German philosopher. *b.* Rammenau. Expounded Kantian system in *Kritik Aller Offenbarung* (1792); professor of philosophy at Jena (1793–99); charged with atheism; left for Berlin; first rector of University of Berlin (1810–14); modified Kantian metaphysics in later works by making the conscious ego, rather than Kant's "thing-in-itself," the primary reality; by basing transcendental idealism on subjective self-affirmation, foreshadowed existentialism; in *Address to the German Nation* (1807–1808), articulated philosophy of German nationalism.

Field *(fēld),* **Cyrus West** 1819–1912. American merchant. *b.* Stockbridge, Mass. Founded Cyrus W. Field & Company (1841), wholesale paper merchants; in association with Frederick N. Gisborne, promoted project to lay the first submarine telegraph cable between England and U. S. (1854–58, 1866); given gold medal by Congress in recognition of efforts.

Fielding *(fēl dĭng),* **Henry** 1707–54. English writer. *b.* Sharpham Park. With Richardson, Smollett, and Stern, considered one of the major novelists of 18th-century English literature. Reputation rests on novels *Joseph Andrews* (1742), *Jonathan Wild* (1743), *Tom Jones* (1749), and *Amelia* (1751); plays *Love in Several Masques* (1728), *The Temple Beau* (1730), *Tom Thumb* (1730), *Rape Upon Rape* (1730), *The Modern Husband* (1731) *Pasquin* (1736), and *The Historical Register for the Year 1736* (1737); also wrote prose essays, poems, and the autobiographical *Journal of a Voyage to Lisbon* (1755).

Fillmore *(fĭl mōr),* **Millard** 1800–1874. 13th president of the U.S. *b.* Locke, N.Y. U.S. Congressman on Whig ticket (1833–35, 1837–43); vice-president of U.S. (1849–50); succeeded to presidency on Zachary Taylor's death (1850); adopted a moderate conservative stand on slavery issue and promoted Compromise of 1850; failed to receive Whig presidential nomination (1852); unsuccessful presidential candidate of American (Know-Nothing) party (1856).

Finlay *(fĭn lī),* **Carlos Juan** 1833–1915. Cuban physician. *b.* Puerto Príncipe. First to suggest that yellow fever is transmitted by the mosquito (1881); chief sanitary officer of Cuba (1902–1909).

Finsen *(fĭn sən),* **Niels Ryberg** 1860–1904. Danish physician. *b.* Thorshavn, Faroe Islands. Founded the science of phototheraphy; discovered therapeutic power of chemical rays of sunlight and artificial light; awarded Nobel Prize in physiology and medicine (1903).

Firdausi *(fər dou sē)* real name: ABUL KASIM MANSUR or HASAN. c941–c1020. Persian poet. *b.* near Tus. Court poet to Mahmud of Ghazni, spent 35 years composing the epic *Shah Namah (Book of Kings)* in 60,000 couplets; received the name "Firdausi" (Native of Paradise) for his skill; quarrelled with the sultan when cheated of the promised reward; left Ghazni after writing bitter satire on Mahmud; spent rest of life in Herat, Mazanderan, and Baghdad; reconciled with Mahmud and returned home to die; also wrote *Yusuf and Zuleikha.*

Fischer *(fĭsh ər),* **Emil** 1852–1919. German chemist. *b.* Euskirchen. Professor of chemistry at Munich (1879–82), Erlangen (1882–85), Würzburg (1885–92), and Berlin (1892–1919); determined structure of sugars, proteins, and purines and synthesized most of them; awarded Nobel Prize in chemistry (1902).

Fischer, Hans 1881–1945. German chemist. *b.* Höchst. Professor of chemistry at Munich (1915, 1921), Innsbruck (1916), and Vienna (1919); synthesized hemin (1928); investigated chlorophyll, porphyrins, and pyrolle; awarded Nobel Prize in chemistry (1930); died by own hand.

Fish *(fĭsh),* **Hamilton** 1808–93. American statesman. *b.* New York, N.Y. Congressman on Whig ticket (1843–45); governor of N.Y. (1849–50); senator (1851–57); secretary of state (1869–77); signed the Washington Treaty of 1871, which settled Alabama claims with Great Britain.

Fisher *(fĭsh ər),* **Andrew** 1862–1928. Australian statesman. *b.* Crosshouse, Scotland. Member of Queensland legislative assembly (1893–1901); Federal House of Representatives (1901–16); member of first Labor government of Australia as minister of trade and customs (1904); leader of Labor party in Parliament (1907); prime minister (1908–1909, 1910–13, 1914–15); Australian high commissioner in England (1916–21).

Fisher, Saint John 1459–1535. English ecclesiastic and martyr. *b.* Beverley. Professor of divinity at Cambridge (1503) and chancellor (1504); bishop of Rochester (from 1504); president of Queen's College (1505–1508); favored New Learning but opposed Reformation; refused to recognize validity of Henry VIII's marriage with Anne Boleyn; refused to comply with Act of Supremacy and Act of Succession; convicted of treason and committed to the Tower; created cardinal by Pope Paul III (1535); beheaded (1535); canonized (1935). Feast day: July 9.

Fitzgerald *(fĭts jĕr əld),* **Edward** 1809–83. English poet. *b.* near Woodbridge. Known for free rendering of quatrains of Omar Khayyam, the 11th-century Persian astronomer-poet, in the *Rubáiyát of Omar Khayyám* (1859); also translated Sophocles, Calderón, and Jami's *Salámán and Absál.*

Fitzgerald, F. Scott full name: Francis Scott Key Fitzgerald. 1896–1940. American writer. *b.* St. Paul, Minn. Popular novelist who chronicled the jazz age in his novels; also known for living the extravagant life of the golden youth of the twenties with his wife Zelda. Principal works: *This Side of Paradise* (1920), *The Beautiful and Damned* (1922), *The Great Gatsby* (1925), *Tender is the Night* (1934), *Taps at Reveille* (1935), *Tales of the Jazz Age* (1922), *All the Sad Young Men* (1926), and *The Last Tycoon* (1941).

Flaccus, Alcuin. *See* **Alcuin**

Flammarion *(flȧ mȧ ryôN),* **Nicolas Camille** 1842–1925. French astronomer. *b.* Montigny-le-Roi. On staff of Paris Observatory (1858–62, 1867) and Bureau of Longitudes (1862–65); founded observatory at Juvisy (1882); French Astronomical Society (1887), and the monthly *L'Astronomie* (1883). Published *Les Merveilles Célestes* (1865), *Astronomie Populaire* (1880), *Les Étoiles* (1881), *Le Monde Avant la Création de l'Homme* (1886), *Uranie* (1889), *La Fin du Monde* (1893), and *La Planète Mars et Ses Conditions d'Inhabitabilité* (1909).

Flamsteed *(flăm stēd),* **John** 1646–1719. English astronomer. *b.* Denby. First astronomer royal (1675); director of Greenwich Observatory (from 1676); recorded astronomical observations (1676–89) in *Historia, Coelestis Britannica* (3 vols., 1725); took holy orders (1684); at first assisted by, but later turned against, Isaac Newton.

Flanagan *(flăn ȧ gən),* **Edward Joseph** 1886–1948. American clergyman. *b.* Roscommon, Ireland. Founded Father Flanagan's Home for Boys in Omaha, which sheltered the homeless (1917), and later grew into an incorporated village known as Boys Town.

Flaubert *(flō bâr),* **Gustave** 1821–80. French novelist. *b.* Rouen. Achieved success with *Madame Bovary* (1857), followed by *Salammbô* (1862), *L'Éducation Sentimentale* (1869), *The Temptation of St. Anthony* (1874), and *Trois Contes* (1877); considered a pioneer of realism because of the wealth of detail and minutiae of observation; influenced Zola, Daudet, and Turgenev with his stylistic perfectionism and objectivity; combined a romantic love of the exotic with an aversion for bourgeois society.

Fleming *(flĕm ĭng),* **Sir Alexander** 1881–1955. British bacteriologist. *b.* Lochfield, Scotland. Working as professor of bacteriology at St. Mary's Hospital, London, discovered penicillin (1928) and lysozyme (1929); shared Nobel Prize in physiology and medicine with Howard Florey and Ernest B. Chain (1945).

Fletcher *(flĕch ər),* **John** 1579–1625. English playwright. *b.* Rye. Wrote plays alone and in collaboration, primarily with Francis Beaumont and Philip Massinger. Works include *The Faithful Shepherdess* (1609), *Bonduca* (1619), *Valentinian* (1614), *Women Pleased* (1620), *The Pilgrim* (1621), *The Wild Goose Chase* (1621), *A King and No King* (1611), *The Maid's Tragedy* (1611), *Philaster* (1608–11), *The Spanish Curate* (1622), *Honest Man's Fortune* (1613), *The Prophetess* (1622), *Thierry and Theodoret* (1616), and *The Knight of Malta* (1616); wrote *The Two Noble Kinsmen* (1634) and *Henry VIII* with Shakespeare.

Fleury *(flû rē),* **André Hercule de** 1653–1743. French prelate and statesman. *b.* Lodève. Bishop of Frejus (1698); as tutor of King Louis XV (from 1715), acquired ascendancy at court; member of council of state (1723); cardinal (1726); prime minister and virtual ruler of France (1726–43); tried to maintain peace and restore national finances; ousted at outset of the War of Austrian Succession.

Florey *(flō rĭ),* **Sir Howard Walter** 1898–1968. British pathologist. *b.* Adelaide, Australia. Professor of pathology at Oxford (1935–62); shared Nobel Prize in physiology and medicine with Alexander Fleming and E. B. Chain for discovery of penicillin (1945); president of Royal Society (1940–45).

Foch *(fôsh),* **Ferdinand** 1851–1929. French general. *b.* Tarbes. Professor (1808) and commandant of École Supérieure de la Guerre (1907); on outbreak of World War I, commanded 20th Army Corps at Nancy; helped devise strategy that stopped Germans at Marne (1914); directed French offensives (1915) culminating in Battle of the Somme (1916); president of inter-Allied Council at Versailles (1917); commander in chief of Allied armies (1918); marshal of France; led Allies' victorious offensive and received German surrender (1918); chairman of supreme war council (from 1919). Author of *Principles of War* (1919) and *Memoirs* (1931).

Fokine *(fô kyĭn),* **Michel** 1880–1942. Russian choreographer. *b.* St. Petersburg. Considered the creator of modern ballet; directed Diaghilev's company (1909–14) and founded own in U.S. (from 1925); naturalized American citizen (1932). Principal choreographies include *The Dying Swan, Blue Beard, Cleopatra, Petrouchka, Scheherazade, Papillons,* and *Paganini.*

Fonteyn *(fôn tān),* **Margot** Full name: Dame Margot Fonteyn de Arias; *née* Margaret Hookham. 1919–. English ballerina. *b.* Reigate. Joined Sadler's Wells Ballet (now the Royal Ballet) in 1934, making her first appearance in *The Haunted Ballroom;* best remembered for her classic roles in *Giselle* and *Sleeping Beauty.*

Ford *(fōrd),* **Ford Madox** original surname: Hueffer. 1873–1939. English writer. *b.* Merton. Founded *English Review* and *Transatlantic Review;* author of *The Fifth Queen* (1906), *The Half Moon* (1909), *The Good Soldier* (1915), *Collected Poems* (1913), *New Poems* (1927), a cycle of four novels titled *Parade's End* (1950), critical studies *Joseph Conrad* (1924), *Rossetti* (1902), *Henry James* (1913), and *Hans Holbein the Younger* (1905); collaborated with Conrad on *The Inheritors* (1901) and *Romance* (1903).

Ford, Gerald Rudolph 1913–. 38th president of U.S. *b.* Omaha, Neb. Member, House of Representatives (1948–73); House Republican minority leader (1965–73); appointed vice-president under 25th Amendment following Spiro Agnew's resignation (1973); raised to presidency on resignation of Richard Nixon (1974); continued economic and foreign policies of predecessor; defeated by Jimmy Carter (1976).

Ford, Henry 1863–1947. American industrialist. *b.* Greenfield, Mich. Founded Ford Motor Company (1903); introduced pioneering assembly-line mass-production techniques; achieved phenomenal success with Model-T cars, selling 15 million (up to 1928); chartered Peace Ship (1915) in a futile effort to end World War I; yielded presidency to son Edsel Bryant (1893–1943) in 1918, but resumed it on Edsel's death (1943). Author of *My Life and Work* (1925) and *Today and Tomorrow* (1926).

Ford, John c1586–c1640. English dramatist. *b.* Ilsington. Principal dramatic works include *The Lovers*

Melancholy (1628), *'Tis Pity Shee's a Whore* (1626), *Love's Sacrifice* (1630), *Chronicle Historie of Perkin Warbeck* (1634), *The Ladies Triall* (1638), and *The Witch of Edmonton* (1621).

Ford, John real name: Sean O'Feeney. 1895–1973. American motion picture director. *b.* Cape Elizabeth, Me. Received Academy Awards for *The Informer* (1935), *The Grapes of Wrath* (1940), and *How Green Was My Valley* (1941). Other notable films include *Stagecoach* (1939), *Tobacco Road* (1941), and *Fort Apache* (1948).

Forester *(fôr əs tər),* **Cecil Scott** 1899–1966. English writer. *b.* Cairo, Egypt. Works include the *Captain Horatio Hornblower* trilogy (1937–39), and later Hornblower stories, *Payment Deferred* (1926), *The African Queen (1935), The Good Shepherd* (1955), and *The Sky and the Forest* (1948); also wrote biographies of Napoleon, Josephine, Victor Emmanuel, Louis XIV, and Nelson; published autobiography *Long Before Forty* (1967).

Forrestal *(fôr ĕst əl),* **James Vincent** 1892–1949. American statesman. *b.* Beacon, N.Y. President of the New York investment house of Dillon, Read & Company (1937–40); entered public service as an assistant to Franklin D. Roosevelt (1940); secretary of the Navy (1944–47); secretary of newly established Department of Defense (1947–49); committed suicide (1949). *The Forrestal Diaries* were published posthumously.

Forssmann *(fôrs mən),* **Werner Theodor Otto** 1904–. German physician. *b.* Berlin. Developed new techniques in heart surgery, including cardiac catheterization; co-winner of Nobel Prize in physiology and medicine (1956) with A. Cournand and D. Richards.

Forster *(fôr stər),* **Edward Morgan** usually E.M. FORSTER. 1879–1970. British novelist. *b.* London. Member of the Bloomsbury group; best known for *Passage to India* (1924), which explored the clash of English and Indian civilizations; other works include *The Longest Journey* (1907), *Where Angels Fear to Tread* (1905), *A Room with a View* (1908), *Howard's End* (1910), *The Celestial Omnibus* (1914), *The Eternal Moment* (1928), *Aspects of the Novel* (1927), *Abinger Harvest* (1936), *Virginia Woolf* (1942), and *Maurice* (1971).

Fortescue *(fôr təs kū),* **Sir John** c1394–c1476. English jurist. *b.* in Somerset. Lord chief justice of the king's bench (1442); as a loyal Lancastrian, attainted by Edward IV (1462); fled with Margaret of Anjou to Scotland and then to Flanders (1463); fought on losing side at Tewkesbury and captured (1471); submitted to Edward IV and granted pardon; notable in English legal history for *De Laudibus Legum Angliae* (1537) and *On the Governance of England* (1714).

Fosdick *(fŏz dĭk),* **Harry Emerson** 1878–1969. American clergyman. *b.* Buffalo, N.Y. Ordained (1903); professor of theology, Union Theological Seminary (1915–46); pastor, Riverside Baptist Church, New York City (1926–46); prominent as a radio preacher; defended modernist theology against Fundamentalism. Author of *The Second Mile* (1908), *The Assurance of Immortality* (1913), *The Meaning of Prayer* (1915), *Twelve Tests of Character* (1923), *A Guide to Understanding the Bible* (1938), *On Being A Real Person* (1943), and *The Living of These Days* (1956).

Foster *(fôs tər),* **John Watson** 1836–1917. American statesman. *b.* Pike County, Ind. Secretary of state (1892–93); U.S. agent at Bering Sea Arbitration in Paris (1893) and before Alaskan Boundary Tribunal in London (1903); represented emperor of China in Sino-Japanese peace negotiations (1894) and at second Hague Conference (1907). Author of *A Century of American Diplomacy* (1900), *American Diplomacy in the Orient* (1903), *The Practice of Diplomacy* (1906), *Diplomatic Memoirs* (1909), and other books.

Foster, Stephen Collins 1826–64. American composer. *b.* Pittsburgh, Pa. Wrote over 200 songs, some of them still among the world's best-loved, including "Old Folks at Home," "My Old Kentucky Home," "Old Black Joe," "Camptown Races," "Oh! Susannah," "Massa's in de Cold, Cold Ground," "Jeanie with the Light Brown Hair," "Beautiful Dreamer," and "Louisiana Belle"; songs popularized by Negro minstrel bands; died in poverty.

Foucault *(fo͞o kō),* **Jean Bernard Léon** 1819–68. French physicist. *b.* Paris. Made important discoveries in optics and mechanics; determined velocity of light using a rotating mirror and proved that light travels more slowly in water than in air; proved axial rotation of the earth; discovered Foucault or eddy currents surrounding noninsulated conductors; invented Foucault prism (1857) and the gyroscope (1852); improved mirrors of reflecting telescopes.

Fourier *(fo͞o ryā),* **François Marie Charles** 1772–1837. French socialist. *b.* Bensançon. Served in army as a chasseur (1793–95); worked thereafter as a commercial traveler; founded Fourierism, a utopian social philosophy. It projected a cooperative community consisting of self-sufficient units (phalanges), each consisting of 1500 people housed in a common dwelling, with freedom to change professions and marriage partners at will; expounded in *Théorie des Quatre Mouvements et des Destinées Générales* (1808), *Traité d'Association Domestique Agricole* (1822), and *Le Nouveau Monde Industriel et Sociétaire* (1829).

Fourier, Baron Jean Baptiste Joseph 1768–1830. French scientist. *b.* Auxerre. Accompanied Napoleon to Egypt (1798); governor of lower Egypt and permanent secretary of the Institute at Cairo; published *Description de l'Égypt;* returned to France; appointed prefect of Isère and later Rhône; conducted research on heat and numerical equations; originated Fourier's theorem and the Fourier series. Author of *Théorie Analytique de la Chaleur* (1822) and *Analyse des Équations Déterminées* (1831).

Fournier d'Albe *(fo͞or nyā dălb),* **Edmund Edward** 1868–1933. English inventor. *b.* London. Invented the optophone, an instrument that converted light into sound, enabling blind people to read by ear (1914); founded telephotography by transmitting first photographic portrait broadcast from London (1923); invented wireless telewriting based on acoustic resonance (1925); compiled an English-Irish dictionary (1903). Author of *The Electron Theory* (1906), *Contemporary Chemistry* (1912), *The Moon Element* (1924), and other books.

Fox *(fŏks),* **Charles James** 1749–1806. English statesman. *b.* London. Entered Parliament at age 19; lord of admiralty (1770–72) and of treasury (1772–74) in the North ministry; earned lifelong hostility of George III by opposition to royal policies; championed the cause of American colonies and vigorously opposed North's colonial policy and the tea duty; foreign secretary (1782–83); resigned on defeat of India Reform Bill; prosecutor in impeachment of Hastings; (1788); employed powers of oratory to advocate Test Acts repeal, abolition of slave trade, parliamentary reform, Canadian self-government, and to oppose treason and sedition bills; defended French Revolution and hailed the fall of the Bastille as "the greatest event that ever happened in the world"; opposed war with France and demanded nonintervention in French affairs; broke with Edmund Burke over French issue; led opposition to William Pitt's foreign policies; withdrew from political life (1797), faced with growing unpopularity of views; toured Netherlands and France (1802) and met with Napoleon; on death of Pitt, appointed foreign secretary in All-the-Talents ministry (1806); initiated peace negotiations with France; buried in Westminster Abbey.

Fox, George 1624–91. English religious leader. *b.* Fenny Drayton. Felt divine call (1643); preached direct and personal relationship with God through inward light of Christ; denounced organized religion, social conventions, and idle amusements; founded (1647–48) the Society of the Friends of Truth (called Quakers) and gained many converts among lower-middle class; made missionary journeys to Scotland (1657), Ireland (1669), West Indies and North America (1671–72), Holland and Germany (1677, 1684); undeterred by persecution and imprisonment, completed organization of sect (1669). Writings include *Journal* (1694), *A Collection of . . . Epistles* (1698), and *Gospel Truth* (1706).

Foxe *(fŏks),* **John** 1516–87. English martyrologist. *b.* Boston. Ordained deacon (1550) and priest (1560). Best known as author of *History of the Acts and Monuments of the Church* popularly known as *Foxe's Book of Martyrs* (1563).

Fragonard *(frȧ gô nȧr),* **Jean Honoré** 1732–1806. French painter. *b.* Grasse. Painted genre pictures of the amorous life at French court, especially a series for Madame du Barry known as *Romance of Love and Youth.* Works include *Bathers, The Swing, Fountain of Love, Music Lesson, Instant Desire,* and *Billet Doux;* also painted landscapes notable for techniques that foreshadowed Impressionism.

France *(frȧNs),* **Anatole** pseudonym of JACQUES ANATOLE FRANÇOIS THIBAULT. 1844–1924. French writer. *b.* Paris. Served on *Le Temps* as literary critic (1888–92); joined Zola in defense of Dreyfus and emerged as an opponent of church and state; principal works include *The Crime of Sylvestre Bonnard* (1881), *Thaïs* (1890), *La Rôtisserie de la Reine Pédauque* (1893), *Histoire Contemporaine* (4 vols., 1896–1901), *Penguin Island* (1908), *Les Dieux Ont Soif* (1912), *The Revolt of the Angels* (1914), and *La Vie in Fleur* (1922). Awarded Nobel Prize in literature (1921) and elected to French Academy (1896).

Francis I *(frȧn sĭs)* 1494–1547. King of France (1515–47). *b.* Cognac. Began reign with victorious Marignano campaign in northern Italy and conquest of Milan (1515); as candidate for imperial crown, lost to Charles V (1519); waged in four wars against Charles V; in first war (1521–26), defeated and taken prisoner at Pavia and released by the surrender of Burgundy, Milan, Genoa, and Naples; second war (1527–29), in alliance with England, Milan, Venice, Florence, Genoa, and the pope, ended by Peace of Cambrai (1529), the so-called "Ladies' Peace," signed for Francis by his mother Louise of Savoy and for Charles by his aunt Margaret of Austria; third war (1536–38) ended by Peace of Nice; fourth war (1542–44) ended, despite victory at Ceresole Alba (1544), by Treaty of Crespy, which continued the antebellum status quo; during last two wars, allied with Suleiman the Magnificent; presided over a brilliant court; patron of Marot, Cellini, and Rabelais; founded Collège de France; built palaces at Fontainebleau, St.-Germain, Cambord, and Villers-Cotterets; sponsored French colonization of Canada.

Francis of Assisi, Saint lay name: Giovanni Francesco Bernardone. 1182–1226. Italian friar. *b.* Assisi. After recovering from a serious illness, had a dream which led him to give up his inheritance and dedicate himself to ascetic devotion, poverty, and care of the poor; gathered eleven disciples and drew up a rule for the Franciscan order, informally approved by Innocent III (1209); rules modifed (1221, 1223) and confirmed by Pope Honorius III (1226); with followers, began preaching a gospel of joyful humility, poverty, and love that extended to birds, beasts, and natural elements; established Second Order of Franciscans for nuns (1212) under Saint Clare, and the Third Order, the Secular Tertiaries (1221); made pilgrimage to Holy Land during Fifth Crusade and secured for the order the right of guardianship of the Holy Sepulchre (1219–20); gave up position as head of the order (1221) and retired to preaching and contemplation; received miracle of the stigmata at Mount Alverno (1224); acknowledged as a saint during his lifetime; canonized (1228); legends of his life collected as *Little Flowers of Saint Francis*. Feast day: Oct. 4.

Francis of Sales, Saint 1567–1622. French prelate. *b.* Sales, Savoy. Ordained (1593); converted the Protestants of Chablais through eloquent sermons; bishop of Nicopolis (1599); bishop of Geneva (1602); helped found Order of the Visitation (1610); canonized (1665); declared Doctor of the Church (1877); patron saint of Catholic writers (1922). Works include *Introduction to a Devout Life* and *Treatise on the Love of God*. Feast day: Jan. 29.

Franck *(fräNk),* **César Auguste** 1822–90. French composer. *b.* Liège, Belgium. Professor of the organ at Paris Conservatory (1872); produced best works after age 50. Compositions include *Hulda* (1895), *Ghisèle* (1896); *Ruth* (1846), *Rédemption* (1872), *Les Béatitudes* (1880), *Rébecca* (1881), *Les Éolides* (1876), *Le Chasseur Maudit* (1883), *Les Djinns* (1884), *Symphony in D Minor* (1886–88), and *Variations Symphoniques.*

Franco *(fräng kō),* **Francisco** full name: FRANCISCO PAULINO HERMENEGILDO TEÓDULO FRANCO-BAHAMONDE. 1892–1975. Spanish statesman. *b.* El Ferrol. Distinguished in campaign against Abd-el-Krim in Morocco (1926); appointed general at age 32; army chief of staff under Robles (1935); on outbreak of Civil War, reinforced insurgents with foreign legionnaires and Moorish troops from Morocco; after death of General Sanjurjo, succeeded as civil and military leader of Nationalists (1936); proclaimed caudillo, generalissimo, and head of state (1938); with aid from Nazi Germany and Fascist Italy, wore down Republican Loyalists in a long bloody struggle; captured Madrid, Barcelona, and Valencia (1939), ending Civil War; signed concordat with the Vatican (1941); kept Spain out of World War II; occupied Tangier (1941) and sent Blue Division of Spanish volunteers to aid Germans on Russian front; exercised absolute power until death; by law of succession of 1947, restored Spanish monarchy (1975).

Frank *(frangk),* **Ilya Mikhailovich** 1908–. Soviet physicist. Shared (with P. A. Cherenkov and I. Y. Tamm) Nobel Prize in physics (1958) for studies of high-energy particles and cosmic radiation, particularly the Cherenkov effect.

Franklin *(frăngk lin),* **Benjamin** 1706–90. American statesman. *b.* Boston, Mass. Apprenticed (1718) as printer to brother James; drifted to Philadelphia (1723); went to London (1724) as master printer; returned to Philadelphia as printer and publisher; published (1730–48) *The Pennsylvania Gazette* and *Poor Richard's Almanack* (1732–57); helped found American Philosophical Society (1743), Philadelphia Library (1742), and University of Pennsylvania (1751); commenced scientific experiments as a member of Junto Club; invented Franklin stove and Ferguson's clock; investigated electricity and proved that lightning and electric current are identical; plotted courses of North American storms and the Gulf Stream; entered public life (1754) as member of Albany Congress, proposing plan of union for colonies; agent for Pennsylvania and other colonies in England (1757–62, 1764–75); made plea against stamp tax before House of Commons (1766); returned on outbreak of hostilities; member of Second Continental Congress (1775); member of committee to draft Declaration of Independence and one of its signatories; one of three men sent to Paris to negotiate treaty with France (1776) and to obtain supplies; ambassador to France (1778–85); commissioner, with John Jay and John Adams, to negotiate peace with Great Britain (1781–83); returned to Philadelphia (1785); president of Pennsylvania executive council (1785–87); member of Constitutional Convention (1787); urged Congress to abolish slavery (1790). Complete works collected and edited by A. H. Smyth (10 vols., 1905–1907).

Franklin, Sir John 1786–1847. English explorer. *b.* Spilsby. Commanded *Trent* in arctic expedition under Captain Buchan; headed expeditions to northern coast of North America (1819–22, 1825–27); commanded ill-fated *Erebus* and *Terror* on an expedition to discover the Northwest Passage (1845); ships crushed by thick ice in Victoria Strait (1846); perished with other members of the expedition; remains found (1859).

Fraunhofer *(froun hō fər)*, **Joseph von** 1787–1826. German physicist and optician. *b.* Straubing, Bavaria. Founded optical institute at Munich; discovered the dark lines in solar spectrum called Fraunhofer lines; made improvements in telescopes and other optical instruments; invented various meters to measure wavelengths of light.

Frazer *(frā zər)*, **Sir James George** 1854–1941. Scottish anthropologist. *b.* Glasgow. Professor of social anthropology at Liverpool (from 1907); published *The Golden Bough* (12 vols., 1900) and a supplement, *Aftermath* (1936), both historical and comparative studies of primitive rites, myths, magic cults, and customs. Other works include *Totemism and Exogamy* (4 vols., 1910); *The Belief in Immortality and the Worship of the Dead* (3 vols., 1913–24), *Folklore in the Old Testament* (1918), and *Anthologia Anthropologica* (1938–39).

Frederick I *(frĕd ər ĭk)* also FREDERICK BARBAROSSA. c1123–90. Holy Roman emperor (1152–90). Succeeded father Frederick II as Frederick III, duke of Swabia, and uncle Conrad III as king of Germany (1152–90); pacified Germany by proclaiming general land peace (1152); crowned emperor by Pope Adrian IV (1155); led six expeditions to Italy (1154–55), 1158–62, 1163, 1166–68, 1174–77, 1184–86) to subdue republican cities of Lombardy; defeated at Legnano (1176) by Lombard League; granted autonomy to Lombardian cities by Peace of Constance (1183); made peace with Pope Alexander IV; broke power of Guelphic leader Henry the Lion (1180–81); asserted sovereignty over Poland, Hungary, Denmark, and Burgundy; died while leading Third Crusade (1190).

Frederick II 1194–1250. Holy Roman emperor (1215–50) and king of Sicily as Frederick I (1198–1250). *b.* Jesi, Italy. Son of Henry VI; ascended throne of the Two Sicilies (1208); helped by Pope Innocent III to wrest imperial crown from Otto IV at Battle of Bouvines; crowned at Aachen (1215); crowned emperor at Rome by Pope Honorius III (1220); led Fifth Crusade (1228–29); captured Jerusalem (1229) and concluded truce with the sultan of Egypt; crowned king of Jerusalem; began struggle with the popes and Lombard League in attempting to unite Germany and Italy; thrice excommunicated by popes Honorius III and Gregory IX; remembered as a patron of art and literature and for legal, fiscal, and commercial reforms.

Frederick II also FREDERICK THE GREAT. 1712–86. King of Prussia (1740–86). *b.* Berlin, Germany. Son of Frederick William I; at age 18, attempted to flee from father's control and barely escaped execution; king (1740); on the accession of Maria Theresa, laid claim to Silesia and began First Silesian War (1740–42); defeated Austrians at Mollwitz (1741) and Chotusitz (1742) and concluded Treaty of Breslau and Berlin, in which Austria yielded Upper and Lower Silesia to Prussia; in Second Silesian War, defeated Austrians at Hohenfriedburg (1745), Soor (1745), Kesseldorf (1745) and concluded Peace of Dresden which confirmed the cession of Silesia (1745); in Seven Years' War, against combined forces of Austria, Russia, France, Sweden, and Saxony, won great victories at Lobositz (1756), Prague (1757), Rossbach (1757), Leuthen (1757), Zorndorf (1758), Leignitz (1759), and Torgau (1759), but later suffered reverses ended by Peace of Hubertusburg (1763); emerged as great military commander, with Prussia as a major European power; acquired Polish Prussia and a piece of greater Poland by joining Russia in first partition of Poland (1772); took part in War of Bavarian Succession (1778); organized Furstenbund (league of German princes) against Austria (1785); laid foundation of Prussian greatness; was a patron of arts and letters and a lover of French culture, writing all his works in French; invited Voltaire to court (1750–53); champion of religious tolerance and a passable musician; began to codify Prussian law; modernized Prussian army; voluminous writings published (33 vols., 1846–57).

Frederick William known as THE GREAT ELECTOR. 1620–88. Elector of Brandenburg (1640–88). *b.* Berlin, Germany. Son of Elector Geoge William; on accession, found the state ravaged by Thirty Years' War; rid country of foreign soldiers, rebuilt cities, restored economy, and built up army of 30,000 men; by Treaty of Westphalia (1648), recovered eastern Pomerania, Halberstadt, and Minden; by siding with Sweden, secured independence of the duchy of Prussia from Poland (1657); by Treaty of Oliva (1660), obtained full sovereignty over Prussia; after 15-year peace, entered into alliance with the emperor, Holland, Spain, and Denmark against France; defeated Swedes at Fehrbellin (1675), but forced to give in to Treaty of St. Germain (1679), by which all conquests were restored to the Swedes; devoted remainder of reign to consolidation of dominions; encouraged immigration, founded royal library in Berlin, improved the treasury, reorganized universities, and built Prussian army into an efficient military machine; laid foundations of Prussian absolute monarchy.

Frémont *(frē mŏnt),* **John Charles** 1813–90. American explorer. *b.* Savannah, Ga. Officer with U.S. Topographical Corps; accompanied Nicollet on exploration of the region between the upper Mississippi and Missouri

Rivers (1838–39); married Jessie Benton, daughter of Senator Thomas Hart Benton (1841); led surveying expedition to Iowa (1841); expedition to Wind River Range of the Rockies (1842) and another that reached northern Colórado, Nevada, and crossed Rockies into California (1843); explored Great Salt Lake and penetrated to mouth of Columbia River; reached California (1845); on outbreak of war with Mexico, took part in annexation of California and helped to capture Los Angeles; arrested for refusing to obey orders of Stephen W. Kearny; court-martialed and convicted, but sentence remitted by President Polk; resigned from army; led private expedition along upper Rio Grande to locate passes for railroad line to California (1848–49); made fortune as a gold digger; one of first two senators from California (1850–51); nominated for president by Republican party and National American (Know-Nothing) party (1856), but defeated by Buchanan; on outbreak of Civil War, appointed major general in charge of the department of the West, headquartered in St. Louis; transferred to command mountain department in western Virginia under Pope, but relieved at own request and resigned; presidential candidate of western convention of Republican party (1864), but withdrew in favor of Lincoln; governor of Arizona (1878–82); died in relative penury; published *Memoirs of My Life* (1886).

Frémy *(frā mē),* **Edmond** 1814–94. French chemist. *b.* Versailles. Director of Museum of Natural History in Paris (1879–91); did important research on ferric, osmic, palmitic, and sulphuric acids, the coloring matter of leaves and flowers, bone composition, cellulose, iron and steel, and saponification of fats; discovered process for making artificial rubies. Author of *Traité de Chimie Générale* (6 vols., 1854–57) and *Encyclopédie Chimique* (10 vols., 1881–94).

French *(frĕnch),* **Daniel Chester** 1850–1931. American sculptor. *b.* Exeter, N.H. Principal works include *Minute Man, John Harvard, Statue of the Republic, Death and the Young Sculptor, Abraham Lincoln* (in Lincoln Memorial), *John Hancock,* and portrait busts of Poe, Emerson, and Hawthorne in the Hall of Fame.

French, John Denton Pinkstone title: Earl of Ypres. 1852–1925. British general. *b.* Ripple. Entered navy (1866) and army (1874); gained spurs in Sudan (1884–85); cavalry commander in Boer War (1899–1901); general (1907); chief of imperial general staff (1912–14); supreme commander of British Expeditionary Forces in France (1914–15); hero of Ypres; resigned (1915); commander in chief of Home Forces; lord lieutenant of Ireland (1918–21). Author of *1914.*

Freneau *(frə nō),* **Philip Morin** 1752–1832. American poet. *b.* New York, N.Y. Propagandist of colonial causes as editor of *Freeman's Journal* in Philadelphia; commanded privateer in War of Independence; captured by British and imprisoned (until 1780); returned to journalism and founded *National Gazette* (1791–93) and *Time-Piece and Literary Companion* (1797–98). Works include *The*

American Village (1772), *The British Prison-Ship* (1781), and *Poems Written and Published During the American Revolutionary War* (2 vols., 1809). Known as poet of the American Revolution.

Fresnel *(frā něl),* **Augustin Jean** 1788–1827. French physicist. *b.* Broglie. Established wave theory of light, invented Fresnel compound lens for use in lighthouses, and devised Fresnel's rhomb (for circularly polarized light by means of a rhomb-shaped prism).

Freud *(froid),* **Sigmund** 1856–1939. Austrian physician and psychiatrist. Founder of psychoanalysis. *b.* Freiburg, Moravia. Studied hysteria under Joseph Breuer and worked with J.M. Charcot in Paris (1885); with Breuer, published *Studien über Hysterie* (1895) on treatment of hysteria by hypnosis; discontinued hypnosis and developed own psychoanalytic method of free association of ideas directed by an analyst; postulated concepts of undischarged mental energy (conversion), primacy of narcissism and sexual urges, particularly infantile sexuality, and dreams as a reservoir of the unconscious; investigated mechanisms of psychic trauma, repression, projection, sublimation, and catharsis; defined three forces of the mind as id (primal element), ego (rational element), and superego (disciplinary element); believed in constant opposition of two basic human drives, the life force and the death wish; discovered Oedipus and Electra complexes; extended psychoanalysis to study of art, culture, anthropology, and literature; founded Vienna Psychoanalytical Society (1908), gathering a circle of brilliant psychoanalysts, including Adler, Jung, and Rank; professor (1902); broke with Jung and Adler on emphasis on sexuality; fled Hitler's Reich and settled in England (1939); called "the Copernicus of the Mind" for initiating revolution in the understanding of the mind. Author of *The Interpretation of Dreams* (1900), *The Psychopathology of Everyday Life* (1904), *Three Contributions to the Theory of Sex* (1905), *Wit and Its Relation to the Unconscious* (1905), *Totem and Taboo* (1913), *A General Introduction to Psychoanalysis* (1920), *The Ego and the Id* (1927), *New Introductory Lectures in Psychoanalysis* (1933), *Moses and Monotheism* (1939), *An Analysis of Psychoanalysis* (1949), *The Future of an Illusion* (1927), and *Beyond the Pleasure Principle* (1919).

Frick *(frĭk),* **Henry Clay** 1849–1919. American industrialist. *b.* West Overton, Pa. Founded Frick and Company (1870), which operated coke ovens in Connellsville coal area; began association with Carnegie (1881); chairman of Carnegie Brothers and Company (1889); ruthlessly suppressed the Homestead labor strike (1892) and became anathema to the unions; active in organizing United States Steel Corporation, becoming its director; gave residence and art collection in New York City to public.

Fried *(frēt),* **Alfred Hermann** 1864–1921. Austrian pacifist. *b.* Vienna. Settled in Berlin (1883); founded (1892) German Peace Society and the pacifist paper *Die Waffen Nieder!* (1891); name changed to *Die Friedenswarte* (1899). Author of *Grundlagen der Ursächlichen Pazifismus* (1916) and *Kriegstagbuch* (4 vols., 1918–20); awarded Nobel Peace Prize (1911).

Frisch *(frēsh),* **Ragnar** 1895–1973. Norwegian economist. *b.* Oslo. Professor of economics at Oslo (from 1931); founder of Econometrics Society and editor-in-chief of *Econometrica* (1931, 1933); co-winner of first Nobel Prize in economics with J. Tinbergen (1968).

Frobisher *(frō bĭsh ər),* **Sir Martin** c1535–94. English sailor. *b.* Altofts. Commanded three expeditions in search of Northwest Passage (1576, 1577, 1578), on first voyage discovering Frobisher Bay; vice-admiral under Drake on expedition to West Indies (1588); as commander of *Triumph* fought against Armada (1588); wounded in sea battle at Crozon off Brest (1594). Author of *Three Voyages.*

Froebel *(frû bĕl),* **Friedrich** 1782–1852. German educator and founder of the Kindergarten system. *b.* Oberweissbach. Teacher in Frankfurt-am-Main (1805); studied and worked under Johann Pestalozzi at Yverdon (1808–10); with Heinrich Langethal and Wilhelm Middendorf, founded school at Griesheim (1816); moved to Keilhau (1817); began training school for teachers at Liebenstein; opened first kindergarten at Blankenburg (1837) and duplicated it throughout Germany; educational theory emphasized developing children's natural aptitudes through spontaneous activity; by decree of Prussian government banned from establishing schools (1851). Author of *The Education of Man* (1826) and *Autobiography* (1886).

Froissart *(frwȧ sȧr),* **Jean** c1333–c1405. French historian. *b.* Valenciennes. Began writing the classic history *Chronique de France, d'Angleterre, d'Écosse et d'Espagne* at age 19; visited England (1360), Scotland (1364), Italy (with Chaucer and Petrarch, 1368), and other countries; entered the church (c1372); settled in Flanders (1390) and completed the history, which covered the period from 1325 to 1400.

Fromm *(frŏm),* **Erich** 1900–1980. American psychoanalyst. *b.* Frankfurt, Germany. Immigrated to U.S. (1934); professor at New York University (from 1962); one of the major 20th-century figures in psychoanalysis; specializing in application of psychoanalytic theory to problems of culture and society. Major works include *Psychoanalysis and Religion (1950); Escape from Freedom* (1941), *The Art of Loving* (1956), and *Beyond the Chains of Illusion* (1962).

Frontenac *(frôNt nȧk),* **Comte de Palluau et de** original name: LOUIS DE BUADE. 1620–98. French colonial governor. b. Paris. Governor of New France (1672–82, 1689–98); defended Quebec successfully against English (1690); broke power of Iroquois (1696); vigorously pursued policy of exploration and expansion; reestablished Fort Frontenac on site of Kingston, Ontario (1696).

Frost *(frôst),* **Robert Lee** 1874–1963. American poet. *b.* San Francisco, Calif. Worked as farmer, cobbler, and English teacher (1900–1912); lived in England

(1912–15), gaining recognition with *A Boy's Will* (1913) and *North of Boston* (1914); professor of English at Amherst (1916–20, 1923–25, 1926–38); poet-in-residence at University of Michigan (1921–23); professor of poetry at Harvard (from 1939); awarded Pulitzer Prize in poetry (1924, 1931, 1937, 1943); U.S. Senate citation of honor (1950). Author of *Mountain Interval* (1916), *New Hampshire* (1923), *Westrunning Brook* (1928), *A Further Range* (1936), *From Snow to Snow* (1936), *A Witness Tree* (1942), *A Masque of Reason* (1945), *A Masque of Mercy* (1947), *A Steeple Bush* (1947), *Complete Poems* (1949), and *In the Clearing* (1962).

Froude *(frōōd),* **James Anthony** 1818–94. English historian. *b.* Dartington. Took deacon's orders (1844); associated with High Church party under Newman; underwent change of faith and resigned from orders (1872); Regius Professor of Modern History at Oxford (1892–94); as Thomas Carlyle's literary executor, edited his *Reminiscences* and *Life* (1881–84). Author of *History of England from the Fall of Wolsey to the Spanish Armada* (12 vols., 1856–69), *The English in Ireland in the Eighteenth Century* (1872–74), *Caesar* (1879), *Oceana* (1886), *The English in the West Indies* (1888), *The Two Chiefs of Dunboy* (1889), *The Earl of Beaconsfield* (1890), and *Life and Letters of Erasmus* (1894).

Frumentius *(frōō mĕn shĭ əs),* **Saint** *d.* c383. Phoenician apostle of Ethiopia. *b.* Tyre. Shipwrecked on voyage in Red Sea; captured by Abyssinians and sent to royal court; became king's favorite and secretary and evangelized the kingdom; consecrated bishop of Axum by Athanasius at Alexandria (c326).

Fry *(frī),* **Christopher** 1907–. English dramatist. *b.* Bristol. Director of Tunbridge Wells Repertory Players (1932–36) and of Playhouse at Oxford (1940); noted for verse plays, such as *A Phoenix Too Frequent* (1946), *The First-born* (1946), *The Lady's Not for Burning* (1949), *Thor, with Angels* (1949), *Venus Observed* (1950), *A Sleep of Prisoners* (1951), and *The Dark Is Light Enough* (1954); also produced a number of translations and film scripts.

Fry, Roger Eliot 1866–1934. English art critic. *b.* London. Director of Metropolitan Museum of Art, New York City (1905–10); organized first exhibition of Post-Impressionists in London (1910); gained reputation as an international authority on art and aesthetics through his works *Vision and Design* (1920), *Cézanne* (1927), *Flemish Art* (1927), *Henri Matisse* (1930), *Characteristics of French Art* (1932), *Reflections on British Painting* (1934), *Last Lectures* (1939), and other books.

Fugger *(fōōg ər),* Family of German financiers whose fortunes were founded by JOHANNES FUGGER (1348–1409), a weaver of Augsburg, and his sons ANDREAS (*d.* 1457) and JAKOB I (*d.* 1469), and Jakob's three sons ULRICH (1441–1510), GEORG (1453–1506), and JAKOB II (1459–1525); the three brothers acted as bankers to popes and the Hapsburgs, traded in spices and textiles with India, and owned mines in Spain, Tirol, and Hungary; all ennobled by the emperor Maximilian, who mortgaged to Jakob the county of Kirchberg and the lordship of Weissenhorn for 10,000 gold gulden; backed the successful candidacy of Charles V as emperor, and during his reign, the house, run by Georg's sons RAYMUND (1489–1535) and ANTON (1493–1560), reached its zenith; given rights of princes and right to coin money; as zealous Catholics supported Eck against Luther; expanded business to New World and had vast land holdings, palaces, and merchant fleets; noted also as patrons of art and learning; family fortunes declined with the Hapsburgs.

Fuller *(fo͞ol ər)*, **Buckminster** full name: RICHARD BUCKMINSTER FULLER. 1895–. American inventor. *b.* Milton, Mass. Innovative thinker and inventor, first gained recognition in the early fifties; known for his complete acceptance of industrialization, and his philosophy that man must adopt his technology to work with his universe; designed Dymaxion structures, including prefabricated houses suspended from central posts and geodesic domes formed of lightweight triangular sections. Author of, among many other works, *Ideas and Integrities* (1963), *Beyond Left and Right* (1968), *Earth, Inc.* (1972), and *Synergetics.*

Fuller, Margaret full name: SARAH MARGARET; title: MARCHIONESS OF OSSOLI. 1810–50. American woman of letters. *b.* Cambridgeport, Mass. Member of Transcendentalist Circle and editor (1840–42) of its magazine *The Dial*; conducted literary conversations with Boston women (1839–44); joined Horace Greeley's *Tribune* as literary critic (1844); went to Europe as *Tribune* correspondent (1846); married Marquis Giovanni Angelo Ossoli (1847) and became involved in Mazzini's movement; took part in Revolution of 1848; lost, with husband and son, in a shipwreck on return to U.S. Author of *Summer on the Lakes in 1843* (1844) and *Woman in the Nineteenth Century* (1845).

Fuller, Melville Weston 1833–1910. American jurist. *b.* Augusta, Me. Practiced law in Chicago (1856-88); chief justice of U.S. (1888–1910); reputation as strict constructionist; arbitrator in Venezuelan boundary dispute; member of International Court of Arbitration at The Hague (1900–1910).

Fulton *(fo͞ol tən)*, **Robert** 1765–1815. American inventor. *b.* Fulton, Pa. Began as a painter; lived in England (1786–97); abandoned painting (from 1793) and turned to mechanical engineering, built the *Clermont* (1807), first commercially successful steamboat, which had its first run from New York City to Albany; other inventions include a machine for spinning flax, a machine for sawing and polishing marble, and a machine for making rope from hemp; also built a canal lock, torpedo, a dredging machine, and a submarine.

Funk *(foongk)*, **Casimir** 1884–1967. American biochemist. *b.* Warsaw, Poland. Engaged in research in Paris, London, Berlin, Warsaw, and New York; founded own laboratory, Casa Biochemica, in Rueil-Malmaison, France (1928–39); consultant to U.S. Vitamin Corporation, New York City, (from 1936); discovered and named vitamins (1911).

Furnivall *(fûr nĭ vəl),* **Frederick James** 1825–1910. English scholar and editor. *b.* Egham. One of the founders (with Ruskin) of London Working Men's College (1849); secretary of Philological Society (1862–1910) and editor of its dictionary project eventually published as the *Oxford English Dictionary*; founder of the Chaucer, Ballad, New Shakespeare, Browning, Shelley, Wycliffe, and Early English Text Societies; editor of over one hundred works in English literature, including *Canterbury Tales* and *Percy Ballads.*

Fust *(fo͞ost),* **Johann** also FAUST. c1400–1466. German printer. *b.* Mainz. Partner and financier of Gutenberg (c1450–c1455); on dissolution of partnership, sued Gutenberg for payment and obtained possession of Gutenberg's printing press in lieu of payment; began own printing business; first to print in color; issued first printed book with a complete date (1457).

G

Gabo *(gȧ bə),* **Naum** original name: NAUM PEVSNER. 1890–. American sculptor. *b.* Bryansk, Russia. Brother of Antoine Pevsner, with whom he issued *Realistic Manifesto of Constructivism* (1920) and founded the non-representational art called "Constructivism"; worked in Germany, France, and England; immigrated to U.S. (1946); works include geometrical constructions in space, made mainly of transparent plastic, such as *Column, Monument for an Airport,* and *The Red Cavern;* drawings include *Still Life with Lamp* and *Head*; also designed (with Antoine Pevsner) the ballet *La Chatte* (1927).

Gabor *(gä bôr),* **Dennis** 1900–. British physicist. *b.* in Hungary. Discovered the holograph; awarded Nobel Prize in physics (1971) for work in three-dimensional photography.

Gage *(gāj),* **Thomas** 1721–87. British general. *b.* Firle. Served in expeditions against Fort Duquesne under Edward Braddock (1755), against Ticonderoga under James Abercrombie (1758), and against Montreal under Jeffrey Amherst (1760); succeeded Amherst as commander in chief in North America, headquartered in New York (1763); governor and captain general of Massachusetts (1774); sent forces to seize store of arms at Concord, precipitating the Revolutionary War; after the Battles of Bunker Hill and Lexington, superseded by William Howe; returned to England.

Gahn *(gän),* **Johan Gottlieb** 1745–1818. Swedish chemist and mineralogist. *b.* Voxna. Discovered method for large-scale preparation of metallic manganese; with Karl Scheele, discovered phosphoric acid in bones (1770).

Gainsborough *(gānz bûr ō),* **Thomas** 1727–88. English painter. *b.* Sudbury. Worked in Ipswich, (1745–60), Bath (1760–74), and London (from 1784); one of 36 original members of Royal Academy (1768); painted over 300 pictures, 220 of which were portraits; considered one of the founders and leading representatives of the English school; principal works include *Mrs. Siddons, George III, Garrick, Richardson, Sterne, Chatterton, Girl with Pigs, The Harvest Wagon, The Blue Boy, The Market Cart,* and *The Shepherd's Boy.*

Galen *(gā lən)* *fl.* 2nd century. Greek physician. *b.* Pergamum, Asia Minor. Studied medicine at Smyrna, Corinth, and Alexandria; became surgeon to the gladiators at Pergamum (158); went to Rome (c164) and was physician to four emperors: Marcus Aurelius, Commodus, Sextus, and Severus; believed to have written over 500 books on medicine, philosophy, and grammar, of which 83 are extant; work on anatomy, medicine, and physiology remained standard for over 1000 years.

Galilei *(gä lə lâ ē),* **Galileo** 1564–1642. Italian astronomer. *b.* Pisa. Professor of mathematics at University of Pisa (1589–91) and at Padua (1592–1610) and Florence; philosopher and mathematician to Grand Duke of Tuscany (1610); published (1613) *Letters on the Solar Spots* accepting Copernican system; summoned to Rome, condemned for heresy and admonished by pope (1616); published *Dialogue on the Two Chief Systems of the Universe* (1632), again provoking the church's wrath; called before Inquisition at Rome and, under threat of torture, forced to renounce belief in Copernican theory (1633); retired to Arcetri, near Florence, and continued research depite almost total blindness (from 1637); principal discoveries and inventions include isochronic swing of the pendulum, hydrostatic balance, equal velocity of falling bodies, open-air thermometer, improved refracting telescope, four large satellites of Jupiter, sun spots, phases of Venus, the law of uniformly accelerated motion toward earth, parabolic paths of projectiles, libration of the moon, existence of stars in the Milky Way, and a proportional compass; summed up experiments and theories in mechanics in *Dialoghi della Nuove Scienzi* (1638).

Gall *(gäl),* **Franz Joseph** 1758–1828. German physician. *b.* Tiefenbrunn. Settled in Vienna (1785); investigated the relationship between mental faculties and cranial forms, thus founding the pseudoscience of phrenology; when banned as an atheist, took up residence in Paris (1807). Principal work was *Anatomie et Physiologie du Système Nerveux en Général* (1810–19).

Gallatin *(găl ə tĭn),* **Albert** full name: Abraham Alfonse Albert. 1761–1849. American statesman. *b.* Geneva, Switzerland. Immigrated to U.S. (1780); entered politics as member of Harrisburg Conference of 1788; Republican senator (1793) but unseated next year on technical grounds; helped put down Whiskey Rebellion (1794); member of House of Representatives (1795–1801) and leader of the Republican minority (1797); instrumental in establishing the finance committee that eventually became the Ways and Means Committee; secretary of treasury (1801–14), with fiscal policies on Jeffersonian principles; key figure in negotiations leading to Treaty of Ghent (1814); founder of American Ethnological Society (1842).

Gallaudet *(găl ə dĕt),* **Thomas Hopkins** 1787–1851. American teacher of deaf and dumb. *b.* Philadelphia, Pa. Founded (1817) first U.S. deaf-mute institution, in Hartford, and served as principal (1817–30); chaplain in the Connecticut institution for the insane at Hartford (1838–51); his two sons, THOMAS GALLAUDET, (1822–1902) and EDWARD MINER GALLAUDET (1837–1917) worked for deaf-mutes. Thomas was the founder of St. Anne's Church for Deaf-Mutes (1852) in New York City and the Gallaudet Home in Poughkeepsie for aged and infirm deaf-mutes (1858). Edward was the founder and president (1864–1910) of the Columbia Institution for the Deaf and Dumb, Washington, D.C., which later became Gallaudet College.

Galle *(gäl ə),* **Johann Gottfried** 1812–1910. German astronomer. *b.* Pabsthaus. Director of observatory at Breslau (1851–57); discovered planet Neptune, working from the calculations of Urbaine Leverrier.

Gallup *(găl əp),* **George Horace** 1901–. American public opinion pollster. *b.* Jefferson, Iowa. Head of journalism department of Drake University; as director of research at Young and Rubicam advertising agency (1932–39) and president of Audience Research Institute, which he founded in 1939, perfected techniques of measuring and polling public opinion; founded (1935) the American Institute of Public Opinion, introducing Gallup polls nationwide.

Galsworthy *(gôlz wûr thĭ),* **John** 1867–1933. English writer. *b.* Coombe. Described the Victorian, upper-middle-class life of the Forsyte family in three trilogies: *The Forsyte Saga* (1922), *A Modern Comedy* (1928), and *End of the Chapter* (1934); other works include *Jocelyn* (1898), *The Island Pharisees* (1904), *The Country House* (1907), and *The Patrician* (1911); among his plays are *The Silver Box* (1906), *Strife* (1909), *Justice* (1910), *The Skin Game* (1920), *Loyalties* (1922), and *Escape* (1926); awarded Nobel Prize in literature (1932).

Galton *(gôl tən),* **Sir Francis** 1822–1911. English scientist. *b.* Birmingham. Founded science of eugenics and wrote extensively on it; devised technique of fingerprint identification; developed questionnaire system of collecting statistical data and tests of physical and mental measurements; laid basis of modern weather map with publication of *Meteorographica* (1863). Author of *Hereditary Genius* (1869), *Natural Inheritance* (1889), *Inquiries into Human Faculty and its Development* (1883), *Noteworthy Families* (1906), and *Finger Prints* (1892), among others.

Galvani *(gäl vä nē),* **Luigi** also ALOISIO. 1737–98. Italian scientist. *b.* Bologna. Professor of anatomy at Bologna (from 1762); discovered that the muscle cut from a frog's leg contracts when placed in contact with metals; believed wrongly that this was caused by animal electricity; galvanism named after him.

Gálvez *(gäl vāth),* **José de** title: MARQUÉS DE LA SONORA. c1729–87. Spanish statesman and colonial administrator. *b.* Vélez-Málaga. Visitador general of Mexico and West Indies (1761–74) and of Sonora (1767–72); sponsored Spanish settlements in Upper California (1769); president of the Council of Indies and minister of Charles III (1776); his brother MATIAS DE GÁLVEZ (1731–84) was captain general of Guatemala (1779) and viceroy of Mexico (1783–84); Matias's son BERNARDO DE GÁLVEZ (1746–86) was governor of Louisiana (1777), commander in chief of the West Indies; aided patriots in American Revolution; in war with Great Britain, captured Baton Rouge and Natchez (1779), Mobile (1780), and Pensacola (1781); annexed Florida under peace pact terms (1783); captain general of Florida and Louisiana; captain general of Cuba (1784); viceroy of Mexico (1785–86); Galveston is named after him.

Gama *(gă mə),* **Vasco da** c1469–1524. Portuguese navigator. *b.* Sines. Chosen by King Emanuel to command expedition to discover an ocean route to East Indies; sailed from Lisbon (1497) with four vessels, rounded Cape of Good Hope, reaching Calicut on Indian west coast (1498); commanded second expedition to India (1502–1503), founded colonies of Mozambique and Sofala, bombarded Calicut in a vengeful act, and collected booty by raiding coastal shipping in Indian Ocean; viceroy of Portuguese Asia (1524); celebrated in Camoëns's *Lusiad.*

Gambetta *(găm bĕt ə),* **Léon Michel** 1838–82. French statesman. *b.* Cahors. Elected to Corps Législatif as deputy (1869) and joined the opposition; one of the proclaimers of the Republic on surrender of Napoleon III at Sedan; minister of interior in Government of National Defense; escaped from Paris in a balloon and organized resistance in provinces (1871); on capitulation of Paris, retired to Spain; elected to National Assembly and Chamber of Deputies (1876); president of Chamber of Deputies (1879–81); premier (1881–82). Author of *Discours Politiques* and *Dépêches* (1880–92).

Gandhi *(gän dē),* **Indira Nehru** 1917–. Indian political leader. *b.* Allahabad. Daughter of Jawaharlal Nehru; educated in India, in Switzerland, and at Oxford; married Feroze Gandhi (1942); aide to Nehru (1947–64); president of Indian National Congress party (1959–60); minister of information (1964–66); prime minister, (1966) succeeding Shastri; stressed socialist domestic policies; defeated Pakistan in war (1971), causing establishment of State of Bangladesh; after a political scandal, introduced semi-autocratic government, suspending most constitutional liberties (1975); defeated when free elections were re-instated (1977).

Gandhi, Mohandas Karamchand called MAHATMA (Great Soul) and BAPU. 1869–1948. Indian statesman. *b.* Porbandar. Studied law in London (1888); went to South Africa (1893), championing rights of Asiatic settlers and using, for the first time, the technique of passive resistance (later known as *satyagraha,* desire for truth); returned to India (1914); severe critic of British rule (after 1919), made common cause with Muslims during Caliphate agitation; as head of nationalist movement, demanded full independence from Britain; urged boycott of British goods and revival of home industries; launched nonviolent campaign of civil disobedience, undertook several fasts in protest, and was imprisoned many times; president of Indian National Congress party (1924–34, 1940–41); sought to reconstruct Indian society on basis of ancient Indian religious and social ideals; captured imagination of western political activists and Indian masses through extreme asceticism, his use of the spinning wheel as a symbol of economic independence, and his opposition to such Hindu social rules as the caste system; last days clouded by partition of India and Hindu-Muslim riots; assassinated by a Hindu fanatic (1948). Author of *The Story of My Experiments with Truth* (1949), *Young India* (1922), and other books.

Garamond *(găr ȧ mŏnd),* **Claude** *d.* 1561. French type designer. *b.* Paris. Commissioned by Francis I to design and cut three fonts for the editions of Greek classics by Robert Estienne; his roman type replaced the Gothic commonly used until then; designed types for Christophe Plantin, Giambattista Bodoni, and Simon de Colines.

García Márquez *(gär sēə mär kĕs),* **Gabriel** 1928–. Colombian writer. *b.* Aaracataca. Work combines magic, myth, and metaphor; best known for the saga *100 Years of Solitude* (1970), which became an international best seller and has been compared to the works of Faulkner, Joyce, and Günter Grass; also published *No One Writes to the Colonel and Other Stories* (1968), *Leaf Storm and Other Stories* (1972), and *The Autumn of the Patriarch* (1977).

Garcilaso de la Vega *(gär sə lä sō thā lä vā gä)* called EL INCA. c1539–1616. Peruvian historian. *b.* Cusco. Son of a Spanish conquistador and an Inca princess; went to Spain (c1506); settled at Cordoba with a pension given by Philip II. Author of *La Florida del Inca: Historia del Adelantado Hernando de Soto* (1605) and *Comentarios Reales Que Tratan del Origen de los Incas* (2 parts, 1609, 1617); considered first South American Spanish writer.

Gardner *(gärd nər),* **Erle Stanley** pseudonym: A. A. FAIR. 1889–1970. American mystery writer. *b.* Malden, Mass. Admitted to the California bar (1911); engaged in practice of law and in business (until 1934); created Perry Mason, one of the most popular fictional detectives, who first appeared in *The Case of the Velvet Claws* (1932); began writing full time (from 1934); in the next 36 years, published hundreds of books under a variety of pseudonyms.

Gardiner *(gärd nər),* **Stephen** c1483–1555. English ecclesiastic and statesman. *b.* Bury St. Edmunds. Emissary of Henry VIII to pope in negotiations to obtain divorce from Catherine of Aragon; secretary of state on fall of Wolsey (1529), and bishop of Winchester

(1531); defended royal supremacy in *De Vera Obedientia* (1535); instrumental in fall of Cromwell and proclamation of Six Articles; committed (1552) to Tower and deprived of bishopric for opposition to Cranmer's doctrinal innovations; freed on accession of Mary; lord high chancellor (1553); encouraged severe persecution of Protestants; attempted to exclude Elizabeth from throne.

Garfield *(gär fēld),* **James Abraham** 1831–81. 20th president of U.S. *b.* Orange, Ohio. Joined the army during Civil War and rose to major general of volunteers; member of House of Representatives from Ohio (1863–80); Republican House leader (from 1876); elected president (1880) after being chosen as Republican compromise candidate; soon after inauguration, antagonized New York Stalwarts led by Roscoe Conkling by attempting to reform civil service; assassinated by a disappointed office-seeker (1881).

Garibaldi *(găr ĭ bôl dĭ),* **Giuseppe** 1807–82. Italian hero of the Risorgimento. *b.* Nice, France. As member of Mazzini's Young Italy movement, exiled for taking part in an attempt to seize Genoa (1834); went to South America and fought in civil wars of Brazil and Uruguay (1835–46); returned to Italy, fighting with Sardinian army against Austria (1848–49) and with Mazzini's short-lived Roman Republic against the French and Neapolitans (1849); fled to U.S. (1850), became naturalized, and lived in Staten Island as a candlemaker; returned to Italy (1854); commanded independent corps, the Hunters of the Alps, in Sardinian service against Austrians (1859); with Victor Emmanuel II's connivance, led expedition of 1000 volunteers against Kingdom of the Two Sicilies; liberated Sicily (1860), crossed to mainland, expelled Francis II, and entered Naples in triumph; foiled in two expeditions against Rome (1862, 1867); suffered defeats at Aspromonte and Mentana; commanded volunteer force in French army during Franco-Prussian War (1870–71); elected deputy in Italian parliament (1874). Author of *Autobiography* (1889) and three novels.

Garner *(gär nər),* **John Nance** 1868–1967. American statesman. *b.* Red River County, Tex. Member of House of Representatives (1903–33); Speaker of the House (1931–33); vice-president of U.S. in first two administrations of Roosevelt (1933–41).

Garrick *(găr ik),* **David** 1717–79. English actor. *b.* Hereford. Studied under Samuel Johnson at Edial; accompanied Johnson to London (1737); took London stage by storm as Richard II (1741), introducing new natural style of acting; joint manager of Drury Lane Theater with Lacy; in a 35-year career, acted 98 roles, including 18 Shakespearean ones, and brought out 56 plays, of which 27 were by Shakespeare; had extensive library on drama, later bequeathed to the British Museum; amassed a vast fortune, retired to Hampton (1776) and was buried with great honor in Westminster Abbey.

Garrison *(găr ĭ sən),* **William Lloyd** 1805–79. American abolitionist. *b.* Newburyport, Mass. Editor of *Newburyport Herald* (1824) and

National Philanthropist (1828); founded the *Liberator* (1831), an anti-slavery weekly, published until 1865; founder of American Anti-Slavery Society (1833) and its president (1843–65); constantly threatened with mob violence and the target of an attempted lynching (1835); antagonized moderates by intransigence and by such acts as burning of the Constitution at Framingham (1854); urged separation between North and South and opposed Civil War; later championed the causes of women, Indians, and prohibition.

Garvey *(gär vĭ),* **Marcus** 1887–1940. American black-nationalist leader. *b.* in Jamaica. Founded Universal Negro Improvement Association in Jamaica (1914); immigrated to U.S (1917), settling in New York City; published (1918–23) the weekly *Negro World,* advocating a "Back to Africa" movement for resettling blacks in independent African states; founded two black-owned steamship lines whose failure led to his conviction for fraud (1925); on release from jail, deported to Jamaica (1927).

Gary *(gâr ĭ),* **Elbert Henry** 1846–1927. American industrialist. *b.* Wheaton, Ill. President of Federal Steel Company (1898); one of the founders of United States Steel Corporation (1901) and its chairman (1903–27); town of Gary, Ind., is named after him.

Gascoigne *(găs koin),* **George** c1525–77. English poet. *b.* Cardington. Credited with first book of prosody in English, the *Posies of G. Gascoigne* (1575), the second tragedy in blank verse, *Jocasta* (1566), the first English prose comedy, *Supposes* (1566), the first English satire, *The Steel Glass* (1576), one of the first English novels, *The Adventures of Master F.J.*, and the first English critical essay, *Certayne Notes of Instruction Concerning the Making of Verse or Ryme in English;* other works include *The Droomme of Doomesday* (1576), *A Glass of Government* (1575), and *The Complaynt of Phylomene* (1563).

Gaskell *(găs kəl),* **Elizabeth Cleghorn** *née* STEVENSON. 1810–65. English novelist. *b.* Cheyne Row. Married William Gaskell (1832); lived a small-town family life in Manchester; wrote about middle-class village life and working-class urban settings; wrote excellent but controversial *Life of Charlotte Brontë* (1857). Novels include *Mary Barton* (1848), *Cranford* (1853), *North and South* (1855), *Lizzie Leigh* (1855), *Sylvia's Lovers* (1853), and *Wives and Daughters* (1865).

Gassendi *(gȧ săN dē),* **Pierre** 1592–1655. French philosopher. *b.* Champtercier. Professor of theology at Digne (1613), of philosophy at Aix (1616), and of mathematics at Paris (1645); opposed Aristotelianism, scholasticism, and Cartesianism; sought to revive atomic theory and Epicureanism, and to reconcile them with Christian theology. Author of *Exercitationes Paradoxicae Adversus Aristoteleos* (1624), *Disquisitiones Anticartesianae* (1643), and *De Vita, Moribus, et Placitis Epicuri* (1647).

Gasser *(găs ər),* **Herbert Spencer** 1888–1963. American physiologist. *b.* Platteville, Wis. Director of Rockefeller Institute for Medical

Research (from 1935); cowinner, with Joseph Erlanger, of Nobel Prize in physiology and medicine (1944) for work on electrophysiology of nerves, recorded in *Electrical Signs of Nervous Activity* (1937).

Gates *(gāts),* **Horatio** c1728–1806. American general. *b.* Maldon, England. Entered English army and fought at Fort Duquesne (1755), Fort Herkimer (1758), and Martinique (1762); retired and settled in W. Va. (1772); on outbreak of War of Independence, joined Continental Army; major general (1776); in command of Northern Department (1776–77) and won brilliant victory over Burgoyne at Saratoga; Conway Cabal failed in its attempt to make him commander in chief, replacing Washington; president of Board of War (1777); as commander of Southern Department, lost disastrous Battle of Camden (1780); relieved of command; spent remainder of war under Washington at Newburgh.

Gaudier-Brzeska *(gō dyā brzhĕs kä),* **Henri** 1891–1915. French sculptor. *b.* St.-Jean-de-Braye. Principal exponent of vorticism. Works include *The Dance, The Embracers,* and *Fawn;* killed in World War I.

Gauguin *(gō găN),* **Eugène Henri Paul** known as PAUL. 1848–1903. French painter. *b.* Paris. Exhibited first painting (1875); abandoned career in banking to devote time to painting (1883); lived in Tahiti (1891–93, 1895–1903); during French period, became leader of Pont-Aven school of Symbolist painters, but later evolved style called synthetism; during Tahitian period, developed consciously primitive style with tapestried canvases in brilliant colors. Principal works include *Where Do We Come From? What Are We? Where Are We Going?, Landscape in Brittany, Riders by the Sea, Ta Matete, An Interior in Tahiti, Arii Matamoe, Portrait of a Breton Woman,* and *Tehamana's Farewell.*

Gauss *(gous),* **Karl Friedrich** 1777–1855. German mathematician. *b.* Brunswick. Pioneer in the application of mathematical theory to electricity and magnetism; contributed to development of modern theory of numbers and curved-surface geometry; solved binomial equations and advanced method of least squares; invented the heliograph, the declination needle, and a magnetometer; investigated the passage of light through dioptric lenses; author of *Disquisitiones Arithmeticae* (1801), *Theoria Motus Corporum Coelestium* (1809), and *Dioptrische Untersuchungen* (1843).

Gautama Buddha. *See* **Buddha, Gautama**

Gautier *(gō tyā),* **Théophile** 1811–72. French writer. *b.* Tarbes. Leader of the Romantic Parnassian movement, which believed in art for art's sake; excelled as critic, poet, and novelist. Novels and stories include *Jeune France* (1833), *Mademoiselle de Maupin* (1835), *La Morte Amoureuse* (1836), *Fortunio* (1837), *Une Larme du Diable* (1839), *Militona* (1847), *La Peau du Tigre* (1852), *Le Roman de la Momie* (1856), *Jettatura* (1857), *Le Capitaine Fracasse* (1863), *La Belle Jenny* (1865), *Spirite* (1866); poems include *Premières Poésies* (1830),

Albertus (1833), *Comédie de la Mort* (1832), *Voyages en Espagne* (1843); and *Émaux et Camées* (1850–65); literary criticism includes *L'Histoire du Romantisme* (1854), *Les Beaux-Arts en Europe* (1852) and *L'Histoire de l'Art Dramatique en France* (6 vols., 1858–59); plays include *Le Tricorne Enchanté* (1845) and *La Juive de Constantine* (1846); wrote an informal autobiography *Ménagerie Intime* (1869).

Gay *(gā),* **John** 1685–1732. English playwright and poet. *b.* Barnstaple. Author of *The Shepherd's Week* (1714), *The What-D'ye-Call-It* (1715), *Trivia, or the Art of Walking the Streets of London* (1716), *Polly* (1729), *Fables* (1727, 1738), *Acis and Galatea* (1732), and *The Beggar's Opera* (1728), the work by which he is best remembered.

Gay-Lussac *(gā lü sȧk),* **Joseph Louis** 1778–1850. French scientist. *b.* St.-Léonard-le-Noblat. Professor of physics at the Sorbonne (1808-32) and chemistry at Jardin des Plantes (from 1832); investigated laws of terrestrial magnetism and established the law of volumes (Gay-Lussac's Law); with Alexander von Humboldt, determined the ratio of hydrogen and oxygen two to one in water; isolated cyanogen and the element boron; devised the Gay-Lussac Tower for manufacturing sulphuric acid; first to prepare iodic and hydriodic acids; invented the hydrometer and the alchoholometer.

Gell-Mann *(gĕl män),* **Murray** 1929–. American physicist. *b.* New York, N.Y. Awarded Nobel Prize in physics (1969) for work on elementary particles.

Genet *(zhə nā),* **Jean** 1910–. French writer. Sentenced to life imprisonment (1948), but pardoned after a petition to the president by French writers; member of the Decadent school. Works include the plays *The Maids* (1947), *The Balcony* (1956), *The Blacks* (1959), and the novels *The Thief's Journal* (1949), *The Miracle of the Rose* (1946), and *Our Lady of the Flowers* (1944).

Genghis Khan *(jĕng gĭs kän)* also Jenghiz or Chinghiz Khan; original name: Temujin. 1162–1227. Mongol conqueror. *b.* Deligun Bulduk. At age 13, succeeded father Yekusai as ruler; brought Naimans and Uigurs, neighboring tribes, into Mongol confederacy; proclaimed khan of the Mongols (1206) with title of Genghis Khan, using Karakorum as capital; conquered northern China with the capture of Peking (1215); conquered Korea (1218); conquered central Asia and the Kara Chitai Empire, from Lake Balkash to Tibet (1218–21); overran Khwarazm (Khiva), plundered northern India, and subdued Iran and Iraq; defeated Russians at Battle of Kalka River (1223) and carried arms as far as Bulgaria.

Geoffrey *(jĕf rĭ)* **of Monmouth** c1100–1154. English chronicler. *b.* Monmouth. Bishop of St. Asaph (1152–54); sometime between 1139 and 1147, published *Historia Regum Britanniae,* an important source of Arthurian and other early British legends, possessing little historical value but quite influential in English literature.

Geoffroy Saint-Hilaire *(săN tē lâr),* **Étienne** 1772–1844. French zoologist. *b.* Étampes. Professor of zoology at Jardin des Plantes (from

1793); member of scientific commission that accompanied Napoleon to Egypt (1798); professor of zoology at Faculty of Sciences in Paris (from 1809); in *Philosophie Anatomique* (2 vols., 1818–20), proposed that all animals conform to a single organic structure; other works include *Philosophie Zoologique* (1830) and *Études Progressives d'un Naturaliste* (1835); his son ISIDORE GEOFFROY SAINT-HILAIRE (1805–61), French zoologist and authority on teratology and animal domestication, published *Histoire Générale des Règnes Organiques* (3 vols., 1854–62) and *Domestication et Naturalisation des Animaux Utiles* (1854).

George Name of six kings of England, the first four of the House of Hanover and two of the House of Windsor:

GEORGE I (GEORGE LOUIS) 1660–1727. King of Great Britain and Ireland (1714–27) and elector of Hanover (1698–1727). *b.* Hanover, Germany. Son of Ernest Augustus, elector of Hanover, and Sophia, granddaughter of James I of England; succeeded Queen Anne (1714) to the British throne under terms of Act of Settlement; spoke no English and entrusted administration to chief ministers Charles Townshend, James Stanhope, and Robert Walpole; favored Whigs over Tories; concluded Triple Alliance with France and Holland (later joined by the emperor) to secure his line on the throne.

GEORGE II (GEORGE AUGUSTUS). 1683–1760. King of Great Britain and Ireland (1727–60) and elector of Hanover (1727–60). *b.* Hanover, Germany. Continued father's policy of supporting Whigs; ended Jacobite hopes at Battle of Culloden (1745) when the duke of Cumberland defeated the Young Pretender, Charles Edward; drawn into wars on Continent to protect Hanoverian interests; sided with Maria Theresa in First and Second Silesian Wars (1740–42, 1744–45) and with Frederick II in Seven Years' War (1756–63); reign witnessed great imperial expansion with foundation of British power in India and Canada. GEORGE III (GEORGE WILLIAM FREDERICK). 1738–1820. King of Great Britain and Ireland (1760–1820), Elector (1760–1815) and King of Hanover (1815–20). *b.* London, England. Attempted to govern as well as reign; responsible for policies leading to American Revolution and the loss of American colonies; by Peace of Paris (1763), acquired Canada from France; supported union of Great Britain and Ireland, but blocked Catholic emancipation; aided by two notable prime ministers, Lord North (1770–82) and Pitt the Younger (1783–1801, 1804–1806) who shaped policy in accordance with his wishes; presided over golden age of English literature; suffered attacks of insanity (1765, 1788–89, 1803, 1804), becoming blind and permanently deranged (after 1811).

GEORGE IV (GEORGE AUGUSTUS FREDERICK). 1762–1830. King of Great Britain and Ireland (1820–30). *b.* London. As prince of Wales, was regent for his father (1811–20); opposed reform movement, but signed Catholic Emancipation Act; supported Tory party after accession.

GEORGE V (GEORGE FREDERICK ERNEST ALBERT). 1865–1936. King

of Great Britain and Northern Ireland and emperor of India (1910–36); changed name of house from Saxe-Coburg-Gotha to Windsor; visited India (1911); saw Britain through World War I; reached agreement with Irish Free State (1921).

GEORGE VI (ALBERT FREDERICK ARTHUR GEORGE). 1895–1952. King of Great Britain and Northern Ireland (1936–52) and emperor of India (1936–48); visited U.S. and Canada (1939); relinquished emperorship of India (1948).

George *(jôr j),* **Saint** *d.* 303. Christian martyr. *b.* Cappadocia, Asia Minor. Military tribune under Diocletian; believed to have been put to death in Nicomedia (303); represented in Christian legends as the slayer of a dragon; adopted as the patron saint of England at the time of Edward III. Feast day: Apr. 23.

George, Henry 1839–97. American economist. *b.* Philadelphia, Pa. Propounded single-tax theory (1868–69), calling for one tax on land and the abolition of all other taxes on industry; developed economic ideas in *Our Land and Land Policy* (1871), *Progress and Poverty* (1876), *Social Problems* (1883), and *Protection or Free Trade* (1886); editor of *San Francisco Times* (1866–68), *Oakland Transcript* (1869), *Daily Evening Post* (1871), and the *Standard* (1886–92); other works include *The Condition of Labor* (1891), and *The Science of Political Economy* (1897).

George, Stefan 1868–1933. German poet. *b.* Büdesheim. Went abroad and associated with Baudelaire, Mallarmé, and other Symbolists in Paris and with Pre-Raphaelites in London; on return to Germany, founded the Symbolist Georgekreis, or Georgecircle, and their review *Blätter für die Kunst* (1892–1919); poems characterized by imagery, beauty, technical perfection, and unusual punctuation. Left Germany after Nazis came to power, but Nazis adopted him as national poet after his death. Works include *Algabal (1892), Das Jahr der Seele* (1897), *Die Bücher der Hirten* (1895), *Der Siebente Ring* (1907), and *Das neue Reich* (1928).

Gerry *(gĕr ĭ),* **Elbridge** 1744–1814. American statesman. *b.* Marblehead, Mass. Member of Continental Congress (1776–79, 1782–85); signed Declaration of Independence and Articles of Confederation; delegate to Federal Convention of 1787 and, as leader of anti-Federalists, opposed the Constitution; House of Representatives (1789–93); member of XYZ mission to France (1797–98); Republican governor of Mass. (1810–12); rearranged electoral districts to secure advantage for his party, a practice now called "gerrymandering"; vice-president under Madison (1813–14).

Gershwin *(gûrsh wĭn),* **George** 1898–1937. American composer. *b.* Brooklyn, N.Y. Works include the opera *Porgy and Bess* (1935), the musical comedies *Lady Be Good* (1924), *Funny Face* (1927), *Girl Crazy* (1930), *Of Thee I Sing* (1931, Pulitzer Prize), and *Let 'Em Eat Cake* (1933), and the jazz symphonies *Rhapsody in Blue* (1923), *Concerto in F* (1925), tone poem *An American in Paris* (1928), and many film scores. His brother

IRA (1896–) wrote lyrics for many of his songs.

Ghazzali *(găz zä lē),* **Abu-Hamid Muhammad al-** 1058–1111. Arab theologian. *b.* Tus, Khorasan. Taught philosophy at Baghdad (1091–95), Damascus, Jerusalem, and Alexandria; opposed Islamic scholasticism. Works include *Opinions of the Philosophers, Tendencies of the Philosophers,* and *Destruction of the Philosophers.*

Ghiberti *(gē bĕr tē),* **Lorenzo** original name: LORENZO DI CIONE DI SER BUONACCORSO. 1378–1455. Italian goldsmith, sculptor, and painter. b. Florence. Painted frescoes for the palace of Pandolfo Malatesta at Rimini; lifework was construction of the two bronze doors of the baptistry of San Giovanni at Florence, which took 44 years to complete (1403–1447); the doors, called "Gates of Paradise" by Michelangelo, comprise some of the finest metalwork of all time; other works include bronze statues of John the Baptist, Matthew, and Stephen for the Or San Michele.

Ghirlandajo *(gēr län dä yō),* **Domenico** also GHIRLANDAIO or GRILLANDAJO; real name: DOMENICO DI TOMMASO BIGORDI. 1449–94. Italian painter and mosaicist. *b.* Florence. Founder of a school of painting and teacher of Michelangelo; principally painted frescoes, of which the most famous are in the Palazzo Vecchio (1481), the church at Ognissanti (1480), the Sassetti Chapel in Santa Trinità (1485), the choir of Santa Maria Novella (1485–88), and the church of the Innocenti (1488); called to Rome by Pope Sixtus IV to paint the fresco *Christ Calling Peter and Andrew* in the Sistine Chapel (1482–84); also painted *Annunciation, Adoration of the Magi,* and *Madonna and Saints,* among others.

Giauque *(jē ōk),* **William Francis** 1895–. American chemist. *b.* Niagara Falls, Canada. Professor of chemistry at University of California (from 1934); co-discoverer with Herrick Lee Johnston of the second and third isotopes of oxygen; discovered (1937) adiabatic demagnetization method of producing temperatures below absolute zero; received Nobel Prize in chemistry (1949) for studies of materials at low temperatures.

Gibbon *(gib un),* **Edward** 1737–94. English historian. *b.* Putney. Converted to Roman Catholicism at age 16 only to renounce it later; at Lausanne (from 1783); began writing his most famous work, *The History of the Decline and Fall of the Roman Empire* (1772); published (6 vols., 1776–88); work marred by unrelieved cynicism and prejudices; defended himself in *Vindication* (1779); also wrote *Autobiography* (1796).

Gibbons *(gib unz),* **Orlando** 1583–1625. English composer. *b.* Oxford. Organist of the royal chapel (1604) and of Westminster Abbey (1623); best known for sacred music. Compositions include anthems *Hosanna, Lift Up Your Heads, O Clap Your Hands,* and *Almighty and Everlasting God,* madrigals *The Silver Swan, O That the Learned Poets,* hymns and fantasies.

Gibbs *(gibz),* **Josiah Willard** 1839–1903. American physicist. *b.* New Haven, Conn. Professor of physics at Yale (1871–1903);

founded the science of physical chemistry with the publication of *On the Equilibrium of Heterogeneous Substances* (1876). Other contributions include *Elementary Principles in Statistical Mechanics* (1902), *Multiple Algebra* (1886), and *Graphical Methods in the Thermodynamics of Fluids* (1873).

Gibran *(jōōb rän),* **Kahlil** 1883–1931. American poet. *b.* Bechari, Lebanon. Resided in U.S. (from 1910); author of such prose poems and mystical works as *The Prophet* (1923), *The Forerunner* (1920), *Sand and Foam: A Book of Aphorisms* (1926), *Jesus, the Son of Man* (1928), and *The Garden of the Prophet* (1933).

Gibson *(gĭb sən),* **Charles Dana** 1867–1944. American illustrator. *b.* Roxbury, Mass. Creator of "the Gibson Girl"; excelled in society cartoons and black-and-white drawings. Author of *The Education of Mr. Pipp, The Americans, The Social Ladder, A Widow and Her Friends,* and other books.

Gide *(zhēd),* **André Paul Guillaume** 1869–1951. French writer. *b.* Paris. Author of over 50 volumes of fiction, poetry, plays, criticism, and biography. Works include *Traité du Narcisse* (1892), *Voyage d'Urien* (1893), *Paludes* (1895), *Fruits of the Earth* (1948), *The Immoralist* (1902), *Strait is the Gate* (1909), *The Vatican Swindle* (1914), *The Counterfeiters* (1926), and *Lest it Die* (1920); critical works include *Prétextes* (1903), *Nouveaux Prétextes* (1911), *Dostoievski* (1923), and *Incidences* (1924); two verse dramas, *Le Roi Candaule* (1901) and *Saul* (1903), and *Journals* (3 vols., 1939); cofounder of influential literary journal *Nouvelle Revue Français* (1909); awarded Nobel Prize in literature (1947).

Gilbert *(gĭl bərt),* **Sir Humphrey** c1539–83. English navigator. *b.* Buxham. Served in the Netherlands and Ireland; published *Discourse* (1576) on the possibility of a Northwest Passage to India; obtained royal patent to set out on voyage of discovery and colonization; sailed from Plymouth (1583) with five ships; after 48 days at sea, landed in Newfoundland and claimed it in the name of Queen Elizabeth; founded first North American English colony at St. John's; perished at sea on return voyage.

Gilbert, William 1540–1603. English scientist. *b.* Colchester. Practiced medicine in London (from 1573); president of College of Physicians (1600); physician to Queen Elizabeth and King James I; published *De Magnete, Magneticisque Corporibus,* the first important scientific work published in England, establishing terrestrial magnetism; first to use the terms electricity, electric force, and magnetic pole; considered "the father of electricity"; gilbert, a unit of magnetomotive power, is named after him.

Gilbert, Sir William Schwenck 1836–1911. English librettist. *b.* London. Began career as a parodist and writer, writing humorous verse under the pseudonym Bab, later collected as *Bab Ballads* (1869); collaborated with Sir Arthur Sullivan on a series of light operas performed by D'Oyly Carte's Opera Company including *Trial by Jury* (1875), *The Sorcerer*

(1877), *H. M. S. Pinafore* (1878), *The Pirates of Penzance* (1879), *Patience* (1881), *Iolanthe* (1882), *Princess Ida* (1884), *The Mikado* (1885), *Ruddigore (1887), The Yeomen of the Guard* (1888), *The Gondoliers* (1889), *Utopia, Limited* (1893), and *The Grand Duke* (1896); broke with Sullivan (1896); independently wrote *Dulcamara* (1866), *The Palace of Truth* (1870), *Pygmalion and Galatea* (1871), *The Wicked World* (1873), *The Happy Land* (1873), *Charity* (1874), *Broken Hearts* (1875), *Engaged* (1877), *The Mountebanks* (1891); considered a master of satirical wit and paradox.

Giles, Blessed. *See* **Aegidius of Assisi**

Gill *(gĭl),* **Eric** 1882–1940. English sculptor, engraver, and typographer. *b.* Brighton. Stone figures include *Madonna and the Child* (1909), *Stations of the Cross* (1913) in Westminster Cathedral, and *Mankind* (1928) in Tate Gallery; type designs include Perpetua, Bunyan, and Gill Sans-Serif. Author of *Autobiography* (1940), *Sculpture . . .* (1917), *Christianity and Art* (1927), *Money and Morals* (1934), and *Letters* (1948).

Ginsberg *(gĭnz bûrg),* **Allen** 1926–. American poet. *b.* Paterson, N.J. Poet and controversial figure; considered leader of the beat poets of the fifties; the most talented poet of protest against the impersonal modern society. Author of *Howl* (1956) and *Kaddish and Other Poems* (1961).

Giorgione, Il *(ēl jōr jō nā)* also, GIORGIONE DA CASTELFRANCO; original name: GIORGIO BARBARELLI. c1478–1511. Italian painter. *b.* Castelfranco. Considered an innovative and romantic Venetian painter; works characterized by rich colors and poetic sensibility; of the many pictures attributed to him, only a few have been authenticated; including *The Tempest, The Family of Giorgione, The Three Philosophers, Sleeping Venus,* the altarpiece *Enthroned Madonna, Gypsy and Soldier, Evander Showing Aeneas the Site of Rome, Venus and Cupid in a Landscape, The Concert, The Knight of Malta,* and *The Judgment of Solomon.*

Giotto *(jôt tō),* **Di Bondone** 1267–1337. Italian painter. *b.* Vespignano. Appointed chief master of the works of Florence Cathedral (1334), for which he designed the facade and campanile; among his great frescoes are 28 from *Life of St. Francis* at Assisi, frescoes of the Bargello at Florence with the portrait of Dante, frescoes in the Arena chapel at Padua including *Life of Christ, Life of the Virgin, Last Judgment,* and *Allegories, Marriage of St. Francis with Poverty, Triumph of Charity, Triumph of Obedience, Glorification of St. Francis, Saint John the Baptist, Saint John the Evangelist, Coronation of the Virgin, Last Supper, Presentation of Christ in the Temple, Madonna with Angels,* and *Two Apostles;* humanized art by achieving lifelike emotions in faces and illusion of movement in figures.

Giraudox *(zhē rō do͞o),* **Jean Hippolyte** 1882–1944. French dramatist and novelist. *b.* Bellac. Combined literary and diplomatic careers, serving as propaganda chief for the French government (1939–

40). Works include *The Madwoman of Chaillot* (1945), *Amphitryon 38* (1929), *La Guerre de Troie n'Aura pas Lieu* (1935), *Provinciales* (1909), *Simon le Pathetique* (1918), *Retour d'Alsace* (1917), *Eglantine* (1927), *Le Sport* (1928), and *Adorable Clio* (1920).

Gissing *(gĭs ĭng),* **George Robert** 1857–1903. English writer. *b.* Wakefield. Portrayed poverty and its misery in *New Grub Street* (1891), *Born in Exile* (1892), *The Odd Women* (1893), and the autobiographical *The Private Papers of Henry Ryecroft* (1903).

Gladstone *(glăd stōn),* **William Ewart** 1809–98. British statesman. *b.* Liverpool. Entered Parliament (1832) as Tory; president of Board of Trade (1843–45); colonial secretary (1845–46) under Peel; chancellor of exchequer (1852–55, 1859–66); leader of House of Commons on death of Palmerston; succeeded Lord Russell as leader of Liberal party (1867); prime minister (1868-74, 1880–85, 1886, 1892–94); disestablished Irish church (1869), notable reforms include reforming civil service, Irish land act, vote by secret ballot, abolition of sale of army commissions, introduction of national education, extended suffrage, and parliamentary reform; on retirement, declined peerage, preferring to remain "the Great Commoner"; unrivaled as parliamentary debater; served in House of Commons for 61 years; extended liberal principles into foreign affairs by denouncing Turkish atrocities in Bulgaria and Armenia. Author of *The State in Its Relations to the Church* (1838), *Studies on Homer and the Homeric Age* (1858), and *Gleanings of Past Years* (1879).

Glaser *(glä zər),* **Donald Arthur** 1926–. American physicist. *b.* Cleveland, Ohio. Professor at University of California (from 1960); devised bubble chamber for observing paths of atomic particles; awarded Nobel Prize in physics (1960).

Gluck *(glo͝ok),* **Christoph Willibald** 1714–87. German composer. *b.* Erasbach. Produced successful operas in Milan beginning with *Artaserse* (1741); went to England (1745) as operatic composer for Haymarket Theater; returned to Vienna (1746) as singing master to Marie Antoinette; met Raniero Calzabigi, the librettist, in Florence (1761) and collaborated with him on a series of masterpieces whose new style revolutionized opera; lived in Paris (1769–79). Celebrated works include *Orfeo ed Euridice* (1762), *Alceste* (1766), *Paride ed Elena* (1769), *Iphigénie en Aulide* (1774), *Armide* (1777), and *Iphigénie en Tauride* (1779).

Gobat *(gô bȧ),* **Charles Albert** 1843–1914. Swiss lawyer and statesman. *b.* Bern. President of Bern International Peace Bureau (1906–14) and administrative head of Interparliamentary Union (from 1892); cowinner with Élie Ducommun of Nobel Peace Prize (1902).

Gobineau *(gô bē nō),* **Comte Joseph Arthur de** 1816–82. French writer. *b.* Bordeaux. In major work *Essai sur L'Inégalité des Races Humaines* (4 vols., 1853–55), propounded theory of racial superiority of blond Nordics, later known as theory of Gobinism. Also wrote *Les Religions et les*

Philosophies dans l'Asie Centrale (1865) and *Nouvelles Asiatiques* (1876).

Goddard *(gŏd ərd),* **Robert Hutchings** 1882–1945. American space scientist. *b.* Worcester, Mass. Conducted rocket experiments and designed early high-altitude rockets in Roswell, N.M. (from 1934); successfully fired world's first liquid-fuel rocket (1926).

Godfrey of Bouillon *(gŏd frĭ əv bo͞o yôN)* c1061–1100. French crusader. *b.* Baisy, Belgium. Served under Emperor Henry IV; duke of Lower Lorraine, with Bouillon as capital (1088); joined First Crusade (1096–99); king of Jerusalem (1099) but relinquished title for that of Protector of the Holy Sepulcher; defeated sultan of Egypt at Ascalon (1099) and completed conquest of Holy Land; celebrated in legends and *chansons de geste* as a great Christian warrior.

Godin *(gô dăN),* **Jean Baptiste André** 1817–88. French social reformer. *b.* Esqueheries. Founder of a successful Fourierist industrial union, or *familistère,* at Guise (1859). Author of *Solutions Sociales* (1871), *Le Gouvernement et la Vrai Socialisme en Action* (1883), and other books.

Godunov *(gŭ do͞o nôf),* **Boris Fëdorovich** c1551–1605. Czar of Russia (1598–1605). Principal member of regency during reign of the imbecile Fyodor Ivanovich; chosen czar on death of Fyodor (1598); believed to have murdered Fyodor's brother Dmitri (1591); regained territories from Sweden and recolonized Siberia; challenged by imposter Dmitri, who claimed to be Fyodor's brother; died during false Dmitri's invasion; subject of a poem by Pushkin and an opera by Moussorgsky.

Godwin *(gŏd wĭn),* **Mary** *née* WOLLSTONECRAFT. 1759–97. English writer. *b.* London. Literary advisor and reader to Samuel Johnson; after liaison with Gilbert Imlay (1793–95), who deserted her, married William Godwin; died giving birth to a daughter, Mary, who later became Shelley's second wife. Author of *Vindication of the Rights of Women* (1792), one of the earliest manifestos of feminism.

Godwin, William 1756–1836. English philosopher. *b.* Wisbeach. After five years at Ware, Stowmarket, and Beaconsfield, as a dissenting minister, became an atheist; gained reputation as spokesman of English radicalism with publication of *Enquiry Concerning Political Justice* (1793); mentor to Coleridge, Wordsworth, Southey, and Shelley; married Mary Wollstonecraft (1797), who died the same year in childbirth. Other works include *Adventures of Caleb Williams* (1794), *Of Population* (1820), and *A History of the Commonwealth* (1824–28).

Goebbels *(gûb əls),* **Paul Joseph** 1897–1945. German Nazi leader. *b.* Rheydt. Joined Nazi party (1922); head of Nazi Party Organization in Berlin (1926); founder and editor of the Nazi journals *Der Angriff* and *Voelkische Freiheit* (1927); Minister of Public Enlightenment and Propaganda (1929); virtually ran the country while Hitler was directing the war; committed suicide (1945). Parts of his *Diaries* found in Berlin were published in 1948.

Goering *(gĕr rĭng),* **Hermann Wilhelm** 1893–1946. German Nazi leader. *b.* Rosenheim. Joined Nazi party (1922) after distinguished service as an aviator in World War I; organized the notorious Sturm-Abteilungen (S.A.) and was wounded in the abortive beer hall putsch (1923); deputy to the Reichstag (1928); elected president of the Reichstag (1932); served successively as Commissioner for Air, Minister of the Interior, economic dictator of Germany (1937), Marshal of the Reich (1938), and president of the Council for War Economy (1940); helped found the Gestapo and build concentration camps; fell into disgrace and condemned to death by Hitler (1945); escaped, but captured by the Allies; tried as principal defendant at Nuremburg War Crimes Tribunal; cheated gallows by committing suicide.

Goethals *(gō thəlz),* **George Washington** 1858–1928. American engineer. *b.* Brooklyn, N.Y. Chief engineer and chairman of the Panama Canal Commission (1907–14); successfully carried out construction of the Canal, opened to shipping in 1914; governor of the Canal Zone (1914–16).

Goethe *(gû tə),* **Johann Wolfgang von** 1749–1832. German poet. *b.* Frankfurt-am-Main. As a student at Strasbourg, influenced by Herder; returned to Frankfurt (1772) where he published *Götz von Berlichingen,* launching the literary movement called Sturm und Drang (1773); inspired by a hopeless love affair, published *Sorrows of Werther* (1774), whose morbid romanticism started a cult of despair; settled at Weimar at invitation of Karl August, prince of Weimar (1776); ennobled, created privy councillor and minister of state, and entrusted with important administrative posts; visited Italy (1768–88, 1790) and gained lasting enthusiasm for classical ideals; conducted scientific research into botany and comparative anatomy, discovering the intermaxillary bone; productive friendship with Schiller (1794–1805); created *Wilhelm Meister's Apprenticeship* (1795–96) and *Hermann and Dorothea* (1797); attained Olympian stature with publication of masterpiece, *Faust* (Part 1, 1808; Part 2, 1832); throughout life, formed intimate and inspiring associations with a number of women, including Charlotte Buff, Charlotte von Stein, Bettina von Arnim, Minna Herzlieb, Marianne von Willemer, Ulrike von Levetzow, and Christiane Vulpius, whom he eventually married (1806). Other major works include *Iphigenie auf Tauris* (1787), *Egmont* (1788), *Torquato Tasso* (1790), *Roman Elegies* (1795), *Reineke Fuchs* (1794), *Die Wahlverwandtschaften* (1809), the autobiography *From My Life* (4 vols., 1811–33), *Italian Journeys* (3 vols., 1816–29), *Westöstlicher Diwan* (1819), *Wilhelm Meister's Travels* (2 vols., 1821–29), *Trilogie der Leidenschaft* (1822), *Die Natürlichte Tochter* (1803), and poetic dramas *Clavigo* and *Stella.*

Gogh *(ğoK),* **Vincent Willem van** 1853–90. Dutch painter. *b.* Groot-Zundert. Began as itinerant preacher possessed of religious fervor; began to draw seriously (1880); after a series of unrequited love affairs, settled at The Hague;

helped by brother Théo, an art dealer; went to Paris, where he became acquainted with Pissarro, Degas, Toulouse-Lautrec, Seurat, and Gauguin; tried to form community of painters with Gauguin at Arles; association with Gauguin ended by a tragic quarrel, in which he cut off his own ear; institutionalized in asylum at St. Rémy (1889–90); went to live at Auvers under supervision of a physician; took own life (1890); considered a pioneer of Expressionism and post-impressionism; used intense and searing colors and free distortions. Notable works include *The Vegetable Gardens, The Potato Eaters, Sunflowers, Starry Night, Boots, Restaurant on Montmartre, Cornfields with Flight of Birds, The Chair and the Pipe, Cypress Road, Bridge at Arles, Vincent's House at Arles, Asylum Corridors, Ravine, Berceuse, L'Arlésienne,* and several self-portraits.

Gogol *(gô gŭl),* **Nikolai Vasilievich** 1809–1852. Russian writer. *b.* Sorochintsi. Settled in St. Petersburg (1829), devoting himself to writing (from 1835); left Russia (1836) and lived for ten years abroad, mostly in Rome; during later years, manifested increasing religious fervor, heightened by a pilgrimage to Jerusalem (1848); considered the father of Russian realism for his works *Dead Souls* (1842), *The Inspector General* (1836), *Evenings on a Farm near Dikanka* (1831), *Mirogorod* (1835), *Taras Bulba* (1842), and *The Cossack Tales* (1836); best known for short stories "*The Overcoat*" and "*The Diary of a Madman.*"

Goldoni *(gōl dō nē)* **Carlo** 1707–93. Italian playwright. *b.* Venice. Wrote over 250 plays in Italian, French, and Venetian dialect, creating modern Italian comedy; from 1761 until the Revolution, lived in Paris. Principal plays include *I Rusteghi, Il Vero Amico, Zelinda e Londoro, La Locandiera, Ventaglio, La Baruffe Chiozzotte,* and *Il Vecchio Bizzarro.*

Goldsmith *(gōld smĭth),* **Oliver** 1728–74. English writer. *b.* near Ballymahon, Ireland. Turned to writing after failing in law, church, teaching, and medicine; became Samuel Johnson's intimate friend and an original member of "The Club," which included Johnson, Garrick, Burke, Boswell, Reynolds, and Gibbon (1764). Most famous works are *The Vicar of Wakefield* (1766), *The Deserted Village* (1770), and *She Stoops to Conquer* (1773); other works include *Enquiry into the Present State of Polite Learning in Europe* (1759), *The Citizen of the World* (1762), *The Traveller* (1764), *The Goodnatured Man* (1768), *A History of England* (1771), and *The History of Greece* (1774).

Goldwater *(gōld wô tər),* **Barry Morris** 1909–. American statesman. *b.* Phoenix, Ariz. U.S. Senator (1953–64; 1968–); unsuccessful Republican candidate for the presidency (1964); identified with Goldwaterism, a far-right brand of conservative Republicanism.

Golgi *(gôl jē),* **Camillo** 1844–1926. Italian physician. *b.* Corteno. Professor of pathology and histology at Pavia; demonstrated structure of the nervous system as an interlacement rather than a network; the Golgi method for staining cells, the Golgi bodies in animal cells, the Golgi material in the cytoplasm, and Golgi's organ are named after him; shared the Nobel Prize for physiology and medicine (1906) with Ramón y Cajal for work on the nervous system.

Gompers *(gŏm pərz),* **Samuel** 1850–1924. American labor leader. *b.* London, England. Immigrated to U.S. (1863); apprenticed to a cigarmaker; joined Cigarmakers' Union (1864) and was its president (1877); chairman of Committee on Constitution that created Federation of Organized Trades and Labor Unions (1881), reorganized as American Federation of Labor (1886); president of Federation (1886–1924, except for 1895); directed and shaped labor movement in America during formative years. Author of *Labor in Europe and America* (1910) and *Seventy Years of Life and Labor* (2 vols., 1925).

Goncourt *(gôɴ ko͞or),* **Edmond Louis Antoine de** 1822–96. French writer. *b.* Nancy. With brother JULES ALFRED HUOT DE GONCOURT (1830–70), wrote naturalistic novels in a style known as *écriture artiste,* combining experimental words with impressionistic narration of facts; their work together includes *Charles Demailly* (1860), *Soeur Philomène* (1861), *Renée Mauperin* (1864), and *Madame Gervaisais* (1869); after Jules's death published *La Fille Élisa* (1878), *La Faustin* (1882), and *Chérie* (1885); documented Parisian society in *Le Journal des Goncourt* (9 vols., 1887–96); founded and endowed the Goncourt Academy, which awards the annual Goncourt prize.

Gonzaga, Luigi. *See* **Aloysius, Saint**

Goodyear *(go͝od yēr),* **Charles** 1800–1860. American inventor. *b.* New Haven, Conn. Discovered and patented the vulcanization process for rubber (1844) based on N.M. Hayward's sulfur treatment process; died in impoverished circumstances as a result of troubles in establishing his business.

Gordon *(gôr dən),* **Charles George** also called CHINESE GORDON, GORDON PASHA. 1833–85. British general. *b.* Woolwich. Went to China (1860) and took part in capture of Peking and destruction of Summer Palace; as commander of a Chinese force called "Ever Victorious Army," suppressed Taiping rebels in 33 engagements; created mandarin of the first class by the emperor (1865); entered service of khedive of Egypt (1874–76, 1877–80) as governor of Equatorial Provinces of central Africa and governor general of the Sudan; suppressed slave trade; pasha (1877); resigned (1880); sent (1884) to Khartoum to relieve Egyptian garrisons threatened by rebels under the Mahdi; city besieged by the Mahdi, but held off besiegers for ten months; killed two days before relief arrived (1885).

Gorki *(gôr kĭ),* **Maksim** also MAXIM GORKY; pseudonym of ALEKSEI MAKSIMOVICH PESHKOV. 1868–1936. Russian writer. *b.* Nizhni Novgorod (renamed Gorki in 1932). Spent early years as a laborer; began writing (1892); involved in Marxist activities as a spokesman of Socialist realism; lived abroad (1905–14, 1922–28); chief of Soviet Propaganda Bureau

(1918); supported official Soviet line on literature and art. Principal works include *The Lower Depths* (1903), *The Night Lodgings* (1905), *The Judge* (1924), *Foma Gordeyev* (1900), *Mother* (1907), *Decadence* (1927), *Forty Years: The Life of Klim Smagin* (1927–36), *My Childhood* (1913), *My Universities* (1913–1923), *Reminiscences of My Youth* (1924), and *Fragments from My Diary* (1924).

Gottfried von Strassburg *(gōt frēt fōn shträs bo͝orK)* *fl.* 1200. German epic poet. Best known as author of the epic *Tristan und Isolde,* incomplete at his death; work celebrated for lyrical beauty, polished style, and narrative power.

Gounod *(go͞o nō),* **Charles François** 1818–93. French composer. *b.* Paris. Fame rests chiefly on opera *Faust* (1859). Other operas include: *Philémon et Baucis* (1860), *La Reine de Saba* (1862), *La Colombe* (1866), *Le Médicin Malgré Lui* (1858), *Roméo et Juliette* (1867), *Sapho* (1851), *Mireille* (1864), *Cinq-Mars* (1877), and *Polyeucte* (1878); also wrote oratorios and church music, including *Messe de Sainte Cécile, La Rédemption* (1882), *Mors et Vita* (1885) and *Ave Maria* or *Meditation on the First Prelude of Bach.*

Goya y Lucientes *(gō yä ē lo͞o thyān tās),* **Francisco José de** 1746–1828. Spanish painter. *b.* Fuendetodos. Court painter to Charles IV (1786); produced a number of satiric etchings in series called *Caprices, The Bullfighters,* and *The Disasters of War;* during French occupation (1808–13), supported Bonapartists; abandoned post as royal painter to Ferdinand VII and left Spain to settle in Bordeaux (1814). Principal works include *Maja Nude, Maja Clothed, Saturn Devouring His Children,* and *Family of Charles IV.*

Graham *(grā əm),* **Martha** 1894–. American dancer and choreographer. *b.* Pittsburgh, Pa. Pupil of Ruth St. Denis; debuted in 1920; formed her own company (1929), becoming a major force in modern dance, particularly noted for the strength and individuality of her performance. Works include *Letter to the World, Appalachian Spring, A Time of Snow,* and *Archaic Hours.*

Graham, Thomas 1805–1869. Scottish chemist. *b.* Glasgow. Professor of chemistry at University College, London (1837–55) and later master of the mint; discovered dialysis for separation of colloids; conducted research on molecular diffusion of gases, formulating Graham's Law. Author of *Elements of Chemistry* (1842) and other books.

Graham, William Franklin known as BILLY GRAHAM. 1918–. American evangelist. *b.* Charlotte, N.C. Conducted Crusades for Christ worldwide (from 1949). Author of *Peace With God* (1954), *Angels* (1975), and other books.

Granit *(grä nēt),* **Ragnar Arthur** 1900–. Swedish scientist. *b.* Finland. Shared (with H. Hartline and G. Wald) Nobel Prize in physiology and medicine (1967) for research on visual mechanisms.

Grant *(grănt),* **Ulysses Simpson** 1822–85. 18th president of U.S. (1869–77). *b.* Point Pleasant, Ohio. Served in Mexican War under Zachary Taylor, but resigned commission (1854); rejoined army as colonel on outbreak of Civil War (1861); commanded Union forces, capturing Fort Henry and Fort Donelson (1862); besieged and took Vicksburg (1863); victorious at Chattanooga, expelling Braxton Bragg from Lookout Mountain and Missionary Ridge (1863); general in chief in command of Union armies (1864); developed strategy resulting in fall of Petersburg and Richmond and leading to Lee's surrender at Appomattox (1865); general (1866); elected president on Republican ticket (1868); re-elected (1872); administration marked by punitive Reconstruction programs in the South, inflation favoring industrial interests, and political and financial scandals; on leaving office, went on a world tour (1877–79). Author of *Personal Memoirs of U.S. Grant* (2 vols., 1885–86).

Grass *(grăs),* **Günter Wilhelm** 1927–. German author. *b.* Danzig. Achieved literary recognition with *The Tin Drum* (1958); later works include *Cat and Mouse* (1961), *Dog Years* (1962), and *The Flounder* (1979); actively associated with German Socialist Democratic Party; elected to German Academy of Arts (1963).

Gratian *(grā shĭ ən)* Latin: FLAVIUS GRATIANUS. 359–83. Roman emperor (375–83). *b.* Sirmium, Pannonia. Made augustus with share in government, by father Valentinian I (367); succeeded father as emperor of the West (375) and uncle Valens as emperor of the East (378); delegated government of the East to Theodosius; persecuted non-Christians and heretics, helping to establish Christianity as universal religion; defeated near Paris by usurper Maximus; killed at Lugdunum.

Graves *(grāvz),* **Robert Ranke** 1895–. English poet and critic. *b.* London. Son of ALFRED PERCEVAL GRAVES (1846–1931), leader of the Irish literary and musical renaissance and of the Pan-Celtic movement. Author of *Poems 1914–1926, Poems 1926–1930, Poems 1930–1933, Goodbye to All That, Autobiography* (1929), *I, Claudius* (1934), *Claudius the God* (1934), *Count Belisarius* (1938), *But It Still Goes On, a Miscellany* (1930), *The White Goddess* (1947), and *Occupation: Writer* (1950).

Gray *(grā),* **Asa** 1810–88. American botanist. *b.* Paris, N.Y. Fisher professor of natural history at Harvard (1842–88); helped popularize the study of North American flora and fauna; established systematic taxonomy as important tool of botany; strong defender of Darwinian theory of evolution. Author of *Elements of Botany* (1836), *Manual of the Botany of the Northern United States* (1848), *Statistics of the Flora of the Northern United States* (1856), *Synoptical Flora of North America* (1878), and *Darwiniana* (1876).

Gray, Thomas 1716–71. English poet. *b.* London. Resident at Cambridge (from 1742); professor of history and modern languages at Cambridge (from 1768); regarded as one of the finest letter-writers in English literature and as forerunner of Romantic poets. Principal works include "Elegy Written in a Country Churchyard" (1751), "Ode on a Distant Prospect of Eton College" (1747), "Progress of Poesy" (1754), "The Bard" (1758); complete works published (5 vols., 1884).

Greco *(grĕk ō),* **El** real name: KYRIAKOS THEOTOKOPOULOS. c1548–1614. Greek-Spanish painter. *b.* Candia, Crete. Studied in Venice under Titian; settled (c1577) in Toledo. Works characterized by vibrant colors and distorted, elongated figures imbued with religious ecstasy; principal works include *St. Martin and the Beggar, View of Toledo, Burial of Count Orgas, Christ Healing the Blind Man, Assumption of the Virgin, Adoration of the Shepherds, Christ Despoiled of His Garments, Baptism of Christ, Crucifixion, Purification of the Temple, Resurrection, The Pentecost,* and *Portrait of a Man.*

Greeley *(grē'lĭ),* **Horace** 1811–72. American journalist and statesman. *b.* Amherst, N.H. Founded the weekly *New Yorker* (1834) and the daily *New York Tribune* (1841); used journals as forums of liberal ideas including Fourierism, homesteading, abolitionism, tariff protection, temperance, and antinativism; important influence on American public opinion during Civil War; influential in founding the Republican party and in the nomination of Lincoln at Chicago convention (1860); credited with hastening Emanicipation Proclamation with publication of the "Prayer of Twenty Millions" in the *Tribune*; after Civil War, advocated universal amnesty and defied public opinion to sign bail bond for Jefferson Davis; nominated by Liberals and Democrats as presidential candidate (1872) but was beaten by Grant. Author of *The American Conflict* (2 vols., 1864–66), *Recollections of a Busy Life* (1868), and other books.

Green *(grēn),* **William** 1873–1952. American labor leader. *b.* Coshocton, Ohio. Began as a miner; president of Ohio District Mineworkers' Union (1906–10); succeeded Gompers as president of American Federation of Labor (1924–52). Author of *Labor and Democracy (1939).*

Greene *(grēn),* **Graham** 1904–. English writer. *b.* Berkhamsted. Major novelist whose works explore basic religious problems of evil, sin, suffering, and salvation, generally employing topical settings and melodramatic thriller techniques. Principal works include *Stamboul Train* (1932), *A Gun for Sale* (1936), *Brighton Rock* (1938), *The Confidential Agent* (1939), *The Power and the Glory* (1940), *The Heart of the Matter* (1948), *The Third Man* (1950), *The End of the Affair* (1951), *The Quiet American* (1955), *Our Man in Havana* (1958), *A Burnt-Out Case* (1961), and *The Comedians* (1966).

Greene, Nathanael 1742–86. American Revolutionary general. *b.* Warwick, R.I. Commissioned brigadier general in Continental army; took part in siege of Boston, and battles at Trenton, Princeton, Brandywine, and Germantown; in supreme command of Continental army during Washington's absence (Sept. 1780); succeeded Gates as commander of the Army of the South (1780); expelled British from South Carolina and Georgia; his son GEORGE WASHINGTON GREENE (1811–83), published *Life of Nathanael Greene* (3 vols., 1867–71).

Gregory I *(grĕg ō rĭ),* **Saint** called GREGORY THE GREAT. c540–604. Pope (590–604). *b.* Rome, Italy.

Descended from noble family; prefect of Rome; retired to devote himself to religious work as monk in one of seven monasteries he established with his wealth; pope (590); restored monastic discipline, enforced rule of celibacy, systematized Gregorian chant and public rituals, and defended papal supremacy against claims of Constantinople; sent Augustine as missionary to Kent; wrote extensively on dogma and scriptures, including *Moralia, Liber Pastoralis Curae,* and *Dialogues*; Fourth Doctor of the Church. Feast day: Mar. 12.

Gregory VII, Saint real name: HILDEBRAND. c1020–85. *b.* near Soana, Italy. Entered Benedictine order; chaplain of Gregory VI, accompanying him in exile to Germany; recalled and made cardinal by Leo IX (1050); influential figure in curia under popes Victor II, Stephen IX, Benedict X, Nicholas II, and Alexander II; pope (1073); launched the Hildebrandine reforms aimed at correcting abuses of simony, lay investiture, and clerical concubinage; efforts to enforce reforms led to conflict with Henry IV, emperor; excommunicated Henry twice, compelling Henry to humiliate himself in penance at Canossa (1077); later deposed by Henry, who set up Clement III as antipope; driven from Rome, spending last days in exile in Salerno.

Gregory XIII real name: UGO BUONCOMPAGNI. 1502–85. Pope (1572–85). *b.* Bologna, Italy. Active in Council of Trent (1545, 1569–73); pope (1572); vigorously opposed the Protestants and supported Jesuits and Capuchins; introduced Gregorian calendar (1582); issued new edition of the canon law and a revised martyrology.

Gregory, Lady Augusta *née* PERSSE. 1852–1932. Irish playwright. *b.* in County Galway. Founder (with W.B. Yeats and others) of Abbey Theater and Irish National Theater Society. Author of "The Rising of the Moon," "Spreading the News," and "The Workhouse Ward," published in *Seven Short Plays* (1909), and a number of books on Irish folklore and legends, including *Poets and Dreamers* (1903), *Cachulain of Muirthemne* (1902), and *Gods and Fighting Men* (1904).

Grenville *(grĕn vĭl),* **George** 1712–70. British statesman. Entered Parliament (1741); leader of House of Commons (1761), first lord of admiralty (1762); prime minister (1763-65); administration notable for the prosecution of Wilkes and the passing of the American Stamp Act.

Grey *(grā),* **Charles** title: 2ND EARL GREY. 1764–1845. British statesman. *b.* Fallodon. Entered Parliament (1786); first lord of the admiralty (1806); foreign secretary (1806–1807); out of office until 1830; prime minister (1830–34) whose policy was peace, retrenchment, and reform; produced first Reform Bill (1832), a bill abolishing slavery throughout the empire (1833), and the Poor Law Amendment Act (1834); resigned (1834).

Grey, Sir Edward title: VISCOUNT GREY OF FALLODEN. 1862–1933. British statesman. *b.* Northumberland. Entered Parliament (1885); secretary of state for foreign affairs (1905–19); during critical period preceding World War I, strengthened Triple Entente with France and Russia, attempted to pacify the Balkans, and tried to reach agreement with Germany. Author of *Twenty-Five Years, 1892–1916* (2 vols., 1925) and *Falloden Papers* (1926).

Grey *(grā),* **Lady Jane** 1537–54. English queen. *b.* Broadgate. Daughter of Henry Grey (Earl of Dorset and later Duke of Suffolk) and Henry VIII's niece Frances Brandon; a precocious child, she was fluent in six languages by age 15; married Lord Guildford Dudley, son of the duke of Northumberland; on death of Edward VI, unwillingly proclaimed queen of England by conspirators, including her father-in-law; reigned for nine days until Mary, supported by the powerful Earl of Oxford, wrested the crown; renounced her claim, but was arrested and condemned for treason; refused to abjure Protestantism; following Thomas Wyatt's Rebellion, beheaded along with her father and her husband.

Grieg *(grēg),* **Edvard Hagerup** 1843–1907. Norwegian composer. *b.* Bergen. Studied at Leipzig and Copenhagen, but emerged as strongly national composer using folk elements in his work. Composed incidental music for Ibsen's *Peer Gynt,* Piano Concerto in A minor, three violin sonatas, choral works, and piano pieces.

Grieve, Christopher Murray. *See* **McDiarmid, Hugh**

Griffith *(grĭf ĭth),* **Arthur** 1872–1922. Irish revolutionary leader. *b.* Dublin. Founded the journal *United Irishmen* (1899); organized Sinn Fein (1906); president of Sinn Fein (1910); founded newspapers to advance cause of Irish nationalism, including *Eire, Sinn Fein, Nationality, Scissors and Paste,* all of which were suppressed; had no part in Easter Rebellion, but was nonetheless imprisoned; deputy president of self-proclaimed Irish Republic in the absence of De Valera (1919); led delegation concluding Irish Free State treaty with England (1921); president of Dail Eireann (1922); died in office.

Griffith, David Lewelyn Wark known as D.W. GRIFFITH. 1875–1948. American motion-picture producer. *b.* La Grange, Ky. Began as an actor; director with Biograph Film Company (1908); independent producer and one of the founders of United Artists (1919); best known for development of new techniques of motion-picture photography including cross-cutting, flashbacks, fade-ins, fade-outs, close-ups, and juxtaposition. Principal films include two masterpieces, *The Birth of a Nation* (1915) and *Intolerance* (1916), as well as *Hearts of the World* (1918), *Broken Blossoms* (1918), and *Orphans of the Storm* (1922).

Grignard *(grē nyär),* **François Auguste Victor** 1871–1935. French chemist. *b.* Cherbourg. Discovered the Grignard reagents, organomagnesium compounds used to synthesize organic compounds; awarded (with Paul Sabatier) Nobel Prize in chemistry (1912) for this discovery.

Grillparzer *(grĭl pär tsər),* **Franz** 1791–1872. Austrian playwright. *b.* Vienna. Best known for dramas blending classical themes and romanticism, such as *Die Ahnfrau* (1817), *Sappho* (1819), the trilogy

The Golden Fleece (1821), *King Ottokar's Fortune and End* (1825), *A True Servant of His Master* (1828), *The Waves of Love and of the Sea* (1831), and three posthumous tragedies *Ein Bruderzwist in Habsburg, Libussa,* and *Die Jüdin von Toledo*; considered Austria's greatest playwright.

Grimm *(grĭm),* **Jacob** 1785–1863. German philologist and folklorist. *b.* Hanau. Best known as collaborator with brother WILHELM KARL (1786–1859) on collection of fairy tales *Kinder und Hausmärchen* (3 vols., 1812, 1815, 1822); both brothers had been librarians to Jerome Bonaparte, king of Westphalia, and later professors and librarians at Kassel, Gottingen, and Berlin; together worked on *Deutsches Wörterbuch* (1854); independently published *Deutsche Grammatik* (1819), regarded as one of the greatest works on philology, in which he formulated Grimm's law, *Deutsche Rechtsalterthümer* (1828), *Deutsche Mythologie* (1835), *Geschichte der Deutschen Sprache* (1848), and *Reinhart Fuchs* (1834).

Gris *(grēs),* **Juan** real name: JOSÉ VICTORIANO GONZÁLEZ. 1887–1927. Spanish painter. *b.* Madrid. Went to Paris (1905) and began painting (1910); emerged with Picasso and Braque as a leader of the Cubist movement and, theoretically, the purest; began designing for Diaghilev (1923); later modified deliberate mathematical distortions of his early phase with representational forms. Best examples of his work are *Still Life with Flowers, Landscape, Homage to Picasso, Harlequin, Still Life with Dice, The Violin,* and *The Guitar.*

Grolier de Servières *(grô lyā də sĕr vyâr),* **Jean** 1479–1565. French bibliophile. *b.* Lyons. Served as treasurer and diplomat at court of Francis I; collected one of the finest libraries of the age, containing 3000 magnificently bound books with personally designed inscriptions and decorations; library dispersed (1675) but over 350 copies survive.

Gromyko *(grō mē kō),* **Andrei Andreevich** 1909–. Soviet diplomat. *b.* Gromyki. Held top positions in the Soviet ministry of foreign affairs, including ambassador to U.S. (1943–46), delegate to U.N. Security Council (1946), and foreign minister (1957).

Gropius *(grō pĭ ŭs),* **Walter** 1883–1969. German architect. *b.* Berlin. In Weimar, founded Bauhaus school of architecture (1919), which aimed at a functional synthesis of the applied arts and bold experimentation with unusual materials; transferred to Dessau (1925–28); lived in England (1934–38); settled in U.S.; chairman and professor of school of architecture at Harvard (1938–52); partner of Marcel Breuer and advisor to New Bauhaus, Chicago (from 1937). Principal buildings include the Bauhaus at Dessau, theater at Jena, and Harvard Graduate Center. Author of *New Architecture and the Bauhaus* (1937) and *Rebuilding Our Communities* (1946).

Grosz *(grōs),* **George** 1893–1959. American artist. *b.* Berlin, Germany. Began as a music-hall performer of songs of his own composition; studied art; became interested in Dadaism (1917) and was a leader of that movement until 1920; associated with the school of New Objectivity; earned the displeasure of the Nazis, who burned some of his works, including *Ecce Homo*; immigrated to U.S. (1932), where he employed art as a mode of social protest. Best examples of his work are *The Survivor, The Couple, Robbers, The Pimps of Death,* and *A Piece of My World.*

Grotius *(grō shĭ ŭs),* **Hugo** Dutch form: Huig van Groot. 1583–1645. Dutch jurist. *b.* Delft. Began practice at the bar at Delft (1599), becoming interested in international law and law of the sea; historiographer of States-General (1603); pensionary of Rotterdam (1613); leader of the Remonstrants (Arminians), arrested by Prince Maurice of Nassau, and sentenced to life imprisonment (1618); escaped and fled to France (1621); published (1625) *De Jura Belli et Paci,* which founded the science of international law; Swedish ambassador to Paris (1634–45). Other works include *Adamus Exul* and *Annales de Rebus Christianae.*

Grünewald *(grü nə vält),* **Matthias** real name: Mathis Nithardt or Gothardt. c1480–1528. German artist. *b.* Aschaffenberg. Considered one of the greatest painters of the German school; court painter to archbisop of Mainze (1508–14) and to Cardinal Albrecht of Brandenburg (1515–25); best known for the Isenheim Altarpiece, which consists of nine paintings (1517).

Gryphius *(grĭ fĭ əs),* **Andreas** 1616–64. German lyric poet and dramatist. *b.* Glogau. Considered greatest German baroque dramatist; sometimes called "the German Shakespeare." Principal works include *Leo Arminius* (1650), *Catharina von Georgien* (1657), *Papinianus* (1659), *Cardenio und Celinde* (1647), *Carolus Stuardus* (1657), *Die Geliebte Dornrose* (1660), *Herr Peter Squentz* (1663), and *Horribilicribrifax* (1663).

Guevara *(gā vä rä),* **Che** real name: Ernesto Guevara de la Serna. 1928–67. Cuban revolutionary. *b.* in Argentina. Graduate in medicine (1953); took part in Cuban revolution (1959); director of economic policy under Castro; left to assume leadership of guerrilla movement in South America; killed in Bolivia (1967). Author of *Guerrilla Warfare* (1961) and *Reminiscences of the Cuban Revolutionary War* (1968).

Guggenheim *(go͞og ən hīm),* **Meyer** 1828–1905. American industrialist. *b.* Langnau, Switzerland. Immigrated to U.S. (c1847); made fortune supplying commodities to Union army during Civil War; developed Colorado copper mines into American Smelting and Refining Company (founded 1901); son Daniel (1856–1930) extended mining interests to Africa, Bolivia, Chile, and Alaska; founded Daniel and Florence Guggenheim Foundation (1924).

Guillaume *(gē yōm),* **Charles Édouard** 1861–1938. French physicist. *b.* Fleurier, Switzerland. Director of Bureau of International Weights and Measures at Sèvres (1915); invented Invar, a nickel-steel alloy that does not expand and is therefore ideal for use in precision instruments and standard measures, and platinite, an alloy used in electric bulbs; awarded Nobel Prize for physics (1920).

Guiscard *(gēs kär),* **Robert** c1015–85. Norman warrior. *b.* near Coutances, Normandy. Son of Tancred de Hauteville; successor to brother Humphrey as ruler of Apulia; Duke of Apulia and Calabria; with brother Roger, conquered Palermo (1072) and Salerno (1077) from Saracens, founding the Kingdom of the Two Sicilies; fought against Byzantine emperor Alexius Comnenus, victorious at Durazzo (1081); captured Rome and delivered Pope Gregory VII from the forces of Henry IV (1084); died during second campaign against the East.

Guizot *(gē zō),* **François Pierre Guillaume** 1787–1874. French historian and statesman. *b.* Nîmes. Professor of modern history at the Sorbonne (1812); elected to Chamber of Deputies (1830); after revolution of 1830, minister of the interior and minister of public instruction; prime minister (1840), heading a reactionary government that became increasingly unpopular; opposed electoral reform, countenanced venality of subordinates, and pursued foreign policy of appeasement; escaped with Louis-Philippe to London after February revolution of 1848, but returned (1849); devoted himself to historical studies (after 1851). Author of a number of books including *Histoire de la Révolution d'Angleterre* (6 vols., 1826–56), *Histoire Parliamentaire de France* (1863), *Histoire de la Civilisation en Europe* (3 vols., 1829–32), *Mémoires Pour Servir à l'Histoire de Mon Temps* (8 vols., 1858–67), and *Le Duc de Broglie* (1872).

Gullstrand *(gŭl strănd),* **Allvar** 1862–1930. Swedish scientist. *b.* Landskrona. Made important contributions to the study of dioptrics of the eye; invented the reflexless stationary ophthalmoscope and the slit lamp for examination of eye tissues; awarded Nobel Prize in medicine and physiology (1911).

Gunter *(gŭn tər),* **Edmund** 1581–1626. English mathematician. *b.* Hertfordshire. Invented a portable quadrant, Gunter's chain, Gunter's line, and Gunter's scale; discovered declination of the magnetic compass; coined the trigonometric terms "cosine" and "cotangent."

Gunther *(gŭn thĕr),* **John** 1901–70. American journalist. *b.* Chicago, Ill. Reporter (from 1922) for the *Chicago Daily News;* commentator for the National Broadcasting Company (1939–42); reputation for crisp and lively reporting style built on a series of political studies: *Inside Europe* (1936), *Inside Asia* (1939), *Inside Latin America* (1941), and *Inside U.S.A.* (1947). Other works include *Death Be Not Proud* (1949) and *Eisenhower* (1952).

Gustavus II *(gəs tā vəs)* known as GUSTAVUS ADOLPHUS; called LION OF THE NORTH, SNOW KING. 1594–1632. Swedish king (1611–31). *b.* Stockholm. Helped by chancellor Oxenstierna, restored internal stability by reconciling the nobles, reorganizing the government, and reforming education and local government; ended Kalmar War (1611–13) against Denmark by a treaty (1613) in which Baltic provinces were restored to Sweden; ended war with Russia (1613–17) by Treaty of Stolbova, in which Sweden recieved parts of Finland and Livonia (1617); conducted long war with Poland (1621–29), terminated by truce of Altmark in which Sigismund III of Poland gave up claims to Swedish throne and left Sweden in possession of Pillau and Memel; championed Protestant cause in Thirty Years' War (1630–32); leaving Oxenstierna in Sweden as regent, took 15,000 men to Pomerania, expelled imperial forces, and took Stettin; defeated Tilly at Breitenfeld (1631) and again at Rain on the Lech (1632); took Munich; confronted imperial army under Wallenstein at Lützen (1632); gained victory in hard-fought battle, but died on the battlefield.

Gutenberg *(gōō tən bərg),* **Johann** original surname: GENSFLEISCH. c1400–1468. German inventor of printing. *b.* Mainz. Began as a goldsmith at Strasbourg; believed to have invented printing from movable type (c1439); formed partnership with Johann Fust at Mainz and established a printing press (c1450); partnership terminated (1455) when Fust secured a verdict for the moneys advanced, seized all types and stock, and formed new business; with aid of Conrad Humery, set up another press; printed the *Gutenberg* (or *Mazarin*) *Bible.*

Guthrie *(gŭth rĭ),* **Samuel** 1782–1848. American chemist. *b.* Brimfield, Mass. Invented a process for converting starch into sugar, a percussion priming powder and a punch lock for setting it off, and chloroform.

Guthrie, Woodrow Wilson called WOODY GUTHRIE. 1912–67. American singer and composer. *b.* Okemah, Okla. Wrote over 1000 songs on folk and political themes, including "This Land Is Your Land." The personal philosophy expressed in his songs inspired the folk singers and composers of the 1960s.

Gwyn *(gwĭn),* **Eleanor** called NELL. 1650–87. English actress. *b.* Hereford. Born in poverty; believed to have sold oranges outside Drury Lane Theater, where she gained the attention of actors; first appeared on stage (1665) in Dryden's *Indian Emperor*; popular with London audience for her gay and sprightly roles until she left the stage (1682); after many other lovers, mistress of Charles II (1669–87), bearing him two sons, Charles Beauclerk, Duke of St. Albans, and James.

H

Haber *(hä bər),* **Fritz** 1868–1934. German chemist. *b.* Breslau. Director of Kaiser-Wilhelm Institute at Berlin (1911–33); with Karl Bosch, developed the Haber-Bosch process for nitrogen fixation; produced synthetic ammonia; awarded the Nobel Prize in chemistry (1918).

Hadrian *(hā drĭ ən) also* ADRIAN full Latin name: PUBLIUS AELIUS HADRIANUS. 76–138. Roman emperor (117–138). *b.* Rome. Succeeded uncle Trajan; visited Britain, Spain, Mauretania, Parthia, Asia Minor, Athens, Sicily, Syria, Palestine, Arabia, and Egypt; established Euphrates River as eastern boundary of empire; promulgated Edictum Perpetuum (132), a collection of praetorial edicts; put down Jewish revolt under Bar Cocheba; founded Adrianapolis; built Hadrian's Wall in Britain and numerous public edifices, including pantheons in Rome and Athens, temple of Zeus in Athens, the Aelian bridge, and the villa in Tibur; enlarged imperial powers, reduced taxes, and reorganized army.

Haeckel *(hĕk əl),* **Ernst Heinrich** 1834–1919. German scientist. *b.* Potsdam. Professor of zoology at Jena (1862–1909); studied marine invertebrates on expeditions to Canary Islands, Red Sea, Ceylon, and Java; drew up genealogical tree of animals; developed philosophical theory of materialistic monism; formulated theory that ontogeny recapitulates phylogeny; emphasized importance of sexual selection in organic evolution. Principal works include *Generale Morphologie der Organismen* (1866), *Natural History of Creation* (1868), *On the Origin and Genealogy of the Human Race* (1870), and *Evolution of Man* (1879).

Hafiz *(hä fĭz)* original name: SHAMS UD-DIN MUHAMMAD. *fl.* 14th century. Persian poet. *b.* Shiraz. Belonged to an order of dervishes and was a member of Sufi sect; appointed teacher to royal family and a professor in a college founded especially for him; principal work, *Divan,* consists of a collection of short odes (ghazals) dealing with sensuous themes that are sometimes interpreted allegorically; because of the sweetness of his poetry, called Chagarlab (Sugarlip).

Haggard *(hăg ərd),* **Sir Henry Rider** 1856–1925. English novelist. *b.* Bradenham Hall. Best known for novels of adventure set in Africa, where he was a civil servant (1875–81). Works include *King Solomon's Mines* (1885), *Allan Quatermain* (1887), *Cleopatra* (1889), *Montezuma's Daughter* (1893), *She* (1887), and *Ayesha* (1905).

Hahn *(hän),* **Otto** 1879–1968. German chemist. *b.* Frankfurt. Director of Kaiser Wilhelm Institute in Berlin (from 1927); with Lise Meitner, discovered radioactive protactinium (1917); with Fritz Strassman, split the uranium atom (1939) and discovered chain reaction; president of Max Planck Society in Gottingen (1946–60); awarded Nobel Prize in chemistry (1944).

Hahnemann *(hä nə män),* **Samuel** full name: CHRISTIAN FRIEDRICH SAMUEL. 1755–1843. German physician and founder of homeopathy. *b.* Meissen. Announced new system of medicine (1796) based on two principles: that a curative drug must produce in a healthy person symptoms of the disease which it is supposed to cure and that small doses are more effective than massive ones; driven from Leipzig (1821) and from all other towns, by the hostility of the apothecaries; forced to flee to Paris (1835). Author of *Organon of the Rational Art of Healing* (1810).

Haig *(hāg),* **Douglas** title: 1ST EARL HAIG. 1861–1928. British general. *b.* Edinburgh, Scotland. Saw active service in Sudan, South

Africa, and India; general (1914); succeeded Sir John French as commander in chief of British expeditionary forces in France (1915–19); field marshal (1917); commander in chief of Home Forces (1919–21); helped organize the Imperial General Staff.

Haile Selassie *(hī lə sĭl lä syĕ)* original name: RAS TAFARI or TAFARI MAKONNEN. 1891–1975. Emperor of Ethiopia (1930–74). *b.* Harar. Governor of province of Harar (1910); led revolt that deposed Emperor Lij Yasu (1916); regent of Ethiopia (until 1928); crowned king (1928) and emperor (1930); in exile during Italian occupation (1936–41); played important role in Pan-African movements after World War II; deposed by army coup (1974); stripped of power and possessions; died a prisoner (1975).

Hakluyt *(hăk lo͞ot),* **Richard** c1552–1616. English geographer. *b.* in Herefordshire. Archdeacon of Westminster (1603); noted for the great collection of travels, *Principall Navigations, Voiages, and Discoveries of the English Nation* (1589; 3 vols., 1598–1600), an invaluable sourcebook on English voyages of 16th century; also published *Divers Voyages Touching the Discovery of America* (1582) and *Discourse Concerning Western Discoveries* (1584); the Hakluyt Society was founded (1846) to continue his work.

Haldane *(hôl dān),* **John Burdon Sanderson** 1892–1964. British biologist. *b.* Oxford. Professor of genetics at London (1933–57) and of biometry, University College (1937–57); immigrated to India and adopted Indian nationality. Author of *Possible Worlds* (1927), *Animal Biology* (1927), *The Causes of Evolution* (1933), *Fact and Faith* (1934), and *New Paths in Genetics* (1949).

Haldane, Richard Burdon title: VISCOUNT HALDANE OF CLOAN. 1856–1928. British statesman. *b.* Scotland. Entered Parliament (1885); secretary of state for war (1905–12); reorganized the army and formed territorial reserve; lord high chancellor (1912–15, 1924); minister of labor (1924). Author of *The Pathway to Reality* (1903), *The Reign of Relativity* (1921), *The Philosophy of Humanism* (1922), and *Human Experience* (1926).

Hale *(hāl),* **George Ellery** 1868–1938. American astronomer. *b.* Chicago, Ill. Director of Yerkes Observatory (1895–1905); professor of astrophysics at University of Chicago (1897–1905); founder and director (1904–23) of Mount Wilson Observatory; invented the spectroheliograph, an instrument used to photograph the sun and detect solar prominences (1890). Author of *The Study of Solar Evolution* (1908) and other books; editor (1892–95) of the *Astrophysical Journal.*

Hale, Nathan 1755–1776. American revolutionary. *b.* Coventry, Conn. Commissioned as a lieutenant in Continental army (1775); took part in siege of Boston; promoted to captain; volunteered to infiltrate enemy lines to obtain military intelligence for Washington; detected and executed as a spy; credited with famous last words: "I only regret that I have but one life to lose for my country."

Halévy *(hȧ lā vē),* **Jacques François Fromental Élie** original surname: LEVY. 1799–1862. French composer. *b.* Paris. Professor at Paris Conservatory (from 1827). Principal operas include *La Juive* (1835), *L'Éclair* (1835), and *Le Juif Errant* (1852); author of *Souvenirs et Portraits* (1861).

Halifax, Earl of. *See* **Montague, Charles**

Hall *(hôl),* **Granville Stanley** 1846–1924. American psychologist. *b.* Ashfield, Mass. President of Clark University (1889–1919); founder and editor of *American Journal of Psychology* (from 1887); first president of American Psychological Association (1891); exerted profound influence on growth of educational psychology in U.S.; established experimental psychology laboratory at Johns Hopkins University. Works include *The Contents of Children's Minds* (1894), *Adolescence* (1904), *Educational Problems* (2 vols., 1911), *Jesus, the Christ, in the Light of Psychology* (2 vols., 1917), and *Life and Confessions of a Psychologist* (1923).

Halley *(hăl ĭ),* **Edmund** 1656–1742. English astronomer. *b.* Haggerston. Began astronomical observations as a boy; sailed for St. Helena (1676) to observe the positions of fixed stars in the Southern Hemisphere; made first complete observation of transit of Mercury (1677); fellow of Royal Society (1678); as a friend of Newton, printed *Principia* at his own cost; editor of *Philosophical Transactions* of the Royal Society (1685–93); Savilian professor of geometry at Oxford (1703); secretary of Royal Society (1713); astronomer royal (1721); published research on the orbits of comets (1705) and correctly predicted the return in 1758 of a comet that had previously appeared at intervals of 76 years, (Halley's comet).

Hals *(häls),* **Frans** c1580–1666. Dutch painter. *b.* Antwerp, Netherlands. Lived most of his life in Haarlem; specialized in portraits of groups and low-life sketches characterized by swagger and vivacity. Best-known works include *Laughing Cavalier, Portrait of a Lady, Jolly Trio, Herring Vender, Gypsy Girl, Seated Man, Banquet of the Company of St. Adrian, The Women Guardians of the Haarlem Almshouse, Young Married Couple,* and *Portrait of a Man.*

Halsey *(hôl sē),* **William Frederick** 1882–1959. American naval officer. *b.* Elizabeth, N.J. Graduated from Annapolis (1904); admiral in World War II; commander of Allied Naval Forces in South Pacific; victor of Marshall and Gilbert Islands (1942) and Solomon Islands (1942) engagements; commander of U.S. Third Fleet (1944–45); his flagship, *Missouri,* was the scene of the Japanese surrender; retired (1945); admiral of the fleet (1945).

Hamilcar Barca *(hȧ mĭl kär bär kȧ)* c270–228 B.C. Carthaginian general. Father of Hannibal; during First Punic War (247), landed in Sicily after ravaging the Italian coast and seized the stronghold of Ercte, which he held for three years; later occupied Mount Eryx (244), mounting attacks against Italian mainland; at the close of the war, retired undefeated to Africa, where he suppressed a revolt of mercenary troops and became virtual dictator of Carthage; led campaign to create a new Carthaginian dominion in Spain as a base from which to subdue Rome, but died in battle with mission only partly accomplished.

Hamilton *(hăm ĭl tən),* **Alexander** 1757–1804. American statesman. *b.* Charles Town, West Indies. Natural son of a Scottish father and Huguenot mother; came to U.S. (1772); on outbreak of Revolutionary War, became a captain of the artillery; attracted Washington's attention and became his aide-de-camp (1777); after the war, became a notable lawyer in N.Y.; elected to Congress (1782); took part in Conventions of Annapolis and Philadelphia; articulated the philosophy and theory of Federalism in 51 contributions to *The Federalist* (1787); secretary of the treasury (1789–95); developed a strong national fiscal system based on sound public credit, geared to the growth of commerce and industry; established Bank of the United States; alienated Jeffersonian anti-Federalists with his advocacy of strong central government, Anglophilism, and emphasis on wealth; remained leader of Federalist party after leaving office (1804); earned the animosity of Aaron Burr and was mortally wounded in a duel with him.

Hamlin *(hăm lĭn),* **Hannibal** 1809–91. American statesman. *b.* Paris Hill, Me. Member of Congress on Democratic ticket (1843–47); senator (1848–57, 1857–61, 1869–81); joined Republican party (1856) after passage of Kansas-Nebraska Bill; vice-president under Lincoln (1861–65); U.S. minister to Spain (1881-82).

Hammarskjöld *(häm är shəld),* **Dag Hjalmar Agne Carl** 1905–61. Swedish statesman. *b.* Jönköping. Son of Hjalmar Hammarskjold (1862–1953), prime minister of Sweden (1914–17). Chairman of Bank of Sweden (1941–48); Swedish foreign minister (1951–53), secretary-general of U.N. (1953–61); took an active role in peace-keeping operations in Middle East; died in an air crash near Ndola, Zambia, during negotiations over the Congo crisis; awarded Nobel Peace Prize posthumously (1961).

Hammerstein *(hăm ər stīn),* **Oscar** c1847–1919. American operatic manager. *b.* Berlin, Germany. Immigrated to U.S. (1863); made fortune by inventing machine for making cigars; built and opened theaters in New York, Philadelphia, and London; sold interests to Metropolitan Opera Company (1910); nephew OSCAR HAMMERSTEIN II (1895–1960), American playwright and librettist, wrote lyrics for a number of stage musicals, most of them in collaboration with Richard Rodgers; best known for *Show Boat* (1927), *Rose Marie* (1924), *Desert Song* (1926), *Oklahoma* (1943), *Carousel* (1945), *South Pacific* (1949), *The King and I* (1951), and *The Sound of Music* (1959).

Hammett *(hăm ĕt),* **Dashiell** full name: SAMUEL DASHIELL HAMMETT. 1894–1961. American author. *b.* St. Mary's County, Md. Served with Pinkerton's Private Detective Agency; turned to writing and became one of the earliest and most respected "private eye" crime authors; as a trustee of the Civil Rights Congress during the McCarthy investigations, he was jailed for a short while (1951). Works include *Red Harvest* (1929), *The Maltese Falcon* (1930), *The Glass Key* (1931), and *The Thin Man* (1932).

Hammurabi *(häm o͞o rä bē)* also KHAMMURABI. *fl.* 21st century B.C. King of Babylon. Extended Babylonian empire; conquered Elamites and Amorites; built royal canal of Babylon, nahr-Hammurabi, named after him; built temples and other public structures and set up an efficient administration; drew up a comprehensive code of laws inscribed on a diorite column, which was discovered at Susa (1901).

Hampden *(hăm dĕn),* **John** 1945–1643. English parliamentarian. *b.* London. Entered parliament (1621); leader of anti-Royalist party; helped prepare charges against Buckingham (1626); defied Charles I by refusing to pay forced loan (1626) and ship money writ (1635); imprisoned (1626) and prosecuted (1637–38); impeached for opposition to the king along with Pym, Strode, Lenthall, and Holles, but escaped arrest and helped precipitate the Civil War; commanded a regiment for Parliament (1642–43); mortally wounded in engagement with Royalists at Chalgrove Field (1643).

Hamsun *(häm so͞on),* **Knut** pseudonym of KNUT PEDERSEN. 1859–1952. Norwegian author. *b.* Lom. Spent early years as a vagabond working in Norway and U.S. as farmer, coal miner, teacher, street car conductor, and shoemaker; gained fame with novel *Hunger* (1888); awarded Nobel prize in literature (1920); a recluse in later life; welcomed Nazi invasion of Norway; fined as a collaborator (1948). Works include *The Growth of the Soil* (1917), *Pan* (1894), *Segelfoss Town* (1925), *Vagabonds* (1930), *The Road Leads On* (1934), *The Ring is Closed* (1937), and *Look Back on Happiness* (1940).

Hancock *(hăn kŏk),* **John** 1737–93. American statesman. *b.* Quincy, Mass. Member of Continental Congress (1775–80, 1785, 1786); president of Congress (1775–77); first signer of Declaration of Independence; governor of Massachusetts (1780–85, 1787–93).

Hand *(hănd),* **Learned** 1872–1961. American jurist. *b.* Albany, N.Y. Chief judge of the Second Federal Court of Appeal (1924–51); widely admired and cited for the intellectual quality of his judgments. Published works include *The Spirit of Liberty* (1952) and *The Bill of Rights* (1958).

Handel *(hăn dəl),* **George Frederick** 1685-1759. German composer. *b.* Halle. Turned from study of law to music; joined Hamburg Opera House as violinist and keyboard player; conductor; produced first opera *Almira* (1705); in Italy (1706–10); presented operas *Rodrigo* and *Agrippina* and composed oratorios *Il Trionfo del Tempo* and *La Resurrezione;* accepted position as Kapellmeister to elector of Hanover (1710); went to London, producing *Rinaldo* (1711); settled in London (1712), first as musical director to earl of Burlingham and duke of Chandos, and later as director of Royal Academy of Music, King's Theater, Rich's Theater; experimented with a new form, the English oratorio; became a **naturalized** British subject

(1726); output of over 46 operas, 32 oratorios, 12 concerti grossi, anthems, instrumental music, cantatas, and songs includes *Atalanta, Berenice, Serse, Esther, Saul, Israel in Egypt, The Messiah, Samson, Judas Maccabaeus, Joshua, Jephthah, Fireworks Music,* and *Water Music.*

Handy *(hăn dĭ),* **William Christopher** 1873–1958. American composer. *b.* Florence, Ala. Formed band in Memphis (1903); composed songs that marked transition from ragtime to jazz; formed publishing company in N.Y.; introduced the blues form to the world of popular music. Best-known compositions include "Memphis Blues" (1912) and "St. Louis Blues" (1914).

Hanna *(hăn ə),* **Mark** full name: MARCUS ALONZO HANNA. 1837–1904. American politician. *b.* New Lisbon, Ohio. Republican party boss in Ohio; an early supporter of McKinley, rose to powerful advisory role in McKinley's administration; as chairman of Republican National Committee (from 1896), U.S. Senator (1897–1904), and presidential advisor, he became a powerful dispenser of patronage; retained influence under President Theodore Roosevelt.

Hannibal *(hăn ĭ bəl)* 247–183 B.C. Carthaginian general. Son of Hamilcar Barca; as a youth, swore eternal enmity to Rome; after death of Hamilcar and assassination of brother-in-law Hasdrubal, succeeded to the command of the army in Spain; laid seige to and took the city of Sagentum, an ally of Rome, as a declaration of war; with 100,000 men and many elephants, crossed the Pyrenees, the Rhone, and the Alps into Italy, a feat almost unparalleled in military history (218); inflicted successive defeats on Romans at Ticino River and Trebbia River (218), at Lago di Trasimeno (217), and at Cannae (216); secured control of Po Valley and gained many allies, such as Capua and Syracuse; captured Tarentum (212) and won victory at Herdoniae (210); faced with loss of manpower and lack of reinforcements; suffered major reverse in defeat and death of brother Hasdrubal at Metaurus (207); withdrew to the mountains of Bruttium for four years; recalled from Italy to save Carthage from advancing army of Scipio (203); defeated on field of Zama (202) and compelled to make peace; ruled Carthage as chief magistrate until Rome demanded him as hostage; fled to the court of Antiochus III and later to that of Prusias, king of Bithynia; pursued by the Romans; committed suicide.

Harden *(här dən),* **Sir Arthur** 1865–1940. English chemist. *b.* Manchester. Made important discoveries in alcoholic fermentation; demonstrated the character of zymase and the role of enzymes in fermentation; awarded (with Hans von Euler-Chelpin) Nobel Prize in chemistry (1929).

Hardenberg, Baron Friedrich von. *See* **Novalis**

Harding *(här dĭng),* **Warren Gamaliel** 1865–1923. 29th president of U.S. (1921–23). *b.* Corsica, Ohio. Began as publisher; Ohio state senator (1900–1904), lieutenant governor of Ohio (1904–1906), U.S. senator (1915–21); president of U.S. (1921–23); as a conservative Republican, favored protective tariffs, big business, and reduced taxes on corporate profits; opposed the League of Nations; promised "a return to normalcy" at inauguration; administration clouded by corruption of high-ranking aides, especially Harry Daugherty and Albert Fall, in Teapot Dome Scandal; died during a speaking tour (1923).

Hardy *(här dĭ),* **Thomas** 1840–1928. English novelist. *b.* Higher Bockhampton. Began writing novels (1871) with *Desperate Remedies;* during the next 26 years, produced 14 novels, of which seven are considered masterpieces: *Under the Greenwood Tree* (1872), *Far From the Madding Crowd* (1874), *The Return of the Native* (1878), *The Mayor of Casterbridge* (1886), *The Trumpet-Major* (1880), *Tess of the D'Urbervilles* (1891), and *Jude the Obscure* (1896); began writing poetry (1898) and during the next 30 years produced eight volumes of verse as well as an epic of the Napoleonic Wars, *The Dynasts* (3 parts, 1903–1908).

Harlan *(här lən),* **John Marshall** 1833–1911. American jurist. *b.* Boyle County, Ky. Admitted to the bar (1853); attorney general of Ky. (1863–67); appointed associate justice of the Supreme Court by President Hayes (1877–1911); established reputation as a dissenting justice, a strict constructionist, opponent of judicial legislation, and liberal advocate of federal power; grandson JOHN MARSHALL HARLAN, 1899–71, was an associate justice of the Supreme Court (1955–71).

Harley *(här lĭ),* **Robert** title: 1ST EARL OF OXFORD. 1661–1724. English statesman. *b.* London. Entered Parliament as a Whig (1689); Speaker (1701); secretary of state (1704); forced out of office by Godolphin; restored to royal favor as chancellor of exchequer and head of ministry (1710–14); lord treasurer and prime minister (1711–14); negotiated end of War of Spanish Succession and, through dismissal of Marlborough, managed to carry Treaty of Utrecht; began South Sea Bubble scheme; displaced in struggle for power with Sir John Bolingbroke; on accession of George I, impeached for high treason (1714), but acquitted (1717); left a valuable collection of manuscripts and books which formed nucleus of the Harleian Library.

Harriman *(hăr ə mən),* **William Averell** 1891–. American statesman. *b.* New York, N.Y. Scion of a wealthy family with a fortune founded on railroads; chairman (from 1932) of Union Pacific Railroad; founded Merchant Shipping Corporation, one of the largest units of the American merchant marine; in banking, founded W. A. Harriman and Company, which became Brown Brothers, Harriman and Company (1931); became interested in politics while supporting Alfred E. Smith (1928); entered public service career under Roosevelt, serving successively as chairman of Business Advisory Council, administrator of Lend-Lease, ambassador to U.S.S.R. (1943–46), secretary of commerce under Truman (1946–48), administrator of European Recovery Program (1948–50), special assistant to the president (1950–51), head of Mutual Security Agency (1951–53), Democratic governor of N.Y. (1955–59), and ambassador-at-large (1961–68).

Harris, Joel Chandler 1848–1908. American journalist and author. *b.* Eatonton, Ga. On the staff of the *Atlanta Constitution* (1876–1900); fame associated with the Uncle Remus stories, particularly *Uncle Remus: His Songs and His Sayings* (1880), *Nights with Uncle Remus* (1883), *Mingo and Other Sketches in Black and White* (1884), *Tales of Home Folks in Peace and War* (1898), *Told by Uncle Remus* (1905), and *Uncle Remus and Br'er Rabbit* (1907).

Harrison *(hăr ĭ sən),* **Benjamin** 1833–1901. 23rd president of U.S. (1889–93) Grandson of William Henry Harrison. *b.* North Bend, Ohio. Commissioned first lieutenant in Union army (1862); served in Sherman's Atlanta campaign; brigadier general (1865); resumed law practice at Indianapolis; senator (1881–87); successful Republican presidential candidate (1888); administration marked by passing Sherman Anti-Trust Act, reform of civil service, and development of merchant marine; defeated by Cleveland (1892); returned to private life. Author of *This Country of Ours* (1897).

Harrison, William Henry 1773–1841. Ninth president of U.S. (1841). *b.* Charles City County, Va. Joined the army and fought against the Indians; took part in the battle on the Miami (1794); territorial secretary (1798); territorial delegate to Congress (1799); governor of Indiana Territory (1800–12); in war with Indians, led forces that defeated Tecumseh's uprising, ending in the battle at Tippecanoe (1811); in War of 1812, commanded the northwest and won notable victories over the British at Perry and at Thames; House of Representatives (1816–19); senator (1825–28); president on Whig ticket (1841), but died within a month of inauguration.

Hart *(härt),* **Moss** 1904–61. American librettist and playwright. *b.* New York, N.Y. Collaborated with George S. Kaufman on a number of plays, including *Once in a Lifetime* (1930), *You Can't Take It with You* (1936, Pulitzer prize), *I'd Rather Be Right* (1937), and *The Man Who Came to Dinner*; directed the musicals *My Fair Lady* and *Camelot*; author of *Act One*.

Harte *(härt),* **Bret** real name: Francis Brett. 1836–1902. American writer. *b.* Albany, N.Y. Went to California and worked as a gold miner and typesetter; founded and edited the *Overland Monthly* (1686–70), to which he contributed the best work of this period, including "The Luck of Roaring Camp" and "The Outcasts of Poker Flat"; returned to N.Y. (1871–78); U.S. consul in Krefeld, Germany, and in Glasgow, Scotland (1878–85); spent last years in England. Principal books include *The Luck of Roaring Camp and Other Sketches* (1870), *The Heathen Chinese* (1870), *Stories of the Sierras* (1872), *Tales of the Argonaut* (1875), *Gabriel Conroy* (1876), *California Stories* (1884), and *Some Other People* (1892).

Hartline *(härt līn),* **Haldan Keffer** 1903–. American scientist. *b.* Bloomsburg, Pa. Shared Nobel Prize in physiology and medicine (1967) with G. Wald and

R. Granit for research on the visual processes of the eye.

Harun al-Rashid *(hä ro͞on ăl ră shĭd)* 763–809. Fifth Abbaside caliph (786–809). Gained throne with help of the Barmecide Yahya; raised Eastern caliphate to its height of splendor and power with territories extending from the Indus to Gibraltar; compelled Emperor Nicephorus I to pay tribute after defeating him at Eregli and Tyana (1806); made Baghdad the center of Arab culture; established diplomatic relations with Charlemagne and China; destroyed the power of the Barmecides (803) by killing all members of the family save one; reign celebrated and romanticized in the *Arabian Nights.*

Harvey *(här vĭ),* **William** 1578–1657. English anatomist. *b.* Folkestone. Studied medicine at Padua (1597–1601); graduated M.D. at Cambridge (1602); physician of St. Bartholomew's Hospital (1609); Lumleian lecturer at College of Physicians (1615); published epoch-making book on circulation *Exercitatio de Motu Cordis et Sanguinis (Essay on the Motion of the Heart and the Blood,* 1628); served as physician extraordinary to James I and Charles I; published a further work on comparative anatomy *Exercitationes de Generatione Animalium (Essays on Generation of Animals,* 1651).

Hasan. *See* **Firdausi**

Hasan. Ali Shah. *See* **Aga Khan**

Hassam *(hăs əm),* **Childe** 1859–1935. American painter and etcher. *b.* Boston, Mass. Considered one of the leading American impressionists. Among his numerous canvases are *Evening Bells, Winter, Manhattan's Sunset Towers, Aphrodite, Lorelei,* and *Summer Sea.*

Hastings *(hās tĭngz),* **Francis Rawdon** titles: Marquis of Hastings, Earl of Moira. 1754–1826. British colonial administrator. *b.* Dublin, Ireland. Served with distinction in American Revolutionary War; led forces that defeated Americans at Hobkirk's Hill (1781); commander in chief in Scotland (1803); governor general of India (1813–22); suppressed the Pindaris and defeated the Marathas (1817–18) and the Gurkhas (1814–16); reformed legal system and civil service; promoted education and freedom of the press; purchased Singapore Island (1819); resigned; governor of Malta (1824–26).

Hastings, Warren 1732–1818. British statesman and colonial administrator. *b.* Churchill. Went to Calcutta as a writer in service of English East India Company (1750); governor of Bengal (1772); governor general of India (1773), the first to hold that title and office; embroiled in disputes with a majority of his council, led by Philip Francis; improved the administration of justice, organized revenue system, and brought war with the Marathas to a close; on return to England (1785), impeached by Parliament on a number of charges, including unlawful deposition of Chait Singh, raja of Benares, confiscation of the treasure of the Begums of Oudh, and the conduct of the Rohilla War; acquitted on all charges (1795); granted a generous annuity by the East India Company in recognition of his services.

Hatshepsut *(hăt shĕp so͞ot)* also Hatshepset, Hatasu. c1540–1481

B.C. Queen of Egypt of the XVIIIth Dynasty. Daughter of Thutmose I; co-ruler with half-brother Thutmose III; in accordance with the official fiction, portrayed as a male with beard; abandoned imperialist policy of Thutmose I and set about building the economy; opened silver mines on Sinai peninsula, built great temple at Deir-el Bahri, erected two obelisks at Karnak, and went on an expedition to the land of Punt; mother of Amenhotep II.

Hauptmann *(houpt män),* **Gerhart** 1862–1946. German writer. *b.* Salzbrunn. Began writing naturalistic plays, including *Before Dawn* (1889), *The Weavers* (1892), and *Gabriel Schillings Flucht* (1912); turned to romanticism in *Hanneles Himmelfahrt* (1892), *The Sunken Bell* (1896), and *Und Pippa Tanzt* (1906), but returned to realism in *Drayman Henschel* (1899) and *Rose Bernd* (1903); also wrote fiction: *The Fool in Christ: Emanuel Quint* (1910), *Atlantis* (1912), *The Heretic of Soana* (1918), and *Till Eulenspiegel* (1928); awarded Nobel Prize in literature (1912); published the autobiographical *Buch der Leidenschaft* (1929) and *Das Abenteuer meiner Jugend* (1937).

Hawkins *(hô kĭnz),* **Sir John** 1532–95. British mariner. *b.* Plymouth. Engaged in profitable slave-trading expeditions between Africa and Spain from 1562; attacked by Spanish fleet in Veracruz, losing all but two ships; treasurer and comptroller of the navy (1573); fought against the Armada as rear admiral of the navy (1588); harried Spanish West Indies trade; second in command to Drake on expedition to West Indies (1595), but died en route.

Haworth *(härth),* **Sir Walter Norman** 1883–1950. English chemist. *b.* Chorley. Professor of organic chemistry at Newcastle (1920–25) and Birmingham (1925–48); for important investigations on vitamin C and carbohydrates awarded (with Paul Karrer) Nobel Prize in chemistry (1937).

Hawthorne *(hô thôrn),* **Nathaniel** 1804–64. American writer. *b.* Salem, Mass. In seclusion (1825–37), writing tales and verses; published collection of early stories in *Twice-Told Tales* (1837); served in Boston Custom House as weigher (1839–41); lived for a year in Brook Farm; wrote a series of stories for children; resided at Concord (1842–45); surveyor of port of Salem (1846–49); made consul to Liverpool by friend Franklin Pierce (1853–58); lived in Italy and England (1858–60); best works include *The Scarlet Letter* (1850), *The House of the Seven Gables* (1851), *The Blithedale Romance* (1852), and *The Marble Faun* (1860).

Hay *(hā),* **John Milton** 1838–1905. American statesman. *b.* Salem, Ind. Served as Lincoln's private secretary (1860–65); until 1898, employed in diplomatic service (in London, Madrid, and Vienna) and journalism; secretary of state (1898–1905) under McKinley and Theodore Roosevelt; formulated Open Door Policy, opening trade to China; architect of the Hay-Pauncefote Treaty (1901) concerning the Panama Canal; combined official duties with writing. Works include *Life of Lincoln* (with John Nicolay, 10 vols.,

1886–90), *Pike Country Ballads* (1871), *Castilian Days* (1871), and *Poems* (1890).

Haydn *(hī dən),* **Franz Joseph** 1732–1809. Austrian composer. *b.* Rohrau. Entered service of the Esterhazy family (1760) and for the next 30 years composed some of his greatest chamber and orchestral music, opera, and sacred music; launched modern age in instrumental music, established the sonata form, and perfected the structural forms of symphony and string quartet; visited London (1791–92, 1794–95) and conducted twelve symphonies; taught Mozart and Beethoven and influenced Mozart's string quartets; compositions include 104 symphonies, about 50 concertos, 84 string quartets, 24 stage works, 12 masses, and other pieces, including the Austrian national anthem and the oratorios *The Creation* and *The Seasons.*

Hayek *(hä yĕk),* **Friedrich August von** 1899–. Austrian economist. *b.* Vienna. Professor of economic science at London (1931–50), Chicago (1950–62), and Freiburg (from 1962); wrote extensively on the problems created by economic controls and industrial fluctuation. Author of *Prices and Production* (1931), *Monetary Theory and the Trade Cycle* (1933), *The Pure Theory of Capital* (1941), *Individualism and Economic Order* (1948), *The Constitution of Liberty* (1960); awarded Nobel Prize in economics (1974).

Hayes *(hāz),* **Rutherford Birchard** 1822–93. 19th president of U.S. (1877–81). *b.* Delaware, Ohio. Practiced law in Cincinnati (1849–61); served in Civil War, rising to major general (1865); House of Representatives (1865–67); governor of Ohio (1868–72, 1876–77); Republican candidate for the presidency (1876); won close election against Samuel Tilden when an electoral commission awarded him disputed votes from four states; administration (1877–81) marked by conciliatory policy toward the South and civil service reform; declined second term and dedicated latter years to educational and social work.

Haynes *(hānz),* **Elwood** 1857–1925. American inventor. *b.* Portland, Ind. Designer and builder of the first American automobile (1893); also invented various alloys, including tungsten chrome steel (1881) and patented stainless steel (1919).

Hazlitt *(hăz lĭt),* **William** 1778–1830. English essayist. *b.* Maidstone. Contributed to newspapers and periodicals (from 1814), including *Edinburgh Review, Examiner, Morning Chronicle, London Magazine,* and *Colburn's New Monthly;* with Coleridge, led in popularizing critical appreciation of Shakespeare and other Elizabethan dramatists; noted for essays characterized by lucid style and grace. Principal works include; *Table-Talk* (1821–22), *The Characters of Shakespeare's Plays* (1817), *Views of the English Stage* (1818), *Lectures on the English Comic Writers* (1819), *Dramatic Literature of the Age of Elizabeth* (1821) *Spirit of the Age* (1825), *Life of Napoleon Buonaparte* (4 vols, 1828–30).

Hearst *(hûrst),* **William Randolph** 1863–1951. American publisher. *b.* San Francisco, Calif. Son of George Hearst (1820–91), U.S.

senator and mining magnate. Took over the *San Francisco Daily Examiner* from his father; acquired other newspapers such as the *Chicago American, Boston American, New York American,* and *New York Mirror,* and the magazines *Good Housekeeping* and *Harper's Bazaar;* introduced sensationalist "yellow journalism" techniques; demanded war with Spain and opposed all forms of internationalism.

Heath *(hēth),* **Edward Richard George** 1916–. English statesman. *b.* Broadstairs. Entered Parliament on Conservative ticket (1950); distinguished as one of a new breed of Tory intellectuals; minister of labor and Lord Privy Seal (1959–60); negotiated British entry into Common Market; president of Board of Trade (1963) under Hume; succeeded Hume as conservative party leader (1965); led Conservatives to electoral victory (1969); as prime minister (1969–74), guided Britain into the Common Market; lost office (1974) to Labor party and was rejected as Conservative leader (1975). Author of *Sailing* (1975); also noted as a musician and conductor.

Heaviside *(hĕv ĭ sīd),* **Oliver** 1850–1925. English physicist. *b.* London. Contributed to the development of telephone and electrical communications; pioneered development of operational calculus; suggested (1902) the existence of the Heaviside layer, an ionized conducting layer in the upper atmosphere capable of reflecting radio waves; author of *Electromagnetic Theory* (3 vols., 1893–1912).

Hebbel *(hĕb əl),* **Friedrich** 1813–63. German dramatist. *b.* Wesselburen. Self-educated; influenced by Hegel, his work is a link between realism and romanticism. Chiefly known for *Judith* (1839), *Maria Magdalena* (1844), *Julia* (1851), *Michael Angelo* (1851), *Agnes Bernauer* (1855), *Herodes und Marianne* (1852), *Gyges und Sein Ring* (1856), and the trilogy *Die Nibelungen* (1862).

Hébert *(ā bâr),* **Jacques René** nickname: Père Duchesne. 1755–94. French revolutionary. *b.* Alençon. On outbreak of French Revolution, edited Jacobin paper *Le Père Duchesne;* member of Revolutionary Council and leader of the ultras known as Hébertists or *enragés* (madmen); instrumental in instituting worship of the Goddess of Reason; witness against Marie Antoinette before Revolutionary Tribunal; arrested by Committee of Public Safety and guillotined (1794).

Hecker *(hĕk ər),* **Isaac Thomas** 1819–88. American Catholic religious. *b.* New York, N.Y. Born into a German Protestant family; converted to Catholicism (1844); joined Redemptorist order (1845); priest (1849); founded Congregation of the Missionary Priests of St. Paul the Apostle, known as "Paulists," (1858); emphasized democratic and American elements in Catholicism; founded the *Catholic World* (1865) and Catholic Publication Society (1866). Author of *The Church and the Age* (1888).

Hedin *(hĕ dēn),* **Sven Anders** 1865–1952. Swedish explorer. *b.* Stockholm. Explored Central Asia, Persia, Mesopotamia, Turkestan, Gobi Desert, Tibet, and

Sinkiang (from 1885); discovered the source of the Brahmaputra, Sutlej, and Indus rivers. Author of *Through Asia* (1898), *Mount Everest* (1922), *Overland to India* (1910), *The Silk Road* (1936), and *My Life as an Explorer* (1925).

Hegel *(hā gəl),* **Georg Wilhelm Friedrich** 1770–1831. German philosopher *b.* Stuttgart. Taught philosophy at Jena, Heidelberg, and Berlin universities; formulated Hegelianism, which later influenced existentialism and Marxism; conceived an all-embracing world-view encompassing ethics, aesthetics, theology, history, and politics and based on the idea of an Absolute or World Soul to which all things conform by the scheme of dialectical logic, a process of achieving synthesis through thesis and antithesis; rejected the reality of finite and separate objects and emphasized the importance of the whole; supported authoritarianism and opposed natural science, especially the philosophy of Newton. Author of *Phenomenology of Mind* (1807), *Science of Logic* (1812–16), *Encyclopedia of Philosophical Sciences* (1817) and *Philosophy of Right* (1821).

Heidegger *(hī dĕg ər),* **Martin** 1889–1976. German philosopher. *b.* Messkirch. Professor at Freiburg (1929–45); formulated *Existenzphilosophie,* which was influenced by Husserl and Kierkegaard and in turn influenced such French existentialists as Jean-Paul Sartre. Principal works include *Being and Time* (1927), *Existence and Being* (1949), and *The Question of Being* (1959).

Heidenstam *(hĕ ĭ dən stäm),* **Verner von** 1859–1940. Swedish writer. *b.* Olshammer. Spent many years traveling in southern Europe and the Orient; emerged as a leader of new romantic movement in Swedish literature with collected verse *Pilgrimage and Years of Wandering* (1888); other poetical works include *Endymion* (1889), *Hans Alienus* (1892), *A Nation* (1902), and *New Poems* (1915); prose works include the cycle of stories based on the life of Charles XII, *The Carlists* (1897–98), *The Pilgrimage of Saint Bridget* (1901), and *The Tree of the Folkungs* (1905–1907); awarded Nobel Prize in literature (1916).

Heine *(hī nə),* **Heinrich 1797–1856. German poet.** *b.* Düsseldorf. Of Jewish parentage, became Christian (1925); drawn to revolutionary ideas in politics; left Germany for Paris on outbreak of the July Revolution in France; struck by spinal paralysis (1848) and spent his remaining life in great suffering, confined to a "mattress grave"; considered among the greatest European lyric poets; his works have a musical quality laced with wit, irony, and, later, bitterness. Chief works include *Gedichte* (1822), *Lyrisches Intermezzo* (1823), *Reisebilder* (1826–27), *Book of Songs* (1827), *Neue Gedichte* (1844) and *Romanzero* (1851), *Der Salon* (1835–40) and *Vermischte Schriften* (1854).

Heisenberg *(hī zən bĕrK),* **Werner Karl** 1901–76. German physicist. *b.* Würzburg. Professor at Leipzig (1927–41) and Berlin (1941–45); director of Max Planck Institute at Gottingen (1945–58); formulated the matrix theory of quantum mechanics and the Uncertainty Principle, which states the impossibility of determining simultaneously the position and velocity of electrons; discovered allotropic forms of hydrogen; awarded Nobel Prize in physics (1932).

Heller *(hĕl lər),* **Joseph** 1923–. American author. *b.* Brooklyn, N.Y. Taught at Yale University and University of Pennsylvania; author of *Catch-22* (1961), a novel depicting the absurdity of war, which stirred the American literary imagination with its zaniness and libidinal vitality (1961); also wrote the play *We Bombed in New Haven* (1967) and the novels *Something Happened* (1975) and *Good as Gold* (1979).

Hellman *(hĕl mən),* **Lillian** 1905–. American dramatist. *b.* New Orleans, La. Author of *The Children's Hour* (1934), *The Little Foxes* (1939), *Watch on the Rhine* (1941), and *Toys in the Attic* (1960); wrote several screenplays, including *The Dark Angel* (1935), *Dead End* (1937), *The Searching Wind* (1945), *Montserrat* (1949), and *The Autumn Garden* (1951). Also known for her collections of short pieces, *An Unfinished Woman*, *Pentimento*, and *Scoundrel Time*.

Helmholtz *(hĕlm hōlts),* **Hermann Ludwig Ferdinand von** 1821–94. German physicist. *b.* Potsdam. Professor of physiology, anatomy, and physics at Königsberg (1849), Bonn (1855), Heidelberg (1858), and Berlin (1871); conducted important investigations in nerve impulses, mechanisms of vision and hearing, acoustical, electrical, and electromagnetic phenomena, electrodynamics, and rheology; invented the ophthalmoscope; proposed the theory of conservation of energy. Author of *Manual of Physiological Optics* (1856–66) and *On the Conservation of Force* (1847).

Hemingway *(hĕm ĭng wā),* **Ernest** 1899–1961. American writer. *b.* Oak Park, Ill. Volunteer in American ambulance unit in World War I; European correspondent for the *Toronto Star* and Hearst news service; noted for brilliant short stories and novellas dealing with courage and virility pitted against hostile environments; introduced a laconic, staccato type of dialogue which underplayed emotion. Works include *Torrents of Spring* (1926), *The Sun Also Rises* (1926), *Men Without Women* (1926), *A Farewell to Arms* (1929), *Death in the Afternoon* (1932), *Winner Take Nothing* (1933), *Green Hills of Africa* (1935), *To Have and Have Not* (1937), *For Whom the Bell Tolls* (1940) and *The Old Man and the Sea* (1952); awarded Nobel Prize in literature (1954).

Hench *(hĕnch),* **Philip Showalter** 1896–1965. American physicist. *b.* Pittsburgh, Pa. Head of department of rheumatics at Mayo Clinic in Rochester (1926); professor of medicine (from 1947); discovered the use of cortisone in the treatment of arthritis; awarded Nobel Prize in physiology and medicine with E.C. Kendall and Tadeus Reichstein (1950).

Hendricks *(hĕn drĭks),* **Thomas Andrews** 1819–85. American statesman. *b.* near Zanesville, Ohio. Elected to Congress (1855–59); senator (1863–69); governor of Indiana (1872); vice-president of U.S. (1885) under Grover Cleveland.

Henley *(hĕn lĭ),* **William Ernest** 1849–1903. English playwright, poet, and critic. *b.* Gloucester. Crippled early in life by tuberculosis; cultivated the friendship of Robert Louis Stevenson, with whom he collaborated on three plays: *Deacon Brodie, Beau Austin,* and *Admiral Guinea;* edited the *Scots Observer* and *Magazine of Art* (1882–86). Major collections of verse include *The Song of the Sword* (1892), *Collected Poems* (1898), *For England's Sake* (1900), *Hawthorn and Lavender* (1901), and *Song of Speed* (1903).

Henri *(hĕn rĭ),* **Robert** 1865–1929. American painter. *b.* Cincinnati, Ohio. Opened studio in Philadelphia (1891) and New York (1899); one of the eight organizers of the Armory Show of 1913. Best known canvases include *The Equestrian, Laughing Girl, Spanish Gypsy,* and *Snow.*

Henry *(hĕn rĭ)* Name of eight kings of England:

HENRY I. also HENRY BEAUCLERC. 1068–1135. King of England (1100–1135). *b.* Yorkshire. Elected by the witan to succeed his brother William II; issued charter restoring laws of Edward the Confessor; recalled Archbishop Anselm, who had been exiled in 1097 after dispute with William II over investiture of clergy; invaded Normandy and defeated brother Norman at Battle of Tinchebrai (1106); defended Normandy against Louis of France in two wars (1109–12, 1116–20); introduced reforms in the administration of justice; died without heir.

HENRY II. 1133–89. King of England (1154–89). *b.* Le Mans, France. Succeeded Stephen; re-established royal power by demolishing castles erected in Stephen's reign and by recovering royal estates; also ruled Anjou, Aquitaine, Poitou, Guinne, and Gascony; forced Scotland and Brittany to acknowledge him as overlord; conquered the Welsh and southeastern Ireland; instituted judicial reforms by establishing court of common pleas, the jury system, and common law in place of Roman law; reduced military and financial powers of barons; efforts to reduce church influence ended in the murder of Archbishop Thomas à Becket; later years clouded by revolts of sons.

HENRY III. 1207–72. King of England (1216–72). *b.* Winchester. As a minor succeeded father John; took over government from regents (1232); his misrule, extortion, favoritism toward foreigners, and subservience to pope led to uprising of barons under Simon de Montfort; compelled to accept the Provisions of Oxford, restricting royal powers; repudiated Provisions; defeated in ensuing Barons' War and taken prisoner at Lewes (1264); rescued by Prince Edward, who defeated Simon at Kenilworth and Evesham (1265); left government to Edward for next seven years.

HENRY IV. called BOLINGBROKE, HENRY OF LANCASTER. 1367–1413. King of England (1399–1413). *b.* near Spilsby. Son of John of Gaunt; banished from England by Richard II (1398); landed in England with army (1399), took possession of the kingdom, defeated and captured Richard, and forced him to resign crown; put down revolts led by Richard's supporters, by the Welsh under

Owen Glendower, by the Percys of Northumberland, by the Scots under Douglas, and by earl marshal Mowbray and archbishop of York Scrope; persecuted heretics and burnt William Chatrys for heresy.

HENRY V. 1387–1422. King of England (1413–22). *b.* Monmouth. Won an outstanding victory at Agincourt against France (1415); invaded France (1417) and brought Normandy under English crown; concluded perpetual peace of Troyes (1420), under which he was recognized as heir to the French throne.

HENRY VI. 1421–71. King of England (1422–61, 1470–71). *b.* Windsor. Succeeded to the throne as an infant, under regency of his uncles, the dukes of Bedford and Gloucester; inherited French throne under Treaty of Troyes but lost all French possessions except Calais in war with Charles VII and Joan of Arc; declared of age (1437); married Margaret of Anjou (1445); latter part of reign marked by economic discontent leading to Cade's Rebellion (1450), and a struggle for power between duke of York and duke of Somerset, supported by Queen Margaret; disabled by fits of insanity; in ensuing Wars of the Roses (1455–85) sided with Lancastrians; defeated Yorkists at Ludlow (1459) and St. Albans (1461) but was himself defeated at Mortimer's Cross and Towton (1461); fled to Scotland; deposed (1461) when duke of York was proclaimed King Edward IV; captured and imprisoned; restored to throne by earl of Warwick's forces (1470), but deposed and imprisoned again; probably killed following Warwick's defeat and death at Tewkesbury (1471).

HENRY VII. also HENRY TUDOR, EARL OF RICHMOND. 1457–1509. King of England of house of Tudor (1485–1509). *b.* Pembroke Castle. Descendant of house of Lancaster; spent 14 years in exile in Brittany during ascendancy of house of York; raised army and invaded England; defeated and killed Richard III at Bosworth Field (1485); proclaimed king; by marrying Elizabeth, daughter of Edward IV, united claims of Lancaster and York; restored material prosperity to England; enhanced royal power by instituting Star Chamber, the enforcement of Statute of Liveries against private armies, and by prudent mercantilist and taxation policies.

HENRY VIII. 1491–1547. King of England (1509–47). *b.* Greenwich. Married Catherine of Aragon, widow of his brother Arthur (1509); early success in foreign policy with Thomas Wolsey as principal advisor; joined Holy League; defeated French at Battle of Spurs (1513) and the Scots at Flodden (1513); met Francis I at Field of the Cloth of Gold (1520); strove unsuccessfully to maintain balance of power between France and Spain; received from pope the title "Defender of the Faith"; divorce with Catherine led to conflict and break with Church of Rome; by Act of Supremacy, created national church with the king as its supreme head (1534); suppressed smaller monasteries; put down the pilgrimage of grace; in pursuit of ecclesiastical supremacy, executed Thomas Cromwell and Sir Thomas More; after the dissolution of marriage with Catherine, married five other queens, of whom the last, Catherine Parr, survived him.

Henry Name of four kings of France:

HENRY I. 1008–60. King of France of the Capetian line (1031–60). Put down revolt of the nobles.

HENRY II. 1519–59. King of France of the house of Valois (1547–59). Married Catherine de Médicis (1533); under the influence of Anne de Montmorency and Diane de Poitiers; captured Toul, Metz, and Verdun from the emperor, and Calais and Boulogne from the English; sided with the Guises and oppressed the Protestants.

HENRY III. 1551–89. King of France (1574–89). *b.* Fontainebleau. Succeeded Charles IX; reign marked by strife between the Catholic Guises and the Protestant Huguenots; joined Huguenot faction under Henry of Navarre, whom he nominated as his successor.

HENRY IV. Also HENRY OF NAVARRE, HENRY THE GREAT. 1553–1610. King of France, first of the Bourbon line (1589–1610). *b.* Pau. Reared as a Calvinist; chosen leader of Protestant party in Third Huguenot War; escaped massacre of St. Bartholomew's Day by professing Catholicism; prisoner at French court (to 1576); escaped and resumed leadership of Huguenots; became heir presumptive on death of Francis, Duc d'Alençon (1584); claim denied by Holy League; in the ensuing War of the Three Henrys, won victory at Coutras (1587); proclaimed king on assassination of Henry III (1589); defeated Holy League forces at Ivry (1590), embraced Roman Catholic faith (1593); entered Paris (1594); crowned at Chartres (1594); issued Edict of Nantes granting toleration to Protestants (1594); concluded Peace of Vervins with Philip II (1598); later restored peace and prosperity to France; with Duc de Sully as principal minister, reorganized administration and finances, encouraged agriculture, commerce, and industry, created navy, and sponsored colonization of Canada under Champlain.

Henry the Navigator 1394–1460. Portuguese prince. *b.* Oporto. Fourth son of John I of Portugal; erected observatory and school for navigation at Sagres; sent pupils on voyages of discovery at own cost; his mariners discovered Madeira Islands (1418), sailed round Cape Nun (1433), Cape Bojador (1434), Cape Blanco (1440), reached Cape Verde (1446), discovered Azores (1448), and reached Sierra Leone; stimulated improvements in shipbuilding, navigation, cartography, and exploration.

Henry, Joseph 1797–1878. American physicist. *b.* Albany, N.Y. Professor of natural philosophy at Princeton (1832–48); first secretary and director of Smithsonian Institution (1846); conducted experiments in electromagnetism and discovered the electromagnetic motor; discovered principle of induced current; invented the galvanometer; demonstrated the oscillatory nature of electric discharge; established a system of weather forecasting. Author of *Contributions to Electricity and Magnetism* (1835–42).

Henry, O. pseudonym of WILLIAM SYDNEY PORTER. 1862–1910. American writer. *b.* Greensboro, N.C. Began writing while serving time for embezzlement; after release, went to N.Y.; contributed stories to magazines at the rate of one a week. Works include the novel *Cabbages and Kings* (1904) and the anthologies *Four Million* (1906), *Strictly Business* (1910), *Options* (1909), *Heart of the West* (1907), *The Trimmed Lamp* (1907), *The Voice of the City* (1908), *The Gentle Grafter* (1908), *Roads of Destiny* (1909), *Whirligigs* (1910), *Sixes and Sevens* (1911), *Rolling Stones* (1912), *Waifs and Strays* (1917), *O. Henryana* (1920), *Postscripts* (1923), and *O. Henry Encore* (1939).

Henry, Patrick 1736–99. American revolutionary. Hanover County, Va. Member of Virginia House of Burgesses (from 1765); led radical group opposing Stamp Act and British policies; delegate to First Continental Congress (1774–76); advocated military defense before the Virginia Convention with an eloquent speech that included the oft-quoted words, "Give me liberty, or give me death"; commander-in-chief of Virginia forces (1775-76); governor of Virginia (1776–79, 1784–86); as member of the Virginia Convention for the ratification of the Constitution, led forces opposing adoption and pressed for inclusion of the ten amendments; later supported Federalist party.

Heraclitus *(hĕr ȧ klī təs)* *fl.* 500 B.C. Greek philosopher. *b.* Ephesus, Asia Minor. Known as the "weeping" or "dark" philosopher because of his incurable pessimism; held that fire is the primordial element out of which everything arose, that change is the first principle, that function is more real than substance, and that everything is relative; wrote *On Nature*, fragments of which are extant.

Herbert *(hûr bərt)*, **George** 1593–1633. English poet. *b.* Montgomery Castle, Wales. Elected public orator at Cambridge (1619); resigned (1627); rector of Fugglestone and Bemerton, Wiltshire (1630) after Anglican ordination; principally remembered for the religious poems collected in *The Temple: Sacred Poems and Private Ejaculations* (1633), whose metaphysical intensity has ranked him with Donne, Crashaw, Marvell, and Traherne as one of the great religious poets.

Herder *(hĕr dər)*, **Johann Gottfried von** 1744–1803. German critic. *b.* Mohrungen, East Prussia. Studied theology; court preacher at Weimar (1776) on Goethe's insistence; leader of *Sturm und Drang* movement in German literature; collection of works in 60 volumes includes *On the Origin of Language* (1772), *Stimmen der Völker in Liedern* (1778–79), *Outlines of the Philosophy of Man* (4 vols., 1784–91), and the poem *Der Cid* (1802–1803).

Herod the Great *(hĕr əd)* c73–4 B.C. King of Judea (37–4 B.C.). Son of Antipater, procurator of Judea; governor of Galilee at age 15; later co-tetrarch of Judea; displaced by Antigonus and fled to Rome; regained power with aid of Romans; confirmed as tetrarch by Augustus; reign stained by bloody atrocities including the massacre of the innocents, the murder of his wife Mariamne, his sons Alexander, Aristobolus, and Antipater, and his benefactor Hyrcanus II; built many public buildings, fortresses, and theaters; rebuilt the Great Temple at Jerusalem.

Herodotus *(hə rŏd ə təs)* *fl.* 5th century B.C. Greek historian. *b.* Halicarnassus. Known as the "Father of history" for his great work on the Persian Wars (500–479 B.C.) in nine books; traveled extensively in Persia, Asia Minor, Egypt, and Greece before settling down as a colonist at Thurii in Italy.

Herrick *(hĕr ĭk),* **Robert** 1591–1674. English lyric poet. *b.* London. Member of the literary circle centered around Ben Jonson; accepted a benefice as dean and prior in Devonshire (1629); vicar (1629–47; 1662–74); ejected during Commonwealth for Cavalier sympathies; his metrical diversity and grace is considered to surpass all other Cavalier poets; his collected works, published as the *Hesperides* (1648), contain secular and religious poetry; in his secular poems, he is one of the most pagan of his contemporaries, strongly influenced by Horace and other Augustan Roman poets; best remembered for "To the Virgin to Make Much of Time" and "Gather Ye Rosebuds While Ye May."

Herschel *(hûr shəl),* **Sir William** originally FRIEDRICH WILHELM. 1738–1822. English astronomer. *b.* Hanover, Germany. Immigrated to England as an organist and music teacher took up astronomy; with a reflecting telescope that he built himself, discovered planet Uranus (1781); court astronomer (1782); discovered two satellites of Uranus (Oberon and Titania), a sixth satellite of Saturn (Enceladus), and a seventh satellite of Saturn (Mimas); determined period of rotation of Saturn and the motion of binary stars; demonstrated the shape of the Milky Way; put forward theory that stars evolve from condensation of nebulae; considered the founder of modern stellar astronomy.

Hershey *(hûr shĭ),* **Alfred Day** 1908–. American biologist. *b.* Owosso, Mich. Awarded Nobel Prize in physiology and medicine (1969) with M. Delbruck and S. Luria for investigations on the genetic structure of viruses.

Hertz *(hĕrts),* **Gustav** 1887–1975. German physicist. *b.* Hamburg. Director of Physical Institute, Berlin (from 1928); director of Siemens Research Laboratory (from 1935); director of research laboratory in U.S.S.R. (1945–54); director of Karl Marx University, Leipzig (1954–61); shared Nobel Prize in physics with James Franck (1945) for confirming quantum theory by experiments.

Hertz, Heinrich Rudolph 1857–94. German physicist. *b.* Hamburg. Conducted important investigations in the electromagnetic theory of light, leading to the discovery of Hertzian waves, electromagnetic waves of large amplitude, used in wireless telegraphy.

Hertzog *(hĕr tsŏK),* **James Barry Munnik** 1866–1942. South African statesman. *b.* Wellington. General in Boer army (1899–1902); minister of justice in first Union government (1910); founded Nationalist party, advocating South African independence; opposed cooperation with Britain in World War I; prime minister in coalition governments (1924–39); promoted policy of racial segregation; on outbreak of World War II, favored separate peace with Germany and neutrality; defeated on this issue in Parliament; resigned (1939).

Herzberg *(hûrts bûrg),* **Gerhard** 1904–. Canadian physicist. *b.* in Germany. Awarded Nobel Prize in chemistry (1971) for investigations on the structure of molecules.

Herzl *(hĕr ts əl),* **Theodor** 1860–1904. Zionist leader. *b.* Budapest, Hungary. As correspondent for *Neue Freie Presse,* Vienna, covered the Dreyfus trial; conceived the idea of a Jewish homeland in Palestine as a solution for anti-Semitism; wrote *Judenstaat* (1896) and became the spokesman for the Zionist movement; convened first Zionist Congress at Basel (1897) and spent remainder of life tirelessly seeking to fulfill the dream of a state of Israel.

Hesiod *(hē sĭ əd)* *fl.* 8th century B.C. Greek poet. *b.* Ascra, Boeotia. Considered the founder of didactic poetry; principal extant works are *Works and Days,* composed of moral precepts and advice to farmers, and *Theogony,* an account of the origin of the world and the birth of the gods.

Hess *(hĕs),* **Victor Franz** 1883–1964. Austrian physicist. *b.* Schloss Waldstein. Professor of physics at Graz (1925–31), Innsbruck (1931–37), and Fordham (from 1938); director of the Physical Institute at Graz (1937–38); shared Nobel Prize with C.D. Anderson for pioneer investigations of cosmic radiation (1936). Author of *The Conductivity of the Atmosphere and Its Causes* (1928) and *Cosmic Radiaton and Biological Effects* (1940).

Hess, Walter Rudolf 1881–1973. Swiss physiologist. *b.* Frauenfeld. Professor of physiology at Zurich (1917–51); invented the viscosimeter; conducted investigations on the nervous system and developed techniques of controlling and stimulating areas of the brain by means of needle electrodes; shared the Nobel Prize in physiology and medicine with E. Moniz (1949).

Hess, *(hĕs),* **Walther Richard Rudolf** 1894–1977. German Nazi leader. *b.* Alexandria, Egypt. Joined Nazi party (1920); secretary and confidant of Hitler, assisting in the writing of *Mein Kampf;* took part in abortive Munich rising (1923); deputy führer (1933); named Stellvertreter (third deputy führer) after Goering (1939); in one of the most eccentric acts of the war parachuted into Scotland, allegedly bearing peace proposals; interned during wartime and tried for war crimes (1946); found guilty and imprisoned for life at Spandau prison in Berlin.

Hesse *(hĕs ĕ),* **Hermann** 1877–1962. German author. *b.* Calw. Best known for novels dealing with spiritual quest and man's essential loneliness; awarded Nobel Prize in literature (1946). Works include *Peter Camezind* (1904), *Rosshalde* (1914), *Knulp* (1915), *Demian* (1919), *Siddhartha* (1922), *Death and the Loner* (1930), *Steppenwolf* (1927), *Magister Ludi* (1945), and *Affirmations* (1955).

Hevesy *(hĕ və shĭ),* **George de** 1885–1966. Hungarian chemist. *b.* Budapest. With D. Coster, discovered the element hafnium (1923); served as professor at Freiburg and later Stockholm; awarded Nobel Prize in chemistry

(1943) for work leading to the use of isotopes as tracers of biological and chemical processes.

Hewitt *(hū ĭt),* **Abram Stevens** 1822–1903. American industrialist and statesman. *b.* Haverstraw, N.Y. Established iron manufacturing company which made the first American-made steel by using open-hearth technique; founded Cooper Union in New York City, naming it after his father-in-law, Peter Cooper; helped overthrow the Tweed Ring and reorganize Tammany Hall; mayor of New York City (1887–88).

Heyerdahl *(hī ər däl),* **Thor** 1914–. Norwegian anthropologist. *b.* Larvik. Served with Norwegian Free Military Forces (1940–45); after the war, set out to prove that modern-day Polynesians are the descendants of ancient Peruvians; sailed a balsa raft across the Pacific Ocean from Callao, Peru to Tuamotu Island in the South Pacific; recorded his adventure in the best-selling *Kon-Tiki* (1948); sailed the Atlantic from Morocco to Barbados in a reed boat (1970) to test the hypothesis that the ancient Egyptians could sail beyond the Pillars of Hercules. Other books include *Aku-Aku* and *The Ra Expeditions.*

Heymans *(hī mäns),* **Corneille** 1892–1968. Belgian physiologist. *b.* Ghent. Professor of pharmacodynamics at Ghent; devised technique of cross-circulation of blood; awarded Nobel Prize in physiology and medicine (1938) for demonstrating the role of the carotid sinus and the aorta in the regulation of breathing.

Heyrovsky *(hā rôf skĭ),* **Jaroslav** 1890–1967. Czech chemist. *b.* Prague. Discovered the polarograph, an electrochemical device for analysis of highly pure substances (1925); awarded the Nobel Prize in chemistry (1959) for his discovery.

Heyse *(hī zĕ),* **Paul Johann von** 1830–1914. German writer. *b.* Berlin. Chiefly known as the master of the novella or short story; collected and edited nearly 40 volumes of stories, including *Gesämmelte Novellen in Versen* (1864), *Meraner Novellen* (1867), *Deutscher Novellenschatz* (1870–76), *Das Buch der Freundschaft* (1883–84), *Novellen vom Gardasee* (1902); of his many novels *Children of the World* (1873) is still popular; his more than 60 dramas are mostly forgotten; awarded Nobel Prize in literature (1910).

Heyward *(hā wərd),* **DuBose** 1885-1940. American novelist. *b.* Charleston, S.C. Author of *Angel* (1926), *Porgy* (1925), the basis of George Gershwin's musical *Porgy and Bess, Peter Ashley* (1932), *Lost Morning* (1936), and *Star Spangled Virgin* (1939); most of his works are set in the city of Charleston.

Hickok *(hĭ kôk),* **Wild Bill** real name: JAMES BUTLER HICKOK. 1837–76. American soldier, scout, and border marshal. *b.* Troy Grove, Ill. Constable of Monticello township (1856); stage driver on Santa Fe Trail; active in Civil War as a Union scout and spy; became U.S. marshal at Ft. Riley, Kansas (1866), an area infested by horse thieves and outlaws; scout with Indian expeditions under Generals Custer, Hancock, and Sheridan; marshal of Hays City, Kansas (1869–71), and Abilene, Kansas (1871–76); shot dead (1876) by Jack McCall.

Hicks *(hĭks),* **John Richard** 1904–. British economist. *b.* near Stratford. Professor at London, Cambridge, Manchester, and Oxford; author of *Value and Capital* and other works; awarded Nobel Prize in economics with Kenneth J. Arrow (1972).

Hideyoshi *(hē dĕ yō shē),* **Toyotomi** 1536–98. Japanese statesman. *b.* Owari. Began as common soldier, but rose to become lord of Chikuzen (1575); named dictator by the mikado (1585) in succession to Nobunaga; completed unification of Japan (1590); froze and legalized social class divisions; developed a maritime code; beautified Osaka, the capital; issued edict against Christian missionaries and executed Japanese Christians.

Hilbert *(hĭl bərt),* **David** 1862–1943. German mathematician. *b.* Königsberg. Known for research on integral equations, the theory of numbers, the theory of invariants; sought to axiomatize arithmetic. Author of *Grundlagen der Geometrie* (1899), *Methoden der Maethematischen Physik* (1924), and other works.

Hill *(hĭl),* **Archibald Vivian** 1886–. English physiologist. *b.* Bristol. Conducted research on the thermochemical dynamics of muscle movement; awarded Nobel Prize in physiology and medicine with Otto Meyerhof (1923). Author of *Living Machinery* (1927) and *Muscular Movement in Man* (1927).

Hill, James Jerome 1838–1916. American financier. *b.* near Rockwood, Canada. Settled in St. Paul, Minn. (1856); gained control of the bankrupt St. Paul and Pacific Railroad and extended it to West Coast (1878); consolidated lines in the Hill system as the Great Northern Railway Company (1890); helped organize Canadian Pacific Railroad; with J.P. Morgan, purchased controlling interest in Chicago, Burlington, and Quincy Railroad (1901); stock market battle with Edward H. Harriman for control of Northern Pacific led to stock market panic of 1901; created Northern Securities Company as holding company for all properties, later declared illegal by the Supreme Court (1904); also active in banking and mines.

Hillary *(hĭl ə rĭ),* **Sir Edmund Percival** 1919–. New Zealand mountaineer. Member of Sir John Hunt's Everest expedition (1953); with Tenzing Norgay, was first to reach summit of Mount Everest. Author of *High Adventure* (1955) and *East of Everest* (1956); later explored Antarctica with Vivian Fuchs (1958).

Hillel *(hĭ lĕl)* also HABABLI THE BABYLONIAN; HAZAKEN THE ELDER. *fl.* 30 B.C.–A.D. 10. Jewish theologian. *b.* in Babylonia. As leader of the Sanhedrin during the reign of Herod, formulated hermeneutic principles of scriptural interpretation; founded Talmudic Judaism on a rational basis; introduced a new spirit of compassion into the reading of the law; first president of the Sanhedrin to be honored with the title "Nasi" (prince or patriarch), which was restricted to him and his descendants.

Hindemith *(hĭn də mĭt),* **Paul** 1895–1963. German composer. *b.* Hanau. Concertmeister at Frankfurt Opera Orchestra (1915–23); professor at Berlin Hochschule (1927–33); immigrated (1933) to

U.S.; professor at Yale and Berkshire Music Center; identified with the neoclassical or modern baroque school. Best-known compositions include *Mathis der Maler* (1934), *Symphonic Metamorphoses* (1944), *Das Marienleben* (1923), *Trauermusik* (1936), *Sancta Susanna* (1921), *Cardillac* (1926), *Cupid and Psyche* (1943), *Der Schwanendreher* (1935), *Nobilissima Visione* (1938), *Die Harmonie der Welt* (1952).

Hindenburg *(hĭn dən bo͝orK),* **Paul von** full name: PAUL LUDWIG HANS ANTON VON BENECKENDORFF UND VON HINDENBURG. 1847–1934. German general and statesman. *b.* Posen. Fought in Franco-German War (1870–71); general (1903); retired (1901); recalled to active duty on outbreak of World War I; with Ludendorff as chief of staff, won decisive victories over Russians at Tannenberg and Masurian Lakes; succeeded Falkenhayn as supreme commander (1916); led German retreat after defeat in Battle of the Marne (1918); elected Reich president (1925); re-elected (1932), defeating Hitler; appointed Hitler chancellor (1933). Author of *Aus Meinem Leben* (1920).

Hinshelwood *(hĭn shəl wo͝od),* **Sir Cyril Norman** 1897–1967. British chemist. *b.* London. Professor of chemistry at Oxford (1937–64); awarded Nobel Prize in chemistry with N. Semenoy (1956) for studies in kinetics of gaseous reactions.

Hipparchus *(hĭ pär kəs) fl.* 2nd century B.C. Greek astronomer. *b.* Nicaea. Discovered procession of the equinoxes; founded trigonometry; determined distances of sun and moon from earth, and length of solar year; discovered eccentricity of the solar orbit; invented the planisphere, developed method of fixing positions on earth and in the sky by means of longitude and latitude; compiled a catalogue of over 1000 stars; considered the father of systematic astronomy; researches and discoveries recorded in Ptolemy's *Almagest.*

Hippocrates *(hĭ pŏk rə tēz)* c460–c377 B.C. Greek physician known as the father of medicine. *b.* island of Kos. Reputed author of over 87 medical treatises, once preserved in the Alexandrian Library; devised a code of medical ethics on which is based the Hippocratic Oath now administered to medical graduates; held that the four fluids of the body—blood, phlegm, yellow bile, and black bile—are the primary elements of health or disease.

Hirohito *(hē rō hē tō)* reign name: SHOWA. 1901–. Emperor of Japan (1926–). *b.* Tokyo. In the Sun lineage, 124th emperor of Japan; married Princess Nagoko (1924), who bore him two sons and three daughters; renounced divinity following Japan's defeat in 1946.

Hiroshige *(hē rō shē gĕ),* **Ando** 1797–1858. Japanese artist. Pupil of Toyohira; became one of the masters of the Ukiyoye style noted for landscapes and color prints. Best known for paintings *Fifty-three Stages of the Tokaido* and *Famous Views of Kyoto.*

Hiss, *(hĭs),* **Alger** 1904–. American official. *b.* Baltimore, Md. High official in the State Department under Roosevelt; presidential advisor at Yalta Conference; tried (1949, 1950) for perjury for having denied before the House Un-American Activities Committee that he had passed 200 State Department documents to Whittaker Chambers, an editor of *Time* and a former Communist agent; found guilty after second trial and sentenced to five years in prison, but merits of the case are still disputed.

Hitchcock *(hĭch kŏk),* **Alfred Joseph** 1900–. American motion picture director. *b.* London. Entered movies as a junior technician (1920) and was directing by 1925; noted as a master of suspense with a faultless technique. Other films include *The Thirty-nine Steps* (1935), *The Lady Vanishes* (1938), *Rebecca* (1940), *Suspicion* (1941), *Rear Window* (1955), *Vertigo* (1958), *Psycho* (1960), *The Birds* (1963), and *Frenzy* (1972).

Hitler *(hĭt lər),* **Adolf** probable original name: SCHICKLGRUBER. 1889–1945. German statesman. *b.* Braunau, Austria. Began as unskilled laborer and painter; served in World War I in Bavarian regiment, rising to corporal; after war, became an informer for the Reichswehr, spying on small political groups; joined one of them, the National Socialist German Workers (Nazi) party, which he developed into a powerful right-wing organization; editor of *Der Völkische Beobachter* (1922); with Ludendorff, led unsuccessful Beer Hall Putsch in Munich against Bavarian government (1923); sentenced to five years imprisonment at Landsberg fortress, where he wrote *Mein Kampf,* an autobiography and manifesto; released after nine months (1924); extended Nazi influence into north Germany; defeated by Hindenburg in presidential elections (1932); named chancellor (1933); outlawed Communists after the Reichstag fire, and in next election gained absolute majority; granted dictatorial powers; on death of Hindenburg, united offices of president and chancellor and assumed title "Der Führer"; in the blood purge of 1934, crushed all opposition within Nazi party; began to organize Germany as a totalitarian state based on Nazi ideology; incorporated anti-Semitism as official policy of Third Reich; vowed to create an Aryan Herrenvolk (superrace) in Germany; in violation of Treaty of Versailles, reoccupied Rhineland and began remilitarizaton (1936); established Rome-Berlin Axis with Mussolini as partner; annexed Austria (1938), the Sudetanland (1938), and Czechoslovakia (1939); signed non-aggression pact with Stalin (1939); invaded Poland and began World War II (1939); within two years, overran most of Europe and invaded Russia (1941); assumed complete direction of the war as commander in chief (1941); committed suicide just before the fall of Berlin (1945).

Hobbes *(hŏbz),* **Thomas** 1588–1679. English philosopher. *b.* Malmesbury. Entered service of Earl of Devonshire as traveling tutor to his sons; in exile in Paris (1640–51) because of his rationalist convictions; set forth a philosophy of empiricism, nominalism, and materialism; held that power of the state should be absolute, that theology and philosophy should be separate, and that church should be subordinate to the state; characterized the natural state of man as "nasty, brutish, and short," leading to a constant war of everyman with everyman; developed a strongly mechanistic theory of psychology. Chief works include *Elements of Law* (1650), *De Cive* (1642), *Human Nature* (1650), *Leviathan* (1651), and *Of Liberty and Necessity* (1654).

Ho Chi Minh *(hō chē mĭn)* 1890–1969. Vietnamese Communist leader. *b.* North Annam. Lived in France and the Soviet Union, working in underground Communist organizations; president of Provisional Democratic Republic of Vietnam (1945); as a nationalist, led successful military campaigns against the French (1946–54); prime minister (1954–55) and president (1954–69) of North Vietnam; led nation's second successful struggle against U.S.-supported South Vietnam; Saigon renamed Ho Chi Minh City after reunification of the country (1973).

Hodgkin *(hŏj kĭn),* **Alan Lloyd** 1914–. British physiologist. Royal Society research professor (from 1952); awarded (with A. Huxley and J. Eccles) Nobel Prize in physiology and medicine (1963) for explaining the generation of signals through body nerve cells.

Hodgkin, Dorothy Crowfoot 1910–. English chemist. *b.* in Egypt. Awarded Nobel Prize in chemistry (1964) for work on the structure of biochemical substances by means of X-ray techniques.

Hoffa *(hôf ə),* **Jimmy** full name: JAMES RIDDLE HOFFA. 1913–1976?. American labor leader. *b.* Brazil, Ind. Joined International Brotherhood of Teamsters (1932); president of Local 299 (1937), president of Michigan Conference of Teamsters (1942), and general president (1957–71); central figure in Senate investigations into organized crime in labor unions; sent to prison (1967) for jury tampering, but remained president of Teamsters; released from prison by President Nixon under a conditional amnesty; failed to recover power in union politics; disappeared under mysterious circumstances in 1976.

Hoffmann *(hōf män),* **Ernst Theodor** 1776–1822. German artist, musician, and writer. *b.* Königsberg. Studied law; active as a conductor; served as judge; wrote the opera *Undine* (1816), which inspired Offenbach's *Tales of Hoffmann;* possessed an inexhaustible and wild imagination, out of which poured a series of fantastic stories, placing him in first rank of German romantics. Works include *The Serapion Brother* (1819–22), *The Devil's Elixir* (1815–16), *Nachstücke* (2 vols., 1817), *Phantasiestücke* (4 vols., 1814), and *Kater Murr, the Educated Cat* (1820–21).

Hofmannsthal *(hōf mäns täl),* **Hugo von** 1874–1929. Austrian dramatist. *b.* Vienna Member of Jung-Wien (Young Vienna) group; noted for such lyrical dramas as *Electra* (1903), *Oedipus and the Sphinx* (1905), *Death and the Fool* (1913), *The Marriage of Sobeide* (1913), *The Play of Everyman* (1917), *The Salzburg Great Theater of the World* (1922), and *The Tower* (1925); wrote librettos for operas by Richard Strauss, including *The Knight of the Rose* (1912), and *Ariadne on Naxos* (1913); with Richard Strauss and Max Reinhardt, founded the Salzburg Festival.

Hofstadter *(hŏf stăt ər),* **Robert** 1915–. American physicist. *b.* New York, N.Y. Professor of physics at Stanford (from 1954); shared Nobel Prize in physics (1961) with R.L. Mössbauer for research on the structure of the atom.

Hogarth *(hō gärth),* **William** 1697–1764. English painter. *b.* London. Noted for paintings and engravings that satirize the foibles of his age and serve as a social commentary. Best-known works include *The Harlot's Progress* (1730), *The Rake's Progress* (1733), *The Pool of Bethesda* and *The Good Samaritan* (1735), *Marriage à la Mode* (1743), *The Sleeping Congregation* (1736), *The Strolling Actresses* (1738), *Four Times of Day* (1738), *The Enraged Musician* (1741), *Industry and Idleness* (1747), *Four Stages of Cruelty* (1751), *The Distressed Poet* (1735), and *Election* (1755); also painted portraits and self-portraits. Author of *Analysis of Beauty* (1753).

Hokusai *(hō koo sī),* **Katsushika** 1760–1849. Japanese artist. *b.* Yedo (now Tokyo). Began career as a master of traditional surimono paintings, later abandoning it for the expressionist Ukiyoye style; in *Mangwa* (1814–19) illustrated 10,000 scenes from Japanese life. Best known for *Hundred Views of Mount Fuji, Waterfalls, Famous Bridges, Large Flowers,* and *Ghost Stories.*

Holbein *(hōl bīn),* **Hans** called THE YOUNGER. 1497–1543. German painter. *b.* Augsburg. Son of HANS HOLBEIN THE ELDER (1465–1524), German painter whose work includes the *Altar of St. Sebastian* in Munich. Worked at Basel (1520–26); to this period belong portraits of Erasmus, Melanchthon, and Burgomaster Meier, the panel *Passion,* and woodcuts for Old and New Testaments; went to London (1526) and settled there (from 1532); court painter to Henry VIII (from 1536); works in England include the woodcuts *The Dance of Death, The Ambassadors, The Last Supper, The Dead Christ,* and portraits of More, Anne of Cleves, Henry VIII, Cromwell, Archbishop Warham, Jane Seymour, and others.

Holberg *(hōl bârg),* **Baron Ludvig** 1684–1754. Danish poet. *b.* Bergen, Norway. Considered founder of Danish literature. Works include the satirical poem *Peder Paars* (1719–20), the comedies *The Pewterer Politician, The Busy Man, Jeppe of the Mountain, Henrik and Pernille,* and *Jacob von Thybo;* the histories *History of Denmark, General Church History,* and *History of the Jews,* and the romance *Niels Klim's Subterranean Journey.*

Hölderlin *(hûl dər lēn),* **Johann Christian Friedrich** 1770–1843. German poet. *b.* Lauffen. Studied theology but turned to poetry; wrote philosophical novel *Hyperion* (1797); became insane (1802) and spent 36 years (from 1807) in an asylum; considered one of Germany's great poets, blending classicism and romanticism; left an unfinished tragedy, *The Death of Empedocles;* best-known odes and elegies collected and published in *Selected Poems* (1954).

Holiday *(hŏl ĭ dā),* **Billy** 1915–59. American singer. *b.* Baltimore, Md. Achieved success as a jazz singer with the great bands of the 1930s; with her inimitable style and melody, captivated night club audiences in the 1940s; her career began to decline as her addiction to narcotics increased; known as Lady Day.

Holinshed *(hŏl ĭnz hĕd),* **Raphael** *d.* c1580. English historian. *b.* Sutton Downes. Employed by Reginald Wolfe, a London printer, to continue writing a history of the British Isles begun by him; completed the undertaking as *The Chronicles of England, Scotland, and Ireland* (2 vols., 1577); work gained fame as source for Shakespeare's historical plays.

Holland *(hŏl ənd),* **John Philip** 1840–1914. American inventor. *b.* Liscanor, Ireland. Immigrated to U.S. (1873); built and launched first successful submarine (with financial aid from the Fenian Society), called *Fenian Ram* (1878); launched the *Holland* (1898), first underwater vessel capable of cruising while submerged.

Holley *(hŏl ĭ),* **Robert William** 1922–. American biochemist. *b.* Urbana, Ill. Awarded Nobel Prize in physiology and medicine (1968) with H. Khorana and M. Nirenberg for discovering the process in which enzymes consisting of a sequence of amino acids determine a cell's function in genetic development.

Holmes *(hōmz),* **Oliver Wendell** 1809–94. American writer and physician. *b.* Cambridge, Mass. Studied medicine; professor at Dartmouth (1839–41) and Harvard (1847–82); gained literary fame with a series of light books, including *The Autocrat of the Breakfast Table* (1858), *The Professor at the Breakfast Table* (1860), and *The Poet at the Breakfast Table* (1872); also wrote poems, essays, novels, and biographies; noted for discovery that childbed fever is contagious. His son was OLIVER WENDELL HOLMES (1841–1935), American jurist. *b.* Boston, Mass. Editor of *American Law Review* (1870–73); Weld Professor of Law at Harvard (1882); associate justice (1882–99) and chief justice (1899–1902) of Supreme Court of Massachusetts; associate justice of U.S. Supreme Court (1902–32). Author of *Common Law* (1881), originally lectures delivered at the Lowell Institute in Boston.

Home *(hūm),* **Sir Alec Frederick Douglas-** 1903–. British statesman. *b.* London. Entered Parliament (1931); secretary of state for Commonwealth Relations (1955–60); secretary of state for foreign affairs (1963); relinquished hereditary earldom and succeeded Macmillan as prime minister (1963); secretary of state for foreign affairs under Edward Heath (1970–73).

Homer *(hō mər)* *fl.* between 9th and 13th centuries B.C. Greek poet. Birthplace claimed by seven cities. Author of the epics *Iliad* and *Odyssey,* and the putative author of "Homeric Hymns"; according to tradition lived on the island of Chios and was blind in old age.

Homer, Winslow 1836–1910. American painter. *b.* Boston, Mass. Contributing artist to *Harper's Weekly* (1859–67); resided at Scarboro, Me. (from 1884). Best known for such seascapes as *The Gulf Stream, Northeaster, Searchlight, Launching the Boat, Cannon Rock,* and *Maine Coast;* also painted war scenes as in *Prisoners from the Front* and rural scenes as in *Visit from an Old Mistress.*

Hood *(hŏŏd),* **Thomas** 1799–1845. English poet. *b.* London. Subeditor of *London Magazine* (1821); began the *Comic Annual* (1830) and *Hood's Monthly Magazine* (1844); gained recognition with anonymously published *Odes and Addresses to Great People* (1825); followed with *Whims and Oddities* (1826), *National Tales* (1827), *Tylney Hall* (1834), *Miss Kilmansegg,* and *Whimsicalities* (1844); invented and popularized picture puns; best known for poems, including "Eugene Aram's Dream" (1829), "The Plea of the Midsummer Fairies" (1827), "Song of the Shirt" (1843), and "The Bridge of Sighs" (1844).

Hooke *(hŏŏk),* **Robert** 1635–1703. English chemist. *b.* Freshwater. Curator of experiments (1662) and secretary (1667) of Royal Society; Gresham Professor of Geometry at Oxford (from 1665); city surveyor of London after the Great Fire; published *Micrographia* on botany and chemistry; formulated Hooke's Law—the expansion of a spring will be in direct proportion to the force applied to it; one of the greatest mechanical geniuses of his age; invented the Gregorian telescope, the marine barometer, the first computing machine and other devices; discovered the fifth star in Orion; expounded law of inverse squares, the kinetic theory of gases, the theory of cells, and the true nature of combustion.

Hooker *(hŏŏk ər),* **Richard** 1554–1600. English theologian. *b.* near Exeter. Chiefly known as the author of *Of the Laws of Ecclesiastical Polity* (9 books, 1594–97; 3 more books published posthumously), a defense of the Anglican Church against its Presbyterian critics; it was a masterpiece of Elizabethan prose and a great religious document noted for its masterly logic and scholarship.

Hoover *(hōō vər),* **Herbert Clark** 1874–1964. 31st president of U.S. (1929–33). *b.* West Branch, Iowa. Trained as a mining engineer and served worldwide as engineer and consultant; chairman of American Relief Commission in London (1914–15), in Belgium (1915–19); chairman of Interallied Food Council and director general of Relief and Reconstruction; founded American Relief Administration (1918); directed relief work in Russia (1921–23); secretary of commerce under Harding (1921–28); initiated work on Hoover Dam on Colorado River; elected president (1928), defeating Democrat Alfred E. Smith by a large majority; created the R.F.C. and the Home Loan Banks; initiated reforms in social service programs, conservation, banking, civil service, tariffs, and business; work undone by Great Depression and Panic of 1939; defeated decisively by Franklin D. Roosevelt in presidential election (1932). Author of *Problems of Lasting Peace* (1942), *American Individualism* (1922), *The Challenge to Liberty* (1934), *America's First Crusade* (1941), and *The Memoirs of Herbert Hoover* (3 vols., 1951–52); also translated Agricola's *De Re Metallica,* a treatise on mining.

Hoover, John Edgar 1895–1972. American administrator and criminologist. *b.* Washington, D.C. First director of the Federal Bureau of Investigation (1924–72), serving under eight presidents and creating a legendary reputation as a public servant with one of the longest tenures; made the FBI one of the most disciplined and efficient law enforcement agencies in the world. Author of *Persons in Hiding* (1938) and other books.

Hopkins *(hŏp kĭnz),* **Sir Frederick Gowland** 1861–1947. English biochemist. *b.* Eastbourne. Professor at Cambridge (from 1914); conducted investigations leading to the discovery (1906) of "accessory food factors," later called vitamins; isolated glutathione (1921) and, with S.W. Cole, tryptophan; studied carbohydrate metabolism and muscular activity, and discovered (with Walter Fletcher) the role of lactic acid in muscular contraction; awarded, with Christian Eijkman, Nobel Prize in physiology and medicine (1929).

Hopkins, Gerard Manley 1844–89. English poet. *b.* Stratford. Converted to Roman Catholicism (1866); ordained as Jesuit priest (1874); professor of classics and Greek at Dublin (1882–89); published no poems in his lifetime; the first edition of his *Poems* appeared in 1918, edited with notes and an introduction by Robert Bridges; soon acknowledged as a major poet, noted for his technical experiments, such as sprung rhythm and outrides. Poems most acclaimed for their intensity and imagery include "The Wreck of the Deutschland," "The Windhover," "Felix Randall," "Vision of the Mermaids," "Pied Beauty," "The Habit of Perfection," "The Golden Echo," "Spring," and "Peace."

Hopkins, Mark 1802–87. American educator. *b.* Stockbridge, Mass. Trained as a physician; professor of moral philosophy and rhetoric at Williams College (1830); later its president (1836–72); ordained as Congregational minister (1836); president of American Board of Commissioners for Foreign Missions (1857–87); gained legendary fame as teacher, causing James A. Garfield to remark that the ideal college is a log of wood with a student at one end and Mark Hopkins at the other. Author of *Lectures on the Evidences of Christianity* (1846), *Teachings and Counsels* (1884), and other books.

Hopper *(hŏp ər),* **Edward** 1882–1967. American painter. *b.* Nyack, N.Y. Studied painting at New York School of Art; first gained national recognition with his one-man exhibition at the Museum of Modern Art (1933); frequent subjects of his paintings are old mansions, city street scenes, lonely figures at cheap hotels and theaters; known for patterning of light and shade; best known paintings include *Light House at Two Lights, House by the Railroad, Corner Saloon, Cape Cod Afternoon,* and *Lighthouse Hill.*

Horace *(hŏr ĭs)* Latin name: QUINTUS HORATIUS FLACCUS. 65–8 B.C. Roman poet and satirist. *b.* Venusia, Italy. Educated at Rome and Athens; served in Republican army under Brutus; returned to Rome; introduced by Vergil to Maecenas, who became his patron; considered poet laureate of the Augustan Age, a master of the quotable phrase, and simple, bright humor. Works include *Satires* (35–30), *Epodes* (29), *Odes* (23–13), *Epistles* (23–8), *Carmen*

Seculare (17), and *Ars Poetica* (13–8).

Horney *(hōr nī),* **Karen** 1885–1952. American psychiatrist. *b.* Berlin, Germany. Immigrated to U.S. (1932); taught at New York Psychoanalytic Institute (1934–41), and New York Medical College (from 1942); founded (1941) and became dean of the American Institute of Psychoanalysts; emphasized the role of social factors in neurosis. Author of *Self-Analysis* (1942), *Our Inner Conflicts* (1945), and other books.

Horowitz *(hô rō vĭts),* **Vladimir** 1904–. American concert pianist. *b.* Kiev, Russia. First appeared in concert in 1924; married Toscanini's daughter, Wanda; resident in U.S. (from 1940); noted for technical virtuosity and vigor, particularly in romantic repertoire; retired from the concert stage in 1953, but returned in 1965.

Houdini *(hōō dē nī),* **Harry** real name: EHRICH WEISS. 1874–1926. American magician. *b.* Appleton, Wis. Specialized in daring, sensational escapes while manacled, chained, and underwater. His feats and showmanship continued to capture the public imagination long after his death.

Housman *(hous mən),* **A.E.** full name: ALFRED EDWARD. 1859–1936. English essayist and poet. *b.* near Bromsgrove. Professor of Latin at University College, London (1892-1911); edited the works of Manilius, Juvenal, and Lucan; better-known as a poet and the author of *Shropshire Lad* (1896), *Last Poems* (1922), *More Poems* (1936), and *The Name and Nature of Poetry* (1933); brother LAURENCE (1865–1959), writer and illustrator, wrote plays, including *Little Plays of St. Francis* (1922) and *Victoria Regina* (1937), and the autobiography *The Unexpected Years* (1937).

Houssay *(ōō sī),* **Bernardo Alberto** 1887–1971. Argentinian physiologist. *b.* Buenos Aires. Shared with C. and G. Cori the Nobel Prize in physiology and medicine (1946) for work on the relation between the pancreas and the pituitary gland.

Houston *(hūs tən),* **Samuel** known as SAM. 1793–1863. American statesman. *b.* Rockbridge County, Va. Served in army (1813–18); House of Representatives (1823); governor of Tennessee (1827–29); lived with the Cherokees as Indian agent in Oklahoma (1829–31); settled in Texas (1833); commander in chief of forces of provisional government of Texas; became hero and founder of independent Texas by defeating Mexicans on the San Jacinto (1836); first president of Republic of Texas (1836–38); re-elected (1841–44); senator when Texas joined the Union (1846–59); governor of Texas (1859–61); refused pledge of allegiance to the Confederacy and retired (1861).

Howe *(hou),* **Elias** 1819–67. American inventor. *b.* Spencer, Mass. Built and patented first sewing machine (1846); litigation with manufacturers, especially Isaac Singer, eventually successful.

Howe, Julia Ward 1819–1910. American writer, lecturer, and leader in women's suffrage movement. *b.* New York, N.Y. Best known for "The Battle Hymn of the Republic," which appeared in *Later Lyrics* (1866); wrote other volumes of verse, including *Passion Flowers* (1854) and *Words for* *the Hour* (1857); other works include *Sex and Education* (1874), *Modern Society* (1880), *Reminiscences* (1899), and *At Sunset* (1910). Husband SAMUEL GRIDLEY HOWE (1801–76), American philanthropist, surgeon in Greek army against Turks (1824–30); later directed relief for Crete (1866–67); founded and directed the Perkins Institution for the Blind and devoted life to the care of the deaf, retarded, slaves, and prisoners; editor of *The Commonwealth*.

Howe, Sir William 1729–1814. British general. Served at Louisburg and led defense of Quebec (1759–60); Member of Parliament (1758); as commander of British forces, won Battle of Bunker Hill (1775); commander in chief of British army in America, succeeding Gage; defeated Washington in Battle of Long Island and occupied New York City (1776); victorious at White Plains (1776) and Brandywine (1777); occupied Philadelphia (1777); resigned command; later served in Napoleonic Wars.

Howells *(hou əlz),* **William Dean** 1837–1920. American author and literary critic. *b.* Martin's Ferry, Ohio. Editor of *Atlantic Monthly* (1871–81); associate editor of *Harper's Magazine* (1886–91); editor of *Cosmopolitan Magazine* (1891–92); exerted powerful influence on the development of fiction and literary criticism; novels considered models of realism, including *Their Wedding Journey* (1872) *The Lady of the Aroostook* (1879), *A Modern Instance* (1882), *A Woman's Reason* (1883), *The Rise of Silas Lapham* (1886), *A Hazard of New Fortunes* (1889), *The Quality of Mercy* (1892), *Through the Eye of the Needle* (1907), and *The Leatherwood God* (1916); expounded literary ideas in *Criticism and Fiction* (1891), *My Literary Passions* (1895), and *Literature and Life* (1902); wrote autobiographical works *Literary Friends and Acquaintances* (1900) and *Years of My Youth* (1915); travelogues *Venetian Life* (1866) and *Italian Journeys* (1867); poetry such as *Poems of Two Friends* (1860), *Stops of Various Quills* (1895), and *The Mother and the Father* (1909).

Huayna Capac *(wī nä kä päk)* also HUAINA CAPAC. c1450–1525. Inca ruler. *b.* Tumibamba, Ecuador. Presided over the golden age of Inca empire with capital at Cusco; extended frontiers of the empire south to Chile and conquered Quito province after a bloody campaign; believed to have reigned for nearly 42 years.

Hubble *(hŭb əl),* **Edwin Powell** 1889–1953. American astronomer. *b.* Marshfield, Mo. Astronomer at Mount Wilson Observatory (from 1919); investigated nebulae; name associated with Hubble Constant, the law which describes the apparent velocity of universes receding in proportion to their distance from earth. Author of *The Realm of Nebulae* (1936) and *The Observational Approach to Cosmology* (1937).

Hudson *(hŭd sən),* **Henry** *d.* 1611. English navigator. Commanded four expeditions to discover Northwest and Northeast Passages; commanded the *Hopewell* on first voyage (1607), reaching Spitzbergen; on second voyage in the *Hopewell* (1608), reached Novaya Zemlya; on third voyage, in the *Half Moon* (1609), sailed nearly 150 miles up the Hudson River; on last voyage (1611), in the *Discovery,* reached Hudson Strait and Hudson Bay; iced in while exploring Bay; ran out of food, seized, with son, by mutineers, and set adrift; believed to have perished.

Hudson, William Henry 1841–1922. English naturalist. *b.* near Buenos Aires, Argentina. Immigrated to England (1869). Author of books on nature including *Green Mansions* (1904), *The Purple Land that England Lost* (1885), *The Naturalist in La Plata* (1892), *British Birds* (1895), *A Hind in Richmond Park* (1922), *Far Away and Long Ago* (1918), and *An Old Thorn* (1920).

Hueffer, Ford Madox. *See* **Ford, Ford Madox**

Huggins *(hŭg ĭnz),* **Charles Brenton** 1901–. American surgeon. *b.* Halifax, Canada. Professor of surgery at University of Chicago (from 1936); head of Ben May Laboratory for Cancer Research (from 1951); shared Nobel Prize in physiology and medicine (1966) with P. Rous for discovery of hormonal treatment for cancer of the prostate gland.

Hughes *(hūz),* **Charles Evans** 1862–1948. American statesman and jurist. *b.* Glens Falls, N.Y. Governor of New York (1907–10); associate justice of U.S. Supreme Court (1910–16); unsuccessful Republican candidate for president (1916); secretary of state under Harding (1921–25); judge on Hague Tribunal (1926–30) and on Permanent Court of International Justice (1928–30); chief justice of Supreme Court (1930–41).

Hughes, James Langston 1902–67. American poet. *b.* Joplin, Mo. Raised by his grandmother until the age of twelve; moved to Ohio with mother; B.A. Lincoln University (1929); traveled extensively; writing largely concerned with depicting the life of a black in America. Best-known works include *Not Without Laughter* (1930), *Weary Blues* (1926), *The Dream Keeper* (1932), *Shakespeare in Harlem* (1942), *One-Way Ticket* (1933), *The Way of the White Folks* (1934). Published autobiography *The Big Sea* (1940).

Hughes, William Morris 1864–1952. Australian statesman. *b.* Llandudno, Wales. Immigrated to Australia (1884); as trade union organizer, became one of the founders of Australian Labor party; entered federal House of Representatives (1901); minister for external affairs (1904); attorney general (1908); prime minister (1915–23); Australian delegate to Paris Peace Conference (1919) and at League of Nations Assembly (1932); founded United Australia party (1930s); held various cabinet posts (1934–41).

Hugo *(hū gō),* **Victor Marie** 1802–85. French writer. *b.* Besançon. Began writing at 14, publishing first work, *Odes et Ballades* (1822); founded fortnightly review *Le Conservateur Littéraire* (1819); Royalist (until 1848); member of Constituent Assembly (1848); banished to Channel Islands (1852); returned to Paris (1870); member of National Assembly at Bordeaux (1871); life member of Senate (1876); founded newspaper *L'Événement* (1848); principal poetic works include *Nouvelles Odes* (1824), *Les Orientales*

(1829), *Les Feuilles d'Antomne* (1831), *Les Chants du Crépuscule* (1835), *Les Voix Intérieures* (1837), *Les Rayons et les Ombres* (1840), *Les Châtiments* (1835), *Les Contemplations* (1856–57), *La Légende des Siècles* (three series, 1859–91), *Les Chansons des Rues et des Bois* (1865), *L'Année Terrible* (1872), *L'Art d'être Grandpère* (1877), *Le Pape* (1878), *La Pitié Suprême* (1879), *L'Ane* (1880), *Les Quatre Vents de l'Esprit* (1881), *La Fin de Satan* (1886), and *Dieu* (1891); dramatic works include *Cromwell* (1827), *Marion Delorme* (1829), *Hernani* (1830), *Le Roi S'Amuse* (1832), *Lucrèce Borgia* (1833), *Marie Tudor* (1833), *Angelo* (1835), *Esmeralda* (1836), *Ruy Blas* (1838), and *Torquemada* (1882); prose works include *Hans d'Island* (1823), *Notre Dame de Paris* (1831), *Les Misérables* (1862), *Toilers of the Sea* (1866), *L'Homme qui Rit* (1869), *Ninety-three* (1874), and *Historie d'un Crime* (1877–78).

Hulagu *(hōō lä gōō)* 1217–65. Mongol ruler. Grandson of Genghis Khan and brother of Kublai Khan; besieged and sacked Baghdad (1258); overthrew the Abbasids in Mesopotamia and the Seljuks in Persia; overran Syria and captured Aleppo and Damascus (1260); on the death of Mangu Khan, founded dynasty of Il-Khans; became Muslim after defeat by the Mameluke sultan of Egypt at Ain Jalut (1260).

Hull *(hŭl),* **Cordell** 1871–1955. American statesman. *b.* Overton, Tenn. House of Representatives (1907–21, 1923–31); senator (1931–33); sponsored important income tax laws; secretary of state (1933–44); awarded Nobel Peace Prize (1945). Author of *The Memoirs of Cordell Hull* (2 vols., 1948).

Humboldt *(hŭm bōlt),* **Baron Alexander von** full name: FRIEDRICH HEINRICH ALEXANDER VON. 1769–1859. German naturalist. *b.* Berlin. With Aimé Bonpland, explored South American regions (1799–1804); with Gustav Rose and Christian Ehrenberg, explored Central Asia; published results in *Voyage aux Régions Équinoxiales du Nouveau Continent* (1814–27), *Asie Centrale* (1843), and *Kosmos* (1845–62); discovered use of isothermal lines, use of guano, and the relation between elevation and mean temperature; also studied plant distribution, origin of rocks, tropical storms, and volcanoes. Brother BARON WILHELM VON HUMBOLT (1767–1835), German philologist, authored seminal works on linguistics; a major work was a study on the Kavi language whose introduction, "On the Difference in Construction of Language and Its Influence upon the Intellectual Development of the Human Race" advanced the science of comparative philology.

Hume *(hyōōm),* **David** 1711–76. Scottish metaphysician. *b.* Edinburgh. Founder of a philosophical system of skepticism known as Humism; held that knowledge was restricted to impressions; rejected the possibility of knowing anything certain; denied causation and any logical or necessary connection between cause and effect; exposed the artificiality of the principles of justice and social obligations implicit in theories of natural law. Principal works include *A Treatise of Human Nature* (1739–40),

Essays, Moral and Political (1741–42) *An Enquiry Concerning Human Understanding* (1748), *An Enquiry Concerning the Principles of Morals* (1751), *History of England* (1754–61), *Four Dissertations* (1757), and *Natural History of Religion* (1757).

Humperdinck *(hŏŏm pər dĭngk),* **Engelbert** 1854–1921. German composer. *b.* Siegburg. Composer of *Hänsel and Gretel* (1893), *Die Königskinder* (1910), and lesser-known works.

Humphrey *(hŭm frĭ),* **Hubert Horatio** 1911–78. American statesman. *b.* Wallace, S.D. Entered politics as mayor of Minneapolis (1945–48); senator from Minnesota (1948); vice-president of U.S. under Johnson (1965–69); losing Democratic candidate for presidency (1968); senator (1970–78).

Hunt *(hŭnt),* **Leigh** full name: JAMES HENRY LEIGH. 1784–1859. English man of letters. *b.* Southgate. Editor of *Examiner* (from 1808), *The Reflector* (from 1810), and *The Liberal* (with Lord Byron, 1822–23); introduced Keats and Shelley to English public; wrote poems "Abou Ben Adhem," "Jenny Kissed Me," and "The Glove and the Lions," *Story of Rimini* (1816), *Foliage* (1818), and *Autobiography* (1850), among other works.

Hunter *(hŭn tər),* **John** 1728–93. British surgeon. *b.* Long Calderwood, Scotland. Considered founder of scientific surgery; began surgical practice (1763); surgeon-extraordinary to king (1776); built museum in London for anatomical, physiological, and pathological specimens (1785); performed first operation for aneurism (1785); surgeon-general to the army (1793); revolutionized dentistry with publication of *Natural History of Human Teeth* (1771–78); made important contributions to studies on blood, embryology, and the fetus.

Huntington *(hŭn tĭng tən),* **Collis Potter** 1821–1900. American railway builder. *b.* Harwinton, Conn. Promoted and built railroads, including the Central Pacific (1869), and the Southern Pacific (1884); president of the Chesapeake and Ohio Railroad, Pacific Mail Steamship, and Mexican International Railway Company.

Hunyadi *(hōō nyŏ dĭ),* **Janos** c1387–1456. Hungarian national hero and warrior. *b.* Hunyad, Transylvania. Commander of frontier provinces under Sigismund and Albert II of Germany; appointed voivode (governor) of Transylvania by Ladislas III of Hungary (1442): defeated Turks, driving them from Adriatic (1441–43); defeated by Turks at Varna (1444), where Ladislas was slain; regent for new king, Ladislas V (1446–52); began new struggles against Turks and Frederick III of Germany; defeated by Turks at Kossovo (1448), but gained victory by heroic defense of Belgrade (1456); three weeks later, died of plague.

Husayn Ali. *See* **Bahaullah**

Huss *(hŭs),* **John** German name; JOHANNES HUS VON HUSINETZ; Czech name: JAN HUS. c1369–1415. Bohemian religious reformer. *b.* Husinetz. Rector of University of Prague (1402); ordained priest; influenced by Wycliffe's teachings, began to attack abuses of clergy;

opposed the burning of Wycliffe's books; excommunicated by antipope John XXIII (1412); defied excommunication and continued preaching; placed under interdict, along with the city of Prague; forced to leave Prague and hide; wrote *Simony* and *De Ecclesia,* defining his doctrines; called before Council of Constance and offered safe conduct; nevertheless, thrown into prison, tried for heresy, and burned at the stake.

Husserl *(hōōs ərl),* **Edmund Gustav Albrecht** 1859–1938. German philosopher. *b.* Prossnitz. Professor of philosophy at Gottingen (1900–1916) and at Freiburg (from 1916); formulated the philosophy known as phenomenology, defining the relationship between conscious mind and objective world; profoundly influenced Gestalt and existentialist philosophers. Author of *Ideen zu Einer Reinen Phanomenologie und Phanomenologischen Philosophie* (1913), *Vorlesungen zur Phanomenologie des Inneren Bewusstseins* (1928), and other works.

Hutchinson *(hŭch ĭn sən),* **Anne** *née* Marbury. 1591–1643. American religious preacher. *b.* Alford, England. Immigrated to Mass. colony with husband William Hutchinson (1634); preached salvation by grace alone, without reference to Church doctrines or works; tried and convicted for heresy and banished from Mass. (1637); moved to Rhode Island (1638) and later to Pelham Bay, N.Y. (1642); massacred by Indians.

Huxley *(hŭk slĭ),* **Andrew Fielding** 1917–. British physiologist. Conducted research on nerve transmission; formulated theory of muscle contraction; awarded Nobel Prize in physiology and medicine with A. Hodgkin and J. Eccles (1963).

Huxley, Famous English family including:

Thomas Henry Huxley 1825–95. English scientist. *b.* Ealing. Assistant surgeon on H. M. S. *Rattlesnake,* collecting South Pacific biological specimens (1845–50); professor of natural history at Royal School of Mines (1854), Royal College of Surgeons (1863–69), Royal Institution (1863–67); president of Royal Society (1881–85); eloquent defender of Darwinian theory of evolution; engaged in debates with Bishop Wilberforce. Author of *Zoological Evidence as to Man's Place in Nature* (1863), *On the Causes of the Phenomena of Organic Nature* (1863), *An Introduction to the Classification of Animals* (1869), *Science and Culture* (1881), *Evolution and Culture* (1891);

Leonard 1860–1933. English editor and writer. Son of Thomas; editor of *Cornhill Magazine.*

Sir Julian Sorell 1887–1975. English biologist. *b.* London. Son of Leonard; professor of zoology in London (from 1925); president of National Union of Scientific Workers (1926–29); secretary of Zoological Society (1935–42); director general of UNESCO (1946–48). Author of *Essays of a Biologist* (1923), *The Stream of Life* (1926), *Evolution Restated* (1940), *Evolutionary Ethics* (1943), *Man in the Modern World* (1947), and *Biological Aspects of Cancer* (1957).

Aldous Leonard 1894–1963. English writer. *b.* Godalming. Son of Leonard; gave up study of medicine and turned to literature; in early novels, preoccupied with biological degeneration of the individual; later turned to mysticism and mind-expanding systems. Author of *The Burning Wheel* (1916), *Limbo* (1920), *Crome Yellow* (1921), *Mortal Coils* (1922), *Antic Hay* (1923), *Those Barren Leaves* (1925), *Point Counter Point* (1928), *Jesting Pilate* 1926), *Brave New World* (1932), *Eyeless in Gaza* (1936), *End and Means* (1937), *After Many a Summer Dies the Swan* (1939), *Time Must Have a Stop* (1944), *Ape and Essence* (1948), *The Perennial Philosophy* (1945), *The Gioconda Smile* (1950), *The Devils of Loudon* (1952), *The Doors of Perception* (1954), and *The Genius and the Goddess* (1955).

Huygens *(hoi gəns),* **Christian** 1629–95. Dutch scientist. *b.* The Hague. Built new, powerful telescopes with improved lenses; discovered the rings of Saturn and its sixth satellite (1655); built first pendulum-regulated clock (1657); proposed wave theory of light (1678); invented micrometer and discovered light polarization; stated law governing collision of elastic bodies and Huygens's Principle, according to which every point of a wave front of light acts as source of new waves; worked in Paris for 15 years (1666-81) as member of Royal Academy of Sciences. Author of *Theoremata* (1651), *Horologium Oscillatorium* (1673), and *Traité de la Lumière* (1678).

Huysmans *(hois mäns),* **Joris Karl** pseudonym of CHARLES MARIE GEORGES. 1848–1907. Flemish writer. *b.* Paris, France. From early ultrarealism, moved through diabolism and occultism to Catholicism. Author of *Les Soeurs Vatard* (1879), *À Vau-l'Eau* (1882), *En Rade* (1887), *À Rebours* (1884), *Là-Bas* (1891), *En Route* (1895), *La Cathédrale (1898), L'Oblat* (1903), *Les Foules de Lourdes* (1906), and *Art Moderne* (1882).

Hyde *(hīd),* **Douglas** known as AN CRAOBHÍN AOBHINN (THE FAIR BRANCH). 1860–1949. Irish writer and statesman. *b.* Roscommon county. Founder and first president of Gaelic League (1893–1915); professor of Irish in National University (1909–32); first president of Eire (1938–45). Author of *A Literary History of Ireland* (1899), *Raftery's Poems* (1904), *Legends of Saints and Sinners from the Irish* (1915), and a number of Gaelic plays.

Hyde, Edward. *See* **Clarendon, Earl of**

I

Ibn-Khaldun *(ib ən Kăl dōōn)* full Arabic name: ABD-AL-RAHMAN IBN-KHALDUN. 1332–1406. Arab historian. *b.* Tunis, North Africa. Served in various Arab courts (from 1352); grand cadi of Cairo; as emissary of sultan of Egypt, negotiated surrender of Damascus to Mongols (1400–1402); considered the greatest Arab historian. Author of *Kitab* *al-Ibar,* whose introduction, *Muqaddamah,* is a masterful discussion of the Arab philosophy of history and a description of the rise of Islam.

Ibn-saud *(ib ən soo o͞od),* **Abdul-Aziz** 1880–1953. King of Saudi Arabia (1932–53). *b.* Riyadh, Arabia. Succeeded father, a Wahabi ruler of Nejd (1901); seized Riyadh, the capital; consolidated Wahabi power and expanded kingdom to Persian Gulf; sided with British against Turks in World War I; invaded and conquered the Hejaz and Mecca (1924–25); proclaimed himself king of Hejaz and Nejd (1926), renaming his kingdom Saudi Arabia (1932); replaced old tribal loyalties with a strong sense of nationalism; granted oil concessions to Aramco Oil Company.

Ibsen *(ĭb sən),* **Henrik** 1828–1906. Norwegian dramatist. *b.* Skien. Trained in medicine; turned to playwriting with *Catilina* (1850); director of Ole Bull's Theater in Bergen (1851–57); first significant play was *The Pretenders* (1857); director of National Theater (1857); in voluntary exile in Germany and Italy as a protest against Norway's neutrality in Denmark's struggle with Germany (1863–91); granted pension by Norwegian Parliament (1866); returned to Oslo (1891); revolutionized modern theater with social and psychological dramas dealing with disturbing and controversial themes; considered a master of stagecraft and dialogue. Principal works include *The Banquet at Solhaug* (1856), *The Warriors at Helgoland* (1858), *Love's Comedy (1862), Brand* (1866), *Peer Gynt* (1866–67), *League of Youth* (1869), *Emperor and Galilean* (1873), *The Pillars of Society* (1877), *A Doll's House* (1879), *Ghosts* (1881), *An Enemy of the People* (1882), *The Wild Duck* (1884), *Rosmersholm* (1886), *The Lady from the Sea* (1888), *Hedda Gabler* (1890), *The Master Builder* (1892), *Little Eyolf* (1894), *John Gabriel Borkman* (1896), and *When We Dead Awaken* (1899).

Ignatius *(ĭg nā shĭ əs),* **Saint** surname: Theophorus. c50–c107. Apostolic father. Disciple of St. John; bishop of Antioch; suffered martyrdom under Trajan. Author of *Ignatian Epistles.* Feast day: Feb. 1.

Ikhnaton *(ĭk nä tən)* also known as Akhenaten, Amenhotep IV, Amenophis. *fl.* 14th century B.C. King of Egypt (1375–1358 B.C.) of the XVIII Dynasty. Married Nefertiti, a Hittite princess; heralded a religious revolution by introducing monotheistic worship of Aten, the sun-god, and diminishing power of the priests of Amen; assumed name Ikhnaton meaning "Aten is pleased"; transferred the capital of Egypt from Thebes to Akhetaton (modern Tell el-Amarna); reign called "the Amarna period" from the extensive documentary material inscribed on tablets; neglected imperial provinces which broke away from Egypt and became independent.

Inge *(ĭng),* **William Ralph** 1860–1954. English divine. *b.* Craike. Professor of divinity at Cambridge (1907–11); Dean of St. Paul's Cathedral in London (1911–34); earned the nickname "Gloomy Dean" for his pessimism; examined mysticism, faith, and ethics from a Christian perspective in a number of works, including *Lay Thoughts of a Dean* (1926), *Outspoken Essays* (1919), *Christian Mysticism* (1899), *Faith and Knowledge* (1904), and *Christian Ethics and Modern Problems* (1930).

Ingres *(äN grə),* **Jean Auguste Dominique** 1780–1867. French painter. *b.* Montauban. Studied painting under David; worked in Rome (1806–20, 1834–41); returned to Paris in great favor (1841); acclaimed for classical and historical paintings. Principal works include *Oedipus and the Sphinx* (1808); *Odalisque* (1814), *Apotheosis of Homer* (1826), *Paolo and Francesca* (1819), *Stratonice* (1839), *Joan of Arc* (1854), and *The Spring* (1856).

Innocent III *(ĭn ō sənt)* real name: GIOVANNI LOTARIO DE' CONTI. 1161–1216. Pope (1198–1216). *b.* Anagni, Italy. Brought papacy to zenith of temporal supremacy; established the primacy of church over state in Europe; inspired Fourth Crusade (1202–1204) and crusade against the Albigenses (1208); humbled Philip II of France and John of England and deposed Otto IV, Holy Roman Emperor; presided over Fourth Lateran Council (1215); promoted a spiritual revival and fought simony and other abuses. Author of *Misery of the Condition of Man* and the hymn "Veni, Sancte Spiritus."

Ionesco *(yō nĕs kō),* **Eugène** 1912–. French playwright. *b.* Rumania. Settled in Paris (1940); became one of the foremost exponents of the Theater of the Absurd; exposed the futility of Western materialism in *The Bald Soprano* (1950), *The Lesson* (1951), *The Chairs* (1952), *Rhinoceros* (1960), *Victims of Duty* (1953), and *The Picture* (1960); his dramas have been described as existential burlesque; also wrote short stories, essays, and ballets.

Iqbal *(ĭk bäl),* **Mohammad** 1875–1938. Indian poet and philosopher. *b.* Sialkot, Punjab. As a deeply nationalistic Muslim poet, conceived the idea of a separate homeland for Muslims within the subcontinent, which later materialized as Pakistan; wrote works in Urdu, Persian, and English. Author of *Six Lectures on the Reconstruction of Religious Thought.*

Irving *(ûr vĭng),* **Washington** 1783–1859. American author. *b.* New York, N.Y. Began literary career with satires *The Letters of Jonathan Oldstyle Gent* (1802–1803) and *Salmagundi* (1807), followed by *A History of New York* (1809) under the pseudonym Diedrich Knickerbocker; lived abroad (1815–32); wrote essays for *The Sketch Book* (1820); published *Bracebridge Hall* (1822), *Christopher Columbus* (1828), *A Chronicle of the Conquest of Granada* (1829), and *Alhambra* (1832); lived rest of life at Tarrytown, N.Y., writing *Oliver Goldsmith* (1849), *Mahomet and His Successors* (2 vols., 1849–50), and *Life of Washington* (5 vols., 1855–59); best known for stories "The Legend of Sleepy Hollow" and "Rip Van Winkle."

Isabella *(ĭz ə bĕl ə)* full name: MARIA ISABELLA LOUISA. Called THE CATHOLIC. 1451–1504. Spanish queen (1474–1504). Daughter of John II; married Ferdinand II of Aragon (1469) and ruled as joint sovereign of Castile and Aragon; during their reign war with the Moors was resumed, and ended with their expulsion from Spain in 1492; reign also marked by conquest of Granada (1492) and expulsion of Jews (1492); patron of Christopher Columbus (1492–99) and Cardinal Jimenez.

Isaiah *(ī zā yȧ)* *fl.* 8th century B.C. Hebrew prophet whose discourses are recorded in the Old Testament book of Isaiah; opposed alliance with Egypt; believed to have been sawn to death under Manasseh.

Isherwood *(ĭsh ər wood),* **Christopher William Bradshaw-** 1904–. English writer. *b.* Disley. Published first novel *All the Conspirators* (1928); traveled to Berlin and China; came to U.S. as a scriptwriter for MGM; naturalized (1946); turned to Eastern mysticism; collaborated with W. H. Auden on a number of works, including *The Dog Beneath the Skin* (1935), *The Ascent of F6* (1937), *On the Frontier* (1938), and *Journey to a War* (1939). Other works include *Mr. Norris Changes Trains* (1935), *Goodbye to Berlin* (1939), *Prater Violet* (1945), *The World in the Evening* (1954), and *Meeting by the River* (1967); published the autobiographical *Lions and Shadows* (1938) and *Christopher and His Kind* (1977).

Isidore *(ĭz ə dōr)* **of Seville, Saint** c560–636. Spanish ecclesiastic. *b.* Cartagena. Archbishop of Seville (594); famed as one of the most learned men of the age on the basis of the encyclopedia work *Origines* or *Etymologiae* (622–33), a compendium of classical knowledge. Author of *De Natura Rerum,* histories of the Goths, Vandals, and Suevi, *De Ecclesiasticis Officiis Libri Duo,* and *Sententiarum Sive de Summo Bono.*

Iskander Bey. *See* **Scanderberg**

Islebius, Magister. *See* **Agricola, Johannes**

Isocrates *(ī sŏk rȧ tēs)* 436–338 B.C. Greek orator. *b.* Athens. Pupil of Socrates; founded school for eloquence (390) in Athens; perfected epideictic form of oratory and composed a number of model speeches, of which 21 are extant; starved himself to death after Battle of Chaeronea, where Philip II of Macedon defeated the Athenians and the Boeotians, ending Greek dreams of unity and freedom.

Israel ben Eliezer. *See* **Baal Shem-To**

Ito *(ē tō),* **Marquis Hirobumi** 1841–1909. Japanese statesman. *b.* Choshu. Leader in introducing Western cultural and political ideas to Japan; drafted Constitution of 1889; prime minister (1886–88, 1892–96, 1898, 1900–1901); first president of Seiyukai party; after Sino-Japanese War (1894–95) negotiated the agreement that made Korea a virtual protectorate of Japan; assassinated by a Korean nationalist at Harbin.

Ivan III Vasilevich *(ē vȧn)* also, IVAN THE GREAT. 1440–1505. Russian grand duke (1462–1505). Threw off Tartar yoke and brought independent princes under his sway; conquered and annexed Novgorod (1471–78); married Zoe, niece of the last Byzantine emperor; adopted two-headed eagle of the Byzantine empire to signal his claim as Ruler of All Russia; proclaimed himself protector of Orthodox Church, with Moscow as the third Rome.

Ivan IV Vasilevich called IVAN THE TERRIBLE. 1530–84. Tsar of Russia (1533–84). After regency of his mother (1533–38) and the boyars (1538–44), took power (1544) and crowned himself first tsar of Russia; married Anastasia Romanovna (1547); convened national assembly, the *Zemski Sobor* (1550); conquered Kazan and Astrakhan and began conquest of Siberia; driven insane by deaths of wife and son Dmitri; set up the dreaded *Oprichniki,* who terrorized the kingdom; ravaged Novgorod; killed son Ivan (1580); met reverses in wars with Poland, Sweden and Livonia; despite insanity, fostered arts and industry.

Ives *(īvz),* **Charles Edward** 1874–1954. American composer. *b.* Danbury, Conn. Achieved recognition in 1940s with ultramodern polytonal compositions; composed chamber music, symphonies, organ pieces, choral works, and over 150 songs. Best-known works include *Three Places in New England* (1903–14), *Ragtime Dances* (1900–1911), and the choral works *Harvest Festival* (1898) and *Celestial Country* (1898–99).

Iwasa *(ē wä sä)* **Matabei** c1580–c1650. Japanese genre painter. Founder of the Ukiyoye school. Work includes portraits of over 30 Japanese poets.

Iyeyasu *(ē yě yä so͞o)* 1542–1616. Japanese warrior and statesman. Founder of Tokugawa shogunate; on death of Hideyoshi, became one of four regents of Hideyori; defeated co-regents at Battle of Sekigahara and became sole ruler (1600); commissioned as shogun by emperor (1603); established capital of kingdom at Yedo (Tokyo); abdicated position in favor of son, but remained virtual ruler; unsuccessful in efforts to develop trade relations with Western powers; prohibited all Christian missionaries; anti-Christian policies continued under his successor IYEMITSU (1604–51), shogun (1623–51), under whom the shogunate reached the peak of its power.

J

Jackson *(jăk sən),* **Andrew** 1767–1845. Seventh president of U.S. (1829–37). *b.* Waxhaw, S.C. Took part in Revolutionary War at age 13 and was captured by the British; public prosecutor and planter in Nashville, Tenn. (1788–96); House of Representatives (1796–97); Senate (1797–98); judge, Tennessee Supreme Court (1798–1804); on outbreak of War of 1812, fought as major general in militia; defeated Creek Indians at Horseshoe Bend (1814); appointed to command of the South as major general in U.S. army; became national hero by successfully defending New Orleans against Pakenham's army (1815); invaded Florida (1818) and defeated the Seminoles; first governor of Florida after its purchase from Spain (1821); Senate (1823); unsuccessful candidate for presidency (1824); elected president of U.S. (1828); administration (1829–37) marked by introduction of spoils system ("To the victor belongs the spoils"); vetoed charter of the Bank of the United States; paid off national debt; opposed states rights in the Nullification Doctrine; sponsored Specie Circular (1836) by which all public lands were to be paid for in specie; considered an able and strong president.

Jackson, Thomas Jonathan known as STONEWALL JACKSON. 1824–63. American Confederate general. *b.* Clarksburg, W. Va. Graduated from West Point (1846); professor at Virginia Military Institute (1851–52); resigned commission (1852); commanded Confederate troops at Harper's Ferry on outbreak of Civil War (1861); brigadier general (1861); commanded brigade at Bull Run and won nickname "Stonewall" for unyielding stand (1861); major general (1861); in brilliant Shenandoah Valley campaign, overwhelmed McDowell, Banks, and Frémont and pushed Northern forces back from Virginia with victories at Port Republic and Cedar Run; took part in second Battle of Bull Run and captured Harper's Ferry (1862); saved Lee from disaster at Antietam and commanded right wing at Fredericksburg and Chancellorsville (1863); died of wounds received when accidentally shot by own troops at Chancellorsville.

Jacob *(zhă kôb),* **François** 1920–. French geneticist. *b.* Nancy. Professor of cellular genetics at College of France; shared, with André Lwoff and Jacques Monod, Nobel Prize in physiology and medicine (1965) for research on viral synthesis and regulatory processes in body cells that contribute to genetic control of enzymes.

Jahn *(yän),* **Friedrich Ludwig** 1778–1852. German gymnastics director. *b.* Lanz. Opened (1811) the Turnplatz, the first gymnasium in Germany, where students were trained in physical fitness and patriotism; suppressed on political grounds (1818); arrested and incarcerated (1819–25); released by Frederick William IV and awarded the Iron Cross. Published *Die Deutsche Turnkunst* (1816) describing his system of physical training.

Jalal-ud-Din Muhammad. *See* **Akbar**

Jalal-ud-din Rumi *(ja lä lood dēn rōō mē),* **Mohammed ibn Mohammed** 1207–73. Persian mystic and poet. *b.* Balkh, Afghanistan. Lived at Iconium as director of a college founded by his father; founded the Sufi order of dervishes known as Maulawiyah. Best known as author of an epic collection of verses, *Mesnavi y ma' navi,* highly regarded by the Sufis.

James *(jāmz)* Name of two kings of England:

JAMES I 1566–1625. King of Scotland as James VI (1567–1625) and king of England (1603–25). *b.* Edinburgh, Scotland. Son of Mary, Queen of Scots, and Henry, Lord Darnley; in conflict with Protestant nobles, compelled by them to submit at Stirling Castle and make Treaty of Berwick with England (1586); suppressed Puritans and Catholics, and introduced episcopacy into Scotland; succeeded Elizabeth on throne of England (1603); struggled to assert divine right of kings; ruled with aid of Robert Carr, Earl of Somerset, and George Villiers, Duke of Buckingham; appointed commission that revised the Bible, producing King James Version (1611); in foreign policy, alienated Protestant powers and concluded peace with Spain; granted patent to the London and Plymouth Companies, leading to colonization of North America (1607); dissolved Parliament (1611) and ruled without one for ten years; rejected the Great Protestation, passed by Parliament against his policies; described as the "wisest fool in Christendom" for being a learned but weak and incapable monarch.

JAMES II 1633–1701. King of England, Scotland, and Ireland (1685–88). *b.* London. Brother of Charles II; appointed lord high admiral on Restoration (1660); accepted Roman Catholic faith (c1671); under Test Act, excluded from office; in voluntary exile in Paris after Popish Plot (1678–79); returned to England after defeat of attempts in Parliament to exclude him from line of succession; succeeded Charles as king (1685); published declaration of liberty of conscience for all denominations (1687); renewed persecution of Covenanters; set up the "Bloody Assizes" after the abortive Monmouth Rebellion; arrested and tried seven bishops who opposed Declaration of Indulgences; suspended the Test Act; his efforts to subvert constitution and church aroused indignation of the Whig establishment, which invited William of Orange to accept the throne of England; deposed in the Bloodless Revolution; fled to France when William landed at Torbay (1688) and thereafter lived as a pensioner of Louis XIV.

James, Henry 1843–1916. American author. *b.* New York, N.Y. Son of HENRY JAMES, SR. (1811–82), American Swedenborgian and Sandemanian writer. Brother of William James; lived and wrote in England (from 1869), becoming British subject (1915); considered a master of psychological novels and superb stylist; his prose consisted of long but superbly constructed sentences, delineating character by minute details. Works include *Roderick Hudson* (1875), *The American* (1877), *Daisy Miller* (1879), *Washington Square* (1880), *Portrait of a Lady* (1881), *The Bostonians* (1886), *Princess Casamassima* (1886), *The Tragic Muse* (1890), *The Spoils of Poynton* (1897), *What Maisie Knew* (1897), *In the Cage* (1898), *The Awkward Age* (1899), *The Wings of a Dove* (1902), *The Ambassadors* (1903), *The Golden Bowl* (1904), *Terminations* (1895), *The Two Magics* (1898), and the *Altar of the Dead* (1909); also wrote critical studies, travel sketches, and the autobiographical works *A Small Boy and Others* (1913), *Notes of a Son and a Brother* (1914), and the unfinished *Middle Years* (1917).

James, Jesse Woodson 1847–82. American outlaw. *b.* Centerville, Clay County, Mo. Fought in the guerrilla bands of the Confederacy during the Civil War; with Coleman Younger, brother Frank James, and other outlaws, staged a series of bank and train robberies in the central states; murdered by a member of his own gang.

James, William 1842–1910. American psychologist. *b.* New York, N.Y. Brother of Henry James; graduated in medicine and taught physiology, anatomy, psychology, and philosophy at Harvard (1872–1907); with the publication of *Principles of Psychology* (1890) laid the science of psychology on a physiological foundation; developed C.S. Peirce's pragmatism in *The Will to Believe* (1897), *Pragmatism* (1907), *The Meaning of Truth* (1909), *A Pluralistic Universe* (1909), and *Some Problems of Philosophy* (1911); explored the religious dimensions of philosophy in *Varieties of Religious Experience* (1902).

Janet *(zhä ně),* **Pierre Marie Félix** 1859–1947. French neurologist. *b.* Paris. Director of La Salpêtriere; professor at the Sorbonne (1898) and College of France (1902); founded automatic psychology and described psychasthenia; made important contributions to mental pathology and hysteria; founded and edited *Journal de Psychologie Normale et Pathologique.* Works include *Mental State of Hystericals* (1907), *The Major Symptoms of Hysteria* (1908), *Principles of Psychotherapy* (1924), and *Psychological Healing* (1925).

Jansen *(yän sěn),* **Cornelius** 1585–1638. Dutch theologian. *b.* Acquoi. Professor of theology at Louvain (from 1630); bishop of Ypres (1636); completed his great work *Augustinus* (4 vols., 1640), which formed the basis of Jansenism; held that Jesuit teachings contradicted Augustinian teaching, denying free will and stressing the need for divine grace and the inalterability of predestination; teaching condemned by the Inquisition (1641) and by Pope Urban VIII (1642); Jansenism was espoused by the Arnauld family, Blaise Pascal, and the Port-Royalists, who defied the Church of Rome for many decades.

Jaspers *(yäs pərs),* **Karl** 1883–1969. German philosopher. *b.* Oldenburg. Professor of psychology (1916) and philosophy (1921) at Heidelberg; developed personal form of existentialism which dealt with the authentic self called "being-oneself." Author of *Psychologie der Weltanschauung* (1919), *Philosophie* (1932), *Existenzphilosophie* (1938), *Vernunft und Existenz* (1935), and *The Perennial Scope of Philosophy* (1949).

Jay *(jā),* **John** 1745–1829. American jurist and statesman. *b.* New York, N.Y. Member of Continental Congress (1774–77) and its president (1778–79); minister to Spain (1779); member of commission for negotiating peace with Great Britain (1782); secretary for foreign affairs (1784–89); contributed five papers on the Constitution and foreign affairs to the *Federalist;* chief justice of the United States (1789–95); negotiated Jay's Treaty with Great Britain, settling differences arising out of violations of Treaty of Paris of 1783; governor of New York (1795–1801).

Jeans *(jēnz),* **Sir James Hopwood** 1877–1946. English astonomer. *b.* Ormskirk. Professor of applied mathematics, Princeton (1905–1909); secretary of Royal Society

(1919–29); professor at Royal Institution (1935–46); made important studies of gases, quantum theory, and radiation; developed tidal theory of solar evolution. Best known for popular books on astronomy, including *The Universe Around Us* (1929), *The Stars in Their Courses* (1931), *Through Space and Time* (1934), *The New Background of Science* (1933), *The Mysterious Universe* (1930), and *Physics and Philosophy* (1942).

Jefferson *(jĕf ər sən),* **Thomas** 1743–1826. Third president of U.S. (1801–1809). *b.* Shadwell, Va. Member of Virginia House of Burgesses (1769–75) and Virginia convention (1774); published *A Summary View of the Rights of British America,* in which he wrote eloquently on the cause of Colonial liberties; member of Continental Congress (1775); member and main author on the five-man commission that drafted the Declaration of Independence; governor of Virginia (1779–81); responsible for the abolition of entail and primogeniture and the establishment of a public school system and religious freedom; returned to Congress (1783); secured adoption of decimal system of coinage; minister to France, succeeding Franklin (1785–89); first secretary of state (1790–93); leader of Republicans opposing Hamiltonian Federalists; vice-president (1796) under John Adams; as president of the Senate, wrote *Manual of Parliamentary Practice* (1801); framed the Kentucky Resolutions (1798), denying the federal government powers not specifically delegated to it by the Constitution; elected president of U.S. (1801) by House of Representatives after tying Burr in the popular vote; administration marked by the acquisition of Louisiana (1803), war against Algerian pirates, the Lewis and Clark expedition, the admission of Ohio, and slave trade prohibition; after the presidency, helped found the University of Virginia; president of American Philosophical Society (1797–1815). *The Writings of Thomas Jefferson,* including his *Autobiography,* were edited by Paul L. Ford (10 vols., 1892–99).

Jenner *(jĕn ər),* **Edward** 1749–1823. English physician. *b.* Berkeley. Studied medicine and began practice at Berkeley (1773); after a series of experiments, perfected the vaccination technique (1796). Published *Inquiry into the Cause and Effect of the Variolae Vaccinae* announcing his discovery (1798).

Jensen *(yĕn sən),* **Hans** 1907–1973. German physicist. *b.* Hamburg. Professor at Heidelberg (from 1949); with Eugene Wigner and Maria Goeppert-Mayer, awarded Nobel Prize in physics (1963) for research into atomic nucleus shell structure.

Jensen, Johannes Vilhelm 1873–1950. Danish writer. *b.* Farsø. Best known for his major work *The Long Journey* (6 vols., 1908–22), an epic saga with Darwinian overtones that brought him the Nobel Prize for literature (1944). Other books include *Himmerlandshistorien* (1898–1910), *The Forest, Madama d'Ora* (1904), *The Fall of the King* (1933), and *The Waving Rye* (1959).

Jeremiah *(jĕr ə mī ə) fl.* 7th century B.C. Hebrew prophet whose prophecies and denunciations are recorded in Jeremiah and

Lamentations in the Old Testament; witnessed the siege of Jerusalem by Nebuchadnezzar; after the fall of Jerusalem, lived in Egypt, where he is believed to have died a martyr's death.

Jerome *(jə rōm),* **Saint** Latin name: EUSEBIUS HIERONYMOUS. c340–420. Italian scholar and Father and Doctor of the Church. *b.* Stridon, Pannonia (Yugoslavia). Studied at Rome; left on a tour of the East (373); struck with a dangerous illness at Antioch, received a vision, causing him to live in the desert as an eremite (374–79); ordained priest (379); returned to Rome on a mission against the Meletian schismatics; secretary to Pope Damasus (382); after the death of Damasus, returned to Bethlehem; engaged in literary labors including the Latin version of the Bible known as the Vulgate, polemical works against heretics, commentaries on the Scriptures, and ecclesiastical histories.

Jesus *(jē zəs)* also known as JESUS CHRIST; THE MESSIAH. *b.* 4–8 B.C.; *d.* A.D. c29. Founder of Christianity. *b.* Bethlehem, Palestine. According to New Testament, born of Virgin Mary; baptized by John the Baptist; gathered 12 disciples and preached the kingdom of God; performed miracles; in the revolutionary Sermon on the Mount, proclaimed a set of new commandments to replace the old; entered Jerusalem in triumph during Passover season and drove the moneychangers from the Temple; aroused the hostility of the priesthood; betrayed to them by one disciple, Judas Iscariot; tried and condemned as a blasphemer; crucified on Golgotha and buried in the tomb of Joseph of Arimathea; rose from the dead on the third day and ascended to heaven 40 days after the Resurrection; believed by orthodox Christians to be the Son of God, who will return to earth on the day of Last Judgment; teachings, recorded in the four Gospels of the New Testament, form the foundation of the Christian Church; events of life commemorated in the Christian calendar; birth denotes the beginning of the modern era.

Jimenez *(hē mā nāth),* **Juan Ramón** 1881–1958. Spanish poet. *b.* Moguer. Left Spain during Civil War (1936) and settled in Florida. Best known for the classic *Platero y Yo* (1914); other works include *Almas de Violeta* (1901), *Arias Tristes* (1903), *Jardines Lefanos* (1905), and *El Silencio de Oro* (1922); awarded Nobel Prize in literature (1956).

Jinnah *(jĭn nə),* **Mohammed Ali** 1876–1948. Pakistani statesman. *b.* Karachi. Studied law and established practice in Bombay; joined Muslim League (1913), becoming its president (1916, 1920, 1934–48); cooperated with Indian National Congress (1916–21), but after 1934 began to agitate for separate state for Indian Muslims; won demand for independent Muslim state on the subcontinent on transfer of power (1947); governor general of new state of Pakistan with the title "Quaid-i-Azam" (Great Leader). Author of *Pakistan* and *Nationalism in Conflict in India.*

Joan of Arc or Jeanne D'Arc *(jōn əv ärk, zhän därk),* **Saint** Also MAID OF ORLEANS. 1412–31. French heroine. *b.* Domremy-la-Pucelle. At age 13, heard voices bidding her to liberate France from the English; presented herself before the Dauphin at Bourges (1429); with consent of the Dauphin, led army that lifted the siege of Orleans; routed the English at Patay and persuaded the Dauphin to march on Reims to be crowned as Charles VII; besieged Paris unsuccessfully; captured by the Burgundians, allies of England, during a sortie at Compiègne (1430) and sold to the English for 10,000 crowns; tried for heresy and sorcery, condemned and burned at the stake (1431); trial declared irregular (1456); beatified (1909); canonized (1920).

Joffre *(zhô frə),* **Joseph Jacques Césaire** 1852–1931. French general. *b.* Rivesaltes. Commissioned (1870); chief of staff (1914); commander in chief (1915); won the Battle of the Marne (1914); chairman of the Allied War Council (1916–18); marshal of France (1917).

Johannes Scotus. *See* **Erigena, Johannes Scotus**

John *(jŏn)* **the Baptist** c5 B.C.–A.D. c30. Last Hebrew prophet and forerunner of Christ. Son of Zacharias and Elizabeth; began mission by urging people to repent and prepare the way for the Messiah; baptized Christ; denounced the incestuous marriage of Herod Antipas and Herodias; beheaded by Herod at the instigation of Herodias.

John, Saint also JOHN THE EVANGELIST, JOHN THE DIVINE. One of the 12 apostles of Christ, son of Zebedee, and brother of Saint James; known as the disciple whom Jesus loved and the one to whose care Christ committed His mother on the day of the Crucifixion; identified with the author of the fourth Gospel, the three Johannine Epistles, and the Book of Revelation; by tradition, believed to have lived out his life as an exile on the island of Patmos, dying at Ephesus.

John XXIII real name: ANGELO GIUSEPPE RONCALLI. 1881–1963. Pope (1958–63). *b.* Sotto il Monte, Italy. Ordained (1904); served as military chaplain in World War I; apostolic delegate to Bulgaria, Turkey, and Greece; nuncio to France (1944–53); patriarch of Venice (1953); pope (1958); convened 21st Ecumenical Council and sought unity with all Christian denominations; inspired a modernizing spirit within the Catholic Church.

John Name of six kings of Portugal:

JOHN I called THE BASTARD, THE GREAT. 1357–1433. King of Portugal (1385–1433). Succeeded half-brother Ferdinand as regent (1383–85); with the help of the English, defeated John of Castile at Aljubarrota (1385); proclaimed king (1385); took Ceuta from the Moors.

JOHN II called THE PERFECT. 1455–95. King of Portugal (1481–95). Suppressed the feudal nobility; sponsored the discovery of the Congo by Diogo Cam and the Cape of Good Hope by Dias; concluded Treaty of Tordesillas with Spain dividing the New World between Spain and Portugal.

JOHN III 1502–57. King of Portugal (1521–57). Introduced the Inquisition into Spain; presided over a decadent court at home and an expanding empire abroad; confirmed as ruler of Brazil by the Congress of Badajoz (1524).

JOHN IV called THE FORTUNATE. 1605–56. King of Portugal (1640–56). Threw off Spanish yoke (1640), defeating the Spanish at Montijo (1644); established the house of Braganza.

JOHN V 1689–1750. King of Portugal (1706–50). Ally of England in War of the Spanish Succession; although profligate, received title Most Faithful King from Pope Benedict XIV.

JOHN VI 1767–1826. King of Portugal (1816–26). Ruled Portugal on behalf of insane mother (1792–1807); driven out of kingdom by the French and forced into exile in Brazil (1807–21); declared king of Portugal (1821); accepted the independence of Brazil under son Dom Pedro I.

John of Gaunt *(gônt)* title: 2ND DUKE OF LANCASTER. 1340–99. English prince. *b.* Ghent, France. Fourth son of Edward III; father of Henry IV and progenitor of the House of Lancaster and Tudor; claimed the throne of Castile through marriage with Constance of Castile; unsuccessful in Scottish campaign of 1384 and Castilian campaign of 1387; opposed the clergy and protected Wycliffe.

John of the Cross, Saint real name: JUAN DE YEPIS Y ALVAREZ. 1542–91. Spanish mystic. *b.* Fontiveros. Founded, with St. Theresa, the order of discalced Carmelites; suffered persecution and imprisonment at the hands of other Carmelites. Author of celebrated works on mysticism, including *Ascent of Mount Carmel, Dark Night of the Soul, Spiritual Canticle,* and *Living Flame of Love.*

Johnson *(jŏn sən),* **Andrew** 1808–75. 17th president of U.S. (1865–69). *b.* Raleigh, N.C. Born in humble circumstances and engaged in tailoring business; began political career as alderman and mayor of Greeneville; served in Tennessee state legislature (1835–43); House of Representatives (1843–53); governor of Tennessee (1853–57); senator (1857–62); declared support of the Union and appointed military governor of Tennessee (1862); vice-president on Union ticket under Lincoln; succeeded to presidency on Lincoln's assassination (1865); at odds with Congress over Reconstruction policies; crisis precipitated by removal of secretary of war Edward M. Stanton; impeached by the House but acquitted by Senate (1868).

Johnson *(yôn sən),* **Eyvind Olof Verner** 1900–1976. Swedish novelist. *b.* Overlulea. Worked as a journalist in Germany and France and settled in Switzerland after World War II. Among his numerous works are *City in Light* (1927), *Commentary on a Shooting Star* (1929), *Night March* (1938), *Group Krilon (1941), The Novel About Olof* (1949), *The Surf* (1946), *Return to Ithaca* (1952); awarded Nobel Prize in literature (1974) with Edmund Martinson.

Johnson, *(jŏn sən),* **Lyndon Baines** 1908–73. 36th president of U.S. (1963–69). *b.* Stonewall, Texas. Member of House of Representatives (1937–49); senator (1949–61) and Senate majority leader; vice-president under John Kennedy (1961–63); became president after Kennedy's assassination in Dallas (1963); won landslide victory in presidential election (1964); initiated Great Society programs, including Medicare, civil rights, and education; intensified the American involvement in Vietnam and incurred popular discontent; declined to accept renomination and retired (1968). Author of *Vantage Point.*

Johnson, Richard Mentor 1780–1850. American statesman. *b.* Louisville, Ky. House of Representatives (1807–19, 1829–37); Senate (1819–29); as colonel of a regiment of Kentucky riflemen, killed the Indian chief Tecumseh during War of 1812; active supporter of Andrew Jackson's policies; chosen vice-president of U.S. by Senate (1837–41) after a tie in the Electoral College.

Johnson, Samuel known as DR. JOHNSON; THE GREAT CHAM OF LITERATURE. 1709–84. English literary figure and lexicographer. *b.* Lichfield. Established school at Lichfield (1736), with David Garrick as one of his students; with Garrick left for London (1737); contributor to *Gentleman's Magazine;* worked on his famous *Dictionary of the English Language* (1747–55), one of the monumental accomplishments of English scholarship; published the *Rambler* (1750–52) and wrote *Idler* papers (1758–60); met James Boswell (1763), his future biographer; with Reynolds, Garrick, Goldsmith, Burke, and others formed the Literary Club, of which he was the presiding genius; traveled in Scotland with Boswell and wrote *Journey to the Western Isles* (1775), supplemented by Boswell's *Tour to the Hebrides.* Other works include *London* (1738), *Life of Savage* (1744), *The Vanity of Human Wishes* (1749), *Rasselas, Prince of Abyssinia* (1759), *Lives of the Poets* (10 vols., 1779–81), and a number of political pamphlets; his wit and wisdom are recorded in Boswell's celebrated biography.

Joliot-Curie *(zhô lyō kü rē),* **Frédéric** 1900–58. French physicist. *b.* Paris. Assistant to Marie Curie (1925); married IRÈNE (1897–1956), French physicist and daughter of Marie Curie (1926). Discovered induced radioactivity and synthesized new elements, including radioactive nitrogen and phosphorus; with Irene, awarded Nobel Prize in chemistry (1935); high commissioner for atomic energy (1946–50); dismissed from post for Communist affiliations; on death from cancer, awarded state funeral.

Jolliet *(jŏl ĭ ĕt),* **Louis** 1645–1700. French explorer. *b.* Quebec, Canada. Commissioned by Frontenac to find the Mississippi River, which had been reported by Indians but never sighted by a white man (1672); with the Jesuit missionary Jacques Marquette and five other Frenchmen, discovered the Mississippi, Fox, Wisconsin, and Illinois rivers (1673); made explorations of Gulf of St. Lawrence and Hudson Bay regions.

Jones *(jōnz),* **Inigo** 1573–1652. English architect. *b.* London. Studied art and architecture in Italy; on return to England (1605) became court architect to Queen Elizabeth, and later James I and Charles I; designed sets and staging for court masques by Jonson, Shirley, Heywood, Davenant, and other playwrights; surveyor general of works (1615); introduced the classical style of Palladio into England. Principal works include the Whitehall Banqueting Hall, the portico of old St. Paul's, Marlborough Chapel, the Ashburnham house, Lincoln's Inn Chapel, and the Covent Garden piazza.

Jones, John Paul original name: JOHN PAUL. 1747–92. American naval hero. *b.* Kirkbean, Scotland. Began sailing at age 12; master of West Indian merchantman; after killing a crew member on the *Betsey,* left for the Colonies and settled in Virginia, adding Jones as surname to foil detection; on outbreak of Revolutionary War, offered services to Continental Congress; lieutenant (1775); commanded the first vessel to fly the Continental flag, the *Alfred* (1775); captain (1776); as commander of the *Providence, Ranger, Bonhomme Richard,* and *Ariel,* performed daring exploits including the capture of the British naval sloop *Drake,* a descent on the *Solway,* and the capture of two British men-of-war at Flamborough Head; received formal thanks of Congress (1781) and a gold medal (1787); entered Russian service as rear admiral (1788); returned to Paris where he died (1792).

Jones, Sir William 1746–94. English Orientalist. *b.* London. Called to the bar (1774); judge of the high court at Calcutta (1783–94); laid foundations of modern comparative philology with studies in Sanskrit and other Oriental languages; translated *Sakuntala, Hitopadesa,* and other Sanskrit works; other works include *Persian Grammar* (1772), *Moallakat* (1781), and *Poems, Consisting Chiefly of Translations from Asiatick Languages* (1772); also famous in jurisprudence as author of *Institutes of Hindu Law, Mohammedan Law of Succession,* and *Mohammedan Law of Inheritance;* founded the Bengal Asiatic Society (1784).

Jonson *(jŏn sən),* **Ben** 1572–1637. English playwright. *b.* Westminster. Began association with the stage (c1595); friend of Shakespeare, Donne, and other poets; wrote *Every Man in His Humour* (1598), in which Shakespeare acted; followed with *Every Man Out of His Humour* (1599), *Volpone* (1606), *Epicoene* (1609), *The Alchemist* (1610), *Bartholomew Fair* (1614), *Cynthia's Revels* (1600), *The Poetaster* (1601), *The Devil is an Ass* (1616), *The Staple of News* (1625), *The Magnetic Lady* (1632), *Tale of a Tub* (1633), and nearly 30 masques, of which *The Masque of Queens* (1609) and *Oberon* (1611) are the best-known; produced two Roman tragedies, *Catilene* (1611) and *Sejanus* (1603); ranks second only to Shakespeare among English lyrical poets; remembered for the poems "Drink to Me Only With Thine Eyes," "Hymn to Diana," "The Triumph of Charis," and "Epitaph on Salathiel Pavy"; prose writings collected in *Timber, or Discoveries Made Upon Men and Matter* (1640); conversations recorded by William Drummond, published (1832); regarded as the first, though unofficial, poet laureate; exerted dominant influence on a group of younger poets, the "tribe of Ben."

Joseph *(jō zəf),* **Chief** Indian name: HINMATON-YALAKTIT. 1840-

1904. Leader of the Nez Percé Indians. Refused to recognize treaty with white men; on the breakout of conflict, led a march of retreat with his men toward the Canadian border, but was defeated and captured by Gen. Nelson A. Miles (1877).

Joséphine *(zhō zä fēn)* full name: MARIE JOSÉPHINE ROSE TASCHER DE LA PAGERIE. 1763–1814. French empress (1804–1809). *b.* Martinique. Married Vicomte Alexandre de Beauharnais (1779); gained the affections of Napoleon and married him (1796), two years after the execution of Beauharnais; accompanied Napoleon on Italian campaigns; in Paris, attracted a brilliant circle of friends and contributed to her husband's growing power; the marriage, being childless, was dissolved (1809); retained the title of Empress until the fall of Napoleon.

Josephus *(jō sē fəs),* **Flavius** original name: JOSEPH BEN MATTHIAS. 37–c100. Hebrew historian. *b.* Jerusalem. Proficient in Hebrew and Greek literature; a leader of the Pharisees, chosen as delegate to Nero (64); appointed governor of Galilee by the Sanhedrin; joined last insurrection of the Jews against the Romans (66); valorously defended Jotapata for 47 days before surrendering to Vespasian; gained Vespasian's favor as a soothsayer; witnessed the destruction of the Temple (70) by Titus; later became a Roman citizen. Writings include *History of the Jewish War* (seven books), *Antiquities of the Jews* (20 books), *Autobiography,* and *Against Apion.*

Jouhaux *(zhōō ō),* **Léon** 1879–1954. French labor leader. *b.* Paris. Secretary-general of the French General Confederation of Labor (1909–40, 1945–47); president of the Economic Council of France (1947–54); awarded Nobel Peace Prize (1951).

Joule *(joul),* **James Prescott** 1818–89. English physicist. *b.* Salford. First to determine the mechanical equivalent of heat and to demonstrate that heat is a form of energy; with Lord Kelvin, formulated absolute scale of temperature; described the phenomenon of magnetostriction of an iron bar; formulated the First Law of Thermodynamics and Joule's Law; studied compressed gases and surface condensation; measured an electric current by a definite unit; the joule, a unit of work equivalent to ten million ergs, is named after him. Author of *Electro-Magnetic Forces* (1840), *On the Production of Heat by Voltaic Electricity* (1840), *On the Heat Evolved During the Electrolysis of Water* (1843), and other works.

Joyce *(jois),* **James Augustine Aloysius** 1882–1941. Irish writer. *b.* Dublin. Spent most of life as a voluntary exile in Switzerland, France, and Italy; published a collection of lyrics, *Chamber Music* (1907). Succeeding works include *Pomes Penyeach* (1927), *Collected Poems* (1927), *Dubliners* (1914), *Exiles* (1918), *A Portrait of the Artist as a Young Man* (1916), *Ulysses* (1922), and *Finnegans Wake* (1939); later works characterized by experimental prose techniques, labyrinthine allusions, and multiple puns; created words whose sounds expressed many levels of meaning, though they lack linguistic sense; abandoned sequential form of novel for stream of consciousness; with *Finnegans Wake* achieved a literary black hole, a phenomenon so dense with meaning that no light can escape from it; considered one of the authentic literary geniuses of modern times.

Juárez *(hwä rās),* **Benito Pablo** 1806–72. Mexican statesman. *b.* Guelatao. Born of Indian parents; governor of Oaxaca (1847); banished by Santa Anna (1853); joined Alvarez in deposing Santa Anna (1855); as minister of justice under Alvarez, authored Juarez Law abolishing religious orders, confiscating church property, abolishing special courts, and reducing power of the army; elected by the Liberals to succeed Ignacio Comonfort, who had been forced to flee the capital (1857); provisional president of Mexico (1857–61) with capital at Vera Cruz; victorious in civil war known as War of the Reform; elected president (1861) and reentered Mexico City; driven out by the invasion of Mexico by the French, English, and Spanish and the proclamation of an empire under Maximilian (1863); on withdrawal of the French and the execution of Maximilian (1867) regained Mexico City; elected president for two terms (1867–72) but faced continued insurrections; died in office while suppressing the revolt of Porfirio Díaz.

Judas Iscariot *(jōō däs ĭs kâr ĭ ət)* New Testament *fl.* 1st century. One of the 12 Apostles. *b.* Kerioth. The only non-Galilean among the Apostles of Christ; betrayed Christ to the Sanhedrin for 30 pieces of silver; believed to have committed suicide.

Julian *(jōōl yən),* Latin name: Flavius Claudius Julianus; called Julian the Apostate. 331–63. Emperor of Rome (361–63). *b.* Constantinople. Nephew of Constantine the Great; escaped the general massacre of males of the younger line of the Flavians; educated as a Christian but delighted in the study of Greek philosophy; created caesar and invested with the rule of Gaul, Spain, and Britain; defeated the Alemanni (357); proclaimed Augustus by the troops (360); set out for Constantinople with army; proclaimed himself a pagan at Sirmium; succeeded Constantius; granted toleration to all religions and stripped the Church of all its privileges; led campaign against Persia and died in battle.

Jung *(yōōng),* **Carl Gustav** 1875–1961. Swiss psychiatrist. *b.* Basel. Studied medicine and worked under Bleuler at Zurich; became associate of Freud and leading exponent of his theories (1907–13); president of International Psychoanalytic Association (1910–14); opposed Freud's emphasis on the sex instinct as the primary element in the libido and broke with him (from 1913); founded the analytical school of psychology; developed the concepts of complexes to signify clusters of emotional ideas, introverted and extroverted psychological types, symbols as transformers of psychic energy, the collective unconscious containing archetypes of inherited tendencies, and individuation as the process by which the psyche regulates itself; saw neurosis as evidence of a healthy though frustrated drive to achieve maturity; stressed the active role of the psychoanalyst.

Author of *Psychology of Dementia Praecox* (1906–1907), *The Theory of Psychoanalysis* (1912), *Psychology of the Unconscious* (1916), *Studies in Word Association* (1918), *Contributions to Analytical Psychology* (1928), *Modern Man in Search of a Soul* (1933), *On Psychic Energy* (1928), *Psychology and Religion* (1937), *Psychology and Alchemy* (1944), *Aion* (1951), *The Undiscovered Self* (1957), *Psychological Factors Determining Human Behavior* and *Essays on Contemporary Events* (1947).

Justinian I *(jŭs tĭn ĭ ən)* full name: Flavius Anicius Sabbatius Justinianus; also called Justinian the Great. 483–565. Eastern Roman Emperor (527–65). *b.* Tauresium, Illyria. Named consul (521); admitted as co-caesar by uncle Justin I; succeeded Justin as emperor; aided by generals Narses and Belisarius, extended the empire to its former limits; destroyed the Vandal and Ostrogothic power in Italy, North Africa, and Spain and restored these territories to the empire; after two inconclusive wars, made peace with Persia (531); suppressed the Green and Blue factions which had rent Constantinople; sponsored a vast building program throughout the empire that included forts, monasteries, and churches, especially the Santa Sophia at Constantinople and the San Vitale in Ravenna; issued the celebrated *Corpus Juris Civilis,* the foundation of Roman law, containing all imperial statutes *(Codex Constitutionem),* commentaries of jurists *(Digesta* or *Pandectae),* textbooks for legal students *(Institutes),* and new laws and constitutions *(Novellae).*

Juvenal *(jo͞o vĕ nəl)* full name: Decimus Junius Juvenalis. c60–c140. Roman satirist. *b.* Aquinum, Italy. Author of 16 extant satires denouncing the corruption, vice, and extravagance of Roman society under Trajan.

K

Kafka *(käf kä),* **Franz** 1883–1924. Austrian writer. *b.* Prague, Czechoslovakia. An introspective writer who explored the metaphysical dilemmas of the human condition; established a genre of writing that combines clarity of style with a febrile and surrealist imagination. Principal works include *The Trial* (1937), *The Castle* (1937), *Amerika* (1937), *Diaries, 1914–1923* (1949), *Letters* (1953), *Conversations* (1953), and short stories, including "Metamorphosis," "The Judgment," "In the Penal Colony," and "The Boilerman"; works have exerted a deep influence on later existentialist writers.

Kalidasa *(kä lĭ dä sä) fl.* 5th century. Indian poet and dramatist. One of the Nava Ratna (nine gems) of the court of King Vikramaditya. Author of the great Sanskrit drama *Sakuntala;* also wrote *Vikramorvasi;* other works ascribed to him include ***Raghu-***

vamsa, Kumarasambhava, Meghaduta, Ritusamhara, Nalodava, and *Srutabogha.*

Kamerlingh Onnes *(kȧ mər ling ôn ĕs),* **Heike** 1853–1926. Dutch physicist. *b.* Groningen. Professor of physics at Leiden; conducted important investigations into the properties of matter at low temperatures; liquefied helium and obtained temperature within one degree of absolute zero, a state in which certain metals have nil electrical resistance; awarded Nobel Prize in physics (1913).

Kandinski *(kŭn dyə̄n skĭ),* **Vasili** also WASSILY KANDINSKI. 1866–1944. Russian painter. *b.* Moscow. Studied painting in Munich (1900); formulated principles of nonrepresentational art in essay "On the Spiritual in Art" (1910); painted first nonobjective work (1911); with Franz Marc, founded the Blue Rider school and wrote *Blaue Reiter;* exhibited in Berlin and other cities; returned to Russia (1914) and founded the Russian Academy and the Institute of Artistic Culture; returned to Germany (1921); taught at the Bauhaus (until 1933); settled in Paris; wrote *Autobiography, Point, Line, and Plane,* and other books.

Kant *(känt),* **Immanuel** 1724–1804. German philosopher. *b.* Königsburg. In three major works, *Critique of Pure Reason* (1781), *Critique of Practical Reason* (1788), and *Critique of the Power of Judgment* (1790), formulated a comprehensive system of philosophy whose principal purpose was to define the nature and limits of knowledge; distinguished sharply between the world of phenomena, which we can experience, and the noumenal world of things-in-themselves, which reason and intellect cannot fathom; held that God, the world as a whole, and soul belonged to the second world; held that moral conduct rested on the categorical imperative: Act as if the maxim from which you act were to become, through your will, a universal law; held liberal religious and political views, but steered philosophy away from both skepticism and dogmatism. Other principal works include *General History of Nature and Theory of the Heavens* (1755); *Observations on the Sense of the Beautiful and the Sublime* (1764), *On the Form and Principles of the Sensible and Intelligible World* (1770), *Principles of the Metaphysics of Ethics* (1785), *Religion within the Limits of Mere Reason* (1793), and *Metaphysics of Morals* (1797).

Kapitza *(kȧ pyĭ tsə),* **Peter Leonidovich** 1894–. Russian physicist. *b.* Kronstadt. Worked under Lord Rutherford at Cambridge (1924–32); returned to Russia to head the Institute for Physical Problems (1935); conducted researches on atomic structure, magnetism, low temperature, and cosmic rays.

Karlfeldt *(kärl fĕlt),* **Erik Axel** 1864–1931. Swedish poet. *b.* Folkärna. Noted for robust descriptions of nature and rustic life. Principal works include *Dalecarlian Frescoes in Rhyme* (1901), *Songs of Love and the Wilderness* (1895), *The Songs of Fridolin and Other Poems* (1898), *Flora and Pomona* (1906), *Flora and Bellona* (1918), and *Autumnal Cornucopia* (1927); declined Nobel Prize in literature (1918) and was awarded it posthumously (1931).

Karo, Joseph ben Ephraim. *See* **Caro, Joseph Ben Ephraim**

Karrer *(kär ər),* **Paul** 1889–1971. Swiss chemist. *b.* Moscow, Russia. Professor at Zurich (1918–59); contributions to chemistry include determination of the structures of vitamin A, carotene, lycopene, xanthophyll, crocetin, and riboflavin; isolation of vitamin K, and synthesis of vitamin E; shared Nobel Prize in chemistry (1937) with W.N. Haworth.

Kastler *(kȧst lâr),* **Alfred** 1902–. French physicist. Awarded Nobel Prize in physics (1966) for the development of lasers and atomic clocks, and the discovery of optical methods for studying Herzian resonances in atoms.

Katsura *(kä tsö rä),* **Taro** 1847–1913. Japanese statesman and prince. Studied in Germany; minister for war (1898–1900); premier (1901–1906, 1908–11, 1912–13); concluded Anglo-Japanese Treaty (1902), which later contributed to the Japanese victory over Russia (1904).

Katz *(kăts),* **Sir Bernard** 1911–. British physiologist. *b.* in Germany. Immigrated to England (1935); taught at the University College (from 1950); shared, with J. Axelrod and Ulf von Euler, Nobel Prize in physiology and medicine (1970) for determination of the nature of substances found at the end of nerve fibers.

Kaufman *(kôf mən),* **George Simon** 1889–1961. American playwright. *b.* Pittsburgh, Pa. Principal dramatic works include *You Can't Take It with You* (1936), *The Man Who Came to Dinner* (1939), *The Solid Gold Cadillac* (1953), *Beggar on Horseback* (1924), *Of Thee I Sing*, (Pulitzer Prize 1931), *Stage Door* (1936), *Dinner at Eight* (1932), *June Moon* (1929), *I'd Rather Be Right* (1937), *Once in a Lifetime* (1930), *Park Avenue* (1946); collaborated with Marc Connelly, Edna Ferber, Ring Lardner, and Moss Hart; author of *The Butter and Egg Man* (1925).

Kawabata *(kä wä bä tä),* **Yasunari** 1899–1972. Japanese writer. *b.* Osaka. Gained recognition with the novel *Dancer of Izu Province* (1925); experimented with Western modes of fiction but later returned to Japanese traditional story techniques. Best works include *Red Group of Asakusa* (1930), *Snow Country* (1947), *Thousand Cranes* (1949), and *Kyoto* (1962); awarded Nobel Prize in literature (1968).

Keats *(kēts),* **John** 1795–1821. English poet. *b.* London. Studied medicine but abandoned it for poetry; encouraged by Leigh Hunt, wrote early sonnets in Hunt's *Examiner;* early works largely neglected and somewhat savagely attacked; later work, beginning with *Lamia, Isabella, The Eve of St. Agnes, and Other Poems,* considered some of the finest poetry in English for its matchless perfection, gemlike beauty, and sensuous imagery; the Miltonic *Hyperion,* unfinished at death, the great odes—on melancholy, on a Grecian urn, to Psyche, to Autumn, and to a nightingale—constitute the best expression of his genius; letters to friends and family regarded as models of literary correspondence; having no taste for metaphysics or utopias, believed that truth is beauty and beauty truth; struck with tuberculosis; sailed to Italy to recuperate but died in Rome (1820). Other works include "On First Looking into Chapman's Homer," "Endymion," and "La Belle Dame Sans Merci."

Kefauver *(kē fä vûr),* **Estes Carey** 1903–63. American statesman. *b.* Madisonville, Tenn. Democratic member of House of Representatives (1939–49); U.S. Senate (1949–63); headed the Senate Crime Investigating Committee (1950–51); unsuccessful candidate for the vice-presidency (1952, 1956).

Kekule von Stradonitz *(kā ko͞o lā fōn shträ dō nĭts),* **Friedrich August** 1829–96. German chemist. *b.* Darmstadt. Professor of chemistry at Bonn (1895–96); demonstrated the tetravalency of carbon; explained stability of aromatic compounds by the formula of benzene rings, or closed chains, which laid the foundation of synthetic chemistry.

Keller *(kĕl ər),* **Gottfried** 1819–90. Swiss poet and novelist. *b.* Zurich. Considered one of the greatest German prose writers; employed brilliant powers of description, irony, and characterization to portray Swiss provincial life. Author of the autobiographical *Der Grüne Heinrich* (4 vols., 1854–55), *Martin Salander* (1886), *People of Seldwyla* (1856), *Sieben Legenden* (1872), *Zuricher Novellen* (1878), and *Das Sinngedicht* (1881).

Keller, Helen Adams 1880–1968. American author. *b.* Tuscumbia, Ala. Noted for her heroic efforts to overcome effects of complete loss of sight and hearing at the age of two; personal courage served as inspiration for many Americans; lectured widely for the cause of the deaf and blind. Author of *The Story of My Life* (1902), *Optimism* (1903), *The World I Live In* (1908), *Out of the Dark* (1913), *My Religion* (1927), *Helen Keller's Journal* (1938), *Let Us Have Faith* (1940), and *Autobiography and Letters* (1946).

Kellogg *(kĕl ôg),* **Frank Billings** 1856–1937. American statesman. *b.* Potsdam, N.Y. Prominent corporation lawyer and, later, special counsel for government in antitrust cases; senator (1917–23); ambassador to Great Britain (1924–25); secretary of state (1925–29); negotiated nearly 80 treaties, especially the Briand-Kellogg Pact (with Aristide Briand) outlawing war (1928); judge of the permanent Court of International Justice at Hague (from 1930); awarded Nobel Peace Prize (1929).

Kelvin *(kĕl vĭn),* **Baron William Thomson** 1824–1907. British scientist. *b.* Belfast, Ireland. Professor of natural philosophy at Glasgow (1846–99); proposed the Kelvin (absolute) scale of temperature; formulated two great laws of thermodynamics, including the doctrine of dissipation of energy; developed theory of electrical oscillations; invented over 56 telegraphic, navigational, mechanical, and electrical instruments, such as the electrometer, tide predictor, mirror galvanometer, siphon recorder, and curb transmitter; investigations on the transmission of electric currents in submarine cables helped make the Atlantic cable a reality; made important investigations in thermodynamics, hydrodynamics, electrostatics, magnetism, elasticity, and electrometry. Principal scientific works include *Treatise on Natural Philosophy* (1867–74), *On Vortex Atoms* (1867), *On Molecular Dynamics and the Wave Theory of Light* (1884), *On the Electrodynamic Properties of Metals* (1885), *Navigation* (1876), *Mathematical and Physical Papers* (1882–90), and *Lectures and Addresses* (1889–91).

Kemal Ataturk *(kĕ mäl ä tä türk)* also Mustafa Kemal, Kemal Pasha; title: Ghazi. 1881–1938. Turkish general and statesman. *b.* Salonika. Entered army as lieutenant; engaged in radical left-wing politics at Damascus, Jaffa, and Salonika; fought in Turkish-Italian War (1911); commanded Turkish defenses on the Gallipoli peninsula, in Caucasus, and in Palestine; awarded title of Pasha; organized Nationalist party to oppose terms of armistice; established provisional government at Ankara with himself as head (1920); led Turkish resistance to Greek occupation of Asia Minor; defeated Greeks at Sakarya River and drove them from Anatolia and Thrace after murdering millions (1921); took Smyrna (1922); named Ghazi (Victorious); obtained favorable terms from the Allies by Treaty of Lausanne (1923); on deposition of sultanate, elected president (1923); introduced domestic reforms including the dissolution of the caliphate and monasteries, adoption of monogamy, equal inheritance rights for women, the Gregorian calendar, the Swiss civil code, Latin script, enforced registration of family names, prohibited the use of fez by men and veils by women; granted the title of Ataturk by the National Assembly.

Kendall *(kĕn dəl),* **Edward Calvin** 1886–1972. American biochemist. *b.* South Norwalk, Conn. Professor of biochemistry at University of Minnesota and head of chemical section at Mayo Clinic (1914–51); isolated thyroxin, glutathione, and cortisone; established efficacy of cortisone and ACTH in alleviating rheumatism and arthritis; with P.S. Hench and T. Reichstein, shared Nobel Prize in physiology and medicine (1950).

Kendrew *(dĕn drü),* **John Cowdery** 1917–. British scientist. *b.* Oxford. With Max Perutz, investigated the chemistry of the blood and discovered the structure of myoglobin; shared Nobel Prize in chemistry (1962) with Perutz.

Kennedy *(kən ə dĭ),* **Edward Moore** 1932–. American statesman. *b.* Brookline, Mass. Brother of John F. Kennedy and Robert F. Kennedy; son of Joseph P. Kennedy; U.S. senator (1964); articulate spokesman of liberal Democratic senators, pushing reforms in the fields of health care and welfare.

Kennedy, John Fitzgerald 1917–63. 35th president of U.S. (1961–63). *b.* Brookline, Mass. House of Representatives (1947–53); Senate (1953–60); elected president on Democratic ticket (1961), the first Roman Catholic to hold that office; launched ambitious domestic program known as the New Frontier; inspired space program with the goal of placing a man on the moon by the end of the decade; established Peace Corps; in memorable confrontation with U.S.S.R., forced Russians to remove missiles from Cuba; concluded Nuclear Test Ban Treaty; advocated strong civil rights legislation, medical care for the aged, and increased federal aid to education; enhanced prestige of the presidency with a new vision and style; assassinated in Dallas (1963). Author of *Profiles in Courage* (1957).

Kennedy, Joseph Patrick 1888–1969. American businessman and diplomat. *b.* Boston, Mass. Built up a massive fortune in banking, real estate, shipping, liquors, and motion picture distribution; chairman of Securities and Exchange Commission (1934–35) and U.S. Maritime Commission (1936–37); ambassador to Great Britain (1937–40); transmitted his ambition to his four sons, producing one U.S. president and two U.S. senators.

Kennedy, Robert Francis 1925–68. American statesman. *b.* Brookline, Mass. Brother of John F. Kennedy and Edward M. Kennedy; son of Joseph P. Kennedy; served at sea during World War II (1944–46); helped to prosecute top union leaders as a member of the Senate Select Subcommittee on Improper Activities (1957–59); managed John's presidential campaign (1960); named attorney general (1961–64), retaining office under President Lyndon B. Johnson; initiated the major civil rights reforms; elected senator from N.Y. (1965–68) on the Democratic ticket; candidate for Democratic presidential nomination (1968); assassinated by Sirhan Bishara Sirhan (1968).

Kenny *(kĕn ē),* **Elizabeth** 1886–1952. Australian nurse. *b.* Warrialda. Developed a new method of treating infantile paralysis using hot moist applications and passive exercise; method adopted by Australian hospitals; came to U.S. (1940); established the Elizabeth Kenny Institute under the auspices of the University of Minnesota. Author of *And They Shall Walk* (1934).

Kent *(kĕnt),* **James** 1763–1847. American jurist. *b.* Fredericksburgh, N.Y. Professor of law at Columbia (1793–98, 1823–26); N.Y. Supreme Court (1798), becoming chief judge (1804); chancellor of N.Y. Court of Chancery (1814–23); laid the basis of the American system of equity jurisdiction. Wrote *Commentaries on American Law* (4 vols., 1826–28), a standard authority that has guided generations of lawyers.

Kepler *(kĕp lər),* **Johannes** 1571–1630. German astronomer. *b.* Weil der Stadt. Educated at University of Tubingen; professor at Graz (1593–99); published treatise *Mysterium Cosmographicum* (1596), which caught the attention of Tycho Brahe; at Prague, as assistant to Brahe (1600); on Brahe's death (1601), became imperial astronomer and court mathematician; also worked at Linz, Ulm, and Sagan; announced three laws of planetary motion in *Astronomia Nova de Motibus Stellae Martis* (1609) and *Harmonice Mundi* (1619); also wrote on optics, calculus, geometry, and novae, and published an expanded edition of Brahe's *Rudolphine Tables* (1627).

Kerenski *(kyĭ ryān skĭ),* **Alexandr Feodorovich** 1881–1970. Russian statesman. *b.* Simbirsk. Elected to Duma as member of Labor party

(1912), gaining reputation as an orator; after February Revolution (1917), served as minister of justice and minister of war in provisional government; succeeded Prince Lvov as prime minister (1917); ousted by Bolsheviks; in exile in Paris and U.S. Author of *The Prelude to Bolshevism* (1919), *The Catastrophe* (1927), *The Road to Tragedy* (1935), and *The Kerensky Memoirs* (1966).

Kern *(kûrn),* **Jerome David** 1885–1945. American composer. *b.* New York, N.Y. Best known for musical scores *Sally* (1920), *Sunny* (1925), *Show Boat* (1927), *Sweet Adeline* (1929), *The Cat and the Fiddle* (1931), *Music in the Air* (1932), and *Roberta* (1933), and for the songs "Ol' Man River," "Smoke Gets in Your Eyes," "Look for the Silver Lining," and "All the Things You Are."

Kerouac *(kĕr ə wăk),* **Jack** 1922–69. American novelist. *b.* Lowell, Mass. Known as laureate of his generation, for which he coined the term "beat," and which he described in *On the Road* (1957), *The Town and the City* (1950), *The Subterraneans* (1958), and *Big Sur* (1962).

Kesey *(kĕ sĭ),* **Ken** 1935–. American writer. *b.* La Junta, Colo. Author of *One Flew Over the Cuckoo's Nest* (1962), which was successfully dramatized, and *Sometimes a Great Notion* (1964).

Key *(kē),* **Francis Scott** 1779–1843. American lawyer. *b.* Frederick County, Md. While negotiating the exchange of an American prisoner-of-war during War of 1812, detained overnight on a British man-of-war; witnessed the bombardment of Fort McHenry at Baltimore; moved by the sight of U.S. flag still flying over the fort, he scribbled the verses of "The Star-Spangled Banner" on the back of an envelope; song officially adopted as the national anthem (1931).

Keynes *(kānz),* **John Maynard** title: BARON KEYNES OF TILTON. 1883–1946. British economist. *b.* Cambridge. A leading member of the Bloomsbury group; member of Royal Commission on Indian Finance and Currency (1913); editor of the *Economic Journal* (1912–46); principal representative of the British Treasury at Paris Peace Conference (1919); resigned from Versailles Commission and strongly opposed terms of Versailles Treaty in *Economic Consequences of the Peace* (1919); published *Treatise of Probability* (1921); criticized restoration of the gold standard (1925); during Great Depression, developed Keynesian theory of planned economy and controlled capitalism in two landmark works: *A Treatise on Money* (1930) and *General Theory of Employment, Interest, and Money* (1936); advocated large-scale government spending to overcome unemployment and business stagnation; theories influenced Roosevelt's New Deal; active in creation of the Bretton Woods Agreement and establishing the International Monetary Fund. Other works include *A Tract on Monetary Reform* (1923), *The End of Laissez-Faire* (1926), *How to Pay for the War* (1940), *Essays in Persuasion* (1931), and *Essays in Biography* (1933).

Keyserling *(kī sər lĭng),* **Count Hermann Alexander** 1880–1946.

German philosopher. *b.* Koenno, Livonia. Achieved fame with journal of a trip around the world, *The Travel Diary of a Philosopher* (1925); established School of Wisdom at Darmstadt, which taught a synthesis of Western and Eastern thought. Principal works include *Creative Understanding* (1922), *The Recovery of Truth* (1927), *The Art of Life* (1936), *Immortality* (1937), and *From Suffering to Fulfillment* (1938).

Khachaturian *(käch ə to͝or ĭ ən),* **Aram Ilich** 1903–78. Russian composer. *b.* Tiflis. Best known for rhythmic and colorful compositions based on folk songs and Oriental themes. Works include the ballets *Gayne* and *Masquerade,* two symphonies, *Piano Concerto, 'Cello Concerto, Toccata, Violin Concerto in D Minor,* and *Happiness.*

Khorana *(kō rä nȧ),* **Har Gobind** 1922–. American scientist. *b.* Punjab, India. Shared, with Robert W. Holley and Marshall W. Nirenberg, Nobel Prize in physiology (1968) for discovery of the process by which enzymes, consisting of a sequence of amino acids, determine a cell's function in genetic development.

Khosrau I *(kŏ srou)* also Chosroes, Khosru; called Khosrau Anushirvan. *d.* 579. 21st Sassanian king of Persia (531–79). In two wars with Justinian (531–32, 540–45), forced Byzantium to pay tribute; renewed war against Justin II; extended Persian empire from Indus River to Red Sea and Central Asia; reign marks the flowering of Pahlavi literature and the renaissance of Zoroastrianism; encouraged trade and agriculture.

Khowarizmi, al-. *See* **al-Khowarizmi**

Khrushchev *(kro͞osh chôf),* **Nikita Sergeevich** 1894–1971. Soviet statesman. *b.* Kalinovka. Joined Communist party (1918) and fought in Civil War; full member of Politburo and presidium of the Supreme Soviet (by 1939); in charge of Soviet agricultural reorganization (1949); first secretary of Communist party on Stalin's death (1953); denounced Stalinism and the cult of personality at 20th Congress of Communist party (1956); premier (1958); visited Western countries, including U.S. (1959); signed Test-Ban Treaty (1963); brutally suppressed the Hungarian Revolution (1956); policies led to rift with China; deposed (1964).

Kierkegaard *(kĭr kə gôr),* **Sören Aabye** 1813–55. Danish philosopher. *b.* Copenhagen. Opposed both Hegelianism and organized forms of religion with his "existential dialectic"; emphasized individual moral loneliness and the dilemmas of religious commitment; defined faith as a leap across a chasm and explored the fear of an individual alone before God; greatly influenced religious and secular philosophers. Principal works include *Either/Or* (1843), *Philosophical Fragments* (1844), *Concluding Unscientific Postscript* (1846), *Stages on Life's Way* (1845), *Works of Love* (1817), *Training in Christianity* (1815), and *Sickness Unto Death.*

Kilmer *(kĭl mər),* **Alfred Joyce** 1886–1918. American poet. *b.* New Brunswick, N.J. Best remembered as the author of "Trees" in *Trees and Other Poems* (1914).

Other works include *Summer of Love* (1911), *Main Street and Other Poems* (1917), *The Circus and Other Essays* (1916), and *Literature in the Making* (1917); killed in action in World War I.

Kim Il Sung *(kĭm ĭl sûng)* 1912– . Korean statesman. *b.* Mangyongdoe, Pyongyang. Organized Communist Youth League (1927); founded the Fatherland Restoration Association (1936) and the Working Party of Korea (1945); organized the Korean People's Army (1948); first head of state of the Democratic People's Republic of Korea (1948), serving as its premier (1948–72) and president (from 1972); headed North Korean army during Korean War (1950–53).

King *(kĭng),* **Martin Luther, Jr.** 1929–68. American clergyman and civil rights leader. *b.* Atlanta, Ga. Minister in Montgomery, Ala.; rose to national fame as leader of a bus boycott; founder and president of the Southern Christian Leadership Conference; spearheaded civil rights agitation with Gandhian techniques of passive resistance and nonviolent demonstrations; led historic march on Washington (1964); received Nobel Peace Prize; assassinated in Memphis, Tenn. (1968). Author of *Where Do We Go from Here?* (1967).

King, Rufus 1755–1827. American statesman. *b.* Scarboro, Me. Member of the Continental Congress (1784–87) and Constitutional Convention (1787); U.S. senator (1789–96, 1813–25) U.S. minister to Great Britain (1796–1803, 1825–26); unsuccessful candidate for the vice-presidency (1804, 1808), and for the presidency (1816).

King, William Lyon Mackenzie 1874–1950. Canadian statesman. *b.* Kitchener, Ont. Entered Dominion Parliament (1908); minister of labor (1909–14); succeeded Sir William Laurier as leader of Liberal party (1919); prime minister (1921–26, 1926–30, 1935–48); advocated dominion autonomy; led Canada during World War II; active in San Francisco Conference (1945).

King, William Rufus DeVane 1786–1853. American statesman. *b.* Sampson County, North Carolina. Entered U.S. House of Representatives (1810); U.S. senator from Alabama (1820–44, 1846–53); U.S. minister to France (1844–46); elected to the vice-presidency just before his death.

Kingsley *(kĭngz lĭ),* **Charles** 1819–75. English novelist. *b.* Holne. Studied for the Church and became rector of Eversley and canon of Middleham (1845), Chester (1869), and Westminster (1873); chaplain to Queen Victoria (1859); professor of literature at London and of modern history at Cambridge (from 1860); as a Christian socialist leader, wrote tracts and two novels, *Alton Locke* (1850) and *Yeast* (1851), dealing with social themes. Best known for historical novels *Hypatia* (1853), *Westward Ho!* (1855), *Two Years Ago* (1857), *Hereward the Wake* (1866); other works include *Glaucus* (1855), *Prose Idylls* (1873), and the poem "The Saint's Tragedy" (1848).

Kipling *(kĭp lĭng),* **Rudyard** 1865–1936. English novelist. *b.* Bombay, India. Educated in England (1871–82); returned to India as journalist on *Civil and Military Gazette* of Lahore; began writing stories and poems; left India (1889); in England (1889–92); in Brattleboro, Vt. (1892–97); lived rest of life in England; identified with the Tory jingoism of imperial Britain, but also recognized as a master of the short adventure story; awarded Nobel Prize in literature (1907). Works include *Departmental Ditties* (1886), *Plain Tales from the Hills* (1888), *Soldiers Three, In Black and White, Wee Willie Winkie* (1888), *The Light That Failed* (1891), *Barrack-Room Ballads* (1892), *Many Inventions* (1893), *The Jungle Book* (1894), *The Second Jungle Book* (1895), *The Seven Seas* (1896), *Captains Courageous* (1897), *The Day's Work* (1898), *Stalky and Co.* (1899), *Kim* (1901), *Just-So Stories* (1902), *The Five Nations* (1903), *Traffics and Discoveries* (1904), *Puck of Pook's Hill* (1906), *Actions and Reactions* (1909), *Rewards and Fairies* (1910), *A Diversity of Creatures* (1917), *The Years Between* (1918), *Debits and Credits* (1926), *A Book of Words* (1928), *Limits and Renewals* (1932), and *Something of Myself* (1937).

Kirchhoff *(kĭrch hōf),* **Gustav Robert** 1824–87. German physicist. *b.* Königsberg. Professor of physics at Heidelberg (1854–74) and Berlin (1874–87); with R. W. Bunsen, discovered method of spectrum analysis (1859), leading to discovery of the elements cesium and rubidium; investigated solar spectrum; founded the science of astrophysics; formulated Kirchhoff's law; conducted research on electricity and optics.

Kissinger *(kĭs ĭn jər),* **Henry Alfred** 1923–. American statesman. *b.* Fürth, Germany. Immigrated to U.S. (1938); taught at Harvard (1951–69); special assistant to the president for national security affairs (1969); secretary of state (1973–77); negotiated Treaty of Paris, which ended Vietnam War (1973); awarded Nobel Peace Prize (1973); conducted "shuttle diplomacy" that restored peace to the Middle East after the October War; by untiring efforts, maintained détente with Soviet Union and helped open diplomatic doors to China.

Kitasato *(kē tä zä tō),* **Shibasaburo** 1856–1931. Japanese bacteriologist. *b.* Kumamoto. Studied in Berlin under Robert Koch (1886–91); on return to Japan, became director of the Institute for Infectious Diseases at Shiteta (from 1896); isolated plague bacillus (1894), tetanus bacillus (1889), dysentery bacillus (1898), and anthrax bacillus (1889); produced a diphtheria antitoxin (1890).

Kitchener *(kĭch ə nər),* **Horatio Herbert** title: EARL KITCHENER OF KHARTOUM AND OF BROOME. 1850–1916. British general. *b.* County Kerry, Ireland. Commissioned (1871); served in expedition for relief of General Gordon at Khartoum (1884): sirdar (commander in chief) of Egyptian army (from 1890); reconquered the Sudan from the Mahdi and reoccupied Khartoum (1898); governor general of the Sudan (1899); chief of staff and commander in chief in South Africa during Boer War (1900–1902); after Boer War, appointed commander in chief of Indian army; on outbreak of World War I, made secretary of state for war (1914); expanded British army from 20 to 70 divisions; lost aboard ship *H. M. S. Hampshire* (1916).

Klaproth *(kläp rōt),* **Martin Heinrich** 1743–1817. German chemist. *b.* Wernigerode. First professor of chemistry at Berlin University; discovered the elements uranium, zirconium, and titanium; pioneered chemical analysis; named tellurium; called Father of analytical chemistry.

Klee *(klā),* **Paul** 1879–1940. Swiss painter. *b.* Münchenbuchsee. With Marc and Kandinsky, founded Blue Rider group at Munich (1911–12) and with Kubin, Macke, Feininger, and others founded the Blue Four movement (1926); professor at the Bauhaus (from 1920); with the rise of Nazi Germany, returned to Switzerland (1933); work combined surrealist and dadaist elements in a highly individual style. Best-known works include *Twittering Machine, Landscape with Yellow Birds, Musical Dinner Party, Mask of Fear, Triumph of Wit Over Suffering, Pastorale,* and *Man on a Tightrope;* author of *Pädagogisches Skizzenbuch* (1925).

Kleist *(klīst),* **Heinrich von** 1777–1811. German dramatist and poet. *b.* Frankfurt-on-the Oder. In the army (1795–99); devoted himself to pamphleteering and literature (from 1799); edited *Phöbus* (1808) and *Berliner Abendblätter* (1811); after period of despondency and neglect, committed suicide; gained posthumous fame for *Die Familie Schroffenstein* (1803), *Penthesilea* (1808), *Das Käthchen von Heilbronn* (1810), *Die Hermannsschlacht* (1821), *Der Zerbrochene Krug* (1811), *Der Prinz von Homburg* (1821), and *Michael Kohlhaas* (1808).

Klopstock *(klōp shtōk),* **Friedrich Gottlieb** 1724–1803. German poet. *b.* Quedlinburg. Best known for religious epic *Der Messias* (1748–73), written in hexameters in 20 cantos; wrote religious dramas *Der Tod Adams* (1757), *David* (1772), and *Salomo* (1772), historical dramas *Hermannsschlacht* (1769), *Hermann und die Fürsten* (1784), and *Hermanns Tod* (1787); introduced bardic choruses called bardietes; other works include *Die Gelehrtenrepublik* (1774), *Oden* (1771), and *Geistliche Lieder* (1758).

Knox *(nŏks),* **John** 1505–72. Scottish reformer. *b.* Haddington. Ordained Roman Catholic priest (1530); through association with George Wishart, became a Protestant (1547); made common cause with the assassins of Cardinal Beaton; captured by French and incarcerated in France (1548); on release (1549), returned to England as chaplain to Edward VI; assisted Cranmer in drafting the 42 articles and in revising the Book of Common Prayer; on accession of Mary, fled to the Continent (1553); strengthened connection with Calvin; published *First Blast of the Trumpet Against the Monstrous Regiment of Women* (1558), *Treatise on Predestination* (1560), and other works; issued the prayer book *Book of Common Order* (1564); returned to Scotland on invitation of the Protestant signatories of the First Covenant; aided establishment of Presbyterianism as dominant church of Scotland; maintained unyielding hostility to Mary, Queen of Scots; wrote *History of the Reformation of Religioun Within the Realme of Scotland* (1584); before death, realized ambition of making Calvinism secure in Scotland.

Koch *(kōK),* **Robert** 1843–1910. German bacteriologist. *b.* Klausthal. Professor of medicine at Berlin (1800), director of the Institute of Health (1885), and director of the Institute for Infectious Diseases (1891); developed techniques of bacteriological culturing and identified the causative bacilli of anthrax (1876), tuberculosis (1882), Asiatic cholera (1883), and rinderpest (1896); investigated bubonic plague, malaria, and sleeping sickness; developed vaccine against rinderpest and anthrax; obtained tuberculin used in diagnosis of tuberculosis; awarded Nobel Prize in physiology and medicine (1905).

Kocher *(kō Kər),* **Emil Theodor** 1841–1917. Swiss surgeon. *b.* Berne. Professor at Berne (from 1872); contributed to the study of the thyroid gland and was the first to conduct successful goiter operations; awarded Nobel Prize in physiology and medicine (1909).

Kodaly *(kō dī),* **Zoltán** 1882–1967. Hungarian composer. *b.* Kecskemét. With Béla Bartók, collected nearly 4000 Hungarian folk melodies; in own music, combined folk music with ultramodern harmonies. Principal works include *Summer Evening* (1906), *Háry János* (1927), *Dances of Galanta* (1933), *Psalmus Hungaricus,* and *Missa Brevis.*

Koestler *(kĕst lər),* **Arthur** 1905–. English writer. *b.* Budapest, Hungary. Worked as a journalist in Palestine, Paris, and Berlin; became a Communist, but after visiting U.S.S.R. (1932–33) repudiated Stalinism; covered Spanish Civil War; imprisoned by Franco and later by Vichy France and the British; enlisted in British army during World War II. Author of *Spanish Testament* (1938), *The Gladiators* (1939), *Darkness at Noon* (1941), *Scum of the Earth* (1941), *Dialogue with Death* (1942), *Arrival and Departure* (1943), *Thieves in the Night* (1946), *Yogi and the Commissar* (1945), *Insight and Outlook* (1949), *Promise and Fulfilment* (1949), *The Trail of the Dinosaur* (1955), *The Sleepwalker* (1959), *The Age of Longing* (1952), *Arrow in the Blue* (1952), *The Act of Creation* (1964), *The Ghost in the Machine* (1967), and *The Call Girls* (1973).

Koffka *(kôf kə),* **Kurt** 1886–1941. American psychologist. *b.* Berlin, Germany. Emigrated to U.S. (1927); taught at Smith College (from 1928); with Max Wertheimer and Wolfgang Köhler, founded Gestalt psychology. Author of *Growth of the Mind* (1924) and *Principles of Gestalt Psychology* (1935).

Köhler *(kû lər),* **Wolfgang** 1887–1967. German psychologist. *b.* Reval, Estonia. Professor of psychology at Grottingen (1921) and Berlin (1922); emigrated to U.S. (1935); professor at Swarthmore College; conducted benchmark investigations with apes; one of the founders of Gestalt psychology. Author of *The Mentality of Apes* (1925), *Gestalt Psychologie* (1929–30), *The New Psychology and Physics* (1930), *The Place of Value in a World of Facts* (1938), *Dynamics in Psychology* (1940), and *Gestalt Psychology* (1947).

Kokoschka *(kō kōsh kä),* **Oskar** 1886–. Austrian painter and dramatist. *b.* Pöchlarn. Professor at Dresden Academy of Art

(1919–24); sought political asylum in England (1938); naturalized as British subject (1947); noted for expressionistic paintings and dramas. Paintings include *Woman with Parrot, Elbe at Dresden, Port of Dover,* and *The Arabs;* poetic dramas include *Mörder, Hoffnung der Frauen* (1907), *The Burning Thornbush* (1911), *Hiob* (1917), and *Orpheus und Eurydike* (1923).

Kollwitz *(kōl vĭts),* **Käthe** 1867–1945. German painter. *b.* Königsburg. Best known for superb lithographs depicting the horrors of war, the grief of poverty, and the tragedy of death; contributed to *Simplicissimus* (from 1910); silenced by the Nazis. Principal works are *The Weavers* (etchings), *War* (woodcuts), *Death* (lithographs), *Bread,* a self-portrait, and two sculptures for a military cemetery in Belgium.

Komensky, Jan Amos. *See* **Comenius, John Amos**

Kornberg *(kôrn bûrg),* **Arthur** 1918–. American biochemist. *b.* Brooklyn, N.Y. Professor of biochemistry at Stanford (from 1959); shared, with Severo Ochoa, Noble Prize in physiology and medicine (1959) for biological synthesis of nucleic acids.

Korzeniowski, Teodor Josef Konrad. *See* **Conrad, Joseph**

Korzybski *(kôr zĭp skē),* **Alfred Habdank Skarbek** 1879–1950. American scientist. *b.* Warsaw, Poland. Immigrated to U.S. (1916); naturalized (1940); pioneered in the science of general semantics, concerned with the logical distinctions between words and the objects they signify; founded Institute of General Semantics at Chicago (1938), later moved to Lakeville, Conn. (1946). Author of *Manhood of Humanity* (1921), *Science and Sanity, An Introduction to Non-Aristotelian Systems and General Semantics* (1933), and *Time-Binding: The General Theory* (1924).

Kosciusko *(kôsh cho͞osh kō),* **Tadeusz Andrzej Bonawentura** 1746–1817. Polish general and patriot. *b.* Mereczowszczyzna. On outbreak of American Revolution, offered services against the British (1776); as colonel of engineers in Continental army, fortified West Point (1778) and fought in military engagements in South Carolina; a founder of Society of the Cincinnati (1783); brigadier general (1783); returned to Poland (1784); as major general, fought in Polish army against Russians (1791); after second partition of Poland (1794), led national resistance as commander in chief and dictator, but was defeated by combined Russian and Prussian forces and captured (1794); released from captivity (1797); spent later years in exile in England, America, and France.

Kossel *(kōs əl),* **Albrecht** 1853–1927. German biochemist. *b.* Rostock. Conducted important investigations on proteins, cell nuclei, albumins, and nuclear substances; discovered enzyme arginase and the pruine theophylline; awarded Nobel Prize in physiology and medicine (1910).

Kossuth *(kŏs o͞oth),* **Louis** Hungarian name: Lajos. 1802–94. Hungarian patriot. *b.* Monok. As member of the Diet (1825–27, 1832–36) and editor of radical journal *Pesti Hirlap* (1841– 44), campaigned for independence of Hungary from Austria; re-elected to Diet (1847,

1848); on fall of Metternich, became finance minister of an independent cabinet and head of committee of national defense (1848); elected president of Hungarian Republic (1849); overthrown following defeat by allied Russian and Austrian forces; resigned office and fled into exile in Turkey; spent rest of life in England, U. S., and Italy, while continuing his efforts to liberate Hungary.

Kosygin *(kủ sē gən),* **Aleksei Nikolayevich** 1904–. Soviet statesman. *b.* Leningrad. Appointed by Stalin to the Central Committee (1939); youngest member of Politburo (1946); renamed to presidium (1957); second in power to Khrushchev as first deputy prime minister (from 1960); on the rise of Brezhnev, named Soviet premier (1964); considered a brilliant, if colorless, expert on economic planning and Soviet industry.

Kraepelin *(krâ pə lēn),* **Emil** 1856–1926. German psychiatrist. *b.* Neustrelitz. Pioneered in experimental psychiatry; classified mental diseases into two groups: manic-depressive and dementia-praecox; conducted researches on brain fatigue and the influence of alcohol in motor functions.

Krafft-Ebing *(kräft ā bĭng),* **Baron Richard von** 1840–1902. German neurologist. *b.* Mannheim. Professor of psychiatry at Strassburg (1872–73), at Graz (1873–79), and at Vienna (1889–1902); published a number of authoritative studies on forensic psychiatry, sexual perversions, hypnotism, and neurology, including the famous *Psychopathia Sexualis* (1886).

Kranach; Kronach. *See* **Cranach**

Krebs *(krĕbz),* **Sir Hans Adolf** 1900–. British biochemist. *b.* Hildesheim, Germany. Shared, with F. A. Lipmann, Nobel Prize in physiology and medicine (1953) for studies in cell metabolism, including the discovery of coenzyme A.

Krogh *(krôg),* **Schack August Steenberg** 1874–1949. Danish physiologist. *b.* Grenaa. Professor of physiology at Copenhagen (from 1916); awarded Nobel Prize in physiology and medicine (1920) for discovery of the mechanism that regulates blood capillary action. Author of *The Anatomy and Physiology of Capillaries* (1922), among other books.

Kropotkin *(krə pôt kĭn),* **Prince Peter Alekseevich** 1842–1921. Russian anarchist. *b.* Moscow. Scion of old Russian nobility; educated as a geographer, and explored Manchuria, Finland, and Sweden; joined radical faction of International Workingmen's Association (1872); arrested for promoting anarchist activities (1874) but escaped to England (1876); condemned at Lyons (1883), receiving a five-year sentence; on release (1886), settled in England; returned to Russia after the Revolution (1917); wrote on anarchism and nihilism. Works include *Mutual Aid* (1902), *Memoirs of a Revolutionist* (1899), *The Conquest of Bread* (1888), *Modern Science and Anarchism* (1903).

Kruger *(kroo̅ gər),* **Stephanus Johannes Paulus** Also OOM PAUL. 1825–1904. South African Boer statesman. *b.* Colesberg. As a boy, participated in Great Trek to Transvaal (1836–40); helped obtain independence of Transvaal from Great Britain according to the Sand River Convention (1852) and became its leader; on annexation of Transvaal by the British, dismissed from office (1878); led Boer rebellion of 1880, with Petrus Joubert and Marthinus Pretorius, negotiated the Pretoria agreement by which independence was restored (1881); president of the Transvaal (1883–1900); anti-British policies led to Boer War (1899); in exile in Europe (1900–1904). Wrote *Memoirs* (1902).

Krupp *(kro͞op),* **Alfred** 1812–87. German industrial magnate. *b.* Essen. Succeeded father Friedrich Krupp (1787–1826) as head of an iron forge; established first Bessemer steel plant and became arms supplier to Germany and the world; gained the nickame Cannon King; led in the development of the breech-loading rifle; control of the company passed to his son Friedrich Alfred (1854–1902) and granddaughter Bertha (1886–1957); her husband, Gustav Krupp von Bohlen und Halbach (1870–1950), was indicted on charges of being an accessory to Nazi war crimes (1945) and divested of management of Krupp industries.

Kublai Khan *(ko͞o blī kän)* 1216–94. Mongol ruler. Grandson of Genghis Khan; founder of Yüan dynasty; with brother Mangu Khan, completed conquest of China (1252–59); succeeded Mangu as khan; founded city of Khanbalik, identified as modern Peking (1264–67); defeated in campaigns against Japan, Southeast Asia, and Indonesia, but conquered Burma and Korea; adopted Chinese culture, making Buddhism the state religion; ruled over one of the largest empires in history, extending from the Pacific to the Black Sea; received Marco Polo at court.

Kuhn *(ko͞on),* **Richard** 1900–67. Austrian chemist. *b.* Vienna. As professor at Kaiser Wilhelm Institute, conducted important investigations on the structure and synthesis of vitamins A and B_2 (riboflavin) and carotinoids; declined the Nobel Prize in chemistry (1938) under Nazi pressure.

K'ung Ch'iu. *See* **Confucius**

K'ung Fu-tzu. *See* **Confucius**

Kusch *(ko͝osh),* **Polycarp** 1911–. American physicist. *b.* Blankenburg, Germany. Professor of physics at Columbia (from 1949); shared Nobel Prize in physics (1955) with W. E. Lamb for precise measurement of the electron's electromagnetic properties.

Kuznets *(kŭz nĕts),* **Simon** 1901–. American economist. *b.* Kharkov, Russia. Immigrated to U.S. (1907); professor at the University of Pennsylvania (1930–54), Johns Hopkins (1954–60), and Harvard (from 1960); winner of Nobel Prize in economic science (1971) for studies using gross national product as a measurement of national economic growth. Author of *National Income and Its Composition, 1919–1938* (1942).

Kyd *(kĭd),* **Thomas** 1558–94. English dramatist. *b.* London. One of best-known tragic poets of the late sixteenth century. The only play definitely attributed to him is *The Spanish Tragedy,* considered one of the most sensational and popular of the Elizabethan period; imprisoned (1593) on a charge of unitarianism and atheism; died in poverty.

L

La Farge *(lä färzh),* **John** 1835–1910. American artist. *b.* New York, N.Y. Gained reputation as a landscape and figure painter, decorator, and stained-glass worker; best known for mural decorations in Trinity Church, Boston (1876–77), the altarpiece for St. Peter's Church, New York (1863), panels in St. Thomas's Church, New York (1877), the altarpiece in Church of the Ascension, New York, and the peacock window in the Worcester Museum. Painted *Christ and Nicodemus, The Three Kings,* and *The Muse of Painting;* author of *Lectures on Art* (1895), *Great Masters* (1903), *Higher Life in Art* (1908), and other books. Son Christopher Grant (1862–1938) was an architect.

Lafayette *(lä fĭ ĕt),* **Marquis de** full name: Marie Joseph Paul Yves Roch Gilbert du Motier. 1757–1834. French soldier. *b.* Château de Chavaniac. Sailed for America (1777) to join Continental army and was commissioned major general; saw action at Brandywine, Gloucester, Barren Hill, Monmouth, Rhode Island, Yorktown, and Valley Forge; present at surrender of Cornwallis; returning to France, served in Assembly of Notables (1787), in States General, and in National Assembly (1789); sponsored adoption of the tricolor; drafted Declaration of Rights (1789); commander in chief of the National Guard; sought to establish constitutional monarchy (1790); in command of army in war with Austria; won victories at Philippeville, Maubeuge, and Florennes (1792); forced by increasing hostility of Jacobins to flee France; imprisoned by Prussians and, later, Austrians; released on Bonaparte's request (1797); inactive in politics until fall of Bonaparte (1815); Chamber of Deputies (1815, 1818–24) as member of liberal faction; made triumphal tour of U.S. on invitation of Congress (1824) and was given $200,000 and a township by Congressional vote; leader of opposition in National Assembly (1825–30); took part in Revolution of 1830 as commander of National Guard.

La Follette *(lä fŏl ət),* **Robert Marion** 1855–1925. American statesman. *b.* Primrose, Wis. House of Representatives (1885–91); governor of Wisconsin on Progressive ticket (1900–1906); senator (1906–25); opposed all forms of international involvement, particularly U.S. entry into World War I, ratification of Covenant of League of Nations, and U.S. admission to World Court; a founder of National Progressive Republican League (1911); espoused a radical political program known as the Wisconsin Idea, which included political and tax reforms and curtailment of corporate power; unsuccessful presidential candidate (1924) of the League for Progressive Political Action.

Lafontaine *(lȧ fôN tĕn),* **Henri** 1854–1943. Belgian jurist. President of the International Peace Bureau (from 1907); awarded Nobel Peace Prize (1913).

La Fontaine *(lȧ fôN tĕn),* **Jean de** 1621–95. French writer. *b.* Château-Thierry. Went to Paris and found patrons in Fouquet and Mme. de la Sablière; achieved recognition with 12 books of *Fables* (1668–94); also wrote comedies, poems, and stories, including *Contes* (1664–74), *Amours de Psyché et de Cupidon* (1669), *Nouveaux Contes* (1671), and *La Captivité de Saint Malo* (1673).

Lagerkvist *(lä gər kvĭst),* **Pär Fabian** 1891–1974. Swedish novelist. *b.* Växjö. Works portray own inner struggle for faith and certainty in a world corrupted by the pessimism bred by violence, evil, and death; combined realism and symbolism; early poems *Angst* (1916) and *Kaos* (1918) adopted expressionism as a vehicle; pursued moral concerns in *The Eternal Smile* (1920), *Evil Stories* (1924), *Guest of Reality* (1925), *The Hangman* (1933), *The Dwarf* (1944), *Barabbas* (1951), *Pilgrim at Sea* (1964), and *Let Man Live* (1949); awarded Nobel Prize in literature (1951).

Lagerlöf *(lä gər lûv),* **Selma Ottiliana Lovisa** 1858–1940. Swedish novelist and poet. *b.* Mårbacka. First woman member of Swedish Academy (1914); awarded Nobel Prize in literature (1909). Works include *Gösta Berling* (1891), *The Miracles of Antichrist* (1897), *Jerusalem* (2 vols., 1901–1902), *Liljecrona's Home* (1911), *The Emperor of Portugallia* (1914), *The Outcast* (1918), *The Ring of the Löwenskölds* (1931), *The Wonderful Adventures of Nils* (2 vols., 1906–1907), *Trolls and Men* (2 vols., 1915–21), *Mårbacka* (1922), and *Diary of Selma Lagerlöf* (1937).

Lagrange *(lȧ gräNzh),* **Joseph Louis** 1736-1813. French mathematician. *b.* Turin, Italy. Appointed by Frederick the Great to succeed Euler as director of Berlin Academy of Sciences (1766–87); solved the isoperimetrical problem; completed the calculus of variations and applied the differential calculus to the theory of probabilities; investigated the libration of the moon and studied the motions of the planets and the satellites of Jupiter; called to Paris by Louis XVI (1789); instrumental in causing adoption of metric system in France (1793); made senator and count by Napoleon. Works include *Mécanique Analytique* (1788), *Théorie des Fonctions Analytiques* (1799), and *Calcul des Fonctions* (1806).

La Guardia *(lȧ gwär dĭ ə),* **Fiorello Henry** 1882–1947. American politician. *b.* New York, N.Y. House of Representatives (1917–21, 1923–33); sponsored prolabor legislation; mayor of New York City on Fusion ticket (1934–45); launched an ambitious program of municipal improvement and curtailed the Tammany Hall bosses; headed the U.S. Office of Civilian Defense (1941–42).

Lamarck *(lȧ märk),* **Chevalier de** full name: Jean Baptiste Pierre Antoine de Monet. 1744–1829. French naturalist. *b.* Bazentin. After a few years in the army, began to study medicine and natural sciences; named custodian of herbarium and later professor of zoology at Jardin du Roi, later, Jardin des Plantes (1793–1818); sought to explain evolution and transformation of animals and plants by the theory of inheritance of acquired characteristics; first to classify animals into vertebrates and invertebrates. Principal works include *Flore Française* (1778), *Dictionnaire de Botanique, Illustrations de Genres, Système des Animaux Sans Vertèbres* (1801), *Philosophie Zoologique* (1809), and *Histoire Naturelle des Animaux Sans Vertèbres* (1815–22).

Lamartine *(lȧ mär tēn),* **Alphonse Marie Louis de Prat de** 1790–1869. French poet and statesman. *b.* Mâcon. With the publication of his first book, *Méditations Poétiques* (1820), acclaimed as a foremost French Romantic poet; later works include *Les Nouvelles Méditations* (1823), *La Mort de Socrate* (1823), *Harmonies Poétiques et Religieuses* (1829), *Jocelyn* (1836), *La Chute d'un Ange* (1838), and *Recueillements Poétiques* (1839); *Histoire des Girondins* (1846), and *Graziella* (1852); active in French politics; minister of foreign affairs in provisional government (1848).

Lamb *(lăm),* **Charles** 1775–1834. English essayist. *b.* London. Life scarred by personal tragedies including his own insanity and that of sister MARY ANN (1764–1847), for whom he acted as guardian; early sonnets published by Coleridge in *Poems of Various Subjects* (1796); contributed "Old Familiar Faces" for *Blank Verse* (1798). Other works include *A Tale of Rosamund Gray* (1797), *Tales from Shakespeare* (with Mary, 1807), and *Specimens of English Dramatic Poets* (1808); wrote for Leigh Hunt's quarterly *The Reflector* and contributed the celebrated *Essays of Elia* and *Last Essays of Elia* to *London Magazine;* admired for human and incisive quality of prose.

Lamb, William title: VISCOUNT MELBOURNE. 1779–1848. British statesman. *b.* London. Entered Parliament (1805); chief secretary of Ireland (1827–28); home secretary (1830–34); prime minister (1834, 1835–41); mentor to young Queen Victoria; career touched by two scandals, the liaison of his wife Caroline with Lord Byron and the charge of his own improper conduct with Caroline Norton.

Lamb, Willis Eugene 1913–. American physicist. *b.* Los Angeles, Calif. Professor of physics at Columbia (1948), Stanford (1951), Oxford (1956), and Yale (1962); shared, with Polycarp Kusch, Nobel Prize in physics (1955) for discoveries concerning the structure of the hydrogen spectrum.

Lambert *(lăm bərt),* **Johann Heinrich** 1728–77. German scientist. *b.* Mülhausen. Developed seminal concepts in mathematics, astronomy, and physics; discovered technique of measuring the intensity and absorption of light in *Photometria* (1760); the lambert, a unit of brightness, named after him; contributed to analytical logic and philosophy in *Neues Organon* (1764). Other works include *Freie Perspective* (1774), *Pyrometrie* (1779), *Theorie der Parallellinien* (1786), *Deutscher Gelehrter Briefwechsel* (4 vols., 1781–84), and *Opera Mathematica.*

Lancaster, 2nd Duke of. *See* **John of Gaunt**

Landau *(län dou),* **Lev Davidovich** 1908–68. Soviet physicist. *b.* Baku. Awarded Nobel Prize in physics (1962) for work on condensed gases, especially liquid helium.

Landor *(lăn dôr),* **Walter Savage** 1775–1864. English man of letters. *b.* Warwick. From early age noted for intractable temper; ran through inheritance and thereafter lived unsettled life in Spain, France, and Florence; reputation rests on poetic and prose works including *Poems* (1795), *Gebir* (1798), *Count Julian* (1812), *Imaginary Conversations* (5 vols., 1824–29), *Pericles and Aspasia* (1836), *The Pentameron* (1837), *Hellenics* (1847), *Italics* (1848), *The Last Fruit Off an Old Tree* (1853), and *Heroic Idylls* (1863).

Landseer *(lănd syər),* **Sir Edwin Henry** 1802–73. English painter. *b.* London. Best known as a painter of animals. Works include *Fighting Dogs* (1818), *The Cat's Paw* (1824), *Chevy Chase* (1826), *High Life and Low Life* (1829), *Jack in Office* (1833), *Sir Walter Scott and His Dogs* (1833), *Dignity and Impudence* (1839), *Monarch of the Glen* (1851), and *Flood in the Highlands* (1860); also sculpted massive lions in the Nelson Monument in Trafalgar Square, London.

Landsteiner *(lănd stī nər),* **Karl** 1868–1943. American pathologist. *b.* Vienna, Austria. Professor of pathological anatomy at Vienna (1909–19); member of Rockefeller Institute of Medical Research (1922–39); established that there are four main types of human blood and that in transfusions blood types must be identical; discovered Rh factor; awarded Nobel Prize in physiology and medicine (1930).

Lang *(lăng),* **Andrew** 1844–1912. Scottish scholar and writer. *b.* Selkirk. Contributed to the study of mythology in *Myth, Ritual, and Religion* (1887), *The Making of Religion* (1898), and *Magic and Religion* (1901); books of verse include *Ballads in Blue China* (1880), *Helen of Troy* (1882), and *Grass of Parnassus* (1888); biographies include *J. G. Lockhart* (1896), *Prince Charles Edward* (1900), *John Knox and the Reformation* (1906), *Maid of France* (1908), and *Sir Walter Scott* (1910); history books include *Pickle the Spy* (1897), *History of Scotland* (4 vols., 1900–1907), and *The Mystery of Mary Stewart* (1901); literary criticism includes *History of English Literature* (1912), *The World of Homer* (1910), *Books and Bookmen* (1886), *Letters to Dead Authors* (1886); also wrote *The Blue Fairy Book* (1889) and its successors; founded the Society of Psychical Research.

Lange *(läng ə),* **Christian Louis** 1869–1938. Norwegian statesman and author. *b.* Stavanger. Secretary of the Nobel Commission of the Norwegian Parliament (1900–1909); represented Norway at the International Peace Conference (1907) and the League of Nations (1920–38); secretary-general of the International Parliamentary Union (1909–33); with K. H. Branting, awarded Nobel Peace Prize (1921). Author of *History of Internationalism* (1919), *Imperialism and Peace* (1938), and other books.

Langley *(lăng lĭ),* **Samuel Pierpont** 1834–1906. American astronomer and aviation pioneer. *b.* Roxbury, Mass. As director of Allegheny Observatory, invented the bolometer for measuring heat distribution in solar spectrum; secretary of Smithsonian Institution (from 1887); began experiments in mechanical flight; built first heavier-than-air flying machines, of which one unmanned model flew 4200 feet propelled by own engine (1896). Author of *Researches on Solar Heat* (1884), *The New Astronomy* (1887), *Experiments in Aerodynamics* (1891), and *The Internal Work of the Wind* (1894).

Langmuir *(lăng mūr),* **Irving** 1881–1957. American chemist. *b.* Brooklyn, N. Y. Associated with the Research Laboratory of General Electric Company (1909–50); developed Lewis-Langmuir atomic theory (with Gilbert N. Lewis); inventions include the gas-filled tungsten lamp, atomic hydrogen welding, electron discharge apparatus, and high-vacuum pump; developed techniques of cloud seeding; awarded Nobel Prize in chemistry (1932) for work on fundamental properties of absorbed films and surface chemistry.

Lanier *(lə nēr),* **Sidney** 1842–81. American poet. *b.* Macon, Ga. Served in Confederate army and was captured and imprisoned; beset by ill health and poverty; worked as hack writer, musician, and teacher of English literature; explored the relationship between music and poetry in *The Science of English Verse* (1880); beginning with *Tiger Lilies* (1867), gained recognition as major poet; published other collections of poetry (1877; 1884). Best-known poems include "Corn," "The Symphony," "Song of the Chattahoochee," "The Marshes of Glynn," "Sunrise," and "Revenge of Hamish."

Lao-tzu *(lou dzŭ)* also LAO-TSE; original name: LI ERH. c604–531 B.C. Chinese philosopher. *b.* in Honan province. Curator of royal library at Loh; believed to be the author of *Tao Teh King,* the Bible of Taoism, teaching the Tao or right path of living by which one becomes attuned to the rhythms of nature by giving up striving.

Laplace *(lä pläs),* **Marquis Pierre Simon de** 1749–1827. French astronomer and mathematician. *b.* Beaumont-en-Auge. Professor of mathematics at Royal Military School, Paris; minister of interior under Napoleon (1799); Senate (from 1799) and its chancellor (from 1803); president of French Academy (from 1817); demonstrated stability of solar system with Three Laws of Laplace; studied motions of the moon, Jupiter, and Saturn; codified the theory of probability, the Nebular hypothesis, and tidal theory. Principal scientific works include *Théorie du Mouvement et de la Figure Elliptique des Planètes* (1784), *Système du Monde* (1796), *Traité de Mécanique Céleste* (5 vols., 1799–1825), and *Théorie Analytique des Probabilités* (1812–20).

Lardner *(lard nər),* **Ring** full name: RINGGOLD WILMER LARDNER. 1885–1933. American humorist. *b.* Niles, Mich. Best known for his sports stories in the authentic vernacular of baseball players. Works include *You Know Me, Al* (1915), *Gullible's Travels* (1917),

Treat 'Em Rough (1918), *The Real Dope* (1918), *The Big Town* (1921), *What of It* (1925), and *Round Up* (1929); also collaborated with George S. Kaufman on *June Moon* (1929).

La Rochefoucauld *(lȧ rôsh f**oo** kō),* **Duc François de** 1613–80. French writer. *b.* Paris. Intrigued against Cardinals Richelieu and Mazarin; fought with the Frondeurs and was wounded at siege of Paris; enjoyed friendship with Mme. de Longueville, Mme. de Sévigné, and Comtesse de La Fayette; gained fame as author of *Réflexions ou Sentences et Maximes Morales* (1665) and *Mémoires sur la Régence d'Anne d'Autriche* (1662); he was an incisive, cynical analyst of human behavior, who held that self-love inspired all social transactions.

La Salle *(lȧ sȧl),* **Robert Cavelier, Sieur de** 1643–87. French explorer. *b.* Rouen. Went to Canada (1666), settling on island of Montreal; explored Lake Ontario region and claimed to have discovered Ohio River (1669); backed by Count de Frontenac, governor of Quebec, granted fur-trade monopoly and patent for exploring and colonizing the West (1678); sailed by St. Joseph, Kankakee, and Illinois rivers to Green Bay, Lake Michigan, and Lake Peoria, where he founded Fort Crèvecoeur (1679); set out to explore the Mississippi (1682) and reached the Gulf of Mexico, taking possession of the river valley in the name of Louis XIV, and christening the territory Louisiana; deprived of command by Frontenac's successor (1682); returned to France and obtained new charter as viceroy of North America; set out (1684) on last expedition to the Mississippi region; landed in Texas; after two years of unsuccessful journeys, murdered by embittered mutineers.

Las Casas *(läs kä säs),* **Bartolomé de** 1474–1566. Spanish missionary and historian. *b.* Seville. Sailed with Columbus on third voyage and went to Hispaniola as a planter (1502); accompanied Diego Velasquez during conquest of Cuba; priest (1510), first to be ordained in New World; champion of Indians and began lifework to abolish Indian slavery; interceded for them before Ferdinand and Cardinal Jimenez and was named Protector of the Indians; began unsuccessful Indian colony at Cumaná (1521); instrumental in passage of "New Laws" to protect Indian rights; as a missionary, traveled in Mexico, Nicaragua, Peru, and Guatemala; bishop of Chiapa (1547); resigned and returned to Spain (1547); an important source to Latin American historians as the author of *Brief Relation of the Destruction of the Indies* (1552) and *Historia General de las Indias* (first printed 1875); known as Apostle of the Indians.

Laski *(lăs kī),* **Harold Joseph** 1893–1950. English political scientist. *b.* Manchester. Professor of political science at London School of Economics (from 1926); chairman of British Labor party(1945–46); a brilliant thinker, influenced evolution of British socialism; propounded a modified form of Marxism. Author of *Authority in the Modern State* (1919), *A Grammar of Politics* (1925), *Communism* (1927), *Liberty in the Modern State* (1930), *Democracy in Crisis* (1933), *Parliamentary*

Government in England (1938), *The American Presidency* (1940), and *The American Democracy* (1948).

Lassalle *(lä säl),* **Ferdinand** 1825–64. German statesman. *b.* Breslau. Entered politics as disciple of Karl Marx (1848); defined "Iron Law of Wages," by which workingmen were trapped in a wage system that always fell to subsistence level; set up first workers' cooperative, the Allgemeiner Deutscher Arbeiterverein (1863), the nucleus of the German Social Democratic party; advocated a modified form of Marxism in which state action was substituted for revolution; killed in a duel. Author of *System der Erworbenen Rechte* (1861), *Capital and Labour* (1864), and *Autobiography* (1910).

Lassus *(läs ûs),* **Orlandus** also ORLANDO DI LASSO, ROLAND DE LASSUS; original name: ROLAND DE LATTRE. c1532–94. Belgian musician. *b.* Mons. Director of chamber music to Albert V, Duke of Bavaria (1560); Kapellmeister (1562); created noble by Maximilian II and pope; composed over 2000 works, sacred and secular, including nearly 60 masses, and madrigals, motets, Magnificats, villanelles, chansons, and songs; considered, with Palestrina, the outstanding composer of 16th century.

Latimer *(lăt ĭ mər),* **Hugh** c1485–1555. English Protestant martyr. *b.* Thurcaston. Noted preacher of reformed doctrines; sided with Henry VIII on validity of marriage to Catherine of Aragon and repudiation of papal authority; bishop of Worcester (1535); sent to the Tower (1539, 1546) for opposition to Act of Six Articles, resigned bishopric (1539), but resumed preaching during reign of Edward VI; on accession of Mary, arrested with Ridley and Cranmer, found guilty of heresy, and burned.

La Tour d'Auvergne, Henri de. *See* **Turenne, Vicomte de**

Latrobe *(lă trōb),* **Benjamin Henry** 1764–1820. American architect. *b.* Fulneck, England. Immigrated to U. S. (1796); appointed surveyor of public buildings by Jefferson (1803); designed south wing of the Capitol and, after War of 1812, rebuilt it; introduced Greek and classical style with his design of the Bank of the U. S., which was based on the Parthenon; built first American cathedral at Baltimore (1805–18) and first water supply system at Philadelphia (1799).

Laud *(lôd),* **William** 1573–1645. English ecclesiastic. *b.* Reading. Ordained (1601); privy councillor (1626); bishop of London (1628); chancellor of Oxford (1630); archbishop of Canterbury (1633); one of the triumvirate with Charles I and Earl of Strafford that worked to strengthen absolutism in church and state; using the Star Chamber and the Court of High Commission sought to extirpate Presbyterianism in Scotland and Calvinism in England; precipitated Bishops' Wars by decreeing Anglican prayer book compulsory in Scotland; impeached by Long Parliament and committed to the Tower (1641); tried, condemned, and beheaded (1645).

Laue *(lou ə),* **Max von** 1879–1960. German physicist. *b.* Pfaffendorf. Discovered method of measuring wave lengths of X-rays by passing them through crystals;

contributed to the theory of relativity, the diffraction of light, and electromagnetism; awarded Nobel Prize in physics (1914). Author of *Die Relativitätstheorie* (2 vols., 1911), *Über die Auffindung der Röntgenstrahlinterferenz* (1920), and other books.

Laurier *(lô ri ā),* **Sir Wilfrid** 1841–1919. Canadian statesman. *b.* St. Lin. Entered Dominion House of Commons (1874); succeeded Edward Blake as leader of Liberal party (1888); prime minister (1896), the first French-Canadian and the first Catholic to hold that office; supported Canadian autonomy within the empire; granted import preference to English goods; hastened building of Grand Trunk Railway and settlement of western lands; established provinces of Alberta and Saskatchewan; cabinet defeated (1911) over reciprocity tariff agreement with U. S.

Laveran *(là vräN),* **Charles Louis Alphonse** 1845–1922. French bacteriologist. *b.* Paris. Professor of military medicine and epidemic diseases at Val de Grâce (1874–78, 1884–94) and at Pasteur Institute, Paris (from 1896); studied malaria, sleeping sickness, and kala-azar; discovered blood parasite that causes malaria (1880); awarded Nobel Prize in physiolgy and medicine (1907) for study of the role of protozoa in causing disease.

Lavoisier *(là vwà zyā),* **Antoine Laurent** 1743–94. French chemist. *b.* Paris. Director of government powder mills (1776); farmer general (1779); commissary of treasury (1791); condemned to death as member of *ancien régime* by the Convention and guillotined (1794); identified and named oxygen and explained its function in respiration and combustion; disproved phlogiston theory; developed modern chemical nomenclature and divided chemical substances into five classes: gas, metal, acidifiable substances, carbon, earthlike substances, and alkalis; developed agricultural chemistry and gunpowder chemistry. Author of *Traité Elémentaire de Chimie* (1789) and *Méthode de Nomenclature Chemique* (1787); considered father of modern chemistry.

Law *(lô),* **Andrew Bonar** 1858–1923. British statesman. *b.* New Brunswick, Canada. Entered British Parliament (1900); succeeded Balfour as Unionist leader in House of Commons (1911); colonial secretary (1915–16); chancellor of the exchequer (1916–18); lord privy seal (1919–21); prime minister (1922–23).

Lawrence *(lô rəns),* **D. H.** full name: DAVID HERBERT. 1885–1930. English novelist. *b.* Eastwood. Son of a miner; afflicted with tuberculosis throughout life; gained success with first novel *White Peacock* (1911); shocked society by preoccupation with physical aspects of love and its frank description in his novels; often prosecuted for obscenity; lived mostly abroad (from 1919); work uneven and humorless, but always iconoclastic. Principal books include *Sons and Lovers* (1913), *The Rainbow* (1915), *The Lost Girl* (1920), *Women in Love* (1920), *Kangaroo* (1923), *Aaron's Rod* (1922), *The Plumed Serpent* (1926), *Lady Chatterley's Lover* (1928), *The Virgin and the Gypsy* (1930,) *Psychoanalysis of the Unconscious* (1921), *Fantasia of the Uncon-*

scious (1922), *Studies in Classic American Literature* (1923), and *Pornography and Obscenity* (1929), as well as short stories, plays, poems, travel narratives, and *Letters.*

Lawrence, Ernest Orlando 1901–58. American physicist. *b.* Canton, S. D. Director of radiation laboratory at University of California (from 1936); consultant at Knolls Atomic Power Laboratory; invented the cyclotron (1930); by investigating the structure of atoms, produced artificial radioactivity and the transmutation of elements; awarded Nobel Prize in physics (1939).

Lawrence, T. E. full name: THOMAS EDWARD; also called LAWRENCE OF ARABIA; changed surname to SHAW (1927). 1888–1935. British adventurer and author. *b.* Portmadoc. Trained as an archaeologist; joined British Museum expedition in Mesopotamia (1910–14); on outbreak of World War I, joined General Wingate's Hejaz expeditionary force (1917) and General Allenby's staff (1918); engaged in promoting, clandestinely and then openly, Arab guerrilla operations against Turks; outstanding as leader of Faisal's levies in the liberation of Arabia; attended Paris Peace Conference (1919); declined all honors, including peerage, in protest against British government's nonfulfillment of pledges to Arabs; advisor to Middle East division of Colonial Office (1921–22); withdrew from public life and died in a motorcycle accident (1935). Author of *The Seven Pillars of Wisdom,* an extraordinary account of the Arab revolt (1926).

Laxness *(läks nĕs),* **Halldór Kiljan** 1902–. Icelandic novelist. *b.* Reykjavik. Converted to Catholicism (1923), and later espoused a form of Christian Communism. Author of *The Great Weaver of Cashmere* (1927), *Salka Valka* (1934), *Independent People* (1939), *Islands Klukkan* (1943), *Gerpla* (1955), and other books; won Nobel Prize in literature (1955).

Layard *(lā ərd),* **Sir Austen Henry** 1817–94. English archaeologist. *b.* Paris. Carried out archeological excavations in Kuyunjik, identified as site of ancient Ninevah, and Nimrud (1845–47); found remains of four palaces and cuneiform inscriptions of Assyrian city of Calah. Author of *Ninevah and Its Remains* (1848), *Monuments of Ninevah* (1850), and other books.

Leakey *(lē kĭ),* **Louis Seymour Bazett** 1903–72. British anthropologist. *b.* Kabete, Kenya. Returned to Africa after education at Cambridge; curator of Coryndon Memorial Museum at Nairobi (1945–61); led anthropological excavations to East Africa, particularly Olduvai Gorge, and unearthed human skeletal remains that helped advance the human evolution chronology: *Zinjanthropus* (1959), 1.75 million years old; *Homo habilis* (1964), two million years old; and *Kenyapithecus africanus* (1967), 20 million years old. Author of *Stone-Age Africa* (1936), *Adam's Ancestors* (1953), *The Progress and Evolution of Man in Africa,* and other books.

Lear *(lēr),* **Edward** 1812–88. English painter and writer. *b.* London. Best known as the author of *Book of Nonsense* (1846), *Non-*

sense Songs, Stories, Botany, and Alphabets (1870), *More Nonsense* (1871), and *Laughable Lyrics* (1876); also wrote a series of *Illustrated Journals of a Landscape Painter*, after a visit to Mediterranean countries (1836–70).

Lecky *(lĕk ĭ),* **William Edward Hartpole** 1838–1903. Irish historian. *b.* near Dublin. Gained fame as a historian with *Leaders of Public Opinion in Ireland* (1861), *A History of the Rise and Influence of Rationalism in Europe* (2 vols., 1865), *A History of European Morals from Augustus to Charlemagne* (2 vols., 1869), *A History of England in the Eighteenth Century* (8 vols., 1878–90), and *Democracy and Liberty* (2 vols., 1896); active as Unionist Member of Parliament (1895–1902).

Leconte de Lisle *(lə kôNt də lēl),* **Charles Marie** 1818–94. French poet. *b.* island of Réunion. Settled in Paris and identified himself with Parnassian poets; disillusioned by the modern age, and turned to antiquity for inspiration. Principal poetic works include *Poèmes Antiques* (1852), *Poèmes et Poésies* (1854), *Le Chemin de la Croix* (1859), *Poèmes Barbares* (1862), *Kaïn* (1869), and *Poèmes Tragiques* (1884); published translations of Greek and classical authors.

Le Corbusier *(lə kôr bü zyā)* pseudonym of CHARLES ÉDOUARD JEANNERET. 1887–1965. French architect. *b.* La Chaux-de-Fonds, Switzerland. One of the founders of modern functional architecture; defined a house as a machine for living; with Ozenfant, issued the Purist Manifesto on the use of machine forms in architecture (1919); devised the *modulor* system of standard-size units; projects include the main buildings of the city of Chandigarh, India; the chapel at Ronchamp (1950–55); the convent of La Tourette near Lyons (1955–60); the Visual Arts Center, Harvard University (1961–62); and the Palace of the League of Nations at Geneva (1927). Author of *Vers une Architecture* (1923), *Propos d'Urbanisme* (1947), and *My Work* (1961).

Lederberg *(lĕd ər bûrg),* **Joshua** 1925–. American geneticist. *b.* Montclair, N. J. With George W. Beadel and Edward L. Tatum, awarded Nobel Prize in physiology and medicine (1958) for experiments establishing that sexual recombination of bacteria results in the exchange of genetic material.

Lee *(lē),* **Ann** 1736–84. American religious mystic. *b.* Manchester, England. Illiterate textile worker, married to a blacksmith; turned to religion and joined Society of Shaking Quakers or Shakers (United Society of Believers in Christ's Second Appearing), becoming their leader; imprisoned for street preaching immigrated to American colonies (1774) with seven followers and on arrival formed Shaker settlement at Watervliet, N. Y. (1776); arrested for treason (1780), but released; established 19 other Shaker communities in New England; known as Ann the Word or Mother Ann.

Lee *(lē),* **Richard Henry** 1732–94. American statesman. *b.* Stratford, Va. As member of the Virginia House of Burgesses (from 1758), gained prominence in defending colonial rights; with Patrick Henry and Thomas Jefferson, initiated Committees of Correspondence

(1773); as Virginia delegate to the Continental Congress (1774–76), moved the Declaration of Independence resolution and was one of its signatories; member of Continental Congress (1784–89) and its president (1784–85); U. S. senator (1789–92).

Lee, Robert Edward 1807–80. American Confederate leader. *b.* Stratford, Va. Commissioned (1829); served in Mexican War (1847); superintendent at West Point (1852); commanded detachment that suppressed John Brown's raid at Harper's Ferry (1859); on secession of seven states, resigned from U. S. army, becoming military advisor to Jefferson Davis and commander of the army of northern Virginia (1862); in engagement known as the Seven Days, pushed back McClellan (1862), and in second Battle of Bull Run (Manassas) defeated John Pope; lost Battle of Antietam (1862), but defeated Union forces at Fredericksburg (1862) and Chancellorsville (1863); never regained initiative after defeat at Gettysburg (1863); repulsed Grant's attacks in Wilderness Campaign (1864); with the fall of Petersburg, found Southern army reduced to 30,000 soldiers; general in chief of all Confederate armies; surrounded at Appomattox and surrendered to Grant (1865); president of Washington (now Washington and Lee) College (1865–70); acclaimed as hero for qualities in the field and for exalted character.

Lee, Tsung Dao 1926–. American physicist. *b.* Shanghai, China. Immigrated to U. S. (1946); professor at Columbia (1956); member of Institute of Advanced Studies at Princeton (1960–63); with C. N. Yang, awarded Nobel Prize in physics (1957) for work disproving the parity conservation laws of nuclear physics.

Leeuwenhoek *(lā vən hōōk),* **Anton van** 1632–1723. Dutch naturalist. *b.* Delft. Built a simple microscope for biological observation and with its aid described red blood corpuscles, blood capillaries, spermatozoa, muscle fibers, lens of the eye, hydra, rotifers, bacteria, yeast plants, and epidermis; disproved spontaneous generation.

Léger *(lā zhā),* **Alexis Saint-Léger** full name: MARIE RENÉ AUGUSTE ALEXIS SAINT-LÉGER LÉGER; pseudonym: SAINT-JOHN PERSE. 1887–1975. French diplomat and poet. *b.* West Indies. Entered service of French foreign ministry, becoming secretary-general (1933–40); in exile in U. S. during World War II; poetry noted for visionary themes, panoramic imagery, and neologisms. Best-known works include *Images à Crusoë* (1909), *Éloges* (1910), *Amitié du Prince* (1924), *Anabase* (1924), *Exil* (1942), *Pluies* (1944), *Amers* (1957), and *Chroniques* (1960); awarded Nobel Prize in literature (1960).

Lehman *(lē mən),* **Herbert Henry** 1878–1963. American statesman. *b.* New York, N. Y. Partner in Lehman Brothers, stock brokers on Wall Street (1908); governor of N. Y. (1932–42); director of U. N. Relief and Rehabilitation Administration (1942–46); Democratic U. S. senator (1949–56).

Leibnitz *(līp nĭtz),* **Baron Gottfried Wilhelm von** 1646–1716. German philosopher and mathematician. *b.* Leipzig. Received doctorate from University of Altdorf at age 20 (1666); the publication of *Nova Methodus* (1667) led to employment at court of elector of Mainz; visited France and England; began to study mathematics; worked out infinitesimal calculus and published theories (1684), four years before Newton; in Hanover as librarian to duke of Brunswick (1676–1716); instrumental in persuading Frederick I to found the Academy of Sciences in Berlin (1700), becoming its first president; wrote books on mathematics, natural science, theology, philosophy, history, logic, and politics; elaborated a complex philosophic system, now known as Leibnitzianism, which held that the universe was composed of an aggregate of substances called monads, infinite in number and indivisible, each a soul preset to mirror the universe and arranged in a hierarchy, with the highest being God; held that between physical and moral realms there is a preestablished harmony so that the universe is the best of all possible worlds. Works include *Systema Theologicum* (1686), *Hypothesis Physica Nova* (1671), *Théodicé* (1710), *La Monadologie* (1714), *Principes de la Nature et de la Grace* (1714), and *Nouveaux Essais* (1704).

Leicester, Earl of. *See* **Dudley, Robert; Montfort, Simon de**

Leloir *(lə lwär),* **Luis Federico** 1906–. Argentine biochemist. *b.* Paris, France. Awarded Nobel Prize in chemistry (1970) for the discovery of sugar nucleotides and their role in the biosynthesis of carbohydrates.

Lenard *(lä närt),* **Philipp** 1862–1947. German physicist. *b.* Pozsony, Czechoslovakia. Professor of physics at Heidelberg (1896–98), 1907–31); discovered Lenard rays emitted through foil-covered window in a Crookes tube; demonstrated emission of electrons from substances by the action of light; awarded the Nobel Prize (1905) for work on cathode rays. Author of *Über Kathodenstrahlen* (1906), *Probleme Komplexer Moleküle* (1914), and *Über das Relativitätsprinzip* (1918).

Lenin *(lĕn ĭn),* **Vladimir Ilyich** original name: ULYANOV. Often called NIKOLAI LENIN. 1870–1924. Russian statesman. *b.* Simbirsk. Studied law at Kazan and St. Petersburg; gave up practice for Marxist agitation and to organize the Union for the Liberation of the Working Class (1894); arrested (1895); exiled to Siberia (1897–1900); in prison, completed *The Development of Capitalism in Russia* (1899); left Russia (1900); settled in Switzerland; founded *Iskra (The Spark),* a revolutionary organ, at Munich; with Plekhanov, drafted program of Social Democratic party; at Socialist Congress (1903), assumed leadership of radical Bolsheviks; returned to Russia to guide Bolsheviks (1905), remaining until 1907; on outbreak of World War I, denounced it as an imperialist outrage, calling on all workers to refuse to support it and to seize power in their own countries; convened Third International in Switzerland (1915) to reaffirm revolution as goal of Communism; permitted by Germans to return to Russia to lead Bolsheviks in February Revolution (1917); overthrew moderate reformers under Kerenski and seized power as head of Soviet of People's Commissars; dissolved Constituent Assembly and established dictatorship of the proletariat; premier (1918); made humiliating peace with Germany by Treaty of Brest-Litovsk (1918); led Bolsheviks to victory in civil war (1918–20); founded Union of Soviet Socialist Republics; introduced New Economic Policy; encouraged atheism and persecuted all religions; suppressed all opposition and reshaped social and political institutions to conform to Marxism; died in Gorki (1924).

Leo *(lē ō)* Name of 13 popes, including:

LEO I, Saint. Called the Great. c390–461. Pope (440–61). *b.* Tuscany. Restored primacy of bishop of Rome over other bishops; with aid of Valentinian III, suppressed Manichaeism; condemned proceedings of "Robber Synod" of Ephesus (449); convened Council of Chalcedon (451); interceded with Attila and Genseric to spare Rome.

LEO XIII. real name: GIOACCHINO VINCENZO PECCI. 1810–1903. Pope (1878–1903). *b.* Carpineto. Through a series of encyclicals, guided Catholic Church into the modern age; in *Immortale Dei,* defined public duties of Catholics as citizens; in *Rerum Novarum* (1891), outlined Catholic social philosophy to meet the challenge of communism and capitalism; other encyclicals dealt with marriage, freemasonry, and Bible study; proclaimed Thomism (the philosophy of St. Thomas Aquinas) as official Church philosophy.

Leonardo da Vinci *(lā ō när dō dä vēn chē)* 1452–1519. Florentine painter, engineer, and scientist. *b.* Vinci, Tuscany. Apprentice in Andrea Verrocchio's workshop in Florence (c1469–82); entered service of Ludovico Sforza, Duke of Milan (1482–99); military engineer to Cesare Borgia (1502); engaged in engineering, architectural projects, and study of hydraulics, mechanics, anatomy, geology, and botany; in service of Louis XIII (1506–13), Pope Leo X (1513–16), and Francis I (1516–19). Principal paintings include *Adoration of the Kings, St. Jerome, Virgin of the Grotto, Last Supper, Mona Lisa, Baptism of Christ, Annunciation, St. John the Baptist,* and *St. Anne;* designed cities, fortifications, and canals; built first revolving stage, devised an armored tank, a guided projectile, a breech-loading cannon, and anticipated theories and discoveries of Newton, Galileo, and aerodynamics of airplane; in notebooks and drawings, left a vast amount of recorded investigations into science and art.

Leopardi *(lā ō pär dē),* **Conte Giacomo** 1798–1837. Italian poet. *b.* Recanati. Sick and deformed from early childhood; expressed despondency and anguish of his own life in some of the finest lyrics in the Italian language; tended to unrelieved philosophical pessimism; wrote essays, dialogues, satires, and letters; distinguished as a philologist and classicist. Works include *Operatti Morali* (1827), *Canzoni* (1824), *Versi* (1826), and *Canti* (1836).

Lepidus *(lĕp ĭ dəs),* **Marcus Aemilius** *d.* c77 B.C. Roman statesman. Praetor of Sicily (81); consul (78);

after attempt to subvert the Sullan Constitution demoted by Senate to the provinces; defeated by Pompey and Catullus. Son MARCUS AEMILIUS LEPIDUS (*d.* 13 B.C.), sided with Caesar in war with Pompey; consul (46); on Caesar's assassination joined Antony and Octavius, becoming member of Second Triumvirate (43), with Africa as his portion of empire; led abortive revolt against Octavius in Sicily (36) and was deposed.

Lermontov *(lyār mən tôf)*, **Mikhail Yurievich** 1814–41. Russian poet. *b.* Moscow. Commissioned in the Guards (1834); wrote ode of protest to czar on death of Pushkin and was penalized by transfer to the Caucasus (1837); fought two duels and was killed in the second. Works include *A Hero of Our Time* (1839), "The Demon" (1829–41), "Ismail Bey," "Hadji Abrek," "Valerik," "The Novice," and "The Song of the Czar Ivan Vasilievich."

Lesseps *(lĕ səps)*, **Vicomte Ferdinand Marie de** 1805–94. French engineer. *b.* Versailles. In French foreign service (from 1825); conceived plan of building a canal across isthmus of Suez (1854); organized Suez Canal Company and obtained concession from Said Pasha, viceroy of Egypt (1859); began construction (1860) and completed the canal (1869); organized company for constructing canal across isthmus of Panama; on its failure, charged with misappropriation of funds (1881–88). Author of *Histoire de Canal de Suez* (1876) and *Souvenirs de Quarante Ans* (1887).

Lessing *(lĕs ĭng)*, **Doris** 1919–. British author. *b.* Kermanshah, Persia. Lived in Southern Rhodesia (1924–49); noted for the literary quality of her works as well as a left-wing bias and a concern with women. Author of *The Grass Is Singing* (1950), *The Golden Notebook* (1962), *African Stories* (1964), *The Four-Gated City* (1969), *Briefing for a Descent into Hell* (1971), and *The Summer Before the Dark* (1973).

Lessing, Gotthold Ephraim 1729–81. German man of letters. *b.* Kamenz. Studied theology (1746); abandoned it to study theater in Leipzig, Berlin (1748), and Wittenberg (1751); lived in Berlin (1752–55, 1758–60, 1765–66) and Leipzig (1755–57); secretary to General Tauentzien in Breslau (1760–65); collaborated with Nicolai and Moses Mendelssohn to found journal *Briefe, die Neueste Litteratur Betreffend* (1759-67); as playwright for German National Theater (1767–69), wrote criticism, collected as *Hamburgische Dramaturgie* (1769); ducal librarian at Wolfenbüttel (1769–81); considered a principal architect of the Enlightenment in Germany; introduced Shakespeare to the German public; promoted religious freedom and toleration. Works include *Kleinigkeiten* (1751), *Laokoon* (1766), *Miss Sara Sampson* (1755), *Minna von Barnhelm* (1763), *Emilia Galotti* (1772), *Nathan the Wise* (1779); *Erziehung des Menschengeschlechts* (1780), and *Beiträge zur Geschichte und Litteratur* (1773–81); published *Fragmente eines Wolfenbüttelschen Ungenannten*, involving him in a bitter theological controversy.

Leverrier *(lə vĕr ryā)*, **Urbain Jean Joseph** 1811–77. French astronomer. *b.* St. Lô. Director of Paris Observatory (from 1854); while attempting to explain the motion of planet Uranus, calculated and predicted the existence of another planet, later discovered and named Neptune (1846); published a revision of planetary theories (1875).

Lewis *(lū ĭs),* **Cecil Day** 1904–72. British poet. *b.* Ballintubber, Ireland. Poet laureate of England (from 1968); like Auden and other political poets of the 1930s, passed through Communism to Christian faith. Author of *Transitional Poems* (1929), *From Feathers to Iron* (1931), *The Magic Mountain* (1933), *The Friendly Tree* (1936), *Overtures to Death* (1938), *Child of Misfortune* (1939), *Word Over All* (1943), *Poetry for You* (1944), *The Poetic Image* (1947); published detective fiction under pseudonym Nicholas Blake.

Lewis, Clive Staples Pseudonym: CLIVE HAMILTON. 1898–1963. English essayist and Christian apologist. *b.* Belfast, Ireland. Professor of Mediaeval and Renaissance English at Cambridge (from 1954); literary studies include *The Allegory of Love* (1936); explored the foundations of Christian belief in *The Screwtape Letters* (1942), *The Problem of Pain* (1940), *Christian's Regress* (1935), *Beyond Personality* (1944), *Miracles* (1947), and *Transposition* (1949); also wrote science fiction and the widely read children's books, *The Chronicles of Narnia.*

Lewis, John Llewellyn 1880–1969. American labor leader. *b.* Lucas, Iowa. Began as coal miner; president of United Mine Workers' Union (1920–60); organized Congress of Industrial Organizations (1935), but left it (1941); returned to American Federation of Labor (1946–47), but left (1947) to become independent; though a maverick, remembered as an effective labor organizer who placed the interests of his union above all else.

Lewis, Meriwether 1774–1809. American explorer. *b.* in Albermarle County, Va. Appointed by Jefferson to conduct exploratory expedition to find route to the Pacific and to gather information about Indians and the Far West (1803); with William Clark, set out from St. Charles, Mo. (1804); followed the Missouri to its source, crossed the Great Divide, and descended Columbia River to Pacific coast; returned to St. Louis (1806); governor of Louisiana (1807–1809). Account recorded in *History of the Expeditions Under the Command of Captains Lewis and Clark* (2 vols., 1814).

Lewis, Sinclair 1885–1951. American writer. *b.* Sauk Centre, Minn. Noted for realistic and satirical novels dealing with American middle class; first American to receive Nobel Prize in literature (1930). Author of *Our Mr. Wrenn* (1914), *The Trail of the Hawk* (1915), *The Job* (1917), *Main Street* (1920), *Babbitt* (1922), *Arrowsmith* (1925), *Mantrap* (1926), *Elmer Gantry* (1927), *The Man Who Knew Coolidge* (1928), *Dodsworth* (1929), *Ann Vickers* (1933), *Work of Art* (1934), *It Can't Happen Here* (1935), *The Prodigal Parents* (1938), *Bethel Merriday* (1940), *Gideon Planish* (1943), *Cass Timberlane* (1945), *Kingsblood Royal* (1947), *The Godseeker* (1949), and *World So Wide* (1951).

Lewis, Wyndham full name: PERCY WYNDHAM LEWIS. 1884–1957. English writer. *b.* Bay of Fundy, Me. Gained recognition as a painter of the Vorticist school and, with Ezra Pound, founded the journal *Blast* (1914–15); turned to satirical writing after World War I, publishing *Tarr* (1918), *The Art of Being Ruled* (1926), *Time and Western Man* (1928), *Childermass* (1929), *The Apes of God* (1930), *The Wild Body* (1931), *The Doom of Youth* (1932), *Men Without Art* (1934), *The Revenge for Love (1937), The Mysterious Mr. Bull* (1938), *The Vulgar Streak* (1941), *America and Cosmic Man* (1948), *Blasting and Bombardiering* (1937), and *Rude Assignment* (1950).

Libby *(lĭb ĭ),* **Willard Frank** 1908–. American chemist. *b.* Grand Valley, Col. Professor of chemistry at Chicago (1945–54); member of Atomic Energy Commission (1954–59); professor of chemistry at UCLA (1959–62); director of Institute of Geophysics (from 1962); awarded Nobel Prize in chemistry (1960) for development of the atomic time clock for determining geological age by measuring the amount of radioactive carbon-14 in organic substances. Author of *Radiocarbon Dating* (1955).

Lie *(lē),* **Trygve Halvdan** 1896–1968. Norwegian statesman. *b.* Oslo. Labor member of Parliament and cabinet member (1935–41); foreign minister of Norwegian government-in-exile in England (1940–45); secretary-general of U. N. (1946); resigned (1952). Author of *In the Cause of Peace* (1951).

Liebig *(lē bĭK),* **Baron Justus von** 1803–73. German chemist. *b.* Darmstadt. Professor of chemistry at Giessen (1824); expanded frontiers of chemistry, making important contributions to almost every field, including organic chemistry, animal chemistry, and alcohols; considered father of agricultural chemistry; developed artificial fertilizers; established first practical chemical laboratory and invented instruments for organic analysis, including Liebig's condenser; discovered chloroform and chloral, and, with Wohler, the benzoyl radical; demonstrated transformation of inorganic to organic substances in plants. Author of *Dictionary of Chemistry* (1837–64), *Organic Chemistry in Its Relation to Agriculture* (1840), *Animal Chemistry* (1842), *Organic Chemistry* (1843), *Agricultural Chemistry* (1855), and *Familiar Letters on Chemistry* (1844).

Lincoln *(lĭng kən),* **Abraham** 1809–65. 16th president of U. S. (1860–65). *b.* Hardin, Ky. Moved to Indiana (1816) and to Macon County, Ind. (1830); mostly self-schooled; performed frontier jobs such as river work, splitting rails, and clerking in a store; studied law; member of Illinois legislature (1834–41); moved to Springfield, Ill., and began law practice (1837); House of Representatives (1846–49); Illinois circuit lawyer (1849–54); leader of Republican party (1856); received 110 votes for vice-president on Frémont ticket (1856); defeated as Republican candidate for Senate (1858) by Stephen A. Douglas; nominated for presidency by Republicans (1860); in a four-candidate contest, carried every Northern state except N. J.; inauguration (1861) followed by secession of Southern states and outbreak of Civil War; issued Emanicipation Proclamation (1863); delivered celebrated Gettysburg Address (1863); reelected (1864); led the Union to victory (1865); five days after Lee's surrender, assassinated in Ford's Theater, Washington, D.C., by John Wilkes Booth.

Lind *(lĭnd),* **Johanna Maria** called Jenny Lind. 1820–87. Swedish singer. *b.* Stockholm. Celebrated in the musical world as the Swedish Nightingale; one of the most admired coloratura sopranos of her day; popular in Britain (1847–48) and in the U. S. (1850–52); became a naturalized British subject (1859); retired from the operatic stage (1849) and thereafter appeared only in concerts and oratorios.

Lindbergh *(lĭn bərg),* **Charles Augustus** 1902–74. American aviator. *b.* Detroit, Mich. Commissioned member of air force corps (1925); made first transatlantic New York-Paris solo flight (1927), in *The Spirit of St. Louis,* a monoplane, in 33 hours and 39 minutes; made other pioneering flights; after kidnap-murder of his son and the sensational trial that followed, moved to England (1935); with Alexis Carrel, devised a mechanical heart and a pump to circulate the blood; opposed American entry into World War II; civilian consultant to Army Air Force during wartime; in later life, espoused environmental causes. Author of *We* (1936), *Of Flight and Life* (1948), and *The Spirit of St. Louis* (1953; Pulitzer prize).

Lindsay *(lĭn zĭ),* **Vachel** full name: Nicholas Vachel. 1879–1931. American poet. *b.* Springfield, Ill. Lived most of adult life as a troubadour chanting and selling own verses for bed and board; introduced colloquial idioms and rhythms into poetry. Works include *Rhymes to Be Traded for Bread* (1912), *General William Booth Enters Into Heaven* (1913), *The Congo* (1914), *The Chinese Nightingale* (1917), *The Golden Whales of California* (1920), *The Daniel Jazz* (1920), *Going-to-the-Sun* (1926), and *Candle in the Cabin* (1926).

Linnaeus *(lĭ nē əs),* **Carolus** 1707–78. Swedish botanist. *b.* Råshult. Assistant to Olaf Rudbeck at Uppsala (1730); made botanical field trips to Lapland, Dalecarlia, Holland, England, France, Öland, and Gotland; practicing physician at Stockholm (1738); professor of botany at Uppsala (from 1742); published over 180 works; developed a system of scientific nomenclature based on relationships within the natural kingdom, thus considered founder of systematic botany. Works include *Systema Naturae* (1737), *Fundamenta Botanica* (1736), *Bibliotheca Botanica* (1736), *Critica Botanica* (1737), *Genera Plantarum* (1737), *Classes Plantarum* (1738), *Philosophia Botanica* (1751), and *Species Plantarum* (1753).

Lin Piao *(lən bē ä ō)* 1908–1971. Chinese Communist general. Took part in Northern Expedition under Chiang Kai-shek (1924–27); broke with Kuomintang to join Communists (1927); aide to Chu Teh; participated in the Long March

(1934–35); succeeded Chu as minister of defense; emerged as leader of the Cultural Revolution (1966–69) and was acknowledged as Mao's heir; his power began to wane after the Cultural Revolution; disgraced and ousted from office; died in unexplained circumstances, possibly after attempting a coup to regain power.

Lipmann *(lĭp mən),* **Fritz Albert** 1899–. American biochemist. *b.* Königsberg, Germany. Professor of biochemistry at Harvard (1949–57); made important contributions to the study of cell metabolism and the vitamin B complex; with Hans Krebs, awarded Nobel Prize in physiology and medicine (1953) for discovery of coenzyme A.

Li Po *(lē bô)* also LI T'AI-PO or LI TAI-PEH. c700–762. Chinese poet of T'ang dynasty. *b.* in Szechwan. Considered greatest poet in Chinese literature; wrote of the frailty, mystery, felicity, and unity of human life in verses celebrated for cadence and imagery; believed to have written over 20,000 poems, of which nearly 2000 are extant; led a dissipated life at the imperial court and as a member of a wandering band known as the Eight Immortals of the Wine Cup.

Lippi *(lēp pĭ),* **Fra Filippo** also LIPPO; sometimes called FRA FILIPPO DEL CARMINE. c1406–69. Florentine painter. *b.* Florence. Carmelite monk (1421–61). Works include frescoes in Prato and Spoleto cathedrals, especially *Life of St. John the Baptist, Life of the Virgin, Relaxation of the Carmelite Rule,* and a series of nativities and madonnas noted for graceful lines and sharp colors. His illegitimate son FILIPPINO or LIPPINO LIPPI (c1457–1504), noted for frescoes in Brancacci chapel, in Strozzi chapel at Florence, in Caraffa chapel at Rome, the altarpiece in church of San Michele at Lucca, and *The Virgin and the Saints, The Adoration of the Magi, Crucifixion,* and *The Vision of St. Bernard.*

Lippmann *(lēp mån),* **Gabriel** 1845–1921. French physicist. *b.* Hallerich, Luxembourg. Professor of physics at Sorbonne (from 1886); invented instruments, including a capillary electrometer and galvanometer; formulated the theory of conservation of electricity; invented a method of color photography by interference process; awarded the Nobel Prize in physics (1908). Author of *Cours de Thermodynamique* (1886) and *Cours d'Acoustique et d'Optique* (1888).

Lister *(lĭs tər),* **Joseph Jackson** 1786–1869. English optician. *b.* London. Discovered the principle of aplanatic foci, forming the basis of improved object-glasses of microscopes; son JOSEPH LISTER, BARON LISTER OF LYME REGIS, (1827–1912). *b.* Upton. Studied medicine; professor of surgery at Glasgow (1860), Edinburgh (1867), and London (1877); founded antiseptic surgery; began heat-sterilization of instruments and the use of carbolic acid as antiseptic; introduced drainage tube and absorbent ligatures in surgery; by improved surgical techniques, reduced gangrene infections following compound bone fractures.

Liszt *(lĭst),* **Franz** 1811–86. Hungarian composer. *b.* Raiding. Began playing in public (1820);

studied in Vienna and Paris; gave concerts throughout Europe and was regarded as the finest pianist of his age; retired from stage (1848) to become musical director at Weimar (1848), devoting himself to composition and teaching; resigned (1861); in Rome, became member of the third order of Franciscans, known as Abbé Liszt; spent rest of life in Rome, Weimar, and Budapest; led a life as romantic as his music; creations included over 1000 compositions, including *Les Préludes, Orpheus, Mazeppa,* the Dante and Faust symphonies, piano concertos in E flat and A, 19 Hungarian rhapsodies, three Liebesträume, sonata in B minor, masses, cantatas, oratorios, and religious music; author of books on Wagner, Chopin, Schumann, and Hungarian music.

Littleton *(lĭt əl tən),* **Sir Thomas** c1407–81. English jurist. *b.* Frankley. Named justice of Common Pleas (from 1466); noted in English legal history as the author of *Tenures,* one of the earliest treatises on English law and the basis of Edward Coke's *Institute of the Lawes of England* (1628), also known as *Coke Upon Littleton.*

Liu Shao-chi *(lə͞oo shou chē)* 1898?–1969. Chinese Communist leader. Gained reputation as an able Communist party organizer and theoretician; succeeded Mao as chairman of the Chinese government; fell into disgrace and was dismissed during the Cultural Revolution (1969).

Liverpool *(lĭv ər po͝ol),* **Earl of** title of Robert Banks Jenkinson. 1770–1828. British statesman. Entered Parliament (1790); foreign secretary in Addington's ministry (1801–1803); home secretary (1804–1806, 1807–1809); secretary for war and colonies (1809–12); prime minister (1812–27); led Britain through Napoleonic Wars and War of 1812; ended slave trade by European powers; introduced severe repressive measures at home, including increased duty on corn, passage of the Six Acts, and suspension of Habeas Corpus Act; supported reactionary governments abroad; died of apoplexy.

Livingston, Robert R. 1746–1813. American statesman. *b.* New York, N. Y. As member of the Continental Congress (from 1775), he was one of five charged with drawing up the Declaration of Independence; first secretary of state (1781–83); as chancellor of New York (1777–1801), administered oath of office to Washington (1789); as minister plenipotentiary in Paris, negotiated the cession of Louisiana; introduced the merino sheep into the colonies and helped Fulton construct the first steamer; his grandfather was Robert Livingston, 1654–1728. *b.* Ancrum, Scotland. Founded the Livingston Manor of 160,000 acres (now in Dutchess and Columbia Counties in N.Y.); secretary for Indian Affairs in N.Y. (1695–1728); Robert R. Livingston's brother was Edward Livingston, 1764–1836. *b.* Livingston Manor. Mayor of New York City (1801–1803); U. S. House of Representatives (1822–28); U. S. Senate (1828–31); secretary of state (1831–33); and minister to France (1833–35). His *Complete Works in Criminal Jurisprudence* (2 vols., 1873) earned him international fame.

Livingstone *(lĭv ĭng stən),* **David** 1813–73. Scottish missionary explorer. *b.* Low Blantyre. Began as factory worker; studied medicine, intending to be a medical missionary; ordained by the London Missionary Society (1840); went to Bechuanaland in South Africa (1841); led exploratory expeditions into undiscovered country north of Transvaal; discovered Lake Ngami (1849); crossed the Kalahari Desert, traveled down the Zambesi, and discovered Victoria Falls (1855); recorded discoveries in *Missionary Travels* (1857); on return to England, resigned from London Missionary Society and accepted government commission to continue Zambesi explorations; discovered (1858) Lakes Shirwa and Nyasa and explored the Zambesi, Shire, and Rovuma rivers; wrote *The Zambesi and Its Tributaries* (1865); returned to Africa (1866) on behalf of Royal Geographical Society to determine the exact source of the Nile and the watershed of central Africa; discovered Lakes Mweru and Bangweulu (1867–68); reached the Lualaba River, but was driven back to Ujiji by ill health and the hostility of slavers; met at Ujiji by H. M. Stanley in a famous encounter (1871); died at Old Chitambo in Zambia (1873); published *Last Journals* of the years 1866–73 (1874).

Livy *(lĭv ĭ),* **Titus** proper name: Titus Livius. 59 B.C.–A.D. 17. Roman historian. *b.* Padua. Noted as the author of *The Annals of the Roman People* in 142 books, of which 35 are extant; the work, commissioned by Augustus, describes the history of Rome from its foundation to the death of Drusus (9 B.C.).

Lloyd *(loid),* **Harold Clayton** 1894–1971. American film comedian. *b.* Burchard, Neb. First appeared as Lonesome Luke in one-reel comedies; created the comic character of a shy, bespectacled boy in a series of popular comedies, such as *Grandma's Boy, Safety Last, Girl Shy,* and *The Freshman;* continued to appear in such talkies as *Feet First, The Cat's Paw,* and *The Milky Way;* later founded the Harold Lloyd Corporation and produced films.

Lloyd George *(loid jôrj),* **David** title: Earl of Dwyfor. 1863–1945. British statesman. *b.* Manchester. Entered Parliament (1890); president of Board of Trade (1905–1908); as chancellor of exchequer (1908–15) sponsored the People's Budget of 1909 with its inroads into wealth and monopoly and led the fight to curtail veto power of House of Lords; responsible for passage of Old Age Pensions Act and National Insurance Act (1911); minister of munitions (1915–16); secretary of state for war (1916); prime minister (1916–22); led Britain to victory in World War I; headed British delegation to Versailles; instrumental in establishment of Irish Free State. Author of *War Memoirs* (6 vols., 1933–36) and *The Truth About the Peace Treaties* (2 vols., 1938).

Locke *(lŏk),* **John** 1632–1704. English philosopher. *b.* Wrington. Studied philosophy and medicine; found patron in Baron Ashley, Earl of Shaftesbury; suspected of complicity in Shaftesbury's Monmouth plot (1684) and forced to live in exile in Holland (1684–88);

on return, became commissioner of appeal and advisor on coinage (1689–1704). Best known as author of *An Essay Concerning Human Understanding* (1690) which denied the existence of innate ideas and declared that the mind was a *tabula rasa* written upon by sense experience alone; postulated the possibility of rational demonstration of moral principles and the existence of God; by insisting that all knowledge was solely based on sensation, laid the foundation of empiricism; as a political philosopher, made an influential defense of the right of the ruled to depose the rulers if they offend natural law; believed in natural goodness of man in presocial state and the need for governments to secure morality, stability, and moderation in public life. Other works include *An Essay Concerning Toleration* (1667), *Some Thoughts Concerning Education* (1693), *The Reasonableness of Christianity* (1695), and *Two Treatises on Government* (1689).

Lodge *(lôj),* **Henry Cabot** 1850–1924. American statesman. *b.* Boston. Scion of one of the most influential families in New England; member, House of Representatives (1887–93); U. S. Senate (1893–1924); as leader of Senate's isolationist group, helped thwart Wilson's international programs and U. S. entry into the League of Nations; recorded his conflict with the administration in *The Senate and the League of Nations* (1925). Other works include *Early Memoirs* (1914), and *The Story of the Revolution* (2 vols., 1898).

Lodge, Sir Oliver Joseph 1851–1940. English physicist. *b.* Penkhull. Professor of physics at Liverpool (1881–1900) and principal of University of Birmingham (1900–1919); made important contributions to wireless telegraphy; studied electrons, electromagnetic waves, ether theory, and lightning; active in psychical research and in reconciling religion and science. Author of *Signalling Across Space Without Wires* (1897), *Modern Views of Electricity* (1889), *Man and the Universe* (1908), *The Ether of Space* (1909), *Science and Mortality* (1908), *Advancing Science* (1931), and *Past Years* (1931).

Loeb *(lûb),* **Jacques** 1859–1924. American physiologist. *b.* Mayen, Germany. Immigrated to U. S. (1891); professor at University of California (1902–10); member of Rockefeller Institute of Medical Research (1910–24); did pioneer research in parthenogenesis, egg fertilization, and regeneration of broken parts by chemical stimulus; developed tropism theory to explain certain types of behavior. Author of *Dynamics of Living Matter* (1906), *Artificial Parthenogenesis and Fertilisation* (1913), *The Mechanistic Conception of Life* (1912), *The Organism as a Whole* (1916), *The Heliotropism of Animals* (1890), and *Physiological Morphology* (1891–92).

Loewe *(lō),* **Frederick** 1904–. American composer. *b.* in Austria. Collaborated with Alan Jay Lerner on a number of very successful musicals, such as *My Fair Lady* and *Camelot,* which set the standards for popular American show tunes.

Loewi *(lû vē),* **Otto** 1873–1961. American pharmacologist. *b.* Frankfurt-am-Main, Germany. Professor of pharmacology at Graz

(1909–38); came to U. S. (1940); professor of pharmacology at New York University (from 1940); investigated digitalis, transmission of nerve impulses, and carbohydrate metabolism; with Sir H. H. Dale, awarded Nobel Prize in physiology and medicine (1936).

Lombard *(lŏm bärd),* **Peter** c1100–1164. Italian theologian. *b.* Novara. Consecrated bishop of Paris (1159); called Magister Sententiarum (Master of Sentences) from his authorship of *Sententiarum Libri IV,* a collection of sentences from Church fathers on Christian doctrine, used as a textbook of Catholic theology during the Middle Ages.

Lomonosov *(lŭ mə nô sôf),* **Mikhail Vasilievich** 1711–65. Russian scholar and scientist. *b.* Denisovka. Professor of chemistry at University of St. Petersburg and later its rector; achievements as a scientist in the study of heat and gases overshadowed by contributions to Russian language and literature; systematized the grammar and orthography of Russian language and introduced tonic rather than syllabic versification into Russian prosody; made the reformed language standard throughout Russia; author of works on rhetoric, grammar, and Russian history.

London *(lŭn dən),* **Jack** 1876–1916. American writer. *b.* San Francisco, Calif. a sailor, hobo, gold miner, newspaperman, longshoreman, Socialist, and salmon fisher; wrote over 43 books, most dealing with romantic adventures based on own experience. Works include *The Son of the Wolf* (1900), *The God of His Fathers* (1901), *A Daughter of the Snows* (1902), *The Call of the Wild* (1903), *The People of the Abyss* (1903), *The Sea-Wolf* (1904), *White Fang* (1907), *Martin Eden* (1909), *When God Laughs* (1911), *Adventure* (1911), *The Cruise of the Snark* (1911), *The Abysmal Brute* (1913), *The Valley of the Moon* (1913), *The Strength of the Strong* (1914), *Jerry of the Islands* (1917), and *John Barleycorn* (1913).

Long *(lông),* **Huey Pierce** 1893–1935. American politician. *b.* Winnfield, La. Governor of Louisiana (1928); won the support of the poor and disadvantaged by demagoguery; created a powerful but corrupt political machine; launched a popular program of public works; U. S. Senate (1931–35); opposed the New Deal, proposing an alternative Share-the-Wealth program; assassinated (1935). Wrote *My First Years in the White House;* his brother Earl Long (1895–1960) was governor of Louisiana (1936–40, 1948–52, 1956–60), until removed from office by reason of insanity; Huey's son, Russell B. Long (1918–) was elected to Senate from Louisiana (1948).

Longfellow *(lông fĕl ō),* **Henry Wadsworth** 1807–82. American poet. *b.* Portland, Me. Professor of modern languages and literature at Bowdoin College (1829–35) and at Harvard (1835–54); gained popular recognition with *Ballads and Other Poems* (1841) that included "The Wreck of the Hesperus," "The Village Blacksmith," "The Skeleton in Armor," "The Rainy Day," and "Maidenhood"; gave up post at Harvard to devote himself to writing; first American poet to achieve wide recognition abroad; excelled in long narrative poems, such as *Evangeline* (1847), *The Song of Hiawatha* (1855), and *The Courtship of Miles Standish* (1858), that combined folkloric quality, idealism, craftsmanship, simple themes, quotable lines, and sentimental romance. Other works include *The Belfry of Bruges* (1846), *Tales of a Wayside Inn* (1863), *New England Tragedy* (1868), *Christus* (1872), *The Masque of Pandora* (1875), *Voices of the Night* (1839), *The Seaside and the Fireside* (1850), *The Golden Legend* (1851), *Three Books of Song* (1872), *The Hanging of the Crane* (1874), *Ultima Thule* (1880), *Hyperion Outre Mer* (1835), and *Poems on Slavery* (1842).

Longinus *(lôn jī nəs),* **Dionysius Cassius** *fl.* 3rd century. Greek philosopher. Taught rhetoric at Athens; later moved to Palmyra and became tutor and political advisor; in the court of Zenobia influenced Zenobia to revolt against Rome; on the suppression of the revolt, executed by Emperor Aurelian. Works include *Philological Discourses, On the First Principles,* and *On the Chief End;* long regarded as the author of *On the Sublime,* written by Longus, a 1st-century Greek writer.

Lopez de Legazpe *(lō pāth dā lā gāth pā),* **Miguel** 1510–72. Spanish conqueror of the Philippines. *b.* Zumarraga. Commanded the forces which conquered the Philippine Islands (1564); conquered Luzon (1571); founded the cities of San Miguel and Manila (1572).

Lorca *(lôr kä),* **Federico Garcia** 1899–1936. Spanish playwright and poet. *b.* Fuente Vaqueros. Balladeer and dramatist; combined Spanish folk themes with elements of classical Greek tragedy. Principal works include *Romancero Gitano* (1929), *Bodas de Sangre* (1938), *Canciones* (1927), *Yerma* (1934), and *La Casa de Bernarda Alba* (1936).

Lorentz *(lō rənts),* **Hendrik Antoon** 1853–1928. Dutch physicist. *b.* Arnhem. Professor of mathematical physics at Leiden (from 1878); one of the first physicists to describe the concept of electrons; developed Maxwell's electromagnetic theory of light; propounded the Lorentz transformation, the Lorentz principle of correlation, and the Fitzgerald-Lorentz contraction, all crucial in the theory of relativity; with Pieter Zeeman, discovered the Zeeman effect, a change in spectrum lines in magnetic fields; with Zeeman, awarded Nobel Prize in physics (1902) for work on the influence of magnetism on radiation. *Collected Papers* published at The Hague (9 vols., 1934–39).

Lotze *(lōt sĕ),* **Rudolf Hermann** 1817–81. German philosopher. *b.* Bautzen. Professor of philosophy at Leipzig (1842) and Göttingen (1844); founded the science of physiological psychology with *Medicinische Psychologie* (1852), opposing the theory of vital force; as a philosopher, developed a system of ideal-realism in which natural laws were described as functions of a world mind. Author of *General Physiology of Bodily Life* (1851), *Metaphysik* (1841), *Microcosmos* (1856–64), and *Systeme der Philosophie* (2 vols., 1874, 1879).

Louis *(lwē)* Name of eighteen kings of France including:

LOUIS IX also called SAINT LOUIS. 1214–70. King of France (1226–70) of the Carolingian line. *b.* Poissy. Considered perfect example of a medieval Christian monarch; took part in Sixth Crusade; landed in Egypt with 40,000 men (1249); defeated and captured at El Mansura (1250), but later ransomed; returned to France (1254); remainder of reign peaceful and prosperous; gained reputation for piety, charity, justice, and asceticism; by Treaty of Paris (1259) and Treaty of Corbeil (1258), made territorial adjustments with Spanish and English; built great cathedrals, including Chartres; helped found the Sorbonne; authorized new code of laws and set up royal courts in provinces, with right of appeal to the Crown; embarked on a new Crusade (1270), but died in Tunis of the plague; canonized (1297). Feast day: Aug. 25.

LOUIS XIV. also called THE GREAT, LE GRAND MONARQUE, THE SUN KING. 1638–1715. King of France (1643–1715) of the Bourbon line. *b.* Saint-Germain-en-Laye. Ascended throne at age five; until 1661, reign dominated by Cardinal Mazarin, queen mother Anne of Austria; chief events included Thirty Years' War, ending with Treaty of Westphalia (1648), the civil wars of the Fronde (1648–53), and war with Spain ended by Peace of the Pyrenees (1659); on death of Mazarin, assumed power (1661); aided by able ministers, including Colbert as comptroller general of finance (1661–83) and Louvois as minister of war (1666–91); engaged in ruinous foreign wars, including Queen's War (1667–68) ended by Treaty of Aix-la-Chapelle, the Dutch War (1672–78) ended by Treaty of Nijmegen, War of the League of Augsburg (1688–97) ended by Treaty of Ryswick, War of the Spanish Succession (1701–14) ended by Treaties of Utrecht (1713) and Rastatt (1714); under Edict of Nantes, resumed persecution of Huguenots (1685); invested the office of the king with almost divine status, epitomized in the words *"L'état, c'est moi"*; reign, longest in the history of Europe, called the Augustan Age in France; witnessed the flowering of French literature and art with such artists as Corneille, Racine, Molière, Pascal, and Fénelon.

LOUIS XV. 1710–74. King of France (1715–74) of the Bourbon line. *b.* Versailles. Ascended throne as a minor; during minority, under the regency of Philippe II, Duc d'Orleans, assisted by Guillaume Dubois; succeeding advisors and ministers included the duke of Bourbon, Cardinal Fleury, duc de Choiseul, and duc d'Aiguillon; involved France in War of the Polish Succession (1733–35), ended by the Treaty of Vienna, War of the Austrian Succession (1740–48), ended by Treaty of Aix-la-Chapelle, and the Seven Years' War (1756–63), ended by the Treaty of Versailles; wars ruined the treasury and caused the loss of Canada and India.

LOUIS XVI. 1754–93. King of France (1774–92) of the Bourbon line. *b.* Versailles. Aided at first by able ministers Chrétian Malesherbes, Anne Robert Turgot, Jacques Necker, and Charles Vergennes; introduced reforms and abolished taxes and laws; failed, however, to stem the tide of popular discontent; aided the Revolutionary cause in American War of Independence (1778–81); convened the States-General (1789), which signalled the beginning of French Revolution; tried to escape from France, but was arrested and brought back to Paris (1791); deposed, tried for treason, found guilty, and guillotined (1793).

Louis Napoleon. *See* **Napoleon III**

Louis Philippe *(fə lēp)* also known as the Citizen King. 1773–1850. King of France (1830–48). *b.* Paris. Son of Louis Philippe Joseph (Philippe-Égalité), Duc d'Orléans; on outbreak of French Revolution, renounced titles and joined revolutionaries; colonel in the Revolutionary Army; joined Charles Dumouriez in an attempted counterrevolution, and on its failure fled to Austria; spent Napoleonic era in exile in Switzerland, U.S., and England; on return to France (1814), estates restored; after July Revolution (1830) against Charles X, proclaimed king of the French by the liberal monarchists—Adolphe Thiers, Lafayette, and others—and elected by National Chamber of Deputies; affected bourgeois manners; reign marked by conquest of Algeria and commercial prosperity following the spread of Industrial Revolution; with François Guizot as principal minister, tried to restore absolute monarchy but alienated liberal supporters; weakened by Bonapartist intrigues and the rise of socialism; overthrown by the Revolution of 1848 and compelled to abdicate and flee to England.

Lowell *(lō əl),* **Amy** 1874–1925. American poet and critic. *b.* Brookline, Mass. Joined the Imagists and experimented with polyphonic prose and free verse. Author of collections of verse including *A Dome of Many-Colored Glass* (1912), *Sword Blades and Poppy Seeds* (1914), *Men, Women, and Ghosts* (1916), *Can Grande's Castle* (1918), *Pictures of the Floating World* (1919), *Legends* (1921), *A Critical Fable* (1922), *What's O'Clock* (1925, Pultizer Prize), *East Wind* (1926), and *Ballads for Sale* (1927), critical studies of French and American poets, and *John Keats* (2 vols., 1925).

Lowell, James Russell 1819–91. American man of letters. *b.* Cambridge, Mass. Editor of *Atlantic Monthly* (1857–61); associate editor of *North American Review* (from 1864); professor of literature at Harvard (1856–86); U. S. minister to Spain (1877–80) and Great Britain (1880–85); fame rests on poetic and critical works, including *A Year's Life* (1841), *Poems* (1844, 1848), *The Vision of Sir Launfal* (1848), *A Fable for Critics* (1848), *The Bigelow Papers* (1848–67), *Under the Willows* (1869), *The Cathedral* (1869), *Three Memorial Poems* (1876), *Heartsease and Rue* (1888), *Conversations on Some of the Old Poets* (1845), *Among My Books* (1870, 1876), *Democracy* (1886), and *Political Essays* (1888).

Lowell, Percival 1855–1916. American astronomer. *b.* Boston, Mass. Established and headed the Lowell Observatory at Flagstaff, Ariz. (1894); conducted studies of planet Mars and predicted existence of planet Pluto; lived in Japan (1877–93) and wrote extensively on the Far East, including *Choson—The Land of the Morning Calm* (1885), *Soul of the Far East*

(1888), and *Occult Japan* (1895); astronomical works include *Mars* (1895), *The Solar System* (1903), *Mars and Its Canals* (1906), *Mars as the Abode of Life* (1908), *The Evolution of Worlds* (1909), and *The Genesis of the Planets* (1916).

Lowell, Robert Traill Spence 1917–77. American poet. *b.* Boston, Mass. Noted for highly individualistic and intense poetry. Works include *Lord Weary's Castle* (1946), *The Mills of the Cavanaughs* (1951), *For the Union Dead* (1964), *Imitations* (1961), *Life Studies* (1959), and *The Old Glory* (1965).

Loyola *(loi ō lə),* **Saint Ignatius of** original name: INIGO DE ONEZ Y LOYOLA. 1491–1556. Spanish churchman. *b.* Guipúzcoa. Began as courtier in court of Ferdinand and Isabella; joined military service (1521); wounded at siege of Pampeluna and crippled for life; while recovering, read *Life of Christ* and *Flowers of the Saints;* converted to religion; fired by intense spiritual enthusiasm, made barefoot pilgrimage to the shrine of the Virgin at Montserrat, renounced the world, and swore himself a knight of the Virgin (1522); made barefoot pilgrimage to Jerusalem (1523–24); as preparation for career of religious teaching, studied at universities of Barcelona Alcalá, Salamanca, and Paris (1524–34); with six companions, founded the Society of Jesus (Jesuits), devoted to the conversion of infidels; took vows of chastity, obedience, and special submission to the pope; ordained priest (1537); the Society of Jesus and its constitution officially recognized by Pope Paul III (1540); elected superior, or general, of the order (1541–46). Author of *Constitutions of the Order, Spiritual Exercises* (1548), and *Letter on Obedience* (1533); canonized (1628). Feast day: July 31.

Lucan *(lu kən)* Latin name: MARCUS ANNAEUS LUCANUS. 39–65. Roman poet. *b.* Córdova, Spain. Enjoyed the friendship of Nero for a brief period, but later led Pisonian conspiracy against him; betrayed and forced to commit suicide; author of *Bellum Civile* or *Pharsalia* (10 books), an epic poem on the civil war between Caesar and Pompey.

Luce *(lo͞os),* **Henry Robinson** 1898–1967. American publisher. *b.* Shantung, China. Cofounder of *Time* magazine and founder of Time-Life publishing empire, which included *Life* (1936–72) and *Fortune* (from 1930) magazines; imbued publishing with a missionary zeal for presenting news in a vivid and colorful manner; one of the most successful media barons of the 20th century.

Lucian *(lū shən)* called THE BLASPHEMER. c120–c200. Greek satirist. *b.* Samosata, Syria. Noted as the author of romances, dialogues, poems, and works on criticism, rhetoric, biography, and, above all, satires on the dying religions and philosophies of his time. Works include *The True History, Dialogues of the Gods, Dialogues of the Dead, Auction of Philosophers, Demonax, Peregrine,* and *Timon.*

Lucretius *(lū krē shi əs)* full name: TITUS LUCRETIUS CARUS. c96–55 B.C. Roman poet. *b.* Rome. Best known as the author of *De Rerum Natura,* a philosophical poem in hexameter celebrating Epicurean philosophy; upheld materialism and denounced religious belief; committed suicide.

Luke *(lūk),* **Saint** *fl.* 1st century. Evangelist and author of the third Gospel and Acts of the Apostles. According to tradition, a physician of non-Jewish origin and companion of St. Paul; symbolized by the ox. Feast day: Oct. 28.

Lully *(lü lē),* **Jean Baptiste** 1632–87. French composer. *b.* Florence, Italy. Went to Paris as a boy; won favor of Louis XIV; became court composer and director of Académie Royale de Musique, later renamed Grand Opéra (1672–87); regarded as founder of national French opera; with Philippe Quinault as librettist, wrote many operas incorporating ballet; developed operatic overture and combined recitative and aria. Works include *Alceste* (1674), *Thésée* (1675), *Atys* (1676), *Proserpine* (1680), *Persée* (1682), *Armide et Renaud* (1686), *Cadmus et Hermione* (1673), *Psyché* (1678), *Phaeton* (1683), *Roland* (1685), and *Acis et Galathée* (1686).

Lully *(lŭl ĭ),* **Raymond** Catalan name: RAMÓN LULL; also known as DOCTOR ILLUMINATUS. c1235–1315. Catalan philosopher and missionary. *b.* Palma, Majorca. Became a Franciscan (1266) after having visions of the crucified Christ; resolved to become missionary to the Muslims; studied Arabic and taught it at Miramar (1275–85); teacher in Paris (1287–89); went to Algeria to convert Muslims (1291); twice banished, and on third trip stoned to death; known for the Lullian method enunciated in *Ars Magna,* a systematic reduction of all knowledge to certain fundamental categories. Other works include *Blanquerna, Libre de Maravelles, Lo Cant de Ramon,* and *Libre de Contemplacio.*

Luria *(lo͞o ryə),* **Salvador Edward** 1912–. American biologist. *b.* Italy. Immigrated to U.S. (1940); with Max Delbrück and Alfred D. Hershey, awarded Nobel Prize in physiology and medicine (1969) for discoveries concerning the replication mechanism and the genetic structure of viruses.

Luther *(lo͞oth ər),* **Martin** 1483–1546. German religious reformer. *b.* Eisleben. Entered Augustinian order at Erfurt (1505); ordained priest (1508); lecturer (1508–11); professor (1511–46) at Wittenberg; visited Rome (1511) and was appalled by the spiritual laxity there; began preaching against sale of indulgences; nailed 95 Theses condemning indulgences to church door at Wittenberg (1517); joined by Melanchthon and later Erasmus and Hutten; summoned to Rome to answer charges but refused (1518); defended position before Cardinal Cajetan at Augsburg; denied supremacy of the pope; published (1520) "Primary Works," three tracts containing the first principles of the Reformation: *Address to the Christian Nobles of the German Nation, On the Babylonian Captivity of the Church of God,* and *Christian Liberty;* enunciated justification by faith alone, the primacy of the Bible as sole authority in matters of faith and practice, and the priesthood of believers; excommunicated by Pope Leo X (1520); publicly burned the bull, an act of defiance that convulsed Germany; appeared before Diet of Worms (1521) but refused to recant; placed under ban; remained under protection of the elector of Saxony (1521–22); translated New Testament and composed *On Monastic Vows* and other tracts; returned to Wittenberg (1522); published translation of *Old Testament,* a hymnbook, and two catechisms; engaged in controversies with Erasmus, Zwingli, and Calvin; guided Melanchthon in drawing up Augsburg Confession (1530), which marked the culmination of the Reformation; regarded as founder of New High German, the modern literary language of Germany. Works include *Table-Talk* and *Diary;* complete works published in Erlangen (67 vols., 1826–57).

Luthuli *(lə too li),* **Albert John** 1898–1967. South African statesman. *b.* in South Africa. Son of a Zulu chief and a Christian missionary; elected tribal chief of Groutville, Natal, but deposed by South African government; president of African National Congress (1952–60); led a campaign of nonviolent resistance to apartheid, prosecuted, and interned; awarded Nobel Peace Prize (1960). Author of *Let My People Go* (1962).

Lwoff *(lə wôf),* **André Michel** 1902–. French microbiologist. *b.* Allier. Professor of microbiology at Pasteur Institute (from 1921); with François Jacob and Jacques L. Monod, awarded Nobel Prize in physiology and medicine (1965) for discovery of the regulatory processes in body cells that contribute to genetic control of enzymes and virus synthesis.

Lydgate *(lĭd gāt),* **John** c1370–c1451. English poet. *b.* Lydgate. Benedictine monk and disciple of Chaucer; court poet to Henry IV, V, and VI; tried to imitate Chaucer's style but is generally prolix and pedestrian. Works include *Falls of Princes* (1430–38), *Troy Book* (1412–20), *The Story of Thebes* (1420), *The Life of Our Lady* (printed 1484), *The Dance of Death* (printed 1554), *The Court of Sapience* (printed 1481), *The Temple of Glass* (printed 1479), and *The Complaint of the Black Knight.*

Lyell *(lī ĕl),* **Sir Charles** 1797–1875. British geologist. *b.* Kinnordy, Scotland. Studied law and was called to the bar but devoted life to geology; considered father of modern geology; opposed the ruling theory of catastrophism and developed theory of uniformitarianism on which modern geology is based. His *Principles of Geology* (1830–33) is ranked with Darwin's *Origin of Species* as a seminal scientific work; other works include *The Elements of Geology* (1838), *The Geological Evidences of the Antiquity of Man* (1863), *Travels in North America* (1845), and *A Second Visit to the United States* (1849).

Lyly *(lĭl ĭ),* **John** c1554–1606. English man of letters. *b.* in Weald of Kent. Originated literary style known as euphuism, marked by affected elegance; employed such style in *Euphues, the Anatomy of Wit* (1579) and *Euphues and His England* (1580); also wrote plays, including *The Woman in the Moone* (c1583), *Alexander and Campaspe* (1584), *Sapho and Phao* (1584), *Endymion* (1591), *Midas* (1592), *Galathea* (1592), *Mother Bombie* (1594), and *Love's Metamorphosis* (1601).

Lynen *(lü nən),* **Feodor** 1911–. German biochemist. Professor of biochemistry at Munich University and director of Max Planck Institut für Zelichemie (from 1942); with Konrad E. Bloch, awarded Nobel Prize in physiology and medicine (1964) for discovery of the mechanism and control of cholesterol and of the biochemistry of the vitamin biotin.

Lyons *(lī ənz),* **Joseph Aloysius** 1879–1939. Australian statesman. *b.* Stanley, Tasmania. Entered Tasmanian House of Assembly (1909); premier of Tasmania (1923–29); sat in Federal House of Representatives (from 1929); held cabinet posts (until 1931); broke away from government and founded United Australia party; as its leader, won general election (1931); prime minister (1932–39); administration restored economic solvency after the Depression.

Lysander *(lī săn dər)* *d.* 395 B.C. Spartan commander. As admiral of Spartan fleet, won victories of Notium (407) and Aegospotami (405); captured Athens (404) and brought the Peloponnesian War to a close; recalled to Sparta by ephors jealous of his supremacy; commanded forces against Boeotians and was killed near Haliartus.

Lysenko *(lĭ sĕng kō),* **Trofim Denisovich** 1898–1976. Soviet biologist. *b.* Karlovka. President of the Academy of Agricultural Sciences (1938–56, 1958–62); officially repudiated Mendelian theory and asserted that environmentally caused traits can be transmitted genetically; developed the theory of vernalization and new varieties of summer wheat and cotton; lost influence after being relieved as head of the Institute of Genetics (1965).

Lytton *(lĭt ən),* **Edward George Earle Lytton Bulwer-** title: BARON LYTTON OF KNEBWORTH. 1803–73. English man of letters. *b.* London. Sat in Parliament (1831–41, 1852–66); colonial secretary (1858–59); prolific output includes *Eugene Aram* (1832), *The Last Days of Pompeii* (1834), *Rienzi* (1835), *The Last of the Barons* (1843), *Harold* (1848), *The Caxtons* (1850), *The Coming Race* (1871), and *Pausanias* (1876); wrote poetry and dramas, including *The Lady of Lyons* (1838), *Richelieu* (1839), *Money* (1840), and *Cromwell* (1842). Son EDWARD ROBERT LYTTON BULWER-LYTTON, 1ST EARL OF LYTTON (1831–91), English statesman and writer, was governor general and viceroy of India (1878–80); under the pseudonym OWEN MEREDITH, wrote *Clytemnestra* (1855), *Lucile* (1860), *The Ring of Amasis* (1863), *Poems* (1867), *Fables in Song* (1874), *Glenaveril, or the Metamorphoses* (1885), and *King of Poppy* (1892).

M

MacArthur *(mək är thər),* **Arthur** 1845–1912. American general. *b.* Springfield, Mass. Fought in Civil War; major general (1898–99); military governor of the Philippines (1900–1901). Son DOUGLAS

MacArthur (1880–1964), American general. *b.* Little Rock, Ark. Commander of 42nd Division in France during World War I; superintendent of U. S. Military Academy at West Point as brigadier general (1919–22); commanding general of Philippine Department (1928); general and chief of staff of U. S. army (1930–35); military advisor to Philippine Commonwealth (1935–37); retired from service (1939); recalled and named general in command of U.S. forces in the Far East (1941); supreme commander of Allied forces in Southwest Pacific (1942); general of the army (1944); directed leap-frogging strategy that pushed Japanese back from the Philippines; accepted surrender of Japan (1945); supreme commander of occupation forces in Japan (1945–51); on outbreak of Korean War, supreme commander of UN forces in Korea (1950–51); pressed the war into North Korea; publicly in conflict with President Truman over military policies, and dismissed (1951); widely admired as one of the ablest commanders in U.S. military history.

Macaulay *(mə kô lĭ),* **Thomas Babington** 1800–1859. English statesman and historian. *b.* Rothley Temple. Sat in Parliament (1830–34, 1839–47, 1852–56); raised to peerage as Baron Macaulay (1857); member of Supreme Council in India (1834–38); drafted Indian Penal Code; secretary of war (1839–41); paymaster general (1846–47); principal literary work *History of England from the Accession of James II* begun (1845) but unfinished at death after publication of five volumes; also wrote *Lays of Ancient Rome* (1842) and numerous essays and historical sketches, as a master of historical narrative.

Maccabaeus *(măk ə bē əs),* **Judas** also Jehudah Maccabaeus ("the hammerer"). *fl.* 2nd century B.C. Jewish national hero. Son of Mattathias, founder of the Hasmonaeans; led the Jewish nation in a war of liberation against Antiochus Epiphanes; defeated four Syrian armies, reconquered Jerusalem, and purified the Temple in 164 B.C.; event commemorated in the feast of the Hanukkah; defeated the Syrians at Nicanor (161) but fell in battle (160).

Macdonald *(mək dŏn əld),* **James Ramsay** 1866–1937. British statesman. *b.* Lossiemouth, Scotland. Entered Parliament (1906); leader of Labor party (1911–14, 1922–31); as a pacifist, opposed England's entry into World War I; lost Khaki Election (1918); prime minister of first British Labor ministry (Jan–Oct., 1924); formed second Labor ministry (1929); introduced progresssive legislation on insurance and public housing; split with Labor party over economic measures to combat the Depression; formed National Labor party; headed a national government in alliance with Conservatives (1931–35). Author of *Socialism* (1907), *Socialism and Government* (1909), and other books.

Macdonald, Sir John Alexander 1815–91. Canadian statesman. *b.* Glasgow, Scotland. Immigrated to Canada (1820); sat in House of Assembly (1844–54, 1856–91); premier of Upper Canada (1857); instrumental in securing passage of British North America Act (1867); first prime minister of Dominion of Canada (1867–73); prime minister (1878–91); promoted construction of Pacific Railway.

Macdonald, John Sandfield 1812–72. Canadian statesman. *b.* St. Raphael. Prime minister of Canada (1862–64); opposed Federation movement but, after Federation, served as first premier of Ontario (1867–71).

Macdowell *(mək dou əl),* **Edward Alexander** 1861–1908. American composer. *b.* New York, N. Y. Studied and taught at Paris, Wiesbaden, Frankfurt, and Zurich; returned to U. S. (1888); first professor of music at Columbia (1896–1904). Best known for *Woodland Sketches, Sea Pieces, Hamlet, Ophelia, Lancelot and Elaine, Lamia, The Saracens, Tragica, Eroica, Norse,* and *Keltic.*

Mach *(mäK),* **Ernst** 1838–1916. Austrian physicist and philosopher. *b.* Turas, Moravia. Carried out experiments on supersonic flight, the flow of gases, shock waves, and the perception of rotation; contribution to aeronautical design acknowledged in the Mach number and the Mach angle, both named after him; as a philosopher, founded *Empiriokritizismus,* a form of logical positivism based on sensations; attempted to correlate psychology and physics. Author of *The Science of Mechanics* (1883), *Beiträge zur Analyse der Empfindungen* (1897), and *Perception and Error* (1905).

Machiavelli *(mä kyə vĕl lĭ),* **Niccolò** 1469–1527. Florentine statesman and political philosopher. *b.* Florence. Leading official under the Florentine Republic (1492–1512); secretary to the Dieci di Libertà e Pace (1498–1512); shaped political and diplomatic policy of the Republic; dismissed from office when Medici regained power (1512); devoted rest of life to literature; wrote *The Prince,* the most important work on the art of government in Middle Ages. Other works include *Art of War, Discourse on the First Ten Books of Livy, History of Florence* and *La Mandragola.*

Mackenzie *(mə kĕn zĭ),* **Alexander** 1822–92. Canadian statesman. *b.* Perthshire, Scotland. Immigrated to Canada (1842); elected to Provincial Parliament of Ontario (1861) and to first Dominion House of Commons (1867); prime minister (1873–78).

Macleish *(məc lēsh),* **Archibald** 1892–. American poet, playwright, and librarian. *b.* Glencoe, Ill. Professor of rhetoric at Harvard (1949–62); assistant secretary of state (1944–45); librarian of Congress (1939–44); won Pulitzer Prize for poetry for *Conquistador* (1933) and *Collected Poems, 1917–52* (1953); achieved Broadway success with *J. B.* (1958). Other volumes of verse include *The Happy Marriage* (1924), *The Pot of Earth* (1925), *Streets in the Moon* (1926), *New Found Land* (1930), *America Was Promises* (1939), and *Actfive* (1948); also wrote the verse plays *Nobodaddy* (1925), *Panic* (1935), *The Fall of the City* (1937), *Herakles* (1967), and collected essays on aesthetics, *Poetry and Experience* (1961).

Macleod *(mək loud),* **John James Rickard** 1876–1935. Scottish physiologist. *b.* near Dunkeld. Professor of physiology at Western

Reserve, Cleveland (1903–18), University of Toronto (1918–28), and University of Aberdeen (1928–35); shared Nobel Prize in physiology and medicine (1923) for discovery of insulin with F. G. Banting (1922). Author of *Practical Physiology* (1903), *Diabetes, Its Pathological Physiology* (1913), *Fundamentals of Human Physiology* (with R. G. Pearce, 1916), *Physiology and Biochemistry in Modern Medicine* (1941), and *Carbohydrate Metabolism and Insulin* (1926).

Macmillan, *(mək mĭl lən),* **Maurice Harold** 1894–. British statesman. Entered Parliament (1924); remained a backbencher (until 1940); held minor positions in Churchill's war cabinet; minister of housing (1951–54); minister of defense (1954–55); secretary of state for foreign affairs (1955); chancellor of the exchequer (1955–57); prime minister (1957–63); worked to improve England's domestic economy and relations between Western and Soviet blocs. Author of a number of books including his autobiography (6 vols., 1966–73).

Madison *(măd ə sən),* **James** 1751–1836. Fourth president of U. S. (1809–17). *b.* Port Conway, Va. Member of Virginia Convention (1776); member of Continental Congress (1780); with Jay and Hamilton, helped frame the Federal Constitution during Constitutional Convention (1787); contributed essays on the meaning of popular government to *The Federalist;* elected to first Congress (1789–97); took leading role in drafting the Bill of Rights; leader of Jeffersonian Republicans opposed to Hamilton; with Jefferson, drafted Virginia Resolutions against the Alien and Sedition Acts; secretary of state under Jefferson (1801–1809); succeeded Jefferson as president (1809); adopted firm policy toward Great Britain, leading to the War of 1812 and the capture of Washington by the British; concluded war by Treaty of Ghent (1814); toward end of administration espoused some Federalist planks; rector of University of Virginia (1826); *Writings of James Madison,* edited by Gaillard Hunt, published (9 vols., 1900–10).

Maeterlinck *(mā tər lĭngk),* **Count Maurice** 1862–1949. Belgian dramatist. *b.* Ghent. Settled in Paris (1896) becoming part of the Symbolist group; published first volume of poetry *Les Serres Chaudes,* and the prose play *La Princess Maleine* (1889); awarded Nobel Prize in literature (1911). Principal works include *Twelve Chansons* (1896), *The Intruder* (1890), *The Blind* (1890), *Pelléas et Mélisande* (1892), *Monna Vanna* (1902), *Joyzelle* (1903), *The Blue Bird* (1909), *The Betrothal* (1918), *Mary Magdalene* (1910), *Wisdom and Destiny* (1898), *The Life of the Bee* (1901), *The Double Garden* (1904), *Life and Flowers* (1907), *The Great Secret* (1921), *The Life of Space* (1927), *The Magic of the Stars* (1930), and *Before God* (1937).

Magellan *(mə jĕl ən)* **Ferdinand** c1480–1521. Portuguese navigator. *b.* Saborosa. In service of King Manuel I of Portugal; in East Indies (1505–12) and Morocco (1513–14); fell out of favor and offered services to Charles V; obtained Charles's backing to find western passage to the Moluccas; commanded five ships and 265 men and left Spain (Sept. 1519); reached bay of Rio de Janeiro (1519) and Rio de la Plata (1520); sailed through what is now known as the Strait of Magellan into Pacific ocean (1920); discovered the Philippines (1521); received the allegiance of the chief of Cebu, who was baptized; killed on expedition to island of Mactan; survivors attacked by chief of Cebu but resumed voyage in two vessels, discovering Borneo and the Moluccas; the *Victoria* sailed around Africa and reached Sanlucar (Sept. 1522), completing the first circumnavigation of the world.

Magritte *(mȧ grēt),* **René** 1898–1967. Belgian Surrealist painter. *b.* Lessines. Best known for his canvases *The Path of the Air, The Voice of the Winds, The False Mirror, Mental Calculus, The State of Man,* and *The Eye.*

Mahavira *(mȧ hä vē rȧ),* **Vardhamana** *fl.* 6th century B.C. Founder of Jainism. Contemporary of Buddha; 24th jina of the Jain scriptures; principal teachings and practices recorded in the *Kalpasutra* and *Mahaviracharita.*

Mahler *(mä lər),* **Gustav** 1860–1911. Austrian conductor and composer. *b.* Kalischt, Bohemia. Chief conductor at Imperial Opera in Vienna (1897–1907), Metropolitan Opera, New York (1908–10), and New York Philharmonic (1908–11). Best-known works include ten symphonies (the last unfinished), *Das Lied von der Erde, Kindertotenlieder, Humoresken,* and *Das Klagende Lied;* works characterized by unconventional methods and structure, anticipating the works of Schoenberg.

Mailer *(mā lər),* **Norman Kingsley** 1923–. American writer. *b.* Long Branch, N. J. Won fame with his first novel, *The Naked and the Dead* (1948); later works include *The Deer Park* (1955), *An American Dream* (1964), *Advertisements for Myself* (1959), *Why Are We in Vietnam?* (1967), *A Fire on the Moon* (1971), *The Prisoner of Sex* (1971), and *Marilyn* (1973); won Pulitzer Prize for *The Armies of the Night* (1968); writings characterized by brilliant journalistic gifts; generally identified with the counterculture.

Maillol *(mȧ yôl),* **Aristide** 1861–1944. French sculptor. *b.* Banyuls-Sur-Mer. In early life, designed tapestries and was a painter; turned to sculpture at age 40; best known for simple, massive nudes in the neoclassical tradition. Works include *Flora, Pomona, Venus, Three Graces, Fame, Torso,* and *Kneeling Woman.*

Maimonides *(mī mŏn ə dēz),* **Rabbi** also MOSES BEN MAIMON, RAM BAM. 1135–1204. Jewish philosopher. *b.* Córdoba, Spain. Fled Spain with parents to escape the Almohades; after few years in Fez, settled in Cairo, becoming physician to the Sultan; feigned conversion to Islam but eventually became chief rabbi of Cairo; lifework was the reconciliation of Judaism and Aristotelian philosophy and the codification of Jewish oral law. Major writings include the *Mishneh Torah (Repetition of the Law),* the *Sefer ha-Micvoth (Book of Precepts), Dalalt al Hairin (Guide of the Perplexed),* and *Siray (Illumination);* minor works include treatises on Moses, happiness,

Unity of God, epistles to Yemenites, and apostasy; wrote on medicine, mathematics, logic, and law; considered most influential exponent of Judaism next to Moses; his 13 articles of Jewish dogma form part of the Jewish liturgy; greatly influenced later Christian thinkers, including Aquinas.

Maine *(mān),* **Sir Henry James Sumner** 1822–88. English jurist. Regius Professor of Civil Law at Cambridge (1847–54); legal member of Council in India (1863–69); planned codification of Indian law; member of secretary of state's council for India (1871–88); professor of jurisprudence at Oxford (1869–78); master of Trinity (1877–88); professor of international law at Cambridge (1887–88). Famed for works on legal history and philosophy, including *Ancient Law* (1861), *Early History of Institutions* (1875), *Early Law and Custom* (1883), and *International Law* (1888).

Makarios III *(mə kär ĭ ōs)* real name: MICHAEL CHRISTODOULOS MOUSKOS. 1913–77. Archbishop and Cypriot statesman. *b.* Ano Panciyia, Greece. Ordained (1946); archbishop (1950); acknowledged leader of Cypriot independence movement; exiled to Seychelles by the British (1957); returned (1959) as national hero and chief minister in the provisional government; elected first president of Cyprus Republic (1960–74); opposed Enosis (union of Cyprus with Greece) and thus antagonized the pro-Greek faction, who drove him from office (1974) in a short-lived coup; after the ensuing Turkish invasion, restored to office (1974–77) but did not succeed in reunifying the island.

Malamud *(ma lə mōōd),* **Bernard** 1914–. American novelist. *b.* Brooklyn, N. Y. Leader of a new school of Jewish writing whose works are concerned with Jewish tradition. Author of *The Natural* (1952), *The Assistant (1957), A New Life* (1961), *The Magic Barrel* (1958), *Pictures of Fidelman* (1969), *The Tenants* (1971), *Rembrandt's Hat* (1973); won Pulitzer Prize for *The Fixer* (1966).

Malcolm X *(măl kəm ĕks)* original name: MALCOLM LITTLE. 1925–65. American Black Muslim leader. *b.* Omaha, Neb. Became a leader of the Black Muslim sect (1963); assassinated by a dissident group within this sect; collaborated with Alex Haley on *The Autobiography of Malcom X,* documenting his career and his alienation from white society.

Malebranche *(mȧl bränsh),* **Nicolas de** 1638–1715. French philosopher. *b.* Paris. Developed the philosophical school of occasionalism, which attempted to overcome Cartesian dualism by attributing man's knowledge of the physical world to God and stressed the separateness of mind and matter. Principal works include *Recherche de la Vérité* (1674), *Traité de la Nature et de la Grâce* (1680), *Meditations Chrétiennes et Métaphysiques* (1683), and *Traité de Morale* (1684).

Malenkov *(mäl yĕn kôf),* **Georgi Maximilianovich** 1902–. Soviet statesman. *b.* Orenburg. Succeeded Stalin as prime minister (1953); compelled to resign (1954) following failure of agricultural policy; demoted to minor post (1957) and expelled from party (1961).

Mallarmé *(mȧ lȧr mā),* **Stéphane** 1842–98. French poet. *b.* Paris. Leader of the Symbolists and the Decadents; attempted to liberate poetry from the limitations of language by introducing word music. Best known for *L'Après Midi d'un Faune* (1876), *Vers et Prose* (1893), *Les Dieux Antiques* (1800), *Poésies* (1887), *Pages* (1890), and *Les Divagations* (1897).

Malory *(măl ə rĭ),* **Sir Thomas** *fl.* 1470. English author. Best known as the compiler of the English prose epic *Le Morte d'Arthur,* a collection of Arthurian legends; believed to have been a retainer of Earl of Warwick; may have written his classic work in prison.

Malpighi *(mäl pē gē),* **Marcello** 1628–94. Italian anatomist. *b.* Bologna. Professor at Pisa, Bologna, and Messina (1657–91); physician to Pope Innocent XII; considered a pioneer in microscopic anatomy; discovered Malpighian layer (epidermis), Malpighian corpuscle (spleen), and Malpighian tufts (kidney); first to describe structure of lungs, brains, spinal cords, and secreting glands; studied chicken embryology and silkworm metamorphosis; furnished proof of the circulation theory by observing blood in capillaries.

Malraux *(mäl rō),* **André** 1901–76. French writer and politician. *b.* Paris. Went to Indochina (1924) as an archaeologist and took part in the revolutionary struggles in the Far East, serving with Chiang Kai-shek as a member of the Committee of Twelve; served with the Republican aviation in the Spanish Civil War; during World War II served with French army and in the Resistance; after the war became adviser to Charles de Gaulle; appointed minister of cultural affairs (1960); recorded his early experiences in *Man's Fate* (1933) and *Man's Hope* (1937); wrote seminal work on art criticism entitled *The Voices of Silence* (1954); his meditations on the human condition and destiny are summed up in the autobiographical *Anti-Memoirs* (1967).

Malthus *(măl thəs),* **Thomas Robert** 1766–1834. English economist. *b.* near Dorking. Took holy orders (1798); curate at Albury, Surrey; published *An Essay on the Principle of Population* (1798) expounding the Malthusian doctrine: population increases geometrically, the means of subsistence arithmetically, and vice, crime, war, disease and moral restraint are necessary checks on this increase. Also published *The Nature and Progress of Rent* (1815) and *Political Economy* (1820).

Manes *(mā nēz)* also MANI, MANICHAEUS. c216–c276. Persian sage. *b.* near Baghdad. Founder of Manichaeanism at age 25 or 30, at court of Shapur I, announced himself as the final prophet and preached a blend of Zoroastrian dualism and Christian salvation from evil; journeyed to Turkestan, India, and China to spread the faith; imprisoned by Shapur and crucified by Bahram I at the instigation of the Magians (276); the Holy Gospel of the Manichaeans is believed to have consisted of seven works, six in Syriac and one in Perisan; until the 5th century, Manichaeanism posed a threat to Christianity, and even later reappeared in the Paulician, Bogomil, Cathari, and Albigensian heresies.

Manet *(mȧ nĕ),* **Édouard** 1833–83. French painter. *b.* Paris. Pupil of Couture; founder and leader of the Impressionists; became controversial by rejecting the classicists and by portraying scenes of everyday life. Best-known works include *Olympia, Déjeuner sur l'Herbe,* and *Bar at the Folies Bergères;* works characterized by effective use of light and color.

Mann *(măn),* **Horace** 1796–1859. American educator. *b.* Franklin, Mass. As secretary of Mass. State Board of Education (from 1837), reorganized the school system and teaching methods, built better schools and equipment, and improved teacher training and salaries; helped establish the first normal school in U.S. (1839); House of Representatives (1848–53); first president of Antioch College (1852–59).

Mann *(män),* **Thomas** 1875–1955. German writer. *b.* Lübeck. Gained recognition with first novel, *Buddenbrooks* (1903); followed with novelettes dealing with themes that preoccupied him—death, decay, neurosis, genius, disease; wrote *Tonio Krüger* (1902), *Tristan* (1903), *Death in Venice* (1912); awarded Nobel Prize in literature (1929) for *The Magic Mountain* (1924); opposed Nazism and immigrated to U.S. (1938), becoming a citizen (1940); returned to Germany (1953). Other major works include *Royal Highness* (1916), *The Beloved Returns* (1940), *Joseph and His Brethren* (4 vols., 1934), *Doktor Faustus* (1947), *The Holy Sinner* (1951), *Confessions of Felix Krull, Confidence Man* (1955), *Essays of Three Decades* (1947), *Die Betrogene* (1953), and *Last Essays* (1959).

Mansfield *(măns fēld),* **Katherine** Pseudonym of KATHLEEN BEAUCHAMP MURRY. 1888–1923. English writer. *b.* Wellington, New Zealand. Settled in Europe (1908); married critic John Middleton Murry (1918); wrote sensitive, penetrating short stories. Used stream-of-consciousness techniques that greatly influenced later writers; succumbed to tuberculosis at age 35. Principal works include *In a German Pension* (1911), *Prelude* (1918), *Je ne Parle pas Français* (1919), *Bliss* (1920), *The Garden Party* (1922), *The Doves' Nest* (1923), *Something Childish* (1924). *Poems* (1923), *Journal* (1927), *Letters* (1928), and *Scrapbook* (1940) were edited by her husband and published posthumously.

Manson *(măn sən),* **Sir Patrick** 1844–1922. British parasitologist. *b.* Aberdeen, Scotland. Engaged in medical missionary work in China (to 1889); on return (1890), founded the London School of Tropical Medicine; called the father of tropical medicine for pioneering work on the transmission of malaria by mosquitoes.

Mantegna *(män tā nyä),* **Andrea** 1431–1506. Italian court painter. *b.* near Padua. Protégé of Lodovico Gonzaga, Duke of Mantua; painted frescoes in private chapel of Pope Innocent VIII; a scrupulous draftsman, whose human figures have a bronze-like sculptural solidity; often achieved technical excellence at the expense of beauty and grace; was also an engraver, architect, sculptor, and poet. Among his canvases are *The*

Triumph of Caesar, a series of nine tempera pictures, *Triumph of Virtue Over Vice, Parnassus, Triumph of Scipio, St. Sebastian, St. George, Adoration of the Magi, Infancy of Christ, Flagellation of Christ, Christ at the Gates of Hell, Resurrection of Christ, Sts. Bernardinus and Antonius,* and *St. Euphemia.*

Manutius, Aldus. *See* **Aldus Manutius**

Manzoni *(män dzō nē),* **Alessandro Francesco Tommaso Antonio** 1785–1873. Italian writer. *b.* Milan. Leader of Italian Romantic school with *I Promessi Sposi (The Betrothed),* considered one of the finest models of Italian prose style (1825–27); abandoned earlier Voltairism for Catholic orthodoxy; advocated and fought for Italian unity. Other works include *Il Conte di Carmagnola* (1820), *Adelchi* (1823), *The Fifth of May* (1821), *Inni Sacri* (1810), and *Osservazione Sulla Morale Cattolica* (1819), a defense of Catholicism.

Mao Tse-Tung *(mou dzŭ doong)* 1893–1976. Chinese statesman. *b.* Hsiangtan, Hunan. Helped found Chinese Communist party (1921); set up a Chinese Soviet Republic in southeast China and led the Communist forces on the Long March (1934–35); cooperated with Kuomintang in united resistance to Japanese army; after defeat of Japan, led Red army in the civil war that expelled Nationalist forces from the mainland; set up People's Republic of China (1949); relinquished position as head of state, but retained chairmanship of Communist party (1959); directed Cultural Revolution (1966).

Marat *(mȧ rȧ),* **Jean Paul** 1743–93. French revolutionary. *b.* Boudry, Switzerland. Studied medicine and practiced in Paris and London; on outbreak of the French Revolution, founded the journal *L'Ami du Peuple* (1789), inciting the populace to violence; elected to National Assembly as a radical Jacobin (1792); joined Danton and Robespierre in overthrowing the moderate Girondists; assassinated by Charlotte Corday in his bath; first buried with honors in the Pantheon (1793) but cast out on the fall of the Jacobins.

Marcion *(mär shĭ ŏn)* c110–c165. Christian heresiarch. *b.* Sinope, Asia Minor. Went to Rome (c140) and began preaching a semi-Gnostic doctrine that rejected the Yahweh of the Old Testament, denied the full Incarnation and Resurrection of Christ, and stressed asceticism; founded the sect of Marcionites, who were very influential in North Africa and the Near East until the 7th century; author of a recension of the Gospel of Luke and the Epistles of Paul, and *Antitheses.*

Marconi *(mär kō nĭ),* **Marchese Guglielmo** 1874–1937. Italian inventor. *b.* Bologna. Conducted experiments with wireless telegraphy; made first successful transmission of long-wave signals (1895); went to England (1896) and formed Marconi's Wireless Telegraph Company Ltd. (1897); transmitted signals across English Channel (1898) and across the Atlantic (1901); invented a directional antenna (1905) and the timed-spark system of generation of continuous waves (1912); with Karl Ferdinand Braun, shared Nobel Prize in physics (1909).

Marcus Aurelius *(mär kəs ô rē lĭ əs)* surnamed ANTONINUS; original name MARCUS ANNIUS VERUS. 121–80. Roman emperor (161–80). *b.* Rome. Nephew of Emperor Antoninus Pius and adopted by him (138); created caesar (139); married Faustina, daughter of the emperor; succeeded Antoninus as emperor with Lucius Verus as colleague (161); after death of Verus, became sole emperor (169); successfully defended the imperial frontiers by subduing the Parthians, Pannonians, Marcomanni and Quadi, and the barbarians in the north; opposed Christianity, instituting anti-Christian persecutions; known as a philosopher and as the author of *Meditations,* a classic work on Stoicism.

Marcus Aurelius Antoninus. *See* **Caracalla**

Maria Theresa *(mə rē ȧ tə rē sə)* 1717–80. Queen of Hungary and Bohemia (1740–80). *b.* Vienna, Austria. Daughter of Emperor Charles VI; married Francis of Lorraine, who became Francis I; on her father's death, succeeded to Hapsburg throne by the Pragmatic Sanction; accession led to War of the Austrian Succession (1741–48) and the Seven Years' War (1756–63), in which Austria lost Silesia and parts of Italy; gained South Poland in the Polish partition of 1772; with the help of Anton Kauntiz, introduced financial reforms and fostered agriculture and commerce; after death of husband, ruled as coemperor with son Joseph II; considered one of the greatest and most popular of the Hapsburg rulers.

Marie Antoinette *(mə rē än twȧ nĕt)* full name: JOSÈPHE JEANNE MARIE ANTOINETTE. 1755–93. Queen of France. *b.* Vienna, Austria. Daughter of Empress Maria Theresa; married Louis XVI while he was Dauphin (1770); disliked by the French for her extravagance, interference in politics, opposition to reform, and contempt for the poor; after fall of the Bastille and the storming of Versailles, urged Austrian intervention and was instrumental in the attempted royal flight to the frontier; imprisoned with king and children (1793); tried by Revolutionary Tribunal and subjected to insults, which she bore with dignity; found guilty of treason, and guillotined (1793).

Maritain *(mȧ rĭ tăN),* **Jacques** 1882–1973. French philosopher. *b.* Paris. Converted to Roman Catholicism (1906); professor at Institut Catholique in Paris (1913–40), later at Toronto and Princeton; developed neo-Thomist teachings and modernized them to serve contemporary intellectual needs. Principal works include *Art and Scholasticism* (1932), *Introduction to Philosophy* (1937), *Degrees of Knowledge* (1938), *True Humanism* (1938), *Art and Poetry* (1943), *Man and the State* (1951), *On the Philosophy of History* (1957), and *On the Use of Philosophy* (1961).

Mark *(märk),* **Saint** full name: JOHN MARK. One of the four Evangelists. Considered the author of the second canonical Gospel; companion of Paul and Barnabas on their first missionary journey; interpreter of Peter in Rome; believed to have established the church at Alexandria and is venerated as founder of the Coptic Christian Church. Feast day: Apr. 25.

Marlowe *(mär lō),* **Christopher** 1564–93. English dramatist. *b.* Canterbury. Began as dramatist to Admiral's Men, the earl of Nottingham's theatrical company; regarded as first English dramatist to use blank verse. Principal works include *Tamburlaine the Great* (1587), *The Tragical History of Dr. Faustus* (1601), *The Jew of Malta* (1588), *Edward II* (1590), *Hero and Leander* (1598), and short poems, of which the most famous is "The Passionate Shepherd to His Love" (1599); lived a roistering life and was condemned for holding atheistic opinions; stabbed in a tavern brawl at age 29.

Marquette *(mär kĕt),* **Père Jacques** 1637–75. French missionary and explorer. *b.* Laon. Went to New France (1666) on mission to Ottawa Indians; founded mission of St. Ignace on north shores of Straits of Mackinac (1671); accompanied Louis Jolliet on voyage to discover the Mississippi (1673); died while establishing a mission among the Illinois Indians. Author of *Voyage et Découverte de Quelques Pays et Nations de l'Amérique Septentrionale.*

Marryat *(măr ĭ ăt),* **Frederick** often known as CAPTAIN MARRYAT. 1792–1848. English sailor and novelist. *b.* London. Entered navy (1806); saw action during Burmese War; resigned commission to devote time to literature (1830). Best-known works include *Frank Mildmay* (1829), *Peter Simple* (1833), *Jacob Faithful* (1834), *The Phantom Ship* (1839), *Masterman Ready* (1841), and *The Children of the New Forest* (1847).

Marshall *(mär shəl),* **George Catlett** 1880–1959. American general and statesman. *b.* Uniontown, Pa. Commissioned in U.S. army (1901); chief of staff of U.S. army (1939–45); general of the army (1944); on retiring (1945), appointed special representative to China; recalled (1947) to become secretary of state (1947–49); secretary of defense (1950–51); initiated the European Recovery Program, commonly known as the Marshall Plan; received Nobel Peace Prize (1953).

Marshall, John 1755–1835. American jurist. *b.* near Germantown, Va. After serving in Revolutionary army, studied law, establishing practice at Richmond (1783); member of Virginia Executive Council (1782–95) and of House of Burgesses (1782–88); spokesman of Federalist party; member of the XYZ mission to France (1797); House of Representatives (1799–1800); secretary of state (1800–1801); chief justice of the United States (1801–35); by his decisions and interpretations, founded the American system of judicial review and constitutional law; established the right of the Supreme Court to review the constitutionality of state and federal laws and transformed it into the final arbiter of the Constitution. Author of *The Life of George Washington* (5 vols., 1804–1807).

Marti *(mär tĭ),* **José Julian** 1853–95. Cuban patriot. *b.* Havana. Exiled from Cuba at 16; professor of literature and philosophy at University of Guatemala; consul in New York for Argentina, Uruguay, and Paraguay; founder of Cuban Revolutionary party (1892); with three armed vessels, landed at Cabonico in Cuba and marched inland in command of a rebel group; killed in an action with Spanish troops at Dos Rios; regarded as one of the finest prose writers of Hispanic America.

Martial *(mär shəl)* full name: MARCUS VALERIUS MARTIALIS. 43–c104. Latin poet. *b.* Bilbilis, Spain. Went to Rome (64), gained friendship of Lucan and Seneca and patronage of emperors Titus and Domitian; returned to Spain (98); his epigrams, collected in 14 books, were highly regarded as models by later epigrammatists.

Martin *(mär tĭn),* **Archer John Porter** 1910–. British chemist. Awarded Nobel Prize in chemistry (1952) with R. L. M. Synge for discovery of partition chromatography, a technique for separating compounds in chemical analysis.

Martin Du Gard (mär tăn dü gȧr) **Roger** 1881–1958. French novelist. *b.* Neuilly-sur-Seine. Gained fame with eight-novel series *The World of the Thibaults* (1939–41), the story of an early-20th-century traditional bourgeois family. Other works include *Devenir* (1909), *Jean Barois* (1913), *La Gonfle* (1928), and *Un Taciturne* (1931). Awarded Nobel Prize in literature (1931).

Marvell *(mär vəl),* **Andrew** 1621–78. English poet, satirist, and pamphleteer. *b.* Holderness. During the Commonwealth he was a moderate puritan who supported individual liberties; Milton's assistant (1657); considered one of the greatest English masters of the eight-syllable couplet. Best-known poems include *Horatian Ode upon Cromwell's Return, To His Coy Mistress,* and *The Garden;* Member of Parliament from 1659, but accepted the Restoration; turned to politics (after 1660) and wrote tracts against the monarchy, arbitrary government, and intolerance.

Marx *(märks),* **Karl** 1818–83. German political philosopher. *b.* Trier, Prussia. Born into a Jewish family, but was baptized a Protestant; received a Ph.D. degree at University of Jena; founded the liberal *Rheinische Zeitung* at Cologne (1842); when this was suppressed, went to Paris, where he began lifelong association with Friedrich Engels; edited *Vorwärts* (1844); settled in Brussels on expulsion from Paris and wrote *Misère de la Philosophie,* a refutation of the socialist ideas contained in Proudhon's *Philosophie de la Misère;* organized the Communist League with Engels; wrote the *Communist Manifesto* (1848); returned to Cologne to edit the *Neue Rheinische Zeitung* and to promote revolution; arrested and expelled; went to London in exile for remainder of life; began work on *Das Kapital,* the first volume of which was published in 1867, and the second and third, edited by Engels, were published posthumously; founded and dominated the International Working Men's Association, also known as First International (1864–75); considered the founder of modern Communism and its most vigorous and relentless polemicist.

Mary *(mâr ĭ)* also BLESSED VIRGIN MARY. Mother of Jesus Christ. (New Testament) Daughter of St. Joachim and St. Anne; presented and dedicated at the Temple as a virgin; married Joseph, a carpenter of Nazareth; in accordance with an annunciation by the archangel Gabriel, bore the Savior, conceived of the Holy Ghost; after the Crucifixion of Christ, was cared for by St. John the Divine. (Roman Catholic Church) The mother of God, conceived immaculately and assumed directly into Heaven; venerated under various names as Queen of Heaven, Star of the Sea, and Our Lady of Sorrows. (Orthodox Church) The most exalted of all created beings. Principal feast day: Annunciation (May 31).

Mary I also MARY TUDOR; known as BLOODY MARY. 1516–58. Queen of England and Ireland (1553–58). *b.* Greenwich Palace. Daughter of Henry VIII by first wife, Catherine of Aragon; succeeded to the throne on death of half-brother Edward VI; married Philip II of Spain (1554); repealed the established status of Protestant Church and reimposed Catholicism; launched systematic persecution of Protestant leaders who opposed her; sent over 300 martyrs, including Ridley, Latimer, and Cranmer, to the stake; in war with France, lost Calais, the last English territory on the Continent.

Mary Stuart known as MARY, QUEEN OF SCOTS. 1542–87. Queen of Scotland. *b.* Linlithgow Palace. Daughter of James V of Scotland and Mary of Guise; became queen of Scotland when one week old, and crowned at Stirling Castle at age 1 (1543); brought up in Catholic faith at French court; married the Dauphin (later Francis II) (1558); on his death (1560) and the death of her mother, returned to Scotland; married Henry Stewart, Lord Darnley, a Catholic; provoked rebellion of James Stewart, Earl of Moray, which was easily suppressed; sought to impose Catholicism on the kingdom and to restore royal absolutism; formed liaison with David Rizzio, a French counselor; alienated from husband because of her refusal to grant him the crown of Scotland in perpetuity; after a group of nobles led by Darnley murdered Rizzio, she fled to Edinburgh, aided by James Hepburn, Earl of Bothwell; reconciled with Darnley and secured banishment of Rizzio's murderers; gave birth to a son, later James VI of Scotland (1566); growing estrangement with Darnley was leading to a divorce when he was murdered (1567), an act universally ascribed to Bothwell, though he was tried and acquitted; abducted by Bothwell, probably at her own instigation, and became his wife (1567); provoked nobles to rebel and her army to desert her; surrendered to the confederate lords and abdicated in favor of her son (1567); escaped from imprisonment, gathered an army, but was defeated at Langside (1568); sought asylum in England; held prisoner by Elizabeth for the rest of her life; implicated in plots against Elizabeth: the Ridolfi (1570–71) and Throckmorton Plots (1582) and Babington's Plot (1586); tried and found guilty of being an accomplice in an attempted assassination of Elizabeth; beheaded at Fotheringay (1587).

Masaryk *(mȧ sȧ rĭk),* **Tomas Garrigue** 1850–1937. Czechoslovak statesman. *b.* Hodonin, Moravia. Professor at Charles University (from 1882); leader in Czech national movement; founded and edited *The Athenaeum* (1883) and *Our Epoch* (1893); elected to Austrian Parliament by Young

Czech party (1891) and the Progressive party (from 1907); organized Czech independence movements in England, France, U. S., and Russia; first president of Czechoslovakian Republic (1918–35); known as a philosopher and writer whose principal works include *Spirit of Russia* (1919), *The Making of a State* (1927), *Ideals of Humanity* (1938), and *Modern Man and Religion* (1938).

Masefield *(măs fēld)*, **John** 1878–1967. English poet. *b.* Ledbury. Published first poetical work, *Salt Water Ballads* (1902); best known for narrative poems *The Everlasting Mercy* (1911), *The Widow in the Bye Street* (1912), *Dauber* (1913), *The Daffodil Fields* (1913), *Reynard the Fox* (1919), and *The Wanderer of Liverpool* (1930); also wrote novels *Sard Harker* (1924), *Odtaa* (1926), *The Hawbucks* (1929), *The Bird of Dawning* (1933), *Dead Ned* (1938), *Live and Kicking Ned* (1939), and *Basilissa* (1940); published the autobiographical *In the Mill* (1941) and *So Long to Learn* (1952); poet laureate of England (1930–67).

Massenet *(mȧs nĕ)* **Jules Émile Frédéric** 1842–1912. French composer. *b.* Montaud. Professor of composition at Paris Conservatory (1878–96). Works include *Don César de Bazan* (1872), *Herodiade* (1884), *Manon* (1885), *Le Cid* (1885), *Werther* (1892), *Thaïs* (1894), *Sapho* (1897), *Le Jongleur de Notre Dame* (1902), *Don Quichotte* (1910), *Amadis* (1922), *Marie Madeleine* (1873), *Éve* (1875), and *La Vierge* (1879), as well as cantatas, masses, overtures, ballets, and orchestral suites.

Massinger *(măs ĭn jĕr)*, **Philip** 1583–1640. English dramatist. *b.* Salisbury. Collaborated with Thomas Dekker, John Fletcher, Nathaniel Field, and Cyril Tourneur; succeeded Fletcher as chief dramatist for the King's Men (1625); noted for skill in building plots and his fluent, flexible style. Author of *The Duke of Milan* (1623), *The Unnatural Combat* (1639), *The Parliament of Love* (1624), *The Roman Actor* (1629), *The Maid of Honor* (1632), *The Great Duke of Florence* (1635), *The Emperor of the East* (1631), *The City Madam* (1658), *The Bashful Lover* (1655), and *A New Way to Pay Old Debts* (1632).

Mata Hari *(mä tȧ hä rĭ)* real name: GERTRUD MARGARETE ZELLE. 1876–1917. Dutch spy. *b.* Leeuwarden, Netherlands. Became a dancer in Paris; during World War I, became a spy in German service; exposed, convicted, and shot. Her name has become synonymous with—dangerous, beautiful, female spy.

Mather (măth ər), **Richard** 1596–1669. American clergyman. *b.* Lowton, England. Suspended from ministry for nonconformity (1634); sailed to New England, settled at Dorchester (1636); became leader of the Congregational church in the New World. Father of INCREASE MATHER (1639–1723), American clergyman. *b.* Dorchester, Mass. Preached in England (1658–61); ordained minister of North Church in Boston (1664); president of Harvard (1685–1701); went to England to plead for new charter and new governor to replace Sir Edmund Andros (1688–92); wrote books and treatises, of which *Cases of Conscience Concerning Evil Spirits* (1693) and *A Brief History of the War with the Indians* (1676) are the best known. Father of COTTON MATHER (1663–1728), American clergyman. *b.* Boston, Mass. Ordained (1685); associated with his father as copastor of Boston North Church (from 1681); though he believed that the Salem witchcraft trials (1692) were unfair, did not oppose them. Author of over 400 works, including *Wonders of the Invisible World* (1693), *Magnalia Christi Americana* (1702), *The Christian Philosopher* (1721), *Manuductio ad Ministerium* (1726), and *Memorable Providences Relating to Witchcraft and Possessions* (1685).

Matisse *(mȧ tēs),* **Henri** 1869–1954. French painter. *b.* La Cateau. Leader and pioneer in the Fauve movement (from 1904); created a style characterized by brilliant color, rhythm, and design; designed decorative panels and windows in the Dominican chapel at Vence in France. Best-known works are *Joie de Vivre, The Dance, Piano Lesson, Young Sailor with a Cap, Still Life with Oranges, Window at Nice, Odalisque, Anemones and Women, Harmony in Blue, Spanish Girl with White Dress,* and *Cap d'Antibes Road.*

Matthew *(măth ū),* **Saint** *fl.* 1st century. Apostle of Jesus Christ and one of the four Evangelists. A tax-gatherer by profession, called by the name of Levi in Mark and Luke; believed to have carried the Gospel to the Black Sea region or to Ethiopia. Feast day: Sept. 24.

Maugham *(môm),* **William Somerset** 1874–1965. English writer. *b.* Paris, France. Studied medicine, but turned to literature; published first novel, *Liza of Lambeth* (1897); began playwrighting after success of *Of Human Bondage* (1915); secret agent in Geneva and Petrograd, writing *Ashenden* (1928) based on his experiences; after a visit to Tahiti, wrote *The Moon and Sixpence* (1919) and a number of short stories; explored mysticism in *The Razor's Edge* (1945); considered a master of the short story, of which the best-known is "Rain," published in *The Trembling of a Leaf* (1921); settled in the south of France and wrote nonfiction, including *The Summing Up* (1938), *A Writer's Notebook* (1949), and *Points of View* (1958); other works include *Mrs. Craddock* (1902), *On a Chinese Screen* (1922), *Cakes and Ale* (1930), *First Person Singular* (1931), *Theatre* (1937), *The Hours Before Dawn* (1942), *Casuarina Tree* (1926), *The Merry-Go-Round* (1904); most important plays are *A Man of Honor* (1903), *Lady Frederick* (1907), *Penelope* (1909), *Smith* (1909), *Home and Beauty* (1919), *The Circle* (1921), *Our Betters* (1923), *The Letter* (1927), *East of Suez* (1922), *The Constant Wife* (1927), *The Sacred Flame* (1929), *The Breadwinner* (1930), and *Sheppey* (1933).

Maupassant *(mō pȧ säN),* **Guy de** full name: HENRI RENÉ ALBERT GUY DE MAUPASSANT. 1850–93. French writer. *b.* Château de Miromesnil. Began writing, encouraged by his godfather, Gustave Flaubert; gained fame with first short story, "Boule de Suif";

wrote nearly 300 short stories and a number of full-length novels, including *Bel-Ami* (1885) and *Une Vie* (1883); succumbed to insanity and committed suicide (1891).

Mauriac *(mô ryäk),* **François** 1885–1970. French writer. *b.* Bordeaux. Considered one of the world's foremost Catholic writers, his books include *Le Baiser au Lépreux* (1922), *Genitrix* (1923), *The Desert of Love* (1929), *Thérèse* (1928), *Vipers' Tangle* (1933), *Woman of the Pharisees* (1947), *The Lamb* (1955); also wrote such verse as *Les Mains Jointes* (1909) and *Adieu à l'Adolescente* (1911); awarded Nobel Prize in literature (1952).

Maurice *(mô rĭs)* known as MAURICE OF NASSAU. 1567–1625. Dutch statesman, Stadholder of Dutch Republic (1587–1625). *b.* Dillenburg, Prussia. Succeeded father William the Silent as leader of United Provinces in their struggle for independence from Spain; in brilliant campaigns, defeated Spaniards at Turnhout (1597) and Nieuwpoort (1600), defended Ostend for three years, seized Zutphen, Deventer, and Nimeguen (1591), Gertruydenberg (1593) and Groningen (1594); concluded 12-year truce with Spain that virtually established Dutch independence (1609); turned against chief advisor, Johan van Olden Barneveldt, in the struggle between Calvinists and Remonstrants; caused Barneveldt's death (1619); renewed struggle with Spain (1621); but met with only moderate success.

Maurice, John Frederick Denison 1805–72. English theologian and political philosopher. *b.* Normanston. Began literary career with *Eustace Conway* (1834), but turned to theology, influenced by Coleridge; accepted holy orders (1837); professor of literature at King's College (1840); of theology (1846–53) and moral philosophy at Cambridge (1866); founded Workingman's College (1854) and Queen's College (1848); important in the founding and development of Christian Socialist movement. Author of *Theological Essays* (1853), *Moral and Metaphysical Philosophy* (1848), *The Doctrine of Sacrifice* (1854), and *Social Morality* (1869).

Maximilian *(mäk sĭ mĭl yən),* **Ferdinand Joseph** 1832–67. Emperor of Mexico (1864–67). *b.* Vienna, Austria. Brother of Francis Joseph I, Emperor of Austria; archduke and viceroy of Lombardo-Venetia (1857–59); installed as emperor of Mexico by Napoleon III of France (1864); drove Juárez out of Mexico; U. S. refused to recognize the new Mexican kingdom and forced France to withdraw her troops; deprived of French support, found himself overwhelmed by Juárez's force; made a valiant effort to defend Queretaro, his last outpost, with 8000 men but was defeated, captured, tried, and shot; after this tragedy his empress, Charlotte, daughter of Leopold I of Belgium, became insane.

Max Müller *(mäks mül ər),* **Friedrich** 1823–1900. British philologist. *b.* Dessau, Germany. Settled at Oxford (1850), becoming professor of modern language and literature (1854) and professor of comparative philology (1868–1900); prepared Sanskrit edition of *Rig Veda* for East India Company

(1849–73); edited *Sacred Books of the East* (51 vols., from 1875); published works on comparative mythology, linguistics, and religion including *A History of Ancient Sanskrit Literature* (1859), *Lectures on the Science of Language* (1861–64), *Lectures on the Science of Religion* (1890), and *Chips from a German Workshop* (4 vols., 1867–75).

Maxwell *(măks wĕl),* **James Clerk** 1831–79. Scottish scientist. *b.* Edinburgh. Presented first scientific paper to Royal Society of Edinburgh at age 15; professor of physics at Aberdeen (1856–60), London (1860–65), and Cambridge (from 1871), where he was responsible for building the Cavendish Laboratory; developed theory of electromagnetic field in *Treatise on Electricity and Magnetism* (1873); demonstrated that light and electricity are the same and travel in similar transverse waves; studied heat, kinetic theory of gases, color, and color blindness; wrote *Matter and Motion* (1876) and *Theory of Heat* (1871).

May *(mā),* **Rollo** 1909–. American psychoanalyst. *b.* Ada, Ohio. Leading exponent of existential psychiatry. Author of *Existence* (1958), *Man's Search for Himself (1953), Love and Will* (1974), and *Psychology and the Human Dilemma* (1966).

Mayer *(mī ər),* **Maria Goeppert** 1906–72. American physicist. *b.* Germany. Awarded Nobel Prize in physics (1963) with J. H. Jenson and E. P. Wigner for research in atomic nuclei.

Mayo *(mā ō),* **William Worrall** 1819–1911. American physician. *b.* Manchester, England. Immigrated to U. S., settling at Rochester, Minn. (1863); head of an emergency hospital erected by the Order of St. Francis, which later became St. Mary's Hospital; his sons William James (1861–1939) and Charles Horace (1865–1939), both surgeons, were cofounders of the Mayo Clinic and the Mayo Foundation for Medical Education and Research (1915).

Mazarin *(mȧ zȧ răN),* **Jules** 1602–61. French cardinal and statesman. *b.* Pescina, Italy. Papal nuncio to France (1634–36); became a naturalized Frenchman and entered service of Louis XIII as protégé of Richelieu; succeeded Richelieu as prime minister (1642); made cardinal, though never ordained as a priest (1641); after death of Louis XIII, continued to dominate the queen-regent, Anne of Austria, possibly becoming her lover; by Treaty of Pyrenees (1659) and Peace of Westphalia, consolidated French power in Europe; domestic policy of destroying the nobility and strengthening the Crown led to Wars of the Fronde (1648–53), during which he was twice expelled from court; amassed an immense fortune and collected a fabulous library, which included the famous Mazarin Bible.

Mazzini *(mät tsē nē),* **Giuseppe** 1805–72. Italian patriot. *b.* Genoa. Studied law; joined the Carbonari, the underground Italian organization (1830); arrested, briefly imprisoned, and released; left Italy and went into exile in France; addressed an incendiary appeal to Charles Albert of Piedmont to spearhead the struggle for independence, earning himself perpetual banishment; expelled from France, went to Paris and London; took part in abortive invasion of Savoy (1834); founded the secret society Young Italy, whose object was to unite Italy under a Republican form of government; on outbreak of Lombard revolt (1848), plunged into the fight and was appointed, with Saffi and Armellini, to the triumvirate of the Roman Republic; went into exile on fall of Republic (1849); planned and directed further revolts in Mantua (1852), Milan (1853), Genoa (1857), and Leghorn (1857); supported Garibaldi's expeditions against Sicily and Naples; elected to Italian Parliament four times, but refused to take oath of allegiance to monarchy, preferring to remain abroad; captured while leading an insurrection at Palermo (1870); until death, remained a tireless, uncompromising, and sincere agitator and idealist. Works include *On the Duties of Man* and *Thoughts Upon Democracy in Europe.*

McCarthy, Eugene Joseph 1916–. American statesman. *b.* Watkins, Minn. Member, House of Representatives (1949–59); U. S. Senate (1959–70); catalyzed liberal opinion against the Vietnam War by seeking Democratic nomination for the presidency against incumbent Lyndon Johnson (1968); became an idol of the youth and the left-leaning intellectuals; after leaving the Senate, turned to editing and poetry. Author of *A Liberal Answer to the Conservative Challenge* (1964), *Year of the People* (1969), and *Other Things and the Aardvark* (1970).

McCarthy *(mȧ kär thĭ),* **Joseph Raymond** 1908–57. American politician. *b.* Grand Chute, Wis. Senator from Wisconsin on Republican ticket (1947–57); encouraged by Cold War atmosphere to launch full-scale inquisition into Communists, left-wingers, and fellow travelers within and without the administration; as chairman of the Permanent Senate Subcommittee on Investigations accused and interrogated many citizens, including members of the army; made the term *McCarthyism* a synonym for political witch-hunting; censured by the Senate (1954).

McClellan *(mȧ klĕl ən),* **George Brinton** 1826–85. American general. *b.* Philadelphia, Pa. On outbreak of Civil War, appointed major general of Ohio volunteers; in the Rich Mountain campaign, cleared Virginia of Confederate forces; commanded the Division of the Potomac (1861); for five months, general in chief of Union forces (1861); suffered reverses in the Seven Days' Battles (1862) and at Bull Run; regrouped at Washington and stopped Lee's progress after a bloody victory at Antietam (1862); relieved of command for failure to follow through on this victory; Democratic presidential opponent of Lincoln (1864); governor of New Jersey (1878–81).

McCormick *(mȧ kôr mĭk),* **Cyrus Hall** 1809–84. American inventor. *b.* Rockbridge County, Va. Patented the first successful reaping machine (1834); moved to Chicago and began large-scale manufacture (1847); made substantial bequests to Presbyterian causes.

McCullers *(mə kŭl ərz),* **Carson** 1917–67. American author. *b.* Columbus, Ga. The recurrent theme of her work was the loneliness and anguish of grotesque characters set in small Southern towns. Author of *The Heart Is a Lonely Hunter* (1940), *Member of the Wedding* (1946), *Ballad of the Sad Cafe* (1951), *Reflections in a Golden Eye* (1941), and *Clock Without Hands* (1961).

McDiarmid *(mək dûr mĭd),* **Hugh** pseudonym of CHRISTOPHER MURRAY GRIEVE. 1892–. Scottish poet. *b.* Langholm. Rejuvenated the Scottish tongue with poetic works; identified with Scottish nationalist and Marxist causes. Works include *Sangschaw, Penny Wheep, A Drunk Man Looks at the Thistle, Stony Limits, First Hymn to Lenin, Cornish Heroic Song for Valda Trevlyn,* and *A Kist for Whistles;* prose works include *Lucky Poet* (1943) and *The Company I've Kept* (1966).

McKinley *(mə kĭn lĭ),* **William** 1843–1901. 25th president of U. S. (1896–1901). *b.* Niles, Ohio. Served in Civil War; practiced law at Canton; House of Representatives (1877–83, 1885-91); chairman of Ways and Means Committee (1889–91); instrumental in passing the McKinley Tariff Act (1890); governor of Ohio (1892–96); in alliance with Marcus Hanna, won Republican presidential nomination (1896) on a platform of protection and prosperity; elected after a front-porch campaign; administration marked by victorious conclusion of Spanish-American War and the annexation of Hawaii, Guam, Puerto Rico, and the Philippines, and the relinquishing of sovereignty over Cuba by Spain; supported Open-Door policy in China; reelected (1900) with Theodore Roosevelt as vice-president; assassinated (1901) by an anarchist in Buffalo; policies established America as a major international power.

McLuhan *(mək lōō ən),* **Herbert Marshall** 1911–. Canadian author. *b.* Edmonton, Alberta. Gained fame as an authority on mass media and as a prophet of electronic journalism; books include *Understanding Media* (1964) and *The Medium is the Message* (1967).

McMillan *(mə mĭl ən),* **Edwin Mattison** 1907–. American physicist. *b.* Redondo Beach, Calif. On the staff of the Radiation Laboratory of the University of California (from 1934); played key role in the development of artificial radioactivity and the cyclotron; co–discoverer of the two transuranium elements neptunium and plutonium; conducted research leading to the development of radar and sonar; with Glenn Seaborg, awarded Nobel Prize in chemistry (1951).

Mead *(mēd),* **Margaret** 1901–78. American anthropologist. *b.* Philadelphia, Pa. Assistant curator of ethnology at American Museum of Natural History (1926) and curator (1964); at Fordham University (from 1968); established reputation as a pioneering anthropologist of primitive societies with *Coming of Age in Samoa* (1928), *Growing Up in New Guinea* (1930), *Male and Female* (1949), *Growth and Culture* (1951), *Sex and Temperament in Three Primitive Societies* (1935) and *And Keep Your Powder Dry* (1942).

Meade *(mēd),* **George Gordon** 1815–72. American gener-

b. Cadiz, Spain. Graduated from West Point (1835) and served in the war against the Seminoles and in the Mexican War; on outbreak of Civil War, joined the Peninsular campaign under McClellan (1862); saw action at Mechanicsville, Gaines's Mill, Glendale, the second Battle of Bull Run, and Antietam; led the 5th Corps to victory at Chancellorsville (1863); commander of the Army of the Potomac (1863); gained memorable victory at Gettysburg, for which he received the thanks of the Congress (1864) and the rank of brigadier general; promoted to major general (1864).

Meany *(mē nĭ),* **George** 1894–. American labor leader. *b.* New York, N. Y. A plumber by profession, rose to become president of the New York Federation of Labor (1934); succeeded William Green as president of the American Federation of Labor (1952); head of the American Federation of Labor-Congress of Industrial Organizations (1955–79).

Medawar *(mĕd ə wär),* **Peter Brian** 1915–. British biologist. *b.* in Brazil. Professor of zoology at Birmingham (1947–51), and of comparative anatomy at London (1951–62); director of National Institute for Medical Research (from 1962); awarded Nobel Prize in physiology and medicine (1960) with Macfarlane Burnet for discovery of acquired immunological tolerance.

Medici *(mĕd ē chē)* Name of Florentine family, noted for their wealth, political power, and patronage of the arts; members include: GIOVANNI DE MEDI-CI 1360–1429. Florentine merchant. Virtual ruler of Florence (1421–29). COSIMO also known as COSIMO THE ELDER. 1389–1464. Son of Giovanni; patron of art, founder of the Medici library and ruler of Florence. LORENZO also known as LORENZO THE MAGNIFICENT. 1449–92. Grandson of Cosimo, ruler of Florence jointly with brother Giuliano (1469–78) and solely, after Giuliano's murder (1478); engaged in long struggle with Pope Sixtus IV, but was later reconciled with him (1480); a distinguished lyric poet and a patron of arts and literature, he made the Laurentian age the golden age of Florentine history. COSIMO I also known as COSIMO THE GREAT. 1519–74. A descendant of the younger branch of the Medicis, gained title of Duke of Florence (1537) and established a dynasty that lasted until the 18th century; conquered Siena (1555) and obtained the title Grand Duke of Tuscany from Pope Pius V (1569).

Meighen *(mē ən),* **Arthur** 1874–1960. Canadian statesman. *b.* Anderson. Elected to Canadian House of Commons (1908); served in various ministries (from 1913); prime minister (1920–21, 1926).

Meiji. *See* **Mutsuhito**

Meir *(mā ēr),* **Golda** *née* MABOVICH. 1898–1978. Israeli stateswoman. *b.* Kiev, Russia. Emigrated to Milwaukee, Wis. (1906); settled in Palestine (1921); joined the Labor government as minister of labor (1949–56); foreign minister (1956-66); prime minister (1969); retired (1974); administration marked by the Yom Kippur War of 1973 and growing diplomatic isolation of Israel; credited with keeping the Labor party together in the face of growing internal opposition.

Melanchthon *(mē lăngk thən)* original name: Philipp Schwarzert. 1497–1560. German Protestant reformer. *b.* Bretten. Professor of Greek at Wittenberg and Luther's collaborator in the translation of the Bible; wrote *Loci Communes Rerum Theologicarum* (1521), the first great exposition of Protestant theology; composed the Augsburg Confession (1530); more moderate and conciliatory than Luther, he was a compromiser who genuinely tried to reach common ground with other theologians for the sake of church unity; though lacking in leadership, provided scholastic framework of the Reformation.

Mellon *(mĕl ən),* **Andrew William** 1855–1937. American financier. *b.* Pittsburgh, Pa. Joined father's banking business in Pittsburgh; founded the Union Savings Bank and the Union Trust Company; held large interests in key industries, especially aluminum, coal, railroads, steel, oil, and electricity; secretary of the treasury under Harding, Coolidge, and Hoover (1921–32); numerous endowments include the National Gallery of Art.

Melville *(mĕl vĭl),* **Herman** 1819–91. American novelist. *b.* New York, N. Y. Went to sea as a boy (1839), sailing on the *Acushnet,* the *United States,* and other ships; lived in Polynesia and the South Sea Islands; on return to U. S. wrote *Typee* (1846), based on his experiences; after its success, followed with *Omoo* (1847), *Mardi* (1849), *Redburn* (1849), *White-Jacket* (1850), *Pierre* (1852), *Israel Potter* (1855), *The Piazza Tales* (1856), and *The Confidence Man* (1857); his greatest book, *Moby Dick* (1851) was regarded as a relative failure on its publication, but was rediscovered and accepted as a classic in the 20th century; turned to verse and published *Battle Pieces and Aspects of the War* (1866) and *Clarel* (1876); toward end of life wrote *Billy Budd, Foretopman* (1924).

Menander *(mə năn dər)* c343–c291 B.C. Greek poet. *b.* Athens. Reputed author of more than 100 comedies, of which the titles of nearly 80 are known and fragments of a few have been discovered, including *Epitrepontes, Perikeiromene,* and *Dyskolos;* a number of plots were adapted by Plautus and Terence, thus helping to preserve his reputation as the greatest Greek poet of the New Comedy.

Mencius *(mĕn shĭ əs)* Chinese form: Meng-tzu or Meng-tse. c372–c289 B.C. Chinese Confucian philosopher. *b.* Shantung province. Traveled from one province to another for twenty years expounding Confucian doctrines for princes; after his death, sayings collected by his disciples under the title *Book of Meng-Tse;* postulated innate goodness of man and stressed the four cardinal virtues: benevolence, righteousness, moral wisdom, and proper conduct; applying these doctrines to politics, advocated free trade, deposition of tyrants, poor laws, education, and abolition of war.

Mencken *(mĕng kən),* **Henry Louis** 1880–1956. American editor and satirist. *b.* Baltimore, Md. On staff of *Baltimore Sun* and *Baltimore Herald* (1899–1941);

coeditor of *Smart Set* (1908–23); cofounder (with George Nathan) and coeditor of *American Mercury* (1924–33); contributing editor of *The Nation* (1921–32); gained reputation for iconoclasm, and influence as a literary arbiter; of his numerous works, the most important was *The American Language* (1918); other works include *In Defense of Women* (1917), *Prejudices* (six series, 1919–27), *Treatise on the Gods* (1930), *Treatise on Right and Wrong* (1934), and *Days of H. L. Mencken* (3 vol., 1939–43).

Mendel *(mĕn dəl),* **Gregor Johann** 1822–84. Austrian botanist. *b.* Heinzendorf. Entered order of Augustinians at Brünn (1843), eventually becoming its abbot; conducted painstaking experiments with plants through systematic crossbreeding and recording of plant characteristics over several generations; on the basis of these experiments, formulated Mendel's Law of heredity and transmission of traits. Published *Versuche über Pflanzenhybriden* (1865) and *Über Einige aus Kunstlicher Befruchtung Gewonnene Hieracium-Bastarde* (1869).

Mendeleev *(myĕn dyĭ lyā yəf),* **Dmitri Ivanovich** 1834–1907. Russian chemist. *b.* Tobolsk. Professor of chemistry at St. Petersburg (from 1866); formulated the periodic law of classification of elements, enabling him to predict the existence and properties of a number of elements subsequently discovered by later scientists. Author of *Principles of Chemistry* (1868–70).

Mendelssohn *(mĕn dəls zōn),* **Felix** in full: Jakob Ludwig Felix Mendelssohn-Bartholdy. 1809–47. German composer. *b.* Hamburg. Grandson of Moses Mendelssohn; first appearance as a pianist at age 10; conducted Bach in Berlin (1829); musical director at Dusseldorf (1833); conductor of Gewandhaus concerts at Leipzig (from 1835); founder and director of Leipzig Conservatory (1843); founder and member of Berlin Academy of Fine Arts (1841); visited England ten times; produced over 100 works, among which are *Symphony in C Minor* (1824), *Indian Symphony* (1833), *Scotch Symphony* (1842), *Reformation Symphony, Hebrides* (1830), *Trumpet Overture* (1844), concertos, music for *A Midsummer Night's Dream, Antigone, Oedipus at Colonus,* and *Athalie, Wedding of Camacho* (1827), *Son and Stranger* (1829), *Songs without Words* (1830–45), sonatas, preludes and fugues, the oratorios *Elijah* (1846) and *St. Paul* (1836), and fragments of *Die Lorelei* and *Christus.*

Mendelssohn, Moses 1729–86. German philosopher. *b.* Dessau. Made significant contributions to aesthetics and Jewish studies; first great champion of Jewish emancipation; translated the Pentateuch and the Psalms into German; advocated religious tolerance in *Jerusalem oder über Religiöse Macht und Judentum* (1783) and monotheism in *Morgenstunden oder über das Dasein Gottes* (1785); as a philosopher, wrote *Philosophische Schriften* (1761), *Philosophische Gespräche* (1755), and *Phädon* (1767); gained friendship and admiration of such contemporaries as Kant and Lessing, who depicted him in *Nathan the Wise;* grandfather of Felix Mendelssohn.

Mengs *(mĕngs),* **Anton Raphael** 1728–79. German painter. *b.* Aussig, Bohemia. Court painter to Augustus III, king of Poland (1745); court painter to Charles III of Spain (1761–69, from 1774); director of school of painting in Rome (from 1754); did best work in Spain. Works include *Apotheosis of the Emperor Trajan,* the *Ascension, Holy Family, Antony and Cleopatra,* and *Nativity.*

Meng-tse; Meng-tzu. *See* **Mencius**

Menninger *(mĕn ĭng ər),* **Karl Augustus** 1893–. American psychiatrist. *b.* Topeka, Kans. With father CHARLES FREDERICK MENNINGER (1862–1953), and brother WILLIAM CLAIRE MENNINGER (1899–), founded the Menninger Clinic at Topeka, which became a center of psychiatric research; established Menninger Foundation (1941). Author of *The Human Mind* (1930), *Man Against Himself* (1938), and *Love Against Hate* (1942).

Menzies *(mĕn zēz),* **Sir Robert Gordon** 1894–1978. Australian statesman. *b.* Jeparit, Victoria. Member of Victoria Parliament (1928); Federal House of Representatives (1934); prime minister (1939–41, 1949–66).

Mercator *(mûr kā tər),* **Gerhardus** original name: GERHARD KREMER. 1512–94. Flemish geographer. *b.* Rupelmonde, Belgium. As founder of Cartographical Institute at Louvain (from 1534), produced maps of the Holy Land (1537), Flanders (1540), the world, showing northern and southern hemispheres (1538), and Europe (1554); commissioned by Charles V to make terrestrial and celestial globes; went to Duisburg (1559) to become cosmographer to duke of Jülich and Cleves; devised the flat projection that bears his name, using it in his map of 1568. Principal works are *Tabulae Geographicae* (1578–84) and the *Atlas* (1595), which was completed by his son.

Mercier *(mĕr syā),* **Désiré Joseph** 1851–1926. Belgian cardinal and writer. *b.* Braine-l'Alleud. Ordained (1874); professor of philosophy at Louvain (1882); founded Institute Supérieur de Philosophie, which developed into an international center of Thomist studies; founder and editor of *Revue Nëo-Scolastique* (1894–1906); archbishop of Malines (1906); cardinal of Belgium (1907); fearless spokesman of the Belgians during German occupation; advocated dialogue with Protestants. Author of *Cours de Philosophie* and other works on psychology, logic, and philosophy.

Meredith *(mĕr ə dĭth),* **George** 1828–1909. English novelist. *b.* Portsmouth. Began as journalist and publisher's reader; achieved popularity as a novelist with *Diana of the Crossways* (1885), continuing with *The Ordeal of Richard Feverel* (1859), *The Shaving of Shagpat* (1856), *Evan Harrington* (1861), *Rhoda Fleming* (1865), *The Adventures of Harry Richmond* (1871), *Beauchamp's Career* (1876), *The Tale of Chloe* (1879), *The Egoist* (1879), *The Tragic Comedians* (1880), and *The Amazing Marriage* (1895); works in verse include *Poems* (1851), *Modern Love* (1862), *A Reading of*

Earth (1888), *A Reading of Life* (1901), and *Last Poems* (1910); works noted for wit and insight but marred by obscurity and dated ideas; president of Society of Authors (1892–1909).

Mérimée *(mā rē mā),* **Prosper** 1803–70. French writer. *b.* Paris. Inspector general of historical monuments (1841); senator (1853); published fiction, including *La Jacquerie* (1828), *Colomba* (1830), *Carmen* (1845), *L'Abbe Aubain* (1846), and *Les Cosaques d'Autrefois* (1865); wrote historical works, including *La Chronique du Temps de Charles IX* (1829), *Essai sur la Guerre Sociale* (1841), *La Conjuration de Catalina* (1844), and *Le Faux Demetrius* (1852); translated Russian classics; correspondence published posthumously as *Lettres à une Inconnue* (1873), and *Lettres à une Autre Inconnue* (1875).

Mesmer *(mĕs mər),* **Franz Anton** also FRIEDRICH. 1734–1815. Austrian physician. *b.* near Konstanz, Germany. Studied theology and medicine; founded mesmerism, a theory of animal magnetism based on supposed curative powers of the magnet; published *Send schreiben an einen Auswärtigen Arzt Über die Magnetkur* (1775); settled in Paris (1778); discredited by a commission appointed by the French government (1785) to investigate his system; died in obscurity in Switzerland.

Mestrovic *(mĕsh trō vĭch),* **Ivan** 1883–1962. Yugoslav sculptor. *b.* Otavitze, Dalmatia. Studied in Vienna and Paris; became friend and follower of Rodin; emigré in London during World Wars I and II; went to U. S. (1947); noted for monumental sculptures depicting religious and mythological subjects in Greek and Byzantine traditions. Principal works include the national temple at Kossovo (1907–12), memorial chapel to unknown soldier in Belgrade, *The Archangel Gabriel,* and busts of Masaryk and Beecham.

Metchnikoff *(mĕch nē kôf),* **Élie** 1845–1916. Russian scientist. *b.* Ivanovka. Professor of zoology and comparative anatomy at Odessa (1870); concentrated exclusively on research (from 1882); went to Paris (1888) and worked with Pasteur; succeeded Pasteur as director of the Pasteur Institute (1895); formulated theories of phagocytosis and intracellular digestion; laid foundation of theory of immunity by establishing the role of cells in fighting bacteria; studied longevity, comparative embryology, and inflammation; with Paul Ehrlich, awarded Nobel Prize in physiology and medicine (1908). Author of *Immunity in Infectious Diseases* (1905), *The Nature of Man* (1903), and *Bactériothérapie, Vaccination, Sérothérapie* (1908).

Metternich *(mĕt ər nĭK),* **Prince Klemens Wenzel Nepomuk Lothar von** family name: METTERNICH-WINNEBURG. 1773–1859. Austrian statesman. *b.* Coblenz, Germany. Scion of a noble family and related by marriage to Count von Kaunitz, Austrian chancellor under Maria Theresa; ambassador to Berlin (1803) and to Paris (1806); minister of foreign affairs (1809–48); negotiated marriage of Marie Louise to Napoleon (1810); signed treaty of alliance with France (1812) but joined the opposing Quadruple

Alliance (1813); at Congress of Vienna (1815), sought to establish the principle of balance of power in Europe and the dominance of Austria; for three decades, the principal architect of the Holy Alliance and champion of the reactionary status quo; advocated suppression of liberal ideas and movements through censorship, espionage, and repression; became such a dominating figure in European politics that the period 1815–48 has been called the Age of Metternich; ousted following French Revolution (1848). Author of *Autobiography* (1880–83).

Meyerhof *(mī ər hōf),* **Otto Fritz** 1884–1951. German scientist. *b.* Hanover. Professor of physiology at Kiel (1918–24), at Berlin (1924–29), at Heidelberg (1930–38), and at University of Pennsylvania (from 1940); with A.V. Hill, received Nobel Prize in physiology and medicine (1922) for investigations on cellular oxidation and transformation of lactic acid in muscles.

Michelangelo *(mī kəl ăn jə lō)* full name: MICHELANGELO BUONARROTI. 1475–1564. Italian artist. *b.* Caprese. Introduced by his master Ghirlandajo to Lorenzo de Medici, who engaged him to work in art school in the Medici gardens (1490–92); after expulsion of the Medici, lived in Bologna (1494–95); summoned to Rome by Cardinal San Giorgio (1496–1501); in Florence (1501–1505); recalled to Rome by Pope Julius II, commissioned to design the papal tomb, intermittently working on it for 40 years; decorated ceiling of the Sistine Chapel (1508–12); on death of Julius (1513), commissioned by Pope Leo X to build façade of Church of San Lorenzo (until 1520); by order of Cardinal Giulio de Medici, completed the tombs of Giuliano and Lorenzo de Medici with the famous reclining figures; assisted in defense of Florence as an engineer (1529); left Florence for Rome (1534), never to return; served popes Clement VII and Paul III; painted *The Last Judgment* in the Sistine Chapel (1535–41); executed frescoes for the Pauline Chapel (1541–50); succeeded Antonio da Sangallo as chief architect of St. Peter's (1546). Principal works include *Battle of the Centaurs* and *Madonna of the Steps,* reliefs in the Casa Buonarroti, *Kneeling Angel* of Bologna, *Bacchus, Cupid, Pietà di San Pietro, David,* statue of Pope Julius II (destroyed, 1511); the Julius tomb with the statue of Moses, *Victory, Christ Risen, Youth Crouching, Cupid Kneeling, Deposition from the Cross, Belvedere Torso,* and the second *Pietà;* principal paintings include *Holy Family of the Tribune, Madonna,* the cartoon of the *Battle of Cascina,* and numerous pen and chalk drawings; planned and designed the Laurentian Library at Florence, the façade for the Medici Chapel, Capitoline Palace, Porta Pia, the Farnese Palace, and St. Peter's; poetic works include sonnets to the poet Vittoria Colonna.

Michelet *(mēsh lĕ),* **Jules** 1798–1874. French historian. *b.* Paris. Professor of College of France (from 1838); wrote romanticized historical works, of which the greatest are *History of France* (17 vols., 1833–67) and *History of the Revolution* (7 vols., (1847–53);

began but did not complete *History of the 19th Century* (1872–73).

Michelson *(mī kəl sən),* **Albert Abraham** 1852–1931. American physicist. *b.* Strelno, Germany. Immigrated to U. S. (1854); professor of physics at Chicago University (1892–1929); determined the speed of light; invented the Michelson interferometer for measuring distances in terms of light-wave length; with E. W. Morley, carried out Michelson-Morley experiments, which demonstrated the nonexistence of universal ether and inspired Einstein to develop theory of relativity; first American scientist to win Nobel Prize in physics (1910).

Mickiewicz *(mēts kyə vēch),* **Adam** 1798–1855. Polish poet. *b.* Zaosie. Exiled from Poland as a revolutionary (1824); in St. Petersburg, Odessa, Moscow, and Paris, worked and wrote tirelessly and eloquently for Polish freedom; died in Constantinople while engaged in raising a Polish legion against Russia. Considered the greatest Polish national poet. Principal works include *Crimean Sonnets, Dziady, Grażyna, Konrad Wallenrod, Forefather's Eve, Pan Tadeusz,* and *Books of the Polish Nation.*

Middleton *(mĭd əl tən),* **Thomas** c1570–1627. English dramatist. *b.* London. Collaborated with Dekker, Drayton and others on realistic, satiric comedies of London life, including *Michaelmas Term* (1607), *A Trick to Catch the Old One* (1607), *A Mad World, My Masters* (1608), *The Roaring Girl* (1611). Later wrote tragedies, such as *A Chaste Maid in Cheapside* (1630), *Women Beware Women* (1622), *The Spanish Gipsy* (1653), *The Changeling* (1621), and *Anything for a Quiet Life* (1662).

Mies Van Der Rohe *(mēs văn dər rō),* **Ludwig** 1886–1969. American architect. *b.* Aachen, Germany. Began as a furniture designer; director of the Bauhaus at Dessau (1930–32); immigrated to U. S. (1937); professor at Chicago (now Illinois) Technical Institute; pioneered functional design with expressive use of glass and steel. Principal buildings include Tugendhaut House at Brno, German Pavilion for Barcelona World Exhibition, and the Seagram Building, New York City.

Milhaud *(mē yō),* **Darius** 1892–1974. French composer. *b.* Aix-en-Provence. Began musical career as a member of *Les Six;* visiting conductor (1923) and lecturer (from 1940) in U. S. Works combine simple diatonic melodies in polytonic counterpoint and include *Les Malheurs d'Orphée* (1926), *Pauvre Matelot* (1926), *Maximilien* (1930), *Médée* (1938), *Christophe Colomb* (1928), *Le Boeuf sur le Toit* (1919), *La Création du Monde* (1923), *Salade* (1924), *Le Train Bleu* (1924), and *Les Songes* (1933); wrote novel *La Brebis Égarée* (1923).

Mill *(mĭl),* **James** 1773–1836. Scottish historian and philosopher. *b.* Northwater Bridge. Official in East India Company; author of *History of India* (1818); with Jeremy Bentham, one of the chief apostles of Utilitarianism; co-founder of and contributor to *The Westminster Review* (1824); assisted in establishing University of London (1825); originator of philosophic radicalism. Author of *Elements of Political Economy* (1829), *Analysis of the Mind* (1829), and *Fragment of Mackintosh* (1835); father of John Stuart Mill.

Mill, John Stuart 1806–73. English philosopher. *b.* London. Son of James Mill; as a precocious child, read Greek and Latin classics at age 10; educated systematically by his father; raised as an agnostic and Utilitarian; worked at India House (1823–58); formed Utilitarian Society (1823); infused Utilitarianism with idealism and humanism; contributed to *London Review* and *Westminster Review;* Member of Parliament (from 1865). Principal works include *Principles of Political Economy* (1848), *System of Logic* (1843), *On Liberty* (1859), *Thoughts on Parliamentary Reform* (1859), *Representative Government* (1861), *Utilitarianism* (1863), *Auguste Comte and Positivism* (1865), *England and Ireland* (1868), *The Subjection of Women* (1869), *The Irish Land Question* (1870), *Three Essays on Religion* (1874), and *Autobiography* (1873).

Millais *(mĭ lā),* **Sir John Everett** 1829–96. English painter. *b.* Southampton. Exhibited first painting, *Pizarro Seizing the Inca of Peru,* at age 17; cofounder (with D. G. Rossetti and Holman Hunt) of Pre-Raphaelite Brotherhood (1848); president of Royal Academy (from 1896). Chief works include *Christ in the House of His Parents, Ophelia, The Order of Release, Autumn Leaves, Blind Girl, The Boyhood of Raleigh, Chill October, The Northwest Passage, Rosalind and Celia, Bride of Lammermoor, Effie Deans, Jephthah,* and *Eve of St. Agnes.*

Millay *(mĭ lā),* **Edna St. Vincent** 1892–1950. American author. *b.* Rockland, Me. Works consist of short lyrics, sonnets, and verse plays, including *Fatal Interview,* (1931), *The Harp-Weaver* (1923), *Renascence* (1917), *A Few Figs from Thistles* (1920), *Second April* (1921), *The Buck in the Snow* (1928), *Wine from These Grapes* (1934), *Conversation at Midnight* (1937), *Huntsman, What Quarry?* (1939), *Make Bright the Arrows* (1940), *There are No Islands, Any More* (1940), *Collected Poems* (1941), and *Collected Lyrics* (1943).

Miller, *(mĭ lər)* **Arthur** 1915–. American dramatist. *b.* New York, N.Y. Noted for social and intellectual dimensions of his plays. Works include *All My Sons* (1947), *After the Fall* (1963), *The Crucible* (1953), and *Incident at Vichy* (1964); *Death of a Salesman* (1949) and *A View From the Bridge* (1955) won Pulitzer prizes.

Miller, Henry 1891–. American author. *b.* New York, N. Y. Spent most of his adult life as an expatriate in Paris; gained a certain notoriety through the pornographic tendencies of his novels, as in *Tropic of Cancer* (1934), *Tropic of Capricorn* (1938), *Airconditioned Nightmare* (1945), and *Selected Prose* (2 vols., 1965).

Millet *(mē lĕ),* **Jean François** 1814–75. French painter. *b.* Gruchy. Came to Paris (1837); settled in Barbizon (from 1849). Among his paintings are *Sower, Peasants Grafting, Angelus, The Gleaners, Death and the Woodcutter, Waiting, The Sheep Shearers, The Man with the Hoe, Shepherds and Sheep, Goose Girl, Evening*

Prayer, and *Potato Planters;* received public recognition as one of the great landscape painters after 1870.

Millikan *(mĭl ĭ kən),* **Robert Andrews** 1868–1953. American physicist. *b.* Morrison, Ill. Professor at Chicago (from 1910); director of Norman Bridge Laboratory of Physics at California Institute of Technology (from 1921); isolated the electron and measured its charge, investigated cosmic rays, Brownian movement in gases, X-rays, photoelectric determination of Planck's Constant, and extension of ultraviolet spectrum. Author of *Electricity, Sound and Light* (1908), *The Electron* (1917), *Science and Life* (1923), *Time, Matter and Value* (1932), *Cosmic Rays* (1939), and *Autobiography* (1951).

Milne *(mĭln),* **Alan Alexander** 1882–1956. British author. *b.* St. John's Wood, London. On the staff of *Punch;* famed for juvenile classics *Winnie-the-Pooh* (1926) and *The House at Pooh Corner* (1928). Also wrote verse collections *Now We Are Six* (1927) and *When We Were Very Young* (1924); books for adults include *Mr. Pim Passes By* (1919), *The Romantic Age* (1920), and *Gentleman Unknown* (1938); published autobiography *It's Too Late Now* (1939).

Miltiades *(mĭl tī ə dēz)* c540–c489 B.C. Athenian general. Participated in Ionian revolt against the Persians (499); led Greek army, winning a great victory at Marathon (490) against the Persians led by Datis and Artaphernes; unsuccessful in expedition against Paros (489).

Milton *(mĭl tən),* **John** 1608–74. English poet. *b.* London. Wrote earliest poems while at Cambridge, including "On the Death of a Fair Infant" (1626) and "On the Morning of Christ's Nativity" (1629); creative works in the early period include "L'Allegro", "Il Penseroso" (1632), "Arcades" (1633), "Comus" (1634), and "Lycidas" (1637); visited Italy (1638–39); on outbreak of Civil War, returned to England (1639); plunged into political and religious polemics with *Reformation of Church Discipline in England* (1641), *Apology for Smectymnuus* (1642), *Areopagitica* (1644), *Tractate of Education* (1644), and *The Tenure of Kings and Magistrates* (1649); as secretary for foreign tongues in Cromwell's government, became principal propagandist of the Protectorate; wrote *Eikonoklastes* (1649) and *Pro Populo Anglicano Defensio* (1650); became blind (1652); break with first wife Mary Powell led to publication of *The Doctrine and Discipline of Divorce* (1643) and *Tetrachordon* (1645); published sonnets on his blindness and to Fairfax and Cromwell (1645); on Restoration, went into hiding until amnestied by Act of Oblivion; devoted rest of life to poetry; wrote his most important works, *Paradise Lost* (12 books, 1674), *Paradise Regained* (1671), and *Samson Agonistes* (1671), in sonorous blank verse with the stated intention of justifying the ways of God to men; wrote the Arian treatise *De Doctrina Christiana* (1823).

Minot *(mī nət),* **George Richards** 1885–1950. American physician. *b.* Boston, Mass. Professor of medicine at Harvard

(1928–48); shared Nobel Prize in physiology and medicine with William P. Murphy and George H. Whipple for research on the treatment of pernicious anemia. Author of *Pathological Physiology and Clinical Description of the Anemias* (1936).

Minuit *(mĭn ū ĭt),* **Peter** also MINNEWIT. c1580–1638. Dutch colonial official. *b.* Wesel Duchy of Cleves, Netherlands. As Dutch governor general of the Colony of New Netherland (1626–31), purchased Manhattan Island from the Indians for 60 gilders ($24); established the Swedish colony on Delaware Bay, near Trenton (1638), and built Fort Christina in Wilmington.

Mirabeau *(mē rə bō),* **Comte de** full name: HONORÉ GABRIEL VICTOR RIQUETI. 1749–91. French Revolutionary leader. *b.* Bignon. Youth spent in wild excesses, leading to repeated jailings and exile; built reputation as a radical writer with *Essai sur le Despotisme, Essai sur les Lettres de Cachet,* and *De la Monarchie Prussienne sous Frédéric le Grand* (1788); elected to Estates General (1789), emerging as dominant figure in the French Revolution in its first two years; as a moderate, worked to establish constitutional monarchy and by his oratory prevented extremists from taking control; probably in the service of the king (from 1790); president of National Assembly (1791) and of Jacobin Club (1790).

Merisi, Michaelangelo. *See* **Caravaggio, Michelangelo Amerighi da**

Miro *(mē rô),* **Joan** 1893–1974. Spanish artist. *b.* Montroig, Catalonia. First exhibition in Barcelona (1918); went to Paris (1919), and allied himself with dadaists, cubists, and surrealists; noted for brilliant colors and whimsical forms. Best-known paintings include *Catalan Landscape, Nude with Mirror, Self-Portrait, The Farm, Dutch Interior, Dog Barking at Moon, Rope and Personages, Person Throwing Stone at a Bird, In Reverse, Still Life with Old Shoe,* and *Maternity.*

Mistral *(mēs trȧl),* **Frédéric** 1830–1914. Provençal poet. *b.* Maillane. Leader of the Félibrige movement promoting Provençal as a literary language. Works include *Tresor dou Félibrige* (2 vols., 1879–86), *Mirèio* (1859), *Lis Isclo d'Or* (1875), *Calendau* (1867), *Nerto* (1884), *La Rèino Jano* (1890), *Lou Pouèmo dou Rose* (1897), and *Memoirs* (1906); with José Echegaray, awarded Nobel Prize in literature (1904).

Mistral, Gabriela original name: LUCILA GODOY DE ALCAYAGA. 1889–1957. Chilean poet. *b.* Vicuña. Chilean consul in Portugal, Spain, France, and U. S. (from 1933); visiting professor in U. S.; noted for intense lyricism and mysticism. Works include *The Voice of Elqui, Children's Songs, Desolation, Vida de San Francisco d'Asis, Rondas Para Niños;* awarded Nobel Prize in literature (1945).

Mitchell *(mĭch əl),* **John** 1870–1919. American labor leader. *b.* Braidwood, Ill. Began as coal miner (1882); one of the founding members of United Mine Workers of America (1890); president of UMW (1898–1908); organized miner's strike (1902). Author of *Organized Labor* (1903), and *The Wage Earner and His Problems* (1913).

Mithridates VI Eupator *(mĭth rə dā tēz)* called THE GREAT. c132–63 B.C. King of Pontus (120–63 B.C). Succeeded to throne at age 13; invaded Crimea and southern Russia, subduing Paphlagonia, Cappadocia, and Bithynia, client states of Rome; waged war with Rome: in the first, defeated by Sulla and forced to submit to the humiliating peace of Dardanus (84); defeated Romans in the second, but defeated by Pompey in the third (66); fled to Crimea (65), where he committed suicide.

Modigliani *(mō dē lyä nē),* **Amedeo** 1884–1920. Italian painter and sculptor. *b.* Leghorn. Influenced by primitivism, Fauvism, and Brancusi, began producing elongated figures, mostly nudes. Works include *Peasant Boy, The Rose Nude, The Blue Child, Recumbent Nude, The Green Corsage, Girl with Rose, Anna de Zborowska, Redhead, Woman Seated,* and *Woman with Necklace.*

Mohammed *(mə hăm ĕd)* 570–632. Founder of Islam; Arabian prophet. *b.* Mecca. Born an orphan in Koreish tribe; married Khadija, a rich widow, 15 years his senior; as a merchant, traveled to Syria and other places; heard a call (c610), described in the Koran as from the angel Gabriel, to preach a new religion with himself as apostle and prophet; gained a small band of converts including wife Khadija, cousin Ali, adopted son Zeid, and Abu-Bakr, future father-in-law and first successor; forced to flee to Taif because of hostility of Meccans (620); attracted adherents among pilgrims from Medina; sought refuge in Medina after hegira, or flight from Mecca (622), marking the beginning of the Islamic era; built first mosque in Medina (623); warrior and legislator, with the sword as the principal weapon of his evangelism; drove out and executed Jews for opposing and ridiculing doctrines; in battles against Meccans, destroyed their power, finally conquering Mecca and becoming its acknowledged master (630); extended sway over all Arabia (630–32); had nine wives and a number of concubines; though simple and frugal in habits, he was also intolerant and brutal; his doctrines, though unoriginal, are accepted by Muslims as revelation.

Moira, Earl J. *See* **Hastings, Francis Rawdon**

Moiseyev *(moi sə yĕf),* **Igor Alexandrovich** 1906–. Russian choreographer. Organized the Moiseyev Dance Company (1936), which is the most avant-garde of the Russian companies and has successfully toured in the West.

Moissan *(mwȧ säN),* **Henri** 1852–1907. French chemist. *b.* Paris. Professor of toxicology and inorganic chemistry at the Sorbonne (from 1889); isolated fluorine; invented the electric arc furnace; devised a system for making tiny artificial diamonds; discovered carborundum; awarded Nobel Prize in chemistry (1906).

Molière *(môl yâr)* pseudonym of JEAN BAPTISTE POQUELIN. 1622–73. French dramatist. *b.* Paris. Formed theater company, L'Illustre Théâtre, and performed in Paris and the provinces; gained patronage of the Prince de Conti, Philippe d'Orleans, and Louis XIV; organized a regular theater, with troupe known as King's Comedians;

founded Comédie Français (1690). Works include *Le Dépit Amoureux* (1658), *Les Précieuses Ridicules* (1659), *Sganarelle* (1660), *L'École des Maris* (1661), *Les Fâcheux* (1661), *L'École des Femmes* (1662), *Le Mariage Force* (1664), *Tartuffe* (1664), *L'Amour Médecin* (1665), *Le Misanthrope* (1666), *Le Médecin Malgré Lui* (1666), *Amphitryon* (1667), *L'Avare* (1668), *Monsieur de Pourceaugnac* (1669), *Le Bourgeois Gentilhomme* (1671), *Les Fourberies de Scapin* (1671), *Les Femmes Savantes* (1672), and *La Malade Imaginaire* (1673).

Mommsen *(mōm zən),* **Theodor** 1817–1903. German historian. *b.* Garding. Professor of law at Leipzig (1848), of Roman law at Zurich (1852) and Breslau (1854), and of ancient history at Berlin (1857); active in anti-Bismarck politics in the Progressive party (1863–66), the National Liberal party (1873–79), Liberal Union (from 1881), and the German Liberal party (from 1884); editor-in-chief of *Corpus Inscriptionum Latinarum* (from 1854). Known for *History of Rome* (4 vols., 1854–56, 1885), and *History of Roman Coinage* (1860); wrote over 920 works on epigraphy, archaeology, numismatics, law, and dialects; awarded Nobel Prize in literature (1902).

Mondriaan *(mŏn drē ȧn),* **Piet** Dutch name: PIETER CORNELIS MONDRIAAN. 1872–1944. Dutch painter. *b.* Amersfoort. With Van Doesburg, became outstanding member of De Stijl group (1917); founded neoplasticism (1920); influenced Bauhaus movement with concept of chromoplasticism; a leader of the Abstraction-Creation group in Paris (1932); painted only in primary colors, and typical paintings were composed of rectangles and bars. Author of *Plastic Art and Pure Plastic Art* (1951); best-known works include *Broadway Boogie-Woogie, Victory Boogie-Woogie, New York City,* and *Composition.*

Monet *(mô nĕ),* **Claude** 1840–1926. French painter. *b.* Paris. Exhibited at first Impressionist exhibition (1874), his canvas *Impression: Soleil Levant* lending its name to the movement; associate of Pissarro, Renoir, and Sisley in developing technique of painting almost exclusively with unmixed colors. Best-known works include *Haystacks, Rouen Cathedral, Waterlilies, The Seine at Givery, Bordighera, Cape Martin, Snow at Port Villers, Un Déjeuner sur l'Herbe, Gare St. Lazare, Venice, Camille, ou la Dame en Vert, Le Jardin de l'Infante,* and *Le Meules.*

Moneta *(mâ nā tä),* **Ernesto Teodoro** 1833–1918. Italian pacifist. *b.* Milan. Editor of *Il Secolo* (1867–96); president of International Peace Congress at Milan (1906); with Louis Renault, awarded Nobel Peace Prize (1907) for his book *Le Guerre, le Insurrezioni, e la Pace nel Secolo XIX* (3 vols., 1903).

Moniz *(mōō nĕsh),* **Antonio Caetano de Abreu Freire Egas** 1874–1955. Portuguese surgeon. *b.* Avanca. Director of the Lisbon Institute of Neurology; introduced cerebral angiography and developed prefrontal lobotomy or leucotomy for treatment of schizophrenia; awarded Nobel Prize in physiology and medicine with

Walter Hess (1949); minister of foreign affairs (1918–19).

Monod *(mô nō),* **Jacques** 1910–76. French biochemist. *b.* Paris. Director of Pasteur Institute and professor of molecular biology at Collège de France (from 1967); with François Jacob and Andre M. Lwoff, awarded Nobel Prize in physiology and medicine (1965) for the discovery of regulatory processes in body cells that contribute to genetic control of enzymes and virus synthesis. Author of *Chance and Necessity* (1971).

Monroe *(mən rō),* **James** 1758–1831. Fifth president of U. S. (1817–25). *b.* Westmoreland County, Va. Served in Revolutionary War, leaving the army as a major; studied law under Jefferson; elected to Va. legislature (1782); member of Continental Congress (1783–86), where he championed states' rights; U. S. senator (1790–94); minister to France (1794–96); governor of Virginia (1799–1802); sent to France as a negotiator of Louisiana Purchase (1803); engaged in diplomatic negotiations in England and Spain (until 1807); governor of Virginia (1811); Madison's secretary of state (1811–17); secretary of war (1814–15); president (1817–25); administration marked by successes in foreign policy, including settlement of disputes with Great Britain and Canada, the acquisition of Florida from Spain, the settlement of Liberia, and formulation of Monroe Doctrine; signed Missouri Compromise (1820); because of success in ending factional strife, administration is known as the era of good feeling; reelected president with overwhelming majority (1820). *Writings* edited by S. M. Hamilton (7 vols., 1898–1903).

Montague *(mŏn tȧ gū),* **Charles** title: EARL OF HALIFAX; BARON HALIFAX. 1661–1715. English statesman. *b.* Horton. Entered Parliament (1689); lord of treasury (1692); responsible for introduction of national debt, formation of Bank of England, issue of first exchequer bills, and currency reform (1695) with aid of Isaac Newton; by a general mortgage scheme, created a consolidated fund to meet interest on public loans; chancellor of the exchequer (1694); first lord of the treasury and prime minister (1697); unpopular and compelled to resign (1699); impeached (1701, 1703) but not prosecuted; out of office during reign of Queen Anne; supported Hanoverian succession (1714), rewarded on accession of George I by being created earl of Halifax and appointed prime minister; noted as a wit, man of letters, and patron of literary establishment. Coauthor of *The City Mouse and the Country Mouse* (1687) with Matthew Prior.

Montaigne *(môn tān),* **Michel Eyquem de** 1533–92. French essayist. *b.* Dordogne. Studied law; joined court of Francis II (from 1571); traveled in Germany, Switzerland, and Italy (1580); mayor of Bordeaux (from 1581); succeeded to family estate (1571), becoming a rural recluse. Author of *Essais* (1580–81), in which he develops a philosophy of skepticism born of his original and searching mind, considered one of the finest examples of essay-writing; its direct style, humor, imagery, and subtlety influenced many succeeding writers.

Montcalm *(mŏN kȧm),* **Louis Joseph de** title: Marquis de Gezan de Saint-Véran. 1712–1759. French general. *b.* near Nîmes. Assumed command of French troops in Canada as field marshal (1756); captured Oswego and Fort William Henry (1758) and defended Ticonderoga; after losing Fort Duquesne and Louisburg, withdrew to Quebec, which he defended with 16,000 troops; defeated by English general James Wolfe at the Battle of the Plains of Abraham; mortally wounded.

Montesquieu *(môN təs kyû),* **Baron de La Brede et de** title of Charles de Secondat. 1689–1755. French political philosopher. *b.* near Bordeaux. President of Bordeaux Parliament (1716); withdrew from political life to devote himself to writing. Author of *Lettres Persanes* (1721) and *Considérations sur les Causes de la Grandeur et de la Décadence des Romains* (1734); in *L'Esprit des Lois* (1748), a study of political institution, he developed a theory of checks and balances that was incorporated into the U. S. Constitution.

Montessori *(mōn tə sō rĭ),* **Maria** 1870–1952. Italian educator. *b.* near Ancona. Studied medicine and became the first Italian woman to receive a medical degree (1894); as physician at the university psychiatric clinic, developed methods of teaching defective children; founded Orthophrenic School to put her principles into practice; encouraged by its success, extended efforts to normal children; opened the first *case dei bambini* (children's school) at Rome (1907); her system of preschool education featured development of individual initiative and freedom of action, of coordination through exercise and games, and of sense perception, with teacher as guide rather than instructor; established Montessori institutes and training centers throughout Europe, Asia, and the Americas; director of Montessori Institute at Barcelona (1917) and founder of Montessori Training Center at Laren (1938). Author of *The Montessori Method* (1912), *Pedagogical Anthropology* (1913), *The Advanced Montessori Method* (1917), and other books.

Monteverdi *(mōn tə vār dī),* **Claudio** 1567–1643. Italian composer. *b.* Cremona. Published first choral piece, *Cantiunculae Sacrae,* at age 15; court musician (from 1590) and maestro di cappella (from 1602) to duke of Mantua; on Duke's death, appointed maestro di cappella at St. Mark's, Venice (1613); considered great innovator and the founder of opera; reduced orchestral accompaniment and stressed vocal virtuosity; introduced the ritornello and the use of tremolo and pizzicato; composed 11 books of madrigals, canzonets, *Orfeo* (1607), *Il Ritorno d'Ulisse* (1641), *L'Incoronazione di Poppea* (1642), *Il Combattimento di Tancredi e Clorinda,* and the mass and vespers of the Virgin (1610); ordained priest (1633).

Montezuma *(mŏn tə zōō mə)* original Nahuatl name: Motecuhzoma (He Who Shoots Arrows to the Sky). Name of two Aztec emperors:

Montezuma I c1390–c1464. Succeeded to throne (1440); extended empire from Atlantic to Pacific through successful wars with the Miztecs and Tlascalans.

MONTEZUMA II c1480–1520. Succeeded to throne (1502); received Cortes into Mexico City (1519); held hostage by Spaniards; when the Aztecs rose, was killed either by Spaniards or Indians.

Montfort *(mŏnt fərt),* **Simon de** title: EARL OF LEICESTER. c1208–65. English statesman. *b.* Normandy, France. Son of SIMON DE MONTFORT (c1160–1218), French soldier and leader in crusade against the Albigenses. Married Eleanor, sister of Henry III; one of king's favorites; governor of Gascony (1248); put down seigneurial disaffection with a heavy hand; antagonized Henry, who forced him to resign (1252); on return to England joined popular camp in Parliament (1254) against Henry's taxation; sided with opposition in Mad Parliament (1258); signed Provisions of Oxford, placing the kingdom under control of 15 barons with himself as leader; when Henry revoked assent to Provisions (1261), led nobles in Barons' War (1263–65); after rejecting arbitration of Louis IX, defeated royal forces and took the king, Prince Edward, and earl of Cornwall prisoners at Lewes (1264); became virtual ruler of kingdom; summoned Model Parliament, consisting of 120 churchmen, 23 barons, 2 knights from every shire, and 2 subjects from each borough (1265); faced with new dissensions in baronial ranks, especially following alliance with the Welsh Llewelyn; defeated and killed at Evesham (1265) by the combined armies of Prince Edward, the Welsh Marchers, and Gilbert, Earl of Gloucester.

Montgolfier *(môN gôl fyā),* **Joseph Michel** 1740–1810. French inventor. *b.* Vidalon-les-Annonay. With brother JACQUES ÉTIENNE (1745–99), French mechanic, invented one of the first air balloons (1782), which in a demonstration (1783) stayed up for ten minutes; a later experiment (1783) was attended by a large crowd at Versailles, including Louis XVI, Marie Antoinette, and Benjamin Franklin.

Montgomery *(mənt gŭm ər ĭ),* **Sir Bernard Law** title: VISCOUNT MONTGOMERY OF ALAMEIN. 1887–1976. British general. *b.* Kennington Oval. Served in World War I; commanded 3rd Division in its retreat from Dunkirk (1940); commanded 8th Army in North Africa and with brilliant offensive at El Alamein, drove Rommel's forces back to Tunis; field marshal in charge of ground forces in invasion of Europe (1944); commanded 21st Army Group, composed of British, Canadian, and U. S. forces; commander of British-occupied zone in Germany (1945–46); chief of imperial general staff (from 1946); created viscount (1946). Author of *Normandy to the Baltic* (1946), *Memoirs* (1958), *The Path to Leadership* (1961), and *History of Warfare* (1968).

Moody *(mo͞o dĭ),* **Dwight Lyman** 1837–99. American evangelist. *b.* Northfield, Mass. Gave up a career as salesman to do missionary work (1860); with Ira D. Sankey, held evangelical meetings throughout U. S. and England; founded Northfield School (1879), Mount Hermon School (1881), and Bible Institute for

Home and Foreign Missions (1889), now the Moody Bible Institute.

Moore *(mŏŏr),* **George** 1852–1933. Irish writer. *b.* Moore Hall, County Mayo. Spent early years as a dilettante artist in Paris; wrote *Flowers of Passion* (1878) and *Pagan Poems* (1882); influenced by Flaubert and Zola, wrote realistic novels, including *A Modern Lover* (1883), *A Mummer's Wife* (1885), *Esther Waters* (1894), *Evelyn Innes* (1898), and *Sister Teresa* (1901); championed Impressionist painters in *Modern Painting* (1893); with Edward Martyn and W. B. Yeats, founded the Irish Literary Theater at Dublin; wrote plays *The Strike at Arlingford* (1893) and *The Bending of the Bough* (1900); returned to London (1911) and wrote *Hail and Farewell* (1911–14), *The Brook Kerith* (1916), *Héloise and Abélard* (1921), *Daphnis and Chloe* (1924), *Aphrodite in Aulis* (1930). Other works include *Confessions of a Young Man* (1888), *Memoirs of My Dead Life* (1905), *The Untilled Field* (1903), *Celibates* (1895), and *Vain Fortune* (1891).

Moore, George Edward 1873–1958. English philosopher. *b.* London. Professor of philosophy at Cambridge (1925–39); editor of the journal *Mind* (1921–47); concerned himself with ethical theory, nature of judgment, theory of knowledge, the problem of goodness, and the problem of perception. Principal works include *Principia Ethica* (1903), *Ethics* (1912), *Philosophical Studies* (1922), *The Philosophy of G. E. Moore* (1943), and *Some More Problems in Philosophy* (1954).

Moore, Henry Spencer 1898–. English sculptor. *b.* Castleford. Considered one of the most original and powerful modern sculptors; characteristic works are reclining figures and groups molded in simple, massive, organic shapes, often with holes and wires in them. Best-known work is *Madonna and Child* (1943–44).

Moore, Marianne Craig 1887–1972. American poet. *b.* St. Louis. Editor of *The Dial* (1925–29); author of *Collected Poems* (1952, Pultizer Prize). Other works include *Poems* (1921), *Observations* (1924), *Selected Poems* (1935), *What Are Years?* (1941), *Nevertheless* (1944), and *Complete Poems* (1967).

Moore, Stanford 1913–. American biochemist. *b.* Chicago, Ill. Shared Nobel Prize (1972) in chemistry with C. B. Anfinsen and W. H. Stein for investigations into the chemical structure of the protein ribonuclease.

Moore, Thomas 1779–1852. Irish poet. *b.* Dublin. In admiralty service in Bermuda; turned to poetry and published *Irish Melodies* (1807–34), *Lalla Rookh* (1817), and *Twopenny Post Bag* (1813); friend and biographer of Byron; prose works include *History of Ireland* (1827) and biographies of Sheridan, Byron, and Fitzgerald; minor poetic works include *Odes and Epistles* (1806), *National Airs* (1818–27), and *The Epicurean* (1827); *Memoirs* edited by Lord John Russell (8 vols., 1852–56).

More *(mōr),* **Sir Thomas** also SAINT THOMAS MORE. 1478–1535. English statesman and martyr. *b.* London. Studied at Oxford and called to the bar; considered the ministry and lived in Charterhouse Carthusian monastery as a lay monk (1499–1503); elected to Parliament (1504); envoy to Flanders; on accession of Henry VIII, appointed undersheriff of London (1510); introduced to Henry VIII by Wolsey; treasurer of the exchequer (1521); chancellor of duchy of Lancaster (1525); speaker of the Commons (1523); high steward of Oxford (1524) and Cambridge (1525); special envoy to Madrid and Paris; on fall of Wolsey, appointed chancellor against his wishes; retired (1532), disagreeing with Henry over the oath requiring renunciation of spiritual allegiance to the pope; charged with high treason on refusal to recognize the king as head of Church of England (1634); committed to the Tower; beheaded (1535); beatified (1886); canonized (1935); acknowledged as a great humanist and writer, whose principal works include *Utopia* (1516), *History of King Richard III* (1513), *Dialogue of Comfort Against Tribulation* (1534), and *Life of John Picus, Earl of Mirandula* (1510). Feast day: July 6.

Morgan *(môr gən),* **John Pierpont** 1837–1913. American financier and philanthropist. *b.* Hartford, Conn. As head of J. Pierpont Morgan & Co., was New York agent of the international banking firm J. S. Morgan & Co., founded by his father; formed Drexel, Morgan and Co. (1871), in association with the Drexels of Philadelphia; founded J. P. Morgan & Co. (1895); leader in government financing through marketing of treasury loans and railway reorganization; built industrial and financial empire in which he and his partners controlled 47 of the largest corporations, including U. S. Steel; collector of art and rare books, most of which were donated to the Morgan Library in New York City.

Morgan, Thomas Hunt 1866–1945. American zoologist. *b.* Lexington, Ky. Professor of zoology at Columbia (1904–28); director of Kerckhoff Laboratories at California Institute of Technology (from 1928); through research on the fruit fly *Drosophila,* established the significance of chromosomes in heredity and sex; awarded Nobel Prize in physiology and medicine (1933). Author of *Mechanism of Mendelian Heredity* (1915), *The Physical Basis of Heredity* (1919), *Evolution and Genetics* (1925), and *Embryology and Genetics* (1933).

Morison *(mŏr ĭ sən),* **Samuel Eliot** 1887–1976. American historian. *b.* Boston, Mass. Professor of American history at Harvard (from 1915) and Oxford (1922–25); historian of U. S. naval operations (1942). Author of *Oxford History of the United States* (1927), *Puritan Pronaos* (1936), *Second Voyage of Columbus* (1939), *Admiral of the Ocean Sea* (1942), and *John Paul Jones* (1959).

Morris *(mŏr ĭs),* **William** 1834–96. English poet and artist. *b.* Walthamstow. Studied architecture and painting, but had a growing interest in practical and decorative arts; founded, with Edward Burne-Jones, the firm of Morris, Marshall Faulkner & Company (later Morris & Company) and revived an interest in design, handicrafts, ceramics, textiles, and stained glass (1861); founded the Arts and Crafts Society and the Society for the Protection of Ancient Buildings (1877); advocated a return to medieval craftsmanship with its pride in work, love of beauty for its own sake, and freedom from mass production techniques; to revive the typographical arts, founded the Kelmscott Press, for which he designed typefaces, ornamental borders, and initials (1890); advocated a doctrine of Utopian socialism; joined Social Democratic Federation (1883); founded the Socialist League (1884), and edited its organ, *The Commonweal;* member of the Socialist Society; a prolific writer, wrote poetry, socialist tracts, and romances; writing includes *The Dream of John Ball* (1888), *News from Nowhere* (1891), *The Defense of Guinevere* (1858), *The Life and Death of Jason* (1867), *The Earthly Paradise* (1868), *Socialism: Its Growth and Outcome* (1893), *Three Northern Love Songs* (1875), *The House of the Wolfings* (1889), *The Roots of the Mountains* (1890), *The Story of the Glittering Plain* (1890), *The Wood Beyond the World* (1894), *The Well at the World's End* (1896), *The Water of the Wondrous Isles* (1897), *The Story of the Sundering Flood* (1898), *Poems by the Way* (1891), *Sigurd the Volsung* (1876), and *Love Is Enough* (1873).

Morse *(môrs),* **Samuel Finley Breese** 1791–1872. American artist and inventor. *b.* Charlestown, Mass. Studied painting and opened studio in N.Y. (1823); founder and first president of National Academy of Design (1826–42); gave up painting (1837) for inventing; developed the magnetic telegraph and Morse code; filed caveat at patent office in Washington (1837); financially beset until Congress voted $30,000 to build a telegraph line from Washington, D.C. to Baltimore (1843); sent first message (1844) on this line, "What hath God wrought!"; successful in litigation to establish patent rights and honored in later years.

Morton *(môr tən),* **Levi Parsons** 1824–1920. American statesman. *b.* Shoreham, Vt. Established banking firm in N.Y. (1863); House of Representatives (1879–81); minister to France (1881–85); vice-president of U.S. (1889–93); governor of N.Y. (1895-96).

Moses *(mō zəz)* *fl.* c12th or 13th century B.C. Hebrew prophet. (Old Testament) Born in Egypt to Hebrew parents but adopted and reared in palace of the pharaoh; commanded by Yahweh to lead the Israelites out of bondage in Egypt to the Promised Land; led the Exodus (emigration of Jews from Egypt and through the wilderness) for 40 years; received Ten Commandments on top of Mount Sinai; sometimes regarded as author of Pentateuch.

Moses, Anna Mary Robertson called GRANDMA MOSES. 1860-1961. American primitive artist. *b.* Greenwich, N.Y. Began painting at the age 75 (1935); her subjects were mainly old country scenes, all from memory. Author of *My Life's History* (1952).

Mossadegh *(mō sa dėk),* **Mohammad** 1881–1967. Iranian statesman. *b.* Tehran. Held several cabinet posts (1920–22); retired after coup of Reza Shah deposed

Qajar dynasty; returned to politics as leader of Iranian National Front; prime minister (1951); created international crisis by nationalizing the British-owned Iranian Oil Company; became the focus of an anti-Shah movement that took control of the government and caused the Shah to flee; overthrown by a pro-Shah coup led by General Zahedi (1953); imprisoned for a few years but later amnestied.

Mössbauer *(mûs bou ər),* **Rudolf Ludwig** 1929–. German physicist. *b.* Munich. Professor of physics at Munich and visiting professor at California Institute of technology (from 1964); shared Nobel Prize in physics (1961) with R. Hofstater for discovery of the Mössbauer effect, which produces and measures recoil-free gamma rays.

Motley *(mŏt lĭ),* **John Lothrop** 1814–77. American historian. *b.* Dorchester, Mass. In diplomatic service as secretary to U.S. legation in St. Petersburg (1841), minister to Austria and Great Britain; noted chiefly as historian and as author of *The Rise of the Dutch Republic* (1856), *The History of the United Netherlands* (4 vols. 1860—68), and *The Life and Death of John of Barneveld* (1874).

Mott *(mŏt),* **John Raleigh** 1865–1955. American Christian leader. *b.* Livingston Manor, N.Y. General secretary (1895–1920) and chairman (1920–28) of World's Student Christian Federation; foreign secretary of International Committee of the Young Men's Christian Association (from 1898); general secretary (1915–31) and chairman (1926) of the World's Committee of the Y.M.C.A.; chairman of International Missionary Council (from 1921); with Emily G. Balch, awarded the Nobel Peace Prize (1946).

Mountbatten, Prince Philip. *See* **Edinburgh, Duke of**

Moussorgsky *(mōō sôrg skû ĭ),* **Modest Petrovich** also **Musorgski** 1835–81. Russian composer. *b.* Karevo. Self-taught musician; gained fame with the opera *Boris Godunov* (1874) and the piano suite *Pictures from an Exhibition* (1874); style characterized by colorful, fiery folk harmonies and melodies; toward end of life, became chronic alcoholic. Left a number of incomplete works, some later finished by his friend Rimski-Korsakov.

Moyano, Sebastian. *See* **Belalcázar, Sebastián de**

Mozart *(mō tsärt),* **Wolfgang Amadeus** original name: JOHANNES CHRYSOSTOMUS WOLFGANGUS THEOPHILUS MOZART. 1756–91. Austrian composer. *b.* Salzburg. A musical prodigy, first performed in public at age 5; accompanied his father on concert tours of Munich, Paris, London, and other places; settled in Salzburg and composed the opera *La Finta Semplice* (1768) for Emperor Joseph II; traveled with his father to Italy (1769–73) and received award of the Golden Spur from pope; concertmaster to archbishop of Salzburg (until 1781); settled in Vienna and became royal chamber composer to the emperor (1790); lived in penury; died while composing *Requiem;* wrote over 600 works, including *Mithridate, Rè di Ponto* (1770), *Idomeneo Rè di Creta* (1781), *Die Entführung aus dem Serail* (1782),

Le Nozze di Figaro (1786), *Don Giovanni* (1787), *Così fan Tutte* (1790), *Die Zauberflöte* (1791), 48 symphonies, 33 cassations, 29 orchestral sets, 47 arias, oratorios, and cantatas, including 15 orchestral masses, 39 litanies, vespers, kyries, and hymns, serenades, piano works, and chamber music.

Mühlenberg *(mū lən bûrg),* **Henry Melchior** 1711–87. American clergyman. *b.* Einbeck, Germany. Immigrated to U.S. (1742); organized first Lutheran Synod (1748); considered the founder of American Lutheran Church.

Muller *(mŭl ər),* **Hermann Joseph** 1890–1967. American scientist. *b.* New York, N.Y. Professor of zoology at Texas (1925–36), Amherst (1942–45), and Indiana (1945–64); awarded Nobel Prize in physiology and medicine (1946) for research on transmutation of genes and chromosome changes by X-rays; coauthor of *Genetics, Medicine, and Man* (1947).

Müller *(mül ər),* **Paul Hermann** 1899–1965. Swiss chemist. Work helped to develop DDT as an insecticide; awarded the Nobel Prize in physiology and medicine (1948).

Mulliken *(mŭl ĭ kən),* **Robert Sanderson** 1896– . American chemist. *b.* Newburyport, Mass. Professor at Chicago (1921–23, 1928–); won Nobel Prize in chemistry (1966) for work on chemical bonds and the study of the electronic structure of molecules by the molecular orbital method.

Munch *(moongk),* **Edvard** 1863–1944. Norwegian artist. *b.* Löten. Studied art in Paris (1889–92), Italy, and Germany; settled in Oslo (1908); from the 1890s, obsessively concerned with themes of death, fear, and angst, portraying them in expressionist and symbolic styles, using bright colors and curved design. Best-known works are *Puberty, Spring, The Sick Child, Ashes, The Scream, Death in the Room, Jealousy, Summer Night, Girls on the Bridge, Dance of Life, The Tree, Girls on the Beach, Old Woman in Hospital, The Kiss,* and *The Stormy Night.*

Munro *(mən rō),* **Hector Hugh** pseudonym: SAKI. 1870–1916. British writer. *b.* Akyab, Burma. Political correspondent of *Westminster Gazette* and *Morning Post* (1902–1908); best known as a writer of witty and bizarre short stories, collected in *The Chronicles of Clovis* (1911), *Beasts and Super Beasts* (1914), *The Square Egg* (1924), *Reginald* (1904), and *Reginald in Russia* (1910); wrote two novels, *The Unbearable Bassington* (1912) and *When William Came* (1913).

Murat *(mü rȧ),* **Joachim** c1767–1815. French general. *b.* Bastide. Entered French army as a volunteer, serving in Italy and Egypt (1796-99); rose to rank of general; aided Napoleon in coup d'état (1799); married Napoleon's sister Maria Annunciata (Caroline) Bonaparte (1800); governor of Paris and marshal of France (1804), prince and high admiral (1805); commanded cavalry at Marengo (1800), winning at Austerlitz (1805), Jena (1806), Eylau, and Friedland (1807); grand duke of Berg and Cleve (1806); king of the Two Sicilies as Joachim I Napoleon (1808); commanded cavalry on Russian campaign (1812); saved his crown after Battle of

Dresden (1813) by a treaty with the Austrians, which he broke to rejoin Napoleon (1815); defeated by Austrians at Tolentino (1815); escaped to Corsica; made a final attempt to regain his kingdom by landing with followers on Calabria but was captured and executed.

Murillo *(mōō rē lyō),* **Bartolomé Esteban** 1617–82. Spanish painter. *b.* Seville. Influenced by Velásquez at Madrid (1643–45); head of the Seville school (1654); founded Academy of Seville (1660); during last period (1661–74), produced a series of brilliant religious paintings including some on his favorite subject, Virgin of the Conception; also painted scenes of low life. Best-known paintings include *Moses Striking the Rock, Abraham and the Angels, Miracle of Loaves and Fishes, Saint Peter Released from Prison, Adoration of the Shepherds, St. John on Patmos, Birth of the Virgin, Vision of St. Anthony, Flight into Egypt,* and *St. Elizabeth.*

Murphy *(mûr fĭ),* **William Parry** 1892– . American physician. *b.* Stoughton, Wis. With George R. Minot and George H. Whipple, awarded Nobel Prize in physiology and medicine (1934) for discovery that administration of liver extract increases activity in the bone marrow where red cells are formed; noted for research into the etiology of pernicious anemia.

Murray *(mûr ĭ),* **Gilbert** full name: George Gilbert Aimé. 1866–1957. British scholar. *b.* Sydney, Australia. Immigrated to England at age 11; professor of Greek at Glasgow (1889) and Oxford (from 1908); foremost Greek scholar of the age, with verse translations of Greek classics and a number of works on Greek culture, including *History of Ancient Greek Literature* (1897), *Rise of Greek Epic* (1907), *Four Stages of Greek Religion* (1913), *Euripides and His Age* (1913), *Classical Tradition in Poetry* (1927), *Aristophanes* (1933), and *Aeschylus, Creator of Tragedy* (1940); also noted as an internationalist; president of League of Nations Union (1923–38) and first president of the general council of the United Nations Association; memoirs published as *Unfinished Autobiography* (1960).

Murray, Sir James Augustus Henry 1837–1915. British lexicographer. *b.* Denholm, Scotland. Established reputation as philologist with *Dialect of the Southern Counties of Scotland* (1873); began lifework (1879), editing the Philological Society's *A New English Dictionary on Historical Principles,* also known as *Oxford English Dictionary;* edited volumes up to T, creating the system underlying this monumental work.

Murrow *(mûr ō),* **Edward R.** original name: Egbert Roscoe Murrow. 1908-65. American broadcast journalist. *b.* Greensboro, N.C. With CBS (1935–61); television narrator on *See It Now* (1951–58) and *Person to Person* (1953–59); director of United States Information Agency (1961–64); remembered for his vivid World War II broadcasts from London.

Murry *(mûr ĭ),* **John Middleton** 1889–1957. English author. *b.* London. Editor of the *Athenaeum* (1919–21), the *Adelphi* (1923–30), and *Peace News* (from 1940); wrote critical and biographical works on Dostoevsky, Keats, Shakespeare, Blake, and Swift, as well as on his wife, Katherine Mansfield; wrote *Poems* (1919), essays, and the autobiographical *Between Two Worlds* (1934).

Musset *(mü sĕ),* **Alfred de** full name: LOUIS CHARLES ALFRED DE 1810–57. French poet. *b.* Paris. Published first collection of poems *Contes d'Espagne et d'Italie* (1830); friend of Victor Hugo's; admitted to the Cénacle, a circle of Romantic poets; abandoned the movement and turned to drama, conceiving the armchair theater—plays meant for reading only, published as *Comédies et Proverbes;* wrote *On ne Saurait Penser de Tout* (1849), *Carmosine* (1850), and *Bettine* (1851) for actual performance; published *Poésies Diverses;* much of his melancholy poetry reflects the disillusionment of an unhappy love affair with George Sand; published the autobiographical *Confessions d'un Enfant du Siècle* (1835); his last publication was *Contes* (1854).

Mussolini *(mōōs sō lē nē),* **Benito** 1883–1945. Italian dictator. *b.* Dovia. Began career as a socialist agitator; arrested several times as secretary of Socialist party; edited the socialist *Avanti!* (1912–14); founded and edited *Il Popolo D'Italia* (1914); fought on Allied side in World War I; at end of war, organized Fascio di Combattimento (1919), a militant nationalist and anti-Bolshevist party consisting mostly of war veterans, shaping it into a political movement whose members were tough, disciplined, and black-shirted; led Fascist march on Rome (1922); when summoned by king to form ministry, did so, allowing dictatorial powers for himself as Il Duce and prime minister; suppressed all opposition parties and newspapers; abolished Chamber of Deputies; signed Lateran Treaty establishing the Vatican State (1929); formed the Axis with Germany; invaded and annexed Ethiopia (1936) and Albania (1939); aided Franco in Spanish Civil War; entered World War II with Germany (1940); following Allied invasion of Italy, deposed and imprisoned (1943); dramatically rescued by the Germans (1943); attempted to return as head of German-supported puppet government but was captured and shot by partisans (1945).

Mutsuhito *(moo tsoo hētō)* reign name: MEIJI (ENLIGHTENED PEACE). 1852–1912. Japanese emperor. *b.* Kyoto. Ascended throne (1867); began reforms, called the Restoration, which brought Japan into the 20th century; transferred capital to Tokyo (1869); abolished feudal system of the shogunate, adopted Gregorian calendar (1873), promulgated new Constitution (1889); abolished torture and established a judicial code; introduced English language in schools; put down Satsuma Rebellion (1877); built railways; formed alliance with England (1902); won notable victories in Sino-Japanese War (1894–95) and Russo-Japanese War (1904–1905).

N

Nabokov *(nə bô kəf; nă bə kəf),* **Vladimir Vladimirovich** 1899–1977. American author. *b.* St. Petersburg, Russia. Fled Russia after Revolution, settling in the U.S. (1940); professor of Russian literature at Cornell (1948–59); moved to Switzerland (1959). Fiction includes *Lolita* (1955), *Pale Fire* (1962), *Ada* (1969), *Pnin* (1957), *Bend Sinister* (1947), *Mary* (1926), *Despair* (1936), *King, Queen, Knave* (1928), *Laughter in the Dark* (1932), *Transparent Things* (1972), *Look at the Harlequins* (1974), and *The Real Life of Sebastian Knight* (1941); translated Russian poetry, wrote short stories collected in *Nabokov's Dozen* and *Spring in Fialta,* and poetry, collected in *A Cluster* and *Poems.*

Nadir Shah *(nä dĭr shä)* called The Conqueror. 1688–1747. King of Persia (1736–47). *b.* Khorasan. Helped Shah Tahmasp expel the Afghan rulers of Persia (1726–31); restored Tahmasp to the throne; defeated Turks (1731); imprisoned Tahmasp (1732) and elevated Tahmasp's infant son to the throne as Abbas III; on death of the puppet (1736), assumed the crown; conquered Afghanistan and drove back the Uzbeks; ravaged North India and took Delhi (1739); left with rich booty including the Peacock Throne studded with diamonds; reduced Khiva, Bokhara and other towns; assassinated.

Nanak *(nä nȧk)* called Guru (Teacher). 1469–1538. Indian religious leader. *b.* Talvandi. A Hindu by birth; influenced by Muslim theology to preach a monotheistic religion (Sikhism) composed of both Hindu and Islamic elements; sayings and teachings compiled as the *Granth* or *Adigranth,* the scripture of the Sikhs.

Nansen *(nän sən),* **Fridtjof** 1861–1930. Norwegian explorer and statesman. *b.* near Oslo. Curator of Natural History Museum at Bergen (from 1882); on Arctic expedition in the *Fram,* reached northernmost point explored up to that time (1895); active in Norwegian independence movement; first Norwegian minister to Great Britain (1906–1908); engaged in oceanographic expeditions to North Atlantic (1910–14); worked for repatriation of World War I prisoners, heading relief work for Russian, Armenian, and Greek refugees (1918–23); Nansen international passport named after him, honoring his work for the stateless and dispossessed; awarded Nobel Peace Prize (1922). Author of *Farthest North* (1897), *Norway and the Union with Sweden* (1905), *Russia and Peace* (1923), *Through Siberia* (1914), *Armenia and the Near East* (1928), *Eskimo Life* (1891), *In Night and Ice* (1897), and *Across Greenland* (1891).

Napier *(nā pĭ ēr),* **John** 1550–1617. Scottish mathematician. *b.*

Merchiston Castle. Invented logarithms and described them in *Mirifici Logarithmorum Canonis Descriptio* (1614); invented a mechanical computer, described in *Rabdologiae seu Numerationis per Virgulas Libri Duo* (1617); pioneered use of decimal notation; wrote a religious work, *A Plaine Discouery of the Whole Reuelation of St. John,* which was widely translated.

Napoleon, I *(nä pō lē ən)* also NAPOLEON BONAPARTE. 1769–1821. Emperor of the French (1804–14). *b.* Ajaccio, Corsica. Joined French army as second lieutenant in the artillery (1785-91); commanded Revolutionary force against Bourbon attack on Toulon (1793); general of brigade; imprisoned as friend of Robespierre during Thermidorian reaction (1794); with a "whiff of grapeshot" subdued mob that had attacked the Tuileries (1795); commander of the Army of the Interior (1795); sent to conduct Italian campaign (1796); married Josephine de Beauharnais (1796); victorious at Lodi and Arcole (1796), occupied Milan and Mantua (1797), expelled Austrians from Italy, and negotiated Treaty of Campoformio, ending Revolutionary War on the Continent and obtaining Belgium and Lombardy for France (1797); planned to defeat England by invading India through Egypt; sailed for Egypt with 35,000 men, occupied Malta, and landed at Alexandria; twice defeated the Mamelukes in Battle of the Pyramids, and entered Cairo; cut off from France when fleet was destroyed by Nelson in Battle of the Nile (1798); invaded Syria (1799); repulsed in attempt to capture Acre; returned to Egypt, defeating Turkish army at Aboukir (1799); leaving Kléber in command of Egypt, secretly embarked for France, to lead her against the Second Coalition; with aid of Abbé Siyes, Lucien Bonaparte, and Roger Ducos, effected the coup d'état of 18th Brumaire, ending the discredited Directory and establishing a consulate with himself as first consul under the Constitution of Year VIII (1799); crossed the Alps, occupied Milan, defeated Austrians at Marengo and Hohenlinden, and dictated Treaty of Lunéville (1801), which ended Second Coalition; secured peace with England by Treaty of Amiens (1802); established Bank of France; by Concordat of 1801, restored privileges to Catholic Church; founded Legion of Honor; reorganized educational system; promulgated the Code Napoléon; made consul for life, later crowning himself emperor of France (1804) and king of Italy (1805); faced with Third Coalition (1805); gave up projected invasion of England after Nelson's victory at Trafalgar (1805); invaded Austria, occupied Vienna, and crushed Austrians at Austerlitz; by Treaty of Pressburg, ended Third Coalition and dissolved Holy Roman Empire (1806); consolidated power by appointing brother Joseph king of Naples and brother Louis king of Holland; confronted with Fourth Coalition; defeated Prussians at Jena and Auerstadt and Russians at Friedland (1807); by Peace of Tilsit, deprived Prussia of half her territory, humbled Russia, and ended Fourth Coalition; entered Berlin, issuing Berlin Decree

(1806), later reinforced by Milan Decree, both enforcing the Continental System (blockade of British commerce); reached zenith of power (1807) as master of Europe; when Portugal refused to conform to Continental System, sent French army under Junot into Portugal and under Murat into Spain; imprisoned Ferdinand of Spain and proclaimed Joseph Bonaparte king of Spain (1808), thus precipitating Peninsular War: entered Madrid in triumph (1808); opposed by Fifth Coalition (1809); led army to Austria; entered Vienna, defeated Archduke Charles at Wagram, and concluded Peace of Schönbrunn (1809); divorced Josephine and married Mary Louisa of Austria (1809); annexed Papal States (1809) and Holland (1810); after two years of peace, the refusal of Czar Alexander to adhere to the Continental System caused him to lead the Grande Armée, 600,000 strong in an invasion of Russia; won Battle of Borodino against Kutuzov (1812) and entered Moscow; forced to retreat, suffering the loss of over three-fourths of his men and matériel; nevertheless, defeated allies at Lutzen and Bautzen; confronted with Sixth Coalition; won last military victory at Dresden (1813); defeated by allies in Battle of Nations at Leipzig (1813); on fall of Paris (1814), forced to abdicate; exiled to Elba by terms of Treaty of Fontainebleau, which allowed him to retain title of emperor and an annual allowance of two million francs; escaped from Elba and reentered Paris (1815); raised new army but was defeated decisively at Waterloo; surrendered to British; banished to St. Helena, where he spent the last six years of life as a prisoner.

Napoleon III also known as Louis Napoleon; full name: Charles Louis Bonaparte. 1808–73. Emperor of the French (1852–70). *b.* Paris. Son of Louis Bonaparte, King of Holland, and nephew of Napoleon (Bonaparte) I; lived early life in exile; on death of Napoleon II, became head of dynasty; engaged in revolts and conspiracies and was imprisoned many times; settled in London; on outbreak of Revolution of 1848, returned to France and was elected deputy; as candidate for presidency of the Republic, elected by overwhelming vote; suppressed constitutional liberties and freedom of press; by coup d'état of 1851, proclaimed himself dictator and president for ten years, dissolved the National Assembly, and promulgated new constitution; brutally put down a workers' uprising; assumed title of emperor of the French as Napoleon III (1852); annexed Savoy and Nice (1860); joined Crimean War on the side of Sardinia against Austria; restored Pope Pius IX to throne (1849); sent Archduke Maximilian of Austria to Mexico to establish French empire in New World (1863–67); sent expeditions to China (1857–60); annexed Cochin China and participated in construction of Suez Canal; ruled as absolute dictator until 1860; sought to regain popularity (1860–67) by restoring some civil liberties and rights of National Assembly; the period 1867–70 is known as the Liberal Empire; worsening relations with Prussia led to Franco-

Prussian War (1870–71); led the army himself, but was defeated and captured at Sedan (1870); deposed by National Assembly in bloodless revolution; exiled to England. Author of books on military and political subjects, including *Idées Napoléoniennes* (1838), *Dictionnaire de la Conversation* and *Histoire de Jules César* (1865–66).

Nash *(năsh),* **Ogden** 1902–71. American humorist. *b.* Rye, N.Y. Created a brand of humor characterized by outrageous puns and unusual rhymes. Author of *Versus* (1949), *Hard Lines* (1931), *I'm a Stranger Here Myself* (1938), *Happy Days* (1933), *The Primrose Path* (1935), *Good Intentions* (1942), *You Can't Get There from Here* (1957), *Many Long Years Ago* (1945), *Family Reunion* (1950), and *The Private Dining Room* (1953); coauthored the musical comedy *One Touch of Venus* (1943) and wrote the lyrics for *Two's Company* (1952).

Nashe *(năsh),* **Thomas** 1567–1601. English satirist and dramatist. *b.* Lowestoft. First known work is *Anatomie of Absurdities* (1589); plunged into Marprelate Controversy against the Puritans, employing invective satire under the pseudonym Pasquil; engaged in battle of polemics with Gabriel Harvey, during which he wrote *Pierce Pennilesse* (1592), *Christes Teares* (1593), and *Have With You to Saffron Walden* (1596); wrote the first English adventure novel, *The Unfortunate Traveller* (1594); thrown into prison for his comedy *Isle of Dogs* (1597); last work was *Lenten Stuffe* (1599).

Nasser *(nä sər),* **Gamal Abdel** 1918–70. Egyptian statesman. *b.* Bani Mor, Egypt. Founder of military junta that overthrew King Farouk (1952); deposed General Neguib and assumed presidency (1954); elected president (1956); symbol of Pan-Arabism and its most articulate spokesman; expropriated Suez Canal and gained prestige through the humiliation of Britain and France in the war that followed (1956); tried but failed to create a union of Arab republics including Syria and Yemen; initiated radical land reforms and undertook the construction of Aswan Dam; lost considerable influence after suffering defeat in Six-Day War (1967) but remained popular with Egyptians until death.

Nation *(nā shən),* **Carry Amelia** *née* MOORE. 1846–1911. American temperance agitator. *b.* Garrard County, Ky. With the hatchet as her symbol and weapon, embarked on a career of wrecking saloons; suffered imprisonment several times. Author of *Autobiography* (1904).

Natta *(nät tä),* **Giulio** 1903–. Italian chemist. Professor of industrial chemistry at Milan Institute of Technology (from 1939); with Karl Ziegler, awarded Nobel Prize for chemistry (1963) for work enabling transformation of simple hydrocarbons into complex molecular substances.

Nebuchadnezzar II *(nĕb ū kəd nĕz ər)* Babylonian name: NABUKUDURRIUSUR. *d.* 562 B.C. Chaldean king of Babylon (605–562 B.C.). Son of Nabopolassar; as crown prince, defeated Necho II of Eygpt at Carchemish (605); conquered Palestine (597), occupied Jerusalem, and took Jehoiachin, king of the

Jews, prisoner, placing Zedekiah in his stead; when Zedekiah revolted (588), besieged and retook Jerusalem, destroyed the city, and carried the Jews into the Babylonian Captivity; took Tyre after 13-year siege; invaded Egypt (572); considered one of the greatest rulers of the ancient world; built the Hanging Gardens, restored the temples, beautified Babylon; achievements recorded in cuneiform inscriptions.

Necker *(nĕ kâr),* **Jacques** 1732–1804. French statesman. *b.* Geneva, Switzerland. Founded own London and Paris banking business (1762), making a fortune by speculation during Seven Years' War (1756–63); director of the treasury (1776); director general of finances (1777); introduced financial reforms and retrenchments but was dismissed; published *Compte Rendu au Roi* (1781) defending his measures; recalled (1788); became a popular hero by recommending the summoning of the States General; king's attempt to dismiss him a second time led to the storming of the Bastille; resigned, faced with increasing unpopularity and powerlessness (1790); retired to Geneva. Among his works are *De l'Administration des Finances de la France* (3 vols., 1784), *Sur l'Administration de M. Necker par Lui-même* (1791), and *De la Révolution Française* (4 vols., 1797).

Neel *(nā əl),* **Louis Eugene Félix** 1904–. French physicist. Professor of physics at Strasbourg (1928–45) and Grenoble (from 1945); awarded Nobel Prize in physics (1970) with H. Alfven for discoveries relating to ferromagnetism, antiferromagnetism, and magnetohydrodynamics.

Negrín *(nā grēn),* **Juan** 1887–1956. Spanish statesman. *b.* Tenerife, Canary Islands. Began career as a physician; professor of physiology at the universities of Laguna and Madrid; fought on the socialist side in establishing the Spanish Republic; minister of finance (1936–37); prime minister (1937); led the Republican government during the Spanish Civil War, moving it to Valencia, Barcelona, and back to Madrid; after the Civil War, set up Republican government-in-exile in Mexico; organized España Combatiente and moved to London.

Nehru *(nā ro͞o),* **Jawaharlal** 1889–1964. Indian statesman. *b.* Allahabad. Studied in England, but on return to India joined Gandhi's nationalist movement; imprisoned (1921) and spent 18 of the next 25 years in jail; president of Indian National Congress (1929, 1936, 1937, 1946; intermittently after Independence); opposed Gandhi's approach to social problems, adopting a secular outlook in politics; first prime minister of India (1950–66); wielded undisputed authority over subcontinent until death; promoted nonalignment internationally and unity of Third World nations; daughter INDIRA GANDHI continued many of his policies as prime minister. Author of works, including *Autobiography* (1936), *Glimpses of World History* (1939), and *The Discovery of India* (1946).

Nelson *(nĕl sən),* **Horatio** title: VISCOUNT NELSON. 1758–1805. British naval hero. *b.* Burnham Thorpe. Entered navy (1770); fought in American Revolutionary War; lost right eye at Calvi (1794);

won laurels by defeating Spanish and French fleets off Cape Vincent (1797); rear admiral (1797); lost right arm in attempt to capture Santa Cruz de Tenerife (1797); won first great victory in Battle of the Nile at Aboukir Bay (1798), ending Napoleon's ambitions in Near East; made Baron Nelson of the Nile and showered with honors and rewards; scandalized English society by liaison with Emma Hamilton; vice admiral (1801); gained hard-won victory in Copenhagen (1801) after ignoring superior's order to retire by putting blind eye to telescope; blockaded Toulon for two years; in final engagement with French off Cape Trafalgar (1805), won greatest victory of career but was mortally wounded and died at moment of triumph.

Nernst *(nĕrnst),* **Walther Hermann** 1864–1941. German scientist. *b.* Briesen, Prussia. Head of Institute for Physics at Berlin (from 1933); invented Nernst lamp; investigated osmotic pressure, electroacoustics, and the specific heat of solids at low temperature; proposed the Third Law of Thermodynamics, known as the Nernst heat theorem; awarded Nobel Prize in chemistry (1921).

Nero *(nē rō)* full name: NERO CLAUDIUS CAESAR DRUSUS GERMANICUS; original name: LUCIUS DOMITIUS AHENOBARBUS 37–68. Roman emperor (54–68); *b.* Antium, Italy. Adopted by stepfather Claudius, on whose death he succeeded to the imperium; reign stained with debauchery, extravagance, and tyranny; responsible for deaths of his brother Britannicus, his mother Agrippina, his wives Octavia and Poppaea, and his advisor Seneca; accused of kindling the fire that destroyed much of Rome (64); ordered systematic persecution of Christians in which many, including Peter and Paul, perished; overthrown in revolt of the Praetorians and committed suicide.

Neruda *(nā rōō thä),* **Pablo** original name: NEFTALÍ RICARDO REYES BASUALTO. 1904–73. Chilean poet. *b.* Parral. In Chilean diplomatic service (1940–42); noted for poems of melancholy despair and Marxist sympathies. Author of *Crepusculario (1923), Veinte Poemas de Amor y una Canción Desesperada* (1924), *Residencia en la Tierra* (1933), and *Odas Elementales* (1937); awarded Nobel Prize in literature (1971).

Nestorius *(nĕs tō rĭ əs)* *d.* c451. Syrian heresiarch. *b.* Syria. Selected patriarch of Constantinople for his eloquence, asceticism, and zeal (428); defended doctrine of Anastasius that the divinity and humanity of Christ were discrete though joined in perfect harmony; deposed for heresy at Council of Ephesus (431); banished to Petra and later to the Egyptian desert; the heresy took deep roots in Persia and in the Assyrian Church, which extended as far as India and China until wiped out by the Muslims.

Neumann *(noi män),* **Johann von** 1903–57. American mathematician. *b.* Budapest, Hungary. Fled Hungary during Bela Kun Communist regime (1919); Professor at Berlin (1927–29), Hamburg (1929–30), and Princeton (from 1930); worked on atomic bomb project at Los Alamos; pioneered in developing high-speed computers, beginning with

M.A.N.I.A.C.; founded the theory of games and contributed to point-set theory, theory of continuous groups, operator theory, and mathematical logic. Works include *Mathematische Grundlagen der Quantenmechanik* (1932), *Functional Operators* (1933–34), and *Theory of Games and Economic Behavior* (1944).

Newman *(nū mən),* **Cardinal John Henry** 1801–90. English Catholic theologian and churchman. *b.* London. Ordained as Anglican priest (1824); vicar of university church (1828–43); leader of Oxford Movement and of Tractarians; contributed to *Tracts for the Times,* especially the climactic *Tract XC* (1841) in which he stated that the Thirty-Nine Articles were in conflict only with the abuses and not with the doctrines of the Catholic Church; edited the *British Critic* until forced out by bishop of Oxford (1833–41); resigned vicarage of St. Mary's (1843); after a two-year seclusion, was received into Roman Catholic Church (1845); ordained priest in Rome (1847); on return to England, established a branch of the Oratorian Congregation; rector of Dublin Catholic University (1851–58); sided with Inopportunists and opposed Ultramontanes; created cardinal by Pope Leo XIII (1879); unequalled as a writer for the lucidity of his logic and for the irony and delicacy of his style. Other works include *Apologia Pro Vita Sua* (1864), *The Idea of a University* (1873), *The Dream of Gerontius* (1866), *The Grammar of Assent* (1870), *The Arians of the Fourth Century* (1833), *Essay on Development of Christian Doctrine* (1845), *Verses on Various Occasions* (1874), and *Sermons* (1849, 1857).

Newton *(nū tən),* **Sir Isaac** 1642–1727. English scientist. *b.* Woolsthorpe. Lucasian professor at Cambridge (from 1669); made three fundamental discoveries which revolutionized science: set forth the theory of universal gravity (1665) and proved on the basis of Kepler's law of planetary orbits that the attraction of the sun upon the planets and that of the earth upon the moon varies inversely as the square of their distances; second, by the mathematical method of fluxions formulated the laws of motion; third, originated the emission or corpuscular theory of light and laid the basis of spectroscopy. Also credited with the invention, independently of Leibnitz, of differential calculus (1665) and integral calculus (1666); constructed a reflecting telescope. Author of *De Mortu Corporum* and *Philosophiae Naturalis Principia Mathematica* (1687), *Optics* (1704), *Optical Lectures* (1728), *Fluxions* (1736), and *Arithmetica Universalis.*

Ney *(nā),* **Michel** titles: Duc d' Elchingen, Prince de La Moskava. 1769–1815. French general. *b.* Saarlouis, Prussia. General, given command of the army of the Rhine (1799); won at Elchingen (1805); fought in battles of Jena (1806), Eylau (1807), Friedland (1807), and Borodino (1812); commanded rear guard in retreat from Moscow; created peer by Louis XVIII at the Restoration (1814), but rejoined Napoleon during the Hundred Days; shared defeat at Waterloo; tried, condemned for treason, and shot.

Nicholas *(nĭk ō ləs)* Name of two czars of Russia:
NICHOLAS I Russian name: NIKOLAI PAVLOVICH. 1796–1855. Czar of Russia (1825–55). *b.* near St. Petersburg. Engaged in wars with Persia (1826–28), Turkey (1827–29), and Britain and France (Crimean War, 1853–56); an opponent of liberal movements, suppressed insurrection in Poland (1830–31) and helped Austria put down revolt in Hungary (1849); led by Pan-Slav sympathies to Russianize all subjects of the empire.
NICHOLAS II Russian name: NIKOLAI ALEKSANDROVICH. 1868–1918. Czar of Russia (1894–1917). *b.* St. Petersburg. Last of the Romanov rulers; responsible for convening the International Peace Conference at The Hague (1898) and founding the Hague Tribunal (1899); established the Duma (1906); humiliated in Russo-Japanese War (1904–1905); alienated the masses with bloody suppression of Revolution of 1905; built Trans-Siberian Railway; introduced moderate reforms with Peter Stolypin as premier; joined Allies against Germany in World War I (1915); military disasters and collapse of domestic economy led to Russian Revolution; abdicated (1917); executed by Bolsheviks (1918).

Nicolle *(nē kôl),* **Charles Jean Henri** 1866–1936. French bacteriologist. *b.* Rouen. Director of Pasteur Institute at Tunis (1903); professor at Collège de France (1932); demonstrated the infectious nature of typhus and its transmission by body lice; awarded Nobel Prize in physiology and medicine (1928).

Niebuhr *(nē boor),* **Reinhold** 1892–1971. American theologian. *b.* Wright City, Mo. Ordained (1915); professor of applied Christianity (from 1930) and dean (from 1950) at Union Theological Seminary; advocated liberalism and social activism. Author of *Does Civilization Need Religion?* (1927), *Moral Man and Immoral Society* (1932), *Beyond Tragedy* (1937), *The Nature and Destiny of Man* (2 vols., 1941–43); *The Children of Light and the Children of Darkness* (1944), and *The Irony of American History* (1952).

Nietzsche *(nē chə),* **Friedrich Wilhelm** 1844–1900. German philosopher. *b.* Röcken. Professor of classical philology at Basel (1869–79); follower of Wagner and Schopenhauer, but later opposed them; spent last 12 years in total insanity; denounced Christianity; proposed a transformation of values based on will to power and an affirmation of strength and virility; held that the strong ought to survive and inherit the earth; conceived the idea of a race of supermen; influenced 20th-century German attitude in World War I and in Third Reich. His works include *Thus Spake Zarathustra* (1883–92), *The Birth of Tragedy* (1872), *Genealogy of Morals* (1887), *Human, All Too Human* (1878–80), *Joyful Wisdom* (1882), *Beyond Good and Evil* (1886), *The Antichrist* (1888), and *Ecce Homo* (1888).

Nightingale *(nīt ĭn gāl),* **Florence** 1820–1910. English nurse. *b.* Florence, Italy. Received training as a nurse (1851); on outbreak of Crimean War (1854), organized a nursing department at Scutari and founded a hospital;

against great odds, continued to minister to the sick and wounded, and worked on reform of hospital sanitation; with funds donated after war, established Nightingale Home at St. Thomas's Hospital, for nurses' training; known as the Lady with the Lamp for her tireless service; awarded Order of Merit (1907); engaged in public health projects in India. Author of *Notes on Hospitals* (1859) and *Notes on Nursing* (1860).

Nijinsky *(nĭ zhĭn skĭ),* **Waslaw** 1890–1950. Russian dancer. *b.* Kiev. Made debut at St. Petersburg (1907); joined Diaghilev's Ballet Russe; first to dance *Petrouchka* in Stravinsky's ballet (1911); noted for roles in *The Afternoon of a Faun, The Specter of the Rose, Cleopatra, Les Sylphides,* and *Scheherazade;* became insane (1917).

Nimitz *(nĭm ĭts),* **Chester William** 1885–1966. American admiral. *b.* Fredericksburg, Tex. Graduated from Annapolis (1905); rear admiral (1938); chief of Bureau of Navigation (1939–41); commander in chief of U.S. Pacific fleet (1941–45); admiral of the fleet (1944); chief of naval operations (1945–47).

Nirenberg *(nĭr ən bûrg),* **Marshall Warren** 1927–. American biochemist. *b.* New York, N. Y. On staff of National Institutes of Health (from 1957); shared Nobel Prize in physiology and medicine (1968) with R. W. Holley and H. Khorana for discovery of the process by which enzymes, consisting of a sequence of amino acids, determine a cell's function in genetic development.

Nitze *(nĭt zə),* **Max** 1848–1906. German urologist. *b.* Berlin. Designed the first modern electrically lighted cystoscope (1877) for endoscopic examination of the urethra, bladder, and rectum.

Nixon *(nĭk sən),* **Richard Milhous** 1913–. 37th president of U. S. (1969–74). *b.* Yorba Linda, Calif. House of Representatives (1947–51); gained national prominence as a red-baiter in the Alger Hiss trial; senator (1951–53); vice-president (1953–61); lost Republican presidential campaign against John F. Kennedy (1960); defeated for governorship of California (1962); successful Republican presidential candidate against Hubert Humphrey (1968); initiated bold foreign policy that brought Cold War to an end, reestablishing relations with People's Republic of China; reelected with overwhelming majority (1972); accused of obstruction of justice and cover-up of evidence in the criminal break-in and burglary at the Democratic National Committee headquarters at Watergate complex in Washington, D.C., known as Watergate Scandal (1972–74); also accused of abuse of power and tax irregularities; faced with almost certain impeachment by the House and conviction by the Senate, resigned (1974), the first president in U. S. history to do so.

Nkrumah *(ən kro͞o mə),* **Kwame** 1909–72. Ghanaian statesman. *b.* Ankroful. Studied at London School of Economics; on return to Ghana, formed Convention People's party, demanding Ghanaian self-government (1949); first prime minister of independent Commonwealth state of Ghana (1957); first president of Republic of Ghana (1960); prime mover in the Charter of African States and spokesman of Pan-African movement; called Osagyefo (the Savior); became increasingly dictatorial, set up one-party state, interfered with judiciary, and imprisoned political opponents; overthrown in a military coup and exiled to Guinea (1966). Author of *Autobiography* (1957) and *Africa Must Unite* (1963).

Nobel *(nō bĕl),* **Alfred** 1833-96. Swedish inventor and philanthropist. *b.* Stockholm. Studied mechanical engineering (1850–54); invented dynamite, explosive gelatin, ballistite, and artificial gutta percha; held over 100 patents; acquired large wealth through his inventions, manufacturing industries, and interest in Baku oil wells; left fortune of $9,200,000 for the establishment of Nobel Prizes in five areas: peace, physics, chemistry, physiology and medicine, and literature.

Noel-Baker *(nō ĕl bā kər),* **Philip John** original name: PHILIP JOHN BAKER. 1889–. British statesman. Captain of British Olympic team (1912); Labor Member of Parliament (from 1929); professor of international relations at London (1924–29) and Yale (1934); cabinet member in Labor governments (1946–51). Author of *Disarmament* (1926) and *The Arms Race* (1958); awarded Nobel Peace Prize (1959).

Noguchi *(nə gōō chĭ),* **Hideyo** 1876–1928. American bacteriologist. *b.* Inawashiro, Japan. Immigrated to U. S. (1899); on the staff of Rockefeller Institute (from 1904); made important contributions to study of etiology and treatment of diseases, including syphilis, yellow fever, Oroya fever, smallpox, and trachoma; invented Noguchi test for diagnosis of syphilis; discovered the parasite of yellow fever and developed a treatment vaccine. Author of *The Action of Snake Venom Upon Cold-Blooded Animals* (1904).

Noguchi, Isamu 1904–. American sculptor. *b.* Los Angeles. Son of Yone Yoguchi, Japanese poet; studied under Brancusi; known for his abstract sculptures of primitive elegance; also known as a landscape architect and set designer.

Nordau *(nōr dou),* **Max Simon** original surname: SÜDFELD. 1849–1923, German writer. *b.* Budapest, Hungary. Settled in Paris (1880); emerged as a Zionist leader and associate of Herzl. Author of books on social and moral problems, including *Conventional Lies of Society* (1883), *Degeneration* (2 vols. 1892–93), *Paradoxes* (1885), *The Malady of the Century* (1888), *The Interpretation of History* (1909), and *Biology of Ethics* (1921), as well as novels, essays, plays, fairy tales, and travel books.

Norris *(nôr ĭs),* **Benjamin Frank** 1870–1902. American novelist. *b.* Chicago. Correspondent in South Africa for *San Francisco Chronicle* (1895–96) and in Cuba for *McClure's Magazine* (1898–99); on the staff of Doubleday, Page & Company (from 1899). Author of *McTeague* (1899), *The Octopus* (1901), and *The Pit* (1903).; the last two forming the first two volumes of a trilogy called *The Epic of the Wheat; Collected Works* published (10 vols., 1928).

Norris, George William 1861–1944. American statesman. *b.* Sandusky County, Ohio. Moved to Nebraska (1885); U. S. House of Representatives (1903–13); U. S. senator (1913–43); leader of the liberal Republican faction; led Republican-Democratic coalition that broke the control of Speaker Joseph G. Cannon on House procedures; opposed Wilson's foreign policy, U. S. entry into World War I, the Versailles Treaty, and the League of Nations; helped establish the Tennessee Valley Administration, the Norris Dam being named in his honor; expelled from the Republican party (1936) for supporting the New Deal; author of the 20th Amendment, which moved forward the date of presidential inauguration and the meeting of Congress; with Fiorello La Guardia, sponsored the anti-injunction labor act; won reelection as an independent (1936) but lost in 1942.

Norrish *(nôr ĭsh),* **Ronald George Wreyford** 1897–1978. British chemist. Professor of chemistry at Cambridge (1930–55); with Manfred Eigen and George Porter, awarded Nobel Prize in chemistry (1957) for studies of extremely fast chemical reactions effected by disturbing equilibrium by very short energy pulsations.

Northrop *(nôr thrəp),* **John Howard** 1891–. American scientist. *b.* Yonkers, N. Y. On staff of Rockefeller Institute (from 1916); first to isolate trypsin and pepsin in crystalline form (1930); discovered fermentation process for acetone manufacture; proposed theory that all proteins are derived from a substance that he called proteinogen; shared Nobel Prize in chemistry (1946) with J. N. Sumner and W. M. Stanley. Author of *Crystalline Enzymes* (1939).

Nostradamus *(nŏs trä dā məs)* original name: Michel de Notredame. 1503–66. French astrologer and physician. *b.* St.-Remy. Physician to Charles IX; became an astrologer and predicted a number of events correctly, including the death of Henry II of France; published a book of prophecies, *Centuries* (1555), written in rhymed quatrains.

Novalis *(nō vä lĭs)* pseudonym of Baron Friedrich von Hardenberg. 1772–1801. German lyric poet. *b.* Wiederstedt. Studied law and worked as a mining engineer; best known as the Prophet of Romanticism, a reputation based on his novel *Heinrich von Ofterdingen* (1802) and lyric poems collected as *Hymns to the Night* (1800); also wrote *Poems, Sacred Songs,* and *Lehrlinge zu Sais.*

Noyes *(noiz),* **Alfred** 1880–1958. English poet. *b.* Wolverhampton. Published first volume of verse, *The Loom of Years* (1902); wrote best work on favorite themes, the sea and the Elizabethans; visiting professor of poetry at Princeton (1914); published the blank verse epic trilogy *The Torchbearers* (1922); shied away from experimentation and upheld conventional poetic techniques. Works include *The Flower of Old Japan* (1903), *The Forest of Wild Thyme* (1905), *Forty Singing Seamen* (1908), *Drake* (1908), and *Tales of Mermaid Tavern* (1912); also wrote plays, novels, short stories, criticism, and *Two Worlds for Memory* (1953).

Nureyev *(nōō rā yəf)*, **Rudolf Hametovich** 1939–. Russian ballet dancer. *b.* Ufa. A soloist with the Leningrad Kirov Ballet; defected to the West in Paris (1961); became a member of Le Grand Ballet du Marquis de Cuevas; joined the Royal Ballet (1962); teamed with Margot Fonteyn in a series of ballets that electrified the ballet world. Author of *Autobiography* (1962).

O

Oates *(ōts)*, **Titus** 1649–1705. English conspirator. *b.* Oakham. In collusion with London clergyman Israel Tonge invented a story, using forged documents, of a Jesuit plot to murder Charles II, place Catholic duke of York on the throne, murder Protestants, and burn London (1678); gained credence when Sir Edmond Berry Godfrey, the judge investigating the charges, was mysteriously murdered; in the ensuing frenzy nearly 35 Catholics were either lynched or executed; on accession of James II, tried for perjury, found guilty (1685), pilloried, and imprisoned for life; pardoned and released on accession of William of Orange (1689).

O'Casey *(ō kā sĭ)*, **Sean** 1880–1964. Irish playwright. *b.* Dublin. Wrote early plays for Abbey Theater; adopted impressionistic techniques; noted for using lower-class speech patterns in his plays. Chief works include *The Shadow of a Gunman* (1923), *Juno and the Peacock* (1924), *The Plough and the Stars* (1926), *The Silver Tassie* (1928) *Within the Gates* (1933), *Purple Dust* (1940), *Red Roses For Me* (1946), *Cockadoodle Dandy* (1949), and *The Bishop's Bonfire* (1955); published autobiography *Mirror in My House* (2 vols., 1956).

Ochoa *(ō chō ä)*, **Severo** 1905–. American biochemist. *b.* Spain. Immigrated to U.S. (1940); on staff of New York College of Medicine (from 1942); with Arthur Kornberg, shared Nobel Prize in physiology and medicine (1959) for synthesis of DNA and RNA, two of the most important nucleic acids.

Ockham *(ŏk əm)*, **William of** Also Occam; also known as Doctor Invincibilis, Venerabilis Inceptor. c1300–c1349. English scholastic philosopher. *b.* Ockham. Entered Franciscan order; at Franciscan assembly at Perugia, defended principle of evangelical poverty against Pope John XXII (1322); imprisoned for heresy at Avignon, but escaped to Bavaria; gained protection of Emperor Louis, whom he defended against temporal claims of the papacy; general of the order (1342); upheld nominalism, according to which the individual is real and universals are only abstracts and knowledge of God, the soul, and immortality can be obtained not through the intellect but through faith and intuition; developed the principle of logic known as Occam's Razor, that entities must not be multiplied beyond what is necessary and that an argument must be reduced to its simplest terms. Author of *Opus Nonaginta Dierum* (1330), *Dialogues* (1343), *Super Potestate Papali, Summa Logices* (1488), and *Tractatus de Sacramento Altaris* (1516).

Oehlenschläger *(ûlən shlā gər),* **Adam Gottlob** 1779–1850. Danish poet. Poet laureate of Scandinavia. *b.* Vesterbro. Professor of aesthetics at Copenhagen (from 1810); crowned king of Scandinavian singers at Lund (1829) and proclaimed national poet (1849); wrote over 24 tragedies regarded as among the greatest dramas in Scandinavian literature. *Hakon Jarl* (1807), *Baldur hin Gode* (1808), *Palnatoke* (1809), *Axel og Valborg* (1810), *Correggio* (1809), *Nordens Guder* (1819), *Helge* (1814), *Regnar Lodbrok* (1848), and *Thors Resje til Jothunhejm* are the works by which he is best known; other works include *Guldhornene* (1803), *Sanct-Hansaften-Spil* (1803), *Aladin* (1805), *Digte* (1803), *Autobiography* (1830–31), and *Reminiscences* (1850).

Oersted *(ûr stĭth),* **Hans Christian** also ÖRSTED 1777–1851. Danish physicist. *b.* Rudkøbing. Established relationship between magnetism and electricity; founded science of electromagnetism; isolated aluminum. Author of *Spirit in Nature* (1850) and other books.

O'Faoláin *(ō fā lən),* **Seán** 1900–. Irish writer. *b.* Cork. Author of collections of short stories *Midsummer Night's Madness* (1932) and *A Purse of Coppers* (1937), novels *A Nest of Simple Folk* (1933), *A Born Genius* (1936), and *Come Back To Erin* (1940), and biographies; wrote a history of his own people, *The Irish* (1947).

Offenbach *(ôf ən bäK),* **Jacques** 1819–80. German composer. *b.* Cologne. Went to Paris (1833); conductor at Théâtre Français (1848); opened own theater, Bouffes Parisiens (1855), for which he composed operas and operettas, among them *Orpheus in the Underworld* (1858), *Le Mariage aux Lanternes, Les Deux Aveugles, Les Violoneux, Ba-ta-clan, Croquefer, La Belle Hélène, Barbe Bleue, La Vie Parisienne, La Grande Duchesse de Gérolstein, Genevieve de Brabant, Roi Carotte, Madame Favart;* his only serious opera, *The Tales of Hoffmann,* was produced after his death.

O'Higgins *(ō hĭg ənz),* **Bernardo** 1778–1842. Chilean statesman. *b.* Chilián. Son of AMBROSIO O'HIGGINS (c1720–1801), Irish-born viceroy of Peru (1796–1801) and Chile (from 1789). Military leader of Chilean patriots (1810); commander of the army (1813); with Jośe Carrera, defeated at Rancagua by Spaniards and forced to flee to Argentina; joined San Martín's invasion of Chile and shared in victory at Chacabuco (1817); dictator of Chile (1817–23); proclaimed Chile independent and gained victory at Maipo (1818); found resistance to his progressive reforms; deposed by revolution, and retired to Peru.

Ohm *(ōm),* **Georg Simon** 1787–1854. German physicist. *b.* Erlangen, Bavaria. Professor at Munich (from 1849); studied galvanism and formulated Ohm's Law; ohm, the electrical unit of resistance, and mho, the unit of conductance, are named after him. Author of *The Galvanic Current Investigated Mathematically* (1827)[1] and other books.

Olmsted *(ōm stĕd),* **Frederick Law** 1822–1903. American landscapist. *b.* Hartford, Conn. Best known as the designer, with Calvert Vaux, of Central Park in New York City (1857); also designed the Boston Park system, Capitol grounds in Washington, Prospect Park in Brooklyn, South Park in Chicago, Fairmount Park in Philadelphia, Riverside and Morningside Parks in New York City, Jackson Park in Chicago, and Mount Royal Park in Montreal; instrumental in converting Yosemite into a national park. Author of travel books, including *Walks and Talks of an American Farmer in England* (1852) and *A Journey in the Seaboard Slave States* (1856).

Omar Khayyam *(ō mär kī äm) d.* c1123. Persian poet, mathematician, and astronomer. *b.* Nishapur. Author of a series of astronomical tables, *Ziji Malikshahi,* and a treatise on algebra; contributions as an astronomer and mathematician eclipsed by fame as the author of *Rubaiyat,* or *Quatrains,* especially in the translation by Edward Fitzgerald.

Omodeo. *See* **Amadeo**

O'Neill *(ō nēl),* **Eugene Gladstone** 1888–1953. American playwright. *b.* New York, N.Y. Abandoned studies at Yale for a roving life as a prospector, sailor, and reporter; began writing plays (1914), especially for the Provincetown Players, which he managed (until 1927); gained fame with Pulitzer prize-winning *Beyond the Horizon* (1919). Works include *Emperor Jones* (1921), *Diff'rent* (1920), *Anna Christie* (1922), *The Hairy Ape* (1922), *Desire Under the Elms* (1924), *The Great God Brown* (1925), *Lazarus Laughed* (1926), *Strange Interlude* (1927), *Mourning Becomes Electra* (1931), and *Ah, Wilderness!* (1932); after 12-year hiatus, presented *The Iceman Cometh* (1946), *A Moon for the Misbegotten* (1947), *Long Day's Journey into Night* (1957, Pulitzer prize), *Hughie* (1942), *A Touch of the Poet* (1958). Other works include *Marco Millions* (1931), *Days Without End* (1934), and *More Stately Mansions* (1962); awarded Nobel Prize in literature (1936); plays characterized by masks, melancholy vision of the human condition, and an unfailing sense of theater.

Onsager *(ŏn sä gər),* **Lars** 1903–. American chemist. *b.* Norway. Immigrated to U.S. (1928); professor at Yale (from 1933); awarded Nobel Prize in chemistry (1968) for discovery of the reciprocal relations between voltage and temperature, fundamental for the thermodynamics of irreversible processes in living cells.

Oppenheimer *(ôp ən hī mər),* **Julius Robert** 1904–67. American nuclear physicist. *b.* New York, N.Y. Professor of physics at California (1929–43); director of Los Alamos laboratory that developed the atomic bomb (1943–45); chairman of advisory committee to U.S. Atomic Energy Commission (1946–52); director of Institute for Advanced Study at Princeton (from 1947); suspended from secret nuclear research and denied access to classified information as "poor security risk"; awarded many honors, including the Fermi Award (1963).

Orfila *(ôr fē lä),* **Matthieu Joseph Bonaventure** 1787–1853. French chemist. *b.* Mahón, Balearic Islands. Considered founder of toxicology; professor of medical jurisprudence (from 1819) and chemistry (from 1823); founded Musée Orfila of comparative anatomy. Author of *Traité de Toxicologie Générale* (1813).

Orford, Earl of. *See* **Walpole, Sir Robert**

Origen *(ŏr ə jən)* surname: ADAMANTIUS: Latin name: ORIGENES. c185–c253. Greek father of the Church. *b.* Alexandria, Egypt. Head of Catechetical School in Alexandria (c211–32); when demoted, founded school in Caesarea; tortured during Decian persecution and died in Tyre; believed to have written over 800 works on dogmatics and textual and exegetic criticism, of which only a few are extant, mostly in garbled recensions; attempted reconciliation of Christian, Stoic, and Neoplatonic ideas. Works include the *Hexapla,* containing six parallel versions of the Bible, *Contra Celsum, De Principiis, Tetrapla,* and *Peri Archon.*

Ortega y Gasset *(ôr tā gä ē gä sət),* **José** 1883–1955. Spanish philosopher. *b.* Madrid. Professor at University of Madrid (from 1911); editor of *El Sol* (from 1917); active in Spanish politics until Civil War, when he went into exile. Best known as the author of *The Revolt of the Masses* (1932), *Meditaciones del Quijote* (1914), *España Invertebrada* (1922), *El Tema de Nuestro Tiempo* (1923), *Espiritu de la Latra* (1927), and *On Love* (1959).

Orwell *(ôr wĕl),* **George** pseudonym of ERIC BLAIR. 1903–50. English writer. *b.* Motihari, India. Policeman in Burma (from 1922); quit the job in disgust, lived in England and France, writing *Down and Out in Paris and London* (1933) based on his experiences; joined Republican army in Spanish Civil War (1936); wounded; wrote one of the best accounts of the war in *Homage to Catalonia* (1938); a dedicated Marxist, he retained a horror of totalitarianism and a concern for human liberty, reflected in two brilliant satires, *Animal Farm* (1945) and *1984* (1949). Other works include *Clergyman's Daughter* (1935), *Keep the Aspidistra Flying* (1936), *The Road to Eigan Pier* (1937), *Coming Up for Air* (1939), *Inside the Whale* (1940), *The Lion and the Unicorn* (1941), *Dickens, Dali and Others* (1946), and *Shooting an Elephant* (1950).

Osler *(ōs lər),* **Sir William** 1849–1919. British physician. *b.* Bond Head, Canada. Studied medicine; professor at McGill University (1874–84), at University of Pennsylvania (1884–89), and at Johns Hopkins (1889–1905); achieved great reputation as a writer, teacher, and researcher. Author of *Principles and Practice of Medicine* (1892), *Science and Immortality* (1904), *Modern Medicine* (1907–1909), and other books.

Ossietzky *(ôs ə ĕts kĭ),* **Carl von** 1889–1938. German pacifist. *b.* Hamburg. Secretary of the German League for Peace; organized "No More War" movement; edited antimilitaristic weekly *Welt-*

bühne (from 1928); in prison for denouncing German secret rearmament (1931–32); in a concentration camp as an enemy of state (1933–36); awarded Nobel Peace Prize (1935); released but died of tuberculosis contracted in prison.

Ostwald *(ôst wält),* **Wilhelm** 1853–1932. German scientist. *b.* Riga, Latvia. Professor of physical chemistry at Leipzig (1887–1906); first exchange professor at Harvard (1905); founded first chemical journal, *Zeitschrift für Physikalische Chemie* (1887), and *Annalen der Naturphilosophie* (1902); formulated Ostwald's Dilution Law; invented Ostwald process for making nitric acid by oxidation of ammonia; did fundamental work on electrical conductivity, equilibrium, rates of reaction, chemical dissociation, and catalysts; developed new theory of color; awarded Nobel Prize in chemistry (1909).

Otis *(ō tĭs),* **James** 1725–83. American statesman. *b.* West Barnstable, Mass. Studied law and practiced in Boston (from 1750); king's advocate general (until 1760); resigned to defend Boston merchants against enforcement of Sugar Act; elected to Massachusetts legislature (1761); championed natural rights of colonists; wrote *The Rights of the Colonies Asserted and Proved* (1764), one of the seminal works of the American Revolution; suffered head injuries during a brawl and thereafter lost his reason.

Otto I *(ŏt ō)* called OTTO THE GREAT. 912–73. King of Germany and Holy Roman Emperor (936–973). Succeeded father Henry I as king of Germany (936); subdued the Bohemians, Wends, Danes, and Magyars; put down rebellious nobles led by Duke Eberhard at Andernach (939); helped Pope John XII against Berengar II (951); crowned emperor by the pope, founding the Holy Roman Empire (962); deposed Pope John XII (963); had son Otto crowned coemperor by John XIII (967); revived forms and ceremonies of Carolingian court.

Ovid *(ŏv ĭd)* full name: PUBLIUS OVIDIUS NASO. 43 B.C.–A.D. c17. Roman poet. *b.* Sulmona, Italy. Abandoned law practice for poetry; works consist of erotic and mythological poetry, including; *Art of Love, Remedia Amoris, Metamorphoses, Fasti, Medicamina Faciei, Amores, Medea,* and *Epistolae;* for unknown reasons, exiled to the Black Sea region (A.D. 8), where he remained until death.

Owen *(ō ən),* **Robert** 1771–1858. Welsh socialist. *b.* Newtown. Self-made businessman and cotton manufacturer; made his New Lanark mills into a model industrial community with schools, adult-education programs, nonprofit stores, medical and social insurance, improved working conditions, recreational facilities, and ban on employment of children; attempted to establish other socialist communities, but failed, notably in U.S.; in *A New View of Society* (1813), stated that man's character is wholly formed by environment; instrumental in passage of Factory Act (1819); built up Socialist movement in England by sponsoring National Equitable Labor Exchange (1832–34) and Grand National Consolidated Trades Union (1834); antagonized people with attacks on organized religion and marriage; discouraged by failure of Harmony Hall (Queenwood) in Hampshire (1839–45), but continued preaching his gospel of social reconstruction until death. Author of *Revolution in Mind and Practice* (1849) and *Autobiography* (1857–58).

Oxenstierna *(ŏŏk sən shâr nȧ),* **Count Axel Gustafsson** also OXENSTIERN, OXENSTJERNA. 1583–1654. Swedish statesman. *b.* Fano. Entered royal service (1602); appointed chancellor by Gustavus Adolphus (1612); negotiated peace treaties with Denmark, Russia, and Poland (1613, 1617, 1626); held supreme control in Rhine region (from 1631); directed foreign policy of Sweden after death of Gustavus Adolphus (1632); director of Evangelical League (1633); guardian and counselor of Queen Christina during her minority (1632–44); negotiated treaties with France (1636) and Denmark (1645); remained in office until death.

Oxford, 1st Earl of. *See* **Harley, Robert**

P

Paderewski *(pä də rĕf skē),* **Ignace Jan** 1860–1941. Polish pianist and composer. *b.* Kurylowka. Began playing piano at age 3; professional debut at Vienna (1887); made concert tours of Paris, Russia, London, and New York; wrote *Manru,* symphony in B Minor, concertos, and piano pieces, of which his minuet is the best known. An ardent patriot, he represented Poland at Versailles Peace Conference (1919); after war, formed coalition ministry, serving as prime minister and foreign minister for ten months (1919); retired from politics and settled in Switzerland.

Paine *(pān),* **Thomas** 1737–1809. American political philosopher. *b.* Thetford, England. Immigrated to America (1774); contributed to *Pennsylvania Magazine;* published pamphlet *Common Sense* (1776), urging immediate independence from Great Britain; it sold between 200,000 and 300,000 copies and became one of the manifestoes of the American Revolution; served in Continental army; published 12 issues of the *Crisis* during the war; brought out *Public Good* (1780); returned to Europe (1787); on outbreak of French Revolution, became its apologist, writing *The Rights of Man* in reply to Burke's *Reflections* (1791–92); tried and convicted for treason and outlawed from England; fled to France and was elected to the Convention (1792); joined Girondist faction; on the fall of Girondists, arrested by the Robespierre faction and imprisoned; released on intercession of James Monroe (1794); remained in France (until 1802). Wrote *The Age of Reason* (2 parts, (1794–96), an exposition of deism;

returned to America (1802) and died in relative obscurity.

Palestrina *(pä lə strē nä),* **Giovanni Pierluigi da** c1526–94. Italian composer. *b.* Palestrina. Organist and maestro di canto of the cathedral of St. Agapit at Palestrina; invited to Rome by Pope Julius III; master of the Julian choir at St. Peter's (1551); choirmaster at St. John Lateran (1555–61) and Santa Maria Maggiore (1561–65); music master at seminary set up by Council of Trent; worked on revision of the Gradual (from 1577); called the Prince of Music and the first Catholic church musician. Works include over 90 masses, 60 motets, hymns, lamentations, and litanies, including *Missa Papae Marcelli* and *Stabat Mater.*

Palladio *(päl lä dyō),* **Andrea** 1518–80. Italian architect. *b.* Vicenza. Founded modern Italian architectural style, modeled on the ancient Roman; among his buildings are Barbarano and Tiene palaces and Olympic theater in Vicenza, the cathedral of Brescia, church of San Giorgio Maggiore in Venice, Palazzo Aldrighelli Casa Adriani at Padua, and the atrium of the Monastery Della Carita at Venice; style imported into England by Inigo Jones and widely copied under the name Palladian. Wrote *The Four Books of Architecture* (1716).

Palmerston *(päm ər stən),* **Viscount** title of HENRY JOHN TEMPLE; nickname: PAM. 1784–1865. English statesman. *b.* Broadlands. Entered Parliament (1807); held minor offices in various ministries (1809–28); left Tory party (1928) and joined Whigs; minister of foreign affairs under Grey (1830–41); secured independence of Belgium and placed Leopold of Saxe-Coburg on Belgian throne; supported constitutional thrones of Isabella of Spain and Maria of Portugal; buttressed Turkey against Russian expansionism; annexed Hong Kong and opened the five ports (1840–41); out of office (1841–46); in foreign office under Lord John Russell (1846); continued support of Continental revolutionary movements; alienated France in the David Pacifico affair (1850); aroused opposition by high-handed, arbitrary procedures; dismissed for approving Louis Napoleon's coup d'état without consulting prime minister (1851); returned as home secretary under Aberdeen (1853); prime minister (1855–58, 1859–65); ended Crimean War; suppressed Indian Mutiny and secured the transfer of British Indian possessions from East India Company to the Crown; remained neutral in U.S. Civil War; supported Italian independence.

Panini *(pä nĭ nĭ)* *fl.* 4 century B.C. Sanskrit grammarian. *b.* Shalatura, India. Author of the earliest Sanskrit grammar and the earliest work on descriptive linguistics, *Ashtadhyayi;* it contains nearly 4000 aphorisms that detail every form of inflection and syntactic usage of Sanskrit.

Pankhurst *(păngk hûrst),* **Emmeline** *née* GOULDEN. 1858–1928. English woman-suffragist. *b.* Manchester. Founded the Women's Social and Political Union (1903), a militant organization which adopted sensational means to press for women's suffrage; often jailed and released, but achieved her goal when women were granted right to vote (1928).

Papadopoulos *(pä pä dō pə lōs),* **George** 1919–. Greek statesman. *b.* Eleochorion. Joined Greek army as a second lieutenant (1940) and rose to commander by mid-1960s; as one of the prime movers of the army coup of 1967, headed the military government (from 1967), serving also as minister of foreign affairs (1970–73); named regent on the flight of King Constantine (1972–73); on the establishment of a republic after a national referendum (1973), became president; toppled in a bloodless coup (1973); arrested after the restoration of democracy (1974).

Papandreou *(pä pən drē ō),* **George** 1888–1968. Greek statesman. *b.* Patras. Founded Democratic Socialist party (1935); exiled by dictator Joannes Metaxas and imprisoned during World War II; escaped from prison (1944); prime minister in exile; deputy premier (1950) and later premier; opposed King Constantine as well as the military regime that seized power in 1967.

Papin *(pȧ păN),* **Denis** c1647–1712. French physicist. *b.* Blois. Assistant to Huygens and Boyle; credited with inventing the steam digester, the condensing pump, steam cannon, paddlewheel boat, and safety valve; member of Royal Society (from 1680); worked at Venice (1680–84), London (1684–87), Marburg (1687–96), and Cassel (1696–1707).

Papini *(pä pē nē),* **Giovanni** 1881–1956. Italian philosopher. *b.* Florence. As an atheist, denounced Christianity, but later was converted to Roman Catholicism. Works include *Pragmatismo* (1913), *Stroncature* (1918), *L'Esperienza Futurista* (1919), *Life of Christ* (1923), *Pane e Vino* (1926), *Gog* (1929), *Italia Mia* (1939), *Figure Umani* (1940), and *Un Uomo Finito* (1913).

Paracelsus *(păr ə sĕl səs),* **Philippus Aureolus** original name: THEOPHRASTUS BOMBASTUS VON HOHENHEIM. 1493–1541. German physician and alchemist. *b.* Maria-Einsiedeln, Switzerland. Spent years in travel, acquiring a vast medical knowledge, especially on chemical properties of minerals; began medical practice at Basel, also lecturing at university (1526–28); driven out of city for unorthodox teachings and intemperate habits; wandered on the Continent (1528–41), eventually settling in Salzburg (1541); held that diseases were caused by specific problems and could be cured by specific remedies; introduced the medical use of opium, mercury, sulphur, iron, lead, arsenic, and copper sulphate; practiced alchemy and occultism. Author of *Die Grosse Wundartznei* (1530) and *Practica D. Theophrasti Paracelsi* (1529).

Paré *(pə rā),* **Ambroise** c1517–90. French surgeon. *b.* Laval. Army surgeon and physician to Henry II, Francis II, Charles IX, and Henry III; introduced the use of ligatures in surgery, thus eliminating cauterization. Author of *Cinq Livres de Chirurgie* (1562); called the father of modern surgery.

Pareto *(pə râ tō),* **Vilfredo** 1848–1923. Italian economist. *b.* Paris, France. Professor at University of Lausanne (from 1894); turned from a career in engineering to the study of economics and society; leader of the mathematical school of economics; ideas incorporated in the Fascist movement. Author of *Mind and Society* (4 vols., 1935), *Course on Political Economics* (1896–97), *The Socialist Systems* (1902), and *Manual on Political Economics* (1906).

Paris *(păr ĭs),* **Matthew** c1200–1259. English historian. Entered Benedictine monastery of St. Albans (1217); succeeded Roger of Wendover as chronicler (1236); continued and expanded Roger's *Historia Major,* a chronicle of events from the creation of the world; published an abridged version, *Historia Minor* or *Historia Anglorum* (3 vols., 1866–69); also wrote lives of abbots and *Additamenta.*

Park *(pärk),* **Mungo** 1771–1806. Scottish explorer. *b.* Foulshiels. Studied medicine and visited Sumatra (1792); explored course of River Niger for the African Association (1795–96); first European to reach the Niger at Sego; ascended to Bamako; narrated his adventures in *Travels in the Interior of Africa* (1799); took second journey to the Niger (1805), drowned near Boussa during an attack by natives; *Journal* of second expedition published (1815).

Parker *(pär kər),* **Dorothy** *née* ROTHSCHILD. 1893–1967. American humorist and writer. *b.* West End, N.J. Prose works include *Here Lies* (1939), *Sunset Gun* (1928), and *Not So Deep As a Well* (1936); verse collections include *Enough Rope* (1926) and *Death and Taxes* (1931); member of the famous literary group known as the Algonquin Wits.

Parker, Matthew 1504–75. English ecclesiastic. *b.* Norwich. Chaplain to Anne Boleyn (1533); vice chancellor of Cambridge (1545); resigned on accession of Mary Tudor; reinstated by Elizabeth and consecrated archbishop of Canterbury (1559); defined Anglicanism as middle course between Catholicism and Puritanism; revised the 42 Articles and reduced them to 39 (1562); directed publication of *Bishop's Bible* (1572); regulated Anglican ecclesiastical service through enactments known as *Advertisements* (1565); edited and published works of early chroniclers. Author of *Antiquitae Britannicae Ecclesiae* (1572).

Parkman *(pärk mən),* **Francis** 1823–93. American historian. *b.* Boston. Studied law, turned to horticulture, but abandoned both for history; traveled over the old Oregon Trail and wrote a classic account of his journey in *The Oregon Trail* (1849); writings characterized by vigor and meticulous accuracy. Author of *History of the Conspiracy of Pontiac* (2 vols., 1851), *Pioneers of France in the New World* (1865), *The Jesuits in North America* (1867), *The Discovery of the Great West* (1869), *Count Frontenac and New France under Louis XIV* (1877), *Montcalm and Wolfe* (1884), and *A Half-Century of Conflict* (1892).

Parmenides *(pär mĕn ĭ dēz) fl.* 5th century B.C. Greek philosopher. *b.* Elea, Italy. Head of Eleatic school of philosophy; went to Athens (c450); set out principal doctrines in the poem *Nature,* divided into two parts, the way of truth and the way of opinion; held that only "being" is eternal reality; change or "non-being" is illusory; Zeno was his disciple and Plato named one of his dialogues after him.

Parnell *(Pär nĕl),* **Charles Stewart** 1846–91. Irish nationalist leader. *b.* Avondale. Elected to Parliament as a Home Ruler (1875); gained popularity among Irishmen by a policy of deliberate obstruction of Parliamentary proceedings; organized the Irish National Land League, becoming its first president (1878); succeeded William Shaw as leader of Home Rule party (1880); devised system of boycotting as political weapon; imprisoned under Coercion Act (1882); issued a No-Rent manifesto from prison; when Land League was banned, formed National League; obtained Gladstone's commitment to Home rule; charged with complicity in Phoenix Park murders in a series of articles in *The Times,* but exonerated and awarded a settlement of £5000; named respondent in a divorce suit by one William Henry O'Shea; ostracized by his party and deposed as a consequence of this scandal.

Parrish *(păr ĭsh),* **Maxfield** 1870–1966. American painter and illustrator. *b.* Philadelphia. Noted for murals, posters, magazine covers, and book illustrations. Among books illustrated by him are *Mother Goose in Prose* and *Knickerbocker's History of New York;* among his murals are *Old King Cole* and *The Pied Piper.*

Pascal *(pȧs kȧl),* **Blaise** 1623–62. French scientist and philosopher. *b.* Clermont. A mathematical prodigy, published *Traité des Sections Coniques* at age 17; other contributions to mathematics include formulation of probability theory, development of differential calculus, and the demonstration of Pascal's arithmetical triangle, Pascal's law, and Pascal's mystic hexagram; on Nov. 23, 1654, had a revelation that made him renounce the world and become a religious mystic; joined forces with the Jansenists and against the Jesuits with 18 brilliant pamphlets, the *Lettres Provinciales* (1656–57), couched in superb ironic prose; his *Apologie de la Religion Catholique* was left unfinished; manuscript notes were collected and published as *Pensées* (1669).

Passfield, Baron. *See* **Webb, Sidney James**

Passy *(pȧ sē),* **Frédéric** 1822–1912. French statesman. *b.* Paris. Member of Chamber of Deputies (1881–89); one of the founders of International Peace League (1867) and of Interparliamentary Peace Union (1888); member of International Peace Bureau at Bern (1892); with J. H. Dunant, awarded Nobel Peace Prize (1901). Author of *Mélanges Économiques* (1857), *Les Machines et Leur Influence sur le Progrès Social* (1866), *L'Histoire du Travail* (1873), and *Vérités et Paradoxes* (1894).

Pasternak *(pă styər nȧk),* **Boris Leonidovich** 1890–1960. Russian poet and novelist. *b.* Moscow. Principally a poet, but also noted as a translator of Shakespeare, Verlaine, Goethe, and Kleist, and as a prose writer who defies classification; awarded Nobel Prize in literature (1958). Works include *Above the Barriers* (1931), *My Sister, Life* (1922), *Themes and Variations* (1923), *The Year 1905* (1927), *Lieutenant Schmidt* (1927), *Spectorsky* (1932), *Second Birth* (1932),

Aerial Ways (1933), *In Early Trains* (1936), *The Sapper's Death* (1943), *Safe Conduct* (1931), *Essay in Autobiography* (1954), and *Dr. Zhivago* (1958).

Pasteur *(päs tûr),* **Louis** 1822–95. French scientist. *b.* Dôle. Professor of physics at Dijon (1848), Strasbourg (from 1849), Lille (1854–57); director of École Normale Supérieure (1857–63) and professor at Sorbonne (1867–89); founded Institut Pasteur at Paris, and was its director (1886–95); demonstrated that lactic, butyric, and acetic fermentation is due to microorganisms; refuted theory of spontaneous generation of disease; effected practical application of fermentation discoveries to manufacture of vinegar, wine, and beer and to the preservation of food by a process of controlled heating, called pasteurization; discovered the causative bacilli of silkworm disease, anthrax, Swine erysipelas, fowl cholera, streptococcus, and rabies; developed vaccination techniques using living but attenuated forms of the disease; aided adoption of prophylactic inoculation as a standard medical technique, especially against rabies; considered the founder of bacteriology.

Pater *(pā tər),* **Walter Horatio** 1839–94. English man of letters. *b.* London. Leader of devotees of Renaissance humanism who stressed artistic perfection as an end in itself and who held that one "should burn with a hard, gemlike flame"; writings noted for clarity and luster. Works include *Imaginary Portraits* (1887), *Appreciations* (1889), *Plato and Platonism* (1893), *History of the Renaissance* (1873), *Marius the Epicurean* (1885), and *The Child in the House* (1894).

Patmore *(păt môr),* **Coventry Kersey Dighton** 1823–96. English poet. *b.* Woodford. Best known for *The Angel in the House* (4 parts, 1854–62). Other works include *Tamerton Church Tower* (1853), *The Unknown Eros* (1877), *Amelia* (1878), and *Rod, Root, and Flower* (1895); after death of wife, became a Roman Catholic and wrote chiefly on religious themes.

Patrick *(păt rĭk),* **Saint** c385–c461. Apostle and patron saint of Ireland. *b.* Nemthur, Scotland. Captured by the Picts (411) and sold as a slave into Ireland; escaped after six years and went to Gaul, where he became a monk; received call to convert Ireland; consecrated bishop (432); received the pallium from pope (441); charged with mission of converting the Irish by Pope Celestine I; landed at Wicklow; preached throughout Ireland despite opposition from the druids; founded church and monastery at Armagh; completed the conversion of Ireland before retiring (457). Wrote books in Latin including *Confession, Epistle,* and *The Cry of the Deer.* Feast day: Mar. 17.

Patton *(păt ən),* **George Smith, Jr.** called OLD BLOOD AND GUTS. 1885–1945. American general. *b.* San Gabriel, Calif. Graduated from U.S. Military Academy (1907); as major general, led U.S. forces in Morocco (1942), Tunisia (1943), and Sicily (1943); led Third Army in France in the legendary Battle of Bastogne and the capture of Metz; commander of the 15th Army; full general (1945); received an enduring reputation as a disciplinarian and a martinet of the old school. Author of *War As I Knew It* (1948).

Paul *(pôl),* **Saint** original name: SAUL. *fl.* 1st century. Apostle to the Gentiles. Jewish-Christian missionary. *b.* Tarsus, Asia Minor. Born a "Hebrew of Hebrews"; trained as a rabbi with Gamaliel; a devout Pharisee and a persecutor of Christians; converted to the Christian faith after having a vision on the road to Damascus; undertook first missionary tour in Cyprus, Pisidia, Pamphylia, and Lycaonia, the second to Asia Minor, Galatia, Phrygia, Macedonia, and Achaia, and the third to Galatia and Phrygia; tried before Felix the procurator for instigation of the Jews and imprisoned; in Rome (from 61); met martyrdom in Rome, perhaps by decapitation (c67); considered the greatest missionary in the history of the Christian church. Author of 13 New Testament *Epistles,* though the authorship of some is even now disputed. Feast day: June 29.

Paul VI real name: GIOVANNI BATTISTA MONTINI. 1897–1978. Pope (1963–1978). *b.* Concesio, Italy. Ordained (1920); archbishop of Milan (1954); cardinal (1958); made tradition-breaking visits to Africa, Asia, Australia, and the Americas; reconvened Vatican II called by John XXIII.

Pauli *(pou lĭ),* **Wolfgang** 1900–1958. Austrian-Swiss physicist. *b.* Vienna. Professor of physics at Zurich (from 1928); visiting professor at Institute of Advanced Study at Princeton (1935, 1939–46); discovered the Exclusion Principle (1924), which states that no two electrons can be in the same quantum state; predicted the existence of a neutral particle in subatomic physics, later confirmed by Fermi; awarded Nobel Prize in physics (1945). Author of *Relativitätstheorie* (1920), *Quantentheorie* (1926), and *Allgemeine Prinzipien der Wellenmechanik* (1933).

Pauling *(pô lĭng),* **Linus Carl** 1901–. American chemist. *b.* Portland, Ore. Professor of chemistry at California Institute of Technology (from 1931) and at University of California, San Diego (from 1967); awarded Nobel Prize in chemistry (1954) for studies in molecular structure, especially the nature of atomic bonding; opponent of American nuclear policy, which he denounced in *No More War* (1958); awarded Nobel Peace Prize (1963). Author of *Structure of Line Spectra* (1930), *Introduction to Quantum Mechanics* (1935), and *Nature of the Chemical Bond* (1939).

Pausanias *(pô sā nĭ əs)* *d.* c466 B.C. Spartan general. Regent of Sparta; commander of the allied Greek Army that triumphed over the Persians at Plataea (479); won Cyprus and Byzantium; alienated Athenians and other allies by overbearing manner; thrice accused of treasonable conduct and twice recalled; on return to Sparta, tried to instigate helots to revolt, but plot was exposed; took refuge in the temple of Athena and starved to death.

Pavlov *(pä vlôf),* **Ivan Petrovich** 1849–1936. Russian scientist. *b.* Ryazan. Professor of physiology and director of the physiological laboratory in the Imperial Academy of Sciences (from

1891); director of department of physiology of the Imperial Institute of Experimental Medicine (from 1913); by studying the physiological nature of stomach juices, was led to the discovery of the conditioned reflex; awarded Nobel Prize in physiology and medicine (1904).

Pavlova *(pä vlô və),* **Anna** 1885?–1931. Russian ballet dancer. *b.* St. Petersburg. Member of the Imperial Ballet, soon becoming its most celebrated dancer; made New York debut (1909–10); best remembered for her role in *The Dying Swan,* a ballet composed for her by Michel Fokine; also performed in *Giselle, Don Quixote,* and her own ballet *Autumn Leaves.*

Peabody *(pē bŏd ĭ),* **George** 1795–1869. American philanthropist. *b.* South Danvers, Mass.; now called Peabody. Merchant and banker in London, achieving a position of leadership in the banking world; devoted his wealth to philanthropy; donated $2.5 million for workers' tenements in London; among his other benefactions are the Peabody Museum of Natural History and Natural Science at Yale, Peabody Museum of Archaeology and Ethnology at Harvard, and Peabody Institute at Baltimore.

Peacock *(pē kŏk),* **Thomas Love** 1785–1866. English man of letters. *b.* Weymouth. Combined a career as examiner at India House with a literary productivity as a satiric novelist. Author of *Headlong Hall* (1816), *Melincourt* (1817), *Nightmare Abbey* (1818), *Maid Marian* (1822), *The Misfortunes of Elphin* (1829), *Crotchet Castle* (1831), *Gryll Grange* (1860), and *Rhododaphne* (1818).

Pearson *(pēr sən),* **Lester Bowles** 1897–1972. Canadian statesman. *b.* Toronto. After distinguished career in Canadian foreign service, became secretary of state for external affairs (1948); Canadian House of Commons (1948); leader of Liberal opposition (from 1958); prime minister (1963); resigned (1968); awarded Nobel Peace Prize (1957).

Peary *(pēr ĭ),* **Robert Edwin** 1856–1920. American Arctic explorer. *b.* Cresson, Pa. Made six voyages to the Arctic to discover the North Pole (1891, 1893, 1898, 1902, 1905, 1908), reaching it on the final one. Author of *Northward Over the Great Ice* (1898), *Nearest the Pole* (1907), and *The North Pole* (1910).

Pedersen, Knut. *See* **Hamsun, Knut**

Peel *(pēl),* **Sir Robert** 1788–1850. English statesman. *b.* near Bury. Entered Parliament (1809); colonial undersecretary (1811); as secretary for Ireland (1812–18), strongly opposed Catholic emancipation; out of office (1818–22); home secretary (1822–27); secured reform of English penal laws; home secretary and leader of House of Commons under Wellington (1828–30); reversed stand on emancipation and sponsored legislation (1829) abolishing Catholic disabilities; consolidated local London constabularies into the Metropolitan Police force, their members thereafter called Peelers or Bobbies; led Tory opposition to Reform Bill sponsored by the Whig ministry of Grey; prime minister (1834–35, 1841); during the next five years, sponsored progressive legislation, including the imposition of income tax, removal of penal laws against Catholics, reorganization of Bank of England, and repeal of the hated corn laws; these moves, which constituted a complete break with conventional Tory stands, led to a split in the party, with Bentinck, Disraeli, and others forming a "no-surrender" faction; resigned (1846).

Péguy *(pā gē),* **Charles Pierre** 1873–1914. French poet and publisher. *b.* Orléans. With Léon Blum and others, founded the journal *Cahiers de la Quinzaine* (1900), which published new French writers; abandoned earlier socialism for orthodox Catholicism; imbued with a hunger for justice and truth. Works include *La Mystère de la Charité de Jeanne d'Arc* (1910), *L'Argent* (1912), *Ève* (1913), *La Porche du Mystère de la Deuxième Vertu* (1911), *La Tapisserie de Notre Dame* (1913), and *La Mystère des Saints-Innocents* (1912); died in World War I.

Peirce *(pûrs),* **Charles Sanders** 1839–1914. American mathematician and logician. *b.* Cambridge, Mass. Son of BENJAMIN PEIRCE, (1809–80), American astronomer. Like his father, member of U.S. Coast Survey (1861–91); in history of logic, important as the founder of pragmatism; also made contributions to mathematical logic, the theory of probability, and scientific methodology. Author of *Studies in Logic* (1883); *Collected Papers* (8 vols., 1931–58).

Pelagius *(pe lā jĭ əs)* original name: MORGAN (?) c360–c420. British monk and heretic. Lived in Rome (c400); acquired Celestius as friend and disciple with whom he went to North Africa and Palestine; founder of Pelagianism, which held that there was no original sin, that the human will is free to choose good or evil, that even pagans can enter into heaven; condemned and anathematized by a number of councils, including Ephesus (431); banished from Rome (418). Author of *On the Trinity, On Free Will, On Testimonies,* and *On the Pauline Epistles.*

Penn *(pĕn),* **William** 1644–1718. English colonizer. *b.* London. Born to wealth; acquired an unflagging interest in religion; became a Quaker and was intermittently imprisoned for nonconformity; published Quaker tracts including *The Sandy Foundation Shaken, No Cross, No Crown,* and *Innocency with her Eyes Open;* on death of his father, petitioned the Crown for a grant of land in New World in payment of a debt owed by Charles II; received grant of territory known as Pensilvania (1681); proposed to establish a home for his persecuted correligionists; visited the colony (1682), laid out the city of Philadelphia, and secured trust of Indian tribes by drawing up a treaty whose conditions he scrupulously honored; gave Pennsylvania a civil government with guaranteed religious freedom; formed a separate colony along lower Delaware River with lands obtained from duke of York; returned to England (1684); continued to work for Quaker cause; after the accession of William III, accused of Jacobite sympathies and was deprived of proprietorship of Pennsylvania (1692–94); put forward a scheme for the union of all American colonies (1697); visited Pennsylvania (1699–1701); modified colony charter and renewed treaties with Indians. Author of *Fruits of Solitude* (1693).

Pepin *(pĕp ĭn)* **The Short** *d.* 768. King of the Franks (751–68). Son of Charles Martel and father of Charlemagne; founded Carolingian dynasty after deposing Childeric III; aided Pope Stephen II in struggle with Lombards (754–55); granted pope the exarchate of Ravenna and the territory of Bologna and Ferrara (known as the Donation of Pepin), which later became the Papal States.

Pepys *(pēps),* **Samuel** 1633–1703. English diarist. *b.* London. Joined the Admiralty (1660); secretary to the Admiralty (1672); imprisoned during Popish Plot scare (1679), but reinstated (1684); president of the Royal Society (1684); dismissed from all offices after Revolution of 1688; principal claim to fame is the *Diary,* which he maintained in Sheltonian shorthand from January 1, 1660, to May 31, 1669; provides a unique commentary on the Restoration, particularly the great plague, the fire of London, and the Dutch Armada; some passages were considered too lurid and were bowdlerized in many editions; the *Diary* was discovered by Baron Braybrooke at Magdalen College, Cambridge, deciphered by Thomas Shelton, and published (1825).

Perceval *(pûr sə vəl),* **Spencer** 1762–1812. English statesman. *b.* London. Entered Parliament (1796); solicitor general (1801); attorney general (1802); chancellor of the exchequer (1807); succeeded Portland as prime minister (1809); uncompromising foe of Catholic emancipation; made bank notes legal tender (1811); assassinated (1812).

Perelman *(pûrl mən),* **Sidney Joseph** 1904–79. American writer and humorist. *b.* Brooklyn, N.Y. Began as artist and writer for *Judge* magazine; frequent contributor to *The New Yorker.* Major works include *Parlor, Bedlam, and Bath* (1930), *Strictly from Hunger* (1937), *Look Who's Talking* (1940), *The Dream Department* (1943), *Crazy Like a Fox* (1944), *Keep It Crisp* (1946), *Acres and Pains* (1947), *Swiss Family Perelman* (1950), and *The Ill-Tempered Clavichord* (1952).

Pericles *(pĕr ĭ klēz)* c490–29 B.C. Athenian statesman. Born into the distinguished Alcmaeonidae family; entered Athenian politics as leader of democratic party; undisputed master after he secured the ostracism of his opponents Cimon and Thucydides; stripped the aristocratic Aeropagus of its political powers; made Athens the dominant naval power through successful expeditions to the Thracian Chersonese and Sinope; made peace with Persia (448); completed fortification of Athens and Piraeus; a patron of art and literature, presided over the Golden Age of Athens, whose principal figures were Aeschylus, Sophocles, Euripides, Anaxagoras, Zeno, Protagoras, Socrates, Myron, and Phidias; beautified Athens with the Parthenon, Erechtheum, the Propylaea, the Odeon, and other public buildings; led Athens during Peloponnesian War (431–429); delivered famous funeral oration; died of plague (429).

Perón *(pə rôn),* **Juan Domingo** 1895–1975. Argentine statesman. *b.* Lobos. Began career in army; member of group of army officers known as GOU, who deposed President Castillo (1943); elected president and virtual dictator of Argentina (1946); organized the Peronistas and emerged as champion of the *decamisados* (shirtless ones); deposed by military coup (1955) and forced into exile; recalled by the military, reelected, and returned to power as president (1973); died within a year of return; succeeded by wife Isabella. Peron's early popularity was partly due to wife EVA DUARTE DE PERÓN (1919–52) who became an important political figure in her own right with a large following among labor.

Perrin *(pĕ răN),* **Jean Baptiste** 1870–1942. French physicist. *b.* Lille. Professor of physical chemistry at Paris (from 1910); investigated Brownian movement in particles, making possible the accurate measurement of atomic size; awarded Nobel Prize in physics (1926) for work on the discontinuous structure of matter and for the discovery of equilibrium of sedimentation. Author of *Traité de Chimie Physique* (1903), *Les Atomes* (1913), and *Les Éléments de la Physique* (1930).

Perry *(pĕr ĭ),* **Matthew Calbraith** 1794–1858. American naval officer. *b.* Newport, R.I. Commanded *Fulton,* the first naval steamship (1837); served in War of 1812 and the Mexican War; commanded expedition to Japan (1852–54), concluding the treaty that opened Japan to Western powers; brother of OLIVER HAZARD PERRY (1785–1819), American naval officer, victor in the naval battle with the British on Lake Erie (1813).

Perse, Saint-John. *See* **Léger, Alexis Saint-Léger**

Pershing *(pûr shĭng),* **John Joseph** 1860–1948. American general. *b.* in Linn County, Mo. Entered the army (1886); served in campaigns in Cuba (1898) and the Philippines (1899–1903); commanded U.S. expeditionary force against Pancho Villa in Mexico (1916); commander in chief of American Expeditionary Force in World War I (1917–19); chief of staff (1921–24); general of the armies (1919). Wrote Pulitzer-Prize-winning *My Experiences in the World War* (1931).

Perugino *(pā rōō jē nō),* **Il** real name: PIETRO VANNUCCI; also called PIER DELLA PIEVE. 1446–1523. Italian painter. *b.* Citta della Pieve. Best known for frescoes of deep delicacy and grace, represented by *Christ Giving the Keys to Peter* in the Sistine Chapel; other works include *Entombment* in the Pitti Palace, *Stanza del Incendio* in the Vatican, and *Crucifixion;* Raphael was among his pupils.

Perth, Earl of. *See* **Drummond, Sir Eric Henry**

Perutz *(pə rōōts),* **Max Ferdinand** 1914–. British biochemist. *b.* Austria. Immigrated to England (1936); worked at the Cavendish Laboratory; director of the Medical Research Council's division of molecular biology; awarded Nobel Prize in chemistry (1962) with C. Kendrew for discovery of the molecular structure of hemoglobin and myoglobin.

Pestalozzi *(pĕs tä lōt sē)*, **Johann Heinrich** 1746–1827. Swiss educator. *b.* Zurich. Influenced by Rousseau's *Émile,* founded a school at Neuhof (1775) to put into practice his innovative educational ideas; undeterred by its failure, headed schools at Stanz (1798), Burgdorf (1799–1804), Münchenbuchsee (1804), and Yverdon (1805–25); expounded pedagogical system in books, collected in 16 volumes (1869–72), including *Evening Hours of a Hermit* (1780), *Leonard and Gertrude* (1781), *How Gertrude Teaches Her Children* (1801), *Meine Lebensschicksale* (1826); stressed educational development based on concrete experiences, direct observation, and clear reasoning.

Pétain *(pā tăN)*, **Henri Philippe Benoni Omer Joseph** 1856–1951. French general and statesman. *b.* Cauchy-à-la-Tour. Graduated from St.-Cyr military academy (1878); became national hero as commanding general of the defense of Verdun (1916); commander in chief under Marshal Foch (1918); marshal of France (1918); minister of war (1934); commanded successful French-Spanish campaign against the Riffs in Morocco (1926); after French collapse (1940), succeeded Reynaud as premier and arranged capitulation to Germany, at which time he became chief of state; fled to Switzerland after liberation of France, but was brought back, tried for treason, convicted, and sentenced to life imprisonment.

Peter *(pē tər)*, **Saint** also SIMON PETER, CEPHAS, and PETRUS. One of the 12 Apostles of Christ, and their acknowledged leader. A fisherman by occupation; after the Resurrection, appointed by Christ as his vicar on earth and charged with feeding His sheep; nicknamed Cephas (Rock) by Jesus; first to baptize a gentile convert; took a leading part in the Council of Jerusalem; imprisoned by Herod Agrippa I, but escaped to found the See of Antioch; by tradition, went to Rome and founded the See of Rome; martyred at the time of Nero by being crucified head downwards; regarded by some as the author of two canonical Epistles in the New Testament. Feast day: June 29.

Peter I original name: PETR ALEXSEEVICH; also called PETER THE GREAT. 1672–1725. Czar of Russia (1682–1725). *b.* Moscow. Son of Alexis; ruled jointly with his half-brother Ivan V, with sister Sophia Alekseyyevna as regent; began personal rule (1689) after overthrowing Sophia; captured Azov (1696) from the Turks; traveled in Western Europe studying European methods (1696–97); returned to suppress revolution of the Strelitzi (1698); in the course of the Northern War (1700–1721), defeated Charles XII at Poltava (1709), and concluded Peace of Nystadt with Sweden, by which he obtained Livonia, Estonia, Ingermanland, and part of Karelia; married Catherine (1712) and made her joint ruler; built St. Petersburg (1703), moving the imperial capital there from Moscow; emperor (1721); brought Russia out of the middle ages with radical reforms; introduced universal taxation, created new bureaucracy, reformed calendar and alphabet, unified currency, introduced western dress, founded medical schools, encouraged industry, emancipated women, abolished patriarchate of Moscow, replacing it with the holy synod with czar as its head, established state control over monastic estates, and sponsored exploration by Vitus Bering and others; put down opposition, including that of his own son Alexis, with a heavy hand.

Petöfi *(pĕ tû fĭ)*, **Sándor** 1823–49. Hungarian poet. *b.* Little Cumania. Author of epics, lyrics, and the national song "Up, Magyar"; with his patriotic war songs, played an important role in the Hungarian Revolution of 1848. Wrote the novel *Hangman's Rope* and volumes of verse, including *Cypress Leaves on Etelka's Grave, Pearls of Love, Starless Nights,* and *Clouds;* killed in the battle of Schässburg (1849).

Petrarch *(pĕ trärch)*, **Francesco Petrarca** 1304–74. Italian lyric poet. *b.* Arezzo. Took minor orders (1326); at Avignon met Laura, who served as his ideal and the inspiration of his later sonnets (1327); became an avid student of the classics; received patronage of the Colonna and Visconti families; with publication of epic *Africa* (1338–42), fame spread throughout Italy and he was crowned poet laureate by senate of Rome (1341); resided at Parma (1347), Milan (1353), Padua (1362), Venice (1362), and Arquà (1370), where he died; considered the first and greatest humanist of the Renaissance and, next to Dante, the greatest Italian poet; influential in setting standards of perfection and harmony in verse form and style. Principal works include *De Viris Illustribus* (1338), *Canzoniere or Rime, Epistles* (1326–74), *Secretum* (1343), *De Vita Solitaria* (1346–56), *I Trionfi* (1352–74), *De Otio Religiosorum* (1347–56), *De Remediis Utriusque Fortunae* (1350–66), *De Contemptu Mundi, De Vera Sapientia,* and *Bucolica.*

Petrie *(pē trĭ)*, **Sir William Matthew Flinders** 1853–1942. English archaeologist. *b.* Charlton. Conducted early excavations at Stonehenge (1875–80); explored Egypt (1880–1914) for the Egypt Exploration Fund and the Palestine Exploration Fund, with principal excavations at Fayum, Naucratis, Daphnae, Nagada, Tanis, Koptos, Thebes, Hawara, Kahun, Lachish, and Abydos; professor of Egyptology in London (1892–1933); founder of British School of Archaeology at Cairo (1894). Author of *Pyramids and Temples of Gizeh* (1883), *Hawara, Biahmu, and Arsinoë* (1889), *Ten Years' Digging in Egypt, 1881–1891* (1892), *History of Egypt* (6 vols., 1923–27), *Methods and Aims in Archaeology* (1904), *Religion in Ancient Egypt* (1906), *Egypt and Israel* (1911), and *Seventy Years of Archaeology* (1931).

Petty *(Pĕt ĭ)*, **Sir William** titles: 2ND EARL OF SHELBURNE; 1ST MARQUIS OF LANSDOWNE. 1737–1805. English statesman. *b.* Dublin, Ireland. President of Board of Trade (1763) under Grenville; lost office for opposing the expulsion of Wilkes; attacked the Stamp Act; secretary of state under Pitt (1766–68); advocated conciliatory policy toward American colonies (1766–82); home secretary under Rockingham (1782); prime minister (1782–83); conceded independence to the American colonies;

made peace with France and Spain; patronized fine arts.

Pfeiffer *(p fī fər)*, **Richard Friedrich Johannes** 1858–1945. German bacteriologist. *b.* Zduny. Professor of hygiene at Königsburg (1899) and Breslau (1909–26); investigated plague and malaria; discovered bacteriolysis (1894) and reported the use of blood agar for the cultivation of bacteria; introduced the Pfeiffer reaction for determining cholera, identified the Pfeiffer bacillus in influenza, produced a serum against cholera, and worked on immunization techniques against typhoid; missing and presumed dead (1945).

Phidias *(fĭd ĭ əs)* *fl.* 5th century B.C. Greek sculptor. *b.* Athens. Received commission from Pericles to carve the monuments to adorn Athens and to serve as general superintendent of public works; among works attributed to him are the memorial to the victory of Marathon at Delphi, Athena Areia at Plataea, Athena Promachos at Athens, the Olympian Zeus at Elis, Athena Parthenos in the Parthenon at Athens, and the Amazon at Ephesus; accused by Pericles' enemies of misappropriating gold intended for the statue and of sacrilege in sculpting himself and Pericles on the shield of the goddess Athena; thrown into prison, where he probably died.

Philip, Prince. *See* **Edinburgh, Duke of**

Philip *(fĭl əp)* **II** also PHILIP AUGUSTUS. 1165–1223. King of France of the Capetian line (1180–1223). Son of Louis VII; succeeded to throne (1180); engaged in wars against the barons, gaining Amiens from count of Flanders (1181–85); persecuted the Jews; fought with Henry II of England (1187–89), forcing him to acknowledge French lordship over English possessions on the Continent; set out on Third Crusade (1190) with Richard I of England, but quarrelled with him and returned to France (1191); allied with Richard's brother John to partition Normandy, leading to a bitter struggle with Richard (1194–99) and John (1202–1208), ending with Philip securing Maine, Touraine, Anjou, Poitou, Normandy, and Brittany—quadrupling the kingdom; attacked Flanders (1213–14) and at Bouvines, defeated princes, including Otto IV, John, and the count of Flanders (1214); thereafter devoted himself to building and civil reform; established royal court of justice; made Paris the administrative center of France; built the Louvre and the cathedral of Notre Dame; chartered the University of Paris.

Philip II 1527–98. King of Spain (1556–98). *b.* Valladolid. Only son of Charles V; on ascending the throne, was the most powerful ruler in Europe, possessing Franche-Comté, Spain, the Two Sicilies, Milan, the Low Countries, Mexico, and Peru; crushed alliance of France and the Papacy at St. Quentin (1557), securing peace by Treaty of Câteau-Cambrésis (1559); emerged as leader of Catholic Europe; suppressed the Moriscos and expelled them from Spain (1569–70); won greatest triumph by destroying Turkish naval power at Lepanto with the Christian force led by John of Austria (1571); conquered and annexed Philippine Islands; founded the Inquisition for maintaining Catholic hegemony in Europe; conquered Portugal (1580–81) and had himself crowned Philip I of Portugal; aided the Guises against Henry of Navarre (1592–98); by attempting to introduce the Inquisition into the Netherlands, touched off a revolt (1567); tried to put down the revolt with bloody measures, but the resistance of the Dutch led to formation of independent Seven United Provinces (1579); created the Invincible Armada for the invasion of England (1588); its defeat marked the beginning of the decline of Spanish naval supremacy; built the Escorial and encouraged art and architecture.

Philip II 382–336 B.C. King of Macedonia (359–336 B.C.). Son of Amyntas II; set out on a career of aggression with the goal of ruling all Greece; beginning with Greek towns on the Macedonian coast, took Crenides in Thrace, renaming it Philippi (356); defeated the Illyrians and the Paeonians (358), captured Amphipolis (358), Potidaea (356), and Methone (353); subdued all of Thessaly (352); took Olynthus and all towns of Chalcidice (347); in sacred war against the Phocians, destroyed all their cities; traveled to Peloponnesus as the champion of the Argives and Messenians against Sparta; appointed commander in chief of the Amphictyonic League in holy war against the Locrians; crushed the alliance of Thebes and Athens at Chaeronea (338); completed the conquest of Greece by subduing Peloponnesus; began preparations for the invasion of the Persian Empire, but was assassinated before they were completed; work carried forward by son Alexander the Great.

Philip Neri *(nā rē)*, **Saint** original name: FILIPPO ROMOLO NERI. 1515–95. Italian ecclesiastic. *b.* Florence. Went to Rome (1533); worked among the poor and founded the Confraternity of the Most Holy Trinity (1548) to aid the sick; ordained (1551); founded a secular community of priests to engage in works of charity and instruction (1564), recognized by Pope Gregory XIII as the Congregation of the Oratory (1575); canonized (1622). Feast day: May 26.

Philo *(fī lō)* **of Alexandria** also PHILO JUDAEUS. 1st century B.C. Jewish philosopher. *b.* Alexandria, Egypt. Sought to reconcile Platonic and Aristotelian philosophy with Hebrew faith; led a delegation of Jews to Rome to plead with Caligula for exemption from the requirement to pay divine homage to the emperor; three of his works on the Pentateuch are extant.

Phyfe *(fīf)*, **Duncan** 1768–1854. American furniture maker. *b.* Scotland. Came to the U.S. (1784); founded the concern of Duncan Phyfe and Son, furniture makers (1840) employing over 100 craftsmen; known for his beautifully designed chairs, sofas, and tables in mahogany.

Piaf *(pē äf)*, **Edith** original name: EDITH GIOVANNA GASSION. 1915–63. French singer. *b.* Paris. Born destitute and began singing in streets and, later, cafés; became a musical legend in her lifetime; life marked by personal tragedy and illness.

Piaget *(pyə zhā)*, **Jean** 1896–. Swiss psychologist. *b.* Neuchâtel. Professor of psychology at Geneva (from 1929) and director of Institut des Sciences de l'Education; studied, by intensive case study method, the development of intellect, conceptual thinking, perception, and language in children. Author of *La Gènese du Nombre Chez l'Enfant* (1941), *Le Développement de la Notion de Temps Chez l'Enfant* (1946), *La Représentation de l'Espace Chez l'Enfant* (1947), *Logic and Psychology* (1957), and other books.

Picasso *(pə kä sō),* **Pablo Ruiz y** 1881–1973. Spanish painter. *b.* Málaga. First exhibited in Barcelona (1897); settled in Paris (1904); with Braque, founded the Cubist movement in Paris (1907–1908); some creative work divided into the Blue (1902–1904), the Pink (1904–1906), and the Brown (1905–1906) periods; ceaselessly experimented with all kinds of materials, forms, and techniques; achieved a breakthrough in modern art with *Les Demoiselles d'Avignon* (1906–1907), considered the first Cubist painting; thereafter began to use deliberate, grotesque distortions and three-dimensional geometric forms; worked on many sculptures and constructions; designed costumes and sets for Diaghilev's Russian Ballet (1917); explored analytic, hermetic, synthetic, and rococo phases of cubism and worked in collage; painted the immense canvas *Guernica* to express his horror of war; his style became Neoclassical during the 1920s and surrealistic after 1925; during the last period of his life, worked with ceramics, graphic arts, lithographs, and etchings; his productivity over the years was prodigious and the output enormous.

Piccard *(pē kär),* **Auguste** 1884–1962. Swiss physicist. *b.* Basel. Professor of physics (1922–40) at University of Brussels; devised a special balloon and airtight gondola for exploring the stratosphere and set a record by ascending 55,577 feet over Zurich (1932); designed and constructed a bathyscaphe in which to explore ocean depths (1948). Author of *In Balloon and Bathyscape* (1956); brother of JEAN FELIX PICCARD (1884–1963), American engineer, who ascended 57,549 feet over Dearborn, Mich. (1934).

Pierce *(pērs),* **Franklin** 1804–69. 14th president of U.S. (1853–57) *b.* Hillsboro, N.H. House of Representatives (1833–37); Senate (1837–42); served in Mexican War (1846–47), becoming brigadier general; nominated as a compromise democratic candidate in presidential election (1852); elected by a small majority; administration marked by the Gadsden Purchase, treaty with Japan, and expeditions to Cuba and Nicaragua; signing the Kansas-Nebraska Bill and repealing the Missouri Compromise began the train of events that led to the Civil War; failed to secure renomination and retired (1856).

Piero della Francesco *(pyē rō dĕl lə frän chās kə)* c1420–92. Umbrian painter. *b.* Borgo San Sepolcro, Italy. Considered one of the foremost exponents of the geometrical design of art. Major canvases include *Resurrection, Flagellation, Nativity,* and *Baptism of Christ;* known especially for his fresco *The Story of the True Cross;* wrote a treatise on geometry and a manual on perspective.

Pieve, Pier della. *See* **Perugino, Il**

Pike *(Pīk),* **Zebulon Montgomery** 1779–1813. American explorer. *b.* Lamberton, N.J. Commanded an expedition to explore the headwaters of the Mississippi (1805–1806), Arkansas, and the Red rivers (1806–1807); reached site of Pueblo, Colo., and discovered a mountain, named Pikes Peak in his honor; killed in the War of 1812, leading an assault against York, Canada (1813).

Pilsudski *(pēl sōōt skē),* **Józef** 1867–1935. Polish general and statesman. *b.* Zulów. Joined Polish revolutionary movement as a youth; exiled to Siberia for attempting to kill Czar Alexander II (1887); on release, renewed struggle as leader of Socialist party and editor of the *Robotnik* (1894); arrested, but escaped abroad; organized clandestine army, known as the Polish Legion, which fought with Austria against Russia at the beginning of World War I; interned by Germany; after the war returned to Warsaw, elected president of newly formed Polish Republic and generalissimo of Polish army (1918); as marshal of Poland (from 1920), led military operations against Bolsheviks, Lithuania, and Ukraine; secured favorable Treaty of Riga (1921); retired after the adoption of Constitution of 1921, but returned in a coup d'état (1926) to form a new government with himself as minister of war and virtual dictator; premier (1926–28, 1930); concluded ten-year non-aggression pact with Hitler (1934); sponsored adoption of a fascist constitution (1935).

Pindar *(pĭn dər)* c522–443 B.C. Greek lyric poet. *b.* Cynoscephalae. Resided at Thebes; extant works include 44 epinicia (odes) celebrating athletic victories in the Olympian, Pythian, Nemean, and Isthmian games; also composed hymns, paeans, choral dithyrambs, processional songs, choral songs for maidens, choral dance-songs, encomia, scolia (festival) songs, and dirges; songs characterized by high-flown diction and religious imagery.

Pinter *(pĭn tər),* **Harold** 1930–. British dramatist. *b.* London. Using superb dramatic idiom, explores the menacing presence of the illogical in human life. Author of *The Birthday Party* (1957), *The Caretaker* (1958), *The Collection* (1961), *The Homecoming* (1965), *The Servant* (1963), *The Pumpkin Eater* (1964), and *No Man's Land;* considered one of Britain's angry young men of the late 1950s and early 1960s.

Pinzón *(pən thôn),* **Martín Alonso** 1441–93. Spanish navigator. *b.* Palos de la Frontera. Head of a family of shipbuilders at Palos; joined and aided Columbus on his historic voyage (1491), commanding the *Pinta;* independently discovered Hispaniola (1493); brother of VICENTE YÁÑEZ PINZÓN (1460–1524), Spanish navigator, who commanded the *Niña* on first voyage of Columbus (1492); in a later voyage (c1500), crossed the equator, reached coast of Brazil, and discovered mouth of the Amazon; in last voyage (1508–1509), may have discovered La Plata.

Pirandello *(pē rän dĕl lō),* **Luigi** 1867–1936. Italian dramatist. *b.* Agrigento, Sicily. Works include novels, short stories, and plays, characterized by intense and grotesque irony; founded own theatrical troupe, which produced his works in Europe and America; awarded Nobel Prize in literature (1934). Among his novels are *The Outcast* (1901), *The Late Mattia Pascal* (1923), *The Old and the Young* (1928), *One, None, and a Hundred Thousand* (1933); short story collections include *The Horse in the Moon* (1932), *Better Think Twice About It* (1935), and *The Medals* (1939); among his most successful plays are *Right You Are If You Think You Are* (1917), *Six Characters in Search of an Author* (1921), *Henry IV* (1922), and *As You Desire Me* (1930).

Piranesi *(pē rä nā sē),* **Giambattista** 1720–78. Italian engraver. *b.* Venice. Went to Rome (1738), becoming fascinated with its glorious monuments and ruins; decided to devote himself to making an engraved record of the grandeurs of Rome; made over 1000 copperplates, of which the most memorable are in the series known as *Carceri (Prisons);* work gave impetus to the study of classical art and design.

Pire *(pēr),* **Dominique Georges** 1910–69. Belgian humanitarian priest. *b.* Dinant. Lecturer at the Louvain (1937–47); worked in the French Resistance during World War II; awarded Nobel Peace Prize (1958) for work among destitute children and elderly refugees, especially the building of European and Anne Frank villages.

Pisanello *(pē sä nĕl lō)* original name: ANTONIO PISANO; also VITTORE PISANO. 1380/97–1455/56. Italian painter and medalist. *b.* San Visilio, near Verona. Patronized by a number of the rulers and nobles of his time, especially Lionello d'Este, Lord of Ferrara; of his numerous frescoes, only two survive: *St. George Mounting His Horse* and *The Miraculous Stag Appearing to St. Eustace;* his medals, considered the finest struck in the 14th and 15th centuries, represent his many patrons as well as John Palaeologus, emperor of the Byzantine Empire.

Pissarro *(pē sä rō),* **Camille** 1830–1903. French Impressionist painter. *b.* St. Thomas, West Indies. Lived in Paris (from 1855); associated with Monet and the Pointillists; as leader of the original Impressionists, influenced Cézanne and Gauguin; most of his works portray the countryside around Paris. Among his canvases are *Boulevard Montmartre, Vues de Paris, Quais de la Seine,* and *Marchés à Rouen.*

Pitman *(pĭt mən),* **Sir Isaac** 1813–97. English phoneticist. *B.* Trowbridge. Published new system of shorthand stenography based on phonetics in *Stenographic Soundhand* (1837); established first school for teaching his system at Bath (1839–43); advocated spelling reform; founded Phonetic Society (1843) and *Phonetic Journal* (1842); credited with the suggestion to the British government to use postage stamps on prepaid letters (1840). Author of *Phonography* (1840).

Pitt *(pĭt),* **William** title: EARL OF CHATHAM; called THE ELDER PITT. 1708–78. English statesman. *b.* London. Entered Parliament (1735); created a powerful impression with his imposing appearance and a magnificent voice suited to parliamentary oratory; opposed Walpole; joined Pelham's ministry (1746) as paymaster general (1746–55); lost office for attacking duke of Newcastle's foreign policy (1755), but returned as leader of House of Commons and virtual prime minister (1756); with Newcastle as nominal head of administration, took over conduct of Seven Years' War; led England to brilliant victories, defeating the French on three continents and on the seas; resigned (1761) when the cabinet overruled his demand for war with Spain; prime minister (1766–68), but prevented from taking an active part in government by poor health; opposed George III's policy toward the American colonies but did not support their independence; known as the Great Commoner for his advocacy of constitutional rights.

Pitt, William called THE YOUNGER PITT. 1759–1806. English statesman. *b.* Hayes. Entered Parliament (1780); leader of House of Commons and chancellor of the exchequer in Shelburne's ministry (1782); on downfall of Fox-North coalition, was invited to form a ministry (1783); received overwhelming majority in general election (1784), enabling him to form a government which lasted almost 20 years; supported major reforms, including the creation of a sinking fund for paying national debt, abolition of sinecures, and revision of taxation and revenue systems; with the outbreak of French Revolution (1789), foreign policy claimed all his attention; fear of revolutionary excesses led him into sterner domestic measures, including suspension of habeas corpus; principal architect of First and Second Coalitions against Napoleon (1793, 1798); resigned (1801) over the king's veto of Catholic emancipation; on declaration of war against France, returned to office (1804); formed Third Coalition against Napoleon (1805); hailed as savior of Europe after victory at Trafalgar; prostrated by news of Napoleon's victories at Ulm and Austerlitz, died brokenhearted.

Pius *(pī əs)* Name of 12 popes, of whom the most important are: PIUS II original name: ENEA SILVIO DE PICCOLOMINI. 1405–64. Pope (1458–64). *b.* near Siena. Tried in vain to unite Europe against the Turks; also distinguished as a poet and writer; wrote *Lucretius et Euryalus* and *Commentaries*.

PIUS V, Saint. original name: MICHAEL GHISLIERI. 1504–72. Pope (1566–72). *b.* Bosco. Led an austere and holy life; promoted the Holy League against the Turks, winning the famous naval battle of Lepanto (1571); revised the breviary (1568) and the missal (1570); canonized (1712).

PIUS VI original name: GIOVÁNNI ANGELO BRASCHI. 1717–99. Pope (1775–79). *b.* Cesena. Established first American see at Baltimore (1789); in conflict with Emperor Joseph, the king of Naples, and the French; deprived of States of the Church by the French and carried as prisoner to Valence in France (1798), where he died.

PIUS VII original name: LUIGI BARNABA CHIARAMONTI. 1742–1823. Pope (1800–1823). *b.* Cesena. Ratified Concordat with France (1801); crowned Napoleon emperor (1804); opposed Napoleon's

Articles Organiques; stripped of papal states and taken prisoner to France; restored to Vatican on fall of Napoleon (1814); suppressed Carbonari.

PIUS IX original name: GIOVANNI MARIA MASTAI-FARETTI. 1792–1878. Pope (1846–78). *b.* Senigalia. Began longest pontificate in papal history as a champion of constitutional reform; turned into an uncompromising reactionary after his flight to Gatea on the proclamation of the Republic at Rome (1848) and his subsequent restoration by the French (1850); deprived of temporal power and territories by Victor Emmanuel (1870); convened Vatican Council (1869–70); proclaimed dogmas of Immaculate Conception (1854) and Papal Infallibility (1870); issued Syllabus of Errors (1864).

PIUS X original name: GIUSEPPE MELCHIORRE SARTO. 1835–1914. Pope (1903–14). *b.* Riese. Promoted liturgical reform and authorized revision of canon law; issued encyclical against modernism.

PIUS XI original name: ACHILLE AMBROGIO DAMIANO RATTI. 1857–1939. Pope (1922–39). *b.* Desio. Noted as a great linguist and scholar; reformed Vatican library; signed Lateran Treaty with Mussolini (1929), by which pope became sovereign of Vatican State; condemned communism in *Divini Redemptoris* (1937) and Nazism in *Mit Brennender Sorge* (1937).

PIUS XII original name: EUGENIO PACELLI. 1876–1958. Pope (1939–58). *b.* Rome. Proclaimed dogma of Assumption of the Virgin Mary.

Pizarro *(pĭ zär ō),* **Francisco** c1470–1541. Spanish conquistador. *b.* Trujillo. Sailed to New World (c1509) and was with Balboa when he discovered the Pacific (1513); with Diego de Almagro and Fernando de Luque, charted a plan for the exploration and conquest of the rich empires of South America; made two expeditions to collect information (1524, 1526); went to Spain and received authority to conquer and govern Peru (1529) with himself as captain general and Almagro as marshal; set sail from Panama (1531) with three vessels; landed at Tumbes and marched inland; reached Cajamarca (1532), where the Inca Atahualpa was seized and massacred after the Spaniards extorted gold and silver worth 4.5 million ducats; marched to Cuzco (1533); received submission of Manco Inca, who was made a puppet ruler; founded Lima as his capital (1535); created marquis by Charles V; took possession of Quito; suppressed Indian revolt under Manco (1536); in dispute over division of territory and spoils, defeated and killed Almagro (1538); was in turn assassinated by followers of Almagro (1541).

Planck *(plängk),* **Max Karl Ernst Ludwig** 1858–1947. German physicist. *b.* Kiel. Professor of physics at university of Kiel (1885–89) and Berlin (1889–1926); on the basis of investigations into radiation from black bodies, formulated the quantum theory, which held that energy transfer is discontinuous and takes place in abrupt installments or quanta; awarded Nobel Prize in physics (1918). Author of *Law of Radiation* (1901), *Vorlesungen über Thermodynamik* (1897), *Vorlesungen über die Theorie der Wärmestrahlung*

(1906), Einführung in die Theoretische Physik (5 vols., 1916–30), and *Das Weltbild der Neueren Physik* (1929).

Plath *(pläth),* **Sylvia** 1932–1963. American author. *b.* Boston, Mass. Explored female consciousness in the novel *The Bell Jar* (1963); also published two books of poetry: *Colossus* (1960) and *Ariel* (1965); committed suicide.

Plato *(plā tō)* original name: ARISTOCLES. c427–347 B.C. Greek philosopher. *b.* Athens. Disciple of Socrates; on the latter's trial, conviction, and death (399), spent some years in travel, visiting Megara, Egypt, Cyrene, Sicily, and Italy; returned to Athens, never to leave it again, except for two brief visits to Syracuse; founded the Academy (388); wrote over 35 extant *Dialogues*, with Socrates appearing in them as locutor and as spokesman of Platonic ideas; expounded a system of philosophy so inclusive and complete that it touches on every aspect of life; held that ideas and the ideal forms are the underlying basis of reality; that the supreme idea is the idea of the good; that true knowledge consists of the apprehension of these ideal and universal forms; that virtue consists of harmony with the universe of ideas; that the rational soul is immortal; also dealt with love, justice, order, laws, rhetoric, and health. Principal dialogues are *Republic, Laws, Phaedrus, Timaeus, Symposium, Apology, Phaedo, Charmides, Cratylus, Critias, Crito, Euthydemus, Georgias, Ion, Laches, Lesser Hippias, Lysis, Menexenus, Meno, Parmenides, Philebus, Politicus, Protagoras, Sophist,* and *Thaettus.*

Plautus *(plô təs),* **Titus Maccius** c254–184 B.C. Roman dramatist. *b.* Sarsina. Author of 21 extant plays, though 131 plays were once attributed to him; his plays, characterized by robust, coarse humor, were immensely popular in his day; Shakespeare, Molière, and Jonson have borrowed from them. Works include *Amphitryon, Captivi, Aulularia, Trinummus, Rudens, Mercator, Persa, Miles Gloriosus, Rudens, Stichus,* and *Curculio.*

Plekhanov *(plĕ Kăg nôf),* **Georgi Valentinovich** 1857–1918. Russian political philosopher. *b.* Tambov. Though born into an aristocratic family, joined the Narodnist (Populist) movement; one of the leaders of the first popular demonstration in St. Petersburg (1876); founded League for the Emancipation of Labor (1883), after being exiled (1880); intellectual leader of Russian Marxists and delegate to Second International (1889–1904); associate of Lenin in the 1890s and early 1900s; cofounder of *Iskra*, the Bolshevik journal; broke with Lenin over Russian participation in World War I, and thereafter drifted away from Bolsheviks; when Bolsheviks seized power, exiled to Finland. Author of over 26 books on Marxism.

Pliny *(plĭn ĭ)* also called PLINY THE ELDER; full name: GAIUS PLINIUS SECUNDUS. 23–79. Roman naturalist. *b.* Como. Served in the army in Africa and Germany; procurator in Spain (70–72); engaged in the study of history, grammar, rhetoric, and natural science; of his writings, which filled 160 volumes, only the *Historia Naturalis*, a scientific encyclopedia in 37 books, survives; his adopted son and nephew was PLINY, also called PLINY THE YOUNGER; full name: GAIUS PLINIUS CAECILIUS SECUNDUS. 62–c114. Roman author and statesman. *b.* Como. Held offices of military tribune, quaestor, praetor, consul propraetor, and governor of Bithynia and Pontica; known as the author of *Epistles*, which has gained him a place in Roman literature as a master stylist.

Plotinus *(plō tī nəs)* c205–70. Roman philosopher. *b.* Lycopolis, Egypt. Studied philosophy at Alexandria under Ammonius Saccas, later in Persia and India; settled in Rome (c244); foremost exponent of Neopythagorean and Neoplatonic philosophy; founded a Platonic Republic in Campania; left 54 works, arranged in six groups of nine books, called *Enneads*; his system was composed of Platonism infused with Oriental beliefs and was antimaterialistic and mystical; postulated a single transcendent great cause or principle from which the Divine Mind, the World Soul, particular souls, and finally material things emanated; greatly influenced Christian thinkers and Idealist schools of philosophy.

Plutarch *(plo͞o tärk)* c46–c120. Greek biographer. *b.* Chaeronea, in Boeotia. Extant works consist of a collection of historical biographies entitled *Parallel Lives: Lives of Illustrious Greeks and Romans*, and a lesser-known collection of short essays, entitled *Opera Moralia*, dealing with religion, ethics, politics, history, and philosophy; his *Lives* was used as source material by later writers, including Shakespeare.

Poe *(pō),* **Edgar Allan** 1809–49. American poet and writer. *b.* Boston. An orphan adopted by John Allan, a merchant in Richmond, Va.; entered University of Virginia, but left after one term (1826); quarrelled with foster father and left home for Boston; published first literary work *Tamerlane and Other Poems* (1827); enlisted in the army (1827–29); cadet at U.S. Military Academy at West Point (1830–31), but dismissed for neglect of duty; published *Al Aaraaf, Tamerlane, and Minor Poems* (1829) and *Poems by Edgar A. Poe* (1831); began earning a living as a writer with *"A MS Found in a Bottle"* (1833); on staff of *Southern Literary Messenger* (1835–37), *Gentleman's Magazine* (1839), and *Graham's Magazine* (1841–42); editor of *Evening Mirror* and editor and owner of *Broadway Journal;* resided at Philadelphia, Baltimore, and New York; increasingly became alcoholic and, particularly after the death of his wife (1847), subject to fits of despondency and insanity. Works include *Tales of the Grotesque and Arabesque* (1840) and *The Raven and Other Poems* (1845); his poems "The Raven," "Ulalume " Annabel Lee," "Lenore," and "To Helen" are among his best known; he established the macabre as a literary genre, and is considered the first mystery story writer; influenced many writers, including the French Symbolists.

Poincaré *(pwäɴ kȧ rā),* **Jules Henri** 1854–1912. French mathematician. *b.* Nancy. Professor at University of Paris (from 1881); made important contributions to physical mechanics, mathematical physics, and astronomy; developed the theory of functions, the electromagnetic theory of light, and the theory of orbits. Author of *Science and Hypothesis* (1903), *Science and Method* (1908); *Calcul des Probabilitiés* (1896), *Les Oscillations Électriques* (1894), *Les Méthodes Nouvelles de la Mécanique Céleste* (1892), and *Électricité et Optique* (1890).

Poincaré, Raymond Nicolas Landry 1860–1934. French statesman. *b.* Bar-le-Duc. Elected to Chamber of Deputies (1887); senator (1903); minister of public instruction (1893, 1895); minister of finance (1894, 1906); premier (1911–13, 1922–24, 1926–29); president of the Republic (1913–20); responsible for the French occupation of the Ruhr. Author of *How France Is Governed* (1913) and *Au Service de la France* (1926).

Polk *(pōk),* **James Knox** 1795–1849. 11th president of U.S. (1845–49). *b.* Mecklenburg County, N.C. House of Representatives (1825–39); Speaker of the House (1835–39); governor of Tenn. (1839–41); presidential nominee of the Democratic Party (1844); elected by narrow margin over Henry Clay; during his administration, achieved all four goals he had set for himself: reduction of tariffs, establishment of independent U.S. treasury, settlement of Oregon boundary dispute, and acquisition of California; by able conduct of the Mexican War, forced Mexico to cede New Mexico as well; did not run for reelection and died within months of leaving office.

Pollock *(pŏl ək),* **Jackson** 1912–56. American painter. *b.* Cody, Wyo. Foremost exponent of Tachism, or action painting, in which paint is dripped and splashed on canvas, a technique he developed (1947) after passing through surrealist and abstract phases. Principal works include *No. 32, Echo, Blue Poles,* and 17-foot-long *One.*

Polo *(pō lō),* **Marco** c1254–c1324. Italian traveler. *b.* Venice. At age 17, accompanied his father and uncle from Acre to court of Kublai Khan in Shangtu, China, passing through Khorasan, up the Oxus to the Pamir, Kashgar, Yarkand, and Khotan, to Lop Nor, across the Gobi Desert, to Tangut (1271–75); employed in the Khan's diplomatic service; rose in favor and was sent as emissary to Yunnan, Burma, Karakorum, Cochin China, and South India; governor of Yang Chow; participated in taking the city of Saianfu; left China (1292) as escort of a Mongol bride for the khan of Persia, and after many adventures reached Venice (1295); taken prisoner in Battle of Curzola between the Venetians and the Genoese; in prison, dictated the story of his travels, published as *The Book of Marco Polo*, one of the world's most celebrated travel accounts.

Polybius *(pō lĭb ĭ əs)* c205–c125 B.C. Greek historian. *b.* Megalopolis. Fought against Rome in the Achaean League and was one of the 1000 Achaean nobles who were captured and taken to Rome; befriended the younger Scipio Africanus and followed him in the African campaign that ended in the destruction of Carthage (146); began collecting materials for his history of the ancient world, journeying to Asia Minor, Egypt, Italy, France, and Spain; completed *His-*

tories, (40 volumes, of which only five survive), a history of Rome and its neighbors from 220 to 146 B.C.

Pomeranus; Pommer, Dr. *See* **Bugenhagen, Johann**

Pompadour *(pôN pȧ do͞or),* **Marquise de** full name: JEANNE ANTOINETTE POISSON LE NORMANT D'ÉTOILES. 1721–64. French beauty, mistress of Louis XV. *b.* Paris. Became a favorite of Louis XV (1745); duchess (1752); dominated Louis and the government of France (1745–64), retaining the affection of Louis to the end; also known as a patroness of art.

Pompey *(pŏm pĭ)* full name: GNAEUS POMPEIUS MAGNUS; also POMPEY THE GREAT. 106–48 B.C. Roman general and statesman. Fought in Social War as a partisan of Sulla against Marius and Cinna (89); pursued and liquidated the Marian faction in Spain and Africa; crushed Servile Revolt of Spartacus (71); elected consul (70); cleared Mediterranean Sea of pirates (67); commander of the East (66); subdued Mithridates of Pontus, Tigranes of Armenia, Antiochus of Syria, and the Jews of Palestine; annexed Syria and Palestine; entered Rome in triumph (61); formed First Triumvirate with Crassus and Caesar (60); married Caesar's daughter, Julia; after her death (54) and that of Crassus (53), turned against Caesar; consul (55); as leader of Conservative faction in senate, required Caesar to disband his army, thus beginning the Civil War (49); defeated by Caesar at Pharsala (48); sought asylum in Egypt but was murdered on orders of Ptolemy.

Pompidou *(pōN pē do͞o),* **Georges Jean Raymond** 1911–74. French statesman. *b.* Montboudif. Trained as banker; director general of the Rothschild banking house; joined De Gaulle's staff (1944); prime minister (1962–68); resigned following the May disturbances; succeeded De Gaulle as president (1969–74).

Ponce de León *(pôn thā thā lā ôn),* **Juan** c1460–1521. Spanish explorer. *b.* San Servas. Accompanied Columbus on second voyage (1493); appointed governor of eastern Hispaniola after taking part in its conquest (1502–1504); as conqueror of Puerto Rico, appointed governor (1510); on quest for the fountain of Perpetual Youth on Bimini Island, discovered Florida (1513); on an expedition to colonize Florida (1521), wounded in a battle with Indians; died on return to Cuba.

Pontoppidan *(pŏn tŏp ē dän),* **Henrik** 1857–1943. Danish novelist. *b.* Fredericia. Abandoned an engineering career for writing; awarded Nobel Prize (with Karl Gjellerup) in literature (1917). Among his novels are *Land of Promise* (1891–95), *Dommens Dag* (1895), *Lykke-Per* (3 vols., 1898–1905), *Kingdom of the Dead* (5 parts, 1912–16); and memoirs *Back to Myself* (1941).

Pope *(pōp),* **Alexander** 1688–1744. English poet. *b.* London. As a Catholic, denied a formal education; gained entry into London literary circles with the publication of *Pastorals* in Tonson's *Miscellany* (1709); won Addison's approval with *Essay on Criticism* (1711); associate of Swift, Bolingbroke, Oxford, and other prominent

Tories; established reputation as a satirist with the mock-heroic *Rape of the Lock* (1714); demonstrated talent for romantic poetry in "Elegy to the Memory of an Unfortunate Lady" and "Eloisa to Abelard" (1717); translated the *Iliad* (1715–20) and the *Odyssey* (1725–26), which earned him over £9000 and made him independently wealthy; in *The Dunciad* (1728), lampooned his detractors with devastating wit; in *Essay on Man* (1733–34) and *Moral Essays* (1731–35), delved into ethics and deism; in last work, *The Satires and Epistles of Horace Imitated* (1733–39), returned to satire; formed the Scriblerus Club with Swift and collaborated on the *Memoirs of Martinus Scriblerus* (1741); vigorously conducted some of the most notorious quarrels in literary history with Addison, John Dennis, Lewis Theobold, and others; considered the greatest satirist in English literature.

Popper *(pôp ər),* **Karl Raimund** 1902–. Austrian philosopher. *b.* Vienna. Left Vienna before the Anschluss and taught in New Zealand and London; revolutionized scientific methodology with *The Logic of Scientific Discovery* (1934), which established falsifiability as the test of a true scientific theory. Other works include *The Poverty of Historicism* (1957), *The Open Society and Its Enemies* (1945), *Conjectures and Refutations* (1963), and *British Philosophy in the Mid-Century* (1957).

Poquelin, Jean Baptiste. *See* **Molière**

Porcupine, Peter. *See.* **Cobett, William**

Porter *(pôr tər),* **Cole** 1892–1964. American composer and lyricist. *b.* Peru, Ind. Best known for his lyrics in the musical comedies *Fifty Million Frenchmen* (1929), *Red, Hot, and Blue* (1936), *Dubarry Was a Lady* (1939), *Mexican Hayride* (1943), *Kiss Me, Kate* (1948), *Out of This World* (1950), and *Can Can* (1953); among his best-known songs are "Begin the Beguine" and "Night and Day."

Porter *(pōr tər),* **George** 1920–. British chemist. Professor at Cambridge (1949–54), Sheffield (1955–63), and London (from 1963); with Manfred Eigen and Ronald Norrish, awarded Nobel Prize in chemistry (1967) for studies of extremely fast chemical reaction effected by disturbing equilibrium by very short energy pulsations.

Porter, Katherine Anne 1894–. American novelist. *b.* Indian Creek, Tex. Major novels include *Flowering Judas* (1930), *Hacienda* (1934), *Noon Wine* (1937), *Pale Horse, Pale Rider* (1939), *The Leaning Tower* (1944), and *Ship of Fools* (1962); a collection of her short stories was published in 1965.

Porter, Rodney Robert 1917–. English biochemist. Professor of biochemistry at Oxford (from 1967); with G.M. Edelman, shared Nobel Prize in physiology and medicine (1972) for research into the chemical structure of antibodies.

Porter, William Sydney. *See* **Henry, O.**

Portland, Third Duke of. *See* **Bentinck, William Henry Cavendish**

Potemkin *(pə tyôm kyĭn),* **Grigori Aleksandrovich** 1739–91. Russian statesman. *b.* Smolensk. As an officer in the Horse Guards, distinguished himself in campaigns against Turks (1769); of handsome and dashing appearance, gained notice and favor of Catherine II (from 1774); field marshal (1784); built the Black Sea fleet and annexed Crimea (1783); founded the cities of Sebastopol, Nikolaev, and Ekaterinoslav; Russian commander in chief in Russo-Turkish War (1787–91); though able and ambitious, he was corrupt, licentious, and unscrupulous. Wrote *Memoirs* (1812).

Pound *(pound),* **Ezra Loomis** 1885–1972. American poet. *b.* Hailey, Idaho. Expatriate in Europe, traveling in Italy, Spain, and France (1909–24); edited the influential *Poetry, Little Review*, and *The Blast*; credited with being the motivating force behind modern poetry and the literary godfather of T.S. Eliot and James Joyce; broadcast Fascist propaganda from Italy during World War II; brought to U.S. (1945) and tried for treason; incarcerated in a mental hospital (1945–58); released (1958) and allowed to return to Italy; principal poetic work is *Cantos* (1925), completed with *Pisan Cantos* (1948). Other volumes of poetry include *A Lume Spento* (1908), *Personae* (1909), *Exultations* (1909), *Provenca* (1910), *Canzoni* (1911), *Ripostes* (1912), *Lustra* (1916), *Homage to Sextus Propertius* (1919), and *Umbra* (1920); also published translations from Chinese, *Literary Essays* (1954), criticism, and books on politics and economics.

Pound, Roscoe 1870–1964. American legal scholar. *b.* Lincoln, Neb. Professor of law at Northwestern University (1907–1909), Chicago (1909–10), and Harvard (1910–37); influential as a teacher and writer. Author of *Outlines of Lectures on Jurisprudence* (1914), *The Spirit of the Common Law* (1921), *Introduction to the Philosophy of Law* (1922), *Law and Morals* (1924), and *Criminal Justice in America* (1930).

Poussin *(pōō săN),* **Nicolas** 1594–1665. French painter. *b.* Grand Andelys. Went to Rome and gained recognition for classical landscapes (1624); received commissions from Cardinal Berberini; returned to Paris (1640) and was appointed, through the influence of Richelieu, painter to Louis XIII; returned to Rome (1643). Principal works include *The Deluge, Plague of the Philistines, Rape of the Sabines, Triumph of Pan, Golden Calf, Moses,* and *Triumph of Truth.*

Powell *(pou əl),* **Cecil Frank** 1903–69. British physicist. *b.* Tonbridge. Professor of physics at Bristol (from 1948); pioneered in tracking of subatomic particles by means of a photographic emulsion viewed through a microscope; awarded Nobel Prize in physics (1950).

Powys *(pō ĭs),* **John Cowper** 1872–1963. English man of letters. *b.* Shirley. Author of novels including *Wolf Solent* (1929), *A Glastonbury Romance* (1933), *Maiden Castle* (1937), and *Owen Glendower* (1941); poetry includes *Mandragora* (1917) and *Samphire* (1922); philosophical works *The Religion of a Sceptic, The Complex Vision*, and *In Defense of Sensuality* (1930); criticism *Visions and Revisions, The Mean-*

ing of Culture (1930) and *Rabelais* (1947); also published *Autobiography* (1934).

Praxiteles *(prăk sĭt əl ēz)* *fl.* 4th century B.C. Athenian sculptor. *b.* Athens. Creator of Aphrodite of Cnidus, one of the most admired statues of the ancient world; other representative extant work is *Hermes with the Infant Dionysus on His Arm*; credited by ancient writers with over 60 statues.

Pregl *(prā gə l),* **Fritz** 1869–1930. Austrian chemist. *b.* Laibach, Yugoslavia. Professor at Innsbruck and at Graz; developed quantitative microanalyis of organic compounds; awarded Nobel Prize in chemistry (1923).

Prescott *(prĕs kət),* **William Hickling** 1796–1859. American historian. *b.* Salem, Mass. Though nearly blind, devoted life to historical research and writing; produced three masterpieces of scholarship: *History of the Reign of Ferdinand and Isabella the Catholic* (3 vols., 1838), *History of the Conquest of Mexico* (3 vols., 1843), and *History of the Conquest of Peru* (1847); began work on and published three volumes of *History of the Reign of Philip II* (1855–58), but did not live to complete it.

Pretorius *(prĕ tōō rē ûs),* **Andries Wilhelmus Jacobus** 1799–1853. South African Boer leader. *b.* Cape Colony. Joined the Great Trek (1838); as commandant general of the Boers, repulsed the Zulus and led Boer resistance to British domination; when his protests to the British governor against British immigration policies went unheeded, organized a second trek across the Vaal River (1848); in ensuing war, defeated at Boomplats; gained British recognition of the independence of Trans-Vaal Republic (1852); Pretoria, the capital of the Republic, named in his honor; his son was MARTINIUS WESSELS PRETORIUS (1819–1901). Boer statesman. *b.* Cape Colony. President of South African Republic (1857–71); president of Orange Free State (1859–63); with Paul Kruger and Piet Joubert, organized Boer resistance after British annexation of Orange Free State (1877); won second recognition of Boer independence from Great Britain (1880).

Prévost *(prā vō),* **Abbé** full name: ANTOINE FRANÇOIS PRÉVOST D'EXILES. 1697–1763. French novelist. *b.* Artois. Attracted to both the contemplative and the active life, spent many years in the barracks and in the cloister before settling down to a literary life in London (1727); wrote *Manon Lescaut* (1731); *Histoire de Cleveland* (1732–39), *Les Mémoires d'un Homme de Qualité (7 vols., 1728–32). Compagnes Philosophiques* (1741), *Mémoires d'un Honnête Homme* (1745), and *Le Monde Moral* (1760); edited *Le Pour et le Contre* (1733–40).

Priestley *(prēst lĭ),* **John Boynton** 1894–. English novelist, playwright, and critic. *b.* Bradford. His vast output of novels includes *Good Companions* (1929), *Angel Pavement* (1930), *Faraway* (1932), *Let the People Sing* (1939), *Blackout in Gretley* (1942) and *Festival* (1952); as a playwright, wrote *Dangerous Corner* (1932), *Laburnum Grove* (1933), *Time and the Conways* (1937), *I Have Been Here Before* (1937), *Music at Night* (1938), *The Long Mirror* (1940),

An Inspector Calls (1946), and *the Linden Tree* (1947); published autobiography *Rain Upon Gadshill* (1939).

Priestley, Joseph 1733–1804. English minister and chemist. *b.* Fieldhead. Nonconformist minister (1755); gradually accepted Socinian and Unitarian doctrines; wrote a number of theology books, including *The Scripture Doctrine of Remission* (1755), *Letters to a Philosophical Unbeliever* (1774), *History of Early Opinions Concerning Jesus Christ* (1786), *A General History of the Christian Church* (4 vols., 1790–1802), and *History of the Corruption of Christianity* (1782), the last of which was burned as atheistic; expressed political philosophy in *Essay on the First Principles of Government* (1768); important in the history of science as the discoverer of dephlogisticated air, later called oxygen; other chemical discoveries included isolation of nitrous oxide, carbon monoxide, and ammonia; demonstrated the decomposition of ammonia by electricity and explained the phenomenon of Priestley rings in *History and Present State of Electricity* (1767); immigrated to U.S. (1794), after his house in Birmingham was burned by a mob because of his pro-French Revolutionary sympathies.

Primrose, Archibald Philip. *See* **Roseberry, Earl of**

Proclus *(prō klŭs)* c410–85. Greek Neoplatonic philosopher. *b.* Constantinople, Byzantium. Head of Academy at Athens (from 450); tried to evolve a comprehensive theology by combining the best pagan traditions of Rome, Greece, Syria, and Egypt to effectively combat the spread of Christianity; developed the concept of triads, consisting of God as the first cause, emanations from that source, and return to it; besides treatises on mathematics and astronomy, wrote *Providence and Fate, Doubts About Providence*, and *The Nature of Evil*.

Prokhorov *(prô Kə rôf)*, **Alexander Mikhailovich** 1916–. Russian physicist. Professor at Lebedev Physics Institute, Moscow; with Charles H. Townes and Nikolai G. Basov, awarded Nobel Prize in physics (1964) for fundamental research in quantum electronics leading to the development of maser-laser principle.

Prokofiev *(prə kôf yĕf)*, **Sergei Sergeevich** 1891–1953. Russian composer. *b.* Sontsovka. Studied under Rimsky-Korsakov at St. Petersburg Conservatory; lived in England and in U.S. (1914–34). Works include symphonies, concertos, *Love for Three Oranges, Lieutenant Kije, Alexander Nevsky, Romeo and Juliet, Scythian Suite, Classical Symphony, Overture on Hebrew Themes*, and *Peter and the Wolf*; published *Autobiography* (1960).

Protagoras *(prō tăg ō rəs)* *fl.* 5th century B.C. Greek philosopher. *b.* Abdera, Thrace. Known as first of the Sophists; banished from Athens for questioning the gods in *On the Gods*, which was publicly burned; to him belongs the statement, "Man is the measure of all things."

Proudhon *(proo dôN)*, **Pierre Joseph** 1809–65. French anarchist. *b.* Besancon. Employed himself throughout life in providing the theoretical framework of anarchism; briefly active in practical politics after Revolution of 1848; edited the journals *Le Peuple* (1848–49), *La Voix du Peuple* (1849–50), and *Le Peuple de 1850* (1850); imprisoned (1849–52) and amnestied (1850); opposed all forms of authority and held that private property was theft since it appropriated the labor of others in the form of rent. Author of *de la Justice dans la Révolution et dans l'Église* (1858), *What Is Property*? (1840), *Système des Contradictions Économiques* (1846), *Les Idées Révolutionnaires* (1849), *Confessions d'un Révolutionnaire* (1849), *Actes de la Révolution* (1849), and *Gratuité du Crédit* (1850).

Proust *(pro͞ost),* **Marcel** 1871–1922. French novelist. *b.* Paris. Withdrew from society (1905) after the death of his mother, the central figure in his life; began working on a multivolume novel that would picture the death of a society through the psychological analysis of his own inner life; completed 13 volumes of this novel, *À la Recherche du Temps Perdu,* known in English as *Remembrance of Things Past*, but left it incomplete at death; an earlier novel *Jean Santeuil* (1899), reconstructed from manuscripts, was published in three volumes (1951).

Prudentius *(pro͞o dĕn shĭ ŭs),* **Aurelius Clemens** 348–c410. Latin Christian poet. *b.* probably in Spain. Considered principal poet of early Christian Church for *Cathemerinon Liber, Peristephanon, Apotheosis, Hamartigeneia, Psychomachia, Contra Symmachum, Diptychon*; served as high official in imperial court.

Przhevalski *(pər zhĕ väl skĭ),* **Nikolai Mikhailovich** 1839–88. Russian explorer. *b.* Smolensk. Began early explorations in Ussuri River region (1867–69); conducted expeditions to Mongolia and China (1870–73), East Turkestan and Tibet, reaching within 160 miles of Lhasa (1876–77, 1879–80), and Mongolia and Tibet (1883–85); explored upper Hwang-Ho and Lake Lop Nor; amassed a large collection of plants and animals and discovered a previously unknown wild camel and a wild horse, named Przhevalsky's horse. Author of *Mongolia, the Tangut Country, and the Solitudes of Northern Tibet* (1876) and *From Kulja Across the Tian Shan to Lob-nor* (1879).

Ptolemy I *(tŏl ə mĭ)* also PTOLEMY SOTER. c367–283 B.C. King of Egypt and founder of Macedonian dynasty. General in the army of Alexander the Great and one of the Diadochi who carved up his empire, receiving Egypt and Libya in the partition; engaged in wars against Perdiccas and Antigonus; assumed title of king (305); made Alexandria the capital of Egypt and endowed it with the celebrated library; received title of Soter (Preserver) by aiding the Rhodians against Demetrius; wrote a life of Alexander the Great; his son was PTOLEMY II. also, PTOLEMY PHILADELPHUS. 309–246 B.C. Annexed Phoenicia; encouraged literature, science, and art; enlarged Alexandrian Library; built the Pharos; developed trade.

Ptolemy in Latin: CLAUDIUS PTOLEMAEUS. *fl.* 2nd century. Alexandrian astronomer, geographer, and mathematician. *b.* Alexandria.

Author of *Almagest*, the compendium of astronomic knowledge, which dominated astronomy until the Copernican system superseded it; described a geocentric system in which the sun, planets, and stars revolved around the earth. Wrote *Geographical Treatise*, a catalogue of 1028 stars, *Tetrabiblos Syntaxis*, and *Karpos* (*Centriloquium*).

Puccini *(po͞ot chē nē),* **Giacomo** *Antonio Domenico Michele Secondo Maria* 1858–1924. Italian operatic composer. *b.* Lucca. Beginning with his first success, *Manon Lescaut* (1893), composed well-known operas including *La Bohème* (1896), *Tosca* (1900), *Madame Butterfly* (1900), and *Turandot*, which was left incomplete and was finished by Alfano; works characterized by exotic melodic innovations.

Pulaski *(pū lăs kĭ),* **Casimir** c1748–79. Polish general. *b.* Podolia. Fought in the insurrection against Russia (1768) and was outlawed from Poland; lived in France and became interested in the cause of the colonists through Benjamin Franklin; went to the Colonies with a letter from Franklin to Washington; entered Revolutionary army (1777), served at Brandywine and Germantown, and organized Pulaski's Legion (1778); defended Charleston (1779) and was mortally wounded at the siege of Savannah (1779).

Pulitzer *(po͝ol ĭt sər),* **Joseph** 1847–1911. American journalist. *b.* Makó, Hungary. On discharge from the Union army, obtained job as reporter on *Westliche Post* (1868); elected to Missouri legislature (1869); police commissioner of St. Louis; part-owner of *Westliche Post* (1871–73); acquired the *St. Louis Staats-Zeitung* (1874); laid the foundation of his fortune by taking over the *St. Louis Dispatch* and merging it with the *Post* to form the *Post-Dispatch* (1878); moved to New York and bought the *World* from Jay Gould (1883); founded *Evening World* (1887); endowed the school of journalism at Columbia and established the Pulitzer Prizes.

Pupin *(po͞o pēn),* **Michael Idvorsky** 1858–1935. American physicist and inventor. *b.* Idvor, Yugoslavia. Professor of electromechanics at Columbia (1901–31); discovered method for tuning oscillating currents; invented the Pupin Coil, a loading coil which extended the range of telephone and telegraphy; developed short-exposure X-ray photography. Author of Pulitzer prize-winning *Immigrant to Inventor* (1923), *Electro-Magnetic Theory* (1895), and *Romance of the Machine* (1930).

Purcell *(pər sĕl),* **Edward Mills** 1912–. American physicist. *b.* Taylorville, Ill. Professor of physics at Harvard (from 1949); investigated radiation phenomena; with Felix Bloch, awarded Nobel Prize (1952) in physics for work on the measurement of atomic nuclei magnetic fields through nuclear resonance method.

Purcell *(pûr səl),* **Henry** 1659–95. English composer. *b.* London. Composer for king's violins (1677), organist of Westminster Abbey (1679), and of Chapel Royal (1682); began composing (from 1680); produced vocal and choral works, including odes and athems; wrote chamber music (from 1683); created the opera *Dido and Aeneas*

(1689); composed the music for Dryden's *Aurengzebe*, Betterton's *Diocletian*, Fletcher's *Prophetess, The Faery Queen,* and Dryden's *Tyrannic Love* and *King Arthur*; greatest work considered to be *Te Deum and Jubilate* for St. Cecilia's Day (1694).

Purkinje *(pŏŏr kĭn yā),* **Johannes Evangelista** 1787–1869. Czech physiologist. *b.* Libochowitz, Bohemia. Entered the cloister, but left it for medicine; professor of physiology at Breslau (1823–50) and Prague (from 1850); made fundamental discoveries in physiology and microscopic anatomy, especially relating to embryology and ophthalmology; work eponymized in Purkinje's fibers, Purkinje's cells, and Purkinje image; coined word "protoplasm" for embryonic nucleus; also noted as a Czech patriot.

Pushkin *(pōōsh kyĭn),* **Aleksander Sergeevich** 1799–1837. Russian national poet. *b.* Moscow. A mulatto by birth, being the grandson of Hannibal, the Negro general of Peter the Great; exiled to south Russia for writing *Ode to Liberty* (1820); dismissed from service, but restored to post (1832); considered as greatest Russian poet; killed at age 38 in a duel. Works include *Ruslan and Lyudmila* (1820), *Fountain of Bakchisarai* (1826), *Tzigani* (1827), *The Captive of the Caucasus* (1822), *Boris Godunov* (1825), *The Gipsies* (1822–24), *Eugene Onegin* (1831), *Poltava* (1829), *The Bronze Horseman* (1833), *The Golden Cockerel* (1833), *The Queen of Spades* (1834), *History of the Revolt of Pugachev* (1834), and *Captain's Daughter* (1836).

Pym *(pĭm),* **John** 1584–1643. English statesman. *b.* Brymore. Entered Parliament (1614); leader in impeachment of Buckingham (1626); with Sir John Eliot, principal signatory of Petition of Right (1628); eloquent spokesman of parliamentary rights in Short Parliament (1640) and Long Parliament (1640); led impeachment of Strafford and Laud; helped carry through the Grand Remonstrance (1641); one of the five members of Parliament whose attempted arrest by the king touched off Civil War (1642); lieutenant of the ordinance on the Parliamentary side (1643), but died soon after.

Pythagoras *(pĭ thăg ə rəs)* *fl.* 6th century B.C. Greek philosopher. *b.* Samos. Settled at Crotona (530), where he founded a school; inspired a movement for religious and moral reformation with emphasis on purity and self-regulation; left no writings, yet under the name Pythogoreanism are grouped doctrines attributed to him, especially the doctrine of transmigration of souls; extended investigations to mathematics, which he raised to a science; believed to have founded the theory of numbers, studied acoustics, and taught that the earth was a globe; persecuted with followers for opposition to organized religion.

Q

Quasimodo *(kwä zē mô dō),* **Salvatore** 1901–68. Italian poet. *b.* Syracuse. Professor of literature at Conservatory of Music, Milan; awarded Nobel Prize in literature (1959). Author of *The Promised Land and Other Poems* (1958), *La Vita Non E' un Sogno* (1949), and *Ed e Subito Sera* (1942); also noted as a translator of Shakespeare and Greek classics.

Quesnay *(kə nā),* **François** 1694–1774. French economist. *b.* Mérey. Studied medicine and became physician to Louis XV; leader of group of economists, called the Physiocratic school, who advocated extreme laissez-faire; formulated doctrines in *Tableaux Économiques,* (1758), all copies of which are now lost; also published *Maximes* (1758) and *Physiocratie* (1678).

Quevedo y Villegas *(kə vā thō ē və lyā gäs),* **Francisco Gómez de** 1580–1645. Spanish writer. *b.* Madrid. Rose to favor in service of duke of Osuna and at court of Philip IV; imprisoned twice (1620–23, 1639–42); one of the most prolific Spanish poets and satirists. Works include *Vida del Buscón Pablos* (1626), *Visions, or Hell's Kingdom* (1640), and *Hell Reformed* (1641).

Quidde *(kvĭd ə),* **Ludwig** 1858–1941. German historian. *b.* Bremen. President of German Peace Society (1914–29) and German Peace Cartel (1920–29); edited *Deutche Zeitschrift für Geschichtswissenschaft* (1889–95); shared Nobel Peace Prize (1927) with Ferdinand Buisson; went into exile in Switzerland on rise of Hitler. Author of *Völkerbund und Demokratie* (1920), *Völkerbund und Friedensbewegung* (1920), *Caligula* (1894), and *Die Schuldfrage* (1922).

Quisling *(kwĭz lĭng),* **Vidkun Abraham Lauritz** 1887–1945. Norwegian political leader. *b.* Fyresdal. Formed Nasjonal Samlung (National Union), a Fascist organization (1933) and entered into secret agreement with Alfred Rosenberg (1936); assisted German invasion of Norway (1940) by proclaiming himself premier, but was deprived of all power and office by the Nazis until 1942; restored to premiership (1942–45); surrendered to Allied forces after liberation of Norway; tried for high treason and shot; his name has become a synonym for traitor to one's country.

R

Rab. *See* **Abba Arika**

Rabelais *(răb ə lā),* **François** pseudonym: Alcofribas Nasier. 1494–c1553. French satirist. *b.* near Chinon. Entered Franciscan monastery at Puy-Saint-Martin (1520), later transferring to Benedictine convent near Orleans; studied medicine at University of Montpellier (1530); practiced as physician at Lyons (from 1532); physician to Jean du Bellay, bishop of Paris, and accompanied him to Rome (1534–37); taught at University of Montpellier (1537–38); in service of Guillaume du Bellay-Langey, governor of Piedmont (1540–43); when his *Tiers Livre* was condemned by Sorbonne (1546), fled to Metz; called to Rome again by Jean du Bellay (1548–49); famous as author of *Gargantua* (1535) and *Pantagruel* (1533), accepted as masterpieces of grotesque invention, broad erudition, esoteric allegory, riotous humor, and humanism.

Rabi *(rā bĭ),* **Isidor Isaac** 1898–. American physicist. *b.* Rymanow, Austria. Professor of physics at Columbia (from 1937); made important contributions to the study of quantum mechanics, molecular beams, magnetism, and radio-frequency spectra of atoms and molecules; awarded Nobel Prize in physics (1944) for discovery of resonance method of recording the magnetic properties of atomic nuclei.

Rabinowitz, Solomon, *See* **Sholem Aleichem**

Rachmaninoff *(rəK mȧ nyĭ nôf),* **Sergei Wassilievitch** 1873–1943. Russian composer. *b.* Nijni-Novogorod. Conductor of Imperial Theater at Moscow (1904–1906); left Russia (1907) and resided in Dresden (until 1918) and in U.S. (from 1918). Compositions include *Prelude in C Sharp Minor, The Cliff, Isle of the Dead, Rhapsody on a Theme of Paganini* (1934), *Aleko, The Miser Knight, Francesca da Rimini, The Bells,* and piano pieces and songs.

Racine *(rȧ sēn),* **Jean Baptiste** 1639–99. French poet and dramatist. *b.* La Ferté-Milon. Gained notice of the court with the ode "La Nymphe de la Seine"; admitted to select literary group known as the Four, with Molière, La Fontaine, and Boileau; first two plays, *Thébaïde* (1664) and *Alexandre* (1665), produced by Moliere's company; achieved first success with *Andromaque* (1667), followed by *Britannicus* (1669), *Bérénice* (1670), *Bajazet* (1672), *Mithdridate* (1673), *Iphigénie* (1674), and *Phèdre* (1677); wrote comedy *Les Plaideurs* satirizing law courts (1668); mortified by adverse criticism of his plays by followers of Nicolas Pradon, gave up the theater until persuaded by Mme. de Maintenon to write two plays for performance at her school, *Esther* (1689) and *Athalie*

(1691); composed four hymns and *Histoire Abrégée de Port Royal;* as a dramatist, unequalled in sweetness of rhythm and cadence, exquisiteness of verse, harmony of dramatic construction, grace of diction, and depth of psychological insight.

Raleigh *(rô lĭ; rä lĭ),* **Sir Walter** also RALEGH. c1552–1618. English courtier, historian, and explorer. *b.* Hayes Barton. Joined half-brother Sir Humphrey Gilbert in piracy against Spaniards (1578); commanded English force against the Desmonds in Munster, Ireland (1580); attracted notice of Elizabeth as a protégé of Robert Dudley, Earl of Leicester; became her favorite, receiving such royal favors as estates, a licensing patent, a woolen export monopoly, office of warden of the stanneries, vice-admiral of Devon and Cornwall, and captain of the guard (1586); under royal charter sent fleet (1584) to explore Atlantic coast of North America; took possession of Virginia; spent over £40,000 in attempt to colonize the region (1584–90); introduced potatoes and tobacco into England; displaced as queen's favorite by Essex, and imprisoned in Tower (1592) for seduction of and marriage to a royal maid; banished from court for four years; associated with group of poets called School of Night, including Marlowe and Chapman; with other members, charged with atheism and forced to defend himself (1594); fitted out expedition to Guiana and Trinidad (1595), sailed up the Orinoco, and narrated his exploits in *The Discovery of Guiana* (1596); gained brilliant naval successes by destroying Spanish fleet at Cadiz (1597) and by capturing Fayal in the Azores (1597); recorded his success in *Relation of Cadiz Action;* governor of Jersey (1600); suppressed rebellion of his rival Essex and served as captain of the guard at his execution; on accession of James I (1603), stripped of all offices and sentenced to death on a charge of plotting against the king; sentence commuted to life imprisonment in the Tower; in prison, devoted himself to chemical experiments and to writing *History of the World;* sent on an ill-fated expedition to seek gold along the Orinoco in Guiana; bedeviled by storms, desertions, sickness, and disease, returned in total failure; arrested again and executed. Author of *The Prerogative of Parliaments* (1615) and *A Discourse of War,* both written in prison.

Raman *(rä män),* **Sir Chandrasekhara Venkata** 1888–1970. Indian scientist. *b.* Tiruchirapally. Professor at Calcutta (1917–33); founded and served as director of Indian Institute of Science at Bangalore (1943); awarded Nobel Prize in physics (1930) for the discovery of the Raman effect (1928), which enables the determination of the nature of a transparent substance by changing the frequency of a light ray passing through it. Author of *Molecular Diffraction of Light.*

Ramon y Cajal *(rä mōn ē kä häl),* **Santiago** 1852-1934. Spanish histologist. *b.* Petilla de Aragon. Professor at Valencia (1881–86), Barcelona (1886–92), and Madrid (1892); did fundamental work on the nervous system; isolated the neuron and determined its functional changes; described the nerve endings and connection of nerve cells in the brain and spinal cord; invented a new method of staining nerve tissue; awarded Nobel Prize with Camillo Golgi (1906). Author of. *Manual of Histology* (1889), *Textura del Sistema Nervioso de Hombre y de los Vertebrados* (2 vols, 1899–1905), *Estudios Sobra la Degeneration del Sistema Nervioso* (2 vols., 1913–14) and *Recollections* (1937).

Ramsay, James Andrew Brown. *See* **Dalhousie, Earl and Marquis of**

Ramsay *(răm zĭ),* **Sir William** 1852–1916. British chemist. *B.* Glasgow, Scotland. Professor of chemistry at London (1887–1913); discovered argon (with Lord Rayleigh), xenon (with Morris W. Travers), neon, krypton, and helium; determined the emanation of helium during the disintegration of radium; for these discoveries, awarded Nobel Prize in chemistry (1904). Author of *The Gases of the Atmosphere, Elements and Electrons,* and *Essays Biographical and Chemical.*

Ramses II *(răm sēz)* usually RAMSES THE GREAT; also RAMESES. *fl.* 13th century B.C. Egyptian king of XIX Dynasty (1292–25). After extended warfare, made peace with the Hittites (1272); spent remainder of reign in a vast building program, of which the monumental remains include temples at Karnak, Luxor, Abu Simbel, and Abydos, and the colossal statue of himself at Thebes.

Rancé *(rän sā),* **Armand Jean Le Bouthillier de** 1626–1700. French monk. *b.* Paris. As abbot of La Trappe monastery instituted reform of the monastic system that resulted in the establishment of a new order, called the Trappists, with emphasis on perpetual prayer and self-denial; forbade intellectual work and permitted only manual labor. Author of *Traité de la Sainteté et des Devoirs de la Vie Monastique* (1683).

Randolph *(răn dôlf),* **Edmund Jennings** 1753–1813. American statesman. *b.* Tazewell Hall, near Williamsburg, Va. Elected to Continental Congress (1779); governor of Virginia (1786); delegate to the Constitutional Convention (1787); refused to sign the Constitution, but advocated its ratification at the Virginia Convention (1788); first U.S. attorney general (1789–94); secretary of state (1794–95); charged with bribery and resigned (1795); defended Aaron Burr as chief counsel.

Ranke *(räng kə),* **Leopold von** 1795–1886. German historian. *b.* Wiehe. Professor of history at Berlin (1825–71); historiographer of Prussia (1841); developed modern historical writing based on research and original documents. These methods and theories have influenced generations of modern historians. Few of his works have been translated into English. Works include *Geschichte der Romanischen und Germanischen Völker von 1494–1535* (1824), *Die Römischen Päpaste* (3 vols., 1834-39), *Deutsche Geschichte im Zeitalter der Reformation* (1839–47), *Neun Bücher Preussicher Geschichte* (1847–48), *Französische Geschichte Vornehmlich im 16 und 17 Jahrhundert* (1852-61); *Englische Geschichte im 16 und 17 Jahrhundert* (1859–67); *Universal History* (1881–88), *Geschichte Wallensteins* (1869), and *Die*

Deutschen Mächte und der Fürstenbund (1872); published autobiography *Zur Eigenen Lebensgeschichte* (1890).

Raphael *(răf ĭ əl)* full name: RAFFAELLO SANTI. 1483–1520. Italian painter. *b.* Urbino. Studied art under his father and later at Perugia under Perugino; went to Florence (1504); invited to Rome to paint the Vatican for Julius II (1508); his prodigious and mature work at Rome is divided into five main groups: the Stanze of the Vatican, the Loggie of the Vatican, decoration of Villa Farnesina, cartoons for the Sistine Chapel and work at St. Peter's; on death of Julius, appointed by Leo X to succeed Bramante as chief architect of St. Peter's (1514). Among his most famous works are *Holy Family, Entombment, The Knight's Dream, St. Catherine, La Spasimo, Vision of Ezekiel, The Transfiguration, Apollo and Marsyas, Saint George and the Dragon, Saint Michael, St. John, The Resurrection, The Crucifixion, Coronation of the Virgin, La Belle Jardinière, La Fornarina, Marriage of the Virgin, School of Athens, The Three Graces, Holy Family, Adoration of the Trinity, Leo X, Violin Player,* and Madonnas, frescoes, and portraits.

Rasmussen *(räs mo͞o sən),* **Knud Johan Victor** 1879–1933. Danish explorer. *b.* Jacobshavn, Greenland. Led expeditions to Greenland (from 1902) and the American Arctic; established (1910) Cape York station at Thule and made first crossing by sledge across Melville Bay; originated the theory that Eskimos and North American Indians belonged to the same racial stock. Author of *Lapland* (1907), *The People of the Polar North* (1908), *Myths and Legends from Greenland* (3 vols., 1921–25), *Greenland by the Polar Sea* (1921), *In the Home of the Polar Eskimos* (1923), *Across Arctic America* (1927), and *The Eagle's Gift* (1932).

Rasputin *(rŭs po͞o tyĭn),* **Grigori Efimovich** c1871–1916. Russian monk. *b.* Pokrovskoe. An illiterate peasant who turned to religion and gained a reputation as a faith healer; of virile and hypnotic appearance, he gathered a considerable following; through the royal chaplain, was introduced to imperial court, influencing the czar and czarina, whose son was "miraculously" cured through his healing powers; as his sinister ascendancy grew into religion and politics, he acquired many enemies, some of whom assassinated him (1916); he was so hated by the people that his body was dug up and burned after the Revolution (1917).

Ravel *(rȧ vĕl),* **Maurice Joseph** 1875–1937. French composer. *b.* Ciboure. Works for the piano include *Le Tombeau de Couperin* (1917), *Gaspard de la Nuit* (1908), *Pavane pour une Infant Défunte* (1899), *Ma Mère l'Oye* (1908), *Sonatina* (1905), *Miroirs* (1905), *Jeux d'Eau* (1901); *L'Heure Espagnole* (1907) and *L'Enfant et les Sortilèges* (1925); for the ballet, *Daphnis et Chloé* (1912), *Boléro* (1928), and *La Valse* (1920); for the orchestra, *Rapsodie Espagnole* (1907).

Rawdon-Hastings, Francis. *See* **Hastings, Francis Rawdon-**

Ray *(rā),* **John** also WRAY. 1627–1705. English naturalist. *b.*

Black Notley. Called the father of English natural history; his classification of plants laid the basis for the Natural System and his zoological studies laid the basis for modern zoology; with Francis Willoughby, toured England and the Continent collecting specimens of animal and vegetable life; first to define the term species in the modern sense and to divide flowering plants into dicotyledons and monocotyledons; classified animal kingdom including insects. Author of *Methodus Plantarum Nova* (1682), *Historia Generalis Plantarum* (3 vols., 1686–1704), *Catalogus Plantarum Angliae* (1670), *Synopsis Methodica Animalium* (1693), *Methodus Insectorum* (1705), *The Wisdom of God Manifested in the Works of the Creation* (1691), and *Miscellaneous Discourses* (1692); the Ray Society was established (1844) to memorialize his work.

Rayleigh *(rā lĭ),* **Baron John William Strutt** 1842–1919. English physicist. *b.* near Maldon. Professor at Cambridge (1879–84) and Royal Institution (1888–1905); chancellor of Cambridge (from 1908); president of Royal Society (1905–1908); principal areas of research were vibratory motion, the theory of sound, and wave theory of light; awarded Nobel Prize in physics (1904) for discovery of argon. Author of *The Theory of Sound* (1877–78) and *Scientific Papers* (1899–1900).

Reade *(rēd),* **Charles** 1814–84. English novelist. *b.* Ipsden. After writing some mediocre plays, turned to novels; achieved fame with *The Cloister and the Hearth* (1861); a social reformer in the Dickensian tradition, wrote novels to expose abuses and injustices of society: the penal system in *It Is Never Too Late to Mend* (1856), insane asylums in *Hard Cash* (1863), insurance frauds in *Foul Play* (1868), trade unions in *Put Yourself in His Place* (1870), medical schools in *A Woman-Hater* (1877), and marriage in *Griffith Gaunt* (1866); also wrote the autobiographical *A Terrible Temptation* (1871).

Réaumur *(rā ō mür),* **René Antoine Ferchault de** 1683–1757. French scientist. *b.* La Rochelle. Conducted investigations into various natural phenomena and developed an improved method of making iron and steel; best known as the inventor of the Réaumur thermometer and Réaumur porcelain. Principal scientific work was *Memoires pour Servir a l'Histoire Naturelle des Insectes* (1734–42).

Récamier *(rä kä myā),* **Jeanne Françoise Julie Adélaïde Bernard** 1777–1849. French socialite. *b.* Lyons. At age 15, married Jacques Récamier, a banker three times her age; remained attached to him until his death in poverty (1830); attracted a brilliant circle to her salon through her wit and beauty; exiled from France by Napoleon, who considered her subversive; her friends included Chateaubriand, Constant, and Madame de Staël; her *Souvenirs et Correspondence* records her reflections on her times.

Reed *(rēd),* **Walter** 1851–1902. American surgeon. *b.* Belroi, Va. Entered army medical corps (1875); professor of bacteriology at Army Medical College, Washington, D.C. (from 1893); member of a commission to determine the agent and mode of transmission of yellow fever; proved that the original hypothesis of Carlos Finlay—that yellow fever is transmitted by the mosquito *Aëdes Aegypti*—was correct.

Reichstein *(rīk stīn),* **Tadeus** 1897–. Swiss chemist. *b*. Wloclawek, Poland. Professor of pharmacy at University of Basel (from 1946); synthesized 1-ascorbic acid; investigated secretions of the suprarenal glands; synthesized adrenal hormones, including cortisone; for this last work received, with E. C. Kendall and P. S. Hench, Nobel Prize in physiology and medicine (1950).

Rembrandt *(rĕm bränt)* full name: REMBRANDT HARMENSZOON VAN RIJN. 1606–69. Dutch painter. *b*. Leiden. Established studio at Amsterdam (from 1630); paintings of early period were bright with dramatic chiaroscuro and brought financial success; later works, mysterious and golden-hued, cost him his popularity and led to his bankruptcy; no artist combined skill and a sense of humanity more powerfully; left over 650 canvases, 200 drawings, and 300 etchings, including over 40 self-portraits. Best-known works include *Christ Presented at the Temple, Supper at Emmaus, The Anatomical Lesson, Night Watch, Pilate Washing His Hands, Aristotle Contemplating the Bust of Homer, Descent from the Cross, The Syndics, Simeon in the Temple, Christ as the Gardener, St. Thomas, The Windmill, Carcass of Beef, The Woman Taken in Adultery, The Auctioneer, Toilet of Bathsheba, Christ Healing the Sick,* and *Burgomaster Jan Six.*

Remington *(rĕm ĭng tən),* **Frederic** 1861–1909. American painter. *b*. Canton, N.Y. Known as the painter of the American West, an area he knew intimately as a cowboy. Works include the bronze sculpture *Bronco Buster* and the canvases *A Dash for the Timber, The Last Stand, Past All Surgery,* and *The Emigrants.*

Renan *(rə näN),* **Joseph Ernest** 1823–92. French philologist and historian. *b*. Tréguier. Trained for the church, but abandoned it as a rationalist and entered a career of scholarship; early treatises reflected the interest in religion and language that occupied him throughout his life: *Averröès et l'Averroïsme* (1852): *Études d'Histoire Religieuse* (1857), *De l'Origine du Langage* (1858), and *Essais de Morale et de Critique* (1859); wrote his major work, *Histoire des Origines du Christianisme,* in five volumes, of which *La Vie de Jésus* (1863) was the first and the most controversial; supplemented his work on Christianity with *Histoire du Peuple d'Israel* (5 vols., 1887–94).

Renault *(rə nō),* **Louis** 1843–1918. French jurist. *b*. Autun. Professor of international law at University of Paris (from 1873); member of the International Court of Arbitration at The Hague (1907); awarded Nobel Peace Prize with Ernesto T. Moneta (1907). Author of *Introduction à l'Étude du Droit International* (1879) and *Précis de Droit Commercial* (1879–82).

Renoir *(rĕ nwär),* **Jean** 1894–1979. French film director. *b*. Paris. Won Croix de Guerre in World War I; turned from script-writing to filmmaking; became naturalized American citizen (1941). Major films include *Nana* (1926), *La Grande Illusion* (1937), *La Bête Humaine* (1946), *The Golden Coach* (1953), and *Le Déjeuner sur l'Herbe* (1959).

Renoir, Pierre Auguste 1841–1919. French painter. *b.* Limoges. Deeply influenced by impressionism and perfected many impressionist techniques; exhibited at first Impressionist show (1874), but achieved first success (1879) with *Portrait of Mme. Charpentier and Her Children;* his canvases are colorful, sensuous, and lyrical. Representative works include *Le Moulin de la Galette, Dans le Loge, Baigneuses, Lise, A Winter Day on the Bois de Boulogne, The Blond Bather, Judgment of Paris, Still Life with Peaches, Girl with Chrysanthemum, Odalisque, Dancer, Harvesters, In the Meadow, The Artist's Studio, The Pont Neuf, Boating Party, Mme. Monet, The Swing,* and *Sisley and His Wife.*

Reuter *(roi tər),* **Baron Paul Julius von** original name: ISRAEL BEER JOSAPHAT. 1816–99. German news agency pioneer. *b.* Kassel. Established—first a pigeon post connection between terminals of German and French telegraph lines at Aachen (1849); developed it into a telegraphic bureau for collecting and transmitting news; transferred headquarters to London (1851); gained acceptance by obtaining news of the American Civil War by cable, which he laid from Cork to Crookhaven; later established branches worldwide.

Reuther *(ro͞o thər),* **Walter Philip** 1907–70. American labor leader. *b.* Wheeling, W. Va. Began as a tool and die worker, but was discharged for union activities; led first major strike in Detroit against automobile manufacturers; president of United Automobile Workers (1946–70) and Congress of Industrial Organizations (1952–55); died in aircraft accident (1970).

Revere *(rə vēr),* **Paul** 1735–1818. American patriot. *b.* Boston, Mass. A goldsmith and copperplate printer by profession; participated in Boston Tea Party, the news of which he carried to N.Y.; as official courier to Congress for the Massachusetts provincial assembly, made a number of rides on horseback carrying important messages, including the famous one on March 29, 1776, to warn John Hancock and Samuel Adams at Lexington that the British were on the march, rousing the Minutemen on the way; during the Revolution, designed and printed the first issue of Continental money and created the official seal of Mass. and the colonies; founded Revere Copper Company at Canton, Mass. (1801).

Reymont *(rā mônt),* **Wladyslaw Stanislaw** 1867–1925. Polish novelist. *b.* Kobiele Wielkie. Best known for the tetralogy *The Peasants* (1904–1909), for which he was awarded the Nobel Prize (1924). Other books include *Comedienne* (1896), *The Promised Land* (1899), *The Year 1794* (1914–19), *Before Sunrise* (1902), and *The Last Polish Parliament* (1917).

Reynolds *(rĕn əldz),* **Sir Joshua** 1723–92. English painter. *b.* Plympton. Visited Rome and studied painting (1749–52); returned to London and by 1760 had become the most famous painter of his time; suggested the establishment of the Literary Club, of which Johnson, Burke, Goldsmith, Garrick, and Sheridan became members; first president of Royal Academy; painter to the king (1784); among his two to three thousand works, the best known are *The Age of Innocence, Mrs. Siddons as the Tragic Muse, The Strawberry Girl, Simplicity, Garrick Between Tragedy and Comedy* and portraits of Johnson, Sterne, Goldsmith, Burke, Fox, and Gibbon.

Reza Shah Pahlavi *(rē zä shä päh lëv ē)* 1877–1944. Shah of Iran (1925–41). *b.* Mazenderan. An Iranian military officer of Cossack origin, he led a successful coup (1921), deposing the Qajar dynasty; prime minister (1923); Shah (1925); crowned (1926); changed name of Persia to Iran; modernized the country and instituted reforms; suspected of Nazi sympathies during World War II; forced to abdicate by British and Russian forces who, in a combined operation, occupied Iran (1941); exiled himself to South Africa, where he died (1944).

Rhodes *(rōdz),* **Cecil John** 1853–1902. British empire-builder. *b.* Bishop Stortford. Went to South Africa for health reasons (1870); made a fortune in Kimberley diamond fields; entered Cape House of Assembly (1881); consolidated diamond interests in the De Beers Company, which gained a monopoly on South African diamond production and became one of the world's richest companies (1888); annexed Bechuanaland to the colony (1884); by treaty with Lobengula, king of the Matabele, obtained vast territory north of Bechuanaland, later known as Rhodesia; founded British South Africa Company with himself as manager (1889); prime minister and virtual dictator of the colony (1890–96); instrumental in Cape-to-Cairo railway project; implicated in Jamieson Raid on Transvaal and forced to resign office (1896); began to develop Rhodesia; during Boer War, took part in siege of Kimberley (1899–1900); died before end of war; left bulk of fortune for the endowment of scholarships.

Ricardo *(rĭ kär dō),* **David** 1772–1823. English economist. *b.* London. Made a fortune in the stock market and retired at 25 to pursue the study of economics; published pamphlet *The High Price of Bullion: a Proof of the Depreciation of Bank-Notes* (1810); his most influential book, *Principles of Political Economy and Taxation* (1810), founded the classical school of economics and determined 19th-century economic thinking on rent, taxes, currency, profits, and trade; formulated the iron law of wages, by which wages cannot rise above the lowest level necessary for subsistence.

Richard *(rĭch ərd)* Name of three kings of England: RICHARD I Surname: COEUR DE LION (LION-HEARTED). 1157–99. King of England (1189–99). *b.* Oxford. Joined with brothers Henry and Geoffrey (1173–74) and Philip Augustus (1188–89) of France against father Henry II; succeeded to throne of England (1189), also becoming duke of Normandy and count of Anjou; took Crusader's vows and set out for Palestine (1190) on Third Crusade; conquered Cyprus

(1191), defeated Saracens at Arsuf, and captured Acre (1191) and Jaffa (1192); made truce with Saladin and returned to England; en route, imprisoned in Austria and Germany and released only on payment of heavy ransom; suppressed rebellion of brother John and defeated John's ally, Philip II of France, at Gisors (1195); mortally wounded while besieging the castle at Chaluz; celebrated in legend for his colorful deeds.

RICHARD II 1367–1400. King of England (1377–99). *b.* Bordeaux, France. Succeeded Edward III (1377); minor (until 1389); helped to suppress revolt of peasants under Wat Tyler (1381); after assuming control of government, ruled as a moderate constitutional monarch (until 1397); engaged in attempts to enlarge royal authority against baronial opposition led by earl of Gloucester; banished Gloucester and dukes of Hereford and Norfolk (1398–99); overthrown by Hereford forces, captured, deposed, imprisoned, and probably murdered (1400).

RICHARD III 1452–1485. King of England (1483–85). *b.* Fotheringhay. On death of Edward IV (1483), seized the young Edward V and proclaimed himself protector; assumed crown shortly after announcing deaths of Edward V and his brother Richard, duke of York (1483); put down revolt of duke of Buckingham; lost life at Bosworth Field in battle against Henry Tudor, earl of Richmond, who later became Henry VII (1485).

Richards *(rĭch ərdz),* **Dickinson Woodruff** 1895—. American surgeon. *b.* Orange, N.J. Professor of medicine at Columbia (from 1947); developed, with A. Cournand and W. Forssmann, technique of inserting catheter tube into heart; with them, awarded Nobel Prize in physiology and medicine (1956).

Richards, Theodore William 1868–1928. American chemist. *b.* Germantown, Pa. Professor at Harvard (from 1901); besides important investigations in thermochemistry, thermodynamics, and thermometry, accurately determined atomic weights of elements; awarded Nobel Prize in chemistry (1914).

Richardson *(rĭch ərd sən),* **Sir Owen Williams** 1879–1959. British physicist. *b.* Dewsbury. Professor of physics at Princeton (1906–14), at King's College, London (1914–24), and at Royal Society, (1924–44); conducted investigations in thermionics and described the phenomenon of emission of electricity from hot bodies, known as Richardson effect; awarded Nobel Prize in physics (1928). Author of *The Electron Theory of Matter* (1914), *The Emission of Electricity from Hot Bodies* (1916), and *Molecular Hydrogen and Its Spectrum* (1933).

Richardson, Samuel 1689–1761. English novelist. *b.* Derbyshire. Apprenticed to a printer and became official printer to House of Commons and master of Stationers Company; came to be regarded as master of the epistolary style and a polished letter-writer with *Familiar Letters* (1741); published *Pamela, or Virtue Rewarded* (1741), the first English domestic novel, in the form of a series of letters; encouraged by its popularity, wrote *Clarissa, or the History of a Young Lady* (7 vols., 1747–48) and *Sir*

Charles Grandison (1754); correspondence published in seven volumes.

Richelieu *(rē shə lyû),* **Cardinal** full name: ARMAND JEAN DU PLESSIS; known as ÉMINENCE ROUGE (Red Eminence). 1585–1642. French statesman and prelate. *b.* Paris. Consecrated bishop (1607); named cardinal (1622); gained favor of Marie de Médicis and was appointed chief minister of Louis XIII (1624–42); appointed prime minister (1629); principal achievements of his administration were suppression of Huguenots with the destruction of La Rochelle and Montauban (1627–28), and alliance with Protestants of the North under Gustavus Adolphus against Catholic Hapsburgs; assured French ascendancy in Europe by constant intrigues, subsidies, alliances, and treaties; declared war on Spain, ended by Treaty of Pyrenees (1659); survived plots against him, including those of Gaston d'Orleans (1626), Henri, duc de Montmorency (1632), and Cinq Mars (1642); foiled attempt of Marie de Médicis to dislodge him (1630); principal architect of French absolutism, enlarged powers of the crown at the expense of the nobles; a patron of literature, founded French Academy (1635) and published *Mémoires* and other books.

Richet *(rē shĕ),* **Charles Robert** 1850–1935. French physiologist. *b.* Paris. Professor at University of Paris (1887–1927); discovered and studied anaphylaxis, investigated serum therapy, and conducted research into physiology of nerves, muscles, and psychical phenomena; awarded Nobel Prize in physiology and medicine (1913). Author of *Les Poisons de l'Intelligence* (1877), *Dictionnaire de Physiologie* (4 vols., 1895–1906), and *L'Anaphylaxie* (1911).

Riemann *(rē män),* **Georg Friedrich Bernhard** 1826–66. German mathematician. *b.* Breselenz. Professor at Göttingen (from 1857); developed the theory of the functions of complex variables; represented them on coincident planes or sheets, known as Riemann's surfaces; founded non-Euclidean geometry, representing elliptical space; contributed to mathematical physics.

Riis *(rēs),* **Jacob August** 1849–1914. American journalist. *b.* Ribe, Denmark. Immigrated to U.S. (1870); served on staffs of *New York Tribune* and *New York Evening Sun* (1877–99); championing the cause of the poor and the dispossessed, gained national fame as a crusading reformer; founded the Jacob A. Riis Neighborhood House. Author of *How the Other Half Lives* (1890), *The Children of the Poor* (1892), *Out of Mulberry Street* (1898), *The Making of an American* (1901), *The Battle with the Slum* (1902), and *Children of the Tenement* (1903).

Riley *(rī lĭ),* **James Whitcomb** 1849–1916. American poet. *b.* Greenfield, Ind. Became known as the Hoosier Poet for homely philosophy and use of Indiana dialect and rural themes. Works include *The Old Swimmin' Hole and 'Leven More Poems* (1883), *Old Fashioned Roses* (1888), *Rhymes of Childhood* (1890), *An Old Sweetheart of Mine* (1902), *Afterwhiles* (1887), *Green Fields and Running Brooks* (1892),

Farm-Rhymes (1901), *Book of Joyous Children* (1902), *The Raggedy Man* (1907), *While the Heart Beats Young* (1906), *Morning* (1907), *Little Orphant Annie Book* (1908), *Songs of Summer* (1908), and *Old Times* (1915).

Rilke *(rĭl kĕ),* **Rainer Maria** 1875–1926. German poet. *b.* Prague, Czechoslovakia. Lived in Paris, Italy, Austria, Scandinavia, and Switzerland; works reflect a profound, lyrical, and mystical quest of a spiritual and aesthetic ideal; now acknowledged as greatest lyric poet of the 20th century on the strength of *Tale of Love and Death of Cornet Christophe Rilke* (1899), *Poems from the Book of Hours* (1899–1902), *Book of Pictures* (1902), *The Life of the Virgin Mary* (1913), *Duino Elegies* (1923), and *Sonnets to Orpheus* (1923); prose works include *The Notebook of Malte Laurids Brigge* (1909), *Stories of God* (1900), *Rodin* (1903), and *Letter to a Young Poet* (1929).

Rimbaud *(răN bō),* **Jean Nicolas Arthur** 1854–1891. French poet. *b.* Charleville. Published first poem at age 16; began wandering by running away to Paris at the invitation of Verlaine; two years of boisterous life ended when he was shot and wounded by Verlaine; during this period, wrote *Illuminations,* in verse and prose; reached peak of creativity (1873) with *Season in Hell;* bitter at its disappointing reception, burned his manuscripts and rejected literature; embarked on a career as soldier, trader, gunrunner, and slaver in Arabia, Egypt, and Ethiopia; contracted an incurable disease which led to amputation of leg and death; published *Lettres de Jean Arthur Rimbaud, Egypte, Arabie, Éthiopie* (1899); *Le Dormeur du Val*, and *Le Bateau Ivre*; macabre and hallucinatory quality of his poems makes him one of the greatest symbolists.

Rimski-Korsakov *(ryēm skû ĭ kŭr sə kôf),* **Nikolai Andreevich** 1844–1908. Russian composer. *b.* Tikhvin. Following family tradition entered navy; professor at St. Petersburg Conservatory (1871) and inspector of naval bands (1873–84); musical interest stimulated by friendship with Borodin, Moussorgsky, and Glazunov; before 1888, produced his orchestral triumphs *Sadko* (1867), *Capriccio Espagnol, Easter Festival,* and *Scheherazade;* produced great operas *The Maid of Pskov* (later *Ivan the Terrible,* 1873, 1892), *The Snow Maiden* (1882), *The Tsar Saltan* (1900), *The Invisible City of Kitesh* (1906), *Mlada* (1893), *La Nuit de Noël* (1895), *La Fiancée du Tsar* (1898), *Mozart and Salieri,* and *The Golden Cockerel* (1906). Author of *My Musical Life* (1942).

Ripley *(rĭp lĭ),* **George** 1802–80. American social reformer and critic. *b.* Greenfield, Mass. Unitarian minister (1826–41); left the ministry to found the Transcendentalist group with Emerson, Alcott, and Margaret Fuller; founded *The Dial* (1840); organized and promoted Brook Farm (1841–47), an experiment in communal living; editor of the *Harbinger* (1845–49), *Harper's New Monthly Magazine* (founded by him in 1850), and (with Charles A. Dana) *New American Cyclopedia* (16 vols., 1858–63).

Rivera *(rē vä rä),* **Diego** 1886–

1957. Mexican mural painter. *b.* Guanajuato. Toured Italy, Spain, and France (1907–21); helped to launch a Mexican government-sponsored project for the decoration of public buildings with frescoes; chose themes based on Mexican life and history; worked in the U.S. (1930–34); his great mural at Rockefeller Center, *Man at the Crossroads,* provoked national controversy because of its inclusion of a portrait of Lenin; as a proletarian artist, generally identified with Communist causes.

Rivera y Orbaneja *(rē vā rä ē ôr bä ne hä),* **Miguel Primo de** title: Marques de Estella. 1870–1930. Spanish dictator. *b.* Cádiz. Entered military academy (1884); served in the Philippines and in Morocco in Spanish-American War; captain general of Barcelona (1922); in bloodless revolution supported by King Alfonso XIII, dismissed civil government and established military directorate (1923–25) and civil dictatorship (1925–30); with the help of France, subdued Abd-el-Krim in Moroccan War (1926); forced to resign after losing support of army (1930); died in exile in Paris. His son José Antonio Primo de Rivera, (1903–36), Spanish ideologue and founder of the Falange, was executed in Civil War (1936).

Robbins *(rŏb ĭnz),* **Frederick Chapman** 1916–. American physician. *b.* Auburn, Ala. Shared, with J. F. Enders and T. H. Weller, Nobel Prize in physiology and medicine (1954) for successfully growing poliomyelitis virus in tissue culture.

Robert VIII *(rŏb ərt)* also Robert Bruce; Robert the Bruce. 1274–1329. King and liberator of Scotland. *b.* Lochmaben or Turnberry or in Essex. As earl of Carrick, swore fealty to Edward I at Berwick (1296); took oath of homage to English king at Carlisle (1297); joined Wallace in revolt against English, but made peace by Capitulation of Irvine; rose again against Edward (1298, 1306); crowned king at Scone (1306); defeated by English army under Earl of Pembroke and driven to refuge in Rathlin off the north coast of Ireland; returned to recover kingdom (1307) after defeating English at Loudon Hill; completed expulsion of English from Scotland through memorable victory at Bannockburn (1314); went to Ireland and defeated Anglo-Irish at Slane (1317); subdued Hebrides (1316); repeatedly invaded England until Treaty of Northampton (1328) recognized the independence of Scotland and Bruce's title to the throne; died of leprosy; interred in Abbey of Dunfermline.

Roberts *(rŏb ərts),* **Frederick Sleigh** title: Earl Roberts of Kandahar, Pretoria, and Waterford. 1832–1914. British general. *b.* Kanpur, India. Entered British Indian army (1851); participated in suppression of Indian Mutiny (1857–58); won Victoria Cross for role in relief of Lucknow, siege of Delhi, and battle of Kanpur; served in Abyssinian and Lushai campaigns; as commander of British forces in Second Afghan War, defeated the Afghans at Charasia (1879) and took Kabul; made celebrated march from Kabul to Kandahar in three weeks with 10,000 men, routing Ayub Khan; commander in chief of India

(1885–93); field marshal and commander in chief of Ireland (1895); commander in chief of British forces in Boer War (1899–1900); raised sieges of Kimberley and Ladysmith, annexed Orange Free State and Pretoria, occupied Transvaal, captured Piet Cronjé, took Bloemfontein, and relieved Mafeking; commander in chief of British Army (1900–1904). Author of *The Rise of Wellington* (1895) and *Forty-One Years in India* (1897).

Robespierre *(rōbz pēr),* **Maximilien François Marie Isidore de** known as THE INCORRUPTIBLE. 1758–94. French revolutionary. *b.* Arras. Elected to States-General (1789), where he became a leader of the extreme left in the Constituent Assembly; appointed public accuser and, with Pétion de Villeneuve, nicknamed Incorruptible Patriots (1791); leader of Jacobin Club (1791–92); elected deputy to National Convention (1792), where he sat with the Montagnards and Danton against Girondists; demanded execution of Louis XVI; after destroying the Girondists, elected to Committee of Public Safety (1793); as its leader and virtual dictator, unleashed the Reign of Terror, sending Hébert, Danton, Desmoulins, and hundreds of others to the guillotine; with Georges Couthon and Louis de Saint-Just as his lieutenants, assumed complete control of the Revolutionary Tribunal, which was made the supreme body in the land by law of 22 Prairial; instituted worship of the Supreme Being (1794); his excesses united his opponents to rally against him in self-defense; arrested by the Convention (9 Thermidor) and, after a summary trial, guillotined with 21 followers.

Robinson *(rŏb ən sən),* **Edwin Arlington** 1869–1935. American poet. *b.* Head Tide, Me. Won Pulitzer Prize for poetry for *Collected Poems* (1921), *The Man Who Died Twice* (1924), and *Tristram* (1927); work marked by wry humor, irony, and melancholy at the passing scene. Other volumes of verse include *The Torrent and the Night Before* (1896), *The Children of the Night* (1897), *The Town Down the River* (1910), *The Man Against the Sky* (1916), *Lancelot* (1920), *Avon's Harvest* (1921), *Dionysius in Doubt* (1925), *Sonnets* (1928), *Matthias at the Door* (1931), *Nicodemus* (1932), and *King Jasper* (1935); also wrote the plays *Van Zorn* (1914) and *The Porcupine* (1915).

Robinson, Sir Robert 1886–1975. British chemist. *b.* Chesterfield. Professor of organic chemistry at Sydney (1912–15), and later at Liverpool, St. Andrews, Manchester, London, and Oxford (1930–55); noted for research on plant pigments, alkaloids, and penicillin; awarded Nobel Prize in chemistry (1947).

Rochambeau *(rô shäN bō),* **Comte de** title of JEAN BAPTISTE DONATIEN DE VIMEUR 1725–1807. French soldier. *b.* Vendôme. Entered army (1742); served with distinction in War of Austrian Succession and Seven Years' War; commander of 6000 men sent to aid colonists in American Revolution (1780); landed at Newport, R.I., and joined Washington at White Plains, N.Y.; rendered effective help in Yorktown campaign, leading to capitulation of Cornwallis (1781); created marshal during French Revolution (1791), but imprisoned during Reign of Terror; served under Napoleon. Author of *Mémoires* (1809).

Rockefeller *(rŏk ə fĕl ər),* **John Davison** 1839–1937. American industrialist and philanthropist. *b.* Richford, N.Y. Entered oil business as member of Clark and Andrews (1861), later Rockefeller, Andrews, and Flagler (1867); with brother WILLIAM (1841–1922), organized Standard Oil Company (1870); through establishment of Standard Oil Trust Agreement, secured near-monopoly on oil production and sales (1882); trust dissolved by court decree (1892), and its successor, Standard Oil of New Jersey, dissolved under Sherman Anti-Trust Act (1911); retired (1911); established charitable trusts including the Rockefeller Foundation, to which he left the bulk of his wealth. His son JOHN DAVISON (1874–1960), American philanthropist, continued his father's philanthropic programs; built Rockefeller Center in New York City and donated the land for the United Nations Building. His grandson JOHN DAVISON (1906–78), American philanthropist, was noted for philanthropic support of population control programs and Asian art. His grandson NELSON ALDRICH (1908–79), American statesman, was governor of N.Y. (1959–73) and vice-president of U.S. (1974–77).

Rockingham *(rŏk ĭng əm),* **Marquis of** title of CHARLES WATSON-WENTWORTH. 1730–82. English statesman. As leader of Whig party, formed first ministry (1765); obtained repeal of Stamp Act; prime minister (1782); consistently opposed royal policy toward American colonies.

Rodin *(rô dăN),* **François Auguste René** 1840–1917. French sculptor. *b.* Paris. Beginning with *The Broken Nose* (1864), aroused controversy with tradition-breaking sculptures; visited Italy (1875); in the Salon of 1877, exhibited *The Age of Bronze*, which was so naturalistic that he was accused of making a cast from life; published *The Cathedrals of France* (1914), revealing Gothic influences on his work. Principal sculptures include *The Kiss, The Thinker, Saint Jean Baptiste, Porte de l'Enfer, Ugolin, Les Bourgeois de Calais, Creation of Man, The Hand of God, L'Homme Qui Marche,* and busts of Laurence, Hugo, Proust, Shaw, and Mahler.

Roebling *(rōb lĭng),* **John Augustus** 1806–69. American engineer. *b.* Mühlhausen, Germany. Immigrated to U.S. (1831); founded factory for manufacturing wire ropes (1841); pioneered in the construction of bridges using wire ropes; principal projects include bridges over the Niagara and over the Ohio at Cincinnati; his bridge over the East River, now known as the Brooklyn Bridge, was completed by his son, WASHINGTON AUGUSTUS (1837–1926).

Roentgen *(rûnt gən),* **Wilhelm Conrad** also RONTGEN. 1845–1923. German physicist. *b.* Lennep, Prussia. Professor at Strasbourg, Giessen, Würzburg, and Munich; discovered electromagnetic rays called X-rays, or Roentgen rays (1895); awarded Nobel Prize in physics (1901); other contributions include specific heat of gases, conductivity of crystals, and polarized light.

Roethke *(rĕt kē),* **Theodore** 1908–63. American poet. *b.* Saginaw, Mich. Published his first book of poems *The Waking* (1941); followed with *Words for the Wind* (1957) and *Collected Poems* (1966); won Pulitzer Prize for poetry (1954) and National Book Award (1965); noted for his surrealistic images and lyric simplicity.

Rogers *(rŏj ərz),* **Will** full name, WILLIAM PENN ADAIR ROGERS 1879–1935. American humorist and showman. *b.* Oologah, Okla. Began stage career with a vaudeville lasso act later combined with a humorous monologue, thus receiving the nickname Cowboy Philosopher; successful with Ziegfeld Follies (from 1914) and starred in motion pictures; wrote a nationally syndicated newspaper column, giving free rein to his salty, homespun philosophy (from 1926); produced similar radio broadcasts. Author of *The Cowboy Philosopher on Prohibition* (1919), *What We Laugh At* (1920), *The Illiterate Digest* (1924), *There's Not a Bathing Suit in Russia* (1927), and *Will Rogers's Political Follies* (1929).

Rolland *(rô läN),* **Romain** 1866–1944. French writer. *b.* Clamecy. Teacher at Superior Normal School in Paris (1891–1912); a pacifist, opposed French participation in World War I and lived in self-exile in Switzerland; espoused many social and political causes, including Gandhism and Communism. Best known as author of *Jean Christophe* (10 vols., 1904–12), *The Soul Enchanted* (7 vols., 1922–33), *The Wolves* (1937), *Danton* (1900), *The Fourteenth of July* (1918), *The Game of Love and Death* (1926), *Beethoven* (1903), *Michel-Ange* (1905), *Vie de Tolstoi* (1911), and *Mahatma Gandhi* (1926); awarded Nobel Prize for literature (1915).

Romains *(rô mäN),* **Jules** pseudonym of LOUIS FARIGOULE. 1885-1972. French writer. *b.* Saint-Julien Chapteuil. In plays, novels, and poems, developed theory of unanimism, which holds that group principles are more important than individual ones. Principal works include *Le Bourg Régénéré* (1906), *Death of a Nobody* (1914), *Men of Good Will* (27 vols., 1932–47), *L'Armée dans le Ville* (1911), *Cromedeyre-le-Vieil* (1920), *Knock, ou le Triomphe de la Médicine* (1923), *Le Mariage de M. Trouhadec* (1925), *Le Dictateur* (1926), *Le Roi Masqué* (1931), *L'Âme des Hommes* (1904), *Odes et Prières* (1913, and *Chants des Dix Années, 1914–1924* (1928).

Romanes *(rō mä nēz),* **George John** 1848–94. British biologist. *b.* Kingston, Canada. Fullerian professor of physiology in London (from 1889); associate of Darwin and developer of theory of evolution; established Romanes Lectures at Oxford (1891). Works include *Jellyfish, Starfish, and Sea Urchins* (1885), *Animal Intelligence* (1881), *Mental Evolution in Man* (1888), *Examination of Weismannism* (1892), and *The Philosophy of Natural History Before and After Darwin* (1888).

Romano *(rō mä nō),* **Giulio** real name: GIULIO DI PIETRO DI FILIPPO DE'GIANUZZI. 1499–1546. Italian painter and architect. *b.* Rome.

Pupil and successor of Raphael; architect to duke of Mantua (1524), for whom he designed and built the ducal palace; built church of San Benedetto and Palazzo del Tè, both at Mantua; besides the *Madonna,* painted frescoes in the Vatican, *Apollo and the Muses* in the Pitti Palace, and *Story of Psyche* and *Fall of Titans* at Mantua.

Rommel *(rōm əl),* **Erwin** called THE DESERT FOX. 1891–1944. German general. *b.* Heidenheim. Fought in World War I; joined Nazi party and participated in Austrian, Sudetenland, and Prague occupations; commanded armored division in invasion of France (1940) with such spectacular success that he was named commander of Afrika Korps; improvised brilliant military tactics that drove British army to El Alamein (1942); field marshal; halted at El Alamein, where he suffered the first of a series of reverses that forced him out of Africa and his command; commander during Allied invasion of France; died, perhaps by own hand.

Ronsard *(rôN sàr),* **Pierre de** 1524–85. French poet. *b.* Vendôme. Gave up life at French court on becoming deaf (1542); began to study and write; joined scholars, including Jean Antoine Baïf, in study of Greek and French (1542–49); began publishing great poems to demonstrate the power, nobility, and refinement of French language, such as *Odes* (1550), *Amours de Cassandre* (1552), *Hymnes* (1555–56), *Bocage* (1554), *Élégies Mascarades, et Bergeries* (1565), and *La Françiade,* unfinished at death; founded the Pléiade, a group of poets devoted to the regeneration of French as a literary language; court poet to Charles IX; wrote two prose works deploring the Wars of Religion: *Discours des Misères de ce Temps* and *Remonstrances au Peuple de France* (1582).

Roosevelt *(rō zə vĕlt),* **Franklin Delano** 1882–1945. 32nd president of U.S. (1933–45). *b.* Hyde Park, N.Y. Entered politics as a Democratic state senator (1910–13); assistant secretary of the navy under Wilson (1913–20); Democratic vice-presidential candidate (1920); stricken with infantile paralysis (1921), but recovered partial use of legs; governor of N.Y. (1929–33); elected president (1932) by defeating incumbent Herbert Hoover on a platform of a "New Deal" for the "forgotten man"; set stage for national recovery during the Hundred Days by vigorously pushing through legislation that brought the economy firmly under the control of the federal government; created farm subsidies; established Securities and Exchange Commission, Civilian Conservation Corps, Tennessee Valley Authority, National Recovery Administration, and Works Projects Administration; reelected three times; defeated in attempt to reorganize Supreme Court and to purge opponents of New Deal in Congress (1940); with entry of U.S. into Second World War, turned energies as commander in chief to victory; with Winston Churchill, issued the eight-point Atlantic Charter (1941); took part in wartime conferences at Casablanca (1943), Cairo (1943), Tehran (1943), and Yalta (1945);

died of a stroke at Warm Springs, Ga. His wife ANNA ELEANOR (1884–1962), was also prominent in public affairs; U.S. representative to U.N. General Assembly (1945). Author of *This is My Story* (1937), *My Days* (1938), and *This I Remember* (1949).

Roosevelt, Theodore 1858–1919. 26th president of U.S. (1901–1909). *b.* New York, N.Y. Entered politics as a Republican in the N.Y. state legislature (1882–84); civil service commissioner (1889–1895); president of New York Board of Police Commissioners (1895–97); assistant secretary of the navy (1897–98); resigned to organize the Rough Riders, a cavalry regiment that he led to Cuba during Spanish-American War; on return, elected governor of N.Y. (1899–1900); as McKinley's running mate, elected vice-president (1900); on McKinley's assassination, succeeded to the presidency (1901); a progressive champion of the little man, denounced the malefactors of great wealth; successfully introduced some social responsibility into American business, broke up monopolies, and regulated the trusts; policies earned him antagonism of right-wing Republicans; as a conservationist, remembered for his efforts for public control over natural resources and appointment of a conservation commission, headed by Gifford Pinchot; in foreign affairs, secured the Panama Canal Zone for U.S.; advocated the "big stick" policy toward Latin America, claiming powers of intervention in the affairs of nations south of the border; received Nobel Peace Prize (1906) for role in bringing about Peace of Portsmouth, ending Russo-Japanese War; introduced "dollar diplomacy" in the Caribbean, built up U.S. Navy, and established the army general staff; on leaving office (1909), went on an African tour, but returned (1912) to seek Republican nomination for president; on failing to receive it, formed the Progressive (Bull Moose) party and ran as its presidential candidate; defeated by Wilson; explored Brazil (1914). Author of books on hunting and politics, including *The Winning of the West* (4 vols., 1889–96), *Life of Oliver Cromwell* (1900), *The Strenuous Life* (1900), *Theodore Roosevelt: An Autobiography* (1913), and *Through the Brazilian Wilderness* (1914).

Root *(rōōt),* **Elihu** 1845–1937. American statesman. *b.* Clinton, N.Y. Secretary of war (1899–1904); reorganized war department and established governments in territories acquired from Spain; as secretary of state (1905–1909), attempted to shore up relations with Latin America and Japan; senator (1909–15); member of Hague Tribunal (1910); president of Carnegie Endowment for International Peace (from 1910); awarded Nobel Peace Prize (1912); U.S. commissioner plenipotentiary at Washington Conference on Limitation of Armaments (1921–22). Author of *Military and Colonial Policy of the United States, Russia and the United States,* and *Latin America and the United States.*

Rosebery *(rōz bər ĭ),* **Earl of** title of ARCHIBALD PHILIP PRIMROSE; also EARL OF MIDLOTHIAN. 1847–1929. British statesman. Held cabinet posts under Gladstone, principally foreign secretary (1886, 1892–94); succeeded Gladstone as prime minister (1894); resigned (1895); leader of Liberal opposition (1895–96); headed imperialist wing within Liberal party. Author of *William Pitt* (1891), *Sir Robert Peel* (1899), *Oliver Cromwell* (1900), *Lord Randolph Churchill* (1906), and *Lord Chatham* (1910).

Ross *(rôs)*, **Sir James Clark** 1800–1862. British polar explorer. *b.* London. With uncle SIR JOHN ROSS (1777–1856), English admiral, went on two arctic expeditions and on four with W. E. Parry (1819–27); discovered north magnetic pole (1831); commanded *Erebus* and *Terror* in Antarctic expedition (1839) and the *Enterprise* in search of Sir John Franklin (1848); discovered Victoria Land, Ross Sea, Ross Island, and other parts of Antarctica. Published *Voyage of Discovery and Research to Southern and Antarctic Regions* (1847).

Ross, Sir Ronald 1857–1932. British physician. *b.* Almora, India. In Indian Medical Service (1881–99); investigated malaria and the life cycle of the anopheles mosquito, the malarial parasite; on return to England, professor of tropical medicine, at Liverpool (1902–12); awarded the Nobel Prize in physiology and medicine (1902) for studies in malaria. Author of *Memoirs* (1923), *The Prevention of Malaria* (1910), and other books.

Rossetti *(rə sĕt ĭ)*, **Dante Gabriel** 1828–82. English painter and poet. *b.* London. With Holman Hunt, Thomas Woolner and others, founded Pre-Raphaelite Brotherhood, whose purpose was to resist the spirit of modernism in art and to return to the purity and simplicity of art in the period before Raphael (1850); painted some of the best representative works in *The Girlhood of Mary Virgin, Beata Beatrix, Lady Lilith, The Beloved, The Annunciation, The Infant Christ adored by a Shepherd and a King, Monna Vanna, Pandora, Proserpina in Hades, La Ghirlandata, Dante's Dream, My Sister's Sleep*, and *The Portrait;* published early poetical works in *The Germ;* among poems collected in *Poems* (1870) and *Ballads and Sonnets* (1881) are "The House of Life," "The Blessed Damozel," "Sister Helen," "Rose Mary," "The White Ship," and "The King's Tragedy." His sister CHRISTINA GEORGINA (1830–94), English poet, *b.* London, wrote a number of intensely religious works; spent last years in seclusion afflicted by serious illnss. Works include *Goblin Market* (1862), *The Prince's Progress* (1866), *Sing-Song, a Nursery Rhyme Book* (1872), *A Pageant and Other Poems* (1881), *Time Flies* (1885), *New Poems* (1896), *Commonplace and Other Stories* (1870), and *The Face of the Deep* (1892).

Rossini *(rəs sē nĭ)*, **Gioacchino Antonio** 1792–1868. Italian composer. *b.* Pesaro. First musical work, a cantata, performed in public (1808); director of San Carlo and Del Fondo theaters in Naples (1815); wrote 20 operas (1815–25); visited Vienna, London, and Paris, and served as director of Théâtre Italien in Paris for 18 months; lived in Bologna (1836–47) and Florence

(1847–55), returning to Paris (1855–68). Among his 39 operas are *Tancredi* (1813), *Elisabetta* (1815), *The Barber of Seville* (1816), *Otello* (1816), *La Cenerentola* (1817), *La Gazza Ladra* (1817), *Armida* (1817), *La Donna del Lago* (1819), *Maometta Secondo* (1820), *Zelmira* (1821), *Semiramide* (1823), *Il Califfo di Bagdad* (1818), and *William Tell* (1829); wrote *Mosè in Egitto* (1818) and *Stabat Mater* (1841).

Rostand *(rôs täN),* **Edmond** 1868–1918. French poet and dramatist. *b.* Marseilles. Best known for *Les Romanesques* (1894), *La Princesse Lointaine* (1895), *La Samaritaine* (1897), *Cyrano de Bergerac* (1898), *L'Aiglon* (1900), *Chantecler* (1910), *Les Mots* (1905), *Un Soir à Hernani* (1902), *Le Bois Sacré* (1909), and *Les Musardises* (1890).

Rothschild *(rōt shīlt; rôth(s) chīld)* Family of German Jewish financiers founded by Meyer Amschel 1743–1812. *b.* Frankfurt, Germany. Trained as a rabbi but turned to money-lending, becoming financial advisor of the landgrave of Hesse; made a fortune during Napoleonic Wars as agent for the British government's financial transactions on the Continent; of his five sons, the most successful were Nathan Meyer, (1777–1836), founder of the British branch, and James (1792–1868), founder of the Paris branch; their descendants still control one of the largest financial empires in Europe.

Rouault *(rwō),* **Georges** 1871–1958. French painter. *b.* Paris. Early training in stained glass shows in all his work, which glows with rich colors outlined in black; themes are often religious and display an intense concern with the suffering and injustice of common life. Among his best-known works are *Christ, The Clown, The Judges, The Girls, Misère et Guerre, Baptism of Christ, The Prodigal Child, Self-Portrait, The Suburbs, Intimate Memories, Circus, Passion,* and *Autumn.*

Rous *(rous),* **Francis Peyton** 1879–1970. American pathologist. *b.* Baltimore, Md. Professor (1920–45) of Rockefeller Institute for Medical Research; discovered (1910) a virus to induce malignant tumors in hens, for which he was awarded Nobel Prize (1966) in physiology and medicine, with C. B. Huggins.

Rousseau *(rōō sō),* **Henri** also known as Le Douanier. 1844–1910. French painter. *b.* Laval. Self-trained as a painter; developed a primitive style and used exotic and vivid colors to paint jungles and everyday scenes. Works include *The Artillery Battery, Monkeys in the Orange Trees, Jungle with a Lion, The Dream, The Muse and the Poet, Exotic Landscape, Banks of the Oise, La Charmeuse de Serpents, Sleeping Gipsy,* and *The Cascade.*

Rousseau, Jean Jacques 1712–78. French philosopher. *b.* Geneva, Switzerland. Orphaned in childhood; began a wandering life at age 14; renounced Calvinism for Catholicism (1728); lived with notorious Mme. Louise Éléanore de Warens at Annecy and at Chambéry (1729–41); lived in Paris and Geneva (until 1766), taking a mistress and fathering five illegitimate children whom he placed in a foundlings home; gained fame by winning (1754) first prize in a competition sponsored by the Academy of Dijon; works condemned by Parliament of Paris (1762) and Genevan Consistory for their antimonarchical and antireligious bias; secured protection of Frederick the Great at Neuchâtel; settled in England at the invitation of David Hume (1766); quarreled with Hume and returned to France (1767); lived last years in partial insanity and paranoia; philosophical reputation based on a number of unorthodox ideas, collectively known as Rousseauism. Principal works include *Discours sur les Arts et Sciences* (1750), *Discours sur l'Origine de l'Inégalite Parmi les Hommes* (1755), *Julie, ou la Nouvelle Héloïse* (1761), *Le Contrat Social* (1762), *Émile, ou Traité de l'Education* (1762), *Confessions* (1781), *Dialogues, Rêveries du Promeneur Solitaire* (1782); also wrote the operetta *Le Devin du Village* (1752); theories influential in providing ideological framework of French Revolution; among his seminal ideas are the noble savage, social contract, and general will; considered the father of romanticism; although most of his political and pedagogical theories proved impractical in application, his reputation has not diminished.

Roux *(rōō),* **Pierre Paul Émile** 1853–1933. French bacteriologist. *b.* Confolens. Joined Pasteur Institute (1888) and became its director (1904–18); discovered antitoxic method of treating diphtheria (1894); conducted important investigations of syphilis, anthrax, tetanus, cholera, tuberculosis, and hydrophobia; discovered pneumococcus bacteria.

Royce *(rois),* **Josiah** 1855–1916. American philosopher. *b.* Grass Valley, Calif. Professor at Harvard (from 1892); developed idealistic philosophy that stressed individuality. Author of *The Spirit of Modern Philosophy* (1892), *The Conception of God* (1897), *Studies of Good and Evil* (1898), *The World and the Individual* (1899), *The Conception of Immortality* (1900), *Herbert Spencer* (1904), *Philosophy of Loyalty* (1908), *Sources of Religious Insight* (1911), *The Problem of Christianity* (1913), and *The Hope of the Great Community* (1916).

Rubens *(rōō bənz),* **Peter Paul** 1577–1640. Flemish painter. *b.* Siegen, Germany. After Jesuit education at Antwerp, went to Italy (1600), service of Vincenzo Gonzaga, duke of Mantua (until 1608); settled in Antwerp and became a prosperous painter, employing a number of assistants; invited to Paris by Marie de Médicis to decorate the Luxembourg, and commissioned to paint 24 paintings on her life; on diplomatic mission to Philip IV of Spain at Madrid (1628) met Velásquez and painted the royal family; sent to England as envoy to Charles I, who knighted him; returned to Antwerp (1630); a prolific painter, he produced more than 2000 works, of which the most noble are *Descent from the Cross, Venus and Adonis, Elevation of the Cross, Rape of the Sabines, The Fall of the Damned, Baptism of Christ, Adoration of the Magi, The Assumption of the Virgin, Helen Fourmont and Her Children, Peace and War, St. George, Battle of the Amazons, The Crucifixion of St. Peter,* and *The Castle of Steen.*

Rubinstein *(ro͞o bən stīn),* **Artur** 1886–. American pianist. *b.* Lodz, Poland. Made his first public appearance at age 12; lived in the U.S. after World War II; one of best known and most beloved concert pianists; among his compositions are piano pieces and chamber music.

Runeberg *(ro͞o nə băr K),* **Johan Ludvig** 1804–77. Finnish poet. *b.* Pietarsaari. Published first volume of poems (1830); his epic *The Elk-Hunters* published (1832), followed by *Hanna* (1836), *Christmas Eve* (1841), *Nadeschda* (1841), *King Fjalar* (1844), and *Ensign Stål's Stories* (1848); founded *Helsingfors Morganblad*, to which he contributed literary criticism; wrote *Can't* (1862) and *The Kings at Salamis* (1863); edited the *Psalm Book* for the Lutheran Church; considered national poet of Finland.

Ruskin *(rŭs kĭn),* **John** 1819–1900. English critic and man of letters. *b.* London. Developed a comprehensive philosophy of art in *Modern Painters* (4 vols., 1843), *Seven Lamps of Architecture* (1849), and *Stones of Venice* (3 vols., 1851–53); gained authority as a cultural arbiter, publishing books on art and nature, including *The Elements of Drawing* (1857), *The Elements of Perspective* (1859), *The Queen of the Air* (1869), *The Laws of Fesole* (1877–78), *Proserpina* (1875–86), *Love's Meinie* (1873–78), *Deucalion* (1875–83), *St. Mark's Rest: The History of Venice* (1877–84), *Mornings in Florence* (1875–77), and *The Bible of Amiens* (1880–85); professor of fine arts at Oxford (1869–79, 1883–84); delivered lectures on art, later published; turned his attention to social and economic reform, issuing manifestoes calling for radical changes in society (from 1860); a critic of squalor, ugliness, and injustice, began to espouse a form of Christian communism. Works in this period are *A Joy Forever* (1880), *The Two Paths* (1859), *Unto This Last* (1860–62), *Munera Pulveris* (1872), *Sesame and Lilies* (1875), *The Ethics of the Dust* (1866), *The Crown of Wild Olive* (1866), *Time and Tide* (1867), *Fors Clavigera* (1871–84); spent much of his own fortune in philanthropy; published autobiography *Praeterita* (24 parts, 1886–88).

Russell *(rŭs əl),* **Bertrand Arthur William** title: 3rd Earl Russell. 1872–1970. English philosopher and mathematician. *b.* Ravenscroft. Elected fellow of Trinity College (1895) and pursued studies in mathematical logic: published *Principles of Mathematics* (1903), *Principia Mathematica* (with A.N. Whitehead, 1910–13), and *Introduction to Mathematical Philosophy* (1919); dismissed from fellowship and imprisoned for pacifist beliefs during World War I; extended intellectual inquiry into general philosophy and science with *Philosophical Essays* (1910), *The Problems of Philosophy* (1911), *Our Knowledge of the External World* (1914), *Mysticism and Logic* (1918), *The Analysis of Mind* (1921), *The Prospects of Industrial Civilization* (1923), *The A B C of Relativity* (1925), *An Inquiry Into Meaning and Truth* (1940), *A History of Western Philosophy* (1945), and *Why I Am Not a Christian* (1957); briefly flirted with Communism but later opposed it with *Theory and Practice of Bolshevism* (1919); stated ideas on education and morals in *On Education* (1926), *Education and the Social Order* (1932), *Marriage and Morals* (1932), *The Conquest of Happiness* (1930), renounced pacifism in *In Praise of Idleness* (1936), but later became opponent of nuclear armament and American military hegemony; awarded Nobel Prize in literature (1950); as a passionate skeptic, opposed all religions; published the autobiographical *Portraits from Memory* (1956), *My Philosophical Development* (1959), and *Autobiography* (2 vols., 1967–68).

Russell, George William Pseudonym: AE. 1867–1935. Irish writer. *b.* Lurgan. Studied art at Dublin; converted to theosophy through Yeats and gave up painting; lectured extensively on Irish nationalism and economics, and founded agricultural societies; edited *The Irish Homestead* (1904–23) and *The Irish Statesman* (1923–30); writings consist of poems *Homeward: Songs by the Way* (1894), *The Earth Breath* (1897), *The Divine Vision* (1904), *New Poems* (1904), *Gods of War* (1915), *Midsummer Eve* (1928), *Vale* (1931), *House of the Titans (1934); religious and mystical works such as The Candle of Vision* (1918); the play *Deirdre* (1907); and works on Irish nationalism and literature.

Russell, Lord John also EARL RUSSELL OF KINGSTON; VISCOUNT AMBERLEY. 1792–1878. English statesman. *b.* London. Entered Parliament (1813); joined Grey's ministry as paymaster of the forces (1830); one of the framers of Reform Bill (1831), securing its passage (1832); leader of Whig party (1834); home secretary (1835–39) and colonial secretary (1839–41); on the fall of Peel, prime minister (1846–52); resigned office because of Palmerston's opposition; foreign secretary under Aberdeen (1852–53); president of council (1854–55); out of office (1855–59), having become unpopular over mismanagement of Crimean War and bungling at Congress of Vienna (1855); foreign secretary (1861); supported Italian unity and kept Britain out of American Civil War; on death of Palmerston, prime minister (1865–66), but forced out of office on defeat of new reform bill. Author of *Life and Times of Fox* (1859–67), *Recollections and Suggestions* (1875), and other books.

Rutherford *(rŭth ər fərd),* **Ernest** title: BARON RUTHERFORD OF NELSON. 1871–1937. British scientist. *b.* Nelson, New Zealand. Went to England on a scholarship, studying at Cambridge; professor at McGill University, Montreal (1898–1907) and Manchester (1907–19); succeeded J.J. Thomson as director of Cavendish Laboratory, Cambridge (from 1919); awarded Nobel Prize in chemistry (1908) for studies in radioactivity; with Frederick Soddy, developed theory of radioactive decay, disproving the classical law of conservation of matter; discovered alpha particles (1904), protons (1920), and predicted existence of neutrons (1920); put forward revolutionary theory that the atom is divisible and that it consists of a concentrated-mass nucleus surrounded by planetary electrons; contributed to structural model of the atom, known as Rutherford-Bohr atom; obtained the first nuclear reaction by bombarding hydrogen atoms with alpha-rays. Published over 150 papers and books including *The Newer Alchemy* (1937), *Radioactivity* (1904), *Radioactive Transformations* (1906), and *Radioactive Substances and Their Radiations* (1912).

Ruzicka *(rōō zhēch kä),* **Leopold** 1887–1976. Swiss chemist. *b.* Bukovar, Yugoslavia. Professor of chemistry at Utrecht (1926) and Zurich (1929); work on steroids includes synthesis of musk and the establishment of the structure and synthesis of sex hormones androsterone and testosterone; with A.F.J. Butenandt, received Nobel Prize in chemistry (1939).

S

Saadi *(sä dē)* also SADI; original name: MUSLIH-UD DIN. c1184–c1291. Persian poet. *b.* Shiraz. Celebrated in Islamic annals as a saint and poet; author of writings in prose and verse, in Persian, Hindustani, and Arabic; the best known are *Gulistan, Diwan, Pendnameh,* and *Bustan.*

Saarinen *(sä rĭ nĕn),* **Gottlieb Eliel** 1873–1950. Finnish architect. *b.* Helsinki. Immigrated to U.S. (c1927). Principal buildings include the national museum in Helsinki, the Cranbrook School, and the Tabernacle Church in Columbus, Ind.. His son EERO (1910–61), American architect, designed the TWA terminal at Kennedy Airport and the CBS building in New York, U.S. embassy buildings in London and Oslo, General Motors Technical Center in Warren, Mich., Morse and Style colleges at Yale, and the opening of the West Arch in St. Louis, Mo. Wrote *Eero Saarinen on His Work* (1963).

Saavedra Lamas *(sä ä vā thrä lä mäs),* **Carlos** 1880–1959. Argentine statesman. *b.* Buenos Aires. Minister of foreign affairs (from 1932); president of League of Nations Assembly (1938); awarded Nobel Peace Prize (1936) for role in negotiations leading to the end of the Chaco War between Paraguay and Bolivia.

Sabatier *(sȧ bȧ tyā),* **Paul** 1854–1941. French chemist. *b.* Carcassonne. Professor at Toulouse (from 1882); studied catalysis and developed a process for the catalytic hydrogenation of oils; with Victor Grignard, shared Nobel Prize in chemistry (1912).

Sabatini *(sä bä tē nē),* **Rafael** 1875–1950. Italian writer. *b.* Jesi. Best known as the author of novels of high adventure and historical romance such as *The Tavern Knight* (1904), *Bardleys the Magnificent* (1906), *The Sea Hawk* (1915), *Scaramouche* (1921), *Captain Blood* (1922), and *The Lost King* (1937).

Sabbatai Zevi *(sə băt ə ī tsə vē)* also **SHABBETHAI. 1626–76. Jewish mys-**

tic. *b.* Smyrna, Turkey. Proclaimed himself the messiah and founded the Sabbatean sect (1648); gained a large following among Jews in Eastern Europe; arrived in Constantinople (1666), but was arrested by Sultan Mohammed IV, given the choice of conversion to Islam or death, chose Islam.

Sachs *(zäks),* **Hans** 1494–1576. German meistersinger. *b.* Nürnberg. Perfected the art of meistersong during years of wandering through Germany as a journeyman shoemaker; settled in Nürnberg (1515); wrote over 6000 works (1514–67), including over 4000 meistersongs, 200 dramas, 1500 narrative fables, and 7 prose dialogues; an adherent of Luther, wrote works advancing the Protestant cause, including *Wittenbergisch Nachtigall* (1523); appears as the central figure in Wagner's opera *Die Meistersinger von Nürnberg.*

Sachs *(săks),* **Nelly** 1891–1970. German poet. *b.* Berlin. Fled Nazi Germany (1940) and found asylum in Sweden. Author of *Legends and Tales* (1921), *Eclipse of the Stars* (1949), *Flight and Metamorphosis* (1959), and other lyrical and dramatic works; with S.Y. Agnon, awarded Nobel Prize in literature (1966).

Sade *(säd),* **Comte Donatien Alphonse François de** called MARQUIS DE SADE. 1740–1814. French soldier. *b.* Paris. Imprisoned for many years at Vincennes and in the Bastille for unnatural sexual practices; died in the insane asylum at Charenton; described sexual perversions associated with his name in *La Philosophie dans le Boudoir* (1793), *Juliette* (1798), *Justine (1791), and Les Crimes de l'Amour* (1800).

Sainte-Beuve *(săNt bûv),* **Charles Augustin** 1804–69. French critic. *b.* Boulogne-sur-Mer. Began literary career as critic for *Le Globe*; contributed to *Revue de Paris*, *National*, *Revue des Deux Mondes*, *Constitutionnel*, *Moniteur*, and *Temps*; articles collected and published as *Portraits Littéraires* (2 series, 1832–44), *Portraits de Femmes* (1844), *Portraits Contemporains* (1846), *Causeries du Lundi* (15 vols., 1849–61), *Nouveaux Lundis* (13 vols., 1863–72), and *Premiers Lundis* (1875). Other works include *Tableau de la Poésie Française au Seizième Siècle* (1828), *Vie et Poésies de Joseph Delorme* (1829), *Volupté* (1834), *Consolations* (1830), and *Pensées d'Août* (1837); considered greatest and most prolific critic of his time.

Saint-Gaudens *(sānt gô dənz),* **Augustus** 1848–1907. American sculptor. *b.* Dublin, Ireland. Studied in Paris and in Rome; on return to America, became foremost sculptor of his time. Works include *Hiawatha, The Puritan,* the bas-relief *Adoration of the Cross*, and statues of Lincoln, Farragut, Sherman, and General Logan. Published *Reminiscences* (1913).

Saint-Just *(săN zhüst),* **Louis Antoine Léon de** 1767–94. French revolutionary. *b.* Décize. Elected to National Convention, where he became a follower of Robespierre (1792); as member of the Committee of Public Safety, backed Robespierre's excesses during Reign of Terror; shared Robespierre's fall and was arrested with him; executed (10 Thermidor 1794).

St. Laurent *(săN lô räN),* **Louis Stephen** 1882–1973. Canadian statesman. *b.* Compton. Entered Parliament (1914); served in Mackenzie King's cabinets as minister of justice and attorney general (1941–46) and minister of external affairs (1946–48); on King's resignation, assumed leadership of Liberal party and became prime minister (1948–57).

Saint-Saëns *(săN säNs),* **Charles Camille** 1835–1921. French composer. *b.* Paris. Composed first symphony (1851); organist of the Madeleine (1858–77); founded the Société Nationale de Musique (1871); composed symphonies, *Samson et Dalila* (1877) and other operas, symphonic poems *Le Rouet d'Omphale* (1871), *Phaëton* (1873), *Danse Macabre* (1874), and *La Jeunesse d'Hercule* (1877), piano, violin, and cello concertos, *Carnaval des Animaux* (1886), chamber music, and church music, including *Messe Solennelle* (1856); music criticism collected in *Harmonie et Mélodie* (1885), *Portraits et Souvenirs* (1899), and *Au Courant de la Vie* (1914).

Saint-Simon *(săN sē môN),* **Comte de** title of CLAUDE HENRI DE ROUVROY. 1760–1825. French socialist. *b.* Paris. Born to a noble but impoverished family; imprisoned as an aristocrat during French Revolution, but accumulated small fortune by speculating in confiscated lands; wasted this fortune and spent later years in poverty; author of socialist system known as Saint-Simonism, which sought to reorganize society by vesting all property in the state, directed by industrial chiefs and men of science; developed his theories in *Lettres d'un Habitant de Genève à ses Contemporains* (1802), *L'Industrie* (1817), *Système Industriel* (1820–23), and *Nouveau Christianisme* (1825).

Saki. *See* **Munro, Hector Hugh**

Sakyamuni; Sakyasimha. *See* **Buddha, Gautama**

Saladin *(săl ə dĭn)* full name: SALAH-AL-DIN YUSUF IBN-AYYUB. 1138–93. Sultan of Egypt. *b.* Tekrit, Mesopotamia. Entered service of Nur-eddin, emir of Syria; accompanied uncle Shirkuh, lieutenant of Nur-eddin, in an expedition against Egypt (1167–68); stayed in Egypt when Shirkuh became grand vizier to the Fatimid caliph and later succeeded to that post; overthrew the Fatimid ruler and proclaimed himself sultan (1171); on Nur-eddin's death annexed Syria; extended empire west to Tunisia, east to Yemen, and north to Asia Minor; in conflict with Crusaders, defeating them at Tiberias (1187); stormed Jerusalem, and captured all towns on Syrian coast; defeated by army of Third Crusade (1189–92) and forced to accept truce.

Salazar *(să lə zär),* **Antonio de Oliveira** 1889–1970. Portuguese statesman. *b.* Vimiero. Professor of economics at University of Coimbra; named minister of finance by Antonio Carmona (1928); financial reforms saved Portugal from economic chaos; elected prime minister and virtual dictator (1932); converted Portugal into a corporate state and drafted constitution for *Novo Estado* (1933), based on encyclicals of Pope Leo XIII; kept Portugal out of Spanish Civil War and World War II; eased out of power after suffering a stroke (1968).

Salinger *(săl ən jər),* **Jerome David** known as J.D. SALINGER. 1919–. American novelist and short-story writer. *b.* New York, N.Y. His first novel, *Catcher in the Rye* (1951), which displayed his keen ear and eye for adolescent idioms and concerns, received popular and critical acclaim. Later works include *Nine Stories* (1953), *Franny and Zooey* (1962), *Raise High the Roof Beams, Carpenters* and *Seymour: An Introduction* (1963).

Salisbury, Marquis of. *See* **Cecil, Robert Arthur Talbot Gascoyne**

Salk *(sôk),* **Jonas Edward** 1914–. American physician. *b.* New York, N.Y. Director of virus research (1947–49) and research professor (1949–54) at Pittsburgh; discovered antipoliomyelitis vaccine (1954), now known as the Salk vaccine; director of Salk Institute for Biological Studies (from 1964).

Sallust *(săl əst)* full name: GAIUS SALLUSTIUS CRISPUS. c86–c34 B.C. Roman historian. *b.* Amiternum, Italy. Tribune (52); expelled from senate (50) for immorality; a partisan of Caesar, restored to office as quaestor (49) and praetor (46); after serving in Caesar's African campaigns, named governor of Numidia, amassing immense wealth; on return to Rome, began historical study, culminating in *Catilina (Bellum Catilinarium)* and *Jugurtha (Bellum Jugurthinum).*

Samuelson *(săm ū əl sən),* **Paul Anthony** 1915–. American economist. *b.* Gary, Ind. Professor at M. I. T. (from 1940); awarded Nobel Prize in economic science (1970). Author of *Foundations of Economic Analysis* (1947) and *Economics: An Introductory Analysis* (1974).

Sand *(sănd),* **George** pseudonym of AMANDINE AURORE LUCIE DUPIN, BARONNE DUDEVANT. 1804–76. French writer. *b.* Paris. Went to Paris (1831), leaving husband Casimir, to earn her living from literature; flouted society by forming liaisons with well-known artists, such as Sandeau, de Musset, Chopin, Delacroix, Liszt, Balzac, Lamennais, Leroux, and de Bourges. Wrote over 100 works, including *Indiana* (1831), *Valentine* (1832), *Lélia* (1833), *Le Secrétaire Intime* (1834), *Jacques* (1834), *Mauprat* (1836), *Consuelo* (1842), *La Mare au Diable* (1846), *La Petite Fadette* (1848), *Jeanne* (1844), *Les Maîtres Sonneurs* (1853), *Mont-Revêche* (1855), *Elle et Lui* (1858), *Jean de la Roche* (1860), *Mlle. de la Quintinie* (1864), *Pierre Qui Roule* (1869), *Le Marquis de Villemer* (1860), and *Nanon* (1872); many of her works are autobiographical, including *Lettres d'un Voyageur* (1830–36), *Un Hiver à Majorque* (1841), *François le Champi* (1849), and *L'Histoire de Ma Vie* (1847); in later life, espoused socialism and republicanism.

Sandburg *(săn bûrg),* **Carl** 1878–1967. American poet and biographer. *b.* Galesburg, Ill. After brief stint as a journalist, turned to poetry, establishing reputation with *Chicago Poems* (1916); developed a robust, homespun vocabulary and idiom, taking his themes from rural and industrial America. Poetic works include *Cornhuskers* (1918), *Smoke and Steel* (1920), *Slabs of the Sunburnt West* (1922), *Good Morning, America* (1928),

Early Moon (1930), *The People, Yes* (1936); also wrote the life of *Abraham Lincoln* (6 vols., 1926–39), *Rootabaga Stories* (1922), *Potato Face* (1930), and *Rootabaga Pigeons* (1923), *Remembrance Rock* (1948), and *Always the Young Strangers* (1953).

Sanger *(săng ər),* **Frederick** 1918– . British biochemist. Professor at Cambridge (from 1940); received Nobel Prize in chemistry (1958) for isolating and identifying the amino acid components of the insulin molecule.

Sanger, Margaret 1883–1966. American leader of the birth-control movement. *b.* Corning, N.Y. Founded magazine *Woman Rebel* to promote birth control; indicted for sending birth control literature through the mails; arrested for running birth-control clinic in Brooklyn, N.Y.; organized first American Birth Control Conference in New York (1921); traveled around the world to publicize the movement (1922); founder and president of the American Birth Control League (until 1928). Author of *What Every Girl Should Know* (1916), *My Fight for Birth Control* (1931), and *Margaret Sanger: An Autobiography* (1938), among other books.

San Martín *(sän mär tēn),* **José Francisco de** 1778–1850. South American statesman. *b.* Yapeyú, Argentina. As officer in Spanish army, fought in Europe and Africa (1789–1811); returned to Argentina to lead the struggle for independence from Spain (1812); defeated Spaniards and assumed rank of commander in chief (1814); conceived bold idea of overthrowing Spanish power in Peru through Chile; with Bernardo O'Higgins, crossed the Andes (1817) with 4000 men; defeated Spaniards at Chacabuco and Maipo, and occupied Santiago (1818); after installing O'Higgins as supreme director of Chile, began plans for invasion of Peru; with support of British admiral Lord Thomas Cochrane, transported his men by sea to the coast of Peru; occupied Lima (1821); proclaimed protector of Peru; on a collision course with Simón Bolívar; after a celebrated interview with Bolívar, yielded office and left the country; spent later years in exile in Europe; honored throughout Latin America as a courageous, unselfish hero.

Santa Anna *(sän tä ä nä),* **Antonio López de** also SANTA ANA. 1797–1876. Mexican statesman. *b.* Jalapa. Began military career in Spanish army; supported Augustín de Iturbide (1821), but later led revolt against him as well as against Manuel Pedraza (1828) and Anastasio Bustamente (1832); seized the presidency (1833–35, 1841–45, 1846–47, 1853–55); as a military leader, was uniformly unsuccessful, suffering defeats by Sam Houston at San Jacinto (1836), by Zachary Taylor at Buena Vista, Cerro Gordo, and Pueblo, and by General Scott at Mexico City; lost power in the Revolution of Ayutla (1855), and died in obscurity.

Santayana *(sän tä yä nä),* **George** 1863–1952. Spanish philosopher. *b.* Madrid. Immigrated to U.S. (1892); professor of philosophy at Harvard (1907–12); returned to Europe (1912) and settled in a convent in Italy; gained a wide audience with his polished literary style. Works include *The Sense of*

Beauty (1896), *Interpretations of Poetry and Religion* (1900), *The Life of Reason* (5 vols., 1905–1906), *Winds of Doctrine* (1913), *Scepticism and Animal Faith* (1923), *The Realms of Being* (4 vols., 1928–40), *Dominations and Powers* (1951), *The Last Puritan* (1935), and *Persons and Places* (3 vols. 1944–53).

Santillana *(sän tē lyä nä)*, **Marqués de** title of ÍÑIGO LÓPEZ DE MENDOZA. 1398–1458. Spanish poet. *b.* Carrion de los Condes. First Spanish poet to use sonnet form in Spanish; tried to introduce poetic techniques of Petrarch and Dante into Spanish. Works consist of short poems called serranillas, *Bias Contra Fortuna, Los Proverbios, Comedieta de Ponza*, and *Carta Proemio*.

Santos-Dumont *(säN tōōz dü môNt)*, **Alberto** 1873–1932. Brazilian aeronaut. *b.* Sao Pãolo. Made first flight in a gasoline-powered lighter-than-aircraft (1898); first flight in an airship from St. Cloud around the Eiffel Tower and back (1901); built first airport at Neuilly (1903); first success in a heavier-than-aircraft (1906), three years after Wright Brothers' flight at Kitty Hawk, flying 715 feet in an airplane shaped like a boxkite; built a successful light monoplane (1909).

Sappho *(săf ō)* *fl.* 7th century B.C. Greek poet. *b.* Lesbos. Believed to have lived on the island of Lesbos with female pupil-companions; only a few facts are known of her personal life: that she had a husband named Cercolas, a daughter, Cleis, and two brothers, Larichus and Charaxus; wrote with lyrical power and emotional fervor; of her nine books, only fragments, including a hymn to Aphrodite, survive; called the tenth Muse by Plato; in legend, represented as immoral and lascivious; considered the first woman poet and one of the most important in the classical world.

Sargent *(sär jənt)*, **John Singer** 1856–1925. American painter. *b.* Florence, Italy. Worked in England, U.S., Italy, and Spain, with studios in London and Boston. Among his better known works are the murals *Evolution of Religion* in the Boston Library, *Carmencita, El Jaleo, Gitana, Hermit, Padre Sebastiano, Lake O'Hara, The Wyndham Sisters*, and a number of portraits.

Sargon *(sär gŏn)* Assyrian name: SHARRU-KENU. Name of two kings of Mesopotamia:

SARGON I. *fl.* between 24th and 28th centuries B.C. Akkadian ruler of Babylon; founder of dynasty of Akkad; believed to have conquered West Syria and Elam.

SARGON II. *fl.* 8th century B.C. King of Assyria (722–705) B.C.). Founder of Sargonid dynasty; consolidated Assyrian empire; conquests include Samaria, northern kingdom of Israel, Hama, Damascus, Armenia, Carchemish, Urartu, Philistia, Cyprus, and Babylon; adopted policy of transporting conquered peoples to remote provinces, in order to destroy their national spirit; built capital at Dur-Sharrukin (Khorsabad).

Saroyan *(sä roi yən)*, **William** 1908–. American writer. *b.* Fresno, Calif. Works include short stories, novels, and plays characterized by subtle humor and concern for the frailties and foibles of ordinary people. Best known for *The Daring Young Man on the Flying Trapeze* (1934), *The Time of Your Life* (1939), *My Heart's in the Highlands* (1939), *The Human Comedy* (1942), *Here Comes, There Goes, You Know Who* (1961), and *Not Dying* (1963).

Sarto *(sär tō),* **Andrea del** original name: ANDREA DOMENICO D'AGNOLO DI FRANCESCO. 1486–1531. Florentine painter. *b.* near Florence. Worked primarily on religious themes; famous for both frescoes and oils. Principal works include *Birth of Saint John, Last Supper, Procession of the Magi, Nativity of the Virgin, Deposition from the Cross,* and a number of Holy Families and Madonnas.

Sartre *(sår trə),* **Jean-Paul** 1905–. French writer. *b.* Paris. A lycée professor of philosophy; comparatively unknown until the end of World War II, when he emerged as an existential anarchist and left-wing intellectual; briefly affiliated with Communist party; developed Heidegger's existentialism into a passionate rejection of God and external values; beginning with the premise that existence is prior to essence and that existence is meaningless per se, proceeded to define the despair and anguish of human freedom; awarded but declined Nobel Prize in literature (1964). Works include *Being and Nothingness* (1943), *No Exit* (1945), *Nausea* (1949), *The Flies* (1948), *The Red Gloves* (1949), *Existentialism* (1946), *The Age of Reason* (1945), *The Reprieve* (1947), *Dirty Hands* (1948), *The Condemned of Altona* (1956), *Troubled Sleep* (1951), *Critique of Dialectical Reason* (1964) and *Words* (1964).

Satchmo. *See* **Armstrong, Louis**

Satie *(sə tē),* **Erik** full name: ALFRED ERIKIT LESLIE-SATIE. 1866–1925. French composer. *b.* Honfleur. Central figure of the group known as The Six, which included Arthur Honegger, Francis Poulenc, and Darius Milhaud; his piano compositions, such as *Gymnopedies* and *Three Pieces in the Shape of a Pear,* are characterized by an eccentric simplicity; also composed the ballets *Parade* and *Mercure.*

Saul. *See* **Paul, Saint**

Savonarola *(sä vō nä rô lä),* **Girolamo** 1452–98. Italian religious reformer. *b.* Ferrara. Entered Dominican order (1475); moved to Florence, becoming prior of St. Mark's (1491); in fiery sermons, denounced vice and corruption of church and state; acknowledged leader of the Piagnoni (the Weepers), the democratic party of Florence; continued polemics against papal party even after being named vicar general of Dominican order (1493); instrumental in overthrow of the Medicis and restoration of the Republic (1494); as virtual dictator, set up a puritan regime that lasted until the Arrabbiati (aristocrats) regained power; forbidden to preach by Pope Alexander VI; disregarded the ban and was excommunicated (1497); claimed the gift of prophecy and visions; enforced enactments against vice and frivolity with two bonfires of vanities; lost hold on the populace after return of the Medici party; lost prestige when a promised ordeal by fire did not occur; captured, imprisoned, tried for sedition and heresy, found guilty, tortured, hanged, and burned to death.

Savoy, Prince of. *See* **Eugene**

Saxe *(säks),* **Hermann Maurice de** 1696–1750. French marshal. *b.* Goslar, Germany. Natural son of Augustus II, elector of Germany. Served under Marlborough in War of the Spanish Succession and under Prince Eugene against the Turks; entered French service (1720); in War of the Austrian Succession, took Prague (1741) and Eger (1742); marshal of France (1744); military successes include victories at Fontenoy (1745), Raucoux (1746), and Laffeld (1747); captured Bergen-on-Zoom and Maestricht (1748). Author of *Mes Réveries* (1757) and *Lettres et Mémoires* (1794).

Saxe-Coburg-Gotha, Albert of. *See* **Albert, Prince**

Say *(sā),* **Jean Baptiste** 1767–1832. French economist. *b.* Lyons. During French Revolution, edited *La Decade* (1794–1800), popularizing theories of Adam Smith; member of the Tribunate (1799–1804); professor at Collège de France (from 1831). Principal works include *Traité d'Économie Politique* (1803), *Catéchisme d'Économie Politique* (1815), *De l'Angleterre et des Anglais* (1815), *Letters à Malthus* (1820), *Cours Complet d'Économie Politique Pratique* (1828–30). Father of Jean Baptiste Léon (1826–1896), French economist. *b.* Paris. Finance minister (1872–73, 1875–76, 1876–79, 1882). Author of *Le Socialisme d'État* (1884), *Dictionnaire des Finances* (1889), and other books.

Sayers *(sā ərz),* **Dorothy Leigh** 1893–1957. English writer. *b.* Oxford. Best known as the creator of the detective Lord Peter Wimsey, whose adventures are chronicled in *Whose Body?* (1923), *Strong Poison* (1930), *Hangman's Holiday* (1933), *Murder Must Advertise* (1933), *The Nine Tailors* (1934), *Gaudy Night* (1935), *Busman's Honeymoon* (1937), and *The Teeth of the Evidence* (1939); later became an apologist for the Christian Church with *The Man Born to Be King* (1943), *The Zeal of Thy House* (1937), and *The Devil to Pay* (1939); also known for her translation of Dante.

Scanderbeg *(skăn dər bĕg)* Turkish name; Iskander Bey; original name: George Castriota. c1403–68. Albanian hero. Son of Ivan Castriota, an Albanian chief; sent to Ottoman court as hostage as a youth; brought up a Muslim; entered Turkish army and became favorite of Murad II; on outbreak of Albanian revolt against the Turks, returned to native country, declared himself a Christian, proclaimed Albanian independence, and began struggle in which he expelled Turks from Albania and maintained independence for 20 years; in the end, deserted by his allies, held out alone in the fortress of Kroia; with his death, the Albanian resistance movement collapsed.

Scarlatti *(skär lät tē),* **Alessandro** 1659–1725. Italian composer. *b.* Palermo, Sicily. Produced first opera in Rome (1680); maestro di cappella to Queen Christina of Sweden and later musical director to court of Naples (1693–1703); regarded as founder of modern opera and inventor of accompanied recitatives and the da capo;

wrote nearly 120 operas, including *Tigrane,* 200 masses, 10 oratorios, 500 cantatas, as well as motets and madrigals. His son DOMENICO (1685–1757), Italian musician. *b.* Naples. Official composer to queen of Poland, king of Portugal, and king of Spain; choirmaster of St. Peter's (1714–19); wrote 545 harpsichord sonatas in florid rococo style.

Scheele *(shā lĕ),* **Karl Wilhelm** 1742–86. Swedish chemist. *b.* Stralsund, Germany. Discoveries include chloride, manganese, barium, ammonia, glycerine, tartaric acid, prussic acid, hydrofluoric acid, benzoic acid, molybdic acid, lactic acid, malic acid, citric acid, oxalic acid, malic acid, arsenious acid, Scheele's green (arsenite of copper), scheelite (tungsten), and (independent of Priestley) oxygen.

Schelling *(shĕl ĭng),* **Friedrich Wilhelm Joseph von** 1775–1854. German philosopher. *b.* Leonberg. Professor at Jena (1798), Würzberg (1803), Munich (1827), and Berlin (from 1847); began as a Fichtean and developed Fichte's principle of the ego and pantheism in *Philosophy of Nature* (1799) and *Transcendental Philosophy* (1800); developed a philosophy of identity; held that both mind and nature were manifestations of the absolute and that all existence is a unity. Principal works include *Der Erste Entwurf eines Systems der Naturphilosophie* (1799), *Bruno oder über das Natürliche und Göttliche Prinzip der Dinge* (1802), *Philosophie und Religion* (1804), and *Menschliche Freiheit* (1809); collected works published (14 vols., 1856–61).

Schiaparelli *(skyä pä rĕl lē),* **Giovanni Virginio** 1835–1910. Italian astronomer. *b.* Savigliano. Director of Milan Observatory (1862–1900); discoveries include the asteroid Hesperia, the canals of Mars, and a number of double stars; demonstrated that Mercury and Mars rotate on their axes in the same period as their revolution around the sun and thus always present the same face to the sun. Author of *Rubra Canicola* (1896–97), *Note e Reflessioni sulla Teoria Astronomica della Stelle Cadenti* (1870), and other books.

Schiller *(shĭl ər),* **Johann Christoph Friedrich von** 1759–1805. German poet. *b.* Marbach. A medical student at Stuttgart, began literary career with the play *Die Räuber* (1781), staged at Mannheim (1782) and earning the displeasure of the duke of Württemberg; escaped from duke's restraints to Mannheim (1783–85); completed *Fiesko* and *Kabale und Liebe* (1784); theater poet at Mannheim; founded the journal *Die Rheinische Thalia;* moved to Leipzig and Dresden, where he completed *Don Carlos* (1887); also wrote the poem *An die Freude,* the hymn to joy used by Beethoven in the Ninth Symphony; removed to Weimar (1787); wrote his first historical work, *Geschichte des Abfalls der Vereinigten Niederlande,* and poems *Die Götter Griechenlands* and *Die Künstler;* professor of history at Jena (from 1789); published his second historical work, *Geschichte des Dreiszigjährigen Kriegs,* and the treatise *Naive und Sentimentalische Dichtung;* formed celebrated friendship with Goethe (from 1794), from which was born the journal *Die Horen* (1795–98);

began the annual *Der Musenalmanach* (1796), contributing to it some of his most popular poems; wrote the trilogy *Wallenstein* (1796), *Maria Stuart* (1801), *Die Jungfrau von Orleans* (1802), *Die Braut von Messina* (1803), *Wilhelm Tell* (1804), and *Demetrius* (incomplete at death); ranked second only to Goethe in German literature and first among German dramatists.

Schlegel *(shlā gəl),* **August Wilhelm von** 1767–1845. German critic. *b.* Hanover. Professor of literature and fine art at Jena (1798), Berlin (1801), Vienna (1808), and Bonn (1818–45); translated Shakespeare, Dante, Calderón, Cervantes, and Camoens, the Hindu scriptures, *Bhagavad-Gita* and the *Ramayana;* cofounder with brother Friedrich of the journal *Athenaeum,* the organ of the Romantic movement. Contributions to literary history include *Spanisches Theater* (1803–09) and *Vorlesungen Über Dramatische Kunst und Litteratur* (1809–11). Brother of FRIEDRICH (1772–1829), German philosopher. *b.* Hanover. In Paris, studied philology and published a pioneering study of Sanskrit *Über die Sprache und Weisheit der Indier* (1808); converted to Catholicism (1803); employed at Vienna in Austrian service (from 1808); Austrian counselor at Frankfurt (1815–18); with his writings in the *Athenaeum,* helped to launch Romantic movement. Works include *Philosophy of History* (2 vols., 1829), *History of Literature* (2 vols., 1815), *Philosophy of Life* (1828), *Lucinde* (1799), and *Alarcos* (1802).

Schleiden *(shlī dən),* **Matthias Jakob** 1804–81. German botanist. *b.* Hamburg. Best remembered for his discovery (1838) that certain plant tissues are composed of cells; recognized the importance of the nucleus of the cells and contributed to the cell theory of living matter; professor at Jena (1839–62) and Dorpat (1863–64). Author of *Principles of Scientific Botany* (1849).

Schliemann *(shlē män),* **Heinrich** 1822–90. German archaeologist. *b.* Neubuckow. Acquired a large fortune in business; retired early to undertake excavations at his own expense in Hissarlik, Turkey, to find Troy and other Homeric sites; discovered nine superimposed city sites, some going back to pre-Homeric times; conducted excavations in Mycenae (1876), Orchomenus (1881), Ithaca (1869, 1878), and Tiryns (1884–85). Author of *Ithaka, der Pelopennes und Troja* (1869), *Trojanische Altertümer* (1874), *Mykenä* (1878), *Ilios* (1881), *Orchomenos* (1881), *Reise in der Troas* (1881), *Troja* (1883), and *Tiryns* (1886).

Schnitter, Johannes. *See* **Agricola, Johannes**

Schnitzer, Eduard. *See* **Emin Pasha**

Schnitzler *(shnits lər),* **Arthur** 1862–1931. Austrian dramatist. *b.* Vienna. Member of Jung Wien (Young Vienna) group of writers who represented impressionism as opposed to naturalism. Works include *Anatol* (1911), *Liebelei* (1895), *The Green Cockatoo* (1913), *Professor Bernhardi* (1913), *The Lonely Way* (1915), *Reigen* (1900), *Leutnant Gustl* (1901), *Casanova's Homecoming* (1921), *Flight into Darkness* (1931), *Traumnovelle* (1926), and

Theresa, the Chronicle of a Woman's Life (1928).

Schönberg *(shûn běrK),* **Arnold** 1874–1951. Austrian composer. *b.* Vienna. Founder and exponent of serial music; abandoned traditional tonality and experimented with atonal music; by 1914 had devised the 12-tone technique, by which the 12 chromatic tones are arranged in a chromatic row without a harmonic center and the tone row used in various forms; professor of music at Prussian Academy of Arts (until 1933); immigrated to U.S. 1933); professor at University of California (1936–44). Works include *Erwartung* (1909), *Die Glückliche Hand* (1913), *Von Heute auf Morgen* (1929), *Pelleas und Melisande* (1905), *Pierrot Lunaire* (1912), *Vorgefuehl* (1912), *Verklärte Nacht* (1899), and *Gurrelieder* (1901).

Schopenhauer *(shō pən hou ər),* **Arthur** 1788–1860. German philosopher. *b.* Danzig. Taught at Berlin (1819–21), but found himself ignored; retired to Frankfurt, where he lived in seclusion until death; in principal work, *The World as Will and Idea,* held that the will, rather than the intellect, is the creative and primary force in nature and that the insatiable passions and appetites of the will form the basic human motivations and the source of all knowledge; accepted the Buddhist doctrine that happiness lies in the negation of will through asceticism; believed that artistic experience provided the only escape from the blind, impelling force of will; espoused the view that this is the worst of all possible worlds since if it were any worse no one would be willing to live in it. Other works include *On the Will to Nature* (1836), *The Two Fundamental Problems of Ethics* (1841), and *Parerga und Paralipomena* (1851).

Schottky *(shōt kē),* **Friedrich Hermann** 1851–1935. German mathematician. *b.* Breslau. Professor at Breslau (1878–82), Zurich (1882–92), and Marburg (1892–1902); noted for contributions to the theory of Abelian functions. Author of *Abriss einer Theorie der Abelschen Functionen von drei Variabeln* (1880). Father of WALTER (1886–), American physicist. Invented the screen-grid tube (1915); the Schottky effect, an irregularity in the emission of thermions in a vacuum tube, named after him.

Schrieffer *(shrē fər),* **John Robert** 1931–. American physicist. *b.* Oak Park, Ill. Awarded Nobel Prize in physics (1972) with John Bardeen and Leon Cooper for theory explaining the superconductivity of metals.

Schrödinger *(shrû* dĭng ər), **Erwin 1887–1961. Austrian physicist.** *b.* Vienna, Austria. Professor at Stuttgart, Breslau, Zurich, Berlin, Dublin, and Vienna; formulated wave theory of matter (Schrödinger dynamics) and applied wave mechanics to explain atomic structure; with P.A.M. Dirac, awarded Nobel Prize in physics (1933). Author of *Collected Papers on Wave Mechanics* (1927), *Science and the Human Temperament* (1935), and *Science and Man* (1958).

Schubert *(shōō* bərt), **Franz Peter** 1797–1828. Austrian composer. *b.* Vienna. Composed first symphony at age 16 and an opera, a Mass in F, and the song *Gretchen am Spinnrad* at age 17; wrote *Erlkönig* (1815); with Vogl, formed a company to tour Vienna; briefly served as tutor to Esterházy family; before he succumbed to typhus (1828), wrote over 600 songs, including "Who is Sylvia?," "Hark, Hark, the Lark," and the song cycles *Die Schöne Mullerin* and *Die Winterreise,* chamber works, such as *Trout Quintet* and *Death and the Maiden,* 9 symphonies, *Moments Musicaux* and other piano works, overtures, and masses.

Schumann *(shōō män),* **Robert Alexander** 1810–56. German composer. *b.* Zwickau. Studied music in Leipzig under Wieck; founded and edited the journal *Die Neue Zeitschrift für Musik* (1834–44); married CLARA WIECK (1819–96), German pianist and composer; professor at Leipzig Conservatoire (from 1843); moved to Dresden (1844); on outbreak of Dresden Revolution (1849), moved to Düsseldorf as musical director; succumbed to mental illness and spent last years in an asylum. Principal works include piano works *Papillons, Carnaval, Kinderszenen,* and *Kreisleriana,* piano concerto in A Minor, Spring Symphony, Third (Rhenish) Symphony, Fourth Symphony in D Minor, the opera *Genoveva,* choral works *Paradise and the Peri,* music to Byron's *Manfred* and Goethe's *Faust,* and over 150 songs.

Schwann *(shvän),* **Theodor** 1810–82. German physiologist. *b.* Neuss. Professor of anatomy at Louvain (1838–48) and Liége (from 1848); established the cell as the fundamental unit of animal and plant tissue; discovered the enzyme pepsin; other research included action of nerves and muscles, spontaneous generation, and putrefaction and fermentation. Author of *Microscopical Researches* (1839).

Schwarzert, Philip. *See* **Melanchthon**

Schweitzer *(shvī tsər),* **Albert** 1875–1965. French missionary, physician, and philosopher. *b.* Kaysersberg, Alsace. Studied philosophy and theology; after obtaining a doctorate (1899), became principal of theological college at Strasbourg (1903); achieved international reputation as theologian with *The Quest of the Historical Jesus* (1910) and as a musicologist with *J.S. Bach, le Musician–Poète* (1905); to fulfill a vow made as a youth to serve humanity after age 30, resigned his position, studied medicine, qualified as a physician, and set out for Africa; established hospital (1913) at Lambarene, French Equatorial Africa, where he lived for the remainder of his life; continued to write extensively on ethics and religion; admired for the nobility of his ideals and the strength of his commitment to them; awarded Nobel Peace Prize (1952). Author of *The Mysticism of Apostle Paul* (1930), *On the Edge of the Primeval Forest* (1922), *More From the Primeval Forest* (1931), *Out of My Life and Thought* (1931), *From My African Notebook* (1938), *The Philosophy of Civilization* (1923), and *The Decay and Restoration of Civilization* (1923).

Schwinger *(shwĭng ər),* **Julian Seymore** 1918–. American physicist. *b.* New York, N.Y. Professor at

Harvard; shared Nobel Prize in physics (1965) with R. P. Feynman and S. Tomonaga for research in quantum electrodynamics that contributed to the understanding of elementary particles in high-energy physics.

Scipio Africanus *(sĭp ĭ ō ăf rĭ kā nəs)* full name: PUBLIUS CORNELIUS SCIPIO AFRICANUS; also SCIPIO THE ELDER. 237–183 B.C. Roman general. As commander and proconsul in Spain (210), defeated Hasdrubal (209) and expelled Carthaginians from Spain; elected consul (205); sailed with 30,000 men to carry Second Punic War to Africa (204); defeated Hannibal at Zama (202) and crippled the power of Carthage; accepted surname Africanus in acknowledgment of this triumph, but refused post of consul and dictator for life; accompanied brother Lucius in campaigns against Antiochus; on return to Rome, hostile senatorial oligarchy led by Cato the Elder accused him of taking bribes from Antiochus, but he was vindicated. Adopted grandson SCIPIO AEMILIANUS NUMANTINUS, PUBLIUS CORNELIUS, AFRICANUS MINOR; known as SCIPIO THE YOUNGER, (185–129 B.C.). Roman general. Commanded Roman army against Carthage in Third Punic War (149); captured and razed Carthage (146); as consul, dispatched to Spain to quell the Numantians (133); on return to Rome, headed the aristocratic party; found dead in mysterious circumstances; believed to have been assassinated by adherents of the Gracchi.

Scott *(skŏt),* **Dred** 1795–1858. American slave. *b.* Southampton County, Va. Central figure in the abolitionist controversy; suit on his behalf was instituted by Henry T. Blow, who sought to secure his freedom on the grounds that a slave who had resided in a free territory was free even after his return to the slave states; case came up before the Supreme Court (1857) and the majority opinion of Chief Justice Roger Brooke Taney held that Scott, as a Negro, was not a U.S. citizen and could not bring suit in a federal court; further, that his status as a slave was not altered by his residence in a free state and that Congress could not deprive citizens of their slave-owning rights.

Scott Robert Falcon 1868–1912. English explorer. *b.* Devonport. Entered navy (1882); commanded Antarctic expedition (1901–1904) in the *Discovery* and second expedition (1910–12) in *Terra Nova;* on second expedition, reached South Pole with four companions (1912), only to discover that the Norwegian expedition under Amundsen had preceded them by a month; perished with companions on return journey. Account of first voyage published in *The Voyage of the Discovery* (1905) and of second in *Scott's Last Expedition* (1913).

Scott, Sir Walter 1771–1832. Scottish author. *b.* Edinburgh. Grew up in Border country that forms the locale of many of early works; read voraciously, acquiring an interest in ballads, collected and published as *Minstrelsy of the Scottish Border* (1802); published first original work *The Lay of the Last Minstrel* (1805); achieved success with *Marmion* (1808) and *The Lady of the Lake* (1810); wrote prose romances beginning with *Waverley* (1814); believing that writing fiction was beneath his dignity, issued early novels under various pseudonyms. *Guy Mannering* (1815), *Lord of the Isles* (1815), *The Antiquary* (1815), *The Black Dwarf* (1816), *Old Mortality* (1816), *Rob Roy* (1817), *The Heart of Midlothian (1818)*, *The Bride of Lammermoor* (1819), *The Legend of Montrose* (1819); *Ivanhoe* (1820), *The Monastery* (1820), *The Abbot* (1820), *Kenilworth* (1821), *The Pirate* (1822), *The Fortunes of Nigel* (1822), *Peveril of the Peak* (1822), *Quentin Durward* (1823), *St. Ronan's Well* (1824), *Red Gauntlet* (1824), *The Betrothed* (1825), *The Talisman* (1825), and *Tales of the Crusaders* (1825); at peak of fame, met serious financial losses when the Ballantyne publishing house, in which he had heavily invested, failed (1825); to pay off indebtedness of over £130,000, wrote *Woodstock* (1826), *Chronicles of the Canongate* (1827), *The Fair Maid of Perth* (1828), *Anne of Geierstein* (1829), *The Two Drovers* (1827), *The Highland Widow* (1827), *The Surgeon's Daughter* (1827), *Tales of a Grandfather* (1828–30), *Count Robert of Paris* (1831), and *Castle Dangerous* (1831). Miscellaneous works include *Border Antiquities of England and Scotland* (1814–17), *Life of Napoleon Buonaparte* (1827), and *History of Scotland* (1830).

Scriabin *(skry ä byĭn)*, **Aleksandr Nikolayevich** 1872–1915. Russian composer and pianist. *b.* Moscow. Teacher at the Moscow Conservatory (1898–1903); later devoted himself to composition; appeared in the U.S. (1906–1907); best known compositions include *Prometheus* and *Divine Poem.*

Seaborg *(sē bôrg)*, **Glenn Theodore** 1912–. American chemist. *b.* Ishpeming, Mich. Professor of chemistry at University of California (1937–42, 1946–61, 1971–); associated with Manhattan project (1942–46); discovered transuranic elements plutonium (1940), americium and curium (1944), berkelium (1949), and californium (1950); with E.M. McMillan, awarded Nobel Prize in chemistry (1951); chairman of Atomic Energy Commission (1961–71).

Seferiades *(sĕf ĕr yä thēs)*, **Giorgos Stylianou** pseudonym: George Seferis. 1900–1971. Greek poet. *b.* Smyrna, Turkey. In Greek diplomatic service. Works include *Mythistorema* (1935), *The Thrush* (1947), *Log Book I, II, III* (1940–55), and *The Turning Point* (1931); awarded Nobel Prize in literature (1963).

Segrè *(sə grā)*, **Emilio** 1905–. American physicist. *b.* Italy. Immigrated to U.S. (1938); professor of physics at University of California (from 1938); with Owen Chamberlain, awarded Nobel Prize (1959) for discovery of the antiproton.

Seleucus I *(sə lū kəs)* surname: Nicator. c358–280 B.C. Macedonian general and founder of Seleucid dynasty; satrap (321–312) and king (312–280) of Babylon; ruler of Seleucid empire (306–280). One of the most ambitious of the Diadochi (successors of Alexander the Great); secured Babylon as his share of Macedonian empire (321); built city of Seleucia as capital; invaded India to complete Alexander's mission, but was defeated by Chandragupta Maurya and forced to conclude peace (305);

following defeat and death of Antigonus at Battle of Ipsus (301), received Syria and Asia Minor in division of spoils; made Antioch his capital, proclaiming himself king of Macedon after defeating Lysimachus (281); assassinated at instigation of Ptolemy II (280).

Semenov *(syə myô nôf),* **Nikolai Nikolaevich** 1896–. Soviet chemist. *b.* Saratov. Director of Institute of Chemical Physics of Soviet Acadmey of Sciences; awarded Nobel Prize in chemistry (1956) with C.N. Hinshelwood, for studies on kinetics of chemical reactions.

Semmelweis *(zĕm əl vīs),* **Ignaz Philipp** 1818–65. Hungarian physician. *b.* Budapest. Pioneered the use of antisepsis in obstetrics; established contagious nature of puerperal fever. Author of *The Cause Concept, and Prophylaxis of Childbed Fever,* whose findings were accepted by the medical community years later.

Seneca *(sĕn ə kə),* **Lucius Annaeus** called SENECA THE YOUNGER. c5 B.C.–A.D.65. Roman philosopher, statesman, and dramatist. *b.* Corduba (now Córdoba), Spain. Brought to Rome as a child and trained in law; senator under Caligula; banished to Corsica (41–49) at instigation of Empress Messalina; recalled (49) and entrusted by Empress Agrippina with the education of her son Domitius, who later became the emperor Nero; on accession of Nero (54), wielded considerable power; consul (57); fell from imperial favor; accused and condemned for complicity in Pisonian conspiracy; took own life by opening his veins on Nero's orders; influential in Roman literature as a Stoic philosopher and playwright. Works include *De Clementia, De Beneficiis, Epistolae ad Lucilium, Apocolocyntosis, Quaestionum Naturalium* and the plays *Hercules, Troades, Phoenissae, Medea, Phaedra, Oedipus, Agamemnon, Thyestes,* and *Hercules Oetaeus.*

Senefelder *(zā nə fĕl dər),* **Aloys** 1771–1834. Bavarian inventor. *b.* Prague, Czechoslovakia. Best known as the inventor of the process of lithography (1796); opened printing establishment in Munich (1806).

Sennacherib *(sə năk ər ĭb)* Assyrian name: SIN—AHE-ERBA. *fl.* 7th century B.C. Sargonid king of Assyria (705–681 B.C.). Continued father Sargon II's campaigns against Babylonians and Elamites; captured and destroyed Babylon (689) and Elam (691); carried his arms to Cilicia in Asia Minor, where he founded Tarsus; took Sidon and subdued Ashdod, Ammon, and Moab; invaded Palestine, captured many cities and besieged Jerusalem; rebuilt his capital Ninevah, and restored its splendor and glory; murdered by his son.

Seton *(sē tən),* **Saint Elizabeth Ann** 1774–1821. American religious. *b.* New York, N.Y. Married William Seton (1794); founded Society for Relief of Poor Widows with Small Children in New York (1797); after death of husband (1803), converted to Catholicism (1804); founded Sisters of Charity of St. Joseph (1809), of which she was the first mother superior; opened first Catholic free school at Emmitsburg, Md. (1809); beatified (1963); canonized (1974).

Seurat *(sə rä),* **Georges Pierre** 1859–91. French painter. *b.* Paris. Systematized the Impressionist techniques of broken color by using patterns of tiny dots of pure color that merge when viewed from a distance, establishing a new school called Pointillism; among his works are *Le Cirque, Sunday Afternoon on the Grand Jatte, Poseurs, Fishing Fleet at Port en Besson,* and *The Circus Parade;* wielded important influence on Expressionism, Fauvism, Cubism, and Neoplasticism.

Seward *(sū ərd),* **William Henry** 1801–72. American statesman. *b.* Florida, N.Y. State senator in N.Y. (1830); governor of N.Y. (1839–43); U.S. senator (1849-61); opposed compromise measures on slavery, citing a higher law than the Constitution; on formation of Republican party, became one of its leaders; failed to attain Republican nomination for presidency; secretary of state under Lincoln (1861-69); handled delicate foreign relations matters such as the Trent Affair; after assassination of Lincoln, became staunch supporter of Johnson's reconstruction policies; negotiated purchase of Alaska from Russia (1867).

Shackleton *(shăk əl tən),* **Sir Ernest Henry** 1874–1922. British explorer. *b.* Kilkee, Ireland. Accompanied Robert Scott on Antarctic expedition (1901) in the *Discovery;* led three more Antarctic expeditions: in *Nimrod* (1907), which located the south magnetic pole, in *Endeavour* (1915) on a trans-Antarctic journey, and the final one (1920) in which he died at South Georgia. Author of *The Heart of the Antarctic* (1909) and *South* (1919).

Shakespeare *(shāk spēr),* **William** 1564–1616. English dramatist and poet. *b.* Stratford-on-Avon. Third child of John Shakespeare, a glover and leather worker; married Anne Hathaway (1582), by whom he had three children; moved to London (1588); produced first drama—either *The Comedy of Errors* or *Henry VI Part 1* (c1589); by 1594 associated as actor or author with Pembroke's, Strange's and possibly Queen's and Sussex Players (1594); acquired Henry Wriothesley, earl of Southampton, as patron; member of Lord Chamberlain's Players, which, after accession of James I, became the King's Men; his name heads the list of actors licensed as Grooms of the King's Chamber; partner, with Burbage and others, in Globe Theater (1599) and in Blackfriars Theater (1609); returned to Stratford-on-Avon (1610), but continued occasional writing and visits to London. His plays are *Henry VI* (Part 1, 1591–92; parts 2 and 3, 1590–91), *Richard III* (1592–93), *Comedy of Errors* (1592–94), *Titus Andronicus* (1593–94), *Taming of the Shrew* (1593–94), *Two Gentlemen of Verona* (1594–95), *Love's Labour's Lost* (1594–95), *Romeo and Juliet* (1594–96), *Richard II* (1595–96), *Midsummer Night's Dream* (1595–96), *King John* (1596–97), *Merchant of Venice* (1596–97), *Merry Wives of Windsor* (1597–1601), *Henry IV* (2 parts 1597–98), *Much Ado About Nothing* (1598–99), *Henry V* (1598–99), *Julius Caesar* (1599–1600), *As You Like It* (1599–1600), *Twelfth Night* (1599–1600), *Hamlet* (1600–1601), *Troilus and Cressida* (1598–1601), *All's Well That Ends Well* (1602–1604), *Othello* (1602), *Measure for*

Measure (1604–1605), *King Lear* (1605), *Macbeth* (1605–1606), *Antony and Cleopatra* (1606–1607), *Coriolanus* (1607–1608), *Timon of Athens* (1605–1608), *Pericles* (1607–1608), *Cymbeline* (1609–10), *Winter's Tale* (1610–11), *The Tempest* (1611–12), *Henry VIII* (1612–13), and *Two Noble Kinsmen* (1612–13); his poems are *Venus and Adonis* (1593), *The Rape of Lucrece* (1594), *The Passionate Pilgrim* (1599), *The Phoenix and the Turtle* (1601), and *Sonnets* (1609).

Shapley *(shăp lĭ),* **Harlow** 1885–1972. American astronomer. *b.* Nashville, Tenn. Director of Mount Wilson Observatory (from 1921); conducted important investigations in photometry, spectroscopy, and cosmogony. Author of *Starlight* (1926), *Star Clusters* (1930), *Galaxies* (1943), and *The View from a Distant Star* (1963).

Sharru-kenu. *See* **Sargon**

Shaw *(shô),* **George Bernard** 1856–1950. British playwright. *b.* Dublin, Ireland. Went to London (c1876); spent early years in impoverished circumstances; converted to socialism by reading Henry George and Karl Marx; remained a vigorous and provocative publicist for radical ideas throughout life; as music critic for the *Star* (1888) and for the *World* (1890), and drama critic for the *Saturday Review* (1895), did much to enhance the reputations of Wagner and Ibsen in England; wrote *The Quintessence of Ibsenism* (1891), and *The Perfect Wagnerite* (1898), as tributes to these two "fellow artist-philosophers"; founded Fabian Society (1884), for which he worked as an unpaid orator; edited *Fabian Essays* and other socialist tracts; produced first play *Widowers' Houses* (1892), but gained first substantial success with *Mrs. Warren's Profession* (1924); wrote over 45 plays, mostly philosophical comedies, constituting a theater of ideas; explored such themes as politics, family life, prostitution, war, religion, and vaccination; through plays and prefaces, upheld a number of causes, including vegetarianism, pacifism, and spelling reform; awarded Nobel Prize for literature (1925). Major plays include *Arms and the Man* (1894), *Candida* (1897), *You Never Can Tell* (1900), *The Devil's Disciple* (1897), *Caesar and Cleopatra* (1899), *Captain Brassbound's Conversion* (1899), *John Bull's Other Island* (1904), *Man and Superman* (1903), *The Doctor's Dilemma* (1906), *Major Barbara* (1907), *Getting Married* (1908), *Misalliance* (1910), *The Showing Up of Blanco Posnet* (1909), *Fanny's First Play* (1911), *Androcles and the Lion* (1912), *Pygmalion* (1912), *Great Catherine* (1913), *O'Flaherty, V.C.* (1915), *Heartbreak House* (1917), *Back to Methusaleh* (1921), *Saint Joan* (1923), *Too True To Be Good* (1932), *Geneva* (1938), *King Charles's Golden Days* (1939); prose works include *The Intelligent Woman's Guide to Socialism and Capitalism* (1928), and *The Black Girl in Search of God* (1932).

Shaw, Thomas Edward. *See* **Lawrence, Thomas Edward**

Shays *(shāz),* **Daniel** c1747–1825. American revolutionary. *b.* Hopkinton, Mass. Fought in Revolutionary War, rising to the rank of captain (1777); led the insurrection in western Mass. known as Shays' Rebellion (1786–87) against heavy taxes and mortgages; led over 1000 followers in attacks against the Supreme Court at Springfield and the Continental arsenal; repulsed and forced to flee to Vermont; sentenced to death, but ultimately pardoned.

Shelekhov *(shē lyə Kôf),* **Grigori Ivanovich** 1747–95. Russian merchant and colonizer. *b.* Rylsk. Organized first Russian expedition to Alaska (1783); founded Russian colony on Kodiak Island (1784) that expanded into the mainland and formed the nucleus of the Russian province of Alaska.

Shelley *(shĕl ĭ),* **Mary Wollstonecraft** 1797–1851. English novelist. *b.* London. Daughter of William Godwin and Mary Wollstonecraft; second wife of Percy Bysshe Shelley. Best known for her novel *Frankenstein* (1818); other works include *Valperga* (1823), *The Last Man* (1826), *Lodore* (1835), *Falkner* (1837), and *Rambles in Germany and Italy* (1844).

Shelley, Percy Bysshe 1792–1822. English poet. *b.* Warnham. Expelled from University College, Oxford, for issuing a pamphlet entitled *The Necessity of Atheism* (1811); married Harriet Westbrook (1811); espoused radical ideas of William Godwin; eloped to Switzerland with Godwin's daughter Mary (1814); married Mary after Harriet's suicide (1816); left England for Italy, and spent rest of life in Venice, Naples, Leghorn, Florence, Rome, and Pisa; formed an intimate association with Lord Byron and his group; died by drowning when his boat sank in a storm; works permeated by idealism, belief in the perfectibility of humanity, love of liberty; distinguished by mastery of every poetic form. Works include *Queen Mab* (1813), *The Revolt of Islam* (1818), *Alastor* (1816), *Prometheus Unbound* (1820), *Hymn to Intellectual Beauty, Mont Blanc* (1816), *The Cenci* (1819), *Epipsychidion* (1821), *Adonais* (1821), *The Triumph of Life* (1824), *The Masque of Anarchy* (1832), *Peter Bell the Third* (1839), *The Witch of Atlas* (1824), *Oedipus Tyrannus* (1820), *Hellas* (1822), *Julian and Maddalo* (1824), *Rosalind and Helen* (1819), and prose works *A Defense of Poetry* (1840), *Essay on Christianity* (1859), and *A Philosophical View of Reform* (1920); letters edited and published posthumously by Mary Shelley.

Sheridan *(shĕr ĭ dən),* **Richard Brinsley** 1751–1816. Irish dramatist. *b.* Dublin. Began writing (1773); established reputation by producing *The Rivals, St. Patrick's Day,* and *The Duenna* (all 1775); succeeded Garrick as manager of Drury Theater (1776); gained full ownership (1778); produced *The School for Scandal* (1777), followed by *The Critic* (1779); retired from theater after *Pizarro* (1799); entered political career (1780) as Whig Member of Parliament; undersecretary of foreign affairs (1782); secretary to treasury (1783); high in favor and confidence of prince regent (later George IV); as manager of the impeachment against Warren Hastings, delivered two great orations in the House; supported American and French Revolutions; lost fortune in the burning Drury Lane Theater (1809); died brokenhearted and in poverty; given a magnificent funeral in Westminster Abbey.

Sherman *(shûr mən),* **James Schoolcraft** 1855–1912. American statesman. *b.* Utica, N.Y. Member of Congress (1887–91, 1893–1909); vice-president of U.S. under Taft (1909–12).

Sherman, William Tecumseh 1820–91. American general. *b.* Lancaster, Ohio. On outbreak of Civil War, commissioned colonel of 13th Infantry; brigadier general (1863); major general (1864); lieutenant general (1866); commander of the army (1869); commanded division at Shiloh (1862), Vicksburg (1863), and Chattanooga (1863); succeeded Grant as commander of Military Division of the Mississippi (1864); began Atlanta Campaign (1864), reaching Atlanta after winning battles at Dalton, Resaca, New Hope Church, Kennesaw Mountain, and Peachtree Creek; from Atlanta began March to the Sea, cutting a swath of destruction through Georgia, and entering Savannah (1864); moved north through South and North Carolina; after victories of Averysboro and Bentonville, accepted surrender of Johnston's army (1865); retired (1884). Author of *Memoirs of General William T. Sherman* (2 vols., 1875).

Sherrington *(shĕr ĭng tən),* **Sir Charles Scott** 1861–1952. English physiologist. *b.* London. Professor of physiology at Liverpool (1895–1913), at Royal Institution (1914-17), and Oxford (1917–35); with Edgar Douglas Adrian, discovered the function of the neuron, sharing Nobel Prize in physiology and medicine (1932) with him. Author of *The Integrative Action of the Nervous System* (1906), *Mammalian Physiology* (1916), *Man on His Nature* (1946), and *The Endeavour of Jean Fernel* (1946).

Shockley *(shŏk lĭ),* **William Bradford** 1910–. American physicist. *b.* England. Awarded Nobel Prize in physics (1956) with J. Bardeen and W. Brattain for work in developing the transistor.

Sholem Aleichem *(shō ləm ə lā Kĕm)* pseudonym of SOLOMON RABINOWITZ. 1859–1916. Yiddish writer. *b.* Kiev, Russia. Immigrated to U.S. (1906). Author of stories and plays on Russian Jews, such as *Tevye der Milchiger,* adapted as *Fiddler on the Roof.*

Sholokhov *(shô lə Kôf),* **Mikhail Aleksandrovich** 1905–. Russian writer. *b.* near Veshenskaya. Best known for the epic novel on the Don Cossacks, *The Silent Don* (1942). Other works include *Seeds of Tomorrow* (1935) and *One Man's Destiny* (1967); awarded Nobel Prize in literature (1965).

Shostakovich *(shŭ stə kô vyĭch),* **Dimitri Dimitrievich** 1906–75. Russian composer. *b.* St. Petersburg. Composed symphonies, the most popular of which are the fifth, on the Russian Revolution of 1917, the seventh, commemorating the siege of Leningrad, and the tenth and eleventh, on the Revolution of 1905; condemned as a deviationist under Stalin. Other works include the operas *The Nose* (1929) and *Lady Macbeth of Mtensk* (1934), the ballets *The Golden Age* and *Bolt,* piano pieces, chamber music, and a violin concerto.

Showa. *See* **Hirohito**

Sibelius *(sĭ bā lĭ əs),* **Jean** 1865–

1957. Finnish composer. *b.* Tavastehus. A passionate nationalist, regarded as the founder of Finnish music; many compositions are based on Finnish legends. Works include seven symphonies, the tone poem *The Swan of Tuonela,* the symphonic poems *En Saga* and *Finlandia, Valse Triste* and *Valse Romantique,* and the opera *The Maiden in the Tower;* wrote last work, *Tapiola* (1926).

Siddhartha. *See* **Buddha, Gautama**

Sidgwick *(sĭj wĭk),* **Henry** 1838–1900. English philosopher. *b.* Skipton. Professor at Cambridge (1883–1900); developed J.S. Mill's utilitarianism by discriminating between altruism and egoism as the means of producing pleasure; founder of the Society for Psychical Research and its first president (1882–85, 1888–93). Works include *The Methods of Ethics* (1874), *Principles of Political Economy* (1883), *Outlines of the History of Ethics* (1886), *The Elements of Politics* (1891), and *Practical Ethics* (1898).

Sidmouth, First Viscount. *See* **Addington, Henry**

Sidney *(sĭd nĭ),* **Sir Philip** 1554–86. English poet. *b.* Penshurst, Kent. Son of SIR HENRY SIDNEY, (1529–86), lord deputy in Ireland and president of the Council of Wales. Served as ambassador to Emperor Rudolf and prince of Orange (1577); member of the Aeropagus, a group of poets writing verse in classical meters; honored as the dedicatee of Spenser's *The Shepheardes Calendar* (1579); after fall of uncle Leicester, lost favor in Elizabeth's court and retired (1580); wrote *Arcadia* (1590), a prose romance, and *Apologie for Poetrie* (later *Defence of Poesie*), one of the earliest examples of English literary criticism; addressed 108 sonnets, collected with 11 songs in *Astrophel and Stella* (1591); accompanied Leicester in campaign in Netherlands against Spain; governor of Flushing (1585); killed in Battle of Zutphen (1586); considered exemplar of Elizabethan gentleman.

Siegbahn *(sēg bän),* **Karl Manne Georg** 1886–1978. Swedish physicist. *b.* Örebro. Professor at Lund (1920–23), Uppsala (1923–26), and Stockholm (from 1937); made precise measurement of X-ray wave lengths; discovered the M series in X-ray spectroscopy; awarded Nobel Prize in physics (1924). Author of *Spektroskopie der Röntgenstrahlen* (1931).

Siemens *(zē məns),* **Ernst Werner von** 1816–92. German inventor and manufacturer. *b.* Lenthe. Established the firm of Siemens and Halske (1847); constructed first telegraph line in Germany, from Berlin to Frankfort; discovered the use of gutta percha as an insulator, improved the galvanometer, and constructed the self-acting dynamo and the selenium photometer; invented the dial telegraph; the Siemen's unit, a mercury unit of resistance, is named after him. His brother SIR WILLIAM (1823–83), English physicist. *b.* Lenthe, Germany. Immigrated to England (1844); invented a water-meter, pyrometer, and bathometer; devised the regenerative furnace and advanced the manufacture of steel; designed the ship *Faraday,* which laid the transatlantic cable.

Sienkiewicz *(shĕn kyə vēch),* **Henryk** 1846–1916. Polish writer. *b.* near Łuków. Active in Polish resistance to Russian occupation; lived in U.S. (1876–78); gained international fame with the publication of *Quo Vadis?* (1896). Other works include the trilogy *With Fire and Sword, Deluge,* and *Wolodyjowski* (1886), *With Dogma* (1891), *Children of the Soil* (1893), *The Crusaders* (4 vols., 1900), *Desert and Wilderness* (1892), and *The Teutonic Knights;* awarded Nobel Prize in literature (1905).

Sieyès *(syā yâs),* **Emmanuel Joseph Comte** usually ABBÉ SIEYÈS. 1748–1836. French revolutionary. *b.* Fréjus. Canon of Tréguier and vicar general to bishop of Chartres; deputy of third estate to States-General (1789); with three sensational pamphlets, *Vues sur les Moyens d'Exécution* (1788), *Essai sur les Privilèges* (1788), and *Qu'est-ce que le Tiers État?* (1789), offered constructive programs for the Revolution; edited the Declaration of the Rights of Man and Citizen; responsible for the division of France into departments; led Thermidorian reaction after fall of Robespierre (1794); member of Council of Five Hundred (1795–99) and of the Directory (1799); with Napoleon, executed coup d'état of 18 Brumaire (1799) and was one of three consuls in the Consulate; rewarded by Napoleon with title of count, an estate, and 600,000 francs; exiled at Bourbon Restoration, but returned to France (1830).

Sikorsky *(sə kôr skĭ),* **Igor Ivanovich** 1889–1972. American aeronautical engineer. *b.* Kiev, Russia. Immigrated to U.S. (1919); founded Sikorsky Aero Engineering Corporation (1923); achievements in aeronautics include building of first four-engined plane (1913), production of first commercial amphibian airplane (1928), and manufacture of first air-worthy helicopter (1939). Author of *Story of the Winged-S* (1938) and *Message of the Lord's Prayer* (1942).

Sillanpää *(sĭl lən pă),* **Frans Eemil** 1888–1964. Finnish writer. *b.* Hameenkyro. Author of *The Maid Silja* (1931), *Meek Heritage* (1938), *Life and the Sun* (1916), *The Pious Misery* (1919), *Hiltu and Ragnar* (1923), *A Man's Way* (1932), *People in the Summer Night* (1934), and *Harvest Month* (1941); awarded Nobel Prize in literature (1939).

Silva Leitão. *See* **Almeida-Garrett**

Simeon Stylites *(sĭm ē ən stī lī tēz),* **Saint** c390–459. Syrian ascetic. *b.* Sisan. Spent 30 years perched on the top of a 72-foot pillar, preaching to multitudes; gained fame for sanctity and asceticism; most widely known pillar saint.

Sinclair *(sən klĕr),* **Upton Beall** 1878–1968. American writer. *b.* Baltimore, Md. Noted writer of novels of social protest beginning with *The Jungle* (1906), which drew public attention to conditions in Chicago stockyards; socialist candidate for public office; founded a commune in Englewood, N.J. (1906). Works include *The Industrial Revolution* (1907), *King Coal* (1917), *The Profits of Religion* (1918), *The Brass Check* (1919), *100%, the Story of a Patriot* (1920), *The Goose-step* (1923), *Oil* (1927), *Boston* (1928), *The Way Out* (1933), and the Lanny Budd series, of which *Dragon's Teeth* (1942), was awarded the Pulitzer prize.

Sitter *(sĭt ər),* **Willem de** 1872–1934. Dutch astronomer. Professor at Leiden (from 1908); proposed theory of an expanding universe; computed size of the universe as 2000 million light years in radius, with about 80,000 million galaxies.

Sitting Bull *(sĭt ĭng bool)* 1834–90. American Indian chief. Grand River, S.D. One of the commanders of the Dakota Sioux in the Sioux War (1876–77) and at Battle of Little Big Horn, where Custer was defeated and killed (1876); escaped to Canada at end of war; returned to surrender (1881); took part in the Ghost Dance uprising (1890) and died while resisting arrest.

Sitwell *(sĭt wĕl)* English literary family including:

DAME EDITH. 1887–1964. poet, critic, and novelist. *b.* Scarborough. Author of *Gold Coast Customs* (1929), *Alexander Pope* (1930), *The English Eccentrics* (1933), *Aspects of Modern Poetry* (1934), *I Live Under a Black Sun* (1937), *Street Songs* (1942), *A Poet's Notebook* (1943), *Collected Poems* (1954), *The Outcasts* (1962), *The Queen and the Hive* (1962), and the autobiography *Taken Care of* (1965).

SIR OSBERT 1892–1969. *b.* London. Author of *Argonaut and Juggernaut* (1919), *Before the Bombardment* (1926), *Triple Fugue* (1924), *England Reclaimed* (1927), *The Man Who Lost Himself* (1929), *Dumb Animals* (1930), *Collected Poems and Satires* (1931), *Penny Foolish* (1935), *Those Were the Days* (1938), *A Place of One's Own* (1942), *Collected Stories* (1953) and *Pound Wise* (1963); published autobiography (5 vols., 1944–50).

SACHEVERELL 1897–. Art critic. Works include *Southern Baroque Art* (1924), *Gothick North* (1929), *Canons of Giant Art* (1933), *Narrative Pictures* (1937), *Poltergeists* (1940), *Valse des Fleurs* (1941), *The Hunters and the Hunted* (1947), the unfinished poem *Gargantua and Dr. Donne, Liszt* (1936), *Mozart* (1932), and the autobiography *Journey to the Ends of Time* (1959).

Smith *(smĭth),* **Adam** 1723–90. Scottish economist. *b.* Kircaldy. Professor of logic (from 1751) and of moral philosophy (1752–64) at Glasgow; intimate of David Hume; began literary career with *Theory of Moral Sentiments* (1759); published magnum opus *Wealth of Nations* (1776), a seminal work that postulated the fundamental theories of value, division of labor, money, prices, wages, and distribution, and opposed mercantilism; laid foundations of political economy and the laissez–faire doctrine on which capitalism was built.

Smith, Joseph 1805–44. American Mormon prophet. *b.* Sharon, Vt. Received divine call as a prophet to restore church of Christ at Manchester, N.Y. (1820); according to his account, received a book written in hieroglyphics on golden plates from an angel (1827); translated it with Urim and Thummim, a pair of magic spectacles; published it (1830) as *The Book of Mormon,* which along with *A Book of Commandments* (1833) and *Doctrine and Covenants* (1835), provides the canons of the Church of Jesus Christ of Latter-Day Saints, founded 1830; rapidly gained converts despite ridicule and hostility; moved to Kirtland,

Ohio (1831), and then to Missouri (1838); left because of a general uprising against him; settled at Commerce, Ill., renaming it Nauvoo (1840); received a revelation authorizing polygamy (1843); opposition to this new doctrine led to schism in the church; resulting violence culminated in his arrest; lynched by a mob while in jail at Carthage.

Smollett *(smŏl ət),* **Tobias George** 1721–71. British novelist. *b.* Dalquhurn, Scotland. Turned from medicine to literature; achieved success with *Roderick Random* (1748). Also wrote *Peregrine Pickle* (1751), *Humphrey Clinker* (1771), *Complete History of England* (1757–58); as editor of *Critical Review,* involved in controversies and libel suits.

Smuts *(smŭts),* **Jan Christiaan** 1870–1950. South African soldier and statesman. *b.* Malmesbury. Gave up British citizenship and fought on Boer side in Boer War (1899–1902); commander of Republican forces in Cape Colony (1901–1902); at end of the war, entered Assembly (1907); with Louis Botha, was instrumental in the creation of the Union of South Africa (1910); in World War I, conquered German South West Africa (1914–15); commanded British troops in East Africa (1916–17); succeeded Botha as prime minister (1919–24); signed Treaty of Versailles for South Africa (1918); minister of justice (1933–39); prime minister (1939–48); field marshal (1941); one of the founders of South African United party.

Smyth, Robert Stephenson. *See* **Baden-Powell of Gilwell, Baron**

Sneider, Johannes. *See* **Agricola, Johannes**

Snow *(snō),* **Charles Percy, Baron** 1905–. English novelist and scientist. *b.* Leicester. Chief scientist for the Ministry of Labor in World War II; editor of *Discovery* (1938–40); portrayed English society in an 11-novel series known as *Strangers and Brothers* (1940–68), in which the central character is Lewis Eliot; explored the moral concerns of a scientific age; in the controversial *Two Cultures* (1959), examined the dichotomy between science and the humanities; made a life peer (1964).

Socrates *(sŏk rə tēz)* c470–399 B.C. Greek philosopher. *b.* Athens. Son of a sculptor and in early life a sculptor himself; fought bravely in Peloponnesian War at Potidaea (432–29), Delium (424), and Amphipolis (422); became teacher of philosophy, gathering a group of disciples that included Plato, Xenophon, and Alcibiades; devised question-and-answer method of inquiry, known as maieutic or Socratic method, in which he acted as the midwife rather than as teacher of knowledge; held that knowledge was identical with virtue; maintined that wisdom consisted of the acknowledgment of ignorance (the Socratic irony); claimed that his mission was to develop honesty and self-awareness; proclaimed the wisest man in the world by the Delphic oracle; accused of impiety and corruption of youth (399); described by his enemies as "an evildoer and a curious person"; defended himself in a famous speech, but was condemned; ended his life by drinking hemlock in prison; left no writings; teachings known wholly through the dialogues of Plato and the *Memorabilia* of Xenophon.

Soddy *(sŏd i),* **Frederick** 1877–1956. English chemist. *b.* Eastbourne. Professor at Aberdeen (1914–19) and Oxford (1919–36); Worked with Rutherford in establishing theory of atomic disintegration of radioactive elements; discovered and coined the term *isotope*; winner of Nobel Prize in chemistry (1921). Author of *Radioactivity* (1904), *The Interpretation of Radium* (1909), *Chemistry of the Radio-Elements* (1912), *Matter and Energy* (1912), *The Wrecking of a Scientific Age* (1927), and *The Story of Atomic Energy* (1949).

Söderblom *(sû dər bloom),* **Nathan** 1866–1931. Swedish theologian. *b.* Trönö. Archbishop of Uppsala (1914–31) and primate of Swedish Lutheran Church; leader in the ecumenical and peace movements; awarded Nobel Peace Prize (1930). Author of books on history of religion, including *The Religions of the World* (1905), *Introduction to the History of Religion* (1920), and *Christian Fellowship* (1923).

Solomon *(sŏl ə mən)* c973–c933 B.C. King of Israel. Son of David and Bathsheba. Noted for his wisdom and wealth; brought Israel to peak of greatness; reputed author of the *Proverbs, The Song of Songs, Ecclesiastes*, and (in the *Apocrypha*), the *Wisdom of Solomon*; built temple at Jerusalem that became center of Jewish civilization and religion.

Solon *(sō lən)* c638–c559 B.C. Athenian lawgiver. Elected archon (c596); laid foundations of Athenian democracy by reforms in which he reorganized the Boule (Senate), the popular assembly, and the council of the Aeropagus, set free the indebted, reformed the currency, and divided the population into four classes with the Thetes as the fourth class; left Athens in a ten-year self-exile; died soon after return.

Soloviëv *(sə ləv yôf),* **Sergei Mikhailovich** 1820–79. Russian historian. Rector of University of Moscow; author of *History of Russia* (29 vols., 1851–79). Father of VLADIMIR SERGEEVICH (1853–1900), Russian philosopher. *b.* Moscow. Noted as a Christian intellectual. Works include *War, Progress, and the End of History* (1900), *The Justification of the Good* (1898), *Lectures on Godmanhood* (1894), *The Meaning of Love* (1947), and *Russia and the Universal Church* (1889).

Solzhenitsyn *(sôl zhə nēt sən),* **Alexander Isayevich** 1918–. Russian writer. *b.* Kislovodsk. Imprisoned in concentration camps for many years; became an impassioned critic of the Soviet system. Wrote *One Day in the Life of Ivan Denisovich* (1962), *The First Circle* (1968), *Cancer Ward* (1970), *The Gulag Archipelago* (1973) and *Lenin in Zurich* (1975); awarded Nobel Prize in literature (1970); exiled from Soviet Union (1974).

Sonora, Marqués de la. *See* **Gálvez, José de**

Sophocles *(sŏf ə klēz)* c496–406 B.C. Greek dramatist. *b.* Colonus Hippius. Gained victory over Aeschylus in a drama contest (468); won the prize at Great Dionysia 18 times; believed to have written over 120 tragedies, of which seven are extant: *Oedipus Tyrannus*

(Oedipus Rex), Oedipus at Colonus, Antigone, Electra, Philoctetes, Ajax, and *Maidens of Trachis.*

Sorel *(sô rəl),* **Georges** 1847–1922. French Syndicalist philosopher. *b.* Cherbourg. Abandoned a career in engineering to take up political philosophy; propounded theory of social change through violence, becoming the most brilliant advocate of anarchosyndicalism; believed that collective action and general strikes are the only means of bringing about social and political change; influenced Mussolini and the evolution of fascism. Wrote *Reflections on Violence* (1908), *L'Avenir Socialiste des Syndicats* (1898), *De l'Utilité du Pragmatisme* (1921), and *Matériaux pour une théorie du Proletariat* (1919).

Soubirous, Bernadette. *See* **Bernadette of Lourdes**

Sousa *(soo zə),* **John Philip** 1854–1932. American bandmaster and composer. *b.* Washington, D.C. Played with the U.S. Marine Band (1880–1892); formed his own band (1892) and toured the world gaining the nickname March King; his more than 100 marches include "Stars and Stripes Forever," "Semper Fidelis," "Washington Post March," "King Cotton," and "Manhattan Beach" also wrote 10 comic operas including *The Bride-Elect, The Smugglers, The Queen of Hearts, El Capitan* and *The Charlatan*; published autobiography *Marching Along* (1928).

Southey *(sou thĭ; sŭ thĭ),* **Robert** 1774–1843. English poet. *b.* Bristol. Began career as a radical; after tours of Spain and Portugal, settled in Lake District with Coleridge and Wordsworth; mellowed into a high Tory; poet laureate (1813). Epic poems include *Vision of Judgment* (1821), *Thalaba* (1801), *Madoc* (1805), *The Curse of Kehama* (1810) and *Roderick, the Last of the Goths* (1821); shorter poems include: "The Holly Tree," "The Battle of Blenheim," and "Stanzas Written in My Library"; historical works include *History of Brazil* (1810), *Life of Nelson* (1813), *Life of John Wesley* (1820), *History of the Peninsular War* (1823), *Book of the Church* (1824), and *Sir Thomas More* (1829); miscellaneous prose works include *Common-Place Book* (1849–51) and *Espriella's Letters from England* (1807).

Spartacus *(spär tə kəs)* *d.* 71 B.C. Roman gladiator. A Thracian shepherd who was sold as a slave to a gladiatorial school; escaped and headed the insurrection of slaves known as the Servile War (73 B.C.); repulsed several Roman armies before being overcome and killed by Crassus.

Speke *(spēk),* **John Hanning** 1827–64. English explorer. *b.* Jordans. Joined Richard Burton in expedition to Somaliland (1854); in a second expedition (1857), discovered Victoria Nyanza and the Kagera (Alexandra) Nile, which he identified as the source of the Nile; with James Grant, sailed down the Nile to Egypt (1860–63). Author of *Journal of the Discovery of the Source of the Nile* (1863).

Spemann *(shpā män),* **Hans** 1869–1941. German zoologist. *b.* Stuttgart. Director of Institute of Biology at Rostock (1914); professor at Freiburg (from 1919);

working in the field of developmental physiology, discovered the organizer effect, the mechanism reponsible for cell differentiation; awarded Nobel Prize in physiology and medicine (1935).

Spencer *(spĕn sər),* **Herbert** 1820–1903. English philosopher. *b.* Derby. Left engineering (1845) to devote himself to a systematic study of nature and society; began with *The Proper Sphere of Government* (1842) urging limitation of governmental authority, a theme he continued in *Social Statics* (1851) and *Man Versus the State* (1854); published *Principles of Psychology* (1855), four years before Darwin's *Origin of Species*, applying the doctrine of evolution to social growth; attempted major synthesis of scientific knowledge in *System of Synthetic Philosophy* (11 vols., 1860–96). Other books include *Education* (1861), *Classification of the Sciences* (1864), *Illustrations of Universal Progress* (1864), *The Study of Sociology* (1873), *Progress* (1881), and *The Philosophy of Style* (1882).

Spengler *(shpĕng lər)* **Oswald** 1880–1936. German historical philosopher. *b.* Blankenburg. In his classic work, *The Decline of the West* (2 vols., 1926–28), traced the cycle of growth and decay of civilizations according to a predetermined historical destiny; predicted the fall of Western civilization and the rise of a new Asiatic one; influenced Nazism. Other works include *Preussentum und Sozialismus* (1920), *Der Mensch und die Technik* (1931), and *Jahre der Entscheidung* (1933).

Spenser *(spĕn sər),* **Edmund** 1552–99. English poet. *b.* London. Educated at Cambridge; gained friendship of Sir Philip Sidney and admission to the circle of poets known as Aeropagus; first work, *The Shepheardes Calendar* (1579), a pastoral poem, is dedicated to Sidney; held a minor civil office in Ireland; began *The Faerie Queene* (1590), an epic allegory for which he developed the Spenserian stanza form rhyming *ababbcbcc*; wrote elegy on death of Sidney, *Astrophel* (1586); visited London to present *Faerie Queene* to Elizabeth (1590); on return to Ireland, wrote minor works "Mother Hubbard's Tale," "The Early Tears of the Muses," and other pieces (collected in *Complaints,* 1591), *Colin Clouts Come Home Againe* (1595), *Amoretti, Epithalamion* (1595), *Four Hymnes* (1596), *Prothalamion* (1596), and *View of the Present State of Ireland* (1596); fled with family to London when his castle at Kilcomen was burned by Irish rebels (1598); considered second only to Shakespeare for poetic imagery and melody.

Spinoza *(spĭ nō zə),* **Baruch** also BENEDICT. 1632–77. Dutch philosopher. *b.* Amsterdam. Received rabbinical training, but his questioning mind, independence, and interest in science made his orthodoxy suspect; excommunicated (1656); made a living by grinding lenses; began formulating his philosophic system with *Tractatus Theologica Politicus* (1670), based on Cartesian philosophy; completed it with *Ethica Ordine Geometrico Demonstrata* (1677); in these two works furnished a brilliant exposition of pantheism; conceived of a universal religion based on eternal verities and uncorrupted by theological speculation; resolved Cartesian dualism of mind and matter by conceiving of an eternal *natura naturans*, of which bodies and minds are only modes and extensions; believed that everything happens according to logical necessity and that people are free in so far as they act in accordance with God's will.

Spitteler *(shpĭt ə lər)*, **Carl** 1845–1924. Swiss writer. *b.* Liestal. Received Nobel Prize in literature (1919) for his epic *Der Olympische Frühling* (1900–1903). Other works include *Prometheus der Dulder* (1924); *Prometheus and Epimetheus* (1881), *Extramundana* (1883), *Schmetterlinge* (1889), *Conrad der Leutnant* (1898), *Imago* (1906), *Lachende Wahrheiten*, and *Meine Frühesten Erlebnisse* (1914).

Spurgeon *(spûr jən)*, **Charles Haddon** 1834–92. English preacher. *b.* Kelvedon. Accepted call to pastorate and gained fame as a preacher (from 1851); so large was his congregation that a 6000-seat church, the Metropolitan Tabernacle, was built for him (1861); edited monthly magazine *The Sword and the Trowel;* preached fundamentalist Calvinist orthodoxy and opposed liberal theology; sermons collected in 50 volumes; also wrote *John Ploughman's Talks* (1869) and other books.

Staël *(stäl)*, **Madame de** full name: ANNE LOUISE GERMAINE NECKER, BARONNE DE STAEL-HOLSTEIN. 1766–1817. French woman of letters. *b.* Paris. Daughter of Jacques Necker; brought up in intellectual society; first work was *Lettres sur le Caractère et les Écrits de J.J. Rousseau* (1788); married (1786) Baron de Staël Holstein, Swedish ambassador, but formally separated (1798); conducted brilliant salon that made her an influential and well-known figure; exiled during French Revolution, returning to Paris in 1795; published *Réflexions sur la Paix Intérieure* (1795) and *Influence des Passions* (1796); allowed to return to Paris by Napoleon (1797), but became object of his dislike and was forced to resume exile (1803); at Weimar, met Goethe and Schiller; until fall of Napoleon, lived in Italy, Austria, Sweden, Russia, and England; published *Littérature et ses Rapports avec les Institutions Sociales* (1800), *Delphine* (1803), *Corinne* (1807), and *De l'Allemagne* (1810), a manifesto of Romanticism, gaining her a European reputation; last works were *Considérations sur la Revolution Française* (1818), *Dix Années d'Exil* (1821), and *Essais Dramatiques* (1821).

Stagarite, the. *See* **Aristotle**.

Stalin *(stȧ lyĭn)*, **Joseph** real name: IOSIF VISSARIONOVICH DZHUGASHVILI. 1879–1953. Russian political leader. *b.* Gori. Trained for priesthood, but expelled from seminary for Marxist activities; joined Social Democratic party (1896) and Bolshevik faction (1903); adopted pseudonym Stalin (Man of Steel); arrested often, but always managed to escape; became associate of Lenin; joined Bolshevik Central Committee (1912); founded (1911) and edited *Pravda*; led Communist bloc in the Duma; in prison during February Revolution (1917); amnestied and took active part in October coup; member of Revolutionary Military Council (1920–23) and People's Commissar for Nationalities (1921–23); organized Red terror in Tsaritsin, later Stalingrad; became dominant force in Communist party by being named general secretary of Central Committee (1922); in struggle following Lenin's death (1924), eliminated all his rivals and emerged as virtual dictator; scrapped Lenin's New Economic Policy and replaced it with a collectivization program; crushed opposition to his economic policy by mass deportation and slave camps; launched five-year plans that enabled Russia to gain impressive industrial and military strength; liquidated remnants of opposition to Stalinism in purge trials; achieved monolithic unity (by 1938); concluded nonaggression pact with Hitler (1938); annexed eastern Poland, part of Finland, Latvia, Estonia, Lithuania, and Bessarabia (1940); on Hitler's invasion of Russia, assumed direction of the war as commissar for defense and prime minister (from 1941); marshal of Soviet Union (from 1943) and generalissimo (from 1945); met with Churchill and Roosevelt at Tehran, and Yalta, and with Truman at Potsdam; achieved vast territorial gains to establish Eastern Europe as a Soviet sphere of influence, making the U.S.S.R. a world power; cut off Soviet Union and her satellites with closed borders; adulated as a demigod; ruled with an iron hand; much of his excesses exposed in the de-Stalinization speech of successor Khrushchev.

Stanhope, Philip Dormer. *See* **Chesterfield, Earl of**

Stanley *(stăn lĭ)*, **Edward George Geoffrey Smith:** title: EARL OF DERBY. 1799–1869. English statesman. *b.* Knowsley. Entered Parliament (1822); chief secretary for Ireland (1830–33); as colonial secretary, emancipated West Indian slaves; prime minister (1852, 1858–59, 1866–68); during last ministry, carried the Reform Bill (1867); noted for his parliamentary eloquence, his Greek scholarship and his translation of the *Illiad.*

Stanley, Sir Henry Morton Original name: JOHN ROWLANDS. 1841–1904. English explorer. *b.* near Denbigh, Wales. Of illegitimate birth and abandoned by parents; sailed to New Orleans as a cabin boy, where he adopted the name of his employer, Stanley; served in Confederate and Union armies, but found true profession as correspondent for *New York Herald* (from 1867): covered Spain and Abyssinia; received (1869) the commission from Gordon Bennett, owner of the *Herald:* "Find Livingstone"; starting from Zanzibar (1871), found Livingstone at Ujiji, greeting him with the now-famous remark, "Dr. Livingstone, I presume?"; published *How I Found Livingstone* (1872); led second expedition to Central Africa under the sponsorship of *Herald* and *London Daily Telegraph* to carry on Livingstone's work; leaving Bagamayo (1874), circumnavigated Victoria Nyanza, explored Lakes Albert and Tanganyika, and sailed down Lualaba to Nyangwe and to mouth of the Congo at Boma (1876–77); published *Through the Dark Continent* (1878); went to Africa (1879–84) in service of King Leopold of Belgium; helped to open the Congo region and to found Congo Free State, described in *The Congo and the Founding of Its Free State* (2 vols., 1885); in final expedition (1887–89) for the relief of Emin Pasha, who had been cut off by the Mahdists in Equatoria, rescued Emin and discovered Ruwenzori (Mountains of the Moon) and Lake Edward; became naturalized British subject (1895). Also published *My Dark Companions* (1893), *Slavery and the Slave Trade in Africa* (1893), and *Autobiography* (1909).

Stanley, Wendell Meredith 1904–1971. American biochemist. *b.* Ridgeville, Ind. Director (from 1948) of Virus Research Laboratory of the University of California; with John H. Northrop and James Sumner, shared Nobel Prize in chemistry (1946) for preparation of enzymes and virus proteins in pure form.

Stanton *(stăn tən),* **Elizabeth** *nee* **Cady** 1815–1902. American woman-suffrage leader. *b.* Johnston, N.Y. Held first woman's rights convention at her house at Seneca Falls, N.Y. (1848); first president of National Woman Suffrage Association (1869–90); with Susan B. Anthony, wrote *History of Woman Suffrage* (3 vols., 1881–86).

Stark *(shtärk),* **Johannes** 1874–1957. German physicist. *b.* Schickendorf, Bavaria. Professor at Aachen (1909–17), at University of Greifswald (1917–20), and Würzburg (1920–22); discovered the Doppler effect in channel rays and the Stark effect, which produces splitting of spectrum lines when the light source is subjected to a strong electric field; awarded Nobel Prize in physics (1919). Author of *Prinzipien der Atom-Dynamik* (3 parts, 1910–15) and *Atomstruktur und Atom-bindung* (1928).

Staudinger *(shtou dĭng ər),* **Hermann** 1881–1965. German chemist. *b.* Worms. Professor of organic chemistry at Freiburg (1926–51); awarded Nobel Prize in chemistry (1953) for research on the chemistry of macromolecules.

Steele *(stēl),* **Sir Richard** 1672–1729. British essayist and dramatist. *b.* Dublin. Gained fame with *The Christian Hero* (1701), written while in the army; followed with *The Funeral* (1702), *The Tender Husband* (1703), and *The Lying Lover* (1704); gazetteer (from 1707); founded *The Tatler* (1709–11), a triweekly journal of news and essays by himself and, from the 18th issue, by Addison; contributed to *The Spectator* (1711–12); launched the periodicals *The Guardian* (1713), *The Englishman* (1713), *Town Talk, The Tea Table, Chit Chat, The Plebeian* (1718), and *The Theatre* (1720); as a partisan of the House of Hanover, expelled from House of Commons (1714), but on Hanoverian succession, rewarded with managership of the Drury Lane Theatre and a knighthood; broke with Addison (1718) and lost his office; beset by financial worries, retired to Wales (1722), where he died seven years later.

Stefansson *(stĕ fäns sən),* **Vilhjalmur** 1879–1962. Icelandic explorer. *b.* Arnes, Canada. Studied anthropology at Harvard; led ethnological expeditions to Canadian far north studying Eskimo mode of life (from 1908); during second expedition, stayed north of Arctic Circle (1913–18) using Eskimo techniques of survival. Author of *My Life with the Eskimo* (1913), *Friendly Arctic* (1921), *The Hunters of the Great North* (1922), *The Adventures of Wrangell Island* (1925), *Unsolved Mysteries of the Arctic* (1939), *Ultima Thule* (1940), *Greenland* (1942), and *Northwest to Fortune* (1958).

Steichen *(stī kən)*, **Edward** 1879–1972. American photographer. *b.* Luxembourg. Chief photographer of Condé Nast publications (1923–38); head of U.S. Navy photographic unit in World War II; director of photography at the Museum of Modern Art, organizing the *Family of Man* exhibition. Author of *A Life in Photography* (1968).

Stein *(stīn)*, **Gertrude** 1874–1946. American author. *b.* Allegheny, Pa. Studied psychology under William James, and later medicine; resided in Paris (from 1903); returned to the U.S. only once (1934); her associations with artists and writers, such as Hemingway and Picasso, have overshadowed her literary works; her prose is obscure, repetitious, and almost unintelligible through a play on sounds and images. Works include *Three Lives* (1908), *Tender Buttons* (1915), *Ten Portraits* (1930), *The Autobiography of Alice B. Toklas* (1933), *Four Saints in Three Acts* (1934), *The World Is Round* (1939), and *Brewsie and Willie* (1946).

Stein, Sir Mark Aurel 1862–1943. British archaeologist. *b.* Budapest, Hungary. In service of archaeological department of government of India; made important explorations in Chinese Turkestan and Central Asia, recorded in *Ancient Khotan* (1907), *The Thousand Buddhas* (1921), *On Alexander's Track to the Indus* (1929), and *Old Routes of Western Iran* (1940).

Stein, William Howard 1911–. American biochemist. *b.* New York, N.Y. With C.B. Afinsen and Stanford Moore, awarded Nobel Prize in chemistry (1972) for research into the chemical structure of the protein ribonuclease.

Steinbeck *(stīn bĕk)*, **John Ernst** 1902–68. American novelist. *b.* Salinas, Calif. Best known for his compassionate, realistic novels portraying the struggles of the poor and disadvantaged, including *Tortilla Flat* (1935), and the Pulitzer-prize-winning *The Grapes of Wrath* (1940) and *Of Mice and Men* (1937). Other works include *In Dubious Battle* (1936), *The Red Pony* (1937), *The Long Valley* (1938), *Cannery Row* (1944), *The Wayward Bus* (1947), *The Moon Is Down* (1942), *East of Eden* (1952), *Sweet Thursday* (1954), *The Winter of Our Discontent* (1961), *The Short Reign of Pippin* (1957), and *Travels with Charley* (1962); awarded Nobel Prize in literature (1962).

Steiner *(shtī nər)*, **Rudolf** 1861–1925. Austrian philosopher. *b.* Kraljevica, Croatia. Drawn into the Theosophy movement (from 1902), becoming a follower of Annie Besant; evolved spiritualistic doctrine called anthroposophy, which he founded as a movement (1912); established Goetheanum, a center near Basel, for promoting his theories; believed in the perfectibility of man's inner nature through release of creative and artistic energy. Author of *Wie Erlangt man Erkenntnisse der Höheren Welten?* (1909) and *Mein Lebensgang* (1925).

Steinmetz *(stīn mĕts),* **Charles Proteus** original name: KARL AUGUST RUDOLF. 1865–1923. American engineer and scientist. *b.* Breslau, Germany. Immigrated to the U.S. (1889); consulting engineer for General Electric in Schenectady (from 1893); professor of electrical engineering at Union College (from 1903); contributions in electrical engineering include discovery of hysteresis, production of artificial lightning, and development of notation for calculating problems in alternating current; held over 200 patents. Author of *Alternating Current Phenomena* (1897), *Theoretical Elements of Electrical Engineering* (1900–1902), and *Engineering Mathematics* (1910).

Stendhal *(stăN dàl)* pseudonym of MARIE HENRI BEYLE. 1783–1842. French novelist. *b.* Grenoble. Served in Napoleonic wars; lived in Italy (1814–21, 1830–42); relatively unknown and unread during his own lifetime, but gained recognition in the 1880s for *Le Rouge et le Noir* (1831) and *La Chartreuse de Parme* (1839); also wrote biographies of Haydn (1814), Rossini (1824), Napoleon (1876), and others, and the autobiography *Life of Henry Brulard* (trans. 1958).

Stephen *(stē vən),* **Saint** also STEPHEN I; called APOSTLE OF HUNGARY. c975–1038. King of Hungary (997–1038). Founder of Arpád dynasty; duke of Hungary (997–1001); crowned king of Hungary with title Apostolic King; suppressed paganism and promoted Christianization of the Magyars; introduced the German form of government with an advisory council of nobles and churchmen; honored as patron saint of Hungary; canonized (1087). Feast day: Sept. 2.

Stephenson *(stē vən sən),* **George** 1781–1848. English inventor. *b.* Wylam. Working as a fireman in a colliery, invented a colliery safety lamp; constructed first locomotive, *My Lord*, running six miles an hour, for the Killingworth Colliery railway; built an improved one with steam blast (1815); engineer for Stockton and Darlington mineral railway (1821) and for Liverpool and Manchester railway (1830); won locomotive engine competition with the *Rocket*, which attained 30 miles an hour; work carried on by son Robert (1803–1859) and nephew GEORGE ROBERT (1819–1905).

Stern *(shtern),* **Otto** 1888–1969. American physicist. *b.* Sohrau, Germany. Professor at Pittsburgh (from 1933); discovered the magnetic moment of protons; developed the molecular-beam method of studying atomic particles; awarded Nobel Prize in physics (1943).

Sterne *(stûrn),* **Laurence** 1713–68. English novelist. *b.* Clonmel, Ireland. Best known for *Tristram Shandy*, a whimsical novel that gained immediate popularity (9 vols., 1760–67), and *A Sentimental Journey Through France and Italy* (1768); considered a master of situational humor and a brilliant satirist and stylist.

Steuben *(stū bən),* **Baron Friedrich Wilhelm Ludolf Gerhard Augustin von** 1730–94. American soldier. *b.* Magdeburg, Germany. Entered

Prussian army (1747); distinguished himself at Prague, Rossback, Kunowice, and Swidnica; offered services to George Washington through Franklin; reached America (1777); appointed inspector general of Continental army and charged with its training; wrote a manual of army regulations and improved military discipline and staff organization; saw action at Monmouth and Yorktown; granted pension and grants of land by Congress; died in Steubenville, N.Y., named for him.

Stevens *(stē vənz),* **Thaddeus** 1792–1868. American statesman. *b.* Danville, Vt. Whig member of the Pennsylvania legislature (1833–42); Whig Congressman (1849–53); Republican Congressman (1859–68); noted for his defense of banking interests and public education and his opposition to slavery; by means of his parliamentary talents and his position as chairman of the Ways and Means and Appropriations committees during the Civil War and Reconstruction, he was influential in making national economic policies; as a leader of the radical wing of the Republican party, he sponsored the harsh features of the Reconstruction program; helped to write the 14th Amendment ensuring supremacy of the Republican party; urged confiscation of all Confederate party estates; one of the managers of the impeachment of President Johnson.

Stevens *(stē venz),* **Wallace** 1879–1955. American poet. *b.* Reading, Pa. Combined the writing of poetry with career as an insurance executive. Works include *Harmonium* (1923), *Ideas of Order* (1935), *Owl's Clover* (1936), *The Man with the Blue Guitar* (1937), *Parts of a World* (1942), *Transport to Summer* (1947), *The Auroras of Autumn* (1950), *The Necessary Angel* (1951), and *Opus Posthumous* (1947); *Collected Poems* (1945) won Pulitzer Prize.

Stevenson *(stē vən sən),* **Adlai Ewing** 1835–1914. American statesman. *b.* Christian County, Ky. Vice-president of U.S. under Cleveland (1893–97). Grandson was ADLAI EWING (1900–1965). American statesman. *b.* Los Angeles, Calif. Entered government service (1933), occupying offices under Roosevelt and Truman; governor of Illinois (1947); nominated as Democratic presidential candidate (1952, 1956), but was defeated both times by Eisenhower; U.S. ambassador to U.N. (1961–65). Author of *Friends and Enemies* (1959) and volumes of speeches *Call to Greatness* (1954) and *What I Think* (1956).

Stevenson, Robert Louis Balfour 1850–94. Scottish writer. *b.* Edinburgh. A frail, sickly child, he waged a lifelong struggle against tuberculosis; trained as a lawyer, but began literary career with travel books *An Inland Voyage* (1878) and *Travels with a Donkey in the Cévennes* (1879); married on trip to California (1879) and, on return, settled in Scotland (1880–87); wrote *The New Arabian Nights* (1882), *Treasure Island* (1883), *The Strange Case of Dr. Jekyll and Mr. Hyde* (1886), *Kidnapped* (1886), *Virginibus Puerisque* (1881), *Familiar Studies of Men and Books* (1882), *A Child's Garden of Verses* (1885), *The Body Snatcher* (1885), and *Prince Otto* (1885); immigrated to U.S., living at Saranac Lake; left U.S. for South Sea Islands, settling at Samoa (1888–94); later works include *The Merry Men* (1887), *The Black Arrow* (1888), *Master of Ballantrae* (1888), *Pulvis et Umbra* (1888), *Catriona* (1893), *The Weir of Hermiston* (incomplete), and *Island Nights' Entertainments* (1893).

Stewart, Robert. *See* **Castlereagh, Viscount**

Stieglitz *(stēg lĭtz),* **Alfred** 1864–1946. American photographer. *b.* Hoboken, N.J. Celebrated as one of the pioneers in developing photography as an art; directed the Photo-Secession Gallery; editor of *Camera Notes, Camera Work,* and *American Amateur Photographer.*

Stoker *(stō kər),* **Bram** real name: ABRAHAM. 1847–1912. Irish writer. *b.* Dublin. Secretary to Sir Henry Irving (from 1878). Wrote the classic horror story *Dracula* (1897).

Stopes *(stōps),* **Marie Carmichael** 1880–1958. English birth-control advocate. *b.* near Dorking. Unhappiness of first marriage caused her to write books on marriage, of which *Married Love* (1918) is the best known; with second husband, Humphrey Verdon Roe, founded Mothers' Clinic for Constructive Birth Control (1921); one of the first birth control clinics, president of Society for Constructive Birth Control and Racial Progress.

Story *(stō rĭ),* **Joseph** 1779–1845. American jurist. *b.* Marblehead, Mass. House of Representatives (1808–1809); associate justice of Supreme Court (1811–45); professor of law at Harvard (1829–45); writings and decisions have become part of American jurisprudence; with John Marshall, shaped and defined constitutional powers of Supreme Court. Works include *Commentaries on the Constitution of the U.S.* (1833), *Commentaries on the Law of Bailments* (1832), *On the Conflict of Laws* (1834), *On Equity Jurisprudence* (1836), *Equity Pleading* (1838), *Law of Agency* (1839), *Law of Partnership* (1841), *Law of Bills of Exchange* (1843), and *Law of Promissory Notes* (1845).

Stowe *(stō),* **Harriet Beecher** 1811–96. American author. b. Litchfield, Conn. Daughter of Lyman Beecher and sister of Henry Ward Beecher; published *Uncle Tom's Cabin* (1852), which achieved phenomenal success and became one of the most influential American books, arousing intense antislavery sentiments in the North; also wrote *Dred* (1856), *The Minister's Wooing* (1859), and *Old Town Folks* (1869); collected works published (16 vols., 1896).

Strabo *(strā bō)* c63 B.C.–A.D. c24. Greek geographer. *b.* Amasia, Pontus. Traveled widely and wrote *Geography* in 17 books, a rich sourcebook of knowledge of the ancient world; also wrote a *History* in 47 books, now lost.

Strachey *(strā chĭ),* **Giles Lytton** 1880–1932. English writer. *b.* London. Member of the Bloomsbury Group; noted for witty and irreverent biographies that made literary history, including *Eminent Victorians* (1918), *Queen Victoria* (1921), *Pope* (1925), *Elizabeth and Essex* (1928), *Portraits in Miniature* (1931), *Characters and Commentaries* (1933), and *Landmarks in French Literature* (1912).

Stradivari *(strä də vä rē),* **Antonio** 1644–1737. Italian violin-maker. *b.* Cremona. Pupil of Nicolo Amati; perfected the Cremona violas and violoncellos, over 1000 in number (1666–1737); work continued by sons Francesco (1671–1743) and Omobono (1679–1742); his instruments are now priceless treasures.

Strauss *(shtrous),* **Johann** 1804–49. Austrian composer. *b.* Vienna. Noted as a conductor and composer of dance music; compositions include 150 waltzes, 14 polkas, 28 galops, 35 quadrilles, and 19 marches; best known of his waltzes are *Lorelei* and the *Donaulieder*. His son JOHANN, called THE YOUNGER, (1825–99), composed nearly 400 pieces of dance music, including *The Blue Danube, Artist's Life, Tales from the Vienna Woods, The Emperor, Wine, Woman, and Song, Morning Papers Waltz, Voices of Spring, Southern Roses*; also wrote operettas *Indigo (1871), Die Fledermaus* (1874), *Cagliostro* (1875), *Prinz Methusalem* (1877), *A Night in Venice* (1883), and *Der Ziegeunerbaron* (1885).

Strauss, Richard 1864–1949. German composer. *b.* Munich. Began composing at age 6, publishing first composition at 11; conductor at Wagner Festival (from 1891); conductor of the Berlin Philharmonic Orchestra (from 1894); produced first opera, *Guntram* (1894); headed music department of Third Reich as Reichmusikkammer (from 1933); headed state opera at Vienna (1919–24); Operas include *Feuersnot* (1901), *Salome* (1905), *Elektra* (1908), *Der Rosenkavalier* (1911), *Ariadne auf Naxos* (1912), *Die Frau ohne Schatten* (1919), *Intermezzo* (1925), *Arabella* (1933), *Die Schweigsame Frau* (1935), *Daphne* (1938), and *Capriccio*, his last work; tone poems include *Don Juan* (1888), *Aus Italien* (1889), *Macbeth* (1890), *Tod und Verklärung* (1890), *Till Eulenspiegels Lustige Streiche* (1895), *Also Sprach Zarathustra* (1896), *Don Quixote* (1897), *Ein Heldenleben* (1898), and *Sinfonia Domestica* (1904).

Stravinsky *(strȧ vĭn skĭ),* **Igor Fëdorovich** 1882–1971. Russian composer. *b.* Oranienbaum. Studied under Rimsky-Korsakov; took musical world by storm with ballets written for Diaghilev's ballet company: *The Firebird* (1910), *Petrouchka* (1911), and *The Rite of Spring* (1913); settled in France (1934) and eventually in U.S. (from 1945); from the 1950s, began using 12-tone technique, bold rhythms, and dissonant harmonies, producing striking and colorful works; a restless experimenter, he developed a neoclassical style that blended 18th century music and jazz. Other works include *Les Noces* (1917), *Pulcinella* (1919), *Le Baiser de la Fée* (1928), *Agon* (1957), *The Rake's Progress* (1951), *The Nightingale* (1914), *Apollo Musagète* (1928), *The Card Game* (1937), *Orpheus* (1948), *The Soldier's Tale* (1918), *Renard* (1917), *Oedipus Rex* (1927), *Fireworks, Symphony of Psalms* (1930), *Threni* (1958), *Requiem Canticles* (1966), *Septuor* (1953), *Symphonies of Wind Instruments* (1921), *Symphony in C Major* (1940), *The Flood* (1962), *In Memoriam Dylan Thomas* (1954),

Elegy for J.F.K. (1964), and *Variations* (1965). Author of *Chronicles of My Life* (1936) and *Conversations* (3 vols., 1959–62).

Stresemann *(shtrā zə män),* **Gustav** 1878–1929. German statesman. *b.* Berlin. Entered Reichstag (1907); founder and leader of German People's party after World War I; chancellor of Weimar Republic (1923); minister of foreign affairs (1923–29); negotiated Locarno mutual security pact with France and England, secured admission of Germany into League of Nations, signed Kellogg-Briand Pact, obtained evacuation of the Ruhr and the Rhineland, and accepted the Dawes and Young Plans for reparations; awarded Nobel Peace Prize (1926) with Aristide Briand.

Strindberg *(strĭnd băr y),* **August** 1849–1912. Swedish playwright. *b.* Stockholm. Wrote first play *Mäster Olof* (1872); in the 69 plays that followed, ranged through realism, naturalism, mysticism, pessimism, and romanticism; wrote historical dramas, novels, social criticism, and short stories; suffered periodic onsets of insanity; tortured by morbid despair, misogyny, and spiritual unrest; much of his antifeminism was attributed to his three unhappy marriages; provoked by criticism to leave Sweden (1882); recalled (1884) to stand trial for blasphemy; founded Intimate Theatre (1907) and wrote plays for it; *Collected Works* in 55 volumes includes the plays *The Secret of the Guild* (1880), *Sir Bengt's Wife* (1882), *The Father* (1887), *Lady Julia* (1888), *To Damascus* (1898–1904), *Crimes and Crimes* (1899), *Gustavus Vasa* (1899), *Gustavus Adolphus* (1900), *The Dance of Death* (1901), *Carl XII* (1901), and *A Dream Play* (1902); novels *The Red Room* (1879), *Swedish Fates and Adventures* (1882–83), *Realized Utopias* (1885), *Married* (1884–86), *The People of Hemso* (1887), *In the Outer Skerries* (1890), and *A Blue Book* (1907–1908); the autobiographies *Tjänstekvinnansson* (1886), *Inferno* (1897), and *Legender* (1898).

Stuart *(stū ərt),* **Gilbert Charles** 1755–1828. American painter. *b.* Narragansett, R.I. Worked his passage to London (1775); established as a fashionable portrait painter (1778); opened studio in Dublin (1787–93); on return to America, opened studios in New York (1793), Philadelphia (1794–96), Germantown (1796–1803), Washington, D.C. (1803–1805), and Boston (1805–28); best known for portraits of Washington, Judge Stephen Jones, F.S. Richards, John Adams, John Quincy Adams, Jefferson, Madison, George III, and Louis XVI.

Sturm *(shtoorm),* **Johannes** 1507–89. German educator. *b.* Schleiden. Professor at Paris (from 1530); invited to reorganize the educational system at Strasbourg (1536); established a gymnasium there (1538) and an academy (1564); introduced teaching methods that were later adopted throughout Europe; sided with Zwingli against Luther and was briefly driven from Strasbourg by the Lutherans (1581).

Stuyvesant *(stī və sənt),* **Peter** 1592–1672. Dutch colonial administrator. *b.* West Friesland. In service of Dutch West India

Company (1635); governor of Curaçao (1643); lost a leg in engagement with Portuguese on St. Martin Island (1644); director general of New Netherlands (1646); assumed office in New Amsterdam (1647); during his administration, promoted commerce, conciliated the Indians, and established boundary with English colonists at Hartford; seized New Sweden (1655); opposed religious and political freedom for the colonists; surrendered city to the English after surprise attack (1664).

Südfeld, Max Simon. *See* **Nordau, Max Simon**

Suleiman *(sü lā män)* known as THE MAGNIFICENT. c1496–1566. Ottoman sultan (1520–66). Succeeded father Selim I; under his expansionist rule, Ottoman empire reached its zenith; added Belgrade, Budapest, Rhodes, Tabriz, Baghdad, Aden, and Algiers to his dominions, while his fleet, under Barbarossa, became the terror of the Mediterranean; suffered serious reverses at Vienna (1529), Malta (1565), and Tunis (1535); promulgated a system of laws that earned him the title Kanuni (Lawgiver); with the help of his architect, Selim Sinan, created notable mosques and palaces; organized the college of Muslim theologians; killed son Mustafa (1553) and prime minister Ibrahim (1536).

Sulla *(sŭl ə),* **Lucius Cornelius** surname: FELIX. 138–78 B.C. Roman statesman. Born of noble family; as quaestor, served under Marius in Africa (107) and helped capture Jugurtha; fought against the Cimbri and the Teutones (104–101); praetor (93); propraetor (92) in Cilicia, where he restored Ariobarzanes to throne of Cappadocia; captured Bovianum in the Social War (90–89); consul (88); earned hostility of Marius by being named commander in the war against Mithridates VI; expelled from Rome by the Marians, but returned heading six legions; took Rome, and with the first proscription overthrew the Marian party (88); fought against Mithridates (87–84); won at Chaeronea (86) and Orchomenus (85), and defeated Marian general Fimbria (84); returned to Rome (83) after imposing peace in the East; brought Civil War to an end by crushing Marian opposition (83–82) and defeating Samnites at Colline Gate; proclaimed himself dictator (82–79), proscribed and killed followers of Marius and expropriated their property; effected important constitutional changes including reorganization of the senate and judiciary; founded miliary colonies throughout Italy; resigned (79).

Sullivan *(sŭl ə vən),* **Sir Arthur Seymour** 1842–1900. English composer. *b.* London. Began career with *Cox and Box*, a comic opera (1867); after writing overtures and oratorios, joined in celebrated partnership with librettist Sir William Gilbert with *Thespis* (1871); went on to produce 13 other comic operas with Gilbert: *Trial by Jury* (1875), *The Sorcerer* (1877), *H.M.S. Pinafore* (1878), *The Pirates of Penzance* (1880), *Patience* (1881), *Iolanthe* (1882), *Princess Ida* (1884), *The Mikado* (1885), *Ruddigore* (1887), *The Yeoman of the Guard* (1888), *The Gondoliers* (1889), *Utopia Limited* (1893), and *The Grand Duke* (1896); composed songs and hymns, including "*Onward, Christian Soldiers*," incidental music for Shakespeare's plays, and cantatas.

Sullivan, Louis Henri 1856–1924. American architect. *b.* Boston, Mass. Considered the father of modernism in American architecture; first to design a skyscraper; notable buildings include Gage Building, the Auditorium, Transportation Building, the Stock Exchange, and the Carson, Pirie, Scott and Company building at Chicago, the Wainwright building and the Union Trust building in St. Louis, and the Bayard building in New York.

Sully Prudhomme *(sü lē prü dôm),* **René François Armand** 1839–1907. French writer. *b.* Paris. Member of the Parnassian group; received first Nobel Prize in literature (1901). Works include *Stances et Poèmes* (1865), *Les Épreuves* (1866), *Les Solitudes* (1869), *Les Destins* (1872), *Les Vaines Tendresses* (1875), *La Justice* (1878), *Le Prisme* (1886), *Le Bonheur* (1888), *Reflections on the Art of Verse* (1892), *Testament Poétique* (1901), *La Vraie Religion Selon Pascal* (1905), and *Que Sais-je? Examen de Conscience* (1895).

Sumner *(sŭm nər),* **James Batcheller** 1887–1955. American biochemist. *b.* Canton, Mass. Professor at Cornell (from 1929); shared Nobel Prize in chemistry (1946) with John H. Northrop and Wendell M. Stanley for discovering the crystallization of enzymes.

Sunday *(sŭn dĭ),* **William Ashley** called BILLY SUNDAY. 1862–1935. American evangelist. *b.* Ames, Iowa. After career as professional baseball player (1883–90), turned to evangelism (after 1896) and became one of the most popular preachers of his day; ordained (1903).

Sun Yat-sen *(so͞on yət sĕn)* **also** SUN WEN, CHUNG SHAN. 1866–1925. Chinese statesman. *b.* Tsuiheng. Studied medicine and practiced at Macao and Canton; led abortive uprising against Manchus in Canton (1895); On its failure, fled, living in U.S., England, and Japan (until 1911); from abroad, engineered ten revolts against the Manchus and was finally successful (1911); first president of Provisional Republican government of China (1911); founded Kuomintang, a national people's party based on principles of nationalism, democracy, and people's livelihood; yielded office to Yüan Shi-kai (1912), against whom he organized a new republic in South China (1921) with himself as president; receiving no help from Western powers, turned to Soviet Union; reorganized the Kuomintang as a revolutionary party with Communist alliance, friendship with U.S.S.R. and support of workers and peasants as its principal policies; died before achieving unification of China. Author of *San Min Chu I* (*The Three Principles of the People*) (1927).

Sutherland *(suth ər lənd),* **Earl Wilbur** 1915–1974. American physiologist. *b.* Burlingame, Kans. Professor at Vanderbilt University (from 1963); awarded Nobel Prize in physiology and medicine (1971) for discoveries concening the mechanism of hormone action.

Suttner *(zo͞ot nər),* **Bertha von** 1843–1914. Austrian pacifist. *b.* Prague, Czechoslovakia. Founded Austrian Society of

Friends of Peace (1891) and, as its president, attended peace congresses at Rome (1891), Bern (1892), Antwerp (1894), and Hamburg (1897); edited journal *Die Waffen Nieder* (from 1892); advanced antiwar cause through her books, including *Lay Down Your Arms* (1889), *Inventarium Einer Seele* (1883), *Trente et Quarante* (1893), *Einsam und Arm* (2 vols., 1896), *Das Maschinenzeitalter* (1899), *Marthas Kinder* (1902), *Briefe an einen toten* (1904), and *Memoirs* (1910); awarded Nobel Peace Prize (1905).

Suvorov *(sōō və rôf),* **Count Aleksandr Vasilievich** 1729–1800. Russian marshal. *b.* Finland. Fought in Seven Years' War (1756–63) and in Russo-Turkish War (1773–74); put down the Pugachev Rebellion (1775); led Russian army in Russo-Turkish War (1787–92); victorious in battles of Kinburn, Focsani, and Rimnik and Ismail; put down Kosciusko's rebellion in Poland (1794); recalled from retirement to fight against the French Revolutionary army which he defeated in Cassano d'Adda, the Trebbia River, and Novi; never defeated in battle; commander in chief (1800).

Svedberg *(svād bărK),* **Theodor** 1884–1971. Swedish chemist. *b.* Valbo. Professor at Uppsala (from 1949); developed the ultracentrifuge for determining molecular weight of large molecules; won Nobel Prize in chemistry (1926) for contributions to colloid chemistry.

Sverdrup *(svăr drōōp),* **Otto Neumann** 1855–1930. Norwegian explorer. *b.* Sogndal. Member of Nansen's polar expedition and commander of the *Fram* on the return journey (1893–96); led expedition in unsuccessful attempt to circumnavigate Greenland (1898–1902); conducted three more expeditions into the Arctic (1914, 1920, 1928). Author of *Nyt Land* (1903).

Swedenborg *(svā dən bôrK),* **Emanuel** 1688–1772. Swedish scientist, mystic, and philosopher. *b.* Stockholm. Studied science and spent 12 years abroad in scientific pursuits; on return, appointed assessor on Swedish Board of Mines (1716); invented machines for carrying boats overland, frustrating the Danish blockade at Fredrikshald (1718); contributed to the fields of chemistry, physics, mathematics, astronomy, geology, engineering, and mining. Published *Opera Philosophica et Mineralia* (1734), *Oeconomia Regni Animalis* (1740), and *Regnum Animali* (1740); designed an airplane with stationary wings; began receiving visions and the call to reveal a new Christian doctrine (1743); devoted rest of life to preaching the knowledge revealed to him; wrote over 40 books on theology, of which the most important are *Heavenly Arcana* (1749–56), *Heaven and Hell* (1758), *Divine Love and Wisdom* (1763), and *True Christian Religion* (1771); after death, his teachings formed the basis of the Church of New Jerusalem, or New Church, organized in London (1778).

Swift *(swĭft),* **Jonathan** 1667–1745. English satirist. *b.* Dublin. Educated at Dublin; went to London (1688), becoming secretary to Sir William Temple; took orders (1695); first literary efforts, *Battle of the Books* and *Tale of a Tub*, were published in 1704; vicar of a parish in Laracor, near Dublin (1700); during this period, published the poem *"Baucis and Philemon"* and tracts and pamphlets, including *Arguments against Abolishing Christianity* (1708); spent time in London (from 1708) in political and literary circles; abandoned Whig stands to become a Tory; through pamphlets and articles in the *Examiner*, contributed to the return of Harley, the Earl of Oxford and to the fall of Marlborough; joined with Arbuthnot and Pope to form the Scriblerus Club (1713); wrote *Journal to Stella* (1710–13); dean of St. Patrick's, Dublin (1713); on death of Queen Anne and the return to power of the Whigs, retired to Dublin (1715); plunged into a campaign for Irish liberties; in *Drapier's Letters*, attacked the patent granted to William Wood for minting copper coins for Ireland, forcing withdrawal of the patent (1724); published his greatest work, *Gulliver's Travels*, in 1726, followed by the mordant *Modest Proposal* (1729); before succumbing to insanity, spent last years on poetic works such as *Verses on the Death of Dr. Swift* and *Rhapsody on Poetry*.

Swinburne *(swĭn bûrn)*, **Algernon Charles** 1837–1909. English poet. *b.* London. Achieved success with poetic drama *Atalanta in Calydon* (1865); poems censured for their paganism and sensuality; favorite themes were those of a classical romantic: liberty, sea, progress, children; principal strengths were imagination and metrical skill. Works include *Poems and Ballads* (1865), *Chastelard* (1865), *Bothwell* (1874), *Mary Stuart* (1881), *A Song of Italy* (1867), *Songs Before Sunrise* (1871), *Erechtheus* (1876), *Poems and Ballads* (1878), *Tristram of Lyonesse* (1882), *Songs of the Springtides* (1880), *Studies in Song* (1880), *A Midsummer Holiday* (1884), *Marino Faliero* (1885), *Poems and Ballads* (1889), *The Tale of Balen* (1896), *Astrophel* (1894), and *A Channel Passage* (1899); wrote such plays as *Locrine* (1887), *The Sisters* (1892), and *Rosamund, Queen of the Lombards* (1899); critical studies on Blake, George Chapman, Charlotte Brontë, Shakespeare, Hugo, and Jonson; *Essays and Studies* (1875); and *Studies in Prose and Poetry* (1894).

Sydenham *(sĭd ən əm)*, **Thomas** 1624–89. English physician. *b.* Wynford Eagle. Studied medicine and practiced in London (from 1655); called the English Hippocrates for his clinical studies and observations, including descriptions of gout, venereal disease, hysteria, Sydenham's chorea, malaria, and smallpox; introduced medical use of opium. Author of *Methodus Curandi Februs* (1666), *Epistolae Responsoriae* (1680), and *Tractatus de Podagra et Hydrope* (1683).

Symonds *(sĭm əndz)*, **John Addington** 1840–93. English man of letters. *b.* Bristol. Fame rests on a monumental study, *The Renaissance in Italy* (5 vols., 1875–86); also published *An Introduction to the Study of Dante* (1872), *Studies of the Greek Poets* (1873–76), and lives of Shelley (1878), Sir Philip Sydney (1886), Ben Jonson (1886), and Michelangelo (1892).

Synge *(sĭng)*, **John Millington** 1871–1909. Irish dramatist.

b. near Dublin. Induced by W.B. Yeats to live in the Aran Islands and to write about Irish peasant life using the expressive language of the natives (1898–1902); wrote *The Aran Islands* (1907), *Kerry and Wicklow, The Shadow of the Glen*, and *Riders to the Sea* (1904); with Lady Augusta Gregory, founded the Abbey Theatre, serving as its director until his death; contributed *The Well of the Saints* (1905), *The Playboy of the Western World* (1907), and *The Tinker's Wedding* (1907); *Deirdre of the Sorrows*, unfinished at his death, was produced posthumously (1910).

Synge *(sĭng),* **Richard Laurence Millington** 1914–. British biochemist. With A.J.P. Martin, received Nobel Prize in chemistry (1952) for discovery of partition chromatography, a method of separating compounds in chemical analysis.

Szent-Gyorgyi von Nagyrapolt *(sənt dyûr dyĭ fən nŏd yrŏ pōlt),* **Albert** 1893–. Hungarian chemist. *b.* Budapest. Professor at Szeged (1931–45) and Budapest (1945–47); immigrated to U.S. (1947); director of Institute of Muscle Research in Woods Hole, Mass.; isolated actin, the fundamental muscle protein, and vitamin C; studied cellular oxidation, muscle contraction, and biological combustion; awarded Nobel Prize in physiology and medicine (1937).

Szilard *(zĭ lärd),* **Leo** 1898–1964. American physicist. *b.* Budapest, Hungary. Immigrated to U.S. (1940); professor at Chicago (1946–53); with Enrico Fermi, developed the fundamental chain reaction that led to the atom bomb; later protested nuclear warfare.

T

Tacitus *(tăs ĭ təs),* **Cornelius** c55–c117. Roman historian. *b.* Rome (?). Quaestor (79); praetor (88); consul (97); compiled works on Roman history and biography notable for their austere moral tone and polished style: *Dialogus de Oratoribus* on the decline of eloquence, *Life of Agricola, Germania* on Germanic tribes, *Historiae* on the Roman Empire from the accession of Galba (68) to the assassination of Domitian (96), and *Annales*, a history of the Julians from Tiberius to Nero.

Taft *(tăft),* **Robert Alphonso** 1889–1953. American statesman. *b.* Cincinnati. Son of William Howard Taft; U.S. senator (1939–53); Senate Republican leader (1947–49); principal exponent during the post-World War II years of conservative and isolationist philosophy; widely respected for his integrity and acumen; cosponsor of the Taft-Hartley Act; sought Republican presidential nomination unsuccessfully (1940, 1944, 1948, 1952).

Taft, William Howard 1857–1930. 27th president of U.S. (1909–13) *b.* Cincinnati. Entered politics in Ohio (1880), holding judicial offices before becoming solicitor general under Harrison (1890); president of Philippine Commission (1900); first civil governor of the Islands (1901); Theodore Roosevelt's secretary of war (1904–1908); as Roosevelt's handpicked successor, won presidential election (1908) over William Jennings Bryan; continued Roosevelt's domestic and international policies, especially trust-busting and dollar diplomacy; unpopular for defense of Payne-Aldrich Tariff Act (1909); antagonized Roosevelt by dismissal of the conservationist Gifford Pinchot and by his philosophic antipathy to labor; renominated but lost to Wilson in a three-way election, with Roosevelt heading a third-party ticket; chief justice of Supreme Court (1921–30).

Tagore *(tə gōr),* **Rabindranath** 1861–1941. Indian poet. *b.* Calcutta. Scion of a noble Indian family of bankers and mystics; founded Santiniketan, an international school in a rural setting (1901); set over 3000 songs to music, wrote over 50 dramas, 100 books of verse, and 40 volumes of fiction, as well as writing on politics and philosophy; translated many of his own works from Bengali into English; awarded Nobel Prize in literature (1913), the first Asian to be so honored. Works include *Mashi* (1918), *Gitanjali* (1912), *The Gardener* (1913), *Sadhana* (1914), *Songs of Kabir* (1915), *Nationalism* (1917), *Parrot's Training* (1918), *Creative Unity* (1922), *Fireflies* (1928), *Red Oleander* (1924), and the autobiographical *My Reminiscences* (1917) and *The Religion of Man* (1931); writings imbued with oriental pantheism and the sense of unity of all living things.

Taine *(tĕn),* **Hippolyte Adolphe** 1828–93. French philosopher. *b.* Vouziers. Professor at École des Beaux Arts (from 1864); with *Histoire de la Littérature Anglaise* (1856–65), established himself as the foremost literary critic of his age; sustained the thesis that heredity, environment, and historic time-frame determine a man's ideas and actions, providing the philosophic basis of naturalism. Other works include *Essai sur les Fables de la Fontaine* (1853) *Essai de Critique et d'Histoire* (1855), *Idéalisme Anglaise* (1864), *De l'Intelligence* (1870), and *Les Origines de la France Contemporaine* (1871–94).

Talbot *(tôl bət),* **William Henry Fox** 1800–1877. English inventor and antiquary. *b.* Evershot. Invented a process of making photographic prints on silver chloride paper (c1839) and the calotype, or Talbotype, process (1841); received Royal Society medal (1838); deciphered the cuneiform inscriptions of Ninevah. Published *Pencil of Nature* (1844), one of the earliest photographic books, *Hermes* (1838–39), and *English Etymologies* (1847).

Talleyrand-Périgord *(tȧ lā räN pā rē gôr),* **Charles Maurice de** title: PRINCE DE BÉNÉVENT. 1754–1838. French statesman. *b.* Paris. Trained for the church; abbot of St. Denis (1775); general agent of the French clergy, (1780); bishop of Autun (1788); elected to States-General from the first estate (1789); Constituent Assembly (1789); proposed confiscation of church property and accepted civil constitution of the clergy, for which acts he was excommunicated; escaped the Terror as envoy in England; traveled in U.S.; returned to France after fall of Robespierre (1796); with the help of Paul Barras, became foreign minister under the Directory (1797); gained confidence of Napoleon, becoming foreign minister under the Consulate; helped Napoleon consolidate his power as consul for life (1802) and emperor (1804); rewarded with title of Prince Bénévent and office of grand chamberlain (1804); opposed Napoleon's expansionism and megalomania and was dismissed (1809); opened secret negotiations with enemies of France; on fall of Napoleon, instrumental in securing Bourbon Restoration and winning peace terms favorable to the maintaining of France's territorial integrity; minister of foreign affairs (1814); prime minister (1815); defended French interests at Congress of Vienna (1814–15); forced into retirement through hostility of royalists (1815); returned to public office (1830) as an ally of Louis Philippe; ambassador to England (1830–34); organized Quadruple Alliance (1834). Published *Mémoires* (5 vols., 1891–92).

Tamerlane *(tăm ə lān)* also TAMBURLAINE, TIMUR. c1336–1405. Mongol conqueror. *b.* Kesh, near Samarkand, Central Asia. Descendant of Genghis Khan; inherited or seized a kingdom whose capital was Samarkand (1369); controlled all of Turkestan (1370), and Khorasan, Azerbaijan, Kurdistan, Afghanistan, and Fars (by 1387); embarked on invasions of Persia, Georgia, and the Tatar empire; penetrated Russia as far as Moscow (1381); crushed the Golden Horde (1395); invaded India, took Delhi (1398); descended on Syria and added Damascus to his conquests; on plains of Angora, scattered the Turks and captured Bejazet (1402); died en route to invasion of China; considered a scourge of god by his contemporaries; conquests were marked by the slaughter of thousands; remembered in Samarkand as a patron of art and architecture.

Tamm *(tȧm),* **Igor Yevgenyevich** 1895–1971. Soviet physicist. With P. Cherenkov and I. Frank, shared Nobel Prize in physics (1958) for discovery of the Cherenkov effect.

Tanguy *(tȧNgē),* **Yves** 1900–1955. American artist. *b.* Paris, France. Settled in U.S. (1939); best known as a leader of the Surrealists. Works include *In Place of Fear, The Witness, Papa Is Wounded, From the Other Side of the Bridge, Black Landscape*, and *Heredity of Acquired Characteristics.*

Tarkington *(tärk ĭng tən),* **Booth** 1869–1946. American novelist. *b.* Indianapolis, Ind. Noted for novels of Indiana life. *The Gentleman from Indiana* (1899), *The Turmoil* (1915), *The Magnificent Ambersons* (1918), *The Midlander* (1923), and *Alice Adams* (1921); also wrote the historical romance *Monsieur Beaucaire* (1900), the popular Penrod books, beginning with *Penrod* (1914); *Seventeen* (1916); the trilogy *Growth* (1927); and the autobiography *The World Does Move* (1928).

Tasso *(täs sō),* **Torquato** 1544–95. Italian poet. *b.* Sorrento. Studied law and philosophy at Padua; as a student published *Rinaldo* (1562); entered service of house of Este (1565) and began work on his epic *Jerusalem Delivered*; accompanied Cardinal Luigi d'Este to Paris (1570), where he met Ronsard and the Pléiade; returned to employ of Duke of Ferrara, Alfonso d'Este; completed *Aminta* (1573) and *Jerusalem Delivered* (1575); beset by persecution mania and delusions, spent remaining years in restless wandering; summoned to Rome by Pope Clement VIII to be crowned poet laureate (1595), but fell ill and died on the way. Other works include *Torrismondo* (1586), *Il Mondo Creato*, and *Discorsi dell'Arte Poetica*.

Tatum *(tāt əm),* **Edward Lawrie** 1909–75. American biochemist. *b.* Boulder, Colo. Professor at Stanford (1937–45, 1948–56), Yale (1945–48), and Rockefeller (1957) universities; awarded Nobel Prize in physiology and medicine (1958), with Joshua Lederberg and G.W. Beadle, for establishing that genes in bread mold transmit hereditary characters by controlling specific chemical reactions.

Tawney *(tô nē),* **Richard Henry** 1880–1962. English economist. *b.* Calcutta, India. Professor of economic history at London (1931–49); president of Workers' Educational Association (1928–44); founded the Christian Socialist tradition in modern economic thinking; influential in councils of British Labor party. Works include *The Acquisitive Society* (1926), *Religion and the Rise of Capitalism* (1926), *Equality* (1931), and *Business and Politics Under James I* (1958).

Taylor *(tā lər),* **Frederick Winslow** 1856–1915. American efficiency and management expert. *b.* Germantown, Pa. As a consulting engineer, developed time and work studies and the concept of scientific management, known as Taylorism. Author of *Principles of Scientific Management* (1911) and other books.

Taylor, Jeremy 1613–67. English prelate. *b.* Cambridge. Chaplain to Archbishop Laud; chaplain in ordinary to King Charles II; on the losing Royalist side in Civil War; went to Wales as chaplain to Richard Vaughn, earl of Carbery, whose home, *Golden Grove*, furnished the title of one of his devotional manuals (1655); at Restoration, appointed bishop of Down and Connor in Ireland (1661); vice-chancellor of Dublin University; as bishop, struggled to enforce conformity, bringing conflict with Presbyterian clergy; noted as author of classics of Christian eloquence; Works include *The Liberty of Prophesying* (1646), *The Life of Christ, or the Great Exemplar* (1649), *Holy Living* (1650), *Holy Dying* (1651), *The Worthy Communicant* (1660), and *Ductor Dubitantium* (1660); *Whole Works* (10 vols.), published 1847–52.

Taylor, Zachary 1784–1850. 12th president of the U.S. (1849–50) *b.* Montebello, Va. Entered army (1808); fought War of 1812, becoming major; fought in wars against Seminoles and in Black Hawk War, winning the nickname **Old Rough and Ready**; when

Texas was invaded by Mexico, advanced to Rio Grande and defeated Mexican forces at Palo Alto (1846) and Resaca de la Palma (1846), occupying Matamoros; commander of Army of the Rio Grande as major general; took Monterey and, with victory at Buena Vista (1847), ended the war; nominated for presidency by Whigs (1847), winning easily; his administration witnessed the beginning of struggle over extension of slavery and the admission of Calif. and New Mexico into the Union; died after sixteen months in office.

Tchaikovsky *(chī kôf skĭ),* **Petr Ilich** 1840–93. Russian composer. *b.* Kamsko-Votinsk. Studied at St. Petersburg Conservatory under Anton Rubinstein; received an annuity (from 1878) from patroness Nadejda von Meck, whom he never met; suffered mental breakdown after disastrous marriage (1877); made trips to England and U.S. as conductor; used Russian and Slavic themes and folk material, but considered himself a cosmopolitan rather than a nationalist musician. Works include six symphonies, three piano concertos, a violin concerto, 11 operas, including *Eugene Onegin, The Queen of Spades, Iolanthe, Joan of Arc*, and *Vakula the Smith*, the ballets *Swan Lake, Sleeping Beauty*, and *Nutcracker*, overtures to *Hamlet* and *Romeo and Juliet*, the orchestral works *Marche Slave, 1812 Overture, Capriccio Italienne, Francesca da Rimini*, and *Manfred*, the suite *Mozartiana,* and songs.

Teilhard de Chardin *(tā yär də shär dăN),* **Pierre** 1881–1955. French Jesuit paleontologist and mystic. *b.* Auvergne. Professor of geology at Institut Catholique in Paris (1918); took paleontological expeditions to China and central Asia, where his studies on the history of early man attracted worldwide attention; developed theological view of evolution that caused his superiors in the Jesuit order to forbid him to teach or publish; writings published posthumously reveal a brilliant and original mind trying to understand evolution through the concepts of noosphere, involution, nonfinality, and complexification. Works include *Phenomenon of Man* (1959) and *The Divine Milieu* (1960).

Telemann *(tĕ lə män),* **Georg Philipp** 1681–1767. German composer. *b.* Magdeburg. Kapellmeister at Sorau, Eisenach, and Bayreuth (1704–21); music director of the Johanneum at Hamburg (1721–67); one of the most prolific of composers, his works include church music, 44 passions, 40 operas, and oratorios including *Der Tag des Gerichts* and *Die Tageszeiten;* also wrote three autobiographies; though unoriginal and lacking in depth, he was technically proficient and introduced grace and richness into German music; ranked above Bach in his lifetime but lost popularity after death until rediscovered in 1930.

Teller *(tĕl ər),* **Edward** 1908–. American physicist. *b.* Budapest, Hungary. Studied in Germany and Denmark; left Germany (1933); Professor at George Washington University (1936–41), Chicago (1946–49), and California (from 1953); worked on Manhattan Project (1941–46); director of Livermore Nuclear Laboratory

(1958–60); foremost advocate of American nuclear superiority in the scientific community; one of the architects of Truman's crash program to build first hydrogen bomb. Author of *Our Nuclear Future* (1958).

Temple, Henry John. *See* **Palmerston, Viscount**

Tennyson *(tĕn ĭ sən),* **Alfred** title: BARON TENNYSON; known as ALFRED, LORD TENNYSON. 1809–92. English poet. *b.* Somersby. Began writing poetry at Trinity College, Cambridge, winning Chancellor's Medal with *"Timbuctoo"* (1829); his *Poems, Chiefly Lyrical* (1830) and *Poems* (1832), containing "The Lady of Shalott," "The Lotus Eaters," and "Oenone," received indifferent reception, but *Poems* (2 vols., 1842) gained acclaim; after publication of *In Memoriam* (1850), was made poet laureate; wrote verse novelettes *Charge of the Light Brigade* (1854), *Maud* (1855), *Idylls of the King* (1859–1888), *Enoch Arden* (1864), and *Aylmer's Field* (1864); wrote historical dramas *Becket* (1884), *Queen Mary* (1875), *Harold* (1876), *The Falcon* (1879), and *The Cup* (1881); later ballads and lyrical narratives collected in *Ballads* (1880), *Tiresias* (1885), *Locksley Hall Sixty Years After* (1886), *Demeter* (1889), and *Death of Oenone* (1892); wrote *The Princess* (1847) on woman's emancipation; as a poet, perfectly suited to Victorian tastes; considered the most popular and widely read poet of his time.

Terence *(tĕr əns)* Latin name: PUBLIUS TERENTIUS AFER. 185–159 B.C. Roman dramatist. *b.* Carthage, North Africa. Taken to Rome as the slave of Publius Terentius Lucanus, whose name he adopted; published first play, *Andria*, in 166; its success gave him entry into Roman society and gained him the friendship of Laelius and the younger Scipio; moved to Greece, where he died; his six extant plays were freely adapted from Menander and Apollodorus: including *Andria, Hecyra, Heautontimoroumenos, Eunuchus, Phormio,* and *Adelphi*.

Tertullian *(tûr tŭl yən)* Latin name: QUINTUS SEPTIMIUS FLORENS TERTULLIANUS. c160–c230. Carthaginian theologian. *b.* Carthage, North Africa. Converted to Christianity (c192) and ordained as a presbyter; drifted from strict orthodoxy to Montanism, a heresy that stressed ecstatic prophecy and severe asceticism; honored as a father of the Latin Church for his eloquent and highly intellectual defense of the Christian faith; his vigorous and vivid style abounds in epigrammatic phrases. Author of *Ad Martyres*, *De Patientia*, *De Prescriptione*, *Apologeticum*, *Ad Nationes*, and *De Anima*; second only to St. Augustine in his influence on Christian theology.

Tesla *(tĕs lə),* **Nikola** 1857–1943. American inventor. *b.* Smiljan, Croatia. Immigrated to U.S. (1884); made important contributions to fields of high-tension electricity, wireless and radio communication, and alternating-current transmission; his inventions include the Tesla coil, the induction motor, electric bulbs without filaments, and a high-frequency generator.

Thackeray *(thăk ər ĭ),* **William Makepeace** 1811–63. English novelist *b.* Calcutta, India. Left university without a degree (1830); tried painting in Paris; reduced to indigence after losing his inheritance, returned to London as a literary hack; contributed regularly to *The Times, New Monthly*, and *Fraser's Magazine*; published first book, *The Paris Sketch-book*, in 1840 and its sequel, *The Irish Sketch-book*, in 1843; successful with pen-and-pencil sketches on snobs of England in *Punch*, contributing over 400 pieces (1842–54); with publication of *Vanity Fair* (1847–48), established literary reputation, confirmed by *Pendennis* (1848), *Henry Esmond* (1852), and *The Newcomes* (1853–55); retired from *Punch* (1854); editor of *The Cornhill Magazine* (1859–62); lesser-known works include *The Virginians* (1857–59), *Philip* (1861–62), and *The Four Georges* (1860).

Thales *(thā lēz)* c640–c546 B.C. Greek philosopher. *b.* Miletus, Asia Minor. One of the Seven Wise Men of Greece; predicted the solar eclipse of 585 B.C.; founder of abstract geometry; based his philosophy on the doctrine that water is the first principle of life and the primal substance of the earth.

Thant *(thănt)*, commonly **U** (or Mr.) Thant. 1909–74. Burmese statesman. *b.* Pantanaw. Burmese ambassador to the U.N. (1957–61); elected acting secretary-general on death of Dag Hammarskjold (1961); served two terms as secretary-general (1962–71); played major role in defusing the Cuban crisis (1962) and the Cyprus crisis (1964).

Thayer *(thâr)*, **Sylvanus** 1785–1872. American military educator. *b.* Braintree, Mass. In War of 1812 in the Corps of Engineers; superintendent of U.S. Military Academy (1817–33); established principles of organization, instruction, and discipline that have made the Academy an outstanding institution of its kind; called Father of the Military Academy; founded Thayer School of Engineering at Dartmouth.

Theiler *(tī lər)*, **Max** 1899–1972. American physiologist. *b.* Pretoria, South Africa. Immigrated to U.S. (1922); on staff of Rockefeller Foundation (from 1930); discovered first effective vaccine against yellow fever (1939); awarded Nobel Prize in physiology and medicine (1951).

Themistocles *(thē mĭs tə klēz)* c527–c460 B.C. Athenian statesman. As archon (493), instrumental in building a strong Athenian fleet; commanded Athenian squadron at battle of Salamis, and though nominally under the Spartan Eurybiades, was responsible for the strategy that led to victory; acclaimed as a hero; at his urging, the Athenians rebuilt fortifications of Athens and Piraeus; ostracized through the machinations of his enemies; as an exile, sought asylum in Argos, Corcyra, Epirus, and eventually at court of Artaxerxes in Persia, where he lived until death.

Theodoric *(thē ŏd ə rĭk)* usually THEODORIC THE GREAT. c454–526. King of the Ostrogoths. *b.* Pannonia. Founder of Ostrogothic dynasty; succeeded father as king (475); after warring with Emperor Zeno, was made master of soldiers (483) and consul (484); obtained Zeno's consent to wrest Italy from the Scythian Odoacer; heading

250,000 troops, defeated Odoacer at Aquileia and Verona (489) and on the Adda (490), completing the conquest of Italy (493) after murdering Odoacer with his own hands; issued Edict of Theodoric (506); with Ravenna as capital, ruled Italy for 33 years; added Sicily, Dalmatia, and parts of Germany to his empire; though an Arian, permitted full civil and religious liberties to Catholics and Jews; stains on his reign are the judicial murders of Boethius and Symmachus.

Theodosius I *(thē ə dō shĭ əs)* full name: FLAVIUS THEODOSIUS; called THE GREAT. c346–95. Roman emperor (379–95). *b.* Cauca, Northern Spain. Co-augustus with Gratian (379) and emperor of the East; after defeating the Goths, restored peace south of the Danube with generous peace terms (379–82); led forces to Italy to depose and slay the usurper Maximus and to restore Valentinian II (388) and to overthrow Eugenius and Arbogast, who had murdered Valentinian (394); publicly humiliated himself before Bishop Ambrose as penance for the massacre of 7000 Thessalonican citizens (390); baptized as a Catholic (380); noted in ecclesiastical history for his efforts to root out Arianism and for summoning the first Council of Constantinople (381); after victory at Aquileia (394), ruled as sole emperor for four months until death; succeeded by his son Arcadius in the East and Honorius in the West.

Theophrastus *(thē ə frăs təs)* *d.* c287 B.C. Greek philosopher. *b.* Eresus, Lesbos. Disciple and successor of Aristotle as head of the Peripatetic School at Athens; reputed author of over 227 works; those extant include *History of Plants* and *Characters*, a series of 30 short vignettes.

Theorell *(tā ə rĕl),* **Axel Hugo Theodor** 1903–. Swedish biochemist. *b.* Linköping. Director of Nobel Institute of Biochemistry (from 1937); first to produce pure form of myoglobin; awarded Nobel Prize in physiology and medicine (1955) for discoveries on the nature of oxidation enzymes.

Theresa *(tə rē sə),* **Saint** also TERESA. 1515–82. Spanish mystic. *b.* Ávila. Entered Carmelite order (1534); rigorous devotions and ascetic exercises gained her mystic visions of divine ecstasy; as the fame of her sanctity spread, she was granted permission by the pope to found a new order of Discalced Carmelites following more rigorous rules (1562); her books, written in simple language, are considered among the greatest in spiritual literature. Wrote *Autobiography, The Way of Perfection, The Interior Castle, Foundations,* and *Exclamations of the Soul to God*; canonized (1622); patron saint of Spain (1814). Feast day: Oct. 15.

Thérèse *(tā râz),* **Saint** also TERESA OF LISIEUX; real name: THÉRÈSE MARTIN. 1873–97. French nun. *b.* Alençon. Entered Carmelite order (1888); her spiritual autobiography reflects her shining purity, love of god, and simplicity; known as the Little Flower of Jesus from her promise at death that "After my death I will let fall a shower of roses"; her path toward sanctity through humble, common tasks is called the Little Way; canonized (1925); Feast day: Oct. 3.

Thévenin, Denis. *See* **Duhamel, Georges**

Thiers *(tyâr),* **Louis Adolphe** 1797–1877. French statesman and historian. *b.* Marseilles. Began political career as an ardent Orleanist and opponent of Polignac ministry (1829–30); supporter of Louis Philippe; foreign minister (1836, 1840); prime minister (1836, 1840); arrested by Louis Napoleon (1851) and banished for a year; led opposition to Second Empire in Corps Législatif (1863–70); opposed declaration of war against Prussia (1870); on fall of the Empire, elected head of provisional government, negotiating peace with Germany and suppressing the Commune of Paris (1871); first president of Third Republic (1871–73); secured withdrawal of Prussian forces by speedy payment of war indemnity; faced with the combined opposition of right and left, retired from public life. Wrote *Histoire de la Révolution Française* (10 vols., 1823–27) and *Histoire du Consulat et de l'Empire* (20 vols., 1845–62).

Thomas *(tŏm əs),* **Saint** also Didymus. One of the 12 Apostles of Jesus Christ; by tradition, evangelized India and Parthia and died in Mylapore, India, as a martyr. Feast day: Dec. 21.

Thomas, Dylan Marlais 1914–53. British poet. *b.* Swansea, Wales. Acclaimed modern poet known for impassioned, intemperate, exuberant language. Published first book of verse, *Eighteen Poems,* in (1934); followed with *Twenty-five Poems* (1936), *Map of Love* (1939), *Portrait of the Artist as a Young Dog* (1940), *The World I Breathe* (1940), *Deaths and Entrances* (1946); turned to drama with *Under Milk Wood* (1954), whose success made him popular; prose works include the autobiographical *Adventures in the Skin Trade* and *A Prospect by the Sea,* both published posthumously (1955).

Thomas, Isaiah 1750–1831. American printer. *b.* Boston. Founded *Massachusetts Spy,* a principal colonial newspaper, in Boston (1770), transferring it to Worcester, Mass., (1775); after Revolutionary War, launched *Massachusetts Magazine* (1789–96); set himself up as a book publisher and pioneered in many facets of publishing: reference books, Bibles, children's books, music books, hymns, medical and legal books, almanacs, and fiction; his books, particularly Bibles, were noted for their typographical excellence; published over 900 titles (1784–1802); after retirement (1802), founded American Antiquarian Society (1812). Wrote *History of Printing in America* (2 vols., 1810), long a standard work.

Thomas A Kempis *(tŏm əs ə kĕm pĭs)* Also Thomas Hamerken, Thomas Hammerlein. 1380–1471. German mystic. *b.* Kempen. Entered Augustinian order (1407); ordained (1413) and rose to superior; traditionally regarded as author of the classic of Christian devotion, *On the Imitation of Christ* (1486).

Thompson *(tŏm sən),* **Francis** 1859–1907. English poet. *b.* Preston. Studied for Catholic priesthood, but left it for medicine; failing that, turned to a vagrant life and odd jobs; reduced to poverty and starvation, debilitated by tuberculosis, and wasted by drug addiction, attempted suicide (1888); in the midst of misery, composed first poems, gaining the attention of Wilfred Meynell, editor of *Merry England*; spent rest of life in the care of the Meynells or in monasteries. Wrote *Poems* (1893), containing "The Hound of Heaven," *Sister Songs* (1895), and *New Poems* (1897).

Thomson *(tŏm sən)*, **Elihu** 1853–1937. American inventor. *b.* Manchester, England. Immigrated to U.S.; obtained over 700 patents for electrical inventions, including electric welding, a three-phase alternating current dynamo, a wattmeter, a cream separator, and the arc lamp; with E.J. Houston, founded the Thomson-Houston Electric Company, which later merged with Edison Electric to form General Electric (1892).

Thomson, Sir George Paget 1892–1975. English physicist. *b.* Cambridge. Son of Sir Joseph John Thomson; professor of natural philosophy at Aberdeen (1922–30), London (1930–52), and master of Corpus Christi College, Cambridge (1952–62); with Clinton Joseph Davisson, awarded Nobel Prize in physics (1937) for the discovery, independently and by different methods, of electron diffraction by crystals. Author of *The Atom* (1937), *Applied Aerodynamics* (1919), *Wave Mechanics of the Free Electron* (1930), and *Theory and Practice of Electron Diffraction* (1939).

Thomson, James 1700–1748. Scottish poet. *b.* Ednam. Best-known works are *The Seasons* (1726–30), which anticipated the Romantic poets, and *The Castle of Indolence*, a long allegorical poem in Spenserian stanzas (1748); wrote minor verse, including *Liberty* (1735–36), *The Masque of Alfred* (1740) containing the song "Rule Britannia," the plays *Sophonisba* (1730), *Agamemnon* (1738), *Edward and Eleanora* (1739), *Tancred and Sigismunda* (1745) and *Coriolanus* (1748).

Thomson, James known as B.V. for his pseudonym, BYSSHE VANOLIS. 1834–82. Scottish poet. *b.* Port Glasgow. Known as the poet of despair, from the sustained melancholy and pessimism of his greatest work, *The City of Dreadful Night* (1874); other works include *Vane's Story* (1881), *Essays and Phantasies* (1881), *A Voice from the Nile* (1884), and *To Our Ladies of Death* (1861).

Thomson, Sir Joseph John 1856–1940. English physicist. *b.* Cheetham Hill. Professor at Cambridge (1884–1918) and London (1905–18); as head of the Cavendish Laboratory in Cambridge, helped make it the greatest research institution of his time; experiments led to his discovery of the electron and the measurement of its mass and charge (1897), and the discovery of the isotope (1911); awarded Nobel Prize in physics (1906). Author of *Elements of the Mathematical Theory of Electricity and Magnetism* (1895), *Conduction of Electricity Through Gases* (1903), *Electricity and Matter* (1904), *The Electron in Chemistry* (1923), and *Recollections and Reflections* (1936).

Thoreau *(thôr ō)*, **Henry David** 1817–62. American writer. *b.* Concord, Mass. After leaving Harvard, taught school (1838–41); gave up teaching to join the Transcendental Club, making a living by lecturing and writing for such journals as *The Dial, Boston Miscellany*, and *Putnam's*; lived alone in a cabin he built at Walden Pond, Concord (1845–47), writing his classic *Walden, or Life in the Woods* (1854); thereafter lived in his father's house, except for brief excursions; arrested and jailed for refusing to pay poll tax; justified his action in *Resistance to Civil Government* (1849), which later inspired Gandhism; the only other book published during his lifetime was *A Week on the Concord and Merrimack Rivers* (1849); prized independence above money and possessions; guiding principles were hatred of slavery, contempt for property, and love of nature; guided and influenced by friendship with Ralph Waldo Emerson; his daily journal (from 1835) formed material for the posthumously published *Maine Woods* (1863), *Cape Cod* (1865), *A Yankee in Canada* (1866), *Poems of Nature* (1895), *Early Spring in Massachusetts* (1881), *Summer* (1884), *Winter* (1887), *Excursions in Field and Forest* (1863), and *Letters to Various Persons* (1865).

Thorvaldsen *(tŏŏr väl sən),* **Albert Bertel** 1768–1844. Danish sculptor. *b.* Copenhagen. Worked in Rome (1797–1819, 1820–38, 1841–44). Principal sculptures include *Lion of Lucerne, Night and Morning, Triumphal Entry of Alexander into Babylon, Christ and the Twelve Apostles, Preaching of John the Baptist*, and mythological figures of Jason, Ganymede, Venus, Psyche, and the Graces.

Thucydides *(thū sĭd ə dēz),* c471–c400 B.C. Greek historian. *b.* Athens. Served in Peloponnesian War; on the failure of his expedition to relieve Amphipolis, condemned and forced into exile for 20 years (until 404); during exile, wrote the monumental *History of the Peloponnesian War*, establishing his claim as the greatest historian of ancient times.

Thurber *(thûr bər),* **James Grover** 1894–1961. American writer. *b.* Columbus, Ohio. On staff of *The New Yorker* (from 1923), contributing humorous sketches and cartoons. Works include *The Owl in the Attic* (1931), *The Seal in the Bedroom* (1932), *My Life and Hard Times* (1934), *Let Your Mind Alone* (1937), *The Thurber Carnival* (1935), *The White Deer* (1945), *The Thirteen Clocks* (1950), *Thurber Country* (1953), and *Vintage Thurber* (1963); wrote plays *The Male Animal* (with Elliott Nugent, 1940) and *Fables for our Times* (1941).

Thutmose III *(thōōt mō sə) fl.* 15th century B.C. Egyptian ruler. Ascended to throne after deposing father; ruled jointly with wife and half-sister Hatshepsut (1501–1496); yielded power to father (1496), but regained it (1493); after death of Hatshepsut (1481), ruled alone, for a total of 54 years; made 17 campaigns into Asia, enlarging the empire to include Abyssinia, Sudan, Nubia, Syria, Mesopotamia, Arabia, Kurdistan, and Armenia; built the great temple of Amen at Karnak and restored the temples at Memphis, Heliopolis, and Abydos.

Tibaldi *(tē bäl dĭ),* **Pellegrino** 1527–96. Italian painter and architect. Municipal architect at Milan (1561) and architect of Milan Cathedral (1567); went to

Spain in employ of Philip II (1586); in addition to frescoes and churches in Bologna, Milan, Novara, and Madrid, fame rests on such paintings as *Adoration of the Shepherds* and *St. Jerome*.

Tiberius *(tī bēr ē əs)* full name: TIBERIUS CLAUDIUS NERO CAESAR. 42 B.C.–A.D. 37. Roman emperor (14–37 A.D.). Stepson of Augustus; fought in Spain, Armenia, Gaul, Pannonia, Germany, on the Danube, and against the Rhaetians and the Vindelicians; forced by Augustus to divorce Vipsania Agrippina to marry Julia, dissolute daughter of Augustus; consul (13, 7 B.C.), tribune (6 B.C.); retired in exile to Rhodes (6 B.C.–A.D. 2); on his return, made official heir by Augustus (4 A.D.); led Roman legions into Germany on a seven-year campaign, returning in triumph (12 A.D.); succeeded Augustus (14); reign marked by justice, frugality, and tax reforms until 22; thereafter, under influence of ministers Sejanus and Macro, became paranoid, tyrannical, and vicious; lived in Capreae (Capri) leading a vice-ridden life (from 27); the murders of Agrippa Postumus, Germanicus, and his son Drusus are attributed to him.

Tiepolo *(tyâ pō lō),* **Giovanni Battista** 1696–1770. Italian painter. *b.* Venice. Executed frescoes at Milan, Würzburg, and the royal palace at Madrid; director of the Academy of Painting at Venice (from 1753). Canvases include *Adoration of the Kings, Crucifixion*, and *Apotheosis of Aeneas*.

Tiffany *(tĭf ə nĭ),* **Charles Lewis** 1812–1902. American jeweler. *b.* Killingly, Conn. Founded a stationery and fancy-goods store in New York (1837), named Tiffany & Company (1851); specialized in the manufacture of sterling silver and jewelry. His son LOUIS COMFORT, (1848–1933), American painter and craftsman, discovered a process for making decorative glass in iridescent colors, known as Tiffany Favrile glass; founded the Tiffany Studios for its production.

Tigranes *(tī grā nēz)* **The Great** c140–c55 B.C. King of Armenia. Son-in-law of Mithridates the Great; placed on the throne with the help of Parthian troops; conquered Syria, Asia Minor, and northern Mesopotamia; founded capital at Tigranocerta (Siirt); conquests alarmed the Romans, who sent an army under Lucullus against him (69); surrendered to Pompey and ruled as vassal of Rome.

Tilden *(tĭl dən),* **Samuel Jones** 1814–86. American statesman. *b.* New Lebanon, N.Y. Elected to N.Y. State Assembly (1845); as chairman of the State Democratic Committee (1866), helped expose and destroy the corrupt Tweed Ring; governor of N.Y. (1875-76); Democratic candidate for president (1876); in one of the most controversial presidential elections, lost to Rutherford B. Hayes by one electoral vote, although he received 250,000 more popular votes; established a trust fund for the New York Public Library.

Tillich *(tĭl ĭK),* **Paul Johannes** 1886–1965. American theologian. *b.* Starzeddel, Germany. Chaplain in German army in World War I; professor of theology at Berlin (1919–24), Marburg, Dresden, Leipzig (1924–29), and Frankfurt

(1929–33); dismissed by Nazis (1933); immigrated to U.S. and taught at New York (1933–55), Harvard (1955–62), and Chicago (1962–65); founder of religious socialism, his theology blended scientific method, psychoanalysis, and philosophic realism with faith. Author of *The Interpretation of History* (1936), *The Protestant Era* (1948), *The Courage to Be* (1952), *Systematic Theology* (3 vols., 1953–63), and *Theology of Culture* (1959).

Tilly *(tĭl ĭ)*, **Count of** title of JOHANN TSERCLAES. 1559–1632. Flemish general. *b.* castle of Tilly, Belgium. Fought in Hungary against the Turks; field marshal of Bavarian army (1610); on outbreak of Thirty Years' War, commander in chief of Catholic League; lifetime record of 36 victories includes White Mountain (1620), Wimpfen and Höchst (1622), and Lutter am Barenberge (1626); replaced Wallenstein as imperial generalissimo (1630); subdued Bohemia (1621) and Palatinate (1622); stormed Magdeburg (1631); suffered defeats by Gustavus Adolphus at Breitenfeld (1631) and near Lech River (1632), where he died in battle.

Timur. *See* **Tamerlane**

Tinbergen *(tĭn bər Kən)*, **Jan** 1903–. Dutch economist. Professor at Netherlands School of Economics (from 1933); with R. Frisch, awarded Nobel Prize in economic science (1969) for development of econometrics and the application of mathematical models to the analysis of economic processes.

Tintoretto *(tĭn tō rĕt ō)*, **Il** real name: JACOPO ROBUSTI. 1518–94. Italian painter. *b.* Venice. Studied under Titian; received as his first major commission the decoration of the choir of Santa Maria dell'Orto (1546); completed works over 50 feet high; worked on cycle of paintings in Scuola di San Rocco in Venice (1564–87) which includes *Crucifixion* (1565), *Annunciation* and *Massacre of the Innocents* (both 1583–87); painted the *Paradiso*, the largest oil canvas in the world, in ducal palace at Venice (1588); replaced Titian as court painter (from 1560) and was in charge of the restorations after the fires of 1574 and 1577. Paintings include *The Miracle of the Slave* (1548), *The Miracle of St. Agnes* (1550), *St. Louis and St. George with the Princess* (1552), *The Last Judgment* (1560), *The Golden Calf* (1560), *The Marriage of Cana* (1561), *The Finding* (1562), *The Removal of the Body of St. Mark* (1562), *The Origin of the Milky Way* (1570), *The Last Supper* (1592–94), and *The Entombment* (1594), as well as *Self Portrait, Tommaso Contarini,* and *Portrait of a Venetian.*

Tiselius *(tĭ sā lĭ əs)*, **Arne Wilhelm Kaurin** 1902–1971. Swedish biochemist. *b.* Stockholm. Professor at Uppsala (from 1938); head of Biochemical Institute (from 1948); president of Nobel Foundation (1960–64); developed quantitative electrophoresis for analyzing serum proteins; devised an improved chromatography for observing colorless substances; awarded Nobel Prize in chemistry (1948).

Titian *(tĭsh ən)* full name: TIZIANO VECELLI. 1477–1576. Italian painter. *b.* Pieve di Cadore. Studied under Giorgioni and Giovanni Bellini; earliest works are three frescoes of scenes in the life of St. Anthony of Padua; collaborated with Giorgione in decoration of Fondaco de Tedeschi at Venice (1508); succeeded Bellini as painter to the Doges of Venice; enjoyed patronage of such rulers and nobles as Alphonse d'Este, Duke of Ferrara (1516), Charles V (1532), and Philip II; lived at Bologna (from 1532) and at Augsburg (1547–48, from 1550); on a visit to Rome, met Michelangelo and painted *Pope Paul III and his Nephews;* when he died, at age 99 during the Plague, he left a vast collection of works including *Alessandro de' Medici, Holy Family, Assumption of the Virgin, Ecce Homo, Medea and Venus, Rape of Europe, Worship of Venus, Bacchus and Ariadne, Sacred and Profane Love, Entombment of Christ, Martyrdom of St. Lawrence, Last Supper, Christ Crowned with Thorns, Titian and His Mistress, Three Ages of Man, Charles V at the Battle of Muhlberg, Danaë, The Fall of Man,* and *Perseus and Andromeda.*

Tito *(tē tō),* **Marshal** original name: Josip Broz. 1892– . Yugoslav statesman. *b.* near Klanjec. Served in Austro-Hungarian army during World War I and was taken prisoner by the Russians; converted to Communism; fought in Red army; returning to Yugoslavia (1921), became a Communist leader; imprisoned (1928–34); leader of International Brigade in Spanish Civil War; after fall of Yugoslavia in World War II, organized underground resistance (from 1941); discredited his rival Draja Mikhailovich, and obtained support of both the Soviet Union and the Allies; at the end of the war, virtually controlled the country with an army of over 200,000 and won overwhelming victory in elections (1945); elected premier of People's Republic of Yugoslavia; secured the abdication of Peter II; became dictator with titles president, minister of defense, and secretary general of the Communist party; expelled from the Cominform for defying Stalin (1948); successfully maintained Yugoslavia's independence as a Communist but nonaligned nation; assumed title of president for life (1963).

Titus *(tī təs)* full name: Titus Flavius Sabinus Vespasianus. c40–81. Roman emperor of the Flavian line (79–81). *b.* Rome. Son of Vespasian; most notable achievement was siege and capture of Jerusalem (70); the Arch of Titus was erected by Domitian to commemorate this event; gave up his dissolute habits on succeeding to throne (79); through his benevolence, gained the title Delight of Mankind; completed the Colosseum and built the baths that bear his name; died suddenly, perhaps poisoned by his brother Domitian.

Tocqueville *(tôk vēl),* **Alexis Charles Henri Maurice Clérel de** 1805–59. French historian. *b.* Verneuil. Sent to U.S. by French government (1831) to study American penitentiary system; extended study to the political system and on return published a classic description and analysis of American democracy, *De la Démocratie en Amérique* (2 vols., 1835–40); elected to Chamber of Deputies (1839), where he opposed both

Socialists and Royalists; minister of foreign affairs for five months (1849); after Louis Napoleon's coup d'état, imprisoned briefly; retired from political life and wrote *L'Ancien Régime et la Révolution* (1856), unfinished at death.

Todd *(tŏd),* **Lord Alexander Robertus** 1907– . British chemist. *b.* Glasgow, Scotland. Professor at Manchester (1938) and Cambridge (1944); awarded Nobel Prize in chemistry (1957) for studies of the structure of nucleic acids.

Togo *(tō gō),* **Marquis Heihachiro** 1847–1934. Japanese admiral. *b.* Kagoshima. Entered navy (1868); as commander of Japanese fleet in Russo-Japnese War (1904–1905), attacked Port Arthur (1904) and won a great sea battle, scattering the Russian naval squadron; annihilated Russian fleet at Tsushima (1905).

Tojo *(tō jō),* **Eiki** also **Hideki.** 1885–1948. Japanese general and statesman. *b.* Tokyo. Chief of staff of Japanese Kwantung army in China (1937–40); minister of war (1940–41); leader of the militarists, as premier led Japan in World War II (1941–44); resigned after loss of Saipan; hanged as a war criminal.

Toller *(tōl ər),* **Ernst** 1893–1939. German poet and dramatist. *b.* Samotschin. Sentenced to five years in prison (1919) for leading social revolutionary agitation in Germany; in prison began career as a dramatist of social protest with *Transfiguration* (1919), *Man and the Masses* (1920), *Swallow Book* (1923), *Brokenbow* (1923), and *The Machine-Wreckers* (1922); after Hitler's rise, left Germany and settled in U.S. (1939); died by suicide (1939). Among other works are *Pastor Hall* (1939), and *I Was a German* (1934).

Tolstoy *(təl stoi; tŏl stoi),* **Count Leo Nikolaevich** 1828–1910. Russian novelist. *b.* Yasnaya Polyana. Spent youth as Russian noble devoted to pleasure; served in army (1851–54); retired to his estates, and, after liberating his serfs, devoted himself to writing; underwent spiritual conversion (c1876), abandoning his Orthodox faith for a primitive Christianity, renouncing materialism, property, and hubris; his central creed was nonviolence and nonresistance to evil. Wrote *War and Peace* (1866), often considered the greatest novel ever written, and *Anna Karenina* (1874), a supreme moral tragedy that forms the dividing line between his earlier and later works; early writings are *Sevastopol* (1853–55), *The Cossacks* (1863), *Two Pilgrims* (1852), *Childhood* (1852), *Boyhood* (1852), *Youth* (1856), *Three Deaths* (1859), and *Kholstomer* (1861); books written after his religious conversion include *A Confession* (1879), *The Death of Ivan Ilyich* (1886), *The Kreutzer Sonata* (1889), *The Power of Darkness* (1889), *The Fruits of Enlightenment* (1891), *The Kingdom of God Is Within You* (1893), *Master and Man* (1894), *My Religion* (1885), *War* (1892), *What Is Art?* (1896), *Resurrection* (1900), *Hadji Murad* (1896), *The End of the Age* (1906), and *The Living Corpse* (1911).

Tomonaga *(tō mō nä gȧ),* **Sin-Itiro** 1906– . Japanese scientist. *b.* Kyoto. With R. Feynman and J. Schwinger, received Nobel Prize in physics (1965) for research in quantum electrodynamics that contributed to the understanding of elementary particles in high-energy physics.

Tonatiuh. *See* **Alvarado, Pedro de**

Torquemada *(tôr kā mä tä),* **Tomás de** c1420–98. Spanish inquisitor. *b.* Valladolid. Entered Dominican order; through Ferdinand and Isabella, obtained sanction from the pope for setting up Holy Office of the Inquisition; appointed first inquisitor general (1483); created grand inquisitor by Pope Innocent VIII (1487); made the Inquisition an instrument of terror; responsible for the expulsion of Jews from Spain.

Torricelli *(tōr rə chĕl lē),* **Evangelista** 1608–47. Italian mathematician and physicist. *b.* Piancaldoli. After publication of the mathematical treatise *Trattato del Moto* (1641), served as amanuensis to blind Galileo; succeeded Galileo as mathematician to grand duke of Tuscany and professor at the Florentine Academy; improved the telescope and microscope, and invented the barometer. Author of *Opera Geometrica* (1644).

Toscanini *(tōs kə nē nē),* **Arturo** 1867–1957. Italian conductor. *b.* Parma. Conductor at La Scala, Milan (1898–1907, 1921–31), Metropolitan Opera, New York (1907–21), New York Philharmonic Orchestra (1928–33); guest conductor at Bayreuth (1930–31) and Salzburg Festivals (1934–36); organized the National Broadcasting Company Symphony.

Toulouse-Lautrec *(to͞o lo͞oz lō trĕk)* full name: Henri Marie Raymond de Toulouse-Lautrec Monfa. 1864–1901. French painter. *b.* Albi. Grotesquely deformed from childhood accident; settled in Montmartre (1884) and began painting; deeply influenced by Degas and Japanese woodcuts; his bohemian life led him to paint the Parisian demimonde, producing posters and sketches of music hall, circus, and theater habitués, clowns, barmaids, prostitutes, and cabaret stars; died of alcoholism and venereal disease. Works include *Dolly the English Barmaid, Jane Avril, Le Promenoir, The Bar, Monsieur Boileau at the Café,* and *At the Races.*

Toussaint L'Ouverture *(to͞o săN lo͞o vĕr tür),* **Pierre Dominique** 1743–1803. Haitian liberator. *b.* near Cape François. Joined slave revolt first on royalist and later on Republican side (1791–94); deputy governor and commander in chief with real authority; forced withdrawal of British from eastern Haiti (1798); conquered Santo Domingo (1801); overcame the mulatto leader Rigaud in civil war (1799); threw off French yoke, proclaiming new constitution with himself as president for life; defied Napoleon's efforts to re-establish slavery; overthrown by French forces under Leclerc, arrested, and sent to prison in France, where he died.

Townes *(tounz),* **Charles Hard** 1915– . American physicist. *b.* Greenville, S.C. Professor at Columbia (1948–61), M.I.T. (1961–67), and California (from 1967); shared Nobel Prize in physics (1964) with Nikolai G. Basov and Aleksander M. Prokhorov for fundamental research in quantum electronics which led to the discovery of maser and laser.

Toynbee *(toin bĭ),* **Arnold Joseph** 1889–1975. British historian. *b.* London. Professor at University of London (from 1919); director of Royal Institute of International Affairs (1925–55); wrote the monumental *A Study of History* (10 vols., 1934–54); rejected historical determinism and emphasized psychic and cultural forces as governing the rise and fall of civilizations. Wrote *Nationality and the War* (1915), *Greek Historical Thought* (1924), and *War and Civilization* (1951).

Trajan *(trā jən)* Latin name: MARCUS ULPIUS TRAJANUS; surname: DACICUS, PARTHICUS. c52–117. Roman emperor (98–117). *b.* Italica, Spain. Spent youth fighting enemies of Rome in Syria and Spain; consul (91); adopted by Nerva as colleague and successor; emperor (98); in two campaigns, (101–103, 104–106), subdued the Dacians, and made Dacia a Roman province; erected Trajan's Column to commemorate triumph; after relative peace (107–14), battled against the Parthians and Armenians; brought Damascus and part of Arabia into the empire; captured Ctesiphon (115); faced with Jewish revolts in Cyprus and Cyrene; on return to Rome, died in Cilicia; noted as a great builder and as an efficient and just administrator.

Trevelyan *(trə vĕl yən),* **George Macaulay** 1876–1962. British historian. *b.* Stratford-on-Avon. Son of SIR GEORGE OTTO TREVELYAN (1838–1928), English statesman and historian, and grandson of SIR CHARLES EDWARD TREVELYAN (1807–86), British administrator in India. Regius Professor of Modern History at Cambridge (1927–40); master of Trinity College (1940–51). Author of distinguished works on social and political history, including *Garibaldi and the Making of Italy* (1911), *British History in the Nineteenth Century, 1782–1901* (1922), *History of England* (1926), *England Under Queen Anne* (3 vols., 1930–34), *The English Revolution, 1688* (1938), *English Social History* (1942), and biographies of John Bright and Lord Grey.

Trollope *(trŏl əp),* **Anthony** 1815–82. English novelist. *b.* London. Joined postal service (1834), performing official duties as roving inspector in Ireland, Egypt, West Indies, U.S., New Zealand, and South Africa; attained success with *The Warden* (1855), the first of the six-volume Barchester Towers series of which the other five are *Barchester Towers* (1857), *Doctor Thorne* (1858), *Framley Parsonage* (1861), *The Small House at Allington* (1864) and *The Last Chronicle of Barset* (1867); his six-volume series of Parliamentary novels deals with the life of Plantagenet Palliser, heir to the Duke of Omnium: *Can You Forgive Her?* (1864), *Phineas Finn* (1869), *The Eustace Diamonds* (1873), *Phineas Redux* (1874), *The Prime Minister* (1876), and *The Duke's Children* (1880); he wrote 38 other novels, including *The Bertrams* (1859), *Castle Richmond* (1860), *The Claverings* (1867), *The American Senator* (1877), *An Eye for an Eye* (1879), and *Marion Fay* (1882); helped to found the *Fortnightly Review* (1865) and edited *St. Paul's Magazine* (1867–70); autobiography published posthumously (1883).

Trotsky *(trôt ski),* **Leon** original name: LEV DAVYDOVICH BRONSTEIN.

1879–1940. Russian statesman. *b.* Yanovka, Ukraine. Began revolutionary career as a youth; first imprisoned at age 19; exiled to Siberia, escaping under the alias Trotsky; first met Lenin in London (1902), later collaborating with him and Plekhanov on *Iskra;* returned to Russia (1905) as president of first soviet in St. Petersburg in the abortive revolution (1905); arrested, exiled, but escaped again; spent 12 years abroad as propagandist and agitator; returned to Russia as Lenin's lieutenant in November Revolution (1917); appointed first people's commissar for foreign affairs (1917) and later commissar of war; negotiated Treaty of Brest-Litovsk; built up Red army from 7000 to 5,000,000 men, organizing labor battalions to rebuild railways; on collision course with Stalin after death of Lenin (1924); lost struggle for dominance in the Party; expelled from Politbureau (1927); exiled to Alma Alta, and finally ordered to leave U.S.S.R. (1929); sentenced to death in absentia (1937) for anti-Stalin activities; found asylum in Mexico, where he was assassinated (1940); before his death, founded the Fourth International, a group of "pure" communists; respected as a powerful writer and orator. Author of *History of the Russian Revolution* (1932).

Trudeau *(trōō dō),* **Pierre Elliott** 1919– . Canadian statesman. *b.* Montreal. Began political career as one of the founders of Rassemblement, a left-wing group opposed to Maurice Duplessis, premier of Quebec; elected to House of Commons (1965) on Liberal ticket; minister of justice and attorney general (1967); succeeded Lester Pearson as federal leader of Liberal party (from 1968) and prime minister (1968–79).

Truman *(trōō mən),* **Harry S** 1884–1972. 33rd president of U.S. (1945–53). *b.* Lamar, Mo. Began as a machine politician, protégé of Tom Pendergast, with whose help he won a Senate seat (1934); gained national attention as chairman of a special committee to investigate defense spending; replaced Henry Wallace as Roosevelt's running mate (1944); succeeded to presidency on Roosevelt's death (1945); attended Potsdam Conference (1945); won surprising reelection over Republican Thomas E. Dewey (1948); his administration saw the dropping of the first atomic bomb, U.S. support for Israel, enunciation of Truman Doctrine (the U.S. policy giving assistance to countries resisting attempted subjugation by armed minorities or outside pressures), and establishment of the North Atlantic Treaty Organization and the Marshall Plan for European recovery; sent American troops into Korea, dismissed General MacArthur, and ordered development of hydrogen bomb; his Fair Deal programs died in Congress; declined renomination (1952). Published *Memoirs* (2 vols., 1955–56).

Trumbull *(trŭm bəl),* **John** 1756–1843. American painter. *b.* Lebanon, Conn. After studying portraiture under Benjamin West in London, opened studios in New York (1789, 1804) and Philadelphia (1792); George Washington was one of many notables who sat for him; commissioned by Congress (1817) to paint four large pictures for the rotunda of the Capital in Washington, D.C. Among his historical paintings are *Battle of Bunker Hill, Death of General Montgomery, Death of General Mercer, Declaration of Independence, Surrender of Lord Cornwallis at Yorktown, Capture of the Hessians at Trenton,* and portraits of Timothy Dwight and Stephen van Rensselaer. Author of *Autobiography* (1841).

Tserklaes, Jan. *See* **Tilly, Count of**

Tubman *(tŭb mən),* **Harriet** 1820–1913. American abolitionist. *b.* Dorchester County, Md. An escaped slave, she helped free over 300 slaves through the legendary Underground Railroad; during the Civil War, served as nurse, laundress, and spy.

Turenne *(tü rĕn),* **Vicomte de** title of Henry de La Tour d' Auvergne. 1611–75. French general. *b.* Sedan. Grandson of William the Silent; brought up as a Reformed Protestant; served under his uncle Maurice of Nassau in Dutch War of Independence; received commission from Cardinal Richelieu (1630), commanding a French regiment; marshal of France (1643); his brilliant victories in Thirty Years' War, especially at Casale Monferrato (1640), Nördlingen (1645), and Roussillon (1642), were responsible for Peace of Westphalia (1648), ending the war; joined the Fronde (1649) but later commanded royalist forces that defeated Condé (1652) in third civil war of the Fronde (1651–58); again defeated Condé, now in command of the Spaniards, at Dunes (1658), ending that threat forever; marshal general of armies of France (1660); conquered Flanders (1667); converted to Catholicism (1668); led French army to success in Holland (1672) in the Third Dutch War, and in Palatinate and Alsace against Imperial forces; killed in action; considered the greatest military leader in French history. Author of *Mémoires*.

Turgenev *(toor gyā nyəf),* **Ivan Sergeevich** 1818–83. Russian novelist. *b.* Orel. Served in Russian civil service (1840–52); spent most of later life abroad; his works provide a social commentary on 19th-century Russia. Wrote novels *Rudkin* (1855), *A Nest of Gentlefolk* (1858), *On the Eve* (1860), *Fathers and Sons* (1862), *Smoke* (1867), and *Virgin Soil* (1876), short story collections *A Quiet Backwater, Asya*, and *First Love*, and plays *A Month in the Country* (1850) and *A Provincial Lady* (1851); writings distinguished by controlled style and balanced objectivity.

Turgot *(tür gō),* **Anne Robert Jacques** title: Baron de l'Aulne. 1727–81. French statesman. As intendant of Limoges (from 1761), attracted attention by radical reforms in financial administration; on accession of Louis XVI, appointed comptroller general of finance (1774–76); launched comprehensive reform scheme based on the principles "No bankruptcy, no increase in taxation, no borrowing"; a physiocrat, practiced theories of free trade, reformed interest rates, and even distribution of taxation; introduced economy in administration, abolished the corvée (cumpulsory feudal service), improved agriculture, and established comprehensive education system; gained powerful enemies, including Marie Antoinette, as a result of his policies; dismissed (1776); engaged in writing his classic works on economics and politics, *Réflexions sur la Formation et la Distribution des Richesses* (1766), *Lettres sur la Tolérance* (1753–54), *Mémoire sur les Prêts à Intérêt* (1769), and in retirement, *Les Six Édits* (1776).

Turner *(tûr nər)*, **Joseph Mallord William** 1775–1851. English painter. *b.* London. Entered school of the Royal Academy at 14, exhibiting at 15; worked as a water colorist (to 1796), later working in oils; beginning with historical and mythological subjects in his first period, turned to abstract and poetic sceneries rendered in shifting gradations of color; gained critical acceptance after Ruskin's *Modern Painters* acclaimed his art (1843); at death, bequeathed 300 canvases and 20,000 watercolors to the nation. Principal works include *Calais Pier Sun Rising in the Mist*, *Liber Studiorum*, *Shipwreck*, *Crossing the Brook*, *Dido Building Carthage*, *Dido Directing the Equipment of the Fleet*, *Ulysses Deriding Polyphemus*, *The Fighting Téméraire*, *The Slave Ship*, *The Approach to Venice*, *Rain, Steam and Speed*, and *The Exile*; also illustrated books such as *The Rivers of England* and *The Rivers of France*.

Turner, Nat 1800–1831. American slave. *b.* Southampton County, Va. Claimed divine inspiration to lead Negro slaves to freedom; together with 70 other slaves, led an insurrection (1831) in which 50 whites, including his master, were murdered; captured after six weeks in hiding; tried, convicted, and hanged.

Tutankhamen *(tōō ängk ä mən)*, *fl.* 14th century B.C. Egyptian king of XVIII Dynasty. Son-in-law of Ikhnaton; ascended throne at age 12, and died at age 18; returned to the worship of Amon; restored the capital to Thebes; his tomb, discovered in 1922 in the Valley of the Kings near Luxor, is one of the great archaeological monuments of the world.

Twain *(twān)*, **Mark** pseudonym of SAMUEL LANGHORNE CLEMENS. 1835–1910. American writer. *b.* Florida, Mo. Lived youth at Hannibal, Mo. (1839–53), where he was a printer's apprentice (1847); journeyman printer at St. Louis, New York, and Philadelphia (1853–55), river pilot on the Mississippi (1857–61), prospector in Carson City, Nev. (1861), newspaper reporter in Virginia City, Nev; adopted Mark Twain as his pseudonym (a term meaning two fathoms deep); as a reporter in California (1864), published his first book, *The Celebrated Jumping Frog of Calaveras County and Other Sketches* (1867); published *The Innocents Abroad* (1869), based on a visit to the Mediterranean and the Holy Land; lived in Buffalo (1869–71) and Hartford, Conn. (1871–88); suffered heavy financial losses in failure of his publishing house, Charles L. Webster & Co. (1896) and made a round-the-world lecture tour to clear debts; last days clouded by despair and agnosticism. Principal works include *The Adventures of Tom Sawyer* (1876), *A Tramp Abroad* (1880), *The Prince and the Pauper*

(1882), Adventures of Huckleberry Finn (1885), *A Connecticut Yankee at King Arthur's Court* (1889), *The Tragedy of Pudd'n'head Wilson* (1894), *The Mysterious Stranger* (1916), *Life on the Mississippi* (1883), and *Mark Twain's Autobiography* (2 vols., 1924).

Tweed *(twēd),* **William Marcy** called Boss Tweed. 1823–78. American politician. *b.* New York, N.Y. Served in Congress (1853–55); chairman of Board of Supervisors of New York City (1856); school commissioner (1856–57); commissioner of public works (1870); chairman of the General Committee of Tammany Hall; gained control of city's finances and swindled the treasury of millions; corruption exposed by Thomas Nash's cartoons in *Harper's Weekly*; arrested in civil and criminal suits (1871); sentenced to 12 years in prison; escaped and fled to Spain; deported from Spain and again imprisoned; died in jail.

Tweedsmuir, Baron. *See* **Buchan, Sir John**

Tyler *(tī lər),* **John** 1790–1862. Tenth president of U.S. (1841–45). *b.* Greenway, Va. Began political career in Virginia legislature (1811–16); House of Representatives (1817–21); governor of Virginia (1825–27); Senator (1827–36); vice-president of U.S. (1841); succeeded to the presidency on death of Harrison (1841), becoming first vice-president to do so; administration troubled by party conflicts; principal achievements were the annexation of Texas, treaty with China, the Webster-Ashburton Treaty delimiting U.S.-Canadian boundary, and reorganization of the navy; a states-rights champion, was denied the cooperation of his own party, becoming a "president without a party"; vetoed Whig bill permitting national banks to establish branches in the states; declined renomination and retired at end of term; remained loyal to Virginia when it seceded from the Union, but died before taking his seat in the Confederate Congress.

Tyler, Wat also Walter. *d.* 1381. English rebel. Leader of a movement in Kent to protest the Statute of Laborers (1351) and the imposition of poll tax; marched to London through Blackheath and Canterbury, burning prisons and public buildings; while negotiating with King Richard II at Smithfield, wounded by William Walworth, mayor of London; later beheaded.

Tyndale *(tĭn dəl),* **William** c1492–1536. English Protestant reformer. *b.* Slymbridge. Ordained (1521); as a Greek scholar and friend of the New Learning, undertook the task of translating the New Testament into English; meeting with opposition in England, went to the Continent (1524); met Luther at Wittenburg; began printing the translation at Cologne (1525), completing it in Worms, where persecution had driven him; of 3000 printed copies, all but a few were burned; banned by Cardinal Wolsey; found refuge in Marburg under protection of Landgrave of Hesse, Philip the Magnanimous (1527); published the *Pentateuch* (1530–31) and *Jonah* (1531); lived chiefly in Antwerp (after 1530); issued revised version of New Testament (1534) and a further revision without marginal notes (1535); wrote tracts defining his theological position as a Zwinglian, attacking Henry VIII in *The Practyse of Prelates* (1536); seized by treachery, imprisoned, and strangled to death after trial for heresy. Other works include *The Parable of the Wicked Mammon* (1528) and *The Obedience of a Christian Man* (1528).

Tyndall *(tĭn dəl),* **John** 1820–93. British physicist. *b.* Leighlin-Bridge, Ireland. Professor of natural philosophy at Royal Institution (from 1853); investigated radiant heat, vapors, gases, glaciers, light, and sound. Principal works include *Heat Considered as a Mode of Motion* (1863), *Faraday as a Discoverer* (1868); *Contributions to Molecular Physics in the Domain of Radiant Heat* (1872), *On the Transmission of Sound by the Atmosphere* (1874), *Fermentation* (1877), and *Fragments of Science* (1892).

U

Unamuno y Jugo *(o͞o nä mo͞o nō ē ho͞o gō),* **Miguel de** 1864–1936. Spanish philosopher. *b.* Bilboa. Professor of Greek (from 1892) and rector and professor of Spanish literature at University of Salamanca (1901–14, 1930–36); in exile as a Republican in the Canary Islands and Paris (1924–30). Author of *The Life of Don Quixote and Sancho Panza* (1905), *Mi Religión y Otros Ensayos* (1910), *Rosario de Sonetos Líricos* (1911), *Contra Esto y Aquello* (1912), *The Tragic Sense of Life* (1913), *Niebla* (1914), *Ensayos* (7 vols., 1916–19), *El Cristo de Velásquez* (1920), *Three Exemplary Novels* (1921), *De Fuerteventura a París* (1925), and *La Agonio del Cristianismo* (1925).

Undset *(o͝on sĕt),* **Sigrid** 1882–1949. Norwegian novelist. *b.* Kalundborg, Denmark. Earlier works reflect her interest in medieval Norway and later ones reveal the intense religiosity that followed her conversion to Roman Catholicism (1924); awarded Nobel Prize in literature (1928). Works include the classic trilogy *Kristin Lavransdatter* (1920–22), the tetralogy *Master of Hestviken*, the trilogy *Saga of Saints* (1934), and the novels *The Axe, Snake Pit, In the Wilderness, The Son Avenger*, and *The Burning Bush*.

Updike *(ŭp dīk),* **John Hoyer** 1932– . American writer. *b.* Shillington, Pa. Works characterized by sensuous apprehension of detail and elaborate, imagistic prose; prolific output includes *Rabbit, Run* (1960), *Poorhouse Fair* (1959), *The Centaur* (1963), *Couples* (1968), and *Rabbit Redux* (1971); also published *Telephone Poles and Other Poems* (1963); his short stories have been collected as *Pigeon Feathers* and *Carpentered Hen*.

Urey *(ū rĭ),* **Harold Clayton** 1893– . American chemist. *b.* Walkerton, Ind. Professor at Columbia (from 1934) and Chicago (from 1945); isolated heavy water and helped to separate uranium isotopes to produce U-235 for making the atomic bomb; discovered deuterium, the heavy hydrogen isotope; investigated entropy of gases, absorption spectra, and the structure of atoms; awarded Nobel Prize in chemistry (1934). Author of *Atoms, Molecules, and Quanta* (1930).

Utrillo *(o͞o trē lō)*, **Maurice** 1883–1955. French painter. *b.* Montmartre, Paris. Son of painter Suzanne Valadon and adopted by Spanish writer Miguel Utrillo, whose name he took; best known for Parisian streetscapes, especially those of the White Period (1908–14) with their subtle coloring and sensitivity; suffered periodic bouts with alcoholism, yet managed to produce a prodigious number of works. Among his canvases are *Notre Dame de Paris, Parisian Suburbs, Reims Cathedral,* and *Moulin de la Galette.*

V

Vail *(vāl)*, **Theodore Newton** 1845–1920. American telephone pioneer. *b.* Minerva, Ohio. Cousin of Alfred Vail (1807–59), partner of Samuel F.B. Morse. Began as telegraph operator; became general manager of Bell Telephone Company (1878–87); founded American Telephone and Telegraph Company and served as its first president (1885–89, 1907–19).

Valdivia *(väl dē vyä)*, **Pedro de** c1500–1553. Spanish conquistador. *b.* near La Serena. Went to Venezuela (c1534) and distinguished himself at Battle of Las Salinas under Pizarro (1538); placed in command of expedition to complete the conquest of Chile (1540); founded Santiago (1541), Concepción (1550), Valparaíso (1544), Imperial (1552), and Valdivia (1552); governor of Chile (1549); slain in revolt of Indians.

Valéry *(vȧ lā rē)*, **Paul Ambroise** 1871–1945. French philosopher and poet. *b.* Cette (Sète). Joined Stéphane Mallarmé's group of poets in Paris, but after early success, abandoned poetry for philosophy, returning to poetry only in 1917. Among his books of verse are *La Jeune Parque* (1917), *Le Cimetière Marin* (1920), *Charmes* (1922), *Album de Vers Anciens* (1920), *L'Ébauche d'un Serpent, Au Platane*; prose works include *An Evening with Mr. Teste* (1925), *Eupalinos* (1923), *L'Âme et la Danse* (1924), and *Reflections on the World of Today* (1948).

Van Allen *(văn ăl ən)*, **James Alfred** 1914– . American physicist. *b.* Mt. Pleasant, Iowa. Professor at University of Iowa (1951); pioneered in high-altitude rocket research; discovered Van Allen radiation belts outside earth's atmosphere, extending from 400 to 40,000 miles above the earth.

Vanbrugh *(văn bro͞o)*, **Sir John** 1664–1726. English playwright. *b.* London. Joined William Congreve (1697) as theater manager and as playwright, producing coarse but witty comedies such as *The Relapse* (1697), *Aesop*

(1697), *The Provoked Wife* (1697), and *The Confederacy* (1705); turned to architecture, achieving success by designing Castle Howard (1702) and Blenheim Palace (1705) in the fashionable baroque style.

Van Buren *(văn bū rən),* **Martin** 1782–1862. Eighth president of U.S. (1837–41) *b.* Kinderhook, N.Y. Member of N.Y. state senate (1812–20); U.S. Senate (1821–28); member of N.Y. political machine known as the Albany Regency; governor of N.Y. (1828); resigned to become Jackson's secretary of state (1829–31); vice-president of U.S. (1833–37); as Jackson's handpicked successor, won presidential nomination and election (1836); major achievement was setting up an independent treasury system; defeated by Harrison in presidential election (1840); unsuccessful candidate for presidency (1844, 1848).

Vancouver *(văn ˊkōō vər),* **George** 1757–98. English explorer. Sailed with Captain Cook on second and third voyages; commanded expedition (1791–94) that explored the Strait of Juan de Fuca, the Gulf of Georgia, New Zealand, and the Hawaiian Islands, and circumnavigated Vancouver Island. Published *Voyage of Discovery to the North Pacific Ocean and Round the World* (3 vols., 1798).

Vanderbilt *(văn dər bəlt),* **Cornelius** 1794–1877. American financier. *b.* Port Richmond, N.Y. Began as owner of a ferry service between Staten Island and New York City; expanded operations by establishing steamboat lines on the Hudson, Long Island Sound, and to California through Lake Nicaragua (1849); at age 70, turned attention to railroads, acquiring New York and Harlem, Hudson River, and New York Central railroads, and after bitter stock market struggles, the Erie Railroad (1862–68); known as a ruthless and wily competitor; at death left a fortune estimated at over $100 million.

Vandyke *(văn dīk),* **Sir Anthony** also VAN DYCK. 1599–1641. Flemish painter. *b.* Antwerp, Belgium. Pupil and assistant of Rubens; lived in Italy (1621–26) and in England (after 1632) as court painter to Charles II; noted for portraits of Charles II and the English nobility in patrician settings. Religious canvases include *Ascension, Adoration of the Magi, Ecstasy of St. Augustine, Christ Crucified Between Thieves, The Deposition*, and *Elevation of the Cross*.

Vanolis, Bysshe. *See* **Thomson, James**

Van Rensselaer *(văn rĕn sə lăr),* **Kiliaen** 1595–1644. Dutch merchant. *b.* Amsterdam. A jeweler by profession; one of the founders of Dutch West India Company (1621); from the Indians, bought a vast tract of land comprising the present counties of Albany, Columbia, and Rensselaer (1635), naming it Rensselaerwyck; descendants enjoyed manorial rights over this territory as patroons.

Van'T Hoff *(vänt hŏf),* **Jacobus Hendricus** 1852–1911. Dutch scientist. *b.* Rotterdam. Professor at Amsterdam (1878–87), Leipzig (1887), and Berlin (1896–1911); considered the founder of physical chemistry and stereochemistry;

pioneered in chemical thermodynamics and osmotic electrical conductivity; studied formation and decomposition of double salts; demonstrated the asymmetric carbon atom, in which the bonds are tetrahedrally arranged; awarded first Nobel Prize in chemistry (1901). Author of *Études de Dynamique Chimique* (1884) and other books.

Varèse *(vă rāz),* **Edgard** 1883–1965. American composer. *b.* Paris, France. Settled in U.S. after World War I; founded New Symphony Orchestra in New York (1919) and International Composers' Guild (1921); his music is characterized by the use of electronic instruments and of the extreme ranges of standard instruments to produce harsh, dissonant effects. Among his works are *Ionisation* (1931), *Density 21.5* (1935), *Poème Electronique* (1958), *Nuit* (1965), and *Arcana* (1927).

Vargas *(vär gäs),* **Getulio Dornelles** 1883–1954. Brazilian statesman. *b.* São Borja. Entered politics as federal deputy (1923); minister of finance (1926–27); governor (1928–30) of the state of Rio Grande do Sul; seized power in a coup d'état (1930) after losing election for presidency; provisional president (1930–34) and president of the second republic and virtual dictator under new constitution promulgated by himself (1934); resigned (1945); but reelected (1951); committed suicide (1954) after forced resignation. Author of *A Nova Política do Brasil* (9 vols., 1938).

Varro *(văr ō),* **Marcus Terentius** 116–27 B.C. Roman scholar. *b.* Reate, Italy. A partisan of Pompey in Civil War, but was restored to Caesar's favor after Battle of Pharsalus (48); appointed Caesar's librarian; in disfavor during Second Triumvirate, but survived and regained property under Augustus; considered the most learned man of his time, whose knowledge embraced history, jurisprudence, grammar, philosophy, husbandry, rhetoric, geometry, dialectics, arithmetic, astrology, music, medicine, archaeology, and architecture; of the 74 works comprising 620 books that he wrote, *De Lingua Latina* and *De Re Rustica* are the only two that survive.

Vasari *(vä zä rē),* **Giorgio** 1511–74. Italian painter and art historian. *b.* Arezzo. Studied under Andrea del Sarto and Michelangelo; as an architect, built part of the Uffizi Palace; as an artist, painted murals in the Vatican and in Palazzo Vecchio at Florence; fame rests primarily on the authorship of *Vite de' Piu Eccelenti Pittori, Scultori, e Architetti Italiani* (1550), one of the earliest works on artistic biography and criticism.

Vaughan *(vôn),* **Henry** known as THE SILURIST. 1622–95. British poet. *b.* Newton-by-Usk, Wales. Studied and practiced medicine; first collection of poems, *Olor Iscanus*, was published in 1651; followed with *Silex Scintillans* (1650–55), *The Mount of Olives* (1652), *Flores Solitudinis*, (1654), and *Thalia Rediviva* (1678); important in literature as one of the earliest metaphysical poets.

Vaughan Williams *(vôn wĭl yəmz),* **Ralph** 1872–1958. English composer. *b.* Down Ampney.

Emerged early in career as exponent of British traditions in music; a leader of English folksong movement, he incorporated folk and church music into his works; compositions range from hymns to music for stage and screen. Best-known works are nine symphonies, including *London Symphony* (1914) and *Pastoral Symphony* (1922), *Hugh the Drover* (1911–14), *Sea Symphony* (1910), *Job* (1930), *Fantasia on a Theme of Tallis*, *Pilgrim's Progress* (1948–49), *Flos Campi* (1925), *The Lark Ascending* (1921), *Five Variants on Dives*, *Sir John in Love* (1929), *Dona Nobis Pacem* (1936), and *Flourish for a Coronation* (1937). Author of *National Music* (1934) and *Beethoven's Choral Symphony and Other Papers*.

Veblen *(vĕb lən),* **Thorstein Bunde** 1857–1929. American social philosopher. *b.* Cato, Wis. Taught at Chicago (1892–1906), Stanford (1906–1909), Missouri (1911–18), and New York (from 1919); one of the first to apply psychology to the study of business and economic institutions; studied the acquisitive society, business cycles, the price system, and other aspects of capitalism; beginning with *The Theory of the Leisure Class* (1899), mercilessly dissected and exposed practices of the established economic order. Other books include *The Instinct of Workmanship and the State of the Industrial Arts* (1914), *The Theory of Business Enterprise* (1904), *Imperial Germany and the Industrial Revolution* (1915), *The Higher Learning in America* (1919), *The Vested Interests and the State of the Industrial Arts* (1919), *The Engineers and the Price System* (1921), and *Absentee Ownership and Business Enterprise in Recent Times* (1923).

Vega *(vā gä),* **Lope de** full name: Lope Félix de Vega Carpio. 1562–1635. Spanish dramatist. *b.* Madrid. Served in Spanish Armada (1588); wrote first full-length poem "Angelica" (1588); on return, settled in Madrid (1596); after death of second wife, took holy orders (c1614), becoming an officer of the Inquisition; considered the founder of Spanish national drama; contributions include 1800 plays and 400 autos, of which 431 plays and 50 autos are extant; inventor of a comic character known as gracioso, later used by other dramatists; wrote mainly cloak-and-sword dramas, heroic comedies and histories, and domestic dramas. Among his plays are *Noche de San Juan, El Castigo sin Venganza, La Estrella de Sevilla, El Mejor Alcalde el Rey, El Acero de Madrid, La Noche Toledana,* and *La Fuente Ovejuna;* other works include *Rimas* (1602), *Peregrino en su Patria* (1604), *Jerusalén Conquistada* (1609), *Corona Trágica* (1627), *Dorotea* (1632), and *La Hermosura de Angélica* (1602), a continuation of Ariosto's *Orlando Furioso*.

Velasquez *(vā läth kāth),* **Diego Rodríguez de Silva y** 1599–1660. Spanish painter. *b.* Seville. Set up studio (1618); court painter to Philip IV; apart from visits to Rome (1629–31, 1649–51), worked in Madrid; portraits include over 40 of his master Philip IV, Pope Innocent X, the Infante Baltasar Carlos, the Infantas Margarita and Maria Theresa, court dwarfs, and jesters. Among other works are *The Water-Carrier of Seville, The Adoration of the Shepherds, Los Borrachos, The Maids of Honor, The Tapestry Weavers, The Expulsion of the Moriscos, Forge of Vulcan, Surrender of Breda, Joseph's Coat, Venus and Cupid, Boar Hunt, St. John the Evangelist, Lot and His Daughters*, and *Crucifixion.*

Venizelos *(vâ nyē zâ lôs),* **Eleutherios** 1864–1936. Greek statesman. *b.* near Canea, Crete. Leader in Greco–Turkish War (1896–97) and in movement for union of Crete and Greece; prime minister (1910–15, Aug.–Oct. 1915, 1917–20, 1924, 1928–32, 1933); organized Balkan League (1912); led Greece in Balkan War (1913); on outbreak of World War I, forced to resign by pro-German King Constantine; established pro-Allied rival government in Salonika (1917); with Allied support, compelled king to resign; secured further territories from Turkey at Versailles Peace Conference; defeated in general election (1920), which brought back King Constantine and the royalists; after Constantine's second abdication, returned to office, establishing Greek Republic (1924); resigned before its proclamation; recalled (1928); defeated in elections (1933) and retired; organized unsuccessful military and naval revolt, and on its failure fled to Paris, where he died in exile. Author of *Vindication of Greek National Policy* (1910).

Verdi *(vār dē),* **Giuseppe** 1813–1901. Italian composer. *b.* Roncole. Achieved first success with *Nabucco* (1842) and thereafter produced a succession of masterpieces, dominating Italian opera. Works include *I Lombardi, Ernani, I due Foscari, Attila, Macbeth, Giovanna d'Arco, La Battaglia di Legnano, Luisa Miller, Rigoletto, Stiffelio, Il Trovatore, La Traviata, I Vespri Sicihani, Simone Boccanegra, Un Ballo in Maschera, La Forza del Destino, Don Carlos, Aïda, Otello, Falstaff,* and *Requiem Mass.*

Vergil *(vûr jəl)* also Virgil; Latin name: Publius Vergilius Maro. 70–19 B.C. Roman poet. *b.* Andes, Gaul. Lived in Mantua, Rome, and Campania; enjoyed patronage of Maecenas, Asinius Pollio, and Octavius (Augustus); principal works are the *Eclogues* or *Bucolics*, consisting of ten pastoral poems (42–37), the *Georgics* (or *Art of Husbandry*) in four books (37–30), and the national epic of Rome, the *Aeneid,* commissioned by Augustus (19); unequalled for the profundity, nobility, and harmony of his verse.

Verhaeren *(vər hȧ rən),* **Émile** 1855–1916. Belgian poet. *b.* St. Amand. One of the symbolist group of poets; works include *Les Flamandes* (1883), *Les Moines* (1886), *Les Débâcles* (1888), *Les Soirs* (1887), *Les Flambeaux Noirs* (1890), *Les Campagnes Hallucinées* (1893), *Les Heures Claires* (1896), *Les Aubes* (1898), *Les Apparus dans mes Chemins* (1891), *Les Villages Illusoires* (1895), *Les Villes Tentaculaires* (1895), *Petites Légendes* (1900), *Forces Tumultueuses* (1902), *Tendresses Premières* (1904), *Les Ailes Rouges de la Guerre* (1916), and *La Multiple Splendeur* (1906).

Verlaine *(vĕr lân),* **Paul** 1844–96. French poet. *b.* Metz. Beginning as a Parnassian, later became a Symbolist and one of the principal Decadents; turning point was his association with Rimbaud, which ended in Brussels (1873) when he tried to prevent Rimbaud from leaving by shooting him; after spending two years in jail, tried to reform himself by turning Catholic (1874); relapsed into abject drunkenness during last years; transformed his experiences into profoundly evocative and sensitive works as *Poèmes Saturniens* (1867), *Fêtes Galantes* (1869), *La Bonne Chanson* (1870), *Romances sans Paroles* (1874), *Sagesse* (1881), *Parallèlement* (1889), *Jadis et Naguère* (1885), *Femmes* (1890), *Bonheur* (1891), *Amour* (1888), *Poètes Maudits* (1884), *Liturgies Intimes* (1892), *Elégies* (1893), *Mes Hôpitaux* (1892), *Mes Prisons* (1893), *Confessions* (1895), and *Mort* (1895).

Vermeer *(vər mār),* **Jan** also, Jan van der Meer van Delft. 1632–75. Dutch painter. *b.* Delft. Little-known until rediscovered in 19th century; now ranks as one of the foremost Dutch painters; slow and meticulous, he painted only about 40 canvases, including *The Allegory of Painting, Young Woman with a Water Jug, The Allegory of Faith, The Procuress, Christ in the House of Martha and Mary, Diana at her Toilet, The Milk Woman, The Lace Maker*, and *Woman Reading a Letter*.

Verne *(vĕrn),* **Jules** 1828–1905. French writer. *b.* Nantes. One of the founders of science fiction, his enormously popular novels anticipated later scientific inventions. Author of *Five Weeks in a Balloon* (1863), *Journey to the Center of the Earth* (1864), *A Trip to the Moon* (1865), *Twenty Thousand Leagues Under the Sea* (1870), *The Mysterious Island* (1870), *Around the World in Eighty Days* (1872), *Michael Strogoff* (1876), *Le Rayon Vert* (1882), *Le Sphinx des Glaces* (1897).

Veronese *(vā rō nā sə),* **Paolo** real name: Paolo Cagliari. 1528–88. Italian painter. *b.* Verona. Called the Painter of Pageants for his lavish crowd scenes; settled at Venice (1555) and completed commissions at the Library of St. Mark and the Convent of St. Sebastian; worked in Rome (1565); painted the ceiling of the ducal palace at Venice. Other works include *Marriage at Cana, The Family of Darius Before Alexander, The Adoration of the Magi, Feast in the House of Levi, Temptation of St. Anthony, Coronation of the Virgin, Deposition from the Cross, Supper at Emmaus, Holy Family, Raising of Lazarus, Mars and Venus, Rape of Europe, Leda and the Swan*, and *Death of Adonis*.

Verrazano *(vār rä tsä nō),* **Giovanni da** c1480–1528. Italian navigator. Commanded a French expedition of exploration (1523), sailing along the North American coast from Newfoundland to North Carolina, discovering New York and Narragansett bays; died in a skirmish with Indians in the West Indies.

Verrocchio *(vər rôk kyō),* **Andrea del** real name: Andrea di Michele Cione. 1435–88. Italian sculptor. *b.* Florence. Adopted the name of his teacher, Giuliano Verrocchio. Among his works are the statue of David, bronze figures for the Medici tombs in San Lorenzo, *Christ and St. Thomas, Boy with a Dol-*

phin, and an equestrian statue of Bartolommeo Colleoni; only one painting survives, *The Baptism of Our Lord*, which was completed by his pupil Leonardo da Vinci.

Vesalius *(və sā lĭ əs)*, **Andreas** 1514–64. Belgian anatomist. *b.* Brussels. Professor of anatomy at Padua, Bologna, Pisa, and Basel; physician to Charles V and Philip II; his famous work *De Humani Corporis Fabrica* is a benchmark in the annals of anatomy (1543); condemned to death by the Inquisition for body-snatching and for making anatomical dissections of the human body; sentence commuted to pilgrimage to the Holy Land; on his return, died in a shipwreck on the island of Zante.

Vespasian *(vĕs pā zhən)* full name: TITUS FLAVIUS SABINUS VESPASIANUS. 9–79. Roman emperor (69–79), first of the Flavian line. *b.* Reate, Italy. Served as tribune in Thrace, and as quaestor in Crete and Cyrene; commanded a legion in Germany and Britain; under Nero, became consul (51) and proconsul in Africa (63); sent to Palestine to suppress Jewish revolt (67); proclaimed emperor by legions at Alexandria (69); after defeating Vitellius, returned to Rome, becoming emperor (70); reign marked by destruction of Jerusalem by Titus, conquest of Britain by Agricola, suppression of the Batavian revolt, and beginning construction of the Colosseum.

Vespucci *(ves po͞o chē)*, **Amerigo** 1451–1512. Italian navigator. *b.* Florence. Member of a firm of provision contractors at Seville who fitted out Columbus's second expedition (1493); by his account, made four expeditions to New World (1497, 1499, 1501, 1503); in the first, holding position of astronomer, touched coast of North American continent perhaps a week or two earlier than the Cabots; later explored mouth of the Amazon (1499); first to describe South America as a separate continent; based on the account of his expeditions, now lost, the German geographer Martin Waldseemüller coined the name America for the new continents.

Vico *(vē kō)*, **Giovanni Battista** 1668–1744. Italian philosopher. *b.* Naples. Professor of rhetoric at Naples and royal historiographer; first to apply scientific method to study of history; developed cyclical theory of civilization, in which he envisioned three stages: the age of gods (theocracy), the age of heroes (aristocracy), and the age of men (democracy), each containing the seeds of its dissolution and the rise of the next. Principal works include *De antiquissimi Italorum Sapientia* (1710), *De Universi Juris uno Principio et Fine Uno* (1720), and *Principii di una Scienza Nuovo d'Intorño alla Commune Natura Delle Nazioni* (1744).

Victoria *(vĭk tō rĭ ə)* full name: ALEXANDRINA VICTORIA. 1819–1901. Queen of England (1837–1901). *b.* London. Daughter of George III's fourth son, Edward, Duke of Kent; succeeded to throne on death of William IV (1837); married Albert, Prince of Saxe-Coburg-Gotha (1840); principal events of her 64-year-long reign were transfer of power over Indian territories from East India Company to the Crown (1858), assumption of title of Empress of India (1876), Crimean War (1853–56), and Boer War (1899); served by 10 prime ministers: Viscount Melbourne, Peel, Earl Russell, earl of Derby, earl of Aberdeen, Viscount Palmerston, Disraeli, Gladstone, marquis of Salisbury, and earl of Rosebery; her long political experience endowed her with an innate judgment of men and events that was rarely incorrect; through the marriages of her nine children, gained dynastic relations with almost all European royal houses; stamped her personality on the age now known as Victorian.

Vigeland *(vē gə län),* **Adolf Gustav** 1869–1943. Norwegian sculptor. *b.* Oslo. Most famous work consists of 100 bronze and granite figures in Frogner Park, Oslo, depicting human development from infancy to old age; also did busts of Ibsen, Björnson, and others.

Vigneaud, Vincent du. *See* **du Vigneaud, Vincent**

Vigny *(vē nyē),* **Comte Alfred Victor de** 1797–1863. French man of letters. *b.* Loches. Entered army at age 16; began active literary career when he published *Poëmes Antiques et Modernes* (1822); before he resigned from the army (1828), published *Le Trappiste* (1822), *Éloa* (1824), and *Cinq-Mars* (1826); meanwhile, his stoicism and mild pessimism began to permeate his writings as in *Chatterton* (1835), *Stello* (1832), *Servitude et Grandeur Militaires* (1835), *Poëmes Philosophiques* (1843), *Les Destinées* (1864), *Daphné* (1912), and *Journal* (1867); also translated Shakespeare into French.

Villa *(vē yä),* **Francisco** usually PANCHO VILLA; original name: DOROTEO ARANGO. 1877–1923. Mexican revolutionary. *b.* Rio Grande. Organized bandits and cattle rustlers into a revolutionary force that aided Francisco Madero to seize power (1910); when Victoriano Huerta overthrew Madero (1913), joined Carranza against Huerta, but later turned against Carranza, who drove him to Northern Mexico; raided border cities in New Mexico in retaliation for U.S. recognition of Carranza regime; pursued by General Pershing and driven back; assassinated, but lives on in Mexican peasant legends.

Villiers, George. *See* **Buckingham**

Villiers, George William Frederick. *See* **Clarendon, Earl of**

Villon *(vē yôN),* **François** real name: FRANCOIS DE MONTCORBIER 1431–63?. French poet. *b.* Paris. On death of father, was adopted by Guillaume de Villon, canon and relative, whose name he adopted; obtained master's degree from Sorbonne (1452); joined a band of criminals and wastrels known as Brotherhood of the Coquille and was imprisoned many times for robbery, assault, and disorderly conduct; convicted of attempted murder and sentenced to be hanged (1463), but, on appeal, sentence was reduced to banishment from Paris for ten years; considered one of the greatest French medieval poets. Principal works are *Le Petit Testament* (1456) and *Le Grand Testament* (1461); many of his ballads convey searing irony, a haunting preoccupation with death and decay, and gentle compassion; his emotions alternated between realism and passion, piety and ribaldry, rebellion and repentance; best-known ballads are *The Ballad of Dead Ladies* (with the refrain "But where are the snows of yester-year?") and *Ballad of the Hanged.*

Vincent de Paul *(văn sän də pôl),* **Saint** c1581–1660. French Catholic priest. *b.* Pouy. Captured by pirates on a voyage from Marseilles and sold into slavery (1605); escaped and returned to France (1607); thereafter devoted his life to charitable work; appointed almoner at French court (1608); founded (1625) Congregation of the Priests of the Mission (also known as Lazarists or Vincentians) and Sisters of Charity (1634); work continued by Society of St. Vincent de Paul, founded by Frédéric Ozanam (1833); canonized (1737). Feast day: July 19.

Vinson *(vĭn sən),* **Frederick Moore** 1890–1953. American jurist. *b.* Louisa, Ky. House of Representatives (1923–29, 1931–37); associate justice, U.S. Court of Appeals (1937–43); director of Office of Economic Stabilization (1943–45); secretary of treasury (1945–46); chief justice of the United States (1946–53).

Virchow *(fĭr kō),* **Rudolf** 1821–1902. German pathologist and statesman. *b.* Schivelbein, Pomerania. Professor of pathological anatomy at Würzburg (from 1849) and Berlin (from 1856); one of the founders of cellular pathology; contributed to study of tumors, leukemia, hygiene, sanitation, anthropology, and ethnology; conducted archaeological excavations with Heinrich Schliemann at Troy; leader of the Progressists and German Liberal party; opponent of Bismarck in Prussian National Assembly (from 1862) and in the Reichstag (1880–93). Author of *Die Cellularpathologie* (1858) and other books.

Virtanen *(vĭr tə nən),* **Artturi Ilmari** 1895–1973. Finnish biochemist. *b.* Helsinki. Professor of biochemistry at Helsinki (from 1939); discovered the A.I.V. method for making silage; conducted experiments in the chemical mechanism of nitrogen-fixation in root nodules; awarded Nobel Prize in chemistry (1945).

Vischer *(fĭsh ər),* **Peter** usually THE ELDER. 1455–1529. German sculptor. *b.* Nuremburg. His architectural sculptures include the statue of King Arthur at Innsbruck, the tomb of Archbishop Ernst at Magdeburg, the tomb of Eitel Friedrich I and his wife at Hechingen, the *Crowning of the Virgin* at Erfurt Cathedral, and the tomb of St. Sebaldus at Nuremburg; work continued by his sons, of whom the best known is Peter the Younger (1487–1528).

Virtruvius Pollio *(vĭ tro͞o vĭ əs pŏl ĭ ō),* **Marcus** *fl.* 1st century B.C. Roman architect. *b.* Verona. Served under Augustus as engineer and architect; wrote *De Architectura*, a treatise on architecture dedicated to Augustus; accepted as an authority on architecture until Middle Ages.

Vivaldi *(vē väl dē),* **Antonio** c1675–1741. Italian violinist. *b.* Venice. Ordained priest (1703); perfected the *Concerto Grosso* as a three-form movement. Compositions include *L'Estro Armonico* (1712) and *The Four Seasons* (1725), as well as sonatas, operas, chamber music, sacred music, and violin concertos.

Vladimir I *(vlăd ĭ mĭr)* also SAINT VLADIMIR, VLADIMIR THE GREAT. c956–1015. First Christian ruler of Russia (980–1015). Varangian grand prince of Kiev (c978–1015); converted to Christianity (c988) and thereafter promoted Christianization of Russia; enlarged kingdom by annexing Lithuania, Galicia, and Livonia.

Vlaminck *(vlə măɴk),* **Maurice de** 1876–1958. French painter. *b.* Paris. Self-taught painter, known for his landscapes; for a time, a leading Fauvist; influenced by Van Gogh and Cezanne. Works include *Village Square, Village Street, Thatched Cottages*, and *The Storm*; published autobiography, *Communications* (1921).

Volta *(vôl tä),* **Count Alessandro** 1745–1827. Italian physicist. *b.* Como. Professor at Pavia (1774–1804); among his inventions are the electrophore, the electroscope, the condenser, and the voltaic pile; summoned by Napoleon to demonstrate his discoveries; the volt, standard electrical unit, is named after him.

Voltaire *(vŏl târ),* real name: FRANÇOIS MARIE AROUET. 1694–1778. French writer. *b.* Paris. Began writing as a college student; unrestrained and scathing satires got him in trouble with the authorities; thrice banished from Paris and twice imprisoned in the Bastille (1716–26); completed tragedy *Oedipe* (1718) in prison, adopting the nickname Voltaire, perhaps an anagram; released from second imprisonment on condition that he would leave France; in England (1726–29) made the acquaintance of English scientists and deists; on return to France, lived with Marquise du Châtelet (until 1749); through influence of Madame de Pompadour, secured the king's favor; appointed historiographer royal and gentleman of the bedchamber (1745–46); accepted Frederick the Great's invitation to visit Prussia, living in Berlin (1750–53); broke with the king and parted bitter enemies; prevented from living in Paris, settled in Geneva (1755–59) and later in Ferney (1759–78); defended victims of religious intolerance and wrote against the Church (from 1762); returned to Paris (1778) to enjoy a triumphal welcome, but died shortly thereafter; important as the most representative figure of the Enlightenment and as a vigorous champion of rationalism and liberty; his enormous literary output published in 72 volumes in 1784 includes *Brutus, Zaïre, Mérope, Mahomet, Alzire, La Henriade, Discours sur l'Homme, La Loi Naturelle, Le Désastre de Lisbonne, Le Mondain, Charles XII, Essai sur les Moeurs, Le Siècle de Louis XIV, Lettres Anglaises ou Philosophiques, Histoire de Russie sous Pierre le Grand, Dictionnaire Philosophique, Essai sur la Poésie Epique, Candide, Zadig,* and *La Princesse de Babylone*.

von Braun, Wernher. *See* **Braun, Wernher von.**

Vondel *(vôn dəl),* **Joost van den** 1587–1679. Dutch poet and dramatist. *b.* Cologne, Germany. Called the Dutch Shakespeare for his poems, dramas, and translations; conducted a prosperous business whose bankruptcy (1657) led him into later poverty; converted to Roman Catholicism (1641) and wrote a number of devotional poems; translated Vergil, Ovid, Seneca, Sophocles and Euripides. Principal dramas include *Jerusalem Destroyed* (1619), *The Amsterdam Hecuba* (1625), *Gysbreght van Aemstel* (1637), *Lucifer* (1654), *Batavian Brothers* (1662), *Faeton* (1663), and *Adam in Exile* (1664).

Vonnegut *(vôn i gət),* **Kurt** 1922–. American author. *b.* Indianapolis, Ind. Began as science fiction writer; established literary reputation and recognition as writer with unique vision with *Slaughterhouse-Five* (1969); also wrote *Player Piano* (1951), *The Sirens of Titan* (1959), *Mother Night* (1962), *Cat's Cradle* (1963), *Welcome to the Monkey House* (1969), *Breakfast of Champions* (1973), *Wampeters, Foma & Granfalloons* (1974), and *Slapstick* (1976).

W

Waals *(väls),* **Johannes Diderik van der** 1837–1923. Dutch physicist. *b.* Leiden, Netherlands. Professor at Amsterdam (1877–1908); among his discoveries are the van der Waals equation of the physical state of a gas or liquid, the van der Waals force, the weak force of attraction between molecules, and the law of corresponding states; awarded the Nobel Prize in physics (1910).

Wagner *(väg nər),* **Wilhelm Richard** known as Richard Wagner. 1813–83. German composer. *b.* Leipzig. Began composing music (c1832); music director of theaters in Magdeburg (1834–36), Königsburg (1836), and Riga (1837–39); moved to Paris in an unsuccessful effort to break into the theater; produced the operas *Rienzi* and *Der Fliegende Holländer* in Dresden, and became Kapellmeister (1843–49); during his Dresden period, composed *Tannhäuser* (1845) and *Lohengrin* (1848); accused of participating in the abortive Dresden Revolution of 1849 and forced to flee to Zurich, where he resided until 1858; returned to Germany under an amnesty (1864); called to Munich by Ludwig II of Bavaria (1864) to produce *Tristan* (1865); aroused hostility at Bavarian court through his tactlessness and extravagance; retired to Switzerland (1865); married Cosima, daughter of Liszt (1870); built theater at Bayreuth (1876), producing first complete performance of the *Ring* tetralogy and *Parsifal* (1882); spent last years in Italy, and died in Venice; reformed operatic structure by introducing music drama (word-tone-drama), fusion of poetry, music, and action, in which a continuous flow of synchronized dialogue and melody, sustained by orchestral leitmotifs, constitutes the unifying principle; expounded his theory of opera in *Das Kunstwerk der Zukunft* (1850) and *Oper und Drama* (1851); emphasized dramatic potential of myth and symbols; Composed *Tristan und Isolde* (1859), *Der Meistersinger von Nürnberg* (1867); *Der Ring des Nibelungen*, consisting of *Das Rheingold* (1854), *Die Walküre* (1856), *Siegfried* (1871), and *Götterdämmerung* (1874); writings include the anti-Semitic *Judaism in Music* (1850), *Art of the Future* (1849), *Communications to My Friends* (1851–52), and *Mein Leben* (1911).

Wagner von Jauregg *(väg nər fən you rĕk)*, **Julius** 1857–1940. Austrian neurologist. *b.* Wels. Work on endemic goiter yielded the discovery that the addition of potassium iodide or sodium to salt can arrest progress of this disease; introduced treatment of general paralysis by inoculation of organisms causing malaria; awarded Nobel Prize in physiology and medicine (1927).

Wakefield *(wāk fēld)*, **Edward Gibbon** 1796–1862. English colonial statesman. *b.* London. In *A Letter from Sydney* (1829), *England and America* (1833), and *A View of the Art of Colonization* (1849), developed principles of scientific colonization including sale rather than grant of lands, cessation of transportation of criminals, regulation of immigration, and distribution of sexes; manager of the South Australian Association that founded South Australia (1834); founder of New Zealand Land Company, which by sending English colonists to New Zealand hastened English annexation of the Islands (1839); founded Anglican colony at Canterbury (1850); helped develop New Zealand (1853–54).

Waksman *(wăks mən)*, **Selman Abraham** 1888–1973. American microbiologist. *b.* Priluka, Ukraine. Immigrated to U.S.; professor of microbiology at Rutgers (from 1942); originated the term *antibiotics*; investigated soil molds and breakdown of organic substances by microorganisms; discovered streptomycin; awarded Nobel Prize in physiology and medicine (1952). Author of *Enzymes* (1926), *Principles of Soil Microbiology* (1927), *Humus* (1936), *Streptomycin* (1949) and *My Life with the Microbes* (1954).

Wald *(wôld)*, **George** 1906–. American biologist. B. New York, N.Y. Professor at Harvard (from 1934); awarded Nobel Prize in physiology and medicine (1967), with Haldan K. Hartline and Ragnar A. Granit, for discoveries pertaining to the eye's primary chemical and physiological processes, including work on color reception.

Wald, Lillian D. 1867–1940. American social worker. *b.* Cincinnati. Activity in all branches of social work bore fruit in the Henry Street Settlement in New York (1893); introduced the first city school nursing service in New York (1902); pioneered the organization of public health nursing; promoted the idea of a federal children's bureau, receiving congressional approval (1908). Author of *House on Henry Street* (1915) and *Windows on Henry Street* (1934).

Waldheim *(vält hīm)*, **Kurt** 1918–. Austrian statesman. *b.* lower Austria. Joined Austrian foreign service (1945); Austria's permanent representative at U.N. (from 1955); ambassador to Canada (1956–60); foreign minister in Conservative People's party government

(1968–70); unsuccessful candidate in Austrian presidential election (1971); secretary-general of U.N. (1972).

Waldo *(wôl dō),* **Peter** *fl.* 12th century. French preacher. A merchant by profession, renounced his riches and through his preaching gathered a group of people around him known at first as the poor men of Lyons, later as the Waldenses; excommunicated as a heretic; persecuted and suppressed for centuries, the movement eventually merged with the Protestant churches.

Wallace *(wŏl ĭs),* **Alfred Russel** 1823–1913. English naturalist. *b.* Usk. Accompanied Henry Walter Bates to the Amazon (1848–50) to collect animal and plant specimens; continued in the Malay Archipelago (1854–62); independently discovered the principle of natural selection through his own research; communicated his thesis to Charles Darwin, who presented it to the Linnaean Society with his own paper on natural selection (1858); pioneered the study of zoogeography and postulated the existence of a division (called Wallace's line) between Asian and Australian animal and plant life. Author of *Travels on the Amazon and Rio Negro* (1853), *Contributions to the Theory of Natural Selection* (1870), *Geographical Distribution of Animals* (1876), *Island Life* (1880), *Darwinism* (1889), and *The World of Life* (1910).

Wallace, Henry Agard 1888–1965. American statesman. *b.* Adair County, Iowa. Son of HENRY CANTWELL WALLACE (1866–1924), secretary of agriculture under Harding and Coolidge. Editor of the journal *Wallace's Farmer* and its successor *Iowa Homestead* (1924–33); a New Dealer, appointed secretary of agriculture under Roosevelt (1933–40); vice-president of U.S. under Roosevelt (1941–45); failing to obtain renomination (1944), returned as secretary of commerce (1945–46); dismissed for opposing Truman's foreign policies (1946); editor of *New Republic* (1946–48); unsuccessful Progressive party presidential candidate (1948). Author of *Price of Freedom* (1940) and other books.

Wallace, Sir William c1272–1305. Scottish national hero. Headed a small band of insurgents and outlaws; began Scottish War of Independence (1297) by driving the English out of Perth, Sterling, and Lanark; victorious over the English army under Earl of Surrey at Stirling Bridge (1297); expelled English from Scotland and elected governor of the realm; defeated by English army under Edward I at Falkirk (1298); waged guerrilla warfare for years, visiting France and Rome to seek aid; betrayed at Glasgow, taken to London, tried, beheaded, and quartered.

Wallach *(väl äĸ),* **Otto** 1847–1931. German chemist. *b.* Konigsburg. Professor at Göttingen (1889–1915); conducted important research in alicyclic compounds such as terpenes, essential oils, and camphors; awarded Nobel Prize in chemistry (1910).

Wallenstein *(wŏl ən stīn),* **Albrecht Eusebius Wenzel von** title: DUKE OF FRIEDLAND AND MECKLENBURG, PRINCE OF SAGAN. 1583–1634. Austrian general. *b.* Herrmanic, Bohemia. Born a Protestant, became

Catholic and was educated by Jesuits; served in Hungary under Rudolf II; helped crush Bohemian revolt (1618–20); commander in chief of Imperial forces (1625); defeated army of Peter Ernst Mansfeld at Dessau Bridge (1626); pacified Hungary and subdued Silesia (1627); after unsuccessful siege of Stralsund and invasion of northern Germany by Gustavus Adolphus, deprived of command (1630); reinstated (1632); defeated at Lützen by Gustavus Adolphus; began secret negotiations with Protestants; dismissed (1634); assassinated.

Walpole *(wôl pōl),* **Horace** 1717–1797. English writer. *b.* London. Son of Sir Robert Walpole; on father's death, purchased a former coachman's cottage, which he remodeled in neo-Gothic style and named Strawberry Hill; the building, decorated with curios and works of art, is considered a landmark in English architecture, influencing taste away from classical and Italianate styles; best-known of his many books is *The Castle of Otranto* (1764), popular as the first Gothic romance; literary fame rests chiefly on his over 2700 letters, principally to Madame du Deffand and Sir Horace Mann.

Walpole, Sir Robert title: Earl of Orford. 1676–1745. English statesman. *b.* Houghton. Entered Parliament (1701); member of the council to Prince George (1705); secretary at war (1708); treasurer of the navy (1710); expelled from House and sent to Tower for corruption (1712); a Hanoverian partisan, restored as paymaster of the forces (1714); conducted impeachment of Bolingbroke and Harley; served as England's first prime minister, holding offices of chancellor of the exchequer and first lord of the treasury (1715–17); introduced the sinking fund (1717); out of office (1717–20); paymaster general (1720); prime minister (1720–42) with Charles Townshend as secretary of state (until 1730) and as sole head of government thereafter; shifted center of power from House of Lords to House of Commons and from king to prime minister; reduced import and export duties, encouraged free trade, and cut land tax; successfully avoided foreign entanglements and wars until forced into War of Austrian Succession (1739); following military reverses, lost support in the House and resigned.

Walsingham *(wôl sĭng əm),* **Sir Francis** c1530–90. English statesman. *b.* Chislehurst. Ambassador to France (1570–73); one of the principal secretaries of state to Queen Elizabeth (1573); organized an elaborate espionage system which is credited with having uncovered the Babington Plot (1586); forewarned the queen of Spanish plans for the invasion of England; died in debt.

Walton *(wôl tən),* **Ernest Thomas Sinton** 1903–. Irish physicist. *b.* Dungarran. With J.D. Cockcroft, assistant to Ernest Rutherford at Cavendish Laboratory in Cambridge; professor at Dublin (from 1946); shared Nobel Prize in physics (1951) with Cockcroft for pioneering work in smashing atomic nuclei with artificially accelerated atomic particles.

Walton, Izaak 1593–1683. English author. *b.* Stafford. Best known as the author of *The Compleat Angler, or the Contemplative Man's Recreation* (1653), a series of dialogues on the pleasures of fishing; wrote biographies of noted authors; known as the Father of Angling.

Warburg *(wôr bûrg),* **Otto Heinrich** 1883–1970. German physiologist and chemist. *b.* Freiburg Baden. Professor at University of Berlin and director of the Kaiser Wilhelm Institute for Biology (from 1914); conducted important investigations on cancerous cells; awarded Nobel Prize in physiology and medicine (1931) for work on respiratory enzymes.

Warhol *(wôr hôl),* **Andy** 1930?–. American artist. *b.* McKeesport, Pa. Known for his pictures of soup can labels and collages of newspaper photographs, which shocked and amused the art world; leading proponent of the Pop Art movement; as a film director, produced the avant garde movies *The Chelsea Girls, Trash, Sleep, Frankenstein*, and *Dracula*; editor of *Interview* magazine.

Warren *(wôr ən),* **Earl** 1891–1971. American jurist. *b.* Los Angeles, Calif. Governor of California (1943–53); Republican vice-presidential nominee (1948); chief justice of the United States (1953–69); during his tenure as chief justice the Court made a series of socially significant decisions concerning civil rights and the rights of defendants.

Warren, Robert Penn 1905–. American poet and novelist. *b.* Guthrie, Ky. Professor at Minnesota (1942–50) and Yale (from 1951); editor of *Southern Review* (1935–42). Poetry includes *Thirty-Six Poems* (1936), *Selected Poems* (1944), and *Selected Poems, Old and New, 1923–66* (1966); novels include *Night Rider* (1939), *At Heaven's Gate* (1943), *All the King's Men* (1943), *World Enough and Time* (1950), and *Wilderness* (1961).

Warville, de. *See* **Brissot, Jacques Pierre**

Washington *(wôsh ĭng tən),* **Booker Taliaferro** 1856–1915. American educator. *b.* Hales Ford, Va. Born into a mulatto slave family; after years of hardship, founded the Tuskegee Institute (1881) for the practical training of blacks in business, trade, and the professions; became an effective speaker and writer. Author of *Up from Slavery* (1900), *The Story of My Life and Work* (1903), and other books.

Washington, George 1732–99. First president of U.S. (1789–97). *b.* Westmoreland County, Va. Schooled by eldest half-brother Lawrence, whose estate, Mount Vernon, he later inherited; employed by Lord Fairfax as surveyor (1748); joined army (1752), first mission being to bear an ultimatum from Governor Robert Dinwiddie to the French at Ohio (1754); commissioned lieutenant colonel and led an attack on French at Fort Duquesne (1754); as aide on Braddock's staff, shared defeat at Monongahela (1755); as colonel, appointed commander in chief of Virginia forces during French and Indian Wars; resigned (1758); married Martha Custis, a rich widow, their combined wealth making him one of the richest men in the colonies; gentleman farmer, hunter, and burgess, and justice (1759–74); early supporter of the patriot cause; represented Virginia in the First and Second Continental Congresses (1774, 1775); commander in chief of Continental army (1775); forced British evacuation of N.Y. (1776); defeated at New York City, Brandywine, and Germantown (1777); after heroic crossing of the Delaware, victorious at Trenton and Princeton (1776); spent bitter winter at Valley Forge (1777–78); strengthened by French alliance, ended revolution by forcing surrender of Cornwallis at Yorktown (1781); resigned commission (1783) and retired to Mount Vernon; recalled as president of Federal Convention (1787); unanimously elected first president of U.S. under the new Constitution, taking oath of office at N.Y. (1789); reelected (1793); above party politics during his first term, veered toward Federalism during second; declined third term and, after historic farewell address, retired from public life (1797); complete writings published (39 vols., 1931–44).

Wassermann *(väs ər män),* **August von** 1866–1925. German bacteriologist. *b.* Bamberg. Professor at Robert Koch Institute of Infectious Diseases (from 1902); director of Institute for Experimental Therapy at Dahlem, near Berlin (from 1913); noted for discovery (1906) of the Wasserman test for the diagnosis of syphilis.

Wassermann, Jakob 1873–1934. German novelist. *b.* Fürth, Bavaria. Chief works include *Die Juden von Zirndorf* (1897), *Caspar Hauser* (1908), *The World's Illusion* (1919), *The Maurizius Case* (1928), *Etzel Andergast* (1931), *Joseph Kerkhovens dritte Existenz* (1934), *The Goose Man* (1915); described his life and work in *My Life as German and Jew* (1921), *Selbstbetrachtungen* (1933), and *Die Kunst der Erzählung* (1904).

Watson *(wŏt sən),* **James Dewey** 1928–. American biochemist. *b.* Chicago, Ill. Professor at Harvard (from 1955); shared Nobel Prize in physiology and medicine (1962) with Francis Crick and Maurice Wilkins for determining the molecular structure of deoxyribonucleic acid (DNA) and its significance for information transfer in living material. Author of *The Double Helix* (1968).

Watt *(wŏt),* **James** 1736–1819. Scottish inventor. *b.* Greenock. Mathematical-instrument maker to University of Glasgow (1757); began experiments toward an improved steam engine (c1760) and invented (1765) and patented (1769) a condensed steam engine; made other improvements, as the sun and planet wheels, the double engine, the governor, and a smokeless furnace (1718–85); one of the first to use the term *horsepower*; the watt, a unit of power, is named after him; with Matthew Boulton, formed a partnership in Birmingham for the manufacture of steam engines (1775).

Watteau *(wȧ tō),* **Jean Antoine** 1684–1721. French painter. *b.* Valenciennes. Excelled in garden landscapes and pastoral idylls, with gay shepherds and shepherdesses and rustic dances; gained fame and membership in the Academy with *Embarkation for Cythera*; also painted *Fêtes Gallantes* and *Le Mezzetin.*

Watts *(wŏts),* **George Frederic** 1817–1904. English painter and sculptor. *b.* London. First notable work was *Caractacus*, a mural for the new Houses of Parliament; became very popular with allegorical paintings and portraits. Among his works are *St. George and the Dragon, The School of Legislation, Sir Galahad, Alfred the Great, Echo, Life's Illusions, Watchman, What of the Night?, Love and Death, Paola and Francesca, Fata Morgana, Hope, Love and Life, Orpheus and Eurydice, She Shall Be Called Woman, Sic Transit*, and *Physical Energy*.

Watts, Isaac 1674–1748. English theologian and hymn-writer. *b.* Southampton. Composed over 700 hymns, including "When I Survey the Wondrous Cross", "O God, Our Help in Ages Past", and "Jesus Shall Reign Where'er the Sun"; religious poems were collected in *Horae Lyricae* (1706), *Hymns and Spiritual Songs* (1707–1709), *Psalms of David Imitated* (1719), and *Divine and Moral Songs for Children* (1720).

Waugh *(wô)*, **Arthur** 1866–1943. English critic and publisher. *b.* Midsomer Norton. Editor, correspondent, literary agent, book critic, and chairman of Chapman and Hall, London publishers (1926–36); wrote biographies of Gordon, Tennyson, and Browning. Son ALEC OR ALEXANDER RABAN (1898–), English author. *b.* London. Author of *The Loom of Youth* (1917), *Wheels Within Wheels* (1933), *Where the Clock Chimes Twice* (1952), and *Island in the Sun* (1956). Another son EVELYN ARTHUR ST. JOHN (1903–1966), English author. *b.* London. Achieved reputation as a stylist and sardonic wit with *Decline and Fall* (1928), *Black Mischief* (1932), *Vile Bodies* (1930), *Scoop* (1938), *A Handful of Dust* (1934), *Edmund Campion* (1935), *Waugh in Abyssinia* (1936), *Put Out More Flags* (1942), *Brideshead Revisited* (1945), *The Loved One* (1948), *Men at Arms* (1952), *Officers and Gentlemen* (1955), *Unconditional Surrender* (1961), *Gilbert Pinfold* (1957), and *A Little Learning* (1964).

Wayne *(wān)*, **Anthony** 1745–96. American Revolutionary officer. *b.* Waynesboro, Pa. Member of Pennsylvania legislature (1774); colonel in Continental army; covered retreat from Canada at Three Rivers (1776) and commanded Ticonderoga; joined Washington's army as brigadier general (1777); served in all important engagements thereafter: Brandywine (1777), Germantown (1777), Monmouth (1778), and Green Spring and Yorktown (1781); in a brilliant attack, took Stony Point (1779); earned the name "Mad Anthony" for his exploits; after retiring (1783), returned (1792) to command forces that defeated Indians at Fallen Timbers (1794); built Fort Wayne and negotiated treaty with Indians (1795).

Webb *(wĕb)*, **Sidney James** title: BARON PASSFIELD. 1859–1947. English socialist. *b.* London. One of the founders of the Fabian Society and a prolific ideologue; entered Parliament (1922); held cabinet offices (1924, 1929–31). Author of *Socialism in England* (1890); married BEATRICE POTTER (1858–1943), English socialist. Together wrote *The History of Trade Unionism* (1894), *Industrial Democracy* (1897), *English Local Government*

(9 vols., 1906–29), Decay of Capitalist Civilization (1921), *English Poor Law History* (3 vols., 1927–29), and several books on Soviet Communism; founded *The New Statesman* (1913), and took an active role in establishing the London School of Economics and Politics (1895); Beatrice was the author of *My Apprenticeship* (1936) and the posthumous *Our Partnership* (1948).

Weber *(vēb ər),* **Baron Karl Maria Friedrich Ernst von** 1786–1826. German composer. *b.* Eutin. Wrote first opera at age 13; first conducted at Breslau (1804–1806); music conductor to duke of Württemberg at Stuttgart (1807–10); Kapellmeister at Prague (1813–17); director at Dresden (1817) and London (1826); considered a founder of German romantic opera. Works include operas *Das Waldmädchen* (1800), *Peter Schmoll* (1803), *Rübezahl* (1804), *Abu Hassan* (1811), *Der Freischütz* (1821), *Euryanthe* (1823), and *Oberon* (1826), music to *Preciosa*, symphonies, concertos, chorales, cantatas, songs, and *Invitation to the Dance*.

Weber, Max 1864–1920. German sociologist. *b.* Erfurt. Professor at Berlin (1893), Freiburg (1894), Heidelberg (1897), and Munich (1919); developed a methodology for the social sciences by synthesizing studies in religion, economics, politics, and law. Most important works are *Protestant Ethic and the Spirit of Capitalism* (1920), *Gesämmelte Aufsätze zur Religionsoziologie* (3 vols., 1920–21), and *Economy and Society* (1925).

Weber, Wilhelm Eduard 1804–91. German physicist. *b.* Wittenberg. Professor at Göttingen (from 1831) and Leipzig (from 1843); invented the electrodynamometer; introduced the absolute scale of electrical units; the weber, a magnetic unit, named after him. Brother of Ernst Heinrich (1795–1878), German physiologist and anatomist. *b.* Wittenberg. Investigated the sense organs, especially those of hearing and touching; formulated Weber's law on the relation of intensity of two sensations.

Webern *(vā bərn),* **Anton von** 1883–1945. Austrian composer. *b.* Vienna. Became one of the principal disciples of Schönberg, developing the twelve-tone technique beyond his master. Among his atonal works are *Passacaglia for Orchestra* (1908), *Geistliche Lieder, Entflieht auf Leichten Kähnen* for chorus, *Five Pieces for Orchestra*, a symphony, and three cantatas.

Webster *(wĕb stər),* **Daniel** 1782–1852. American statesman. *b.* Salisbury, N.H. Gained fame as lawyer in the Dartmouth College case and *McCulloch* vs. *Maryland*; member of House of Representatives from N.H. (1813–17) and from Mass. (1823–27); a founder of the Whig party formed to oppose Jacksonian Democrats and to support vested interests; U.S. Senater (1827–41, 1845–50); secretary of state (1841–43, 1850–52); an avowed presidential candidate in every election from 1836 to 1852; as secretary of state, successfully negotiated Webster-Ashburton Treaty with Britain (1842); lukewarm opponent of slavery, placed unity of the country above abolitionist principles and thus supported Compromise of 1850; fame rests on his great orations, especially the Reply to Hayne, with its impassioned plea for "liberty and union, now and forever, one and inseparable," the oration at second centennial of the landing of Pilgrims at Plymouth, two at Bunker Hill, orations on the deaths of Thomas Jefferson and John Adams, and the oration at the cornerstone ceremony at the Capitol (1851).

Webster, John c1580–c1625. English dramatist. *b.* London. Collaborated with Dekker, Marston, Heywood, Chettle, Drayton, Middleton, and others. Best known for *The White Devil, or Vittoria Corombona* (c1610) and *The Duchess of Malfi* (1614).

Webster, Noah 1758–1843. American lexicographer. *b.* West Hartford, Conn. After serving in Revolutionary War, became a teacher; after being admitted to the bar (1781), combined law and teaching; determined to develop a national language in America, published *A Grammatical Institute of the English Language* including the *Blue-Backed Speller* (1782–83), a grammar (1784) and a reader (1785); enlarged ideas on the Americanization of English in *Dissertations on the English Language* (1789); turned to journalism, becoming editor of *The American Magazine* (1787–88); published newspapers *The American Minerva* (1793–98) and *The Herald*; produced his first dictionary, *A Compendious Dictionary of the English Language* (1806), followed with its abridgment, *A Dictionary for the Use of Common Schools* (1807); founded Amherst College (1819); wrote *An American Dictionary of the English Language* (2 vols., 1828), *History of the United States* (1832), and *Brief History of Epidemic and Pestilential Diseases* (2 vols., 1799); earned the title Father of American Copyright by tirelessly campaigning for legal rights of authors and for securing passage of Copyright Act (1870); his contributions to lexicography have made Webster and dictionary synonymous.

Wedgwood *(wĕj wood),* **Josiah** 1730–95. English potter. *b.* Burslem. Known for major advances in pottery-making, including cream-colored queen's ware, blue jasper ware, Egyptian or black basalt ware, and veined ware in imitation of granite; produced copies of classical vases.

Wegener *(vā gə nər),* **Alfred Lothar** 1880–1930. German geophysicist. *b.* Berlin. Professor at Hamburg (from 1919) and Graz (from 1924); conducted expeditions to Greenland (1906–1908, 1912–13, 1929, 1930); noted for theory of continental drift (the Wegener hypothesis) describing how the present continents broke off from a supercontinent eons ago and are still changing in relation to one another. Published *The Origin of Continents and Oceans* (1924) and *Thermodynamics of the Atomosphere* (1911).

Weill *(vīl),* **Kurt** 1900–1950. German-American composer. *b.* Dessau. Immigrated to U.S. (1935) as a refugee from the Nazis; collaborated with Bertolt Brecht on *The Threepenny Opera*; wrote musical scores for *Lady in the Dark* (1941), *One Touch of Venus* (1943), *Knickerbocker Holiday* (1938), *Lost in the Stars* (1949), *Johnny Johnson* (1936), and *The Eternal Road* (1938).

Weizmann *(vīts män),* **Chaim** 1874–1952. Russian Zionist leader. *b.* near Pinsk. Studied in Germany but became a British subject (1910); a chemist by profession, he created synthetic acetone for the manufacture of explosives; active in Zionist movement (from 1898); his tireless advocacy was responsible for Balfour Declaration (1917), affirming British support for a Jewish homeland in Palestine; president of World Zionist Organization (1920–31), Jewish Agency (1929–31, from 1935), Hebrew University (from 1932), and the Republic of Israel (1948–52).

Weller *(wĕl ər),* **Thomas Huckle** 1915–. American biologist. *b.* Ann Arbor, Mich. Professor at Harvard (from 1940); with J.F. Enders and F.C. Robbins, shared Nobel Prize in physiology and medicine (1954) for successfully growing poliomyelitis virus in cultures of different tissues outside a living organism.

Wellesley *(wĕlz lĭ),* **Marquis Richard Colley** title: EARL OF MORNINGTON. 1760–1842. British statesman. *b.* County Meath, Ireland. Elder brother of Arthur Wellesley, Duke of Wellington; entered House of Commons (1784); lord of the treasury, member of the privy council, and member of the Board of Control of East India Company; governor general of India (1797); his administration, considered brilliant, eliminated France as a rival, overthrew the anti-British Tipu Sultan of Mysore, and punished the Maratha Confederacy; ambassador to Madrid (1808–1809); foreign secretary (1809–12); lord lieutenant of Ireland (1821–28, 1833–34).

Wellington *(wĕl ĭnn tən),* **Duke of** title of ARTHUR WELLESLEY. 1769–1852. British general and statesman. *b.* County Meath, Ireland. Entered army (1787); preceded brother Richard Colley Wellesley to India as colonel (1799); appointed by his brother to supreme command in the Deccan; took part in wars against Mysore and the Marathas (1803); on return to England, entered House of Commons (1806); secretary for Ireland (1807–1809); in victorious expedition against Danes (1807); with commencement of Peninsular War (1808), sent to aid Portuguese against the French; gained victories at Rolica and Vemeiro; on death of Sir John Moore, given chief command (1809); pushed French back from Portugal (1810–11), winning at Talavera (1809); with victory at Salamanca (1812), entered Madrid; expelled French from Spain after defeating them at Vitoria (1813); invaded France, winning at Orthez and Toulouse(1814); made duke of Wellington (1814); ambassador to Paris (1814–15); British representative at Congress of Vienna (1815); on Napoleon's return from Elba, assumed command (1815) and, at Waterloo, ended Napoleon's power; negotiated Peace of Paris (1815); commander in chief of allied army of occupation in France (1815–18); attended congresses of Aix-la-Chapelle (1818) and Verona (1822); master general of the ordinance (1818); emissary to Moscow (1826); named commander in chief (1827) and confirmed in that office for life (1842); prime minister (1828–30); opposed Reform Bill, but supported Catholic emancipation; foreign secretary (1834–35); minister without portfolio (1841–46); retired from public life (1846).

Wells *(wĕlz),* **Herbert George** known as H.G. WELLS. 1866–1946. English writer. *b.* London. A prolific writer of science fantasies and novels of contemporary mores, he used his books as vehicles for his radical and utopian ideals. Among his works are *Time Machine* (1895), *The Island of Doctor Moreau* (1896), *The Wheels of Chance* (1896), *The Invisible Man* (1897), *The War in the Air* (1908), *The War of the Worlds* (1898), *The Food of the Gods* (1904), *A Modern Utopia* (1908), *Love and Mr. Lewisham* (1900), *Kipps* (1905), *The History of Mr. Polly* (1910), *Ann Veronica* (1909), *Tono-Bungay* (1909), *The New Machiavelli* (1911), *Mr. Britling Sees It Through* (1916), *Joan and Peter* (1918), *Marriage* (1912), *The Outline of History* (1920), *The Science of Life* (1929–30), *The World of William Clissold* (1926), *The Work, Wealth, and Happiness of Mankind* (1932), *The Shape of Things to Come* (1933), *Experiment in Autobiography* (1934), *Fate of Homo Sapiens* (1939), *The New World Order* (1940), and *Phoenix* (1942).

Wentworth *(wĕnt wûrth),* **William Charles** 1793–1872. Australian statesman. *b.* Norfolk Island. Founded the newspaper *The Australian* (1824), advocating self-government and the rights of landholders; active in securing passage of the constitutions of 1842 and 1854; founded Sydney University (1852). Author of *Statistical Account of the British Settlements in Australasia* (1819).

Werfel *(vĕr fəl),* **Franz** 1890–1945. Austrian writer. *b.* Prague, Czechoslovakia. Immigrated to U.S. (1940). Author of plays *Good Song* (1926), *Juarez and Maximilian* (1926), *Paul Among the Jews* (1928), *The Eternal Road* (1936), and *Jacobowski and the Colonel* (1944), and novels *Verdi* (1925), *The Man Who Conquered Death* (1926), *The Class Reunion* (1928), *The Forty Days of Musa Dagh* (1934), *The Song of Bernadette* (1942), and *The Star of the Unborn* (1946).

Werner *(vĕr nər),* **Alfred** 1866–1919. Swiss chemist. *b.* Mülhausen, Alsace. Professor in Zurich (from 1893); formulated the coordination theory of complexes, a fundamental discovery in inorganic chemistry which led to the study of isomerism; awarded Nobel Prize in chemistry (1913). Author of *Lehrbuch der Stereochemie* (1904).

Wesley *(wĕs lē),* **John** 1703–91. English theologian. *b.* Epworth. Ordained (1728); joined a small group of men (including James Hervey and George Whitefield) gathered by his brother Charles, conspicuous for their piety and methodical observance of religious duties (hence called Methodists); accompanied Charles to Georgia as missionary among colonists and Indians (1735–38); influenced by the Moravians, and underwent religious conversion (1738) that brought him assurance of salvation through Jesus Christ alone; excluded from preaching from the pulpit, began preaching outdoors at Bristol (1739), where he founded the first Methodist chapel; converted a ruined London foundry into a chapel and made it his headquarters; held first conference of Methodists (1744); remaining loyal to the Church of England, ordained ministers for the colonies and appointed Francis Asbury general superintendent in America (1772); found most converts in the working class; later broke with Whitefield, the Moravians, and the Calvinists; along with his missionary work, wrote histories, treatises, grammars, translations, biblical commentaries, biographies, hymns, and an English dictionary; his *Journal* was published (8 vols., 1909–16). His brother CHARLES (1707–88), English preacher and hymn-writer. *b.* Bristol. Accompanied his brother to Georgia (1735); ordained (1735); underwent religious conversion (1738); actively associated with the Methodist movement as a preacher (1739–56). Author of over 6500 hymns, including"Hark! The Herald Angels Sing" and "Jesus, Lover of My Soul."

West *(wěst),* **Benjamin** 1738–1820. American painter. *b.* Springfield, Pa. Worked in Philadelphia and New York (to 1760); in Italy (1760–63); settled in London (1763); gained patronage of George III, was appointed court painter (from 1772); charter member of the Royal Academy and its president (1792–1820). Among his noted paintings are *The Death of Wolfe, Christ Healing the Sick, Death on the Pale Horse, Alexander the Great and His Physicians, Penn's Treaty with the Indians*, and *Battle of La Hogue.*

West, Nathanael Original name: Nathan Weinstein. 1903–40. American novelist. *b.* New York, N.Y. Satirized and indicted American popular culture in *A Cool Million* (1934), *Miss Lonelyhearts* (1933), and *The Day of the Locust* (1939).

Westermarck *(věs tər märk),* **Edward Alexander** 1862–1939. Finnish anthropologist. *b.* Helsinki. Professor at University of London (from 1907). Author of works on human morals, including *The History of Human Marriage* (1891), *The Origin and Development of the Moral Ideas* (2 vols., 1908), *Early Beliefs and Their Social Influence* (1932), *Christianity and Morals* (1939), and *Autobiography* (1929).

Westinghouse *(wěs tĭng hous),* **George** 1846–1914. American inventor. *b.* Central Bridge, N.Y. Inventor of the air brake and automatic railroad signal devices; pioneer in the introduction of high-voltage alternating current single-phase electrical transmission; held over 400 patents in the field of electricity and mechanics; founded Westinghouse Air Brake Company (1869), Westinghouse Electric Company (1886), and other concerns.

Wharton *(hwôr tən),* **Edith Newbold** 1862–1937. American novelist. *b.* New York, N.Y. Born into a wealthy New York family; noted for her novels dealing with high society, and her acute portrayal of its civilized manners and resulting narrowness; highly acclaimed writer by such critics as Henry James. Notable works: *The Valley of Decision* (1902), *The House of Mirth* (1905), *Ethan Frome* (1911), *The Custom of the Country* (1913), *The Age of Innocence* (1920, Pulitzer prize), *Old New York* (4 vols., 1924), *Certain*

People (1930), and *A Backward Glance* (1934).

Wheatstone *(hwēt stōn),* **Sir Charles** 1802–75. English physicist. *b.* Gloucester. Professor at King's College, London (from 1834); with W.F. Cooke, invented the electric telegraph (1837); among his other inventions are the stereoscope (1838), the concertina (1829), an automatic telegraph, and a kaleidophon; coined the term microphone; popularized a device, now known as Wheatstone bridge, for accurate measurement of electrical resistance.

Wheeler *(hwē lər),* **William Almon** 1819–87. American statesman. *b.* Malone, N.Y. Republican member of House of Representatives (1861–63, 1869–77); author of the Wheeler Compromise (1874); vice-president of U.S. (1877–81).

Whipple *(hwĭ pəl),* **George Hoyt** 1878–1976. American pathologist. *b.* Ashland, N.H. Professor in California (1920–21) and at Rochester (1921–55); with George Minot and William P. Murphy, received Nobel Prize in physiology and medicine (1934) for discovery that administering liver extract increases activity in the bone marrow where red cells are formed.

Whistler *(hwĭs lər),* **James Abbott McNeill** 1834–1903. American painter. *b.* Lowell, Mass. Left America (1855), settling first in Paris and later in London; pugnacious, flamboyant, witty, he became known as much for his eccentricities as for his art; stung by Ruskin's criticisms, filed a libel suit against him and won a farthing damages; produced over 400 superb etchings. Among his noted works are *Portrait of My Mother, Peacock Room,* the *Nocturnes* series, *Harmony in Gray and Green*, the *Thames* series, the *Venice* series, *At the Piano, Blue Wave, Biarritz, Trafalgar Square, Westminster Bridge, Battersea Bridge*, and portrait of Carlyle; his *Gentle Art of Making Enemies* (1890) contain essays and aphorisms.

White *(hwīt),* **Edward Douglass** 1845–1921. American jurist. *b.* La Fourche Parish, La. Senator from Louisiana (1891–94); associate justice of Supreme Court (1894–1910); chief justice of the United States (1910–21); laid down the rule of reason as the guiding principle in decisions in antitrust cases.

White, Patrick 1912– . Australian author. *b.* London, England. Awarded Nobel Prize in literature (1973), the first Australian to be so honored. Author of *Happy Valley* (1939), *The Living and the Dead* (1941), *The Aunt's Story* (1946), *The Tree of Man* (1954), *Riders in the Chariot* (1961), *The Solid Mandala* (1966), *Voss* (1957), and *The Burnt One* (1964).

White, William Allen 1868–1944. American journalist. *b.* Emporia, Kans. As editor and owner of *Emporia Gazette*, became famous for his sage editorials articulating grassroots republicanism. Among his many books are *A Certain Rich Man* (1909), *The Editor and His People* (1924), *Forty Years on Main Street* (1937), *A Puritan in Babylon: The Story of Calvin Coolidge* (1938), and *The Autobiography of William Allen White* (1946).

Whitefield *(hwīt fēld),* **George** 1714–70. English evangelist. *b.* Bell Inn. At Oxford, joined Methodist group led by Charles and John Wesley; followed Wesley to Georgia (1738); on return to England, ordained priest; began preaching in open fields in Bristol (1739); parted company with Methodists over their repudiation of strict Calvinism; leader of Calvinistic Methodists; actively supported by countess of Huntingdon; during his apostolate, made seven visits to America; founded Bethesda College at Savannah; died in Newburyport, Mass.

Whitehead *(hwīt hĕd),* **Alfred North** 1861–1947. English mathematician and philosopher. *b.* London. Professor at London (1914–24) and Harvard (1924–36); collaborated with Bertrand Russell on *Principia Mathematica* (1910); developed an idealistic philosophy based on mathematical concepts; explored the interrelation of time, space, and matter. Principal works include *The Principles of Natural Knowledge* (1919), *Science and the Modern World* (1925), *Process and Reality* (1929), *Adventures of Ideas* (1933), *Nature and Life* (1934), *Modes of Thought (1938), and Religion in the Making* (1926).

Whitman *(hwīt mən),* **Walt** 1819–92. American poet. *b.* West Hills, N.Y. Worked as a typesetter, teacher, journalist, hospital nurse, and clerk; principal work, *Leaves of Grass* (1855), originally 95 pages, grew to over 400 pages through eight editions; his favorite themes were democracy, celebration of physical love, dignity of man, and pantheism; denounced as author of an indecent work, he received little recognition in U.S. until after he received critical acclaim in England (1876). Other poetic works include *Drum-Taps* (1865), *Sequel to Drum-Taps* (1866), and *November Boughs* (1888); prose works include *Democratic Vistas* (1871) and *Specimen Days and Collect* (1883).

Whitney *(hwĭt nĭ),* **Eli** 1765–1825. American inventor. *b.* Westborough, Mass. Went to Georgia as teacher; found patron, in widow of General Nathanael Greene; on her suggestion, invented the cotton gin for cleaning seed from cotton fibers (1793), but invention was stolen before he could secure a patent (1794); engaged in lawsuits to defend his rights; voted $50,000 by state of South Carolina; moved to Connecticut, where he started a factory for the manufacture of firearms with standardized, interchangeable parts.

Whittier *(hwĭt ĭ ər),* **John Greenleaf** 1807–92. American poet. *b.* Haverhill, Mass. Known as poet laureate of abolitionism; editor (from 1829) of journals, including *The National Era* (1847–59); poems evoked a vanished past of New England and the simple faith of New Englanders. Works include *Legends of New England* (1831), *Moll Pitcher* (1832), *Lays of My Home* (1843), *The Voices of Freedom* (1846), *Songs of Labor* (1850), *Home Ballads* (1860), *In War Time* (1864), *Snow-Bound* (1866), *Among the Hills* (1869), *Miriam* (1869), *Pennsylvania Pilgrim* (1872), *Hazel Blossoms* (1875), and *At Sundown* (1890).

Wieland *(vē länt),* **Christoph Martin** 1733–1813. German poet. *b.* near Biberach. Early works showed promise of a didactic and mystic writer in *Die Natur der Dinge* (1751), *Der Geprufte Abraham* (1753), and *Empfindungen des Christen* (1753); under the influence of Voltaire and others, wrote satiric dramas and romances; translated Shakespeare and Horace; wrote novel *Don Sylvio von Rosalvo* (1765) on the model of Cervantes; published first German bildungsroman *Die Geschichte des Agathon* (1766–67); professor of philosophy and literature at University of Erfurt (1769–72); on publication of *Der Goldene Spiegel* (1772), invited to Weimar as tutor to dukes Charles Augustus and Constantine; joined Weimar Group that included Goethe, Schiller, and Herder; edited *Der Teutsche Merkur* (1773–1809) and *Das Attische Museum* (1796–1809); collected works in 45 volumes include *Lady Johanna Gray* (1758), *Idris and Zenide* (1768), *Musarion* (1768), *Oberon* (1780), *The Republic of Fools* (1774), *Aristipp* (4 vols., 1800–1801), and *Dschinnistan*.

Wien *(vēn)*, **Wilhelm** 1864–1928. German physicist. *b.* Gaffken, Prussia. Professor of physics at Aachen (from 1896), Giessen (from 1899), Würzburg (from 1900), and Munich (from 1920); investigated X-rays, cathode rays, hydrodynamics, and positive rays; formulated Wien's Displacement Law; awarded Nobel Prize in physics (1911) for discovery of radiation of energy from black bodies.

Wiener *(wē nər)*, **Norbert** 1894– . American mathematician. *b.* Columbia, Mo. Worked on computers and electronic calculators; made pioneering contributions to a new field of study known as cybernetics, dealing with control and communications in men and machines; known also for work on probability and mathematical logic; professor of mathematics at M.I.T. (from 1919). Author of *Cybernetics* (1948), *I Am a Mathematician* (1956), and *The Fourier Integral and Certain of Its Applications* (1933).

Wigner *(wĭg nər)*, **Eugene Paul** 1902– . American physicist. *b.* Budapest, Hungary. Professor at Princeton (from 1938); contributions to nuclear physics include the Breit-Wigner formula governing resonant nuclear reactions, the Wigner theorem, and the Wigner nuclides; awarded Nobel Prize in physics (1963).

Wilberforce *(wĭl bər fōrs)*, **William** 1759–1833. English humanitarian. *b.* Hull. Entered Parliament (1780); worked for legislation abolishing slavery; secured abolition of slave trade (1807); founded Anti-slavery Society (1823) and began work for universal abolition of slavery; converted to evangelical Christianity under influence of Dean Isaac Milner, becoming a central figure in the Clapham sect; founded *The Christian Observer* (1801). Author of *Practical View of Christianity* (1797).

Wilde *(wīld)*, **Oscar Fingal O'Flahertie Wills** 1854–1900. Irish poet. *b.* Dublin. Brilliant epigrams, studied eccentricities, and sparkling wit made him a cult figure in Victorian England; cultivated an art for art's sake philosophy and aesthetic insouciance. Principal works are *Lady Windermere's Fan* (1892), *A Woman of No*

Importance (1893), *An Ideal Husband* (1895), *The Importance of Being Earnest* (1895), *Salomé, The Picture of Dorian Gray* (1891), *Lord Arthur Savile's Crime* (1891), *The Duchess of Padua* (1891), and *Collected Poems* (1892); in one of the sensational trials in 19th-century England, found guilty on morals charge (1895) and imprisoned for two years; out of this experience came *De Profundis* (1905) and *Ballad of Reading Gaol* (1898); spent last years in Paris under an assumed name, spiritually and financially broken.

Wilder *(wĭl dər),* **Thornton Niven** 1897–1975. American writer. *b.* Madison, Wis. Noted as author of both novels and plays; three-time Pulitzer Prize winner; with publication of *The Bridge of San Luis Rey* (1927) instituted genre of characters brought together by dramatic accident. Other works include *Heaven's My Destination* (1935), *The Ides of March* (1948), *The Angel That Troubled the Waters* (1928), *Our Town* (1938), *The Skin of Our Teeth* (1942), and *A Life in the Sun* (1955).

Wilkes *(wĭlks),* **John** 1727–97. English politician. *b.* London. Entered Parliament (1762); founded journal *North Briton* (1762), in which he attacked the prime minister and George III; seized and committed to the Tower under a general warrant, but released after trial and obtained damages for illegal arrest; expelled from Parliament as author of the obscene *Essay on Woman* (1764); took refuge in France and was outlawed for nonappearance at trial; returned to England (1768) and gained a reversal of his banishment but was imprisoned for 22 months; elected to Parliament (1769), but denied seat; reelected four times and repeatedly ejected from Parliament; became a popular hero and martyr in the cause of freedom; lord mayor of London (1774); allowed to take seat in Parliament (1774–90); championed American colonies and causes of parliamentary reform and freedom of the press.

Wilkins *(wĭl kənz),* **Maurice Hugh Frederick** 1916– . British biophysicist. *b.* New Zealand. Did research at University of California (1944) and in Medical Research Council at London (from 1946); with F. Crick and James Watson, shared Nobel Prize in physiology and medicine for discovery of the helical structure of DNA (1962).

Willard *(wĭl ərd),* **Emma** 1787–1870. American educator. *b.* Berlin, Conn. Pioneer in higher education for women, founding a school for girls at Middlebury, Vt. (1814), Waterford Academy (1819–21), and the Troy Female Seminary, later known as Emma Willard School (1821–38). Among her works is *Plan for Improving Female Education.*

Willard, Frances Elizabeth Caroline 1839–98. American temperance leader. *b.* Churchville, N.Y. Professor of aesthetics at Evanston, Ill. (1874); secretary of the Woman's Christian Temperance Union (1874) and its president (from 1879); helped found Prohibition party (1884) and the International Council of Women (1887). Author of *Women and Temperance* (1883), *How to Win* (1886), *Glimpse of Fifty Years*

(1889), and *My Happy Half-Century* (1894).

William I *(wĭl yəm)* called WILLIAM THE CONQUEROR. 1027–87. King of England (1066–87). *b.* Falaise, Normandy. Natural son of Robert the Devil, Duke of Normandy, but succeeded to duchy as William II on father's death without legitimate issue (1035); suppressed revolt of nobles at Val es Dunes (1047); visited cousin Edward the Confessor (1051) and received promise of English succession, reinforced by an oath extracted from Harold, Earl of Essex (1064); repulsed two French invasions (1054, 1058); conquered Maine (1063), extending kingdom to the Loire; on death of Edward the Confessor and election of Harold as king by the witan, enforced his claim by force after obtaining a bull from Pope Alexander II acknowledging him as rightful heir to English throne; invaded England, defeated and killed Harold at Battle of Hastings (1066); crowned at Westminster; took four years to complete conquest by suppressing English uprisings and Danish invasion; compelled homage from Scottish King Malcolm at Abernethy (1072); occupied with Continental wars and the revolts of son Robert and half-brother Odo; established feudal system in England; eliminated power of the nobles by making land titles based on his grant, scattering feudal estates, exercising power in each shire through the sheriff, requiring an oath of fealty from all landowners, and setting royal courts alongside of manorial courts; with aid of Lanfranc, whom he appointed archbishop of Canterbury, reorganized English church, separating spiritual from temporal courts; built castles, introduced the curfew system, ordered compilation of Domesday Book, a census of the English lands; abolished the four great earldoms of Anglo-Saxon England; died at Mantes, France, at war with Philip I.

William I also WILLIAM THE SILENT 1533–84. Founder of Dutch Republic and first stadholder (1579–84). *b.* Dillenburg. Son of William, count of Nassau; educated in Catholic faith at court of Emperor Charles V; inherited principality of Orange as prince (1544–84); commander of imperial army in Netherlands and governor of northern Holland (1555); succeeded father as count of Nassau (1559); protested persecution of Protestants by Granvella; supported League of the Gueux against Spanish encroachments; resigned offices (1567); proclaimed a traitor by duke of Alva and put under ban by Philip; refused to appear before Council of Blood (1568); proclaimed adherence to Protestant cause and took up arms against Spain (1568) as commander of Dutch War of Liberation; suffered initial reverses but captured Briel (1572); converted to Calvinism (1573); by Pacification of Ghent, united Holland, Zealand, and southern provinces (1576), and, by Union of Utrecht, the seven northern provinces (1579); on declaration of independence of United Provinces (1581), made stadholder; assassinated by a Catholic fanatic.

William III 1650–1702. Stadholder of Holland (1672–1702) and king of England (1689–1702). *b.*

The Hague, Netherlands. Spent early years in struggles with Jan de Witt, leader of aristocratic Republicans; at war with Louis XIV, terminated by Treaty of Nijmegen (1673); married his cousin, Mary, the eldest daughter of duke of York, later James II of England (1677); invited by seven English patriots to overthrow James II, headed an army of 15,000; landed at Torbay (1688); after flight of James and the Bloodless (Glorious) Revolution, accepted the crown offered by Parliament; proclaimed joint sovereign with Mary; accepted Declaration of Rights (1689) and assented to Act of Settlement (1701); Jacobite resistance in Scotland was ended with Battle of Killiecrankie (1689) and Massacre of Glencoe (1692); invaded Ireland, defeating James at Battle of Boyne (1690); formed Grand Alliance against France and, with allied victory at La Hogue (1692), frustrated Louis's projected invasion of England; after Mary's death, became sole ruler (1694); ended war with France with Treaty of Ryswick (1696), in which Louis recognized him as king of England; resumed war with France with second Grand Alliance (1701); during reign, the Bank of England was established and the present system of ministerial responsibility was introduced.

Williams *(wĭl yəmz),* **Roger** c1603–83. American clergyman. *b.* London, England. Sailed for New World (1630); banished from Salem for outspoken opposition to New England theocracy; moved first to Plymouth (1631–33) and, after banishment, to R.I. (1635); founded Providence (1636); established complete religious freedom, a human code of laws, and a primitive form of democracy; as a missionary to the Indians, gained their friendship and confidence, enabling him to mediate between them and the colonists to avert war; founded first Baptist church in America (1639); withdrew from organized religion and became a seeker without formal creed; obtained Rhode Island's first charter from England and served as governor (1644–47) and president (1654–58). Author of *Key into the Language of America* (1643), *The Bloody Tenent of Persecution* (1644), and other books.

Williams, Tennessee original name: THOMAS LANIER WILLIAMS. 1911– . American playwright. *b.* Columbus, Miss. Major American literary figure, noted as the author of plays with a Southern setting, including *The Glass Menagerie* (1945), *A Streetcar Named Desire* (1947), *Cat on a Hot Tin Roof* (1955), *Sweet Bird of Youth* (1959), *The Night of the Iguana* (1961), *Orpheus Descending* (1957), *Suddenly Last Summer* (1958), and *The Milk Train Doesn't Stop Here Anymore* (1963); also wrote the novel *The Roman Spring of Mrs. Stone* (1950), short stories, poetry, and memoirs.

Williams, William Carlos 1883–1963. American poet. *b.* Rutherford, N.J. Practiced as a physician; as a poet, developed a free-verse style close to colloquial speech. Poetic works include *The Tempers* (1913), *The Complete Collected Poems, 1906–1938* (1939), *The Wedge* (1945), and *Paterson* (1946–50), a five-volume personal epic; prose works include *The*

Great American Novel (1923), *White Mule* (1937), *In the Money* (1940), and *The Autobiography of William Carlos Williams* (1951); awarded the Dial Prize for service to American literature.

Willstätter *(vĭl shtĕt ər),* **Richard** 1872–1942. German chemist. *b.* Karlsruhe. Professor at Zurich (from 1905), Berlin (from 1912), and Munich (1915–25); considered a foremost researcher into alkaloids and plant pigments; determined the structure of chlorophyll (1906), anthocyanins (1913), tropine, and cocaine, synthesizing the last two; awarded Nobel Prize in chemistry (1915).

Wilson *(wĭl sən),* **Charles Thomas Rees** 1869–1959. Scottish physicist. *b.* Glencorse. Professor of natural philosophy at Cambridge (1925–34); conducted research on atmospheric electricity, condensation nuclei, and ions; developed Wilson's cloud chamber (1897) for photographing and studying ionized particles; awarded Nobel Prize in physics with A.H. Compton (1927).

Wilson, Edmund 1895–1972. American critic. *b.* Red Bank, N.J. Editor of *Vanity Fair* (1920–21) and book review editor for *The New Yorker* (from 1944). Principal works include *Axel's Castle* (1931), *I Thought of Daisy* (1929), *The Wound and the Bow* (1941), *The Triple Thinkers* (1938), *To the Finland Station* (1940), *Memoirs of Hecate Country* (1946), *The Shores of Light* (1952), *The Scrolls from the Dead Sea* (1955), *Patriotic Gore* (1962), *A Piece of my Mind: Reflections at Sixty* (1956), and *A Prelude (1967).*

Wilson, Harold full name: James Harold. 1916– . British statesman. *b.* Huddersfield. Entered Parliament on Labor ticket (1945); became youngest cabinet minister since Pitt when he became president of Board of Trade (1947–51); succeeded Gaitskell as leader of Labor party (1963); prime minister (1964–70, 1973–76); followed moderate socialist policies at home; administration marked by periodic economic crises and high inflation.

Wilson, Henry original name: Jeremiah Jones Colbath. 1812–75. American statesman. *b.* Farmington, N.H. An ardent Abolitionist, led the group that withdrew from the Whig convention (1848) because of its refusal to take a firm stand against slavery; founded Free-Soil party and edited its journal *Republican* (1848–51); transferred loyalty to the Know-Nothing party, on whose plank he was elected senator (1855–73); withdrew from Know-Nothing party (c1855) to become a founder of the Republican party; chairman of military affairs committee through Civil War; vice-president of U.S. (1873–75). Author of *History of the Rise and Fall of Slave Power in America* (3 vols., 1872–75).

Wilson, Woodrow 1856–1924. 28th president of U.S. (1913–21). *b.* Staunton, Va. Professor (1890–1902) and president (1902–10) of Princeton University, where he introduced important administrative reforms; governor of New Jersey, opposing machine politicians (1911–13), but gaining national attention for his vigor and honesty; secured Democratic presidential nomination on 46th ballot (1912); elected president with a large electoral majority; inaugurated a series of reforms called the New Freedom; administration noted for the passage of three constitutional amendments (prohibition, woman's suffrage, and popular election of senators), the Underwood Tariff Act, the Clayton Antitrust Act, Workman's Compensation Act, the Child Labor Law, and the establishment of the Federal Trade Commission and the Federal Reserve Banking System; on outbreak of World War I, sought to maintain an impartial neutrality; after repeated German attacks on U.S. shipping, requested and obtained a declaration of war from Congress (1917); outlined the Fourteen Points forming the basis for armistice (1918); took part in the Peace Conference and succeeded in incorporating League of Nations Covenant in the peace treaty; awarded Nobel Peace Prize (1919); failed to obtain Senate ratification of Treaty; embarked on a nationwide tour to gain popular support, suffering a breakdown (1919); remained paralyzed physically and officially through remainder of term. Author of *Congressional Government* (1885), *A History of the American Peoples* (5 vols., 1902), and *Constitutional Government in the United States* (1908).

Winckelmann *(vĭng kəl män)*, **Johann Joachim** 1717–68. German archaeologist. *b.* Stendal, Saxony. Began study of archaeology as librarian at Dresden (1748); converted to Roman Catholic Church (1754); went to Italy (1755), where he became papal antiquary; studied the remains of Pompeii, Naples, Herculaneum, and Paestum. Author of *History of the Art of Antiquity* (1764), *Gedanken über die Nachahmung der Griechischen Werke* (1755), and *Monumenti Antichi Inediti* (1767); murdered by a robber at Trieste; considered founder of archaeology.

Windaus *(vĭn dous)*, **Adolf** 1876–1959. German chemist. *b.* Berlin. Professor at Innsbruck (1913) and Göttingen (1915); discovered and synthesized vitamin D_3 from ergosterol through the action of ultraviolet light; investigated cardiac poisons, cholesterin, sterins, digital glucosides, colchicine, and imidazoles; awarded Nobel Prize in chemistry (1928).

Winfrid; Wynfrith. *See* **Boniface, Saint**

Winslow *(wĭnz lō)*, **Edward** 1595–1655. American Pilgrim father. *b.* Droitwich, England. Sailed on the *Mayflower* (1620); one of the founders of Plymouth colony (1620); governor of Plymouth (1633, 1636, 1644), which he described in *A Relation or Journall of the Beginning and Proceedings of the English Plantation Setled at Plimoth in New England* (1622), *Good News from New England* (1624), and *New England's Salamander* (1647); went back to England several times on behalf of the colony; appointed by Oliver Cromwell as commissioner of an expedition to Spanish West Indies (1655); captured Jamaica; his son Josiah (c1629–80), American colonial statesman. *b.* Plymouth, Mass. Was the first native-born governor of New Plymouth (1673–80).

Winthrop *(wĭn thrəp)*, **John** 1588–1649. American Colonial statesman. *b.* Groton, England.

Governor of the Massachusetts Bay Colony (1629); arrived in Salem on the *Arbella* (1630); governor (1630–34, 1637–40, 1642–44, 1646–49); one of the organizers and first president of United Colonies of New England (1645); autocratic rule was one of the formative influences in establishing a theocratic government. Wrote *Journal* (1825–26). His son JOHN (1606–76), American Colonial statesman. B. Groton, England. Colonized Ipswich, Mass. (1633); founded Saybrook, Conn. and New London, Conn.; governor of Conn. (1657, 1659–76), obtaining a charter for the colony (1662). Grandson JOHN also FITZ-JOHN, (1638–1707), American colonial statesman. *b.* Ipswich, Mass. Settled at New London, Conn.; fought against Dutch, Indians, and French (1673–90); governor of Conn. (1698–1707).

Wise *(wīz),* **Stephen Samuel** 1874–1949. American Jewish leader. *b.* Budapest, Hungary. Founded and served as rabbi of the Free Synagogue at New York (1907–49); as an active Zionist, became spokesman of the American Jewish community; founded and was president of Zionist Organization of America (1917, 1936–38); president of the American Jewish Congress and its representative at the Versailles Peace Conference; founder and president of the Jewish Institute of Religion (1922); one of the organizers of the World Jewish Congress.

Wittgenstein *(vĭt gən shtīn),* **Ludwig Josef Johann** 1889–1951. Austrian philosopher. *b.* Vienna. Born Jewish, but was baptized Roman Catholic; studied in Cambridge under Bertrand Russell and G.E. Moore; taught at Cambridge (1930–47); considered a seminal 20th-century thinker; founder of logical positivism, which condemns speculative philosophy in general and holds that the function of metaphysics is to analyze and clarify language. Principal works are *Tractatus Logico-Philosophicus* (1921), which he completed as a prisoner of war in Italy, and *Philosophical Investigations* (1953); true to his beliefs, renounced philosophy for a while and served as gardener, porter, and schoolmaster.

Wodehouse *(wood hous),* **Pelham Grenville** 1881–1975. British humorist. Noted for hilarious caricatures of English stock figures; a prolific writer, he produced over a hundred novels in a career that spanned over 50 years; immigrated to U.S. (1947); became an American citizen (1955); published autobiographies *Performing Flea* (1953) and *Over Seventy* (1957). Principal works include: *The Intimate Jeeves* (1924), *Meet Mr. Mulliner* (1927), *The Mulliner Omnibus* (1935), and *The Code of the Woosters* (1938).

Wöhler *(vû lər),* **Friedrich** 1800–1882. German chemist. *b.* Eschersheim. Professor at Göttingen (from 1836); his contributions to organic chemistry include discovery of aluminum, beryllium, and yttrium, development of a process for manufacturing nickel, synthesis of urea from ammonium cyanate, the first synthesis of an organic compound from an inorganic material, and study of isomerism. Author of *Grundriss der Chemie* (1831).

Wolf *(vôlf),* **Friedrich August** 1759–1824. German classical scholar and philologist. *b.* Hagewrode. Professor at Halle (from 1783) and at Berlin (from 1806); in his chief work, *Prolegomena ad Homerum*, advanced the thesis that the *Iliad* and *Odyssey* are the works of not one but of a number of bards; edited works of Homer, Plato, Cicero, and other classical scholars. Wrote *Darstellung der Alterthumswissenschaft* (1807); regarded as the founder of scientific philology.

Wolf, Hugo 1860–1903. Austrian composer. *b.* Windischgraz. Lived in poverty in Vienna, working as music teacher and critic; died insane; most of his compositions came to be widely known only after his death. Works include more than 300 lieder, many of them settings of poems by Goethe, Mörike, Eichendorff, translations of the *Italienisches Liederbuch* of Heyse and Geibel, the opera *Der Corregidor* (1895), the symphonic poem, *Penthesilea* (1883), and *Italian Serenade* (1894).

Wolfe *(wo͝olf),* **James** 1727–1759. British general. *b.* Westerham. Entered army (1742); distinguished himself at Dettingen (1743), Louisburg (1758), and against the Jacobites in Scotland; entrusted by William Pitt to command the force charged with expelling the French from Canada (1759); sailed with 9000 men and landed below Quebec; led men up the Heights of Abraham by night; surprised, routed, and killed Montcalm in the fateful battle that decided the ownership of Canada; mortally wounded in battle and died in the hour of victory.

Wolfe, Thomas Clayton 1900–1938. American novelist. *b.* Asheville, N.C. Considered by many critics one of the greatest prose writers in America, though others have called his works blank verse bombast and apocalyptic delirium; his relationship with Maxwell Perkins, his editor at Scribner's, is one of the legends of American publishing. Author of *Look Homeward, Angel* (1929), *Of Time and the River* (1935), *The Web and the Rock* (1939), and *You Can't Go Home Again* (1940); *Story of a Novel* (1936) is a critical analysis of his own work.

Wollaston *(wo͝ol əs tən),* **William Hyde** 1766–1828. English chemist and physicist. *b.* East Dereham. Devoted himself to research (from 1880); made important contributions to chemistry, optics, and physics; discovered palladium (1804) and rhodium (1805); invented method of making platinum ductile; discovered the dark Fraunhofer lines in the solar spectrum and ultraviolet rays; invented the camera lucida, goniometer, and Wollaston's doublet, important in optics.

Wolsey *(wo͝ol zĭ),* **Thomas** c1475–1530. English prelate and statesman. *b.* Ipswich. Studied divinity at Oxford; came to attention of Henry VII as chaplain of Calais; chaplain to the king (1507); conspicuous by acumen and skill in negotiations displayed on missions to Scotland and the Low Countries; on accession of Henry VIII, progressed in royal favor; privy councilor (1511); archbishop of York (1514); cardinal (1515); papal legate (1518); lord chancellor (1515–29); amassed more power and wealth than any minister before him, virtually controlling the realm, determining domestic and foreign policies; built Hampton Court, one of his many palaces, and lived in a style that rivaled the king's; gained strategic leverage for England on the Continent by maintaining delicate balance of power between Francis I of France and Charles V of Spain; his fall was as rapid as his rise; failing to secure the annulment of Henry's marriage with Catherine, he was stripped of all offices and properties and arrested for high treason; died en route to London to face trial.

Wood *(wŏŏd),* **Grant** 1892–1942. American painter and lithographer. *b.* Anamosa, Iowa. Often called Painter of the Soil. Best-known works include *American Gothic* (1930), *Daughters of the Revolution* (1932), and *Woman with Plants* (1929).

Woodward *(wŏŏd wərd),* **Robert Burns** 1917– . American chemist. *b.* Boston, Mass. Professor at Harvard (from 1953); director of Woodward Research Institute at Basel (from 1963); awarded Nobel Prize in chemistry (1965) for synthesis of organic compounds including chlorophyll, cortisone, and quinine.

Woolf *(wŏŏlf),* **Virginia** full name: ADELINE VIRGINIA. 1882–1941. English author. *b.* London. Married LEONARD SIDNEY (1880–1969), English man of letters (1912); together they founded Hogarth Press (1917). Member of the Bloomsbury Group; developed an impressionistic stream-of-consciousness technique, producing prose of a dreamlike quality. Among her works are *The Voyage Out* (1915), *Night and Day* (1919), *Jacob's Room* (1922), *Mrs. Dalloway* (1925), *To the Lighthouse* (1927), *Orlando* (1928), *The Waves* (1931), *The Years* (1937), *Between the Acts* (1941), *Monday or Tuesday* (1921), and *A Room of One's Own* (1929); suffered periodic breakdowns, eventually drowning herself; *A Writer's Diary* was published posthumously (1953).

Woolley *(wŏŏl ĭ),* **Sir Charles Leonard** 1880–1960. English archaeologist. *b.* London. Conducted excavations in Nubia (1907–11, 1912), Carchemish (1912–14, 1919), Sinai (1914), Tell el-Amarna (1921–22), Ur (1922–34), Syria (1937–39), and Atchana (1937–39, 1946–49). Author of *The Sumerians* (1929), *Digging Up the Past* (1930), *Ur of the Chaldees* (1934), *Abraham* (1936), and *Alalakh* (1955).

Worde *(wôrd),* **Wynkyn de** real name: JAN VAN WYNKYN. *d.* c1535. English printer. *b.* Alsace. Went to England and became assistant to William Caxton (1476), succeeding him (1491); made improvements in printing and typecutting; printed over 400 books.

Wordsworth *(wûrds wûrth),* **William** 1770–1850. English poet. *b.* Cockermouth. After finishing at Cambridge, traveled in France; engaged in love affair with Annette Vallon, who bore him a daughter; returned to England on declaration of war (1793); for a few years toyed with Godwin's anarchism and rationalism; enabled by a legacy to settle with sister Dorothy at Racedown, Dorsetshire; moved to Alfoxden to be nearer Coleridge, whose influence was critical in turning him away from radicalism into romanticism; collaborated with Coleridge on *Lyrical Ballads* (1798, 1800, 1802, 1805), in which they explored the lives of rustic people living close to nature; visited Germany with Coleridge (1798–99); on return, lived with sister in Lake District; married Mary Hutchinson (1802); in later years adopted extreme conservative political positions, opposing parliamentary reforms, Catholic emancipation, and other liberal measures; succeeded Southey as poet laureate (1843); his own philosophy of poetry was to write "in the real language of men in a state of vivid sensation." Works include "Tintern Abbey," "Ode to Duty," "Michael," "Ruth," "The Solitary Reaper," "Intimations of Immortality," "Yarrow Revisited," "Prelude," the *Lucy* poems, "Afflictions of Margaret," "The Excursion," "The River Duddon," "Ecclesiastical Sketches," and "Dion."

Wrangell *(vrang gəl),* **Baron Ferdinand Petrovich von** 1794–1870. Russian explorer. *b.* Pskov. Accompanied two expeditions around the world (1817–19, 1825–27); led expedition to the Arctic (1820–24); governor of Russian colonies in Alaska and director of Russian-American Trading Company; Wrangell Island named after him. Author of *Polar Expedition* (1840).

Wray, John. *See* **Ray, John**

Wren *(rĕn),* **Sir Christopher** 1632–1723. English architect. *b.* East Knoyle. Professor of astronomy at London (1657–60) and Oxford (1661–73); one of the founders of Royal Society and its president (from 1680); began career as architect with design for chapel at Pembroke College (1663); drew plans for rebuilding London after Great Fire (1666), but they were never implemented; designed over 52 churches, including St. Paul's, his most enduring monument. Other buildings include the Royal Exchange, Custom House, Temple Bar, the College of Physicians, Greenwich Observatory, Chelsea Hospital, Oxford Ashmolean Museum, Hampton Court additions, Greenwich Hospital, Buckingham House, Marlborough House, Sheldonian Theater, Trinity College library, chapel of Brasenose College at Oxford, Drury Lane Theater, and the spires of Litchfield Cathedral and Westminster Abbey.

Wright *(rīt),* **Frank Lloyd** 1869–1959. American architect. *b.* Richland Center, Wis. Introduced Prairie Style homes, designed to harmonize with the surrounding landscape and built with low horizontal lines and projecting eaves; also experimented with open planning in houses; to extend the influence of his architectural ideas founded and directed the Taliesin Fellowship. Among his renowned buildings are Larkin Company building in Buffalo, Robie House in Chicago, Taliesin I, II, and III at Spring Green, Wisc. and Taliesin West at Phoenix, Ariz., Imperial Hotel in Tokyo, Guggenheim Museum, New York, Falling Water home near Pittsburgh, and S.C. Johnson & Son building in Racine, Wisc. Author of *Modern Architecture* (1931) and *Autobiography* (1932).

Wright *(rīt),* **Richard** 1909–60. American novelist. *b.* Natchez, Miss. Employed by Federal Writers' Project. Author of *Uncle Tom's Children* (1938), a collection of short stories; *Native Son* (1940), a novel; *12 Million Black Voices* (1941); and *Black Boy (1941)*, an autobiography.

Wright, Wilbur 1867–1912. American aviation pioneer. *b.* Millville, Ind. With brother ORVILLE (1871–1948), American aviation pioneer, *b.* Dayton, Ohio, founded Wright Cycle Company (1892); became interested in gliders, perfecting them after many experiments; made first successful flight in a heavier-than-air machine (1903) at Kitty Hawk; using a biplane powered by a four-cylinder motor and launched by a catapult, stayed in the air for 59 seconds, traveling 852 feet; improved the machine and made a circular flight of 24 miles (1905); received patent for the invention (1906); successfully competed for a plane for the War Department (1909); and formed the Wright Company for manufacture of airplanes (1909). On death of Wilbur (1912), Orville sold interest in the company. Orville is the author of *How We Invented the Airplane* (1953).

Wycliffe *(wĭk lĭf)*, **John** c1320–84. English religious reformer. *b.* Hipswell. Studied at Oxford, becoming a popular preacher; directed early attacks on the secular power of the Church and the worldliness and arrogance of clergy; justified the refusal of tribute demanded by Rome; summoned before the bishop of London in St. Paul's to answer charge of heresy, but escaped trial; condemned in five papal bulls; with election of antipope Clement VII, threw off allegiance to the papacy; emboldened to strike at such fundamental doctrines of the Church as absolution, confession, penances, indulgences, and transsubstantiation; condemned by council convened by archbishop of Canterbury (1382); forced into retirement, began writing tracts in English rather than Latin and organized a body of "poor priests" to spread his teachings; translated Gospels into English from the Vulgate; 44 years after his death his body was disinterred and burned and the ashes cast into the River Swift in execution of an order by Council of Constance; called the Morning Star of the Reformation.

Wyeth *(wī əth)*, **Andrew** 1917– . American painter. *b.* Chadds Ford, Pa. One of most successful 20th-century American painters; painter of landscapes in acutely defined detail, with striking effects of light, perspective, and texture reflecting life in the country; known for *Christina's World, Corner in a Barn,* and *Wind From the Sea*.

X

Xavier *(zā vĭ ər)*, **Saint Francis** 1506–52. Spanish Apostle to the Indies. *b.* Pamplona. Friend and associate of Ignatius Loyola and with him founder of the Society of Jesus; ordained priest (1537); worked in Italy (1537–40); sent by John III of Portugal as missionary to Goa (1541); preached at Goa and Kerala, India (1542–45), Malacca and the Moluccas (1545–46), Ceylon (1547), and Japan (1549–52); canonized (1622). Feast day: Dec. 3.

Xenophon *(zĕn ə fən)* c434–c355 B.C. Greek historian. *b.* Athens. Joined Greek mercenaries serving Persian prince Cyrus the Younger in an expedition against Artaxerxes II; after death of Cyrus in battle of Cunaxa (401) and the murder of Greek commanders by Persians, was chosen to lead "the Ten Thousand Greeks" 1500 miles to Scutari (399); offered service to Lacedaemonian Army and for this was exiled from Athens; took side of Sparta in the battle of Coronea against alliance of Athens, Corinth, and Thebes (394); spent later years at Scillus and Corinth in literary labors. Works include *Hellenics, Anabasis, Encomium of Agesilaus, The Lacedaemonian Polity, The Cyropaedeia, Athenian Finance, Memorials of Socrates, Symposion, Oeconomics, Hieron,* and *Apology of Socrates.*

Xerxes I *(zûrk sēz)* called THE GREAT; properly KHSAYARSHA; in the Bible: AHASUERUS. c519–465 B.C. King of Persia (486–465 B.C.). Son of Darius Hystaspes, whom he succeeded on the eve of his third expedition to Greece; assembled forces estimated by Herodotus at over 2 million men and 1200 warships; built a bridge across the Hellespont consisting of a double line of boats to transport his army to Europe; crossed Thrace, Macedonia, and Thessaly, overwhelmed Leonidas at Thermopylae, and took and pillaged Athens; withdrew after defeat of Persian fleet at Salamis, leaving his army in Greece under Mardonius, whose defeat at Plataea (479) brought Persian Wars to a close; assassinated.

Y

Yang *(yäng),* **Chen Ning** 1922– . American physicist. *b.* Hofei, China. Professor at Princeton (1955–65) and at Stony Brook (from 1965); with Tsung-Dao Lee, disproved the law of parity conservation in nuclear physics; awarded Nobel Prize in physics (1957).

Yeats *(yāts),* **William Butler** 1865–1939. Irish poet. *b.* Dublin. Began literary career as a member of the Yellow Book group of artists and writers; his great interests were Celtic mythology, theosophy, mysticism, spiritualism, and the Irish theater; books contributed to the Irish literary revival in drama and poetry. His poetic works include *The Wanderings of Oisin* (1889), *The Wind Among the Reeds* (1899), *Responsibilities* (1914), *The Wild Swans at Coole* (1917), *The Tower* (1927), *The Winding Stair* (1929), *Wheels and Butterflies* (1934), *Dramatis Personae* (1936), and *Last Poems* (1940); with Lady Gregory and Edward Martyn, founded Irish

Literary Theater (1899) which, as the Abbey Theater (from 1904) became the home of modern Irish drama. Among his plays are *The Countess Kathleen* (1892), *The Land of Heart's Desire* (1894), *The Shadowy Waters* (1900), *Cathleen ni Houlihan* (1902), *The Pot of Broth* (1902), *The Hour Glass* (1903), *On Baile's Strand* (1904), *The King's Threshold* (1904), *Deirdre* (1907), *Plays for an Irish Theater* (1912), *The Player Queen* (1919), *Four Plays for Dancers* (1921), *The Cat and the Moon* (1924), *The Herne's Egg* (1938), and *Purgatory* (1938); his prose works include *The Celtic Twilight* (1893), *The Secret Rose* (1897), *Ideas of Good and Evil* (1903), *In the Seven Woods* (1903), *Stories of Red Hanrahan* (1904), *The Cutting of an Agate* (1912), *Per Amica Silentia Lunae* (1918), and *A Vision* (1926); published autobiographies *Reveries Over Childhood* (1915) and *The Trembling of the Veil* (1922); awarded Nobel Prize in literature (1923).

Young *(yŭng)*, **Brigham** 1801–77. American Mormon leader. *b.* Whitingham, Vt. Converted to Mormonism (1831), becoming an apostle (1835); missionary to England (1839–41); successor to Joseph Smith (1844); led great trek of Mormons to Utah (1847); elected governor of State of Deseret (1849); founded Salt Lake City; confirmed as governor of Utah by President Fillmore (1850); proclaimed polygamy and thus defied law of U.S.; removed from office and indicted (1871), but not convicted; laid foundation of Mormon prosperity by encouraging agriculture and manufacturing.

Young, Thomas 1773–1829. English physicist. *b.* Milverton. Professor at Royal Institution (from 1801); suggested the law of the interference of light (the foundation of the wave theory of light), the theory of color sensation (later developed by Hermann Helmholtz), and the theory of capillarity; helped decipher the Rosetta Stone.

Younghusband *(yŭng hŭz bənd)*, **Sir Francis Edward** 1863–1942. British explorer. *b.* Murree, India. Opened Tibet to the West as head of British mission to Lhasa (1902–1904), securing an Anglo-Tibetan treaty; explored Manchuria (1886) and discovered route from Kashgar to India through the Mustagh Pass. Author of *The Relief of Chitral* (1895), *The Heart of a Continent* (1896), and *India and Tibet* (1910).

Yuan Shih-k'ai *(yü än shĭ kī)* 1859–1916. Chinese statesman. *b.* Hsiangcheng. Entered army (1882); governor of Shantung (1900); viceroy of Chihli (1901–1907); dismissed from office on death of dowager empress (1908); on outbreak of Revolution, recalled to office, becoming commander in chief of northern forces (1912) and premier; elected president of China after Sun Yat-sen yielded office to him (1912–16); sought unsuccessfully to set up a dictatorship and reestablish monarchy; died in unknown circumstances.

Yukawa *(yo͞o kä wä)*, **Hideki** 1907– . Japanese scientist. *b.* Tokyo. Professor at Kyoto

(1939–50), Princeton, and Columbia (1948–53); director of Kyoto Research Institute (from 1953); predicted the existence of the meson (1935), a subatomic particle smaller than a proton and larger than an electron; awarded Nobel Prize in physics (1949), the first Japanese to be so honored.

Z

Zamenhof *(zä mən hôf),* **Lazarus Ludwig** 1859–1917. Polish philologist and oculist. *b.* Bialystok. Invented Esperanto, an artificial international language (1887).

Zangwill *(zăng gwĭl),* **Israel** 1864–1926. English writer. *b.* London. Best known for his tales and plays on Jewish themes; including *Children of the Ghetto* (1892), *Ghetto Tragedies* (1894), *The Melting Pot* (1908), and *We Moderns* (1926).

Zapata *(sä pä tä),* **Emiliano** c1877–1919. Mexican revolutionary. *b.* Morelos. With a band of peasants, led the revolution in south Mexico for agrarian reform against all regimes of Mexican presidents from Porfirio Diaz; his movement, called zapatismo, was a threat to organized institutions, but made him a legend among the dispossessed; occupied Mexico City three times (1914–15); assassinated by agents of President Carranza.

Zarathustra. *See* **Zoroaster**

Zeeman *(zā män),* **Pieter** 1865–1943. Dutch physicist. *b.* Zonnemaire. Professor at Amsterdam (from 1900); discovered the Zeeman effect, the splitting of lines in a spectrum of light placed in a strong magnetic field; with H.A. Lorentz, awarded Nobel Prize in physics (1902). Author of *Researches in Magneto-Optics* (1913).

Zenger *(zĕng ər),* **John Peter** 1680–1746. American journalist. *b.* Germany. Immigrated to the American colonies at age 13; established a printing business in New York; in his *New York Weekly Journal*, attacked the government of Governor William Cosby and was consequently brought to trial on a charge of libel; defended in court by Andrew Hamilton and acquitted; case celebrated as a landmark in the history of press freedom.

Zeno *(zē nō)* *fl.* 5th century B.C. Greek philosopher. *b.* Elea, Italy. A pupil of Parmenides; noted for his famous paradoxes; appears in Plato's *Parmenides* as teacher of Socrates.

Zeno *d.* c264 B.C. Greek philosopher. *b.* Citium, Cyprus. After studying under the Cynics at Athens, opened his own school at the Stoa (Poecile) or the Painted Porch, from which his philosophy, Stoicism, derives its name; taught that nature is morally indifferent and that the only virtues are self-sufficiency and endurance; based his doctrines on determinism and materialism; wrote 18 books, including the *Republic*; committed suicide.

Zenobia *(zə nō bĭ ȧ)* *fl.* 3rd century. Queen of Palmyra. Wife of Odenathus; acknowledged by Gallienus as ruler of the East (264); on assassination of Odenathus, succeeded to the throne (c267) as regent for her son and as queen; extended rule over Asia Minor, Syria, Mesopotamia, and Egypt, and openly defied Rome; defeated by Aurelian (271); after fall of Palmyra, captured and taken to Rome to grace the emperor's triumph.

Zeppelin *(tsĕp ə lēn),* **Count Ferdinand von** 1838–1917. German aeronaut. *b.* Constance. Constructed the first airship (dirigible) of rigid type, named zeppelin (1897–1900); established factory for their manufacture at Friedrichsshafen.

Zernike *(zĕr nĭ kə),* **Frits** 1888–1966. Dutch physicist. *b.* Amsterdam. Professor at Groningen (1910–58); invented the phase contrast microscope (1932); awarded Nobel Prize in physics (1953).

Ziegler *(zē glər),* **Karl** 1898–1973. German chemist. *b.* Helsa. Professor at Marburg (from 1920) and Heidelberg (from 1936); director of Max Planck Carbon Research Institute at Mulheim (from 1943); with Giulio Natta, received Nobel Prize in chemistry (1963) for research that developed a system for changing simple hydrocarbons into complex molecular substances.

Zola *(zô lȧ),* **Émile** 1840–1902. French novelist. *b.* Paris. One of the leading practitioners of naturalism in literature; first work, *Contes à Ninon* (1874), followed by *Nouveaux Contes à Ninon* (1874), *La Confession de Claude* (1865), *Le Voeu d'une Morte* (1866), *Les Mystères de Marseille* (1867), *Thérèse Raquin* (1867), and *Madeleine Férat* (1868); published a cycle of 20 novels under the collective title of *Les Rougon-Macquart* (from 1871), including *Le Ventre de Paris* (1873), *La Conquête de Plassans* (1874), *L'Assomoir* (1877), *Nana* (1880), *Pot-Bouille* (1882), *La Joie de Vivre* (1884), *Germinal* (1885), *La Bête Humaine* (1890), *L'Argent* (1891), *La Débâcle* (1892), and *Le Docteur Pascal* (1893); also *Trilogy of the Three Cities, Lourdes* (1894), *Rome* (1896), and *Paris* (1898); in his novels, explored almost every aspect of French life and the human condition; as an anticlericalist and social reformer, espoused the cause of Dreyfus and became his foremost defender; also published works on criticism, politics, and drama.

Zoroaster *(zō rō ăs tər)* Greek form of Persian ZARATHUSTRA. *fl.* c6th century B.C. Religious teacher and prophet. *b.* northwest Persia. Belonged to a family called Spitama; believed to have lived during the reign of King Vishtaspa (Hystaspes?); led struggle against the polytheism of Vedic Aryans from India; founded Zoroastrianism, conceiving of the universe as consisting of two warring principles, the gods of goodness led by Ahura Mazda and the gods of evil led by Ahriman (Angra Maniyu); proclaimed doctrines in the *Avesta* in hymns known as *Gathas*; theology later developed by the Magis into a system known as Mazdaism; dominant under the Achaemenidae and the Sassinidae; almost eliminated by Islam.

Zsigmondy *(zhig mən dĭ),* **Richard** 1865–1929. German chemist. *b.* Vienna, Austria. Professor at Göttingen (from 1907); did fundamental research on colloidal solutions and ultrafiltration; with H.F.W. Siedentopf, designed the ultramicroscope (1903); awarded Nobel Prize in chemistry (1925).

Zweig *(tsvīk),* **Arnold** 1887–1968. German author. *b.* Glogau. Exiled from Nazi Germany (1934); lived in Palestine (after 1934). Author of *The Case of Sargent Grischa* (1927), *Young Woman of 1914* (1931); *De Vriendt Goes Home* (1932), and *Education Before Verdun* (1936). Brother of STEFAN (1881–1942), Austrian writer. *b.* Vienna. Author of *Amok* (1923), *Conflicts* (1926), *Kaleidoscope* (1934), *Beware of Pity* (1939), and *The World of Yesterday* (1943).

Zwingli *(tsvĭng lĭ),* **Huldreich** 1484–1531. Swiss Protestant reformer. *b.* Wildhaus. Pastor at Glarus, Einsiedeln, and Zurich; successfully disputed with vicar general of Constance, gaining public support for Reformation; set forth doctrines in the Sixty-seven Theses, adopted by Zurich (1523); opposed doctrine of transsubstantiation and broke with Luther on this issue at the Council of Marburg (1529); died at Battle of Cappel in war with the Catholic cantons; translated the Bible into Swiss German. Principal work is *Of True and False Religion* (1525).